Admiralty Record®

Volume 10

PUBLISHED ADMIRALTY OPINIONS OF
THE SUPREME COURT OF THE UNITED STATES AND
THE UNITED STATES COURTS OF APPEALS ISSUED DURING
THE CALENDAR YEAR

2022

Cite as: 10 Adm. R. ____

REPORTED BY KIRK N. AURANDT, ESQ.
MEMBER OF THE BAR IN LOUISIANA AND PENNSYLVANIA

ADMIRALTY RECORD PUBLISHING COMPANY, L.L.C.
MANDEVILLE, LOUISIANA, U.S.A.

ISSN 2334-5411
ISBN 978-1-7337790-8-1

Admiralty record: published admiralty opinions of the Supreme Court of the United States and the United States Courts of Appeals issued during the calendar year ... Mandeville, Louisiana, U.S.A.: Admiralty Record Publishing Company, LLC, 2014-

KF1104.A75
ISSN: 2334-5411

https://lccn.loc.gov/2014200303

PREFACE

Volume 10—the tenth annual edition of the Admiralty Record®—reports the published admiralty opinions of the Supreme Court of the United States and the United States Courts of Appeals that were issued during the calendar year 2022. The opinions reported are the original majority, concurring, and dissenting opinions of the Court, with only minor changes in formatting to better suit a dual-column presentation. The pagination found in the Court's original opinion is indicated by the number contained inside of black brackets, *see, e.g.*, **[—15—]**. The pagination found in the official Reporter is indicated by the number contained inside of black braces, *see, e.g.*, **{–15–}**. Also, where applicable, I have added parallel citations to opinions reported in this Volume and in prior Volumes of the Admiralty Record®.

The decision to select an opinion to appear in Volume 10 of the Admiralty Record® was made solely by me following an examination of those opinions that each of the above-named courts designated for publication in 2022. Every effort has been made to ensure inclusion of all 2022 federal appellate court admiralty opinions that were designated for publication; however, to the extent that a relevant admiralty opinion has been inadvertently overlooked or otherwise mistakenly omitted, the error is regretted and is solely my own. A few opinions from appeals in civil cases that technically may not have fallen under a federal district court's admiralty or maritime jurisdiction have been reported if they touched upon admiralty matters, or were otherwise deemed to be of potential interest to the admiralty practitioner. Additionally, several opinions from criminal cases involving maritime crimes and civil cases arising under the Federal Employers' Liability Act have been included.

To assist the reader in locating those opinions from 2022 involving subject matters of interest, I have prepared an Index to the opinions. I have also prepared Tables of Authority, which supply page references to the cases, statutes, and rules cited in each opinion. Prior to relying upon any of the opinions reported herein, the reader is reminded to verify the current status of any particular case as valid precedent by checking the case with a reliable citator.

Additional copies of the Admiralty Record® may be ordered at www.admiraltyrecord.com. I hope that the Admiralty Record® will continue to be a valuable and ready reference source for not only the admiralty practitioner, but for anyone who is interested in reading the published admiralty opinions of the federal appellate courts.

KIRK N. AURANDT, ESQ.

This page intentionally left blank

Table of Contents[1]

(Cases arranged chronologically by Court)

[1] In 2022, there were no published admiralty opinions from the United States Courts of Appeals for the Sixth, Seventh, Eighth, Tenth, and Federal Circuits.

Supreme Court of the United States

Supreme Court of the United States

No. 20-807

LEDURE
VS.
UNION PAC. R.R. CO.

On Writ of Certiorari to the United States Court of Appeals for the Seventh Circuit

Decided: April 28, 2022

Citation: 596 U.S. ____, 142 S.Ct. 1582, 10 Adm. R. 2 (2022) (Per Curiam).

[—1—] {–1582–} PER CURIAM:

The judgment is affirmed by an equally divided Court.

JUSTICE BARRETT took no part in the consideration or decision of this case.

(Reporter's Note: Affirmed LeDure v. Union Pac. R.R. Co., 962 F.3d 907, 8 Adm. R. 278 (7th Cir. 2020)).

United States Court of Appeals for the First Circuit

United States Court of Appeals
for the First Circuit

No. 21-1566

MOORE
vs.
ELECTRIC BOAT CORP.

Appeal from the United States District Court for the District of Rhode Island

Decided: January 31, 2022

Citation: 25 F.4th 30, 10 Adm. R. 4 (1st Cir. 2022).

Before **LYNCH, KAYATTA,** and **GELPI,** Circuit Judges.

[—3—] {-32-} LYNCH, Circuit Judge:

Electric Boat Corporation is a federal contractor which has built submarines for the United States Navy for more than 100 years, including the submarine involved in this case: the USS *Francis Scott Key*. Michael Moore, who was enlisted in the Navy, was assigned to work as an electronics technician aboard the USS *Francis Scott Key* from 1965 to 1969. Decades after he was exposed to asbestos during construction of the submarine, Michael Moore and his wife Rose (collectively, "Moore") filed suit against Electric Boat and other defendants alleging the various state claims described further below.

In October 2020, Electric Boat removed the case to federal court under 28 U.S.C. § 1442, the federal officer removal statute. In response, Moore filed a motion before the district court to remand to state court. After full briefing, in July 2021, the district court granted Moore's remand motion, finding that Electric Boat had failed to satisfy the § 1442(a)(1) requirements for federal officer removal. *See Moore v. Crane Co.*, No. 20-cv-00466-LDA, 2021 WL 2719258, at *5 (D.R.I. July 1, 2021).

The district court interpreted the statute in a manner inconsistent with the 2011 congressional amendment to § 1442(a)(1). Removal Clarification Act of 2011, Pub. L. No. 112- 51, 125 Stat. 545. We reverse and hold that Electric Boat has established the statutory requirements for removal. **[—4—]**

I.

A. Factual Background

During the mid-1960s, Electric Boat built the USS *Francis Scott Key* for the Navy at its shipyard in Groton, Connecticut. **{-33-}** The Electric Boat shipyard operated "in accordance with government contracts, in conformance with military specifications, and under Navy oversight." The Navy supervised Electric Boat's operations, had designated officials present at the Electric Boat shipyard to oversee Electric Boat's employees, and maintained a substantial presence at the shipyard, including offices, sleeping quarters, training centers, and other facilities. The Navy oversaw every aspect of the design, construction, maintenance, and modernization of its submarines like the USS *Francis Scott Key*.

Michael Moore, who was serving in the Navy at the time, worked as an electronics technician aboard the USS *Francis Scott Key* from 1965 to 1969. He alleges that he was exposed to asbestos and asbestos-containing products while at the "premises owned and/or controlled" by Electric Boat. In September 2018, he was diagnosed with lung cancer caused by exposure to asbestos.

B. Procedural History

In Rhode Island state court, Moore brought several claims against all defendants, including failure to warn, negligence, strict product liability, breach of warranty, and **[—5—]** conspiracy. As to Electric Boat specifically, Moore also alleged that Electric Boat "fail[ed] to provide safe equipment," "fail[ed] to provide adequate safety measures and protection," "fail[ed] to adequately warn . . . of the inherent dangers of asbestos," "fail[ed] to maintain . . . proper and safe condition[s]" on the premises, and "fail[ed] to follow and adhere" to state and federal laws and regulations.

After Electric Boat removed the case to federal court under § 1442(a)(1), Moore moved to remand to state court. Electric Boat opposed and submitted several exhibits in support of removal, including affidavits from Bradford Heil, a retired Electric Boat employee, and Admiral John B. Padgett, III, a retired Rear Admiral in the Navy. Padgett's affidavit stated that the Navy "directed, controlled and approved any warnings relating to health or safety to its servicepersons such as Mr. Moore." Moore did not submit any affidavits in response.

In July 2021, the district court granted the motion to remand. The district court first held that, to satisfy the requirements for removal under § 1442(a)(1), Electric Boat must demonstrate that "it was acting 'under color' of a federal official or agency" and that there was "a causal link between the 'acting under' restrictions and the cause of plaintiff's injury." *Moore*, 2021 WL 2719258, at *2. Applying this standard to the facts of the case, the court held that Electric Boat failed to satisfy the **[—6—]** § 1442(a)(1) requirements because Electric Boat's proffered evidence "fail[ed] to address the premises theory of liability." *Id.* at *4.

The court also held that, to defend removal, Electric Boat would need to "demonstrate that the Navy controlled the *warnings* at the shipyard itself, to such an extent as to preclude Electric Boat from fulfilling its duty to warn." *Id.* (emphasis in original). The court then found that "there is no support here for the proposition that the Navy prohibited workplace warnings." *Id.* at *5.[1]

Electric Boat timely appealed. **{–34–}**

II.

We review de novo the district court's jurisdictional determination on removal. *See Romulus v. CVS Pharmacy, Inc.*, 770 F.3d 67, 73 (1st Cir. 2014). Where the district court resolves disputed issues of fact, we review those factual findings for clear error. *See id.*; *Amoche v. Guar. Tr. Life Ins. Co.*, 556 F.3d 41, 48 (1st Cir. 2009). To the extent the district court found that the Navy did not control any and all warnings concerning the health **[—7—]** and safety of servicepersons working on the USS *Francis Scott Key* and at the Electric Boat shipyard, that finding was clear error.

A. Federal Officer Removal Under § 1442(a)(1)

The federal officer removal statute provides that a civil action commenced in state court may be removed if it is against or directed to:

> The United States or any agency thereof or any officer (or any person *acting under* that officer) of the United States or of any agency thereof, in an official or individual capacity, *for or relating to* any act under color of such office or on account of any right, title or authority claimed under any Act of Congress for the apprehension or punishment of criminals or the collection of the revenue.

28 U.S.C. § 1442(a)(1) (emphases added).

The district court erred by applying the "causal link" standard to federal officer removal, which is far narrower than the proper standard under § 1442(a)(1), as amended in 2011 when Congress changed the provision to reach removal based on a suit "for *or relating to* any act under color of [federal] office." *See* Removal Clarification Act of 2011, Pub. L. No. 112-51, 125 Stat. 545 (emphasis added); *see Latiolais v. Huntington Ingalls, Inc.*, 951 F.3d 286, 292–96, 8 Adm. R. 155, 157–61 (5th Cir. 2020) (en banc) (rejecting the "causal connection" requirement and instead applying the "relating to" standard); *Sawyer v. Foster Wheeler LLC*, 860 F.3d 249, 258, 5 Adm. R. 167, 172–73 (4th Cir. 2017) (same). **[—8—]**

[1] Electric Boat vigorously disputes this finding. The record supports Electric Boat's contention that the Navy did, in fact, control any and all warnings that concerned the health and safety of servicepersons working on the USS *Francis Scott Key* and at the shipyard. Moore did not offer any evidence to the contrary.

Electric Boat bears the burden under § 1442(a)(1), *see Bor-Son Bldg. Corp. v. Heller*, 572 F.2d 174, 181 n.13 (8th Cir. 1978), to establish: (1) that it was "acting under a federal officer's authority," *Rhode Island v. Shell Oil Prods. Co., L.L.C.*, 979 F.3d 50, 59 (1st Cir. 2020), *summarily vacated on other grounds*, 141 S. Ct. 2666 (2021) (Mem.); (2) that the charged conduct was carried out "for or relating to" the asserted official authority, 28 U.S.C. § 1442(a)(1);[2] and (3) that it "will assert a colorable federal defense to the suit," *Shell Oil Prods.*, 979 F.3d at 59.

B. Electric Boat Satisfies the Standard for Federal Officer Removal Under § 1442(a)(1)

Moore does not dispute that Electric Boat has shown that it was "acting under a federal officer's authority."[3] We **{-35-}** focus on the second two requirements for removal. **[—9—]**

[2] We have also described the "relating to" requirement as a "nexus" between "the allegations in the complaint and conduct undertaken at the behest of a federal officer." *Shell Oil Prods.*, 979 F.3d at 59. This nexus requirement is not a causation requirement, as the district court erroneously held. *Moore*, 2021 WL 2719258, at *4.

[3] In the context of § 1442(a)(1), the Supreme Court has interpreted "acting under" a federal officer to contemplate a relationship where the private party engages in an effort "to *assist*, or to help *carry out*, the duties or tasks of the federal superior." *Watson v. Philip Morris Co.*, 551 U.S. 142, 151–52 (2007) (emphasis in original). The relationship typically involves "subjection, guidance, or control." *Id.* at 151 (quoting *Webster's New International Dictionary* 2765 (2d ed. 1953)). And the words "acting under" are "broad" and "liberally construed." **[—9—]** *Id.* at 147 (third quoting *Colorado v. Symes*, 286 U.S. 510, 517 (1932)).

Courts have consistently held that the "acting under" requirement is easily satisfied where a federal contractor removes a case involving injuries arising from a product manufactured for the government. *See Genereaux v. Am. Beryllia Corp.*, 577 F.3d 350, 357 n.9 (1st Cir. 2009) (recognizing federal officer removal based on defendant's assertion that it was "acting under" a federal officer because "the beryllium-containing products it supplied to Raytheon were used in manufacturing 'military hardware'"); *see also Latiolais*, 951 F.3d at 291, 8 Adm. R. at 156 (holding that federal contractor that repaired Naval vessels was "acting under" a federal officer's authority); *Sawyer*, 860 F.3d at 255, 5 Adm. R. at 170 (holding that federal contractor that assembled boilers for Naval vessels was "acting under" a federal officer's authority); *Papp v. Fore-Kast Sales Co.*, 842 F.3d 805, 813 (3d Cir. 2016) (holding that federal contractor that constructed military aircrafts for the government was "acting under" a federal officer's authority).

1. *"For or relating to"*

In 2011, Congress amended § 1442(a)(1) to reach removal based on a suit "for or relating to any act under color of [federal] office." *See* Removal Clarification Act of 2011, Pub. L. No. 112-51, 125 Stat. 545 (adding "or relating to" language to the provision).[4] Circuits have consistently given this requirement a broad reading and held that no causal link is required. *See Latiolais*, 951 F.3d at 292–96, 8 Adm. R. at 157–61 ("[W]e overrule *Bartel[v. Alcoa Steamship Co.*, 805 F.3d 169, 3 Adm. R. 422 (5th Cir. 2015)] and its progeny to **[—10—]** the extent that those cases erroneously relied on a 'causal nexus' test after Congress amended section 1442(a) to add 'relating to.'" (footnote omitted)); *Sawyer*, 860 F.3d at 258, 5 Adm. R. at 173 ("The district court imposed a stricter standard of causation than that recognized by the statute . . . which is only that the charged conduct *relate to* an act under color of federal office." (emphasis in original)). The First Circuit nexus standard is not a causal requirement and is not to be understood as anything more than a "related to" nexus. *See Shell Oil Prods.*, 979 F.3d at 59.

Any single claim is independently sufficient to satisfy the "for or relating to" requirement under § 1442(a)(1). *See Baker v. Atl. Richfield Co.*, 962 F.3d 937, 945 (7th Cir. 2020); C.A. Wright & A.R. Miller, *Federal Practice and Procedure* § 3726 (4th ed., Apr. 2021 update) ("Because Section 1442(a)(l) authorizes

[4] The amended language "broaden[ed] the universe of acts that enable Federal officers to remove to Federal court." H.R. Rep. No. 112–17, at 6 (2011). The Supreme Court has stated in other contexts that the ordinary meaning of the phrase "relating to" is "a broad one," holding that it normally means in "association with or connection with." *Morales v. Trans World Airlines, Inc.*, 504 U.S. 374, 383–84 (1992) (third quoting *Black's Law Dictionary* 1158 (5th ed. 1979)).

removal of the entire action even if only one of the controversies it raises involves a federal officer or agency, the section creates a species of statutorily-mandated supplemental subject-matter jurisdiction."). Here, all of Moore's claims against Electric Boat are "for or relating to" Electric Boat's actions taken under color of federal office.

Moore brought claims against all defendants for failure to warn, negligence, strict product liability, breach of warranty, and conspiracy. The Navy assigned Moore, an enlisted Navy serviceman, to the Electric Boat shipyard where Electric Boat built **[—11—]** the USS *Francis Scott Key* while "acting under" the authority of naval officers and in relation to that authority. The Navy oversaw every aspect of the design, construction, **{-36-}** maintenance, and modernization of the submarine, including the use of asbestos in the construction of the submarine. The undisputed record demonstrates that Moore's claims clearly "relate to" Electric Boat's contracted work while "acting under" the Navy.

Moore tries to defend against removal with more specific allegations that Electric Boat in particular failed to provide safe equipment, provide adequate safety measures and protection, maintain proper and safe conditions on the premises, and follow state and federal laws and regulations. The Navy dictated the use of asbestos, workplace safety measures, and the posting of warnings both on the submarine and at the Electric Boat shipyard. Thus, all of Moore's claims as to Electric Boat, too, clearly "relate to" Electric Boat's actions taken while "acting under" color of federal office. *See Latiolais*, 951 F.3d at 296, 8 Adm. R. at 161 (holding that claims for failure to warn about asbestos and failure to take measures to prevent exposure were "connected with the installation of asbestos during the refurbishment of the USS *Tappahannock* . . . pursuant to directions of the U.S. Navy," and thus, the "civil action relates to an act under color of federal office"); *Sawyer*, 860 F.3d at 258, 5 Adm. R. at 173 (explaining that "Foster Wheeler's alleged failure **[—12—]** to give warnings to Shipyard employees is therefore clearly related to Foster Wheeler's performance of its contract with the Navy.").

As to the claim that Electric Boat failed to adequately warn of the dangers of asbestos, the district court and Moore posit a purported distinction between "premises liability" and liability arising from harms caused from constructing the submarine itself. We doubt that a premises liability claim is different from Moore's other claims because the premises were under Navy control. At oral argument, Moore's counsel conceded that there is no assertion that Moore worked in an isolated part of the shipyard, outside Navy control. Nor is there any assertion that Moore's injuries did not stem from the various activities mandated by the Navy.

The district court applied the "causal link" standard rather than the "related to" nexus standard to its analysis of the premises liability claims. The record does not support the district court's statement that the Navy did not preclude Electric Boat from posting additional workplace warnings. Even assuming it does, § 1442(a)(1) does not "demand[] a showing of a specific government direction," which goes well beyond the "relating to" requirement. *Sawyer*, 860 F.3d at 258, 5 Adm. R. at 173. Moore's premises liability claims are clearly "related to" Electric Boat's construction of the USS *Francis Scott Key* which took place while "acting under" the Navy because the Navy oversaw and directed the workplace safety **[—13—]** measures and the posting of warnings at the Electric Boat shipyard premises.

2. *"Colorable federal defense"*

The district court did not decide whether Electric Boat has a "colorable defense" but did observe that the "burden is low," and the requirement "has generally not proven an obstacle in similar litigation." *Moore*, 2021 WL 2719258, at *2 n.5. Moore asks that if we find that Electric Boat has satisfied the "relating to" requirement, this matter should be remanded to the district court. Moore does not identify any unresolved findings of fact that would be essential to resolving this question. Based on the record, it is clear that there are multiple colorable defenses available to Electric Boat. We may reach the issue as a matter of discretion. *See Singleton v. Wulff*, 428 U.S. 106, 121 (1976). **{-37-}**

Under § 1442(a)(1), a "colorable federal defense" need not be "clearly sustainable." *Willingham v. Morgan*, 395 U.S. 402, 407 (1969). The Supreme Court has rejected a "narrow, grudging interpretation" of the requirement. *Id.* Rather, a federal defense is colorable unless it is "immaterial and made solely for the purpose of obtaining jurisdiction" or "wholly insubstantial and frivolous." *Latiolais*, 951 F.3d at 297, 8 Adm. R. at 161 (quoting *Zeringue v. Crane Co.*, 846 F.3d 785, 790, 5 Adm. R. 193, 194–95 (5th Cir. 2017)). Electric Boat asserts several colorable defenses to the claims against it. **[—14—]**

Electric Boat first asserts the government contractor immunity defense outlined in *Boyle v. United Technologies Corp.*, 487 U.S. 500, 512 (1988). Courts applying *Boyle* to failure-to-warn cases have held that the immunity applies where: "(1) the government exercised its discretion and approved certain warnings; (2) the contractor provided the warnings required by the government; [and] (3) the contractor warned the government about dangers in the equipment's use that were known to the contractor but not to the government." *Sawyer*, 860 F.3d 249, 256, 5 Adm. R. at 171 (quoting *Oliver v. Oshkosh Truck Corp.*, 96 F.3d 992, 1003–04 (7th Cir. 1996)) (alteration in original).

Electric Boat offered evidence colorably showing that all three *Boyle* conditions have been met in this case. Electric Boat submitted affidavits stating that the Navy controlled the use and content of the warnings on the USS *Francis Scott Key* and at the Electric Boat shipyard. Moore does not dispute these facts. The affidavits support the argument that the Navy "exercised its discretion and approved certain warnings" related to asbestos. The affidavits also support, and Moore does not dispute, that Electric Boat complied with the Navy's requirements and "provided the warnings required by the government." And Electric Boat presented the colorable argument that there were no dangers "that were known to the contractor but not to the government" because the government knew more than Electric Boat about asbestos-related **[—15—]** hazards and safety measures. *See Sawyer*, 860 F.3d at 256, 5 Adm. R. at 171 ("Foster Wheeler credibly demonstrated . . . that the Navy's knowledge of asbestos-related hazards exceeded Foster Wheeler's during the relevant time period."); *Latiolais*, 951 F.3d at 298, 8 Adm. R. at 162 ("Avondale's evidence tends to support that the federal government knew more than Avondale knew about asbestos-related hazards and related safety measures.").

In light of the evidence submitted by Electric Boat, the government contractor immunity defense is not "wholly insubstantial and frivolous." Electric Boat has made at least a colorable showing that the Navy exercised discretion in requiring Electric Boat to provide certain warnings while fully aware of the dangers of asbestos. Whether or not the government prohibited Electric Boat from posting additional warnings speaks to the merits of the defense but does not undermine the colorability of the immunity defense.

Electric Boat also asserts that it is entitled to derivative sovereign immunity under *Yearsley v. W.A. Ross Construction Co.*, 309 U.S. 18 (1940). Under *Yearsley*, "a government contractor is not subject to suit if (1) the government authorized the contractor's actions and (2) the government 'validly conferred' that authorization, meaning it acted within its constitutional power." *Cunningham v. Gen. Dynamics Info.* **[—16—]** *Tech., Inc.*, 888 F.3d 640, 643 (4th Cir. 2018) (quoting *In re KBR, Inc., Burn Pit Litig.*, 744 F.3d 326, 342 (4th Cir. 2014)).

Electric Boat likewise has made a colorable showing that it satisfied the *Yearsley* **{-38-}** requirements to assert the derivative sovereign immunity defense. Electric Boat's proffered evidence colorably shows that it acted at the direction of the Navy, which "authorized [Electric Boat's] actions." And the Navy clearly "acted within its constitutional power" to contract with Electric Boat to build submarines.

Electric Boat lastly asserts that it is protected by the Federal Tort Claims Act's combatant activities exception. *See* 28 U.S.C. § 2680(j) (barring suit for "[a]ny claim arising out of the combatant activities of the military or naval forces, or the Coast Guard, during time of war"); *see also Saleh v. Titan Corp.*, 580 F.3d 1, 9 (D.C. Cir. 2009) ("During wartime, where a private service contractor is integrated into combatant activities over which the military retains command authority, a tort claim arising out of the contractor's engagement in such activities shall be preempted.").

Electric Boat built and maintained submarines, including the USS *Francis Scott Key*, during the Vietnam War. Those submarines were used by the Navy in its "combatant activities . . . during time of war." Thus, Electric Boat has presented at least **[—17—]** a colorable argument in support of the combatant activities exception.

III.

Reversed and Remanded.

United States Court of Appeals
for the First Circuit

No. 19-1818

RHODE ISLAND
vs.
SHELL OIL PRODS. CO.

Appeal from the United States District Court for the District of Rhode Island

Decided: May 23, 2022

Citation: 35 F.4th 44, 10 Adm. R. 10 (1st Cir. 2022).

Before **THOMPSON** and **HOWARD**, Circuit Judges.*

* Judge Torruella heard argument in this appeal. But he did not participate in the decision, which is being rendered by a "quorum" of the panel. *See* 28 U.S.C. § 46(d).

[—5—] **{-48-}** **THOMPSON**, Circuit Judge: **{-49-}**

This is our second pass at a climate-change case that requires us to explore the mind-numbing complexities of federal removal jurisdiction. *See Rhode Island v. Shell Oil Prods. Co.*, 979 F.3d 50, 54 (1st Cir. 2020) ("*Shell Oil*"). We start by bringing the reader up to speed.[1]

Like other state and local governments across the country, Rhode Island claims that the Energy Companies named in our **{-50-}** caption knew for decades that burning fossil fuels is damaging the earth's atmosphere but duped the public into buying more and more of their products (consequences be damned)—all to line their very deep pockets. *See id.* at 53. Seeking relief for the catastrophic harm they supposedly have done (and will do) to its non-federal property and natural resources, Rhode Island—also like other governments elsewhere—sued the Energy Companies in state court. *See id.* at 53-54. And its longish complaint alleges state-law causes of action for public nuisance, strict-liability design defect, negligent design defect, negligent failure to warn, impairment of public-trust resources, and violations of the state's Environmental Rights Act.

Not eager to try this case in a Rhode Island court, the Energy Companies removed the matter to federal court under the federal-officer removal statute, the federal-question doctrine, **[—6—]** the Outer Continental Shelf Lands Act (just "OCSLA" from now on), the admiralty-jurisdiction statute, and the bankruptcy-removal statute. But to their disappointment, the district judge thought that none of those grounds could provide a hook on which removal could hang. *See id.* And so he remanded the case to state court. *See id.*

On the Energy Companies' appeal—in our first go-around—we concluded that we could only review the federal-officer removal ground. *See id.* at 58–60. And ruling that the Energy Companies had not satisfied the requirements of the federal-officer removal statute, we affirmed the judge's remand order. *See id.* at 60. But on the Energy Companies' petition for *certiorari*, the Supreme Court (without reversing our decision on the merits) GVR'd us (short for **g**ranted certiorari, *v*acated, and *r*emanded) and instructed that we give "further consideration in light of *BP p.l.c. v. Mayor & City Council of Baltimore*, 141 S. Ct. 1532 (2021)"—a then-hot-off-the-presses opinion requiring courts of appeals to review the judge's entire remand order and consider all of the defendants' removal grounds, not just the part of the order resolving the federal-officer removal ground.[2] *See* **[—7—]** *Shell Oil Prods. Co. v. Rhode Island*, 141 S. Ct. 2666 (2021) (Mem.).

Pleased to oblige, we requested and received supplemental briefs from counsel.[3] In them, the parties continue battling over whether the Energy Companies can remove the case on various bases. And it is to this dispute that we turn to below, using a *de novo* standard (which gives zero deference to the judge's views) and adding more details when needed to put the arguments into workable

[1] For efficiency's sake, we assume the reader's general familiarity with our *Shell Oil* opinion.

[2] For a good discussion of the GVR mechanism, *see Gonzalez v. Justices of the Municipal Court of Boston*, 420 F.3d 5, 7–8 (1st Cir. 2005). As a heads-up, today's opinion requires some tolerance for acronyms.

[3] We wish to thank the amici and their attorneys for their helpful insights as well.

perspective. *See Amoche v. Guarantee Tr. Life Ins. Co.*, 556 F.3d 41, 48 (1st Cir. 2009). But to give away the opinion's ending up front: leaning hard on our sibling circuits' analyses in comparable climate-change cases—particularly *County of San Mateo v. Chevron Corp.*, Nos. 18-15499, 18-15502, 18-15503, 18-16376, 2022 WL 1151275, 10 Adm. R. 284 (9th Cir. Apr. 19, 2022) ("*San Mateo*"); *Mayor & City Council of Baltimore v. BP P.L.C.*, 31 F.4th 178 (4th Cir. 2022) ("*BP P.L.C.*"); *Board of County Commissioners of Boulder County v. Suncor Energy (U.S.A.) Inc.*, 25 F.4th 1238 (10th Cir. 2022) ("*Suncor*"); *City of Oakland v. BP PLC*, 969 F.3d 895, 907 (9th Cir. 2020) ("*Oakland*"), *cert. denied*, **{-51-}** 141 S. Ct. 2776 (2021)—we once more *affirm* the judge's remand order. **[—8—]**

Overarching Considerations

Federal courts have limited jurisdiction, charted (within constitutional limits) by federal statute. *See, e.g., López-Muñoz v. Triple-S Salud, Inc.*, 754 F.3d 1, 5 (1st Cir. 2014); *Fayard v. Ne. Vehicle Servs., LLC*, 533 F.3d 42, 48 (1st Cir. 2008) (noting that "[b]oth jurisdiction and removal are primarily creatures of Congress"). And as we are about to see, lots of statutes control removal of state-filed cases to federal court.

A generalized removal statute says that a defendant can remove a state-filed case to federal court only if the plaintiff could have brought the case there originally. *See* 28 U.S.C. § 1441(a). Pertinently here, a federal court has original jurisdiction over cases that "aris[e] under" federal law—*i.e.*, "the Constitution, *laws*, or treaties *of the United States*," *see* 28 U.S.C. § 1331 (emphases added), plus "claims founded upon federal common law," *see Illinois v. City of Milwaukee*, 406 U.S. 91, 100 (1972). Section 1441 is known as the general-removal statute. *See, e.g., Home Depot U.S.A., Inc. v. Jackson*, 139 S. Ct. 1743, 1746 (2019) ("*Home Depot*"). And section 1331 is known as the general federal-question jurisdiction statute. *See, e.g., Holmes Grp., Inc. v. Vornado Air Circulation Sys., Inc.*, 535 U.S. 826, 829 (2002).

Specialized removal statutes exist too. Take, for instance, the bankruptcy-removal statute, which (in broad strokes) **[—9—]** allows removal to a district court of any claim of which that court would have jurisdiction under another provision that (generally speaking) creates federal jurisdiction for disputes "arising under" the bankruptcy code, disputes "arising in" a bankruptcy case, and disputes "related to" the resolution of a bankruptcy case. *See* 28 U.S.C. §§ 1452(a), 1334(a)–(b).

Whether a case arises under federal law typically is "determined from what necessarily appears" on the face of a plaintiff's complaint, "unaided by anything alleged in anticipation or avoidance of defenses which it is thought the defendant may interpose." *See Taylor v. Anderson*, 234 U.S. 74, 75–76 (1914); *see also Franchise Tax Bd. v. Constr. Laborers Vacation Tr.*, 463 U.S. 1, 9–12 (1983). This is known as the well-pleaded-complaint rule, because it concentrates our attention on the complaint's terms. *See Franchise Tax Bd.*, 463 U.S. at 9–10. And in most instances, that rule makes plaintiff the "master" of the complaint—including the master of "what law" plaintiff "will rely upon." *See The Fair v. Kohler Die & Specialty Co.*, 228 U.S. 22, 25 (1913) (Holmes, J., for the Court).

As with many rules, however, exceptions exist. *See Rose v. RTN Fed. Credit Union*, 1 F.4th 56, 59–60 (1st Cir. 2021). One exception applies when "a state-law claim necessarily raise[s] a stated federal issue," which is "actually disputed and substantial," and which a federal court can consider "without **[—10—]** disturbing any congressionally approved balance" between state and federal power. *See Grable & Sons Metal Prods., Inc. v. Darue Eng'g & Mfg.*, 545 U.S. 308, 313–16 (2005) ("*Grable*"); *accord R.I. Fishermen's All., Inc. v. R.I. Dep't of Envtl. Mgmt.*, 585 F.3d 42, 49 (1st Cir. 2009). Only a "*slim* category" of state-law claims satisfies *Grable*, however. *See Empire Healthchoice Assurance, Inc. v. McVeigh*, 547 U.S. 677, 701 (2006) ("*Empire Healthchoice*") (emphasis added); **{-52-}** *San Mateo*, 2022 WL 1151275, at *4, 10 Adm. R. at 286. Another exception applies when federal law has completely displaced state law and so "provide[s] the exclusive cause of action for such claims"—thus making the asserted claim necessarily federal. *See Beneficial Nat'l Bank v. Anderson*, 539 U.S. 1, 11 (2003) ("*Beneficial*"); *accord Caterpillar Inc. v. Williams*, 482 U.S. 386, 393 (1987); *Lawless v. Steward Health Care Sys., LLC*, 894 F.3d 9, 17 (1st Cir. 2018); *López-Muñoz*, 754 F.3d at 5.[4] Complete **[—11—]** preemption is a "narrow exception." *Beneficial*, 539 U.S. at 5.[5] But in the rare situations when it applies, courts sometime derisively describe the complaint as "artfully pleaded" to sidestep the federal claim. *See, e.g.*, *Rivet*, 522 U.S. at 475.

As the parties trying to remove the case from state to federal court, the Energy Companies must prove that the federal court has original jurisdiction. *See* 28 U.S.C. § 1441(a); *see also Danca v. Private Health Care Sys., Inc.*, 185 F.3d 1, 4 (1st Cir. 1999). And because removal jurisdiction raises serious federalism concerns, we construe removal statutes *strictly* and *against* removal. *See, e.g.*, *Syngenta Crop Prot., Inc. v. Henson*, 537 U.S. 28, 32 (2002); *Rosselló-González v. Calderón-Serra*, 398 F.3d 1, 11 (1st Cir. 2004). So if federal jurisdiction is doubtful, a federal court must remand to state court. *See, e.g.*, *Rosselló-González*, 398 F.3d at 11. **[—12—]**

Issues in Play

The Energy Companies argue for removal based on federal-question jurisdiction, which they think exists because (as they tell it) Rhode Island artfully pleaded state claims that are at bottom governed by federal common law; completely preempted by federal law; necessarily dependent on substantial and disputed federal issues; and based on injuries or conduct on federal enclaves. They also argue for removal based on other jurisdictional and removal statutes, namely the OCSLA-jurisdiction statute, the admiralty-jurisdiction **{-53-}** statute, and the bankruptcy-removal statute.[6] **[—13—]**

---

4 Anything involving "preemption" can be confusing. And in this setting, the word itself can cause even the most sophisticated readers to scratch their collective heads over the difference between "complete preemption" and "ordinary preemption." *See Rueli v. Baystate Health, Inc.*, 835 F.3d 53, 57 (1st Cir. 2016). As a sort of cheat sheet: Only complete preemption affects the court's jurisdiction. *See id.* Where it exists, "there is . . . no such thing as a state-law claim" in the regulated area because Congress intended federal law to provide the *exclusive* cause of action for that claim. *See Beneficial*, 539 U.S. at 9, 11. And a court thus treats the complaint as if a federal claim appears on the face of it. *See Rivet v. Regions Bank of La.*, 522 U.S. 470, 476 (1998). Ordinary preemption, contrastingly, "refer[s] to certain *defenses*" to the claim's merits, "of which a classic example is a state claim foreclosed because its assertion conflicts with a federal statute or falls within a field preempted by federal **[—11—]** law." *See Cavallaro v. UMass Mem'l Healthcare, Inc.*, 678 F.3d 1, 4 n.3 (1st Cir. 2012) (emphasis added). And as a mere defense, ordinary preemption—according to the well-pleaded-complaint rule—"will *not* provide a basis for removal." *See Beneficial*, 539 U.S. at 6 (emphasis added).

5 Because complete preemption affects plaintiffs' usual ability to plead the law they want, the Supreme Court is "reluctant" to find the exception applies. *See Metro. Life Ins. v. Taylor*, 481 U.S. 58, 65 (1987) ("*Metro. Life*"). The Court, in fact, has found complete preemption in only *three* statutes, *see San Mateo*, 2022 WL 1151275, at *6, 10 Adm. R. at 287–88: (1) *Beneficial*, 539 U.S. at 10–11 (National Bank Act §§ 85 and 86); (2) *Metro. Life*, 481 U.S. at 66–67 (Employee Retirement Income Security Act § 502(a)); and (3) *Avco Corp. v. Aero Lodge No. 735*, 390 U.S. 557, 560 (1968) (Labor Management Relations Act § 301).

6 A word about the federal-officer removal statute—which, like the bankruptcy-removal statute, is a specialized removal statute. This provision allows private actors "acting under" color of federal authority to remove a state-court action "for or relating to any act under color of such office." *See* 28 U.S.C. § 1442(a)(1). And per our precedent, the Energy Companies must show that they acted under a federal officer, that the claims against them are "for or relating to" the alleged official authority, and that they will raise a colorable federal defense. *See Moore v. Elec. Boat Corp.*, 25 F.4th 30, 34 & n.2, 10 Adm. R. 4, 6 & n.2 (1st Cir. 2022) (noting that *Shell Oil* "described the 'relating to' requirement as a 'nexus' between 'the allegations in the complaint and conduct undertaken at the behest of a federal officer,'" but stating that "[t]his nexus requirement is not a causation requirement" (quoting *Shell Oil*, 979 F.3d at 59)).

As reported in *Shell Oil*, the Energy Companies direct "us to three contracts with the federal government related to the production of oil and

In the pages that follow, we discuss and reject each of the Energy Companies' arguments (again, all in keeping with the recent decisions of other circuit courts).

Federal-Question Jurisdiction

Federal Common Law

Citing the artful-pleading doctrine, the Energy Companies argue that even though Rhode Island's complaint says nothing about federal common law, the claims alleged "are inherently federal" and necessarily arise under federal law because they are "based on interstate and international emissions" (excess capitalization removed)—*i.e.*, uniquely federal interests, the theory goes, that must be governed by federal common law. To their way of thinking then, Rhode Island's claims amount to federal claims in disguise. Noting our "skepti[cism]" about "the applicability of the artful pleading doctrine outside of complete federal preemption of a state cause of action," *see Rosselló-González*, 398 F.3d at 12 (citing *Franchise Tax Bd.* and *Rivet*), Rhode Island protests that the well-pleaded-complaint rule **[—14—]** (which—as already explained—generally bars removal unless a federal question appears on the complaint's face) stops us from looking behind the complaint and construing the state-law theories as federal common-law ones. But as a fallback, Rhode Island argues that even if the Energy Companies could get around that rule, they would still lose because Congress has replaced the federal common law that they rely on.

Avoiding the kerfuffle over the parties' artful pleading-based arguments—our credo is that "if it is not necessary to decide more, it is necessary not to decide more," *see PDK Labs. Inc. v. U.S. D.E.A.*, 362 F.3d 786, 799 (D.C. Cir. 2004) (Roberts, J., concurring in part and concurring in the judgment)—we take the "even if" approach and ultimately conclude the Energy Companies cannot premise removal on a federal common law that no longer **{–54–}** exists, *see generally* 14C Charles A. Wright, *Federal Practice and Procedure* § 3722.1 (Rev. 4th ed. Apr. 2022) ("*Federal Practice and Procedure*") (lamenting that "the artful-pleading doctrine lacks precise definition and has bred considerable confusion"). Why we so rule requires some unpacking, however.

While there is no general common law, pockets of federal judge-made law exist that bind the states. *See BP P.L.C.*, 31 F.4th at 200 (providing examples). But the circumstances where the "judicial creation of a special federal rule" ought to displace state law are "few and restricted," *see O'Melveny & Meyers v.* **[—15—]** *F.D.I.C.*, 512 U.S. 79, 89 (1994) ("*O'Melveny*") (quotation marks omitted)—limited to those "extraordinary cases," *see id.*, involving both "uniquely federal interests" *and* a "significant conflict . . . between some federal policy or interest and the use of state law," *see Boyle v. United Tech. Corp.*, 487 U.S. 500, 506 (1988) (quotation marks omitted). That makes sense because where federal common law exists, it "preempt[s] and replace[s]" state law, *see id.* at 504—which raises sensitive issues of separation of powers and federalism, *see Rodriguez v. F.D.I.C.*, 140 S. Ct. 713, 717 (2020) (underscoring that "[j]udicial lawmaking in the form of federal common law plays a necessarily modest role under a Constitution that vests the federal government's 'legislative Powers' in Congress and reserves most other regulatory authority to the States" (quoting U.S. Const. art. 1, § 1)). Critically as well, the side pushing a theory of

---

argue that they were 'acting under' a federal officer because they 'help[ed] the Government to produce an item that it needs.'" *See* 979 F.3d at 59 (alteration in original and quoting *Watson v. Philip Morris Cos.*, 551 U.S. 142, 153 (2007)). But Rhode Island's complaint, we said, alleges that the Energy Companies "produced and sold oil and gas products in Rhode Island that were damaging the environment and engaged in a misinformation **[—13—]** campaign about the harmful effects of their products on the earth's climate." *Id.* at 60. And, we ruled, the trio of contracts "mandate[s] none of those activities"—thus making the case unremovable under the federal-officer removal statute. *See id.* Because nothing in the Supreme Court's *BP p.l.c.* opinion undermines that holding (*BP p.l.c.*, remember, only requires us to consider the Energy Companies' other removal grounds), we "adhere to" *Shell Oil*'s rejection of federal-officer removal jurisdiction (and for what it is worth, the Energy Companies identify no shortcomings with that rejection).

federal common law must show a "*specific, concrete* federal policy or interest" with which state law directly conflicts "as a *precondition* for recognition of a federal rule of decision." *See O'Melveny*, 512 U.S. at 87–88 (emphases added).[7]

The Energy Companies spend a lot of time on the "uniquely federal interests" point, highlighting (for instance) the federal government's special concern with "controlling interstate **[—16—]** pollution, promoting energy independence, and negotiating multilateral treaties addressing global warning"—interests, they continue, that call for the application of a "uniform federal rule of decision," which makes the case "removable under 28 U.S.C. §§ 1331 and 1441." But even "[a]ssuming" (without granting) that these concerns constitute "uniquely federal interests," *see BP P.L.C.*, 31 F.4th at 202, we—like the Fourth Circuit in *BP P.L.C.*—find that the Energy Companies (despite being the burden-bearer on the removal issue) never adequately describe how "any significant conflict exist[s] between" these "federal interests" and the state-law claims, which (again) seek to hold them liable for the climate change-related harms they caused by deliberately misrepresenting the dangers they knew would arise from their deceptive hyping of fossil fuels, *see id.* at 203–04. Not only does this "misstep" raise a waiver problem. *See, e.g.*, *Rodríguez v. Mun. of San Juan*, 659 F.3d 168, 175–76 (1st Cir. 2011) (discussing how to set an issue up for decision); *United States v. Zannino*, 895 F.2d 1, 17 (1st Cir. 1990) (doing the same and stressing that "[i]t is not enough merely to mention a possible argument in the most skeletal way, leaving the court to do counsel's work"). It also deals a "fatal" blow to the Energy Companies' bid to base federal-question **{–55–}** jurisdiction on federal common law. *See BP P.L.C.*, 31 F.4th at 202 (quoting *O'Melveny*, 512 U.S. at 88); *see Atherton v. F.D.I.C.*, 519 U.S. 213, 218 (1997) **[—17—]** (confirming that "the guiding principle is that a significant conflict between some federal policy or interest and the use of state law . . . must first be *specifically shown*" (omission in original, emphasis added, and quoting *Wallis v. Pan Am. Petroleum Corp.*, 384 U.S. 63, 68 (1966))).

To the extent the Energy Companies rely on *City of New York v. Chevron Corp.*, 993 F.3d 81 (2d Cir. 2021), to hint at a conflict between the federal government's relations with foreign countries and the rights of states, they are unable to do so. *See BP P.L.C.*, 31 F.4th at 202–03 (rebuffing a similar suggestion in a similar case); *Suncor*, 25 F.4th at 1262 (same). *City of New York*, after all, is distinguishable in at least one key respect. There, unlike here, the government "filed suit in *federal court* in the *first instance*" (relying on diversity jurisdiction)—so the court considered the fossil-fuel producers' "preemption defense on its own terms, not under the heightened standard unique to the removability inquiry." *See* 993 F.3d at 94 (emphases added). And the court found that its ordinary preemption analysis did not clash with the "fleet of cases" (among them *Oakland*) recognizing that "anticipated defenses"—including those based on federal common law—could not "singlehandedly create federal-question jurisdiction under 28 U.S.C. § 1331 in light of the well-pleaded complaint rule." *See id.* **[—18—]**

Ignoring these problems just for discussion purposes, we still say the Energy Companies fall short. Instead of handling "the threshold inquiry above," they here—like the energy companies in *BP P.L.C.*—shine a spotlight on some old Supreme Court cases "that once (or possibly) recognized federal common law in the context of interstate pollution and greenhouse-gas emissions." *See* 31 F.4th at 204. And from there, they intimate that applying state law in this area would upset our constitutional scheme. Put aside how the federal common law they bring up does not address the type of acts Rhode Island seeks judicial redress for.[8] Even accepting the

[7] Courts use "federal rule of decision" to mean "federal common law," and vice versa. *See BP P.L.C.*, 31 F.4th at 200 n.3.

[8] Rhode Island (to repeat) seeks to hold "[d]efendants" liable for their "tortious conduct" that "deliberately and unnecessarily deceived" consumers about the scientific consensus on climate change and its devastating effects, and about the starring role their products play in causing it (quotes taken from the complaint), *not* to

Energy Companies' description of Rhode Island's claims as being "transboundary pollution" claims (again, just for argument's sake), we know that "[w]hen Congress addresses a question previously governed by a decision rested on federal common law . . . the need for such an unusual exercise of lawmaking by federal courts disappears." *See Am. Elec. Power Co. v. Connecticut*, 564 U.S. 410, 423 (2011) ("*AEP*") (quoting *City of Milwaukee v. Illinois*, 451 U.S. 304, 314 (1981)). The Clean Water Act and the Clean Air Act—neither of which Rhode Island invokes **[—19—]** —"have statutorily displaced any federal common law that previously existed." *See BP P.L.C.*, 31 F.4th at 207. So we cannot rule that any federal common law controls Rhode Island's claims. *See id.* at 199, 205–06 (saying that although the energy companies "characterize [the government's] claims as 'interstate-pollution claims' that arise under federal common law," Congress displaced **{-56-}** the federal common law of interstate pollution, and it would "def[y] logic" to base removal on a "federal common law claim [that] has been deemed displaced, extinguished, and rendered null by the Supreme Court").[9]

Grable

The Energy Companies next argue that "[e]ven if" Rhode Island's claims found their origins in state rather than federal law, "removal still would be proper under *Grable*." *Grable*, as we signaled a few pages back, requires us to ask if Rhode Island's claims fall into the very rare class that (1) necessarily raise a **[—20—]** federal issue that is (2) truly disputed and (3) substantial and that (4) a federal court can decide without upsetting the balance between state and federal judiciaries. *See Gunn v. Minton*, 568 U.S. 251, 258 (2013) (discussing *Grable*). Just like other circuits in comparable cases, *see San Mateo*, 2022 WL 1151275, at *4–6, 10 Adm. R. at 286–87; *BP P.L.C.*, 31 F.4th at 208-15, we answer no.

We begin and end at prong (1), the necessarily-raised prong—which the Energy Companies can satisfy only if a federal issue "is a *necessary* element of one of the well-pleaded state claims" in Rhode Island's complaint. *See Franchise Tax Bd.*, 463 U.S. at 13 (emphasis added); *see also Gunn*, 568 U.S. at 258 (stressing that jurisdiction lies under *Grable* only if "all four" prongs "are met"). The best way to wrap one's mind around this prong is to consider what happened in *Grable*. The IRS seized and sold Grable's real property to satisfy a tax lien. *See* 545 U.S. at 310. Grable challenged the sale via a quiet-title suit in state court, calling the buyer's title invalid because the IRS had not complied with federal notice requirements. *Id.* at 311. The buyer removed the case to federal court. *Id.* The only disputed issue concerned whether Grable got "notice within the meaning of the *federal statute*." *See id.* at 315 (emphasis added). And the Supreme Court held that such a claim "arises under" federal law because (among other things) there was *nothing* in the suit but *federal law*: state law provided the remedy, a declaration of **[—21—]** ownership—but ownership could not be decided without deciding if the federal government respected *federal* legal demands. *See id.* In other words, "[d]eciding an issue of federal law was *inescapable*." *Hartland Lakeside Joint No. 3 Sch. Dist. v. WEA Ins. Corp.*, 756 F.3d 1032, 1035 (7th Cir. 2014) (emphasis added). Importantly too, "the national government itself was vitally concerned about the outcome; an adverse decision could undercut its ability to collect taxes." *See id.*

---

regulate greenhouse-gas emissions (Rhode Island challenges no federal contract, permit, regulation, or treaty, for example).

[9] Interestingly—and we think tellingly—some of the Energy Companies successfully argued in another case that "the Clean Air Act *displaces* any federal common law claims potentially arising from greenhouse[-]gas emissions" (excess capitalization omitted but emphasis added). *See* Answering Brief of ExxonMobil et al. at 61, *Native Village of Kivalina v. ExxonMobil Corp.*, 696 F.3d 849 (9th Cir. 2012) ("*Kivalina*") (No. 09-17490), 2010 WL 3299982, at *61. "Displacement of the federal common law does not leave those injured by air pollution without a remedy," wrote a concurring *Kivalina* panelist, because "[o]nce federal common law is displaced, state nuisance law becomes an available option to the extent it is not preempted by federal law." *See Kivalina*, 696 F.3d at 866 (Pro, D.J., concurring) (citing *AEP*, 564 U.S. at 429).

Nothing at all similar is involved here. True, the Energy Companies say that Rhode Island's claims are "bound up with," "implicate," or "seek[] to replace" various "federal interests"—including energy policy, economic policy, environmental regulation, **{–57–}** national security, and foreign affairs. But faced with comparable arguments, cases akin to this one flatly reject the idea that federal law is an *essential element* to the kind of classic state-law claims Rhode Island raises—claims, as we keep saying, that accuse the Energy Companies of contributing to climate change that (per the complaint) is wreaking havoc on the state's infrastructure and coastal communities. *See San Mateo*, 2022 WL 1151275, at *5, 10 Adm. R. at 286; *BP P.L.C.*, 31 F.4th at 208–15. To paraphrase these courts: none of Rhode Island's claims has as an element a violation of federal law; the Energy Companies pinpoint no specific federal issue that must necessarily be decided for Rhode Island to win its case; and their speaking about federal law **[—22—]** or federal concerns in the most generalized way is not enough for *Grable* purposes. *See San Mateo*, 2022 WL 1151275, at *5, 10 Adm. R. at 286; *BP P.L.C.*, 31 F.4th 208–15. Hence Rhode Island's state-law claims—like those in *San Mateo* and *BP P.L.C.*—are not among the rare few that "can[] be squeezed into the slim category *Grable* exemplifies." *See Empire Healthchoice*, 547 U.S. at 701.

Complete Preemption

As intimated above, Congress can pass a statute so broad that any complaint raising claims in that area is necessarily federal in nature and so is removable to federal court. *See, e.g., Beneficial*, 539 U.S. at 8. "Complete preemption," we must say (echoing a circuit relative of ours) "is 'a doctrine only a judge could love'"—"and one only judges could confusingly name." *See Loffredo v. Daimler AG*, 500 F. App'x 491, 495 (6th Cir. 2012) (quoting *Bartholet v. Reishauer A.G. (Zurich)*, 953 F.2d 1073, 1075 (7th Cir. 1992)). "More productively thought of as a jurisdictional rather than a preemptive rule, complete preemption amounts to an exception to the well-pleaded complaint rule that converts a state-law claim . . . into a federal claim." *Id.*

Invoking this doctrine, the Energy Companies contend that the Clean Air Act completely preempts Rhode Island's claims and thus authorizes removal. So having ruled above "that the federal common law does not completely preempt the state-law claims, we now consider whether the federal act that displaced the **[—23—]** federal common law—the [Clean Air Act]—completely preempts them." *See Suncor*, 25 F.4th at 1263. No circuit to consider the kind of argument the Energy Companies press here has accepted it. *See San Mateo*, 2022 WL 1151275, at *6, 10 Adm. R. at 287–88; *BP P.L.C.*, 31 F.4th at 215–17; *Suncor*, 25 F.4th 1263–65. And we will not be the first.

"[T]he Clean Air Act is not one of the three statutes that the Supreme Court has determined has extraordinary preemptive force."[10] *See San Mateo*, 2022 WL 1151275, at *6, 10 Adm. R. at 288 (quoting *Oakland*, 969 F.3d at 907); *BP P.L.C.*, 31 F.4th at 215; *Suncor*, 25 F.4th at 1257. Also—and as noted previously—complete preemption requires that defendants show Congress *clearly intended* to supersede state authority. *See, e.g., Metro. Life*, 481 U.S. at 65–66. But the Clean Air Act says that "pollution prevention . . . and air pollution control at its source is the primary responsibility of *States and local governments*." *See* 42 U.S.C. § 7401(a)(3) (emphasis added); *see also BP P.L.C.*, 31 F.4th at 215; *Oakland*, 969 F.3d at 908. And the Act has two "savings clauses" that expressly preserve non-Clean Air Act claims. *See BP P.L.C.*, 31 F.4th at 216 (discussing "savings clauses that preserve state and local governments' **{–58–}** legal right to impose standards and limitations on air pollution that are stricter than national **[—24—]** requirements"); *see also Oakland*, 969 F.3d at 907–08 (noting that the Act "preserves state-law causes of action pursuant to a saving clause" that "'makes clear that states retain the right to "adopt or enforce" common law standards that apply to emissions' and preserves '[s]tate common law standards . . . against preemption'" (discussing 42 U.S.C.

[10] Recall our earlier footnoted comments about the National Bank Act, the Employee Retirement Income Security Act, and the Labor Management Relations Act.

§ 7416, and quoting *Merrick v. Diageo Ams. Supply, Inc.*, 805 F.3d 685, 690, 691 (6th Cir. 2015), which cites in turn *W. Va. Univ. Hosp., Inc. v. Casey*, 499 U.S. 83, 98 (1991))). All of which takes complete preemption off the table. *See Suncor*, 25 F.4th at 1263; *accord BP P.L.C.*, 31 F.4th at 215–17; *Oakland*, 969 F.3d at 907–08. If more were needed, another prerequisite of complete preemption—do not forget—is that a statute supplies a federal cause of action to replace the state claim. *See, e.g., Beneficial*, 539 U.S. at 9; *López-Muñoz*, 754 F.3d at 5 (commenting that Supreme Court opinions "finding complete preemption share a common denominator: exclusive federal regulation of the subject matter of the asserted state claim, coupled with a federal cause of action for wrongs of the same type"). Accordingly then, the Clean Air Act's not providing an "exclusive federal cause of action for suits against private polluters" makes complete preemption a nonstarter too. *See Suncor*, 25 F.4th at 1263; *accord BP P.L.C.*, 31 F.4th 215–17; *Oakland*, 969 F.3d at 907–08.[11] **[—25—]**

Federal Enclave

Federal courts have federal-question jurisdiction over tort claims arising on federal enclaves. *See, e.g., BP P.L.C.*, 31 F.4th at 217–18; *Suncor*, 25 F.4th at 1271. Rhode Island's complaint, however, specifically avoids seeking relief for damages to any federal lands in the Ocean State.[12] Faced with this reality, the Energy Companies claim that a big chunk of their "operative activities occurred on federal land"—like at the "Elk Hills Naval Petroleum Reserve" in California. *See generally BP P.L.C.*, 31 F.4th at 217 (stating that "naval installations are generally considered federal enclaves"). The problem for them, though, is that "[t]he doctrine of federal enclave jurisdiction generally requires that *all* pertinent events t[ake] place on a federal enclave." *See Suncor*, 25 F.4th at 1271 (alterations by the *Suncor* Court and quotations omitted). And some of the pertinent events—*e.g.*, the Energy Companies' deceptive marketing and Rhode Island's injuries—occurred outside federal enclaves. *See BP* **[—26—]** *P.L.C.*, 31 F.4th at 217–18 (explaining that "federal-question jurisdiction is not conferred merely because *some* of Defendants' activities occurred on military installations"); *see also San Mateo*, 2022 WL 1151275, at *8, 10 Adm. R. at 289–90 (finding that "[t]he connection between conduct on federal enclaves and the Counties' alleged injuries is too attenuated and remote to establish that the Counties' cause of action is governed by federal law **{-59-}** applicable to any federal enclave"). Enough said about that issue.

OCSLA Jurisdiction

Pointing to their "substantial" activities on the outer continent shelf ("OCS")—they say "the five" biggest "operators" there since the mid-1990s "have included at least three entities among the [Energy Companies] here (or a predecessor) or one of their subsidiaries"—the Energy Companies also maintain that federal jurisdiction exists under OCSLA.[13] That statute extends such jurisdiction to "cases and controversies arising out of, or *in connection with*[,] . . . any operation conducted on the [OCS] which involves exploration, development, or production of . . . minerals." 43 U.S.C. § 1349(b)(1) (emphasis added). The italicized phrase—"in connection with"—bears directly on this case. Our circuit (as the parties seem to agree) has not yet **[—27—]** addressed that phrase's meaning.

---

[11] The Energy Companies make much of a Clean Air Act provision that lets states initiate federal-court challenges to actions by **[—25—]** the Environmental Protection Agency regarding nationwide emissions. But that section has nothing to do with Rhode Island's claims here, which (once again) concern the Energy Companies' deceptive promotion of damaging fossil-fuel products. *See BP P.L.C.*, 31 F.4th at 215–17 (rejecting a similar complete-preemption argument); *Suncor*, 25 F.4th at 1264–65 (ditto); *Oakland*, 969 F.3d at 908 (ditto again).

[12] "Ocean State" is a nickname of Rhode Island. "Little Rhody" is another. *See* "List of U.S. state and territory nicknames," Wikipedia, https://en.wikipedia.org/wiki/List_of_U.S._state_and_territory_nicknames.

[13] The OCS includes the seabed and natural resources lying "3 miles to 200 miles off the United States coast." *See Ctr. For Biological Diversity v. U.S. Dep't of Interior*, 563 F.3d 466, 472, (D.C. Cir. 2009); *see also* 43 U.S.C. §§ 1301(a), 1331(a).

Which explains why the Energy Companies rely big time on cases from the Fifth Circuit that have.[14]

OCSLA jurisdiction exists, says the Fifth Circuit, if "(1) the activities that caused the injury constituted an 'operation' 'conducted on the [OCS]' that involved the exploration and production of minerals, and (2) the case 'arises out of, or in connection with' the operation," *In re Deepwater Horizon*, 745 F.3d 157, 163, 2 Adm. R. 171, 172–73 (5th Cir. 2014) ("*Deepwater*") (quoting OCSLA)—a "jurisdictional test" intended "to cover a '"wide range of activity occurring beyond the territorial waters of the states,"'" *Suncor*, 25 F.4th at 1272 (quoting *Barker v. Hercules Offshore, Inc.*, 713 F.3d 208, 213, 1 Adm. R. 206, 207 (5th Cir. 2013), in turn quoting *Texaco Expl. & Prod., Inc. v. AmClyde Engineered Prods. Co.*, 448 F.3d 760, 768 (5th Cir. 2006), *amended on reh'g*, 453 F.3d 652 (5th Cir. 2006)); *accord BP P.L.C.*, 31 F.4th at 219–20. Though the Energy Companies argue otherwise, the test's "second prong"—the only prong in dispute—might require "'a but-for connection.'" *See Suncor*, 25 F.4th at 1272 (quoting *Deepwater*, 745 F.3d at 163, 2 Adm. R. at 173); *accord BP P.L.C.*, 31 F.4th at 220 ("declin[ing] to disrupt th[e] settled and sensible trend" of cases holding that "'arise out of, or in connection with' under the OCSLA . . . imposes a but-for relationship between a party's case and operations on the OCS"). **[—28—]** *Cf. generally Maracich v. Spears*, 570 U.S. 48, 60 (2013) (noting that "[t]he phrase 'in connection with' provides little guidance without a limiting principle").[15] We say "might" because the Ninth Circuit holds "that the language of § 1349(b), 'aris[e] out of, or in connection with,' does not *necessarily* require but-for causation." *See San Mateo*, 2022 WL 1151275, at *10, 10 Adm. R. at 292 (emphasis added). But we need not wrestle the but-for-causation issue to the ground today. And that is because "[d]espite [the] different **{–60–}** approach[es] to construing § 1349(b), our sister circuits' application of § 1349(b) leads to a materially similar result," *see id.*, 10 Adm. R. at 292—as we now explain.

Cases finding OCSLA jurisdiction involve "either . . . a direct physical connection to an OCS operation (collision, death, personal injury, loss of wildlife, toxic exposure) or a contract or property dispute directly related to [that] operation." *See id.*, 10 Adm. R. at 292 (quoting *Suncor*, 25 F.4th at 1273 (stockpiling cases)). The "core" of Rhode Island's suit concerns how the Energy Companies "knew what fossil fuels were doing to the environment and continued **[—29—]** to sell them anyway, all while misleading consumers about the true impact of the products." *See Shell Oil*, 979 F.3d at 54. The Energy Companies talk up how "extensive [their] OCS operations" are. That may be. But Rhode Island's claims concern their "overall conduct, not whatever unknown fraction of their fossil fuels was produced on the OCS." *See Bd. of Cty. Comm'rs of Boulder Cty. v. Suncor Energy (U.S.A.) Inc.*, 405 F. Supp. 3d 947, 979 (D. Colo. 2019).[16] And just because the Energy Companies have "extensive OCS operations" does not mean that Rhode Island's claims satisfy OCSLA's in-connection-with benchmark. If it did then *any* suit against fossil-fuel companies regarding *any* adverse impact linked to their products would trigger OCSLA federal jurisdiction because (to quote Rhode Island's latest brief) "a significant portion" of the oil and gas we use comes from the OCS—a consequence too absurd to be attributed to Congress. *See generally Sheridan v. United States*, 487 U.S. 392, 402 n.7 (1988) (explaining that "courts should strive to avoid attributing absurd designs to Congress").

---

[14] The Fifth Circuit is quite familiar with OCSLA, apparently.

[15] Arguing against the but-for standard, the Energy Companies hype *Ford Motor Co. v. Montana Eighth Judicial District Court*, 141 S. Ct. 1017 (2021). *Ford Motor Co.* held that the "requirement of a 'connection' between a plaintiff's suit and a defendant's activities" for a court to exercise personal jurisdiction is not the same as but-for causation. *See id.* at 1026. Like the Ninth Circuit, however, "we are skeptical that *Ford Motor Co.*'s interpretation of judicial rules delineating the scope of a court's specific personal jurisdiction is pertinent in this different statutory context." *See San Mateo*, 2022 WL 1151275, at *10, 10 Adm. R. at 292.

[16] That is the decision the Tenth Circuit affirmed in *Suncor*.

Anyhow, Rhode Island's allegations "do not refer to actions taken on the [OCS]." *See San Mateo*, 2022 WL 1151275, at *11, 10 Adm. R. at 293. Ergo, the Energy Companies have not shown that Rhode Island's "tort claims 'aris[e] out of'" or are "'in connection with' [their] **[—30—]** operations on the [OCS] for purposes of" OCSLA jurisdiction. *See id.*, 10 Adm. R. at 293.

Pulling out all the stops, the Energy Companies write that "OCSLA jurisdiction is also proper for the additional and independent reason that the relief [Rhode Island] seeks would" present an obstacle to "the efficient exploitation of the minerals from the OCS"—thus jeopardizing "the continued scope and viability of [their] OCS operations and the federal OCS leasing program as a whole." Their theory is that a large monetary judgment against them "would inevitably deter" OCS operations. But like the Tenth Circuit, we fail "to see how such a prospective theory of negative economic incentives—flowing from a lawsuit that does not directly attack OCS exploration, resource development, or leases—is anything other than contingent and speculative." *See Suncor*, 25 F.4th at 1275. And "contingent and speculative" do not suffice for OCSLA jurisdiction purposes. *See id.*; *accord BP P.L.C.*, 31 F.4th at 222.

Admiralty Jurisdiction

The Energy Companies also think they can get the case into federal court under admiralty jurisdiction because (to quote their brief) "fossil-fuel extraction occurs on vessels engaged in maritime commerce." We think not, however.

The Constitution extends federal jurisdiction to "admiralty and maritime" cases. *See* U.S. Const., art. III, § 2, **[—31—]** cl. 1. And Congress grants federal courts jurisdiction over "[a]ny civil case of admiralty or maritime jurisdiction, saving to suitors in all cases all other remedies to which they are **{-61-}** otherwise entitled." *See* 28 U.S.C. § 1333(1).[17] While "not entirely clear," it seems the drafters of the saving-to-suitors clause intended to "preserve[] remedies and the concurrent jurisdiction of state courts over some admiralty and maritime claims." *See Lewis v. Lewis & Clark Marine, Inc.*, 531 U.S. 438, 444, 445 (2001).[18]

The district judge in our case relied on a line of decisions indicating that admiralty issues—without more—cannot make a case removable from state to federal court. The Energy Companies call this reversible error, writing that a recent amendment to section 1441 (the general-removal statute) jettisoned jargon that these courts had used "to block the removal of admiralty claims absent another basis for federal jurisdiction." "[C]ourts," however, "split on whether the working of the amended statute changes the rule for removal of maritime claims." *BP P.L.C.*, 31 F.4th at 226 (quoting Thomas J. Schoenbaum, *Admiralty* **[—32—]** *and Maritime Law* § 4.3, Westlaw (database updated Dec. 2021)). We need not choose sides, because even if saving-to-suitors actions are freely removable under section 1441 (and we are not saying either way), the Energy Companies still face an insurmountable obstacle.

A tort claim comes within our admiralty jurisdiction if the party invoking that jurisdiction "satisf[ies] conditions both of location and of connection with maritime activity." *See Jerome B. Grubart, Inc. v. Great Lakes Dredge & Dock Co.*, 513 U.S. 527, 534 (1995). The test is intricate. But we can make short work of the Energy Companies' effort by focusing on one facet. When, as here, the "injury suffered" is on "land," the jurisdiction-invoking party must show that "a vessel on navigable water" caused the tort. *See id.* So even if the Energy Companies could show that fossil-fuel extraction occurs on "vessels," that

[17] "Suitors" in this context is just another word for "plaintiffs." *See* 14A *Federal Practice & Procedure Jurisdiction* § 3672.

[18] Courts often use "admiralty" and "maritime" synonymously. *See Adamson v. Port of Bellingham*, 907 F.3d 1122, 1125 n.4, 6 Adm. R. 360, 361 n.4 (9th Cir. 2018). *See generally Sisson v. Ruby*, 497 U.S. 358, 362 (1990) (using "admiralty jurisdiction" and "maritime jurisdiction" interchangeably).

gets them nowhere.[19] We say that because Rhode Island does not allege any vessel caused the land-based injuries (the complaint alleges their dangerous products and misleading promotion caused Rhode Island's injuries, not a vessel)—a point made in Rhode Island's brief, without contradiction from the Energy Companies in their reply **[—33—]** brief. And that means no admiralty jurisdiction exists in this case. *See BP P.L.C.*, 31 F.4th at 227.

Bankruptcy Jurisdiction

As we noted a little while ago, a party in a civil suit may remove claims "related to" bankruptcy cases. *See* 28 U.S.C. §§ 1452(a), 1334(b). Seizing on this, the Energy Companies tell us that Rhode Island's complaint is "related to" bankruptcy cases because it "seeks to hold [them] liable for the pre-bankruptcy operations of Texaco Inc. (a subsidiary of Chevron) and Getty Petroleum." "Texaco's confirmed bankruptcy plan," the Energy Companies say, "bars various claims arising against it" before "March 15, 1988." And, they add, Rhode Island's "allegations against Texaco include conduct" before that date. Quoting a Fourth Circuit opinion— **{–62–}** *Valley Historic Ltd. Partnership v. Bank of New York*, 486 F.3d 831, 836–37 (4th Cir. 2007)—they then write that deciding Rhode Island's "claims would 'affect the interpretation, implementation, consummation, execution, or administration of [Texaco's] confirmed plan.'"[20]

But taking another page from the Fourth Circuit's *BP P.L.C.* opinion—which considered and rejected a strikingly similar argument—we rule not only that "there is no indication that the bankruptcy plan involved climate change" but also that the Energy **[—34—]** Companies offer no convincing explanation for "how a judgment more than thirty years later could impact Texaco's estate." *See* 31 F.4th at 223. And even if they think their appellate papers give the needed indication and explanation, we would consider the argument "too skeletal or confusingly constructed and thus waived." *See Págan-Lisboa v. Soc. Sec. Admin.*, 996 F.3d 1, 7 (1st Cir. 2021) (quotation marks omitted). The Energy Companies also vaguely suggest (emphasis ours) that Rhode Island's "theories of liability" are based on the actions of their "predecessors, subsidiaries, and affiliates" and so "affect *additional* bankruptcy matters." But that perfunctory comment is insufficient to preserve the issue for appeal. *See, e.g.*, *Rodríguez*, 659 F.3d at 175–76. The bottom line is that "we find no federal jurisdiction under the bankruptcy[-]removal statute." *See BP P.L.C.*, 31 F.4th at 225.

Final Words

We *affirm* the district judge's order remanding the case to Rhode Island state court. Costs to Rhode Island.

---

[19] Rhode Island apparently disagrees with the Energy Companies' claim that "a floating oil rig," for example, is a vessel used for navigation. Given our "even if" approach, we have no need to wade into that debate.

[20] The internal quotations are from the Fourth Circuit case.

United States Court of Appeals
for the First Circuit

No. 20-2073

AADLAND
VS.
BOAT SANTA RITA II, INC.

Appeal from the United States District Court for the District of Massachusetts

Decided: July 28, 2022

Citation: 42 F.4th 34, 10 Adm. R. 21 (1st Cir. 2022).

Before **BARRON,** Chief Judge, **THOMPSON** and **HAWKINS,*** Circuit Judges.

* Of the Ninth Circuit, sitting by designation.

[—3—] {-37-} BARRON, Chief Judge:

This appeal concerns a suit that Magnus Aadland brought in the United States District Court for the District of Massachusetts against the owners of a fishing vessel on which he was a seaman. He alleges that the owners breached a federal common law obligation under admiralty law that is known as the duty of cure. He contends that they did so by failing to pay him adequately for the costs of the medical care that he received after he fell ill from an infection that he acquired while working aboard their vessel. He further alleges that, even if the defendants did satisfy their duty of cure through various payments that they made to him and his private health insurer, they so delayed in doing so that he is entitled to compensatory damages for emotional distress, punitive damages, and attorney's fees. The District Court granted judgment to the defendants after a bench trial.

We vacate the grant of judgment with respect to Aadland's claim that the defendants' breached their duty of cure and remand for further proceedings consistent with this decision. Our ruling on that score also leads us to vacate the District Court's grant of judgment to the defendants with respect to Aadland's claims for compensatory damages for emotional distress, punitive damages, and attorney's fees for the defendants' alleged delay in fulfilling the duty of cure. Finally, we reverse the District Court's ruling that Aadland had **{-38-}** reached what is known as the "point of maximum **[—4—]** medical recovery," which is a bar to any claim for cure based on the costs of recovery past that point in time.

I.

The following facts are not contested on appeal. On July 9, 2014, the F/V Linda, owned by Boat Santa Rita II ("BSR II"), Boat Santa Rita III, Frank Patania, and Salvatore Patania, left New Bedford, Massachusetts on a commercial scalloping trip. Aadland was the vessel's captain.

A few days into the trip, while at sea, Aadland fell ill. His condition continued to worsen, and the F/V Linda reversed course and traveled back to Massachusetts. Upon arrival in New Bedford on July 18, 2014, Aadland was transported to a hospital. He was diagnosed with a group G Streptococcus infection.

Aadland spent the next six months at various inpatient facilities, receiving medical treatment at them from July 18, 2014, to December 29, 2014. He was then discharged and received outpatient treatment until July 9, 2015, when he was again admitted to the hospital due to health complications that stemmed from the infection. Aadland was released from this second period of hospitalization on September 10, 2015. He thereafter received outpatient treatment for symptoms attributable to the infection.

It is a general principle of admiralty law that if "a seaman falls sick[] or is wounded[] in the service of the ship," "the vessel and her owners are liable . . . to the extent of [the **[—5—]** seaman's] maintenance and cure." *Atl. Sounding Co. v. Townsend*, 557 U.S. 404, 413 (2009) (quoting *The Osceola*, 189 U.S. 158, 175 (1903)). The duty of maintenance and cure is often referred to as a single duty, but there are two distinct aspects of it—"maintenance" and "cure."

"Maintenance" refers to "the provision of, or payment for, food and lodging." *LeBlanc v.*

B.G.T. Corp., 992 F.2d 394, 397 (1st Cir. 1993). "Cure," by contrast, refers to "necessary health-care expenses . . . incurred during the period of [the seaman's] recovery from an injury or malady." *Id.*

The duty of maintenance and cure can be traced back centuries to legal codes of several seafaring nations. *See Vaughan v. Atkinson*, 369 U.S. 527, 532 n.4 (1962); *see also* 1B Erastus Cornelius Benedict, *Benedict on Admiralty* § 42 (2022) (explaining that a shipowner's duty to provide maintenance and cure can be found in the Laws of Oleron, which date to approximately the year 1200); 2 Robert Force & Martin J. Norris, *The Law of Seamen* § 26:6 (5th ed. 2021) (same). The Supreme Court of the United States first formally recognized the duty of maintenance and cure, however, in *The Osceola*, 189 U.S. 158, 172 (1903).

In doing so, the Court echoed Justice Story's oft-quoted passage in *Harden v. Gordon*, 11 F. Cas. 480 (C.C.D. Me. 1823). There, he explained that **[—6—]**

> [s]eamen are by the peculiarity of their lives liable to sudden sickness from change of climate, exposure to perils, and exhausting labour. They are generally poor and friendless . . . . If some provision be not made for them in sickness at the expense of the ship, they must often in foreign ports suffer the accumulated evils of disease, and poverty, and sometimes perish from the want of suitable nourishment. Their common earnings in many instances are wholly inadequate to provide for the expenses of sickness. **{-39-}**

Id. at 483. Justice Story reasoned there that if the "expenses of his [on-ship] sickness [or injury] are a charge upon the ship, the interest of the owner will be immediately connected with that of the seamen" and "[t]he master will watch over their health with vigilance and fidelity[,] . . . tak[ing] the best methods . . . to prevent diseases, [and] to ensure a speedy recovery from them." *Id.*

The parties agree that from December 30, 2014 to October 16, 2020, Aadland was paid maintenance of $84 per day by BSR II,[1] which amounted to $175,664 in total. There is no dispute before us regarding whether the defendants satisfied their duty of "maintenance."

The picture is more complicated with respect to whether the defendants satisfied their duty of "cure." That is in part **[—7—]** because, for a portion of the period that followed Aadland's on-ship infection, he used private health insurance that he had through his wife's employer to pay for the costs of the healthcare that he received related to that infection. It was not entirely clear at the time that the Tufts health insurance plan furnished by his wife's employer covered the costs of treating his on-ship illness, because it was a work-related illness.[2]

In addition, after Aadland's wife lost her job, Aadland personally enrolled in the Tufts COBRA plan, at a cost of approximately $2,000 per month.[3] For most of the period in which Aadland was enrolled in the Tufts COBRA plan, BSR II paid Aadland an "advance" of $114 per day. Aadland began receiving advance payments six months after he fell ill on the ship.[4]

BSR II referred to the payments when made as "advance" payments. BSR II also made these payments with the disclaimer that

[1] Aadland received the first payment from BSR II on February 5, 2015, containing the amount owed by BSR II to Aadland from December 30, 2014 until February 5, 2015.

[2] Aadland's health insurance policy contained a disclaimer that his insurer "will not provide coverage for any injury or illness for which it determines that benefits are available under any workers' compensation coverage or equivalent employer liability."

[3] Since April 2017, Medicare has been Aadland's primary insurer, but Aadland has also purchased a supplemental healthcare plan. Aadland testified that he enrolled in the Tufts COBRA plan in October 2014.

[4] As already discussed, Aadland received the first payment from BSR II in February 2015, which included payments for December 2014-February 2015.

"the amount of any settlement, judgment or award" "resulting [—8—] from [a] claim for personal injuries or illness occurring [in July 2014] while aboard the F/V Linda" "will be reduced by the amount of the advance."

Aadland received a total of $238,374 in advance payments. He used a portion of those payments to pay the premiums for his Tufts COBRA plan, which he in turn relied on to pay for the costs of the treatment that he received for his on-ship illness during this period. There is no indication in the record that Aadland has reimbursed the defendants for any of the funds that he received as "advance payments."

In addition, BSR II reimbursed Aadland for his out-of-pocket medical expenses owing to his on-ship illness. These included expenses such as those he incurred from the co-payments he was required to make under his insurance plan.

Finally, after the commencement of this suit, BSR II paid Aadland's health insurer, Tufts, $400,000 "in full satisfaction of any lien or claim [the insurer, Tufts,] might have against [the] Aadland[s] . . . for coverage **{-40-}** of Aadland's medical expenses." BSR II made this payment on the eve of trial.

Aadland filed his lawsuit against the F/V Linda, BSR II, BSR III, and their owners on July 7, 2017. Aadland's operative complaint alleges that the defendants breached their duty of cure, which he contends his on-ship illness triggered. His complaint claims that he is entitled to damages in the amount of the total **[—9—]** cost of the healthcare that he received to treat his July 2014 infection, as well as compensation for pain and suffering that resulted from the defendants' delay in providing him with the payments for cure that he contends that he is owed. *See Hines v. J.A. LAPorte, Inc.*, 820 F.2d 1187, 1190 (11th Cir. 1987) (affirming an award of compensatory damages for "prolonged . . . pain and suffering" that resulted from the defendant's failure in that case to timely provide maintenance and cure); *Stevens v. Seacoast Co.*, 414 F.2d 1032, 1040 (5th Cir. 1969) (noting that if the delay in providing adequate maintenance and cure "contributed in any degree to additional pain or disability or prolonged the recovery period," "resulting damages [from that delay] are due"). Aadland's complaint further alleges that the defendants' failure to provide him with adequate cure payments was willful and thus that he is entitled to punitive damages, attorney's fees, and costs. *See Atl. Sounding Co.*, 557 U.S. at 407-08 (holding that punitive damages can be awarded if a shipowner's failure to timely pay maintenance and cure was "willful"); *Vaughan v. Atkinson*, 369 U.S. 527, 530-31 (1962) (holding that attorney's fees can be awarded if a seaman proves that a shipowner failed to timely provide maintenance and cure); *Robinson v. Pocahontas, Inc.*, 477 F.2d 1048, 1051 (1st Cir. 1973) (explaining that where a shipowner was "callous, willful, or recalcitrant in withholding [maintenance or **[—10—]** cure] payments," the seaman may recover punitive damages as well as attorney's fees).

The defendants filed their answer to Aadland's complaint on September 11, 2017. They moved thereafter for summary judgment on the issue of whether they "willfully" failed to provide adequate maintenance and cure. They did not, at that time, move for summary judgment on the underlying issue of whether they had fulfilled whatever duty of maintenance and cure they had to Aadland in consequence of his on-ship illness.

The District Court denied the defendants' summary judgment motion on November 25, 2019. The case then proceeded to a three-day bench trial.

At the bench trial, the District Court heard testimony from Aadland, his wife, and Frank Patania, one of the owners of the vessel on which Aadland worked when he fell ill. Evidence admitted into the record included Aadland's medical bills, payments from BSR II to Aadland, communications between Aadland's wife and Frank Patania, and communications between Frank Patania and BSR II's insurance broker regarding Aadland's illness.

The District Court entered judgment on October 16, 2020, in favor of the defendants under Federal Rule of Civil Procedure 58. After finding the facts described above, *see Aadland v. Boat Santa Rita II, Inc.*, No. 17-cv-11248, 2020 WL 6119926, at **[—11—]** *1-3 (D. Mass. Oct. 16, 2020), the District Court issued its legal conclusions.

The District Court first addressed whether the defendants had any ongoing duty of cure or whether they did not because Aadland had reached what is known as the point of maximum medical recovery. That is the point at which the seaman who has suffered an on-ship illness or injury "is **{-41-}** 'so far cured as possible,'" *Whitman v. Miles*, 387 F.3d 68, 72 (1st Cir. 2004) (quoting *Farrell v. United States*, 336 U.S. 511, 518 (1949)), such that the shipowner no longer has a duty of cure to satisfy. The District Court found that "[t]here [was] no evidence that Aadland ha[d] not reached maximum medical recovery," given that Aadland had testified that "he only saw his cardiologist, infectious disease doctor and primary care physician every six months for checkups and . . . was discharged from occupational therapy to begin a home exercise program." *Aadland*, 2020 WL 6119926, at *3. The District Court concluded on that basis that the defendants could "terminate maintenance and cure" to Aadland on a going-forward basis (assuming, that is, that it had satisfied its duty up until that point). *Id.* (quoting *Saco v. Tug Tucana Corp.*, 483 F. Supp. 2d 88, 99 (D. Mass. 2007)).

The District Court next addressed whether the defendants had satisfied their duty of cure up until the point at which **[—12—]** Aadland had reached maximum medical recovery. It ruled that the defendants had. *Id.* at *3-4.

Finally, the District Court concluded that Aadland's claim seeking damages for emotional distress, punitive damages, and attorney's fees could not succeed because Aadland could not establish that the defendants willfully withheld maintenance and cure payments that he was due. *Id.* Thus, the District Court granted judgment to the defendants on these claims as well.

Aadland thereafter timely appealed.

II.

"When a district court conducts a bench trial, its legal determinations engender de novo review," as do its "determinations about the sufficiency of the evidence." *United States v. 15 Bosworth Street*, 236 F.3d 50, 53 (1st Cir. 2001). Its factual findings are reviewed for clear error. *See id.*; *see also* Fed. R. Civ. P. 52(a)(6).

A district court's resolution of mixed questions of law and fact is typically treated with deference. But, if the district court "'premise[s] its ultimate finding . . . on an erroneous interpretation of the standard to be applied,' . . . we treat the trial court's conclusion as a question of law," entitled to no deference. *Vinick v. United States*, 205 F.3d 1, 7 (1st Cir. 2000) (alteration in original) (quoting *United States v. Parke, Davis & Co.*, 362 U.S. 29, 44 (1960)). **[—13—]**

III.

We start with Aadland's challenge to the District Court's grant of judgment to the defendants on his claim that they breached their duty of cure to him. A premise of this challenge is that he is entitled to a cure award that is equal to the cost of the reasonably necessary medical care that he received to treat his on-ship illness, even if he did not personally pay that full cost in receiving that care because he relied on private insurance to pay it. An additional premise of this challenge is that the cost of this care in his case is properly measured by the "sticker price" of $1.2 million that his healthcare providers charged for that care and not some lesser amount, such as the amount that his healthcare providers accepted as payment from his insurer for the care that they provided to him in treating his on-ship illness.

Based on these twin premises, Aadland contends that the District Court erred in granting judgment to the defendants on the breach-of-the-duty-of-cure claim because the defendants did not, and still have not, paid him that $1.2 million amount that he contends that they owe him as cure. And that is so, he contends, notwithstanding **{-42-}** that he acknowledges in pressing this challenge that the defendants have made some payments directly to him and one payment (of $400,000) directly to his insurer in return for its release of his liability to the insurer. **[—14—]**

Of course, as Aadland acknowledges, he did not actually pay $1.2 million for the care that he received to treat his on-ship illness. He instead paid for that care, as we have seen, chiefly through a private insurer, though he did also incur some out-of-pocket expenses in the form of co-pays and the like. He thus does not dispute that he was out-of-pocket for the care only for the amount of the premiums that he had to pay for the insurance and for the costs of the co-payments and the like, and that this amount is far less than the amount of cure that he seeks.

Nor does Aadland dispute that his healthcare providers did not themselves receive $1.2 million for the care that they provided to him. Instead, he concedes that they received as payment for that care only roughly $600,000, which was paid to them by Tufts pursuant to both the Tufts plan that his wife had through her employer and through the Tufts COBRA plan.

Nonetheless, Aadland contends that, based on the logic of a Fifth Circuit ruling whose reasoning he asks us to adopt, *Gauthier v. Crosby Marine Service, Inc.*, 752 F.2d 1085 (5th Cir. 1985), the defendants are still obliged to pay him the $1.2 million pursuant to their duty of cure. For, he contends, that case rightly holds that when "a seaman alone purchase[s] medical insurance," *id.* at 1090, and relies on it to pay the costs of the care that he receives to treat an on-ship illness or injury, then the proper measure of the shipowner's cure obligation is the cost **[—15—]** of that care and not either the out-of-pocket cost to the seaman of receiving it or the amount that the healthcare providers accepted for such care from the insurer.

Moreover, Aadland contends that *Gauthier* also was right in holding one more thing—that, in a circumstance in which the seaman relied on health insurance that he alone purchased to cover the costs of the care that he received for his on-ship illness or injury, the shipowner is not entitled to set off the amount that the healthcare providers received from the seaman's health insurer as payment for that care from the shipowner's obligation to pay cure in the amount of the costs of that care. *Id.* Thus, he contends, based on *Gauthier*, the defendants here may not set off from what he contends is their $1.2 million cure obligation the roughly $600,000 that Aadland's healthcare providers received from the insurer to pay for the treatment of Aadland's on-ship illness.

For these reasons, Aadland contends that the District Court's grant of judgment to the defendants cannot stand because the District Court declined to apply *Gauthier* to his case, based on reasons for doing so that he contends are not sound. For, by failing to apply *Gauthier* here, he contends, the District Court erroneously concluded both that the defendants are entitled to set off from their cure obligation the roughly $600,000 that his healthcare providers received from the insurer and that, given the set-off and the payments made to Aadland by the defendants, Aadland **[—16—]** had incurred no expense for the care that he received for his on-ship illness, he was not entitled to any additional payment as cure. He further contends that there is no alternative ground manifest in the record on which we can affirm the District Court's ruling granting judgment to the defendants on his claim that they are in breach of their duty of cure. And that is so, he contends, even if we were to agree with him that the District Court's reasoning in **{-43-}** so granting judgment on that claim was flawed.

We approach this case, as the parties do and as the District Court did, on the assumption that *Gauthier* guides our analysis—but without barring attention to that issue in the future. As we will explain, we conclude that there is merit to Aadland's challenge to the District Court's ruling granting judgment to the defendants on his breach-of-the-duty-of-cure claim. Moreover, as we will also explain, we agree with Aadland that we cannot affirm the District Court's grant of judgment to the defendants on that claim on an alternative ground, at least given the arguments that the defendants have made to us. Finally, because of these conclusions, we will also address the question of what the proper measure of cure is in this case insofar as there is no basis for applying *Gauthier* here, so that the District Court on remand may determine based on that amount the extent to which all, or any, of the defendants' cure obligation has been satisfied. **[—17—]**

A.

We start with the issue that the District Court found to be dispositive, which concerns the applicability of *Gauthier* to this case. Given that the District Court declined to apply *Gauthier* here because it determined that *Gauthier* was factually distinguishable rather than wrongly decided, a brief review of the facts of that case is in order.

The shipowners in *Gauthier* had initially paid maintenance and cure to the seaman after the seaman had suffered injuries while aboard their vessels. *See Gauthier v. Crosby Marine Serv., Inc.*, 499 F. Supp. 295, 298 (E.D. La. 1980), *on reconsideration*, 536 F. Supp. 269 (E.D. La. 1982). The shipowners had then stopped doing so after the seaman's condition had worsened. *Id.* They stopped doing so, moreover, despite the seaman's affirmative request for continued cure. *Id.*

The seaman in that case, after having had his request for cure rebuffed, turned to his private insurer to pay for the costs of his medical care pursuant to a policy that he had alone purchased with no help from either shipowner. After having used that insurance to pay for his treatment of his on-ship-injuries, he then sued the shipowners who had denied him further cure payment. *Id.*

The shipowners defended against the suit in part by arguing that they were entitled to set off from their cure **[—18—]** obligation the payments that the seaman's insurer had made for the seaman's healthcare attributable to his on-ship injuries. *See Gauthier*, 752 F.2d at 1090. Moreover, the shipowners argued on that basis that they did not owe the seaman the cure that he sought because the costs of the seaman's medical care for his injuries that had been paid for by the insurer was not an "expense" that the seaman had incurred. *Id.*

Gauthier rejected the shipowners' contention. It held instead that the seaman "had incurred expenses" because he alone had paid the premiums that secured the private health insurance that he had used to pay for the healthcare that he had received to treat his on-ship injuries. It further held that "where a seaman has alone purchased medical insurance, the shipowner is not entitled to a set-off from the maintenance and cure obligation moneys the seaman receives from his insurer." *Id.* The court reasoned that "the policy of protecting injured or ill seamen" at the root of maintenance and cure "would be hampered if a shipowner, in hopes of reducing his liability, delayed maintenance and cure payments to force seamen to look first to their private insurer." *Id.* **{-44-}**

In granting judgment to the defendants on Aadland's breach-of-the-duty-of-cure claim, the District Court did not purport to take issue with *Gauthier*'s holding that the shipowners in that case were not entitled to the set-off. Instead, it ruled **[—19—]** that *Gauthier* was distinguishable as a factual matter from Aadland's case and that, in consequence, its no-set-off rule did not apply here. *Aadland*, 2020 WL 6119926, at *4.

The District Court first noted that Aadland, unlike the seamen in the cases on which *Gauthier* relied, had not requested cure from the defendants. It also noted, relatedly, that, as a result, the defendants were "not aware of Aadland suffering any dire financial straits" due to his medical expenses and had not refused any request from Aadland for cure. *Id.* The District Court then explained that while the seaman in *Gauthier* had incurred expenses personally in the form of the payments that he made to cover the costs of the premiums for the insurance he relied on to pay for his care, "Aadland ha[d] not incurred any medical expenses himself and even his health insurance premiums, which were part of the basis of the calculation of the advances he has received from BSR II, have been covered." *Id.* Nor, the District Court noted, are there "outstanding medical expenses or reimbursements for Aadland's medical care that Aadland is obligated to pay." *Id.*

The District Court explained that "*under these circumstances*," *Aadland*, 2020 WL 6119926, at *4 (emphasis added), *Gauthier*'s rule that where a "seaman alone purchase[s] medical insurance," the shipowner cannot reduce its cure obligation by the amount of money the seaman receives from his insurer, *Gauthier*, 752 F.2d at 1090, does not apply. And, after accounting for the **[—20—]** set-off of the roughly $600,000 that Aadland's medical providers accepted as payment for their treatment of his on-ship illness, the District Court then granted summary judgment to the defendants on Aadland's breach-of-the-duty-of-cure claim on the ground that Aadland had incurred no expenses for his treatment, at least given the payments that had been made directly to him by the defendants.

As this recitation of the decision below shows, the District Court's ruling that *Gauthier* could be distinguished from Aadland's case rested, at least in part, on the ground that Aadland failed to request cure as the seaman in that case had. But, the District Court did not hold that a seaman must request cure to be entitled to it. Moreover, the defendants concede on appeal that a shipowner's duty to provide maintenance and cure to a seaman who falls ill or is injured at sea includes the duty to inform the seaman that the shipowner has that duty, and they do not dispute Aadland's contention that they did not inform him of their obligation in that regard.

Thus, we do not see how the fact that Aadland failed to request cure from the defendants provides a basis for concluding that *Gauthier*'s no-set-off rule is inapplicable here, insofar as that no-set-off rule is otherwise applicable. For, if Aadland had no duty to request cure and was not informed by the defendants of their duty to provide cure to him, then his failure to have requested cure could not relieve the defendants of whatever cure **[—21—]** obligation to him that they otherwise would have had. The question thus would remain under *Gauthier*—absent some other reasons for deeming it to be inapplicable—as to whether the defendants were entitled to reduce their cure obligation by setting off the payment that the insurer made to Aadland's healthcare providers to treat his on-ship illness.

But, as we have noted, the District Court did not suggest that *Gauthier* erred **{–45–}** in holding that defendants are not entitled to set off such payments when the seaman alone purchased the health insurance on which he relied to cover the costs of his care. Nor did the District Court find that Aadland did not alone purchase the health insurance on which he relied to obtain his care for his on-ship illness. Nor, finally, did the District Court hold that any of the other unique features of Aadland's case on their own, and without the added feature of his not having requested cure, suffice to render *Gauthier* inapplicable. Thus, the District Court appears to have held that the defendants were entitled to the set-off without finding that Aadland did not alone purchase the insurance that he used to pay for his medical care, and the District Court did so based, at least in part, on a reason that (insofar as *Gauthier*'s rule itself goes unchallenged) does not justify that conclusion—namely, that Aadland did not request cure at any point. **[—22—]**

Accordingly, because the District Court did not hold that the defendants would be entitled to judgment on Aadland's breach-of-the-duty-of-cure claim even if they were not entitled to the set-off, we cannot affirm that ruling. Instead, we must vacate it, because it rests on an impermissible ground for distinguishing *Gauthier* and does not otherwise explain why *Gauthier* does not apply.

B.

The defendants contend, however, that even if the District Court's reasons for distinguishing *Gauthier* do not hold up, there is an alternative ground for affirming the District Court's ruling granting judgment to them on Aadland's breach-of-the-duty-of-cure claim. And that is so, they contend, because the record incontrovertibly shows that Aadland, unlike the seaman in *Gauthier* itself, did not "alone purchase[] [his] medical insurance," *Gauthier*, 752 F.2d at 1090, and so incurred no "expense" for his care (at least given what the record shows regarding the other payments that the defendants made either directly to him or to his insurer). Thus, they argue, even under *Gauthier* itself, Aadland is wrong to contend that the District Court erred in ruling that the defendants were entitled to the set-off and that he has incurred no expenses for the care that he received, at least given the payments that have been made directly to him by the defendants. But, although we may affirm the District **[—23—]** Court on any ground manifest in the record, *see Ungar v. Arafat*, 634 F.3d 46, 51 n.4 (1st Cir. 2011), we cannot do so here for the reasons that we will next explain.

To be sure, the record does show—without dispute—that, just as the District Court found, the premiums for the insurance that Aadland relied on during the first three months following his on-ship illness to pay for the costs of his care attributable to his on-ship illness were deducted directly from his wife's paycheck rather than his own. But, while there is precedent to support the notion that a seaman who receives financial assistance from his parent in the wake of his on-ship illness or injury does not thereby incur an expense that is a "charge" on the shipowner, *see, e.g., Johnson v. United States*, 333 U.S. 46, 50 (1948); *In re RJF Int'l Corp.*, 334 F. Supp. 2d 109, 113 (D.R.I. 2004), we agree with Aadland that the nature of the relationship between the seaman and the person providing financial assistance to him matters. And, given that it is not unusual for a married couple to share finances, we are not persuaded by the defendants' implicit assertion that the use of one spouse's paycheck to fund the insurance of the other is necessarily a "gift" from the one to the other in the same way that perhaps a **{-46-}** parent paying the premiums of an adult child might be viewed. **[—24—]**

Indeed, in the maintenance context, an injured seaman might stay at home to recover, and his spouse might pay the rent or mortgage for that home at that time. But, we do not agree that means that the spouse is "gifting" the seaman shelter, such that the seaman cannot get maintenance to help pay the rent or mortgage. *Cf. Saco*, 483 F. Supp. 2d at 101-02.

Thus, the record does not compel the conclusion that Aadland did not alone purchase his insurance—and so did not incur any expense in consequence of his reliance on it to pay for his care—during this period. Instead, it provides a supportable basis for finding that he did. Accordingly, at least as to this period, we conclude that the District Court's grant of judgment to the defendants on Aadland's breach-of-the-duty-of-cure claim must be vacated, absent a finding about the nature of the financial relationship between Aadland and his spouse that would support a finding that he did not incur an expense from the costs of paying the premiums during this period.

Nor can we agree with the defendants that the record conclusively shows that Aadland did not alone purchase his insurance—and so, for that reason, incurred no expense—during the ensuing period in which he relied on his Tufts COBRA health insurance to pay his healthcare providers for the costs of the care he received to treat his on-ship illness. The defendants point out that the record indisputably shows that, during this **[—25—]** period, Aadland received "advance" payments from the defendants that he then used to pay the premiums for the Tufts COBRA insurance. They go on to contend that, as a result, they, rather than Aadland, purchased that insurance. *See, e.g., Shaw v. Ohio River Co.*, 526 F.2d 193, 200-01 (3d Cir. 1975) (finding that a shipowner was entitled to a set-off for the medical expenses paid for by a health insurance plan it provided to its seamen at no expense to themselves).

But, the District Court did not find, and the record does not incontrovertibly show, that the advance payments were made to Aadland in a form other than as a loan. For, while the

District Court found that Aadland had not paid the defendants back for the advance payments as of the time the District Court issued its judgment, *Aadland*, 2020 WL 6119926, at *2, the relevant question is whether the advance payments were made to Aadland pursuant to an agreement between Aadland and the defendants that Aadland did not need to pay the defendants back for those payments.[5] **[—26—]**

After all, if those payments were not made pursuant to such an agreement, then Aadland was merely loaned money by the defendants that he owed to them. And, in that event, Aadland would have been in all relevant respects "abandon[ed] . . . to his fate" and own devices to cover the costs of caring for his on-ship illness during the period in which he was enrolled in the Tufts COBRA insurance. **{-47-}** *The Dutra Grp. v. Batterton*, 139 S. Ct. 2275, 2286, 7 Adm. R. 43, 50 (2019) (quoting *McBride v. Estis Well Serv., L.L.C.*, 768 F.3d 382, 394 n.12, 2 Adm. R. 320, 329 n.12 (5th Cir. 2014) (Clement, J., concurring)). For, we see no basis for concluding that a shipowner may evade *Gauthier*'s no-set-off rule by making the seaman a loan to cover the costs of the insurance that the seaman then alone purchases and relies on to pay for the healthcare that he needs to treat an on-ship illness.

Indeed, the proposition that a shipowner may not evade *Gauthier*'s no-set-off rule by making a loan to the seaman to cover the costs of his private health insurance is not itself disputed by the defendants. Nor was that proposition rejected by the District Court.

In addition, the proposition accords with—even if it is not compelled by—*Gauthier*'s own rationale for not allowing a set-off of the payments made by an insurer pursuant to insurance that the seaman alone purchased. *Gauthier* cautioned that if a shipowner were able to reduce its cure obligation in such a **[—27—]** fashion, then the shipowner would be incentivized to "delay[] maintenance and cure payments to force seamen to look first to their private insurer"—an outcome the court there concluded was at odds with the duty's aim of "protecting injured or ill seamen." 752 F.2d at 1090.

This proposition draws additional support from the Supreme Court's decision in *Vaughan v. Atkinson*, 369 U.S. 527 (1962). There, the Court held that a shipowner cannot "force the disabled seaman to work, and then evade part or all of their [maintenance] obligation by having it reduced by the amount of the sick man's earnings," because otherwise "unconscionable employers . . . [would] use the withholding of maintenance and cure as a means of forcing sick seamen to go to work when they should be resting, and to make the seamen themselves pay in whole or in part the amounts owing as maintenance and cure." *Id.* at 533. And, we note, this proposition accords as well with the rule that a shipowner may reduce the cost of its cure obligation via the seaman's admission to a public marine hospital that provides medical care only if the shipowner first presents the injured or ill seaman with "a master's certificate carrying admittance to a public hospital." *Kossick v. United Fruit Co.*, 365 U.S. 731, 737 (1961); *see also Calmar S. S. Corp. v. Taylor*, 303 U.S. 525, 531 (1938). **[—28—]**

Thus, insofar as the record may be deemed to show that the "advance payments" were made to Aadland as a loan, there would be no basis for finding that he did not alone purchase the Tufts Cobra Plan insurance and so no basis for affirming the District Court's ruling that the defendants are entitled to the set-off they seek. There then also would be no basis for concluding, given *Gauthier*, that the

---

[5] The defendants argue that because the advance payments are best understood as maintenance and cure payments, there is no expectation that Aadland pay the advance payments back. *See Block Island Fishing, Inc. v. Rogers*, 844 F.3d 358, 366, 4 Adm. R. 47, 53–54 (1st Cir. 2016). But, the defendants do not contend that they represented that the payments were maintenance or cure payments at the time that they were made to Aadland. Instead, they contend that they should be understood as much at present because of the way they were calculated. We thus leave the resolution of this factual dispute about the nature of the payments at the time that they were made to the parties and the District Court on remand.

defendants are entitled to a grant of judgment on Aadland's breach-of-the-duty-of-cure claim.

Accordingly, because of the uncertain nature of the record as to whether Aadland did or did not alone purchase the insurance in question, the defendants' proposed alternative ground for affirming the District Court's grant of judgment to the defendants on Aadland's breach-of-the-duty-of-cure claim fails. We thus vacate and remand the District Court's judgment for the defendants on Aadland's breach-of-the-duty-of-cure claim, so that the District Court may make the findings that have not yet been made but that bear on whether Aadland did alone purchase his insurance during the periods in question. For, we emphasize, if he did alone purchase that **{-48-}** insurance, then the defendants would not be entitled to set off from their cure obligation the roughly $600,000 payment that Aadland's medical providers received from the insurer as payment for their treatment of his on-ship illness. And thus, the determination of whether Aadland was entitled to recover on his breach-of-the-duty-of-cure claim would have to be **[—29—]** assessed on the understanding that no such set-off could be claimed by the defendants, which is an assessment that the District Court has not yet made.[6]

C.

Having determined this much thus far, the question as to what the proper measure of cure is in this case necessarily also presents itself. That question is plainly relevant to the issue that may arise on remand concerning how much of the defendants' cure obligation (if any) has been satisfied (set-off not included) through payments that they have made, either directly to Aadland or to the insurer, Tufts.

As we have noted, with respect to the issue of the amount of cure that is owed, Aadland contends that, if *Gauthier* applies, then he is owed as cure the "sticker price" of the healthcare that he received, which is $1.2 million. That amount, Aadland contends, **[—30—]** represents the reasonable costs of his care, given that it is the amount that his healthcare providers charged for it.[7]

The defendants contend in response, however, that, insofar as *Gauthier* does apply here, the proper valuation of the cure obligation is still at most the amount that Aadland's healthcare providers accepted as full payment from the insurer for his care. And, they assert, that amount comes to approximately $600,000, which is considerably less than the $1.2 million amount that Aadland favors.

In pressing for this lesser amount to measure the cure obligation even under *Gauthier*, the defendants first emphasize, correctly, that *Gauthier* never resolved how much cure the shipowner there owed the seaman; *Gauthier* only determined that the shipowner was not entitled to set off the payments that the insurer made to cover the cost of the seaman's care against its cure obligation. The defendants then further note that it was not until *Manderson v. Chet Morrison Contractors, Inc.*, 666 F.3d 373 (5th Cir. 2012), that the Fifth Circuit reached the question of what the cure obligation would be in a situation in which *Gauthier* applied. They **[—31—]** then contend that *Manderson* undermines Aadland's position that the proper measure of cure is $1.2 million in his case. We agree.

[6] There is a third period concerning Aadland's coverage that is worth noting. Since April 2017, Aadland's healthcare has been paid for through Medicare and a private supplemental health insurance plan he pays for. No party advances a separate reason for distinguishing *Gauthier* based on the source of Aadland's health insurance during this third period. Nor do we purport to comment on whether these facts would provide a basis for distinguishing *Gauthier*. *Compare Moran Towing & Transp., Co. v. Lombas*, 58 F.3d 24 (2d Cir. 1995), *with Gypsum Carrier, Inc. v. Handelsman*, 307 F.2d 525 (9th Cir. 1962).

[7] Aadland does not develop an argument to us that the proper measure of cure in his case is the cost of his care—be it the "sticker price" or the roughly $600,000 his healthcare providers accepted as payment—plus the cost of his premiums and out-of-pocket expenses. We thus deem such an argument waived. *See United States v. Zannino*, 895 F.2d 1, 17 (1st Cir. 1990).

The defendants point out that *Manderson* held that when a seaman alone purchases his medical insurance, such that *Gauthier*'s no-set-off rule applies, "the relevant amount" owed as cure is not the "sticker price" the healthcare providers assign **{–49–}** to the care that they provided to the seaman to treat his on-ship illness or injury. Rather, "the relevant amount is that needed to satisfy the seaman's medical charges," which there was the "lower amount paid by [the seaman's] insurer." *Manderson*, 666 F.3d at 382. Thus, the defendants contend, because "the amount paid by" Aadland's insurer was only approximately $600,000, Aadland cannot, given *Manderson*, be entitled to a cure award that is pegged to the $1.2 million "sticker price" that his healthcare providers assigned to the care that they provided to him to treat his on-ship infection.

Aadland contends otherwise by arguing that, under *Manderson*, the lower measure of cure that the Fifth Circuit there embraced only applies if the shipowner has taken a proactive step toward ensuring that the seaman has a way to pay for the care needed to treat his on-ship injury or illness. And, he contends, the record shows that, unlike in *Manderson*, the defendants in this case "played no part in the proactive procurement or payment of" the health insurance that was used to pay for the care in question. **[—32—]** Thus, he contends, he is entitled to a cure award pegged to the $1.2 million sticker price, notwithstanding that his health care providers in fact accepted a much lower amount.

But, we are not persuaded by Aadland's contention. *Manderson* does not purport to limit its holding regarding the proper measure of cure in a case in which a seaman relies on insurance that he alone purchased to pay for the healthcare that he received for an on-ship illness or injury to the circumstance in which the defendants took steps to ensure that the seaman had a way to pay for his insurance (without, of course, going so far as to pay for that insurance). Moreover, Aadland himself acknowledges that the defendants here knew at the time that they made the advance payments that Aadland had health insurance that he was relying on to pay for his care. And, while the record does show that there are questions about whether the insurance would cover those costs, we see no basis for concluding that the mere possibility that coverage could be denied in and of itself suffices to make *Manderson*'s approach to defining the measure of cure inapplicable in a case like this. That is at least the case given that there is no dispute that the defendants in this case did take some measures to ensure that the seaman to whom the duty of cure would be owed could procure insurance, such as by, at the very least, loaning him money to procure it through the advance payments that they made to him. Nor, we add, did Aadland have his requests **[—33—]** for coverage denied by Tufts during the period in which he was relying on that insurance to pay for his care.[8] **{–50–}**

---

[8] We note that, insofar as the defendants mean also to assert that Aadland is actually entitled only to a much lower amount of cure, as defined chiefly by the costs of the premiums for his health insurance plus any expenses attending to his reliance on that insurance (rather than the cost of the healthcare itself), the District Court did not so hold. (The District Court only determined that *Gauthier* was distinguishable; it did not then reach the issue of what the defendants' cure obligation would be if *Gauthier* was not distinguishable.) Moreover, *Manderson*, applying *Gauthier*, does not hold that the cost of the premiums is the right measure of cure when a seaman alone purchases insurance, *see* 666 F.3d at 382, and the defendants do not develop any argument for why *Manderson*'s reasoning should not apply here. Thus, any such argument is waived. *See Zannino*, 895 F.2d at 17 ("[A] litigant has an obligation 'to spell out its arguments squarely and distinctly,' or else forever hold its peace." (quoting *Rivera–Gomez v. de Castro*, 843 F.2d 631, 635 (1st Cir. 1988))).

We note, too, that insofar as the defendants mean to contend that, if the amount accepted as payment by the healthcare providers is the measure of cure, that amount here is only $400,0000 because that is the amount that they paid directly to the insurer in return for its release of Aadland of any liability owing to the payments that it made to the healthcare providers for that care, we also cannot agree. And that is so, because the defendants do not purport to take issue with *Manderson*, which stated that the correct value of the cure obligation in that case was "the lesser amount those *providers* accepted as full payment

Thus, we conclude that, insofar as *Gauthier* does apply, we cannot agree with Aadland that the duty of cure is defined in his case by the sticker price for the healthcare that he received but that neither he nor his insurer was charged. Instead, insofar as Aadland did alone purchase the insurance in question, such that *Gauthier* applies, the cure owed here is the roughly $600,000 that **[—34—]** his healthcare providers accepted as payment for his care from his insurer.

Of course, there still does remain the question of whether, given that the cure owed would be roughly half of the $1.2 million amount that Aadland is suing to obtain, the defendants have satisfied their duty of cure. The defendants contend that they have done so by virtue of the payments that they made to Aadland and his insurer since Aadland fell ill in July 2014 and the fact that his wife paid for a portion of his health insurance premiums.

But, the District Court has not addressed this question. That is so, because it was of the view—which we have rejected—that the defendants could set off the roughly $600,000 paid for Aadland's care by the insurer because, in part, Aadland failed to request cure.

Thus, we leave to the District Court on remand the assessment of what cure was paid—insofar as, that is, the District Court finds on remand that Aadland did alone purchase the insurance on which he relied to pay for his care for some period of the time in question. Nonetheless, we do make the following observations with respect to that assessment.

First, and by way of recalling our analysis above concerning how *Gauthier* applies here, if the District Court were to find on remand that the advance payments were made with the **[—35—]** understanding that Aadland would not by accepting them incur a debt to the defendants, then, at least as to the period of time for which Aadland used the payments to pay for the premiums for the insurance that he used to pay for the healthcare that he received for is on-ship illness, *Gauthier* would be distinguishable. And, in that event, the defendants, for such period, would appear to have fulfilled their cure obligation, given the set-off to which they would be entitled.

But, if the District Court were to find on remand that Aadland incurred a debt from his receipt of the advance payments, then a distinct set of questions would arise concerning how to calculate what amount of cure was owed and what amount had been satisfied. And, as to that set of questions, we offer the following guidance.

To the extent that the District Court were to find on remand that the debt had been incurred by Aadland from his receipt of the advance payments but that some or all of the debt then had been extinguished, it may be that a portion of the amount of the extinguished debt would satisfy some of the defendants' cure obligation. We say no more on this score, however, because the parties do not develop on appeal an argument as to whether the amount of any extinguished debt incurred from receipt of the advance payments should be credited against the defendants' cure obligation, and if so, in what amount. **[—36—] {-51-}**

Indeed, neither party advances an argument even as to whether any such amount of extinguished debt should be credited against the defendants' cure obligation of roughly $600,000 (as measured by the amount of payment accepted by Aadland's health care providers from the insurer) or viewed as covering the costs of an additional part of the defendants' cure obligation. On the latter view, we note, the amount of the defendants' cure obligation would not be just the roughly $600,000 that the healthcare providers accepted as payment from the insurer. It instead would be that amount *plus* the cost of (at least a portion of) the premiums for the insurance that the insurer provided as well as Aadland's out-of-pocket expenses for the healthcare that he received for his on-ship illness in the form of co-payments and the like.

from *Manderson*'s insurer," 666 F.3d at 381-82 (emphasis added).

We thus leave this nuanced set of questions to the District Court to address on remand. That way the District Court may address those questions after having heard whatever arguments the parties may make to it, including any arguments that the parties may choose to make to it as to whether any arguments pertaining to this set of questions have been waived over the course of this litigation by either party.

There is also the question of whether the defendants' payment of $400,000 to the insurer, or any portion of that payment, may count toward the satisfaction of the defendants' cure obligation and how that payment may bear on the amount of that **[—37—]** obligation. But, here, too we leave these questions to the District Court, given the limited arguments touching on them that have been made to us by the parties on appeal. This approach will enable the District Court to resolve these questions in the first instance with the aid of having heard whatever arguments the parties may choose to make, given that the parties have not developed arguments pertaining to those questions to us on appeal.

Finally, we note that if the District Court were to conclude on remand that Aadland did not alone purchase his health insurance either only during the period in which he received his health insurance through his wife's employer-sponsored plan or, alternatively, only during the period in which he was covered by the Tufts COBRA plan following her termination from her job, then there would remain the question of how much cure Aadland must still be paid by the defendants as cure for that specific period. For, in that event, Aadland would not be entitled to recovery for nonpayment of cure based on *Gauthier* for the other period, precisely because he would not have been found to have alone purchased his insurance for that period.

Aadland has not developed, however, a distinct argument to us as to what amount the defendants would owe him as cure in the event that he were to be found to have alone purchased his insurance for only one of the periods identified above rather than **[—38—]** for the whole of the time spanning both periods. Nor, we should add, have the defendants weighed in on this issue to us.

We do note, though, that, given the episodic way that maintenance and cure payments are customarily calculated, it seems plausible that Aadland would be entitled to cure for the cost of the care that he received for such a limited period, notwithstanding that he did not alone purchase the insurance that he relied on to pay for the healthcare that he received during the whole of the time that he was relying on such healthcare to treat his on-ship illness. But, in all events, we leave this question as well to the District Court to resolve on remand, so that, again, it may do so with the benefit of whatever arguments the parties properly advance below. **{-52-}**

IV.

Having vacated the District Court's grant of judgment to the defendants on Aadland's breach-of-the-duty-of-cure claim, we now come to his additional claim that the defendants' failure to timely pay him adequate cure, to the extent the defendants so failed, was done in "bad faith." Here, Aadland argues that the record shows that the defendants knew of their cure obligation to him and recognized that his health insurance may not cover the costs of his care, yet never communicated its cure obligation to him and waited until "the eve of trial" before reaching an agreement with his insurer to release him from any liability **[—39—]** resulting from his use of his insurance to pay for the care he received to treat his on-ship illness. As a result, Aadland contends that he is entitled to compensatory damages for mental distress for the "mental anguish" that he suffered due to both his need to rely on his insurance to pay for his healthcare despite the ambiguity as to whether the insurance covered those costs, as well as his need to file this suit to receive adequate cure from the defendants. And, Aadland further contends that he is entitled to punitive damages and attorney's fees for the defendants' allegedly willful delay in fulfilling their cure obligation.

As we noted at the outset, the District Court was not persuaded and granted judgment for the defendants on this claim. But, the District Court's judgment in this regard relied on its determination that Aadland was not deprived of any cure owed to him by the defendants because *Gauthier* did not apply, in part because Aadland did not request cure. Nor, in granting judgment to the defendants with respect to these delay-based claims, did it address the fact that, from the time Aadland fell ill at sea to the time of this suit, Aadland faced the risk of a lawsuit by his insurer to recover the cost of the healthcare his insurance had paid for.

We therefore vacate the District Court's grant of judgment on his claim seeking compensatory damages for emotional distress, punitive damages, and attorney's fees. That way, the **[—40—]** District Court may consider those claims in light of our other conclusions regarding Aadland's claim for cure.

V.

We have one final ruling by the District Court to address. It concerns whether the defendants have met their burden of proving that Aadland has reached the point of maximum medical recovery.

"Maximum medical recovery" occurs "[w]hen a seaman's 'condition has stabilized,'" *Whitman*, 387 F.3d at 72 (quoting *In re RJF Int'l Corp.*, 354 F.3d 104, 106 (1st Cir. 2004)), and the seaman is "so far cured as possible," *Ferrara v. A. & V. Fishing, Inc.*, 99 F.3d 449, 454 (1st Cir. 1996) (quoting *LeBlanc*, 992 F.2d at 397). Even when a seaman's "progress ended short of a full recovery, the seaman . . . is no longer entitled to maintenance and cure" once the shipowner has proven by a preponderance of the evidence that the seaman has reached the point of maximum medical recovery. *Whitman*, 387 F.3d at 72 (quoting *In re RJF Int'l Corp.*, 354 F.3d at 106); *see also Johnson v. Marlin Drilling Co.*, 893 F.2d 77, 79 (5th Cir. 1990) (describing the burden of proof by which a shipowner must establish that the injured seaman has reached the point of maximum medical recovery as when it is "probable that further treatment will result in no betterment of the seaman's condition" (quoting *Gaspard v. Taylor Diving & Salvage* **[—41—]** *Co.*, 649 F.2d 372, 374 n.3 (5th Cir. 1981))); 1 *Admiralty & Mar. Law* § 6:33 (6th ed. 2021) (same). **{–53–}**

As part of the defendants' effort to minimize the amount owed to Aadland as cure, if any amount is, the defendants argued to the District Court, as a defense, that Aadland had reached the point of "maximum medical recovery" by July 2019. For that reason, they contend, he is not entitled to cure payments for any healthcare he received for his on-ship illness after that point in time. The District Court agreed, and Aadland now appeals that ruling.

We note at the outset that we are dubious that the issue of maximum medical recovery is properly presented in this case. The defendants, in raising this defense, contend that Aadland reached the point of maximum medical recovery only in July 2019—just three months before trial and well after he first became ill. But, it is not clear to us from either the record or the arguments of the parties whether Aadland sought cure from the defendants to cover the cost of treatment he received in that three-month period as Aadland has been paying for his healthcare, at least in part, through Medicare since April 2017.[9] Nor did the **[—42—]** defendants themselves seek a declaratory judgment of any sort on this issue. Nonetheless, the District Court ruled on this issue, and there is ambiguity as to whether Aadland may seek cure for treatment he received after July 2019. We thus address it, and, as we will explain, we conclude that Aadland is right that the

[9] The record evidence Aadland points to in support of his statement that he incurred approximately $1.2 million in healthcare expenses lists the last expense paid by Aadland's health insurance as being incurred in March 2017. But, the figure Aadland asserts represents the "sticker price" of his healthcare exceeds **[—42—]** the amount billed to his insurance as of March 2017, and other evidence in the record supports the finding that Aadland has been visiting his doctors after that date and paying for that care with some form of insurance.

District Court's maximum-medical-recovery ruling was wrong.

A.

When determining whether a seaman has reached the point of maximum medical recovery, a court must consider whether "further rehabilitation would be more than simply palliative, and would [instead] improve [the seaman's] medical condition." *In re RJF Intern. Corp.*, 354 F.3d at 107 (citations omitted). The burden is on the shipowner to provide evidence that supports, by a preponderance of evidence, its assertions regarding "the earliest time when it is reasonably and in good faith determined by those charged with the seaman's care and treatment that the maximum cure reasonably possible has been effected." *Hubbard v. Faros Fisheries, Inc.*, 626 F.2d 196, 202 (1st Cir. 1980) (quoting *Vella v. Ford Motor Co.*, 421 U.S. 1, 6 n.5 (1975)). It is thus "the medical, not the judicial, determination of permanency that **[—43—]** terminates the right to maintenance and cure" via maximum medical recovery. *Id.*

Here, the District Court determined that, because "[t]here is no evidence that Aadland has not reached maximum medical recovery," the defendants had fulfilled their obligation to provide Aadland with cure. *Aadland*, 2020 WL 6119926, at *3. But, by framing the conclusion in that way, the District Court, as Aadland emphasizes in his arguments to us, "shifted the burden to prove [maximum medical recovery] away from [the defendants] and placed the burden to disprove [maximum medical recovery] onto Aadland," such that the District Court committed "an error of law." *See also Weeks Marine, Inc. v. Watson*, 190 F. Supp. 3d 588, 597 (E.D. La. 2016) ("After a seaman has proved his initial entitlement to maintenance and cure, the **{-54-}** burden shifts to the ship owner to prove that maximum cure has been reached."); *Saco*, 483 F. Supp. 2d at 99 (same); *Smith v. Delaware Bay Launch Serv., Inc.*, 972 F. Supp. 836, 848 (D. Del. 1997) (same); *McMillan v. Tug Jane A. Bouchard*, 885 F. Supp. 452, 459 (E.D.N.Y. 1995) (same); 1 *Admiralty & Mar. Law* § 6:33 (same).

If, when reviewing a district court's judgment following a bench trial, the district court "'premise[s] its ultimate finding . . . on an erroneous interpretation of the standard to be applied,' . . . we treat the trial court's conclusion as a question of law," entitled to no deference. *Vinick*, 205 F.3d at 6 (quoting **[—44—]** *Parke, Davis & Co.*, 362 U.S. at 44). We thus must proceed by reviewing de novo the District Court's determination that the evidence in the record sufficed to show that Aadland had reached a point of maximum medical recovery. *Id.*; *see also Aldridge v. A.T. Cross Corp.*, 284 F.3d 72, 84 (1st Cir. 2002) (explaining that this court can "affirm a district court's judgment on any grounds supported by the record" (quoting *Greenless v. Almond*, 277 F.3d 601, 605 (1st Cir. 2002))).

B.

The defendants support their contention that they can meet their burden to show that Aadland has reached a point of maximum medical recovery, such that we may affirm the District Court's ruling as to maximum medical recovery, with reference to three pieces of evidence in the record. First, they point to a note "discharg[ing] [Aadland] from occupational therapy to begin a home exercise program." Second, they point to Aadland's testimony in his October 12, 2018 deposition that "he only saw his cardiologist, infectious disease doctor and primary care physician every six months for checkups." Finally, they point to Aadland's testimony that he went skiing in Maine in 2016.[10] Aadland contends **[—45—]** that none of these pieces of evidence suffices to permit the defendants to meet their burden of proof as to this affirmative defense,

[10] The defendants, in their briefing to us, also present a series of statements made by Aadland's doctors that could indicate that Aadland has reached a point of maximum medical recovery, but none of those statements were admitted into the record before the District Court. As a result, we cannot affirm **[—45—]** the District Court by referring to any of those documents. *Cf.* Fed. R. App. P. 10(e); *United States v. Rivera-Rosario*, 300 F.3d 1, 9 (1st Cir. 2002) ("[A] 10(e) motion is designed to only supplement the record on appeal so that it accurately reflects what occurred before the district court." (quoting *Belber v. Lipson*, 905 F.2d 549, 551 n.1 (1st Cir.1990))).

because none of them suffices to show that his treating "physicians [have] made an unequivocal diagnosis of . . . permanency." *See Hubbard*, 626 F.2d at 202. We agree.

To be sure, the "discharge note" that the defendants point to was from a treating physician. But, the District Court interpreted this document as "discharg[ing]" Aadland from occupational therapy after fourteen sessions so that he could "begin a home exercise program," even though the record shows, as Aadland emphasizes in his briefing to us, at trial, that Aadland testified that, from September 2015 until March 2020 (when COVID made receiving treatment difficult), he "did each year the amount" of physical and occupational therapy he "was allowed to from the insurance company." Aadland further testified that in 2019, the year the "discharge note" was produced, the maximum number of occupational therapy sessions was fourteen—the same number of sessions he received before the note "discharged" him to proceed with home exercise—and that he had arranged with his occupational therapist to continue treatment with the sessions he **[—46—]** had "saved" for later in the year, and **{–55–}** "then [in] January of 2020[,] [he] would start with new ones." Thus, it is not at all clear that the "discharge note"—once it is considered in combination with Aadland's testimony about his occupational therapy—shows by a preponderance of the evidence that Aadland was receiving "palliative" rather than "rehabilitative" care. *See In re RJF Intern. Corp.*, 354 F.3d at 107.

Nor does Aadland's October 12, 2018 deposition help the defendants to meet their burden of establishing as much. The defendants contend that Aadland's statements that "he only saw his cardiologist, infectious disease doctor and primary care physician every six months for checkups" support a finding that Aadland had reached a point of maximum medical recovery. But, given that Aadland was not asked why he did not see his doctors more frequently at that deposition, it is hard to know whether that frequency of visits speaks to the "palliative" nature of his care or whether that too can be attributed to the limits of his health insurance policy.

It is true that in the same deposition, Aadland did not disagree that his doctors were "not doing anything for [him] at the moment designed for [him] to get . . . better." But, it is not at all clear whether Aadland, in making that statement, was communicating his own opinion of the efficacy of his doctors' care or relaying his doctors' opinions as to his prognosis. And, that **[—47—]** distinction matters as Aadland is not a medical doctor and thus cannot himself make the "medical determination" necessary to determine that he has reached maximum medical recovery—a reality that the defendants' themselves do not dispute. *See Hubbard*, 626 F.2d at 202 (quoting *Vella*, 421 U.S. at 6 n.5).

Finally, the defendants contend that Aadland's testimony at trial that he went skiing in 2016 suffices to show that he has reached a point of maximum medical recovery. But, Aadland testified that he went skiing in 2016 with Maine Adaptive, which he explained is a skiing program for people with disabilities. That fact in and of itself provides no indication of Aadland's prognosis, nor does it suggest whether the treatment he continued to receive in the years that followed was merely "palliative" or was "rehabilitative" in nature. Nor, we add, is the evidence that he went skiing a determination by Aadland's medical doctor that he had recovered to the maximum extent reasonably possible.

C.

We are thus not persuaded that the evidence to which the defendants point—even when viewed together—suffices to meet their burden of demonstrating that Aadland's treating physicians had determined that Aadland had reached maximum medical recovery. Neither the "discharge note" nor Aadland's deposition testimony nor Aadland's time skiing in 2016 suggest that it is more likely than not that, at the time of trial, Aadland's care was **[—48—]** "palliative" rather than "rehabilitative." We thus conclude that the District Court erred in determining that the defendants' duty to provide cure had terminated, and so we reverse that aspect of the District Court's judgment.

VI.

For the foregoing reasons, the judgment of the District Court is reversed in part, vacated in part, and remanded for further proceedings. The parties shall bear their own costs.

This page intentionally left blank

United States Court of Appeals for the Second Circuit

United States Court of Appeals
for the Second Circuit

No. 20-2768

OJEDA
vs.
METROPOLITAN TRANSP. AUTH.

Appeal from the United States District Court for the Southern District of New York

Decided: July 19, 2022

Citation: 41 F.4th 56, 10 Adm. R. 40 (2d Cir. 2022).

Before **POOLER, WESLEY,** and **MENASHI,** Circuit Judges.

[—2—] {–59–} MENASHI, Circuit Judge:

Plaintiff-Appellee Domingo Ojeda was employed as a police officer by the Metropolitan Transportation Authority ("MTA"), the defendant-appellant in this case. While patrolling a railroad station, Ojeda witnessed an incident between a man and a woman in the station's parking lot. After intervening and discovering that the man **[—3—]** had an open order of protection against him, Ojeda handcuffed the man. The arrestee fled, and Ojeda injured himself in pursuit. **{–60–}**

Ojeda sued the MTA under the Federal Employers' Liability Act ("FELA"), 45 U.S.C. § 51, alleging that the MTA's negligence—including its failure to provide him with a prisoner compartment in his patrol car—caused his injuries. A jury ruled in favor of Ojeda and awarded him damages. On appeal, the MTA argues that it is immune from liability pursuant to the governmental function defense and that, in any event, it cannot be held liable without expert testimony. The district court rejected these arguments when it denied the MTA's motion for judgment as a matter of law. We affirm.

BACKGROUND

The MTA was created under New York law as "a body corporate and politic constituting a public benefit corporation." N.Y. Pub. Auth. L. § 1263. Its purpose is "the continuance, further development and improvement of commuter transportation and other services related thereto within the metropolitan commuter transportation district." *Id.* § 1264. Metro-North Commuter Railroad Company ("Metro-North") is a subsidiary of the MTA. N.Y. Comp. Codes R. & Regs. tit. 21, § 1085.1(a). Metro-North "operates and maintains the Hudson, Harlem, New Haven, Port Jervis and Pascack Valley commuter railroad lines." *Id.* § 1085.2(g).

The MTA is "authorized and empowered, to provide and maintain an authority police department and a uniformed authority police force." N.Y. Pub. Auth. L. § 1266-h. According to statute, "[e]ach member of such uniformed police force shall be a 'police officer' for the purposes of the criminal procedure law, with all of the powers of such police officers thereunder." *Id.* The MTA police may **[—4—]** "enforce and prevent violation of all laws and ordinances" "in and about any or all of the facilities owned, occupied and/or operated by the [MTA] and its subsidiary corporations." *Id.*

In 2003, Ojeda joined the MTA police and attended the New York Police Department academy for six months for basic training. In the first part of his thirteen-year career as an MTA police officer, Ojeda worked in the patrol unit. He then joined the emergency services unit ("ESU"), a unit within the police department that, according to Ojeda, "responds to a higher problematic situation that is beyond the scope of the regular police officer." App'x 106-07. Such situations include "barricaded subjects," "emotionally disturbed persons," "extrication from vehicles," and "anything that uses specialized tools or is beyond the capacity of the police officer to handle." *Id.* at 107. To serve in the ESU, Ojeda had to undergo specialized training.

On a typical day, ESU officers are assigned to a particular region of the metro system and either make themselves available for a regular patrol officer's request for assistance or conduct patrol themselves. The standard vehicle provided to ESU officers is a truck with a utility body attached to it. The utility body's contents include medical emergency equipment, protective suits, vehicle extrication equipment, and rope rescue equipment. The truck is not equipped to transport people placed in custody. Instead, if an ESU officer makes an arrest, he must request assistance from another patrol unit to transport the arrestee.

Ojeda and his partner, Officer Gregg Cella, were assigned to patrol Harrison Station, a commuter rail stop on Metro-North's New Haven Line, on the night of October 2, 2013. About two hours into **[—5—]** their patrol, they spotted a vehicle enter the station's parking lot with a female driver and a male passenger. Both occupants exited the car, and the man reentered **{-61-}** the car to sit in the driver's seat. As the woman reached into the car on the passenger side—with the door open—the man drove the car in reverse. As Ojeda tells it, "[t]he door knock[ed] her down and the door literally [went] right over her head." *Id.* at 121.

Ojeda left his own vehicle to address the situation, and Cella followed him. Ojeda directed the driver to pull the car over to the curb, and Ojeda turned off the engine and removed the keys. He then brought the man to the rear of the car and began questioning him. He learned that the man and the woman had a child together. Ojeda also noticed that the woman was "up and screaming and yelling with" Cella and that she "was speaking in both Spanish and English." *Id.* at 123-24.

Because Ojeda spoke Spanish, he traded places with Cella and began questioning the woman. She claimed that there was an order of protection against the man. Ojeda told Cella what the woman said, which prompted Cella to search for any outstanding warrants or orders of protection using the man's driver's license. That review confirmed that there was an open order of protection, and Ojeda proceeded to place the man in handcuffs and arrest him. Ojeda secured the arrestee by holding onto the handcuffs while Cella communicated with dispatch.[1]

At that point, the woman began talking with the man. Ojeda told them to stop speaking with each other. The man asked Ojeda to **[—6—]** loosen the handcuffs. Ojeda requested that the man call him "sir or officer" and said that "officer works," and the man began to refer to Ojeda as "Officer Works." App'x 130. Now suspecting that the man was under the influence, Ojeda turned to the woman and asked if he had a history of using drugs. The woman responded that he did.

Ojeda let go of the handcuffs to approach the woman and ask what drugs the man had been using. At that point, the man took off running. Ojeda pursued him on foot, but as he passed the ESU truck, he felt a "pop" in his leg and slowed down. *Id.* at 131. As the man disappeared, Ojeda encountered another police officer, who called backup to assist in a search. (The search was unsuccessful, but the following day the man turned himself in.)

After backup arrived, Ojeda remained at the scene for another three-and-a-half hours to search for his prisoner. Later that night, he drove himself to a hospital, where doctors determined that he may have torn his Achilles tendon. Because of his injury, Ojeda was placed on restricted duty. After nearly a year passed without a full recovery, Ojeda underwent surgery in September 2014. The following year, the MTA police chief marked Ojeda as "disabled" for pension purposes. Five months later, his employment with the MTA was terminated.

Ojeda filed a complaint against the MTA under the FELA, alleging that the MTA's negligence caused his injuries. Specifically, Ojeda alleged that the MTA negligently (1) failed "to provide the plaintiff with the necessary and proper tools and equipment with which to work," (2) failed "to provide [Ojeda] with an appropriate and timely backup," and (3) "provid[ed] plaintiff with a police partner who left plaintiff alone to manage with two persons." Am. Compl. ¶ 21, *Ojeda v. MTA*, 477 F. Supp. 3d 65 (S.D.N.Y. 2020) (No. **[—7—]** 16-CV-3), ECF No. 29. In

[1] According to Ojeda, Cella was ten to fifteen feet away from Ojeda when he spoke with dispatch on his cell phone. Ojeda also asserts that Cella was on an unrelated second phone call right after he spoke with dispatch.

connection with his injuries, Ojeda sought $5 million in damages. **{–62–}**

Before trial commenced, the MTA moved in limine to exclude evidence regarding the MTA's decision to assign the ESU vehicle to Ojeda and regarding Cella's alleged negligence. *See* Motions in Limine, *Ojeda*, 477 F. Supp. 3d 65, ECF Nos. 103, 104. According to the MTA, the governmental function defense protected it from liability based on its decisions to issue Ojeda equipment or to assign Cella as his partner. The MTA also argued that those claims would require expert evidence, which Ojeda failed to produce. The district court declined to decide whether the governmental function defense is available in a FELA case, but it granted the MTA's motion insofar as Ojeda was not allowed to "testify about the MTA's official policies and practices of assigning police officers to a specific patrol car" or to "state whether Officer Cella acted negligently during the encounter based on the MTA's official policies and practices of detaining an arrestee." App'x 83. However, Ojeda was permitted to "testify about his experience of being assigned to a patrol car as well as what he saw Officer Cella doing during the arrest so long as his testimony is based on his own observations and experiences." *Id.* at 83-84.

The case went to trial, and the only testimony came from Ojeda, Ojeda's treating orthopedist, and Cella. At trial, the parties stipulated that the MTA "does not study response time to requests for backup calls." Trial Transcript at 99, *Ojeda*, 477 F. Supp. 3d 65. Before the case was submitted to the jury, the MTA moved for a directed verdict and reiterated its arguments that Ojeda could not establish liability without expert testimony and that it was immune from liability pursuant to the governmental function defense. The district court **[—8—]** denied the motion. Although the district court "agree[d] ... that there's not a wealth of evidence in this case on certain things," it decided "there's enough to go to the jury." App'x 152. As to the governmental function defense, the district court stated that "[w]hen looking at the case law, it is not clear that it even applies to a FELA case." *Id.* at 151.

The jury found that Ojeda had proven by a preponderance of the evidence that the MTA "was negligent in failing to provide a safe place to work on October 2, 2013," and that such negligence "caused, in whole or in part, [the] injury to" Ojeda. Verdict at 1, *Ojeda*, 477 F. Supp. 3d 65, ECF No. 138. Additionally, the jury determined that eighty percent of Ojeda's damages resulted from his own negligence. *Id.* at 2. Because the jury found that Ojeda's total damages were $2,650,000, judgment was entered in favor of Ojeda for a total award of $530,000. Judgment at 1-3, *Ojeda*, 477 F. Supp. 3d 65, ECF No. 139.

The MTA renewed its motion for judgment as a matter of law pursuant to Federal Rule of Civil Procedure 50 for the same reasons it articulated in its motions in limine and its motion for a directed verdict. The district court denied the motion and again rejected the MTA's arguments. *Ojeda*, 477 F. Supp. 3d at 73-76. First, the district court concluded that, despite the lack of expert testimony, "the evidence presented at trial was sufficient to support the jury's finding that [the MTA] was 20% negligent for failing to provide [Ojeda] with a reasonably safe place to work under FELA." *Id.* at 75. Second, the district court rejected the MTA's argument that the governmental function defense shields the MTA from liability in this case. *Id.* at 76. This time, the district court was less circumspect; it held that "the **[—9—]** governmental function defense does not apply in FELA cases, and that the MTA is not entitled to immunity under such a defense." *Id.*

The MTA timely appealed. **{–63–}**

DISCUSSION

"We review *de novo* the district court's decision on a motion for judgment as a matter of law, applying the same standard that is required of the district court." *Smalls v. Collins*, 10 F.4th 117, 131 (2d Cir. 2021) (internal quotation marks omitted). "[W]e are required to consider the evidence in the light most favorable to the party against whom the motion was made and to give that party the benefit of all reasonable inferences that the jury might have drawn in his favor from the evidence." *Black v. Finantra Cap., Inc.*, 418 F.3d 203, 208-09 (2d Cir. 2005) (internal quotation marks omitted). When reviewing a district court's denial of a Rule 50 motion, we "cannot assess the weight of conflicting evidence, pass on the credibility of the witnesses, or substitute [our] judgment for that of the jury." *Tolbert v. Queens Coll.*, 242 F.3d 58, 70 (2d Cir. 2001) (quoting *Smith v. Lightning Bolt Prods., Inc.*, 861 F.2d 363, 367 (2d Cir. 1988)).

The MTA raises two arguments on appeal. First, it contends that the governmental function defense shields the MTA from liability for its decision to send Ojeda on patrol in a truck without a prisoner compartment, its decision to assign him Cella as a partner, and its failure to study backup response times. Second, the MTA in the alternative argues that the district court erred in permitting a jury to find negligence on the part of the MTA without expert testimony. We address these arguments in turn. **[—10—]**

I

First, the MTA argues that the governmental function defense shields it from liability in this case. In the MTA's view, the alleged negligence occurred in "the exercise of police discretion," which as a "quintessential governmental function[]" cannot form the basis of liability for negligence. Appellant's Br. 16-17. Ojeda contends—and the district court held—that the FELA bars the MTA from asserting the governmental function defense. We hold that the governmental function defense remains available in FELA suits, but it offers no relief to the MTA in this case.

A

We begin with whether the MTA may claim the governmental function defense in FELA cases.[2] The FELA provides that "[e]very common carrier by railroad while engaging in commerce between any of the several States or Territories ... shall be liable in damages to any person suffering injury while he is employed by such carrier in such commerce ... for such injury or death resulting in whole or in part from the negligence of any of the officers, agents, or employees of such carrier." 45 U.S.C. § 51. "In FELA actions, the plaintiff must prove the traditional common law elements of negligence: duty, breach, foreseeability, and causation." *Tufariello v. Long Island R.R.*, 458 F.3d 80, 87 (2d Cir. 2006). **[—11—]**

Though a FELA action may resemble a traditional negligence claim, "the plaintiff's burden in making a showing of causation and negligence is lighter under FELA than it would be at common law because 'the theory of FELA is that where the employer's conduct falls short of the high standard required of him by the Act and his fault, in whole or in part, causes injury, liability ensues.'" *Id.* (quoting **{-64-}** *Kernan v. Am. Dredging Co.*, 355 U.S. 426, 438-39 (1958)). The FELA "does not define negligence, leaving that question to be determined ... by the common law principles as established and applied in the federal courts." *Urie v. Thompson*, 337 U.S. 163, 174 (1949) (internal quotation marks omitted). In other words, "[w]hat constitutes negligence for the statute's purposes is a federal question, not varying in accordance with the differing conceptions of negligence applicable under state and local laws for other purposes. Federal decisional law formulating and applying the concept govern." *Id.*; *see also id.* ("*Erie R. Co. v. Tompkins*, 304 U.S. 64[(1938)], has no application.").

At the same time, the Supreme Court "ha[s] made clear" that what constitutes negligence under the FELA "generally turns on principles of common law." *Consol. Rail Corp. v. Gottshall*, 512 U.S. 532, 543 (1994). The statute "is founded on common-law concepts of negligence and injury, subject to such qualifications as Congress has imported into those terms." *Urie*, 337 U.S. at 182. Accordingly, the Supreme Court has directed us to approach interpretation of the FELA in two steps. First, "we must look to FELA itself,

[2] As a general matter, the MTA is a governmental entity entitled to invoke the governmental function defense. *See Doe v. City of New York*, 890 N.Y.S.2d 548, 550 (N.Y. App. Div. 2d Dep't 2009) (holding the MTA to be "immune from negligence claims arising out of the performance of [its] governmental functions").

its purposes and background, and the construction we have given it over the years." *Gottshall*, 512 U.S. at 541. Second, "because FELA jurisprudence gleans guidance from common-law developments, we must consider the common law's treatment of the right of recovery asserted" by the plaintiff. *Id.* at 541-42 (internal quotation marks and **[—12—]** citation omitted). "[A]lthough common-law principles are not necessarily dispositive of questions arising under FELA, unless they are expressly rejected in the text of the statute, they are entitled to great weight in our analysis." *Id.* at 544; *see also id.* ("Only to the extent of ... explicit statutory alterations is FELA an avowed departure from the rules of the common law.") (internal quotation marks omitted).

Applying that analysis, we hold that the governmental function defense remains available in FELA cases. There is no dispute that the governmental function defense is a creature of the common law. In *Gottshall*, the Supreme Court drew on the common law to define the right to recover under the FELA for negligently inflicted emotional distress. *Id.* at 544-49. It reasoned that "because negligent infliction of emotional distress is not explicitly addressed in the statute, the common-law background of this right of recovery must play a vital role in giving content to the scope of an employer's duty under FELA to avoid inflicting emotional injury." *Id.* at 551. In this case, though the FELA expressly abrogates the common-law defenses of contributory negligence and assumption of risk,[3] the statute says nothing about the governmental function defense. Therefore, as in *Gottshall*, the common-law background means that the governmental function defense remains available in FELA cases.

Ojeda argues that we should understand 45 U.S.C. § 55 expressly to displace the governmental function defense. That section provides that "[a]ny contract, rule, regulation, or device whatsoever, **[—13—]** the purpose or intent of which shall be to enable any common carrier to exempt itself from **{-65-}** any liability created by this chapter, shall to that extent be void." According to Ojeda, the governmental function defense is a "device" within the meaning of § 55 because that section bars "anything" a railroad might use "to evade its liability under the FELA." Appellee's Br. 29.

We disagree that § 55 can be read so broadly. The Supreme Court has already "'cataloged' the ways in which FELA expressly departed from the common law: It abolished the fellow servant rule, rejected contributory negligence in favor of comparative negligence, prohibited employers from contracting around the Act, and abolished the assumption of risk defense." *Norfolk S. Ry. v. Sorrell*, 549 U.S. 158, 168 (2007) (quoting *Norfolk & W. R. Co. v. Ayers*, 538 U.S. 135, 145 (2003)). As noted above, "unless [common-law principles] are expressly rejected in the text of the [FELA], they are entitled to great weight." *Gottshall*, 512 U.S. at 544. Ojeda's interpretation of "device" as including every common-law defense against liability contradicts that presumption. *See also Nordgren v. Burlington N. R.R.*, 101 F.3d 1246, 1251 (8th Cir. 1996) (holding that "any device whatsoever" in 45 U.S.C. § 55 "refers only to any other creative agreements or arrangements the railroad might come up with to exempt itself from liability").

We conclude that the governmental function defense remains available in cases brought under the FELA.

B

That the MTA may claim the governmental function defense in FELA suits, however, does not mean it avoids liability in this case. Because the governmental function defense is an affirmative defense, **[—14—]** *see Ferreira v. City of Binghamton*, 975 F.3d 255, 284 (2d Cir. 2020), the MTA must show its entitlement to the defense's protection. To that end, the MTA argues that its actions are protected under "the common-law doctrine of governmental immunity" that "shield[s] public

[3] *See* 45 U.S.C. § 53 ("[T]he fact that the employee may have been guilty of contributory negligence shall not bar a recovery."); *id.* § 54 ("In any action brought [under the FELA], [an] employee shall not be held to have assumed the risks of his employment.").

entities from liability for discretionary actions taken during the performance of governmental functions." *Valdez v. City of New York*, 18 N.Y.3d 69, 75-76 (2011).

In *Owen v. City of Independence*, 445 U.S. 622, 644-50 (1980), the Supreme Court described the common law as affording municipalities immunity from tort liability by reference to two distinctions. First, under the "governmental-proprietary distinction," a municipality is liable under ordinary tort principles when "performing the same 'proprietary' functions as any private corporation," but it is immune when "acting in [a] 'governmental' or 'public' capacity." *Id.* at 645. Second, under the ministerial-discretionary distinction, a municipality is protected from "suits ... either for the non-exercise of, or for the manner in which in good faith it exercises, *discretionary powers* of a public or legislative character" but not from suits for activities that are "ministerial in nature." *Id.* at 644, 648 (internal quotation marks omitted). Thus, to evaluate whether the governmental function defense applies, we ask two questions. First, was the municipality engaged in a proprietary or a governmental function? Second, if it was engaged in a governmental function, was it exercising discretionary authority or performing a ministerial duty? Only a governmental function performed through discretionary authority receives the protection of the defense.[4] **[—15—] {-66-}**

Courts in this circuit have had few occasions to explore when a municipality may be liable to its police officers under the FELA. This court approached the issue in *Greene v. Long Island R.R.*, an interlocutory appeal of the district court's decision that the MTA was a "common carrier by railroad" within the meaning of the FELA. 280 F.3d 224, 226 (2d Cir. 2002). The case arose from an MTA police officer's suit against the MTA for being "negligent in failing to provide Greene with safe working conditions, including by failing to equip the jeep with a siren and adequate emergency lights and flashers." *Id.* at 227. This court agreed with the district court that the MTA was a common carrier under the FELA but "express[ed] no view as to whether Greene was injured ... by reason of any defect or insufficiency, due to MTA's negligence, in its equipment." *Id.* at 240. On remand, the parties in *Greene* settled before the district court reached the merits. Order of Discontinuance, *Greene v. Long Island R.R.*, No. 98-CV-4316 (E.D.N.Y. Dec. 3, 2003), ECF No. 66.[5] **[—16—]**

As noted above, what constitutes negligence under the FELA is a federal question that depends on the common law generally rather than on "differing conceptions of negligence applicable under state and local laws." *Urie*, 337 U.S. at 174. The MTA, however, argues that it is entitled to the governmental function defense as defined by New York courts. We need not

---

[4] *See* 6 Eugene McQuillin, Treatise on the Law of Municipal Corporations § 2628 (1913) ("As a branch of the rule of nonliability of municipalities for **[—15—]** torts in connection with the exercise of *governmental* functions, is the rule which distinguishes (1) ministerial duties from (2) legislative, judicial and discretionary functions."); *see also* Restatement (Second) of Torts § 895C cmt. g (1979) (observing that "discretionary function" immunity "is based on the theory that some governmental functions are of a type that should not be subject to review and second-guessing by the courts in a tort action"); *Ferreira*, 975 F.3d at 283 n.10 ("When a municipality is engaged in a 'proprietary' rather than a 'governmental' role, it is subject to the ordinary rules of negligence that apply to private parties, so that neither discretionary immunity nor the special duty rule apply.") (describing New York law).

[5] State court cases in which police officers have sued the MTA for negligence under the FELA have been similarly inconclusive. Such suits have been dismissed for failure to show negligence with no suggestion that the claims would be barred by the governmental function defense. *See* **[—16—]** *Curley v. Consol. R. Corp.*, 81 N.Y.2d 746, 747-48 (1992) (dismissing suit alleging a defective police car because the "plaintiff's evidence is insufficient as a matter of law, without total speculation, to permit the inference that any negligent act or omission on Conrail's part caused his injuries") (citation omitted); *Cruz v. MTA*, 963 N.Y.S.2d 18, 19 (N.Y. App. Div. 1st Dep't 2013) (dismissing suit alleging injuries incurred after the MTA negligently summoned the officer to the scene of an assault because "[t]here is no reasonable basis for finding that there was any negligence on the MTA's part that contributed to [the] plaintiff's injuries").

decide the exact contours of the governmental function defense under the FELA because the MTA cannot succeed even under its assumption that we should look primarily to New York law to describe the scope of the defense.

1

Under New York law, "[w]hen a negligence claim is asserted against a municipality, the first issue for a court to decide is whether the municipal entity was engaged in a proprietary function or acted in a governmental capacity at the time the claim arose." *Turturro v. City of New York*, 28 N.Y.3d 469, 477 (2016) (quoting *Applewhite v. Accuhealth, Inc.*, 21 N.Y.3d 420, 425 (2013)). "If the municipality's actions fall in the proprietary realm, it **{-67-}** is subject to suit under the ordinary rules of negligence applicable to nongovernmental parties." *Applewhite*, 21 N.Y.3d at 425. **[—17—]**

The defense is therefore available only if the MTA was engaged in a governmental function. "A government entity performs a purely proprietary role when its activities essentially substitute for or supplement traditionally private enterprises." *Id.* (internal quotation marks omitted). By contrast, "a municipality will be deemed to have been engaged in a governmental function when its acts are undertaken for the protection and safety of the public pursuant to the general police powers." *Id.* (internal quotation marks omitted). Because such functions exist on a "continuum," the "relevant inquiry in determining whether a governmental agency is acting within a governmental or proprietary capacity is to examine the specific act or omission out of which the injury is claimed to have arisen and the capacity in which that act or failure to act occurred." *In re World Trade Ctr. Bombing Litig.*, 17 N.Y.3d 428, 446-47 (2011) (internal quotation marks omitted).

"Police protection" is a "quintessential example of a governmental function." *Id.* at 448. That function "involves the provision of a governmental service to protect the public generally from external hazards and particularly to control the activities of criminal wrongdoers." *Riss v. City of New York*, 22 N.Y.2d 579, 581 (1968). Because "[t]he amount of protection that may be provided is limited by the resources of the community and by a considered legislative-executive decision as to how those resources may be deployed," tort liability based on the failure to provide adequate police protection "could and would inevitably determine how the limited police resources of the community should be allocated and without predictable limits." *Id.* at 581-82. **[—18—]**

Though this case involves the police, Ojeda does not allege that the MTA failed adequately "to protect the public." *Id.* at 581. Instead, Ojeda's claim is that the MTA, in assigning him a patrol car without a prisoner compartment, failed to provide him with a safe workplace or with proper equipment. The claim is not based on the MTA's duties as a governmental entity providing police protection but on the MTA's duties as an employer providing safe working conditions to its employees. When acting as an employer, the MTA "is bound ... to the exercise of reasonable care in providing [its] employee with a safe place in which to work, with proper and adequate tools, appliances and machinery, and with fellow-employees competent for the tasks to which they are assigned." *Marceau v. Rutland R.R. Co.*, 211 N.Y. 203, 209 (1914). For that reason, courts have departed from the general rule of nonliability when a "particular act, although in connection with a governmental function, was itself a corporate duty, so as to render the municipality liable to employees for injuries received." 6 McQuillin, *supra* note 4, § 2620.[6] In this **{-68-}** way, "the varied functions of a

[6] *See also* 63 C.J.S. *Municipal Corporations* § 883 (2022) ("Although the organization and maintenance of a fire department are generally regarded as governmental duties, a municipality is generally held liable in the case of a firefighter injured by defective appliances of the department or by the negligence of others therein in the performance of the firefighter's duties.") (footnote omitted); *MacClave v. City of New York*, 265 N.Y.S.2d 222, 224 (N.Y. App. Div. 1st Dep't 1965) (affirming a jury verdict against the city for negligently furnishing a mask to a firefighter that was "dangerous to use for general fire-fighting purposes").

governmental entity can be interspersed with both governmental and proprietary elements." *World Trade Ctr.*, 17 N.Y.3d at 447.

The jury found, based on the vehicle, partner, and backup the MTA provided to Ojeda, that the MTA "was negligent in failing to **[—19—]** provide a safe place to work on October 2, 2013." Verdict, *supra*, at 1. In its decisions regarding the state of Ojeda's workplace, the MTA was engaged in a proprietary rather than governmental function. It therefore cannot establish a governmental function defense for that conduct.[7]

2

Even if the MTA were engaged in a governmental function when it provided Ojeda a partner, backup, and a patrol car without a prisoner compartment, it still would need to show that its decision was a "discretionary action[]."*Valdez*, 18 N.Y.3d at 75-76. Under New York law, "[a] public employee's discretionary acts—meaning conduct involving the exercise of reasoned judgment—may not result in the municipality's liability even when the conduct is negligent." *Lauer v. City of New York*, 95 N.Y.2d 95, 99 (2000). "In other words, even if a plaintiff establishes all elements of a negligence claim, a state or municipal defendant engaging in a governmental function can avoid liability if it timely raises the defense and proves that the **[—20—]** alleged negligent act or omission involved the exercise of discretionary authority." *Valdez*, 18 N.Y.3d at 76.

New York's protection for discretionary acts is not unlimited. "[T]he governmental function immunity defense cannot attach unless the municipal defendant establishes that the discretion possessed by its employees was in fact exercised in relation to the conduct on which liability is predicated." *Id.* When, "viewing the record as a whole," the plaintiff's claim "essentially arises from a misjudgment that was discretionary," New York courts hold that the municipality is entitled to immunity. *Mon v. City of New York*, 78 N.Y.2d 309, 315 (1991).[8] When "there is no evidence" that the municipality "exercised ... discretion" or "made a judgment of any sort," New York courts hold that governmental function immunity does not apply. **{-69-}** *Haddock v. City of New York*, 75 N.Y.2d 478, 485 (1990).[9] **[—21—]**

In this case, the MTA has failed to establish that it exercised its discretion when, without studying backup response times, it assigned Ojeda to patrol with Cella in a vehicle without a prisoner compartment.

[7] Employees such as Ojeda are not limited to bringing safe workplace suits against their municipal employers. "An employee may recover merely as an individual, on the ground of negligence, in a proper case, without in any way relying on the liability of a master for injuries to his servant." 6 McQuillin, *supra* note 4, § 2620. We need not decide the extent to which the governmental function defense would defeat a FELA claim that in substance asserted the employee's rights as a member of the public. In this case, Ojeda's amended complaint brought claims that no member of the public could bring—that the MTA failed "to provide [Ojeda] with the necessary and proper tools and equipment with which to work," failed "to provide [Ojeda] with an appropriate and timely backup," and "provid[ed] [Ojeda] with a police partner who left plaintiff alone to manage with two persons." Am. Compl., *supra*, ¶ 21.

[8] *See also Johnson v. City of New York*, 15 N.Y.3d 676, 681 (2010) (holding that the governmental function defense barred a claim arising from a stray bullet fired by police because "on this record ... it cannot be said that the officers failed to exercise discretion in discharging their weapons"); *Devlin v. City of New York*, 148 N.Y.S.3d 149, 151-52 (N.Y. App. Div. 2d Dep't 2021) (granting summary judgment to the city because "[t]he evidence ... demonstrated that the officers' decision involved reasoned judgment and an exercise of discretion").

[9] *See also Stevens v. Town of E. Fishkill Police Dep't*, 156 N.Y.S.3d 288, 290 (N.Y. App. Div. 2d Dep't 2021) (affirming the denial of a town's motion to dismiss because it "failed to establish, prima facie, ... that the officers' actions were discretionary, meaning conduct involving the exercise of reasoned judgment"); *Santaiti v. Town of Ramapo*, 80 N.Y.S.3d 288, 296 (N.Y. App. Div. 2d Dep't 2018) (affirming the denial of a town's motion to dismiss because "it cannot be said, as a matter of law, that the discretion possessed by the Town was in fact exercised") (internal quotation marks and alteration omitted).

Given that discretionary immunity is an affirmative defense, *Ferreira*, 975 F.3d at 270, a municipal defendant must "demonstrate[] its prima facie entitlement to judgment as a matter of law by establishing, among other things, that ... [its] decision constituted a discretionary act involving the exercise of reasoned judgment," *Heckel v. City of New York*, 875 N.Y.S.2d 217, 218 (N.Y. App. Div. 2d Dep't 2009). As Ojeda notes, the MTA "does not discuss ... what policies were at issue, nor does it tie those policies to any kind of evidence whatsoever showing that discretionary acts were actually performed." Appellee's Br. 27. The MTA's motion in limine provides only a conclusory assertion that "the MTA exercised discretion in procuring its vehicle fleet and in assigning officers to various duties during any particular shift." Motion in Limine at 3, *Ojeda*, 477 F. Supp. 3d 65, ECF No. 103. In sum, the MTA has not demonstrated that it exercised its "reasoned judgment" when assigning vehicles for patrol or otherwise affecting Ojeda's workplace. *Heckel*, 875 N.Y.S.2d at 218.

The MTA relies on *McCormack v. City of New York*—in which the court dismissed a wrongful death claim based on the city's provision of a faulty bullet-proof vest to the decedent police officer as barred by the governmental function defense—for the proposition that it cannot be held liable for torts relating to a police department's choice of equipment. 80 N.Y.2d 808, 810 (1992). We disagree that *McCormack* stands for so broad a proposition. Unlike in this case, the municipal defendant in *McCormack* met its burden of showing that it exercised its discretion. As the court noted in that case, "the evidence at trial **[—22—]** showed" that "the more protective devices available on the market afford reduced mobility, a disadvantage that might well lead City officials to choose [the bullet-proof vest at issue] over the alternatives." *Id.* at 811. The municipality therefore showed that it had made a reasoned judgment in its choice of equipment.

In order to establish a governmental function defense, a municipality must demonstrate that its action involved "the exercise of discretion or expert judgment in policy matters." *Id.* at 811 (quoting *Haddock*, 75 N.Y.2d at 484). The MTA has not done so in this case, and therefore the governmental function defense does not bar Ojeda's suit.[10] **{-70-}**

II

Second, the MTA argues that the district court erred in permitting the jury to find liability without expert testimony on the standard of care. "[T]he trial judge has broad discretion in the matter **[—23—]** of the admission or exclusion of expert evidence, and his action is to be sustained unless manifestly erroneous." *Salem v. U.S. Lines Co.*, 370 U.S. 31, 35 (1962). The MTA contends that the district court abused that discretion because the jury needed expert testimony to evaluate the choice to assign Ojeda a patrol car without a prisoner compartment, the assignment of Cella as Ojeda's partner, and the failure to study backup response times.

"[C]auses of action in which the law predicates recovery upon expert testimony" are "rare." *Id.* "It is well settled that expert testimony is unnecessary in cases where jurors are as capable of comprehending the primary facts and of drawing correct conclusions from them as are witnesses

---

10 To the extent that the jury attributed Cella's negligent conduct to the MTA—as opposed to finding the MTA negligent for assigning Cella as a partner—the governmental function defense does not bar this aspect of Ojeda's claim either. Insofar as Ojeda alleged that Cella's conduct made it harder for Ojeda safely to perform his work, he did so in the context of his safe workplace claim, which as explained above implicates a proprietary duty. *See supra* Part I.B.1.; *see also Buckley v. City of New York*, 56 N.Y.2d 300, 302 (1982) (upholding a jury verdict finding the city liable for its police officer negligently shooting a fellow police officer). Moreover, the MTA did not request a special verdict or interrogatory and did not otherwise object to the verdict form. It has therefore waived the general-verdict rule. *Morse v. Fusto*, 804 F.3d 538, 551-52 (2d Cir. 2015). Because there are multiple bases to support the jury's verdict apart from Cella's negligence, the MTA would not be entitled to a new trial even if it could not be held liable for Cella's negligence.

possessed of special or peculiar training." *Wills v. Amerada Hess Corp.*, 379 F.3d 32, 46 (2d Cir. 2004) (internal quotation marks omitted). We require expert evidence only when a necessary element of the claim "would not be obvious to the lay juror." *Id.* Thus, we have held that expert testimony was required to establish "the causal link between exposure to toxins and other behavior and squamous cell carcinoma" for a Jones Act claim. *Id.* We have also suggested that "special expertise" was necessary when a claim involved "esoteric" injuries such as "dyscalculia and spelling dyspraxia." *Ulfik v. Metro-North Commuter R.R.*, 77 F.3d 54, 59 (2d Cir. 1996) (discussing *Claar v. Burlington N. R.R. Co.*, 29 F.3d 499 (9th Cir. 1994)). Conversely, we have held that expert testimony was unnecessary in a dispute over whether "prolonged exposure to paint fumes would cause headache, nausea, and dizziness." *Id.* at 59-60.

The district court did not manifestly err in allowing this case to be submitted to the jury without expert testimony. In *Spokane & Inland Empire R.R. Co. v. United States*, the Supreme Court affirmed a jury's **[—24—]** verdict finding that the safety measures placed on a train were an inadequate substitute for the statutorily required handholds and grab-irons. 241 U.S. 344, 347-51 (1916). The railroad argued that the jury should not be permitted to make a finding on that issue without expert testimony. *Id.* at 351. The Supreme Court disagreed, holding that "the question" of whether the train was adequately equipped "was not one for experts and that the jury after hearing the testimony and inspecting the openings were competent to determine the issue." *Id.* Likewise, the Supreme Court in *Salem* permitted a jury to find—after hearing testimony and viewing photographs—that a shipowner was negligent for "having failed to provide railings or other safety devices" without the aid of expert testimony. 370 U.S. at 34 (internal **{-71-}** quotation marks omitted). Because "the potential danger was fairly obvious and a jury should be perfectly competent to decide whether the handholds furnished were sufficient to discharge the owner's duty to provide his seamen with a safe place to work," the Supreme Court held that the jury's verdict "hardly require[d] expert knowledge of naval architecture." *Id.* at 36-37 (quoting *Salem v. United States*, 293 F.2d 121, 126 (2d Cir. 1961) (Smith, J., dissenting)).

As in *Salem*, the "potential danger" of failing to provide Ojeda with a prisoner compartment, a capable partner, or timely backup was "fairly obvious." *Id.* The jury in this case was equipped to evaluate the MTA's actions in sending Ojeda on patrol with Cella in a vehicle lacking a prisoner compartment and without studying backup response times. Those judgments are not the sort that we have held requires expert knowledge. We will not reverse the jury's verdict in this case solely for lack of expert testimony. **[—25—]**

CONCLUSION

A different jury might have reached a different verdict in this case. But in FELA cases "the role of the jury is significantly greater than in common law negligence actions," and its "right to pass upon the question of the employer's liability must be most liberally viewed." *Gallose v. Long Island R.R. Co.*, 878 F.2d 80, 84 (2d Cir. 1989) (internal quotation marks and alteration omitted). We may reverse the denial of a motion for judgment notwithstanding the verdict only if "the evidence is such that, without weighing the credibility of the witnesses or otherwise considering the weight of the evidence, there can be but one conclusion as to the verdict that reasonable men could have reached." *Simblest v. Maynard*, 427 F.2d 1, 4 (2d Cir. 1970).

Though the governmental function defense was available for the MTA to assert, the MTA failed to show that the defense barred liability in this case. Additionally, we cannot say that the evidence supporting the jury's verdict for Ojeda was legally insufficient. We therefore **AFFIRM** the judgment of the district court.

United States Court of Appeals
for the Second Circuit

No. 21-0616

SILVA
vs.
FARRISH

Appeal from the United States District Court for the Eastern District of New York

Decided: August 25, 2022

Citation: 47 F.4th 78, 10 Adm. R. 50 (2d Cir. 2022).

Before **JACOB, WESLEY,** and **MENASHI,** Circuit Judges.

[—3—] {-81-} MENASHI, Circuit Judge:

Plaintiffs-Appellants Gerrod Smith, Jonathan Smith, and David Silva are members of the Shinnecock Indian Nation and reside on the Shinnecock Reservation. They believe that when the Shinnecock ceded land to colonial settlers, the tribe retained the aboriginal right to fish in the Shinnecock Bay without interference and that the Supremacy Clause protects this right from state laws that would abridge it.[1] Over the past decade, however, state officials have ticketed and prosecuted the plaintiffs for violating state laws that regulate fishing in the Shinnecock Bay. Seeking to clarify their fishing rights, the plaintiffs filed this action in the U.S. District Court for the Eastern District of New York against the New York State Department of Environmental Conservation ("DEC"),[2] several DEC officials in **[—4—]** their official and personal capacities,[3] the Suffolk County District Attorney's Office, and Assistant District Attorney Brian Greenwood.[4]

The complaint alleged that the enforcement of state fishing regulations against the plaintiffs in the Shinnecock Bay violates their fishing rights. It also alleged that the defendants' prior enforcement of state fishing regulations amounted to intentional discrimination in violation of 42 U.S.C. §§ 1981 and 1982. The plaintiffs sought declaratory and injunctive relief to prevent the further enforcement of state fishing regulations against them. The plaintiffs sought monetary damages from the individual defendants based on the allegations of discrimination. **{-82-}**

The district court granted summary judgment to the DEC defendants. The district court concluded that state sovereign immunity barred all the claims against the DEC—as well as those against the DEC officials in their official capacities—and that the *Ex parte Young* exception to state sovereign immunity did not apply. The district court additionally held that the plaintiffs lacked standing to bring their claims for declaratory and injunctive relief and that *Younger* abstention precluded consideration of Silva's claims for prospective relief. The district court further held that the plaintiffs' **[—5—]** discrimination claims were either time-barred or failed to allege a prima facie case of discrimination.

We hold that *Ex parte Young* applies to the plaintiffs' fishing-rights claims against the DEC officials—but not against the DEC itself—because the plaintiffs allege an ongoing violation of federal law and seek prospective

---

1 *See* App'x 38 ("The colonial documents ... in which the Shinnecock ceded land and negotiated retained fishing rights are legally enforceable today under state and federal law."); App'x 41 ("The aboriginal right to fish in unrelinquished aboriginal territory and the related retained right to fish in ceded territory is a protected federal right under the Supremacy Clause.").

2 State law empowers the DEC to manage the "fish and wildlife resources" of the state, including the habitats of fish and wildlife. N.Y. Environmental Conservation Law § 11-0303(1).

3 The DEC officials include DEC Conservation Officers Brian Farrish and Evan Laczi and DEC Commissioner Basil Seggos.

4 On appeal, the plaintiffs do not raise any arguments regarding the district court's grant of summary judgment to the Suffolk County District Attorney's Office and Assistant District Attorney Brian Greenwood. Those arguments are therefore waived, *see Graves v. Finch Pruyn & Co.*, 457 F.3d 181, 184 (2d Cir. 2006), and we affirm the judgment of the district court insofar as it granted summary judgment to those defendants.

relief against state officials. We also hold that the plaintiffs have Article III standing to seek prospective relief and that *Younger* abstention no longer bars Silva from seeking prospective relief because his criminal proceedings have ended. We therefore conclude that the district court erred in granting summary judgment to the DEC officials on the plaintiffs' claims for declaratory and injunctive relief. As for the plaintiffs' discrimination claims, we conclude that the district court properly granted summary judgment to the defendants because there is no evidence in the record that would permit an inference of discriminatory intent. Accordingly, we affirm in part and vacate in part the judgment of the district court. The case is remanded for further proceedings consistent with this opinion.

BACKGROUND

I

The plaintiffs are members of the Shinnecock Indian Nation, a federally recognized Indian tribe, and reside on the Shinnecock Reservation. The plaintiffs believe that, based on certain colonial-era deeds, they have the right to fish in the Shinnecock Bay without interference and that the Supremacy Clause protects that right from state abridgment. Over the past decade, however, the state has ticketed and prosecuted the plaintiffs for violating state laws that regulate fishing in the Shinnecock Bay. **[—6—]**

Gerrod Smith was prosecuted in October 2008 for possessing eighteen out-of-season and undersized summer flounder, sixteen out-of-season and undersized porgy, and two undersized blackfish harvested from the Shinnecock Bay in violation of state law. Around the same time, Jonathan Smith received a civil infraction ticket and a criminal summons for operating an "unpermitted aquaculture facility" in the Shinnecock Bay in violation of New York Environmental Conservation Law § 13-0316(2) and for using "improper shellfish tags" in violation of § 13-0319. The cases against Gerrod Smith and Jonathan Smith were ultimately dismissed. In 2017, Silva was charged with fishing without a license as well as unlawful possession of underage eels and possession of eels over the limit. *See* N.Y. Environmental Conservation Law § 13-0355(3); (fishing without a license); 6 N.Y.C.R.R. § 40.1(b)(1)(ii) (undersized eels); *id.* § 40.1(b)(1)(iii) (eels over the limit).

While Silva's criminal prosecution was pending in state court, the plaintiffs filed this action in the U.S. District Court for the Eastern District of New York. The complaint alleged that certain colonial-era deeds establish the plaintiffs' "right to fish in the waters of Shinnecock Bay and its estuary," App'x 16, and that the application of state fishing regulations to the **{-83-}** plaintiffs violates those fishing rights. The complaint also alleged that the defendants' prior enforcement of state fishing regulations amounted to a "continuing pattern and practice of purposeful acts of discrimination based on their race as Native Americans" in violation of 42 U.S.C. §§ 1981 and 1982. App'x 21.

The plaintiffs sought a declaration of their fishing rights and an injunction preventing the defendants from continuing the criminal prosecution against Silva and from otherwise interfering with the plaintiffs' "use of the waters, fishing, taking fish, and holding fish and **[—7—]** shellfish in Shinnecock Bay and its estuary and other usual and customary Shinnecock fishing waters." App'x 22. The plaintiffs sought monetary damages based on the allegations of discrimination.

The plaintiffs moved for a preliminary injunction, and the district court denied their motion. *Silva v. Farrish*, No. 18-CV-3648S, 2018 WL 8967113, at *4 (E.D.N.Y. July 31, 2018). The district court concluded that Silva failed to show a likelihood of success on the merits and that even if he had, abstention was required under *Younger*. *Id.* The district court further held that the Smiths lacked standing because their injuries were "entirely speculative and remote." *Id.* at *5.

II

The defendants moved to dismiss the complaint for lack of subject matter jurisdiction under Federal Rule of Civil

Procedure 12(b)(1) and for failure to state a claim under Rule 12(b)(6). The district court referred the motions to a magistrate judge, who recommended dismissing the plaintiffs' complaint in its entirety. *Silva v. Farrish*, No. 18-CV-3648S, 2019 WL 117602 (E.D.N.Y. Jan. 7, 2019). The magistrate judge held that state sovereign immunity barred the claims against the DEC and its officials in their official capacities. *Id.* at *9-12. In so holding, the magistrate judge rejected the plaintiffs' argument that *Ex parte Young* authorized their claims for prospective relief. *Id.* at *9-12. The magistrate judge concluded—as alternative bases for dismissal—that the plaintiffs lacked standing to seek prospective relief, *id.* at *15 & n.19, and that *Younger* abstention precluded consideration of Silva's claims for prospective relief, *id.* at *14. The magistrate judge further held that the plaintiffs' **[—8—]** discrimination claims against the DEC officials in their individual capacities failed to state a claim. *Id.* at *16.[5]

The district court neither adopted nor rejected the magistrate judge's recommendation but terminated the dismissal motions and set a briefing schedule for summary judgment motions. The district court then referred the summary judgment motions to the magistrate judge for another report and recommendation. The magistrate judge recommended granting summary judgment to the defendants on the claims for declaratory and injunctive relief for the same reasons that were provided in the first report and recommendation. *Silva v. Farrish*, No. 18-CV-3648, 2020 WL 3451344 (E.D.N.Y. May 27, 2020), *report and recommendation adopted*, No. 18-CV-3648, 2021 WL 613092 (E.D.N.Y. Feb. 17, 2021). As for the plaintiffs' claims of racial discrimination, the magistrate judge concluded that the Smiths' claims were time-barred, **{-84-}** *id.* at *11, and that Silva did not make out a prima facie case of discrimination, *id.* at *12.

The district court adopted the report and recommendation "in its entirety" and granted summary judgment to the defendants. *Silva v. Farrish*, No. 18-CV-3648, 2021 WL 613092 (E.D.N.Y. Feb. 17, 2021). In their objection to the report and recommendation, the plaintiffs disclosed that Silva had "abandoned" his state-court criminal appeal and argued that *Younger* abstention no longer barred Silva's claims. The district court rejected this argument, concluding that Silva's **[—9—]** abandonment of his state-court appeal did "not equate to exhausting ... state appellate remedies" so *Younger* still applied. *Id.* at *2 (internal quotation marks omitted).

The plaintiffs timely appealed.

DISCUSSION

I

We begin with the district court's grant of summary judgment on the plaintiffs' claims for declaratory and injunctive relief. We hold that the *Ex parte Young* exception to state sovereign immunity applies to these claims against the DEC officials, that the plaintiffs have Article III standing to pursue prospective relief, and that *Younger* abstention does not bar Silva's claims for prospective relief. Accordingly, the district court erred in granting summary judgment to the DEC officials.

A

States are generally "immune from suit" under "the doctrine of sovereign immunity." *Whole Woman's Health v. Jackson*, 142 S. Ct. 522, 532 (2021). That doctrine recognizes that the states "entered the Union with their sovereign immunity intact, unlimited by Article III's jurisdictional grant." *Va. Off. for Prot. & Advoc. v. Stewart*, 563 U.S. 247, 253 (2011). Here, the plaintiffs do not contest that the DEC and its officials are part of the state and enjoy sovereign immunity from suit. Instead, the plaintiffs invoke *Ex parte Young*, 209 U.S. 123 (1908), which provides a "a

[5] The magistrate judge recommended dismissing the plaintiffs' claims against the Suffolk County District Attorney's Office and Assistant District Attorney Brian Greenwood on the grounds that the District Attorney's Office is not an entity susceptible to suit and that Greenwood was entitled to absolute prosecutorial immunity. *Silva*, 2020 WL 3451344, at *19.

narrow exception grounded in traditional equity practice—one that allows certain private parties to seek judicial orders in federal court preventing state executive officials from enforcing state laws that are contrary to federal law." *Whole Woman's* **[—10—]** *Health*, 142 S. Ct. at 532. *Ex parte Young*, however, has no application to the DEC itself. *See P.R. Aqueduct & Sewer Auth. v. Metcalf & Eddy, Inc.*, 506 U.S. 139, 146 (1993) (explaining that *Ex parte Young* "has no application in suits against the States and their agencies, which are barred regardless of the relief sought"). We therefore consider the plaintiffs' argument as it relates to the DEC officials.

To determine whether *Ex parte Young* applies to a complaint, we conduct a "straightforward inquiry" into whether the complaint (1) "alleges an ongoing violation of federal law" and (2) "seeks relief properly characterized as prospective." *Verizon Md. v. Pub. Serv. Comm'n of Md.*, 535 U.S. 635, 645 (2002); *see also Dairy Mart Convenience Stores, Inc. v. Nickel*, 411 F.3d 367, 372 (2d Cir. 2005). There is no doubt that the plaintiffs' suit satisfies both prongs. The plaintiffs allege that the enforcement of state fishing regulations violates their federally protected fishing rights. Their requested relief—that the DEC officials be enjoined from enforcing the state fishing regulations against them—would prospectively end the alleged violation. Based on this analysis, *Ex parte Young* applies. **{-85-}**

The DEC defendants argue that the Supreme Court's decision in *Idaho v. Coeur d'Alene Tribe of Idaho*, 521 U.S. 261 (1997), and our decision in *Western Mohegan Tribe & Nation v. Orange County*, 395 F.3d 18 (2d Cir. 2004), foreclose the application of *Ex parte Young* in this case. We disagree. In *Coeur d'Alene*, the Supreme Court said that if the effect of the requested relief is "the functional equivalent of quiet title" to land, then the suit has effectively been brought against the state and is barred by state sovereign immunity. 521 U.S. at 282. The suit cannot proceed if it asserts an "entitlement to the exclusive use and occupancy and the right to quiet enjoyment of ... lands." *Id.* at 265. In other words, the suit is effectively one against the state when **[—11—]** "substantially all benefits of ownership and control would shift from the State to the Tribe." *Id.* at 282.

In *Coeur d'Alene*, the tribe requested a declaratory judgment not only to declare invalid any laws "purport[ing] to regulate, authorize, use, or affect in any way the submerged lands" but also to prohibit the state from taking "action in violation of the Tribe's rights of exclusive use and occupancy, quiet enjoyment, and other ownership interest in the submerged lands." *Id.* at 265.[6] In *Western Mohegan*, the tribe sought a declaration that it held "Indian title," which it described as the right "to camp, to hunt, to fish, and to use the waters and timbers" as well as the right "to *exclude all others,* including holders of fee simple title, through state law possessory actions such as ejectment and trespass." 395 F.3d at 22 (alteration omitted).

The plaintiffs here seek a declaration that the law grants them a right to fish in the Shinnecock Bay without interference and that the DEC officials are unlawfully denying them that right. Unlike the tribes in *Coeur d'Alene* and *Western Mohegan*, the plaintiffs' request for relief in this case would not transfer ownership and control of the Shinnecock Bay from the state to an Indian tribe. Nor would it allow the plaintiffs to prevent others from fishing in the Shinnecock Bay. It **[—12—]** would merely resolve the plaintiffs' individual claims that they have their own right to fish there.[7]

---

[6] *See also Stewart*, 563 U.S. at 257 (explaining that *Coeur d'Alene* "refused to allow an Indian Tribe to use *Ex parte Young* to obtain injunctive and declaratory relief establishing its exclusive right to the use and enjoyment of certain submerged lands in Idaho and the invalidity of all state statutes and regulations governing that land").

[7] The DEC defendants argue that the plaintiffs "have at various points ... suggested that ownership of all or part of the Shinnecock Bay is itself 'contested,' or that all or part of the Bay is under Shinnecock 'jurisdiction.'" DEC Defendants' Br. 37. Whatever the plaintiffs may have suggested about the status of the Shinnecock Bay, the relief

A decision of the Sixth Circuit is instructive. In *Hamilton v. Myers*, 281 F.3d 520 (6th Cir. 2002), the court was asked to determine whether the plaintiffs could "seek a judicial declaration of, and an injunction protecting, their alleged exclusive riparian rights over Doherty land grants submerged under [a] Lake." *Id.* at 527. The court observed that "[u]nlike the Tribe in *Coeur d'Alene*, the Hamiltons are not seeking to divest sovereign ownership of [the] Lake from the state, or seeking entitlement to the exclusive use and occupancy of the lake. Nor are the Hamiltons seeking to invalidate the regulatory authority of the [state] agencies" over the lake. *Id.* at 528. If "the Hamiltons prevail at trial," the court explained, the "Lake **{-86-}** will remain within the sovereign control of the State ... and will continue to be subject to [the state's] regulatory authority. At most ..., the State ... will be required to tailor its regulatory scheme to respect the [plaintiffs'] constitutionally protected riparian rights." *Id.* The court held that *Coeur d'Alene* did not "extend" to that case. *Id.* So too here. If the plaintiffs succeed in obtaining their requested relief, at most the state would need to tailor its regulatory scheme to respect the plaintiffs' fishing rights. That is a "typical *Young* action," which seeks to "bring the State's regulatory scheme into compliance with federal law." *Coeur d'Alene*, 521 U.S. at 289 (O'Connor, J., concurring in part and **[—13—]** concurring in the judgment). The requested relief would not divest the state of its ownership of the submerged land or the waters, which means this suit is not effectively one against the state.

We hold that the plaintiffs' claims seeking prospective relief against the DEC officials fall within the *Ex parte Young* exception to state sovereign immunity and accordingly may proceed.

B

Article III of the Constitution limits the jurisdiction of federal courts to "Cases" and "Controversies." U.S. Const., art. III, § 2. The doctrine of standing applies the case-or-controversy requirement by "identify[ing] those disputes which are appropriately resolved through the judicial process." *Lujan v. Defenders of Wildlife*, 504 U.S. 555, 560, (1992) (quoting *Whitmore v. Arkansas*, 495 U.S. 149, 155 (1990)). To establish Article III standing, a plaintiff must have "(1) suffered an injury in fact, (2) that is fairly traceable to the challenged conduct of the defendant, and (3) that is likely to be redressed by a favorable judicial decision." *Spokeo Inc. v. Robins*, 578 U.S. 330, 338 (2016).

An injury in fact must be "concrete and particularized" and "actual or imminent, not conjectural or hypothetical." *Lujan*, 504 U.S. at 560 (internal quotation marks omitted). Those claiming a "risk of future harm" may seek "forward-looking, injunctive relief to prevent the harm from occurring" but only if "the risk of harm is sufficiently imminent and substantial." *TransUnion LLC v. Ramirez*, 141 S. Ct. 2190, 2210 (2021); *see also Lacewell v. Off. of Comptroller of Currency*, 999 F.3d 130, 141 (2d Cir. 2021). **[—14—]**

When a plaintiff seeks relief from a threatened criminal prosecution, the Supreme Court has instructed that imminence does "not require a plaintiff to expose himself to liability before bringing suit to challenge the basis for the threat—for example, the constitutionality of a law threatened to be enforced." *MedImmune, Inc. v. Genentech, Inc.*, 549 U.S. 118, 128-29 (2007). Rather, an imminent injury is apparent when the plaintiff has alleged (1) "an intention to engage in a course of conduct arguably affected with a constitutional interest, but proscribed by a statute," and (2) "a credible threat of prosecution thereunder." *Susan B. Anthony List v. Driehaus*, 573 U.S. 149, 159 (2014).[8] In other words, "a **{-87-}** plaintiff has

they seek in this case is not a "right to *exclude all others*." *Western Mohegan*, 395 F.3d at 22.

[8] "The Supreme Court has not limited standing to pursue pre-enforcement challenges only to plaintiffs intending conduct arguably affected with a constitutional interest." *Knife Rts., Inc. v. Vance*, 802 F.3d 377, 384 n.4 (2d Cir. 2015). In *Cayuga Nation v. Tanner*, for example, the plaintiffs alleged that a federal statute preempted the "application of a local anti-gambling ordinance" to the plaintiffs' gaming facility. 824 F.3d 321, 323 (2d

standing to make a preenforcement challenge 'when fear of criminal prosecution under an allegedly unconstitutional statute is not imaginary or wholly speculative.'" *Hedges v. Obama*, 724 F.3d 170, 196 (2d Cir. 2013) (quoting *Babbitt v. United Farm Workers Nat'l Union*, 442 U.S. 289, 302 (1979)).

In this case, the DEC defendants initially raised the issue of standing in their motion to dismiss and did so again in their motion for summary judgment, arguing in both motions that the plaintiffs' **[—15—]** alleged injury was insufficiently imminent.[9] Because "standing was challenged largely on the basis of the pleadings," we "accept as true all material allegations of the complaint, and ... construe the complaint in favor of the complaining party." *Gladstone Realtors v. Village of Bellwood*, 441 U.S. 91, 109 (1979); *Sullivan v. Syracuse Hous. Auth.*, 962 F.2d 1101, 1106-07 (2d Cir. 1992) (stating in the context of a motion for summary judgment that the "court is constrained" when ruling on standing to "accept as true all material allegations of the complaint, and [to] construe the complaint in favor of the complaining party"). "[A]long with the allegations made in the complaint," we consider "other facts and circumstances as may be evident from the record." *Sullivan*, 962 F.2d at 1107; *see also Cargill Int'l S.A. v. M/T Pavel Dybenko*, 991 F.2d 1012, 1019 (2d Cir. 1993) ("[C]ourt[s] must look at the substance of the allegations to determine jurisdiction.").

The plaintiffs have shown that the threat of enforcement of the state fishing laws amounts to an injury in fact.[10] First, the plaintiffs allege "an intention to engage in a course of conduct" arguably protected by federal law but proscribed by state law. *Babbitt*, 442 U.S. at 298. The plaintiffs previously fished in the Shinnecock Bay in violation of the state fishing regulations, and according to their complaint they are "deterred and chilled" from doing so again because they fear prosecution. App'x 18. The plaintiffs thereby **[—16—]** explain that they would fish if they did not fear prosecution. We have said that "specificity" in such plans is not "essential to standing" when the plaintiffs "have already been subjected to enforcement actions." *Knife Rts.*, 802 F.3d at 386 n.5. Given the plaintiffs' history of fishing in the Shinnecock Bay and their prosecutions for that conduct, their allegation is sufficient to show their intent to fish there again.

Second, the plaintiffs have alleged a "credible threat" of future enforcement of the state fishing regulations. *Babbitt*, 442 U.S. at 298. Each plaintiff has already been subject to fines and enforcement proceedings for violating the fishing regulations, and "past enforcement against the same conduct is good evidence that the threat of enforcement is not chimerical." **{-88-}** *Driehaus*, 573 U.S. at 164 (internal quotation marks omitted). The state has not foresworn enforcement of the fishing regulations, and "courts are generally willing to presume that the government will enforce the law as long as the relevant statute is recent and not moribund." *Cayuga Nation*, 824 F.3d at 331-32 (internal quotation marks omitted). "Where, as here, there is reason to believe that the plaintiffs will be targets of criminal prosecution, and there has been no disavowal of an intention to prosecute those individuals, the plaintiffs have adequately alleged a credible threat of prosecution." *Id.* at 331-32. Under these circumstances, the plaintiffs' "professed fear of prosecution is hardly conjectural or hypothetical." *Knife Rts.*, 802 F.3d at 385.

The DEC defendants argue that a party "cannot rely on past injury to satisfy the injury requirement" but "must show a

Cir. 2016). Applying the *Driehaus* standard, we held that the plaintiffs had standing to bring a pre-enforcement challenge because they "alleged that they intend to conduct bingo games, which is clearly prohibited by the Ordinance, and the Village has announced its intention to enforce the Ordinance against" the plaintiffs. *Id.* at 331.

[9] *See* Motion to Dismiss at 7-9, *Silva*, No. 8-CV-3648, ECF No. 56-3; Motion for Summary Judgment at 8-9, *Silva*, No. 8-CV-3648, ECF No. 84-4.

[10] Judge Wesley would conclude that only Silva has established an injury in fact because the Smiths' criminal proceedings were resolved in 2009 and 2010 and the Smiths do not allege a regular course of conduct. In his view, the following analysis applies only to Silva rather than all three plaintiffs.

likelihood that he ... will be injured in the future." DEC Defendants' Br. 45-46 (quoting *Shain v. Ellison*, 356 F.3d 211, 215 (2d Cir. 2004), and citing *City of Los Angeles v. Lyons*, 461 U.S. 95, 101-02 (1983)). But the plaintiffs have shown such a likelihood by alleging both an intention **[—17—]** to fish and a credible threat of prosecution if they do. The cases on which the DEC defendants rely involved circumstances in which a past injury was unlikely to recur. In *Lyons*, the plaintiff sought declaratory and injunctive relief because he claimed that he had been illegally choked by Los Angeles police officers. 461 U.S. at 98. The plaintiff alleged that the Los Angeles police routinely applied chokeholds and that he faced a threat of being illegally subjected to such treatment in the future. *See id.* at 105-06. The Supreme Court decided that the plaintiff lacked standing to challenge the alleged policy because he failed to identify an imminent threat that he would again be stopped and mistreated by the police; he expressed no intent to violate the law, and he could not establish that arresting police officers would necessarily apply a chokehold in a future encounter. *See id.* It was speculative that the plaintiff would again be stopped by police officers who decided to employ a chokehold. Similarly, in *Shain*, we held that the plaintiff was unable "to establish a sufficient likelihood of a future unconstitutional strip search" because the possibility that he would again be subjected to such a search relied on an "accumulation of inferences" that were "simply too speculative and conjectural." 356 F.3d at 216.

The plaintiffs in this case do not rely on such speculation. The state has promulgated its fishing regulations and does not dispute that it would apply those regulations to the plaintiffs should they fish again without complying. "[N]owhere in the record" have the defendants "disavowed that they would criminally charge [the plaintiffs] again in the same circumstances." *Knife Rts.*, 802 F.3d at 386-87; *see also Holder v. Humanitarian L. Project*, 561 U.S. 1, 16 (2010) (recognizing a threat as imminent because the government had "not **[—18—]** argued ... that plaintiffs will not be prosecuted if they do what they say they wish to do").

The plaintiffs seek to fish in the Shinnecock Bay without complying with state fishing regulations. We do not see a basis in the record for dismissing their claims on the ground that they do not intend to fish or that the state does not intend to enforce its regulations. We hold that the plaintiffs have shown an injury in fact for standing to pursue declaratory and injunctive relief.

C

Last, we address whether *Younger* abstention bars consideration of **{-89-}** Silva's claims for injunctive relief. Silva pursued two different claims for injunctive relief. The first would "enjoin[] the Defendants from enforcing the laws of the State of New York against Plaintiff Silva in Southampton Town Justice Court in Case No. 17-7008." App'x 22. The second would "enjoin[] the Defendants from ... interfering with Plaintiffs' use of the waters, fishing, taking fish, and holding fish and shellfish in Shinnecock Bay and its estuary and other usual and customary Shinnecock fishing waters." App'x 22. Although there was an ongoing state prosecution when Silva filed his federal complaint, that proceeding has now ended. Silva's first claim—and the *Younger* issue associated with it—is therefore moot. Silva may proceed on his second claim for injunctive relief.

We faced a similar situation in *Pathways, Inc. v. Dunne*, 329 F.3d 108 (2d Cir. 2003). In that case, "the lawsuits and litigation efforts initiated by [the defendants] against [the plaintiff] in the state courts ... concluded." *Id.* at 114. We decided that the plaintiff's claims for injunctive relief that implicated "state cases pending when the District Court ruled" were "now moot because those cases are **[—19—]** concluded." *Id.* But, like Silva's claims, the plaintiff's claims included "a prospective component: [the plaintiff] sought to prevent suits that [the defendants] might file in the future, or other obstructive activity in which they might engage." *Id.* Those forward-looking claims were not barred because "*Younger* is not a bar to federal court action when state judicial proceedings have not themselves commenced." *Id.* (quoting

Hawaii Hous. Authority v. Midkiff, 467 U.S. 229, 238-39 (1984)).[11]

Because there is no dispute that Silva's prosecution has ended, we regard his request to enjoin that prosecution as moot. But *Younger* abstention does not affect his other claim for injunctive relief.[12] **[—20—]**

II

As for the plaintiffs' discrimination claims, we conclude that the district court properly granted summary judgment to the defendants because there is no evidence in the record that would permit an inference of discriminatory intent.

Section 1981 provides that "all persons have equal right to make and enforce contracts," and § 1982 "establishes that all persons have equal right to purchase, lease, sell, hold, and convey real and personal property." **{-90-}** *Costello v. Town of Huntington*, No. 14-CV-2061, 2015 WL 1396448, at *12 (E.D.N.Y. Mar. 25, 2015) (citing 42 U.S.C. §§ 1981, 1982). To state a prima facie claim under either provision, plaintiffs must prove: "(1) they are members of a racial minority; (2) an intent to discriminate on the basis of their race by defendant; and (3) the discrimination concerned one or more of the activities enumerated in the statute (i.e., make and enforce contracts, sue and be sued, give evidence, etc.)." *Mian v. Donaldson, Lufkin & Jenrette Sec. Corp.*, 7 F.3d 1085, 1087 (2d Cir. 1993).

The second element of the claim—an intent to discriminate—is the focus of this appeal. To survive summary judgment, the plaintiffs needed to produce enough evidence for a reasonable jury to find that the defendants intentionally discriminated against the plaintiffs based on race. *See Ayissi-Etoh v. Fannie Mae*, 712 F.3d 572, 576 (D.C. Cir. 2013) ("For purposes of summary judgment, the operative question under Section 1981 ... is whether the employee produced sufficient evidence for a reasonable jury to find that ... the employer intentionally discriminated against the employee on the basis of race.") (internal quotation marks omitted). The plaintiffs did not provide evidence from which a rational trier of fact could find racially **[—21—]** discriminatory intent. The record shows that the DEC officials cited the three plaintiffs for violating race-neutral, generally applicable fishing regulations in state waters. There is no evidence that the DEC officials did or said anything that would indicate racial animus. Nor is there evidence that they treated non-Indians more favorably than the plaintiffs.

The plaintiffs point to an email that, they argue, establishes "illegal racial profiling of Shinnecock people of the Native American race." Appellants' Br. 22. The email, dated March 28, 2017, and sent from DEC Captain Dallas Bengel to a large group of DEC employees (including Laczi and Farrish), explained that "[w]ord is out that the Shinnecocks are actively seeking a shipper for glass eels" and noted that the DEC "will have to work the off-reservation areas diligently to prevent illegal harvest." App'x 420. The plaintiffs argue that the email reflects racial animus because it identifies the

---

[11] Presented with a similar situation, the Tenth Circuit "vacate[d] the district court's order dismissing [the plaintiff's] claims on *Younger* grounds and remand[ed] these claims for further consideration." *Columbian Fin. Corp. v. Stork*, 811 F.3d 390, 395 (10th Cir. 2016); *see also Bass v. Butler*, 258 F.3d 176, 179 (3d Cir. 2001); *Davis v. Rendell*, 659 F.2d 374, 376 (3d Cir. 1981); *Wood v. Several Unknown Metro. Police Officers*, 835 F.2d 340, 341-42 (D.C. Cir. 1987).

[12] The DEC defendants argue that *Younger* abstention requires dismissal of Silva's claim for injunctive relief because he did not "exhaust[] his state court appellate remedies." DEC Defendants' Br. 42. To be sure, Silva may not forgo appealing an adverse state-court judgment to pursue a collateral attack on that judgment in federal court. In *Huffman v. Pursue, Ltd.*, for example, the plaintiff did not appeal a state-court judgment issued against him and instead sought to enjoin the execution of that judgment in federal court. 420 U.S. 592, 599 (1975). The Supreme Court said that the plaintiff "must exhaust his state appellate remedies before seeking relief" in federal court. *Id.* at 608. Here, by contrast, Silva's second claim for relief does not collaterally attack his criminal conviction but instead seeks prospectively to prevent the defendants from interfering with his alleged right to fish.

"Shinnecocks." But "Shinnecocks" is not a slur; it describes the tribe and its members. The email does not instruct DEC officials to harass or to profile tribe members; it directs them to work "diligently to prevent [an] illegal harvest" of glass eels—a nondiscriminatory law-enforcement objective.

Without evidence of racial animus, the plaintiffs' discrimination claims cannot survive summary judgment. We affirm the judgment of the district court insofar as it granted of summary judgment on these claims.

CONCLUSION

The district court erred in granting summary judgment to the DEC officials on the plaintiffs' claims for declaratory and injunctive relief with respect to their fishing rights. The district court properly **[—22—]** granted summary judgment to the DEC itself on those claims and to all the defendants on the discrimination claims. Accordingly, we affirm in part and vacate in part the judgment of the district court. The case is remanded for further proceedings consistent with this opinion.

United States Court of Appeals for the Second Circuit

No. 20-3188

TOWN OF SOUTHOLD
vs.
WHEELER[1]

Appeal from the United States District Court for the Eastern District of New York

Decided: September 2, 2022

Citation: 48 F.4th 67, 10 Adm. R. 59 (2d Cir. 2022).

Before **LIVINGSTON,** Chief Judge, and **CARNEY** and **BIANCO,** Circuit Judges.

[—4—] {-70-} LIVINGSTON, Chief Judge:

Along the northern edge of "that slender riotous island which extends itself due east of New York," the aptly named Long Island, lies "the most domesticated body of salt water in the Western hemisphere, the great wet barnyard of Long Island Sound." F. SCOTT FITZGERALD, THE GREAT GATSBY 4–5 (Scribner 2004) (1925). This appeal concerns the efforts of the federal Environmental Protection Agency ("EPA") to designate a new waste disposal site in the Sound—a site for the byproducts of dredging activities undertaken to maintain and improve the Sound's shipping channels and ports, as well as support coastal businesses and other private parties.

The Coastal Zone Management Act ("CZMA") encourages states to develop programs to manage their coastal areas and requires federal activities that affect these areas to be "consistent to the maximum extent practicable with the enforceable policies" of each state's program. 16 U.S.C. § 1456(c)(1)(A). Regulations implementing **{-71-}** the CZMA, in turn, have interpreted that phrase to require "full[] consisten[cy]" with state programs. 15 C.F.R. § 930.32(a)(1). Under these provisions, New York State formally objected to the EPA's proposed activity, asserting that the designation of the new dredging site would not be fully **[—5—]** consistent with its coastal management program and an analogous program developed by the Town of Southold, New York ("Southold," and together with New York, the "Plaintiffs-Appellants"). Responding to the objections, the EPA reiterated its conclusion that the designation would, in fact, be fully consistent with Plaintiffs-Appellants' coastal management programs. After a lengthy dialogue in which New York refused to withdraw its objections, the EPA opted to proceed with the new site designation without New York's assent.

New York then sued in the United States District Court for the Eastern District of New York under the Administrative Procedure Act ("APA"), alleging that the agency's designation violates the Marine Protection, Research and Sanctuaries Act of 1972, 33 U.S.C. § 1411, ("MPRSA") and the CZMA. Southold and the Connecticut Department of Energy and Environmental Protection ("Connecticut," and together with EPA, "Defendants-Appellees") intervened on behalf of New York and the EPA, respectively, and the parties cross-moved for summary judgment. The district court (Korman, *J.*) granted Defendants-Appellees' motions. *See Rosado v. Wheeler*, 473 F. Supp. 3d 115 (E.D.N.Y. 2020). These appeals followed. **[—6—]**

New York principally argues that the district court erred in applying the APA's deferential arbitrary-and-capricious standard for judicial review to its CZMA claim.[2] For the reasons set forth below, we reject that argument. And applying the arbitrary-and-capricious standard, we conclude that the district court properly granted Defendants-Appellees' cross-motions for summary judgment on the CZMA claims because the EPA adequately justified its consistency determination. We also conclude that Southold waived its claim that the EPA's designation of the new site violates the National Environmental Protection Act

[1] The Clerk of Court is directed to amend the official caption as set forth above.

[2] New York does not challenge the district court's dismissal of its MPRSA claims on appeal and has thus abandoned them. *See Major League Baseball Props., Inc. v. Salvino, Inc.*, 542 F.3d 290, 294 (2d Cir. 2008).

("NEPA"). We therefore affirm the judgment of the district court.

I. BACKGROUND

A. Legal Background

Congress enacted the CZMA in 1972 to further the "national interest in the effective management, beneficial use, protection, and development of the coastal zone." 16 U.S.C. § 1451(a). The coastal zone is defined as "the coastal waters (including the lands therein and thereunder) and the adjacent shorelands . . . in **[—7—]** proximity to the shorelines of the several coastal states."[3] *Id.* § 1453(1). Recognizing that then-existing "state and local institutional arrangements for planning and regulating land and water uses" in the coastal zone were "inadequate," *id.* § 1451(h), the Act sought "to encourage the states to exercise their full authority over the lands and waters in the coastal zone," *id.* § 1451(i).

To advance this objective, the CZMA gives states a key role in environmental regulation by allowing them to develop their own coastal zone management programs, which are subject to federal approval **{-72-}** by the National Oceanic and Atmospheric Administration ("NOAA") in the Department of Commerce. *See id.* § 1455(d). Coastal zone management programs include "comprehensive statement[s] . . . prepared and adopted by the state in accordance with the provisions of [the CZMA], setting forth objectives, policies, and standards to guide public and private uses of lands and waters in the coastal zone." *Id.* § 1453(12).

Once a state's program has been approved by NOAA, "[e]ach Federal agency activity . . . that affects . . . the coastal zone" is required to "be carried out in a manner which is consistent to the maximum extent practicable with the **[—8—]** enforceable policies of approved State management programs." *Id.* § 1456(c)(1)(A); *see also* 15 C.F.R. § 930.36(e)(2). NOAA regulations define "consistent to the maximum extent practicable" to mean "fully consistent with the enforceable policies of management programs unless full consistency is prohibited by existing law applicable to the Federal agency." 15 C.F.R. § 930.32(a)(1). The policies enumerated in a state's coastal management program need not be particularly detailed. NOAA regulations explain:

> An enforceable policy [in a State's coastal management program] shall contain standards of sufficient specificity to guide public and private uses. Enforceable policies need not establish detailed criteria such that a proponent of an activity could determine the consistency of an activity without interaction with the State agency. State agencies may identify management measures which are based on enforceable policies, and, if implemented, would allow the activity to be conducted consistent with the enforceable policies of the program.

Id. § 930.11(h).

A federal agency proposing to undertake an activity that affects a state's coastal zone must send the state a determination of whether the activity is consistent with the policies contained in the state's coastal management program "no . . . later than 90 days before final approval of the Federal activity." 16 U.S.C. § 1456(c)(1)(C); *see also* 15 C.F.R. § 930.36(b)(1). The state may then concur with or object to the federal agency's consistency determination. 16 U.S.C. § 1456(c)(3)(A). **[—9—]** Regulations issued by NOAA set forth a limited process for resolving a consistency dispute between a state and federal agency:

> In the event of an objection [to the Federal agency's consistency determination by a State agency], Federal and State agencies should use the remaining portion of the 90-day notice period (*see* § 930.36(b)) to attempt to resolve their differences. If resolution has not been reached at the end of the 90-day period, Federal agencies should consider using the dispute resolution

[3] The term "coastal waters" includes "sounds," and the term "coastal states" includes any state bordering Long Island Sound. 16 U.S.C. § 1453(3)–(4).

mechanisms of this part and postponing final federal action until the problems have been resolved. At the end of the 90-day period the Federal agency shall not proceed with the activity over a State agency's objection unless:

> (1) the Federal agency has concluded that under the "consistent to the maximum extent practicable" standard described in section 930.32 consistency with the enforceable policies of the management program is prohibited by existing law applicable to the Federal agency and the Federal agency has clearly described, in writing, to the State agency the legal impediments to full consistency (*See* §§ 930.32(a) and 930.39(a)), or
>
> (2) the Federal agency has concluded that its proposed action is fully consistent with the enforceable policies of **{–73–}** the management program, *though the State agency objects*.

15 C.F.R. § 930.43(d) (emphasis added). If the federal agency ultimately decides to proceed with the activity to which the state objects, the federal agency "shall notify the State agency of its decision to proceed before the project commences." *Id.* § 930.43(e). **[—10—]**

NOAA regulations "describe mediation procedures which Federal and State agencies may use to attempt to resolve serious disagreements which arise during the administration of approved management programs." *Id.* § 930.110; *see also id.* § 930.44 ("In the event of a serious disagreement between a Federal agency and a State agency regarding the consistency of a proposed federal activity affecting any coastal use or resource, either party may request the . . . mediation services provided for in [15 C.F.R. § 930.110, *et seq.*]"). The regulations contemplate two avenues of mediation: informal mediation by NOAA's Office of Ocean and Coastal Resource Management, *see id.* § 930.111, and formal mediation by the Secretary of Commerce (the "Secretary"), *see id.* § 930.112. A state or federal agency can decline the Secretary's invitation to engage in mediation, *see id.* § 930.112(b), or unilaterally withdraw from mediation at any point, *see id.* § 930.115(b). And state and federal agencies need not exhaust the mediation process described above to seek judicial review. NOAA regulations provide:

> The availability of the mediation services provided in this subpart is not intended expressly or implicitly to limit the parties' use of alternate forums to resolve disputes. Specifically, judicial review where otherwise available by law may be sought by any party to a serious disagreement without first having exhausted the mediation process provided for in this subpart.

Id. § 930.116. **[—11—]**

Finally, the CZMA provides that the President of the United States may exempt a federal agency from the requirement that its actions be consistent with a state's coastal management program.

> After any final judgment, decree, or order of any Federal court that is appealable under section 1291 or 1292 of title 28, or under any other applicable provision of Federal law, that a specific Federal agency activity is not in compliance with subparagraph (A), and certification by the Secretary that mediation under subsection (h) is not likely to result in such compliance, the President may, upon written request from the Secretary, *exempt from compliance those elements of the Federal agency activity that are found by the Federal court to be inconsistent with an approved State program*, if the President determines that the activity is in the paramount interest of the United States.

16 U.S.C. § 1456(c)(1)(B) (emphasis added).

B. Factual Background

Dredging involves the excavation of materials that accumulate on the ocean floor over time. Periodic dredging is essential for the maintenance and improvement of coastal navigation infrastructure, including channels, navigable rivers, harbors, and marinas. Some dredged materials, considered "beneficial," can be used to replenish beach sand, construct wetlands, and cap landfills. Others, however, cannot be put to beneficial use and must be disposed of in open waters. Such open-water disposal is often controversial because dredged materials "may **[—12—]** be contaminated by municipal or industrial wastes or by runoff from **{-74-}** terrestrial sources such as agricultural lands." 40 C.F.R. § 227.13(a).

Long Island Sound is a 110-mile-long tidal estuary that lies between New York, Connecticut, and Rhode Island. The Sound is bounded by the Atlantic Ocean to the east and the East River tidal strait to the west, and the border between Connecticut and New York runs from east to west through the center of the Sound. Over 200 harbors, coves, bays, and navigable rivers around the Sound require periodic dredging. The Army Corps of Engineers (the "Corps") is responsible for fifty-two maintenance and improvement projects in the Sound and adjacent waters, and many other federal and non-federal projects in the area maintain and improve marinas, boat yards, and coastal businesses.

New York submitted a coastal management program to NOAA in August 1982.[4] NOAA approved that program, thus "activat[ing] Federal agency responsibility for being consistent with" its policies. Approval of the New York Coastal Zone Management Program, 47 Fed. Reg. 47,056, 47,056 (Oct. 22, 1982). Two components of New York's coastal management program are relevant to this **[—13—]** appeal: the Long Island Sound Coastal Management Program, which New York authored in 2002 (the "New York Program"), and the Town of Southold Local Waterfront Revitalization Program, which was adopted by the Town of Southold, New York, in 2005 (the "Southold Program") and was "formally approved and incorporated into [the New York Program]." Joint App'x 3107.

1. The Western and Central Sites

While this dispute concerns the EPA's designation of a dredged material disposal site in the *eastern* portion of Long Island Sound, there are existing designated sites in the Sound's western and central portions that we refer to, respectively, as the "Western Site" and the "Central Site." The EPA first published a Notice of Intent to consider designating dredged material disposal sites in the Sound's waters in 1999. *See* Designation of Dredged Material Disposal Sites in Long Island Sound, Connecticut and New York, 64 Fed. Reg. 29,865, 29,865 (June 3, 1999). Four years later, the EPA published a proposed rule seeking to designate the Western and Central Sites. *See* Proposed Designation of Dredged Material Disposal Sites in the Central and Western Portions of Long Island Sound, CT, 68 Fed. Reg. 53,687, 53,687 (Sept. 12, 2003). New York initially objected to the EPA's determination that the Western and Central Site designations would be **[—14—]** consistent with the New York Program, as required under the CZMA. After a period of negotiation, however, the state and the agency agreed to a set of site use restrictions that would "apply to all federal projects, and non-federal projects generating more than 25,000 cubic yards of dredged material" but would "not apply to smaller non-federal projects." Designation of Dredged Material Disposal Sites in Central and Western Long Island Sound, CT, 70 Fed. Reg. 32,498, 32,511 (June 3, 2005).

As relevant here, the restrictions contemplated that the Corps would develop a Dredged Materials Management Plan ("DMMP") for the Sound, a "comprehensive stud[y] carried out by the [Corps], in consultation with the EPA and the affected states, to help manage dredged material in a cost-effective and environmentally acceptable manner." *Id.* The EPA agreed that the DMMP for the Sound would address **{-75-}** the Sound's future dredging needs and the "development of procedures and standards for

[4] *See* NEW YORK STATE COASTAL MANAGEMENT PROGRAM AND FINAL ENVIRONMENTAL IMPACT STATEMENT 4, https://dos.ny.gov/system/files/documents/2021/04/ny_cmp_dec2020_w-bookmarks_working_topost.pdf.

the use of practicable alternatives to open-water disposal" of dredged material "to reduce [it] wherever practicable." *Id.* Once an agreement was in place as to the proposed restrictions, New York withdrew its objection and concurred with the EPA's conclusion that the agency's designation of the Central and Western Sites would be consistent with the New York Program. **[—15—]** The EPA published a final rule in June 2005 that designated the Western and Central Sites and incorporated New York's restrictions. *Id.* at 32,498, 32,511.

Over a decade later, in December 2015, the Corps completed the DMMP. The DMMP "examine[s] possible alternatives to open water placement of dredged material in Long Island Sound and compare[s] the costs and benefits of such alternatives with . . . current practice." Joint App'x 4002. It aims "to provide a 30 year management strategy to add certainty to dredging and placement activities . . . within the Region in an environmentally acceptable and economically practicable manner." *Id.* at 4084. The DMMP estimates that federal, state, local, and private dredging activities in the Sound will generate roughly 53 million cubic yards of dredged material over the 30-year period from 2015 through 2045, approximately 34 million of which will be fine-grained materials suitable for open-water disposal. It notes, however, that "only a portion" of the dredged materials will "likely . . . be dredged in that period, as future actions are contingent on Federal and non-Federal budget decisions." *Id.* at 3952.

2. The Eastern Site

Before the designation of the dredged material disposal site at issue here, no long-term disposal site existed in the eastern portion of the Sound. Two **[—16—]** preexisting disposal sites in the eastern Sound—the New London Disposal Site (the "New London Site") and the Cornfield Shoals Disposal Site (the "Cornfield Shoals Site")—had been authorized only for temporary use and were scheduled to close in December 2016.[5] In 2012, the EPA began exploring whether a new long-term disposal site should be designated to service the eastern Sound.

After screening eleven potential sites and a "no action alternative," the EPA proposed designating a disposal site in the eastern Sound (the "Eastern Site"). Designation of a Dredged Material Disposal Site in Eastern Region of Long Island Sound; Connecticut, 81 Fed. Reg. 24,748, 24,761 (Apr. 27, 2016). The Eastern Site would comprise the western half of the existing New London Site and two new adjacent areas to its west. The agency proposed that the Eastern Site would be governed by the same site use restrictions that it had agreed to with respect to the Western and Central Sites. When New York expressed concern to the EPA about the Eastern Site, the agency asked the Corps to examine the dredged material disposal needs of the eastern portion of the Sound in greater detail. In response, the Corps revised the DMMP, estimating the need for open-water disposal **[—17—]** capacity in the eastern Sound over the next thirty years to be 20.2 million cubic yards.

In July 2016, the EPA submitted a consistency determination pursuant to the CZMA, asserting that the Eastern Site **{–76–}** designation would be fully consistent with the enforceable policies of the New York and Southold Programs. New York disagreed and formally objected to the agency's consistency determination in October 2016. It argued that the Eastern Site designation would be inconsistent with the New York Program and with Policies 5 (water quality), 6 (ecosystem protection), 8 (hazardous waste management), 10 (water-dependent uses), and 11 (living marine resources) of the Southold Program.[6]

[5] The New London and Cornfield Shoals Sites were initially set to close in December 2011, but Congress extended the deadline to December 2016 so that the EPA had additional time to evaluate whether to designate a long-term disposal site in the Sound's eastern portion.

[6] New York asserted to the EPA that it was "bound by the terms of the CZMA" to object to the EPA's designation of the new disposal site on Southold's behalf because the Southold Program has been incorporated into the New York Program. Joint App'x 3107.

The EPA responded to New York's objection in November 2016, concluding that the State's arguments were "unfounded" and that the Eastern Site designation would, in fact, be fully consistent with both Programs. Joint App'x 3222. The agency explained that it "considered whether to seek mediation assistance from NOAA . . . to address this CZMA dispute . . . but . . . decided against" that course because the mediation process might be "lengthy." *Id.* at 3223–24. The EPA **[—18—]** therefore concluded "that it is necessary to proceed with the site designation at this point" despite the ongoing consistency dispute with New York. *Id.* at 3224. Later the same day, the EPA issued a final rule formally designating the Eastern Site as a permanent disposal site under the MPRSA. *See* Designation of a Dredged Material Disposal Site in Eastern Region of Long Island Sound; Connecticut, 81 Fed. Reg. 87,820, 87,820 (Dec. 6, 2016). The rule became effective on January 5, 2017. *See id.* at 87,821.

C. Procedural History

New York sued the EPA in August 2017 and filed the operative complaint in October 2017. New York raised five claims under the APA—four alleging violations of the MPRSA and the fifth alleging a CZMA violation. The State of Connecticut moved to intervene as a defendant, and Southold moved to intervene as a plaintiff. The district court granted both motions.[7]

The parties then cross-moved for summary judgment on the plaintiffs' claims alleging violation of the MPRSA and the CZMA. The plaintiffs advanced several arguments under the MPRSA: (1) that the EPA's determination that a new site was needed in the eastern Sound was arbitrary and capricious; (2) that the EPA **[—19—]** failed to adequately consider whether the Eastern Site would interfere with shipping and navigation on the Sound; (3) that the EPA's decision to designate the new Eastern Site rather than relying on preexisting disposal sites was arbitrary and capricious; and (4) that the EPA had failed to consider the potential pollution arising from the disposal of non-federal projects of less than 25,000 cubic yards. The plaintiffs also asserted that the Eastern Site designation violated the CZMA because it was not consistent to the maximum extent practicable with the New York and Southold Programs.

The district court (Korman, *J.*) denied the plaintiffs' motions for summary judgment and granted Defendants-Appellees' cross-motions in July 2020. The bulk of the district court's opinion addressed whether the EPA's designation of the Eastern Site pursuant to the MPRSA was arbitrary and capricious under the APA. Applying that deferential standard of review, the district court upheld the agency's action.

The district court then turned to the plaintiffs' allegation that the CZMA had **{-77-}** been violated. The district court rejected that claim, drawing on its analysis of the alleged MPRSA violations because "New York rest[ed] its CZMA claim largely on the 'same conduct and actions upon which [its MPRSA] claims for relief' are based." **[—20—]** *Rosado*, 473 F. Supp. 3d at 146 (quoting N.Y. Summ. J. Br., District Court Dkt. No. 71-1, at 84). The district court concluded that "New York has not offered any additional viable explanations for how EPA's designation of the Eastern Site is inconsistent with [the New York or Southold] Programs." *Id.* The district court entered judgment for Defendants-Appellees on July 20, 2020, and Plaintiffs-Appellants timely appealed.

II. DISCUSSION

A. Standard of Review

"On appeal from a grant of summary judgment involving a claim brought under the [APA], we review the administrative record *de novo* without according deference to the decision of the district court." *Karpova v. Snow*, 497 F.3d 262, 267 (2d Cir. 2007). "Under the APA, courts review agency action to determine if it is 'arbitrary, capricious, an abuse of discretion, or otherwise not in accordance with law.'" *Friends of Animals v.*

[7] Suffolk County also intervened below as a plaintiff but did not appeal.

Romero, 948 F.3d 579, 585 (2d Cir. 2020) (quoting 5 U.S.C. § 706(2)(A)). Under this "narrow" standard of review, a "court is not empowered to substitute its judgment for that of the agency." *Friends of Ompompanoosuc v. FERC*, 968 F.2d 1549, 1554 (2d Cir. 1992) (quoting *Citizens to Pres. Overton Park v.* **[—21—]** *Volpe*, 401 U.S. 402, 416 (1971)). Rather, a court will overturn an agency's determination only

> when the agency "has relied on factors which Congress has not intended it to consider, entirely failed to consider an important aspect of the problem, offered an explanation for its decision that runs counter to the evidence before the agency, or is so implausible that it could not be ascribed to a difference in view or the product of agency expertise."

Karpova, 497 F.3d at 267–68 (quoting *Motor Vehicle Mfrs. Ass'n of U.S., Inc. v. State Farm Mut. Auto. Ins. Co.*, 463 U.S. 29, 43 (1983)).

> In other words, so long as the agency examines the relevant data and has set out a satisfactory explanation including a rational connection between the facts found and the choice made, a reviewing court will uphold the agency action, even a decision that is not perfectly clear, provided the agency's path to its conclusion may reasonably be discerned.

Id. at 268.

New York contends on appeal that the district court erred in applying arbitrary-and-capricious review to the CZMA claim. We disagree. At the start, New York argued below that the EPA's consistency determination was "arbitrary and capricious." N.Y. Summ. J. Br. 84. New York's argument that the district court erred by applying that standard of review is thus arguably waived. *See Wal-Mart Stores, Inc. v. Visa U.S.A., Inc.*, 396 F.3d 96, 124 n.29 (2d Cir. 2005) ("[W]here a party **[—22—]** has shifted his position on appeal and advances arguments available but not pressed below, waiver will bar raising the issue on appeal." (citation, internal quotation marks, and alteration omitted)).

In any event, we conclude that the district court correctly applied the arbitrary-and-capricious standard to Plaintiffs-Appellants' CZMA claim. New York advances several counterarguments on appeal, but none is persuasive. First, New York notes that the CZMA requires that federal agency action "be carried out in a **{–78–}** manner which is consistent to the *maximum extent* practicable with the enforceable policies of approved State management programs." 16 U.S.C. § 1456(c)(1)(A) (emphasis added); *see also* 15 C.F.R. §§ 930.32(a)(1), 930.36(e)(2). But this provision is not a standard of review. And New York does not argue that the CZMA or its accompanying regulations set forth a standard of review to displace the APA's arbitrary-and-capricious standard. *See N.Y. Pub. Int. Rsch. Grp., Inc. v. Johnson*, 427 F.3d 172, 179 (2d Cir. 2005) (explaining that when a statute "does not provide a standard of review," we typically "review [the agency's] actions under the Administrative Procedure Act . . . , which contemplates setting aside only agency actions that are 'arbitrary, capricious, an abuse of discretion, or **[—23—]** otherwise not in accordance with law.'" (quoting 5 U.S.C. § 706(2)(A))); *see also Alaska Dep't of Env't Conservation v. EPA*, 540 U.S. 461, 496–97 (2004).

Indeed, because the CZMA does not provide a standard of review, courts have routinely subjected CZMA claims to arbitrary-and-capricious review. *See, e.g., Akiak Native Cmty. v. U.S. Postal Serv.*, 213 F.3d 1140, 1144 (9th Cir. 2000) ("The 'arbitrary or capricious' standard is appropriate for resolutions of factual disputes implicating substantial agency expertise." (citing *Marsh v. Or. Nat. Res. Council*, 490 U.S. 360, 376–77 (1989))); *Del. Dep't of Nat. Res. & Env't Control v. U.S. Army Corps of Eng'rs*, 685 F.3d 259, 286–87 (3d Cir. 2012); *City of Riverview v. Surface Transp. Bd.*, 398 F.3d 434, 439–40 (6th Cir. 2005); *Am. Petroleum Inst. v. Knecht*, 609 F.2d 1306, 1310 (9th Cir. 1979); *see also City of Sausalito v. O'Neill*, 386 F.3d 1186, 1205, 1222 (9th Cir. 2004) (reasoning that a court should "not generally overturn a consistency determination [under the CZMA] just because we might have come to a different conclusion were the determination of 'consistency' before us in the first instance" (citing *Overton Park*, 401 U.S. at 416)). And we are unpersuaded that the CZMA's requirement that federal agency action be "consitent to the maximum extent practicable with the enforceable policies of approved State management programs" draws these decisions into question. 16 U.S.C. § 1456(c)(1)(A). **[—24—]**

Next, New York contends that we must review the EPA's consistency determination *de novo* because the EPA does not "administer" the CZMA. N.Y. Br. 37. But this argument conflates arbitrary-and-capricious review with a different doctrine—*Chevron* deference—which does not apply here. *See Chevron, U.S.A., Inc. v. Nat. Res. Def. Council, Inc.*, 467 U.S. 837 (1984). "We evaluate challenges to an agency's interpretation of a statute that it administers within the two-step *Chevron* deference framework," *Catskill Mountains Chapter of Trout Unlimited, Inc. v. EPA*, 846 F.3d 492, 507 (2d Cir. 2017), but review an agency's "interpretation of . . . a statute that it does not administer[] *de novo*," *N.Y. State Dep't of Env't Conservation v. FERC*, 884 F.3d 450, 455 (2d Cir. 2018). "When the question is not one of the agency's authority but of the reasonableness of its actions," however, "the 'arbitrary and capricious' standard of the APA governs." *N.Y. Pub. Int. Rsch. Grp. v. Whitman*, 321 F.3d 316, 324 (2d Cir. 2003); *see also Judulang v. Holder*, 565 U.S. 42, 52 n.7 (2011) (observing that when the challenged agency action "is not an interpretation of any statutory language," "the more apt analytic framework . . . is standard 'arbitrary or capricious' review under the APA" (brackets omitted)); *Hong v. U.S. Sec. & Exch. Comm'n*, 41 F.4th 83, 93 n.12 (2d Cir. 2022) ("us[ing] the *Chevron* framework to **{-79-}** address the statutory interpretation questions presented" **[—25—]** there but separately evaluating whether "the agency's *application* of the statute and regulations . . . was arbitrary or capricious").

This case does not implicate the *Chevron* doctrine because New York does not challenge the EPA's "authority" to render a consistency determination or its interpretation of the CZMA. Instead, it challenges the "reasonableness" of the EPA's consistency determination under that statute. *N.Y. Pub. Int. Rsch. Grp.*, 321 F.3d at 324. Put another way, New York challenges the EPA's "application" of the CZMA in its consistency determination. *Hong*, 41 F.4th at 93 n.12 (emphasis omitted). And so "the 'arbitrary and capricious' standard of the APA governs." *N.Y. Pub. Int. Rsch. Grp.*, 321 F.3d at 324.

For similar reasons, we reject New York's argument that we must review the EPA's consistency determination *de novo* because it has alleged that this determination was "'not in accordance with' the CZMA." N.Y. Br. 33 (quoting 5 U.S.C. § 706(2)(A)). The Supreme Court rejected a materially identical argument in *Marsh*. In that case, the respondents argued that "strict review is appropriate under the 'in accordance with law' clause of § 706(2)(A)" because they "maintain[ed] that the question for review centers on the legal meaning of [a statutory] term" in NEPA "or, in the alternative, the predominantly legal question **[—26—]** whether established and uncontested historical facts presented by the administrative record satisfy this standard." *Marsh*, 490 U.S. at 376. But the Court rejected that "[c]haracteriz[ation]" of the dispute because the respondents' challenge did not turn on NEPA's "meaning" or any other "predominantly legal" question but instead "involve[d] primarily issues of fact." *Id.* at 376–77. And because "analysis of the relevant documents" for the respondents' NEPA claim "require[d] a high level of technical expertise," the Court held that it "must defer to 'the informed discretion of the responsible federal agencies.'" *Id.* at 377 (quoting *Kleppe v. Sierra Club*, 427 U.S. 390, 412 (1976)). The *Marsh* Court therefore concluded that "review of the narrow question before [it] whether the [agency's] determination . . . should be set aside is controlled by the 'arbitrary and capricious' standard of § 706(2)(A)." *Id.* at 376; *see also J. Andrew Lange, Inc. v. FAA*, 208 F.3d 389, 391 (2d Cir. 2000) (explaining that "[u]nder the APA, this Court reviews errors of law de novo" but reviews "other agency findings, conclusions, and actions" under the arbitrary-and-capricious standard).

Marsh's reasoning applies here. *See Akiak*, 213 F.3d at 1144 (applying *Marsh* to a CZMA claim). Like that case, this case does not turn on predominantly legal issues, such as the EPA's interpretation of the CZMA. It depends instead on the **[—27—]** fact-specific question of whether the EPA adequately responded to New York's objections to its consistency determination. So as in *Marsh*, "[t]he question presented for review in this case is a classic example of a factual dispute the resolution of which implicates substantial agency expertise." 490 U.S. at 376. Thus, we follow *Marsh*'s lead in rejecting Plaintiffs-Appellants' "supposition that review is of a legal question and that the [EPA's] decision 'deserves no deference.'" *Id.* at 377.

Scheduled Airlines Traffic Offices, Inc. v. DOD, on which New York relies, in fact illustrates why the APA's "not in accordance with law" standard is *inapplicable* here. *See* 87 F.3d 1356, 1361 (D.C. Cir. 1996). That case involved "a pure question **{-80-}** of statutory interpretation independent of the complex factual determinations or policy judgments particularly within agencies' expertise." *Id.* For that reason, the court held that the issue there was "not whether the Department acted arbitrarily or capriciously, . . . but rather whether it acted 'in accordance with [federal] law.'" *Id.* (quoting 5 U.S.C. § 706(2)(A)) (alteration in original). And because "the Defense Department ha[d] not been entrusted to administer" the statute at issue in the case, the court reviewed the agency's interpretation *de novo*. *Id.*; *cf. Holland v. Nat'l Mining Ass'n*, 309 F.3d 808, 815 (D.C. Cir. 2002) ("In reviewing an agency's **[—28—]** statutory interpretation under the APA's 'not in accordance with law' standard, we adhere to the familiar two-step test of *Chevron*, provided that the conditions for such review are met."). But unlike *Scheduled Airlines Traffic Offices*, this case turns on "complex factual determinations," not "a pure question of statutory interpretation." 87 F.3d at 1361. Thus, the arbitrary-and-capricious standard applies.

Nor does the presidential waiver provision found in 16 U.S.C. § 1456(c)(1)(B) imply, as New York contends, N.Y. Br. 44, that the CZMA forecloses arbitrary-and-capricious review. Section 1456(c)(1)(B) simply provides that *if* a federal court concludes that an agency's consistency determination was erroneous, the Secretary can seek a waiver of the CZMA's consistency requirement from the President. But this provision does not alter the standard of review by which a court determines *whether* a consistency determination was in error.

B. Application

Because we conclude that the arbitrary-and-capricious standard governs here, we apply that standard in reviewing Plaintiffs-Appellants' claims on the merits. Plaintiffs-Appellants argue that the district court erred by upholding the EPA's determination that its designation of the Eastern Site is consistent to the **[—29—]** maximum extent practicable with the New York and Southold Programs. Southold also challenges the adequacy of the Environmental Impact Statement that the EPA submitted pursuant to NEPA in support of its designation. For the reasons set forth below, we reject these claims.

1. New York's Claims

New York generally asserts that the EPA's designation of the Eastern Site is inconsistent with the following policies of the New York Program:

> to "[p]rotect water quality of coastal waters from adverse impacts associated with excavation, fill, dredging, and disposal of dredged material" (Policy 5, Sub-Policy 5.3); to work towards "reduction or elimination of adverse impacts associated with existing development" (Policy 6, Sub-Policy 6.1); to "[a]void placement of dredged material in Long Island Sound when opportunities for beneficial reuse of the material exist" (Policy 10, Sub-Policy 10.6); and to promote "marine resources by . . . protecting spawning grounds, habitats, and water quality" (Policy 11, Sub-Policy 11.1).

N.Y. Br. 50 (alterations and omission in original) (citations omitted); *see also* Joint App'x 3241–42. But the specific arguments that New York raises on appeal pertain only to Sub-Policy 10.6 of the New York Program, entitled "Provide sufficient infrastructure for water-dependent uses." That policy states:

> Use suitable dredged material for beach nourishment, dune reconstruction, or other beneficial uses. Avoid placement of dredged material in Long Island Sound when opportunities for beneficial reuse of the material exist. Allow placement of **{-81-}** suitable dredged **[—30—]** material in nearshore locations to advance maritime or port-related functions, provided it is adequately contained and avoids negative impacts on vegetated wetlands and significant coastal fish and wildlife habitats. Avoid shore and water surface uses which would impede navigation.

Joint App'x 3214–15.

Relying on Sub-Policy 10.6, New York argues that the EPA did not adequately respond to four of its objections to the EPA's consistency determination: (1) that a new dredging site was not needed in the eastern Sound because the Western and Central Sites have adequate capacity to fulfill the Sound's dredging requirements, (2) that the EPA improperly considered a lack of funding in its consistency determination, (3) that certain waste materials disposed of at the Eastern Site could be subject to environmentally harmful "capping" practices, and (4) that the EPA unreasonably included site use restrictions based on the restrictions for the Western and Central Sites. We are not persuaded. As explained below, the EPA adequately responded to each of these objections.

First, New York argues that the EPA failed to adequately respond to its objection that the Eastern Site is unnecessary because the Western and Central **[—31—]** Sites have adequate capacity to fulfill the Sound's dredging requirements for the next several decades.[8] But the EPA explained that

> [d]isposal capacity at the [Western Site] and [Central Site] does not obviate the need for the [Eastern Site]. [The Corps] projected in the DMMP that dredging in Long Island Sound would generate . . . 49.6 [million cubic yards or "mcy"] of material that could potentially need to be placed at an open-water disposal site. . . .
>
> . . . [T]he [Central Site] and [Western Site] are each estimated to have a disposal capacity of about 20 mcy. This 40 mcy of capacity is not enough to take the entire 49.6 mcy of material that *could* require open-water disposal.

Id. at 3243–44. And it cautioned that

> it must be understood that estimates of the amounts of material of different types needing to be managed in the future are unavoidably imperfect. The actual amount of material that will require management could be higher (or lower) over the 30-year planning horizon. This is especially evident when unpredictable events, such as large storms and possible improvement dredging projects, are considered. **[—32—]**

Id. at 3245.

---

[8] The EPA argues that New York waived this argument by failing to raise it before the district court. As noted above, "where a party has shifted his position on appeal and advances arguments available but not pressed below, waiver will bar raising the issue on appeal." *Wal-Mart Stores*, 396 F.3d at 124 n.29 (citation, internal quotation marks, and alteration omitted). Before the district court, New York argued that the EPA's designation of the Eastern Site is inconsistent with Policy 5 and Sub-Policy 5.3 of the New York Program because there is no need for the Eastern Site. New York did not argue that the designation would be inconsistent with Sub-Policy 10.6 for that reason. Nonetheless, because New York's argument on appeal sufficiently resembles the argument that it advanced before the district court, we do not agree that New York has waived it.

Although New York acknowledges that the Corps estimated that the Sound could generate up to 49.6 million cubic yards of dredged material requiring open-water disposal in the coming decades and that the total capacity of the Western and Central Sites was only 40 mcy, the State notes that the 49.6 figure included 15.5 million **{-82-}** cubic yards[9] of dredged sand that might be put to "beneficial use, such as beach renourishment." N.Y. Br. 18.[10] So New York contends that the EPA should have subtracted out that 15.5 mcy from the topline 49.6 estimate, which would have led it to conclude that the Western and Central Sites had adequate capacity to accept all the dredged material the Corps projected the Sound would generate in the coming decades.

The EPA adequately responded to this objection. It reasoned, first, that there was "no guarantee" that it could find a beneficial use for dredged material **[—33—]** from the Sound. Joint App'x 3244. The agency also noted that because the 49.6 million cubic yards figure was an estimate, the Sound might generate even more dredged material that would require additional disposal capacity. And the EPA's determination that the Eastern Site was necessary did not rest solely on an estimate of the quantity of dredged material the Sound might generate. As the agency explained:

> Beyond the question of disposal capacity, when EPA took into account overall environmental effects, environmental and safety risks, logistical difficulties, and the expense of using such distant sites, EPA concluded that the [Central Site], [Western Site], and [Rhode Island Sound Disposal Site (the "RI Site")] would not reasonably serve the needs of the eastern Long Island Sound region. A key consideration in EPA's determination that a designated site is needed in eastern Long Island Sound is that going outside the region would involve far longer transit distances from dredging centers in the eastern Sound.

Id. at 3245. For those reasons, the EPA's conclusion that it was "reasonable and prudent to designate sites to ensure adequate disposal capacity is available for all the projected material" was not arbitrary and capricious. *Id.*

Second, New York argues that the EPA improperly "invoked the cost savings of having a dumping site proximate to dredging centers in the Eastern Sound" as a "benefit" of designating the Eastern Site. N.Y. Br. 53. That **[—34—]** consideration, New York contends, violates 15 C.F.R. § 930.32(a)(3), which provides:

> Federal agencies shall not use a general claim of a lack of funding or insufficient appropriated funds or failure to include the cost of being fully consistent in Federal budget and planning processes as a basis for being consistent to the maximum extent practicable with an enforceable policy of a management program.

New York misstates the nature of the cost considerations that the EPA considered. In responding to New York's objections, the EPA explained:

> Finally, longer haul distances also would increase the cost both to taxpayers and private entities of completing dredging projects. Using the [Central Site], [Western Site], or [RI Site] would greatly increase the

[9] We observe that New York's brief is inconsistent as to the amount of dredged sand that could be amenable to a beneficial use. *Compare* N.Y. Br. 27–28, 50–51 (15.2 million cubic yards), *with id.* at 18 (15.5 million cubic yards). The record also appears inconsistent on this point. The Corps apparently reported this figure as 15.5 million cubic yards, *see* Joint App'x 3968–69, but the EPA later stated that the Corps had reported it as 15.2 million cubic yards, *see* Joint App'x 3243–44. Because this discrepancy does not affect our conclusions, we use 15.5 million cubic yards without further discussion.

[10] The Corps also estimated that 3.3 million cubic yards of dredged material would be contaminated with dangerous toxins and so would be unsuitable for open-water disposal. Joint App'x 3969.

> transport distance for, **{-83-}** and duration of, open-water disposal for dredging projects from the eastern Long Island Sound region. This, in turn, would greatly increase the cost of such projects. It could also render certain dredging projects too expensive to conduct. . . . EPA is *not* designating the [Eastern Site] solely in order to make dredging less expensive, but it would be irrational to ignore that reducing the cost of necessary dredging is another of the many benefits of designating the [Eastern Site], a site which EPA has determined to be environmentally sound, instead of relying on more distant sites.

Joint App'x 3246. Thus, the EPA did not rely on the agency's *own* cost considerations to support its consistency determination. It instead outlined the costs that would accrue *to taxpayers and private enterprises* from a failure to designate the new site. While 15 C.F.R. § 930.32(a)(3) prevents a federal agency from using its own budgetary constraints as an excuse to avoid complying with a **[—35—]** state's coastal management program, it does not compel the agency to pursue activities that it deems economically wasteful.

Third, New York argues that the EPA ignored its objection that toxic "material from smaller nonfederal projects dumped at the Eastern site could be subject to capping," N.Y. Br. 57–58, a process that involves "using relatively cleaner material to cover relatively less clean material and, thus, isolate the latter from the environment," Joint App'x 3258. The State asserts that dredged material is "often laden" with "toxins," and that nonfederal projects generating less than 25,000 cubic yards of dredged material are subject only to the Clean Water Act ("CWA") rather than the "more stringent" standards of the MPRSA. N.Y. Br. 57.

The EPA explicitly addressed this objection in its November 4, 2016, response letter. The EPA explained that New York's objection rests on a "misguided understanding" of the proposed designation of the Eastern Site. Joint App'x 3258. The agency "would *not* approve of the disposal of toxic sediments at the [Eastern Site] on the grounds that it could later be capped with cleaner material" because "MPRSA regulations clearly dictate that only 'suitable' material may be placed at an open-water disposal site regulated under the MPRSA," and a **[—36—]** proposal to "cap" unsuitable material with cleaner material "does not change that." *Id.*

New York asserts that the EPA's response was inadequate because it failed to address the prospect that "capping" may still occur for smaller, nonfederal projects subject to regulation under the CWA rather than the "more stringent" MPRSA standards. N.Y. Br. 57. But that amounts to an argument that the CWA, which indisputably applies to those projects, does not adequately regulate capping. And as the EPA persuasively argues, that objection lies "with Congress, not EPA." EPA Br. 44. The EPA notes, moreover, that concerns about capping in any hypothetical future project can be addressed during the individual permitting process.

New York also contends that the EPA cannot now respond to New York's argument about small, nonfederal projects because it failed to do so during the notice-and-comment process. *See Michigan v. EPA*, 576 U.S. 743, 758 (2015) ("[A] court may uphold agency action only on the grounds that the agency invoked when it took the action."). But New York, too, did not raise the issue of small, nonfederal projects during the notice-and-comment process, and arbitrary-and-capricious review does not require that an agency respond in advance to every **[—37—]** hypothetical objection that might be raised. *See* **{-84-}** *Appalachian Power Co. v. EPA*, 251 F.3d 1026, 1036 (D.C. Cir. 2001) ("It is black-letter administrative law that absent special circumstances, a party must initially present its comments to the agency during the rulemaking in order for the court to consider the issue." (citation, internal quotation marks, and alteration omitted)).

Finally, New York argues that the EPA erred by "unilaterally" adding conditions to the proposed Eastern Site "and then rely[ing] on those restrictions as evidence of consistency under the CZMA despite the State's objection." N.Y. Br. 61. New York claims that the agency "transpose[d] negotiated restrictions for the Central and Western sites onto the Eastern site, and then use[d] them as a basis for nullifying New York's objection to the Eastern site." N.Y. Reply Br. 33. But the EPA never asserted that the additional site restrictions render its designation of the Eastern Site consistent with the New York Program on their own. Rather, in responding to New York's objections, the agency explained:

> Applying these site use restrictions to the [Eastern Site] should be equally acceptable because the restrictions apply equally well to the eastern Sound and applying the same restrictions across the entire Sound makes good sense. As a result, the entire Sound will be covered by the same regulatory regime applied by the same federal and state regulators. **[—38—]**

Joint App'x 3223. New York therefore fails to show that the EPA's decision to impose additional restrictions on the Eastern Site undermines the agency's efforts to achieve full consistency with the New York Program.

2. Town of Southold's Claims

In a separate brief, Southold challenges the EPA's determination that its designation of the Eastern Site is fully consistent with the Southold Program. Southold also contends that the EPA violated NEPA in designating the Eastern Site. As explained below, we conclude that the EPA's determination that its activity is fully consistent with the Southold Program is not arbitrary and capricious, and that Southold's NEPA claim is waived.

i. CZMA

Southold begins by arguing that the EPA's designation of the Eastern Site is inconsistent with several policies enumerated in the Southold Program. First, Southold claims that the EPA's designation conflicts with Sub-Policy 5.3 of the Southold Program, entitled "Protect and enhance quality of coastal waters." It provides:

> A. Protect water quality based on an evaluation of physical factors (pH, dissolved oxygen, dissolved solids, nutrients, odor, color and turbidity), health factors (pathogens, chemical contaminants, and **[—39—]** toxicity), and aesthetic factors (oils, floatables, refuse, and suspended solids).
>
> C. Protect water quality of coastal waters from adverse impacts associated with excavation, fill, dredging, and disposal of dredged material.

Id. at 3252–53. Southold asserts, without elaboration, that "[c]oncerns regarding [the] extent of the testing and protocols used were raised repeatedly . . . without a satisfactory response." Southold Br. 27. The record demonstrates, however, that the EPA adequately responded to Southold's concerns about the Eastern Site's effect on the Sound's water quality. The agency noted that designating a new disposal site does not affect water quality; only individual projects, which require a permit, can do so. *See* Joint App'x 3254. So, the EPA explained, Southold's concerns **{-85-}** about water quality can be addressed in the permitting process for any hypothetical future project. And the agency reasoned that "the sediment suitability criteria in EPA's MPRSA regulations require the assessment of physical, health and aesthetic factors," ensuring that the designation of the Eastern Site is consistent with the Southold Program. *Id.* Taken together, these two responses adequately addressed Southold's water-quality objection.

Second, Southold argues that the EPA's site designation conflicts with Sub-Policy 6.1 of the Southold Program, which emphasizes protecting "ecological **[—40—]** quality." *Id.* at 3260–61. But the agency explained in detail how the Eastern Site designation would comport with that policy. The EPA highlighted "the aspects of [its] analysis relating to chemistry, toxicity, bioaccumulation, benthic health, aquatic organism impacts, and bathymetry, all of which contribute to the assessment of possible physical, chemical, and biological changes if the site is designated." *Id.* at 3262. Indeed, the agency noted, "[b]enthic analyses within . . . the [Eastern Site] indicate good quality habitats for benthic organisms," and "[t]he data shows rapid recovery of benthic organisms within the disposal sites after the initial effects of sediment placement." *Id.* at 3262 n.27. The EPA also explained that its "assessment is based on over 40 years of monitoring data on chemistry, toxicity, bioaccumulation, benthic health, and bathymetry to assess physical, chemical and biological changes at the [New London Site] and [Cornfield Shoals Site]." *Id.* at 3262–63. Thus, the record shows that the EPA adequately responded to Southold's objections regarding Sub-Policy 6.1.

Third, Southold argues that the EPA's site designation is inconsistent with Sub-Policy 6.2 of the Southold Program, which aims to protect coastal fish and wildlife habitats. But Southold failed to raise that objection during the notice-and-comment process or in the district court. Southold is therefore precluded from **[—41—]** raising that issue for the first time on appeal. *See In re Nortel Networks Corp. Sec. Litig.*, 539 F.3d 129, 132 (2d Cir. 2008) ("It is a well-established general rule that an appellate court will not consider an issue raised for the first time on appeal." (citation, internal quotation marks, and alteration omitted)); *Appalachian Power Co.*, 251 F.3d at 1036 ("[A] party must initially present its comments to the agency during the rulemaking in order for the court to consider the issue." (citation, internal quotation marks, and alteration omitted)).

Fourth, Southold argues that the EPA's site designation conflicts with Sub-Policies 8 and 10 of the Southold Program, which contain Southold's waste policy and water-dependent use policy, respectively. Southold failed to raise those two objections during the notice-and-comment process as well and is barred from doing so now. *See Appalachian Power*, 251 F.3d at 1036.

Fifth and finally, Southold argues that the EPA's site designation is inconsistent with Sub-Policy 11 of the Southold Program, which promotes the sustainable use of living marine organisms and the protection of their habitats. But the EPA's response to this objection, too, was adequate:

> EPA directly considered the question of habitat effects and concluded that the site would not have significant adverse effects on marine habitat. . . . Furthermore, . . . EPA re-delineated the boundaries of the [Eastern Site] to exclude two rocky, hardbottom areas that could **[—42—]** provide relatively higher quality habitat for marine organisms. . . . Thus, EPA remains confident that designation of the [Eastern Site] is consistent with the **{-86-}** Marine Resources Policies to the maximum extent practicable.

Joint App'x 3278. Southold does not explain why this response was inadequate, so its final objection fails as well.

ii. NEPA

Finally, Southold contends that the Environmental Impact Statement the EPA submitted in support of its Eastern Site designation is inadequate because the agency failed to take a sufficiently "hard look" at its environmental impact in violation of the Supreme Court's decision in *Kleppe*, 427 U.S. 390. Southold Br. 20.

Southold abandoned this claim in the district court. Although Southold's complaint raises a NEPA claim, the town did not mention that claim in its summary judgment briefing. And the district court's decision did not discuss it, either. We therefore conclude that Southold is precluded from belatedly asserting its NEPA claim on appeal. *See In re Nortel Networks*, 539 F.3d at 132.

III. Conclusion

For the foregoing reasons, we **AFFIRM** the judgment of the district court.

United States Court of Appeals
for the Second Circuit

No. 20-4248

COMMODITIES & MINERALS ENTER. LTD.
VS.
CVG FERROMINERA ORINOCO, C.A.

Appeal from the United States District Court for the Southern District of New York

Decided: October 3, 2022

Citation: 49 F.4th 802, 10 Adm. R. 73 (2d Cir. 2022).

Before **CABRANES**, **LYNCH**, and **NARDINI**, Circuit Judges.

[—2—] {-806-} NARDINI, Circuit Judge: **{-807-}**

Respondent-Appellant CVG Ferrominera Orinoco, C.A. ("Ferrominera"), appeals from the judgment of the United States **[—3—]** District Court for the Southern District of New York (Andrew L. Carter, Jr., *Judge*) confirming a foreign arbitral award and granting attorney's fees and costs in favor of Petitioner-Appellee Commodities & Minerals Enterprise Ltd. ("CME"). Ferrominera challenges the judgment on three grounds. First, it argues that the district court lacked personal jurisdiction over Ferrominera because CME did not serve a summons when it moved to confirm the arbitral award. Second, Ferrominera contends that the district court erred in confirming the award, pointing to purported defects in the arbitral panel's jurisdiction, issues with the scope of the panel's award, and conflicts with United States public policy. Third, it argues that the district court abused its discretion in awarding attorney's fees and costs in favor of CME.

We hold that a party is not required to serve a summons in order to confirm a foreign arbitral award under the New York Convention, more formally known as the Convention on the **[—4—]** Recognition and Enforcement of Foreign Arbitral Awards, June 10, 1958, 21 U.S.T. 2517, T.I.A.S. No. 6997, 330 U.N.T.S. 38 (as applied through the Federal Arbitration Act ("FAA"), 9 U.S.C. §§ 201-208). We further hold that the district court properly enforced the arbitral award, but that it erred in awarding attorney's fees and costs. Accordingly, we **AFFIRM** in part and **VACATE** in part.

I. Background

A. The commercial relationship

CME is incorporated under the laws of the British Virgin Islands and is in the business of trading commodities and minerals, including iron ore. Ferrominera is a Venezuelan company, owned by the Venezuelan government, that produces and exports iron ore.

The dispute in this case stems from a contract involving a ship named the *General Piar*. In 2010, Ferrominera chartered the *General Piar* from CME to shuttle iron ore from Ferrominera's Venezuelan mines, down the Orinoco River, and to an offshore transfer station **[—5—]** where it would be shipped away by CME.[1] The seventeen-page charter between CME and Ferrominera (the "General Piar Charter") contains a broad arbitration clause, which states, in part:

> This charter shall be governed by and construed in accordance with Title 9 of the United States Code and the maritime law of the United States Code and any dispute arising out of or in connection with this contract shall be referred to three persons at New York . . . ; their decision or that of any two of them shall be final, and for the purposes of enforcing any award, judgement may be entered on an award by any court of competent jurisdiction. The proceedings shall be conducted in accordance with the rules of the Society of Maritime Arbitrators, Inc.

Joint App'x at 215-16.

---

[1] More precisely, in 2010 CME entered a five-year time-charter for the *General Piar* from the ship's owner, and then sub-chartered the ship to Ferrominera. The then-President and Chairman of the Board of Directors of Ferrominera signed the charter, and the Board of Directors formally approved it.

B. The arbitration proceeding

By February 2016, the parties' commercial relationship had deteriorated. Seeking **{-808-}** to recover for unpaid invoices, lost profits, and attorney's fees, CME commenced an arbitration proceeding before a **[—6—]** panel of three arbitrators (the "Panel") in New York City pursuant to the rules of the Society of Maritime Arbitrators (the "SMA Rules").

Ferrominera raised numerous jurisdictional defenses and substantive counterclaims. Among other things, it argued that the Panel lacked jurisdiction over the dispute because the General Piar Charter and its arbitration agreement were obtained through corruption and thus void, and that the arbitration agreement was invalid under Venezuelan law. Ferrominera also argued that CME's claims fell outside the scope of the arbitration clause. In the alternative, Ferrominera argued a variety of set-offs and counterclaims.

On December 20, 2018, the Panel found for CME and rejected Ferrominera's defenses.[2] The Panel concluded that it had jurisdiction over the dispute and that the arbitration agreement covered the **[—7—]** claims and counterclaims. As to the contract defenses, the Panel found that the General Piar Charter was not void or unenforceable, and was not invalid under Venezuelan law. Specifically, the Panel concluded that the evidence Ferrominera presented did not show that CME had engaged in corruption with respect to the General Piar Charter. As to the arguments of invalidity under Venezuelan law, the Panel held that Venezuelan law did not apply because U.S. maritime law was selected in the choice-of-law provision of the General Piar Charter. Even if Venezuelan law did apply, the Panel agreed with an expert in Venezuelan law offered by CME and determined that the Charter and its arbitration agreement would nonetheless be enforceable under the Venezuelan doctrine of "good faith." The Panel found for CME and issued an award for $12,655,594.36, plus post-award interest at an annual rate of 5.5% until the award is fully paid or confirmed and made a judgment of the court. **[—8—]**

C. Court proceedings to confirm the arbitral award

On December 19, 2019, CME brought this action to confirm the arbitral award in the Southern District of New York. CME sought entry of a judgment against Ferrominera, including the Panel's Award of $12,655,594.36 plus interest, as well as costs and expenses in favor of CME, including reasonable attorney's fees.

Ferrominera argued that the award should not be confirmed. It argued, *inter alia,* that the service of notice was defective; that the Panel lacked jurisdiction to arbitrate the dispute; that the Panel's award exceeded the scope of the arbitration agreement by failing to credit Ferrominera for payments it had made to CME under the General Piar Charter, and instead allocating them to different contracts; and that enforcing the award would violate United States public policy because the General Piar Charter was obtained through corruption.

On December 10, 2020, the district court entered judgment in favor of CME, granting CME's application to confirm the award and **[—9—]** its request for attorney's fees and costs. Ferrominera appeals this judgment.

II. Discussion

On appeal, Ferrominera first challenges the district court's exercise of personal jurisdiction based on an alleged defect in **{-809-}** service of notice, namely CME's failure to serve a summons. It next contests the district court's confirmation of the award, arguing (1) that the Panel lacked jurisdiction over the dispute because the parties' arbitration agreement was invalid under Venezuelan law; (2) that the Award exceeded the scope of the arbitration provision because it improperly allocated payments made by

[2] The Panel issued the Final Award on December 20, 2018, which explained the Panel's reasoning in over 150 pages. On February 11, 2019, the Panel issued a Corrected Award, which corrected clerical errors in the Final Award (together, "the Award").

Ferrominera to CME to other contracts; and (3) that enforcement of the Award would violate United States public policy because the General Piar Charter had been obtained through corruption. Finally, it challenges the award of attorney's fees in favor of CME. **[—10—]**

For the reasons discussed below, we affirm the district court's ruling confirming the Award, but hold that it abused its discretion in awarding attorney's fees and costs to CME.

A. Governing legal standards

An application to confirm a foreign arbitral award[3] "'is a summary proceeding that merely makes what is already a final arbitration award a judgment of the court.'" *Yusuf Ahmed Alghanim & Sons v. Toys "R" Us, Inc.*, 126 F.3d 15, 23 (2d Cir. 1997) (quoting *Florasynth, Inc. v. Pickholz*, 750 F.3d 171, 176 (2d Cir. 1984)). "The review of arbitration awards is 'very limited . . . in order to avoid undermining the twin goals of arbitration, namely, settling disputes efficiently and avoiding long and expensive litigation.'" *Yusuf Ahmed Alghanim & Sons*, 126 F.3d at 23 (quoting *Folkways Music Publishers, Inc. v. Weiss*, 989 F.2d 108, 111 (2d Cir. 1993)). That review is **[—11—]** "extremely deferential" to the findings of the arbitration panel. *Porzig v. Dresdner, Kleinwort, Benson, N. Am. LLC*, 497 F.3d 133, 139 (2d Cir. 2007).

The parties do not dispute that this case falls under the New York Convention. *See Bergesen v. Joseph Muller Corp.*, 710 F.2d 928, 932 (2d Cir. 1983) (holding that the New York Convention's application to arbitral awards "not considered as domestic" includes awards "involving parties domiciled or having their principal place of business outside the enforcing jurisdiction"); *see also* 9 U.S.C. §§ 201-208 (incorporating the New York Convention). Article V of the New York Convention governs a district court's review of an application to confirm a foreign arbitral award. That Article contains an exhaustive list of seven defenses to confirmation,[4] and states that the **[—12—]** "party opposing

[3] The New York Convention, also called the Convention on the Recognition and Enforcement of Foreign Arbitral Awards, defines its application, in relevant part, as to "awards not considered domestic." Art. 1. As the Convention's title suggests, such non-domestic awards are also referred to as foreign awards, and we will use the latter term here.

[4] In full, Article V of the New York Convention states:

1. Recognition and enforcement of the award may be refused, at the request of the party against whom it is invoked, only if that party furnishes to the competent authority where the recognition and enforcement is sought, proof that: **[—12—]**

(a) The parties to the agreement . . . were, under the law applicable to them, under some incapacity, or the said agreement is not valid under the law to which the parties have subjected it or, failing any indication thereon, under the law of the country where the award was made; or

(b) The party against whom the award is invoked was not given proper notice of the appointment of the arbitrator or of the arbitration proceedings or was otherwise unable to present his case; or

(c) The award deals with a difference not contemplated by or not falling within the terms of the submission to arbitration, or it contains decisions on matters beyond the scope of the submission to arbitration, provided that, if the decisions on matters submitted to arbitration can be separated from those not so submitted, that part of the award which contains decisions on matters submitted to arbitration may be recognized and enforced; or

(d) The composition of the arbitral authority or the arbitral procedure was not in accordance with the agreement of the parties, or, failing such agreement, was not in accordance with the law of the country where the arbitration took place; or

(e) The award has not yet become binding on the parties, or has been set aside or suspended by a competent authority of the country in which, or under the law of which, that award was made.

2. Recognition and enforcement of an arbitral award may also be refused if the competent authority in the country where recognition and enforcement is sought finds that:

(a) The subject matter of the difference is not capable of settlement by arbitration under the law of that country; or

(b) The recognition or enforcement of the award would be contrary to the public policy of that country.

{-810-} enforcement of an arbitral award has the burden to prove that one of the seven defenses" applies. *Encyclopaedia Universalis S.A. v. Encyclopaedia Britannica, Inc.*, 403 F.3d 85, 90 (2d Cir. 2005) (citing the New York Convention, Art. V(1)); *see also* 9 U.S.C. **[—13—]** § 207 ("The court shall confirm the award unless it finds one of the grounds for refusal or deferral of recognition or enforcement of the award specified in the said Convention."). "The burden is a heavy one, as 'the showing required to avoid summary confirmance is high.'" *Encyclopaedia Universalis*, 403 F.3d at 90 (quoting *Yusuf Ahmed Alghanim & Sons*, 126 F.3d at 23). "In sum, a district court *must* enforce an arbitral award unless a litigant satisfies one of the seven enumerated defenses [under the New York Convention]; if one of the defenses is established, the district court *may* choose to refuse recognition of the award." *Corporación Mexicana de Mantenimiento Integral, S. De R.L. De C.V. v. Pemex-Exploración y Producción ("Pemex")*, 832 F.3d 92, 106 (2d Cir. 2016).

On appeal of a district court's confirmation of an arbitral award, "[w]e review a district court's legal interpretations of the New York Convention as well as its contract interpretation de novo; findings of fact are reviewed for clear error." *Leeward Constr. Co., Ltd.* **[—14—]** *v. Am. Univ. of Antigua-Coll. of Med.*, 826 F.3d 634, 638 (2d Cir. 2016) (quoting *VRG Linhas Aereas S.A. v. MatlinPatterson Glob. Opportunities Partners II L.P.*, 717 F.3d 322, 325 (2d Cir. 2013)); *see also Pemex*, 832 F.3d at 100.

B. Personal jurisdiction

Ferrominera first challenges the district court's exercise of personal jurisdiction in this proceeding, antecedent to the question of whether any of the seven defenses to confirmation under the New York Convention apply. Ferrominera argues that because it is an instrumentality of a foreign state, the Foreign Sovereign Immunities Act ("FSIA"), 28 U.S.C. § 1608, requires the delivery of a summons upon it to properly effect service. Because CME never served a summons, Ferrominera claims, service was fatally deficient and the **[—15—]** district court erred in exercising personal jurisdiction over Ferrominera.[5] **{-811-}**

For the reasons that follow, we are not persuaded by Ferrominera's argument. The FAA explicitly requires only service of notice of the application to confirm the arbitral award, not also a summons. Although the FAA partially incorporates the FSIA (through the Federal Rules of Civil Procedure) to fill gaps in *how* service must be made on a foreign instrumentality, those cross-references do not alter *what* must be served under the FAA. **[—16—]** Accordingly, the district court correctly rejected Ferrominera's service argument and appropriately exercised personal jurisdiction.

To understand how service must be made on an instrumentality of a foreign government in a proceeding to confirm a foreign arbitral award, we must consider a series of cross-references involving the FAA, the Federal Rules of Civil Procedure, and the FSIA.

Our starting point is Chapter 2 of the FAA, which codifies enforcement of foreign arbitral awards under the New York Convention. Chapter 2 instructs parties on how to file an application to confirm such an award, and how to defend against confirmation, but it does not lay out any rules for service of process. Section 207 authorizes a party to "apply" to a competent court "for an order

---

[5] CME mailed the petition to confirm the Award and its supporting documents to the last known addresses of Ferrominera's counsel in the United States, France, and England and to Ferrominera's last known address in Venezuela. It also delivered the petition by hand courier to Ferrominera's Venezuelan address.

CME argues that Ferrominera has waived its service of process objection by failing to raise that argument sufficiently before the district court. We disagree. Ferrominera raised its objection in its initial appearance before the district court and, in its brief opposing CME's petition to confirm the Award, cross-referenced that argument in a footnote. That was enough to put the district court on notice as to Ferrominera's jurisdictional defenses and to preserve the issue for appeal. *See Transaero, Inc v. La Fuerza Aerea Boliviana*, 162 F.3d 724, 729 (2d Cir. 1998).

confirming [an] award." 9 U.S.C. § 207. Such an application must be confirmed unless the court finds "one of the grounds for refusal or deferral of recognition or enforcement of the award specified" in the **[—17—]** New York Convention. *Id.* But aside from requiring the party to file its application to confirm, neither Chapter 2 nor the New York Convention specifies how an adverse litigant must be notified of the new proceeding.

To fill that gap, Chapter 2 resorts (with some caveats) to the rules governing domestic arbitral awards set forth in Chapter 1 of the FAA. Specifically, § 208 incorporates the provisions of Chapter 1, though only "to the extent that [Chapter 1] is not in conflict with [Chapter 2] or the Convention as ratified by the United States." 9 U.S.C. § 208. One of these incorporated provisions is § 9 of the FAA, which sets forth the procedure for confirming domestic awards, including service-of-process rules. Section 9 tells us that "[i]f the adverse party shall be a nonresident [of the district within which the award was made], then the *notice of the application* shall be served by the marshal of any district within which the adverse party may be found *in like manner as other process of the court.*" 9 U.S.C. § 9 (emphasis **[—18—]** added). As the italicized language indicates, § 9 specifies both *what* is to be served ("notice of the application") and *how* it is to be served ("in like manner as other process of the court"). But that latter phrase—"in like manner as other process of the court"—requires us to look elsewhere to understand how "other process" is carried out.[6] **[—19—] {-812-}**

Thus, we turn to the Federal Rules of Civil Procedure, which establish the general mode of serving process in federal courts. It is well established that—with one important qualification—Rule 4 sets forth the basic procedures for serving process in connection with arbitral awards. *Reed & Martin, Inc. v. Westinghouse Elec. Corp.*, 439 F.2d 1268, 1277 (2d Cir. 1971) ("The phrase 'in like manner as other process of the court' found in § 9 of the Arbitration Act refers to Fed. R. Civ. P. 4 on the accomplishment of appropriate service[.]"). That qualification, however, is set forth in Rule 81, which provides that the Federal Rules of Civil Procedure, "to the extent applicable, govern proceedings under the [FAA], except as [that] law[] provide[s] other procedures." Fed. R. Civ. P. 81(a)(6)(B). And so our next question is how Rule 4, only to the extent consistent with the FAA, directs service of process in the circumstances before us. **[—20—]**

Here, where the adverse party is the instrumentality of a foreign state, Rule 4 cross-references special rules of the FSIA. Specifically, Rule 4 provides that "[a] foreign state or its political subdivision, agency, or

---

[6] Although Ferrominera contends that service of a summons was required (in light of further cross-references to the FSIA that we shall discuss shortly), it does not argue that such overseas service had to be accomplished by the U.S. Marshals Service under § 9 of the FAA. Nor would such a contention make any sense. Although § 9 indicates that notice shall be served "by the marshal of any district within which the adverse party may be found," that provision is incorporated into Chapter 2 (governing foreign arbitral awards) only "to the extent" that it does not "conflict" with Chapter 2 or the New York Convention. In a foreign arbitral proceeding where the adverse party is overseas, there is often no "district within which the adverse party may be found," and hence no such marshal to be employed. And in any event, service by the U.S. Marshal—a domestic law enforcement official—would often be impossible on a foreign instrumentality overseas. This is why private process servers are now the norm, even in the context of foreign sovereigns. *See* Foreign Process, U.S. Marshals, https://www.usmarshals.gov/what-we-do/service-of-process/civil-process/foreign-process (last visited on Sept. 2, 2022). Because it would seemingly conflict with the New York Convention to require parties to use a mode of service that cannot be executed, it is hard to imagine how § 9's reference to marshals would be incorporated by reference into Chapter 2's codification of the New York Convention with respect to foreign parties. *See, e.g., In re Arbitration Between InterCarbon Bermuda, Ltd. and Caltex Trading & Transp. Corp.*, 146 F.R.D. 64, 67 n.3 (S.D.N.Y. 1993) ("Section 12 [governing motions to vacate arbitral awards] is an anachronism not only because it cannot account for the internationalization of arbitration law subsequent to its enactment, but also because it cannot account for the subsequent abandonment of United States marshals as routine process **[—19—]** servers."). But Ferrominera does not press the point, and so we need not resolve the issue here.

instrumentality must be served in accordance with 28 U.S.C. § 1608." Fed. R. Civ. P. 4(j)(1). Section 1608(b), in turn, provides a series of cascading alternatives to serve such a foreign instrumentality:

> (1) by delivery of a copy of the summons and complaint in accordance with any special arrangement for service between the plaintiff and the agency or instrumentality; or
> (2) if no special arrangement exists, by delivery of a copy of the summons and complaint either to an officer, a managing or general agent, or to any other agent authorized by appointment or by law to receive service of process in the United States; or in accordance with an applicable international convention on service of judicial documents; or
> (3) if service cannot be made under paragraphs (1) or (2), and if reasonably calculated to give actual notice, by delivery of a copy of the summons and complaint, together with a translation of each into the official language of the foreign state— **[—21—]**
> (A) as directed by an authority of the foreign state or political subdivision in response to a letter rogatory or request or
> (B) by any form of mail requiring a signed receipt, to be addressed and dispatched by the clerk of the court to the agency or instrumentality to be served, or
> (C) as directed by order of the court consistent with the law of the place where service is to be made. **{-813-}**

28 U.S.C. § 1608(b)(1)-(3). It is here, in each of the three options listed in § 1608(b)(1), (2), and (3), that Ferrominera points to the requirement that service be accomplished by "delivery of a copy of the summons and complaint."

Given that wandering path, we pause to briefly restate the journey. Neither Chapter 2 of the FAA nor the New York Convention mention service requirements for an application to confirm an arbitral award. Chapter 2 of the FAA incorporates Chapter 1 as a gap-filler, insofar as the two do not conflict. Chapter 1 of the FAA requires service of a "notice of application," which must be done "in like manner" as other court process. The phrase "in like manner" refers **[—22—]** to Federal Rule of Civil Procedure 4 (which, Rule 81 reminds us, must always be consistent with the FAA). For foreign instrumentalities, Rule 4(j) directs us to § 1608 of the FSIA, which describes various methods of service on foreign instrumentalities or agencies. And it is only at this last stop—§ 1608(b)—that we find the first mention of a "summons and complaint."

Ferrominera argues that because CME failed to serve it with a summons, it failed to comply with the service requirements of the FSIA. It contends that the FSIA dictates "the exclusive means by which service of process may be effected," and that § 1608(b) of the FSIA requires service of "a summons" even in proceedings to confirm an arbitral award. Appellant Br. at 12 (quoting *Seramur v. Saudi Arabian Airlines*, 934 F. Supp. 48, 51 (E.D.N.Y. 1996)). We are not persuaded.

We hold that a summons is not required to properly effect service when seeking confirmation of a foreign arbitral award against **[—23—]** a foreign instrumentality. We reach this conclusion for two principal reasons: (1) the FAA itself defines the *documents* to be served, and cross-references other provisions (including Rule 4 and the FSIA) only to fill gaps in the permissible *manner* of serving those documents; and (2) it would make no sense to import the FSIA's requirement of service of a "summons and complaint" into the FAA because motions to confirm arbitral awards are not commenced by the filing of a complaint.

First, a plain reading of the relevant statutes and rules supports the conclusion that the only thing that must be served is the notice of application. Chapter 1, § 9 of the

FAA specifies that "the *notice of the application* shall be served . . . in like manner as other process of the court." 9 U.S.C. § 9 (emphasis added). The FAA does not require service beyond this. Although the FSIA mentions delivery of something different from a notice of application—a "summons and complaint," 28 U.S.C. § 1608(b)(1)-(3)—recall that procedures **[—24—]** otherwise provided for are not incorporated upstream into the FAA. Rule 81(a)(6)(B) of the Federal Rules of Civil Procedure enables only limited incorporation of the FSIA into Rule 4—that is, "except as [the FAA] provide[s] other procedures." Here, § 9 of the FAA provides a procedure on what notice shall be served upon the opposing party—"notice of the *application"*—thereby triggering the exception to incorporation. 9 U.S.C. § 9 (emphasis added). Because the reference in § 1608(b)(1)-(3) to "the delivery of a copy of the summons and complaint" remains unincorporated, it bears no weight. Moreover, § 9 of the FAA cross-references other provisions only to determine the "manner" in which notice of the application must be served. The FSIA is therefore incorporated into the FAA only to the extent it answers *how* to serve process, not to supplant the FAA's specification of *what* must be served. **{-814-}**

Second, a proceeding to confirm an arbitral award under the FAA is commenced by an application rather than a "complaint"; **[—25—]** accordingly, there is no basis for serving a "summons and complaint," which are the documents referenced in § 1608(b). We have explained that "'confirmation of an arbitration award is a summary proceeding that merely makes what is already a final arbitration award a judgment of the court.'" *Yusuf Ahmed Alghanim & Sons*, 126 F.3d at 23 (quoting *Florasynth, Inc.*, 750 F.2d at 176). Lest there be any doubt, the FAA's provision implementing the New York Convention calls for a party merely to "apply to" the court for an "order confirming the award[.]" 9 U.S.C. § 207; *see* 9 U.S.C. § 9 ("notice of the *application* [to confirm an arbitral award] shall be served" on the adverse party "in like manner as other process of the court") (emphasis added); *accord Int'l Standard Elec. Corp. v. Bridas Sociedad Anonima Petrolera, Industrial y Comercial*, 745 F. Supp. 172, 182 (S.D.N.Y. 1990) ("A confirmation proceeding under the Convention is not an original action, it is, rather in the nature of a post-judgment enforcement proceeding." (internal quotation marks and alterations omitted)). Given the summary **[—26—]** nature of confirmation proceedings, it is unsurprising that the FAA would require only service of notice of an application as opposed to service of a full summons and complaint. *See Teamsters Local 177 v. United Parcel Serv.*, 966 F.3d 245, 252, 254 (3d Cir. 2020) (agreeing with *Florasynth*, 750 F.2d at 176, that confirmation of an arbitration award is a summary proceeding, and noting that summary proceedings may be "conducted without formal pleadings, on short notice, without summons and complaints, generally on affidavits, and sometimes even *ex parte*" (quoting *New Hampshire Fire Ins. Co. v. Scanlon*, 362 U.S. 404, 406 (1960))). And because no "complaint" is involved in a motion to confirm an arbitral award, it would make little sense to read the FAA as incorporating the FSIA's instruction to serve both "a summons and complaint" (and even less sense to conclude that only half of that pair of documents—namely, a summons—must be served). Thus, we hold that the New York Convention and the FAA **[—27—]** require only service of notice of the application to confirm a foreign arbitral award, and not also a summons.[7] **{-815-}**

---

[7] This conclusion is consistent with at least three district courts in this Circuit to have faced similar questions. *See Associated Indus. Ins. Co. v. Excalibur Reinsurance Corp.*, No. 13 CIV. 8239, 2014 WL 6792021, at *4 (S.D.N.Y. Nov. 26, 2014) (service of summons not required to commence proceeding to vacate domestic arbitration award under the FAA); *Scandinavian Reinsurance Co. v. St. Paul Fire & Marine Ins. Co.*, 732 F. Supp. 2d 293, 305-06 (S.D.N.Y. 2010) (service of summons not required to commence proceeding to confirm foreign arbitral award under the New York Convention and FAA), *rev'd on other grounds*, 668 F.3d 60 (2d Cir. 2012); *Home Ins. Co. v. RHA/Pennsylvania Nursing Homes, Inc.*, 113 F. Supp. 2d 633, 635 n.10 (S.D.N.Y. 2000) (service of summons not required for purpose of commencing proceeding to confirm domestic arbitration award under the FAA).

Having reached this legal conclusion, we easily determine that CME properly effected service of notice on Ferrominera. Under the first of the three modes of service listed in § 1608(b) of the FSIA, **[—28—]** service "shall be made . . . in accordance with any special arrangement for service between the plaintiff and the agency or instrumentality." 28 U.S.C. § 1608(b)(1). Here, neither party disputes that the General Piar Charter incorporated the SMA Rules and that those rules constitute a "special arrangement" for the purposes of § 1608.[8] SMA Rule 35 provides that

> Wherever parties have agreed to arbitration under these Rules, they shall be deemed to have consented to service of any papers, notices or process necessary to initiate or continue an arbitration under these Rules or a court action to confirm judgment on the Award issued. Such documents may be served:
>
> a. By mail addressed to such party or counsel at their last known address; or
>
> b. By personal service. **[—29—]**

Joint App'x at 237. The district court found, and the parties do not dispute, that CME complied with this special arrangement. *Commodities & Minerals Enter., Ltd. v. CVG Ferrominera Orinoco, C.A.*, No. 19-cv-11654-ALC, 2020 WL 7261111, at *2, *4 (S.D.N.Y. Dec. 10, 2020) ("CME served the instant petition and supporting documents on arbitration counsel to [Ferrominera] . . . and on [Ferrominera] at its last known address, in Venezuela by mail."). As a result, CME complied with the service of notice requirements of the New York Convention and the FAA, and the district court properly exercised personal jurisdiction over Ferrominera.

C. Confirmation of the Award

Ferrominera next raises three arguments challenging the district court's confirmation of the award: (1) the arbitration agreement was invalid under Venezuelan law, and therefore the panel lacked jurisdiction to hear the dispute; (2) in the alternative, if the arbitration agreement was valid, the Panel nonetheless exceeded the scope of its jurisdiction under the arbitration agreement in its **[—30—]** calculation of damages; and (3) confirming the Award would violate United States public policy because the General Piar Charter was the product of corruption.

We reject all three arguments.

1. Validity of the arbitration agreement

Ferrominera first challenges the confirmation of the Award on the ground that the Panel lacked jurisdiction because the arbitration agreement was invalid under Venezuelan law.

With respect to this challenge, Ferrominera fails to identify what (if any) specific defense it invokes under Article V(1) of the New York

---

Ferrominera points to two district court actions in Florida between these same parties where, in both cases, the courts held that it was improper for CME to fail to serve a summons in filing its application for enforcement of other, related arbitral awards. *See Commodities & Minerals Enterprise Ltd. v. CVG Ferrominera Orinoco, C.A.*, No. 17-20196-CIV, 2017 WL 11625759, at *3 (S.D. Fla. Apr. 4, 2017); *Commodities & Mins. Enter. Ltd. v. CVG Ferrominera Orinoco, C.A.*, 338 F.R.D. 664, 667 (S.D. Fla. 2021); *see also Ballantine v. Dominican Republic,* 19 Civ. 3598, 2020 WL 4597159, at *2-4 (D.D.C. Aug. 11, 2020) (holding that petitioners failed to effect valid service on the Dominican Republic of a motion to vacate an arbitral award for various reasons, including failure to serve a timely summons under the FSIA). Those courts relied on the phrase "summons and complaint" in § 1608(b) of the FSIA to conclude that service of a summons was required. In our view, these courts erred in failing to start their analysis with the FAA, which incorporates the FSIA's requirements only as to the *manner* of service, not *what* must be served.

[8] Ferrominera separately contests whether the arbitration agreement (which incorporates the SMA rules) is valid. This argument is addressed later in this opinion. *See infra* at Section II.C. But that argument aside, Ferrominera does not contest that if the arbitration agreement is valid, it incorporates the SMA Rules, nor that the SMA Rules are an incorporated "special arrangement" under § 1608 of the FSIA.

Convention. This is a serious lapse. Because the defenses listed under Article V are exhaustive and Ferrominera carries a heavy burden to prove such a defense, *see Encyclopaedia Universalis*, 403 F.3d at 90, a party must first identify which defense it is invoking to establish any potential entitlement to that **{–816–}** defense. When faced with this same briefing deficiency at the district court, Judge Carter construed this argument as falling within Article V(1)(a) and **[—31—]** characterized Ferrominera's challenge as against the "validity" of the agreement. *See Commodities & Minerals Enter.*, 2020 WL 7261111, at *4 n.3. On appeal, Ferrominera has not challenged Judge Carter's characterization, and so we limit ourselves to that enumerated defense.[9]

Ferrominera argues that the arbitration agreement was not "valid" because it was not authorized under any of three different Venezuelan laws. Specifically, it argues that various approvals were not in place from different Venezuelan officials, which were necessary for this state-owned business to enter an arbitration agreement. This argument is premised on the notion that the existence of a valid arbitration agreement is governed by Venezuelan law. **[—32—]**

But Article V(1)(a) says otherwise. Whether an arbitration agreement is "valid" is governed by "the law to which the parties have subjected it" (or "failing any indication thereon, under the law of the country where the award was made"). New York Convention, Art. V(1)(a). Consistent with this language, we have repeatedly held that the existence or validity of an arbitration agreement is governed by a choice-of-law clause where one exists, because choice-of-law clauses are separable when the contract's validity is otherwise disputed. *See Motorola Credit Corp. v. Uzan*, 388 F.3d 39, 50-51 (2d Cir. 2004) (applying choice-of-law clause selecting Swiss law to determine validity of international arbitration agreement); *Sphere Drake Ins. Ltd. v. Clarendon Nat'l Ins. Co.*, 263 F.3d 26, 32 n.3 (2d Cir. 2001) (applying New Jersey and New York choice-of-law clauses to a party's claim that the underlying arbitration agreements were void because they were signed by an unauthorized agent); *Int'l Minerals & Res., S.A. v. Pappas*, 96 F.3d 586, 592 (2d Cir. 1996) (applying an English choice-of- **[—33—]** law clause to an issue of contract formation); *see also* 3 Gary Born, *International Commercial Arbitration* § 26.05(C) (3d ed. 2021) ("A choice of law agreement is effective to select the law governing the arbitration agreement even if one party denies the validity or existence of those agreements.").

Ferrominera contends that applying the Charter's choice-of-law clause to questions of validity inappropriately presumes the conclusion—namely, that the dispute resolution provision in which that choice-of-law clause sits is valid. Ferrominera relies on *Schnabel v. Trilegiant Corp.*, 697 F.3d 110, 119 (2d Cir. 2012), to support this argument, but *Schnabel* is readily distinguished from the present case. In *Schnabel*, the Court declined to enforce the choice-of-law clause when considering whether the underlying contract was valid because there was a dispute about whether the choice-of-law clause had been part of the contract at the time of its formation. *Id.* at 114-19. Because the choice-of-law clause was specifically challenged, "[a]pplying [it] **[—34—]** to resolve the contract formation issue would presume the applicability of a provision before its adoption by the parties has been established." *Id.* at 119. Thus, rather than a broad exception to the ordinary rule (that choice-of-law clauses are separable), *Schnabel* presents only a narrow **{–817–}** corollary to the logic of separability: if the validity of the choice-of-law clause is *specifically* challenged, that clause

[9] We note that Article V(1)(a) also provides for another defense, distinct from the invalidity of the arbitration agreement, that "[t]he parties to the [arbitration] agreement . . . were, under the law applicable to them, under some incapacity . . . ." Ferrominera has not cited this provision in its briefing before this Court, nor did it do so before the district court. Accordingly, we limit ourselves to the question of whether the arbitration agreement was "valid" within the meaning of Article V(1)(a).

cannot be evaluated separately from the contract.[10]

Here, unlike in *Schnabel*, there is no dispute that the choice-of-law clause is included in the General Piar Charter, which both parties signed. Therefore, the ordinary rule—that choice-of-law clauses are separated out from contracts for questions of validity—applies in full force. *See Motorola*, 388 F.3d at 50-51. Applying that rule, we find that the General Piar Charter contained a choice-of-law clause, and that **[—35—]** clause opted for U.S. maritime law. Joint App'x at 215-16. Accordingly, U.S. law, and not Venezuelan law, governs the General Piar Charter, including any question about the arbitration agreement's validity.[11]

Ferrominera's arguments as to why there is no valid arbitration agreement, however, are limited exclusively to Venezuelan law. It has made no such arguments under U.S. maritime law. Because a party resisting confirmation of a foreign arbitral award has the burden of establishing a defense under Article V(1), we conclude that Ferrominera has not borne its burden to show that the arbitration **[—36—]** agreement is invalid where, as here, it has put forth no arguments whatsoever under the applicable law.[12] Accordingly, the arbitration agreement is valid and enforceable.

2. The scope of the arbitration agreement

Ferrominera next argues that the Award should not be confirmed under Article **{–818–}** V(1)(c) of the New York Convention because the Panel exceeded its authority in calculating damages. Specifically, Ferrominera contends that the Panel incorrectly allocated past payments it made to CME to contracts other than the General Piar **[—37—]** Charter. In so doing, its argument goes, the Panel violated Ferrominera's right to decide how to allocate payments among these contracts and improperly shifted moneys already paid to the disputed General Piar Charter.

But Ferrominera's claim amounts to nothing more than a quarrel over how much it owes in damages, which was properly a question for the arbitrators. As the district

---

[10] A similar rule exists in the context of arbitration clauses. Although arbitration agreements are ordinarily separable from questions of broader contract validity, *see Prima Paint Corp. v. Flood & Conklin Mfg. Co.*, 388 U.S. 395, 402 (1967), they cannot be separated when the arbitration agreement is itself challenged as invalid. *Buckeye Check Cashing, Inc. v. Cardegna*, 546 U.S. 440, 446-49 (2006).

[11] Although the district court correctly determined that U.S. law applied, it reached that conclusion by finding that the arbitration clause encompassed issues of arbitrability, and therefore deferred to the Panel's findings, even on the choice of law issue. *Commodities & Minerals Enter.*, 2020 WL 7261111, at *5. As outlined here, however, on a motion to confirm a foreign arbitral award the law governing the validity of the arbitration agreement is dictated not by deference to the Panel's decision, but rather by Article V(1)(a) of the New York Convention, which directs the court to review issues of arbitration agreement validity under "the law to which the parties have subjected it or, failing any indication thereon, under the law of the country where the award was made." The district court's deference to the Panel on this point was therefore unwarranted, but we agree with the conclusions of both the Panel and the district court that U.S. maritime law applies.

[12] Ferrominera also argues that the Panel's decision on the validity of the arbitration agreement should have been reviewed *de novo* by the district court. But we need not reach this issue. Regardless of how much (if any) deference might have been warranted, the fact remains that Ferrominera presented no arguments under U.S. maritime law to justify disturbing the Panel's conclusion that it had jurisdiction to arbitrate the dispute.

Furthermore, while it is true that there is caselaw suggesting that a court can review challenges to the validity of an arbitration agreement when those challenges are either to the arbitration agreement itself (rather than the contract as a whole) or to the whole contract as void *ab initio*, *see, e.g.*, *Buckeye Check Cashing*, 546 U.S. at 444 n.1, 446-48; *Sphere Drake Ins. Ltd.*, 263 F.3d at 32, those cases all arose at the threshold stage of arbitration, on motions to compel. Whether those cases also stand for the proposition that a court may (or must) review the validity of an arbitration agreement *de novo* on a motion to confirm (or, for that matter, on a motion to vacate), does not necessarily follow. For the reasons stated above, however, we need not address this question.

court correctly held, Article V(1)(c) provides a defense to confirmation where an arbitration award "deals with a difference not contemplated by or not falling within the terms of the submission to arbitration, or it contains decisions on matters beyond the scope of the submission to arbitration." The question of the correct calculation of damages "falls squarely within the broad arbitration clause in the General Piar Charter." *Commodities & Minerals Enter.*, 2020 WL 7261111, at *5. Ferrominera's argument—which is, at most, that the Panel calculated damages incorrectly—thus falls outside of Article V(1)(c) and, in fact, **[—38—]** outside of any defense listed in Article V. *Cf. Stolt-Nielsen S.A. v. AnimalFeeds Int'l Corp.*, 559 U.S. 662, 671 (2010) ("It is not enough for petitioners to show that the panel committed an error—or even a serious error. It is only when an arbitrator strays from interpretation and application of the agreement and effectively dispenses his own brand of industrial justice that his decision may be unenforceable." (cleaned up)); *Parsons & Whittemore Overseas Co. v. Societe Generale De L'Industrie Du Papier (RAKTA)*, 508 F.2d 969, 976-77 (2d Cir. 1974) (rejecting appellant's attack on money awarded for start-up expenses and costs because the New York Convention "does not sanction second-guessing the arbitrator's construction of the parties' agreement").

3. United States public policy

Ferrominera brings its final argument against confirmation of the Award under Article V(2)(b) of the New York Convention. The thrust of this argument is that the General Piar Charter was procured **[—39—]** through corruption and, therefore, enforcement of the Award would violate United States public policy.

This argument, however, falls outside the narrow public policy exception codified by Article V(2)(b). Article V(2)(b) allows a court to refuse "recognition or enforcement of the award [if such recognition or enforcement] would be contrary to the public policy of that country." *See Telenor Mobile Commc'ns AS v. Storm LLC*, 584 F.3d 396, 405, 411 (2d Cir. 2009) (holding that confirming a foreign arbitral award was not contrary to New York's public policy against compelling a party to violate a foreign judgment). But "Article V(2)(b) must be 'construed very narrowly' to encompass only those circumstances 'where enforcement would violate our most basic notions of morality and justice.'" *Id.* at 411 (quoting *Europcar Italia S.p.A. v. Maiellano Tours, Inc.*, 156 F.3d 310, 315 (2d Cir. 1998)). In reviewing an arbitral award for violations of public policy, a court may not "revisit or question the fact-finding or the reasoning which **[—40—]** produced the award." *IBEW, Local 97 v. Niagara Mohawk Power Corp.*, 143 F.3d 704, 716 (2d Cir. 1998). Instead, "a court's task in reviewing . . . possible violations of public policy is limited to determining whether the award itself, as contrasted with the reasoning that underlies the award, 'create[s] [an] explicit conflict with other laws **{-819-}** and legal precedents' and thus clearly violates an identifiable public policy." *Id.* (quoting *United Paperworkers Int'l Union v. Misco, Inc.*, 484 U.S. 29, 43 (1987)). When a party claims that an underlying contract is invalid for violating public policy, that claim is "to be determined exclusively by the arbitrators." *Europcar Italia*, 156 F.3d at 315.

Ferrominera's public policy argument attacks the General Piar Charter itself, not the Award or its enforcement. The Panel carefully considered Ferrominera's corruption allegations and gave Ferrominera ample opportunity to substantiate its claim. Despite extensive discovery and opportunity to present its case, the Panel concluded that the General Piar Charter was not, as a factual matter, **[—41—]** the product of corrupt acts by CME. Both before the district court and here, Ferrominera merely seeks to relitigate the Panel's factual determination on this point. It offers no argument that enforcement itself, "within the parameters of the arbitrator's interpretation of the facts," *IBEW, Local 97*, 143 F.3d at 726, violates public policy.[13]

---

[13] *Hardy Expl. & Prod. (India), Inc. v. Gov't of India, Ministry of Petroleum & Nat. Gas*, 314 F. Supp. 3d 95 (D.D.C. 2018), relied on by Ferrominera, only highlights the insufficiency of its argument. In *Hardy*, the court found that

In sum, Ferrominera's public policy argument asks this Court to relitigate the Panel's factual determinations underlying the validity of the Charter. But this argument falls outside of Article V(2)(b)'s narrow public policy exception, and the district court properly rejected it. **[—42—]**

D. Attorney's fees

Lastly, Ferrominera challenges the district court's award of attorney's fees in favor of CME.

The district court granted CME's request for attorney's fees "in light of Ferrominera's failure to comply with the award or come forward with a good faith reason for not complying." *Commodities & Minerals Enter.*, 2020 WL 7261111, at *7. Although our review of fee awards is "highly deferential," *Mautner v. Hirsch*, 32 F.3d 37, 39 (2d Cir. 1994), we conclude that the district court abused its discretion here.

Generally, "in a federal action, attorney's fees cannot be recovered by the successful party in the absence of statutory authority for the award." *Int'l Chem. Workers Union (AFL-CIO), Local No. 227 v. BASF Wyandotte Corp.*, 774 F.2d 43, 47 (2d Cir. 1985). Section 9 of the FAA does not provide such statutory authority, because it makes no mention of the recovery of attorney's fees. Still, a court retains "inherent equitable powers" to "award attorney's fees when the **[—43—]** opposing counsel acts 'in bad faith, vexatiously, wantonly, or for oppressive reasons.'" *Id.* (quoting *F.D. Rich Co. v. United States ex rel. Indus. Lumber Co.*, 417 U.S. 116, 129 (1974)). "As applied to suits for the confirmation and enforcement of arbitration awards, the guiding principle has been [that] 'when a challenger refuses to abide by an arbitrator's decision without justification, attorney's fees **{-820-}** and costs may properly be awarded.'" *Int'l Chem. Workers Union*, 774 F.2d at 47 (quoting *Bell Production Engineers Ass'n v. Bell Helicopter Textron*, 688 F.2d 997, 999 (5th Cir. 1982)).

Here, although we ultimately disagree with Ferrominera's arguments, we conclude that those arguments were not presented "without justification," *id.*, and that Ferrominera did not act "in bad faith, vexatiously, wantonly, or for oppressive reasons." *F.D. Rich Co.*, 417 U.S. at 129. In particular, we note that the first question addressed in this opinion—namely, whether service of a summons is required to apply to a court for an order confirming a foreign arbitration award—**[—44—]** is a question of first impression for this Court. Furthermore, we acknowledge that Ferrominera twice achieved some success on this exact argument in another federal district court. *See Commodities & Minerals Enterprise Ltd. v. CVG Ferrominera Orinoco, C.A.*, No. 17-20196-CIV, 2017 WL 11625759 (S.D. Fla. Apr. 4, 2017); *Commodities & Mins. Enter. Ltd. v. CVG Ferrominera Orinoco, C.A.*, 338 F.R.D. 664, 667 (S.D. Fla. 2021). We therefore cannot say that its arguments were brought in bad faith. *See Oliveri v. Thompson*, 803 F.2d 1265, 1272 (2d Cir. 1986) ("[W]e have declined to uphold [fee] awards under the bad-faith exception absent both 'clear evidence' that the challenged actions are 'entirely without color, and [are taken] for reasons of harassment or delay or for other improper purposes' and a 'high degree of specificity in the factual findings of [the] lower courts.'" (quoting *Dow Chemical Pacific Ltd. v. Rascator Maritime S.A.*, 782 F.2d 329, 344 (2d Cir. 1986))). **[—45—]**

Accordingly, we vacate the portion of the judgment that awarded attorney's fees and costs to CME.

---

enforcement of an arbitration award against India would violate public policy. *Id.* at 110-11. But the award at issue was one for specific performance that required India to turn over certain land in that country to the plaintiff. *Id.* In that case, *enforcement of the award itself* violated clear United States policy respecting a sovereign nation's right to control its own land. *Id.* Those facts stand in sharp contrast to Ferrominera's argument here, which is nothing more than a collateral attack on the General Piar Charter and a thinly veiled effort to relitigate factual determinations made by the Panel. Ferrominera makes no argument that enforcing the Award, standing alone, violates public policy.

III. Conclusion

In sum, we hold as follows:

(1) A party applying to a court to confirm a foreign arbitral award under Chapter 2 of the Federal Arbitration Act and the New York Convention is not required to serve a summons on the adverse party to satisfy the FAA's service of notice requirement. CME properly effected service of notice on Ferrominera because its service of notice complied with the parties' "special arrangement" as permitted under 28 U.S.C. § 1608(b)(1).

(2) The district court properly enforced the arbitration award because Ferrominera failed to establish that the arbitration agreement was invalid under U.S. maritime law, the Panel did not exceed its authority under the arbitration agreement **[—46—]** in issuing the Award, and the Award is not contrary to U.S. public policy.

(3) The district court abused its discretion in awarding attorney's fees and costs in favor of CME.

We therefore **AFFIRM** the judgment of the district court to the extent that it recognized and enforced the Award in favor of CME and **VACATE** the judgment of the district court to the extent that it awarded attorney's fees and costs in favor of CME.

This page intentionally left blank

United States Court of Appeals for the Third Circuit

United States Court of Appeals
for the Third Circuit

No. 21-1562

GREAT LAKES INS. SE
vs.
RAIDERS RETREAT REALTY CO.

Appeal from the United States District Court for the Eastern District of Pennsylvania

Decided: August 30, 2022

Citation: 47 F.4th 225, 10 Adm. R. 88 (3d Cir. 2022).

Before **CHAGARES,** Chief Judge, **AMBRO,** and **FUENTES,** Circuit Judges.

[—3—] {-227-} **AMBRO,** Circuit Judge:

A yacht owned by Raiders Retreat Realty Co., LLC ran aground. Luckily (or so it believed), Raiders had insured the vessel with marine insurer Great Lakes Insurance SE ("GLI"). But after Raiders submitted a claim under its policy, GLI left it high and dry. The insurer's reason for denying coverage: the yacht's fire-extinguishing equipment had not been timely recertified or inspected notwithstanding that the vessel's damage was not caused by fire. GLI sued first, seeking in federal court a declaratory judgment that Raiders' alleged failure to recertify or inspect its fire-suppression equipment rendered the policy void from its inception.

Raiders responded with five counterclaims, including three extra-contractual counterclaims arising under Pennsylvania law for breach of fiduciary duty, insurance bad faith, and breach of Pennsylvania's Unfair Trade Practices and Consumer Protection Law, 73 Pa. Stat. Ann. § 201-1, *et seq.* (the "Unfair Trade Practices Law"), respectively. Concluding the policy's choice-of-law provision mandated the application of New York law and thus precluded Raiders' Pennsylvania-law-based counterclaims, the District Court dismissed those claims. In so doing, the Court rejected Raiders' argument that applying New York law would contravene Pennsylvania public policy, thereby making the choice-of-law provision unenforceable under *The Bremen v. Zapata Off-Shore Co.*, 407 U.S. 1, 15 (1972), which held that under federal admiralty law **[—4—]** a forum-selection provision is unenforceable "if enforcement would contravene a strong public policy of the forum in which suit is brought." The District Court held that *The Bremen* did not apply for the choice-of-law issue, such that it need not consider whether there is strong Pennsylvania public policy that precludes applying New York law. We think the answer may be otherwise.

I. Background

Raiders, a Pennsylvania-based company, insured a yacht for up to $550,000 with GLI, a company headquartered in the United Kingdom. That yacht ran aground in June 2019, incurring at least $300,000 in damage. Raiders submitted a claim to GLI for loss of the vessel, but GLI rejected it, claiming that the yacht's fire-extinguishing equipment was not timely recertified or inspected contrary to Raiders' prior statements otherwise. Though the damage to **{-228-}** the yacht was free of fire, GLI maintained Raiders misrepresented the vessel's fire-suppression system's operating ability, thus making the policy void from inception. The insurer then filed an action for declaratory judgment in the U.S. District Court for the Eastern District of Pennsylvania to determine whether the policy was indeed void.

As noted, Raiders contested GLI's allegations and brought five counterclaims. It alleged breach of contract (Count I); breach of the implied covenant of good faith and fair dealing (Count II); breach of fiduciary duty (Count III); insurance bad faith, in violation of 42 Pa. Stat. and Cons. Stat. Ann. § 8371 (Count IV); and violation of Pennsylvania's Unfair Trade Practices Law (Count V). Relying on the policy's choice-of-law provision, GLI moved for judgment on the pleadings under Federal Rule of Civil Procedure 12(c) as to **[—5—]** Counts III through V, which sought relief available against insurance companies under Pennsylvania law (hence not based on the insurance contract and thereby referred to as extracontractual claims), on the ground that New York law, which precludes these claims, governs. The choice-of-law provision in the policy reads:

> It is hereby agreed that any dispute arising hereunder shall be adjudicated according to well established, entrenched principles and precedents of substantive United States Federal Admiralty law and practice[,] but where no such well established, entrenched precedent exists, this insuring agreement is subject to the substantive laws of the State of New York.

App. at 113. The District Court concluded that New York law governed and barred Raiders' Pennsylvania-law-based counterclaims, thereby dismissing Counts III through V. The Court later denied Raiders' motion to reconsider its judgment. Raiders now appeals.

II. Standard of Review

We give a fresh, or plenary, review of the District Court's choice-of-law determination. *See Berg Chilling Sys., Inc. v. Hull Corp.*, 435 F.3d 455, 462 (3d Cir. 2006). We likewise exercise plenary review of the Court's construction of a written contract, *see USX Corp. v. Prime Leasing Inc.*, 988 F.2d 433, 437 (3d Cir. 1993), and apply the same standard to its grant of a motion for judgment on the pleadings, "accept[ing] the nonmoving party's factual allegations as true and constru[ing] all allegations in the light most favorable to **[—6—]** that party," *Fed Cetera, LLC v. Nat'l Credit Servs., Inc.*, 938 F.3d 466, 469 n.7 (3d Cir. 2019).

III. Discussion

A. Our jurisdiction over this interlocutory appeal.

Because this case concerns a maritime insurance contract, it fell within the District Court's maritime jurisdiction. 28 U.S.C. § 1333(1); *AGF Marine Aviation & Transp. v. Cassin*, 544 F.3d 255, 260 (3d Cir. 2008). Our jurisdiction over the appeal is less clear. Though neither party contests it, before reaching the merits of this case we must first independently establish our authority to decide. *In re Klaas*, 858 F.3d 820, 825 (3d Cir. 2017). We have, under 28 U.S.C. § 1292(a)(3), jurisdiction over appeals from "[i]nterlocutory decrees of such district courts or the judges thereof determining the rights and liabilities of the parties to admiralty cases in which appeals from final decrees are allowed." For interlocutory appeals in admiralty cases, our precedent makes this language "appl[y] to situations such as the dismissal of parties from the litigation, grants of summary judgment (even if not to all parties), and **{-229-}** other cases where a claim has somehow been terminated." *In re Complaint of PMD Enters., Inc.*, 301 F.3d 147, 149 (3d Cir. 2002). In short, "the order appealed from must conclusively determine the merits of a claim or defense." *Kingstate Oil v. M/V Green Star*, 815 F.2d 918, 921 (3d Cir. 1987).

In practice, we have allowed interlocutory appeals in admiralty cases where parties' claims against one of the defendants suffered dismissal for lack of subject matter jurisdiction, *see Jones & Laughlin Steel, Inc. v. Mon River* **[—7—]** *Towing, Inc.*, 772 F.2d 62, 64 n.1 (3d Cir. 1985); the grant of judgment on a counterclaim where the principal claim was undecided, *see In re Nautilus Motor Tanker Co.*, 85 F.3d 105, 110 n.3 (3d Cir. 1996); and even in an appeal from an order determining the rights and liabilities of some but not all parties, *see Bankers Tr. Co. v. Bethlehem Steel Corp.*, 761 F.2d 943, 945 n.1 (3d Cir. 1985).

On the other hand, we refused to allow an interlocutory appeal in admiralty where the trial court dismissed one claim on which forfeiture of a vessel was based but three other grounds for that remedy remained. *See United States v. The Lake George*, 224 F.2d 117, 118–19 (3d Cir. 1955). We likewise rejected an interlocutory appeal in admiralty where the District Court denied a plaintiff's motion for summary judgment on the defendant's counterclaim because "no right or liability of the parties ha[d] been 'conclusively determine[d].'" *PMD*, 301 F.3d at 151 (second alteration in original) (quoting *Kingstate Oil*, 815 F.2d at 921). We explained that "[h]ad the District Court denied [the defendant] the right to file the counterclaim or had it granted summary judgment to [the plaintiff] on [the defendant's] counterclaim, the rights and liabilities of the parties may well have been conclusively determined, in which case the District Court's decision would have been appealable." *Id.*

Because it foreclosed certain counterclaims, the District Court's decision to dismiss Raiders' extracontractual counterclaims is analogous to the hypothetical scenarios we outlined in *PMD*. As we explained, "the rights and liabilities of the parties may well have been conclusively determined" and so "would have been appealable." *Id.* **[—8—]**

Applying that logic here warrants interlocutory review. Further, while Raiders still maintains two remaining counterclaims (Counts I and II), the Pennsylvania-law-based counterclaims dismissed by the District Court seek forms of relief unavailable under the surviving counts. *Cf. Lake George*, 224 F.2d at 118–19 (foreclosing appeal in admiralty where remaining claims sought same relief as dismissed claim). Moreover, "[i]n maritime cases, [a] choice-of-law . . . determination," such as the one before us, is deemed a "determination on the merits and may be treated as the equivalent of a motion for summary judgment." *Vasquez v. Bridgestone/Firestone, Inc.*, 325 F.3d 665, 680 n.26 (5th Cir. 2003). For these reasons, we hold that the District Court's dismissal of Raiders' extracontractual counterclaims "determin[ed] the rights and liabilities of the parties" under § 1292(a)(3). Hence we have jurisdiction over this interlocutory appeal.

B. The District Court should have considered whether applying New York substantive law would contravene Pennsylvania's "strong public policy" under *The Bremen*.

As our Court has summarized, the seminal maritime insurance decision in *Wilburn Boat Co. v. Fireman's Fund Insurance Co.*, 348 U.S. 310 (1955), established that "maritime contracts are governed by federal **{-230-}** admiralty law when there is an established federal rule, but absent such a rule, state law applies." *Royal Ins. Co. of Am. v. KSI Trading Corp.*, 563 F.3d 68, 73 (3d Cir. 2009). One such established federal rule is that "[a] choice of law provision in a marine insurance contract will be upheld in the absence of evidence that its enforcement would be unreasonable or unjust." 2 Thomas J. Schoenbaum, **[—9—]** Admiralty and Maritime Law § 19:6 (6th ed. 2020); *see also Great Lakes Reinsurance (UK) PLC v. Durham Auctions, Inc.*, 585 F.3d 236, 242–44 (5th Cir. 2009) (determining whether enforcing identical choice-of-law section in maritime insurance policy "would be unreasonable or unjust"); *cf. Neely v. Club Med Mgmt. Servs., Inc.*, 63 F.3d 166, 197 n.36 (3d Cir. 1995) (observing in dicta that choice-of-law provisions are "typically . . . enforced under federal maritime law").

Raiders, however, contends this presumption of enforceability should not control the choice of law here.[1] Citing *The Bremen*, it argues that enforcing the choice of law in the policy would be unreasonable and unjust, as applying New York law would contravene the strong public policy of Pennsylvania, which protects insureds in Pennsylvania from, among other things, bad faith and unfair trade practices by insurance companies.

The Bremen involved a dispute between an American and a German company about the enforceability of a forum-selection provision in a towing contract drawn up to facilitate **[—10—]** the transport of a drilling rig from Louisiana to the Adriatic Sea off the coast of Italy: "Any dispute arising must be treated before the London Court of Justice." 407 U.S. at 2. When a contractual dispute arose, the

[1] Raiders also maintains the express language of the policy's choice-of-law provision does not mandate applying New York law to preclude its claims arising under Pennsylvania law. But as it failed to raise this argument in the District Court (or, for that matter, the more intriguing argument that the provision is ambiguous and therefore should be construed against GLI as the drafting party), Raiders has not properly preserved this argument for our review. *See Simko v. U.S. Steel Corp.*, 992 F.3d 198, 205 (3d Cir. 2021) ("It is well-established that arguments raised for the first time on appeal are not properly preserved for appellate review.").

American company sued in a federal court. *Id.* at 3–4.

The U.S. Supreme Court ultimately held that the contract's forum selection was facially valid and should be honored unless a compelling and countervailing reason rendered enforcement unreasonable. *Id.* at 10, 15, 20. It explained that that forum-selection articles in maritime cases should be enforced absent a "strong showing" that "enforcement would be unreasonable and unjust, or that the clause [is] invalid for such reasons as fraud or overreaching." *Id.* at 15. It then provided examples of circumstances where enforcement of a choice-of-forum provision would be "unreasonable and unjust," including, among other things, situations where enforcement would "*contravene a strong public policy of the forum in which suit is brought, whether declared by statute or by judicial decision.*" *Id.* (emphasis added). The choice of forum there was enforceable because there was "strong evidence that the forum clause was a vital part of the [parties'] agreement," *id.* at 14, and it was not "an agreement between two Americans to resolve their essentially local disputes in a remote alien forum," *id.* at 17.

Nearly twenty years later, in *Carnival Cruise Lines, Inc. v. Shute*, 499 U.S. 585, 588 (1991), the Supreme Court extended *The Bremen*'s framework to a dispute over **{-231-}** which of two competing states was the proper forum for a tort action in admiralty. *Carnival* stemmed from a suit in Washington State filed by a cruise ship passenger who sustained injuries in international waters off the coast of Mexico. *Id.* The **[—11—]** passenger's ticket contained a forum-selection proviso that "all disputes and matters" be litigated in Florida courts. *Id.* at 587–88.

The Supreme Court analyzed the case under the framework laid out in *The Bremen* to evaluate the "reasonableness of the forum clause," "refin[ing]" the latter case's analysis "to account for the realities of form passage contracts." *Id.* at 593. It noted that "a cruise line has a special interest in limiting the fora in which it potentially could be subject to suit." *Id.* And "[b]ecause a cruise ship typically carries passengers from many locales, it is not unlikely that a mishap on a cruise could subject the cruise line to litigation in several different fora." *Id.* The Court further explained that "a clause establishing *ex ante* the forum for dispute resolution has the salutary effect of dispelling any confusion about where suits arising from the contract must be brought and defended." *Id.* at 593–94. Forum aside, "the fact that [the passenger's] accident occurred off the coast of Mexico" meant "this dispute [was not] an essentially local one inherently more suited to resolution in the State of Washington than in Florida." *Id.* at 594 (quotation marks omitted). In *Carnival*, therefore, the Supreme Court extended *The Bremen*'s framework to disputes over whether one state or another was the proper forum to bring suit under a forum-selection provision.

GLI argues *The Bremen* "is utterly irrelevant because it had absolutely nothing to do with the enforcement of choice of *law* clauses." Ans. Br. at 26 (emphasis added). We do not agree. Though the contract in *The Bremen* "did not specifically provide that the substantive law of England should be applied," the Court nonetheless "conclude[d] that the forum clause was also an effort to obtain certainty as to the applicable substantive **[—12—]** law," as "it is the general rule in English courts that the parties are assumed, absent contrary indication, to have designated the forum with the view that it should apply its own law." *The Bremen*, 407 U.S. at 13 n.15.

The U.S. Court of Appeals for the D.C. Circuit grasped this in *Milanovich v. Costa Crociere, S.p.A.*, 954 F.2d 763, 767 n.7 (D.C. Cir. 1992), by extending *The Bremen*'s framework to the choice of law in a cruise ticket: while "*The Bremen* involved a choice-of-forum clause, . . . the Supreme Court recognized that enforcing the provision would have the effect of subjecting the contract to foreign law." *Milanovich* concerned whether American or Italian law governed a cruise ship passenger's personal injury lawsuit where the contract contained a provision specifying the application of Italian law. *Id.* at 765–66. In resolving this question, the D.C.

Circuit relied on *The Bremen* and *Carnival* to hold that

> courts should honor a contractual choice-of-law provision in a passenger ticket unless the party challenging the enforcement of the provision can establish that "enforcement would be unreasonable and unjust," "the clause was invalid for such reasons as fraud or overreaching," or "*enforcement would contravene a strong public policy of the forum in which suit is brought.*"

Id. at 768 (quoting *The Bremen*, 407 U.S. at 15) (emphasis added). **[—13—]**

In the intervening decades, other circuits have relied on *Milanovich* when considering choice-of-law provisions in maritime contracts. *See* **{-232-}** *Chan v. Soc'y Expeditions, Inc.*, 123 F.3d 1287, 1297 (9th Cir. 1997) (upholding choice of law in cruise ticket over defendants' objections that Liberian law should apply); *Durham Auctions*, 585 F.3d at 243–45 (upholding identical choice-of-law provision where insured did not show applying New York law would contravene strong public policy of Mississippi). We are therefore persuaded that *The Bremen*'s framework is not "utterly irrelevant" in the context of choice-of-law provisions but rather applies equally to them as it does to those provisions selecting a forum.

GLI argues, however, that admiralty law is different: even if *The Bremen* does extend to choices of law in addition to forums, the framework it laid out does not apply here because, based on the Supreme Court's statement in *Wilburn Boat* discussed above, "there is a rule of federal admiralty law that choice of law clauses in policies of marine insurance are presumptively valid and enforceable." Ans. Br. at 29. Hence we "must apply that federal rule, no matter what." *Id.* at 21. This mirrors the District Court's opinion here, which held that the public policy of Pennsylvania could not overcome "the well-established principle that choice-of-law provisions in maritime contracts are presumptively valid." App. at 21.

In reaching its conclusion, the District Court also relied on the U.S. Court of Appeals for the Ninth Circuit's decision in *Galilea, LLC v. AGCS Marine Insurance Co.*, 879 F.3d 1052, 6 Adm. R. 300 (9th Cir. 2018). GLI likewise points to *Galilea* to argue *The Bremen* does not apply here. We disagree. *Galilea*, which does not bind our Court, involved a dispute over the scope of an insurance contract for a yacht owned by a Nevada company. **[—14—]** 879 F.3d at 1054, 6 Adm. R. at 300. The yacht's policy contained a forum-selection provision mandating arbitration in New York and a choice-of-law provision applying federal maritime law, but where no such established principles and precedents exist, New York law applied. *Id.* at 1055, 6 Adm. R. at 301. The yacht's owner sued in federal court in Montana and argued the choice-of-law and choice-of-forum provisions were precluded by Montana law (which purportedly has a strong public policy against enforcement of arbitration agreements) under *The Bremen*. *Id.* at 1055, 1059–60, 6 Adm. R. at 301, 305–06.

The Ninth Circuit disagreed. It first explained that because the arbitration provision was enforceable under the Federal Arbitration Act ("FAA"), 9 U.S.C. § 1, *et seq.*, "there [was] no gap in federal maritime law to fill with law from any state, Montana included, as the FAA supplies the governing arbitration law for maritime transactions." *Id.* at 1060, 6 Adm. R. at 305 (emphasis in original). The Court then reasoned that "*The Bremen* considered whether the public policy of the forum where suit was brought—there, federal public policy as supplied by federal maritime law—outweighed the application of the law of other countries." *Id.*, 6 Adm. R. at 305. The *Galilea* dispute, in contrast, concerned an "unequal, hierarchical relationship between federal maritime law and state law." *Id.*, 6 Adm. R. at 305. Because "[w]ithin federal admiralty jurisdiction, conflicting state policy cannot override squarely applicable federal maritime law," the Ninth Circuit held that the insured's "reliance on Montana law under *The Bremen* [was] misplaced." *Id.* at 1060–61, 6 Adm. R. at 306.

From this, the District Court here "conclude[d] that the public policy of a state where a case was filed cannot override the presumptive validity, under federal maritime choice-of-law principles, of a provision in a marine insurance contract where **[—15—]** the chosen forum has a substantial relationship to the parties or the transaction." App. at 21. "The issue is not," the Court explained, "whether New York law conflicts with Pennsylvania public policy." *Id.* **{-233-}** Rather, it is "whether the well-established principle that choice-of-law provisions in maritime contracts are presumptively valid must yield to the public policy preferences of the particular state in which the case happens to have been brought." *Id.* In holding the answer is no, the Court's opinion (relying on *Galilea*) turned on the view that *The Bremen* and its progeny apply to one set of circumstances whereas there is a separate regime governing choice-of-law concerns in marine insurance contracts. *Id.* at 21–22.

But the principle of generally enforcing choice-of-law provisions in marine insurance contracts is *not* altogether separate from the choice-of-forum/choice-of-law regime set out in *The Bremen* and *Milanovich*. Indeed, the rule that choice-of-law provisions in maritime insurance contracts are presumed enforceable unless "enforcement would be unreasonable or unjust," Schoenbaum, *supra*, § 19:6, is identical to *The Bremen*'s rule that forum-selection provisions should be honored unless "enforcement would be unreasonable and unjust," 407 U.S. at 15. Given this overlap—coupled with *The Bremen*'s "strong public policy" exception comprising but one part of the holding's broader "unreasonable and unjust" standard—we consider it altogether reasonable that a "strong public policy of the forum [state] in which suit is brought" could, as to that policy specifically, render unenforceable the choice of state law in a marine insurance contract. *See id.*

Moreover, the District Court's confining of *The Bremen* and its progeny only to disputes between international fora and **[—16—]** U.S. law is belied by *Carnival* (uncited by the parties), in which the Supreme Court applied *The Bremen* to a dispute over whether Washington State or Florida was the proper forum to decide. Given the broad language in *The Bremen*, its oft-recognized applicability to choice-of-law provisions, *see e.g., Milanovich*, 954 F.2d at 768, and the extension of its holding to a state-versus-state question in *Carnival*, we hold that *The Bremen*'s framework extends to the choice-of-law provision at issue here. Accordingly, the District Court needed to consider whether Pennsylvania has a strong public policy that would be thwarted by applying New York law. We thus vacate and remand for further proceedings consistent with this holding.

This page intentionally left blank

United States Court of Appeals for the Fourth Circuit

United States Court of Appeals
for the Fourth Circuit

No. 20-2275

SYSTEMS APPLICATION & TECHS., INC.
vs.
UNITED STATES

Appeal from the United States District Court for the District of Maryland at Greenbelt

Decided: February 14, 2022

Citation: 26 F.4th 163, 10 Adm. R. 96 (4th Cir. 2022).

Before **GREGORY,** Chief Judge, and **WYNN** and **THACKER,** Circuit Judges.

[—2—] {-166-} WYNN, Circuit Judge:

In 2015, employees of a Navy services contractor, Systems Application & Technologies, Inc. ("SA-TECH"), sued the contractor in California state court for violations of the state's labor laws. Before and during that suit, SA-TECH sought guidance from the Navy as to whether California's labor laws applied to it and its subcontractors, given the federal nature of its service contract. When its requests went unanswered, SA-TECH filed a claim with its contracting officer under the Contract Disputes Act. The contracting officer denied the claim.

SA-TECH then filed a complaint in federal district court in Maryland, seeking declaratory and injunctive relief. The district court dismissed the complaint for lack of subject matter jurisdiction pursuant to the Contract Disputes Act's exhaustion requirements. We agree and affirm.

I.

SA-TECH is a Navy contractor headquartered in Maryland. Under a series of contracts beginning in 2008, SA-TECH has assisted the Navy with training and weapons **{-167-}** testing. SA-TECH primarily provides these services at Navy bases in California and at sea, where the services are often performed aboard Navy vessels operating off the Pacific coast.

Specifically, SA-TECH's contractual duties include captaining certain Navy vessels, launching and recovering targets used in testing, and role-playing hostile forces in training exercises. The Navy determines what services SA-TECH and its subcontractors perform on a week-by-week basis, and the Navy maintains the right to change the duration **[—3—]** of an at-sea mission at its discretion. These missions or exercises may last only a few hours or may span several weeks, thus requiring SA-TECH personnel to spend more than 24 hours at a time aboard the ships. However, SA-TECH "does not pay [its employees] overtime for time spent aboard a vessel asleep or otherwise not working." Opening Br. at 14. Instead, SA-TECH's employees work a "6 on 6 off" schedule each day, for a total of 12 working hours per day, for which they are paid "9 hours of normal time and 3 hours of overtime." *Id.* at 13–14.

SA-TECH's payments under its Navy contracts are determined by a cost-reimbursement system, through which it receives reimbursement for the costs it incurs under the contracts and earns further revenue by collecting a fee for its services. Under this system, labor costs for certain management and technical personnel are part of a fixed price, but "[a]ll other labor categories are cost-reimbursable." S.J.A. 59.[1] The Navy contractually requires some SA-TECH personnel to hold minimum-security clearances or meet minimum education and experience requirements, but the Navy does not otherwise dictate how SA-TECH hires or compensates its employees. Under its contracts, however, SA-TECH must "perform all work in accordance with the contract and all applicable federal, state and local laws, regulations, codes and directives." S.J.A. 52. **[—4—]**

A.

The present dispute between SA-TECH and the Navy can be traced to a shift in understanding of California labor law. In January 2015, the Supreme Court of

[1] Citations to the "J.A." and "S.J.A." refer, respectively, to the Joint Appendix and Sealed Joint Appendix filed by the parties in this appeal.

California held in *Mendiola v. CPS Security Solutions, Inc.* that construction-site security guards who were confined to the premises while on call were entitled to overtime pay—including for time spent asleep. 340 P.3d 355, 358 (Cal. 2015). Because California labor regulations defined hours worked as "the time during which an employee *is subject to the control of* an employer, [including] all the time the employee is suffered or permitted to work, whether or not required to do so," the court ruled that "sleep time" could not be excluded from compensable time during 24-hour shifts. *Id.* at 359, 362, 366 (emphasis added) (citation omitted). The court noted that while federal labor law did not require sleep time to be paid, California was free to offer "greater protection" for employees. *Id.* at 361.

Mindful of the potential impact of *Mendiola* on its employees, SA-TECH quickly contacted the Navy, seeking its guidance on how the ruling might impact employee compensation for SA-TECH's military training services within California. In April 2015, the Navy responded that *Mendiola* does not apply to SA-TECH's contract because (1) state law does not apply to federal enclaves, which the Navy stated would include Navy vessels; and (2) the U.S. **{–168–}** Constitution's Supremacy Clause provides that federal law must govern defense functions, including the operation of public vessels. SA-TECH sought additional guidance from the Navy, but none was provided.

In August 2015, employees of SA-TECH and one of its subcontractors sued SA-TECH and the subcontractor in California state court, alleging seven violations of **[—5—]** California labor law. *Richard v. Sys. Application & Techs., Inc.*, No. 56–2015–00471720–CU–OE–VTA (Cal. Super. Ct. filed Aug. 31, 2015). In the *Richard* case, the employees raised claims under *Mendiola*, contending that they were only compensated for twelve hours in any given workday, even though they often were required to "remain on ships or other vessels at least (or in excess of) 24 hours continuously." J.A. 17, 43.

SA-TECH attempted to remove the case to federal court in California and requested that the Navy enter an appearance and assist with the dismissal or defense of the case. But the Navy declined, and the district court remanded the case to state court in December 2015 after finding that the plaintiffs' claims were "solely based on California wage and hour employment law" and that SA-TECH failed to "demonstrate[] that the Federal Government ha[d] any interest in the resolution of th[e] dispute." J.A. 61.

Two months later, with the litigation back in state court, SA-TECH moved to dismiss for lack of jurisdiction. SA-TECH claimed the case was controlled by two federal statutes that permit suits against the United States under certain maritime circumstances, the Public Vessels Act ("Vessels Act"), 46 U.S.C. § 31101, *et seq.*, and the Suits in Admiralty Act ("Admiralty Act"), 46 U.S.C. § 30901, *et seq.*

Meanwhile, in April 2017, the Navy sent a letter to the *Richard* plaintiffs' counsel, advising them that SA-TECH and its subcontractor were not agents of the United States under the relevant contracts. In August 2018, the state trial court refused to grant SA-TECH the dismissal it sought, finding neither the Vessels Act nor the Admiralty Act to be applicable to the facts of the case. *Richard v. Sys. Application & Techs., Inc.*, No. 56-2015-00471720-CU-OE-VTA, 2018 WL 4354148, at *2 (Cal. Super. Ct. Aug. 14, 2018). **[—6—]**

B.

In June 2017, SA-TECH was still in search of clarity on whether it was an agent of the Government and how the *Mendiola* decision might impact its operations. So, it wrote to the Navy pursuant to the Contract Disputes Act of 1978. That Act provides the procedure by which disputes concerning "any express or implied contract . . . made by an executive agency for . . . the procurement of services" are resolved. 41 U.S.C. § 7102(a). As an initial step, the Contract Disputes Act requires an aggrieved contractor of a federal agency to present a valid claim to the agency's contracting officer in writing for contract interpretation. *See* 41 U.S.C. § 7103(a)(1)–(2); 48 C.F.R. § 52.233-1(d)(1).

In its 2017 letter, SA-TECH purported to seek contract interpretations by requesting, first, that "the Navy confirm that SA-TECH and [its subcontractor] are agents of the Navy for [Vessels and Admiralty Acts] purposes under [its relevant contracts]"; second, that the Navy provide "contractual direction regarding whether SA-TECH and its subcontractors should pay employees wages and overtime for the time they spend asleep at sea," and if so, that the Navy confirm that it would treat those wages "as an allowable cost" under its contracts with SA-TECH; and third, that "the Navy confirm that, if SA-TECH reaches a settlement agreement with the **{–169–}** *Richard* plaintiffs to pay the challenged overtime and other related charges, the Navy will reimburse the charges as allowable costs under the [relevant c]ontracts." J.A. 51–52.

Within two months, the Navy's contracting officer denied each of SA-TECH's requests. On the agency question, the officer wrote that, due to ongoing litigation in another, federal case in which the Government's position was that SA-TECH and its **[—7—]** subcontractor were *not* agents of the United States, it would be inappropriate for the officer to "make the requested determination." J.A. 57 (referencing *Daniels v. United States*, No. 316CV02077BTMDHB, 2017 WL 3478765 (S.D. Cal. Aug. 11, 2017)). The contracting officer also denied the other two requests as insufficient and premature, reasoning that they were monetary claims disguised as contract-interpretation requests. In the officer's view, SA-TECH sought to commit the Navy to covering unknown costs yet to be incurred, or measured, by SA-TECH. The officer also stressed that SA-TECH failed to identify any specific contractual terms "which may be subject to varying interpretations" or to submit any statement of costs. J.A. 56.

Not satisfied by the contracting officer's decision, SA-TECH timely filed suit in federal district court in Maryland. SA-TECH sought declaratory judgment on substantially the same three issues it had presented to the Navy: whether SA-TECH acts as the Navy's agent under the contracts, Vessels Act, and Admiralty Act, including for purposes of overtime claims (Count I); whether the modified understanding of California labor laws after *Mendiola* would control SA-TECH's operations on Navy and Navy-chartered ships, and whether SA-TECH would be permitted or required by the Navy, under its contracts, to pay any sleep-time overtime (Count II); and whether costs incurred by SA-TECH in settling the state-court *Richard* litigation would be allowable costs under its current **[—8—]** contract (Count III).[2] *See Sys. Application & Techs., Inc. v. United States*, 491 F. Supp. 3d 73, 79–80 (D. Md. 2020).

The district court granted the Government's motion to dismiss for lack of subject matter jurisdiction. *Id.* at 87. The district court reasoned that SA-TECH had not exhausted its remedies under the Contract Disputes Act as to any of its claims, so the court could not exercise jurisdiction over them. *Id.* As to Count I, the district court concluded that the agency claim was not asserted "as a matter of right," a threshold requirement for *any* claim raised under the Act. *Id.* at 85–86. Regarding Counts II and III, the court found those claims were properly categorized as monetary claims because their true "gravamen . . . plainly concern[ed] money" damages. *Id.* at 84. But as those monetary claims failed to include a "sum certain"—a requirement of the Act—SA-TECH never properly presented them to the Navy's contracting officer, and thus failed to exhaust its remedies.[3] *Id.* at 84–85.

Its claims dismissed, SA-TECH timely appealed.

---

[2] SA-TECH also requested injunctive relief to enjoin the Navy from asserting that SA-TECH was not its agent. That request is not at issue in this appeal.

[3] The district court also held that even if it had jurisdiction, it would decline to issue a declaratory judgment as to any of the counts on prudential grounds. *Sys. Application & Techs.*, 491 F. Supp. 3d at 87 n.9. Because we conclude that the district court correctly found it lacked jurisdiction, we do not address whether declaratory relief was proper.

II.

We review "the issue of whether a district court possessed jurisdiction in a **{-170-}** declaratory judgment proceeding" de novo. *Volvo Constr. Equip. N. Am., Inc. v. CLM Equip. Co.*, 386 F.3d 581, 591 (4th Cir. 2004). **[—9—]**

III.

The Contract Disputes Act provides a narrow waiver of the United States' sovereign immunity. *Cf. Lane v. Pena*, 518 U.S. 187, 192 (1996) ("[A statutory] waiver of the Government's sovereign immunity will be strictly construed, in terms of its scope, in favor of the sovereign."). The Act "applies to any express or implied contract . . . made by an executive agency for . . . the procurement of services," including contracts sounding in maritime law. 41 U.S.C. § 7102(a); *see, e.g.*, *Sw. Marine ex rel. Universal Painting & Sandblasting Corp. v. United States*, 43 F.3d 420, 424 (9th Cir. 1994); *Bethlehem Steel Corp. v. Avondale Shipyards, Inc.*, 951 F.2d 92, 94 (5th Cir. 1992). Moreover, "[w]hen the Contract Disputes Act applies, it provides the *exclusive* mechanism for dispute resolution." *Dalton v. Sherwood Van Lines, Inc.*, 50 F.3d 1014, 1017 (Fed. Cir. 1995) (emphasis added); *see also id.* (explaining that "the Contract Disputes Act was not designed to serve as an alternative administrative remedy, available at the contractor's option"); *United States v. J & E Salvage Co.*, 55 F.3d 985, 987 (4th Cir. 1995) ("The review procedures under the [Contract Disputes Act] are exclusive of jurisdiction in any other forum.").

An aggrieved contractor who wishes to pursue relief under the Act must first present a valid, written claim to the agency's contracting officer, who will issue a written decision. 41 U.S.C. § 7103(a)(1)–(3) ("Each claim by a contractor against the Federal Government relating to a contract shall be submitted to the contracting officer [in writing] for a decision."). If the officer denies the claim, then generally, the contractor may either appeal to the governing agency board or bring an action in the Court of Federal Claims. *See id.* **[—10—]** § 7104; *J & E Salvage Co.*, 55 F.3d at 987. Either way, further appeals may be pursued in the Federal Circuit. *See* 41 U.S.C. § 7107(a)(1); *J & E Salvage Co.*, 55 F.3d at 987.

But for claims arising under maritime contracts like those ostensibly at issue here, the contractor may appeal the contracting officer's decision instead to a federal district court.[4] 41 U.S.C. § 7102(d); *see E. Coast Repair & Fabrication, LLC v. United States ex rel. Dep't of Navy*, 16 F.4th 87, 90 n*, 9 Adm. R. 166, 167 n.1 (4th Cir. 2021) ("A contractor usually must choose between an agency board and the U.S. Court of Federal Claims. But in maritime cases like this one, a contractor may choose a federal district court."); *Sw. Marine*, 43 F.3d at 423–24 (noting that § 7102(d) "directs jurisdiction for [Contract Disputes Act] appeals [in maritime cases] away from the [Court of Federal Claims] and the Federal Circuit Court of Appeals, in favor of the historic admiralty jurisdiction of the federal district courts").

Before bringing an action in district court, however, the contractor *must* have exhausted its lower-level administrative remedies. The Act states that "[e]ach claim by a contractor against the Federal Government relating to a contract *shall* be submitted to the contracting officer for a **{-171-}** decision."[5] 41 U.S.C.

---

[4] The Navy notes that "jurisdiction in the district court" in this case "may not be entirely free from doubt," suggesting that this case may not, in fact, involve maritime contracts. Response Br. at 11 n.2. We need not reach that question because there are, as the Navy puts it, "more fundamental jurisdictional problems with SA-TECH's claims." *Id.*

[5] This requirement applies equally to maritime contracts. 41 U.S.C. § 7102(d) (maritime contracts are governed by the Vessels and Admiralty Acts only "to the extent that those [statutes] are not inconsistent with [the Contract Disputes Act]"); *see Bethlehem Steel Corp.*, 951 F.2d at 94 ("[R]ather than completely excluding maritime contracts from the Contract Disputes Act, [§ 7102] simply vests appeals from the administrative determination of claims in the district courts." (quoting *River & Offshore Servs. Co. v.* **[—11—]** *United States*, 651 F. Supp. 276, 281 (E.D. La. 1987))); *Sw. Marine*, 43 F.3d at 423 (explaining that the incorporation of the Vessels and Admiralty Acts into the Contract Disputes Act "does not alter the requirement that

§ 7103(a)(1) (emphasis added); *see, e.g.*, **[—11—]** *Bethlehem Steel*, 951 F.2d at 94 (finding a lack of jurisdiction over a maritime contract claim where the contractor "did not file a proper administrative claim against the government"); *Sw. Marine, Inc. v. United States*, 926 F. Supp. 142, 144 (N.D. Cal. 1995) ("The language of [the governing statutes has] been carefully drafted to give jurisdiction to the federal district courts *only after* the administrative remedies mandated by the [Contract Disputes Act] have been exhausted." (emphasis added)); *Sys. Application & Techs.*, 491 F. Supp. 3d at 80 ("Where, as here, the Government conditions waiver on a party's exhausting statutorily [prescribed] administrative remedies, then any failure to exhaust bars suit in this Court.").

To exhaust its administrative remedies, an aggrieved contractor must present to the contracting officer a valid claim that relates to the contract. 41 U.S.C. § 7103(a). As the Contract Disputes Act does not define what a "claim" is, *see id.* § 7101, we follow the Federal Circuit's lead in using the definition of "claim" provided by the Federal Acquisition Regulations, *Securiforce Int'l Am., LLC v. United States*, 879 F.3d 1354, 1359 (Fed. Cir. 2018).[6] Under those regulations, a "claim" is "a written demand or written assertion by one of the contracting parties seeking, as a matter of right, the payment of **[—12—]** money in a sum certain, the adjustment or interpretation of contract terms, or other relief arising under or relating to th[e] contract."[7] 48 C.F.R. § 52.233-1(c).

The Federal Circuit has indicated that "we should read the definition of 'claim' broadly." *Todd Constr., L.P. v. United States*, 656 F.3d 1306, 1311 (Fed. Cir. 2011). Nevertheless, for all claims, the contractor must be seeking some relief "as a matter of right." 48 C.F.R. § 52.233-1(c). This requires that an aggrieved contractor "*specifically assert* entitlement to the relief sought." *Alliant Techsystems, Inc. v. United States*, 178 F.3d 1260, 1265 (Fed. Cir. 1999) (emphasis added). In other words, "the claim must be a demand for something *due or believed to be due* rather **{-172-}** than, for example, a cost proposal for work the government later decides it would like performed." *Id.* (emphasis added). A contractor can satisfy the matter-of-right requirement by, for example, "assert[ing] specific contractual and legal grounds for its interpretation of the [contract]." *Id.* That said, a contractor "need not assert a specific contractual provision to meet the 'matter of right' requirement." *BLR Grp. Of Am., Inc. v. United States*, 84 Fed. Cl. 634, 640 (2008).

Additionally, under the definition in 48 C.F.R. § 52.233-1(c), a contractor's failure to include a "sum certain" in a monetary request renders their submission not a "claim" **[—13—]** under the Contract Disputes Act and is "fatal to jurisdiction under" that Act. *Securiforce*, 879 F.3d at 1360 (quoting *Northrop Grumman Computing Sys., Inc. v. United States*, 709 F.3d 1107, 1112 (Fed. Cir. 2013)). "The Court of Federal Claims has, on several occasions, held that the 'sum certain' requirement is met 'when the amount in dispute can be determined by a simple mathematical calculation.'" *GPA-I, LP v. United States*, 46 Fed. Cl. 762, 766 (2000) (quoting *Hamza v. United States*, 31 Fed. Cl. 315, 322 (1994)).

Of course, a *nonmonetary* claim need not state a "sum certain." *See Securiforce*, 879

---

contract claims be presented to a Contracting Officer in the first instance").

[6] We agree with the district court that, "[s]ince non-maritime [Contract Disputes Act] claims are appealed to either the Federal Circuit or the Court of Federal Claims, their guidance is particularly germane to this dispute." *Sys. Application & Techs.*, 491 F. Supp. 3d at 83 n.7 (citations omitted); *see* 41 U.S.C. §§ 7104, 7107.

[7] In addition to this definition from the Federal Acquisition Regulations, the Federal Circuit has noted that it may be appropriate to look to whether a particular demand constitutes a claim "based on . . . the language of the contract in dispute[] and the facts of the case." *Reflectone, Inc. v. Dalton*, 60 F.3d 1572, 1575 (Fed. Cir. 1995). Because the relevant contract in this case does not specify an alternative definition of "claim" and neither party cites "unusual facts" that should alter our analysis under the regulatory definition of "claim," we need not decide more broadly what factors may be relevant to the definition of "claim" for purposes of the Contract Disputes Act. *See id.* at 1575 n.3; *BLR Grp. of Am. v. United States*, 84 Fed. Cl. 634, 639 (2008).

F.3d at 1360 ("[C]ontractors may in some circumstances properly seek only declaratory relief without stating a sum certain . . . ."); *GPA-I*, 46 Fed. Cl. at 766 (same). Nonmonetary claims can seek "adjustment or interpretation of contract terms, or other relief arising under or relating to th[e] contract." 48 C.F.R. § 52.233-1(c). A nonmonetary claim seeking "'interpretation of a contract term' is a [valid] claim if the contractor 'specifically asserts entitlement to the declaratory relief sought . . . by asserting specific contractual and legal grounds for its interpretation.'" *GPA-I*, 46 Fed. Cl. at 766 (cleaned up) (quoting *Alliant Techsystems*, 178 F.3d at 1265). As for "other relief," the meaning of this third category is expansive. The Federal Circuit has held that "to be a claim 'relating to the contract' under the [Contract Disputes Act], a [contractor's] claim 'must [only] have some relationship to the terms or performance of a government contract.'" *Todd Constr.*, 656 F.3d at 1312 (quoting *Applied Cos. v. United States*, 144 F.3d 1470, 1478 (Fed. Cir. 1998)); *see also id.* at 1313 (holding that the performance evaluations at issue "relate[d]" to the contractor's "performance under the contract," even though they "may not relate to the terms of the contract itself"). **[—14—]**

With these principles in mind, we now turn to the claims before us.

A.

We first consider Count I, SA-TECH's claim concerning whether it is an agent of the Navy. The parties agree that this claim is nonmonetary. SA-TECH therefore could have satisfied the exhaustion requirement by asserting a claim for (1) "the adjustment or interpretation of contract terms" or (2) "other relief arising under or relating to th[e] contract." 48 C.F.R. § 52.233-1(c). Either way, it needed to show that it was entitled to seek the contract interpretation or other relief "as a matter of right." *Id.* We agree with the district court that SA-TECH failed to meet this standard.

Regarding the first option, although SA-TECH styles its agency-status request as one seeking "contract interpretation," it pinpoints no specific contractual term or provision for this Court to interpret. Opening Br. at 35. While a contractor "need not assert a specific contractual provision to meet the *'matter of right'* requirement," *BLR Grp.*, 84 Fed. Cl. at 640 (emphasis added), it must do so to rely on the **{–173–}** "adjustment or interpretation of contract terms" part of the definition of "claim," 48 C.F.R. § 52.233-1(c). But, while SA-TECH may have "invoked provisions of its contract" relating to the use of public vessels and the Navy's ability to control the management of training exercises, Reply Br. at 10, it does so predominately in its factual background sections. And in those sections, as well as within its actual discussion of the agency-status issue, SA-TECH failed to point to a specific **[—15—]** contract term whose meaning required adjustment or interpretation. 48 C.F.R. § 52.233-1(c).[8]

Instead, SA-TECH primarily argues that the control exercised by the Navy over SA-TECH and its operation of some Navy ships, as evidenced by the contracts and other facts in the record, proves that SA-TECH is the Navy's agent under the Vessels and Admiralty Acts. It then demands the Navy confirm, or this Court declare, that position to be true. We agree with the district court that SA-TECH's agency-status claim does not truly seek an interpretation or adjustment of any contractual terms, but instead requests "other relief" relating to the contracts. *Sys. Application & Techs.*, 491 F. Supp. 3d at 85–86 (finding that the agency-status claim fell

[8] The cases SA-TECH cites for its statement that its agency-status claim "is the sort of interpretive question routinely raised and resolved under the [Contract Disputes Act]" do not deal with similar amorphous claims or agency interpretations. Opening Br. at 34, 42–43; *see DaVita, Inc. v. United States*, 110 Fed. Cl. 71, 85–87 (2013) (interpreting payment terms under the contract); *CW Gov't Travel, Inc. v. United States*, 63 Fed. Cl. 369, 371, 389 (2004) (seeking an interpretation of specified exclusivity provisions); *Tiger Nat. Gas, Inc. v. United States*, 61 Fed. Cl. 287, 293 (2004) (contesting an offset claim decision based on a savings guarantee provision in the contract); *Kellogg Brown & Root Servs., Inc.*, ASBCA No. 58578, 13 BCA ¶ 35,411 (seeking an interpretation of a "Tour of Duty/Hours of Work" clause of its contract).

under the portion of the definition of "claim" "seeking, *as a matter of right* . . . other relief . . . relating to th[e] contract" (quoting 48 C.F.R. § 52.233-1(c))).

However, SA-TECH's claim fares no better under the "other relief" prong. Even allowing that the relief sought "relat[es] to th[e] contract[s]," SA-TECH has not shown it is legally entitled to the opinion it seeks "as a matter of right." 48 C.F.R. § 52.233-1(c). **[—16—]**

SA-TECH asserts that courts and Congress have recognized that "agency status under the [Vessels Act and Admiralty Act] is critically important for contractors." Opening Br. at 36. Since agency status impacts the scope of a contractor's liability, SA-TECH's argument goes, an agency determination is critical to its performance. *See Servis v. Hiller Sys. Inc.*, 54 F.3d 203, 207 (4th Cir. 1995) ("Where the [Vessels or Admiralty Acts] provide[] a remedy against the United States, there is no recourse against the government agent whose actions engendered the lawsuit."). Because the question of agency relates to its performance, and was asserted pursuant to the Contract Disputes Act, SA-TECH contends it has satisfied all requirements. We disagree.

Illustrative here is the Court of Federal Claims' decision in *BLR Group of America v. United States*. In *BLR Group*, a contractor whose contract was terminated for convenience by the Air Force submitted two claims under the Contract Disputes Act, requesting that the Air Force (1) correct the ratings and reviews within its contract performance assessment report and (2) delete certain comments from the initial report from the past-performance information-retrieval system.[9] **{-174-}** 84 Fed. Cl. at 635–39. The court explained that as the contractor was "not seeking money damages or the adjustment of **[—17—]** contract terms, [its] claim must be a written demand seeking, as a matter of right, [other] relief arising under or relating to the contract." *Id.* at 639.

Focusing on the "as a matter of right" requirement, the court analyzed each claim separately. For the assessment-report claim, the court explained that while the contractor did not need to assert a specific contractual provision to satisfy the "as a matter of right" requirement, he was required to "assert entitlement that ha[d] some legal basis." *Id.* at 640. Thus, "[a]s a threshold matter," the court needed to decide "whether [the] plaintiff was legally entitled to a[n assessment report]." *Id.* The contractor pointed to specific Federal Acquisition Regulations provisions and Air Force regulations which stated, in part, that "[A]gencies *shall* prepare an evaluation of contractor performance for each contract" which met certain requirements. *Id.* (emphasis added) (quoting 48 C.F.R. § 42.1502(a) (2006)). Because the contract met those requirements, the court found that the contractor was legally entitled to a performance evaluation and, as a "logical corollary," to a correct one. *Id.* at 640–42.

By contrast, the court found the contractor could not assert a claim "as a matter of right" for deletion of certain content from the information-retrieval system. *Id.* at 642–43. The regulations and guidelines cited by the contractor did not address, beyond "general statements," "what must occur after a[n assessment report] has been posted to the [retrieval system] for dissemination." *Id.* at 643. Because the cited authorities did "not address the manner in which a [retrieval system] entry is displayed or formatted," the court concluded that "there [wa]s no legal basis for [the contractor] to assert a [Contract Disputes Act] claim regarding the display or format of its [retrieval system] entry." *Id.* **[—18—]**

---

[9] The Court of Federal Claims later granted a motion for reconsideration as to the first claim, in which it reasserted that the contractor satisfied the "'matter of right' requirement by asserting entitlement to relief with some legal basis; namely, entitlement to a fair and accurate performance evaluation pursuant to [Federal Acquisition Regulations] § 42.1502(a)." *BLR Grp. of Am., Inc. v. United States*, 94 Fed. Cl. 354, 365 (2010), *dismissed*, 460 F. App'x 918 (Fed. Cir. 2011); *see also id.* at 372 (explaining again that "[i]n this case . . . the Air Force was required to prepare and disseminate a fair and accurate evaluation of [the contractor]'s contract performance—a requirement equivalent to a mandatory contract term").

SA-TECH's claims resemble the *BLR Group* contractor's second asserted claim more than the first. SA-TECH has not pointed to any legal authority or provision requiring the Navy to provide a blanket declaration that SA-TECH is or is not its agent under the contracts. The Vessels and Admiralty Acts, upon which SA-TECH relies, provide a potential legal basis for asserting that the proper defendant in *Richard* is the Government, because they waive the Government's immunity in certain actions concerning Government vessels or those of parties acting on the Government's behalf. *See* 46 U.S.C. §§ 30903, 31102; *Manuel v. United States*, 50 F.3d 1253, 1260 (4th Cir. 1995) (holding that the exclusivity provision of the Admiralty Act required a seaman who worked on a ship owned by the United States to bring his action against the Government instead of the ship's private operating agent); *Favorite v. Marine Pers. & Provisioning, Inc.*, 955 F.2d 382, 385–86 (5th Cir. 1992) (finding a privately owned vessel operated for the benefit of the Government to constitute a public vessel under the Vessels and Admiralty Acts because the Government exercised "possession, command, and control" over the vessel). **{-175-}**

But, critically, the Vessels and Admiralty Acts do not establish a legal basis for SA-TECH to assert that *the Navy* must advise SA-TECH as to whether or not it believes SA-TECH to be its carte blanche agent under these statutes.[10] That is, though those statutes **[—19—]** may bear on SA-TECH's potential liability in cases brought by third parties, they have nothing to offer on the question of whether SA-TECH is an agent per se. Consequently, we fail to see how the Vessels and Admiralty Acts entitle SA-TECH to force the Government to name it as an agent because that agency status is "something due" to SA-TECH under its contracts or the acts themselves. *Alliant Techsystems*, 178 F.3d at 1265; *see BLR Grp.*, 84 Fed. Cl. at 640–43 (looking to specific regulations to find legal entitlement to an asserted claim).

SA-TECH disagrees, arguing that the Contract Disputes Act requires only that the claim *relate to* the contract and does not require a separate form of entitlement to relief other than that provided in the Act itself.[11] However, the cases it relies on belie its position.

First, SA-TECH cites *Todd Construction, L.P. v. United States* for its argument that there is no separate "matter of right" requirement and that claims only need to be related to the contract. But *Todd Construction* explicitly noted that the Government did not dispute that the contractor satisfied the "matter of right" requirement in that case. 656 F.3d at 1311. In fact, the requested relief—a judgment stating the contractor's performance review was inaccurate—arose directly from a regulation.[12] *Id.* at 1308–09 (noting that, at the time, the **[—20—]** Federal Acquisition Regulations required provision of a performance report and review of said report to ensure it was accurate (citing 48 C.F.R. § 36.201 (2006))); *see also id.* at 1314 n.6 (noting that "the regulation applies of its own force and directly governs the parties' performance under the contracts"). Thus, the Federal Circuit implicitly acknowledged the

[10] As the Government notes in its Response Brief, both acts primarily function only to waive sovereign immunity. *Cf. Manuel*, 50 F.3d at 1255 n.1 ("Neither the [Admiralty Act] nor the [Vessels Act] create causes of action against the United States. Instead, they act only as a waiver of the sovereign immunity of the United States in admiralty cases. The acts merely provide the jurisdictional hook upon which to hang a traditional admiralty claim.").

[11] Throughout its Opening Brief, SA-TECH stresses that the Contract Disputes Act simply states that claims "relating to the contract" must be presented. *See* Opening Br. at 42; 41 U.S.C. § 1703. Certainly, the claim must be related to the contract. But we still must determine whether it is a valid "claim" at all, as defined by 48 C.F.R. § 52.233-1(c).

[12] Indeed, the lower court had found the "matter of right" requirement to be met since "[f]ederal regulations require[d]" the provision of a fair and accurate performance report and the plaintiff asserted a claim seeking a fair report "prepared in accordance with **[—20—]** the regulations." *Todd Constr. L.P. v. United States*, 85 Fed. Cl. 34, 43 (2008) (citing 48 C.F.R. § 36.201 (2006)).

importance of the existence of a regulation or other legal basis providing a right to the "other relief" sought. *See id.*; *BLR Grp.*, 84 Fed. Cl. at 643 ("So long as [the contractor] grounds its entitlement on *some legal basis*, [it] has met the 'matter of right' requirement for filing a [Contract Disputes Act] claim." (emphasis added)).

Second, relying on *Alliant Techsystems*, SA-TECH argues that by asking whether it asserted a legal entitlement to its claim, we would be placing the cart before the horse by reaching the merits before deciding jurisdiction. This is not so under the facts before us, and the approach described above. **{-176-}**

In *Alliant Techsystems*, the contractor sought a declaration that it was not bound to perform under specified option provisions of its contract because the Government untimely exercised the option and used a delivery rate not included in the option clause. 178 F.3d at 1264. The Federal Circuit held that a contractor asserted a contract interpretation claim as a matter of right where it "asserted specific contractual and legal grounds for its interpretation of the option" clause at issue. *Id.* at 1265. In doing so, the court rejected the Government's argument that the interpretation was not sought as a "matter of right" **[—21—]** because, in the Government's view, another provision of the contract required the contractor to perform first, and only seek an interpretation of the clause *after* performance was completed. *See id.* The court noted that the Government's interpretation would require the court to determine the merits of the claim—whether the contractor had to perform the option—before reaching jurisdiction and thus "reverse[d] the proper sequence." *Id.*

By contrast, here, neither the district court nor this Court has offered any opinion as to whether SA-TECH may qualify as an agent of the Navy pursuant to its current contracts under the Admiralty or Vessels Acts. Indeed, we do not reach the merits of this claim at all. Nor need we do so to determine that SA-TECH failed to assert specific contractual or legal grounds entitling it to force the Navy to issue a blanket declaration as to whether or not SA-TECH is its agent.

Third, *Alliant Techsystems* directly forecloses SA-TECH's argument that it is automatically asserting a claim "as a matter of right" by way of asserting it under the Contract Disputes Act. If that were so, the Federal Circuit in *Alliant Techsystems* would have had no occasion to delve into the question of whether the claim in that case was asserted "as a matter of right," because it, too, was raised pursuant to the Contract Disputes Act. In fact, such an understanding would render the entirety of the definition of "claim" in 48 C.F.R. § 52.233-1(c) superfluous for Contract Disputes Act purposes; all claims under the Act could simply be asserted as claims for other relief relating in some way to the contract. SA-TECH cites no authority to support such a broad understanding of the meaning of "claim." **[—22—]**

Ultimately, because SA-TECH does not specifically assert any legal or contractual grounds entitling it to the Navy's opinion on its agency status under the Admiralty or Vessels Acts, its claim is invalid under the Contract Disputes Act. *BLR Grp.*, 84 Fed. Cl. at 643 (finding there to be no Contract Disputes Act claim where the plaintiff failed to show any legal grounds entitling it to the relief sought). SA-TECH's failure to present a valid claim means that it did not exhaust all administrative remedies, so the federal courts do not have subject matter jurisdiction. We affirm the district court's ruling as to Count I.

B.

That brings us to Counts II and III which are SA-TECH's claims concerning wage and overtime payments under California law, as understood in *Mendiola*. Although the district court acknowledged that "the distinction between monetary and non-monetary claims is not always straightforward," it ultimately concluded that Counts II and III primarily sought monetary payment. *Sys. Application & Techs.*, 491 F. Supp. 3d at 83–85. We agree.

As noted above, a contractor's failure to include a "sum certain" in a monetary request is "fatal to jurisdiction under" the Contract Disputes Act. **{–177–}** *Securiforce*, 879 F.3d at 1360 (citation omitted). And a contractor "may not circumvent the general rule requiring a sum certain by reframing monetary claims as nonmonetary." *Id.* Courts thus must take a close look at "whether a given claim is properly classified as monetary or nonmonetary." *Id.* The Federal Circuit advises courts to "look to the substance of the pleadings[,] rather than their form" to make this determination. *Id.* (quoting *Brazos Elec. Power Co-op. v. United States*, 144 F.3d 784, 787 (Fed. Cir. 1998)). "If 'the only significant consequence' **[—23—]** of the declaratory relief sought 'would be that [the plaintiff] would obtain monetary damages from the federal government,' the claim is in essence a monetary one." *Id.* (quoting *Brazos Elec. Power Co-op.*, 144 F.3d at 787); *see also Weststar Eng'g, Inc.*, ASBCA No. 52484, 02-1 BCA ¶ 31,759 (Armed Services Board of Contract Appeals noting that, "[w]here the gravamen of a claim is money, the contractor cannot avoid the requirement for a sum certain . . . by casting it as a claim for contract interpretation").

However, that the requested relief "has obvious monetary ramifications" does not necessarily morph a claim into a monetary one if the gravamen of the request itself is *not* money. *TRW, Inc.*, ASBCA No. 51172, 99-2 BCA ¶ 30,407. A few examples will help establish the parameters for our analysis of SA-TECH's claims.

In *Securiforce International America, LLC v. United States*, a contractor sought declaratory relief that its fuel delivery contract was improperly terminated. 879 F.3d at 1358. The Federal Circuit held that it lacked jurisdiction because the claim was a monetary one in need of a sum certain. *Id.* at 1360–61. Although the claim was styled as a nonmonetary request for declaratory relief, the Federal Circuit found that relief, if granted, would "yield only one significant consequence: it would entitle Securiforce to recover money damages from the government." *Id.* at 1360. Because the claim was for money damages but involved no timely presentation of a "sum certain" to the contracting officer, the Federal Circuit found the initial claim to have been improperly presented under the Contract Disputes Act. *Id.* at 1360–62.

Similarly, in *Kellogg Brown & Root Services, Inc. v. United States*, the Court of Federal Claims found a service provider's request for indemnification, presented as a **[—24—]** question of contract interpretation, to be a monetary claim. 115 Fed. Cl. 168, 174–79 (2014). While performing services under Government contract, Kellogg personnel were exposed to hazardous chemicals. *Id.* at 170. The personnel sued Kellogg. *Id.* In turn, Kellogg sent numerous letters to the Army Corps contracting officer, seeking the Government's participation in the lawsuit as well as indemnification, which Kellogg asserted it was due under a specific contract clause. *Id.* at 174–79. The court explained that Kellogg "ha[d] experienced and will experience significant costs in the third-party [law]suits, both in defense and settlement" and was "no matter how indirectly" "invoking its right to compensation from the government." *Id.* at 176. In coming to this conclusion, the court reasoned that Kellogg had focused on the "catastrophic financial exposure" resulting from the third-party claim. *Id.* at 175. The court lacked jurisdiction "over what [Kellogg] style[d] as a nonmonetary claim" because Kellogg's "'nonmonetary' claim [was] essentially an invalid [Contract Disputes Act] claim for money damages." *Id.* at 184. As in *Securiforce*, the *Kellogg* court held that the claim was invalid because it was a monetary one that did not state a sum certain. *Id.* at 181–85.

By contrast, in *CW Government Travel, Inc. v. United States*, the Court of Federal Claims held that the contractor had presented **{–178–}** a valid, nonmonetary claim when he requested that the contracting officer "confirm that the travel requirements for all [work] sites . . . [would] continue to be performed by [the contractor] throughout the total contract period, including all options exercised by the Government." 63 Fed. Cl. 369, 382 (2004) (citation omitted). The court disagreed with the Government's assertion that this claim only sought a "guarantee of how the

Government would act if, in the future," a requested transfer **[—25—]** occurred. *Id.* (emphasis omitted). Rather, the court concluded that there was a valid claim since, "[b]y submitting its interpretation of the exclusivity provisions . . . and by asking the Contracting Officer to 'confirm' or refute its interpretation, [the contractor] sought *a contracting officer's interpretation of contract terms*, rather than *a guarantee that the government would behave a certain way* under the contract." *Id.* at 383 (emphases added).

Courts have sometimes applied these principles in a way that seems to blur the line between monetary and nonmonetary claims, but even in those cases, the declaration sought was for relief under a specific pay schedule or on a cost-accounting basis. For example, in *DaVita, Inc. v. United States*, the Court of Federal Claims found that the requested declaratory judgment—that "DaVita is entitled to payment at the rates included in . . . DaVita's [Veterans Affairs] Contract' for 'dialysis services provided pursuant to authorizations issued by Contract"—was not a disguised money claim. 110 Fed. Cl. 71, 86 (2013) (cleaned up). In the court's view, the "gravamen" of this claim was "not a request for a sum certain" but "quintessentially a claim for the interpretation of the contract's payment terms." *Id.* Similarly, in *TRW*, the Armed Service Board of Contract Appeals held that a contractor's declaratory request—seeking contract interpretation on "the allowability and/or allocability of certain costs that TRW included in its final rate submissions for the 1990, 1991, and 1992 cost accounting periods"—was not a request for money damages. 99-2 BCA ¶ 30,407. The Board granted declaratory relief, noting that any "monetary ramifications" of TRW's claim did not supersede the contract interpretation TRW sought concerning its final rate submissions. *Id.* **[—26—]**

SA-TECH maintains that its request—declaratory relief as to whether *Mendiola* applies, and, if so, whether the Government will allow settlement, sleep-time, or other costs—is a valid, future-looking nonmonetary claim like that in *CW Government Travel*. SA-TECH argues that these questions implicate significant consequences, unrelated to money damages, such as an interpretation of governing law. It further contends that the approach adopted by the district court, which looked to whether the "gravamen" of the claim was money, would turn all contract claims into monetary damages claims, since money is inherently at issue in all contracts. Opening Br. at 45.

We disagree. SA-TECH seeks indemnification by another name. Like the service provider in *Kellogg*, both its initial claim and its complaint sought a guaranteed reimbursement for unspecified costs, some of which have yet to be incurred (or may never be). Regarding Count II, when seeking the Government's position on whether *Mendiola* applied to the contracts, SA-TECH stressed that if the Government fails to comply with certain "implied contract obligations, the law recognizes a constructive change, entitling the contractor to an equitable adjustment." J.A. 51. It is unclear what, other than money, that adjustment may be. And in its complaint, SA-TECH insisted that "the Navy must provide **{-179-}** clear contractual direction regarding whether California wage and hour law applies aboard Navy controlled ships and federal enclaves *and support (financially and legally) its interpretation*." J.A. 12 (emphasis added).

In its briefing, SA-TECH warns of dire consequences, arguing that incurring the additional costs required by *Mendiola* would "nearly triple the wages for its personnel's time spent at sea," creating a "multi-million dollar liability" that the Navy will only **[—27—]** consider reimbursing after the fact. Opening Br. at 6. We take SA-TECH at its word—this is a monetary claim. *See Kellogg*, 115 Fed. Cl. at 175 (remarking on the difficulty of "avoid[ing] the monetary aspect" of a contractor's request for indemnification against "catastrophic financial exposure"). And, as the district court aptly put it, "even well-reasoned policy arguments cannot relax jurisdictional requirements." *Sys. Application & Techs.*, 491 F. Supp. 3d at 85.

As for Count III, SA-TECH's initial submission to the contracting officer demanded that the Navy "immediately affirm that it will *reimburse* SA-TECH under the Contracts for costs incurred [in] settling the litigation." J.A. 49 (emphasis added). In its complaint, SA-TECH asked for a declaratory contract interpretation as to whether "if SA-TECH reaches a settlement agreement . . . the Navy will *reimburse the charges* as an allowable cost under the Contracts." J.A. 12 (emphasis added). And throughout its claim, complaint, and briefing, SA-TECH emphasized that without knowing whether the Government will cover such settlement costs, it will "suffer[] severe financial harm." J.A. 47; *see* J.A. 34 ("If SA-TECH settles the employment lawsuit and the Navy subsequently does not allow the settlement costs, SA-TECH will have suffered severe financial harm."); Opening Br. at 4 (stating liability "could total many millions of dollars"), 6 (noting SA-TECH could incur a "multi-million dollar liability," creating "severe financial risk for SA-TECH"), 19–20. Clearly, the gravamen of SA-TECH's claims in Counts II and III is a monetary one.

And, unlike the contractors in *DaVita* and *TRW*, SA-TECH is not asking for payment for services rendered under some contractual pay rate, nor does it seek approval of costs and accounting measures in specific rate submissions. Instead, it seeks a guarantee **[—28—]** for sums unknown and speculative. *Nowhere* in the record does SA-TECH provide even an estimated number for the costs it might incur other than to say such liability would be in the "millions of dollars."[13] J.A. 11. SA-TECH may resubmit a claim at a later date, if and when the sums become more determined and knowable.[14] But it cannot do so based on speculation now.

To be sure, the initial claim and complaint also request a decision regarding whether *Mendiola* or federal law govern wage-time provisions under the contract. However, it is not clear what specific contract clause or rate schedule, if any, SA-TECH requests interpretation of. SA-TECH points to the Federal Acquisition Regulations provision that "contracting officers and contractors should seek advance agreement on the treatment of special or unusual costs," 48 C.F.R. § 31.109(a), as evidence that this is not a monetary claim **{–180–}** but instead an act of regulatory compliance. But what SA-TECH seeks here is an unqualified commitment from the Navy that the Government will pay for any incurred settlement and labor costs, no matter what they may be. That is a claim for money, not an attempt to negotiate an "advance agreement." What's more, the *only* consequences of the issuance of a declaration regarding *Mendiola* that SA-TECH has ever mentioned in this litigation relate to money. **[—29—]**

In sum, what SA-TECH wants this Court to do, either explicitly or in effect, is to declare whether California or federal labor law applies to *all* "future missions under the 2013 Contract," irrespective of any applicable contract provisions or particular SA-TECH subcontractors. J.A. 12. In turn, SA-TECH wishes for the Navy to "support (financially and legally) its interpretation" by guaranteeing any necessary payments of unknown settlement and labor costs. *Id.* But we agree with the district court that Counts II and III are monetary claims for which SA-TECH did not present a requested sum certain, as required to exhaust its remedies. Accordingly, we conclude that the district court correctly dismissed SA-TECH's claims under Counts II and III for lack of subject matter jurisdiction.

IV.

For the reasons stated above, we hold that SA-TECH failed to present valid claims under the Contract Disputes Act and thus did not exhaust its administrative remedies. Accordingly, we affirm the district court's dismissal of SA-TECH's claims for lack of subject matter jurisdiction.

AFFIRMED

[13] In fact, SA-TECH acknowledges that it does not know the "formal claim amount" from the *Richard* plaintiffs and does "not know" what the plaintiffs will claim. Opening Br. at 4–5.

[14] SA-TECH has represented to this Court that it filed a new monetary claim in January 2021.

United States Court of Appeals
for the Fourth Circuit

No. 21-1260

KRUEGER
VS.
ANGELOS

Appeal from the United States District Court for the District of Maryland at Baltimore

Decided: February 15, 2022

Citation: 26 F.4th 212, 10 Adm. R. 108 (4th Cir. 2022).

Before **GREGORY,** Chief Judge, **QUATTLEBAUM,** Circuit Judge, and **FLOYD,** Senior Circuit Judge.

[—3—] {–214–} **QUATTLEBAUM,** Circuit Judge:

Under the Labor Management Relations Act, unions and management can enter into trust agreements to provide employment benefits. And sometimes the management of several employers join together to reach those agreements with a union. When that happens, disputes may arise about adding or removing employers from the trust agreement's coverage. Here, we must decide whether, by statute or agreement, labor unions and management are required to arbitrate disputes about which employers are covered by the trust agreements that create funds for employee benefits.

I.

The Steamship Trade Association of Baltimore, Inc. (STA)—an association of businesses involved with the transport of cargo into and out of the Port of Baltimore—and the International Longshoremen's Association (ILA) entered into four trust agreements to create funds that provide employee benefits in accordance with the Labor Management Relations Act. As required by the Act, the agreements provide an equal number of trustees representing the labor union (Union Trustees) and trustees representing the employers (Management Trustees).

Not all companies that do business at the Port of Baltimore are members of the STA. The dispute here arose when the Union Trustees sought to expand the definition of "Employer" in the trust agreements to include non-STA employers engaged **{–215–}** in the same businesses as STA-affiliated employers at the Port of Baltimore. As currently defined in **[—4—]** the trust agreements, the term "Employer" means "the STA or an Employer-Member or former Employer-Member of the STA." J.A. 44.

During a meeting of the funds' trustees, the Union Trustees moved to adopt such amendments. Under the proposed amendment to the trust agreements, the term "Employer" would include "any employer who signs a CBA [collective bargaining agreement] with the ILA or its [local affiliates] that requires contributions to the Trust." *Id.* at 93. Expanding the definition of "Employer" would increase the number of contributors to the trusts. All Union Trustees voted for the motion and all Management Trustees opposed it, creating a deadlock. The Management Trustees refused the Union Trustees' request to decide the matter by arbitration.

The Union Trustees then sued to compel arbitration under 29 U.S.C. § 186(c)(5)(B). Upon the Management Trustees' motion, the district court dismissed the complaint for failure to state a claim upon which relief can be granted. The Union Trustees timely appealed, and we have jurisdiction under 28 U.S.C. § 1291.[1] **[—5—]**

---

[1] "We review de novo the grant of a motion to dismiss for failure to state a claim, applying the same standards as the district court." *Fairfax v. CBS Corp.*, 2 F.4th 286, 291 (4th Cir. 2021) (quotations omitted). "We take all well-pled facts to be true, drawing all reasonable inferences in favor of the plaintiff, but 'we need not accept the legal conclusions drawn from the facts, and we need not accept as true unwarranted inferences, unreasonable conclusions or arguments.'" *Carey v. Throwe*, 957 F.3d 468, 474 (4th Cir. 2020) (quoting *Giarratano v. Johnson*, 521 F.3d 298, 302 (4th Cir. 2008)). We may also consider "documents integral to and relied upon in the complaint," as long as the plaintiff does not question their authenticity, which here the Union Trustees do not. *See Fairfax*, 2 F.4th at 292.

II.

We begin with the Union Trustees' allegation that 29 U.S.C. § 186(c)(5)(B) compels arbitration of the dispute over amending the definition of "Employer" in the trust agreements. But § 186(c)(5)(B)'s arbitration provision applies only in a narrow set of circumstances. That section provides that in the event of a "deadlock on the administration of such fund," an arbitrator resolves "such deadlock."[2] *See* 29 U.S.C. § 186(c)(5)(B). Thus, to the extent that arbitration must occur under § 186(c)(5)(B), it is only over the "administration" of employee benefit trust funds.

Our Court has not yet interpreted the term "administration" in § 186(c)(5)(B), but some of our sister circuits have. Recently, the Eighth Circuit, in *Gillick v. Elliott*, 1 F.4th 608 (8th Cir. 2021), addressed a similar § 186(c)(5)(B) dispute where the union-appointed trustee sought to compel arbitration so that the arbitrator could amend the trust agreement. *Gillick* rejected the union-appointed trustee's position. "Amending a trust agreement is not 'a matter of day-to-day administration of the trust funds.'" *Id.* at 614 (quoting *Farmer v. Fisher*, 586 F.2d 1226, 1230 (8th Cir. 1978), *overruled on other grounds by Robbins v. Prosser's Moving & Storage Co.*, 700 F.2d 433 (8th Cir. 1983)). The Tenth Circuit reached the same conclusion several years prior. In *Ader v. Hughes*, 570 F.2d 303, 307 (10th Cir. 1978), it held that "[w]hatever else may be meant by trust fund 'administration,' the term does not include decisions to amend or not amend a 302(c)(5) trust agreement." **[—6—] {-216-}**

We agree with these interpretations of § 186(c)(5)(B). Consistent with *Gillick* and *Ader*, multiple dictionaries define "administration" as an executive, management role. *See, e.g., Administration, Black's Law Dictionary* (11th ed. 2019) ("The management or performance of the executive duties of a government, institution, or business; collectively, all the actions that are involved in managing the work of an organization."); *Administration, Merriam-Webster's Collegiate Dictionary* (11th ed. 2020) ("1 : performance of executive duties: MANAGEMENT").[3] Indeed, Merriam-Webster's Collegiate Dictionary explicitly distinguishes the term "administration" from "policy-making," i.e., an act with quasi-legislative functions such as amending an agreement. *See Administration, Merriam-Webster's Collegiate Dictionary*, *supra*. Amending the trust agreements, which would be changing how the trusts are constituted, is not part of managing the trusts or administering the trusts.

This understanding also comports with the rest of the statutory language in § 186(c)(5)(B). In addition to discussing the composition of the trust, § 186(c)(5)(B) focuses on how the written trust agreement must specify "the detailed basis *on which such payments are to be made*." 29 U.S.C. § 186(c)(5)(B) (emphasis added). This indicates that § 186(c)(5)(B) is concerned with the management of the funds, not changing them. **[—7—]**

In arguing that § 186(c)(5)(B) includes amending the definition of "Employee," the Union Trustees primarily rely on two decisions from our sister circuits. *See Barrett v. Miller*, 276 F.2d 429 (2d Cir. 1960); *Emp. Trustees of W. Pa. Teamsters v. Union Trustees of W. Pa. Teamsters* (*Western Pennsylvania Teamsters*), 870 F.3d 235 (3d Cir. 2017). However, these cases do not advance the Union Trustee's position.

In *Barrett*, the union trustees proposed adopting a self-insurance program rather than continuing to pay premiums to independent

[2] To be precise, the statute designates "an impartial umpire." 29 U.S.C. § 186(c)(5)(B).

[3] The dictionary definitions at the time of the enactment are similar. *See Administration, Black's Law Dictionary* (3d ed. 1944) ("[T]he practical management and direction of the executive department . . . also conventionally applied to the whole class of public functionaries, or those in charge of the management of the executive department."); *Administration, Webster's New International Dictionary* (2d ed. 1940) ("2. The managing or conduct of an office or employment; the performance of the executive duties of an institution, business, or the like . . . .").

insurance companies. After concluding that the trustees had no power to make this change, the Second Circuit rejected the union trustees' action to compel arbitration. The court reasoned that an arbitrator's powers extend no further than those of the trustees. *See* 276 F.2d at 431. And since the trustees were not authorized to adopt any self-insurance proposal, an arbitrator could not do so either. From the Second Court's perspective, the inability for an arbitrator to decide on a particular issue provides a "positive assurance that the contract is not susceptible to an interpretation to cover the asserted dispute." *See id.* at 431–33. This decision says nothing about whether amendments to a trust agreement constitute the administration of a trust.

Next, *Western Pennsylvania Teamsters* actually undermines the Union Trustees' position. There, the trustees were deadlocked over a motion to pay compensation to eligible trustees and a motion to clarify and confirm that the term "Employer Trustees" required such trustee to be a full-time employee of a contributing employer to the fund. Of note, the second motion sought "to clarify *and confirm*," in contrast to an earlier "motion to 'clarify **{-217-}** *and amend*.'" 870 F.3d at 238–39 (emphases in original). In affirming the arbitration of these issues, the Third Circuit first emphasized that "the [Labor Management Relations **[—8—]** Act] is restricted to matters involving deadlocks in the 'administration' of the trust fund." *Id.* at 242. The court then emphasized how "no decision by an arbitrator on this motion to 'clarify and confirm' would lead to the amendment of the Trust Agreement." *Id.* at 243. The implication from the Third Circuit's decision, therefore, is that a motion to amend the trust agreement, which is what the Union Trustees seek to do in our case, is not subject to arbitration.

Finally, the Union Trustees also cite to our decision in *United Steel, Paper and Forestry, Rubber, Manufacturing, Energy, Allied Industrial & Service Workers International Union AFL-CIO/CLC, Local No. 850L v. Continental Tire North America, Inc.*, 568 F.3d 158 (4th Cir. 2009), which compelled arbitration under 29 U.S.C. § 185. This decision, however, has no bearing for interpreting § 186(c)(5)(B), which is the statutory provision at issue here. Unlike § 186(c)(5)(B), § 185 permits lawsuits for "violation of contracts between an employer and a labor organization representing employees." 29 U.S.C. § 185(a). Since *United Steel* ultimately deals with a dispute over a contract violation, it provides no basis to assert a cause of action under § 186(c)(5)(B).

In sum, the authority on which the Union Trustees rely is not persuasive. Section 186(c)(5)(B) does not provide a valid reason to compel arbitration over the proposal of the Union Trustees to expand the definition of "Employer" in the trust agreements. **[—9—]**

III.

We next consider whether the terms of the trust agreements compel arbitration. The Union Trustees argue that, independent from § 186(c)(5)(B), arbitration may be compelled by contract. In resolving contractual disputes between employers and unions over questions of arbitrability, the Supreme Court has developed several background principles. *See AT&T Techs., Inc. v. Commc'ns Workers of Am.*, 475 U.S. 643, 648–51 (1986); *see also W. Pa. Teamsters*, 870 F.3d at 240 (discussing *AT&T*'s principles as "long established"). Two of these principles relate to our discussion. First, "arbitration is a matter of contract and a party cannot be required to submit to arbitration any dispute which he has not agreed so to submit." *AT&T*, 475 U.S. at 648. Second, if a contract contains an arbitration clause, "a presumption of arbitrability" exists, and there must be "positive assurance that the arbitration clause is not susceptible of an interpretation that covers the asserted dispute." *Id.* at 650. Doubts are resolved in favor of coverage. *Id.*

Here, the trust agreements contain arbitration clauses. Section 8.01 confers arbitration "[i]n the event the Trustees cannot decide any matter or resolve any dispute because of a tie vote." J.A. 74. But Section 8.01's reach is limited by Section 8.03, which states: "[t]he arbitrator shall not have the power or authority to change or modify the basic provisions of this Agreement." *Id.* at 75.

At oral argument, the Union Trustees' counsel conceded that the term "Employer," which as stated above determines, among other things, who contributes to the trusts, is a "basic provision" of the trust agreements. And for good reason. With no part of the trust agreement defining the term "basic provisions," we look at what the ordinary meaning of **[—10—]** such term would be. *See* **{-218-}** *Mey v. DIRECTV, LLC*, 971 F.3d 284, 289 (4th Cir. 2020) (looking at the dictionary to understand the ordinary meaning because the contract did not define the term in dispute). "Basic" means "of, relating to, or forming the base or essence," or "constituting or serving as the basis or starting point." *Basic, Merriam-Webster's Collegiate Dictionary, supra*. "Basis," in turn, is defined as "the bottom of something considered as its foundation," "the principal component of something" and even "something on which something else is established or based." *Basis, Merriam-Webster's Collegiate Dictionary, supra*. Determining who contributes to the trust funds is a basic provision of the trust agreements. To put it differently, determining which entity must contribute to the trust agreements goes to the "essence" of the trusts, or at the very least qualifies as the "starting point," "foundation" and "principal component" of the trusts.[4] Thus, Section 8.03's express bar of arbitration to amend basic provisions—combined with the fact that the definition of "Employer" is a basic provision—provides the "positive assurance" as required in *AT&T*, 475 U.S. at 650, that the parties never agreed to arbitrate disputes about amending the definition of "Employer." **[—11—]**

Despite their concession about the term "Employer," the Union Trustees insist that any expansion of who may contribute to the funds is a trivial matter that does not amount to amending any basic provision. They offer three reasons for this characterization, none of which are persuasive.

First, the Union Trustees argue that non-STA employers already contribute to the funds, since the current definition of "Employer" includes "former Employer-Member of the STA." Opening Br. 18 (quoting J.A. 131, which in turn quotes Section 1.01 of the trust agreement). Thus, according to the Union Trustees, since some non-STA members are already part of the trusts, adding more non-STA members is a trivial matter. But this is unconvincing. Adding non-STA employers—but only those who used to be STA members *at one point*—might be an important line for the bargaining parties to have drawn. We see no reason to conclude that because the parties included former STA members in the definition of "Employer," including all non-STA members would be trivial.[5]

Second, the Union Trustees argue that the trustees have amended the definition of "Employee" in the past. According to them, since the definition has been amended before, doing it again would be trivial. But we fail to see the logic of this position. Our country has amended its Constitution **{-219-}** 27 times. That hardly means doing it an 28th time is trivial. While **[—12—]** our Constitution and

[4] Dictionary definitions of "basic" and "basis" when the trust agreements were reached are effectively the same. *See Basic, Webster's Third New International Dictionary* (1976) (first and second entries); *Basis, Webster's Third New International Dictionary, supra* (first, second and fourth entries). In addition, the term "provision" is not at issue. As the district court observed: "In a legal document, the word 'provision' refers to a 'clause in a statute, contract or other legal document.' . . . Thus, there is no question as to whether the definition of the term 'Employer' constitutes a provision; the Court must only determine whether it constitutes a 'basic' provision." J.A. 203 (citing *Provision, Black's Law Dictionary* (11th ed. 2019), *supra*).

[5] As discussed above, *Western Pennsylvania Teamsters* bolsters our point. While the Union Trustees argue that the present dispute is comparable to *Western Pennsylvania Teamsters*, the unions in that case made sure that their motion was to "confirm" an already existing provision, not "amend." If the Union Trustees are so confident that this distinction "has no practical difference," Opening Br. 19, they could have easily adopted the same approach—which they did not. *Cf.* Resp. Br. 16 ("[T]he Union Trustees are not requesting an arbitrator to interpret existing language . . . .").

the trust agreements here are very different documents, this analogy reveals that it simply does not make sense that agreeing to prior amendments means any future amendment is trivial. If anything, amending the definition of "Employer" before in a way that does not include non-STA members suggests a conscious decision that such an enlargement of who must contribute to the trusts contravenes the parties' agreement.

Typically, parties expand either the fund contributors or fund beneficiaries through amendments. So was the case in *Bueno v. Gill*, No. 02 Civ. 1000DLC, 2002 WL 31106342, at *1 (S.D.N.Y. Sept. 20, 2002), *opinion adhered to on reconsideration*, 237 F. Supp. 2d 447 (S.D.N.Y. 2002), a case that the Union Trustees cite. *Bueno* held a proposal to carve out assets from the fund so that a portion could be devoted to non-union employees was not only beyond the trustees' power but also "unquestionably beyond the scope of issues that the Trust Agreement permits to be resolved by arbitration." *Id.* at *4. The court there reasoned that such amendment would "require a change and modification of basic provisions of the Trust Agreement." *Id.* While the Union Trustees argue that this case shows how the Union Trustees' proposal is modest in comparison, that is not so. In fact, *Bueno* demonstrates how changing the fundamental nature of who the trust fund recipient would be is changing a "basic provision" of a trust agreement. If the output of a trust fund (trust recipient) is a basic provision, the input (trust contributor) should be as well. **[—13—]**

Third, the Union Trustees argue that, under the trust agreements, an arbitrator steps into the shoes of the trustee.[6] Based on that, they contend that an arbitrator, "rather than making change or modification to the Trust Agreements," would merely step into the shoes of the trustees to "implement its proposed change." Opening Br. 22. But the parties never agreed to amend the definition of "Employer." Absent any such agreement, there is nothing for an arbitrator to implement. And the reason the parties were deadlocked here is that they could not agree on the amendment in the first place.

In conclusion, while it is true that courts incorporate a "presumption of arbitrability" in employer-union arbitration disputes when an arbitration agreement exists, here the trust agreements provide a "positive assurance" that arbitration may not be compelled.

IV.

For the foregoing reasons, the district court's order dismissing the case is

AFFIRMED.

[6] While the Union Trustees' counsel represented to the contrary at oral argument, our review of the case record makes us question whether the Union Trustees truly argued this last point in front of the district court. After all, phrases such as "stand in the shoes" and citations to the Union Trustees' case law and legislative history related to the matter are nowhere to be found in the Union Trustees' district court briefs. Thus, it is highly likely that the Union Trustees waived their third argument. *See United States v. Davis*, 954 F.2d 182, 187 (4th Cir. 1992) ("It is an accepted rule of appellate procedure that ordinarily an appellate court will not consider an issue not raised in the court from which the appeal is taken."). And even if we set aside the waiver issue, the Union Trustees' arguments fail on the merits for all the reasons discussed in this opinion.

United States Court of Appeals
for the Fourth Circuit

No. 21-7089

**UNITED STATES
VS.
SAID**

Appeal from the United States District Court for the Eastern District of Virginia at Norfolk

Decided: February 23, 2022

Citation: 26 F.4th 653, 10 Adm. R. 113 (4th Cir. 2022).

Before **KING** and **WYNN**, Circuit Judges, and **KEENAN**, Senior Circuit Judge.

[—3—] {-655-} WYNN, Circuit Judge:

The question on appeal is whether Petitioner Mohamed Ali Said's convictions on two counts of using and carrying a firearm during and in relation to a crime of violence may stand when some of the predicate convictions that the jury might have **{-656-}** relied on in convicting him of the firearms charges have been invalidated. The district court answered no and vacated the two firearms convictions.

Under this Circuit's precedent, however, Said did not meet his burden of showing that the error in the jury instructions had a "substantial and injurious effect or influence in determining the jury's verdict." *United States v. Smith*, 723 F.3d 510, 512 (4th Cir. 2013) (quoting *Brecht v. Abrahamson*, 507 U.S. 619, 631 (1993)). Accordingly, we reverse the district court's judgment in relevant part and remand with instructions to enter an order denying Said's § 2255 petition as to the two counts in question.[1]

I.

In April 2010, Said and six others—all Somali citizens—attacked the USS *Ashland* (LSD 48), a commissioned ship in the United States Navy with significant armament and a crew that typically includes a Marine Corps Detachment, in the Gulf of Aden.[2] For Said and several of his confederates, this was their second attempt on a vessel in as many months. In late February, they had entered the Gulf "searching for a merchant ship to **[—4—]** seize," but were intercepted by the HMS *Chatham* of the British Royal Navy. *United States v. Said*, 798 F.3d 182, 186, 3 Adm. R. 231, 231–32 (4th Cir. 2015).

Trying their luck again in April, Said and the others loaded "a small wooden skiff . . . with a hooked ladder, three AK–47s, and [a rocket-propelled grenade launcher]." *Id.* at 186–87, 3 Adm. R. at 231–32. They approached the *Ashland*, believing it to be a merchant vessel. Said and one of his co-defendants "held loaded AK–47s," and the codefendant used his weapon to shoot at the *Ashland*. *Id.* at 187, 3 Adm. R. at 232. The *Ashland* returned fire, killing one of the attackers and apprehending the six survivors who were brought to Virginia for prosecution.[3] *Id.* at 188, 3 Adm. R. at 233.

The operative indictment charged Said with ten counts:

- Conspiracy to commit hostage taking, 18 U.S.C. § 1203(a) (Count 1);
- Conspiracy to commit kidnapping, *id.* § 1201(a)(2), (c) (Count 2);
- Conspiracy to perform an act of violence against persons on a vessel, *id.* § 2291(a)(6), (9) (Count 3);
- Conspiracy to use and carry a firearm and a destructive device during and in relation to, and to possess a firearm and a destructive device in

---

[1] The district court also granted relief as to a third count. Both parties agree that was proper. Our opinion does not disturb that relief.

[2] The facts stated herein are taken from our previous decision affirming Said's convictions on direct appeal and are recited in the light most favorable to the Government, as the prevailing party at trial. *See United States v. Said*, 798 F.3d 182, 186 n.2, 3 Adm. R. 231, 231 n.2 (4th Cir. 2015) (citing *United States v. Singh*, 518 F.3d 236, 241 n.2 (4th Cir. 2008)).

[3] Said was tried alongside four of his codefendants. The fifth pleaded guilty shortly after their arrest. *Said*, 798 F.3d at 188–89, 3 Adm. R. at 233–34.

furtherance of, a crime of violence, *id.* § 924(o) (Count 4);
- Piracy, *id.* § 1651 (Count 5);
- Attack to plunder a vessel, *id.* § 1659 (Count 6);
- Assault with a dangerous weapon on a federal officer or employee, *id.* § 111(a)(1), (b) (Count 7);
- Performing an act of violence against persons on a vessel, *id.* § 2291(a)(6) (Count 8);
- Using and carrying a firearm during and in relation to, and possessing a firearm in furtherance of, a crime of **{-657-}** violence, *id.* § 924(c)(1)(A) (Count 9); and
- Using, carrying, and discharging a firearm during and in relation to a crime of violence, *id.* § 924(c)(1)(A)(iii) (Count 10). **[—5—]**

The charges related to the encounter with the HMS *Chatham* in February 2010 and the attack on the USS *Ashland* in April 2010. Counts 1 through 4 encompassed the time periods for both; Count 9 related only to the *Chatham*; and the remaining charges related only to the *Ashland*. Further, Counts 5 through 10 included allegations of aiding and abetting. 18 U.S.C. § 2(a).

Counts 4, 9, and 10 relied on other crimes charged in the indictment as predicate "crime[s] of violence." J.A. 48, 53–54.[4] Specifically, the firearm offenses charged in Counts 4 and 10 of the indictment were predicated on seven alternative crimes of violence: the conspiracy counts charged in Counts 1 through 3, and other crimes charged in Counts 5 through 8. The firearm offense charged in Count 9 was predicated solely on the conspiracy offenses (Counts 1 through 3).

During trial in 2013, the district court provided the jury with a number of instructions that are relevant to this appeal. First, the court instructed the jury that, as to Counts 4 and 10, the Government had to prove beyond a reasonable doubt that Said "committed *any one or more* of the crimes charged in" Counts 1 through 3 and 5 through 8 of the indictment.[5] J.A. 198 (emphasis added); *see also* J.A. 183. The court also gave a "limiting instruction" as to Count 10, instructing that "Count Ten is to be considered only if you have found [Said] guilty of *at least one* of the crimes of violence charged in Counts **[—6—]** One, Two, Three, Five, Six, Seven, or Eight." J.A. 198–99 (emphasis added); *see also* J.A. 74 (Government counsel making the same point in closing). And the court noted that the Government was "required to prove beyond a reasonable doubt that [Said], or another who was aided and abetted by [him,] actively employed the firearms described in" Count 10. J.A. 201. Finally, the court instructed the jury that its "verdict must be unanimous." J.A. 206.

The jury convicted Said on all ten counts, and further unanimously found that "a firearm was discharged during" the crime charged in Count 10. J.A. 218. The verdict form did not require the jury to identify the predicate offenses upon which the convictions for Counts 4, 9, or 10 were based.

In November 2016, the district court sentenced Said to 396 months' imprisonment:[6] 120 months on Counts 1 through 8, all to be served concurrently; 96 months on Count 9, to be served consecutively; and 180 months on Count 10, also to be served consecutively. Said additionally received a total effective supervised release term of five years. Neither party appealed the sentence. **{-658-}**

[4] Citations to the "J.A." refer to the Joint Appendix filed by the parties in this appeal.

[5] In its instructions on Count 10, the district court erroneously listed Count 4 as a possible predicate. However, the court properly omitted Count 4 when listing the possible predicates in several other places in the instructions. Said has not argued that this error prejudiced him.

[6] This followed an original sentencing to an aggregate of 500 months in 2014. *Said*, 798 F.3d at 192, 3 Adm. R. at 237. We vacated that sentence in 2015 upon the Government's appeal, in which the Government successfully argued that the statutorily required sentence of life in prison for the piracy count, Count 5, did not violate the Eighth Amendment. *Id.* at 200, 3 Adm. R. at 243–44. On remand, however, the Government moved for a downward departure for reasons unrelated to this appeal.

In January 2021, Said filed a habeas petition under 28 U.S.C. § 2255 seeking to vacate his convictions on Counts 4, 9, and 10 in light of the Supreme Court's decision in *United States v. Davis*, 139 S. Ct. 2319 (2019), which he argued undermined the predicates **[—7—]** necessary to sustain those convictions, and which we have held applies retroactively on collateral review,[7] *see In re Thomas*, 988 F.3d 783, 790 (4th Cir. 2021). Specifically, 18 U.S.C. § 924(c)—the relevant statute for Counts 4, 9, and 10—prohibits using or carrying a firearm "during and in relation to any crime of violence or drug trafficking crime" or possessing a firearm "in furtherance of any such crime."[8] 18 U.S.C. § 924(c)(1)(A). A "crime of violence" is defined by statute as "an offense that is a felony and" either (A) "has as an element the use, attempted use, or threatened use of physical force against the person or property of another," or (B) "that by its nature, involves a substantial risk that physical force against the person or property of another may be used in the course of committing the offense." *Id.* § 924(c)(3). In *United States v. Davis*, however, the Supreme Court held that the second definitional clause—(B), known as the "residual clause"—is unconstitutionally vague. *Davis*, 139 S. Ct. at 2336. Thus, predicate crimes of violence must fall under clause (A), the "force clause," to be valid. **[—8—]**

Said's § 2255 motion contended that at least three predicates, Counts 1 through 3, were no longer valid after *Davis*, and that therefore the jury was incorrectly instructed that it could consider those charges as predicates for Counts 4, 9, and 10. He further argued that he was prejudiced by this error because there was a reasonable possibility that the jury relied *solely* on those invalid predicates in convicting him of Counts 4, 9, and 10. The district court agreed and granted the § 2255 motion; vacated Said's convictions on Counts 4, 9, and 10; and resentenced Said to 120 months' incarceration, a sentence he had already completed. *Said v. United States*, No. 2:10-CR-57-1, 2021 WL 3037412, at *12 (E.D. Va. July 19, 2021). The Government timely appealed the vacatur of Said's convictions on Counts 4 and 10, while conceding that Count 9 was properly vacated because it was based only on the invalid predicates. We granted the Government's motion to stay the district court's judgment pending appeal.

II.

We begin with a review of the predicate convictions. The Government **{–659–}** concedes that, after *Davis*, Counts 1 through 3—the conspiracy charges—may no longer serve as predicate crimes of violence because they do not categorically require "the use, attempted use, or threatened use of physical force against the person or property of another." 18 U.S.C. § 924(c)(3)(A); *see United States v. Simms*, 914 F.3d 229, 233–34 (4th Cir. 2019) (holding that conspiracy to commit Hobbs Act robbery "does not categorically qualify as a crime of violence under the elements-based categorical approach . . . because to convict a defendant of this offense, the Government must prove only that the defendant *agreed* **[—9—]** *with another* to commit actions that, *if realized*, would violate the Hobbs Act" (emphases added)).

Additionally, the parties and the district court agreed that, at minimum, Counts 7 and

[7] Said originally filed his petition in June 2020, within one year of the Supreme Court's decision in *Davis*. In November 2020, the district court dismissed that petition without prejudice to refiling it within sixty days. Said refiled the petition within that time frame. Said's petition is not a second or successive petition under 28 U.S.C. § 2255(h) because the initial petition was dismissed without prejudice to cure technical deficiencies. *See, e.g.*, *Slack v. McDaniel*, 529 U.S. 473, 485–86 (2000); *Stewart v. Martinez-Villareal*, 523 U.S. 637, 643–45 (1998); *In re Goddard*, 170 F.3d 435, 438 (4th Cir. 1999). Nor did the Government appeal the sixty-day extension or otherwise argue that Said's petition was untimely. *See Miller v. United States*, 735 F.3d 141, 143 (4th Cir. 2013) (Government may waive statute-of-limitations defense under § 2255); Brian R. Means, *Federal Habeas Manual* § 9A:159 (2021) ("The statute of limitations is an affirmative defense that must be asserted by the government.").

[8] While Count 4 charged a violation of 18 U.S.C. § 924(o), that statute is simply the conspiracy form of § 924(c). *See* 18 U.S.C. § 924(o) (providing penalties for "[a] person who conspires to commit an offense under [§ 924(c)]").

8 remained valid predicate crimes of violence after *Davis*.[9] *Said*, 2021 WL 3037412, at *9. Because it is Said's burden to show error, and because the parties have not briefed the crime-of-violence question as to Counts 5 through 8, we assume for purposes of this analysis that they are all valid predicates.[10]

Thus, Said was charged with, and the jury found him guilty of, both valid and invalid predicates. Both parties agree with the district court that instructing the jury that *any* of these crimes could serve as predicates for the § 924(c) charges was error. *See id.* at *10. Nevertheless, a § 924(c) conviction may stand even if the jury based its verdict on an **[—10—]** invalid predicate, so long as the jury *also* relied on a valid predicate. *United States v. Hare*, 820 F.3d 93, 106 (4th Cir. 2016); *see United States v. Crawley*, 2 F.4th 257, 263 (4th Cir. 2021) (reaffirming *Hare* after *Davis*), *cert. denied*, 142 S. Ct. 819 (2022). But here, the verdict form did not specify which predicate or predicates the jury relied upon in finding Said guilty of Counts 4 and 10.

So, we are left with the question of whether Said is entitled to habeas relief because the jury *may* have relied *solely* on one or more of the invalid predicates in rendering guilty verdicts on Counts 4 and 10. We conclude that the answer is no.

III.

In evaluating this issue, we must first determine our standard of review. "In **{-660-}** our consideration of the district court's rulings [on a § 2255 petition], we review its legal conclusions de novo and its findings of fact for clear error." *United States v. Roane*, 378 F.3d 382, 395 (4th Cir. 2004). But how do we evaluate the impact of an instructional error on a conviction? The answer depends on whether a defendant preserved the objection (by raising it before the district court) as well as what stage the case is in (direct appeal or collateral attack).

On direct appeal regarding a preserved, meritorious objection to jury instructions, the defendant is entitled to relief unless the error is harmless beyond a reasonable doubt. *Smith*, 723 F.3d at 512 (citing *Chapman v. California*, 386 U.S. 18, 24 (1967)); *see id.* at 515 ("Under *Chapman*, an error is harmless if it is 'clear beyond a reasonable doubt that a rational jury would have found the defendant guilty absent the error.'" (quoting *Neder v. United States*, 527 U.S. 1, 18 (1999))). **[—11—]**

Where a defendant, like Said, fails to preserve his objection, our review on direct appeal is for plain error.[11] On plain-error

[9] Although Counts 5 through 8 included allegations of aiding and abetting under 18 U.S.C. § 2(a), we have held that "aiding and abetting a crime of violence is also categorically a crime of violence." *United States v. Ali*, 991 F.3d 561, 574 (4th Cir.), *cert. denied*, 142 S. Ct. 486 (2021). To the extent those counts charged crimes of violence, therefore, it is of no moment whether the jury believed Said to have committed them as a principal or as an aider and abettor.

[10] We note that we have suggested, in an unpublished opinion, that the crime charged in Count 7, § 111(b), may be a proper predicate offense for a § 924(c) conviction. *See United States v. Lewis*, 724 F. App'x 269, 270 n.* (4th Cir. 2018) (per curiam) (finding no plain error where § 111(b) was used as a predicate offense for a § 924(c) conviction). Our sister circuits agree that it is. *See United States v. Bryant*, 949 F.3d 168, 181 n.12 (4th Cir. 2020) (noting this agreement); *see also United States v. Taylor*, 848 F.3d 476, 492–93 (1st Cir. 2017); *Gray v. United States*, 980 F.3d 264, 268 (2d Cir. 2020) (per curiam); *United States v. Bullock*, 970 F.3d 210, 213 (3d Cir. 2020) (evaluating Sentencing Guidelines § 4B1.1); *United States v. Hernandez-Hernandez*, 817 F.3d 207, 217 (5th Cir. 2016) (evaluating Sentencing Guidelines § 2L1.2); *United States v. Rafidi*, 829 F.3d 437, 446 (6th Cir. 2016); *United States v. Juvenile Female*, 566 F.3d 943, 947 (9th Cir. 2009) (evaluating 18 U.S.C. § 16); *United States v. Kendall*, 876 F.3d 1264, 1269–70 (10th Cir. 2017); *United States v. Bates*, 960 F.3d 1278, 1285 (11th Cir. 2020); *United States v. Quaglin*, 851 F. App'x 218, 218–19 (D.C. Cir. 2021) (per curiam).

[11] The Government argued below that Said procedurally defaulted his *Davis* challenge by not raising it before his convictions became final, and that he could not establish either cause or prejudice for the default. But the Government has not pursued that argument on appeal, except insofar as it argues Said was not prejudiced because the errors as to Counts 4 and 10 were harmless. We therefore do not address the question of procedural

review, "the defendant rather than the Government bears the burden of proof." *United States v. Hastings*, 134 F.3d 235, 243 (4th Cir. 1998). The defendant must show that the court's jury instructions included an error that was "clear and obvious," and "that the error affected his substantial rights, meaning that it '*affected the outcome of the district court proceedings*.'"[12] *United States v. Ali*, 991 F.3d 561, 572 (4th Cir.) (emphasis added) (quoting *United States v. Catone*, 769 F.3d 866, 871 (4th Cir. 2014)), *cert. denied*, 142 S. Ct. 486 (2021).

An even *more* stringent standard applies in a § 2255 case like the one at bar. On federal habeas review of an instructional error, we apply the "harmless-error standard . . . articulated in *Brecht v. Abrahamson*," in which the Supreme Court held that an "error is harmless if it did not have a 'substantial and injurious effect or influence in determining the jury's verdict.'" *Smith*, 723 F.3d at 512 (quoting *Brecht*, 507 U.S. at 623); *see id.* at 516 (applying *Brecht* to a § 2255 case); *see also Hedgpeth v. Pulido*, 555 U.S. **[—12—]** 57, 58 (2008) (per curiam) (applying *Brecht* in a case where, like this one, "the jury was instructed on alternative theories of guilt and may have relied on an invalid one"). This standard requires the habeas petitioner to show that "[t]here [is] more than a 'reasonable possibility' that the error was harmful." *Davis v. Ayala*, 576 U.S. 257, 268 (2015) (quoting *Brecht*, 507 U.S. at 637). Thus, "mere speculation that the **{–661–}** defendant was prejudiced by trial error" is not enough; "the court must find that the defendant was actually prejudiced by the error." *Id.* (quoting *Calderon v. Coleman*, 525 U.S. 141, 146 (1998) (per curiam)).

Applying this standard, we first evaluate the district court's conclusion that Said has shown prejudicial error because it is impossible to know from the record which predicate or predicates the jury had in mind when it convicted him of Counts 4 and 10. We then turn to Said's assertion that he can show prejudicial error because we do not know whether the jury was unanimous in its decision as to which predicate or predicates applied. We reject both contentions.[13]

A.

The district court concluded that Said could show "substantial and injurious effect" from the instructional error "because there is more than a 'reasonable probability that the **[—13—]** jury would not have convicted [Said] of the § 924 offenses if the invalid [crime-of-violence] predicate [was] not included on the verdict form.'" *Said*, 2021 WL 3037412, at *11 (quoting *United States v. Jones*, 935 F.3d 266, 274 (5th Cir. 2019) (per curiam)). The court indicated that it held "grave doubt" that Said would have been convicted on Counts 4 and 10 "but for the improper jury instructions" because "there is no evidence in the record showing that the jury relied on either an invalid or valid predicate offense to convict" him of those counts. *Id.* at *11 & n.5; *see id.* at *12 (noting that this "grave doubt" arose because the record was "unclear" regarding which predicate or predicates the jury relied upon).

That is not enough. As we have repeatedly held, even under the plain-error standard,

---

default. *See United States v. Harris*, 991 F.3d 552, 558 (4th Cir.) (procedural default is an affirmative defense), *cert. denied*, 142 S. Ct. 379 (2021); *Grayson O Co. v. Agadir Int'l LLC*, 856 F.3d 307, 316 (4th Cir. 2017) (party waives argument by failing to raise it in its opening brief).

[12] Further, even if these elements are established, "we do not correct the error unless it 'seriously affects the fairness, integrity or public reputation of judicial proceedings.'" *Ali*, 991 F.3d at 572 (quoting *United States v. Massenburg*, 564 F.3d 337, 343 (4th Cir. 2009)).

[13] We also note that the district court purported to apply the modified categorical approach to determine which of the "seven alternative potential predicates for Counts Four and Ten . . . were vital for [Said]'s convictions." *Said*, 2021 WL 3037412, at *6. As we explained in *Ali*, "[t]his [analysis] fundamentally misunderstands what the categorical approach accomplishes and the nature of our inquiry" in this case. *Ali*, 991 F.3d at 574. "The purpose of the categorical (and modified categorical) approach is not to determine what the predicate was—a factual question—but rather whether a particular predicate meets the requirements of a 'crime of violence'—a purely legal question" not presently before us. *Id.*

"the defendant bears the burden of showing 'that the erroneous instruction given resulted in his conviction, *not merely that it was impossible to tell under which prong the jury convicted*.'" *Ali*, 991 F.3d at 575 (emphasis added) (internal quotation marks omitted) (quoting *United States v. Robinson*, 627 F.3d 941, 954 (4th Cir. 2010)); *see also Hastings*, 134 F.3d at 243–44 (same). That is, "ambiguity is insufficient" to "establish[] actual prejudice" even under plain-error review. *Ali*, 991 F.3d at 575. Instead, the defendant "must show not only that he *could* have been convicted under the erroneous . . . instruction, but also that he *was not* convicted under the" proper instruction. *Robinson*, 627 F.3d at 955.

Accordingly, mere "uncertainty as to which . . . [predicate or predicates] the jury [relied on] when it found [the defendant] guilty of the § 924(c) counts" does not suffice to demonstrate plain error, let alone the sort of substantial and injurious error required for **[—14—]** habeas relief.[14] **{-662-}** *Ali*, 991 F.3d at 575; *see Davis*, 576 U.S. at 268 (under *Brecht*, "mere speculation" is insufficient). Rather, to meet his burden, Said must show "more than a reasonable possibility" that the jury *only* found him guilty on Counts 4 and 10 because it improperly considered Counts 1 through 3 to be crimes of violence. *Davis*, 576 U.S. at 268 (internal quotation marks omitted).

This he cannot do. Certainly, the record does not indicate which predicates the jury relied on. But, at the risk of repetition, that sort of ambiguity is not enough. Further, common sense supports that a jury that found Said guilty of several substantive crimes of violence, the evidence for all of which showed to involve the use of firearms in an attack against the *Ashland*, had at least one of those crimes in mind when they convicted him of using, carrying, and discharging a weapon (or aiding and abetting the same) during and in relation to a crime of violence that occurred during the time period covering the attack on the *Ashland*.[15] **[—15—]**

Said argues that the Government pointed to the conspiracy predicates in its closing argument, which arguably increases the likelihood that the jury relied on those invalid predicates. But that does nothing to show that

[14] Said directs our attention to cases from other circuits that have found plain error in similar circumstances. *See, e.g.*, *United States v. Capers*, 20 F.4th 105, 123 (2d Cir. 2021); *Jones*, 935 F.3d at 274 (5th Cir.). But, of course, we are bound by our own precedent. And, in any event, this is not a plain-error case; the standard we must apply here is even more difficult for Said to satisfy.

[15] Thus, though the fact that Said can point to nothing more than ambiguity is enough to resolve this case, we note that the facts here strengthen this conclusion even more. The jury found Said guilty of, among other things, assault with a dangerous weapon on a federal officer or employee (Count 7). They convicted him of conspiring to use and carry a firearm and a destructive device during and in relation to, and to possess a firearm and a destructive device in furtherance of, a crime of violence (Count 4). And they found him guilty of discharging a firearm (or aiding and abetting a codefendant who discharged a firearm) during and in relation to a crime of violence (Count 10). All of those charges covered the time period that included the attack on the *Ashland*, and the evidence in the case established that the only weapon discharged in either the encounter with the *Chatham* or the attack on **[—15—]** the *Ashland* was the AK–47 that Said's codefendant fired at the *Ashland*. We struggle to see how the jury could have convicted Said both of (1) assaulting individuals on the *Ashland* with a dangerous weapon and (2) discharging a firearm toward the *Ashland* during and in relation to a crime of violence, without finding that the firearm was discharged during and in relation to said assault. *Cf. Reyes v. United States*, 998 F.3d 753, 759 (7th Cir. 2021) ("[The defendant] was convicted of conspiracy, robbery, and brandishing. The trial evidence showed that he provided the gun and that it was in fact brandished during the robbery. No rational juror could have concluded that the gun was brandished in furtherance of only the conspirators' agreement to commit a robbery, but not in furtherance of the robbery itself, during which the gun was actually brandished."). And while Count 4 is more complicated because it charged *conspiracy* to use and carry a firearm during a crime of violence and covered the encounters with both the *Chatham* and the *Ashland*, we do not think it plausible that the jury could have convicted Said of conspiracy to use and carry a firearm *only* during and in relation to *other conspiracy* charges, and *not* during and in relation to the actual substantive crimes of violence for which the jury also convicted Said.

the jury reached the commonsense-defying conclusion of relying *only* on those predicates, especially given that the Government also reinforced to the jury that it could rely on the valid predicates. So we do not think Said can show that there is *more than a reasonable possibility* that the jury convicted him of Counts 4 and 10 based solely on Counts 1, 2, and/or 3. Put another way, neither Said nor the district court has pointed to any reason why the jury would not have convicted him on Counts 4 and 10 based on at least one of the valid predicates—let alone any evidence that they did not do so. *See Robinson*, 627 F.3d at 955. **{-663-}**

In analyzing these issues, our decision in *Ali* is instructive. In that case, the defendant was convicted, in relevant part, of four counts of Hobbs Act robbery and four counts of carrying a firearm in connection with a crime of violence. *Ali*, 991 F.3d at 564. **[—16—]** Each robbery charge and corresponding firearms charge pertained to one of four separate robberies that took place over the course of roughly three weeks. *Id.* at 564–65; *see* Joint Appendix at 40–47, *Ali*, 991 F.3d 561 (No. 15-4433) [hereinafter *Ali* Joint Appendix]. As to the robberies, the court instructed the jury that they could find the defendant guilty by way of *either* aiding and abetting liability *or* conspiracy liability (or both). *Ali*, 991 F.3d at 572. And the court instructed that a conviction under either theory would suffice for § 924(c) liability. *Id.* The jury found the defendant guilty on all charges. The verdict form did not require the jury to specify the theory of guilt for either the robbery charges or the § 924(c) charges. *Ali* Joint Appendix at 796–98.

On appeal, we found that these instructions were in error and that the error was plain, because while a conviction for aiding and abetting Hobbs Act robbery was a proper § 924(c) predicate, a conviction for *conspiracy* to commit Hobbs Act robbery was not. *Ali*, 991 F.3d at 572–73. But we rejected the defendant's contention that this error "affected [the defendant's] substantial rights, meaning that it 'affected the outcome of the district court proceedings.'" *Id.* at 572 (quoting *Catone*, 769 F.3d at 871). We concluded (1) that "a showing of uncertainty as to 'whether the verdict returned by the jury rested solely on the mis-instruction' does not meet the defendant's burden of establishing actual prejudice" and (2) that the Government presented evidence of "overwhelming weight" that the defendant actually aided and abetted the robberies, rather than merely conspiring to commit them. *Id.* at 575 (quoting *Hastings*, 134 F.3d at 243); *see id.* at 576. Here, too, Said pointed only to "uncertainty" regarding which predicate or predicates the jury relied on. **[—17—]**

Moreover, in this case, we have no occasion to reach the weight of the evidence because the jury *actually convicted* Said of all the possible predicate theories. Put differently, *Ali* involved two levels of ambiguity, but this case involves only one. In *Ali*, it was unclear from the verdict form (1) whether the jury found the defendant guilty of Hobbs Act robbery on the basis of conspiracy, aiding-and-abetting liability, or both, and (2) whether the jury found the defendant guilty of the § 924(c) charges on the basis of a predicate robbery conspiracy, robbery by aiding or abetting, or both. We determined that the overwhelming weight of the evidence showed that the defendant "did more than simply conspire to commit robberies but that he assisted their commission." *Id.* at 576. And we rejected the defendant's instructional-error argument on that basis. We did not then question whether the jury's *§ 924(c)* conviction could have nevertheless been based on mere conspiracy, on the supposition that the jury could have found the defendant guilty of robbery on *both* conspiracy and aiding-and-abetting grounds, and then based the § 924(c) conviction solely on conspiracy.

But that is what Said asks of us here. In this case, we have no ambiguity about the substantive crimes the jury convicted Said of (the first form of ambiguity in *Ali*): the jury found Said guilty of every charge, and he has not pointed to ways in which those individual charges could be split into valid and invalid predicates. Rather, he asks us to hold that the instructional error had a "substantial and injurious effect" on his conviction because the jury did not specify on which predicate or predicates its § 924(c) conclusions were based (the second **{-664-}** form of ambiguity in *Ali*). For the reasons discussed above, we reject that argument. **[—18—]**

To be clear, we do not hold that a challenge such as Said's will *never* succeed when the defendant has been convicted of both a § 924(c) charge and a valid crime-of-violence predicate. Such a broad question is not before us, and another case with a different set of facts may well come out differently, as the Government agreed at oral argument. *See* Oral Arg. at 40:10–43:15, https://www.ca4.uscourts.gov/OAarchive/mp3/21-7089-20211209.mp3; *see also Ali*, 991 F.3d at 575 (noting that the analysis required in this type of case is a "'case-specific and fact-intensive' determination" (quoting *Robinson*, 627 F.3d at 956)). But here, Said has pointed to nothing to eliminate the commonsense prospect that the jury relied on one or more of the valid predicates when it convicted him of the § 924 charges in Counts 4 and 10.

B.

Said further contends that this case involves a second, separate error that was not present in *Ali*: the issue of juror unanimity.[16] The district court agreed. *Said*, 2021 WL 3037412, at *10 ("[T]he Court recognizes that the lack of special instructions also runs afoul of the long-established right of jury unanimity enshrined in the Sixth Amendment . . . because it is unclear which predicate offenses the jurors relied on to convict [Said] on Counts Four and Ten."). We conclude that, even assuming legal error exists, Said's argument still rests on ambiguity, which is not sufficient for the reasons described above. **[—19—]**

Said argues that he is entitled to relief because, while the jurors were told their "verdict must be unanimous," they were not instructed that they must unanimously agree *on the specific predicate or predicates* upon which they based their guilty verdicts for Counts 4 and 10. J.A. 206. He contends that such an instruction was required by *Richardson v. United States*, a continuing-criminal-enterprise case in which the Supreme Court held that the jury must reach unanimous agreement not only as to the fact "that the defendant committed some 'continuing series of violations' but also . . . in respect to each individual violation." *Richardson v. United States*, 526 U.S. 813, 815–16 (1999). For that reason, Said claims, the question before us is whether even a *single juror* based their verdicts for Counts 4 and 10 solely on one or more of the three improper predicates. And, in his view, that issue distinguishes this case from *Ali*, because he says the *Ali* court appropriately required unanimity. He also points out that *Ali* involved only one valid and one invalid predicate, whereas this case involves a total of seven predicates. Thus, he argues, this case presents "exponentially more combinations of how the jury could have properly or improperly convicted Said" than *Ali* did. Response Br. at 13.

Even assuming, arguendo, that (1) the district court's instructions constituted a *Richardson* error and (2) *Ali* did not involve such an error, Said's argument is meritless. We rejected a similar argument in *United States v. Myers*, in which the defendant argued "that the district court committed reversible error by failing to specifically instruct the jury that it must unanimously agree upon which of four drug transactions in evidence satisfied the distribution element necessary for a conviction on the . . . charge of drug trafficking **{-665-}** and on the . . . charge of possession and use of a firearm in furtherance of drug trafficking." **[—20—]** *United States v. Myers*, 280 F.3d 407, 414 (4th Cir. 2002). Reviewing for plain error, we assumed without deciding that *Richardson* could extend to § 924(c) but concluded that the defendant could not show "that the failure to give the instruction *resulted in* his conviction." *Id.* (emphasis added). We held that, "[g]iven the overwhelming evidence of drug distribution . . . , especially with respect to the transaction between [the defendant] and [a specific individual], the likelihood that the jury was confused or less than unanimous on all of the four transactions in evidence is

[16] The Government has not argued that Said procedurally defaulted this claim by failing to raise it before his convictions became final or on direct appeal, or that it is untimely.

exceedingly remote. Indeed, it strains credulity to conclude that, in finding [the defendant] guilty, the jury may not have been unanimous in concluding that he had distributed crack to [the specified individual]." *Id.* at 415.

So too here. The idea that even a single juror relied solely on the conspiracy charges, rather than the other violent crimes *of which the jury unanimously found Said guilty*, in convicting him of the § 924(c) charges in Counts 4 and 10, simply strains credulity for the reasons given above.[17] *See supra* at 14–15 & n.15. Said's assertion that such a counterintuitive vote was *possible* cannot satisfy his steep burden on habeas review.[18] **[—21—]** *Fowler v. Joyner*, 753 F.3d 446, 459 (4th Cir. 2014) (noting that on federal habeas review of constitutional errors, "we apply the more onerous[] harmless error analysis set forth in *Brecht*").

IV.

For the foregoing reasons, Said is not entitled to habeas relief on Counts 4 and 10. Accordingly, we reverse the district court's judgment ordering such relief and remand with instructions to deny Said's habeas petition as to Counts 4 and 10. Because we leave undisturbed the court's grant of habeas relief as to Count 9, however, we leave it to the district court to consider in the first instance whether to resentence Said on any other count under the sentencing-package doctrine, now that we have reinstated Counts 4 and 10.[19] **[—22—] {-666-}**

REVERSED IN PART AND REMANDED WITH INSTRUCTIONS

[17] We do not understand Said to be pressing a claim that there is a *Richardson* error even if all of the jurors *did* rely on at least one valid predicate (i.e., because we cannot know whether they all relied on the *same* valid predicate or predicates). To the extent he makes such an argument, we decline to address it as beyond the scope of his *Davis*-based § 2255 petition.

[18] We are not persuaded by Said's contention that rejecting his habeas claim would "create a deeply problematic loophole in the constitutional guarantee of unanimity in jury verdicts." Response Br. at 17. Any such "loophole" can be closed by a defendant objecting to the instructions and requesting unanimity instructions pursuant to *Richardson*, as Said could have done but failed to do here. Should the court reject the proposed instructions, such a defendant could then raise that preserved issue on direct appeal, subject to a much less stringent standard than the one we must apply in this case.

[19] *See United States v. Chaney*, 911 F.3d 222, 226 (4th Cir. 2018) ("[T]he 'sentence-package theory,' . . . we have recognized, provides that in appropriate circumstances resentencing on all counts is a proper remedy under § 2255 for a single unlawful conviction."); *United States v. Hillary*, 106 F.3d 1170, 1171 (4th Cir. 1997) (holding that § 2255(b) "confers a 'broad and flexible' power to the district courts 'to fashion an appropriate remedy'" (quoting *United States v. Garcia*, 956 F.2d 41, 45 (4th Cir. 1992))); *United States v. Smith*, 115 F.3d 241, 245 (4th Cir. 1997) (holding that since the term "sentence" in § 2255 "must be viewed in the aggregate," a district court has jurisdiction to conduct a resentencing on all surviving counts in a multi-count indictment when only one of the counts has been successfully challenged in a collateral proceeding); *United States v. Ventura*, 864 F.3d 301, 309 (4th Cir. 2017) (noting, in a direct appeal, that "[w]e agree with our sister circuits that 'when a defendant is found guilty on a multicount indictment, there is a strong likelihood that the district court will craft a disposition in which the sentences on the various counts form part of an overall plan,' and that if some counts are vacated, 'the judge should be free to review the efficacy of what remains in light of the original plan'" (quoting *United States v. Townsend*, 178 F.3d 558, 567 (D.C. Cir. 1999))); *cf. United States v. Hadden*, 475 F.3d 652, 669 (4th Cir. 2007) (affirming the district court's decision, in a § 2255 case, *not* to conduct a full resentencing where the district court struck a sentence on one count and "reenter[ed] the remaining sentence," thus "indicat[ing] that it was satisfied with the resulting sentence" (emphasis omitted)).

United States Court of Appeals
for the Fourth Circuit

No. 20-2268

IN RE NEWBROOK SHIPPING CORP.

Appeal from the United States District Court for the District of Maryland at Baltimore

Decided: April 20, 2022

Citation: 31 F.4th 889, 10 Adm. R. 122 (4th Cir. 2022).

Before **MOTZ, DIAZ,** and **RICHARDSON,** Circuit Judges.

[—3—] {–890–} RICHARDSON, Circuit Judge:

Nadella Corporation bought a ship, the MV *Falcon Carrier*, for scrap from Falcon Carrier Shipping Limited. Unbeknownst to Nadella, the ship was encumbered by $368,000 of debt. To recover that **{–891–}** debt, the debt holder "arrested"[1] Nadella's new ship. Nadella then tried to recover that debt from the ship's seller Falcon Carrier Shipping. These efforts have led to actual or planned legal action in four countries across multiple continents and the arrest of two other ships. In the latest legal flare up, Newbrook Shipping—the owner of those two ships arrested by Nadella—sued Nadella in South Africa and was considering another lawsuit in Nevis, a small island nation in the Caribbean. To support those actions, Newbrook applied in Maryland federal court for an ex parte order under 28 U.S.C. § 1782 authorizing discovery from Nadella's purported parent company, Global Marketing Systems. The district court seemed to reject discovery for the speculative "proceeding" in Nevis but then granted the full application. **[—4—]**

Global Marketing argues that the district court substantively erred in granting the entire application for discovery. Global Marketing also argues that the district court erred in approving service of process. We agree, vacating and remanding for further proceedings consistent with this opinion.

I. Background

A. The MV *Falcon Carrier*'s sale

In 2013, Falcon Carrier Shipping Limited sold the MV *Falcon Carrier* ("*Carrier*") to the Nadella Corporation. In doing so, Falcon Carrier Shipping warranted that the *Carrier* was free from liabilities and debts and agreed to indemnify Nadella for any claims. Nadella, a Nevis corporation owned by Global Marketing, bought the *Carrier* for scrap.

B. The MV *Falcon Carrier*'s arrest

After Nadella bought the *Carrier*, another company, Samchira, arrested the *Carrier* in the Supreme Court of Bangladesh. That action sought to recover around $368,000 of pre-sale debt associated with the ship. As a result, Nadella sought recovery for breach of contract from Falcon Carrier Shipping. That breach-of-contract claim is now being arbitrated in Singapore.

[1] Admiralty disputes often involve harm on the high seas or in multiple jurisdictions, and ship ownership can be uncertain. Because this confusion can make recovery difficult in a normal legal proceeding, liability can attach to the ship itself. *Perez & Compania (Cataluna), S.A. v. M/V Mexico I*, 826 F.2d 1449, 1451 (5th Cir. 1987). Parties allegedly harmed by the ship, such as those bringing claims for maritime torts or contract breaches, are said to have a "maritime lien" on the ship (or its cargo), and the maritime lien "confer[s] the right to sue the vessel itself *in rem*." *Bank One, La. N.A. v. Mr. Dean MV*, 293 F.3d 830, 832 (5th Cir. 2002); *see Amstar Corp. v. S/S Alexandros T.*, 664 F.2d 904, 908–09 (4th Cir. 1981); Barry Hunsaker, Jr., *Due Process in Admiralty Arrest and Attachment*, 56 Tex. L. Rev. 1091, 1093 (1978). These liens are enforced by "arresting" ships. In America, when a plaintiff files a complaint in federal court asserting a maritime lien through an *in rem* proceeding against the ship, "the clerk of the admiralty court issues a warrant for the arrest of the property and delivers it to the marshal for service." Hunsaker, *supra*, at 1095 (citing Fed. R. Civ. P. supp. rule C(3)). The marshal then seizes the ship as security to ensure payment from the ship's owner. Fed. R. Civ. P., supp. rule C(3)–(4). Similar procedures exist, as relevant here, in Bangladesh and South Africa.

C. The MV *Falcon Traveller*'s arrest

As security for its claim against Falcon Carrier Shipping, Nadella also began arrest proceedings in South Africa against a different ship, the MV *Falcon Traveller* ("*Traveller*"). The *Traveller* was owned by Newbrook. But Nadella argued that, despite this nominal difference in ownership, the *Traveller* and the *Carrier* were indirectly owned **[—5—]** by the same person and so were "associated" vessels under South African **{-892-}** law.[2] But a South African court disagreed, even though it found the assertion to be "subjectively honest." The court determined that Falcon Carrier Shipping (and thus, before Nadella's purchase, the *Carrier*) was owned by Nico Poons, while Newbrook (and thus the *Traveller*) was owned by Nico's father Ronald Poons. Because the two ships were not "associated," Nadella could not arrest the *Traveller* to cover losses from the bad deal it got on the *Carrier*.

Newbrook then sued Nadella—also in South Africa—seeking damages for the *Traveller*'s wrongful arrest. The South African court ordered Nadella to post a bond to cover its liability to Newbrook and to pay various costs. Nadella, citing a lack of funds, failed to post that bond, or to pay costs as ordered, and that issue apparently is still pending in South Africa. *See Nadella Corp. v. Motor Vessel* 'Falcon Confidence', No. AC5/19, High Court of South Africa (Western Cape Division), 14 para. 43 (Apr. 28, 2021) ("April Judgment") (saved as ECF opinion attachment).[3]

D. The MV *Falcon Confidence*'s arrest

Continuing its effort to secure its claim against Falcon Carrier Shipping, Nadella arrested another ship, the MV *Falcon Confidence* ("*Confidence*"), in South Africa in 2019. The *Confidence* is owned by Newbrook's subsidiary Falcon Confidence Shipping **[—6—]** Limited.[4] Nadella and Falcon Confidence Shipping are now litigating in South African courts whether the *Confidence* is an associated vessel to the *Carrier*. As Newbrook and Falcon Confidence Shipping contend that the vessels are unrelated, they have alleged that the arrest was wrongful.

E. The Federal Court action

That brings this journey to our shores. Newbrook believes that Nadella is owned by Global Marketing Systems, Inc., a Maryland corporation. Newbrook also believes Global Marketing is owned and controlled by Maryland resident Dr. Anil Sharma.[5] So Newbrook filed an ex parte application under 28 U.S.C. § 1782 in Maryland federal district court seeking discovery for use in this ongoing saga.

Under § 1782, a party in a foreign proceeding can obtain a discovery order for materials from an American target for use in the foreign proceeding. These applications are often decided ex parte, with the target having a chance to later challenge the discovery order. *See, e.g.*, **{-893-}** *Brandi-Dohrn v. IKB Deutsche Industriebank AG*, 673 F.3d 76, 82 (2d Cir. 2012). **[—7—]**

Here, Newbrook's application sought information from Global Marketing and Dr. Sharma about "the circumstances surrounding

[2] While we need not dive deep into South African maritime law, roughly speaking, an "associated" ship is one that is owned by the same person or company who owned the "ship concerned" during the time the claim arose. Admiralty Jurisdiction Regulation Act 105 of 1983 § 7.

[3] Global Marketing asked that we supplement the record by taking judicial notice of the April 2021 order by the South African court. We grant that request.

[4] In filing this § 1782 application, Newbrook was joined by its subsidiary. But as the reader will soon learn, the naming conventions used by Newbrook create some confusion. And that confusion ensnares even Newbrook itself. For example, the case's caption on Appellees' brief lists "Falcon *Confidential* Shipping Ltd.," as Newbrook's subsidiary. But their brief's contents—and *most* of the record—refer to "Falcon *Confidence* Shipping Ltd." We assume, for this appeal alone, that this reflects a scrivener's error and not separate entities.

[5] While Sharma was named in the application, he has never been effectively served with a subpoena and has never appeared before the district court. So he could not be subject to discovery yet. He is thus not a party to this appeal, and we do not address issues related to him.

Nadella's claim in the South African Action that the *Falcon Confidence* is a related ship to the *Falcon Carrier*." J.A. 12. Allegedly to support its claims of wrongful arrest—or more precisely, the claims of its subsidiary, Falcon Confidence Shipping—Newbrook requested a broad range of discovery including "documents and communications . . . sufficient to show any basis for Nadella's argument that the *Falcon Confidence* and *Falcon Carrier* are associated ships." J.A. 12. Newbrook also sought to depose Global Marketing and Dr. Sharma about topics including the "relation, affiliation, or connection" between the *Carrier* and the *Confidence*; the "ultimate beneficial ownership of Nadella" and "Sharma's relation, affiliation, or connection with Nadella"; "Nadella's intent or motive in arresting" both the *Confidence* and the *Traveller*; and information about Nadella's and Global Marketing's corporate forms. J.A. 40.

Newbrook's application was not limited to the current South Africa action involving the *Confidence*'s arrest. It also sought discovery for a contemplated action against Nadella in Nevis. But the district court rejected this action as too speculative, and Newbrook does not appeal that decision, so only the South African action is relevant here.

Based on the South Africa action, the district court granted Newbrook's ex parte discovery application in March 2020. Newbrook then tried to serve the subpoenas on Global Marketing by leaving them at Global Marketing's office with a trader—who appears to be involved in the purchase of ships or sale of scrap material. But the trader insisted that he was unauthorized to accept subpoenas. Global Marketing moved to strike service and quash the issued subpoenas on both service-of-process and substantive **[—8—]** grounds, arguing the service was improper because the subpoenas were not served on its registered agent and that the application for discovery was wrongly granted on its merits.

In November 2020, the district court denied Global Marketing's motion and ordered it to respond to the subpoena request within 30 days. Global Marketing timely appealed and persuaded the district court to stay the discovery order.

F. Recent South African court decision

Before this Court heard oral argument, the South African court issued a new ruling in the *Confidence*-arrest litigation. There, Nadella sought to require Falcon Confidence Shipping to "make further and better discovery." April Judgment at 8 para. 24.[6] The court granted that request and directed Falcon Confidence Shipping to produce the documents that Nadella requested. *Id.* at 19 para. 57.1. The court criticized Falcon Confidence Shipping for its "abject failure . . . to produce *any* documents of real substance pertaining to the management and control of the MV *Falcon Confidence*" and entered a punitive costs order against Falcon Confidence Shipping for "obstructing the conduct of the proceedings." *Id.* at 8 para. 23, 13 para. 39. **{-894-}**

In the same order, the court also addressed Falcon Confidence Shipping's request to compel both oral witness testimony and the production of documents in support of its argument that Nadella was a shell company that acted with unclean hands by using its **[—9—]** corporate structure to avoid paying legal costs to Newbrook. *Id.* at 14 para. 41. If Nadella acted with unclean hands, Falcon Confidence Shipping argued that Nadella could not seek relief in South African courts. But the South African court rejected Falcon Confidence Shipping's application, determining that the papers it submitted did not raise a factual dispute justifying further evidentiary factfinding. *Id.* at 15 para. 46. The court found that Falcon Confidence Shipping's discovery requests amounted to no more than a "'fishing expedition' with a view to ascertaining whether there might be a

---

[6] The documents Nadella sought pertained to "(1) the incorporation and business of [Falcon Confidence Shipping] and the purchase, financing and mortgaging of the MV *Falcon Confidence*, and its management, operation and alleged control by the company and/or by Ronald and/or Nico Poons; and (2) various corporate entities or trusts . . . which [Nadella] alleges form the structure in terms of which control of the vessel ultimately vested in Nico Poons." April Judgment at 10 para. 30.

possible defense available to them,'" which could not justify the discovery it sought. *Id.* at 17 para. 51. Finally, while not reaching a firm decision on the issue, the court expressed doubt that an unclean-hands defense was viable under the circumstances given recent amendments to the South African Constitution. *Id.* at 16–17 para. 50.

II. Discussion

The district court's § 1782 order is a final order, so we have jurisdiction under 28 U.S.C. § 1291. *See In re Naranjo*, 768 F.3d 332, 347 (4th Cir. 2014) ("Because the § 1782 order is a sufficiently final order, we have subject matter jurisdiction to hear an immediate appeal from a district court's order granting discovery under that statute."). And that final order encompasses the Global Marketing's challenge to the service of process. *See id. at* 343. We review the § 1782 order for abuse of discretion. *In re Letter of Request from Amtsgericht Ingolstadt, Fed. Republic of Germany*, 82 F.3d 590, 592 (4th Cir. 1996). And we review de novo the district court's denial of the motion to quash for insufficient service of process. *Colleton Prep. Academy, Inc. v. Hoover Univ., Inc.*, 616 F.3d 413, 421 n.9 (4th Cir. 2010). **[—10—]**

A. 28 U.S.C § 1782

Section 1782 represents nearly 150 years of efforts by Congress to encourage collaboration with foreign tribunals. *See* Act of March 3, 1873, ch. 245, 17 Stat. 581. The modern § 1782(a) provides:

> The district court of the district in which a person resides or is found may order him to give his testimony or statement or to produce a document or other thing for use in a proceeding in a foreign or international tribunal, including criminal investigations conducted before formal accusation. The order may be made pursuant to a letter rogatory issued, or request made, by a foreign or international tribunal or upon the application of any interested person and may direct that the testimony or statement be given, or the document or other thing be produced, before a person appointed by the court.

The statute identifies four mandatory conditions that must be satisfied before an application can be granted: (1) The application must be made to the "district court for the district in which the person resides or is found"; (2) the application must come from "an interested person" or a foreign tribunal; (3) the application must seek evidence, including "testimony" or "a document"; and (4) the evidence sought by the application must be "for use in a proceeding in a foreign or international tribunal." § 1782(a); *see Intel Corp. v. Advanced Micro Devices, Inc.*, 542 U.S. 241, 246 (2004).

We agree with the district court that the first three requirements are met here: The application was made to the proper court, **{-895-}** was made "by an interested person,"[7] and seeks **[—11—]** testimonial and documentary evidence. *See In re Clerici*, 481 F.3d 1324, 1331–32 (11th Cir. 2007).

But the last condition—that the evidence sought must be "for use" in a foreign proceeding—is not fully satisfied. The statute refers to each piece of relevant evidence in the singular, stating that a district court may order a person to give "his testimony or statement or to produce *a* document or *other thing* for use in a [foreign] proceeding," § 1782(a), so the applicant must show that each thing (or at least each category of things) sought is "for use" in the foreign proceeding. Merely showing that some evidence sought within the application as a whole has some "use" is not sufficient. That does not mean

---

[7] An "interested person" includes legal persons, such as business associations like Falcon Confidence Shipping and Newbrook. *See Intel*, 542 U.S. at 257. Falcon Confidence Shipping is a party to the proceeding in South Africa and qualifies as an interested party. (That is true so long as our assumption on appeal that references to Falcon *Confidential* Shipping are scrivener's errors.) It is less clear whether Newbrook—the parent company for Falcon Confidence Shipping—is an interested party to that action. But (Continued) **[—11—]** given the application is supported by one interested person, we need not decide whether Newbrook has a legitimate "interest" under § 1782 on appeal.

that each thing or category of things sought must be essential for victory in the foreign proceeding. *Mees v. Buiter*, 793 F.3d 291, 298 (2d Cir. 2015). But the court must find that there is a reasonable possibility that the evidence sought "will be employed with some advantage or serve some use in the proceeding." *Id.*

Two foreign proceedings were identified by Newbrook: the ongoing South African action related to the *Confidence*'s arrest and a proposed action in Nevis. The district court found that the South African action qualified but rejected the Nevis action as too speculative to be a "proceeding," a decision Newbrook does not challenge. But the Nevis action, Newbrook admitted, was the basis for seeking some of the evidence. And the district court seemed to agree that some evidence sought was for use in Nevis. Yet even after finding the Nevis action did not qualify as a proceeding because it was too speculative, **[—12—]** the district court granted the entire § 1782 application, without restricting the evidence sought to what would be "for use" in the South Africa action.

Newbrook suggests that the district court implicitly limited the discovery application to items that would be for use in South Africa. We do not read the district court's order as imposing such a limitation, given that it stated that it was denying Global Marketing's motion to quash and generally ordered Global Marketing to respond. Nor should it fall to Global Marketing to guess at which documents Newbrook wants for which actions; if the district court narrowed the subpoena's scope, it should say so clearly so that Global Marketing knows which documents it must produce and what, if any, deposition questions it must be prepared to answer.

There may well be some overlap between the two actions but satisfying the for-use condition required specifying the evidence sought for the South African action (the only qualifying foreign action). Merely including one permissible category cannot bless a list of other, impermissibly sought evidence. This record's complexity counsels us to vacate and remand this issue to the district court, to determine which evidence, if any, is really "for use" in the South African action. This is particularly appropriate after the recent South African court decision clarified the scope of the South African proceedings and required **{-896-}** Falcon Confidence Shipping to comply with existing discovery requests in that jurisdiction, which may well bear on the "for use" requirement (and also perhaps the discretionary *Intel* factors discussed below).

If the district court determines on remand that certain evidence is "for use" in the South Africa action, that would not end the inquiry. For even where these four statutory **[—13—]** conditions are satisfied, the district court retains discretion in granting or denying these orders. *Intel*, 542 U.S. at 247 ("[Section] 1782(a) authorizes, but does not require, a federal district court to provide judicial assistance."); *see also* § 1782 (stating that a "district court . . . *may* order" the discovery (emphasis added)). The Supreme Court has explained that in exercising its discretion, the court should conduct an equity-like balancing test, paying particular attention to the four factors identified in *Intel*: (1) the involvement of "the person from whom discovery is sought" in the foreign proceeding, (2) "the nature of the foreign tribunal, the character of the proceedings underway abroad, and the receptivity of the foreign government, court or agency to U.S. federal-court judicial assistance," (3) "whether the § 1782(a) request conceals an attempt to circumvent foreign proof-gathering restrictions or other policies of a foreign country or the United States," and (4) whether the request is "unduly intrusive or burdensome" in which case it "may be rejected or trimmed." *Intel*, 542 U.S. at 264–65. Like the threshold requirements, these four discretionary factors should be applied to each thing sought by the application. The ultimate balance remains well within the district court's broad discretion and addresses common discovery concerns. *Cf. Virginia Dep't of Corr. v. Jordan*, 921 F.3d 180, 189 (4th Cir. 2019) (discussing when a Rule 45 subpoena subjects a non-party to undue burden). So we leave this consideration to the district court on remand. **[—14—]**

In remanding, we leave in the district court's capable hands what evidence satisfies the for-use condition and how the discretionary *Intel* factors should be applied to any evidence that does.[8]

B. Adequacy of Service of Subpoenas

Section 1782 orders are generally governed by the Federal Rules of Civil Procedure. § 1782 ("To the extent that the order does not prescribe otherwise, the testimony or statement shall be taken, and the document or other thing produced, in accordance with the Federal Rules of Civil Procedure."); *see Gov't of Ghana v. ProEnergy Servs., LLC*, 677 F.3d 340, 343 (8th Cir. 2012). Though the district judge can prescribe different rules, the court here agreed that the discovery sought "shall be governed by the Federal Rules of Civil Procedure." J.A. 67; *see* 28 U.S.C. §1782 (noting that the district court "may prescribe the practice and procedure, which may be in whole or part the practice and procedure of the foreign country or the international tribunal, for taking the testimony or statement or producing the document or other thing").

The district court's order authorized Newbrook "to use and serve a subpoena on the Discovery Targets" to compel discovery. J.A. 67. Federal Rule of Civil Procedure 45 governs a subpoena's service, and "requires delivering a copy to the named person." Fed. R. Civ. P. 45(b)(1). **{-897-}** But for a corporation or other artificial entity, the entity is not a "person" on whom service can be directly made. *See* 9 James Wm. Moore et al., *Moore's* **[—15—]** *Federal Practice - Civil* § 45.21 (2021). A plaintiff cannot hand a document directly to an abstraction, so that abstraction must be served through an agent. *See Daimler AG v. Bauman*, 571 U.S. 117, 135 n. 13 (2014) ("A corporation is a distinct legal entity that can act only through its agents.") (quoting 1 William Fletcher, *Fletcher Cyclopedia of the Law of Corporations* § 30, at 30 (Supp. 2012–2013)).

But the question remains to which agent the subpoena must be "delivered," and how. Fortunately, the Federal Rules give us some guidance by showing how to serve corporations generally. Rule 4(h)(1) identifies two ways a domestic corporation may be served with a summons and complaint:

> (A) in the manner prescribed by Rule 4(e)(1) for serving an individual; or
>
> (B) by delivering a copy of the summons and of the complaint to an officer, a managing or general agent, or any other agent authorized by appointment or by law to receive service of process and—if the agent is one authorized by statute and the statute so requires—by also mailing a copy of each to the defendant.

Rule 4(e)(1) permits an individual to be served in a manner permitted by "state law for serving a summons in an action brought in courts of general jurisdiction in the state where the district court is located or where service is made." Maryland Rule 2-124(d) first provides for service upon a corporation "by serving its resident agent, president, secretary, or treasurer." But "if a good faith attempt to serve the resident agent, president, secretary, or treasurer has failed, service may be made by serving the manager, any director, vice president, assistant secretary, assistant treasurer, or other person expressly or impliedly authorized to receive service of process." Maryland Rule 2-124(d). **[—16—]**

The second service method for a corporation also expressly permits "delivering" the complaint to certain officers or agents: "an officer, a managing or general agent, or any other agent authorized by appointment or by law to receive service of process." Fed. R. Civ. P. 4(h)(1)(B). So to satisfy Rule 45's mandate of "delivering a copy to the named person" when the "person" is a corporation, there must be delivery to an appropriate agent, as identified by Rule 4(h).

[8] We also note that the order to comply could be read to suggest that Sharma must individually comply with the discovery required from him. But before the court may order discovery from Sharma, he must be served.

Some courts have ventured beyond that required by the Rules to permit service by any means that provides actual notice. Doing so, they have reasoned, conserves resources that would be wasted if compliance with the Rules was required. *Stiles v. Walmart, Inc.*, No. 1:20-mc-002, 2020 WL 1976426, at *4 (S.D. Ohio Apr. 24, 2020); *see Greenway Enterprises, Inc. v. CSI Eng'g, P.C.*, No. AW-07-2762, 2008 WL 11509733, at *1 (D. Md. May 23, 2008). And we do not doubt that broader means of service would save resources—though perhaps imposing other costs. But regardless of its wisdom, Rule 45 requires that the subpoena be served by "delivering a copy to the named person." Actual notice with no delivery to the named person fails to satisfy the Rule's demands.[9] **[—17—] {-898-}**

The district court did not address whether an appropriate agent—as identified in Maryland Rule 2-124(d) or Federal Rule 4(h)(2)—was served in this case. This inquiry depends on applying agency law to the circumstances of service here. And we leave that in the district court's capable hands.

* * *

Section 1782 applications give litigants access to federal courts to obtain discovery for use in international litigation. But that access is not unlimited. Among other threshold requirements, the requested discovery must be for use in a reasonably contemplated, non-speculative proceeding. Because the district court held that the speculative proceeding in Nevis did not provide a basis for § 1782 discovery, the court erred by granting the full application. So we must remand for further proceedings. We also remand for the district court to consider Global Marketing's argument that it was not properly served under the Federal Rules. So the saga does not end here, and the litigants must set out for the district court once more.

VACATED AND REMANDED

---

[9] While we hold that there must be delivery, we need not decide here "how" that delivery must occur. The predominant view appears to be that the delivery must be directly delivered by a process server personally (often referred to as "personal service"). *See* Charles A. Wright & Arthur A. Miller, 9A *Federal Practice and Procedure* § 2454 (3d ed. 2021). But at least one Circuit Court has suggested that delivery under Rule 45 may be accomplished through certified mail by the United States Postal Service. *See Ott v. City of Milwaukee*, 682 F.3d 552, 557 (7th Cir. 2012) (finding certified mail satisfies Rule 45's delivery requirement because the postal agent qualifies as "the person at least 18 years of age" such that the postal proof-of-delivery record shows a "delivery"); *see also Hall v. Sullivan*, 229 F.R.D. 501, 503–06 (D. Md. 2005). Certified mail was not used here so we need not delve into whether delivery methods such as certified mail to a corporate agent would suffice.

United States Court of Appeals for the Fourth Circuit

No. 21-1607

SING FUELS PTE LTD.
vs.
M/V LILA SHANGHAI

Appeal from the United States District Court for the Eastern District of Virginia at Newport News

Decided: July 1, 2022

Citation: 39 F.4th 263, 10 Adm. R. 129 (4th Cir. 2022).

Before **WILKINSON** and **DIAZ,** Circuit Judges, and **FLOYD,** Senior Circuit Judge.

[—2—] {-266-} FLOYD, Senior Circuit Judge:

This dispute concerns whether an international trader of bunker fuel is entitled to a maritime lien on a vessel under the Commercial Instrument and Maritime Lien Act (CIMLA), 46 U.S.C. §§ 31301–43. Because, in this case, the bunker trader failed to show that it procured the vessel's fuel "on the order of the owner or a person authorized by the owner," § 31342(a), we affirm the district court's judgment denying the maritime lien.

I.

A.

Built in 2011, the M/V LILA SHANGHAI (the Vessel) is a gross tonnage bulk carrier owned by Autumn Harvest Maritime Co. (Autumn Harvest).[1] As the owner, Autumn Harvest time-chartered the Vessel to Bostomar Bulk Shipping Pte Ltd. (Bostomar) from April 25, 2019, to December 31, 2019. To memorialize their arrangement, Autumn Harvest and Bostomar entered into a maritime contract known as a time charter party.[2] The time charter party provided "[t]hat whilst on hire the Charterers shall provide and pay for **[—3—]** all the fuel except as otherwise agreed . . . ."[3] J.A. 792. It foreclosed charterers **{-267-}** from unilaterally placing liens on the Vessel, expressly stating: "Charterers will not suffer, nor permit to be continued, any lien or encumbrance incurred by them or their agents, which might have priority over the title and interest of the owners in the vessel." J.A. 795. In the event of "any dispute" between Autumn Harvest and Bostomar about the Vessel and their respective obligations, the time charter party required "the matter in dispute . . . be referred to three persons at [sic] Singapore" for arbitration proceedings. J.A. 795.

After agreeing to those provisions, Bostomar sub-chartered the Vessel to Medmar Inc. (Medmar), a company in Greece known for chartering ships for international voyages.[4] On June 10, 2019, Medmar received the Vessel for an excursion from Argentina to India. While sailing to India, the Vessel needed bunkers to complete its journey.[5] Around June 28, 2019, Costas Mylonakis, an employee of Windrose Marine, contacted Appellant Sing Fuels Pte. Ltd. (Sing Fuels) to order the Vessel's bunkers.

---

[1] Bulk carriers are used to transport large quantities of unpackaged cargo, including, but not limited to, coal, grain, and iron ore. Rosalie Balkin, *The International Maritime Organization and Maritime Security*, 30 Tul. Mar. L.J. 1, 33 (2006).

[2] "A time charter party is a contract between a vessel owner and charterer whereby the charterer pays the owner a fixed monthly sum for the use of the vessel during the period covered by the charter." *Trans-Asiatic Oil Ltd., S.A. v. Apex Oil Co.*, 804 F.2d 773, 775 n.3 (1st Cir. 1986). Also known more simply as "time charter," a time charter party also describes how "the charterer and owner share duties for the carriage of goods for a specified time." *Yeramex Int'l v. S.S. Tendo*, 595 F.2d 943, 946 (4th Cir. 1979). Time charter parties have "commercial objective[s]" and "divide the duties for navigation and seaworthiness of the ship and for the handling of cargo among the owner and charterer, with the expectation that both will benefit from the vessel's earnings." *Id.*

[3] The parties only included a "working copy" of the time charter party within the record, and this "working copy" is not memorialized between Autumn Harvest and Bostomar. J.A. 790–835. In any event, the parties do not contest the existence of a binding time charter party, nor do they disagree over the contents of the "working copy."

[4] The record does not contain any express agreement between Medmar and Bostomar.

[5] Within the maritime industry, "bunkers" is a term referring to "marine fuels of various grades and specifications." J.A. 446.

A worldwide trader of bunkers, Sing Fuels's main office is in Singapore, but it also maintains offices in South Africa, Dubai, Greece, and the United Kingdom. In typical transactions, such as here, a potential customer contacts a salesperson with Sing Fuels and asks about a delivery of bunkers to a given port. After receiving the request, Sing Fuels's **[—4—]** salesperson then contacts physical suppliers who can deliver the bunkers, obtains multiple prices for the customer's consideration, and eventually finds an agreeable price. Sing Fuels then issues a sales and purchase order for both the customer and the physical supplier.

On July 1, 2019, Sing Fuels transmitted its Sales Order Confirmation, which included the Terms and Conditions of Sale for Marine Fuels 2017 (bunker contract), only to Mylonakis's e-mail address affiliated with Windrose Marine. Within the e-mail, which did not copy Medmar, Sing Fuels stated: "MERE RECEIPT OF THIS CONFIRMATION SIGNIFIES ACCEPTANCE OF RESPONSIBILITY FOR PAYMENT OF OUR BUNKER INVOICE BY EACH AND ALL OF THEM." J.A. 522. The e-mail also asked Mylonakis to obtain Medmar's signature and company stamp on the Sales Order Confirmation, which billed the request for bunkers to an account associated with Medmar.[6] Mylonakis never returned any memorialized document from Medmar. Sing Fuels exclusively communicated with Mylonakis for this transaction, considered Mylonakis to be Medmar's fuel broker, and never spoke directly with Medmar. Mylonakis also never communicated with Medmar, he conferred instead with a mysterious entity called M.A.C. Shipping.

When the Vessel reached Port Elizabeth, South Africa, it physically received bunkers on two occasions in July (the July bunkers) from South African Marine Fuels, a subsidiary of Addax Energy SA. First, on July 10, 2019, the Vessel received 595.888 **[—5—]** metric tons, 380 centistokes (cst), of bunkers. Second, on July 12, 2019, the **{–268–}** Vessel received 459.038 metric tons, 380 cst, of bunkers. The Vessel received, in total, 1,049.296 metric tons, 380 cst, of bunkers, amounting to $532,312.48 in fuel. *See* J.A. 551 (tax invoice for the July bunkers). For both deliveries, either the Vessel's Master or Chief Engineer indicated receipt of the bunkers. *See* J.A. 549–50 (Bunker Delivery Notes). All the July bunkers were consumed by the Vessel.

Medmar returned the Vessel to Bostomar on August 12, 2019, with Sing Fuels still awaiting payment for the July bunkers. By October 2019, payment for the July bunkers was still outstanding, so Sing Fuels sent Autumn Harvest a notice of nonpayment, requesting an immediate disbursement in the amount of $540,527.71. *See* J.A. 552–54 (notice to Autumn Harvest requesting payment for the July bunkers). In February 2020, Sing Fuels formally met with Autumn Harvest to discuss the payment for the July bunkers. Autumn Harvest refused to pay. In the wake of the collapsed negotiations, Sing Fuels paid the physical supplier of the July bunkers.

According to Sing Fuels, over the course of 2019, it engaged in eight transactions with Medmar and always obtained timely payments, including for a delivery of bunkers totaling $300,000.00 in May 2019.[7] Yet, Sing Fuels never identified what corporate entity or who within that entity paid those bills for Medmar. Without knowing where to turn after **[—6—]** Medmar's payment default on the July bunkers, and its discussions with Autumn Harvest exhausted, Sing Fuels started tracking the Vessel on a regular basis.[8] Even though Sing Fuels had opportunities to arrest the Vessel at other ports, including in the United Kingdom and India, it declined to do so. Instead, it waited until the Vessel docked

[6] The record does not contain a signed or company-stamped document from either Mylonakis or Medmar because, despite its request, Sing Fuels never received one.

[7] Besides testimony from one of Sing Fuels's witnesses, the record does not contain documentary evidence of these prior transactions, and Sing Fuels never proffered any such evidence at its bench trial. At oral argument, Sing Fuels's counsel confirmed that such documentary evidence was never introduced, let alone admitted, at trial.

[8] The record does not suggest that Sing Fuels ever sought payment directly from Medmar.

in the United States and then availed itself of our federal courts to recoup payment for the July bunkers.

B.

Pursuing an action in rem, Sing Fuels filed its Verified Complaint against the Vessel in the United States District Court for the Eastern District of Virginia on April 22, 2020. It sought two forms of relief against the Vessel. First, moving under Rule C of the Supplemental Rules of Admiralty and Maritime Claims and Asset Forfeiture Actions, Sing Fuels requested the Vessel's arrest at port in the Eastern District of Virginia. Second, upon a successful arrest, it wanted a maritime lien placed on the Vessel pursuant to the CIMLA, 46 U.S.C. §§ 31301–43, for the amount owed on the July bunkers, $532,312.48.

On April 24, 2020, the district court issued a warrant for the Vessel's arrest upon its arrival in Virginia. The United States Marshals Service arrested and seized the Vessel, with the National Maritime Services (NMS) serving as the Vessel's substitute custodian. Four days later, on April 28, 2020, Autumn Harvest posted its Letter of Undertaking to serve as substitute security, allowing it to stand in the Vessel's place. After approving **[—7—]** Autumn Harvest as substitute security, the court ordered NMS to release the Vessel, and Autumn Harvest filed its Answer to the Verified Complaint on June 1, 2020.[9] **{-269-}**

When settlement discussions failed, a bench trial ensued. With the parties stipulating to certain facts and exhibits, the district court held its one-day trial on February 23, 2021. Sing Fuels only proffered two witnesses, both of whom it employed: (1) Ulrich Rasmussen, a vice president of credit risk, and (2) Stella Lykouri, a senior bunker trader. *See* J.A. 446 (Rasmussen's testimony); J.A. 502 (Lykouri's testimony); *see also* Witness List, *Sing Fuels Pte. Ltd. v. M/V Lila Shanghai*, 534 F. Supp. 3d 551 (E.D. Va. 2021) (No. 4:20-cv-00058-RAJ-LRL), ECF No. 41-1. Sing Fuels never called Mylonakis to testify, nor did it call anyone associated with Medmar, Windrose Marine, or M.A.C. Shipping.[10] *See* Witness List, *Sing Fuels Pte. Ltd.*, 534 F. Supp. 3d 551 (No. 4:20-cv-00058-RAJ-LRL), ECF No. 41-1. In terms of exhibits, Sing Fuels submitted the bunker contract, bunker delivery notes, an invoice, and four e-mails, all involving the July bunkers, into evidence. Exhibit List, *Sing Fuels Pte. Ltd.*, 534 F. Supp. 3d 551 (No. 4:20-cv-00058-RAJ-LRL), ECF No. 41-2. It did not provide any other documents showing prior transactions involving Medmar, Mylonakis, Windrose Marine, or M.A.C. Shipping. *See id.* At the trial's conclusion, the court ordered the parties to submit post-trial briefs within thirty days. **[—8—]**

After receiving the parties' post-trial briefs, the district court issued its order and opinion in favor of the Vessel on April 20, 2021, entering a judgment that same day. *Sing Fuels Pte. Ltd.*, 534 F. Supp. 3d at 555. Making findings of fact and conclusions of law, the court first determined that United States law, as opposed to Singapore law, governed the parties' dispute. *Id.* at 563–66. Applying United States law, the court then turned to the existence of a maritime lien and whether equitable laches barred Sing Fuels's action. *Id.* at 566–73.

The court first held that Mylonakis did not possess any actual, apparent, or presumed authority to hold the Vessel liable for the July bunkers. *Id.* at 566–69. Regarding actual authority, the court determined that the time charter party precluded Medmar from placing liens on the Vessel. *Id.* at 566–67. As for apparent or presumed authority, the court held the record, at best, showed a "tenuous relationship" between Mylonakis and Medmar, and "no documentation" demon-

[9] Neither Medmar, Windrose Marine, nor M.A.C. Shipping were ever made parties to the action.

[10] The district court's Final Pretrial Order lists Mylonakis as a fact witness for Sing Fuels, however, Sing Fuels never called him as a witness for the bench trial even though the court conditionally overruled Autumn Harvest's objection to his testimony. *See* Final Pretrial Order, *Sing Fuels Pte. Ltd.*, 534 F. Supp. 3d 551 (No. 4:20-cv-00058-RAJ-LRL), ECF No. 31.

strated Mylonakis as an agent for Autumn Harvest, Bostomar, or Medmar. *Id.* at 567–68. Additionally, the court found that Mylonakis ordered the bunkers for M.A.C. Shipping, not Medmar, with nothing indicating whether those two entities were related. *Id.* As an alternative ground for resolution, the court next held that the doctrine of equitable laches barred Sing Fuels's suit because (1) Sing Fuels never presented a "satisfactory excuse" for its delay in bringing the action, and (2) the Vessel would be unfairly prejudiced if the action continued. *Id.* at 569–73. Accordingly, relying on both distinct conclusions, the district court ruled in the Vessel's favor. **[—9—]**

Sing Fuels timely appeals the district court's judgment, challenging both the maritime lien's existence and application of equitable laches as a bar to suit. We have jurisdiction under 28 U.S.C. § 1291.

II.

"We review a judgment following a bench trial under a mixed standard of **{-270-}** review—factual findings may be reversed only if clearly erroneous, while conclusions of law, including contract construction, are examined de novo." *Roanoke Cement Co., L.L.C. v. Falk Corp.*, 413 F.3d 431, 433 (4th Cir. 2005) (citations omitted). And we will "not disturb the district court's factual findings if they are 'plausible in light of the record viewed in its entirety.'" *Heyer v. U.S. Bureau of Prisons*, 984 F.3d 347, 355 (4th Cir. 2021) (quoting *Anderson v. City of Bessemer*, 470 U.S. 564, 574 (1985)).

"But while clear error review is deferential, it is not toothless." *Butts v. United States*, 930 F.3d 234, 238 (4th Cir. 2019) (citing *United States v. Wooden*, 693 F.3d 440, 452 (4th Cir. 2012)). "Factual findings made by the district court are not 'so sacrosanct as to evade review,' and this Court may reverse those findings when definitely and firmly convinced they are mistaken after a review of the full record." *Heyer*, 984 F.3d at 355 (quoting *Jiminez v. Mary Washington Coll.*, 57 F.3d 369, 379 (4th Cir. 1995)). There are four grounds permitting us to reverse factual findings: "(1) they were derived under an incorrect legal standard, (2) they 'are not supported by substantial evidence,' (3) they were made while ignoring 'substantial evidence' supporting the opposite conclusion, and (4) **[—10—]** they are 'contrary to the clear weight of the evidence.'" *Id.* (quoting *Jiminez*, 57 F.3d at 379).

III.

A.

Before we address Sing Fuels's arguments about its entitlement to a maritime lien, we briefly consider the threshold issue of which country's laws apply to this case. *World Fuel Servs. Trading, DMCC v. Hebei Prince Shipping Co., Ltd.*, 783 F.3d 507, 513, 3 Adm. R. 201, 204 (4th Cir. 2015). Choice-of-law determinations are questions of law that we review de novo. *Richard v. Anadarko Petroleum Corp.*, 850 F.3d 701, 707, 5 Adm. R. 217, 219 (5th Cir. 2017); *Dresdner Bank AG v. M/V Olympia Voyager*, 463 F.3d 1210, 1214 (11th Cir. 2006).

"In the absence of a contractual choice-of-law clause, federal courts sitting in admiralty apply federal maritime choice-of-law principles derived from the Supreme Court's decision in *Lauritzen v. Larsen*, 345 U.S. 571, 73 S. Ct. 921, 97 L. Ed. 1254 (1953), and its progeny." *Chan v. Soc'y of Expeditions, Inc.*, 123 F.3d 1287, 1296 (9th Cir. 1997) (citations omitted). "Where the parties have specified in their contract which law should apply to their transaction, however, 'admiralty courts will generally give effect to that choice.'" *Triton Marine Fuels Ltd., S.A. v. M/V Pac. Chukotka*, 575 F.3d 409, 413 (4th Cir. 2009) (quoting *Hawkspere Shipping Co., Ltd. v. Intamex, S.A.*, 330 F.3d 225, 233 (4th Cir. 2003)). Unless there is a compelling reason of public policy, this Court will enforce a "freely negotiated choice-of-law clause in a maritime contract . . . ." *Id.* (citations omitted). **[—11—]**

Assuming its validity as the parties have, the bunker contract—purportedly for Medmar but only transmitted to Mylonakis—contains a choice-of-law provision permitting Sing Fuels to choose any jurisdiction that it wishes in order to obtain a maritime lien. Clause 23.1 provides: "*Without derogation from Clause 23.7*, the Contract shall be governed by and construed in accordance with the laws of Singapore." J.A. 546 (emphasis added). In turn, and in full, Clause 23.7 clearly states:

> Notwithstanding the Clauses above, the Seller is free to bring suit in any jurisdiction and shall be entitled to avail itself of all remedies under maritime or other law to obtain jurisdiction and/or security for its claims against Buyer, its **{–271–}** agents or affiliates, the Vessel, the Owners and charterers and any of their respective agents, servants or assigns, including but not limited to vessel arrest and attachment procedures, similar laws, rules or statutes in any jurisdiction. *Further, the Seller may apply and benefit from any law in any jurisdiction which grants the Seller a maritime lien* and/or right to arrest the Vessel and the parties' rights and remedies under the Contract shall at the Seller's election be resolved by that law to the exclusion of Singapore law.

J.A. 547 (emphasis added). Clause 23.7 complements clause 12.2, the latter of which discusses liens and guarantees: "The Seller . . . shall, among other things, *enjoy the full benefit of local legislation granting the Seller a maritime lien on the Vessel* and/or providing for the right to arrest the Vessel." J.A. 535 (emphasis added). Clause 12.2 goes on, explaining that "[n]othing in the Contract shall be construed to limit the rights and/or legal remedies that the Seller may enjoy against the Vessel or the Buyer in any jurisdiction." J.A. 535. At first blush, clauses 12.2 and 23.7 provide Sing Fuels with a right to seek a maritime lien in the jurisdiction of its choosing because, under those terms, it can expressly (1) "apply and benefit from any law in any jurisdiction which grants [it] a **[—12—]** maritime lien," and (2) "enjoy the full benefit of local legislation granting [it] a maritime lien on the Vessel . . . ." J.A. 535, 547.

Confronted with these unfavorable provisions and completely ignoring clause 12.2, Autumn Harvest argues that clause 23.7 is invalid and unenforceable under Singapore law because that jurisdiction "does not allow these 'floating' choice of law provisions . . . ." Autumn Harvest's Resp. Br. 39. Without clause 23.7, according to Autumn Harvest, there is "no basis" to apply United States law, and Singapore, whose laws would then apply, does not recognize maritime liens. *Id.* at 37, 40; *see also* Sing Fuels's Reply Br. 19. Although it prefers the adoption of United States law, Sing Fuels maintains that clause 23.7 is valid under Singapore law when characterized as a "variation clause," and, even if clause 23.7 is rendered null, Singapore law still requires we employ United States law as the lex fori.[11] Sing Fuels's Reply Br. 19–21.

In the context of maritime liens, our Court has only addressed the enforceability of a choice-of-law provision containing an explicit reference to United States law and not to "any law in any jurisdiction" or "local legislation." *See Triton Marine*, 575 F.3d at 412–16. Some federal courts have enforced contractual language authorizing parties to enforce maritime liens in "any jurisdiction in accordance with local law in such jurisdiction." *See Liverpool & London S.S. Prot. & Indem. Ass'n Ltd. v. Queen of Leman MV*, 296 F.3d 350, 353 (5th Cir. 2002); *cf. Bominflot, Inc. v. M/V Henrich S*, 465 F.3d 144, 147–48 (4th Cir. 2006) (applying English law when the contracting parties *did not* specify any other law **[—13—]** within the maritime agreement). To be sure, there is little case law ruling on the enforceability of choice-of-law provisions that permit parties to obtain maritime liens under "any jurisdiction's" laws, let alone under Singapore law.

But fortunately, we need not delve into the parties' complex arguments about the choice-of-law question or formally decide whether Singapore law prohibits clause 23.7, precluding its enforcement. Generally, "when the resolution of a choice-of-law determination would not alter **{–272–}** the disposition of a

---

[11] Lex fori refers to "[t]he law of the forum" or, in other words, "the law of the jurisdiction where the case is pending." *Lex Fori*, Black's Law Dictionary (11th ed. 2019).

legal question, a reviewing court need not decide which body of law controls." *Okmyansky v. Herbalife Int'l of Am., Inc.*, 415 F.3d 154, 158 (1st Cir. 2005) (citations omitted); *see also Int'l Adm'rs, Inc. v. Life Ins. Co. of N. Am.*, 753 F.2d 1373, 1376 n.4 (7th Cir. 1985) ("Conflicts rules are appealed to only when a difference in law will make a difference to the outcome." (citation omitted)). In *World Fuel Services Trading, DMCC v. Hebei Prince Shipping Co., Ltd.*, we agreed with a district court that a choice-of-law inquiry, involving Greek law and United States law, was unwarranted when either law's exercise "[made] no discernible difference to the relevant analysis in the case at bar." 783 F.3d at 514–15, 3 Adm. R. at 205 (citations omitted).

In the case at hand, Singapore law prohibits maritime liens on vessels as a means to obtain payment for bunkers.[12] And as we conclude below, the specific facts of this case **[—14—]** do not permit a maritime lien under United States law. *See infra* Part III.B. So regardless of whether we follow Singapore law or United States law, a maritime lien is not permitted, and the outcome is the same. We therefore follow the district court's sound approach and forge ahead with applying United States law regarding the existence of a maritime lien on the Vessel.[13] *See Hebei Prince Shipping*, 783 F.3d at 514–15, 3 Adm. R. at 205–06 (following a district court's employ of Greek law after similarly concluding that the choice-of-law question did not need resolution).

B.

The primary dispute between the parties is whether the district court properly denied Sing Fuels's request for a maritime lien under the CIMLA. Sing Fuels stresses that it provided the July bunkers only because Mylonakis "act[ed] with the apparent authority and as agent [for] Medmar . . . ." Sing Fuels's Opening Br. 25.[14] Autumn Harvest maintains **[—15—]** that the determination of an agency relationship is a question of fact under maritime law, the district court did not clearly err in declining to find such a relationship, and Sing Fuels failed to prove its case. *See* Autumn **{-273-}** Harvest's Resp. Br. 14–23. On the limited facts before us, Autumn Harvest's arguments must carry the day. Sing Fuels failed to carry its evidentiary burden, and we hold that the district court's agency ruling is not clearly erroneous.

1.

"A maritime lien 'is a right in the vessel' that entitles a vessel's creditor to have the vessel sold in order to satisfy an outstanding debt." *Addax Energy SA v. M/V Yasa H. Mulla*, 987 F.3d 80, 86, 9 Adm. R. 156, 159

---

[12] Some federal courts insist: "Singapore law does not recognize maritime liens." *World Fuel Servs. Singapore Pte, Ltd. v. Bulk Juliana M/V*, 822 F.3d 766, 772, 4 Adm. R. 240, 243–44 (5th Cir. 2016) (citing *Sembawang Shipyard, Ltd. v. Charger, Inc.*, 955 F.2d 983, 988 (5th Cir. 1992)). Both parties also believe this is the law of Singapore. *See* Autumn Harvest's Opening Br. 37; Sing Fuels's Reply Br. 19. But we believe that Singapore law is more nuanced. Singapore has traditionally recognized maritime liens but only for "salvage, seamen's wages, master's wages [and] disbursements[,] and liabilities and damage." J.A. 704 (Continued) **[—14—]** (quoting *The 'Halcyon Isle'*, [1977–1978] SLR(R) 11 (Sing.)); *see also Bankers Tr. Int'l Ltd. v. Todd Shipyards Corp.* [1981] AC 221 (PC) (appeal taken from Sing.); 17(2) Halsbury's Laws of Singapore ¶ 220.0168 (2020). However, maritime liens for a ship's liabilities for goods and services, typically called bottomry, are now obsolete. *Bankers Tr. Int'l Ltd. v. Todd Shipyards Corp.* [1981] AC 221 (PC) (appeal taken from Sing.). Thus, under Singapore law, payment for bunkers is not one of the explicit categories where maritime liens are available. Sing Fuels never suggests otherwise.

[13] We further note that Autumn Harvest's briefing primarily rests on United States law, leaving the choice-of-law question as an alternative ground for affirming the district court. Autumn Harvest's Resp. Br. 36–41. And at oral argument, Autumn Harvest focused on United States law and did not press for Singapore law at all.

[14] To the extent Sing Fuels attempts to rely on any other agency theories for its maritime lien, those were never briefed and are now waived. *See Grayson O Co. v. Agadir Int'l LLC*, 856 F.3d 307, 316 (4th Cir. 2017) ("A party waives an argument by failing to present (Continued) **[—15—]** it in its opening brief . . . ." (citation omitted)). Accordingly, we only concern ourselves with apparent agency.

(4th Cir. 2021) (quoting *Itel Containers Int'l Corp. v. Atlanttrafik Express Serv. Ltd.*, 982 F.2d 765, 768 (2d Cir. 1992)). The United States "allow[s] for broader use and enforcement of maritime liens, including the creation of a statutory right to a maritime lien for necessaries . . . ." *Bominflot*, 465 F.3d at 147 (citations omitted). The CIMLA grants parties a statutory avenue to obtain maritime liens:

> (a) . . . [A] person providing necessaries to a vessel on the order of the owner or a person authorized by the owner—
> (1) has a maritime lien on the vessel;
> (2) may bring a civil action in rem to enforce the lien; and
> (3) is not required to allege or prove in the action that credit was given to the vessel. **[—16—]**

46 U.S.C. § 31342(a)(1)–(3). So to prove the existence of a maritime lien under the CIMLA, a party must show the following: (1) "a person providing necessaries"; (2) "to a vessel"; and (3) "on the order of the owner or a person authorized by the owner." § 31342(a); *see also ING Bank N.V. v. Bomin Bunker Oil Corp.*, 953 F.3d 390, 393–94, 8 Adm. R. 169, 171 (5th Cir. 2020) (same).

The CIMLA further states that certain "persons" are "presumed" to possess authority to obtain a vessel's necessaries, including:

> (1) the owner;
> (2) the master;
> (3) a person entrusted with the management of the vessel at the port of supply; or
> (4) an officer or agent appointed by—
> (A) the owner;
> (B) a charterer;
> (C) an owner pro hac vice; or
> (D) an agreed buyer in possession of the vessel.

§ 31341(a)(1)–(4). Section 31341's presumption is not "conclusive" as to a maritime lien's existence because a party can rebut the statutory presumption with competent evidence. *See Lake Charles Stevedores, Inc. v. Professor Vladimir Popov MV*, 199 F.3d 220, 225 (5th Cir. 1999) (citations omitted).

There is no dispute that Sing Fuels was "a person providing necessaries" and those "necessaries" were provided "to a vessel." *Compare* Sing Fuels's Opening Br. 23–24 (arguing Sing Fuels satisfied the first two requirements for a maritime lien), *with* Autumn Harvest's Resp. Br. 13 ("There is no dispute as to the first two factors."). We agree those threshold requirements are fulfilled. Bunkers qualify as "necessaries" under § 31342(a). *See ING Bank N.V. v. M/V Temara*, 892 F.3d 511, 519, 6 Adm. R. 44, 48 (2d Cir. 2018) ("'Necessaries' **[—17—]** include, among other things, bunkers." (citations omitted)). And Sing Fuels is "a person providing necessaries to a vessel" because it specifically ordered the July bunkers for the Vessel in its capacity as a bunker trader. *Id.*, 6 Adm. R. at 48 ("A maritime lien may be asserted by an entity when that entity contracts with a vessel's owner, charterer, or other statutorily-authorized person for the provision of necessaries and the necessaries are supplied pursuant to that agreement even if by another party."). Accordingly, the sole question before this **{-274-}** Court is whether Sing Fuels acted "on the order of the owner or a person authorized by the owner." § 31342(a).

2.

At the outset, we first note that there is no argument or record evidence indicating that Sing Fuels acted "on the order of the owner" when ordering the July bunkers. *Id.* During the bench trial, Rasmussen expressly conceded that Sing Fuels never had any communication with Autumn Harvest, the Vessel's owner, before ordering and supplying the July bunkers. We find the following exchange instructive:

> Q. But you chose never to contact my client, Autumn Harvest, regarding these bunkers, correct?
> [Rasmussen]. Autumn Harvest wasn't -- wasn't our customer. MedMar was our customer.
> . . .

Q. You had no communication of any kind with [Autumn Harvest] before the bunkers were supplied?
[Rasmussen]. Correct.
Q. And you've got no evidence that [Autumn Harvest] ever received a copy of any Sales Confirmation before the bunkers were supplied, correct?
[Rasmussen]. Correct.
Q. You've got no evidence that [Autumn Harvest] ever received a copy of your Terms and Conditions before you supplied the bunkers, correct? **[—18—]**
[Rasmussen]. Correct.
Q. To your knowledge, Mr. Mylonakis never communicated with [Autumn Harvest] regarding these bunkers, did he?
[Rasmussen]. Not to my knowledge.

J.A. 480–81. These concessions make clear that Sing Fuels never ordered the July bunkers "on the order of the owner," Autumn Harvest, as required by the CIMLA. § 31342(a). Autumn Harvest never directly requested the July bunkers from Sing Fuels, and nor did it ever contract with Sing Fuels, so nothing was "on the order of the owner" under § 31342(a). *Cf. Bunker Holdings Ltd. v. Yang Ming Liberia Corp.*, 906 F.3d 843, 845, 6 Adm. R. 386, 386 (9th Cir. 2018) (holding that an order for bunkers was not provided "on the order of the owner" when the vessel's owner only contracted with a fuel broker and not with the physical supplier seeking the maritime lien).

Because Sing Fuels did not provide the July bunkers at Autumn Harvest's request, it is only entitled to a maritime lien if it can show it ordered them "on the order of . . . a person authorized by the owner." § 31342(a). Under these circumstances, Sing Fuels needed to demonstrate that either Mylonakis or Medmar is "a person authorized by the owner," Autumn Harvest. *Id.* It failed to do so. According to Sing Fuels's own theories at trial, Mylonakis was supposedly a fuel broker for Medmar, not Autumn Harvest. *See* J.A. 453 ("This message was sent to Costas Mylonakis, who is the fuel broker for MedMar."); J.A. 472 ("Mr. Mylonakis was the broker for MedMar and acting as their agent."); *see also* J.A. 480–81. Mylonakis *may* have been authorized to procure the July bunkers by Medmar, but he clearly was not permitted to do so by Autumn Harvest, the Vessel's owner. **[—19—]**

As for Medmar, not only did none of its representatives testify at trial, Sing Fuels submitted no evidence suggesting that Autumn Harvest authorized Medmar, as its agent, to order the Vessel's July bunkers. *See Bunker Holdings*, 906 F.3d at 845, 6 Adm. R. at 386–87 (finding that a bunker trader was not acting as a vessel owner's agent when it only contracted with a physical supplier to provide bunkers for a vessel and never submitted evidence to the contrary); *see also* **{-275-}** *Valero Mktg. & Supply Co. v. M/V Almi Sun*, 893 F.3d 290, 295, 6 Adm. R. 205, 208 (5th Cir. 2018) (same). This is unsurprising because Medmar, as a sub-charterer, had no relationship with Autumn Harvest.[15] *See Barcliff, LLC v. M/V Deep Blue*, 876 F.3d 1063, 1071, 5 Adm. R. 518, 523 (11th Cir. 2017) ("[T]he subcontractor is merely a contractual counterparty of the general contractor; it has no relationship with the owner."). In sum, Sing Fuels simply failed to show how it acted "on the order of the owner or a person authorized by the owner" under the CIMLA. § 31342(a).

3.

As opposed to grappling with the CIMLA's explicit requirement under § 31342(a), Sing Fuels rests its entitlement to a maritime lien entirely on Mylonakis being Medmar's **[—20—]** apparent agent, which would trigger the CIMLA's statutory presumption and grant

[15] As an appellate court, we review the district court's decision based upon the record before it below. Fed. R. App. P. 10(a); *Fassett v. Delta Kappa Epsilon (New York)*, 807 F.2d 1150, 1165 (3d Cir. 1986). In the record before us, there is only a contract between Autumn Harvest and Bostomar, which contains a clause expressly prohibiting Bostomar and its agents from placing any liens on the Vessel. *See* J.A. 795. Presumably, Medmar contracted with Bostomar to sub-charter the Vessel, but the contents of that contract, if it exists, are not in the record. Likewise, there is no contract in the record between Autumn Harvest and Medmar, which further suggests Medmar is not "a person authorized" by Autumn Harvest. § 31342(a).

Mylonakis tentative authority to bind the Vessel. As a charterer, Medmar's agents have presumptive authority to procure necessaries on behalf of the Vessel. § 31341(a)(4). But under the CIMLA's terms, the rebuttable presumption of authority to bind a vessel is only applicable if an agency relationship indeed exists, including one involving apparent authority. *See id.*; *see also Lake Charles Stevedores,* 199 F.3d at 226–27 (analyzing whether usual agency theories applied to trigger the CIMLA's statutory presumption); *Crescent City Marine, Inc. v. M/V Nunki,* 20 F.3d 665, 668–69 (5th Cir. 1994) (similar).

We thus begin with the well-known principles of apparent authority. "Apparent authority results from a principal's manifestation of an agent's authority to a third party, regardless of the actual understanding between the principal and agent." *Auvil v. Grafton Homes, Inc.*, 92 F.3d 226, 230 (4th Cir. 1996) (citations omitted). An agent can bind a principal through apparent authority but only when the principal, by her acts or omissions, causes a third party to rely on the agent's authority to act on the principal's behalf. *Id.* The third party must exercise "good faith" and "reasonable prudence" in their reliance upon the apparent agent. *Id.* "From the well-established tenet that an agent cannot create his own authority to represent a principal, it follows that an agent's statements that he has such authority cannot, without more, entitle a third party to rely on his agency." *Id.* (citations omitted) (cleaned up). This is for good reason: "Apparent authority is present only when a third party's belief is traceable to manifestations of the principal." Restatement (Third) of Agency § 3.03 cmt. b (Am. L. Inst. 2006). **[—21—]**

We have previously noted that agency findings involve "factual matters" lying within the jury's province. *Krakauer v. Dish Network, L.L.C.*, 925 F.3d 643, 660 (4th Cir. 2019) (quoting *Metco Prods., Inc., v. Nat'l Lab. Rels. Bd.*, 884 F.2d 156, 159 (4th Cir. 1989)). Because they boil down to the facts, we review findings of apparent agency—even in the admiralty context—under a clearly erroneous standard. **{–276–}** *S.C. State Ports Auth. v. M/V Tyson Lykes*, 67 F.3d 59, 61 (4th Cir. 1995); *Famous Knitwear Corp. v. Drug Fair, Inc.*, 493 F.2d 251, 252 (4th Cir. 1974) ("The finding of apparent authority, including as it must, the reasonableness of Feder's reliance on Drug Fair's manifestations in that regard, is an 'ultimate factual inference' and is to be reviewed under the 'clearly erroneous standard' . . . ." (citations omitted)); *see also Garanti Finansal Kiralama A.S. v. Aqua Marine & Trading Inc.*, 697 F.3d 59, 71 (2d Cir. 2012) ("[T]he existence of either actual or apparent authority is a question of fact, revolving as it does around the actions by, and relationships between, principal, agent, and third parties." (citations omitted)); *Lake Charles Stevedores*, 199 F.3d at 226 (similar); *Equilease Corp. v. M/V Sampson*, 756 F.2d 357, 363 (5th Cir. 1985) (similar).

When analyzing apparent agency, the district court concluded that "Mylonakis, the fuel broker, was not the agent for MedMar Inc., and, thus, could not establish the maritime line [sic] on behalf of Plaintiff." *Sing Fuels Pte. Ltd.*, 534 F. Supp. 3d at 567. To reach that conclusion, the court first considered Sing Fuels's argument that Medmar's alleged payment for bunkers in May 2019 established Mylonakis's apparent authority to bind the Vessel. *Id.* It found Sing Fuels's position "undercut" because Rasmussen later admitted **[—22—]** that he did not know whether or not Medmar even paid for the May 2019 transaction.[16] *Id.*; *see also* J.A. 500 (Rasmussen's concession about the May 2019 bunkers). This finding is not clearly erroneous by any means.

As conceded at oral argument, Sing Fuels never proffered any documents establishing any of its prior dealings with Mylonakis or Medmar, including for the alleged fuel transaction in May 2019. So there is no

[16] During direct examination, Rasmussen expressly testified that Medmar paid for the May 2019 transaction, and he reiterated that belief when he was later questioned. *See* J.A. 451–52, 498. However, during recross examination, Rasmussen then conceded that he did not know who actually paid for the May 2019 transaction at all. *See* J.A. 500.

"substantial evidence" that the district court could have relied upon to either rescue Rasmussen's credibility or support an "opposite conclusion" of the prior transactions justifying apparent authority with respect to the July 2019 bunkers. *Heyer*, 984 F.3d at 355 (quoting *Jiminez*, 57 F.3d at 379). The district court's conclusion about Mylonakis's apparent authority partly rests upon Rasmussen's credibility, and "[w]here a district court's factual finding in a bench trial is based upon an assessment of witness credibility, such finding 'is deserving of the highest degree of appellate deference.'" *F.C. Wheat Maritime Corp. v. United States*, 663 F.3d 714, 723 (4th Cir. 2011) (citation omitted). We see no good reason to disturb that finding here, particularly when Sing Fuels never points to other evidence making it clearly erroneous.

But the district court was not only concerned with Rasmussen's credibility regarding the previous bunker transaction, it also expressly considered the following facts when it rejected Sing Fuels's reliance on Mylonakis's apparent agency: (1) Sing Fuels only **[—23—]** communicated with Mylonakis and never spoke with Medmar about the July bunkers; (2) "no documentation" suggested an agency relationship between Mylonakis and Medmar; (3) Mylonakis never spoke with Medmar but revealed his exclusive dealings with M.A.C. Shipping to Rasmussen; and (4) Sing Fuels failed to "confirm the relationship" between M.A.C. Shipping and Medmar. *Sing Fuels Pte. Ltd.*, 534 F. Supp. 3d at 567–68. Based on those facts, the court arrived at the reasoned **{-277-}** conclusion that Sing Fuels failed to demonstrate that Mylonakis was Medmar's apparent agent, precluding him from having any connection to the Vessel.[17] *Id.* at 568. This is not a clearly erroneous finding because it is "plausible in light of the record viewed in its entirety." *Heyer*, 984 F.3d at 355 (quoting *City of Bessemer*, 470 U.S. at 574).

Besides perplexing testimony from Rasmussen,[18] evidence further showed Sing Fuels transmitted the Sales Order Confirmation to Mylonakis at his account associated with **[—24—]** Windrose Marine, his employer, and not to Medmar directly. Moreover, Sing Fuels emphasized that it *only* worked with Mylonakis for procuring the July bunkers, and never spoke with Medmar. It is hornbook law that Mylonakis cannot deem himself Medmar's apparent agent without any manifestation coming from Medmar. *See Auvil*, 92 F.3d at 230 ("[Because a]n agent cannot create his own authority to represent a principal, it follows that an agent's statements that he has such authority cannot, without more, entitle a third party to rely on his agency." (citations omitted) (cleaned up)); Restatement (Third) of Agency § 3.03 cmt. b (noting that apparent agency must involve the manifestation of a principal). Tellingly, Sing Fuels could not confirm whether Medmar was the corporate entity paying for the previous bunker deliveries that it purportedly supplied. *See* J.A. 499–500. And then, Sing Fuels never established any firm connection between Medmar, Windrose Marine, and M.A.C.

[17] At one point, Sing Fuels's briefing shifts focus from Mylonakis to Medmar, positing that "the lien *was established* simply through the order of bunkers by Medmar (as subcharterer) which were in fact delivered to the Vessel by Sing Fuels." Sing Fuels's Opening Br. 31 (emphasis added). That is not the law. Section 31341(a)(4)(B) only provides a charterer's "officer or agent" with presumptive authority, albeit rebuttable, to procure a vessel's necessaries. *See Hebei Prince Shipping*, 783 F.3d at 521–22, 3 Adm. R. at 211–12 (noting that § 31341(a)'s presumption is rebuttable). And, in this case, Sing Fuels rebuts itself by conceding that it never communicated with any of Medmar's officers about obtaining the July bunkers. *See* J.A. 472–74. It exclusively communicated with who it believed was Medmar's agent, Mylonakis. *Id.* So § 31341(a)'s presumption turns on whether Mylonakis is an agent.

[18] Rasmussen testified that he "believe[d]" M.A.C. Shipping and Medmar were "two of the same" based upon a representation from Mylonakis, but he also admitted that he never reviewed any corporate documents about M.A.C Shipping or asked Medmar whether it was related to M.A.C. Shipping. *See* J.A. 473, 478. We view this as going to the weight of Rasmussen's testimony. *Fed. Trade Comm'n v. Ross*, 743 F.3d 886, 894 (4th Cir. 2014) ("In cases in which a district court's factual findings turn on assessments of witness (Continued) **[—24—]** credibility or the weighing of conflicting evidence during a bench trial, such findings are entitled to even greater deference." (citation omitted)).

Shipping. So we are left wanting for a manifestation from Medmar. Under these circumstances, we believe the district court's decision against apparent authority is well-grounded in the record, particularly with a glaring absence of proof and primarily relying on only witness testimony before it. *See Tramp Oil & Marine, Ltd. v. M/V "Mermaid I"*, 805 F.2d 42, 45 (1st Cir. 1986) (holding that a broker of bunkers was not entitled to a maritime lien when "no relationship existed" between the broker and a vessel, and "neither the vessel owner nor the charterer even knew of [the broker]"). **[—25—]**

In a final attempt to procure its maritime lien, Sing Fuels heavily relies on *Marine Fuel Supply & Towing, Inc. v. M/V Ken Lucky*, 869 F.2d 473 (9th Cir. 1988), but that case is readily distinguishable. In *M/V Ken Lucky*, the Ninth Circuit held that a physical supplier was entitled to a maritime lien when *the parties agreed* that the fuel order originated from a sub-charterer **{-278-}** and that sub-charterer possessed authority to legally bind the vessel. *Id.* at 476–77. Contrary to *M/V Ken Lucky*, Autumn Harvest does not make that crucial factual admission, which is evident by the parties vigorously contesting its existence in this case. We are not in the terrain of *M/V Ken Lucky* and join our sister circuits in distinguishing it on this narrow basis. *See Bunker Holdings*, 906 F.3d at 845–46, 6 Adm. R. at 387 (distinguishing *M/V Ken Lucky* due to the factual admission and concessions); *Valero*, 893 F.3d at 295, 6 Adm. R. at 208 (same); *Barcliff*, 876 F.3d at 1068–69, 5 Adm. R. at 521–22 (same).

In short, based on the limited facts before it, the district court's finding that Mylonakis was not an apparent or presumed agent of Medmar is not clearly erroneous.[19]

IV.

"[M]aritime liens are to be strictly construed, i.e., they are not to be lightly extended by construction, analogy or inference . . . ." *Atl. & Gulf Stevedores, Inc. v. M/V Grand Loyalty*, 608 F.2d 197, 200–01 (5th Cir. 1979) (citations omitted). Given the limited record **[—26—]** before us, we cannot conclude that Sing Fuels is entitled to a maritime lien when it has failed to adequately prove an agency relationship between Medmar and Mylonakis or otherwise show how the district court's agency conclusion is clearly erroneous. Therefore, the district court's judgment against Sing Fuels and in the Vessel's favor is

AFFIRMED.

(Reporter's Note: Concurring opinion follows on p. 140).

---

[19] Because we hold that Sing Fuels failed to show an agency relationship justifying a maritime lien, we need not address the propriety of equitable laches. *Marshall v. Meadows*, 105 F.3d 904, 905 n.4 (4th Cir. 1997). We likewise express no view on other forms of legal relief available to Sing Fuels. *Edwards v. Johnston Cnty. Health Dep't*, 885 F.2d 1215, 1225 (4th Cir. 1989).

[—27—] {-278-} **WILKINSON,** Circuit Judge, concurring:

I agree with the majority that Sing Fuels has failed to show that Mylonakis, the fuel broker with which it dealt, was acting as an agent of anyone with authority to bind the vessel. It therefore is not entitled to a maritime lien, and I concur in the majority opinion. I write, however, to note the pitfalls that may arise in the future with cases like these, which threaten to destabilize the basic principle of admiralty law that suppliers of necessaries such as bunker fuel must be able to rely on maritime liens to ensure payment.

It is no secret that there are real problems with our supply chains today, much of which have to do with increased difficulties in transporting goods over the oceans. Indeed, "[i]nternational shipping costs have swung far more sharply during the pandemic and amid recent supply-chain disruptions than in the wake of the financial crisis." Lydia O'Neal, *Studies Find Supply-Chain Turmoil Had Unprecedented Economic Impact*, The Wall Street Journal, Jan. 10, 2022. To take just one example, prices for transporting goods from China to the United States have peaked at "more than 50% above the long-term trend for container shipping rates." *Id.* The worst thing we could do would be to add legal complications to those disruptions that already exist as a matter of physical logistics.

It is important, therefore, that those who provide bunker fuel or other necessaries to vessels be paid and be paid promptly. Every incentive should be to encourage prompt payment for fuel that was in fact delivered to the vessel, as it was here. Fuel is what keeps ships running and promises of prompt payment are what keep fuel {-279-} flowing. The very purpose of a maritime lien, long a part of our admiralty law, is the "desire to protect the ship," which is "peculiarly subject to vicissitudes which would compel abandonment of [—28—] vessel or voyage, unless repairs and supplies were promptly furnished." *Piedmont & George's Creek Coal Co. v. Seaboard Fisheries Co.*, 254 U.S. 1, 9 (1920).

To be sure, a maritime lien may only exist where a person provides necessaries to a vessel "on the order of the owner or a person authorized by the owner." 46 U.S.C. § 31342(a). The requirement that the supplier deal either with the owner of the ship or with an agent of the owner is a natural one. Yet there is a risk that the agency requirement will be used by unscrupulous parties as a shell game to evade their contractual duties. As this case illustrates, the maritime economy involves complex interrelations between owners of vessels, charterers, subcharterers, fuel brokers, and suppliers. It would only add to supply-side snarls to require entities providing fuel to unravel the particular relationships, contractual or otherwise, that exist between owners and charterers, or between charterers and the brokers they employ.

Instead, suppliers are entitled to rely on multiple presumptions. As a matter of statutory maritime law, they are entitled to rely on the presumption that a charterer or its agents may bind the vessel on behalf of its owner. *See id.* § 31341(a); *World Fuel Servs. Trading, DMCC v. Hebei Prince Shipping Co.*, 783 F.3d 507, 522, 3 Adm. R. 201, 212 (4th Cir. 2015) (stating that this presumption "can be rebutted only by proof that the seller had actual knowledge that the charterer lacked the ability to bind the vessel as part of the contract for necessaries"). And as a matter of agency law, suppliers are entitled to rely on the principle of apparent authority, whereby a charterer may create an agency relationship by manifesting to suppliers, whether "by written or spoken words or any other conduct," that a broker has the authority to represent it in negotiations or in contractual arrangements for [—29—] necessaries. Restatement (Second) of Agency § 27 (1958). So it need not usually be an onerous task for suppliers to obtain maritime liens for fuel delivered to a vessel.

In this particular case, I agree with the majority that Sing Fuels has not met its burden of showing either actual or apparent authority on the part of Mylonakis. As the majority indicates, the supplier in this case did nothing to ascertain an agency relationship between Mylonakis and the owner (Autumn Harvest) or the charterer (Medmar) of the vessel. It did not show this at the time of the transaction nor did it present testimony indicating the existence of such relationship at trial. Nonetheless, I am left with a feeling of unease. It is undisputed that Sing Fuels furnished fuel in Port Elizabeth that enabled the M/V Lila Shanghai to continue on its way. It is undisputed that the vessel consumed this fuel. And it is undisputed that Sing Fuels was never paid for this fuel.

I would not want this ruling to require too much of suppliers. And I hope that courts in the future will review with skepticism attempts to obscure or confuse agency relationships on the part of those who accept necessaries and then resist strenuously any payment for them.

This page intentionally left blank

United States Court of Appeals for the Fifth Circuit

United States Court of Appeals
for the Fifth Circuit

No. 20-30364

O'BRIEN'S RESPONSE MANAGEMENT, L.L.C.
vs.
BP EXPLORATION & PROD., INC.

Appeal from the United States District Court for the Eastern District of Louisiana

Decided: January 19, 2022

Citation: 24 F.4th 422, 10 Adm. R. 144 (5th Cir. 2022).

Before **JONES, CLEMENT,** and **GRAVES,** Circuit Judges.

[—1—] {-425-} JONES, Circuit Judge:

This latest installment of litigation spilling out of the Deepwater Horizon offshore explosion and fire centers on who should pay for personal **[—2—]** injury claims brought by **{-426-}** employees of two companies hired by BP Exploration & Production Inc. and BP America Production Company ("BP") to clean up the oil spill. Specifically, BP claims to be an "additional insured" under two policies obtained by O'Brien's Response Management, L.L.C. ("O'Brien's"). BP also seeks indemnification by O'Brien's and/or National Response Corporation ("NRC," together "Responders") under its contract with each plaintiff.

The issues here require interpretation of BP's contracts with each of the Responders and the related insurance policies in light of sometimes sparse case law. Ultimately, we conclude that BP was an additional insured up to the minimum amount required by its contract with O'Brien's; the two insurance policies maintained by O'Brien's cannot be combined to satisfy the minimum amount; O'Brien's is not required to indemnify BP because BP materially breached its indemnification provision with respect to the Back-End Litigation Option ("BELO") claims brought by O'Brien's employees; and a claim-by-claim analysis is required to determine the materiality of any breach regarding the remaining indemnity claims against both O'Brien's and NRC. Thus, we AFFIRM in part, REVERSE in part, and REMAND for further proceedings.[1]

I. BACKGROUND

BP retained the Responders for nearly $2 billion to assist with clean-up efforts in the aftermath of the April 2010 Deepwater Horizon oil spill. BP and O'Brien's executed a Bridge Agreement in 2010 that incorporated, with modifications, a Master Consulting Services Contract they originally entered **[—3—]** into in 2004 (the "BP-O'Brien's Contract"). BP also entered into an Agreement for the Provision of Response Resources with NRC in 2003 (the BP-NRC Agreement). The relevant provisions are described below.

The Responders and their respective subcontractors employed thousands of workers as part of their clean-up efforts. Thousands among these workers then filed personal injury lawsuits against BP, which were consolidated with the multidistrict litigation ("MDL") arising from the disaster.[2] The district court organized the MDL cases into various "pleading bundles." Relevant here, the B3 bundle included "all claims for personal injury and/or medical monitoring for exposure or other injury occurring after the explosion and fire of April 20, 2010." On the court's instruction, the Plaintiffs' Steering Committee ("PSC") filed a B3 Master Complaint in December 2010 that plaintiffs could join by filing a short form joinder. In April 2012, BP settled the B3 claims ("Medical Settlement") with the PSC and a defined settlement class. The opt-out deadline closed in October 2012. Importantly, the Medical Settlement created a new type of claim for latent injuries—the BELO claims—so long as settlement class members followed certain procedures. BP calls these claims "creature[s] of the Medical Settlement." Although BP

[1] We do not reach any potentially applicable exclusions, such as the "oil rig exclusion" mentioned by Navigators in its briefing, that were not ruled on by the district court in the first instance.

[2] After the district court granted the Responders' motion to lift the MDL stay in 2019, it deconsolidated the case "for organizational purposes[.]"

emphasizes that the Responders were aware of the settlement before the district court approved it in January 2013, BP does not dispute that neither O'Brien's nor NRC had control over the negotiations, nor did either approve the **{-427-}** settlement.[3] **[—4—]**

After the settlement, plaintiffs could bring two relevant types of claims: (1) opt-out B3 claims if they did not participate in the settlement, and (2) BELO claims if they were class members who alleged latent injuries and followed the approved process per the Medical Settlement.[4]

In March 2017, BP notified O'Brien's about a BELO suit filed by an O'Brien's employee and sought indemnification under their Contract for the first time. BP subsequently sought indemnification for approximately 1,800 BELO claims by O'Brien's employees and 200 such claims by NRC employees, as well as a smaller number of opt-out B3 claims against each Responder. The Responders refused to indemnify BP under their respective contracts. Instead, they sued for a declaration that they need not indemnify BP for any BELO or opt-out B3 claims. BP counterclaimed for breach of contract, a declaration in favor of its indemnification rights, and unjust enrichment.

O'Brien's is a named insured on two pertinent policies: (1) a Primary Bumbershoot Liability policy issued by Navigators Insurance Company (the "Primary Bumbershoot" policy)[5] providing marine umbrella insurance with an aggregate limit of $10,000,000; and (2) an Excess Bumbershoot Liability policy (the "First Excess Bumbershoot" policy) issued by Navigators and other insurers, which incorporates the Primary Bumbershoot's policy terms and provides excess coverage up to $90,000,000. **[—5—]**

O'Brien's also maintained marine general liability coverage under a policy issued by Starr Indemnity & Liability Company ("Starr policy") and a contractor's operations and professional services environmental insurance ("COPS") policy that covered liabilities excluded by the Starr policy. Both policies had coverage limits of $1 million per occurrence and $2 million in aggregate and have been exhausted.

In June 2019, O'Brien's notified BP that it was an additional insured under the Primary and First Excess Bumbershoot policies. Navigators, however, refused BP's demands for coverage, prompting BP to amend its counterclaim against the Responders and file a third-party claim against Navigators on its bumbershoot policies.

Navigators, BP, and O'Brien's and NRC filed cross-motions for judgment on the pleadings. The district court ruled against BP on each issue, concluding that (1) BP was not an additional insured under the relevant insurance policies; (2) O'Brien's was not required to indemnify BP because BP violated the consent-to-settle, notice, and control-of-defense provisions of the BP-O'Brien's Contract; and (3) NRC was not required to indemnify BP under their contract because NRC "had no liability under 'Responder Immunity Law.'" The district court also determined that **{-428-}** O'Brien's did not breach its contractual obligation to acquire insurance coverage for BP. BP timely appealed.

[3] In its brief, BP points to a letter from the Responders to the district court that demonstrates the Responders were aware of the settlement and that they were not involved in its negotiation. It states the latter conclusion directly: "The Clean-Up Responder Defendants are not involved in the ongoing settlement negotiations."

[4] To count as a BELO claim the condition must have been *diagnosed* after April 16, 2012. Thus, a condition that manifested before the settlement and was later diagnosed might still qualify as a BELO claim.

[5] "A 'bumbershoot,' the English term for umbrella, is a marine insurance policy covering multiple liability coverages in excess of one or more different underlying policies, comparable to the commercial liability umbrella covering liabilities on land." 15 COUCH ON INSURANCE § 220:32 & n.29 (2021) (citation omitted).

II. DISCUSSION

This court reviews Rule 12(c) judgments on the pleadings *de novo*. *See Garza v. Escobar*, 972 F.3d 721, 727 (5th Cir. 2020) (citations omitted). We accept well-pleaded facts as true and construe them in the light most favorable to the non-moving party. *Edionwe v. Bailey*, 860 F.3d 287, 291 (5th **[—6—]** Cir. 2017) (citation omitted). The parties agree that Texas law applies.[6] As already stated, this appeal turns on whether BP is an additional insured under the Primary and First Excess Bumbershoot policies and on the interpretation of the indemnification provisions of BP's separate contracts with O'Brien's and NRC. We address the issues in turn.

A. Additional Insured Status

BP seeks coverage as an "additional insured" under the Primary and Excess Bumbershoot policies covering O'Brien's. Under Texas law, "[i]nsurance policies are controlled by rules of interpretation and construction which are applicable to contracts generally." *Richards v. State Farm Lloyd's*, 597 S.W.3d 492, 497 (Tex. 2020) (internal quotation marks and citation omitted). Further, to construe contracts, Texas courts "give terms their plain, ordinary and generally accepted meaning . . . . [and] will enforce the unambiguous document as written." *Heritage Res., Inc. v. NationsBank*, 939 S.W.2d 118, 121 (Tex. 1996) (citations omitted). Although insurance coverage analysis "necessarily begins with the four corners of the policies[,] . . . ." the Texas Supreme Court holds that "insurance policies can incorporate limitations on coverages encompassed in extrinsic documents by reference to those documents." *In re Deepwater Horizon*, 470 S.W.3d 452, 460 (Tex. 2015) (citations omitted). If a policy "directs [Texas courts] elsewhere, [they] will refer to an incorporated document to the extent required by the policy[,]" but they "do not consider coverage limitations in underlying transactional documents[]" unless required by the policy. *Id.* **[—7—]**

In a provision similar to one involved in *Deepwater Horizon*, the Primary Bumbershoot policy defined an "assured" to include "any person, organization, trustee or estate to whom the Named Assured is obligated by virtue of a written contract or agreement to provide insurance as is afforded by this policy[.]" *Compare In re Deepwater Horizon*, 470 S.W.3d at 457. And the First Excess Bumbershoot policy was subject to the primary policy's terms, definitions, exclusions, and conditions. BP is thus an additional insured under the two bumbershoot policies to the extent required by the BP-O'Brien's Contract.

The BP-O'Brien's Contract confirms BP's status with regard to at least some of O'Brien's insurance coverage. Section 12.01, entitled "Insurance," required O'Brien's to maintain four types of policies,[7] including:

> 12.01.03 Comprehensive General Liability Insurance, including contractual liability coverage, with minimum limits of US$2,000,000 per occurrence. **{–429–}**

Section 12.02 established BP's additional insured status as to the CGL coverage and marine extension thereof:

> Except for Workers' Compensation Insurance set forth in Section 12.01.01, all policies shall name [BP entities] as additional insureds. In addition, all of the policies listed above, without exception, shall be endorsed to waive subrogation against the [BP entities] . . . . Additionally, if [O'Brien's] shall perform any Services hereunder on navigable waters then each of the policies listed in 12.01.02 [Employer's Liability] and 12.01.03 [Comprehensive General Liability] above shall be endorsed to cover marine operations. **[—8—]**

[6] Navigators reserved the right to contest the Texas choice-of-law provision, contending the BP-O'Brien's Contract was amended post-loss, but decided to accept Texas law here because it did not identify any conflict-of-law issues.

[7] Workers' compensation, employer's liability, and automobile liability insurance are the additional required coverages.

Navigators challenges BP's claim to be an additional insured on the bumbershoot policies for two primary reasons. First, Navigators distinguishes its bumbershoot policies from the CGL coverage referenced in Section 12.01.03 and argues that O'Brien's fulfilled its contractual obligations by naming BP as an additional assured on its Starr and COPS policies that provided GCL-type coverage. Second, once O'Brien's fulfilled its obligations with respect to CGL coverage, Navigators insists that its bumbershoot policies did not provide additional assured coverage to BP. Alternatively, Navigators argues that if BP is entitled to additional assured coverage under its bumbershoot policies, then that coverage is limited to the $2,000,000 minimum required by Section 12.01.03. Navigators' first two arguments do not withstand analysis, but the coverage amount argument must be closely examined.

1. CGL Coverage

To begin, Navigators concedes that the Starr policy provides "standard primary CGL [i]nsurance, modified slightly to cover marine operations." It also agrees that BP is an additional assured under the Starr and COPS policies, and that its Primary Bumbershoot policy provides excess coverage that "expressly includes the Starr Policy and the COPS policy by name." Finally, Navigators describes the First Excess Bumbershoot policy as "follow-form" of its primary policy. To state these facts is to conclude that the bumbershoot policies afford CGL-type coverage as described in the BP-O'Brien's Contract.

Navigators resists the obvious, emphasizing general differences between CGL and bumbershoot policies writ large. General distinctions are unpersuasive here. Undoubtedly, bumbershoot policies can differ from standard CGL policies. *See* Robert T. Lemon II, *Allocation of Marine Risks: An Overview of the Marine Insurance Package*, 81 TUL. L. REV. 1467, 1492 **[—9—]** (2007) (citation omitted) (recognizing that a "CGL policy is not a marine policy and is not intended to cover risks[]"). But the specific coverage overlap of Navigators' bumbershoot policies with the Starr policy (which was modified to cover marine operations, after all), together with the bumbershoot policies' direct reference to the Starr and COPS policies, refutes any meaningful distinction here. Therefore, the specific coverage provided by the policies is the relevant inquiry.[8] The bumbershoot **{-430-}** policies provide CGL-type coverage, so they are best understood as CGL policies under the BP-O'Brien's Contract, and BP is an additional assured.

Navigators also asserts that the BP-O'Brien's Contract limits BP's assured status to "*primary* CGL insurance, not bumbershoot, umbrella or excess insurance." But the word "primary" is nowhere in the text of the Contract, which requires only that O'Brien's "maintain" CGL insurance with a certain minimum limit.[9] **[—10—]**

---

[8] At one point in this litigation, O'Brien's and BP considered the term CGL as used in the agreement to encompass the Primary Bumbershoot policy. In opposing motions for judgment on the pleadings, the Responders stated that "BP was automatically named as an additional insured on the [Primary Bumbershoot policy], which provides CGL insurance." And in their answer to BP's amended counterclaims, the Responders recognized that "[i]n June 2019, O'Brien's notified BP that BP is an additional insured under the [Primary Bumbershoot policy] . . . ." Although the Responders now take "no position" on the insurance issue "because it does not concern them," their prior clear understanding of the Primary Bumbershoot policy supports our conclusion that Navigators' policies provide CGL-type coverage. *See Harris v Rowe*, 593 S.W.2d 303, 306 (Tex. 1979) (recognizing that "[c]ourts rightfully assume that parties to a contract are in the best position to know what was intended by the language employed[,]" and "should adopt the construction of the instrument as placed upon it by the parties unless there is clear language in the instrument indicating an intention to the contrary" (citations omitted)).

[9] To be sure, some contracts include separate provisions requiring CGL insurance and also excess coverage. *See, e.g., Ironshore Specialty Ins. Co. v. Aspen Underwriting, Ltd.*, 788 F.3d 456, 458 (5th Cir. 2015) (requiring CGL insurance and excess liability insurance above the CGL policy in distinct subsections). None of the cases cited by Navigators, **[—10—]** however, concludes that excess coverage mirroring a primary CGL policy does not constitute CGL coverage. And we see no need to draw that conclusion today.

2. Contractual Minimum Coverage

The next question is how much coverage BP is entitled to as an additional assured on the bumbershoot policies. BP contends it is entitled to the full $100,000,000 under these policies notwithstanding that Section 12.01.03 required O'Brien's to purchase CGL with "minimum limits" of $2 million per occurrence.

In re Deepwater Horizon provides the analytical framework, and previous decisions of this court supply a key to the outcome. The *In re Deepwater Horizon* court looked first at the insurance policy, whose language, substantially similar to that before us, defined an additional insured as any entity to whom the named insured was "obliged by oral or written Insured Contract . . . to provide insurance such as afforded by [the] Policy." 470 S.W.3d at 457 (internal quotations omitted and alterations in original). The court then inspected the parties' contract to determine the extent of coverage.

Because the Primary Bumbershoot policy creates an "obligation" that mirrors the obligation in *In re Deepwater Horizon,* we move to the terms of the BP-O'Brien's Contract referenced by the Primary Bumbershoot policy. BP focuses on language in Section 12.02, which states that "[e]xcept for Workers' Compensation Insurance set forth in Section 12.01.01, all policies shall name [the BP entities] as additional insureds." "All policies," it contends, means *all* policies procured by O'Brien's. But the very next sentence in Section 12.02 references "all of the policies listed above" when dealing with waiver of subrogation. And the logical inference from both sentences together is that in excluding Workers' Compensation Insurance, **[—11—]** Section 12.02 cross-references "all" of the policies in Section 12.01.01 and nothing more. BP itself concedes that "all policies" does not literally mean "all," because in context, the phrase "plainly refers to all insurance policies providing the types of 'insurance coverage' listed in the previous section, except for Workers' Compensation Insurance." BP fails to explain how the CGL's minimum coverage limits are not included in the "all policies" language of Section 12.02.

The BP-O'Brien's Contract contraindicates extending BP's additional assured status to the maximum coverage voluntarily purchased by O'Brien's. Our precedent **{-431-}** strongly reinforces that conclusion. In the wake of *In re Deepwater Horizon,* this court made an *Erie* guess in *Ironshore Specialty Ins. Co. v. Aspen Underwriting, Ltd.* that an additional assured was covered only to the minimum *obliged* by the parties' contract and not the maximum obtained by the named insured.[10] 788 F.3d 456, 461-63 (5th Cir. 2015). To be sure, the BP-O'Brien's Contract specifies CGL coverage with $2 million "minimum limits," whereas the policy in *Ironshore* referenced only "$5 million." *Id.* at 458. But that is still a limit, and the parties agreed in *Ironshore* that $5 million was the maximum required by the master service agreement there. *Id.* at 459.[11] **[—12—]**

This court's decision in *Musgrove v. Southland Corp.* also rejects BP's proffered interpretation.[12] 898 F.2d 1041 (5th Cir.

---

[10] The policy in *Ironshore* covered "any person or entity to whom [the insured was] obliged by a written 'Insured Contract . . . .'" 788 F.3d at 458. The court reasoned that because a similar provision was sufficient "in *Deepwater Horizon* to incorporate the Drilling Contract's limitation on coverage[,] . . . . [t]he nearly identical language in [the contractor's] policies . . . compel[led] the same result." *Id.* at 463.

[11] The parties also dispute the commercial context of the BP-O'Brien's Contract. But their arguments amount to a draw. BP claims the "all policies" clause was intended to "hitch[]" BP's wagon to O'Brien's full coverage because O'Brien's managed the cleanup work and "had every incentive to obtain adequate CGL insurance for itself." But Navigators points out that BP did not take this approach with its NRC contract, and argues that it was equally reasonable for BP to require certain minimum coverage from O'Brien's. In short, the commercial context is not decisive here. *Cf. Kachina Pipeline Co., Inc. v. Lillis,* **[—12—]** 471 S.W.3d 445, 450 (Tex. 2015) (permitting consideration of "facts and circumstances surrounding a contract, . . ." but recognizing that "extrinsic evidence can be considered only to interpret an ambiguous writing, not to create ambiguity." (citations omitted)).

[12] Although *Musgrove* arose under Louisiana law, a panel of this court favorably cited the decision while applying Texas law. *See Forest Oil*

1990). A key issue in *Musgrove* was whether a party was an additional insured on an excess policy covering losses greater than $1,000,000. *Id.* at 1043-44. Like the bumbershoot policies here, an excess policy in *Musgrove* limited coverage for additional insureds to those whom the named insured was "obligated by virtue of a written contract." *Id.* at 1043. The relevant contract required primary CGL insurance "of not less than $1 million per occurrence." *Id.* The court rejected drop-down coverage by the excess policy, however, because of its express limitation to losses exceeding $1 million. It also disregarded an additional assured provision that would have required "[a]ll insurance coverages carried by Contractor, *whether or not required hereby* , . . ." to also "extend to and protect Company . . . to the full amount of such coverage, but not less than" $1,000,000 in CGL insurance. *Id.* (emphasis and alterations in original). The panel rejected application of this language, *inter alia,*[13] because the insured "was not contractually **{-432-}** obligated to **[—13—]** obtain excess liability coverage for [the other party.]" *Id.* at 1044 (citation omitted).

As in this case, the insurance policy in *Musgrove* only covered additional insureds as "obligated" by an insured's written contract. *Id.* at 1043. Further, the contract required CGL coverage "of not less than" a certain amount. *Id.* And this court enforced the policy as a limit on excess coverage notwithstanding additional insured language that, if applicable, would have required the company to be named "on all of the above insurance[.]" *Id.* at 1043-44.[14]

BP relies heavily on a Georgia state court's interpretation of a similar additional insured clause, which it describes as the only authority that construed the "all policies" language at issue in this appeal. *See Ins. Co. of Pa. v. APAC-Se., Inc.*, 677 S.E.2d 734 (Ga. Ct. App. 2009). *APAC* is unpersuasive for several reasons. First, as we have explained, this court favors requiring insurance companies to cover only the minimum amount obliged by an underlying referenced contract when the policy contains similar language to the bumbershoot policies at issue here. That legal context influences our interpretation. *Cf.* 8 COUCH ON INSURANCE § 112:31 (2021) (recognizing that "[t]he phrase 'additional insured' is affected by **[—14—]** many sources: (1) definitions contained in the policy, (2) statutory definitions, and (3) case law that has applied the phrase to various fact patterns[]").

Second, the additional insured clause in *APAC* distinguished between "all policies" and "required insurance," and the court characterized the latter term as "setting forth other duties placed upon [the named insured] relating to insurance procurement." 677 S.E.2d at 739. No such distinction exists in the additional insured clause here. BP nonetheless emphasizes the phrase "required

Corp. v. Strata Energy, Inc., 929 F.2d 1039, 1045 (5th Cir. 1991) (citing *Musgrove v. Southland Corp.*, 898 F.2d 1041, 1043 (5th Cir. 1990)). *Forest Oil* construed one policy to the "full extent of its . . . coverage[]" because it lacked language that would provide coverage "only to the extent that [the insured] was contractually required to provide such insurance[,]" but construed another policy, which did express such language, as limited to the amount required by an underlying contract. *Id.* at 1044-45.

[13] Principally, this language appeared in a contractor's manual attached to the contract, and the manual stated that the parties' contract "prevails in any conflict." *Musgrove,* 898 F.2d at 1043-44. Alternatively, the panel held, the manual's language gave the insured the prerogative, but not a duty, to purchase excess insurance on the other party's behalf. *Id.* at 1044.

[14] We recognize that, under Texas law, when two reasonable interpretations of an insurance policy exist the one favoring coverage should be preferred. *Evanston Ins. Co. v. Legacy of Life, Inc.*, 370 S.W.3d 377, 380 (Tex. 2012) (citation omitted). This rule applies even where a policy incorporates another agreement by reference. *Aubris Res. LP v. St. Paul Fire & Marine Ins. Co.*, 566 F.3d 483, 489 n.3 (5th Cir. 2009) (seeing "no reason why the special rules of insurance policy interpretation should not apply where, as here, the insurance policy's additional insured endorsement incorporates section 10.2 by reference[]"). Nevertheless, in light of *Ironshore*, *Forest Oil*, and *Musgrove*, and the BP-O'Brien's Contract itself, we find just one reasonable interpretation. *See In re Deepwater Horizon*, 470 S.W.3d 452, 464 (Tex. 2015) ("Disagreement about a policy's meaning does not create an ambiguity if there is only one reasonable interpretation.").

insurance coverage" in Section 11.07 of the BP-O'Brien's Contract, a separate provision requiring insurance coverage of the parties' mutual indemnity duties. BP would compare that language with the "all policies" language in Section 12.02. The comparison does not work; in *APAC*, the court's interpretation relied on the fact that "all policies" and "required insurance" were "two different terms in short sequence within the same paragraph."[15] *Id.*

Finally, the *APAC* court held a narrow interpretation of "all policies" unlikely because it "would undermine [the named insured's] ability to ensure that it meets its **{-433-}** contractual obligation . . . ." to provide indemnification. *Id.* But, as just noted, that same concern is not present in the BP-O'Brien's Contract, which separately requires coverage for the parties' indemnity obligations and states that indemnity and insurance provisions are independent of each other. **[—15—]**

We conclude that the BP-O'Brien's Contract, read in full, adopts the $2 million minimum CGL coverage as the maximum required to be furnished by each party for the benefit of the other and that Navigators' bumbershoot policies incorporated the limit of the contractual obligation.

3. The Starr and COPS Policies Do Not Satisfy the Minimum

Although the district court correctly concluded that BP was only an additional insured with respect to the $2,000,000 obligated by the BP-O'Brien's Contract, it erred in concluding that amount was fully satisfied by the Starr and COPS policies (each bearing $1,000,000 coverage limits per occurrence).[16] BP is entitled to $2 million of coverage.

The facts speak for themselves. The Starr policy provides CGL-type coverage but excludes pollution and professional liability coverage. The COPS policy fills that gap by covering pollution and professional liability. The two policies cover different sets of risks and each affords a single $1,000,000 layer of complementary CGL-type coverage per occurrence. Allowing Navigators, as it urges, to count the policies together would create an absurd result. A party could obtain primary CGL coverage, subject it to numerous exclusions, obtain separate policies covering only those exclusions, add the total together, and thus circumvent contractual minimum amount requirements.[17] We conclude, instead, that the Starr and COPS policies cannot be combined to meet the minimum CGL coverage **[—16—]** requirement. Together, they only constitute $1,000,000 of the $2,000,000 required by the BP-O'Brien's Contract because they are mutually reinforcing policies designed to satisfy the same obligation by filling in each other's gaps.

B. Indemnification Obligations

Notwithstanding the contractual mutual indemnity obligations between the Responders and BP, the district court concluded that BP was not entitled to indemnification under either contract for any of the claims. Regarding O'Brien's, the district court concluded BP violated the BP-O'Brien's Contract's notice, consent-to-settle, and control-of-defense prerequisites to indem-

---

[15] Additionally, Articles 11 and 12 are completely different from the *APAC* provision. Section 11.07 used "required insurance coverage" to emphasize that the parties' Article 11 "indemnity obligations" are "independent of" the Article 12 "insurance requirements." Thus, the "all policies" language in Section 12.02 was intended to ensure BP was named an additional insured on the policies procured by O'Brien's *to satisfy its coverage obligations* set forth in Section 12.01.03.

[16] According to Navigators, the fact that the Starr and COPS policies are exhausted has no bearing on whether they count toward the minimum CGL coverage required by the BP-O'Brien's Contract. BP does not dispute this point and thus concedes it.

[17] The parties also dispute whether the COPS policy's claims-made coverage for professional liability conflicts with the BP-O'Brien's Contract's requirement that minimum coverage limits be "per occurrence." While this may provide another reason not to consider the COPS policy a separate CGL policy for purposes of complying with the minimum $2,000,000 coverage requirement, we need not reach it.

nification. With respect to NRC, it concluded that no indemnification obligations arose under the contract with respect to any claims because NRC was immune pursuant to applicable federal responder immunity laws. We discuss each contract in turn.

1. BP-O'Brien's Contract BELO claims

Article 11 of the BP-O'Brien's Contract holds each party to mutual indemnity obligations **{-434-}** with regard to injuries to persons within their control. Section 11.02 states that this duty is "[s]ubject to the other provisions of this Article 11[.]" Section 11.04 then articulates notice, control-of-defense, and consent-to-settle requirements for indemnification:

> Contractor or Company as the case may be shall *promptly give to the other party notice in writing of any claim made or proceedings commenced* for which Contractor or Company claims to be entitled to indemnification under this contract. Such notice shall state with as much detail as is reasonably practicable the facts and circumstances giving rise to the claim and shall be given as soon as possible after the party seeking indemnity hereunder . . . becomes aware of such claim or proceeding. The [indemnitor] . . . shall confer with the indemnitee concerning the defense of any such claim or proceedings but, subject to the remainder of this Section 11.04, *the indemnitor or* **[—17—]** *its insurer shall retain control of the conduct of such defense*, including, but not limited to, the selection and management of counsel. *Notwithstanding the foregoing, however, neither party shall effect settlement or compromise of any claim or proceeding without having obtained the prior written consent of the other party*, which shall not be unreasonably withheld . . . . The indemnitee may, upon written notice to the indemnitor and at the indemnitee's sole cost and expense, select its own counsel to participate in and be present for the defense of any such claim or proceeding, *provided such counsel shall not take any action in the course of such claim or proceeding to prejudice the defense of such claim or proceeding.*

(emphasis added).

The district court correctly concluded that BP materially breached the BP-O'Brien's Contract regarding the BELO claims.[18] Those are the claims that BP agreed with the PSC to litigate, if plaintiffs followed certain procedures for claims that arose following the Medical Settlement. Invoking a prior material breach to justify non-performance is an affirmative defense on which O'Brien's bears the burden of proof. *See Tony Gullo Motors I, L.P.* **[—18—]** *v. Chapa*, 212 S.W.3d 299, 314 (Tex. 2006). "A fundamental principle of contract law is that when one party to a contract commits a material breach of that contract, the other party is discharged or excused from any obligation to perform." *Hernandez v.Gulf Grp. Lloyds,* 875 S.W.2d 691, 692 (Tex. 1994) (citations omitted). "By contrast, when a party commits a nonmaterial breach, the other party is not excused from future performance but may sue for the damages caused by the breach." **{-435-}** *Bartush–Schnitzius Foods Co. v. Cimco*

[18] Contrary to O'Brien's' position, the "subject to" preface to Section 11.02 is not best read as turning the subsequent notice, consent-to-settle, and control-of-defense provisions regarding indemnity into conditions precedent, whose non-fulfillment would void the indemnity obligation. In *Cedyco Corp. v. PetroQuest Energy, LLC*, this court observed that "Texas does not generally favor reading conditions precedent into contracts, ..." before finding such a condition although in a much different context. 497 F.3d 485, 488–89 (5th Cir. 2007) (citation omitted). The general rule holds that "language in a contract is not construed to create a condition precedent if another reading of that language is possible." *Marathon E.G. Holding, Ltd. v. CMS Enters. Co.*, 597 F.3d 311, 321-22 (5th Cir. 2010) (citations omitted); *see also Foreca v. GRD Development Co.*, 758 S.W.2d 744, 745–46 (Tex. 1988) (concluding that "'subject to legal documentation' language is not conclusive on intent to contract[]" in rejecting the argument that such a phrase "constitutes an uncomplied with condition precedent[]" (citation omitted)). The remainder of the indemnity obligation is sufficiently open-ended to preclude a condition precedent.

Refrigeration, Inc., 518 S.W.3d 432, 436 (Tex. 2017) (per curiam) (internal quotation marks and citation omitted).

Texas courts consider the following five factors when determining whether a breach is material:

> 1) the extent to which the injured party will be deprived of the benefit which he reasonably expected;
> 2) the extent to which the injured party can be adequately compensated for the part of that benefit of which he will be deprived;
> 3) the extent to which the party failing to perform or to offer to perform will suffer forfeiture;
> 4) the likelihood that the party failing to perform or to offer to perform will cure his failure, taking account of the circumstances including any reasonable assurances; and
> 5) the extent to which the behavior of the party failing to perform or to offer to perform comports with standards of good faith and fair dealing.

Mustang Pipeline Co., Inc. v. Driver Pipeline Co., Inc., 134 S.W.3d 195, 199 (Tex. 2004) (quoting RESTATEMENT (SECOND) OF CONTRACTS § 241 **[—19—]** (1981)); *see In re Dall. Roadster, Ltd.*, 846 F.3d 112, 127–29 (5th Cir. 2017) (recognizing and applying the Restatement factors).[19]

By entering the Medical Settlement without O'Brien's consent, BP breached the control-of-defense and consent-to-settle provisions of the indemnity clause. The consent-to-settle provision states that "neither party shall effect settlement or compromise of any claim or proceeding" without obtaining written consent of the other party. BP failed to include O'Brien's in the negotiation over BELO claims, and it preemptively agreed to deprive the defense of such later-accruing claims of certain defenses while also extending the limitations period to four years.[20]

BP attempts to avoid any finding of breach by emphasizing that it was only obliged to notify O'Brien's, according to their Contract, once there were actual "claim[s] made" or "proceedings commenced." Conversely, it was not required to obtain O'Brien's consent for the Medical Settlement because the BELO claims arose afterwards (and the settlement only resolved B3 claims for which BP does not seek indemnification).

Though chronologically accurate, these arguments are unconvincing. The consent-to-settle provision states that "*[n]otwithstanding the foregoing*, however, neither party shall effect settlement *or compromise* of *any* claim or proceeding . . ." without obtaining written consent of the other party. The lexical range of the word compromise includes "a concession to something **[—20—]** derogatory or prejudicial." Compromise, MERRIAM WEBSTER DICTIONARY, https://merriam-webster.com/dictionary/compromise (last visited Nov. 17, 2021). Nothing in this provision excludes compromising *future* claims, as the Medical Settlement did in significant part. Further, "notwithstanding the foregoing" disclaims reference to prior language in the same provision that might support limiting **{-436-}** O'Brien's right to consent to settle only then-existing claims or proceedings. Finally, the term "any" is one of enlargement and not limitation. The Medical Settlement unambiguously compromised the defense of BELO claims in some respects; BP therefore breached the consent-to-settle provision with respect to the BELO claims.[21]

---

[19] The *Mustang Pipeline* court also noted the Restatement's two additional "circumstances [having to do with delayed performance] that are significant in determining when a party's duties are discharged under a contract due to the other party's material breach[,]" but neither is relevant here. *Mustang Pipeline Co., Inc., Inc.*,134 S.W.3d at 199.

[20] Other "compromising" aspects of the Medical Settlement included no cap on compensatory damages, disallowing defenses like claim splitting and laches, and not requiring proof of elements like exposure to contaminants.

[21] We also conclude that BP breached the notice requirement. Although BP was required to give notice for "any claim made or proceedings commenced," the fact that BELO claims were not in existence at the time of the settlement did not

Finally, the breach was material according to the *Mustang Pipeline* factors.[22] Again, the Medical Settlement undisputedly compromised the defense of BELO claims though it also benefited O'Brien's (e.g., by including it as a released party). BP nonetheless argues that O'Brien's is not prejudiced for *all* BELO claims. For example, a claim brought within the standard **[—21—]** statute of limitations would not benefit from the settlement's extended limitations period, and a claim that does not benefit from claim-splitting would not be prejudiced by the settlement's waiver of that issue. True enough, but O'Brien's is still prejudiced because it did not negotiate and structure the settlement itself, as was its right under the consent-to-settle provision. BP went it alone and created a new class of claims—*all* BELO claims—that were a "creature of" its global settlement. Requiring O'Brien's to independently litigate whether the defense of a given BELO claim was prejudiced by the terms of the Medical Settlement would require inquiry into the "but for" world of whatever settlement O'Brien's might have reached if given the chance.[23] BP's strategy defeated the underlying purpose of the indemnity provisions: to ensure the indemnitor knew about a claim, led the defense, and agreed to all settlements or any compromise of the claims. Because BP's breach was material, O'Brien's is not required to indemnify the BELO claims.

2. BP-O'Brien's Contract Opt-Out B3 Claims

We disagree, however, with the district court's conclusion that BP materially breached the notice and control-of-defense provisions of the BP-O'Brien's indemnity agreement for opt-out B3 claims at this stage. Opt-out B3 claims are those that were not settled by the Medical Settlement and therefore remained for individual plaintiffs to litigate against BP. The district court's reasoning rested almost entirely on the length of time—over six years—between the opt-out deadline and **{-437-}** the tendering of claims to O'Brien's. Contrary to the court's reasoning, it is far from clear that BP **[—22—]** breached the notice provision for all of the opt-out B3 claims, and even less obvious that any such breach was material.

Although BP had a list of 1,638 valid opt-outs by the deadline prescribed by the Medical Settlement, it needed employer information to tender the claims to O'Brien's. The district court provided minimal support for concluding that this "information was almost certainly available to BP for all of these workers."[24] Although the short form joinders that plaintiffs could file to join the B3 Master Complaint required employer information, the district court recognized "there [was] no guarantee that all cleanup workers would have filed a short form joinder or filled out the employer information." No party seems to dispute that at least *some* of the plaintiffs either omitted or erroneously provided their employer information on the short form joinder. Yet, such information was essential to connecting the claimants with BP's contractors for purposes like investigation and

---

obviate BP's obligations in this unique circumstance. As BP concedes, BELO claims are "creature[s] of the Medical Settlement." Any awkwardness about how notice regarding "future" claims works as a practical matter (and as a matter of contractual interpretation) rests squarely on the ingenuity of the settlement terms. At bottom, BP's argument attempts to evade the commonsense purpose of the notice and control-of-defense clauses: to enable the party footing the bill to know of, control, and resolve relevant claims *before* they are settled or otherwise compromised. BP should have notified O'Brien's that it would seek indemnification for newly created BELO claims during the negotiation that settled the initial B3 claims and that spawned the BELO claims.

[22] O'Brien's was entirely deprived of its ability to control the settlement under the first *Mustang Pipeline* factor; it would be difficult for BP to compensate O'Brien's under the second factor given the unknowability of the "but for" world; and BP cannot cure its failure under the fourth factor.

[23] *See Berkley Reg'l Ins. v. Phila. Indem. Ins.*, 690 F.3d 342, 351 (5th Cir. 2012) (finding prejudice in a late-notice case in the insurance context even though "we cannot fully know what effect, if any, [a party's] participation would have had on [the mediation] process").

[24] The district court generally referenced databases that BP could have utilized. BP disputes this point, and O'Brien's does not engage on this factual issue in its briefing.

assessing indemnity duties. Resolving the question of BP's breach requires separate inquiry as to what information BP possessed about each claim, what notice was reasonable under the circumstances, and whether BP could have provided notice to O'Brien's for that claim.[25]

Accordingly, we cannot conclude that opt-out B3 claims were materially compromised by the purported delay in notice. O'Brien's **[—23—]** concedes that "these claims and proceedings were initially stayed against BP and then further sorted out by [Pretrial Order] 63 and 66 . . . ." And, as the district court recognized, this multi-faceted litigation has implicated numerous claims, including B3 claims that "were asserted directly against the Responders." Whether O'Brien's was prejudiced, pursuant to Texas law, with respect to a given claim due to delayed notice is a fact-bound question. *See Bartush-Schnitzius*, 518 S.W.3d at 436 (recognizing that, "[g]enerally, materiality is an issue to be determined by the trier of facts[]" (internal quotation marks and citation omitted)). Developing the factual record is a task for the district court in the first instance.

3. Claims Relating to the BP-NRC Agreement

In relevant part, the NRC-BP Agreement requires NRC to indemnify BP only to the extent a claim is "caused by the gross negligence or willful misconduct of [NRC]," and for which NRC was not entitled to the protection of "Responder Immunity Law."[26] This Agreement lacks notice, control-of-defense, or consent-to-settle provisions.

Under the circumstances presented here, the opt-out B3 and BELO claims **{-438-}** implicating the BP-NRC Agreement must be evaluated on a claim-by-claim basis. We agree with BP that the district court erred by relying on its 2016 orders to conclude that "under no circumstances is BP entitled to indemnity from NRC." The fact that one set of B3 plaintiffs failed to raise a genuine issue regarding whether NRC had disobeyed federal instructions does not mean no plaintiff ever will.[27] NRC appears to recognize as much, **[—24—]** arguing in large part that "BP has yet to identify any actual case" that would fall within the contract's indemnification provisions. NRC acknowledges that if such a case ever materialized "the most that would follow from BP's argument is that it remains able to argue for a different result under those peculiar facts[.]" We agree—BP should be able to make such an argument under appropriate facts. Thus, we conclude that whether a given claim falls within the BP-NRC Agreement's indemnification provision is a claim-specific,

---

[25] To be clear, BP's *post hoc* argument that the claims were "in no shape to be litigated[]" has no mooring in the text of the BP-O'Brien's Contract. Its obligation under the Contract was only to "promptly give to the other party notice in writing of any claim made or proceedings commenced for which [BP] claim[ed] to be entitled to indemnification . . . ." And the notice was required to "state with as much detail as [was] reasonably practicable the facts and circumstances giving rise to the claim and [had to] be given as soon as possible after [BP] bec[ame] aware of such claim or proceeding." This did not create a right for BP to organize the litigation before giving notice.

[26] BP and NRC seem to agree that the immunity question turns on the extent to which NRC was acting "pursuant to the authorization and direction of the federal government."

[27] The 2016 orders referenced by the district court focused only on certain B3 claims directed against the clean-up defendants (including the Responders here), *not* those **[—24—]** directed against BP. *See generally In re Oil Spill by the Oil Rig "Deepwater Horizon" in the Gulf of Mexico*, MDL No. 2179, ECF No. 21406, 2016 WL 4091416 (E.D. La. Aug. 2, 2016) [hereinafter "August Order"]; *In re Oil Spill by the Oil Rig "Deepwater Horizon" in the Gulf of Mexico*, MDL No. 2179, ECF No. 15853, 2016 WL 614690 (E.D. La. Feb. 16, 2016).

In fact, the August Order illustrates how a responder might fail to establish a "derivative immunity defense," and thus at least potentially fall within the relevant indemnity clause here. August Order, 2016 WL 4091416, at *9 (finding a "genuine dispute as to a material fact as to whether [a responder] complied with an applicable and relevant federal regulation or directive during the response[]" based on allegations that the responder "supplied [a plaintiff] with no [personal protective equipment]," as required by the Occupational Safety and Health Administration's Hazardous Waste and Emergency Response Standard).

factual inquiry best resolved by the district court in the first instance.

Alternatively, the district court indicated in a footnote that "the Medical Settlement similarly prejudiced NRC, voiding NRC's duty to indemnify BP against the BELO claims." But because the BP-NRC Agreement did not contain notice, control-of-defense, or consent-to-settle provisions, it is unclear whether NRC's indemnification obligations precisely track the material breach analysis under the BP-O'Brien's Contract. The single case cited by the district court, arising under Louisiana law, is factually far-afield from the one before us. *Hiern v. St. Paul-Mercury Indem. Co.*, 262 F.2d 526, 528–29 (5th Cir. 1959) (involving allegations that an indemnitee's "failure to act, after promising it would do so, permitted [a] co-indemnitor to dispose of misappropriated assets while [the indemnitee] was **[—25—]** making repeated representations that it was doing and would be [doing] everything possible to secure these assets . . ."). The district court must carefully reassess the BELO claims under the BP-NRC Agreement pursuant to Texas law.

III. CONCLUSION

For the foregoing reasons, we AFFIRM the judgment as follows: (1) BP is an additional insured under the relevant policies only to the extent required to meet the BP-O'Brien's Contract's $2,000,000 CGL insurance requirement; and (2) BP materially breached the indemnity provisions under the BP-O'Brien's Contract with respect to BELO claims, excusing O'Brien's from performing its indemnification obligations under the contract for those claims. **{-439-}**

We REVERSE the judgment as follows: (1) The Starr and COPS policies cannot be combined to satisfy the BP-O'Brien's Contract's $2,000,000 CGL insurance requirement; together they constitute $1,000,000 in CGL-type coverage; (2) Determining whether BP materially breached its obligations under the BP-O'Brien's Contract with respect to opt-out B3 claims requires factual development on a claim-by-claim basis; (3) Similarly, the district court must evaluate NRC's indemnification obligations for opt-out B3 and BELO claims under the BP-NRC Agreement on a claim-by-claim basis.

This case is REMANDED to the district court for further proceedings consistent with this opinion.[28]

AFFIRMED IN PART, REVERSED IN PART, and REMANDED.

*(Reporter's Note: Dissenting opinion in part follows on p. **156**).*

[28] These holdings should not be read to limit the ability of the parties to raise on remand other arguments not at issue in this appeal.

[—26—] {-439-} **GRAVES**, Circuit Judge, dissenting in part:

I respectfully dissent from Section II.B.2 of the majority opinion. Because I conclude BP materially breached the BP-O'Brien's indemnity agreement for opt-out B3 claims based on the record before us, I disagree with the majority's contention that those claims require factual development. In my view, O'Brien's is not required to indemnify BP on any claims because BP failed to give reasonably practicable prompt notice to O'Brien's. I would therefore affirm the district court on this issue as well.

BP's failure to tender any of the opt-out B3 claims before March 2019 materially breached the notice provision of the BP-O'Brien's indemnity agreement. The notice provision required BP to provide as much detail as reasonably practicable under the facts and circumstances. At the time of the Medical Settlement in November 2012, BP knew that some of the 1,638 opt-out B3 claims were from O'Brien's employees. Because BP wanted indemnity from O'Brien's, it should have immediately tendered the claims with known employer information. And for the claims without known employer information BP should have tendered the entire list of opt-outs to O'Brien's. Then O'Brien's would have had an opportunity to determine which opt-out claims were made by its employees.

BP simply argues that it did not tender the claims because they were "in no shape to be litigated." But the notice provision says nothing about claims being in shape to be litigated. The notice provision directs notice be given with as much detail as reasonably practicable. Whether BP determined some of the opt-outs belonged to O'Brien's in November 2012, or sometime after, is of no consequence.

So, in my view, remand on this issue is unnecessary. The district court would be tasked with individual inquiries on each of the approximately 400 opt-out B3 claims as to whether BP had employer information for those [—27—] claims at the time of the Medical Settlement, and if not, when did it have that information. But that information makes no difference because BP certainly breached as to the claims with employer information, and there is no reason it took BP nearly seven years to discover O'Brien's was the employer for the claims without employer information.

It is clear BP breached the notice provision for the claims in which BP had the employer information from the complaints or short form joinder and O'Brien's was in fact identified as the employer. The fact that some of the B3 claims were negotiated {-440-} in the Medical Settlement and some were opt-outs does not change the duty to notify O'Brien's as soon as the claims were known to belong to O'Brien's. Insofar as BP had the employer information that identified O'Brien's for some of the opt-out claims, I would affirm the district court's determination that BP breached the BP-O'Brien's indemnity agreement on those claims.

As for the claims in which there was no employer information, remand to determine when BP knew the claims belonged to O'Brien's would likely not result in a finding that BP did not breach the notice provision. Although I do not necessarily agree with the district court's factual contention that BP had readily available databases with employer information, I find it difficult to conclude there is any circumstance that would have taken BP nearly seven years to obtain the necessary employer information (if it was not readily available). BP of course disputes that it had employer information readily available, but even so, BP does not state what steps it took to obtain employer information (or that it could *reasonably* take seven years to do so). Because BP had knowledge that at least some of the opt-out B3 claims belonged to O'Brien's, BP should have then been aware that some of the claims without employer information belonged to O'Brien's as well, and attempted to obtain employer information within a reasonable time. *Cf. Ridglea Est. Condo. Ass'n v. Lexington Ins. Co.*, 415 F.3d 474, 477 (5th Cir. 2005) (concluding party [—28—] should have been aware of likelihood of damage due to presence of other damage and stating the party should have inspected within a reasonable time to provide reasonable notice of damage).

BP strangely argues O'Brien's should have known which opt-outs belonged to it because O'Brien's was a party to the MDL and had access to the list of opt-outs. But that argument ignores the fact that BP didn't notify O'Brien's it would seek indemnity of *any* B3 claims. Certainly O'Brien's would know which claims were brought by its own employees. That, however, does not negate the important point here—BP did not notify O'Brien's that it would seek indemnity of those claims. O'Brien's knowledge of which opt-out B3 claims were from its own employees is just that. It does not also give O'Brien's notice that BP would seek indemnity on those claims.

BP's argument also emphasizes my qualm with what is reasonably practicable notice. If O'Brien's could have "unquestionably" determined in 2012 which of the opt-out B3 claims were brought by its own employees, and BP was going to seek indemnity for any claims that belonged to O'Brien's, why didn't BP notify O'Brien's at that time? It would have been reasonably practicable in November 2012 for BP to inform O'Brien's that "if any of these opt-out B3 claims are from your employees, we want indemnity." O'Brien's would have then known immediately which claims were brought by its own employees (and BP would want indemnification for) and could have shared that information with BP. Instead of acknowledging this simple and reasonable step it could have taken, BP now contends it acted well within the indemnity agreement's terms by sitting on its hands for nearly seven years before saying a word about these opt-out B3 claims to O'Brien's.

Not only did BP breach the notice provision, that breach was material. Most of the *Mustang Pipeline* factors weigh in favor of concluding BP's breach material. Specifically, O'Brien's was deprived of its benefit of the bargain (to **[—29—]** receive prompt notice), BP cannot compensate O'Brien's for that deprivation, BP cannot cure its breach after **{-441-}** so much time has passed, and it does not appear that BP acted in good faith.

O'Brien's was deprived of its right to investigate the opt-out B3 claims from at the latest, November 2012 until March 2019 when they were tendered. Notice requirements afford rights like the right to join in the investigation, to settle a case or claim, and to interpose and control the defense. *See Berkeley Reg'l Ins. Co. v. Phila. Indem. Ins. Co.*, 690 F.3d 342, 348 (5th Cir. 2012). O'Brien's had no notice BP would seek indemnity of these claims and in the interim conducted no investigation while under the impression that these claims would not be tendered. BP's only argument on this is that it is "implausible" to think O'Brien's would investigate these claims while they were stayed or sorted. For the same reasons the majority declines to enter the "but-for" world, I see no need to here. There is no way to know whether O'Brien's would have actually investigated those claims. Regardless, for nearly seven years, O'Brien's was deprived of the opportunity to make a choice on investigating the claims it would ultimately be asked to pay.

I also note that opt-out B3 claims were part of the B3 class. BP attempted to settle those claims through the Medical Settlement. BP negotiated with class counsel and reached the terms of the Medical Settlement. And when the opt-out B3 plaintiffs received notice of the Medical Settlement, they determined they would rather pursue their own claims than agree to the present terms. As a practical matter, the terms of the settlement, which O'Brien's had no participation in, certainly affected opt-out decisions. So up until those opt-out B3 plaintiffs actually opted-out, BP controlled the defense, organized the settlement class, and established the procedure for dealing with opt-outs. All without notifying or allowing O'Brien's to participate. Through this lens, it is obvious that BP's breach **[—30—]** was material and BP failed to act in good faith.[1] The harm created by BP excluding O'Brien's from the early part of the litigation of these claims is

[1] Notably, BP does not seek indemnification for the B3 claims settled in the Medical Settlement. Nor does it seem likely that BP would be able avoid a material breach on those claims settled under the consent-to-settle or notice provisions.

not erased simply because they ultimately opted out. We cannot know what effect O'Brien's participation in the settlement would have had.

When a plaintiff opts out of a class action settlement, it is necessarily a derivative of the settlement terms. Because O'Brien's was not notified before or during the Medical Settlement that BP was going to seek indemnity of any B3 claims or the potential opt-outs, O'Brien's was excluded from the settlement negotiations, lacked the control of the defense, and had no input on the process for handling those potential opt-outs. BP's breach was material on the opt-out B3 claims to the same extent it was on the BELO claims.

BP shut out O'Brien's throughout the entirety of the litigation of these opt-out B3 claims. For BP to seek indemnity from O'Brien's after years of facing these claims, knowing some belonged to O'Brien's, and having the ability to connect the others to O'Brien's, is absurd. The district court concluded the length of time from the time BP had a list of the opt-outs in November 2012, until the first opt-out B3 claim was tendered in March 2019, was prejudicial to O'Brien's. I see no error in this reasoning. Remand is thus unnecessary.

Because BP's delayed notifying O'Brien's of the opt-out B3 claims for nearly seven years, I would conclude BP **{-442-}** materially breached the BP-O'Brien's indemnity agreement. Contrary to the majority, I would affirm the **[—31—]** district court on this issue and hold O'Brien's is not required to indemnify BP on any claims.

United States Court of Appeals
for the Fifth Circuit

No. 20-30019

SCF WAXLER MARINE, L.L.C.
VS.
ARIS T M/V

Appeal from the United States District Court for the Eastern District of Louisiana

Decided: January 24, 2022

Citation: 24 F.4th 458, 10 Adm. R. 159 (5th Cir. 2022).

Before **JONES, SMITH,** and **ELROD,** Circuit Judges.

[—6—] {-465-} ELROD, Circuit Judge: **{-466-}**

On the evening of January 31, 2016, three vessels were travelling on the Mississippi River. Unfortunately, they did not pass peacefully in the night. This case is about why, and how fault should be assigned. Because we hold that the district court did not err in allocating the parties' respective **[—7—]** liabilities, in limiting the parties' liability, or in dismissing the personal injury claim, we AFFIRM.

I.

On the evening of January 31, 2016, the Mississippi River was running high. The weather was fair, and a light surface fog was developing on the portion of river near Hahnville, Louisiana.

The *Aris T* was moving up the Mississippi River at the same time the *Elizabeth* and the *Loretta* were moving down it.[1] The allision occurred as the three vessels were passing each other in the Hahnville Bar, a bend between mile markers 124.5 and 126 in the Mississippi River where a number of moorings are located. In a nutshell, the allision occurred as the *Aris T* was passing the *Loretta* and the *Elizabeth* at the same time as the *Loretta* was overtaking the *Elizabeth*, and given their positioning, there simply was not enough room for the three vessels to be adjacent to each other simultaneously.[2] **[—8—]**

The *Aris T* was mastered by Captain Baltas, but at all relevant times was piloted **{-467-}** by Michael Leone, a compulsory pilot.[3] The *Aris T* was in good working order and its crew was duly trained. It was equipped with two Electronic Chart Display and Information System ("ECDIS") units which could be used for navigation, but at the time were only being used for training purposes and had limited functionality. Instead, the *Aris T* was using radar and paper charts for navigation, and Pilot Leone had a portable Rose Point electronic chart system.

The *Elizabeth* was under the command of Captain Christiansen. The *Elizabeth* was in good working order and navigated with both radar and a Rose Point system.

The *Loretta* was piloted by Captain Sanamo; it too was navigated with radar and a Rose Point system. Unlike the other two

---

[1] The *Aris T* refers to the vessel itself and "*Aris T* Interests" refers collectively to the vessel, its owner Aris T. Ene, and its manager Marmaras Navigation Limited.

The *Elizabeth* refers to the vessel itself and "*Elizabeth* Interests" refers collectively to the co-owners of the defendant vessel: Genesis Marine, L.L.C. and Genesis Marine, L.L.C. of Delaware.

The *Loretta* refers to the vessel itself and "*Loretta* Interest" refers to its owner, Cenac Marine Services, L.L.C. (also referred to as "Cenac"). We also note that Cenac's various insurance companies (collectively, the "Insurance Parties") are involved in this case: Continental Insurance Company, AGCS Marine Insurance Company, New York Marine and General Insurance Company, Stonington Insurance Company, National Specialty Insurance Company, and Lloyd's Syndicates.

[2] A video reconstruction of the allision shows the paths of the vessels and includes relevant audio recorded from the *Aris T*'s VDR, which recorded all VHF transmissions sent or received by the *Aris T*'s VHF radio and all voices recorded on the four microphones located on the *Aris T*'s bridge. This video reconstruction was admitted into evidence, and no party has contested its accuracy.

[3] A compulsory pilot is "one who is legally required to be taken by the vessel owner," typically to guarantee that the pilot has knowledge of the local waters. Guy C. Stephenson, *A Pilot Is A Pilot: Compulsory Pilots—Vessel Owner's Responsibilities for Intervention and Personal Injury*, 70 TUL. L. REV. 633, 634 (1995).

vessels, however, the *Loretta* was not in good working order. The *Loretta* was secured to the barges it was towing by two-part face wires.[4] At some point during these events, this wiring system failed, limiting the *Loretta*'s maneuverability. This was not the first time the *Loretta*'s face-wire system failed, but Cenac chose a band-aid solution rather than redesigning to a three-part face-wire system, which would have run back to the barge an additional time.

As the *Loretta* and the *Elizabeth* were approaching the Hahnville Bar, Captain Christiansen suggested to Captain Sanamo that the *Loretta* overtake the *Elizabeth*. Captain Sanamo had previously asked to overtake the *Elizabeth*, but at that point Captain Christiansen thought the maneuver was **[—9—]** too dangerous. But Captain Christiansen was going to be "stopping and backing up" at the Bayou Fleet, just south of the Hahnville Bar. Because he would be slowing down to back in, he thought that this was a good time for the *Loretta* to overtake him.

Further, Captain Christiansen mistakenly believed there was nothing nearby going upriver; neither he nor Captain Sanamo had heard the *Aris T*'s earlier announcement of its position over the radio, which could be because Pilot Leone transmitted using a handheld VHF radio from within the steel confines of the *Aris T*'s bridge. But the *Aris T*, despite being able to hear Captain Sanamo and Captain Christiansen's communications about the overtaking agreement, did nothing to correct the captains' faulty assumption that nothing was coming upriver towards them. Pilot Leone did not reach out and advise the *Elizabeth* and the *Loretta* of its upbound route, nor did he reduce the *Aris T*'s speed.

It was not until five minutes later, when the *Loretta* was already overtaking the *Elizabeth*, that Captain Christiansen reached out to Pilot Leone to organize the *Aris T*'s passing. They agreed to a one-whistle, port-to-port side passing. Captain Sanamo then reached out to Pilot Leone, and they too organized a port-to-port side passing. This meant that the three vessels agreed to pass each other with the *Elizabeth* on the west moving downriver, the *Aris T* on the east moving upriver, and the *Loretta* in between them moving downriver, overtaking the *Elizabeth*. **{-468-}**

It did not go as planned. Because Captain Christiansen said the *Elizabeth* would be backing into the Bayou Fleet, Captain Sanamo and Pilot Leone expected the *Elizabeth* to be very close to the west bank. But instead, the *Elizabeth* was in the middle of the river, and continuously slid east during the passing due to the four- to five-knot current. This greatly reduced the amount of space the *Loretta* and the *Aris T* had to execute their pass. Captain Sanamo, perhaps realizing there might not be sufficient space, suggested to Pilot Leone that the *Loretta* abandon its attempt to overtake the *Elizabeth*. **[—10—]**

At this point, "the maneuver was so precarious that it could only work if: "(a) the *Elizabeth* somehow stopped its slide and began moving towards the west bank, which it gave no sign of doing; (b) the *Loretta* could somehow push out in front of the *Elizabeth* to complete the overtaking maneuver, which it had not been able to do thus far; and (c) nothing else went wrong." But Pilot Leone told Captain Sanamo there was "plenty of room" and to continue forward, and Captain Sanamo did not protest. Pilot Leone momentarily suggested altering the passing plan so the *Aris T* would pass in between the *Loretta* and the *Elizabeth*, but he quickly recanted that suggestion. And so, despite the limited river space, the boats proceeded with their planned passage.

The *Elizabeth* continued sliding east, which forced Captain Sanamo to slow down to avoid colliding with the *Elizabeth*, and this kept the *Loretta* in the *Aris T*'s path. Further preventing the *Loretta* from getting out of the

[4] Face wires secure the towboat to its tow. A face wire is two-part when it runs from winches on the towboat to terminal fittings welded to the deck of the barge (one part) and then back to the towboat (second part). Three-part face wire would then run back to the barge one more time.

Aris T's path was its face wire breaking.[5] Cenac discarded the face wire before it could be examined.

At some point, Pilot Leone realized the *Aris T* was on course to hit the *Loretta*, so he took emergency evasive maneuvers. The maneuvers avoided a collision with the *Loretta*. But they resulted in the *Aris T*'s colliding with the vessel *SCF Vision*, which was moored at the Valero facility. The *SCF Vision* in turn struck and damaged the Valero facility. The *Aris T*, at this point trying to stop, then collided with the vessels *M/V Pedernales* and *Kirby 28080* and allided with Shell/Motiva Berth 4 and Berth 2, damaging both of them.[6] **[—11—]**

During the failed passing, Captain Christiansen was incommunicado with Captain Sanamo and Pilot Leone. He later testified that their passing each other did not concern his vessel, so there was no need for him to communicate with them, even though his not acting in accordance with his stated intention to back into the Bayou Fleet reduced their maneuvering space. Captain Sanamo was talking on his cell phone with his girlfriend during the accident, in violation of Cenac's cell phone policy. And Pilot Leone failed to react appropriately to the overtaking announcement and kept the *Aris T* going at speed, rather than slowing down.

While this was happening, Antoine Morris, an employee of Shell/Motiva, was working at Shell/Motiva Berth 1, located about 1000 feet from Berth 2. Upon hearing a warning from the Berth 4 operator about the accident, Morris decided to walk to the emergency shutdown device to turn off the dock's product lines. But while on his way, upon seeing the *Aris T* in the **{-469-}** distance, Morris panicked, lost his footing, and fell. Immediately after his fall, he was able to get up and walk.

He remained at work until his shift ended and did not report any symptoms to his coworker or supervisor. He later saw a series of doctors, and was eventually diagnosed with PTSD and a traumatic brain injury by Dr. Axelrad, the third doctor he saw.[7] An independent evaluator, Dr. Ginzburg, testified that Morris did not have either of these ailments.

SCF Waxler Marine, L.L.C., owner of the moored vessel *SCF Vision*, sued the *Aris T, in rem*, for damages caused by the accident. Then, each of the Shore Plaintiffs[8] sued both the *Aris T in rem* and the other *Aris T* Interests *in personam*. Then the *Aris T* filed a complaint under the Limitation of **[—12—]** Liability Act,[9] asserting that the owners were not liable, and the *Loretta* Interest did the same. The cases were consolidated, and thereafter, the *Loretta* Interest and the *Aris T* Interests filed third-party complaints against the *Elizabeth* Interests.

The *Elizabeth* Interests then asserted limitation of liability as a defense. Morris asserted claims in the limitation proceedings, seeking claims for personal injuries. Finally, the Shore Plaintiffs filed third party complaints against the Insurance Parties under "Louisiana's direct-action statute, La. R.S. 22:1269, which allows injured persons to sue the insurers of a person alleged to have caused and accident."

Two bench trials followed under Federal Rule of Civil Procedure 52. First, the district

[5] The parties contest whether the face wire broke before or after the accident occurred. The district court, after hearing testimony and reviewing the *Loretta*'s Rose Point system, camera, and radar footage, concluded that it broke before the passing was complete.

[6] We refer to the owners of vessels that were moored at or near the docks and came into the *Aris T*'s collision course as the "Vessel Plaintiffs."

[7] At the first and second doctor's visits, Morris denied hitting his head or experiencing any concussion symptoms, but he did complain of neck pain.

[8] "Shore Plaintiffs" refers to the owners of the docks and berths damaged by the accident: Valero Refining - New Orleans, L.L.C. ("Valero"), Motiva Enterprises, L.L.C., and Shell Chemical, L.P.

[9] 46 U.S.C. §§ 30501, *et seq.* The Act allows owners of vessels involved in accidents to limit their liability to the value of the vessel and pending freight in certain situations. *See id.* § 30505. It also allows them to proactively bring suits to claim this limited liability. *Id.* § 30511.

court tried the negligence and limitation-of-liability claims over the course of 10 days. Second, the district court tried Morris's personal injury case. Before the bench trials commenced, the district court denied the Shore Plaintiffs motion for partial summary judgment on the issue of whether the Insurance Parties could limit their liability if the *Loretta* Interest could.

The district court found that the *Elizabeth*, *Loretta*, and *Aris T* were all liable for the damages to the Shore Plaintiffs and Vessel Plaintiffs. The court used maritime statutes and regulations, including the U.S. Inland Navigation Rules, 33 C.F.R. §§ 83.01, *et seq.*, to determine the applicable standards of care. Because comparative fault applies to maritime accidents, the district court then described each vessel's faults. It found the *Loretta* and *Elizabeth* primarily and equally at fault for creating the dangerous situation with their overtaking agreement (allocating 45% of the liability to each) and found the *Aris T* at fault to a lesser extent (allocating 10% of the liability). **[—13—]**

The district court ruled that the *Loretta* Interest and the *Elizabeth* Interests could not limit their liability because they were themselves negligent but that the *Aris T* Interests could limit their liability because the culpability rested solely with the compulsory pilot, Pilot Leone.

Finally, the district court dismissed Morris's claims with prejudice. It found **{-470-}** that the cause of his injuries was his own carelessness and inattention, and not the *Aris T*'s alliding with a different berth; therefore, Morris could not establish the duty or cause elements of his claim. It further found that Morris could not recover for emotional injuries under a "zone of danger" theory because he was not in the zone of danger.

II.

Four appeals involving different subsets of the parties were consolidated into this case. The *Elizabeth* Interests appeal the district court's assigning them 45% of the fault and denying its limitation of liability. The *Loretta* Interest appeals on the same grounds as the *Elizabeth* Interests. The Shore Plaintiffs appeal the district court's previous denial of partial summary judgment regarding the Cenac Insurer's ability to limit their liability to that of the *Loretta* Interest. Finally, Morris appeals the district court's dismissal of his case.

A. Allocation of Liability

The first issue in this appeal is whether the district court erred in its allocation of fault among the three vessel defendants: the *Elizabeth*, the *Loretta*, and the *Aris T*.

Negligence in general maritime law operates much like negligence in state tort law. To establish maritime negligence, "a plaintiff must demonstrate that there was [1] a duty owed by the defendant to the plaintiff, [2] breach of that duty, [3] injury sustained by the plaintiff, and [4] a causal connection between the defendant's conduct and the plaintiff's injury." **[—14—]** *GIC Servs., L.L.C. v. Freightplus USA, Inc.*, 866 F.3d 649, 659, 5 Adm. R. 287, 291 (5th Cir. 2017) (quotation omitted).

The appellants, the *Loretta* Interest and the *Elizabeth* Interests, do not contest that they are liable. Instead, they contest how the district court apportioned fault among them and the *Aris T* Interests. "[W]hen two or more parties have contributed by their fault to cause property damage in a maritime collision or stranding, liability for such damage is to be allocated among the parties proportionately to the comparative degree of their fault . . . ." *United States v. Reliable Transfer Co.*, 421 U.S. 397, 411 (1975). "Apportionment is not a mechanical exercise that depends upon counting up the errors committed by both parties. The trial court must determine, based upon the number and quality of faults by each party, the role each fault had in causing the collision." *Stolt Achievement, Ltd. v. Dredge B.E. Lindholm*, 447 F.3d 360, 370 (5th Cir. 2006).

"[W]e review 'a trial court's finding on apportionment of relative fault in a maritime collision' only for clear error." *Deloach Marine Servs., L.L.C. v. Marquette Transp. Co., L.L.C.*, 974 F.3d 601, 609, 8 Adm. R. 228, 233 (5th Cir. 2020) (quoting *In re Settoon Towing, L.L.C.*, 859 F.3d 340, 344, 5 Adm. R. 266, 267 (5th Cir. 2017)). Allocation is treated as a finding of fact. *See Deloach*, 974 F.3d at 607, 8 Adm. R. at 231. "Even if we might have given different weight to different pieces of evidence than did the district court, this is not a reason to disturb that court's findings of relative responsibility, absent a showing of clear error." *Id.* at 609, 8 Adm. R. at 233 (quotation omitted). The exception to this is "when factual findings in an admiralty case are essentially based on an incorrect legal principle, [the] Rule 52(a) clearly erroneous [standard] does not apply and we disregard any such possible findings." *Marine Transp. Lines, Inc. v. M/V Tako Invader*, 37 F.3d 1138, 1142 (5th Cir. 1994) (quotation omitted). **[—15—]**

The *Elizabeth* Interests and the *Loretta* Interest argue that they should be allocated less than 45% of the fault and **{-471-}** that others should be allocated more. The *Aris T* Interests and the Shore Plaintiffs defend the district court's apportionment.

We do not find error in the district court's evaluation of the *Elizabeth*'s violations of the Inland Navigation Rules or in the *Loretta*'s violations of the Inland Navigation Rules.[10] The district court correctly found that the *Elizabeth* violated Inland Rules 2 (prudent seamanship), 5 (lookout), 7 (risk of collision), 8 (action to avoid collision), 9 (keeping to the outer limit of the channel that lies on the vessel's starboard side as is safe and practicable), and 17 (action by stand-on vessel). In addition, the district court properly found that the *Loretta* violated Inland Rules 2 (prudent seamanship), 5 (lookout), 7 (risk of collision), 8 (action to avoid collision), 9 (failure to propose manner of passing in narrow channel), 13 (overtaking), 14 (failure to propose manner of passing in meeting situation), 16 (action by give-way vessel), and 34(d) (danger signal). Finally, the district court properly found that the *Aris T* was liable for violating Inland Rules 2 (prudent seamanship), 6 (safe speed), 7 (risk of collision), and 9 (failure to hold up to allow a safe passing).

Though the district court did not mention whether the *Aris T* violated Inland Rules 8, 14, and 16, we do not consider that to be clearly erroneous. Rather, based on the conflicting evidence presented at trial, we infer that the **[—16—]** district court (based on its ultimate conclusions) did not believe that the *Aris T* violated Inland Rules 8 and 16 because she could not have taken "early and substantial" "positive" action to avoid the incident based on the narrow passage facing the vessels (and the relative positions of the *Elizabeth* and the *Loretta*). *See* 33 C.F.R. §§ 83.08, 83.16. And given that the *Aris T* was entering the outside bend of a west-bound turn in high-current conditions, we infer that the district court concluded that the *Aris T* did not violate Inland Rule 14 because she could not have altered her course any more than she already had leading up to the incident. *See id.* § 83.14. And in any event, the conflicting evidence on what the *Aris T* could have done under those circumstances leaves little room for legal error. Thus, though the district court did not mention these Inland Rules in discussing the *Aris T*'s liability, we find no clear error in its ultimate conclusions.

We thus conclude that the district court did not clearly err in allocating liability as to the *Elizabeth*, the *Loretta*, or the *Aris T*.

B. Limitations of Liability

The *Aris T* Interests, *Elizabeth* Interests, *Loretta* Interest, and the excess insurers for the *Loretta* Interest all claim the right to limit their respective liability to the value of their vessels, plus pending freight at the conclusion

[10] Relatedly, we hold that the district court did not abuse its discretion in relying on undisclosed portions of Cunningham's testimony elicited on cross examination, and that even assuming *arguendo* that it was error to admit the testimony, such error was harmless because the district court only relied upon disclosed portions of his testimony in its Findings of Fact and Conclusions of Law.

We also hold that the district court did not abuse its discretion in determining that the *Loretta*'s face wire was in poor condition.

of the voyage. The district court found that the *Aris T* Interests are able to do so but that the others could not.

There are two distinct ways the owner of a vessel involved in an accident can limit its liability to the value of the vessel and its freight. First, the Limitation of Liability Act, 46 U.S.C. §§ 30501, *et seq.*, provides for such limitation in certain situations. The *Loretta* Interest and the *Elizabeth* **{-472-}** Interests claim their liability should be limited under the Act, an argument addressed in Part II.B.1 below. Second, when the negligence of a vessel is attributable solely to a compulsory pilot, the vessel is only liable *in rem*, **[—17—]** effectively limiting the owner's liability to the same extent as the Limitation of Liability Act. *See Probo II London v. Isla Santay MV*, 92 F.3d 361, 365 (5th Cir. 1996). The *Aris T* Interests assert their liability should be limited in this way, as the district court found. This is addressed in Part II.B.2 below.

1.

The Limitation of Liability Act provides that "the liability of the owner of a vessel for any claim, debt, or liability" "arising from . . . any act, matter, or thing, loss, damage, or forfeiture, done, occasioned, or incurred, without the privity or knowledge of the owner" "shall not exceed the value of the vessel and pending freight." 46 U.S.C. § 30505(a)–(b).

In short, "[u]nder the Act, a party is entitled to limitation only if it is '*without privity or knowledge*' of the cause of the loss." *In re Hellenic Inc.*, 252 F.3d 391, 394 (5th Cir. 2001) (emphasis added) (quoting *Brunet v. United Gas Pipeline Co.*, 15 F.3d 500, 504 (5th Cir. 1994)). Furthermore, "if the vessel's negligence or unseaworthiness is the proximate cause of the claimant's loss, the [ship owner] must prove it had no privity or knowledge of the unseaworthy conditions or negligent acts." *Trico Marine Assets Inc. v. Diamond B Marine Servs. Inc.*, 332 F.3d 779, 789 (5th Cir. 2003). "[K]nowledge, when the shipowner is a corporation, is judged not only by what the corporation's managing officers actually knew, but also by what they should have known." *Id.* at 789–90. That is, if the unseaworthy "condition could have been discovered through the exercise of reasonable diligence," a corporate owner is deemed to have knowledge of it and cannot limit its liability. *In re Omega Protein, Inc.*, 548 F.3d 361, 371 (5th Cir. 2008) (quoting *Brister v. A.W.I., Inc.*, 946 F.2d 350, 356 (5th Cir. 1991)).

Importantly, the owner must have privity or knowledge of the "acts of negligence or conditions of unseaworthiness [that] *caused* the accident." *Farrell Lines Inc. v. Jones*, 530 F.2d 7, 10 (5th Cir. 1976) (emphasis added). **[—18—]** The owner's knowledge of acts of negligence or conditions of unseaworthiness that did not cause the accident does not prevent the owner from limiting liability. *See id.*; *see also In re Omega Protein*, 548 F.3d at 369–70 (finding that the owner's failure to train its employees on a navigation system did not mean they could not limit liability when the failure to use the navigation system did not cause the accident). Similarly, the owner's knowledge of acts that actually caused the accident, but were not acts of negligence or conditions of unseaworthiness, does not prevent the owner from limiting liability. *See Farrell Lines Inc.*, 530 F.2d at 10.

A vessel can be rendered unseaworthy by having either insufficient equipment or an insufficiently competent and trained crew. *See Jackson v. OMI Corp.*, 245 F.3d 525, 527 (5th Cir. 2001). Thus, the privity or knowledge standard "obliges the owner to select a competent master." *In re Omega Protein*, 548 F.3d at 374. It also requires the owner to properly train the master and crew. *See Trico Marine Assets*, 332 F.3d at 790 (finding knowledge when the "captain was improperly trained"). It does not, however, render the owner liable for "mere 'mistakes of navigation' by an otherwise competent crew." *In re Omega Protein*, 548 F.3d at 371 (quoting *Brister*, 946 F.2d at 356). This is because "when the owner is so far removed **{-473-}** from the vessel that he can exert no control over the master's actions, he should not be taxed with the master's negligence." *Cont'l Oil Co. v. Bonanza Corp.*, 706 F.2d 1365, 1377 n.15 (5th Cir. 1983) (en banc).

Therefore, when the cause of the allision was the crew's errors, the owner's ability to limit its liability turns on whether the crew was incompetent, which the owner should have known, or whether the crew made mere mistakes of navigation, which the owner could not have known about. A captain's record and years of experience are relevant to this inquiry. *See Kristie Leigh Enters. v. Am. Com. Lines*, 72 F.3d 479, 482 (5th Cir. 1996). Also relevant is the owner's knowledge of how well trained the captain is. *See* **[—19—]** *Trico Marine Assets*, 332 F.3d at 790. Finally, all of these questions—the cause of the accident, the owner's privity or knowledge, and the crew's competence—are fact-specific, and therefore subject to clear-error review. *See In re Omega Protein*, 548 F.3d at 361.

The district court found that the *Elizabeth* Interests could not limit their liability because they themselves were negligent in: (1) hiring an incompetent master without doing a proper background check; (2) failing to properly train Captain Christiansen in how to use the Rose Point navigation system; and (3) approving Captain Christiansen's decision to maneuver into the Bayou Fleet without an assist tug. Further, the court found that the *Loretta* Interest could not limit its liability because it was negligent in (1) sending the *Loretta* out with an inadequate face-wire system, and (2) not enforcing its cell-phone policy. The district court found that the *Aris T* owners could limit their liability.

In challenging this ruling, the *Elizabeth* Interests contend that the district court's finding that Captain Christiansen was incompetent was error. They point out that the Coast Guard did not cite Captain Christiansen for the incident, but the Coast Guard did cite Captain Sanamo and Pilot Leone. Moreover, Captain Christiansen had years of experience navigating the Hahnville Bar, and his prior suspensions were twenty years before this incident and not at all relevant to evaluating his competence here. Given all this, the *Elizabeth* Interests contend that Captain Christiansen's errors were mere mistakes of navigation that the *Elizabeth*'s owners could not have known of, and not incompetence they should have known about before hiring him. We agree that the district court erred in finding Captain Christiansen incompetent.

Nevertheless, the district court provided two other grounds for not limiting the *Elizabeth* Interests' liability: the *Elizabeth* Interests failed to **[—20—]** provide Captain Christiansen with training on the Rose Point navigation system—which resulted in Captain Christiansen's not using all available means to maintain a proper lookout—and the *Elizabeth* Interests' general manager approved the down-streaming maneuver without a tugboat assist that was employed by Captain Christiansen during the allision sequence. The *Elizabeth* Interests thus had "privity or knowledge" of the conditions that contributed to the *Aris T*s allision. 46 U.S.C. § 30505(b). We affirm on these grounds.

The *Loretta* Interest, Cenac, contends the district court erred in finding that Cenac could not limit its liability. Cenac argues that the factors the district court held that Cenac had knowledge of—the faulty face-wire system and Captain Sanamo's talking on his cell phone—were not *causes* of the accident. Cenac posits that the face wire parting could not have been a cause of the accident because, according **{-474-}** to Cenac, the parting did not occur until after the *Loretta* was mostly past the *Aris T.* Cenac points to Captain Sanamo's testimony as to when he believed it broke, as well as to some expert testimony that the *Loretta* could not have maneuvered as it did if the face wire had broken earlier. Cenac also posits that Captain Sanamo's cell phone call with his girlfriend during the accident was not a cause of the accident because it did not distract him. According to Cenac, though the line was open, Captain Sanamo was not actively talking with his girlfriend and was adequately focused on the task at hand, as evidenced by his active communication with Pilot Leone on the radio. Thus, because Cenac believes these factors were not causes of the accident, Cenac contends that those issues do not preclude it from limiting its liability. **[—21—]**

We affirm the district court because the district court's finding of causality with respect to these issues was not clearly erroneous.[11] It was not error for the district court to discount Captain Sanamo's testimony about the face wire, and instead credit other expert testimony and evidence (*e.g.*, radar and video footage) that it broke earlier, and thus was a cause of the allision. Moreover, it was not error for the district court to conclude that the cell phone was a distraction and a cause of the allision, especially in light of the fact that the Coast Guard sanctioned Captain Sanamo for it.

Thus, we affirm the district court's ruling that the Limitation of Liability Act does not allow the *Elizabeth* Interests or the *Loretta* Interest to limit liability in this case.

2.

The district court determined that the *Aris T* could limit its liability using the "compulsory pilot" defense. "[T]he 'compulsory pilot defense,' can be traced back to" as early as the nineteenth century. *Probo II London*, 92 F.3d at 365. Under it, "the vessel itself is liable *in rem* for a maritime collision caused by the fault of its compulsory pilot; if the pilot alone was at fault, the shipowner will not be liable *in personam*; however, if the negligence of the master or crew contributed to the collision, then in addition to the vessel's liability *in rem* the shipowner also will face *in personam* liability." *Id.*

The negligence of a vessel's master can contribute to an allision either through actions or omissions. Generally, the "master is entitled to assume that the pilot is an expert on local conditions and practices," and defers to his command. *Avondale Indus., Inc. v. Int'l Marine Carriers, Inc.*, 15 F.3d 489, 493 (5th Cir. 1994). But the master may not "regard the presence of a duly- **[—22—]** licensed pilot in compulsory pilot waters as freeing him from every obligation to attend to the safety of the vessel." *The Oregon*, 158 U.S. 186, 195 (1895). Instead, if "it becomes manifest that the pilot is steering the vessel into danger," the master is negligent if he does not timely intervene. *Avondale*, 15 F.3d at 493. This responsibility to intervene places a duty on the ship's master to maintain an "adequate level of information" about the ship's navigation. *Id.*

The *Elizabeth* Interests and the *Loretta* Interest contend the district court erred in allowing the *Aris T* to limit its liability because the negligence contributing to the allision can be attributed to more than just Pilot Leone's decisions. **{-475-}** First, they argue that Captain Baltas, the *Aris T*'s master, agreed with Pilot Leone's decisions and therefore the crew's negligence contributed to the allision. Second, they contend that the shipowner's failure to equip the *Aris T* with a functional ECDIS system was negligent and contributed to the accident. Third, they contend that the shipowner offered no training to its bridge officers on the Inland Rules of Navigation.

We affirm the district court's ruling that the *Aris T* can limit its liability. Captain Baltas was monitoring the situation, and he was entitled to trust Pilot Leone's greater expertise on the spacing in the Hahnville Bar. Moreover, the *Aris T* was adequately equipped; the ECDIS system was not mandatory at the time, and Pilot Leone had the same navigation system as the *Elizabeth* and the *Loretta*. Finally, Pilot Leone had adequate knowledge of the Inland Rules of Navigation; the point of having compulsory pilots for areas with specific navigational rules is to compensate for the crew's lack of knowledge in that area. We conclude that the *Aris T*'s negligence was attributable solely to the compulsory pilot, Pilot Leone, and therefore, the *Aris T* is only liable *in rem*. **[—23—]**

C. The Personal Injury Claim

Antoine Morris, a Shell/Motiva employee was working on a berth when he caught sight of the *Aris T* alliding with a berth over 1,000 feet away. The berth he was standing on was not struck and did not move or shake. Morris simply panicked at the surprising sight of the vessel alliding with another berth, lost his footing, and fell. The district court dismissed

[11] Because we affirm the district court's ruling that Cenac may not limit its liability, we dismiss as moot Cenac's excess insurers' challenge.

his negligence claim, and Morris challenges the dismissal on both procedural and substantive grounds. We affirm the district court's dismissal.

Morris raises four points of error. First, he contends that the district court abused its discretion by denying him a continuance on the morning of the trial because his key expert, Dr. Axelrad, was at his brother's deathbed and would be unable to testify in person. This prejudiced him, Morris says, because the other parties' expert witness sharply criticized Dr. Axelrad's deposition testimony, and Dr. Axelrad could not respond.

The matter of a continuance is reviewed for abuse of discretion. *See Avery v. Alabama,* 308 U.S. 444, 446 (1940). District courts are given "exceedingly wide" discretion in making "scheduling decision[s], such as whether a continuance should be granted." *HC Gun & Knife Shows, Inc. v. City of Hous.*, 201 F.3d 544, 549 (5th Cir. 2000). We determine that the district court did not abuse its discretion in denying the last-minute continuance. The numerous other parties also had expert witnesses who had arranged their schedules around the existing trial dates. Denying the continuance did not prejudice Morris because the trial court admitted Dr. Axelrad's video perpetuation deposition as evidence. As the district court explained, "[the video] was taken for perpetuation purposes, and that's what the rules provide, and for -- just for situations such as this that are unanticipated that render a witness unavailable, and then the deposition becomes the reasonable substitute for that testimony." **[—24—]**

Second, Morris contends that the district court erred by relying on the testimony of Dr. Ginzburg, a forensic psychiatrist retained by the *Aris T* Interests, over Morris's expert, Dr. Axelrad. Under Federal Rule of Civil Procedure 52, "findings of fact are reviewed for clear error and legal issues are reviewed de novo." *Becker v. Tidewater, Inc.*, 586 F.3d 358, 365 (5th Cir. 2009). Because Morris's objection **{-476-}** is about the district court's finding that one expert's account of Morris's injury was factually correct, it is reviewed for clear error. "When findings are based on determinations regarding the credibility of witnesses, Rule 52(a) demands even greater deference to the trial court's findings." *Anderson v. City of Bessemer City,* 470 U.S. 564, 575 (1985). Objective evidence contradicting a witness's testimony or internal inconsistencies can render a district court's accepting a witness's testimony clearly erroneous. *Id.* "But when a trial judge's finding is based on his decision to credit the testimony of one of two or more witnesses, each of whom has told a coherent and facially plausible story that is not contradicted by extrinsic evidence, that finding, if not internally inconsistent, can virtually never be clear error." *Id.*

District courts make credibility decisions, and the district court was well within its discretion to credit Dr. Ginzburg's diagnosis over Dr. Axelrad's. Morris has pointed to no inconsistencies in Dr. Ginzburg's testimony, nor has he pointed to any extrinsic evidence that leaves a firm conviction that the district court's crediting Dr. Ginzburg was error.

Third, Morris asserts that the district court erred in concluding he was not in the zone of danger and therefore could not recover emotional damages. He argues that the district court impermissibly relied on the fortuity that the berth Morris was on was not struck, and that despite this, the *Aris T* was close enough to Morris to put him in immediate danger. Specifically, he argues that the 1,000-foot distance between the *Aris T* and himself was not that large **[—25—]** because the *Aris T* was large, and the poor visibility conditions made it seem closer than it was.

Under a zone-of-danger tort theory, plaintiffs can recover for emotional injuries if they "are placed in immediate risk of physical harm by that conduct." *Consol. Rail Corp. v. Gottshall,* 512 U.S. 532, 548 (1994). The theory extends the ambit of plaintiffs who can recover for emotional injuries from those who sustain a physical impact from the tort to those who were close enough to reasonably be emotionally damaged by it. *See id.* at 547–48.

We have "repeatedly declined to adopt or preclude the zone of danger theory" for general maritime law. *Gough v. Nat. Gas Pipeline Co. of Am.*, 996 F.2d 763, 766 (5th Cir. 1993).[12] Even assuming *arguendo* that plaintiffs can recover under the zone-of-danger theory in general maritime law, analogous case law from other contexts state that a plaintiff must establish that "the claimant was objectively within the zone of danger; claimant feared for his life at the time of the accident or person was in danger, and his emotional injuries were a reasonably foreseeable consequence of the defendant's alleged negligence." *Owens*, 2005 WL 840502, at *3. To be in the zone of danger, a plaintiff must be in "immediate risk of physical harm." *Consol. Rail Corp.*, 512 U.S. at 548. And in determining whether emotional injuries were reasonably foreseeable, **{-477-}** courts can consider the experience seamen are likely to have. *See Plaisance v. Texaco, Inc.*, 966 F.2d 166, 168 (5th Cir. 1992) (en banc). **[—26—]**

We agree with the district court. Morris was never in any danger of being hurt by the *Aris T*, as he had ample time to leave the berth before the *Aris T* would have reached it. The ship was travelling less than 3 miles per hour, giving Morris several minutes to leave the berth, even with his fall. Moreover, Morris remained on the berth after his fall.

Finally, Morris argues that the accident was a substantial cause of his fall, so he can recover physical damages. "Questions of . . . causation[] are factual issues, and may not be set aside on appeal unless clearly erroneous." *In re Omega Protein*, 548 F.3d at 367. Under maritime law, causation requires that the negligence be "a substantial factor" in the injury. *Donaghey*, 974 F.2d at 649 (citation omitted). "The term 'substantial factor' means more than 'but for the negligence, the harm would not have resulted.'" *Id.* (quoting *Spinks v. Chevron Oil Co.*, 507 F.2d 216, 223 (5th Cir. 1975)). In addition, foreseeability is also relevant to the proximate-cause determination. *See In re Signal*, 579 F.3d at 490 n.12.

The district court's determination of causation is subject to clear-error review, and nothing Morris has pointed to leaves a firm conviction that the accident was a substantial factor in his fall. On the contrary, we agree with the district court's conclusion that Morris unreasonably panicked, and that this unforeseeable panic caused the accident. Thus, at a minimum, he cannot meet the proximate-cause element of his negligence case.

III.

For these reasons, we AFFIRM the judgment in all respects.

---

[12] Our court, however, has allowed recovery under a zone-of-danger theory under the Jones Act. *See Naquin v. Elevating Boats, L.L.C.*, 744 F.3d 927, 938, 2 Adm. R. 200, 206–07 (5th Cir. 2014). Moreover, district courts throughout the circuit regularly allow recovery under general maritime law using this theory. *See, e.g., Owens v. Glob. Santa Fe Drilling Co.*, No. Civ. A. 04-702, 2005 WL 840502, at * 3 (E.D. La. Apr. 8, 2005) (citing *Anselmi v. Penrod Drilling Corp.*, 813 F. Supp. 438, 442 (E.D. La. 1993); *Williams v. Treasure Chest Casino, L.L.C.*, Nos. 2:95-CV-3968, 2:97-CV-0947, 1998 WL 42586 (E.D. La. Feb. 4, 1998)).

United States Court of Appeals
for the Fifth Circuit

No. 21-40307

UNITED STATES
vs.
BLANCO

Appeal from the United States District Court for the Southern District of Texas

Decided: March 8, 2022

Citation: 27 F.4th 375, 10 Adm. R. 169 (5th Cir. 2022).

Before **OWEN**, Chief Judge, and **HIGGINBOTHAM** and **ELROD**, Circuit Judges.

[—1—] {-377-} ELROD, Circuit Judge: **{-378-}**

Hector Fernando Blanco was charged with forcibly and intentionally assaulting his then-girlfriend, Morgan Greer, on a Royal Caribbean cruise ship that departed from Galveston, Texas. Blanco subsequently pleaded guilty. Based on his presentence report (PSR), which included a three-level "bodily injury" enhancement and 3 additional criminal history points for a previous conviction, the district court sentenced Blanco to 36 months of imprisonment and 2 years of supervised release. Blanco objected to the bodily injury enhancement and now appeals both the enhancement and the **[—2—]** criminal history points that factored into his PSR. Because the district court erred in assessing 3 criminal history points for a stale 2002 conviction, which affected Blanco's substantial rights, we VACATE his sentence and REMAND for resentencing. We AFFIRM the district court's application of the bodily injury enhancement.

I.

On November 18, 2018, Blanco intentionally assaulted Greer in a cabin the pair shared aboard the Royal Caribbean cruise ship "Liberty of the Seas," while in international waters approximately 45 miles from Galveston, Texas. Blanco and Greer were dating at the time of the assault. At approximately 2:00 a.m. on November 18, Blanco entered the cruise ship cabin highly intoxicated while Greer was asleep. Blanco searched through Greer's cellphone and confronted her about various pictures and text messages that she allegedly sent to her ex-husband.

The confrontation escalated when Blanco put his hands over Greer's mouth, grabbed a bath towel, and told Greer she was going to die or be thrown overboard. Blanco subsequently twisted the bath towel, wrapped it around Greer's neck and began to choke her. Blanco then dragged Greer by the neck on the floor toward the balcony, threatening to throw her overboard. Fearing that she would be strangled, knocked unconscious, or thrown overboard, Greer bit Blanco's hand in an effort to escape.

Greer ultimately escaped and reported the assault to ship personnel. Greer asked to see the ship's doctor and was initially seen by an intake nurse who documented that Greer experienced pain in her neck, but had no bruises, visible marks, or wounds. The ship's doctor also noted that there were no signs of physical abuse but prescribed pain medication and strongly advised Greer to see her home physician at the end of the cruise. The ship's security office began an investigation, which was completed by the Federal Bureau of **[—3—]** Investigation once the ship arrived back in Galveston, Texas. FBI Agent Laura Brunstetter interviewed Greer when the ship docked in Galveston—eight hours after the assault—and saw bruising on Greer's neck, chin, the sides of her face, as well as red marks on her scalp. The FBI also gathered physical evidence, including a towel that contained human hair with the root still attached—which was confirmed to belong to Greer.

Blanco was charged and pleaded guilty to one count of "forcibly and intentionally **{-379-}** assault[ing] Morgan Greer, who was then [his] dating and intimate partner, by attempting to strangle and suffocate her with his hands and a bath towel," while "within the special maritime and territorial jurisdiction of the United States and within the jurisdiction of the [c]ourt," in violation of 18 U.S.C. §§ 7, 113(a)(8), 3238.

The district court ordered and adopted the probation officer's PSR based on the 2018 version of the Sentencing Guidelines, which calculated an offense level of 17. This calculation included a base offense level of 14, a three-level enhancement for strangling or attempted strangling of an intimate partner, a three-level enhancement for bodily injury sustained by Greer, and a three-level reduction for acceptance of responsibility. The PSR also calculated Blanco's criminal history at a category V based on several previous convictions, including a 2002 conviction for operating a motor vehicle after a lifetime forfeiture of his driver's license. Based on the PSR calculations, Blanco faced a Guidelines range of 46–57 months of imprisonment.

Blanco objected to the bodily injury enhancement, arguing that the evidence was insufficient to show that Greer suffered bodily injury as defined by the Guidelines. In support of his objections, Blanco submitted the report of the medical examination that took place just after the assault and photographs taken both before and after the assault. The Government filed a response asserting that forthcoming sentencing testimony from Greer and **[—4—]** Agent Brunstetter would establish that Greer suffered bodily injury that was painful and obvious as a result of the assault.

At sentencing, the district court considered arguments from counsel related to Blanco's objection and the testimony from Greer and Agent Brunstetter. Overruling Blanco's objection, the district court acknowledged the Guidelines range of 46–57 months of imprisonment, granted Blanco's request for a downward variance, and imposed a below-Guidelines sentence of 36 months of imprisonment and 2 years of supervised release. Blanco timely appealed.

II.

For the first time on appeal, Blanco challenges the PSR calculation for his criminal history category that was adopted by the district court. He argues that the district court erred in assessing three criminal history points for a stale 2002 conviction, thereby affecting his substantial rights because the district court used a higher imprisonment range as a starting point. We agree.

Blanco contends that—based on this Court's precedent and the plain language of the criminal history calculations in the Guidelines—his 2002 sentence was too old to receive criminal history points. Blanco claims that the sentence imposed on his 2002 conviction for operating a motor vehicle after forfeiture of his driver's license for life did not total more than 13 months and was originally imposed more than 10 years before the commencement of the assault. He further argues that this improper assessment affected his substantial rights and the fairness of his judicial proceedings because the district court incorrectly used a higher Guidelines range as a starting point to apply its downward variance.

The government concedes that the district court committed clear error in assigning three criminal history points for Blanco's 2002 conviction. **[—5—]** However, the government contends that the error did not affect Blanco's substantial rights because the district court's sentencing decision was based on factors independent of the Guidelines. We agree with Blanco. **{-380-}**

Because Blanco did not raise this objection in district court, we review this issue for plain error. *United States v. Johnson*, 943 F.3d 735, 737 (5th Cir. 2019). To prevail, Blanco "must show a forfeited error that is clear or obvious and that affects his substantial rights." *Id.* Even if Blanco makes the requisite showing, we may exercise our discretion to correct the error "only if it seriously affects the fairness, integrity or public reputation of judicial proceedings." *Id.* (internal quotation marks and citation omitted).

The Sentencing Guidelines direct district courts to calculate a defendant's criminal history score in part by assessing points for each of the defendant's prior sentences of imprisonment. U.S.S.G. § 4A1.1. Three criminal history points are added for each sentence of imprisonment exceeding one year and one month. *Id.* § 4A1.1(a). Further, to qualify as a sentence of imprisonment, the defendant must actually serve a period of imprisonment. *Id.* § 4A1.2, cmt. 2.

Blanco was assigned three criminal history points for a 2002 conviction for operating a motor vehicle after a lifetime forfeiture of his driver's license. This conviction resulted in a four-year prison term, but two years were suspended to at home confinement and two years were probated. Blanco's probation was ultimately revoked, and he was sentenced to a one-year prison term.[1] **[—6—]**

Because Blanco's original sentence was probated, the term of imprisonment used to calculate his criminal history points should have been the one-year term after revocation of his probation. *See Id.* § 4A1.2(k)(1) & cmt. 11; *see also United States v. Rodriguez-Parra*, 581 F.3d 227, 229–30 (5th Cir. 2009) (noting that the suspended part of a sentence is not part of the sentence of imprisonment). Blanco's PSR also indicates that the sentence for his 2002 conviction was originally imposed more than ten years prior to the assault of Greer.

When "a straightforward application of the [G]uidelines" reveals the error in applying a defendant's criminal history points, the error was clear and obvious. *United States v. Torres*, 856 F.3d 1095, 1099 (5th Cir. 2017). Thus, Blanco should not have been assessed any points for the 2002 conviction because he did not receive a term of imprisonment that exceeded one year and one month and his sentence was imposed over ten years before the assault. *See* U.S.S.G. § 4A1.2(e); *see also United States v. Arviso-Mata*, 442 F.3d 382, 385 (5th Cir. 2006) (explaining that if criminal history points are to be assessed for a term of imprisonment less than one year and one month, the term must have been imposed within ten years of the instant offense); U.S.S.G. § 4A1.2(k)(2)(C) (explaining that when a new term of imprisonment is imposed following revocation of probation and the total term is less than one year and one month, the date of the original sentence is used to determine the ten-year period). This is a clear and obvious error by the district court.

Blanco must also show that the error affected his substantial rights and "seriously affect[ed] the fairness, integrity or public reputation of judicial proceedings." *Johnson*, 943 F.3d at 737. The substantial rights prong of our plain error review requires the appellant to "show a reasonable probability, that but for the error, the outcome of the proceeding would **{-381-}** have been different." *Molina-Martinez v. United States*, 578 U.S. 189, 194 (2016) **[—7—]** (internal quotation marks and citation omitted). The district court's reliance on an incorrect Guidelines range will usually suffice to show an effect on the defendant's substantial rights where "the record is silent as to what the district court might have done had it considered the correct Guidelines range." *Id.* at 201. "Even if the sentencing judge sees a reason to vary from the Guidelines, if the judge uses the sentencing range as the beginning point to explain the decision to deviate from it, *then the Guidelines are in a real sense the basis for the sentence.*" *Id.* at 199 (internal quotation marks and citations omitted).

Further, "[i]n the ordinary case . . . the failure to correct a plain Guidelines error that affects a defendant's substantial rights will seriously affect the fairness, integrity, and public reputation of judicial proceedings." *Rosales-Mireles v. United States*, 138 S. Ct. 1897, 1911 (2018). Because of "the role the district court plays in calculating the range and the relative ease of correcting the error," the potential deprivation of liberty from a Guidelines error undermines "the fairness, integrity, or public reputation of judicial proceedings." *Id.* at 1908. As we have also stated, exercising our discretion in correcting a "plain procedural error in sentencing proceedings" is not based upon Blanco's criminal history. *United States v. Sanchez-Arvizu*, 893 F.3d 312, 317–18 (5th Cir. 2018). Thus, where the first three prongs are met, the Supreme Court "expects relief to ordinarily be available to defendants in

---

[1] When computing criminal history points after a defendant's probation is revoked, as here, the original term of imprisonment is added to any term of imprisonment imposed upon revocation. *See* U.S.S.G. § 4A1.2(k)(1).

sentencing cases." *United States v. Urbina-Fuentes*, 900 F.3d 687, 699 (5th Cir. 2018) (internal quotation marks and citation omitted).

The government argues that the district court imposed a downward variance based on Blanco's "history and other characteristics" and other 18 U.S.C. § 3553(a) sentencing factors—independent of the Guidelines. The district court noted Blanco's "long criminal history"—though many of his offenses were traffic-related—and expressed concerns about deterrence based on his repeated driving without a license although he had been **[—8—]** "banned from driving for life." However, in its decision to grant a downward variance from the original Guidelines range, the district court considered Blanco's criminal history as "overrepresented."

While Blanco's criminal history and other characteristics were factors in his below-Guidelines sentence, the Guidelines were still the starting point and basis for his sentence. The record reflects that, at sentencing, the district court expressly and repeatedly mentioned that it considered the Guidelines in its decision. In granting Blanco's request for a downward variance, the court stated that it "considered the [G]uidelines, and based upon the totality of factors . . . sentence[d] the defendant to 36 months." The district court further noted that it "considered the Guidelines" to find that a variance was "consistent with" and had "take[n] into account the purposes of 18 U.S.C. § 3553(a)." Although the district court ultimately varied from the Guidelines range it originally calculated, a defendant's substantial rights are affected if: (1) a district court uses the Guidelines as a starting point; (2) the Guidelines calculation is incorrect; and (3) the record is silent as to what the district court might have done had the Guidelines range been correct. *See Molina-Martinez*, 578 U.S. at 199–200. All three are present in this case.

Had Blanco's PSR been calculated correctly, his resulting criminal history category **{-382-}** would have been IV and not the category V score he was originally assessed. *See* U.S.S.G. ch. 5 pt. A. A category IV score combined with a total offense level of 17 would have produced a Guidelines range of 37 to 46 months rather than the 46 to 57 months the district court calculated. U.S.S.G. ch. 5 pt. A. The record further reflects that the district court's reliance on the Guidelines as a basis for his sentence—although it ultimately departed from them—shows a reasonable probability that his sentence would have been different. *See Molina-Martinez*, 578 U.S. at 194. The failure to correct this error in the Guidelines calculation affected Blanco's substantial **[—9—]** rights and seriously affected the fairness, integrity, and public reputation of his judicial proceedings.[2]

Because the district court erred in assessing three criminal history points for Blanco's 2002 conviction, we therefore vacate his sentence and remand for resentencing.

III.

Blanco also argues that the district court erred by assessing a three-level bodily injury enhancement under U.S.S.G. § 2A2.2(b)(3)(A). We disagree.

Blanco contends that the district court's assessment of the three-level bodily injury enhancement was in error because there was insufficient evidence that Greer sustained a bodily injury as defined by the Guidelines. In particular, he maintains that the evidence failed to show that Greer's injuries were painful and obvious or were the type for which medical care ordinarily would be sought.

The government argues that, in light of the record, it was plausible for the district court to find Greer sustained a bodily injury under § 2A2.2(b)(3)(A). Specifically, the government points to: (1) Greer's testimony related to the pain she sustained during the assault; (2) the forensic evidence of Greer's hair with the root still attached recovered from the bath towel; and (3) Agent Brunstetter's testimony related to her observation and photographing of

[2] We also reject the government's additional argument that because Blanco's sentence was below both the correct and incorrect Guidelines range his substantial rights were not affected.

bruising on Greer's face, neck, and knee and red marks on her scalp. **[—10—]**

We review the "district court's interpretations of Guidelines de novo and its factual findings for clear error." *United States v. Williams*, 610 F.3d 271, 292 (5th Cir. 2010); *see also United States v. Lister*, 229 F. App'x 334, 339 (5th Cir. 2007) (involving bodily injury enhancement). Whether Greer sustained a bodily injury under U.S.S.G. § 2A1.2 is a factual finding that is reviewed for clear error. *United States v. Douglas*, 957 F.3d 602, 607 (5th Cir. 2020); *see also Lister*, 229 F. App'x at 340. A factual finding is not clearly erroneous if it is plausible in light of the whole record. *United States v. Ruiz-Hernandez*, 890 F.3d 202, 211, 6 Adm. R. 199, 203–04 (5th Cir. 2018).

"Sentencing enhancements must be proven by a preponderance of the evidence." *Id.*, 6 Adm. R. at 203 (internal quotation marks and citations omitted). Section 2A2.2(b)(3)(A) applies a three-level enhancement in cases of aggravated assault if the victim sustained bodily injury. The Guidelines define bodily injury as "any significant injury; e.g., an injury that is painful and obvious, or is of a type for which medical attention ordinarily would be sought." U.S.S.G. § 1B1.1, cmt. 1.B; *see also* § 2A2.2, cmt. 1 (stating that, for purposes **{–383–}** of § 2A2.2, the term "bodily injury" has the meaning given that term in § 1B1.1). The enhancement turns on the injury sustained by Greer and not on the actions of Blanco. *United States v. Guerrero*, 169 F.3d 933, 946 (5th Cir. 1999). Further, testimony from the victim about the injury sustained provides strong evidence to support the bodily injury enhancement. *Id.* at 947.

Blanco does not dispute that Greer suffered pain; rather, he contends that her injuries were not sufficient to satisfy § 2A2.2. He argues that Greer only sought medical attention for security purposes and that an evaluation by the ship's doctor and nurse noted neck pain but no visible marks or wounds. Further, he contends that, although photographs taken after the assault appear to show bruises on Greer's neck, cheek, and leg as well as red marks on her neck, cheek, and scalp, they are similar to marks presented in other **[—11—]** photographs taken before the assault took place. This argument not only contradicts properly credited witness testimony, but it also downplays the record's reflection of the brutal nature of the assault.

The district court properly credited Greer's sentence hearing testimony that she experienced pain as a result of the assault; that she had trouble breathing, was dizzy, and saw black spots when she was choked; that her neck was sore for a week; that she had trouble breathing on the second day after the assault; and that she asked to see a doctor while still on the ship. In addition, both Greer and Agent Brunstetter testified that Greer suffered bruises from the assault. In fact, Agent Brunstetter testified that she could still see bruising on Greer's face at the November 21, 2018 initial appearance—which Greer tried to cover with makeup.

The PSR and its Addendum provide further evidence of bruising. Agent Brunstetter also testified that the lighting was poor in the original photographs taken shortly after the assault, so some of the photographs did not accurately portray what she observed during her interview with Greer. The district court was entitled to credit Agent Brunstetter's testimony and the information in the PSR Addendum explaining the lack of obvious bruising in the photographs. *See United States v. Harris*, 740 F.3d 956, 968 (5th Cir. 2014). In addition, the record contains evidence of Greer's hair loss from the root that was found on a towel in the cabin.

We have indicated that the bodily injury enhancement may apply even if the injury is not both painful and obvious and that the absence "of bruising, swelling, or bleeding is not dispositive." *United States v. Washington*, 500 F. App'x 279, 283 (5th Cir. 2012) (affirming the bodily injury enhancement when the victim was punched in the nose, although there was no evidence of physical injury and the victim did not seek medical care); *see also United States v. Smith*, 822 F.3d 755, 765 (5th Cir. 2016) (affirming bodily injury **[—12—]** enhancement where a bank customer was thrown to the ground from a chair and kicked, and a bank employee sustained bruising and a small amount of hair loss).

In light of this evidence, it is plausible that Greer suffered bodily injury as defined by the Guidelines. *See Ruiz-Hernandez*, 890 F.3d at 211, 6 Adm. R. at 203–04. Therefore, we affirm the district court's application of the bodily injury enhancement.

IV.

Because the district court erred in assessing three criminal history points for a stale 2002 conviction, which affected Blanco's substantial rights, we VACATE his sentence and REMAND for resentencing. We AFFIRM the district court's application **{–384–}** of the three-level bodily injury enhancement.

United States Court of Appeals
for the Fifth Circuit

No. 21-10068

TANGO MARINE S.A.
VS.
ELEPHANT GROUP LTD.

Appeal from the United States District Court for the Northern District of Texas

ON PETITION FOR REHEARING

(Opinion, December 3, 2021, 5TH CIR., 19 F.4th 808, 9 Adm. R. 279)

Decided: March 11, 2022

Citation: 28 F.4th 600, 10 Adm. R. 175 (5th Cir. 2022).

Before **JONES, SOUTHWICK,** and **ENGELHARDT,** Circuit Judges.

[—1—] {-600-} PER CURIAM: {-601-}

No member of the panel nor judge in regular active service of the court having requested that the court be polled on Rehearing En Banc (FED. R. APP. P. and 5TH CIR. R. 35), the Petition for Rehearing En Banc is DENIED. **[—2—]**

Because of the absence of a request for a poll of the en banc court, this panel will treat the petition as one for panel rehearing. FED. R. APP. P. 40; 5TH CIR. R. 40. We will deny rehearing and again affirm the district court judgment, but we will also withdraw our prior opinion. Consequently, we address a few points about the effect of our affirmance.

The Plaintiff's amended complaint asserted jurisdiction in the Northern District of Texas despite its acknowledgement that the "Defendants cannot be found in this District within the meaning of Supplemental Rule B." That cited rule allows for suit in a district in which a defendant cannot be found on the basis of a complaint that seeks attachment of a defendant's assets in the district in the hands of garnishees. FED. R. CIV. P., SUPP. RULE B. The amended complaint identified several garnishees in the district and sought issuance of process for attachment and garnishment of the Defendants' property in their possession of a value "up to the amount of at least $4,510,058.20 (principal damages as set out above, $50,000 for interest, costs and attorneys' fees) to secure Tango's claims." The extent of the relief the judgment grants against the Defendants is defined by the jurisdiction asserted under Supplemental Rule B.

After review of the briefs and record and consideration of oral argument, we conclude that the district court committed no reversible error in granting judgment. We AFFIRM.

We withdraw our prior opinion. *See Tango Marine S.A. v. Elephant Grp. Ltd.*, 19 F.4th 808, 9 Adm. R. 279 (5th Cir. 2021). The panel specifically withdraws its interpretation of *Great Prize, S.A. v. Mariner Shipping Party, Ltd.*, 967 F.2d 157, 159 (5th Cir. 1992). *See id.* at 814, 9 Adm. R. at 282. What *Great Prize* means can be left for an appeal in which its meaning matters. It does not in this case.

The petition for rehearing is DENIED.

United States Court of Appeals
for the Fifth Circuit

No. 21-60501

CENTRAL BOAT RENTALS, INC.
vs.
M/V NOR GOLIATH

Appeal from the United States District Court for the Southern District of Mississippi

Decided: April 12, 2022

Citation: 31 F.4th 320, 10 Adm. R. 176 (5th Cir. 2022).

Before **OWEN,** Chief Judge, and **HIGGINBOTHAM** and **ELROD,** Circuit Judges.

[—1—] {-322-} HIGGINBOTHAM, Circuit Judge:

Again, the familiar question of whether provisions were a "necessary" under the Commercial Instruments and Maritime Liens Act ("CIMLA").[1] **[—2—]** To its answer, able counsel bring creative arguments urging that we expand CIMLA's reach. We decline the invitation and affirm the judgment of the district court.[2]

I.

This dispute arose from the bankruptcy of Epic Companies, L.L.C.[3] Epic was a general contractor that decommissioned oil platforms in the Gulf of Mexico, subcontracting with owners of various vessels to complete decommissioning projects, including heavy lift vessels, material barges, and tugboats. The M/V Nor Goliath was a heavy lift vessel hired by Epic to lift oil platform components out of the water and place them onto barges. Tugboats then towed the loaded barges from the Nor Goliath's location in the Gulf to an inland scrapyard for further dismantling, returning to the Nor Goliath with empty barges. These tugboats were owned by various towing companies.[4] **{-323-}**

Upon Epic's bankruptcy, the suppliers looked elsewhere to recoup their costs. The Towing Companies joined a suit filed in the United States District Court for the Southern District of Mississippi, seeking to assert and enforce maritime liens under CIMLA against the Nor Goliath, maintaining that the tugboats provided it necessary services by towing the barges. The Nor Goliath and the Towing Companies each filed motions for summary **[—3—]** judgment. The district court granted summary judgment to the Nor Goliath, holding that the services rendered by the tugboats did not create a lien on the Nor Goliath.[5] The Towing Companies timely appealed.

II.

We review *de novo* a district court's grant of summary judgment.[6] We affirm a summary judgment ruling "when the nonmoving party fails to meet its burden to come forward with facts and law demonstrating a basis for recovery that would support a jury verdict."[7] "Whether a maritime lien exists is a question of law, reviewed *de novo*."[8]

III.

Under CIMLA,

> a person providing necessaries to a vessel on the order of the owner or a person authorized by the owner (1) has a

[1] 46 U.S.C. § 31301 *et seq.*

[2] We have jurisdiction to review this interlocutory appeal under 28 U.S.C. § 1292(a)(3) as the district court's grant of summary judgment determined the rights and liabilities of parties in an admiralty case.

[3] *See In re Epic Companies, LLC,* No. 19-34752 (Bankr. S. D. Tex., filed August 26, 2019).

[4] The Towing Companies are the named Intervenors-Appellants: Central Boat Rentals, Inc.; Global Towing Service, L.L.C.; Offshore Towing Inc.; McAllister Towing of New York, L.L.C.; and Curtin Maritime Corp.

[5] *See Arc Controls, Inc. v. M/V Nor Goliath,* No. 1:19CV391-LG-RPM, 2021 WL 1971485, (S.D. Miss. May 17, 2021).

[6] *World Fuel Servs. Singapore Pte, Ltd. v. Bulk Juliana M/V,* 822 F.3d 766, 770, 4 Adm. R. 240, 242 (5th Cir. 2016).

[7] *Little v. Liquid Air Corp.,* 37 F.3d 1069, 1071 (5th Cir. 1994).

[8] *Comar Marine, Corp. v. Raider Marine Logistics, LLC,* 792 F.3d 564, 575, 3 Adm. R. 371, 377 (5th Cir. 2015) (italicization added).

> maritime lien on the vessel; (2) may bring a civil action in rem to enforce the lien; and (3) is not required to allege or prove in the action that credit was given to the vessel.[9]

"'[N]ecessaries' includes repairs, supplies, towage, and the use of a dry dock or marine railway."[10] **[—4—]**

"We apply the provisions of CIMLA *stricti juris* to ensure that maritime liens are not lightly extended by construction, analogy, or inference."[11] Necessaries "includes most goods or services that are useful to the vessel, keep her out of danger, and enable her to perform her particular function. These are items useful to vessel operations and necessary to keep the ship going."[12] "Necessaries are the things that a prudent owner would provide to enable a ship to perform well the functions for which she has been engaged."[13] We look to the "particular function" and requirements of a ship to determine what is a necessary for that ship.[14]

IV.

First, the Towing Companies argue that the Nor Goliath's particular function **{–324–}** was the entirety of the decommissioning process, therefore every good or service used to decommission an oil platform was a necessary to the Nor Goliath. We disagree. The decommissioning project was Epic's goal as the general contractor. Indeed, Epic hired a fleet of vessels for the project. As the Nor Goliath's role was to lift platform components and place them on the barges,[15] its necessaries are goods or services it used for this particular function. **[—5—]**

Second, the Towing Companies argue their towing services provided the barges to the Nor Goliath, and the barges are equipment necessary for the Nor Goliath's particular function. Not so. In *Trico Marine Operators, Inc. v. Falcon Drilling Co.*, we held that drilling equipment was a necessary for an offshore drilling vessel, for the equipment was necessary for the vessel's particular function—drilling.[16] Then, in *Martin Energy Servs., L.L.C. v. Bourbon Petrel M/V*, we held that gasoline is not a necessary to a vessel tasked with carrying the gasoline as cargo to another vessel for its consumption, only the consuming vessel received a necessary.[17] This is because liens arise when "the good or service was provided for use by the vessel itself."[18]

It is plain that the barges were not equipment for the Nor Goliath, did not help the Nor Goliath's crane raise and lower the platform components, and so the Nor Goliath did not "use" the barges. It follows that the Towing Companies did not provide a service necessary to the Nor Goliath's particular function.

Third, the Towing Companies alternatively contend that they provided a necessary as the decommissioning project would have ground to a halt without the tugboats moving the barges; thus the Nor Goliath indirectly benefitted from the towing of the barges. The argument that maritime liens arise from indirect benefit misapprehends the concept of liens for necessaries. Mutually beneficial conduct is expected when each vessel was hired by the same general contractor. Indeed, every ship in Epic's fleet indirectly benefitted from the barges being towed just as every ship indirectly benefitted from the Nor Goliath's lifting and loading. But mutually beneficial

---

[9] 46 U.S.C. § 31342(a).

[10] 46 U.S.C. § 31301(4).

[11] *Valero Mktg. & Supply Co. v. M/V Almi Sun, IMO No. 9579535*, 893 F.3d 290, 292, 6 Adm. R. 205, 206 (5th Cir. 2018) (internal quotations omitted).

[12] *Martin Energy Servs., L.L.C. v. Bourbon Petrel M/V*, 962 F.3d 827, 831, 8 Adm. R. 196, 197 (5th Cir. 2020) (internal quotations omitted).

[13] *Equilease Corp. v. M/V Sampson*, 793 F.2d 598, 603 (5th Cir. 1986) (en banc).

[14] *Martin*, 962 F.3d at 832–33, 8 Adm. R. at 198–99. *See also Equilease*, 793 F.2d at 603 ("What is a 'necessary' is to be determined relative to the requirements of the ship.").

[15] *See Arc Controls, Inc. v. M/V NOR GOLIATH*, No. 1:19CV391-LG-RPM, 2021 WL 2931426, at *2 (S.D. Miss. July 12, 2021).

[16] 116 F.3d 159, 162 (5th Cir. 1997).

[17] *Martin*, 962 F.3d at 832–33, 8 Adm. R. at 198–99.

[18] *Id.* at 833, 8 Adm. R. at 199.

[—6—] conduct alone cannot give rise to a maritime lien under CIMLA, otherwise multi-ship operations would give rise to an untenable situation where all the ships in a fleet would have liens on the other. In short, maritime liens for necessaries run against the vessel that received the necessary and no further.[19]

V.

Note that the Towing Companies also claim that they are entitled to maritime liens as they protected the Nor Goliath from the hazards of the sea, alleging that the Nor Goliath would be in danger if it was forced to hold an oil platform component suspended by its crane in choppy waters. Whatever its merits, the Towing Companies did not present any evidence of the danger these conditions posed to the Nor Goliath, which previously suspended and transported large loads without the aid of barges. As the nonmovants at the **{–325–}** summary judgment stage, the Towing Companies did not meet their burden to demonstrate that the Nor Goliath was in danger beyond their conclusory allegations and unsubstantiated assertions.[20]

VI.

Ultimately these arguments for extending the protection of liens for necessaries provided by CIMLA fail to accept that the primacy of the lien is essential to its role of securing necessaries for vessels. They require the suppliers of necessaries, as we have defined them, to share pro rata with other creditors, a loss of primacy diluting the incentive to suppliers to the detriment of CIMLA's core mission. These economic realities were not lost on Congress as evidenced by its singular treatment of maritime liens, **[—7—]** providing a separate statutory pathway for enforcement within CIMLA.[21] Attentive to the economic realities to which CIMLA's plain language responds, we apply its language *stricti juris*.[22]

The Towing Companies fail to demonstrate a legal basis for their claimed maritime liens against the Nor Goliath. The district court's grant of summary judgment is AFFIRMED.

---

19 *Id.*, 8 Adm. R. at 199.
20 *Little*, 37 F.3d at 1075.
21 46 U.S.C. § 31342.
22 *Valero*, 893 F.3d at 292, 6 Adm. R. at 206.

United States Court of Appeals
for the Fifth Circuit

No. 21-30594

IN RE N&W TOWING, L.L.C.

Appeal from the United States District Court for the Eastern District of Louisiana

Decided: April 20, 2022

Citation: 31 F.4th 968, 10 Adm. R. 179 (5th Cir. 2022).

Before **HIGGINSON, WILLETT,** and **HO,** Circuit Judges.

[—2—] {-969-} HIGGINSON, Circuit Judge:

After Trey Wooley was injured on board a ship owned by N&W Marine Towing, N&W filed a maritime limitation action in federal district court. Though the district court initially stayed Wooley from prosecuting claims against N&W in other forums, the court lifted its stay after Wooley made certain stipulations. On appeal, N&W argues that the district court abused its discretion by lifting the stay. We AFFIRM.

I.

On August 31, 2020, N&W Marine Towing (N&W), the owner of the vessel M/V *Nicholas*, filed in federal district court a Verified Complaint in Limitation, pursuant to the Limitation of Liability Act of 1851 (the Limitation Act).[1] The complaint alleges **{-970-}** that on February 29, 2020, the *Nicholas* was towing six barges up the Mississippi River when it was overtaken by the *Majesty of the Seas*, a cruise ship. The complaint further alleges that the *Majesty of the Seas*' wake caused one of the *Nicholas*'s face wires to break and that the ship's other face wire broke while the *Nicholas* was maneuvering **[—3—]** towards the riverbank. At this point, a third ship, the M/V *Assault*, offered to assist the *Nicholas* in replacing the face wires. Several *Assault* deckhands then boarded the *Nicholas*, and one of these deckhands, Trey Wooley, offered to remove the broken face wire from the winch. Wooley's hand was injured while he was attempting to remove the wire.

In response to N&W's complaint, the district court issued an order providing that "the commencement or further prosecution of any action or proceeding" against N&W involving claims related to the incident described in the complaint "is hereby stayed and restrained until the hearing and determination of this proceeding." Subsequently, Wooley, Royal Caribbean Cruises (RCC) (the owner of the *Majesty of the Seas*), and Turn Services (Wooley's employer) all filed in the district court claims against N&W. N&W filed counterclaims against RCC and Turn Services.

Wooley also filed a Petition for Damages in Louisiana state court. Wooley's state court petition named as defendants N&W, the *Nicholas*, RCC, and the *Majesty of the Seas*, along with several insurance companies. RCC removed Wooley's petition to federal court, asserting diversity of citizenship as grounds for removal. After the removed case was consolidated with N&W's limitation action, Wooley filed a Motion to Remand. The district court has not ruled on that motion. Wooley also filed a Motion to Bifurcate, which the district court denied.

Wooley and N&W both settled their claims against RCC. Wooley then filed a Motion to Stay Limitation of Liability Proceedings and Motion to Lift Injunction. In support of this motion, Wooley and Turn Services filed a Stipulation of Claimants to Lift Stay. The district court granted Wooley's motion to stay the limitation proceedings and lift the injunction, and it stated **[—4—]** that Wooley could "proceed with the prosecution of his state court suit." N&W appealed.[2]

II.

Under the Limitation of Liability Act, shipowners "may bring a civil action in a district court of the United States for

[1] The Limitation Act, which is discussed in detail below, is codified at 46 U.S.C. §§ 30501-30512. *See also* FED. R. CIV. P. SUPP. R. F.

[2] We have jurisdiction over this appeal from an interlocutory order lifting an injunction under 28 U.S.C. § 1292(a)(1).

limitation of liability." 46 U.S.C. § 30511(a). The Limitation Act allows shipowners to limit their liability for an array of "claims, debts, and liabilities" that might arise from the activities of their vessels to "the value of the vessel and pending freight," as long as the incident giving rise to liability occurred "without the privity or knowledge of the owner." 46 U.S.C. § 30505(a)-(b); *see also Magnolia Marine Transp. Co. v. Laplace Towing Corp.*, 964 F.2d 1571, 1575 (5th Cir. 1992) (summarizing Limitation Act); *Odeco Oil & Gas Co., Drilling Div. v. Bonnette*, 74 F.3d 671, 674 (5th Cir. 1996) (same). When a shipowner brings an action under the Limitation Act, "all claims and proceedings against the owner related to the matter in question shall cease." 46 U.S.C. § 30511(c). Accordingly, after a limitation action is filed, "the limitation court stays all related claims against the shipowner pending in any forum, and requires **{-971-}** all claimants to timely assert their claims in the limitation court." *Magnolia Marine*, 964 F.2d at 1575; *see also* FED. R. CIV. P. SUPP. R. F(3) ("On application of the plaintiff the court shall enjoin the further prosecution of any action or proceeding against the plaintiff or the plaintiff's property with respect to any claim subject to limitation in the action.").[3] **[—5—]**

However, "[a] shipowner's right to limitation . . . is cabined by the 'saving to suitors' clause." *Odeco Oil*, 74 F.3d at 674. Under the Judiciary Act of 1791, federal district courts "have original jurisdiction, exclusive of the courts of the States, of . . . [a]ny civil case of admiralty or maritime jurisdiction, *saving to suitors in all cases all other remedies to which they are otherwise entitled*." 28 U.S.C. § 1333(1) (emphasis added). Thus, although the Limitation Act "gives shipowners the right to seek limitation of their liability exclusively in federal court," the Judiciary Act's saving to suitors clause "affords suitors a choice of remedies." *In re Tetra Applied Techs. L P*, 362 F.3d 338, 340 (5th Cir. 2004) (citing *Lewis v. Lewis & Clark Marine, Inc.*, 531 U.S. 438, 448 (2001)). "This statutory framework has created 'recurring and inherent conflict' between the saving-to-suitors clause of § 1333, with its 'presumption in favor of jury trials and common law remedies,' and the 'apparent exclusive jurisdiction' vested in admiralty courts by the [Limitation] Act." *Magnolia Marine*, 964 F.2d at 1575 (quoting *In re Dammers & Vanderheide & Scheepvaart Maats Christina B.V.*, 836 F.2d 750, 754 (2d Cir. 1988)).

In resolving the tension between the Limitation Act and the savings to suitors clause, "the district court's primary concern is to protect the shipowner's absolute right to claim the Act's liability cap, and to reserve the adjudication of that right in the federal forum." *Odeco Oil*, 74 F.3d at 674 (cleaned up). However, we have recognized "two instances in which a district court must allow a state court action to proceed":

> (1) when the total amount of the claims does not exceed the shipowner's declared value of the vessel and its freight, and (2) when *all claimants* stipulate that the federal court has **[—6—]** exclusive jurisdiction over the limitation proceeding, and that the claimants will not seek to enforce a damage award greater than the value of the ship and its freight until the shipowner's right to limitation has been determined by the federal court.

Id.; *see also In re Tetra*, 362 F.3d at 341 (explaining that "claims may proceed outside the limitation action (1) if they total less than the value of the vessel, or (2) if the claimants stipulate that the federal court has exclusive jurisdiction over the limitation of liability proceeding and that they will not seek to enforce a greater damage award until the limitation action has been heard by the federal court" (citation omitted)).

In maritime limitation of liability actions, "[w]e review a district court's decision to lift a

[3] Because the Supreme Court determined that the Limitation Act is "'incapable of execution' without further instructions to the courts," it "promulgated procedural rules to govern limitation actions," which are "now contained in Supplemental Admiralty and **[—5—]** Maritime Claims Rule F." *In re Tetra Applied Techs. L P*, 362 F.3d 338, 340 (5th Cir. 2004) (quoting *Lewis v. Lewis & Clark Marine, Inc.*, 531 U.S. 438, 447 (2001)).

stay for abuse of discretion." *Odeco Oil*, 74 F.3d at 674. However, "the issue whether a set of stipulations adequately protects a shipowner's rights under the Limitation Act is a question of law **{–972–}** reviewed de novo." *In re Tetra*, 362 F.3d at 340. If a stipulation adequately protects a shipowner's rights, then the district court does not abuse its discretion by lifting a stay against proceedings in other forums. *See Lewis*, 531 U.S. at 454 ("[W]here, as here, the District Court satisfies itself that a vessel owner's right to seek limitation will be protected, the decision to dissolve the injunction is well within the court's discretion."); *In re Two "R" Drilling Co., Inc.*, 943 F.2d 576, 578 (5th Cir. 1991) ("Where the claimant concedes the admiralty court's exclusive jurisdiction to determine all issues relating to the limitation of liability, the district court should lift any stay against the state proceeding."); *In re Tetra*, 362 F.3d at 343 ("Because the proffered stipulations were sufficient to protect the rights of the shipowner to limitation, the court's denial of Leger's right to a choice of forum under the saving to suitors clause constitutes an abuse of discretion.").

Here, after N&W filed its limitation action, three parties filed claims: Wooley, Turn Services, and RCC. However, RCC and N&W settled, and **[—7—]** Turn Services assigned its claims to Wooley, leaving Wooley as the only remaining claimant. Wooley then filed a stipulation stating the following:

> In order to afford sufficient protection from excess liability arising out of third party claims where indemnification or contribution is or may be sought by other defendants pending the resolution of all claims in the limitation proceeding, in the event there is a judgment or recovery by claimant in any state court action or proceeding of any type in excess of the value of the Limitation Fund determined in accordance with 46 U.S.C.A. § 30511 and Supplemental Admiralty and Maritime Claims Rule F, in no event will Claimant seek to enforce such excess judgment or recover against N&W Marine Towing, L.L.C., insofar as such enforcement may expose N&W Marine Towing, L.L.C.'s liability in excess of the adjudicated total Limitation Fund value, until such time as there has been an adjudication of limitation by this Court, which has exclusive jurisdiction and authority to determine all issues relevant to N&W Marine Towing, L.L.C.'s claim for limitation of liability, and Plaintiff further agrees that any claim of res judicata based on judgment in any other Court, with respect to any issue of exoneration from and limitation of liability is reserved to this court, is hereby waived.

The district court concluded that Wooley's "stipulation adequately protects N&W's absolute right to limit its liability in the federal forum." We agree. Because the stipulation both recognized the district court's exclusive jurisdiction over the limitation proceeding and stated that Wooley would not seek to enforce a damage award greater than the value of the ship and its freight[4] until the district court had adjudicated the limitation proceeding, it **[—8—]** meets the requirements set forth in *Odeco Oil. See* 74 F.3d at 674. Accordingly, the district court did not abuse its discretion by lifting the stay and allowing Wooley to pursue remedies in other forums. *See Lewis*, 531 U.S. at 454; *In re Two "R" Drilling Co.*, 943 F.2d at 578; *In re Tetra*, 362 F.3d at 343.[5] **{–973–}**

---

[4] Wooley's stipulation referred to the value of the "Limitation Fund," which contains "an amount equal to the value of the owner's interest in the vessel and pending freight," plus "an amount, or approved security, that the court may fix from time to time as necessary to carry out this chapter." 46 U.S.C. § 30511(b)(1).

[5] N&W briefly argues that Wooley's stipulation is inadequate because "[t]he precise details" of the assignment agreement between Turn Services and Wooley "are unknown." According to N&W, "in order to protect the shipowner's Limitation fund the District Court needs to examine the assignment to ensure it does not allow for a double recovery and the Limitation fund is not impacted by this agreement." However, N&W cites no authority supporting the proposition that the details of an assignment agreement might affect the adequacy of a stipulation. Moreover, because Turn Services

III.

N&W spends the bulk of its brief arguing that the district court abused its discretion by lifting the stay because "Wooley's state court suit . . . was already in federal court after a proper and timely 'SNAP' removal." N&W maintains that even though both N&W and Wooley are Louisiana citizens, Wooley's state court lawsuit against N&W and RCC was properly removed to federal court on diversity of citizenship grounds, under the doctrines of **[—9—]** both snap removal[6] and improper joinder.[7] N&W then reasons that since Wooley's state court lawsuit was properly removed, the question "of whether the proposed Stipulation protects the vessel owner's interest now becomes moot," given that the saving to suitors clause does not guarantee plaintiffs a non-federal forum in cases where there exists some independent basis of federal jurisdiction, such as diversity of citizenship.[8]

Wooley responds that his state court lawsuit was not properly removed because the parties were not completely diverse, **{-974-}** unlike other snap **[—10—]** removal cases.[9] But as a threshold matter, Wooley suggests that N&W's brief "confuses the issues, as this is not truly a removal case." The district court reached a similar conclusion, explaining that even assuming "that snap removal was properly executed, the result would still be the same because the Court is not remanding based on lack of diversity" but rather "simply staying the limitation portion to afford [Wooley's] statutory right to pursue damages in state court." The district court responded to N&W's argument that Wooley violated the stay when he filed his state court petition by stating that N&W "argues that [Wooley] has taken fatal procedural missteps but offers

---

joined Wooley's stipulation, stating that it was doing so "out of an abundance of caution," the requirements of *Odeco Oil* are met even assuming arguendo that the assignment is somehow defective and that Turn Services therefore remains a claimant. *See Odeco Oil*, 74 F.3d at 675 (explaining that a district court should lift a Limitation Act stay if "*all claimants* . . . sign the stipulation protecting the shipowner's rights"). Further, since the district court has retained jurisdiction over N&W's limitation action, it can resolve any issues relating to the assignment that might arise in the future, and presumably a state court could also do so in an appropriate case.

[6] N&W maintains that because RCC removed the case before N&W had been served, snap removal was proper under *Texas Brine Co., L.L.C. v. Am. Arb. Ass'n, Inc.*, which held that "[a] non-forum defendant may remove an otherwise removable case even when a named defendant who has yet to be 'properly joined and served' is a citizen of the forum state." 955 F.3d 482, 487 (5th Cir. 2020).

[7] N&W argues that because Wooley violated the district court's stay by naming N&W as a defendant in his state court suit, N&W's citizenship "is not to be considered when determining complete diversity of the parties following removal." N&W cites a Third Circuit case involving a bankruptcy stay for this proposition. *See Brown v. Jevic*, 575 F.3d 322, 327 (3d Cir. 2009) ("[B]ecause Brown had no reasonable basis to believe that JEVIC was amenable to suit, we hold that JEVIC was a fraudulently joined party and its status as a Defendant could not be used to defeat otherwise proper federal jurisdiction.").

[8] *See Barker v. Hercules Offshore, Inc.*, 713 F.3d 208, 220, 1 Adm. R. 206, 213 (5th Cir. 2013) (explaining that that "the saving to suitors clause under general maritime law does not guarantee plaintiffs a nonfederal forum, or limit the right of defendants to remove such actions to federal court where there exists some basis for federal jurisdiction other than admiralty" (cleaned up)). N&W also argues that Wooley's claims should remain in federal court because he named a vessel in rem in his state court suit, even though federal courts have exclusive jurisdiction over such actions. *See Madruga v. Superior Ct. of State of Cal. in & for San Diego Cty.*, 346 U.S. 556, 560 (1954) (explaining that federal admiralty jurisdiction "is 'exclusive' only as to those maritime causes of action begun and carried on as proceedings *in rem*, that is, where a vessel or thing is itself treated as the offender and made the defendant by name or description in order to enforce a lien"). However, N&W frames this argument in the prudential terms of "[j]udicial economy, fairness, and efficiency," conceding that, by itself, federal jurisdiction over in rem proceedings against vessels "is not a sufficient basis for removal."

[9] Wooley points the court to a district court opinion concluding that "[s]nap removals can occur only in removal cases based solely on diversity jurisdiction where complete diversity exists." *Cox v. J.B. Hunt Transp., Inc.*, No. CV H-20-1454, 2020 WL 3288090, at *2 (S.D. Tex. June 17, 2020) (citation omitted).

nothing concrete as to how or why those missteps outweigh the collective precedents requiring stay [of the limitation proceeding] in factually analogous cases."

We agree with Wooley and the district court that N&W's arguments regarding removal are not relevant to the issue of whether the district court abused its discretion by lifting the stay. N&W cites no authority for the proposition that a district court abuses its discretion if it grants a claimant's motion to lift a stay in a limitation action where a companion case for damages was properly removed to federal court (due to snap removal, improper joinder, or otherwise). Rather, as explained above, our precedents require district courts hearing limitation actions to lift a stay against proceedings in other forums when a claimant makes the appropriate stipulations. *See Odeco Oil*, 74 F.3d at 674; *In re Two "R" Drilling Co.*, 943 F.2d at 578; *In re Tetra*, 362 F.3d at 343. Because Wooley made these stipulations, the district court did not abuse its discretion by granting his motion. **[—11—]**

Based on its briefing, N&W appears particularly troubled by the district court's statement that by lifting the stay it was "permitting Claimant, Trey Wooley, to proceed with the prosecution of his state court suit." However, as previously explained, though Wooley filed a petition for damages in Louisiana state court, that suit was removed to federal court and consolidated with N&W's limitation action. Wooley subsequently filed a motion to remand, but the district court has not yet ruled on the motion. Because Wooley thus does not appear to be currently prosecuting a state court suit, the above-quoted language from the district court's order should be read not as affirmatively authorizing Wooley to proceed with a particular state court suit but rather as simply emphasizing that the district court's stay no longer prevents Wooley from prosecuting an otherwise appropriate state court suit against N&W. Whether Wooley can in fact prosecute such a suit is a question that an appropriate court can determine at the appropriate time. This appeal solely concerns the issue of whether the district court abused its discretion by lifting its stay.[10]

IV.

For the foregoing reasons, we AFFIRM the district court's order granting Wooley's **{–975–}** Motion to Stay Limitation of Liability Proceedings and Motion to Lift Injunction.

---

10 We note that one way in which Wooley might be able to prosecute a state court suit would be if the district court were to decide to grant his motion to remand. However, unless such an event occurs, Wooley's removed suit against N&W will presumably remain in federal court. Of course, if the district court were to grant that motion, N&W could appeal, reiterating its arguments regarding snap removal and improper joinder at that time.

United States Court of Appeals
for the Fifth Circuit

No. 21-30028

UNITED STATES
vs.
ERR, LLC

Appeal from the United States District Court for the Eastern District of Louisiana

Decided: May 26, 2022

Citation: 35 F.4th 405, 10 Adm. R. 184 (5th Cir. 2022).

Before **DAVIS, WILLETT,** and **OLDHAM,** Circuit Judges.

[—1—] {-407-} OLDHAM, Circuit Judge:

The question presented is whether the Seventh Amendment guarantees the right to a jury trial of the Government's claims under the Oil Pollution Act of 1990. The district court said it was a close call but ultimately answered no. We say yes. We therefore reverse in part, vacate in part, and remand. **[—2—]**

I.

A.

First, some background on the legislative scheme. In 1990, Congress enacted the Oil Pollution Act ("OPA"), which amended the Clean Water Act ("CWA"). *See* 33 U.S.C. § 2701 *et seq.* The OPA was Congress's "response to the Exxon Valdez oil spill in Prince William Sound, Alaska, and was intended to streamline federal law so as to provide quick and efficient cleanup of oil spills, compensate victims of such spills, and internalize the costs of spills within the petroleum industry." **{-408-}** *Rice v. Harken Expl. Co.*, 250 F.3d 264, 266 (5th Cir. 2001). The OPA generally imposes strict liability on parties responsible for oil spills, subject to certain complete defenses. *See* 33 U.S.C. §§ 2702, 2703; *see also Rice*, 250 F.3d at 266; *In re Needham*, 354 F.3d 340, 344 (5th Cir. 2003); *United States v. Am. Com. Lines, LLC*, 875 F.3d 170, 174, 5 Adm. R. 324, 326 (5th Cir. 2017).

Congress also created a way for those who clean up an oil spill to get paid quickly. In general, cleaners must first present their claims to the party putatively responsible for the spill. *See* 33 U.S.C. § 2713(a), (b). But if the party denies liability or has not paid the claim within 90 days, the claimant may elect to sue that party or seek repayment from the National Pollution Funds Center ("NPFC"), which administers the Oil Spill Liability Trust Fund ("Fund"). *See generally id.* §§ 2712, 2713; Exec. Order No. 12,777, § 7, 56 Fed. Reg. 54,757, 54,766–68 (Oct. 18, 1991).[1] If the claimant elects **[—3—]** repayment from the NPFC, then it will get all removal expenses that are necessary, reasonable, and consistent with the relevant statutory criteria for such payments. *See* 33 U.S.C. § 2713(c); *see also* 33 C.F.R. §§ 136.105, 136.203, 136.205. And if the Fund pays the removal expenses, then the Government receives by subrogation "all rights, claims and causes of action that the claimant has." 33 U.S.C. § 2715(a); *see also id.* § 2712(f). The NPFC may then seek recoupment from the responsible party, including by filing a lawsuit. *See id.* § 2715(c). The recoupment includes "interest . . . , administrative and adjudicative costs, and attorney's fees." *Ibid.*

B.

Now, the facts and procedural history. ERR owns and operates a wastewater treatment facility on the west bank of the Mississippi River in Louisiana.[2] Throughout May 12,

[1] The Fund's resources generally come from environmental taxes on crude oil and certain petroleum products, payments received from specified environmental fines and penalties, and removal costs paid to the Fund. *See* 26 U.S.C. § 9509; *see also United States v. Hyundai Merch. Marine Co.*, 172 F.3d 1187, 1192 (9th Cir. 1999) ("Funds recovered for removal costs are paid to the Oil Spill Liability Trust Fund, which is available to the President for the payment of removal costs." (citing 33 U.S.C. §§ 2706(f) , 2712(a)(1))).

[2] There are two other defendants in this action, both of which are connected to ERR, LLC. Hugh Nungesser, Jr. is one of ERR's members. Nungesser was also a member of Evergreen Resource Recovery, LLC, which at some point operated the same treatment facility as ERR. Unless otherwise

2015, ERR's facility received a transfer of oily water from a slop-oil barge. While still at the facility, at about 11:45 p.m., the barge tankerman noticed a discoloration in the water near the barge. Just after midnight, the barge left ERR's facility and traveled upstream via a tugboat. The National Response Center that same morning received two reports of oil in the Mississippi River—downstream from ERR's facility.

The Coast Guard and the State of Louisiana sent people to investigate. Their investigation included taking samples of the oil from the river, the barge, and ERR's facility. And they concluded ERR was responsible for the spill. **[—4—]**

Meanwhile, from May 13, 2015, to June 26, 2015, Oil Mop, LLC—one of ERR's designated spill contractors—performed oil removal and soil remediation. On July 22, 2015, Oil Mop submitted its bill of $793,228.74 to ERR. ERR refused to pay. After 90 days passed, Oil Mop submitted a claim of $651,767.26 to the NPFC for reimbursement **{-409-}** of removal costs. The NPFC reimbursed Oil Mop $631,228.74.

On October 20, 2017, the NPFC billed ERR for what it paid Oil Mop. ERR again refused to pay. The Government then sued ERR for what it paid Oil Mop, its administrative-adjudication costs, attorney's fees, and interest.

ERR demanded a jury trial. The Government moved to strike the demand. And the district court agreed with the Government. In general, the Seventh Amendment guarantees a jury "[i]n Suits at common law." U.S. CONST. amend. VII. The district court held, however, that the Government's OPA claims sound not in law but in equity, because the Government sought the equitable remedy of restitution.

In October 2020, the district court held a four-day bench trial. Two months later, the court ruled for the Government and awarded removal costs, administrative-adjudication costs, and attorney's fees. ERR timely appealed, challenging the court's denial of the jury-trial demand, its application of the OPA, and its monetary-compensation determination. We have jurisdiction under 28 U.S.C. § 1291. We address only ERR's Seventh Amendment challenge. Our review is *de novo*. *U.S. Bank Nat'l Ass'n v. Verizon Commc'ns, Inc.*, 761 F.3d 409, 416 (5th Cir. 2014).

II.

We begin with (A) some history on the civil jury right. We then discuss (B) Supreme Court precedent interpreting the Seventh Amendment. Finally, we hold (C) the Seventh Amendment guarantees ERR's right to a jury trial here. **[—5—]**

A.

First, history. The Constitution, as ratified in 1788, did not contain a right to a jury trial in civil cases. *See* U.S. CONST. art. III, § 2, cl. 3 (guaranteeing jury in criminal cases). The omission generated fierce criticism from the Anti-Federalists. As one protested, "jury trials[,] which have so long been considered the surest barrier against arbitrary power, and the palladium of liberty[,] with the loss of which the loss of our freedom may be dated, are taken away by the proposed form of government." Luther Martin's Information to the General Assembly of the State of Maryland, *in* 2 THE COMPLETE ANTI-FEDERALIST 27, 70 (Herbert J. Storing ed., 1981). As another explained: "Judges, unincumbered by juries, have been ever found much better friends to government than to the people. Such judges will always be more desirable than juries to [would-be tyrants], upon the same principle that a large standing army . . . is ever desirable to those who wish to enslave the people." Old Whig No. 8, *in* 3 THE COMPLETE ANTI-FEDERALIST, *supra*, at 49. And another emphasized that the civil jury was essential to preserving "democratical balance in the Judiciary power." Hampden No. 2, *in* 4 THE COMPLETE ANTI-FEDERALIST,

expressly noted, we refer to the defendants collectively as "ERR."

supra, at 200. Many other Anti-Federalists expressed similar concerns.[3] **[—6—]** **{-410-}**

The Federalists recognized this criticism as one of the Anti- Federalists' most trenchant. *See* THE FEDERALIST NO. 83, at 495 (Alexander Hamilton) (Clinton Rossiter ed., 1961) ("The objection to the plan of the convention, *which has met with most success in this State*, and perhaps in several of the other States, is that relative to the want of a constitutional provision for the trial by jury in civil cases." (emphasis added)); *Parsons v. Bedford*, 28 U.S. (3 Pet.) 433, 446 (1830) (Story, J.) ("One of the strongest objections originally taken against the constitution of the United States, was the want of an express provision securing the right of trial by jury in civil cases."). Still, Hamilton tried to defend the omission. He expressed doubts that there was an "inseparable connection between the existence of liberty and the trial by jury in civil cases" and downplayed how much the civil jury trial would be "a security against corruption." THE FEDERALIST NO. 83, *supra*, at 499–500. But his main defense for the omission was practical. Hamilton argued that it'd be too difficult to draft a provision that protected the civil jury right. This is because the States provided radically different rights, so it'd be dangerous to draft a provision that covered one. Instead, Hamilton thought it best for Congress to provide the right to a civil jury trial on a case-by-case basis. In Hamilton's own words:

> From this sketch it appears that there is a material diversity, as well in the modification as in the extent of the institution of trial by jury in civil cases, in the several States; and from this fact these obvious reflections flow: first, that no general rule could have been fixed upon by the convention which would have **[—7—]** corresponded with the circumstances of all the States; and secondly, that more or at least as much might have been hazarded by taking the system of any one State for a standard, as by omitting a provision altogether and leaving the matter, as has been done, to legislative regulation.

Id. at 503.

Hamilton lost, however. The American people recognized the power of the Anti-Federalists' criticisms and ratified the Seventh Amendment in 1791. That Amendment provides:

> In Suits at common law, where the value in controversy shall exceed twenty dollars, the right of trial by jury shall be preserved, and no fact tried by a jury, shall be otherwise reexamined in any Court of the United States, than according to the rules of the common law.

U.S. CONST. amend. VII.

B.

Next, precedent. The Supreme Court has long understood "Suits at common law" to refer "not merely [to] suits, which the *common*

[3] *See, e.g.*, Federal Farmer No. 4, *in* 2 THE COMPLETE ANTI-FEDERALIST, *supra*, at 250 (describing jurors as "centinels and guardians" of the people and stating that he is "very sorry that even a few of our countrymen should consider jurors and representatives in a different point of view, as ignorant troublesome bodies, which ought not to have any share in the concerns of government"); Federal Farmer No. 15, *in* 2 THE COMPLETE ANTI-FEDERALIST, *supra*, at 320 ("The jury trial, especially politically considered, is by far the most important feature in the judicial department in a free country . . . . [B]y holding the jury's right to return a general verdict in all cases sacred, we secure to the people at large, their just and rightful controul in the judicial department. . . . [T]he jury trial brings with it an open and public discussion of all causes, and excludes secret and arbitrary proceedings."); Essay of A Democratic Federalist, *in* 3 THE COMPLETE ANTI-FEDERALIST, *supra*, at 61 ("What refuge shall we then have to shelter us from the iron **[—6—]** hand of arbitrary power?—O! my fellow citizens, think of this while it is yet time, and never consent to part with the glorious privilege of trial by jury, but with your lives."); Observations on the New Constitution and on the Federal and State Conventions by A Columbian Patriot, *in* 4 THE COMPLETE ANTI-FEDERALIST, *supra*, at 276–77 (worrying that the unamended Constitution would lead to "[t]he abolition of trial by jury in civil causes").

law recognized among its old and settled proceedings, but [to] suits in which *legal* rights were to be ascertained and determined, in contradistinction to those where equitable rights alone were recognized, and equitable remedies were administered." *Parsons*, 28 U.S. at 447. So the Seventh Amendment "applies not only to common-law causes of **{–411–}** action, but also to actions brought to enforce statutory rights that are analogous to common-law causes of action ordinarily decided in English law courts in the late 18th century, as opposed to those customarily heard by courts of equity or admiralty." *Feltner v. Columbia Pictures Television, Inc.*, 523 U.S. 340, 348 (1998) (quotation omitted). **[—8—]**

To determine whether a right of action requires a jury trial, we must consider two factors. "First, we compare the statutory action to 18th-century actions brought in the courts of England prior to the merger of the courts of law and equity. Second, we examine the remedy sought and determine whether it is legal or equitable in nature." *Tull v. United States*, 481 U.S. 412, 417–18 (1987) (citation omitted). The second factor is "more important." *Granfinanciera, S.A. v. Nordberg*, 492 U.S. 33, 42 (1989).[4]

[4] The Supreme Court has also asked whether the particular "trial decision" must be decided by the jury to preserve the jury-trial right. *See City of Monterey v. Del Monte Dunes at Monterey, Ltd.*, 526 U.S. 687, 708, 718–21 (1999); *Markman v. Westview Instruments, Inc.*, 517 U.S. 370, 376 (1996) ("If the action in question belongs in the law category, we then ask whether the particular trial decision must fall to the jury in order to preserve the substance of the common-law right as it existed in 1791."); *see also Tex. Advanced Optoelectronic Sols., Inc. v. Renesas Elecs. Am., Inc.*, 895 F.3d 1304, 1319–20 (Fed. Cir. 2018) (noting that the Supreme Court has asked the Seventh Amendment question in "two ways," one of which includes the trial-decision issue). The Court looks principally to history, but if history doesn't provide a "clear answer," it considers "precedent and functional considerations." *Monterey*, 526 U.S. at 718; *see also Markman*, 517 U.S. at 384, 388. Neither party addresses this issue. And for good reason: The Government doesn't dispute that juries resolve complex issues like this all the time, including when the Government (or someone else) under the OPA brings an action for damages.

C.

Here, the Government brought two "alternative" claims. The first is a claim under 33 U.S.C. § 2702(a) ("Recoupment Claim"). The second is a claim under 33 U.S.C. §§ 2712(f) and 2715 ("Subrogation Claim"). We address each claim in turn. We conclude (1) ERR has a Seventh Amendment right to a jury trial for the Recoupment Claim. And because of the overlap between the two claims, this conclusion suffices to reverse the district court. *See, e.g., Beacon Theatres, Inc. v. Westover*, 359 U.S. 500, 508–10 (1959); *Dairy Queen, Inc. v. Wood*, 369 U.S. 469, 472–73 (1962); *Ross v. Bernhard*, 396 U.S. **[—9—]** 531, 542–43 (1970). In any event, we conclude (2) ERR has a right to a jury trial for the Subrogation Claim.

1.

First, the Recoupment Claim. We begin with (a) the nature of the action. We then tackle (b) the type of remedy. We hold both factors support the conclusion that ERR has a right to a jury trial for the Recoupment Claim.

a.

The nature of the action supports a jury right. The Government's action is, at its foundation, one for tort. And historically, tort claimants had two routes to sue a tortfeasor for monetary compensation. Both involved actions at law that were triable to juries.

The first route allowed victims to bring "[c]ommon-law tort actions . . . under the writs of trespass and trespass on the case. **{–412–}** Trespass remedied direct, forcible tortious injuries, while the later developed trespass on the case remedied indirect or consequential harms." *City of Monterey v. Del Monte Dunes at Monterey, Ltd.*, 526 U.S. 687, 729 (1999) (Scalia, J., concurring in part) (citation omitted); *see also* Robert Brauneis, *The First Constitutional Tort: The Remedial Revolution in Nineteenth-Century State Just Compensation Law*, 52 VAND. L. REV. 57, 70–72 (1999). The second route allowed victims "to waive the tort and proceed instead in quasi contract." *Monterey*, 526 U.S. at 716–17 (plurality op.). When victims chose the latter route, they sought "through a writ of assumpsit . . . monetary restitution." *Tex. Advanced Optoelectronic Sols., Inc. v. Renesas Elecs. Am., Inc.*, 895 F.3d 1304, 1323 (Fed. Cir. 2018) (collecting sources); *see also Fed. Deposit Ins. Corp. v. Bank One, Waukesha*, 881 F.2d 390, 393 (7th Cir. 1989) ("No one doubts—though many regret—that the common law allowed the victim of a tort to elect the quasi-contract claim with its longer period of limitations."). **[—10—]**

The OPA mimics these common-law options. The statute first creates a legal duty and then provides a right of action to compensate the injured party for a breach of that duty. *See Curtis v. Loether*, 415 U.S. 189, 195 (1974) ("A damages action under the statute sounds basically in tort—the statute merely defines a new legal duty, and authorizes the courts to compensate a plaintiff for the injury caused by the defendant's wrongful breach."); *Monterey*, 526 U.S. at 727 (Scalia, J., concurring in part) ("Like other tort causes of action, [the applicable law] is designed to provide compensation for injuries arising from the violation of legal duties, and thereby, of course, to deter future violations." (citation omitted)); *see also id.* at 709 (majority op.) ("[C]ommon-law tort actions provide redress for interference with protected personal or property interests."). That's just like torts. The OPA even provides the same two options as the common law to get money: (1) an action for *damages* (akin to a writ of trespass or trespass on the case) or (2) an action for *monetary restitution* (akin to writ of assumpsit/quasi-contract).

Here, the Government chose the second route (quasi-contract). It performed the cleanup and then sought reimbursement from ERR. That is a quintessential quasi-contract action. *Cf., e.g., Process Eng'rs & Const'rs, Inc. v. DiGregorio, Inc.*, 93 A.3d 1047, 1053–55 (R.I. 2014) (cited in 42 C.J.S. IMPLIED CONTRACTS § 17 n.1). And such quasi-contract actions sound in law, not equity. *See Monterey*, 526 U.S. at 717 (plurality op.) ("[Q]uasi contract was itself an action at law."). So the first factor supports a right to a jury.

b.

The type of remedy is "more important." *Granfinanciera*, 492 U.S. at 42. And this more-important factor also supports a jury right. All agree that the reimbursement the Government seeks here is a form of restitution. So we start with (i) some background on restitution. We next explain why (ii) the **[—11—]** remedy here is one *at law*. We last reject (iii) the Government's remaining counterarguments.

i.

Background first. It's well-established that restitution can sound in either law or equity. *See Great-W. Life & Annuity Ins. Co. v. Knudson*, 534 U.S. 204, 212 (2002) ("In the days of the divided bench, restitution was available in certain cases at law, and **{-413-}** in certain others in equity."). Restitution *at law* involved "cases in which the plaintiff could *not* assert title or right to possession of particular property, but in which nevertheless he might be able to show just grounds for recovering money to pay for some benefit the defendant had received from him." *Id.* at 213 (quotation omitted). The plaintiff had a right of action to restitution at law "from the common-law writ of assumpsit." *Ibid.* These claims were "considered legal because [the plaintiff] sought to obtain a judgment imposing a merely personal liability upon the defendant to pay a sum of money. Such claims were viewed essentially as actions at law for breach of contract (whether the contract was actual or implied)." *Ibid.* (quotation omitted).

By contrast, restitution *in equity* ordinarily required identification of particular property or funds in the wrongdoer's possession traceable to the victim. *Ibid.* "A court of equity could then order a defendant to transfer title (in the case of the constructive trust) or to give a security interest (in the case of the equitable lien) to a plaintiff who was, in the eyes of equity, the true owner." *Ibid.* Simply put, for restitution *in equity*, the claim "generally must seek not to impose personal liability on the defendant, but to restore to the plaintiff particular funds or property in the defendant's possession." *Id.* at 214.

There is a "limited exception" for when restitution in equity doesn't require identification of particular property in the defendant's possession: **[—12—]** "an accounting for profits." *Id.* at 214 n.2. An "accounting for profits [is] a remedy closely resembling disgorgement." *Liu v. SEC*, 140 S. Ct. 1936, 1940 n.1 (2020); *see also ibid.* (calling accounting for profits a remedy "parallel[]" to disgorgement). Accounting for profits (and disgorgement) permit the award of the wrongdoer's net profits caused by the wrongdoing to restore the victim to the *status quo ante. See, e.g., id.* at 1940, 1943.[5]

ii.

The removal costs are most analogous to restitution at law. The Government isn't seeking particular property or funds in the defendant's possession caused by the wrongdoing. Nor is the Government seeking ERR's "net profits" caused by the oil spill. So the unjust-enrichment remedy here is akin to restitution *at law*.

Moreover, the Government's Recoupment Claim bears no resemblance to a tort action in equity. As the Supreme Court has explained, "a classic example" of relief given by a court of equity to remedy a tort was injunctive relief to abate a nuisance or to stop a trespass. *Tull*, 481 U.S. at 423. To be sure, sometimes a court of equity awarded monetary relief—but only incident to an injunction. *See id.* at 424 ("A court in equity was empowered to provide monetary awards that were incidental to or intertwined **{-414-}** with injunctive relief."); *see also Tex. Advanced*, 895 F.3d at 1322 **[—13—]** & n.9. Here, the Government never sought any form of injunctive relief. So its monetary claims are not incident to anything; they are the core of the Government's claims *at law*.

iii.

The Government doesn't dispute that the relief here is most like restitution at law as described in *Great-West Life*. Instead, its main argument is that *Great-West Life* is inapposite because it wasn't a Seventh Amendment case. That's both true and irrelevant.

In *Great-West Life*, Justice Scalia analyzed restitution's historical development from the pre-Founding era to the merger of law and equity[6]—the exact same inquiry Supreme Court precedent requires for the Seventh Amendment. Justice Scalia even compared his analysis in *Great-West Life* to the one required by the Seventh Amendment. *See* 534 U.S. at 217 ("It is an inquiry, moreover, that we are accustomed to pursuing, and will always have to pursue, in other contexts," including the Seventh Amendment's right to a civil jury.); *id.* at 213 ("[W]hether [restitution] is legal or equitable depends on the basis for the plaintiff's claim and the nature of the underlying remedies sought." (quotation omitted)). Thus, neither the correctness nor the persuasiveness of *Great-West Life*'s description of restitution at law and in equity turns on the particular context in which Justice Scalia performed it. And in any event, the Supreme Court has directed us to follow its "transsubstantive guidance on broad and fundamental equitable principles." *Liu*, 140 S. Ct. at 1944 (quotation omitted). So we're obligated to follow *Great-West Life*. **[—14—]**

We therefore hold that the Recoupment Claim sounds in law and hence triggers ERR's Seventh Amendment right to a jury.

[5] In certain circumstances, disgorgement (and an accounting for profits) may still be a legal remedy, such as when the defendant's net profits are really used "as a '*proxy*' for actual damages in the form of lost profits or a reasonable royalty." *Tex. Advanced*, 895 F.3d at 1321 (emphasis added); *see also id.* at 1320 ("In some cases, a plaintiff seeking disgorgement as a remedy for trade secret misappropriation might prove that this measure of relief, though focused on the defendant's gains, is good evidence of damages in the form of the plaintiff's losses or of a reasonable royalty for use of the secret."); *TCL Commc'n Tech. Holdings Ltd. v. Telefonaktiebolaget LM Ericsson*, 943 F.3d 1360, 1372–74 (Fed. Cir. 2019) (concluding that a release payment was legal relief because it sought to estimate damages).

[6] Equity and law "merged" or "fused" in 1938. *See, e.g., SCA Hygiene Prod. Aktiebolag v. First Quality Baby Prod., LLC*, 137 S. Ct. 954, 966 (2017); *see also* FED. R. CIV. P. 2 ("There is one form of action—the civil action.").

2.

Next, the Subrogation Claim. This claim is intertwined with the Recoupment Claim, which requires a jury trial. In these circumstances, a jury trial is required on the overlapping issues to preserve the Seventh Amendment right. *See, e.g., Beacon*, 359 U.S. at 508–10; *Dairy Queen*, 369 U.S. at 472–73; *Ross*, 396 U.S. at 537; *Tull*, 481 U.S. at 425 ("[I]f a legal claim is joined with an equitable claim, the right to jury trial on the legal claim, including all issues common to both claims, remains intact. The right cannot be abridged by characterizing the legal claim as incidental to the equitable relief sought." (quotation omitted)).

In any event, even if the claims were not intertwined, the Government's Subrogation Claim still triggers ERR's constitutional right to a jury trial. We first explain (a) that both the nature of the Government's action and the type of remedy sound in law. We then reject (b) the Government's counterarguments.

a.

We again start with the nature of the action and the type of remedy implicated by the Government's Subrogation Claim. Subrogation involves switching one plaintiff for another. *See US Airways, Inc. v. McCutchen*, 569 U.S. 88, 97 n.5 (2013) ("Subrogation **{-415-}** simply means substitution of one person for another; that is, one person is allowed to stand in the shoes of another and assert that person's rights against a third party." (quotation omitted)). But it does not affect the underlying type of remedy; the new plaintiff gets the same remedy (legal or equitable) that the previous one could've gotten. **[—15—]**

Even though subrogation originated in courts of equity, the equitable fiction of substituting the plaintiff for the original rightholder does not, standing alone, make a subrogation action equitable in nature for purposes of the Seventh Amendment. *See* DAN B. DOBBS, LAW OF REMEDIES: DAMAGES, EQUITY, RESTITUTION 411 (3d ed. 2018) [hereinafter DOBBS] ("Subrogation can be compared to an assignment of the creditor's rights to plaintiff, and sometimes subrogation is in fact referred to as an equitable assignment. The assignment, however, is made by the court, not by the parties." (quotation omitted)). That's because two Supreme Court decisions instruct that we should consider whether the *underlying claim* is legal or equitable.

The first decision is *Ross v. Bernhard*, 396 U.S. 531 (1970). There, stockholders brought a derivative suit in federal court against the directors of their closed-end investment company and the corporation's brokers. *Id.* at 531–32. The "derivative suit ha[d] dual aspects": (1) "the stockholder's right to sue on behalf of the corporation, historically an equitable matter"; and (2) "the claim of the corporation against directors or third parties on which, if the corporation had sued and the claim presented legal issues, the company could demand a jury trial." *Id.* at 538.

The Supreme Court concluded that the threshold equitable fiction did not foreclose a Seventh Amendment right to a jury trial. As the Court explained: "If [the action] presents a legal issue, one entitling the corporation to a jury trial under the Seventh Amendment, the right to a jury is not forfeited merely because the stockholder's right to sue must first be adjudicated as an equitable issue triable to the court." *Id.* at 539. That is, "the right to a jury should not turn on how the parties happen to be brought into court." *Id.* at 542 n.15. This principle was a natural consequence of the merger of law and equity because "[p]urely procedural impediments to the **[—16—]** presentation of any issue by any party, based on the difference between law and equity, were destroyed." *Id.* at 539–40.

Or consider *Chauffeurs, Teamsters & Helpers, Local No. 391 v. Terry*, 494 U.S. 558 (1990). There, an employee sued his union for backpay on the ground that the union breached its duty of fair representation. *Id.* at 561. To win, the employee had to prove two things: (1) his employer "breach[ed] the collective-bargaining agreement" and (2) the union breached its duty of fair representation. *See id.* at 569. The Court explained that the collective-bargaining-agreement issue was analogous to a breach-of-contract claim (legal) and the fair-representation issue was analogous to a trust action (equitable). *See id.* at 565–70.

Still, the Supreme Court held there was a right to a jury. As to the nature-of-the-action factor, the Court concluded that it was "in equipoise" because the action "encompasse[d] both equitable and legal issues." *Id.* at 570. As to the nature-of-the-remedy factor, the Court concluded that "the remedy of backpay sought in this duty of fair representation action is legal in nature." *Id.* at 573. With one factor neutral and **{-416-}** one supporting a jury right, the Court held that the employees were "entitled to a jury trial on all issues presented in their suit." *Ibid.*

So too here. Subrogation is merely a procedural fiction created by courts of equity to allow suits involving underlying legal issues and legal relief to proceed. *See US Airways*, 569 U.S. at 97 n.5. The underlying claim here—*i.e.*, the "heart of the action," *Ross*, 396 U.S. at 539—is one that would have been brought in courts at law. It's either a claim identical to the Recoupment Claim or an ordinary breach-of-contract claim seeking monetary damages for the costs of cleaning up the spill. *See supra*, at 9–14 (explaining that the Recoupment Claim sounds at law); *see also AcryliCon USA, LLC v. Silikal GmbH*, 985 F.3d 1350, 1374 (11th Cir. 2021) ("The Seventh Amendment **[—17—]** applies here because breach of contract is a traditional action at law, and a money judgment, even if based on restitution, is generally a legal remedy."); *Bowen v. Massachusetts*, 487 U.S. 879, 917 (1988) (Scalia, J., dissenting). Given *Ross* and *Chauffeurs*, the nature of the action favors a right to a jury. And for the same reasons as the Recoupment Claim, the type of remedy does too.

b.

The Government's principal response is to compare its OPA claims to analogous actions under the Comprehensive Environmental Response, Compensation, and Liability Act ("CERCLA"). And the Government places great weight on authority outside this circuit interpreting CERCLA, which it contends should be extended to the OPA.

The Government mainly relies on *Hatco Corp. v. W.R. Grace & Co. Connecticut*, 59 F.3d 400 (3d Cir. 1995). The court's analysis in that case, however, hinged on the premise that restitution *always* sounds in equity. *See id.* at 412. Whatever the truth of that premise in 1995, it has been squarely foreclosed by subsequent Supreme Court precedent. *See Great-W. Life*, 534 U.S. at 212 ("However, not all relief falling under the rubric of restitution is available in equity. In the days of the divided bench, restitution was available in certain cases at law, and in certain others in equity."); *see also id.* at 215 (explaining "the well-settled principle that restitution is not an exclusively equitable remedy" (quotation omitted)). And as to CERCLA's analogue to the OPA claim for subrogation,[7] the *Hatco* court said nothing about *Ross* and *Chauffeurs*. *Hatco* is thus unpersuasive, and we decline to extend it. **[—18—]**

* * *

We hold that the Seventh Amendment guarantees ERR's right to a jury trial of the Government's OPA claims. For the foregoing reasons, we REVERSE in part, VACATE in part, and REMAND for a jury trial.

---

[7] Contribution and subrogation are of a piece. *See* DOBBS, *supra*, at 414–15 ("The close relationship [between contribution and] subrogation can be seen in such a case **[—18—]** because it would be equally possible to reason that *A*, having paid the debt that *B* owes in equity and good conscience, is subrogated to the creditor's claim against *B*.").

United States Court of Appeals
for the Fifth Circuit

No. 21-30520

XL INS. AM., INC.
vs.
TURN SERVS., L.L.C.

Appeal from the United States District Court for the Eastern District of Louisiana

Decided: June 10, 2022

Citation: 37 F.4th 204, 10 Adm. R. 192 (5th Cir. 2022).

Before **SMITH, WIENER,** and **SOUTHWICK,** Circuit Judges.

[—1—] {–204–} WIENER, Circuit Judge: **{–205–}**

Plaintiff-Appellant XL Insurance America, Inc. ("XL"), as subrogee of Boh Bros. Construction Co., L.L.C. ("Boh Bros."), challenges the district court's summary judgment in favor of Defendant-Appellee Turn Services, L.L.C. ("Turn").

For nearly a century, *Robins Dry Dock & Repair Co. v. Flint*, 275 U.S. 303 (1927), has limited plaintiffs' ability to recover "purely economic claims **[—2—]** . . . in a maritime negligence suit."[1] "[A]bsent physical injury to a proprietary interest"—or one of a few other limited exceptions—plaintiffs asserting such claims are out of luck.[2] As Chief Justice Holmes noted there, "a tort to the person or property of one man does not make the tort-feasor liable to another merely because the injured person was under a contract with that other unknown to the doer of the wrong."[3]

We have faithfully applied this "pragmatic limitation on the doctrine of foreseeability."[4] We have explained in doing so that its purpose is "to limit the consequences of negligence and exclude indirect economic repercussions, which can be widespread and open-ended."[5] Put another way, the "spectre of runaway recovery lies at the heart of the *Robins Dry Dock* rubric."[6]

No such spectre lurks among us today. For that reason—and notwithstanding the district court's thoughtful disposition of the matter—we vacate and remand for further treatment consistent with this opinion.

I. OPERATIVE FACTS

Plains Marketing LP ("Plains") hired Boh Bros. to construct a dock in the Mississippi River. The project required Boh Bros. to install mooring dolphins in the river. It is undisputed that Plains owned the dolphins. **[—3—]**

On the night of February 12, 2019—while the construction project was ongoing—the M/V AFFIRMED, a vessel owned by Turn, allided with MD-9, one of the mooring dolphins. Fortunately, Boh Bros. had procured a builder's risk insurance **{–206–}** policy from XL covering the project. The policy covered Boh Bros. as the named insured and Plains as an additional insured party.

Boh Bros. repaired the dolphin at a cost of $1.254 million and submitted a claim to XL. XL paid Boh Bros. that amount less the deductible. XL also paid Boh Bros. $485,000, which Boh Bros. remitted to Plains after subtracting Plains's share of the deductible.[7]

XL, acting as Boh Bros.'s subrogee, sued Turn in an effort to recover the more than $1.7 million that XL had paid out. The district

---

[1] *In re Taira Lynn Marine Ltd. No. 5, LLC*, 444 F.3d 371, 377 (5th Cir. 2006).

[2] *Id.*

[3] *Robins Dry Dock*, 275 U.S. at 309 (citing *Nat'l Sav. Bank v. Ward*, 100 U.S. 195 (1879)).

[4] *Plains Pipeline, L.P. v. Great Lakes Dredge & Dock Co.*, 620 F. App'x 281, 285 (5th Cir. 2015) (per curiam) (quoting *Louisiana ex rel. Guste v. M/V TESTBANK*, 752 F.2d 1019, 1032 (5th Cir. 1985) (en banc)).

[5] *Catalyst Old River Hydroelectric Ltd. P'ship v. Ingram Barge Co.*, 639 F.3d 207, 210 (5th Cir. 2011) (citing *TESTBANK*, 752 F.2d at 1022).

[6] *Amoco Transp. Co. v. S/S Mason Lykes*, 768 F.2d 659, 668 (5th Cir. 1985).

[7] The record does not establish what this $485,000 payout covered, although common sense and record evidence suggest it was for a loss incurred by Plains, the recipient. XL "concedes that [it] . . . was not for direct physical damage to the dock project/MD-9."

court, however, granted Turn's summary judgment motion, concluding that *Robins Dry Dock* precluded XL from recovering from Turn. XL timely appealed.

II. Standard of Review

We review a summary judgment de novo.[8] Summary judgment is proper only if "the movant shows that there is no genuine dispute as to any material fact and the movant is entitled to judgment as a matter of law."[9]

III. Analysis

A. Repair Costs

As noted, the district court rendered summary judgment for Turn in the belief that *Robins Dry Dock* compelled that outcome. The court concluded **[—4—]** that a decision to the contrary would "undoubtedly contradict the doctrine's [policy against] limitless liability." We disagree. A claim for the costs of repairing damage caused by an allision presents no such risk. *Robins Dry Dock* therefore does not bar XL's claim as it relates to the $1.254 million in repair costs.

"It is unmistakable that the law of this circuit does not allow recovery of purely economic claims absent physical injury to a proprietary interest in a maritime negligence suit."[10] As noted above—and by the district court— this rule exists to avoid the possibility of limitless liability.[11]

We have emphatically rejected calls to abandon the physical injury requirement.[12] In doing so, though, we have explained that the requirement—like the common law principle from which it emerged— applies to claims for "pure economic losses."[13] We have also made clear that "*Robins Dry Dock* is inapposite" when "the risk of double recovery from the tortfeasor is not extant."[14] In *Amoco Transport Co. v. S/S Mason Lykes*—which we decided mere months after *TESTBANK*—we concluded that the owners of cargo aboard a ship involved in a collision could recover their economic losses, despite the cargo's being undamaged.[15] We reached this conclusion because, given a risk-shifting provision in the cargo owners' **[—5—]** agreement with the ship **{-207-}** owner, there was no risk of "double recovery, much less runaway recovery."[16]

If *Robins Dry Dock* was inapposite to that situation, it must also be inapposite to the instant case. Unlike the cargo owners in *Amoco*, Boh Bros. (XL's subroger) did not suffer a "pure economic loss." Rather, the $1.2 million claim was paid for the cost of repairing physical damage to the dolphin. The fact that Plains owned the dolphin is irrelevant: The $1.2 million went towards repairing physical damage, and that is dispositive. As in *Amoco*, there is no risk of "runaway recovery."[17]

On appeal, Turn devotes significant ink to its contention that Boh Bros.'s responsibility for repairing the dolphin does not equate to a proprietary interest in it. Turn similarly contends that the risk of loss for the dolphin was not shifted from Plains to Boh Bros. by virtue of their contract. (If it were, an exception to *Robins Dry Dock* would apply.)[18] We are particularly skeptical of the second claim: If Boh Bros. bore no risk for the project, why would it pay for the repairs? Surely that is enough to warrant applying the risk-shifting exception to *Robins Dry Dock*. We need not answer this question definitively, though, because we hold that *Robins Dry Dock* is not implicated by the $1.2 million that XL paid Boh Bros. to cover the repairs.

---

8 *Taira Lynn*, 444 F.3d at 376 (citing *Am. Home Assurance Co. v. United Space All., LLC*, 378 F.3d 482, 486 (5th Cir. 2004)).

9 Fed. R. Civ. Proc. 56(a).

10 *Taira Lynn*, 444 F.3d at 376.

11 *See, e.g., Catalyst*, 639 F.3d at 210.

12 *TESTBANK*, 752 F.2d at 1032.

13 *Id.* at 1027.

14 *Amoco*, 768 F.2d at 668 (citing *Venore Transp. Co. v. M/V STRUMA*, 583 F.2d 708 (4th Cir. 1978)).

15 *Id.* at 660–62.

16 *Id.* at 668.

17 *Id.*

18 *See id.*

B. Economic Damages

The remaining $485,000 of XL's claim presents a slightly different issue. As noted, the record is less than clear regarding the nature of the damages covered by this payment from XL. It concedes, however, that the **[—6—]** money it paid "was not for direct physical damage to the dock project/MD- 9." We may assume for purposes of this appeal, then, that the subject payment covered some sort of economic damages. Record evidence indicates, however, that Boh Bros. passed the $485,000 along to Plains, subtracting only an agreed-upon portion of the deductible. It is also undisputed that Plains owned the damaged dolphin at the time of the allision. And, as noted, the dolphin suffered extensive damage.

We perceive no reason, then, that *Robins Dry Dock* bars recovery in this situation. It is clear, after all, that the doctrine would be inapplicable here if XL had paid the money directly to Plains, because Plains had a proprietary interest in the damaged dolphin. That the money passes through the hands of an intermediary—here, Boh Bros.—is irrelevant to the concerns animating *Robins Dry Dock*.[19] Regardless, the district court is well-positioned to make any additional findings of fact that may prove necessary regarding such claim.

IV. CONCLUSION

We conclude that the rule of *Robins Dry Dock* does not bar recovery by XL. We therefore VACATE the district court's judgment and REMAND for further proceedings consistent with this opinion.

---

19 *See, e.g., id.* at 668–69.

United States Court of Appeals
for the Fifth Circuit

No. 22-20021

PREBLE-RISH HAITI, S.A.
vs.
BB ENERGY USA, L.L.C.

Appeal from the United States District Court for the Southern District of Texas

Decided: July 14, 2022

Citation: 40 F.4th 368, 10 Adm. R. 195 (5th Cir. 2022).

Before **HIGGINBOTHAM, DENNIS,** and **GRAVES,** Circuit Judges.

[—1—] {-369-} GRAVES, Circuit Judge: **{-370-}**

The Foreign Sovereign Immunities Act provides a foreign state's property with immunity from prejudgment attachment unless an exception applies. The relevant exception in this case requires a foreign state to explicitly waive its immunity from prejudgment attachment. 28 U.S.C. § 1610(d). Although this court has yet to interpret the § 1610(d) exception, today we hold that an explicit waiver must be, well, *explicit*. Anything short **[—2—]** of a foreign state's clearly expressed waiver of immunity from prejudgment attachment will not suffice under § 1610(d). Here, however, the district court entered a writ of attachment based on the erroneous conclusion that Haiti and its agency waived their immunity from prejudgment attachment based on a contract that said nothing about prejudgment attachment. We therefore REVERSE the district court and VACATE the writ.

BACKGROUND

Plaintiff-Appellee Preble-Rish Haiti, S.A. filed this case pursuant to Rule B of the Supplemental Rules for Admiralty or Maritime Claims in the Federal Rules of Civil Procedure. It sought to attach assets to secure a partial final arbitration award against the Republic of Haiti and the Bureau de Monétisation de Programmes d'Aide au Developpement (BMPAD). Garnishee BB Energy USA, L.L.C. admits to holding credits belonging to BMPAD located in the Southern District of Texas.

A. Underlying Facts

In May 2020, Preble-Rish, a Haitian company, entered into three contracts with BMPAD, a Haitian government agency, to deliver fuel. The contracts specified that BMPAD would provide a letter of credit as payment. BMPAD did not provide that letter, so the contracts were amended to permit BMPAD to instead make full prepayment pursuant to an invoice Preble-Rish submitted before each delivery. The contracts stated Preble-Rish would make six deliveries of fuel in response to orders from BMPAD.

Relevant here, the contracts had an arbitration clause stating:

> In the event of a dispute between the [BMPAD] and [Preble Rish] under this Contract, the dispute shall be submitted by either party to arbitration in New York. . . . The decision of the arbitrators shall be final, conclusive and binding on all Parties. **[—3—]** Judgment upon such award may be entered in any court of competent jurisdiction.

Pursuant to the contracts, BMPAD and Preble-Rish executed their duties without issue on four deliveries of fuel. Problems arose on the fifth delivery. To resolve these issues, on November 20, 2020, Preble-Rish sent BMPAD a notice demanding arbitration in New York. BMPAD did not appear in the arbitration and refused to participate. On December 22, 2020, Haiti and BMPAD filed a petition in New York state court to obtain an order to stay the pending arbitration with Preble-Rish. Preble-Rish opposed the petition and filed a cross-motion to compel arbitration.

While Haiti and BMPAD's action was pending in New York state court, on August 6, 2021, the arbitration panel issued a partial final award of security. The award required BMPAD to post approximately $23 million in security. **{-371-}**

On September 27, 2021, the New York state court denied BMPAD's petition to stay the arbitration and granted Preble-Rish's motion to compel arbitration. The order states: "It is beyond dispute that the parties freely and unequivocally agreed to arbitrate all of their disputes in New York." That order was affirmed by the New York Appellate Division on April 12, 2022. The Appellate Division stated BMPAD failed to show the arbitration clause was invalid under Haitian law.

B. Procedural History

On June 15, 2021, Preble-Rish filed this Rule B attachment action in the Southern District of Texas to secure any final award from the pending arbitration and the partial final award of security. In its first complaint, Preble-Rish asserted claims for breach of contract and unjust enrichment. After complying with Rule B, Preble-Rish sought a writ of attachment for property belonging to BMPAD located in the district but in the possession of **[—4—]** BB Energy. Preble-Rish alleged that BMPAD prepays BB Energy for fuel and that the prepaid funds are property of BMPAD present in the district.

The district court issued the writ of attachment and Preble-Rish served BB Energy with the writ on July 1, 2021. BB Energy promptly moved to dismiss and argued the district court lacked jurisdiction over the complaint based on BMPAD's sovereign immunity.[1] BB Energy also moved to vacate the attachment because the contracts at issue were not maritime in nature and therefore precluded admiralty jurisdiction as needed for Rule B attachment. The district court stayed the writ to determine the subject matter jurisdiction issue.

On August 10, 2021, the district court denied BB Energy's motion to dismiss because it concluded BMPAD had waived sovereign immunity by agreeing to arbitrate disputes under the contracts. The district court also concluded BMPAD explicitly waived its sovereign immunity from prejudgment attachment by agreeing to provide letters of credit or prepayment as stated in the contracts and because the property that sought to be attached was "used for commercial activity in the United States." Having concluded that BMPAD waived its sovereign immunity generally and from prejudgment attachment, the district court determined it had subject matter jurisdiction over the case and reinstated the writ of attachment. BB Energy did not appeal this order.

On September 3, 2021, the district court granted BB Energy's motion to vacate the writ of attachment. The district court concluded the contracts **[—5—]** were not maritime in nature and did not satisfy the requirements for admiralty jurisdiction for Rule B attachments.

Preble-Rish filed an amended complaint[2] and added claims for maritime fraud and conversion. BB Energy moved to dismiss and again, raised BMPAD's sovereign immunity by arguing the new maritime tort claims fell outside the scope of the arbitration clause and BMPAD did not waive its immunity from prejudgment attachment. **{–372–}** The district court deferred ruling on the motion to dismiss and directed the parties to discovery. BB Energy appealed and this court remanded the case with instructions for the district court to limit discovery to the sovereign immunity jurisdictional issue. *See Preble-Rish Haiti, S.A. v. BB Energy USA, LLC*, No. 21-20534, 2021 WL 5143757, at *3 (5th Cir. Nov. 4, 2021) (unpublished). On remand, the parties agreed no further discovery was needed to resolve the issue.

---

[1] To date, neither Haiti nor BMPAD has appeared in this case. BB Energy nonetheless has standing to assert the sovereign immunity defense because the property it holds qualifies as "property of a foreign state." *See Walker Int'l Holdings Ltd. v. Republic of Congo*, 395 F.3d 229, 233 (5th Cir. 2004).

[2] Preble-Rish first filed a notice of appeal and a motion for reconsideration, or in the alternative, a motion for leave to file an amended complaint. After the district court granted Preble-Rish leave, Preble-Rish withdrew its notice of appeal and filed its amended complaint.

On January 4, 2022, the district court denied BB Energy's motion to dismiss based on sovereign immunity. The district court relied on its August 10, 2021 decision to conclude that the arbitration clause waived BMPAD's immunity from suit. It therefore only determined whether the arbitration clause covered maritime tort claims in the amended complaint. The court broadly construed the arbitration clause's waiver for disputes "under this contract" to encompass the maritime tort claims in addition to the breach of contract claims. The district court also applied issue preclusion as to whether Haitian law prohibited arbitration against governmental entities and cited the New York state court's order denying BMPAD's motion to stay arbitration. Although BB Energy raised BMPAD's sovereign immunity from **[—6—]** prejudgment attachment again, the district court stated it had already decided that issue and cited its August 10, 2021 order.

BB Energy appeals the January 4, 2022 order pursuant to the collateral order doctrine.[3]

DISCUSSION

This case turns on the interpretation of 28 U.S.C. § 1610(d) which provides a limited exception to the general rule that a foreign state and its property is entitled to sovereign immunity. That exception applies only when "the foreign state explicitly waived its immunity from attachment prior to judgment." § 1610(d). Here, there was no explicit waiver. So we conclude BMPAD did not waive its immunity from prejudgment attachment and the district court erred in concluding otherwise.

Without this waiver, the district court did not have jurisdiction to enter the writ of attachment against BB Energy.[4] We accordingly reverse the district court and vacate the writ.

The denial of sovereign immunity is reviewed de novo. *See Frank v. Commonwealth of Antigua and Barbuda*, 842 F.3d 362, 367 (5th Cir. 2016). A foreign state's sovereign immunity deprives the federal courts of jurisdiction. The Foreign Sovereign Immunities Act (FSIA) therefore "provides the sole source of subject matter jurisdiction in suits against a foreign state." *Id.* **[—7—]** (quoting *Dale v. Colagiovanni*, 443 F.3d 425, 427–28 (5th Cir. 2006)); 28 U.S.C. § 1604. Pursuant to the FSIA, the general rule is that foreign states are immune from suit in American courts. 28 U.S.C. § 1604; *see also Arriba Ltd. v. Petroleos Mexicanos*, 962 F.2d 528, 532–33 (5th Cir. 1992). Along with immunity from suit generally, the FSIA provides a foreign **{-373-}** state's property with immunity from attachment or execution unless an exception applies. 28 U.S.C. § 1609.

The relevant exception here is § 1610(d), which states:

> The property of a foreign state . . . used for a commercial activity in the United States, shall not be immune from attachment prior to the entry of judgment in any action . . . if—
>
> (1) the foreign state has explicitly waived its immunity from attachment prior to judgment . . . and
>
> (2) the purpose of the attachment is to secure satisfaction of a judgment that has been or may ultimately be entered against the foreign state, and not to obtain jurisdiction.

This exception has three conditions: (1) the property must be used for a commercial purpose in the United States; (2) there must be an explicit waiver; and (3) the purpose of

[3] Contrary to Preble-Rish's argument that this court lacks appellate jurisdiction, the collateral order doctrine permits review of the denial of sovereign immunity from writs of garnishment or attachment. *See Stena Rederi AB v. Comision de Contratos del Comite Ejecutivo Gen. del Sindicato Revolucionario de Trabajadores Petroleros de la Republica Mexicana, S.C.*, 923 F.2d 380, 386 (5th Cir. 1991).

[4] Because we resolve this appeal on the prejudgment attachment issue, we assume without deciding that BMPAD implicitly waived its sovereign immunity from suit generally pursuant to 28 U.S.C. § 1605(a)(1).

attachment must be to secure satisfaction of a judgment. *See Pine Top Receivables of Ill., LLC v. Banco de Seguros del Estado*, 771 F.3d 980, 983 (7th Cir. 2014). BB Energy only challenges the first two elements; it argues there is no explicit waiver from prejudgment attachment and the credits it holds for BMPAD are not "used for commercial activity in the United States." **[—8—]**

This court has not yet interpreted the § 1610(d) exception or its requirements. We are confident, however, that the explicit waiver requirement has not been met here.[5]

To interpret § 1610(d), "we begin 'where all such inquiries must begin: with the language of the statute itself.'" *Republic of Sudan v. Harrison*, 139 S. Ct. 1048, 1056 (2019) (alterations and citations omitted). Section 1610(d) revokes sovereign immunity for a foreign state's property "if the foreign state has explicitly waived its immunity from attachment prior to judgment." The key word here is "explicitly." This naturally and ordinarily means in a definite and unambiguous manner. To be unequivocal, express, clear, or plain. Dictionaries contrast "explicitly" with "not merely by implication or implicitly." *E.g., Explicitly*, OXFORD ENG. DICTIONARY (3d ed. June 2016).

We, like other courts, think an explicit waiver must be *explicit* "in the common sense meaning of that term." *S & S Machinery Co. v. Masinexportimport*, 706 F.2d 411, 416 (2d Cir. 1983). While an explicit waiver need not include the words "prejudgment attachment" or the like, an asserted waiver "must demonstrate unambiguously the foreign state's intention to waive its immunity from prejudgment attachment." *Id.* This requires "unmistakable and plain language." *Id.*

The importance of the explicit waiver requirement is also highlighted when we compare § 1610(d) to the language used in other exceptions in the FSIA. For instance, there are several other exceptions that permit a waiver to be explicit *or* implicit. *Compare* §§ 1605(a)(1), 1610(a)(1) (allowing wavier to be explicit or by implication), *with* § 1610(d). *See also S & S Machinery*, 706 F.2d at 416 ("The requirement that the waiver of immunity from **[—9—]** prejudgment attachment be *explicitly* made is underscored both by the plain language of § 1610(d) and by the contrast between § 1610(d) and § 1610(a)." (emphasis in original)).

With this understanding, we can only conclude that BMPAD did not explicitly waive its immunity from prejudgment attachment. The only basis for a waiver of **{-374-}** any immunity is the arbitration clause in the contract between BMPAD and Preble-Rish. The arbitration clause is relevant to whether BMPAD waived its sovereign immunity from suit generally, but a waiver of immunity from suit has "no bearing upon the question of immunity from prejudgment attachment." *S & S Machinery*, 706 F.2d at 417.

Even when we look at the arbitration clause and the contract as a whole, we find nothing to support an explicit waiver of immunity from prejudgment attachment. The clause does not contemplate prejudgment attachment or any other liabilities. Nor does it mention security or letters of credit in the context of disputes between the parties. Although Preble-Rish and BMPAD agreed any arbitration awards would "be final, conclusive and binding," that language does not contemplate any specific remedy or allow the arbitration panel to ignore the immunity from prejudgment attachment as provided by the FSIA.

And in prior cases where this court has concluded the § 1610(d) exception applied, the parties' agreement has *explicitly* said sovereign immunity is waived "including any immunity from the jurisdiction of any court or *from any execution or attachment in aid of execution prior to judgment or otherwise*." *Atwood Turnkey Drilling, Inc. v. Petroleo Brasileiro, S.A.*, 875 F.2d 1174, 1177 (5th Cir. 1989) (emphasis added); *see also Mangattu v. M/V Ibn Hayyan*, 35 F.3d 205, 210 (5th Cir. 1994) (rejecting argument that agreement to laws of another country is sufficient to find an explicit waiver); *id.* ("If the subsequent law of

[5] As for the other two requirements, we find no error in the district court's analysis.

another country in fact waives immunity, it would be an **[—10—]** *implicit waiver . . . .*" (emphasis added)). Such explicit language is absent here.

Preble-Rish urges us to find waiver because, in the contracts, BMPAD agreed to provide letters of credit or full prepayment, i.e., agreed to provide security in Preble-Rish's favor. To support this theory, Preble-Rish points to *Banco de Seguros del Estado v. Mutual Marine Office, Inc.*, 344 F.3d 255 (2d Cir. 2003). In that case, the Second Circuit determined a sovereign entity agreed to "apply for and secure delivery to [the other party] a clean irrevocable Letter of Credit issued by a bank" and therefore demonstrated that the "parties embraced the usefulness of letters of credit as a means of securing their respective rights and obligations and as a means of facilitating the transaction generally." *Mut. Marine Off.*, 344 F.3d at 261 (citations omitted). The parties in that case had also agreed to arbitration and explicitly stated the "arbitrators are relieved of all judicial formalities and may abstain from following the strict rules of law." *Id.* (internal quotation marks and citations omitted). Although the district court accepted this theory, we are unpersuaded.

The Second Circuit in *Mutual Marine* noted the arbitration clause at issue did not *explicitly authorize* the arbitrator to order a letter of credit as security against a possible final award. *See id.* So rather than relying on § 1610(d)'s demand that a waiver be explicit, the court looked to other provisions in the agreement to *infer* a waiver of immunity from prejudgment attachment. If the court needs to infer a waiver, then the waiver is not explicit. *See Pine Top*, 771 F.3d at 985 (concluding a waiver that must be discerned from contract clauses "that do not speak to orders of preanswer security in judicial proceedings" is not explicit). And although BMPAD agreed to provide letters of credit, the contracts in this case lack the same generous arbitration clause that allows arbitrators to "abstain from following the strict rules of law." *Id.* Without such authorization, the contract here **[—11—]** simply provides **{-375-}** for letters of credit during the underlying transaction—not in any disputes that are ultimately submitted to arbitration. *Mutual Marine* is thus distinguishable and unpersuasive on the issue before us.

CONCLUSION

To satisfy § 1610(d), an explicit waiver of immunity from prejudgment attachment must be express, clear, and unambiguous. Anything short of that is insufficient. Because there is no such explicit waiver in the contract or elsewhere, the district court erred in concluding BMPAD waived its sovereign immunity from prejudgment attachment. We accordingly REVERSE the district court and VACATE the writ of attachment.

United States Court of Appeals
for the Fifth Circuit

No. 22-20002

GRAND FAMOUS SHIPPING LTD.
VS.
CHINA NAVIGATION CO. PTE.

Appeal from the United States District Court for the Southern District of Texas

Decided: August 15, 2022

Citation: 45 F.4th 799, 10 Adm. R. 200 (5th Cir. 2022).

Before **SMITH, CLEMENT,** and **HAYNES,** Circuit Judges. *

* Judge Haynes concurs in the judgment only.

[—2—] {-800-} CLEMENT, Circuit Judge:

A time-chartered vessel allided with a barge and a dock in the Houston Ship Channel. The owner of the barge and the lessee of the dock sued both the vessel's owner and her then-time charterer, seeking damages for negligence.

The district court granted summary judgment in the time-charterer's favor. It held that the time charterer did not function as the vessel's de facto owner, nor did it negligently discharge its duties as her time charterer. The lessee of the dock, on behalf of itself and certain other interested parties, timely appealed. We AFFIRM.

I.

On June 13, 2018, while navigating the Houston Ship Channel, the captain of the M/V Yochow ordered a helmsman to turn the vessel hard to starboard (right). The **{-801-}** helmsman, who allegedly was fatigued due to an inadequate work/rest schedule, instead turned the vessel hard to port (left). That mistake caused the Yochow to strike the OSG 243 barge, which was berthed at Dock A. The momentum from the allision pushed the barge into the dock, damaging both substantially.

On June 20, 2018, OSG 243 LLC—the barge's registered owner—and Overseas Shipholding Group, Inc.—the barge's manager—filed a verified complaint against the Yochow, *in rem*, and against Grand Famous Shipping Ltd. and China Navigation Co., *in personam*. *See* Complaint, *OSG 243 LLC v. M/V YOCHOW*, No. 4:18-CV-2046, (S.D. Tex. June 20, 2018), ECF No. 1. Grand Famous is the registered owner of the Yochow. China Navigation was, at the time of the allision, the long-term time charterer of the Yochow pursuant to a Time Charter Party with Grand Famous.

In the verified complaint, OSG 243 LLC and Overseas Shipholding Group, Inc. sought "money damages in excess of $3,300,000.00 **[—3—]** representing the cost to repair the OSG 243, loss of hire, surveying costs, cargo loss, additional operating cost and interest" as a result of the alleged negligence of the "M/V YOCHOW [and] her owner and operator." Complaint at 3, 4:18-CV-2046, ECF No. 1.

In December 2018, Grand Famous and Beikun Shipping Tianjin Co.—the technical manager of the Yochow pursuant to a Ship Management Agreement with Grand Famous—brought a limitation of liability action in federal district court. TPC Group LLC—the lessee of Dock A; OSG 243 LLC; Overseas Shipholding Group, Inc.; and Port of Houston Authority filed answers and claims in limitation in response to Grand Famous and Beikun's limitation action. *See Grand Famous Shipping Ltd. v. Port of Hous. Auth.*, 574 F. Supp. 3d 438, 440 (S.D. Tex. 2021).

The district court consolidated the damages case with the limitation action. China Navigation then filed an answer and, shortly thereafter, filed a motion for summary judgment seeking dismissal of all claims against it. As relevant here, China Navigation argued that it could not be held liable in tort for the allision because, as time charterer, it lacked operational control over the Yochow and was not responsible for the Yochow's safety or the negligence of her crew. Moreover, it argued that there was no evidence that it was negligent in conducting its traditional duties as time charterer.

TPC was the only party that filed a substantive response to China Navigation's motion for summary judgment. *See id.* at 442 n.1. TPC advanced a two-part theory for China Navigation's liability. First, it argued that China Navigation was independently negligent as time charterer by failing to exercise reasonable care in selecting and employing a competent contractor (*i.e.*, Grand Famous and, by extension, Beikun). That was so, TPC argued, because China Navigation failed to ensure that (a) Grand Famous was financially stable, and (b) the Yochow had appropriate safety **[—4—]** management procedures in place. Had China Navigation been more careful in vetting Grand Famous, the argument goes, it would have discovered inadequacies in the Yochow's safety management procedures—in particular, her fatigue management protocols—and the allision would not have occurred.

Second, it argued that China Navigation was the de facto owner of the Yochow and therefore responsible for the Yochow's safety and the negligence of her crew. It even went as far as to argue that China Navigation used Grand Famous as a shell company to shield itself from liability. **{–802–}**

The district court granted summary judgment in China Navigation's favor. It held first that there was no genuine issue of material fact as to whether China Navigation was the Yochow's de facto owner. It next held that China Navigation did not act as a negligent time charterer because it did not owe a duty to vet Grand Famous' finances or the Yochow's safety protocols.

TPC and "certain interested underwriters" timely appealed, as did OSG 243 LLC and Overseas Ship Management, Inc. OSG 243 LLC and Overseas Ship Management, Inc. joined TPC's appellate briefing but did not file briefs of their own.

II.

We review a district court's order granting a motion for summary judgment de novo, applying the same standard as the district court. *Hyatt v. Thomas*, 843 F.3d 172, 176 (5th Cir. 2016). Summary judgment is appropriate when "there is no genuine dispute as to any material fact and the movant is entitled to judgment as a matter of law." FED. R. CIV. P. 56(a). A disputed fact is material if it "might affect the outcome of the suit under the governing law[.]" *Hyatt,* 843 F.3d at 177 (quoting *Anderson v. Liberty Lobby, Inc.*, 477 U.S. 242, 248 (1986)). "We construe all facts and inferences in the light most **[—5—]** favorable to the nonmoving party[.]" *Dillon v. Rogers,* 596 F.3d 260, 266 (5th Cir. 2010) (quoting *Murray v. Earle*, 405 F.3d 278, 284 (5th Cir. 2005)).

III.

There are two questions on appeal. The first is confined to the facts of this case: Did China Navigation exercise sufficient operational control over the Yochow such that it should be considered her de facto owner? No.

The second is more general and, if resolved in TPC's favor, would have potentially far-reaching consequences for the shipping industry: Does a time charterer have a duty to vet a vessel owner prior to executing a charter party? TPC acknowledges that our existing maritime jurisprudence has never explicitly recognized such a duty. Yet, it suggests that one nevertheless exists. We disagree.

A.

A charter party is a maritime contract that describes the "arrangements and contractual engagements entered into when one person (the 'charterer') takes over the use of the whole of a ship belonging to another (the 'owner')." GRANT GILMORE & CHARLES L. BLACK, JR., THE LAW OF ADMIRALTY 193 (2d ed. 1975) (hereinafter "GILMORE & BLACK"). There are three primary kinds of charter parties, which are highly standardized: voyage charters, time charters, and demise or bareboat charters. *Id.* at 193–94.

> In a voyage charter the ship is engaged to carry a full cargo on a single voyage. The owner retains all control over the vessel. In a time charter the ship's

> carrying capacity is taken by the charterer for a fixed time for the carriage of goods on as many voyages as can fit into the charter period. *Again, the owner retains all control for management and navigation.* In a demise or bareboat charter, the charterer takes over full control of the **[—6—]** ship and becomes the owner pro hac vice. The charterer thus assumes control of management and navigation.

Dougherty v. Navigazione San Paolo, S.P.A. Medafrica Line, 622 F. Supp. 1, 3 (E.D. Pa. 1984) (emphasis added) (citing GILMORE & BLACK at 193–94); *see also In re Dann Ocean Towing, Inc.*, No. 1:15-CV-01610-NLH-AMD, 2018 WL 901716, at *3 (D.N.J. Feb. 15, 2018). "The time charter **{-803-}** is used where the charterer's affairs make it desirable for him to have tonnage under his control for a period of time, without undertaking the responsibilities of ship navigation and management or the long-term financial commitments of vessel ownership." GILMORE & BLACK at 194.

This case involves a time charter. In 2013, during the Yochow's construction, China Navigation and Grand Famous executed a standard time charter party,[1] pursuant to which China Navigation could engage the Yochow to carry cargo for a specified duration.[2] Grand Famous and China Navigation contracted at arm's length through an intermediary shipbroker called Taiwan Wallem Transportation Co. Under this time charter, as is customary, Grand Famous retained control over all material aspects of vessel management and navigation:

> Nothing herein stated is to be construed as a demise of the vessel to the Time Charterers. The Owners shall remain responsible for the navigation of the vessel, acts of pilots and tug boats, insurance, crew, and all other similar matters, same as when trading for their own account. **[—7—]**

In addition, Grand Famous remained responsible for ensuring that the Yochow's safety management systems complied with the International Safety Management (ISM) Code. China Navigation, in exchange, was responsible for covering certain of the Yochow's expenses, including fuel and port charges. It also got to rename the Yochow, paint her in its house colors, paint its logo on her funnel, and fly its house flag.

TPC does not attempt to argue that the time charter itself transferred control over the Yochow from Grand Famous to China Navigation. Nor could it; the parties explicitly contracted for a time charter, wherein Grand Famous retained control over the vessel. If the parties had wanted to structure their agreement differently such that responsibility for the Yochow's management, navigation, and safety shifted to China Navigation, they could have done so. There's a charter party for that—a demise charter. But they didn't.

In fact, one of the very reasons why an entity would choose a time charter is precisely to avoid "undertaking the responsibilities of ship navigation and management or the long-term financial commitments of vessel ownership." GILMORE & BLACK at 194. It is therefore clear from the time charter's terms that China Navigation did not assume contractual control over the Yochow.

Even so, TPC argues that the court should treat China Navigation *as if* it were the Yochow's owner because it held itself out to the world as such. For support, TPC relies on the fact that China Navigation was listed as the Yochow's "Manager" in the Lloyd's Register of Ships until this incident; China Navigation listed the Yochow as a vessel that it "operated" in a 2016 Sustainability Report; and China Navigation renamed the vessel, painted her in its house colors, and painted its corporate logo on her funnel. In addition, TPC claims that China Navigation "'stayed involved' with the operation of **[—8—]** the

[1] This agreement was based on a standard form promulgated by the New York Produce Exchange. The parties amended it in a few places to suit their particular needs.

[2] In April 2018, China Navigation sub-chartered the Yochow to Daiichi pursuant to a Fixture Recap. At the time of the allision giving rise to this dispute, the Yochow was under sub-charter to Daiichi.

[Yochow].” It points to the fact that China Navigation directed the Yochow's captain to download its reporting software, **{-804-}** Swirelink, which reports data about the vessel back to China Navigation.

These arguments are unmoored from reality.

First, the time charter explicitly gave China Navigation the privilege of renaming the vessel and painting her in its house colors and with its logo. That had nothing to do with China Navigation's exercising operational control over the Yochow and everything to do with its exercising its rights under the time charter. Second, that China Navigation listed the Yochow as "operated" in its 2016 Sustainability Report should be viewed in the proper context. Its designation of the Yochow as "operated" was to distinguish her from vessels that China Navigation listed as "owned" and/or "managed."

China Navigation treated vessels that it "owned" or "managed" differently from vessels that it listed as "operated." For example, China Navigation maintained its own ISM-compliant safety management system (SMS) on vessels that it managed. But both parties agree that, pursuant to the Ship Management Agreement, Grand Famous made *Beikun* responsible for implementing and maintaining the Yochow's SMS. In fact, the Ship Management Agreement gave Beikun responsibility for nearly all management-related duties, including maintaining an SMS, providing routine maintenance and arranging for repairs, manning the vessel and training her crews, and educating her crews on the SMS. The evidence shows that it was Beikun, not China Navigation, that managed the Yochow.

Third, TPC's argument that China Navigation was the Yochow's de facto owner because it was listed as her manager in the Lloyd's Register of Ships falls flat. TPC cites no authority for the proposition that the way a time charterer *describes* a vessel to third parties is of legal import. And indeed, it is not; the terms of the charter party control, and those terms clearly describe **[—9—]** China Navigation as the time charterer and Grand Famous as the owner with control over the vessel. *See, e.g., Gale-Ebanks v. Chesapeake Crewing, LLC,* 525 F. Supp. 3d 620, 626 (D. Md. 2021) ("Courts are reluctant to determine that a time charterer has operational control over a vessel, which would render it an owner *pro hac vice*."). Again, the touchstone of de facto ownership is *control,* and China Navigation had virtually none.

Finally, TPC's argument that China Navigation "stayed involved" in operating the Yochow because it directed the Yochow's captain to download Swirelink is unpersuasive. Pursuant to the time charter, China Navigation was responsible for certain of the Yochow's expenses, including her fuel costs and port charges. Given that Swirelink tracks "where each and every vessel is" and reports vessels' "time, location, speed, and consumption," it makes perfect sense that China Navigation would require the Yochow to download it. This does not show that China Navigation exercised operational control.

In sum, the facts do not demonstrate that China Navigation retained contractual control over the Yochow. Nor do they suggest that it exercised operational control over the Yochow to such an extent that it should be considered her de facto owner.

B.

The only remaining avenue for relief available to TPC is to show that China Navigation acted as a negligent time charterer. Its ability to do so turns on whether China Navigation owed a duty to vet Grand Famous' finances and safety management protocols prior to executing the charter party. **{-805-}**

TPC argues that, had China Navigation diligently investigated Grand Famous and ensured that Grand Famous diligently investigated Beikun, it would have discovered that neither had the ability to support the Yochow. According to TPC, Grand Famous owns only one vessel and has no **[—10—]** employees, no physical office, and only one (unpaid) director. And Beikun, to whom

Grand Famous delegated technical management responsibility of the Yochow, had only sixteen employees and around $2.8 million in registered capital. TPC says this was woefully insufficient to support the Yochow's operations.

China Navigation's position is that, as a matter of law, it had no duty to vet the Yochow's owners or managers, nor was it obligated to vet the financial stability of Grand Famous or Beikun's safety procedures.[3] The duties of a time charterer to third parties are well defined, it argues, and do not extend beyond certain "spheres" of activity.

We're on board with China Navigation. The general rule under traditional principles of admiralty law is that "a time charterer who has no control over the vessel[] assumes no liability for negligence of the crew or unseaworthiness of the vessel absent a showing that the parties to the charter intended otherwise." *In re P & E Boat Rentals, Inc.*, 872 F.2d 642, 647 (5th Cir. 1989) (cleaned up). As discussed, *supra*, there is no indication that China **[—11—]** Navigation and Grand Famous intended to vary the terms of the time charter such that China Navigation would assume control—and the responsibilities that attend that control—over the Yochow.

Despite the general rule, however, a time charterer may still be liable for negligently "conducting its activities as time charterer." *Id.*; *Graham v. Milky Way Barge, Inc.*, 824 F.2d 376, 388 (5th Cir. 1987); *see also In re Dann Ocean Towing*, 2018 WL 901716, at *5. This circuit recognizes "a distinction between a time charterer's potential liability under the time charter and independent tort liability which is not governed by the time charter." *Milky Way*, 824 F.2d at 388. Thus, even though China Navigation did not assume control over the Yochow by contract or otherwise, it may nevertheless be liable to third parties for negligence. *Milky Way* is instructive on this point.

In *Milky Way*, Chevron time chartered a vessel that capsized and threw four men overboard. *Id.* at 378. Three men survived and sued Chevron and the vessel's owner, claiming, *inter alia*, that Chevron negligently dispatched the vessel into unsheltered waters despite inclement weather. *Id.* at 378–79, 387–88. The district court held that Chevron was negligent, and Chevron appealed, arguing that "as a time charterer it ha[d] no liability for the unseaworthiness of the chartered vessel or the negligence of its crew." *Id.* at 387–88. We rejected Chevron's argument and affirmed the district court. *Id.* Despite recognizing **{-806-}** that it is the "unusual" case in which a time charterer is liable "for an incident concerning the vessel under charter," we held that the district court did not clearly err in finding that Chevron was *independently negligent* in contributing to the vessel capsizing. *Id.* at 388.

Importantly, *Milky Way* teaches that "general principles of negligence govern maritime torts." *Id.* TPC relies on *Milky Way* to argue that, despite China Navigation's role as time charterer, it still owed a duty to third parties **[—12—]** to carefully vet its independent contractor—Grand Famous—before time chartering the Yochow.

But there is more to the story than just *Milky Way*. While time charterers may face

---

[3] This was also the position that China Navigation took in the district court:

> Q. China Navigation, one of the reasons you do a high level check on deficiencies is because China Navigation feels like it's its obligation to make sure that the vessels it charters operate safely. True?
>
> A. There's no obligation to check on that. We're looking to protect our commercial interest.
>
> ...
>
> Q. Do you believe that, as a matter of custom in the industry or just as a matter of safety, pure general safety, that China Navigation had an obligation to make sure that the owner of the Yochow was competent and qualified to perform that mission safely?
>
> A. No, we have no obligation.

some exposure to liability for negligence to third parties, that exposure is not unlimited.

In this circuit, time charterers owe "a hybrid duty arising from contract and tort, to persons with whom [they have] no contractual relationship, including vessel passengers, to avoid negligent actions *within the sphere of activity* over which [they] exercise[] at least partial control." *Hodgen v. Forest Oil Corp.*, 87 F.3d 1512, 1520 (5th Cir. 1996) (emphasis added).[4] "[T]he traditional spheres of activity in which a time charterer exercises control and thus owes a duty include choosing the vessel's cargo, route, and general mission, as well as the specific time in which the vessel will perform its assignment." *Id.* Most importantly for our purposes, "a time charterer owes *no duty* beyond these spheres" unless the parties "vary the traditional assignment of control by contract or custom." *Id.* (emphasis added).

In other words, time charterers *do* owe duties to third parties. Namely, to avoid negligent acts within the traditional spheres of activity over which they exercise control. But those spheres are well defined, and time charterers are not—as a matter of law—liable for acts taken outside those spheres unless the parties agree otherwise by contract or custom.

Ensuring the competence of a contractual counterparty plainly does not fall within a traditional sphere of activity over which time charterers exercise control. And there is no indication that China Navigation and Grand Famous intended to "vary the traditional assignment of control by contract **[—13—]** or custom." *Id.* Thus, China Navigation did not owe a duty to vet Grand Famous' finances or the Yochow's safety management protocols prior to executing the time charter.

IV.

TPC's claim is that China Navigation is responsible for the allision because it failed to diligently vet Grand Famous and the Yochow's safety management protocols. Had it done so, it would have discovered inadequacies in those protocols—primary among them were the Yochow's work/rest standards. Those standards, TPC argues, caused the Yochow's helmsman to turn to port when he should have turned to starboard. Thus, China Navigation is liable for the damages that resulted.

The Yochow crew's alleged failure to abide by Stubb's twelfth commandment does not provide a lifeboat for TPC's theory of liability.[5] The fatal flaw in TPC's argument is that China Navigation did *not*, as a matter of law, owe any duty to vet **{–807–}** Grand Famous or the Yochow's safety procedures. Neither did it assume control over the Yochow as her de facto owner. The district court properly granted summary judgment in China Navigation's favor.

The judgment is AFFIRMED.

[4] *Hodgen* was overruled on other grounds by *Grand Isle Shipyard, Inc. v. Seacor Marine, LLC*, 589 F.3d 778 (5th Cir. 2009) (en banc).

[5] HERMAN MELVILLE, MOBY DICK; OR, THE WHITE WHALE 113 (Dodd, Mead & Co. 1922) (1851) ("Think not is my eleventh commandment; and sleep when you can, is my twelfth[.]").

United States Court of Appeals
for the Fifth Circuit

No. 20-30382

DOUGLASS
vs.
NIPPON YUSEN KABUSHIKI KAISHA

Appeal from the United States District Court for the Eastern District of Louisiana

ON PETITION FOR REHEARING EN BANC

Decided: August 16, 2022

Citation: 46 F.4th 226, 10 Adm. R. 206 (5th Cir. 2022) (en banc).

Before **RICHMAN**, Chief Judge, and **JONES, SMITH, STEWART, DENNIS, ELROD, SOUTHWICK, HAYNES, GRAVES, HIGGINSON, COSTA, WILLETT, HO, DUNCAN, ENGELHARDT, OLDHAM**, and **WILSON**, Circuit Judges.

[—2—] {-229-} **JONES**, Circuit Judge, joined by **RICHMAN**, Chief Judge, and **SMITH, STEWART, DENNIS, SOUTHWICK, HAYNES, COSTA, HO, DUNCAN, ENGELHARDT**, and **WILSON**, Circuit Judges:*

* Judge Haynes concurs in the judgment only. Senior Judge King was a member of the panel but chose not to participate in en banc rehearing.

The issue before the en banc court is whether a federal court may exercise personal jurisdiction over a foreign corporation for federal claims, which arise from injuries and deaths of American naval personnel in a collision in foreign waters. To succeed, the plaintiffs must show either that the foreign corporation is "at home" in the United States or that their claims arise from or relate to the foreign corporation's business activities in the [—3—] United States. The district court rejected the first alternative based on substantial precedent; the plaintiffs foreswore, as they had to, reliance on the second alternative. We AFFIRM.

I. BACKGROUND

Nippon Yusen Kabushiki Kaisha ("NYK"), incorporated and headquartered in Japan, is a major global logistics company that transports cargo by air and sea. For its seaside operations, NYK owns or charters a formidable fleet that includes bulk carriers, container ships (of all sizes), **{-230-}** car transporters, tankers, cruise ships, shuttle tankers, drillships, and LNG carriers, among other vessels.[1] NYK charters more than half of the ships it uses to transport cargo.[2] The vessels call port throughout the world. Between 2017 and 2019, about seven percent of the worldwide port calls made by NYK owned or chartered vessels were in the United States, totaling about 1500 calls annually.

A natural consequence of NYK's handling shipments bound for the United States is that it occasionally litigates in American courts. Since 2010, for example, NYK has filed around thirty lawsuits in federal courts, most involving claims seeking freight charges owed under bills of lading.[3] And every so often, NYK and its ships are sued in American courts, typically for **[—4—]** cargo damaged en route to the United States or for injuries that occurred during cargo operations in the United States.[4]

---

1 NYK Group Fleet, NYK LINE FACT BOOK I 2019, at 8 (Apr. 26, 2019), https://www.nyk.com/english/ir/library/fact/first/2019/__icsFiles/afieldfile/2019/10/28/190426FB1E_1.pdf (last visited Oct. 23, 2021).

2 *Id.*

3 *See, e.g.*, Complaint at 3-5, *Nippon Yusen Kabushiki Kaisha v. GSF Nut Co., LLC*, No. 2:2017-cv-5614 (C.D. Cal. July 28, 2017), ECF No. 1; Complaint at 5-8, *Nippon Yusen Kabushiki Kaisha v. Multi-Trans Shipping Agency, Inc.*, No. 2:2016-cv-9523 (C.D. Cal. Dec. 23, 2016), ECF No. 1; Complaint at 3-5, *Nippon Yusen Kabushiki Kaisha v. Wesmex Inc.*, No. 8:2014-cv-1910 (C.D. Cal. Dec. 3, 2014), ECF No. 1.

4 *See, e.g.*, Complaint at 1-5, *Epperson v. NYK Line*, No. 4:2019-cv-5948 (N.D. Cal. Sept. 24, 2019), ECF No. 1 (negligence claim by American harbor pilot injured in United States waters by allegedly faulty Jacob's ladder); Complaint at 3-5, *Neal v. NYK Line*, No. 4:2013-cv-507 (N.D. Cal. Feb. 5, 2013), ECF No. 1 (negligence claim by longshoreman involved in unloading NYK vessel in the United States); Complaint at 2-3, *Starr Indem. & Liab. Co. v. Yamato Transp. U.S.A., Inc.*, No. 2:2016-cv-4616 (C.D. Cal. June 24, 2016), ECF No. 1 (damaged cargo); Complaint at 2-4, *Great Am. Ins. Co. of N.Y. v. Hanjin Shipping*, No. 2:2015-cv-8798 (C.D. Cal. Nov. 11, 2015), ECF No. 1 (same); Complaint at 2-4, *Beachside Produce, LLC v.*

Among NYK's approximately 1700 employees, about 25 are seconded to NYK subsidiaries in the United States. Overall, NYK's business in the United States and North America makes up less than ten percent of its annual revenue.

On June 17, 2017, the *ACX Crystal*, a 730-foot container ship chartered by NYK,[5] collided with the destroyer *USS Fitzgerald* in Japanese territorial waters.[6] **{-231-}** As the *ACX Crystal*'s bow ripped through the *Fitzgerald*'s **[—5—]** hull at midship, several compartments on the *Fitzgerald* flooded, killing seven American sailors and injuring dozens of others. At the time of the collision, the *ACX Crystal*, then a Philippine-flagged vessel, was on an intra-Asia trade route. It has never called port in the United States.

Personal representatives of the seven sailors killed sued NYK in federal court, asserting wrongful death and survival claims under the Death on the High Seas Act, 46 U.S.C. § 30301 *et seq.* The injured sailors and their family members sued NYK separately, asserting negligence and loss of consortium claims.[7] In both cases, the plaintiffs alleged that NYK, a foreign corporation, is amenable to federal court jurisdiction under FED. R. CIV. P. 4(k)(2) based on its "substantial, systematic and continuous contacts with the United States as a whole." Neither complaint alleges that the injuries at issue arose out of or relate to NYK's contacts with the United States.

NYK moved to dismiss the suits for lack of personal jurisdiction under FED. R. CIV. P. 12(b)(2). The district court obliged, issuing identical opinions. Relying on *Patterson v. Aker Solutions Inc.*, 826 F.3d 231, 4 Adm. R. 259 (5th Cir. 2016), the district court held that the Fifth Amendment due process test for personal jurisdiction governs this admiralty dispute and mirrors the Fourteenth Amendment test. Applying the Fourteenth Amendment standard, the district court concluded that NYK did not have sufficient **[—6—]** contacts with the United States to justify the court's exercising personal jurisdiction over it.

On appeal, the cases were consolidated. The panel affirmed the judgment but suggested it would have reached a different result if not bound by *Patterson*. Concurring, Judges Elrod and Willett opined that "our interpretation of Fourteenth Amendment due process is shaped by federalism concerns that

Nippon Yusen Kabushiki Kaisha, No. 2:2015-cv-4951 (C.D. Cal. June 30, 2015), ECF No. 1 (same).

[5] NYK had a time charter for the *ACX Crystal*. A time charterer obtains use of a ship in only a limited sense: The vessel's owner "provides the vessel's master and crew and (depending on the circumstances) pays the normal operating expenses, while the charterer obtains the commercial benefit of having its cargo carried." DAVID W. ROBERTSON, STEVEN F. FRIEDELL, & MICHAEL F. STURLEY, ADMIRALTY AND MARITIME LAW IN THE UNITED STATES 325 (4th ed. 2020). In other words, time charters "are more like taxis or limousine services or hotels than they are like typical leases." *Id.* Because the time charterer typically has little or no control over the vessel's navigation, it almost never bears liability for a collision stemming from navigational error. *See Moore v. Phillips Petroleum Co.*, 912 F.2d 789, 792 (5th Cir. 1990) ("The vessel owner remains responsible for . . . navigational errors by the pilot and negligence by the crew . . . .") (citation omitted). Thus, even if the plaintiffs could establish personal jurisdiction over NYK, their claims face other substantial hurdles.

[6] The after-accident reports issued by the National Transportation Safety Board and the Japanese Transport Safety Board largely fault the United States Navy for the collision—neither report places any fault on NYK. *See* National Transportation Safety Board, *Marine Accident Report: Collision Between US Navy Destroyer Fitzgerald and Philippine-Fleg Container Ship ACX Crystal Sagami Nada Bay off Izu Peninsula, Honshu Island, Japan July 17, 2017* (2020), https://www.ntsb.gov/investigations-/AccidentReports/Reports/MAR 2002.pdf (last visited Oct. 23, 2021); Japan Transport Safety Board, *Marine Accident Investigation Report* (Aug. 29, 2019), https://www. mlit.go.jp/jtsb/eng-mar_report/2019 /2017tk0009e.pdf (last visited Oct. 23, 2021).

[7] The injured sailors and the personal representatives of the sailors killed also sued the *ACX Crystal*'s owner, Olympic Steamship Company, and its bareboat charterer, Vega Carriers Corporation, both Panamanian corporations, in Japan for the same injuries at issue in this lawsuit. *See* Appellee's Rule 28(j) Letter dated Jan. 29, 2021.

are irrelevant to the Fifth Amendment context," and *Patterson* imposed an "unnecessary limitation" on Rule 4(k)(2). In their view, *Patterson* "unwittingly limited Rule 4(k)(2) by collapsing the Fifth Amendment and Fourteenth Amendment due process analyses."

This court granted plaintiffs' petition for rehearing en banc to consider whether NYK is subject to jurisdiction in these cases.

II. STANDARD OF REVIEW

This court's review of a Rule 12(b)(2) dismissal for lack of personal jurisdiction is de novo. *Patterson*, 826 F.3d at 233, 4 Adm. R. at 259 (citing *Revell v. Lidov*, 317 F.3d 467, 469 (5th Cir. 2002)).

III. DISCUSSION

The Fifth Amendment due process standard governs the personal jurisdiction inquiry in this lawsuit raising federal claims in federal court. The en banc dispute centers on whether the Fifth Amendment standard mirrors the "minimum contacts" and "fair play and substantial justice" **{-232-}** principles underlying the Fourteenth Amendment personal jurisdiction inquiry. Two issues, considered in turn, logically precede that debate. First, we reject the plaintiffs' passing argument that NYK, as a foreign corporation, lacks Fifth Amendment due process rights altogether and therefore cannot object to a federal court's assertion of personal jurisdiction over it. Second, we expose the faulty premise underlying the plaintiffs' contention that applying **[—7—]** Fourteenth Amendment personal jurisdiction standards in Fifth Amendment cases would render Rule 4(k)(2) a nullity.[8]

A. Foreign corporations litigating in federal court may challenge the court's personal jurisdiction under the Fifth Amendment Due Process Clause.

The plaintiffs oddly contend that NYK, as a foreign corporation, has no Fifth Amendment due process rights at all. In support, they cite cases addressing whether constitutional rights extend to foreign persons acting abroad. *See Agency for Int'l Dev. v. All. for Open Soc'y Int'l, Inc.*, 140 S. Ct. 2082, 2088 (2020) (holding that foreign subsidiaries of United States companies do not have First Amendment rights); *United States v. Verdugo-* **[—8—]** *Urquidez*, 494 U.S. 259, 274-75, 110 S. Ct. 1056, 1065-66 (1990) (rejecting contention that DEA's search of a residence in Mexico violated non-citizen's Fourth Amendment rights).[9] Here, however, NYK invokes its

---

[8] This majority opinion addresses the exact arguments raised by the plaintiffs consistently throughout the litigation. But for one point, we will not address the dissents' wholly novel arguments, which pointedly divorce themselves from the parties' theory of the case. *Post* at 47 n.5 ("I disagree with both approaches because both start not with the Fifth Amendment but with inapplicable Fourteenth Amendment case law."). By standing up for the law as it has been accepted unanimously among the circuit courts, we decline to consider adversarially untested propositions. Moreover, the principal dissent's criticism that NYK bore some burden—to anticipate and analyze personal jurisdiction without any reference to well-settled case law—is simply wrong. At the very least, it is the plaintiffs' burden to establish the court's jurisdiction in response to a Rule 12(b)(2) personal jurisdiction challenge by a defendant. *Johnson v. Multidata Sys. Int'l Corp.*, 523 F.3d 602, 609 (5th Cir. 2008).

If we were to address the merits of the principal dissent's theory, however, we would note its repeated insistence that, consistent with the Fifth Amendment, *Congress* could pass a law to subject foreign defendants to American federal court jurisdiction for any injuries inflicted on American citizens or claims arising abroad. Whether this is correct or not, we do not assay. Moreover, we cannot analyze this theory because the dissent posits no rule or limits flowing from the Fifth Amendment. And finally, no court has adopted the dissent's view that Rule 4(k)(2) alone suffices to extend substantive personal jurisdiction to the constitutional limit, and the Rule's language alone suggests otherwise. FED. R. CIV. P. 4(k)(2) ("[S]erving a summons . . . establishes personal jurisdiction over a defendant if . . . exercising jurisdiction is consistent with the United States Constitution and laws.").

[9] The plaintiffs also rely on *Dep't of Homeland Sec. v. Thuraissigiam*, 140 S. Ct. 1959, 1981-83 (2020), to support their claim. That case, however, is inapt here because it addresses whether non-naturalized foreigners have due process rights to judicial review of immigration decisions where

constitutional due process rights in the course of litigation *in the United States*. Therefore, any constitutional violation can occur only in the United States. *Cf. Verdugo-Urquidez*, 494 U.S. at 264, 110 S. Ct. at 1060 (differentiating Fifth and Fourth Amendment violations and concluding that unlike an "unreasonable search and seizure," a violation of the privilege against self-incrimination "occurs only at trial"). The cases the plaintiffs rely on are thus inapposite. **{–233–}**

Further, the plaintiffs' argument is irreconcilable with the countless cases where courts, including the Supreme Court, have afforded foreign corporations due-process-based personal-jurisdiction protections under the Fourteenth Amendment. *See, e.g., Goodyear Dunlop Tires Operations, S.A. v. Brown*, 564 U.S. 915, 131 S. Ct. 2846 (2011); *J. McIntyre Mach., Ltd. v. Nicastro*, 564 U.S. 873, 131 S. Ct. 2780 (2011); *Asahi Metal Indus. Co. v. Superior Ct. of Cal.*, 480 U.S. 102, 107 S. Ct. 1026 (1987). Thus, NYK can object to a federal court's unwarranted exercise of personal jurisdiction to the same extent as a United States citizen.

B. Rule 4(k) is a procedural rule governing the territorial limits of service.

Federal Rule of Civil Procedure 4(k)(2) states that, "[f]or a claim that arises under federal law, serving a summons . . . establishes personal jurisdiction over a defendant if: (A) the defendant is not subject to **[—9—]** jurisdiction in any state's courts of general jurisdiction; and (B) exercising jurisdiction is consistent with the United States Consti-tution and laws."

Throughout their briefing, the plaintiffs present Rule 4(k)(2) as the substantive source of personal jurisdiction over NYK and contend that adopting the Fourteenth Amendment standard would render Rule 4(k)(2) a nullity. That rule-centric view obscures the purely constitutional nature of the personal jurisdiction question at issue here. Rule 4(k)(2) is a procedural rule governing the territorial limits of service. The text is expressly subservient to the constitutional limits of due process. The rule does not— and cannot—control the constitutional inquiry whether due process prohibits a court from exercising personal jurisdiction over the defendant in a given lawsuit.

Congress did not statutorily provide such review. *Id.*

Today, personal jurisdiction is typically exercised through a summons to appear in court on pain of default. The valid exercise of jurisdiction through a summons requires (1) notice of the command and (2) amenability to the command. The notice requirement is procedural, and the amenability requirement is substantive. Historically, those require-ments were inextricably intertwined because federal courts had jurisdiction over only defendants that voluntarily appeared or were personally served in the district.[10] At the advent of the Federal Rules of Civil Procedure, the **[—10—]** procedural limitations on proper notice were basically the same.[11] *See* FED. R. CIV. P. 4(f) (1938).

In 1945, however, the Supreme Court made clear that due process permitted personal jurisdiction over a nonresident defendant as long as the defendant had "certain minimum contacts with [the forum] such that the maintenance of the suit does not offend 'traditional notions of fair play and substantial justice.'" *Int'l Shoe Co. v. Washington*, 326 U.S. 310, 316, 66 S. Ct. 154, 158 (1945) (quoting *Milliken v. Meyer*, 311 U.S. 457, 463, 61 S. Ct. 339, 343 (1940)). After *International Shoe*, states began authorizing

[10] Judiciary Act of 1789, ch. 20, § 11, 1 Stat. 73, 79 ("But no person shall be arrested in one district for trial in another, in any civil action before a circuit or district court. . . . And no civil suit shall be brought before either of said courts against an inhabitant of the United States, by any original process in any other district than that whereof he is an inhabitant, or in which he shall be found at the time of serving the writ .... ").

[11] FED. R. CIV. P. 4(f) advisory committee's note (1937) ("This Rule enlarges to some extent the present rule as to where service may be made. It does not, however, enlarge the jurisdiction of the district courts.").

{-234-} out-of-state service.[12] Rule 4 was amended in 1963 to allow service outside the territorial limits of the state when authorized by state law.[13] As the territorial scope of service expanded, the due process limitations on personal jurisdiction assumed greater independent significance. *See, e.g.*, *Burger King Corp. v. Rudzewicz*, 471 U.S. 462, 105 S. Ct. 2174 (1985); *Helicopteros Nacionales de Colombia, S.A. v. Hall*, 466 U.S. 408, 104 S. Ct. 1868 (1984); *World-Wide Volkswagen Corp. v. Woodson*, 444 U.S. 286, 100 S. Ct. 559 (1980); *Kulko v. Superior Ct. of Cal.*, 436 U.S. 84, 98 S. Ct. 1690 (1978).

Then came the 1993 Amendments. Rule 4 was completely rewritten and what was Rule 4(f) became Rule 4(k). Relevant here, the new Rule 4(k)(2), adopted in response to the Supreme Court's decision in *Omni* **[—11—]** *Capital Int'l v. Rudolf Wolff & Co.*, 484 U.S. 97, 108 S. Ct. 404 (1987), assumed its current wording, although Rule 4(k) retained the old Rule 4(f)'s caption, "Territorial Limits of Effective Service." FED. R. CIV. P. 4(k).

Notwithstanding the amendments, Rule 4(k) is still just a procedural rule about issuing summonses. By law, the Federal Rules of Civil Procedure cannot "abridge, enlarge or modify any substantive right," 28 U.S.C. § 2072(b), and a rule expanding the scope of a court's personal jurisdiction would modify a substantive right no less than a rule expanding subject matter jurisdiction. Further, the Advisory Committee that recommended the 1993 Amendments recognized that "[t]here remain constitutional limitations on the exercise of territorial jurisdiction by federal courts over persons outside the United States." FED. R. CIV. P. 4(k)(2) advisory committee's note to 1993 amendment. No doubt service of a summons under Rule 4(k)(2) establishes personal jurisdiction when procedurally authorized by the Federal Rules and consistent with the Constitution. But as the rule expresses, the efficacy of service remains subject to the constitutional question whether a defendant is amenable to jurisdiction. The plaintiffs' consequentialist argument, that adopting a certain due process test for personal jurisdiction under the Fifth Amendment would render Rule 4(k)(2) a nullity, is textually and logically unsound.

C. The Fifth Amendment due process test for personal jurisdiction mirrors the Fourteenth Amendment test.

This brings us to the heart of the dispute: Determining what standard governs personal jurisdiction over defendants sued on federal claims in federal court under the Fifth Amendment Due Process Clause.

NYK contends that the Fifth Amendment due process test for personal jurisdiction parallels the Fourteenth Amendment test, except that the Fifth Amendment test looks at contacts with the United States as a whole **[—12—]** rather than any one state. On this basis, NYK continues, the tried and true dichotomy between specific and general jurisdiction applies under the Fifth Amendment. Because the plaintiffs do not allege that their claims arise out of or relate to NYK's contacts with the United States, NYK is amenable to the district court's **{-235-}** jurisdiction only under a general jurisdiction theory, which means NYK is amenable to jurisdiction if and only if its contacts are "so continuous and systematic as to render it essentially at home in the" relevant forum, the United States. *Daimler AG v. Bauman*, 571 U.S. 117, 139, 134 S. Ct. 746, 761 (2014) (quoting *Goodyear*, 564 U.S. at 920, 131 S. Ct. at 2851) (cleaned up).

The plaintiffs and their amici[14] key off their interpretation of Rule 4(k)(2) and contend that the Fifth and Fourteenth Amendment due

---

[12] Douglas D. McFarland, *Dictum Run Wild: How Long-Arm Statutes Extended to the Limits of Due Process*, 84 B.U. L. Rev. 491, 492-97 (2004) (discussing the rise of state long-arm statutes after *International Shoe*).

[13] FED. R. CIV. P. 4(f) advisory committee's note (1963) ("The first sentence is amended to assure the effectiveness of service outside the territorial limits of the State in all the cases in which any of the rules authorize service beyond those boundaries.").

[14] Professors Helen Hershkoff, Arthur R. Miller, Alan B. Morrison, John E. Sexton, and Adam N. Steinman filed an *amicus curiae* brief in this case supporting the plaintiffs.

process requirements are critically different. They note first that the Supreme Court has expounded on the Fourteenth Amendment due process requirements for personal jurisdiction but has consistently reserved the Fifth Amendment question. Additionally, while principles of interstate federalism and individual liberty animate the Supreme Court's Fourteenth Amendment personal jurisdiction jurisprudence, the Fifth Amendment focuses on the United States' sovereign limits rather than the states' reciprocal sovereign limits, rendering federalism immaterial. Because the Fifth Amendment is concerned with guaranteeing fairness for defendants rather than circumscribing state court jurisdiction, a distinct and more permissive standard is warranted. What is more, importing the Fourteenth Amendment standards into the Fifth Amendment analysis would render Rule 4(k)(2) **[—13—]** essentially nugatory. Finally, at a minimum, admiralty's unique nature and history necessitate a distinct standard.

In the plaintiffs' view, the Fifth Amendment due process inquiry is simply whether a defendant, sued on a federal claim, was doing enough systematic and continuous business in the United States that it had fair notice it could be subjected to suit in federal courts. Their novel theory eschews the traditional distinction between general and specific personal jurisdiction and, more specifically, advocates against applying recent Supreme Court general jurisdiction cases like *Daimler* in favor of a barebones "continuous and systematic" standard articulated in *International Shoe* and allegedly applied heretofore in this court.

In Fourteenth Amendment vernacular, the plaintiffs' proposed personal jurisdiction test appears to dress a general jurisdiction theory in specific jurisdiction garb. But even if they argued that their claims must in some way be related to the foreign defendant's continuous and systematic contacts with the United States, the "related" prong of their proposed Fifth Amendment personal jurisdiction test is toothless: If personal injury and wrongful death claims caused in foreign waters by a foreign logistics company's chartered, foreign-registered vessel bound for a foreign country are sufficiently related to that corporation's shipping-related contacts with the United States, then what isn't? The plaintiffs' conception of "related" goes far beyond the Fourteenth Amendment's "arise out of or relate to" standard.

We reject the plaintiffs' theory and hold that the Fifth Amendment due process test for personal jurisdiction requires the same "minimum contacts" with the United States as the Fourteenth Amendment requires with a state. Both Due Process Clauses use the same language and serve the same purpose, protecting individual liberty by guaranteeing limits on **[—14—]** personal jurisdiction. Every court that has considered this point agrees that the standards mirror each other. The plaintiffs' **{-236-}** rule-centric argument, that importing the Fourteenth Amendment standards into the Fifth Amendment context renders Rule 4(k)(2) a nullity, is unpersuasive and wrong. Finally, the plaintiffs misinterpret the law underlying their argument about admiralty law's unique nature and history regarding jurisdiction over foreign defendants.

1. The Due Process Clauses.

Limits on the scope of a court's personal jurisdiction "flow[] not from Art. III, but from the Due Process Clause." *Ins. Corp. of Ir. v. Compagnie des Bauxites de Guinee*, 456 U.S. 694, 702, 102 S. Ct. 2099, 2104 (1982). Both Due Process Clauses protect persons from the deprivation of "life, liberty, or property, without due process of law." U.S. CONST. amend. V; amend. XIV, § 1. The clauses differ only in that the Fifth Amendment Due Process Clause limits the federal government, while the Fourteenth Amendment Due Process Clause limits the states. Based on that dissimilarity, the plaintiffs contend that the Fourteenth Amendment Due Process Clause vindicates federalism principles that are irrelevant under the Fifth Amendment. No doubt federalism is immaterial under the Fifth Amendment, but the plaintiffs' myopic emphasis on federalism misses the very core of due process.

"Due process of law" traces its origins to the Great Charter of individual liberty, Magna Carta.[15] Individual liberty is what the Supreme **[—15—]** Court emphasizes as the foundation of the personal jurisdiction requirement. That requirement "represents a restriction on judicial power not as a matter of sovereignty, but as a matter of individual liberty." *Ins. Corp. of Ir.*, 456 U.S. at 702, 102 S. Ct. at 2104; *see also Nicastro*, 564 U.S. at 899-900, 131 S. Ct. at 2798 (Ginsburg, J., dissenting) (citing *Ins. Corp. of Ir.*, 456 U.S. at 703 n.10, 102 S. Ct. at 2104 n.10); *Burger King*, 471 U.S. at 471-72, 105 S. Ct. at 2181-82. *International Shoe*'s minimum contacts test secures defendants' individual liberty by protecting them against (1) the concrete burden of "litigating in a distant or inconvenient forum," *World-Wide Volkswagen*, 444 U.S. at 292, 100 S. Ct. at 564, and (2) the abstract burden of "submitting to the coercive power of a [forum] that may have little legitimate interest in the claims in question." *Bristol-Myers Squibb Co. v. Superior Ct. of Cal.*, 137 S. Ct. 1773, 1781 (2017). A forum's "interest" in the litigation depends on, *inter alia*, the relationship among the defendant, the forum, and the litigation.

To be sure, federalism concerns are central to the Supreme Court's interpretation of the Fourteenth Amendment Due Process Clause.[16] But "federalism" is a proxy for the abstract burden of a defendant's submitting to the coercive power of a forum with little interest in the dispute. In *Insurance Corp. of Ireland*, the Supreme Court explained that the "restriction **{-237-}** on state sovereign power described in *World-Wide Volkswagen*," i.e., the "federalism" aspect of Fourteenth Amendment due process, "must be seen as ultimately a function of the individual liberty interest preserved by the Due **[—16—]** Process Clause." 456 U.S. at 702 n.10, 102 S. Ct. at 2104 n.10. Indeed, "if the federalism concept operated as an independent restriction on the sovereign power of the court, it would not be possible to waive the personal jurisdiction requirement"—an individual's "actions cannot change the powers of sovereignty, although the individual can subject himself to powers from which he may otherwise be protected." *Id.* In short, "federalism" is not the quintessence of the personal jurisdiction analysis under the Fourteenth Amendment Due Process Clause, it is a derivative concern.

Further, an analogous "federalism" dynamic may arise in the Fifth Amendment context under the rubric of "international comity."[17] Just as a state court's exercising coercive power over an out-of-state defendant offends Fourteenth Amendment due process when the relationship among the defendant, the state, and the litigation is insufficient, so, too, may a federal court's exercising coercive power over a foreign non-resident defendant offend Fifth Amendment due process when the relationship among the defendant, the United States, and the litigation is insufficient. Either situation potentially infringes

[15] Magna Carta guaranteed that "[n]o free man shall be taken, imprisoned, disseised, outlawed, banished, or in any way destroyed, nor will We proceed against or prosecute him, except by the lawful judgment of his peers and by the law of the land." A.E. DICK HOWARD, MAGNA CARTA TEXT AND COMMENTARY 45 (rev. ed. 1998). At the time of the Fifth Amendment's ratification, people universally understood "due process of law" to convey "the same meaning as the words 'by the law of the land'" in **[—15—]** Magna Carta. *Murray's Lessee v. Hoboken Land & Improvement Co.*, 59 U.S. (18 How.) 272, 276 (1856).

[16] *See, e.g. Ford Motor Co. v. Mont. Eighth Jud. Dist. Ct.*, 592 U.S. ---, 141 S. Ct. 1017, 1025, 1030 (2021); *Bristol-Myers Squibb*, 137 S. Ct. at 1780-81, 1788; *World-Wide Volkswagen*, 444 U.S. at 293-94, 100 S. Ct. at 565-66.

[17] Consider, for instance, the international comity concerns implicated in this case. Under the plaintiffs' theory, virtually every foreign corporation with more than a nominal amount of business in the United States can be haled into federal court for any federal claim. Such a reading of the Due Process Clause would not "give[] a degree of predictability to the legal system" that would allow corporations to reasonably "structure their primary conduct with some minimum assurance as to where that conduct will and will not render them liable to suit." *World-Wide Volkswagen*, 444 U.S. at 297, 100 S. Ct. at 567. Even if NYK were ultimately held amenable to federal court jurisdiction here, the same international comity concerns may warrant forum non conveniens dismissal—especially because concurrent litigation is pending in Japanese Courts.

individual liberty, though the impact of foreign relations and national security surely can affect the United States' "sovereign reach" in ways irrelevant to this case. **[—17—]**

In any event, the plaintiffs' focus on "federalism" concerns in the Supreme Court's Fourteenth Amendment jurisprudence is beside the point. Federalism concerns are germane to *specific* jurisdiction—not general jurisdiction, which is the only theory the plaintiffs advanced in the district court.[18] "Federalism" cannot matter for general jurisdiction. If a corporate defendant is "at home" in the forum, by incorporation, principal place of business, or otherwise, that forum has "complete and irresistible" jurisdiction over it. J. STORY, COMMENTARIES ON THE CONFLICT OF LAWS 911-12, (3d ed. 1846); *see also Daimler*, 571 U.S. at 127, 134 S. Ct. at 754; *Goodyear*, 564 U.S. at 919, 131 S. Ct. at 2851; *Helicopteros*, 466 U.S. at 414 n.9, 104 S. Ct. at 1872 n.9. Plaintiffs' proffered "federalism" differences between the Fifth and Fourteenth Amendments are superfluous. **{-238-}**

Because the Due Process Clauses use the same language and guarantee individual liberty in the same way, it makes sense that the standards developed in the Fourteenth Amendment context must govern under the Fifth Amendment.

2. Courts all apply the Fourteenth Amendment "minimum contacts" standard in Fifth Amendment cases.

This court and six other circuits apply Fourteenth Amendment due process analysis to determine personal jurisdiction in cases governed by the Fifth Amendment. **[—18—]**

Every Fifth Circuit decision addressing the scope of contacts required for personal jurisdiction under the Fifth Amendment has applied the then-existing Fourteenth Amendment framework.[19] Relatedly, this court's Rule 4(k)(2) cases consistently recognize and invoke the general-specific jurisdiction dichotomy, which the plaintiffs dismiss as irrelevant to the Fifth Amendment.[20] Paradigmatically, in *Patterson*, the court considered whether general jurisdiction existed over a foreign defendant on a federal claim based on its contacts with the United States as a whole. *Patterson*, 826 F.3d at 234, 4 Adm. R. at 259–60. In finding insufficient contacts with the United States to support general jurisdiction, the court squarely relied on a then-recent Supreme Court decision founded on the Fourteenth Amendment. *Id.*, 4 Adm. R. at 260 (citing *Daimler*, 571 U.S. 139, 134 S. Ct. at 761).

In practice, this court has found that a foreign corporation's contacts satisfy Fifth Amendment due process only in cases where the parties' dispute arose out of or related to those United States contacts, that is, where specific jurisdiction existed.[21] The Fifth

---

[18] *Compare Ford Motor Co.*, 141 S. Ct. at 1025, 1030 (raising "federalism" concerns in specific personal jurisdiction case) and *Bristol-Myers Squibb*, 137 S. Ct. at 1780-81, 1788 (same) and *World-Wide Volkswagen*, 444 U.S. at 293-94, 100 S. Ct. at 565-66 (same) *with Daimler*, 571 U.S. 117, 134 S. Ct. 746 (failing to raise "federalism" concerns in general personal jurisdiction case); *Goodyear*, 564 U.S. 915, 131 S. Ct. 2846 (same); *Helicopteros*, 466 U.S. 407, 104 S. Ct. 1868 (1984) (same). *But see Daimler*, 571 U.S. at 157, 134 S. Ct. at 772 (Sotomayor, J., concurring in the judgment).

[19] *See, e.g., Patterson*, 826 F.3d at 234, 4 Adm. R. at 260 (relying on Fourteenth Amendment cases); *Quick Techs., Inc. v. Sage Grp. PLC*, 313 F.3d 338, 343-45 (5th Cir. 2002) (same); *Adams v. Unione Mediterranea di Sicurta*, 364 F.3d 646, 651-52 (5th Cir. 2004) (same).

[20] *See, e.g., Stutzman v. Rainbow Yacht Adventures Ltd.*, 265 F. App'x 402 (5th Cir. 2008) (per curiam); *Quick Techs.*, 313 F.3d at 343-45; *Submersible Sys., Inc. v. Perforadora Cent., S.A. de C.V.*, 249 F.3d 413, 420 (5th Cir. 2001).

[21] *See Nagravision SA v. Gotech Int'l Tech. Ltd.*, 882 F.3d 494 (5th Cir. 2018) (approving personal jurisdiction over foreign defendants where plaintiffs alleged that defendants "use a network of servers located in various cities across . . . the United States to engage in the unauthorized distribution of Nagravision's control words in violation of the DMCA and FCA"); *Adams*, 364 F.3d at 651-652 (finding sufficient contacts for personal jurisdiction where foreign defendant insured steel shipment to United States and "enabled prosecution of claims in the United States by

Circuit has never found that a foreign **[—19—]** corporation's contacts with the United States alone supported general jurisdiction over unrelated lawsuits.[22] **{-239-}**

The plaintiffs' reliance on *Adams v. Unione Mediterranea di Scurta*, 364 F.3d 646 (5th Cir. 2004) is misplaced. This court determined that the defendant, an Italian insurer, had "continuous and systematic contacts with the United States as a whole." *Id.* at 651-52. But the claims stemmed from a cargo insurance policy covering a shipment to the United States. *Id.* at 648. *Adams* represents a straightforward application of *International Shoe*'s specific jurisdiction principles.[23] *See Int'l Shoe*, 326 U.S. at 317, 66 S. Ct. at **[—20—]** 159 (jurisdiction over a corporate defendant is proper "when the activities of the corporation [in the forum] have not only been continuous and systematic, *but also* give rise to the liabilities sued on" (emphasis added)).

Furthermore, the Second, Sixth, Seventh, Eleventh, Federal, and D.C. Circuits all agree that no meaningful difference exists between the Fifth and Fourteenth Amendments' minimum contacts analyses.[24] In *Livnat v. Palestinian Authority*, 851 F.3d 45 (D.C. Cir. 2017), the court rejected the same federalism-based arguments urged here. The court pointed out that the Supreme Court instinctively relied on its Fourteenth Amendment personal jurisdiction jurisprudence when presented with an argument that asserting jurisdiction in a Foreign Sovereign Immunity Act case would violate the Fifth Amendment Due Process Clause.[25] *Id.* at 54 (citing *Republic of Argentina v. Weltover, Inc.*, 504 U.S. 607, 620, 112 S. Ct. 2160, 2169 (1992) (quoting *Burger King*, 471 U.S. at 475, 105 S. Ct. at 2183)). The court noted that every circuit to "expressly analyze[] whether the Fifth and Fourteenth Amend-

providing claims agents and surveyors" in United States).

[22] *See, e.g., De Leon v. Shih Wei Navigation Co.*, 269 F. App'x 487, 490-91 (5th Cir. 2008) (per curiam) (rejecting general personal jurisdiction theory); *Stutzman*, 265 F. App'x at 403-04 (same); *Submersible Sys.*, 249 F.3d at 420-21.

Indeed, our research found no case accepting a general personal jurisdiction theory under the Fifth Amendment like what plaintiffs propose here. *See, e.g., Doe v. Buratai*, 792 F. App'x 6, 9 (D.C. Cir. 2019) (per curiam); *Morris ex rel. Or. Cascade Corp. v. Harley*, 720 F. App'x 326, 329 (9th Cir. 2017) (per curiam); *Wolf v. Celebrity Cruises, Inc.*, 683 F. App'x 786, 793 (11th Cir. 2017) (per curiam); *Schulman v. Inst. for Shipboard Educ.*, 624 F. App'x 1002, 1006 (11th Cir. 2015) (per curiam) (applying *Daimler*'s test to reject general personal jurisdiction under the Fifth Amendment); *Abelesz v. OTP Bank*, 692 F.3d 638, 660 (7th Cir. 2012) (relying on *Goodyear*, 564 U.S. 915); *Fraser v. Smith*, 594 F.3d 842, 850 (11th Cir. 2010); *Synthes (U.S.A.) v. G.M. Dos Reis Jr. Ind. Com. de Equip. Medico*, 563 F.3d 1285, 1297 (Fed. Cir. 2009); *Porina v. Marward Shipping Co.*, 521 F.3d 122, 129 (2d Cir. 2008); *Saudi v. Northrop Grumman Corp.*, 427 F.3d 271, 276 (4th Cir. 2005); *Saudi v. Acomarit Maritimes Servs., S.A.*, 114 F. App'x 449, 456 (3d Cir. 2004); *Base Metal Trading, Ltd. v. OJSC "Novokuznetsky Aluminum Factory"*, 283 F.3d 208, 215 (4th Cir. 2002); *United States v. Swiss Am. Bank, Ltd.*, 274 F.3d 610, 620 (1st Cir. 2001); *Consol. Dev. Corp. v. Sherritt, Inc.*, 216 F.3d 1286, 1292-93 (11th Cir. 2000).

[23] In *Daimler*, the Supreme Court laid to rest the pervasive fallacy that *International Shoe*'s use of the words "continuous and systematic" describes the level of contacts necessary for exercising general personal jurisdiction. The Court explained that "the words 'continuous and systematic' were used in *International Shoe* to describe instances in which the exercise of *specific* jurisdiction would be appropriate." *Daimler*, 571 U.S. at 138, 134 S. Ct. at 761 (citing *Int'l Shoe*, 326 U.S. at 317, 66 S. Ct. at 159). The plaintiffs try to resuscitate that debunked notion.

[24] *Livnat v. Palestinian Auth.*, 851 F.3d 45, 54-55 (D.C. Cir. 2017); *Waldman v. Palestine Liberation Org.*, 835 F.3d 317, 330 (2d Cir. 2016); *Carrier Corp. v. Outokumpu Oyj*, 673 F.3d 430, 449 (6th Cir. 2012); *Abelesz*, 692 F.3d at 660; *Oldfield v. Pueblo de Bahia Lora, S.A.*, 558 F.3d 1210, 1219 n.25 (11th Cir. 2009); *Porina*, 521 F.3d at 127-29; *Deprenyl Animal Health, Inc. v. Univ. of Toronto Innovations Found.*, 297 F.3d 1343, 1350 (Fed. Cir. 2002).

[25] To be sure, the defendants in that case only raised the personal-jurisdiction argument "as an aid in interpreting" FSIA's direct-effect requirement. *Republic of Argentina v. Weltover, Inc.*, 504 U.S. 607, 619 n.2, 112 S. Ct. 2160, 2169 n.2 (1992) (quotation omitted). But that in no way minimizes the significance of the fact that the Supreme Court's first instinct, when presented with a question of Fifth Amendment personal jurisdiction, was to turn to its Fourteenth Amendment precedent.

ment standards differ" agreed "that there is no meaningful difference in the level of contacts required for personal jurisdiction." *Id.* at 54-55 (citations omitted). The court rejected the argument that the Fourteenth Amendment's federalism concerns fundamentally differentiate it from the **[—21—]** Fifth Amendment precisely because a "'vital' purpose of personal-jurisdiction standards is to 'ensure[] fairness to the defendant'" and "protect 'the sovereign concerns of other nations' **{-240-}** whose courts might otherwise adjudicate the claims." *Id.* at 55 (quoting *Stabilisierungsfonds Fur Wein v. Kaiser Stuhl Wine Distribs. Pty. Ltd.*, 647 F.2d 200, 203 n.4 (D.C. Cir. 1981) (per curiam)). Such considerations "weigh at least as heavily in the Fifth Amendment context" as they do in the Fourteenth Amendment context. *Id.* And not insignificantly, the court notes that "[a]pplying consistent personal-jurisdiction standards under the Fifth and Fourteenth Amendments is . . . easier to administer." *Id.* at 55-56.

In the face of consistent authority from this and a large majority of the circuits, we decline to jury rig a novel personal jurisdiction test under the Fifth Amendment. We are not encouraged to do so because the Supreme Court has occasionally reserved deciding the question whether "the Fifth Amendment imposes the same restrictions on the exercise of personal jurisdiction by a federal court" as does the Fourteenth Amendment on state courts.[26] *See Bristol-Myers Squibb*, 137 S. Ct. at 1784; *Nicastro*, 564 U.S. at 885, 131 S. Ct. at 2790; *Omni Capital*, 484 U.S. at 102 n.5, 108 S. Ct. at 408 n.5; *Asahi*, 480 U.S. at 113 n.*. Most recently, members of the Court seemed uncertain about the tried and true Fourteenth Amendment standards. *See Ford Motor Co. v. Mont. Eighth Jud. Dist. Ct.*, 141 S. Ct. 1017, 1032-33 (2021) (Alito, J., concurring); *Id.* at 1034-35, 1038 (Gorsuch, J., concurring). Far be **[—22—]** it for this lower court to muddy the waters further on a critical issue that precedes litigation in every federal court.

3. Rule 4(k)(2) is not rendered a nullity.

To support their proposed test, the plaintiffs contend that employing Fourteenth Amendment personal jurisdiction standards in the Fifth Amendment context renders Rule 4(k)(2) a nullity.[27] The argument is both unpersuasive and belied by a formidable body of precedent.

As already explained, Rule 4(k)(2) is a procedural rule governing the territorial limits of effective service. The Fifth Amendment due process limitations on a federal court's exercising jurisdiction over a foreign defendant exist independently of Rule 4(k)(2) and are indeed contemplated by the Rule itself. Rendering an interpretation of the Fifth Amendment based on the effects that choice has on Rule 4(k)(2) would let the procedural tail wag the constitutional dog.

More important, courts are routinely employing Fourteenth Amendment personal **{-241-}** jurisdiction standards in the Fifth Amendment context, yet Rule 4(k)(2) cases involving specific personal jurisdiction have arisen and continue to arise with regularity. *See, e.g., CGC Holding Co. v. Hutchens*, 974 F.3d 1201 (10th Cir. 2020); *Compania de Inversiones Mercantiles, S.A. v. Grupo*

[26] It appears that the Court reserved only the predicate question whether it is appropriate under the Fifth Amendment to consider "*national* contacts, rather than . . . the contacts between the defendant and the State in which the federal court sits." *Asahi,* 480 U.S. at 113 n.* (emphasis added); *see also Bristol-Myers Squibb*, 137 S. Ct. at 1784 (citing *Omni Capital*, 484 U.S. at 102, n.5, which cites *Asahi*); *Nicastro*, 564 U.S. at 885, 131 S. Ct. at 2790 (citing *Asahi,* 480 U.S. at 113 n.*) (plurality); *Omni Capital*, 484 U.S. at 102 n.5, 108 S. Ct. at 408 n.5 (citing *Asahi,* 480 U.S. at 113 n.*). No one here disputes the applicability of national contacts under the Fifth Amendment.

[27] Although the plaintiffs do not say so explicitly, perhaps their argument is that adopting *Daimler*'s "at home" requirement would render Rule 4(k)(2) inapplicable in general personal jurisdiction cases. That might be true. But even so, it is hardly troubling that federal courts can rarely, if ever, exercise personal jurisdiction over foreign defendants in cases raising claims that do not "arise out of or relate to" their contacts with the United States. *Cf. Daimler*, 571 U.S. at 140-42, 134 S. Ct. at 762-63 (chastising Ninth Circuit for failing to give heed to the "risks to international comity its expansive view of general jurisdiction posed").

Cementos de Chihuahua S.A.B. de C.V., 970 F.3d 1269 (10th Cir. 2020); *Plixer Int'l, Inc. v. Scrutinizer GmbH*, 905 F.3d 1 (1st **[—23—]** Cir. 2018); *M-I Drilling Fluids UK Ltd. v. Dynamic Air Ltda.*, 890 F.3d 995 (Fed. Cir. 2018); *Adams*, 364 F.3d 646; *ISI Int'l, Inc. v. Borden Ladner Gervais LLP*, 256 F.3d 548 (7th Cir. 2001). The plaintiffs' rhetoric fades in the face of reality.

4. No admiralty law exception exists.

At a minimum, the plaintiffs contend, this case warrants a more-indulgent personal jurisdiction standard because it involves admiralty claims and admiralty is special. Admiralty, they point out, is uniquely a creature of federal common law in addition to state and federal statutory law. Admiralty's broad jurisdiction has been described as extending "to all acts and torts done upon the high seas, and within the ebb and flow of the sea." 2 JOSEPH STORY, COMMENTARIES ON THE CONSTITUTION OF THE UNITED STATES 450, § 1665 (4th ed. 1873). Indeed, in no other context do courts "have complete jurisdiction over suits . . . between foreigners." *Langnes v. Green*, 282 U.S. 531, 544, 51 S. Ct. 243, 248 (1931).

The Fifth Circuit has long claimed expertise in and appreciation for admiralty's tradition and peculiar jurisprudence, but shibboleths cannot carry the plaintiffs' argument. In fact, there is no textual support in the Fifth Amendment for the plaintiffs' proffered distinction and no case law favoring their theory. About an admiralty "exception" to principles of personal jurisdiction, no more need be said: The Due Process Clauses contain no exception.

Further, plaintiffs' historical argument misunderstands *The Belgenland*, 114 U.S. 355, 5 S. Ct. 860 (1885), on which they principally rely. In that case, a federal court adjudicated a dispute arising out of a collision on the high seas between a Norwegian ship and a Belgian ship. 114 U.S. at 356-58, 5 S. Ct. at 860-61. The federal courts exercised in rem jurisdiction over the foreign ship, jurisdiction obtained because a U.S. marshal arrested the **[—24—]** vessel at port *in the federal court's district*. 114 U.S. at 356, 5 S. Ct. at 860. Because a court's jurisdiction over a ship arrested in its own district is unassailable, personal jurisdiction there was a nonissue. *Cf. Burnham v. Superior Ct. of Cal.*, 495 U.S. 604, 619, 110 S. Ct. 2105, 2115 (1990) (plurality) (concluding that "jurisdiction based on physical presence alone constitutes due process because it is one of the continuing traditions of our legal system that define the due process standard of 'traditional notions of fair play and substantial justice'").[28] The plaintiffs have confused personal jurisdiction with subject matter jurisdiction, which the Supreme Court discussed in *The Belgenland*. In sum, the plaintiffs' proposed admiralty-exclusive extension of due process standards for personal jurisdiction standard is all wet.

D. NYK is not amenable to jurisdiction in this dispute.

The foregoing discussion explains why the standards governing personal **{-242-}** jurisdiction are essentially the same under the Fifth and Fourteenth Amendment Due Process Clauses. For federal claims filed in federal courts, of course, the relevant minimum contacts are those with the entire United States, not a forum state. The Fifth Amendment Due Process Clause immunizes a non-resident, non-consenting defendant against a federal court's jurisdiction unless that defendant has "certain minimum contacts with [the United States] such that the maintenance of the suit does not offend 'traditional notions of fair play and substantial justice.'" *Int'l Shoe*, 326 U.S. at 316, 66 S. Ct. at 158. Whether a defendant has "minimum contacts" with a forum depends on the nature and extent of "the defendant's relationship to the forum." *Bristol-Myers*, 137 S. Ct. at 1779. The focus on the **[—25—]** defendant's relationship with the forum underlies the general-specific

[28] It is true that *Pennoyer v. Neff*, 95 U.S. 714 (1877), preceded *The Belgenland* by a few years and was the first case in which the Supreme Court linked personal jurisdiction with due process. As explained above, however, the latter case did not impinge on *Pennoyer*'s analysis.

jurisdiction dichotomy. *See Goodyear*, 564 U.S. at 919, 131 S. Ct. 2851.

General jurisdiction is the sole avenue for exercising jurisdiction over NYK here, because that is the only theory argued to the district court.[29] General jurisdiction extends to "any and all" claims against the defendant concerning events and conduct anywhere in the world. *Id.* But that breadth comes with a reciprocal limit: "Only a select 'set of affiliations with a forum' will expose a defendant to such sweeping jurisdiction." *Ford Motor Co.*, 141 S. Ct. at 1024 (quoting *Daimler*, 571 U.S. at 137, 134 S. Ct. at 760). Normally, a corporation is "at home" in its "place of incorporation and principal place of business." *Daimler*, 571 U.S. at 137, 134 S. Ct. at 760. But in an "exceptional case . . . a corporation's operations in a forum other than its formal place of incorporation or principal place of business may be so substantial and of such a nature as to render the corporation at home in [the United States]." *Id.* at 139 n.19.

Exercising general jurisdiction over NYK does not comport with its Fifth Amendment due process rights. NYK is incorporated and headquartered in Japan. As a result, exercising general jurisdiction over NYK would require that its contacts with the United States "be so substantial and of such a nature to render [it] at home" in the United States. *Daimler*, 571 U.S. at 139 n.19, 134 S. Ct. at 761 n.19. *Perkins v. Benguet Consolidated Mining Co.*, 342 U.S. 437, 72 S. Ct. 413 (1952) remains the lodestar for such exceptional circumstances. In *Perkins*, the defendant, **[—26—]** Benguet, was a Filipino corporation that operated gold and silver mines in the Philippines. *Id.* at 439. During World War II, Benguet's president relocated to Ohio and ran the company's operations from there. *Id.* at 447-48. Ohio state courts could exercise jurisdiction over Benguet because "Ohio was the corporation's principal, if temporary, place of business." *Keeton v. Hustler Mag., Inc.*, 465 U.S. 770, 780 n.11, 104 S. Ct. 1473, 1481 n.11 (1984).

Not so with NYK and the United States. No doubt NYK's contacts with the United States are, in absolute terms, substantial. NYK ships call on at least fifty U.S. ports, and NYK even dedicates several ships exclusively to delivering cars between Japan and the United States. At one time, it operated twenty-seven shipping terminals and six air-cargo terminals in the United **{–243–}** States.[30] Overall, its North American entities generate about $1.47 billion in consolidated revenue every year.[31]

But determining whether a defendant's contacts are "so substantial and of such a nature as to render the corporation at home" in the forum is an inherently comparative inquiry. *Daimler*, 571 U.S. at 139 nn.19, 20, 134 S. Ct. at 761-62 nn.19, 20. And comparatively, NYK's contacts with the United States comprise only a minor portion of its worldwide contacts. As the district court recognized: "All of NYK Line's high-level decision-making takes place in Japan, and port calls made to the United States represent just six to eight percent of all port calls made by NYK Line worldwide. **[—27—]** Furthermore, NYK Line's American employees represent less than 1.5 percent of all [its] employees." Therefore, the United States is hardly "the center of [NYK's] activities" or a "surrogate for [NYK's] place of incorporation or head office." *Daimler*, 571 U.S. at 130 n.8, 134 S. Ct. at 756 n.8. The district court's

[29] In the district court, the plaintiffs made clear that they did "not contend that the Court has specific jurisdiction over NYK," rather, they asserted that the court "has general jurisdiction over NYK." To the extent plaintiffs contend for the first time in this court that the district court could exercise specific jurisdiction over NYK, their argument is waived. *FDIC v. Mijalis*, 15 F.3d 1314, 1327 (5th Cir. 1994).

[30] NYK Group, Fact Book I 2017, 13-15 (Apr. 28, 2017), https://www.nyk.com/english/ir/library/fact/first/2017/__icsFiles/afieldfile/2019/10/17/2017_factbook01_all.pdf (last visited Oct. 23, 2021).

[31] The plaintiffs also draw attention to the fact that NYK often litigates in federal court, pointing out that, over the last decade, NYK has filed at least thirty lawsuits in federal district courts, and that over thirty lawsuits were filed against NYK in federal district courts. That a particular corporate defendant frequently litigates in a forum's courts also has no bearing on whether that defendant is essentially "at home" in the forum.

determinations are not clearly erroneous, nor did it apply the law incorrectly. Accordingly, NYK is not amenable to the general jurisdiction of American courts despite its contacts with the United States.

IV. CONCLUSION

Seventy-six years ago, Justice Frankfurter opined that "[t]o suppose that 'due process of law' meant one thing in the Fifth Amendment and another in the Fourteenth is too frivolous to require elaborate rejection." *Malinski v. New York*, 324 U.S. 401, 415 (1945) (Frankfurter, J., concurring). After considerable elaboration, this court confirms his intuition. We reject the plaintiffs' invitation to craft an atextual, novel, and unprecedented Fifth Amendment personal jurisdiction standard. Under the Supreme Court's reigning test for personal jurisdiction, the district court's well-reasoned judgment absolving NYK from appearing in federal court is AFFIRMED.

(Reporter's Note: Concurring opinion follows on p. 219).

[—28—] {-243-} HO, Circuit Judge, joined by **COSTA,** Circuit Judge, concurring:

The Fifth Amendment provides that no person may be "deprived of life, liberty, or property, without due process of law." U.S. CONST. amend. V. Everyone agrees that this language applies only to the federal government, and that that's why we have the Fourteenth Amendment—to ensure that the states too may not "deprive any person of life, liberty, or property, without due process of law." U.S. CONST. amend. XIV.

There's no denying the textual parallel between the Fifth and Fourteenth Amendments. That's why the majority today understandably construes "due process of law" to mean the same thing under the Fifth and Fourteenth Amendments alike.

Moreover, that approach is not only sensible as a textual matter—it also makes for a simpler body of federal constitutional law. Our legal system is already complex enough for litigants and lawyers, without additionally forcing people to navigate two distinct bodies of federal constitutional **{-244-}** rights, depending on who's on the right side of the "v."

Accordingly, the majority reasonably holds—as has every other circuit to have addressed the issue—that, when faced with a Fifth Amendment question concerning personal jurisdiction, we apply Fourteenth Amendment precedent governing personal jurisdiction.

The lead dissent responds that the meaning of words can change over time. *See post*, at 43–44, 63 (Elrod, J., dissenting). As it correctly notes, the Fifth Amendment was ratified in 1791—while the Fourteenth Amendment was not ratified until 1868, three quarters of a century later. So the lead dissent suggests that, whatever "due process" may have meant in 1868, fidelity to original public meaning requires us to separately inquire whether "due process" may have meant something different in 1791. **[—29—]**

That's fair enough, as an intellectual matter. But in fairness to the majority, the lead dissent does not point to a single Supreme Court decision holding that we should interpret Fifth Amendment due process differently from Fourteenth Amendment due process.

It simply says that the Supreme Court has reserved the issue. *See post*, at 43 (Elrod, J., dissenting) (citing *French v. Barber Asphalt Pav. Co.*, 181 U.S. 324, 328 (1901)). For example, it points out that a majority of the Supreme Court once noted the possibility that a situation "may arise" in which it "may be proper" to construe the Fifth and Fourteenth Amendments differently. *French*, 181 U.S. at 328.

But *French* was issued before the Court embraced the doctrine of incorporation. I write separately to explain how the Supreme Court's approach to incorporation is hard to square as a logical matter with the lead dissent's theory of linguistic drift under the Due Process Clause.

I.

Under the doctrine of incorporation, the Supreme Court has repeatedly held that we should interpret the Due Process Clause of the Fourteenth Amendment coextensively with a number of the provisions contained in the Bill of Rights. As a result, when it comes to rights that are incorporated against the states by the Due Process Clause, we apply the same body of law to the states that we do to the federal government.

The Supreme Court most recently reaffirmed these principles in the context of the Second Amendment right to keep and bear arms. Like the Fifth Amendment, "[t]he Second Amendment was adopted in 1791; the Fourteenth in 1868." *N.Y. State Rifle & Pistol Ass'n, Inc. v. Bruen*, _ U.S. _, _ (2022). "For decades, the Supreme Court has referred to the Second Amendment as a fundamental civil right, comparable to other provisions of the Bill of Rights." *Mance v. Sessions*, 896 F.3d 390, 398 (5th Cir. 2018) (Ho, **[—30—]** J., dissenting from denial of rehearing en banc) (citing, *e.g.*, *Johnson v. Eisentrager*, 339 U.S. 763, 784 (1950)).

Yet everyone agrees that the Second Amendment, like the Fifth Amendment, applies only to the federal government—hence the Fourteenth Amendment, which the Supreme Court has interpreted to apply fundamental rights like the Second Amendment to the states. *See McDonald v. City of Chicago*, 561 U.S. 742 (2010).

But if the Second Amendment is just like the Fifth Amendment—because both provisions precede the ratification of the Fourteenth Amendment by 77 years—does that mean that the right to keep and bear **{-245-}** arms might apply differently to the United States than to the several states?

The Supreme Court has repeatedly held that the answer is no: "Bill of Rights protections" like the Second Amendment must "be enforced against the States under the Fourteenth Amendment according to the *same standards* that protect those personal rights against federal encroachment." *McDonald*, 561 U.S. at 765 (cleaned up) (emphasis added). *See also N.Y. State Rifle*, _ U.S. at _ (same).

There is, to be sure, a "scholarly debate" over whether courts should look to "the prevailing understanding of an individual right when the Fourteenth Amendment was ratified in 1868" or "the public understanding of the right when the Bill of Rights was adopted in 1791" when determining the scope of constitutional rights. *Id.* at _.

But the Supreme Court has held on numerous occasions that, whether we define the right as it existed in 1791 or in 1868, the right is the same against the federal government and the states alike. "[W]e have made clear that individual rights enumerated in the Bill of Rights and made applicable against the States through the Fourteenth Amendment have the *same scope* as against the Federal Government." *Id.* (emphasis added). **[—31—]**

The Court cited several examples where it has taken that approach. *See, e.g.*, *Ramos v. Louisiana*, 590 U.S. _, _ (2020) ("This Court has long explained . . . that incorporated provisions of the Bill of Rights bear the *same content* when asserted against States as they do when asserted against the federal government.") (emphasis added); *Timbs v. Indiana*, 586 U.S. _, _ (2019) ("[I]f a Bill of Rights protection is incorporated, there is *no daylight* between the federal and state conduct it prohibits or requires.") (emphasis added); *Malloy v. Hogan*, 378 U.S. 1, 10–11 (1964) ("The Court thus has rejected the notion that the Fourteenth Amendment applies to the States only a watered-down, subjective version of the individual guarantees of the Bill of Rights.") (quotations omitted).

To this list of examples, I'll add one more. The Court has decided various challenges to state abortion laws—including the partial birth abortion law that it held unconstitutional in *Stenberg v. Carhart*, 530 U.S. 914 (2000). In *Gonzales v. Carhart*, 550 U.S. 124 (2007), the Court addressed a constitutional objection to the federal Partial Birth Abortion Act.

Tellingly, the United States government did not even try to defend—and the Court did not uphold—the federal Partial Birth Abortion Act on the ground that Fifth Amendment due process is different from Fourteenth Amendment due process. Not a single justice even flagged it as a potential issue. Justice Thomas wrote separately to reaffirm his longstanding view that "the Court's abortion jurisprudence . . . has no basis in the Constitution" without attempting to draw any distinction between the Fifth and Fourteenth Amendments (as well as to ask, without deciding, whether the Act is allowed under the Commerce Clause). *Id.* at 168–69 (Thomas, J., concurring).[1] **[—32—] {-246-}**

---

[1] Nor was the argument presented by any of the parties in *Carhart*. The argument was made only by amicus, and only in the court of appeals, which rejected the argument on the merits. *See Carhart v. Gonzales*, 413 F.3d 791, 795 n.2 (8th Cir. 2005) ("One amicus [—32—] suggests *Stenberg* does not control because that case was decided under the Fourteenth Amendment, which, of

II.

I see logical difficulties in squaring the dissenters' theory of linguistic drift with the Supreme Court's longstanding incorporation jurisprudence.

To be sure, I'm all for following the text and original understanding of the Constitution to the maximum extent permitted by a faithful reading of Supreme Court precedent, as I've repeatedly noted. *See, e.g., Williams v. Taylor Seidenbach, Inc.*, 958 F.3d 341, 350 (5th Cir. 2020) (en banc) (Ho, J., concurring); *Texas v. Rettig*, 993 F.3d 408, 409, 417–18 (5th Cir. 2021) (Ho, J., dissenting from denial of rehearing en banc); *Williams v. Homeland Ins. Co.*, 18 F.4th 806, 818–19 (5th Cir. 2021) (Ho, J., concurring). And reasonable minds can debate in good faith the Supreme Court's personal jurisdiction precedent, and ask whether it is faithful to the original understanding of the Constitution. *Cf. Ford Motor Co. v. Mont. Eighth Jud. Dist. Ct.*, 592 U.S. _, _ & n.2 (2021) (Gorsuch, J., concurring) (citing differing views).

But the members of this court all agree that fidelity to Supreme Court precedent must trump fidelity to text and original public meaning. And that means reading precedent faithfully. "Lower court judges don't have license to adopt a cramped reading of a case in order to functionally overrule it." *NLRB v. Int'l Ass'n of Bridge, Structural, Ornamental, & Reinforcing Iron Workers, Local 229, AFL-CIO*, 974 F.3d 1106, 1116 (9th Cir. 2020) (Bumatay, J., dissenting from denial of rehearing en banc) (quotations omitted). *See also* **[—33—]** Josh Blackman, *Originalism and Stare Decisis in the Lower Courts*, 13 NYU J.L. & LIBERTY 44, 51 (2019) ("Of course, judges can always draw razor-thin distinctions and contend that a particular issue is not governed by a non-originalist precedent. But judges should resist this temptation."). "[L]ogic [may] demand[] that we extend an [allegedly] atextual body of precedent in order to preserve rationality or consistency in the law." *Williams*, 18 F.4th at 821 (Ho, J., concurring).

Under the doctrine of incorporation, the Supreme Court has repeatedly instructed that we must interpret the Due Process Clause of the Fourteenth Amendment coextensively with various provisions of the Bill of Rights. And therein lies the logical challenge I see with the dissent's proposed framework. For if we accept the dissenters' theory of linguistic drift when it comes to due process, logic would presumably require that we entertain the possibility of linguistic drift in *every* aspect of due process.

For example, what does the First Amendment require when it comes to the states? Well, we know the First Amendment might have meant one thing in 1791, but something quite different in 1868. And so too with the Second Amendment, the Fourth Amendment, the Eighth Amendment, and so on.

So presumably the dissenters would apply a different body of First Amendment law, Second Amendment law, and so on, to the states as opposed to the federal government, in recognition of the possibility of linguistic drift between 1791 and 1868.

But we don't do that. Because the Supreme Court has told us we can't do that—most recently, in *N.Y. State Rifle*. **{–247–}**

And that's the logical problem I see with the dissent's approach. If Supreme Court precedent requires us to apply the *same* standard of "due process" to the states and the federal government when it comes to *other* **[—34—]** constitutional rights like the First and Second Amendments, what's the logic in applying *different* standards when it comes to due process itself?

If we're being principled about linguistic drift, we presumably wouldn't limit it to just

course, does not apply to the federal government. While *Stenberg* was indeed a Fourteenth Amendment case, the Due Process Clause of the Fifth Amendment is textually identical to the Due Process Clause of the Fourteenth Amendment, and both proscribe virtually identical governmental conduct.") (citing *Malloy*, 378 U.S. at 8). The amicus declined to reprise the argument in the Supreme Court.

the Fifth Amendment—or just the Due Process Clause of the Fifth Amendment. We would either allow for linguistic drift with respect to *every* provision of the Bill of Rights—or to *none* of them.

To my mind, logical fidelity to Supreme Court precedent would seem to suggest that the answer must be none.

III.

In response, the lead dissent says that "due process" is different inasmuch as, unlike the incorporated provisions, it's actually codified in the text of the Fourteenth Amendment. *See post*, at 45–46 n.4 (Elrod, J., dissenting).

That's obviously true as far as it goes: due process explicitly appears in the text of the Fourteenth Amendment, while the incorporated provisions are implicit in due process by operation of Supreme Court precedent.

But why should that matter? The dissent doesn't explain. And it's hard to understand, especially considering that Supreme Court precedent essentially directs us to act as if the words of the First Amendment, the Second Amendment, and so on appear alongside the Due Process Clause in the Fourteenth Amendment. *See, e.g., McDonald*, 561 U.S. at 791 ("[A] provision of the Bill of Rights that protects a right that is fundamental from an American perspective applies equally to the Federal Government and the States. We therefore hold that the Due Process Clause of the Fourteenth Amendment incorporates the Second Amendment.") (citation omitted).

Moreover, the dissent's logic, if anything, gets things exactly backwards. The Fifth and Fourteenth Amendment Due Process Clauses use **[—35—]** the same words—and so that's the reason we should apply *different* standards? It's a curious way to split the baby.

Nor do I understand what the dissent hopes to accomplish by drawing a distinction between "reverse" versus "plain-vanilla" incorporation. *See post*, at 45 n.4 (Elrod, J., dissenting). I'll just sum things up this way: Everyone agrees that both the federal government and the states are subject to due process. And everyone agrees that this includes not only due process *qua* due process, but also various other provisions in the Bill of Rights. The only disagreement is whether we should apply the *same* legal standards under various provisions in the Bill of Rights—*except* for "due process" itself. If there's a case for applying one body of law when it comes to all the provisions that due process incorporates, but two bodies of law when it comes to due process itself, I'm not sure what it is, and I'm not sure that the dissenters have made it.

IV.

As for Judge Oldham's solo dissent, I'll begin by noting where we substantially agree. Like me, Judge Oldham makes clear that he does not endorse the lead dissent's theory of linguistic drift. *See post*, at 101 (Oldham, J., dissenting). Like me, Judge Oldham does not say that there are two distinct bodies of due process law, one that governs the states and another that governs the federal government. Rather, he suggests that "*none* of the personal-jurisdiction **{-248-}** limits—for *any* government, state or federal—come from the Fifth or Fourteenth Amendments," but rather, "[t]hey instead come from the common law." *Id.* at 102–03 n.1.

So we agree that there is one body of due process law, not two. Here's where we part company, then: If we're agreed that there's only a single body of due process law, then I don't see how we can ignore Supreme Court precedent under Fourteenth Amendment due process in a case involving **[—36—]** Fifth Amendment due process. And that's where my reference to the doctrine of incorporation comes in.

Judge Oldham dismisses my invocation of the incorporation doctrine on the ground that that is a doctrine of substantive due process—whereas this is a personal jurisdiction case, which implicates procedural due process. *See id.* at 102. He makes the same observation about the judicially-created right to abortion examined in *Carhart*. *See id.* at 103.

He's of course entirely right that both the incorporation doctrine generally, and abortion in particular, are creatures of substantive due process. But I don't see why the substantive/procedural due process distinction should make any difference here.

To explain why, let me first summarize his core argument. It proceeds like this: "The Supreme Court has confessed that its Fourteenth Amendment personal jurisdiction precedents do not rest on original public meaning." *Id.* at 102. Accordingly, he concludes, as originalists, we're allowed to ignore that body of law, which applies only to states, when it comes to Fifth Amendment cases, which involve the federal government. *Id.*

My response is that that is the opposite of what we do under the doctrine of incorporation—where we apply the same body of law to the states and the federal government.

It's also the opposite of what happened in *Carhart*. Just like the Court's personal jurisdiction precedents, the Supreme Court's abortion precedents "do not rest on original public meaning" (at least not before *Dobbs*). *Id.* Yet, as I point out, the federal government did not even bother to argue in *Carhart* that it can ignore the Court's Fourteenth Amendment abortion law when it comes to Fifth Amendment cases. **[—37—]**

Yes, those examples come from substantive due process—whereas this case involves procedural due process. But I'm not sure why we would apply one approach to precedent in substantive due process cases (follow the 14th when it comes to the 5th), and precisely the opposite approach to precedent in procedural due process cases (ignore the 14th when it comes to the 5th). I would have thought that our duty to be faithful to Supreme Court precedent doesn't wax and wane depending on which underlying body of law the precedent entails.

Finally, in a footnote, Judge Oldham notes that the Supreme Court has repeatedly declined to address the question of divergence in personal jurisdiction cases even after it started incorporating various other provisions. *See id.* at 103 n.2. Again, that's true, I just don't know what it proves. The Supreme Court ordinarily does not weigh in on issues absent a circuit split. And here, there is none—every circuit to have addressed the issue has rejected the theory of divergence when it comes to personal jurisdiction.

V.

One final concern before I close: Embracing the linguistic drift theory urged by the lead dissent would involve an additional layer of complication—the launching of **{–249–}** an unprecedented second body of substantive federal constitutional law.

Of course, if text and original understanding compel complexity, then complexity we shall give. But all things equal, we should endeavor to make the law simpler, not more byzantine.

Perhaps the Supreme Court will someday switch gears and embrace the dissent's view that due process under the Fifth Amendment is indeed different from due process under the Fourteenth Amendment. Perhaps the Court will one day hold that fidelity to text and original public meaning **[—38—]** necessitates the complexity of developing two distinct bodies of federal constitutional rights—one against the feds and one against the states.

But until then, I will stick with the simplicity of the approach adopted by the majority of my colleagues—not to mention all of the circuits that have previously addressed the issue. I concur.

(Reporter's Note: Dissenting opinion follows on p. 224).

[—39—] {-249-} **ELROD,** Circuit Judge, joined by **GRAVES, HIGGINSON, WILLETT,** and **OLDHAM,** Circuit Judges, dissenting:*

* Judge Higginson joins Part VI of this opinion. Judge Oldham joins Parts II.B and VI of this opinion.

The majority today holds that the Fifth Amendment's Due Process Clause "immunizes" from suit in federal court a multinational corporation with extensive business dealings in the United States and which litigates here frequently as a plaintiff. Defendant–Appellee Nippon Yusen Kabushiki Kaisha ("NYK"), an international shipping conglomerate, calls regularly on American ports, operates numerous shipping terminals here, and reaps hundreds of millions of dollars in annual revenue in so doing. In the course of its substantial business here, NYK has invoked the power of our federal courts to protect *its* rights as a plaintiff over *seventy-five* times. But today, the *en banc* court holds that it would "offend 'traditional notions of fair play and substantial justice'" for injured United States servicemen and bereaved military families to sue NYK in United States federal court.

Today's result is as needless as it is confounding: The majority opinion fails to prove—as a matter of the Fifth Amendment's text, history, and structure—the existence of a principled limit on Congress's ability to authorize federal courts' personal jurisdiction over a foreign defendant. Relying entirely on inapposite Fourteenth Amendment precedent, the majority opinion arrives at a conclusion that will nullify Federal Rule of Civil Procedure 4(k)(2) in most of its applications, crush the chances of American terror victims seeking recovery in federal court, and, quite anomalously, afford foreign *civil* defendants greater due process protection than foreign *criminal* defendants. [—40—]

Because the Fifth Amendment's Due Process Clause does not shield NYK from suit in United States federal court, I would hold that the district court has personal jurisdiction in this case. I respectfully dissent.

I.

The ACX Crystal, a foreign cargo ship, crashed into the U.S.S. Fitzgerald, a U.S. Navy destroyer, in Japanese waters. Seven sailors were killed. Forty were injured. Seeking damages under admiralty law and the Death on the High Seas Act, the bereaved and injured sued NYK, the foreign shipping company that chartered the vessel, in federal court.

In both cases consolidated before us on appeal, NYK sought and the district court **{-250-}** granted dismissal for lack of personal jurisdiction. The injured Navy sailors and bereaved families appealed. They argued that the Fifth rather than Fourteenth Amendment governed the extent of federal courts' personal jurisdiction over foreign defendants pursuant to Federal Rule of Civil Procedure 4(k)(2). And the Supreme Court's Fourteenth Amendment personal jurisdiction precedents, they argued cogently, neither bind us nor should be imported into the Fifth Amendment context.

Bound by a prior panel opinion, *Patterson v. Aker Solutions, Inc.*, 826 F.3d 231, 4 Adm. R. 259 (5th Cir. 2016), this court affirmed, in keeping with the rule of orderliness. *Douglass v. Nippon Yusen Kabushiki Kaisha*, 996 F.3d 289, 297–300 (5th Cir. 2021). Without discussion of the relevant differences between the Constitution's due process clauses, *Patterson* had applied recent Supreme Court precedents from the Fourteenth Amendment context to a Fifth Amendment case. *Patterson*, 826 F.3d at 234, 4 Adm. R. at 260. The panel in this case noted that it was constrained to do the same. But it added that, absent *Patterson*, plaintiffs–appellants' position was "persuasive," and indeed, "ha[d] merit." *Douglass*, 996 F.3d at 293–97. [—41—]

Two panel members specially concurred. *Id.* at 300–02 (Elrod, J., joined by Willett, J., specially concurring). The concurrence "agree[d] with the majority opinion that the case would be decided differently if we were not bound by *Patterson*," and called all hands on deck to reevaluate our precedent. *Id.* Several important considerations counseled in favor of "apply[ing] a jurisdictional framework that distinguishes between Fifth Amendment and Fourteenth Amendment due process standards." *Id.* at 301. For one thing, "the federalism concerns that animate the Supreme Court's jurisprudence on the jurisdictional limitations of the Fourteenth Amendment's Due Process Clause are irrelevant in the Fifth Amendment context." *Id.* We further warned against "imposing restraints on federal courts' exercise of personal jurisdiction (and . . . Congress's ability to authorize jurisdiction by statute) beyond what the Constitution requires." *Id.* With these concerns in mind, we invited the court to take a different tack *en banc*.

The full court accepted our invitation to reconsider the propriety of applying the Supreme Court's Fourteenth Amendment precedents in the Fifth Amendment context. But today the majority opinion declines to chart a new course, leaving our precedent at sea and the plaintiffs high and dry.

II.

What does the Due Process Clause of the *Fifth* Amendment have to say about personal jurisdiction?

Our circuit's precedents are awash with confusion: On the one hand, we have made clear that the Fifth Amendment—and *not* the Fourteenth Amendment—governs due process challenges to federal courts' exercise of jurisdiction over foreign defendants pursuant to Rule 4(k)(2). *See, e.g., Submersible Sys., Inc. v. Perforadora Cent., S.A. de C.V.*, 249 F.3d 413, 420 (5th Cir. 2001) ("The due process required in federal cases governed by Rule **[—42—]** 4(k)(2) is measured with reference to the Fifth Amendment, rather than the Fourteenth Amendment."). On the other hand, our Rule 4(k)(2) personal jurisdiction cases have generally tracked Supreme Court case law from the Fourteenth Amendment context. *See, e.g., Adams v. Unione Mediterranea Di Sicurta*, 364 F.3d 646, 652 (5th Cir. 2004) (citing Fourteenth Amendment precedent including *Helicopteros Nacionales de Colombia, S.A. v. Hall*, 466 U.S. 408 (1984), and **{-251-}** *World-Wide Volkswagen Corp. v. Woodson*, 444 U.S. 286 (1980)); *Patterson*, 826 F.3d at 234, 4 Adm. R. at 260 (applying *Daimler AG v. Bauman*, 571 U.S. 117 (2014)).

Left entirely unexplained is *why* we have silently imported Fourteenth Amendment jurisprudence into our Fifth Amendment cases. We have assumed, without argument, that the Fifth and Fourteenth Amendment Due Process Clauses operate in exactly the same manner vis-à-vis personal jurisdiction. *See, e.g., Patterson*, 826 F.3d at 234, 4 Adm. R. at 260 (providing no explanation for the case's application of the latest Fourteenth Amendment precedents from the Supreme Court in ruling on a Fifth Amendment question); *World Tanker Carriers Corp. v. M/V Ya Mawlaya*, 99 F.3d 717, 723–24 (5th Cir. 1996) (applying, without explanation, the "now familiar [Fourteenth Amendment] minimum contacts analysis" in a Rule 4(k)(2) personal jurisdiction case, without even mentioning the Fifth Amendment once). But this unspoken assumption is unsound. The Fifth Amendment does not merely carry Fourteenth Amendment ballast. It has its own text, history, and structural implications. Its Due Process Clause need not parrot what the Supreme Court has said about the Fourteenth's.

Perhaps our court has considered the relationship between the Fifth and Fourteenth Amendment Due Process Clauses too obvious to require argument. The majority opinion implies as much with its concluding quotation from Justice Frankfurter's solo concurrence in *Malinski v. New York*, 324 U.S. 401 (1945): "To suppose that 'due process of law' meant one **[—43—]** thing in the Fifth Amendment and another in the Fourteenth is too frivolous to require elaborate rejection." *Id.* at 415 (Frankfurter, J., concurring); *ante* at 27. A six-justice majority of the Supreme Court, however, has taken a different view, writing: "[A]s the[] [Fifth and Fourteenth Amendments] were ingrafted upon the Constitution at different times and in widely different circumstances of our national life, it may be that questions may arise in which different constructions and applications of their provisions may be proper." *French v. Barber Asphalt Pav. Co.*, 181 U.S. 324, 328

(1901);[1] *see also Wight v. Davidson*, 181 U.S. 371, 384 (1901) ("[I]t by no means necessarily follows that a long and consistent construction put upon the 5th Amendment [Due Process Clause] . . . is to be deemed overruled by a decision concerning the operation of the 14th Amendment as controlling state legislation."); *Carroll v. Greenwich Ins. Co. of N.Y.*, 199 U.S. 401, 410 (1905) (Holmes, J.) (refusing to "affirm that in no instance could a distinction [between the amendments] be taken").

The relationship between the amendments' Due Process Clauses and the limits of federal courts' personal jurisdiction clearly merits "considerable elaboration." *Ante* at 27. Far from frivolous, this thorny topic has launched more than a few law review articles.[2] Indeed, the latest originalist scholarship strongly suggests that "'due process of law' has undergone linguistic **{-252-}** drift." Max Crema & Lawrence B. Solum, *The Original Meaning of "Due Process of* **[—44—]** *Law" in the Fifth Amendment*, 108 Va. L. Rev. 447, 453 (2022). That is, "its meaning has changed since the First Congress proposed [the Fifth Amendment] for ratification" in 1789, and before the 39th Congress proposed the Fourteenth Amendment in 1866. *Id.* at 453, 461–524 (examining a wide array of primary sources and conducting rigorous historical and corpus-linguistics analysis). Thus, it is quite reasonable to think that the original public meaning of the Fifth Amendment's Due Process Clause diverges from the Fourteenth Amendment's as it bears upon personal jurisdiction—particularly given the interstate-federalism principles baked into the Fourteenth Amendment.[3]

The Supreme Court itself has specifically flagged and repeatedly reserved the question before us for another day. *See, e.g., Bristol-Myers Squibb Co. v. Sup. Ct. of Cal., S.F. Cnty.*, 137 S. Ct. 1773, 1783–84 (2017) ("[S]ince our decision concerns the due process limits on the exercise of specific jurisdiction by a State, we leave open the question whether the Fifth Amendment imposes the same restrictions on the exercise of personal **[—45—]** jurisdiction by a federal court."); *J. McIntyre Mach., Ltd. v. Nicastro*, 564 U.S. 873, 885 (2011) (plurality op.) (noting that it was unnecessary "to address . . . any constitutional concerns that might be attendant" to more expansive federal court exercises of personal jurisdiction over foreign defendants); *post* at 96 (Higginson, J., dissenting).[4] **[—46—]**

---

[1] *Contra French*, 181 U.S. at 355 (Harlan, J., dissenting) ("[D]ue process of law cannot mean one thing under the 5th Amendment and another thing under the 14th Amendment, the words used being the same in each amendment.").

[2] For just a small sampling, *see generally, e.g.*, Stephen E. Sachs, *The Unlimited Jurisdiction of the Federal Courts*, 106 Va. L. Rev. 1703 (2020); Jonathan Remy Nash, *National Personal Jurisdiction*, 68 Emory L.J. 509 (2019); Wendy Perdue, *Aliens, the Internet, and "Purposeful Availment": A Reassessment of Fifth Amendment Limits on Personal Jurisdiction*, 98 Nw. U. L. Rev. 455 (2004); *see also* Stephen E. Sachs, Pennoyer *Was Right*, 95 Tex. L. Rev. 1249 (2017).

[3] The concurring opinion readily acknowledges the theoretical possibility of linguistic drift over time. *Ante* at 28 (Ho, J., concurring). Although my concurring colleague comes to a different conclusion, he recognizes that it is "fair enough, as an intellectual matter" to account for linguistic drift in discerning constitutional provisions' original public meanings. *Id.* at 29. Our disagreement flows not from our judicial philosophies but from our divergent good-faith readings of Supreme Court precedent. *See, e.g.*, *infra* n.4.

Relatedly, the concurring opinion expresses an additional concern that this theory of linguistic drift would introduce "an additional layer of complication" in federal constitutional law—and "all things equal, we should endeavor to make the law *simpler*, not more byzantine." *Ante* at 37 (Ho, J., concurring) (emphasis added). We ought not opt for Occam over originalism. The concurring opinion agrees. *Id.* ("Of course, if text and original understanding compel complexity, then complexity we shall give."). But *ceteris paribus*, simplicity would weigh in favor of fewer limits on personal jurisdiction, not more. And that simpler result aligns with the original meaning of the Fifth Amendment's Due Process Clause. *See infra* n.35.

[4] *See also, e.g., Omni Cap. Int'l, Ltd. v. Rudolf Wolff & Co., Ltd.*, 484 U.S. 97, 102 n.5 (1987) (stating that the Court had no occasion to address the Fifth Amendment's applicability to personal jurisdiction); *Asahi Metal Indus. Co. v. Superior Ct. of Cal., Solano Cnty.*, 480 U.S. 102, 113 n.* (1987) (same).

In my view, it is precisely our duty as an inferior court to percolate the arguments **{-253-}** raised by this novel constitutional issue for eventual Supreme Court review. *Cf. Dep't of Homeland Sec. v. New York*, 140 S. Ct. 599, 600 (2020) (Gorsuch, J., concurring in grant of stay) (noting that the percolation "process that permits the airing of competing views . . . aids this Court's own decision-making process"); *Box v. Planned Parenthood of Ind. & Ky., Inc.*, 139 S. Ct. 1780, 1784 (2019) (Thomas, J., concurring) ("[F]urther percolation may assist our review of [an] issue of first impression . . . ."). We are asked in this case to interpret the Fifth Amendment's Due Process Clause with respect to federal court personal jurisdiction—a question of first impression that the Supreme Court has repeatedly declined to answer. And when we are called to interpret a constitutional provision without on-point Supreme Court guidance, we should look first to the Constitution's text, history, and structure before we borrow freely from adjacent Supreme Court jurisprudence.[5] **[—47—]**

In the face of the Supreme Court's repeated reservation of this question for a future case, the concurring opinion claims that the Court has already answered it. *Ante* at 29–31 (Ho, J., concurring). It has not.

The concurrence first relies on the Court's statements about incorporation doctrine. The argument seems to go like this: (A) the Supreme Court has held that "incorporated provisions of the Bill of Rights bear the same content when asserted against States as they do when asserted against the federal government," *id.* at 31 (quoting *Ramos v. Louisiana*, 140 S. Ct. 1390, 1397 (2020) (emphasis omitted)); (B) the Fourteenth Amendment's Due Process Clause incorporates the Fifth Amendment's Due Process Clause against the states; thus, the concurrence concludes, (C) any Fifth Amendment rights vis-à-vis personal jurisdiction must "bear the same content" as those under the Fourteenth Amendment's Due Process Clause, *id.* at 29–31.

There are at least two problems with this argument. First, it turns incorporation doctrine upside-down. This case is actually about *reverse* incorporation—that is, reading (newer) *Fourteenth* Amendment jurisprudence into the (older) *Fifth* Amendment Due Process Clause, rather than vice versa. And none of the concurrence's plain-vanilla incorporation cases suggest we must—or even should—transplant the Supreme Court's personal jurisdiction doctrine from the Fourteenth Amendment into the Fifth Amendment. Second, it is hardly obvious that the Fifth Amendment's Due Process Clause is "just like" the Second Amendment or any other provision in the Bill of Rights vis-à-vis incorporation. *Id.* at 30. With due process, the Amenders did something special: they gave the Fourteenth Amendment *its own* Due Process Clause. So, the Fifth Amendment's Due Process Clause never needed to be "incorporated" *through* the Fourteenth Amendment's Due Process Clause. The former never needed to pass through the latter's lens to be refracted against the states. The Fourteenth Amendment's Due Process Clause *already* applied to the states directly. For that reason, it does not follow that the scope of the rights protected by the two clauses must bear the same content. Incidentally, this also explains why linguistic drift is relevant *only* to the Fifth Amendment context—and thus why we **[—46—]** would not "apply a different body of First Amendment law, Second Amendment law, and so on, to the states as opposed to the federal government." *See id.* at 33.

In support of its view, the concurring opinion also points to *Gonzales v. Carhart*, 550 U.S. 124 (2007), where the Court upheld a federal-law abortion restriction without considering whether the Fifth Amendment's Due Process Clause creates a different framework than the Fourteenth Amendment's when it comes to abortion jurisprudence. *See ante* at 31 (Ho, J., concurring). *Carhart* is wholly inapposite. No scholar, litigant, or jurist had offered any plausible reason to think that the original public meaning of the Fifth and Fourteenth Amendments differed as to the permissibility of abortion restrictions. Here by contrast, as multiple scholars have explained in detail, the Fifth and Fourteenth Amendments had distinct original understandings when it came to the jurisdictional restrictions they imposed on federal and state courts, respectively. *See, e.g.*, Sachs, *Unlimited Jurisdiction*, *supra*, at 1708–09, 1710–27. The non-discussion of an irrelevant question in an unrelated case does not prevent us from reaching the right answer to a constitutional question that the Supreme Court has expressly left open.

[5] *Cf.* Antonin Scalia, *Common Law Courts in a Civil-Law System in* A Matter of Interpretation 39 (1997) (disapprovingly describing constitutional analysis that takes as its "starting point" Supreme Court case law and thus removes from focus the Constitution's **[—47—]** "original text and understanding"); *Ford Motor Co. v. Mont. Eighth Jud. Dist. Ct.*, 141 S. Ct. 1017, 1036 n.2 (2021) (Gorsuch, J., concurring in the judgment) (indicating that "the right question" to be asking in

We are bound to apply controlling law as it stands. In this case, there is no {-254-} controlling Supreme Court precedent. What controls is the Fifth Amendment Due Process Clause. If the *en banc* majority is convinced that the Fifth Amendment Due Process Clause, as originally understood, imposes the same set of jurisdictional rules that the Supreme Court has decreed pursuant to the Fourteenth Amendment, then it bears the burden of proving that with reference to the Fifth Amendment's text, history, and structure. The majority opinion has made no such effort. *See ante* at 7 n.8. It fails to meet its burden from the very get-go.[6] Indeed,

---

Fourteenth Amendment personal jurisdiction context is "what the Constitution as originally understood requires").

Both parties in this case ask us to take as our "starting point" Supreme Court personal jurisdiction case law from the Fourteenth Amendment context. Appellees vigorously contend that Fourteenth Amendment personal jurisdiction case law, particularly *Daimler*, 571 U.S. 117, controls our interpretation of the Fifth Amendment's Due Process Clause in this case. Meanwhile, appellants argue that Fourteenth Amendment case law does not bind us in the Fifth Amendment context; but they nonetheless ask us to kick off our analysis with *International Shoe Co. v. Washington*, 326 U.S. 310 (1945), while refraining from relying on its progeny. I disagree with both approaches because both start not with the Fifth Amendment but with inapplicable Fourteenth Amendment case law.

Thus, I agree with the majority opinion that we ought to "reject the plaintiffs' invitation to craft an atextual, novel, and unprecedented Fifth Amendment personal jurisdiction standard" that is not founded upon the amendment's original understanding. *Ante* at 27. But, as I explain in this dissent, we *also* ought to reject NYK's invitation to calcify our current Fifth Amendment precedents, which erroneously import Fourteenth Amendment Supreme Court jurisprudence.

[6] The majority opinion's footnoted response to this dissent is unresponsive on this score: Lacking Supreme Court case law restricting federal courts' exercise of personal jurisdiction under the Fifth Amendment, NYK must convince us, as a matter of text, history, and structure, that the Fifth Amendment's Due Process Clause merely mimes the Fourteenth's as to personal jurisdiction. But NYK has made no such argument, and nor has the majority opinion. *See ante* at 7 n.8. [—48—]

In fact, the majority opinion expressly refuses to engage with the contrary arguments presented in this dissent, declining to address anything but "the *exact* arguments raised by the plaintiffs." *Id.* (emphasis added). Respectfully, I do not think our approach should be so blinkered. Of course we take cases as they are presented to us, but that does not mean that we must parrot parties' "exact" views in our opinions. Our duty is to resolve the appeal correctly and offer our *independent* explanation of the bases for *our* decision. *See United States v. Brace*, 145 F.3d 247, 267 (5th Cir. 1998) (*en banc*) (DeMoss, J., dissenting) ("To refrain from independent analysis is to abdicate the essential function of judging. Just as we do not abdicate our judicial responsibilities and blindly accept the parties' stipulations, neither do we don blinders and confine our consideration to those legal doctrines that are presented by the parties.").

More to the point, however, plaintiffs-appellants themselves raised all the arguments necessary to succeed here on appeal: Although neither they nor their *amici* ground their proposed 'national contacts' test in the original understanding of the Fifth Amendment, they *did* argue—quite correctly—that Fifth Amendment personal jurisdiction standards are not dictated by Fourteenth Amendment jurisprudence. *See* Appellants' *En Banc* Br. 18–20, 18 n.5 (citing, *inter alia*, Sachs, *Unlimited Jurisdiction*, *supra*, and early nineteenth-century cases *Picquet v. Swan*, 19 F. Cas. 609 (C.C.D. Mass. 1828) and *Toland v. Sprague*, 37 U.S. 300 (13 Pet.), 327 (1838)); *En Banc* Oral Argument at 25:20–25:57 (noting but not relying upon originalist scholarship to fashion a middle-ground 'national contacts' test); *id.* at 58:12–58:53 ("It's also important to understand that there is considerable originalist scholarship that the Fifth Amendment does not address personal jurisdiction. I mentioned the Stephen Sachs article, he's actually written several articles to that effect.").

That being the case, the onus was on NYK to persuade us that we should continue to use Fourteenth Amendment jurisprudence to cast light on the Fifth Amendment and restrict the constitutional applicability of Rule 4(k)(2). *Cf. Baldwin v. Missouri*, 281 U.S. 586, 599 (1930) ("As this Court has often held, the burden rests upon him who assails a statute to establish its unconstitutionality."); *Brown v. Maryland*, 25 U.S. (12 Wheat.) 419, 436–37 (1827) ("It has been truly said, that the presumption is in favour of every legislative act, and that the whole burthen of proof lies on him who denies its constitutionality."). In my view, NYK has failed to do so. And, without a reason to affirm the district court's restrictive view of its ability to exercise personal jurisdiction under

{-255-} the majority opinion could **[—48—] [—49—]** not meet its burden if it tried. The text, history, and structural implications of the Fifth Amendment Due Process Clause suggest that its original public meaning imposed few (if any) barriers to federal court personal jurisdiction.

A.

First, the text. The Fifth Amendment Due Process Clause provides: "No person shall be . . . deprived of life, liberty, or property, without due process of law[.]" U.S. Const. amend. V. This provision, Justice Joseph Story explained in 1833, draws upon "the language of magna charta, '*nec super eum ibimus, nec super eum mittimus, nisi per legale judicium parium suorum, vel per legem terrae*,' neither will we pass upon him, or condemn him, but by the lawful judgment of his peers, or by the law of the land."[7] 3 Joseph Story, Commentaries on the Constitution of the United States § 1783 (Hillard, Gray, & Co. 1833). Citing the renowned seventeenth century English jurist Lord Coke, Alexander Hamilton wrote in 1784 that "[i]f we enquire what is meant by the law of the land, the best commentators will tell us, that it means *due process of law, that is, by indictment or presentment of good and lawful men*, and trial and conviction in consequence." Alexander Hamilton, *A Letter from Phocion to the Considerate Citizens of New York* (Jan. 1784), *reprinted in* 3 The Papers of Alexander Hamilton 485, 485–86 (Harold C. Syrett & Jacob E. Cooke eds., 1962) (emphasis in original) (referring to **[—50—]** 2 Edward Coke, Institutes of the Lawes of England 50 (1642)).[8] Indeed, **{-256-}** the relationship between "law of the land" and "due process of law" antedates Lord Coke's magisterial interpretation of Magna Carta by nearly three centuries.[9]

---

the Fifth Amendment's Due Process Clause, we should overrule our misguided precedents in this area and reverse the district court's dismissal for lack of jurisdiction.

The majority opinion further suggests that this dissent fails on its own terms because Congress has not acted to extend federal court jurisdiction. *See ante* at 7 n.8; *infra* section II.B. Not so. Rule 4(k)(2), promulgated and enacted pursuant to the Rules Enabling Act with Congress's imprimatur, plainly supports personal jurisdiction here. *See* Fed. R. Civ. P. 4(k)(2); 28 U.S.C. §§ 2071–2077; *id.* §§ 2074, 2075 (providing Congress **[—49—]** with a statutory window of at least seven months to reject, modify, or defer any proposed rule, after which period proposed rules take effect with Congressional approval).

[7] Up until about a century ago, the predominant spelling of the Great Charter was "*Magna Charta*," pronounced the same as it is today (with a hard -k- sound). *See* Bryan A. Garner, *A Magna Carta Style Guide*, 101 A.B.A. J. 26, 26 (2015). In an "astonishingly swift reversal of linguistic fortune," English speakers in the twentieth century began spelling it "*Magna Carta*," at least in part because of pervasive mispronunciation with a -ch- sound. *See id.*

[8] Justice Story also cited Lord Coke in making the broader assertion that "*per legem terrae* (by the law of the land) mean[s] by due process of law." *See* Story, *supra*, at § 1783; Crema & Solum, *supra*, at 516–24 (arguing that Justice Story may have misread Lord Coke in conflating the broader legal expression "law of the land" with its narrower subset "due process of law"). Mid-nineteenth century cases began to adopt Justice Story's broad equation of "law of the land" with "due process of law." *See, e.g.*, *Den ex dem. Murray v. Hoboken Land & Imp. Co.*, 59 U.S. (18 How.) 272, 276 (1855) ("The words, 'due process of law,' were undoubtedly intended to convey the same meaning as the words, 'by the law of the land,' in *Magna Charta*." (citing, *inter alia*, Lord Coke)). But, as Hamilton's "Letter from Phocion" illustrates, the Founding generation understood "law of the land" to encompass both "due process of law" (*i.e.*, indictment, presentment, service of the proper writ) *and* civil and criminal procedure more generally (*i.e.*, motions practice, trial). *See* Crema & Solum, *supra*, at 504–06. Thus, "due process of law," as originally understood at the time that the Fifth Amendment was proposed and ratified, likely had a narrower meaning than it came to have by the time the Fourteenth Amendment was proposed and ratified. *See also infra* section II.C.1.

[9] *See* 28 Edw. 3, c. 3 (1354) (Eng.) (implementing Magna Carta's thirty-ninth chapter and using "due Process of the Law" (albeit in law French) in place of "law of the land"). Note that Magna Carta's chapter divisions were only standardized in the eighteenth century by Sir William Blackstone. On Blackstone's numbering system, the '*per legem terrae*' chapter is *thirty-nine* in the original 1215 Magna Carta, and *twenty-nine* in the 1225 issue, which is also frequently cited.

Over the course of almost six centuries between the signing of Magna Carta in 1215 and the American Founding in the late eighteenth century, the related phrases "law of the land" and "due process of law" came to signify the procedural protections of the English positive law.[10] Sir William **[—51—]** Blackstone, for instance—another renowned English jurist whose work, like Coke's, deeply influenced American legal thought—wrote of "the affirmative acts of parliament wherein justice is directed to be done according to *the law of the land*," and noted that the law of the land "depends not upon the arbitrary will of any judge; but is permanent, fixed, and unchangeable, *unless by authority of parliament*." 1 William Blackstone, Commentaries *141–42 (emphasis added).

An early eighteenth-century case, *Regina v. Paty* (1704) 92 Eng. Rep. 232 (Q.B.), exemplified the prevailing conception of due process in the years leading up to the American Founding. Petitioners in that case sought *habeas corpus*, having been jailed on a warrant issued by the speaker of the House of Commons for allegedly breaching parliamentary privilege. *Id.* at 232–33. They argued that their incarceration violated Magna Carta's assurance that "no man ought to be taken or imprisoned but by the law of the land." *Id.* at 233 (reporting petitioners' objections). Three of the four justices hearing the case denied the petitioners' claim. *Id.* at 232–33 (Gould, J.), 233–35 (Powys, J.), 235–36 (Powell, J.). As reported, Justice Powys addressed petitioners' argument as follows:

> [T]o this I answer, that *lex terrae* is not confined to the common law, but takes in all the other laws, which are in force in this realm; as the civil and canon law, &c. and among the rest, the *Lex Parliamenti*. By the 28 Ed. 3, c. 3, there the words *lex terrae*, which are used in *Mag. Char.* are explained by the words, *due process of law*; and the meaning of the statute is, that all commitments must be by a legal authority. And the law of Parliament is as much a law as any; nay, if there be any superiority, this is a superior law. **[—52—]**

Id. at 234 (emphasis added). The sole dissenting justice, Chief Justice Holt, did not disagree with this premise; he disagreed only as to the legal status of the House of Commons warrant in question. *Id.* at 236–37 (Holt, C.J., dissenting). Thus, the Queen's Bench was unanimous as to this **{-257-}** central point: Magna Carta's guarantee of due process did not extrinsically constrain the legislative process. It required only that legal deprivation be preceded by lawful process, in keeping with the common law or duly enacted legislation.[11]

Early American colonists quickly transplanted this deeply rooted English legal tradition in their own governing documents. Using variations on the longstanding phrases "law of the land" and "due process of law," the colonists brought with them the legal soil of

[10] *See* Ryan C. Williams, *The One and Only Substantive Due Process Clause*, 120 Yale L.J. 408, 428–34 (2010) ("[A]n eighteenth-century reader well-versed in English law would likely have understood both the law of the land and due process of law to require only compliance with duly enacted positive law...."); *Murray's Lessee v. Hoboken Land & Improvement Co.*, 59 U.S. (18 How.) 272, 276 (1856) ("'[D]ue process of law' generally **[—51—]** implies and includes *actor, reus, judex*, regular allegations, opportunity to answer, and a trial according to some settled course of judicial proceedings....").

[11] Some fifty years earlier, in another English case, a *habeas corpus* petitioner similarly invoked the "29th chapter of Magna Carta" and its statutory complement (42 Edw. 3, c. 3) against the Parliamentary warrant on which he had been arrested, asserting that he had "been proceeded against not according to the law of the land." *Case of Captain Streater*, 5 How. St. Tr. 366, 374–86 (1653); *see also supra* n.9 (explaining Magna Carta's chapter-numbering conventions). The judge in that case was perhaps even less impressed with the argument than the Queen's Bench in *Paty's Case*: "[Petitioner's counsel] says, The parliament hath not the power to alter the laws. Why, they have the legislative power, and may alter and order in such sort as they please; they may daily. It is strange a counsellor should say this." *Captain Streater*, 5 How. St. Tr. at 386. "[I]n all justice, an inferior court cannot controul what the Parliament does. . . . We must submit to the legislative power . . . ." *Id.*

their forebears in their first charters and declarations of rights.[12] The same language carried over into [—53—] state constitutions,[13] the Northwest {-258-} Ordinance,[14] and eventually, the Fifth Amendment to the federal Constitution.[15] [—54—]

B.

In light of the text and history behind the Fifth Amendment's Due Process Clause, what bearing (if any) did the clause have on federal courts' exercise of personal jurisdiction or Congress's ability to expand it? There are relatively few cases from our nation's early constitutional history to serve as waypoints on our interpretive voyage.[16] In any event,

---

[12] *See, e.g.*, The New York Charter of Liberties and Privileges ¶ 13 (1683) ("Noe freeman shall be taken and imprisoned or be disseized of his Freehold or Libertye or Free Customes or be outlawed or Exiled or any other wayes destroyed nor shall be passed upon adjudged or condemned But by the Lawfull Judgment of his peers and *by the Law of this province*." (emphasis added)); An Act Declaring What Are the Rights and Priviledges, of His Majesty's Subjects, Inhabiting Within this Province of East New Jersey (1698) (using both "laws of this Province" and "due course of law").

Quite recently, two scholars have suggested that three interrelated legal phrases stemming from Magna Carta and six subsequent Edwardian statutes—"law of the land," "course of law," and "due process of law"—were in use during the Founding era and [—53—] generally understood to mean somewhat different things: "law of the land" referred most broadly to the English positive law; "course of law" meant legal procedure; and "due process of law" referred rather narrowly to the appropriate "process"—that is, "'writs or precepts that go forth' from a court" by which "[g]overnment officials . . . issue orders, impose obligations, or grant rights." *See* Crema & Solum, *supra*, at 461–525; *id.* at 465 (quoting *Process*, 2 Timothy Cunningham, A New and Complete Law-Dictionary (London, 1765)).

[13] *See, e.g.*, Md. Const. of 1776, Declaration and Charter of Rights, art. 21 ("That no freeman ought to be taken, or imprisoned, or disseized of his freehold, liberties, or privileges, or outlawed, or exiled, or in any manner destroyed, or deprived of his life, liberty, or property, but by the lawful judgment of his peers, or by the law of the land."); N.Y. Const. of 1777, art. XIII ("[N]o member of this state shall be disfranchised, or deprived of any the rights or privileges secured to the subjects of this State by this constitution, unless by the law of the land, or the judgment of his peers."). Some states tailored these provisions more narrowly to the criminal context, *e.g.*, Pa. Const. of 1776, Declaration of Rights, art. IX ("That in all prosecutions for criminal offences, a man . . . [cannot] be justly deprived of his liberty except by the laws of the land, or the judgment of his peers."), while others phrased the provisions to provide protections for criminal defendants but did not expressly cabin the scope to only criminal defendants, *e.g.*, Mass. Const. pt. I, art. XII (1870) ("[N]o subject shall be arrested, imprisoned, despoiled, or deprived of his property, immunities, or privileges, put out of the protection of the law, exiled, or deprived of his life, liberty, or estate, but by the judgment of his peers, or the law of the land."). *See* Williams, *supra*, at 437–38 & nn.120–22; *see also* Edward S. Corwin, *The Doctrine of Due Process of Law Before the Civil War*, 24 Harv. L. Rev. 366, 370–71 (1911) (arguing that "the phrase 'law of the land,' which is the universal form in [early state] constitutions, [did not] import any limitation upon legislative power").

[14] Ordinance of 1787: The Northwest Territorial Government, art. II, U.S.C. LV, LVI (2006) ("No man shall be deprived of his liberty or property but by the judgment of his peers, or the *law of the land* " (emphasis added)).

[15] Notes from the constitutional convention or the ratification debates provide little aid in understanding the Fifth Amendment's Due Process Clause. *See* 1 Annals of Cong. 434 (James Madison introducing the amendment), 753–54 (debating other clauses of the amendment, but not the due process clause). "The immediate inspiration for Madison's proposal was most likely Article II of the Northwest Ordinance," which had a provision like those adopted in state constitutions and which Congress passed a few years earlier. *See* Williams, *supra*, at 446 n.156 (quoting Ordinance of 1787: The Northwest Territorial [—54—] Government, U.S.C. LV, LVI (2006)); *see also* Crema & Solum, *supra*, at 506–07 (noting that New York's 1788 ratification letter—the only one to request a "due process of law" guarantee—was likely "the inspiration for James Madison's decision to include the Due Process of Law Clause"). The lack of debate during the Constitution's framing and ratification is likely due to the fact that 'due process' was well understood at the time as having "a precise technical import" that was, well, beyond debate. *See* Alexander Hamilton, *New York Assembly. Remarks on an Act for Regulating Elections* (Feb. 6, 1787), *reprinted in* 4 The Papers of Alexander Hamilton 34–37 (ed. Harold C. Syrett 1962).

[16] The reason for that, in part, is strict Congressional control over venue for federal civil

"[s]howing that Founding-era due process *didn't* limit federal personal jurisdiction is an exercise in proving a negative." Stephen E. Sachs, *The Unlimited Jurisdiction of the Federal Courts*, 106 Va. L. Rev. 1703, 1710 (2020); *see also Elkins v. United States*, 364 U.S. 206, 218 (1960) ("[A]s a practical matter it is never easy to prove a negative . . . ."). And the majority opinion points us to no case whatsoever from our nation's early history to carry its burden in support of its view. Nor could it: the few relevant cases that we have compellingly suggest that due process had precious little to do with jurisdiction.

1.

Consider *Picquet v. Swan*, 19 F. Cas. 609 (C.C.D. Mass. 1828) (No. 11,134). Antonio Picquet, a Frenchman, sued James Swan, an American expatriate in Paris, in federal court. *Id.* at 609. Swan never appeared, so Picquet sought a default judgment. But Justice Joseph Story, riding circuit, **[—55—]** refused to authorize such "upon the ground[] that there ha[d] been no sufficient service of the process." *Id.* at 619. The problem, Justice Story explained, was that Congress had not authorized extraterritorial process *clearly enough* to overcome the "general principle[]," in keeping with the "law of nations," "that a court created within and for a particular territory is bounded in the exercise of its power by the limits of such territory." *Id.* at 611, 615.

But Congress could have done so. Indeed, Congress *had* expressly authorized more expansive nationwide process in special circumstances, and having done so, Congress itself evidently acknowledged **{-259-}** that it legislated against a restrictive background rule that constrained a federal court's process to its own particular district. *Id.* at 611 (noting examples). Relying both on this "understanding of congress" and "on general principles" of law, Justice Story repudiated a default rule that would permit "an alien, who has never been within the United States" to be "served with a summons or other process by any attachment of his property . . . and be bound thereby to appear and submit to the jurisdiction of [an American federal] court." *Id.* at 615.

If there were a moment in the opinion to mention any lurking Fifth Amendment due process issue, this would have been it.[17] Had Justice Story thought that a *constitutional* provision—not merely a defeasible background principle of the law of nations—demanded narrow statutory construction, "it would have been the simplest thing for him to say so." *See United States v. Zubaydah*, 142 S. Ct. 959, 992 (2022) (Gorsuch, J., dissenting). "Not only do universal principles of law preclude extraterritorial federal court **[—56—]** process," Justice Story might very well have written, "but our own Constitution's Fifth Amendment prohibits it as violative of due process of law." He wrote no such thing, of course—and this is the dog that did not bark.[18] *See id.* at 992 (Gorsuch, J., dissenting) (making the same form of argument based on the "clear implication" of judicial silence).

But Justice Story went even further. He *expressly* contemplated the possibility of vast—perhaps unlimited—federal court jurisdiction, provided that Congress clearly said so: "If congress had prescribed such a[n] [expansive] rule, the court would *certainly be bound* to follow it . . . ." *Id.* (emphasis added).[19] Surely Justice Story would not have said that federal courts would "certainly" be "bound" to exercise constitutionally problematic jurisdiction merely upon

suits. *See, e.g.*, Judiciary Act of 1789, ch. 20, § 11, 1 Stat. 73, 79. This necessarily limited the occasions that could give rise to jurisdictional issues.

17 Sachs, *supra*, at 1716 (discussing this part of *Picquet* and noting that if exercising extraterritorial jurisdiction over foreign defendants violated due process—in addition to common-law and general principles of justice—then "now was the time to say so").

18 *See* Sir Arthur Conan Doyle, *The Adventure of Silver Blaze*, Strand Mag., Dec. 1892, at 645, 656–57, 659 (mystery-solving clue was the "curious incident" of the dog that "did nothing in the night-time").

19 *See also Piquet*, 19 F. Cas. at 613 ("*[I]ndependent of some positive provision to the contrary*, no judgment could be rendered in the circuit court against any person, upon whom process could not be personally served within the district." (emphasis added)).

Congressional say-so. To the contrary, he would have flagged any extrinsic constitutional limits on federal court jurisdiction that would have defeated overly expansive Congressional authorization. After all, whenever an act of Congress and the Constitution conflict, courts are obviously bound to obey the latter. *Marbury v. Madison*, 5 U.S. (1 Cranch) 137, 177 (1803).

But again, Justice Story conspicuously said nothing of this sort. And what he *did* say strongly suggests the *absence* of constitutional constraints on Congress's ability to authorize sweeping federal court jurisdiction over even foreign parties residing abroad. In the course of addressing Piquet's argument that the Judiciary Act of 1789 posed no barrier to extraterritorial **[—57—]** process, Justice Story observed that Picquet relied on an unspoken—and incorrect—premise: namely, that absent affirmative statutory *limitations*, the reach of federal process was unbounded. *Piquet*, 19 F. Cas. at 613. Justice Story held the inverse to be true: absent affirmative *authorization*, the reach of American courts' **{–260–}** process was limited by "general principles of law." *Id.* at 611, 615.

As Justice Story saw it, the "general principles of law" that gave rise to the background presumption against extra-territorial process were not a brooding omnipresence that indefeasibly tied Congress's hands. Congress could act to change the background rule. It just had to do so explicitly. Thus, Justice Story wrote that although "repugnant to the general rights and sovereignty of other nations" and not an intention to be presumed lightly from general congressional language, "a subject of England, or France, or Russia, having a controversy with one of our own citizens, *may* be summoned from the other end of the globe to obey our process, and submit to the judgment of our courts," if Congress's intent is "established by irresistible proof." *Id.* at 613. Importantly, Justice Story made no mention of Fifth Amendment due process.

But there *was* a *different* constitutional problem with Picquet's case. Picquet, it turns out, had described Swan as being "of the city of Boston, in the commonwealth of Massachusetts, one of the United States of America, and a citizen *of the said United States*." *Id.* at 609 (emphasis added). He did not, however, specify that Swan was "a citizen *of Massachusetts*, or of any particular state." *Id.* at 616 (emphasis added). And while the Judiciary Act of 1789 gave circuit courts jurisdiction over cases to which "an alien" like Piquet "is a party," 1 Stat. at 78, § 11, Article III of the Constitution "does not extend the judicial power of the United States to [*all* cases in which an alien is a party], but limits it to controversies between *citizens of a state*, and **[—58—]** foreign citizens or subjects." *Picquet*, 19 F. Cas. at 616 (paraphrasing U.S. Const. art. III, § 2) (emphasis added).

So, Justice Story pedantically engaged in constitutional avoidance to dodge this rigidly formalistic Article III problem. He interpreted the Judiciary Act to mean that "if an alien is one party, a citizen of some particular state must be the other party." *Id.* at 616. Picquet's writ technically did not pass muster because Picquet had not (in so many words) denominated his counterparty, Swan, a "citizen of *a state*"—a fact necessary for the court to exercise diversity jurisdiction according to the letter of the Constitution. If Justice Story was so attuned to this picayune constitutional peccadillo, could he really have overlooked a looming Fifth Amendment due process problem?

Justice Story's failure to make any mention of the Fifth Amendment's Due Process Clause would be glaring *if* Justice Story believed that it constrained courts' exercise of personal jurisdiction. But his omission makes perfect sense if the Clause merely required lawful process in keeping with the common law or duly enacted legislation.

2.

Picquet's silence as to due process is telling. And it does not stand alone. Of the other early cases that we have, none lends support to the view that a string of Supreme Court cases interpreting the Fourteenth Amendment from the mid-twentieth century to the present somehow captured the Fifth Amendment's original public meaning. Just the opposite. Other cases both before and after *Picquet* suggest—in what they *do not* say—that Fifth Amendment due process had no bearing on the extent to which Congress could authorize federal courts to issue process internationally.

A decade before *Picquet*, Justice Bushrod Washington (President George Washington's nephew) already aired much the same reasoning while **[—59—]** riding circuit in **{-261-}** Pennsylvania. In *Ex parte Graham*, which Justice Story cited favorably in *Picquet*, Justice Washington determined that a Philadelphia merchant was improperly arrested in Pennsylvania on the basis of a Rhode Island circuit court order. 10 F. Cas. 911, 911, 913 (C.C.E.D. Pa. 1818) (No. 5,657). "In the exercise of a jurisdiction over persons not inhabitants of, or found within the district where the suit is brought," he wrote, "there are difficulties, which, in the opinion of the court, *nothing but an act of congress can remove*." *Id.* at 913 (emphasis added). And furthermore, he added,

> should it be the will of congress to vest in the courts of the United States an extra-territorial jurisdiction in prize causes, over persons and things found in a district other than that from which the process issued, it would seem to be proper, if not absolutely necessary, at the same time to prescribe the mode of executing the process.

Id. Congress had the power; it simply had to exercise it. And if there were any due process limitations on Congress's power, Justice Washington wholly neglected to mention them.

A decade after *Picquet*, the full Supreme Court endorsed Justice Story's circuit court opinion. *Toland*, 37 U.S. (13 Pet.) at 328, 330. In *Toland*, Justice Barbour described "the reasoning in [*Picquet*], generally, as having great force," and announced that the Court had "arrived at the same conclusions" as Justice Story had in *Picquet*. *Id.* at 328, 330. Toland, a Pennsylvanian plaintiff, sued Sprague, an American denizen of Gibraltar, for stiffing him on a shipment of tobacco and miscellaneous other goods. *Id.* at 302. As in *Picquet*, the question raised was "whether the process of foreign attachment can be properly used by the circuit courts of the United States, in cases where the defendant is domiciled abroad, and not found within the district in which the process issues, so that it can be served upon him." *Id.* at 327. Hewing closely to Justice Story's logic in *Picquet*, the Court held that **[—60—]** Congress's Process Acts, read in light of the Judiciary Act, had not expressly given federal courts the authority to cause process to be personally served upon foreign defendants abroad. *Id.* at 327–30. But, just as in *Picquet*, the Court intimated that express, "special authority of law"—"positive legislation"—*could* grant federal courts that power and thus expand their jurisdiction. *Id.* at 329–30.

Foreign attachment was not invariably doomed for lack of congressional authorization. In a couple other early nineteenth-century cases before *Picquet*, Justice Washington, riding circuit in Pennsylvania, refused to uphold challenges to foreign attachments against a Cantonese tea merchant on claims arising out of business conducted in Canton. *See Fisher v. Consequa*, 9 F. Cas. 120, 121–22 (C.C.D. Pa. 1809) (No. 4,816) (finding "no ground to dissolve [a foreign] attachment," as authorized by a colonial Pennsylvanian law, because that law "has received in practice a liberal construction, so as to embrace debts contracted in foreign countries, by persons who never did reside here, and who, of course, could not properly be said to absent themselves; and which debts, neither by the terms of the contract, nor by the removal of the debtor hither, could be said to be owing here"); *id.* at 121 (noting that the state law providing for foreign attachment was a "remedial law" that "ought . . . to be so extended as to remove the mischief [of absconding foreign debtors], and to advance the remedy" for the "injury of the inhabitants of Pennsylvania"); *Willings v. Consequa*, 30 F. Cas. 52, 52–55 (C.C.D. Pa. 1815) (No. 17,766) (failing to mention any jurisdictional issue with a series of suits brought by American **{-262-}** merchants against a Cantonese merchant on parole contracts "made at

Canton" for the delivery of tea to Amsterdam). Perhaps these cases would have come down differently in light of *Picquet* and *Toland*. But, for our purposes, the key thing to notice is that neither opinion so much as hints at a constitutional due process problem. **[—61—]**

From this brief survey of nineteenth-century case law, a couple of things are reasonably clear: First, so long as a statute or rule provides a means of serving process on civil defendants—even defendants halfway across the globe—a federal court could and should exercise jurisdiction, despite offending the law of nations. Second, so long as Congress expressly authorized such expansive process, Fifth Amendment due process does not impose constitutional limits on federal courts' exercise of personal jurisdiction. Just as Magna Carta's *per legem terrae* clause did not tie Parliament's hands in *Paty*'s case, early American cases show—by what they omit—that the Fifth Amendment's Due Process Clause does not restrict Congress's ability to prescribe, by law, the extent to which federal courts may issue process and thereby acquire personal jurisdiction over even foreign defendants a world away.

C.

The majority opinion hopscotches right over all this history, leaping from Runnymede in 1215 A.D. straight to Washington, D.C. in 1945. *Ante* at 14–15. It turns out, as we have seen, that a good bit happened in the intervening seven centuries that is helpful to discerning what the Fifth Amendment's Due Process Clause, as originally understood, had to say about personal jurisdiction. *Supra* sections II.A–B. But on the majority opinion's abridged telling of the story, "the Great Charter of individual liberty, Magna Carta" gave rise to "due process of law," and (seven centuries later), *International Shoe* and its progeny suddenly elucidated how due process protects individual liberty vis-à-vis personal jurisdiction.[20] *Ante* **[—62—]** at 14–15. As the majority **{-263-}** opinion would have it, *International Shoe et al.*—an extensive line of Fourteenth Amendment case law—apply equally to Fifth Amendment due process, because both "Due Process Clauses use the same language and guarantee individual liberty in the same way." *Ante* at 17.

This is anachronism.[21] Case law applying the Fourteenth Amendment construes a

[20] I agree, of course, with the majority opinion that 'due process of law' protects individual liberty. *Ante* at 14–17. But so does federalism. *See, e.g., Planned Parenthood Gulf Coast, Inc. v. Phillips*, 24 F.4th 442, 450 (5th Cir. 2022) ("Federalism recognizes our dual sovereignties—the states and the federal government—and 'secures to citizens the liberties that derive from the diffusion of sovereign power.'" (quoting *Shelby County v.* **[—62—]** *Holder*, 570 U.S. 529, 543 (2013))); *Williams ex rel. J.E. v. Reeves*, 981 F.3d 437, 439 (5th Cir. 2020) (Jones, J., dissenting) ("Federalism, the principle of dual sovereignties, is a bedrock principle of our Founding and a bulwark of individual liberty because it diffuses the exercise of power by governments."). And so does the separation of powers. *See Bond v. United States*, 564 U.S. 211, 222 (2011) ("The structural principles secured by the separation of powers protect the individual as well."). Indeed, our entire system of government was designed to promote ordered liberty. Yet it is equally clear that not every safeguard of our liberty comes in the form of an inflexible right against the state. Federalism, for instance, protects individual liberty *structurally* by preventing dangerous concentrations of power. Among its many other functions, Fifth Amendment due process likewise protects liberty by guaranteeing that deprivations thereof *only* occur pursuant to the law of the land—which includes statutes and rules that define and delimit federal courts' jurisdictional reach. *Cf. Sachs*, Pennoyer *Was Right, supra*, at 1314 ("[D]ue process requires jurisdiction, full stop[] .... To the extent that Congress has enumerated power to determine [federal courts' jurisdiction], the Due Process Clauses won't stand in the way."); *id.*at 1288 (explaining that because (1) "[d]ue process ... forbid[s] deprivations of liberty or property without the lawful judgment of a properly authorized court," and (2) "a court lacking in personal jurisdiction isn't properly authorized [and] can't issue a lawful judgment," therefore, (3) an unlawful judgment from a court lacking personal jurisdiction constitutes a due process violation).

[21] It also begs the question. The Fifth Amendment only protects individual liberty in the same way as the Fourteenth Amendment if we apply the same precedents from the Fourteenth Amendment context in the Fifth Amendment context—which is precisely the conclusion that the statement is supposed to explain. *See ante* at 17

different text directed at a different audience, and which was written at a different time in our history and, accordingly, under different circumstances. To imbue the older Fifth Amendment with newer glosses on **[—63—]** the more recent Fourteenth Amendment is to put new wine in an old wineskin.[22]

1.

The Fourteenth Amendment was drafted more than seventy-five years after Fifth Amendment, and under quite different historical circumstances. As already discussed, recent originalist scholarship indicates that the phrase "due process of law" underwent substantial linguistic drift over the course of the nineteenth century. *See* Crema & Solum, *supra*, at 509–25; *supra* section II.A & n.8. In 1791, the phrase bore a rather technical legal meaning: namely, service of the proper writ—what we call "service of process" today. But by 1868, "due process of law" had come to refer to procedural fairness more generally. For this reason, Supreme Court precedents interpreting "due process of law" as it was used in 1868 are not dispositive of the phrase's usage in the late eighteenth century.

Still, even if we were to assume *arguendo* that the Fifth and Fourteenth Amendment Due Process Clauses share identical *semantic* content, there remain deeper structural state–federal differences that significantly affect the clauses' legal effect.[23] *International Shoe* and its progeny are concerned not only with due process generally, but also with principles of interstate **[—64—]** federalism. And principles of interstate federalism are irrelevant in the *Fifth* Amendment context of *federal* court personal jurisdiction.[24] **{–264–}**

Federalism concerns animate the Supreme Court's jurisprudence on the jurisdictional limitations of the Fourteenth Amendment's Due Process Clause. *See Ford Motor Co. v. Mont. Eighth Jud. Dist. Ct.*, 141 S. Ct. 1017, 1030 (2021) (noting that "principles of 'interstate federalism'" are central to the Court's analysis of Fourteenth Amendment due process limitations on personal jurisdiction (quoting *World-Wide Volkswagen*, 444 U.S. at 293)).[25] To prevent competing assertions of state court jurisdiction within the federal system, the Supreme Court has fashioned rules under the Fourteenth Amendment to limit state courts to the exercise of general personal jurisdiction over corporate defendants that are incorporated in the state, house their "nerve center" there, or are otherwise "essentially at home" in the state.

These federalism concerns are entirely absent in the Fifth Amendment due process

("Because the Due Process Clauses use the same language and guarantee individual liberty in the same way, it makes sense that the standards developed in the Fourteenth Amendment context must govern under the Fifth Amendment.").

[22] *See* Crema & Solum, *supra*, at 528 (stating that it is most consistent with public meaning originalism to hold the view that "the meaning of the two Clauses are independent of one another" and rejecting the reverse-incorporation view that "[r]atification of the Fourteenth Amendment implicitly amended the earlier Fifth Amendment Due Process of Law Clause").

[23] *Cf. Xitronix Corp. v. KLA-Tencor Corp.*, 916 F.3d 429, 442–43 (5th Cir. 2019) (Higginson, J.) (observing that although "the Supreme Court prefers to construe like text alike[,] [i]t has refused to give identical terms the same meaning . . . when contexts and considerations differ," and holding that the lack of "federalism concerns" present in a different context justified a different interpretation of the same statutory language).

[24] The textual differences between the amendments are also reflective of these deeper structural state–federal differences between the clauses' respective applications. *Contrast* U.S. Const. amend. XIV, § 1 ("[N]or shall any *State* deprive any person of life, liberty, or property, without due process of law[.]" (emphasis added)), *with* U.S. Const. amend. V ("No person shall be . . . deprived of life, liberty, or property, without due process of law[.]").

[25] *See also, e.g.*, *Bristol-Myers*, 137 S. Ct. at 1780 ("[R]estrictions on personal jurisdiction 'are more than a guarantee of immunity from inconvenient or distant litigation. They are a consequence of territorial limitations on the power of the respective States.'" (quoting *Hanson v. Denckla*, 357 U.S. 235, 251 (1958))); *id.* at 1788 (Sotomayor, J., dissenting) ("The majority's animating concern, in the end, appears to be federalism . . . .").

context.[26] Since federal law applies uniformly and **[—65—]** what matters, ultimately, is the sovereignty of the United States, federal courts' personal jurisdiction can properly be much more expansive. As the United States Solicitor General recently argued before the Supreme Court, "the United States' constitutional powers and special competence in matters of foreign affairs and international commerce, in contrast to the limited and geographically cabined sovereignty of each of the several States, would permit the exercise of federal judicial power in ways that have no analogue at the state level." Brief of the United States as *Amicus Curiae* at 32, *Ford Motor Co.*, 141 S. Ct. 1017 (Nos. 19-368, 19-369), 2020 WL 1478612.

This all makes sense as a matter of first principles. Personal jurisdiction is anchored to the concept of sovereignty. *Cf. McIntyre*, 564 U.S. at 883–84 ("[J]urisdiction is in the first instance a question of authority rather than fairness[.]"). A court has personal jurisdiction over a defendant when the state, of which the court is an instrumentality, has sovereign power over a defendant, either generally or with respect to a particular transaction or occurrence. The Constitution's Due Process Clauses come into play indirectly. For a defendant to be "deprived of life, liberty, or property" with **[—66—]** the constitutionally **{–265–}** required "due process of law," a properly authorized court must have rendered a lawful judgment in the proper manner. *See* Sachs, Pennoyer *was Right*, *supra*, at 1314; Sachs, *Unlimited Jurisdiction*, *supra*, at 1726–27. A court is only properly authorized when it is enabled to partake of the state's sovereign power over the defendant. Without authority, the court's judgment is "waste paper," and execution of the judgment would be unconstitutional for lack of due process. *See Voorhees v. Jackson*, 35 U.S. (10 Pet.) 449, 469, 475 (1836).

Domestically, Fourteenth Amendment due process thus prevents states from unjustifiably trenching on others' sovereign prerogative to have their courts hear cases concerning defendants residing or doing business within state borders. *See Pennoyer v. Neff*, 95 U.S. 714, 732–33 (1877). Applicable to state action, and here, *interstate* action, the Fourteenth Amendment necessarily carries federalist cargo.

But in the international sphere, our Constitution dictates no particular ordering of relations with other countries. Rather, the Constitution assigns that job to Congress and the President. *See* U.S. Const. art. I, § 8, cl. 3 (congressional power to "regulate Commerce with foreign Nations"); *id.* art. I, § 8, cl. 10 (congressional power to "define and punish Piracies and Felonies committed on the high Seas, and Offenses against the Law of Nations"); *id.* art. I, § 8, cl. 11 (congressional power to "declare War, grant Letters of Marque and Reprisal, and make Rules concerning Captures on Land and Water"); *id.* art. II, § 2, cl. 1 (presidential designation as "Commander in Chief"); *id.* art. II, § 2, cl. 2 (presidential power "to make Treaties"). The Fifth Amendment, as originally understood, imposes no extrinsic constraint on our coordinate branches' exercise of their prerogatives to conduct foreign relations in and through federal courts. Congress can open the federal courthouse door to lawsuits

---

[26] The United States, intervening in a case pending in the Second Circuit, very recently put it this way: **[—65—]**

> [F]ederalism concerns do not apply to the federal government. Unlike a state, which is subject to "territorial limitations" on its power, *World-Wide Volkswagen*, 444 U.S. at 294, the United States has authority "to enforce its laws beyond [its] territorial boundaries," *EEOC v. Arabian American Oil Co.*, 499 U.S. 244, 248 (1991), *superseded by statute on other grounds.* And rather than the limited and mutually exclusive sovereignty of the several states, the federal government's sovereignty includes authority over foreign commerce and foreign affairs. Indeed, the United States' "powers of external sovereignty" and its ability to conduct its relationships with foreign actors are grounded in the United States' status in international law as an independent state. *United States v. Curtiss-Wright Export Corp.*, 299 U.S. 304, 318 (1936).

Brief of Intervenor–Appellant United States at 35–40, *Fuld v. Palestinian Liberation Org.* (2d Cir. June 24, 2022) (Nos. 22-76, 22-496).

against foreign defendants. The Executive can prosecute or sue foreign actors in federal courts. Because the Fifth **[—67—]** Amendment, unlike the Fourteenth Amendment, applies to federal courts and is not shaped by principles of federalism, it poses no barrier.

2.

Dismissing the interstate federalism concerns that animate much of Fourteenth Amendment personal jurisdiction jurisprudence, the majority opinion leans heavily on the "individual liberty interest[s]" protected by due process to justify extending Fourteenth Amendment due process case law into the Fifth Amendment to protect a foreign corporation. *Ante* at 14–17. This amounts to an improper, unhesitating expansion of substantive due process.

As a preliminary matter, it is not entirely clear whether foreign defendants abroad have due process rights in the first place. On the one hand, the Supreme Court recently emphasized that "it is long settled as a matter of American constitutional law that foreign citizens outside U.S. territory do not possess rights under the U.S. Constitution." *Agency for Int'l Dev. v. All. for Open Soc'y Int'l, Inc.*, 140 S. Ct. 2082, 2086 (2020) (citing, *inter alia*, *Boumediene v. Bush*, 553 U.S. 723, 770–71 (2008), *United States v. Verdugo-Urquidez*, 494 U.S. 259, 265–75 (1990), and *Johnson v. Eisentrager*, 339 U.S. 763, 784 (1950) (opinion of Jackson, J.)).[27] On the other hand, as **{-266-}** the majority opinion correctly notes, a slew of Fourteenth Amendment personal jurisdiction cases has, without question, accepted the premise that foreign corporations have due process rights as to personal jurisdiction. *Ante* at 7–8. **[—68—]** Absent Supreme Court resolution of this perplexing problem, the Supreme Court's Fourteenth Amendment cases suggest that, as to personal jurisdiction, foreign actors abroad do have rights under the United States Constitution, anomalous as that may be. *See, e.g.*, *Daimler*, 571 U.S. at 139–41; *Asahi*, 480 U.S. at 114–15.

For better or worse, the words "due process of law" as used in the Fourteenth Amendment have always had, or else have since acquired, a substantive aspect that was never borne by the words *per legem terrae* in Magna Carta or "due process of law" as they were used at the Founding. *See* Williams, *supra*, at 428–34 (tracing the history of "due process" to explain how the Fourteenth Amendment's Due Process Clause is substantive, whereas the Fifth Amendment's is not); *United States v. Vaello Madero*, 142 S. Ct. 1539, 1535 (2022) (Thomas, J., concurring) ("[T]he Fifth Amendment's text and history provide little support for modern substantive due process doctrine.").[28] The liberty interest that the majority opinion expounds is substantive in character. *Ante* at 8, 24 (concluding that non-resident, non-consenting defendants have a liberty-based right of immunity from suit in United States federal court). *See generally* Wendy Collins Perdue, *Sin, Scandal, and Substantive Due Process: Personal Jurisdiction and* Pennoyer *Reconsidered*, 62 Wash. L. Rev. 479 (1987) (parsing the nature of the liberty interest at stake in the personal jurisdiction analysis under the Fourteenth Amendment and concluding that it is "a substantive due process **[—69—]** right").[29] While the Supreme Court has instructed us

---

[27] *See also Hernandez v. United States*, 785 F.3d 117, 126 (5th Cir. 2015) (Jones, J., concurring) ("The Supreme Court [has] held . . . and has reiterated . . . that as a general matter aliens outside the sovereign territory of the United States are not entitled to Fifth Amendment rights." (citing *Johnson*, 339 U.S. at 782–85)); *Castro v. Cabrera*, 742 F.3d 595, 599 n.5 (5th Cir. 2014) (noting that *Johnson* "reject[ed] extraterritorial application of the Fifth Amendment").

[28] *See also Planned Parenthood of Se. Pa. v. Casey*, 505 U.S. 833, 847 (1992) ("[T]he guaranties of due process, though having their roots in Magna Carta's '*per legem terrae*' and considered as procedural safeguards 'against executive usurpation and tyranny,' have in this country become 'bulwarks also against arbitrary legislation.'" (quoting *Poe v. Ullman*, 367 U.S. 497, 541 (1961) (Harlan, J., dissenting))).

[29] *See also* Jay Conison, *What Does Due Process Have to Do with Jurisdiction?*, 46 Rutgers L. Rev. 1071, 1158, 1192–99, 1209 (1994) ("The constitutional law of personal jurisdiction is a hodge-podge of nineteenth-century natural justice and natural rights, early twentieth-century substantive due process, and general law.").

that the Fourteenth Amendment protects substantive personal-jurisdiction rights, it has not done so with the Fifth Amendment, and extending such a right here does not comport with the Fifth Amendment's meaning at the Founding.

Of course, the Supreme Court has ascribed to the Fifth Amendment Due Process Clause a "substantive" facet alongside the Fourteenth Amendment. *See, e.g., United States v. Salerno*, 481 U.S. 739, 746 (1987) (acknowledging "[s]o-called 'substantive due process'" under the Fifth Amendment); *Wright v. United States*, 302 U.S. 583, 607 (1938) (holding that "[t]he phrase 'due process' in the Fifth and Fourteenth Amendments has **{-267-}** long since been expanded beyond its literal meaning of due procedure"). But the Supreme Court has also limited the expansion of "substantive due process" in recent decades. *See Collins v. City of Harker Heights*, 503 U.S. 115, 125 (1992) (expressing "reluctan[ce] to expand the concept of substantive due process because guideposts for responsible decision-making in this unchartered area are scarce and open-ended"). If, as the majority opinion urges, we are to treat Fourteenth Amendment due process jurisprudence as equally applicable to Fifth Amendment due process, we ought to consider its limits, too.

In the seminal case of *Washington v. Glucksberg*, the Court outlined two limiting factors to assess when faced with a novel substantive due process claim: First, the "fundamental right" asserted must be, "objectively, 'deeply rooted in this Nation's history and tradition.'" 521 U.S. 702, 720–21 (1997) (quoting *Moore v. City of E. Cleveland*, 431 U.S. 494, 503 (1977)). And second, **[—70—]** the "asserted fundamental liberty interest" must be amenable to a "careful description." *Id.* at 527 (quoting *Reno v. Flores*, 507 U.S. 292, 302 (1993)). We have adopted and applied this framework. *See Malagon de Fuentes v. Gonzales*, 462 F.3d 498, 505 (5th Cir. 2006) ("To establish a substantive due process violation, a plaintiff must first both carefully describe that right and establish it as 'deeply rooted in this Nation's history and tradition.'" (quoting *Glucksberg*, 521 U.S. at 720–21)); *see also Cantu-Delgadillo v. Holder*, 584 F.3d 682, 687 (5th Cir. 2009).

In considering whether to introduce into Fifth Amendment Due Process Clause jurisprudence a novel substantive due process right to immunity from personal jurisdiction in federal court, we ought to follow the *Glucksberg* framework. And that framework clearly precludes the majority opinion's expansion of substantive due process by "reverse incorporating" Fourteenth Amendment case law into the Fifth Amendment.

Taking the second factor first, the right that the majority opinion asserts in the name of individual liberty is not amenable to a clear and limited description. The Supreme Court itself has wavered in its articulation of the liberty interest at stake in its Fourteenth Amendment cases and has frequently discussed the issue in terms of "interstate federalism."[30] Case **[—71—]** law in this area is highly fact-specific,[31] and the **{-268-}**

---

[30] *Compare, e.g., Ins. Corp. of Ireland v. Compagnie des Bauxites de Guinee*, 456 U.S. 694, 702 (1982) ("The personal jurisdiction requirement recognizes and protects an individual liberty interest."), *with Hanson*, 357 U.S. at 251 (noting that limits on personal jurisdiction are ultimately a "consequence of territorial limitations on the power of the respective States"), *Bristol-Myers*, 137 S. Ct. at 1780 (same), *and World-Wide Volkswagen*, 444 U.S. at 293 ("The sovereignty of each State . . . implie[s] a limitation on the sovereignty of all its sister States . . . ."). Scholars too have puzzled over the exact nature of the right that the Court's twentieth-century Fourteenth Amendment jurisprudence has wrought. *See, e.g.*, Perdue, *Sin, Scandal, and Substantive Due Process*, *supra*, at 511–19; Conison, *supra*, at 1187–1203.

[31] *See, e.g., Polythane Sys. v. Marina Ventures Int'l, Ltd.*, 993 F.2d 1201, 1207 (5th Cir. 1993) ("Determinations regarding the exercise of personal jurisdiction over non-resident defendants must be made on a case-by-case basis."); *Walker v. Newgent*, 583 F.2d 163, 168 (5th Cir. 1978) ("Of necessity, inquiries into whether the exercise of personal jurisdiction is permissible in a particular case are sensitive to the facts of each case."); *accord uBID, Inc. v. GoDaddy Group, Inc.*, 623 F.3d 421, 433 (7th Cir. 2010) ("[T]his is a field of law where the Supreme Court has repeatedly refused opportunities to draw such bright lines.").

Supreme Court itself has recognized that delimiting defendants' "liberty interest[s]" vis-à-vis personal jurisdiction "necessarily requires determinations 'in which few answers will be written in black and white. The greys are dominant and even among them the shades are innumerable.'" *Burger King Corp. v. Rudzewicz*, 471 U.S. 462, 471, 486 n.29 (1985) (quoting *Kulko v. Super. Ct. of Cal.*, 436 U.S. 84, 92 (1978)). It can hardly be said, therefore, that the right of immunity that the majority opinion inserts into the Fifth Amendment is clearly delimited.

The bigger problem for the majority opinion, though, is *Glucksberg*'s central requirement that newly posited substantive due process rights be objectively deeply rooted in our Nation's history and traditions. 521 U.S. at 720–21. As already discussed at length, *supra* sections II.A–B, longstanding English and antebellum American legal history show that "due process of law" was not considered to impose substantive limits on the legislative body's ability to expand or contract courts' jurisdiction. Rather, centuries of tradition appear to support the view that even the most "repugnant" exercise of jurisdiction over defendants halfway across the globe could very well be authorized by Congress. *See Picquet*, 19 F. Cas. at 613. While there is, of course, a considerable tradition rooted in natural law and the law of nations against expansive extraterritorial exercises of jurisdiction, it is not the role of **[—72—]** the federal judiciary to constitutionalize such under the auspices of 'due process.'[32]

3.

Emphasizing defendants' "individual liberty" interests, *ante* at 14–17, raises another big problem for the majority opinion: Both historically and to the present day, foreign *criminal* defendants have been subjected to federal courts' jurisdiction for crimes committed abroad. This, despite the fact that criminal defendants, whose liberty—and very lives—are on the line, are always entitled to the very strictest due process rights. *See infra* section IV.D.1. The majority opinion wholly neglects to explain why it elevates foreign *civil* defendants above criminal defendants for special due-process solicitude in this context.

Since at least the seventeenth century, English and early American jurisprudence has expressly allowed criminal prosecutions of foreign actors for foreign conduct in domestic courts. In the 1820 case of *United States v. Smith*, Justice Story considered English criminal prosecutions from the late 1690s and early 1700s to be "entitled to great consideration" because of the "universal approbation of the legal principles asserted by them." 18 U.S. (5 Wheat.) 153, 177–80 n.h (1820) (citing *Rex v. Dawson*, 13 How. St. Tr. 451, 454–55 (1696), and *Rex v. Kidd*, 14 How. St. Tr. 123, 147, 180–83 (1701)). Notably, he found it "worthy of remark, that in *none* of these indictments was there any averment that the prisoners were British subjects; and most of them were for piracies committed on *foreign* subjects and vessels." *Id.* (emphases **[—73—]** added).[33] In other words, there was **{-269-}** no jurisdictional problem with prosecuting possible foreigners in domestic court for foreign conduct that injured other foreigners. Even when nothing about the criminal, the crime, or the victim has anything to do with the forum, English courts could hear and adjudicate the prosecutions. Due process interposed no jurisdictional barrier.

In contemporary due process jurisprudence, we and our sister circuits merely

---

[32] *Contra* Lea Brilmayer, *Jurisdictional Due Process and Political Theory*, 39 U. Fla. L. Rev. 293, 313 (1987) (noting the dubious judicial "legitimacy of relying upon natural law arguments" to support limits on personal jurisdiction, but suggesting that they might instead, "with some plausibility, be attributed to the constitutional text," which is "after all, . . . rather vague").

[33] Indeed, in the cited 1696 English case of *Rex v. Dawson*, the jury instructions of the presiding Sir Charles Hedges, the Judge of the High Court of Admiralty, indicated that the extraterritorial piracy prosecution was "cognizable of th[at] Court" because "[t]he King of England hath not only an empire and sovereignty over the British seas" for "the punishment of piracy," but also "an undoubted jurisdiction and power" in "the most remote parts of the world." 13 How. St. Tr. at 455.

require that when the United States prosecutes a non-citizen for foreign conduct there must be "a sufficient nexus between the conduct condemned and the United States" such that it "would not be arbitrary or fundamentally unfair" for our courts to enter judgment against the defendant. *See United States v. Rojas*, 812 F.3d 382, 393 (5th Cir. 2016) (quoting *United States v. Lawrence*, 727 F.3d 386, 396 (5th Cir. 2013)); Restatement (Fourth) of Foreign Relations Law § 403(c) & n.4 (2018) (citing sister circuit cases). And "a jurisdictional nexus exists when the aim of that activity"—or perhaps merely its effect—"is to cause harm inside the United States or to U.S. citizens or interests." *See id.* (quoting *United States v. Al Kassar*, 660 F.3d 108 (2d Cir. 2011)); *United States v. Murillo*, 826 F.3d 152, 157 (4th Cir. 2016) ("[I]t is not arbitrary to prosecute a defendant in the United States if his 'actions affected significant American interests'—even if the defendant did not mean to affect those interests." (quoting *United States v. Brehm*, 691 F.3d 547, 552–53 (4th Cir. 2012))). **[—74—]**

So, even though due process today places more limits perhaps on federal courts' *criminal* jurisdiction than there were historically, this "more expansive due process test in criminal cases" is hardly as constraining as the test that the majority opinion today demands in the *civil* context. *Waldman v. Palestine Liberation Org.*, 835 F.3d 317, 340 (2d Cir. 2016). Thus, our sister circuits have unhesitatingly affirmed convictions in federal district court of Somali pirates for murders committed some thirty nautical miles off the Somali coast, a Spanish illegal weapons trafficker for deals brokered in Spain and Beirut, a Colombian taxicab driver for murdering an undercover American DEA special agent in Bogotá, and a leader of an extensive international criminal drug enterprise for funding terrorism—among others. *See, e.g., United States v. Beyle*, 782 F.3d 159, 165–69, 3 Adm. R. 190, 192–97 (4th Cir. 2015) (opinion of Wilkinson, J.); *Al Kassar*, 660 F.3d at 117–20 (opinion of Jacobs, C.J.); *Murillo*, 826 F.3d at 153–54, 156–57; *In re Sealed Case*, 936 F.3d 582, 593–94 (D.C. Cir. 2019) (opinion of Griffith, J.).[34]

The bottom line is this: We can prosecute foreign pirates, arms traffickers, murderers, and terrorists in our federal courts for criminal conduct abroad; we can condemn them to life imprisonment; we can sentence them even to death; but we *cannot*, on the majority opinion's reasoning, subject them to *civil* suit in United States federal courts without violating due process unless they are "at home" here (or the lawsuit arises out of their purposeful **{-270-}** "minimum contacts" with the United States). It is nonsense on stilts to hold that allowing a civil lawsuit against a foreign defendant for foreign conduct violates due process but that a criminal prosecution against the *same* defendant for the *same* foreign conduct does not. **[—75—]** The Fifth Amendment does not compel us to pronounce such absurdity. As originally and subsequently understood, its Due Process Clause imposes no stricter limit on personal jurisdiction in civil cases than it does in criminal prosecutions; indeed, it imposes *no* limit on Congress's ability to extend the range of federal courts' civil process. *See supra* sections II.A–B.

D.

That the Fifth Amendment's Due Process Clause, as originally understood, imposes no direct constraint on Congress's ability to demarcate the extent of federal courts' power is not necessarily to say that it imposes no constraints whatsoever. Indeed, the Due Process Clause secures individual liberty not just by requiring that "courts have jurisdiction, period." Sachs, *Unlimited Jurisdiction*, *supra*, at 1712 (emphasis removed); *supra* n.20. In my view, it also ensures the rule of law more broadly by guarding against arbitrary, capricious, and *ad hoc* government action.

---

[34] *See also, e.g., United States v. Shibin*, 722 F.3d 233, 1 Adm. R. 138 (4th Cir. 2013); *United States v. Dire*, 680 F.3d 446 (4th Cir. 2012); *Brehm*, 691 F.3d at 552–54; *United States v. Ali*, 718 F.3d 929, 944–47 (D.C. Cir. 2013).

In the context of personal jurisdiction, arbitrary modes of process or nefarious allocations of judicial authority designed to frustrate notice and fair hearing would certainly violate the Due Process Clause. *See* Sachs, *Unlimited Jurisdiction*, *supra*, at 1740. Take the fair-hearing requirement, for example. "Congress could violate the due process clause by requiring all federal cases to be tried in Adak (the westernmost settlement in the Aleutian Islands)," because the arbitrarily distant forum "make[s] the offer of adjudication a mirage." *Bd. of Trs., Sheet Metal Workers' Nat. Pension Fund v. Elite Erectors, Inc.*, 212 F.3d 1031, 1036 (7th Cir. 2000) (Easterbrook, J.).

Now consider the fair notice requirement. Imagine a hypothetical Rule 4(k)(3), which says: "Constructive service of process by posting a complaint and summons in pig Latin on the Court-House door on the island of Tobago establishes personal jurisdiction over any named defendant in any federal district court." This too would obviously founder on Fifth **[—76—]** Amendment due process grounds. *See Potter v. Castle Const. Co.*, 355 F.2d 212, 215 (5th Cir. 1966) ("[D]ue process under the Fifth Amendment . . . [requires] 'notice reasonably calculated, under all the circumstances, to apprise interested parties of the pendency of the action and afford them an opportunity to present their objections.'" (quoting *Mullane v. Cent. Hanover Bank & Tr. Co.*, 339 U.S. 306, 314–315 (1950))).

III.

What does the original understanding of the Fifth Amendment's Due Process Clause mean for these cases before us? The answer is really quite simple: the plaintiffs' cases should go forward. Because the Fifth Amendment's Due Process Clause, as originally understood, poses no extrinsic limit on Congress's ability to authorize expansive personal jurisdiction in federal courts, the district court had personal jurisdiction over NYK pursuant to Rule 4(k)(2).[35] **{-271-}**

The majority opinion instead holds that the Fifth Amendment protects corporate defendant NYK against the "concrete burden of 'litigating in a distant or inconvenient forum' and the abstract burden of 'submitting to the coercive power of a [forum] that may have little legitimate interest in the claims in question." *Ante* at 15 (quoting Fourteenth Amendment cases *World-Wide Volkswagen*, 444 U.S. at 291, and *Bristol-Myers*, 137 S. Ct. at 1781). Even if, *arguendo*, we were to accept as true the existence of these substantive due process rights, in what way does litigating **[—77—]** in the United States burden NYK? Put another way, how has NYK's liberty actually been impinged?

Recall that NYK is a massive multinational corporation—one of the largest shipping and logistics companies in the world. And like any modern multinational conglomerate, NYK is the consummate cosmopolitan: the world is its home. Although formally headquartered in Japan, NYK is perfectly at home here in the United States.[36]

NYK is no stranger to our shores: Its ships regularly call on at least thirty United States ports,[37] averaging about 1,500 calls

[35] Incidentally, the majority opinion quotes with approval the D.C. Circuit's suggestion that "[a]pplying consistent personal-jurisdiction standards under the Fifth and Fourteenth amendments is . . . easier to administer." *Ante* at 20–21 (quoting *Livnat v. Palestinian Auth.*, 851 F.3d 45, 55–56 (D.C. Cir. 2017)). Easier still, I would suggest, is simply applying the Fifth Amendment as originally understood.

[36] The majority opinion correctly cites *Daimler* to remind us that, under governing Fourteenth Amendment jurisprudence, the 'at home' test is "an inherently comparative inquiry." *Ante* at 26. And so it is. But, as this case shows, this "comparative inquiry," which focuses as much on a corporate defendant's immaterial foreign contacts as on its contacts with the United States, ultimately means that "too big to fail" multinational corporations are also "too big for general jurisdiction." *See Daimler*, 571 U.S. at 143 (Sotomayor, J., concurring in the judgment); *cf. id.* at 158 ("[This] proportionality approach will treat small businesses unfairly in comparison to national and multinational conglomerates. Whereas a larger company will often be immunized from general jurisdiction in a State on account of its extensive contacts outside the forum, a small business will not be.").

[37] The record indicates that NYK ships called on forty-one separate United States ports located

annually—more than four calls per day. In a highly fragmented market, it ranked tenth in United States containerized export trade and twelfth in import trade in 2013. Part of its fleet does nothing but deliver cars to the United States. NYK operates twenty-seven shipping terminals in United States ports and air-cargo service at six United States airports. Its employees work at the corporation's American subsidiaries. Shares of NYK stock are deposited at the Bank of New York Mellon and may be purchased by United States investors. All told, NYK reaps roughly $1.5 *billion* in annual revenue in North America. **[—78—]**

In the course of doing business here, NYK has frequently availed itself of the American legal system. The corporation has brought at least seventy-eight lawsuits in federal court since 1993 (almost three per year), thus invoking the power of our courts to demand over $22 million in damages.[38] **[—79—]**

along the east coast, west coast, and Gulf of Mexico between March 2019 and February 2020 alone.

[38] *See* Complaint at 3–5, *Nippon Yusen Kabushiki Kaisha v. Riverside Navigation Ltd.*, No. 3:20-CV-00588 (M.D. La. Sept. 8, 2020), ECF No. 1 (breach of contract suit seeking over $3 million); Complaint at 45–47, *Nippon Yusen Kabushiki Kaisha v. Norfolk S. Ry. Co.*, No. 1:20-CV-00858 (D.D.C. Mar. 31, 2020), ECF No. 1 (antitrust violations under the Sherman Act and Clayton Act); Complaint at 30–32, *Nippon Yusen Kabushiki Kaisha v. BNSF Ry. Co.*, No. 1:20-CV-00790 (D.D.C. Mar. 23, 2020), ECF No. 1 (antitrust violations under the Sherman Act and Clayton Act); Complaint at 30–32, *Nippon Yusen Kabushiki Kaisha v. BNSF Ry. Co.*, No. 2:20-CV-02570 (D.N.J. Mar. 10, 2020), ECF No. 1 (antitrust violations under the Sherman Act and Clayton Act); Complaint at 1–3, *Nippon Yusen Kabushiki Kaisha v. Elite Int'l Corp. L.L.C.*, No. 1:18-CV-02640 (N.D. Ill. Apr. 12, 2018), ECF No. 1 (commercial maritime suit seeking almost $80,000); Complaint at 1–2, *Nippon Yusen Kabushiki Kaisha v. Pactrans Air & Sea, Inc.*, No. 1:18-CV-02331 (N.D. Ill. Mar. 30, 2018), ECF No. 1 (commercial maritime suit seeking almost $30,000); Complaint at 3–6, *Nippon Yusen Kabushiki Kaisha v. GSF Nut Co., LLC*, No. 2:17-CV-05614 (C.D. Cal. July 28, 2017), ECF No. 1 (commercial maritime suit seeking over $20,000); Complaint at 5–10, *Nippon Yusen Kabushiki Kaisha v. Multi-Trans Shipping Agency, Inc.*, No. 2:16-CV-09523 (C.D. Cal. Dec. 23, 2016), ECF No. 1 (commercial maritime suit seeking $50,000); Complaint at 4–10, *Nippon Yusen Kaisha v. BNSF Ry. Co.*, No. 2:16-CV-00208 (W.D. Wash. Feb. 11, 2016), ECF No. 1 (commercial dispute seeking damages or indemnification of up to $1 million); Complaint at 4–7, *Nippon Yusen Kaisha v. Global Fresh Inc.*, No. 2:15-CV-08907 (C.D. Cal. Nov. 16, 2015), ECF No. 1 (commercial maritime suit seeking over $35,000); Complaint at 4–7, *Nippon Yusen Kaisha v. Best Global Logistics USA, Inc.*, No. 2:15-CV-08540 (C.D. Cal. Nov. 2, 2015), ECF No. 1 (commercial maritime suit seeking over $675,000); Complaint at 2–3, *Nippon Yusen Kaisha v. Lincoln Gen. Ins. Co.*, No. 1:15-CV-03231 (S.D.N.Y. Apr. 24, 2015), ECF No. 1 (bond dispute seeking almost $67,000); Complaint at 4–8, *Nippon Yusen Kaisha v. Staudt Int'l Servs. Corp.*, No. 2:15-CV- 02516 (C.D. Cal. Apr. 6, 2015), ECF No. 1 (commercial maritime suit seeking over $32,000); Complaint at 3–5, *Nippon Yusen Kabushiki Kaisha v. Kraiem*, No. 2:15-CV-01364 (D.N.J. Feb. 23, 2015), ECF No. 1 (suit to obtain security against state-court judgment for up to $100,000); Complaint at 3–6, *Nippon Yusen Kaisha v. Wesmex Inc.*, No. 8:14-CV- 01910 (C.D. Cal. Dec. 3, 2014), ECF No. 1 (commercial maritime suit seeking about $28,000); Complaint at 3–6, *Nippon Yusen Kaisha v. Am. Recreation Prods.*, No. 2:14-CV-08428 (C.D. Cal. Oct. 30, 2014), ECF No. 1 (commercial maritime suit seeking around $27,000); Complaint at 3–6, *Nippon Yusen Kaisha v. Pandol Assocs. Marketing, Inc.*, No. 2:14-CV-08055 (C.D. Cal. Oct. 17, 2014), ECF No. 1 (commercial maritime suit seeking **[—79—]** about $70,000); Complaint at 3–5, *Nippon Yusen Kaisha v. Infinity 8 Int'l Trade LLC*, No. 2:14-CV-03419 (C.D. Cal. May 2, 2014), ECF No. 1 (commercial maritime suit seeking approximately $57,000); Complaint at 2–4, *Nippon Yusen Kaisha v. Arch Ins. Co.*, No. 1:14- CV-01369 (S.D.N.Y. Feb. 28, 2014), ECF No. 2 (bond dispute seeking around $75,000); Complaint at 1–2, *Nippon Yusen Kaisha v. Latvian Am. Shipping Line Inc.*, No. 1:13-CV-04592 (S.D.N.Y. July 2, 2013), ECF No. 1 (breach of contract suit seeking almost $25,000); Complaint at 3–4, *Nippon Yusen Kaisha v. Millenium Plus, Inc.*, No. 2:13-CV-03029 (C.D. Cal. Apr. 30, 2013), ECF No. 1 (commercial maritime suit seeking about $32,000); Complaint at 4–6, *Nippon Yusen Kaisha v. Agape Int'l Shipping*, No. 2:12-CV-10068 (C.D. Cal. Nov. 26, 2012), ECF No. 1 (commercial maritime suit seeking about $42,000); Complaint at 1–2, *Nippon Yusen Kaisha v. Shiplane Transport, Inc.*, No. 2:12-CV-05951 (D.N.J. Sept. 21, 2012), ECF No. 1 (breach of contract suit seeking about $62,000); Complaint at 4–6, *Nippon Yusen Kaisha v. Air Sea Cargo Network, Inc.*, No. 2:12-CV-07790 (C.D. Cal. Sept. 11, 2012), ECF No. 1 (commercial maritime suit seeking about $17,000); Complaint at

1–2, *Nippon Yusen Kaisha v. FIL Lines USA Inc.*, No. 1:12-CV-06643 (S.D.N.Y. Aug. 30, 2012), ECF No. 1 (commercial maritime suit seeking almost $48,000); Complaint at 3–5, *Nippon Yusen Kaisha v. Cargo Int'l Forwarders & NVOCC, Inc.*, No. 2:12-CV-07266 (C.D. Cal. Aug. 23, 2012), ECF No. 1 (commercial maritime suit seeking about $22,000); Complaint at 3–5, *Nippon Yusen Kaisha v. Sunshine Shipping, Inc.*, No. 2:12-CV- 05473 (C.D. Cal. June 22, 2012), ECF No. 1 (commercial maritime suit seeking over $151,000); Complaint at 3–5, *Nippon Yusen Kaisha v. TJD Int'l, Inc.*, No. 2:11-CV-07301 (D.N.J. Dec. 16, 2011), ECF No. 1 (breach of contract suit seeking over $110,000); Complaint at 1–3, *Nippon Yusen Kaisha v. Shiplane Transport, Inc.*, No. 1:11-CV-06327 (S.D.N.Y. Sept. 9, 2011), ECF No. 1 (indemnity suit seeking $60,000); Complaint at 4–10, *Nippon Yusen Kaisha v. BNSF Ry. Co.*, No. 2:11-CV-00978 (W.D. Wash. June 10, 2011), ECF No. 1 (commercial dispute seeking damages or indemnification of around $312,000); Complaint at 1–2, *Nippon Yusen Kaisha v. Summer Breeze Transport, Inc.*, No. 1:10-CV-22185 (S.D. Fla. July 2, 2010), ECF No. 1 (commercial maritime dispute seeking almost $287,000); Complaint at 5–10, *Nippon Yusen Kaisha v. BNSF Ry. Co.*, No. 2:10-CV-03190 (C.D. Cal. Apr. 28, 2010), ECF No. 1 (commercial dispute seeking damages or indemnification of around $3.16 million); Complaint at 1–2, *Nippon Yusen Kaisha v. Wing Lee Dev., Inc.*, No. 1:09-CV-09521 (S.D.N.Y. Nov. 16, 2009), ECF No. 1 (commercial maritime dispute seeking $24,540); Complaint at 1–2, *Nippon Yusen Kaisha v. Nick's Int'l Shipping, Inc.*, No. 1:09-CV-09520 (S.D.N.Y. Nov. 16, 2009), ECF No. 1 (commercial maritime dispute seeking just over $95,000); Complaint at 2, *Nippon Yusen Kaisha v. Triship Glob. Logistics, Inc.*, No. 1:09-CV-09519 (S.D.N.Y. Nov. 16, 2009), ECF No. 1 (admiralty suit seeking over $38,000); Complaint at 1–2, *Nippon Yusen Kaisha v. United Trans-Trade, Inc.*, No. 1:09-CV-09518 (S.D.N.Y. Nov. 16, 2009), ECF No. 1 (commercial maritime dispute seeking around $28,000); Complaint at 4–6, *Nippon Yusen Kaisha v. 817 Rolls Knitted Fabric 100% Poly Charmeuse*, No. 1:09-CV-05974 (S.D.N.Y. June 30, 2009), ECF No. 1 (*in rem* admiralty suit seeking around $85,000); Complaint at 1–3, *Nippon Yusen* **[—80—]** *Kaisha v. Baltic Auto Shipping, Inc.*, No. 1:09-CV-05698 (S.D.N.Y. June 22, 2009), ECF No. 1 (suit seeking around $250,000); Complaint at 3–5, *Nippon Yusen Kaisha v. Cargo Int'l Forwarders & NVOCC, Inc.*, No. 1:09-CV-05697 (S.D.N.Y June 22, 2009), ECF No. 1 (breach of contract suit seeking about $50,000); Complaint at 1–3, *Nippon Yusen Kaisha v. Green Vanderbilt Corp.*, No. 1:09-CV-04464 (S.D.N.Y. May 8, 2009), ECF No. 1 (breach of contract suit seeking around $85,000); Complaint at 1–3, *Nippon Yusen Kaisha v. JJB Trucking & Shipping Servs. Corp.*, No. 1:09-CV-04444 (S.D.N.Y. May 8, 2009), ECF No. 1 (breach of contract suit seeking around $14,000); Complaint at 1–3, *Nippon Yusen Kaisha v. Fish On Bait Co., LLC*, No. 1:09-CV-04443 (S.D.N.Y. May 8, 2009), ECF No. 1 (breach of contract suit seeking about $100,000); Complaint at 1–3, *Nippon Yusen Kaisha v. Seaspeed Overseas Shipping Co.*, No. 1:09-CV-04442 (S.D.N.Y. May 8, 2009), ECF No. 1 (breach of contract suit seeking roughly $18,000); Complaint at 1, *Nippon Yusen Kaisha v. Relampago Express Transportes*, No. 1:09-CV-04439 (S.D.N.Y. May 8, 2009), ECF No. 1 (breach of contract suit seeking around $35,000); Complaint at 1–3, *Nippon Yusen Kaisha Line v. EMU Lines PVT LTD.*, No. 1:09-CV-00665 (S.D.N.Y. Jan. 23, 2009), ECF No. 1 (breach of contract suit seeking around $33,000); Complaint at 2–4, *Nippon Yusen Kaisha v. TJD Int'l Inc.*, No. 2:08-CV-06349 (D.N.J. Dec. 24, 2008), ECF No. 1 (admiralty suit seeking around $500,000); Complaint at 2–4, *Nippon Yusen Kaisha v. Fortune Ocean Shipping Ltd.*, No. 1:08-CV-09887 (S.D.N.Y Nov. 14, 2008), ECF No. 1 (commercial maritime suit seeking about $200,000); Amended Complaint at 2–6, *Nippon Yusen Kaisha v. N. China Shipping Ltd. BHM*, No. 1:08-CV-09850 (S.D.N.Y Nov. 13, 2008), ECF No. 3 (commercial maritime suit seeking over $293,000); Complaint at 7–12, *NYK Line (N. Am.) Inc. & Nippon Yusen Kabushiki Kaisha v. New Amera Transit, Inc.*, 2:08-CV-05505 (D.N.J. Nov. 6, 2008), ECF No. 1 (breach of contract suit seeking $265,000); Complaint at 1–2, *Nippon Yusen Kaisha v. Plastic Nation Inc.*, No. 1:08-CV-06736 (S.D.N.Y July 29, 2008), ECF No. 1 (breach of contract suit seeking over $23,000); Complaint at 2–5, *Nippon Yusen Kaisha v. McDonough Indus. LLC*, No. 1:08-CV-03444 (S.D.N.Y Apr. 8, 2008), ECF No. 1 (breach of contract suit seeking attachment of up to $1.3 million); Complaint at 7–12, *NYK Line (N. Am.) Inc. & Nippon Yusen Kabushiki Kaisha v. BNSF Ry. Co.*, 2:08-CV-00320 (W.D. Wash. Feb. 22, 2008), ECF No. 1 (breach of contract suit seeking at least $130,000); Complaint at 1–2, *Nippon Yusen Kaisha v. Am. Heritage Furniture, Inc.*, No. 1:08-CV-00488 (S.D.N.Y Jan. 18, 2008), ECF No. 1 (breach of contract suit seeking about $30,000); Complaint at 1–2, *Nippon Yusen Kaisha v. Q.P.S. Materials, Inc.*, No. 1:08-CV-00487 (S.D.N.Y Jan. 18, 2008), ECF No. 1 (breach of contract suit seeking about $23,000); Complaint at 1–2, *Nippon Yusen Kaisha v. Yanfield Int'l Corp.*, No. 1:08-CV-00486 (S.D.N.Y Jan. 18, 2008), ECF No. 1 (breach of contract suit seeking about $25,000); Complaint at 1–2, *Nippon Yusen Kaisha v. Distrib. I (USA), Inc.*, No. 1:08-CV-00484 (S.D.N.Y Jan. 18, 2008), ECF No. 1 (breach of contract suit seeking almost $100,000); Complaint

[—80—] [—81—] [—82—] It has quite regularly defended itself **{-274-}** from suit here as well[39]—likely at its own invitation: NYK's bills of lading and sea waybills affirmatively select the Southern District of New York as the exclusive forum for all disputes thereunder.

It strains belief to suggest that the United States is really "a distant or inconvenient forum" for NYK or that NYK is abstractly burdened by "submitting to" United States federal courts' "coercive power." For one thing,

---

at 2, *Nippon Yusen Kaisha v. Freight Servs. of W. Coast Corp.*, No. 1:07-CV-07840 (S.D.N.Y Sept. 5, 2007), ECF No. 1 (breach of contract suit seeking just shy of $60,000); Complaint at 1–2, *Nippon Yusen Kaisha v. Fresh W. Exch.*, No. 1:07-CV-07839 (S.D.N.Y **[—81—]** Sept. 5, 2007), ECF No. 1 (breach of contract suit seeking over $36,000); Complaint at 1–2, *Nippon Yusen Kaisha v. Anderson Int'l Global, LLC*, No. 1:07-CV-07838 (S.D.N.Y Sept. 5, 2007), ECF No. 1 (breach of contract suit seeking around $170,000); Complaint, *Nippon Yusen Kaisha v. BNSF Ry. Co.*, No. 2:07-CV-02896 (C.D. Cal. May 2, 2007), ECF No. 1 (docket indicates demand for approximately $225,000); Complaint, *Nippon Yusen Kaisha v. BNSF Ry. Co.*, No. 2:07-CV-02417 (C.D. Cal. Apr. 11, 2007), ECF No. 1 (docket indicates demands for around $13,000); Complaint at 1–2, *Nippon Yusen Kaisha v. Zircon Logistics, Inc.*, No. 1:07-CV-02874 (S.D.N.Y. April 10, 2007), ECF No. 1 (breach of contract suit seeking $135,000); Complaint at 1–2, *Nippon Yusen Kaisha v. Air 7 Seas Trans Logistics*, No. 1:07-CV-02873 (S.D.N.Y Apr. 10, 2007), ECF No. 1 (breach of contract suit seeking $75,000); Complaint at 4–10, *Nippon Yusen Kaisha v. BNSF Ry. Co.*, 3:07-CV-00563 (N.D. Cal. Jan. 26, 2007), ECF No. 1 (commercial dispute seeking damages or indemnification of over $255,000); Amended Complaint at 5–10, *Nippon Yusen Kaisha v. BASF Corp.*, 3:06-CV-03704 (N.D. Cal. June 9, 2006), ECF 43 (suit seeking to avoid or limit liability for loss of goods in transit); Complaint at 6–11, *Nippon Yusen Kaisha v. BNSF Ry. Co.*, 3:05-CV-03609 (N.D. Cal. Sept. 7, 2005), ECF No. 1 (commercial dispute seeking damages or indemnification of over $6 million); Complaint, *Nippon Yusen Kaisha v. Union Pac. Ry. Co.*, 2:04-CV-08861 (C.D. Cal. Oct. 26, 2004), ECF No. 1; Complaint, *NYK Line (N. Am.) Inc. & Nippon Yusen Kaisha v. BNSF Ry. Co.*, 2:00-CV-02728 (C.D. Cal. Mar. 16, 2000), ECF No. 1 (docket indicates demand for around $411,000); Complaint, *Nippon Yusen Kaisha v. Bulktrans (Eur.) Corp.*, No. 1:00-CV-00573 (S.D.N.Y Jan. 27, 2000), ECF No. 1 (docket indicates demand for $500,000); Complaint, *Nippon Yusen Kaisha v. Kellaway Transp., Inc.*, No. 2:99-CV-01441 (D.N.J. Mar. 29, 1999), ECF No. 1; Complaint, *Trans-Pac. Policing Agreement & Nippon Yusen Kaisha, Ltd. v. U.S. Customs Serv.*, No. 1:97-CV-02188 (D.D.C. Sept. 22, 1997), ECF No. 1; Complaint, *Nippon Yusen Kaisha v. Velsicol Chem.*, 2:97-CV-03176 (C.D. Cal. Apr. 30, 1997), ECF No. 1 (docket indicates demand for roughly $168,000); Complaint, *Nippon Yusen Kaisha v. Atlantic Ro/Ro Carriers of Tex., Inc.*, No. 2:96-CV-04020 (D.N.J. Aug. 22, 1996), ECF No. 1 (docket indicates demand for around $2,000); Complaint, *Nippon Yusen Kaisha v. W. Ave. Serv.*, No. 1:96-CV-06137 (S.D.N.Y. Aug. 14, 1996), ECF No. 1 (docket indicates a demand for approximately $14,000); Complaint, *Nippon Yusen Kaisha v. Jeri-Jo Inc.*, 2:95-CV-06287 (D.N.J. Dec. 18, 1995), ECF No. 1 (docket indicates a demand of around $548,000); Complaint, *Nippon Yusen Kaisha v. Kellaway Transp. Inc.*, 2:95-CV-04349 (D.N.J. Aug. 16, 1995), ECF No. 1 (docket indicates a demand for approximately $131,000); Complaint, *Nippon Yusen Kaisha Line v. Packard Bell*, 2:94-CV-03484 (C.D. Cal. May 26, 1994), ECF No. 1; Complaint, *Am. President Lines, Ltd. & Nippon Yusen Kaisha, et al. v. Kirch Indus. Co.*, No. 1:93-CV-00497 (D.D.C. Mar. 9, 1993), ECF No. 1; *see also* Third-Party Complaint, *Tokio Marine & Fire Ins. Co., Ltd. v. M/V Joyous Age*, No. 1:03-CV-06346 (S.D.N.Y. Aug. 22, 2003), ECF 4; Third-Party Complaint, *Thyssen Krupp Steel v. M/V Andorinha*, No. 1:01-CV-04305 (S.D.N.Y. May 21, 2001), ECF No. 10; Third-Party Complaint, *Talatala v. Nippon Yusen Kaisma*, No. 1:94-CV-00340 (D. Haw. May 5, 1994), ECF No. 19 (party name spelled "*Kaisma*" rather **[—82—]** than "*Kaisha*" on the docket); Third-Party Complaint, *Okura & Co. (Am.), Inc. v. M.V. Yamataka Maru*, No. 1:92-CV-03783 (S.D.N.Y. May 26, 1992), ECF No. 6; Complaint at 4–5, *Nippon Yusen Kaisha v. Bankers Ins. Co.*, No. 8:19-CV-01343 (M.D. Fla. June 3, 2019), ECF No. 1-3 (removed from state court).

As matters of public record, complaints filed in federal court are properly subject to judicial notice. *Ruiz v. Brennan*, 851 F.3d 464, 468 (5th Cir. 2017) ("[W]e may take judicial notice of matters of public record.").

[39] *Ante* at 4 n.4 (citing complaints filed against NYK in federal court). NYK also pleaded guilty in 2014 to criminal antitrust charges for its conduct in shipping cargo "to and from the United States and elsewhere." Information, *United States v. Nippon Yusen Kabushiki Kaisha* (D. Md. 2014) (alleging corporate violations of 15 U.S.C. § 1 (Sherman Act)); Plea Agreement at 2, 6, *United States v. Nippon Yusen Kabushiki Kaisha*, 1:14-CR-00612 (D. Md. Mar. 11, 2015), ECF No. 20 (agreeing to a fine of $59.4 million).

it is hardly too distant or inconvenient for NYK to do business here; why, then, is litigation here too distant and inconvenient? It is hardly too distant or inconvenient for NYK to litigate here as a plaintiff; why, then, is it too distant and inconvenient as a defendant? NYK clearly welcomes the opportunity **{-275-}** to take advantage of the United States' robust marketplace, an economy fostered by the rule of law that our judicial system ensures, and the corporation freely avails itself of federal courts as a plaintiff. Can NYK really complain about submitting to federal judicial power when NYK enjoys the security that that power provides? And can NYK really argue that the United States has "little legitimate interest" in adjudicating claims brought **[—83—]** under United States federal law by United States servicemen and their families?

The cases before us present no due process problems. Plaintiffs properly brought suit pursuant to Rule 4(k)(2). NYK has no substantive due process right to be immune from suit here. And even if it did, none of its supposed liberty interests have actually been infringed. The Fifth Amendment's Due Process Clause poses no obstacle, so these suits should proceed.[40]

IV.

The tail should not wag the dog any more than the bow should turn the ship. While the anticipated repercussions of a constitutional ruling should not drive the ultimate determination on the merits, it is nonetheless worth calling attention to the severe and anomalous consequences of today's majority holding. First, it will render most of Rule 4(k)(2)'s intended **[—84—]** applications unconstitutional, thereby reducing the statutorily authorized rule[41] to a virtual nullity.[42] Second, it will similarly choke Rule 4(k)(1)(C), which "establishes personal jurisdiction over a defendant" by "[s]erving a summons or filing a waiver of service . . . when authorized by a federal statute." As a result, American victims of terrorist attacks abroad and Cuban refugees who have lost everything to Communist confiscation will not be able, meaningfully, **{-276-}** to avail themselves of remedial federal legislation. And finally, today's holding also brings about a couple of anomalies: (1) *civil* foreign defendants now have more due process rights than *criminal* foreign defendants; and (2) *foreign* corporations now receive more due process protection than *domestic* corporations under our own Constitution.

---

[40] NYK has not alleged any other due process issues with these cases, and nor could it: The applicable Federal Rules of Civil Procedure are in no way arbitrary or calculated to frustrate notice. Rule 4(k)(2) reasonably addresses the problem that would arise when a plaintiff has federal law claims against a "defendant [who] is not subject to jurisdiction in any state's courts of general jurisdiction." In such a case, it would be absurd if United States *federal* law claims (brought by United States servicemen, no less) could not be heard in United States *federal* court, simply because no individual *state*'s courts had jurisdiction pursuant to *state* long-arm statutes or in keeping with the strictures of the Fourteenth Amendment (which apply to the *states*). *See* Fed. R. Civ. P. 4(k)(1)(A). Rule 4(k)(2) solves the problem by specifying that "serving a summons [per Rule 4(f)] or filing a waiver of service [per Rule 4(d)] establishes [a federal district court's] personal jurisdiction over a defendant" in such a case. In this case, no state had jurisdiction to hear the federal law claims of the plaintiff servicemen and their bereaved families. So, they filed their complaints in federal court, and they successfully obtained waivers of service from NYK in Tokyo. NYK received ample notice of the pending lawsuits. And evidently, this multinational corporate defendant had no more trouble getting a fair hearing here in federal court as a defendant than it has had prosecuting dozens of civil cases as a plaintiff in federal court.

[41] Rule 4(k) was adopted under the Judicial Improvements and Access to Justice Act of 1988. *See* Pub. L. No. 100-702, § 401, 102 Stat. 4642, 4648 (codified as amended at 28 U.S.C. § 2072).

[42] *Cf. Sveen v. Melin*, 138 S. Ct. 1815, 1831 (2018) (Gorsuch, J., dissenting) ("The judicial power to declare a law unconstitutional should never be lightly invoked."); *Lamar Outdoor Advert. v. Miss. St. Tax Comm'n*, 701 F.2d 314, 333 (5th Cir. 1983) ("We recognize that our power to strike down state laws as unconstitutional is strong medicine; we do not administer it lightly."); *El Paso & Ne. Ry. Co. v. Gutierrez*, 215 U.S. 87, 96 (1909) ("It is hardly necessary to repeat what this court has often affirmed, that an act of Congress is not to be declared invalid except for reasons so clear and satisfactory as to leave no doubt of its unconstitutionality.").

A.

Today's majority holding guts Rule 4(k)(2) of virtually all of its intended applications. Instead of examining the Fifth Amendment Due Process Clause's original meaning, the *en banc* court simply rides the wake of inapposite Supreme Court Fourteenth Amendment jurisprudence. Promulgated in 1993 in response to the Supreme Court's decision in *Omni Capital Int'l, Ltd. v. Rudolf Wolff & Co., Ltd.*, 484 U.S. 97 (1987), Rule 4(k)(2) was designed to authorize federal courts to exercise personal jurisdiction over **[—85—]** federal claims that could not otherwise be heard in any state court to the fullest extent consistent with the Constitution. If the Fifth Amendment mirrors the Fourteenth Amendment, Rule (4)(k)(2)'s range of applications nearly vanishes.

Consider first general jurisdiction. The Supreme Court has said that the Fourteenth Amendment only allows the exercise of general personal jurisdiction over a foreign defendant who is "essentially at home" in the United States—an "exceptional case" very seldom encountered in real life. *Daimler*, 571 U.S. at 139 & n.19 (citing *Perkins v. Benguet Consol. Mining Co.*, 342 U.S. 437, 447–48 (1952)). Rarely is a foreign-domiciled corporation deemed "at home" in the United States. Yet these foreign-domiciled corporations are precisely the prospective defendants to whom Rule 4(k)(2) was thought to apply.

The majority opinion suggests *specific* jurisdiction would remain available under Rule 4(k)(2). *Ante* at 22–23 & n.27. Maybe so. A few occasional applications of the Rule could conceivably arise, for instance, when claims arise in states with long-arm statutes that stop short of the constitutional maximum,[43] or when cyber-injuries affect the United States as **[—86—]** a whole and no state in particular. But, as with general jurisdiction, it would still be the "exceptional case."

Because the majority opinion lashes together the Fifth and Fourteenth Amendment personal jurisdiction standards without distinction, Fourteenth Amendment **{-277-}** limitations on *specific* jurisdiction now apply likewise to Fifth Amendment cases. And the Supreme Court has said that for courts to have specific jurisdiction to entertain certain claims, the Fourteenth Amendment requires the underlying injury to have occurred, at least in part, in the forum. *Bristol-Myers*, 137 S. Ct. at 1781–82 ("In order for a court to exercise specific jurisdiction over a claim, there must be an 'affiliation between the forum and the underlying controversy, principally, [an] activity or an occurrence that takes place in the forum State.'" (quoting *Goodyear Dunlop Tires Operations, S.A. v. Brown*, 564 U.S. 915, 919 (2011))); *cf. Ford Motor Co.*, 141 S. Ct. at 1028, 1030–31 (upholding specific jurisdiction in states where Ford "systematically served a market . . . for the very vehicles that the plaintiffs allege malfunctioned and injured them in those States").

Applying *Bristol-Myers*'s forum-injury requirement would squelch federal courts'

[43] Specifically, Rule 4(k)(2) could apply where: (1) a defendant has minimum contacts with a forum state that has a long-arm statute that stops short of the constitutional limit; (2) the defendant's contacts fall between the constitutional and statutory lines; and (3) no other state forum is available.

In our circuit, such applications of the Rule could arguably only arise out of Mississippi, which has a somewhat limited long-arm statute. *Compare* Miss. Stat. § 13-3-57 (2003) (Mississippi long-arm statute); *Gross v. Chevrolet Country, Inc.*, 655 So. 2d 873, 877–78 (Miss. 1995) (analyzing statutory factors to determine that a nonresident corporation was "not amenable to jurisdiction in Mississippi pursuant to [the state] long arm statute"), *with* Tex. Civ. Prac. & Rem. Code § 17.042 (2001) (Texas long-arm statute); *Searcy v. Parex Res., Inc.*, 496 S.W.3d 58, 66 (Tex. 2016) ("The Texas long arm statute provides for personal jurisdiction that extends to the limits of the United States Constitution, and so federal due process requirements shape the contours of Texas courts' **[—86—]** jurisdictional reach."), *and* La. R.S. § 13:3201 (Louisiana long-arm statute); *Bridges v. Autozone Props., Inc.*, 900 So. 2d 784, 803 (La. 2005) ("[T]he limits of Louisiana's long-arm statute [are] coextensive with the limits of constitutional Due Process.").

exercise of *specific* jurisdiction over American injuries sustained abroad, just as *Daimler*'s "at home" test would squash federal courts' exercise of *general* jurisdiction over foreign corporate defendants doing substantial, considerable business in the United States. As a result, Rule 4(k)(2)—a congressionally authorized rule—will indeed be rendered virtually a nullity—and this as a result of casual reliance on inapposite Supreme Court precedent. *Cf. United States v. Morrison*, 529 U.S. 598, 607 (2000) ("Due respect for the decisions of a coordinate branch of **[—87—]** Government demands that we invalidate a congressional enactment *only upon a plain showing* that Congress has exceeded its constitutional bounds." (emphasis added)).

B.

Today's decision also threatens to sink our ability to hear many cases sounding in admiralty—an area of law in which we have long been empowered to adjudicate claims involving far-flung parties aboard vessels in far-flung places on the seven seas. Federal courts hold a unique role in admiralty to define causes of action and to hear cases arising in the world's common areas—the high seas—as the Supreme Court has made clear. *See Fitzgerald v. U.S. Lines Co.*, 374 U.S. 16, 20–21 (1963) ("Article III of the Constitution vested in the federal courts jurisdiction over admiralty and maritime cases . . . . This Court has long recognized its power and responsibility in this area and has exercised that power where necessary to do so."); *The Belgenland*, 114 U.S. 355, 368–69 (1885) (noting that there is "no good reason" why a party injured on the high seas "should ever be denied justice in our courts," even when both parties are "foreigners"); *cf. The Dutra Group v. Batterton*, 139 S. Ct. 2275, 2278, 7 Adm. R. 43, 43–44 (2019) (discussing the history of federal courts "enlarged and liberal" maritime and admiralty jurisprudence (quoting *Brown v. Lull*, 4 F. Cas. 407, 409 (C.C.D. Mass. 1836) (No. 2,018) (Story, J.))).

We and our sister circuits regularly hear cases involving diverse international parties arising out of events occurring on waters far away. *See, e.g., Liaw Su Teng v. Skaarup Shipping Corp.*, 743 F.2d 1140, 1142–43, 1145–46 (5th Cir. 1984) (applying *The Belgenland* to "retain jurisdiction" over an admiralty suit involving Taiwanese and Hong Kong sailors on a Liberian ship that crashed with a Greek ship off the coast of Algeria), *overruled on other grounds by In re Air Crash Disaster Near New Orleans, La. on July 9, 1982*, 821 **[—88—]** F.2d 1147 (5th Cir. 1987); **{-278-}** *Fitzgerald v. Texaco, Inc.*, 521 F.2d 448, 450–54 (2d Cir. 1975) (mentioning no jurisdictional issue in a lawsuit between German and Panamanian interests as to vessels shipwrecked in the English channel); *id.* at 455 (Oakes, J., dissenting) (noting that because the court was "dealing . . . with a transitory action, a collision occurring on the high seas, albeit in the English Channel, between vessels of foreign registry, with foreign nationals as plaintiffs ... we have jurisdiction"); *Gkiafis v. S.S. Yiosonas*, 387 F.2d 460, 462 (4th Cir. 1967) ("A suit in admiralty between foreigners is within the jurisdiction of the District Courts of the United States. Not only does jurisdiction exist, but it will be exercised 'unless special circumstances exist to show that justice would be better subserved by declining it.'" (quoting *The Belgenland*, 114 U.S. at 367)).

Although the present case involves a collision occurring in Japanese territorial waters, the majority holding could impact future cases arising on the briny deep far from any other sovereign. Because the *en banc* majority declines to plumb the Fifth Amendment's original public meaning, we are now stuck with an atextual, ahistorical rule that might constrict our ability even to hear cases that arise beyond any nation's territorial power. Suppose, for instance, the collision that spawned this case took place as the ships were passing Hawaii—but just outside of United States territorial waters. Even though the claims would have arisen on the high seas, and indeed, much closer to the United States than Japan, the holding of the majority opinion would still require the plaintiffs to go all the way to Japan to pursue their claims because NYK is not "at home" in the United States. This should give us pause.

C.

This may seem like an academic debate about the quirks of civil procedure. But consider what this means in the real world. As Judge **[—89—]** Higginson rightly observes, today's holding will "redirect United States citizen-plaintiffs—asserting United States federal law claims and invoking United States federal law service of process—offshore, often to countries with far less developed legal systems than Japan." *Post* at 99. In significantly curtailing plaintiffs' recourse to our nation's federal courts, the majority's decision effectively neuters Congress of its ability to use our own legal system and its well-established rule of law to help right the most grievous wrongs committed against Americans abroad.

Look no further than the *amicus* brief submitted by victims of the Castro regime. In response to Castro's terrorist acts, Congress passed and President Clinton signed the Cuban Liberty and Democratic Solidarity (LIBERTAD) Act of 1996. Pub. L. No. 104-114, 110 Stat. 785 (codified at 22 U.S.C. § 6021, *et seq.*) [hereinafter Helms–Burton Act, as it is commonly known]. The Helms–Burton Act sought to impose international sanctions on the Castro regime. Specifically, under Title III of the Act, Congress provided that "[t]o deter trafficking in wrongfully confiscated property, United States nationals who were the victims of [such] confiscations should be endowed with a judicial remedy in the courts of the United States that would deny traffickers any profits from economically exploiting Castro's wrongful seizures." 22 U.S.C. § 6081(11); *see also id.* § 6082(a)(1)(A).

Despite Congress providing this remedy, every President from 1996 to 2019 lawfully suspended that private right of action. *See id.* § 6085(c) (giving the President such authority). But in 2019, President Trump ended the suspension of Title III, which enabled suits to be filed against those trafficking in this stolen property. *See* **{–279–}** *Glen v. Am. Airlines, Inc.*, 7 F.4th 331, 333 (5th Cir. 2021). As a result, the victims of the Castro regime's pervasive seizure of Cuban assets can seek relief from those foreign actors that reaped profits from the victims' stolen property abroad. *See, e.g.*, *Herederos de Roberto Gomez Cabrera, LLC v. Teck Res. Ltd.*, 535 F. Supp. 3d 1299, 1304–07 **[—90—]** (S.D. Fla. 2021), *appeal filed*, No. 21-12834 (11th Cir. Aug. 18, 2021) (seeking relief under the Helms–Burton Act and presently appealing dismissal for lack of personal jurisdiction).

However, it is an empty gesture here in this circuit. That is because (according to the majority opinion) the Fifth Amendment's Due Process Clause bars Congress from authorizing federal courts to exercise personal jurisdiction unless either (1) the foreign actor is "essentially at home" here, or (2) the foreign actor's trafficking of the stolen property has substantially occurred in the United States. By constitutionally cabining Rule 4(k)(2), and also necessarily limiting Rule 4(k)(1)(C), the victims of the Castro regime are again left empty-handed.

This is not a one-off problem confined to the Helms–Burton Act. Take the Antiterrorism Act, which provided victims of terrorism abroad a private right of action in our federal courts. 18 U.S.C. § 2333(a). Now, so long as foreign sponsors of terrorism target American interests abroad, federal district courts cannot exercise personal jurisdiction over victims' claims, despite Congress's express statutory permission (as recognized by Rule 4(k)(1)(C))—this, supposedly because of the Fifth Amendment's Due Process Clause. *See, e.g.*, Aaron D. Simowitz, *The Private Law of Terror*, 126 Penn St. L. Rev. 159, 192–93 (2021); *see also* Brief of Intervenor–Appellant United States at 35–40, *Fuld v. Palestinian Liberation Org.* (2d Cir. June 24, 2022) (Nos. 22-76, 22-496) (noting that "Congress . . . has enacted numerous laws, including the ATA, combating acts of international terrorism outside the United States that affect U.S. persons and interests" by vesting federal courts with adjudicative authority, and arguing that the Fifth Amendment interposes no obstacle to federal court personal jurisdiction in such cases). **[—91—]**

Consider also the practical effect of the majority opinion's holding on the Executive.

As *amici* civil procedure professors point out, if the United States sued foreign defendants in our federal courts to recover civil damages for injuries sustained abroad (like, for instance, a Navy vessel wrecked in foreign waters), the holding in this case equally precludes us from exercising personal jurisdiction over foreign defendants if they are not "essentially at home" in the United States. Thus, under the majority opinion's reasoning, the federal government is powerless to vindicate American interests and to recoup damages inflicted (ultimately) on the American taxpayer in our own federal courts because the Fifth Amendment's Due Process Clause protects a foreign defendant from being haled into our courts.[44] The harsh absurdity of this conclusion should surely make us think twice.

D.

Not only does the majority opinion virtually erase a Federal Rule of Civil Procedure and squash the real-world ability of **{-280-}** our coordinate branches to pursue legitimate objectives through and in federal court, but, as suggested earlier, *see supra* sections II.C.2–3, this *en banc* holding also creates at least two legal anomalies. First, we now privilege *civil* foreign defendants with a due process right not shared by foreign *criminal* defendants. And second, we privilege foreign corporations over comparable corporations domiciled here: the former can reap the rewards of doing business here without the legal **[—92—]** consequences to which our own corporations must submit. Both anomalies suggest that the *en banc* court has lost its bearings.

1.

"The due process requirements in a *civil* case where only property interests are at stake are, of course, *much less stringent* than in a *criminal* case involving life and liberty interests." *Fehlhaber v. Fehlhaber*, 681 F.2d 1015, 1027 (5th Cir. 1982) (emphases added). These heightened stakes account for the many differences between civil and criminal procedure: Criminal defendants, for instance, must be proven guilty beyond a reasonable doubt, while civil defendants ordinarily need only be found liable by a preponderance of the evidence. *See In re Winship*, 397 U.S. 358, 364 (1970). Criminal defendants are entitled to receive exculpatory evidence from the prosecution without asking for it; civil defendants proactively must use discovery to get the evidence that they need. *See Brady v. Maryland*, 373 U.S. 83, 86 (1963). The list goes on.

Today's majority opinion produces a troubling inversion of this general rule. Along with our sister circuits, we have previously held that federal courts *may* render binding judgments against foreigners in criminal cases, regardless of the defendants' territorial contacts with the United States, so long as the defendants' alleged criminal conduct affected the United States or U.S. nationals abroad.[45] *See, e.g.*, *Rojas*, 812 F.3d at 393 ("In **[—93—]** the context of non-U.S. citizens, due process requires the government to demonstrate that there exists a sufficient nexus between the conduct condemned and the United States

---

[44] *Cf. The Belgenland*, 114 U.S. at 368–69 ("[W]here the parties are not only foreigners, but belong to different nations, and the injury . . . takes place on the high seas, there seems to be no good reason why the party injured, or doing the service, should ever be denied justice in our courts."). If an injured *foreign* party suing another *foreigner* "should [n]ever be denied justice in our courts," *a fortiori*, neither should an injured United States citizen or the United States itself.

[45] Of course, the federal courts' ability to render binding criminal judgments against foreigners also depends upon the existence of a law of Congress enacted pursuant to one of Congress's constitutionally enumerated powers. *See, e.g.*, *United States v. Davila-Mendoza*, 972 F.3d 1264, 1268–78, 8 Adm. R. 513, 514–22 (11th Cir. 2020) (vacating convictions of three foreign nationals for crimes committed in a foreign nation's territorial waters because the Maritime Drug Law Enforcement Act exceeded Congress's enumerated foreign commerce power). But this does not imply that other enumerated powers do not allow Congress to authorize **[—93—]** personal jurisdiction in federal courts over foreign actors for foreign conduct (whether civil or criminal) affecting United States interests.

such that application of the statute would not be arbitrary or fundamentally unfair to the defendant." (quoting *Lawrence*, 727 F.3d at 396 (internal quotation marks omitted))); *Murillo*, 826 F.3d at 157 (finding no Fifth Amendment obstacle to prosecuting a foreign defendant in the United States "if his 'actions affected significant American interests'—even if the defendant did not mean to affect those interests" (quoting *Brehm*, 691 F.3d at 552)).

But now that the Fourteenth Amendment "at home" test applies in the Fifth Amendment context, foreign corporate civil defendants will be "immunize[d]" from suit here. *Ante* at 24. Unlike foreign criminal defendants, whom federal courts can sentence to death or prison even if they have never set foot in the United States or never even intended to affect the United States, civil corporate defendants **{-281-}** will be insulated against federal court personal jurisdiction in cases involving mere money damages if they can simply show that despite doing even extensive business in the United States, they are not "essentially at home" here. *See Waldman*, 835 F.3d at 340 (candidly acknowledging the difference in standards applicable to criminal and civil cases after importing *Daimler*'s "at home" test). This cannot be right.

2.

Yet another anomaly lies in our affording significant due process rights to a foreign corporation. The American Constitution exists primarily to secure the rights of Americans. The Supreme Court has held that foreign **[—94—]** corporations are entitled to less constitutional protection than citizens, if at all—especially when they remain abroad. *See Agency for Int'l Dev.*, 140 S. Ct. at 2086–87 (foreign corporation has no First Amendment rights, despite having domestic affiliates); *see also Douglass*, 996 F.3d at 295; *cf. Dep't of Homeland Sec. v. Thuraissigiam*, 140 S. Ct. 1959, 1981–83 (2020) (alien within U.S. territory not entitled to full range of due process rights); *Verdugo-Urquidez*, 494 U.S. at 264–75 (alien abroad not protected by the Fourth Amendment); *Eisentrager*, 339 U.S. at 784 (aliens abroad not protected by the Fifth Amendment).

Here, NYK would like to have its cake and eat it too. This foreign corporation has frequently reaped the benefits of the American legal system—it has sued nearly *eighty* times in federal district courts in under thirty years—but, having *been* sued, NYK suddenly cries foul. To claim the protection of Fourteenth Amendment due process case law, NYK insists that it is not "at home" in the United States and, therefore, cannot be haled into U.S. court from its residence abroad. In other words, the corporation demands the right to stay home, abroad. But, in asserting that it *has* due process rights under the U.S. Constitution in the first place, NYK acknowledges its presence in the United States and its desire to receive the legal benefits of being "at home" here. This runs up against the principle of noncontradiction: NYK cannot both be "at home" here and not. Something is not quite right.

* * *

All of these troubling consequences and anomalies are big red flags signaling that we have headed down the wrong path. We are better off looking to what the Fifth Amendment's Due Process Clause meant when it was adopted—not what the Supreme Court has said the Fourteenth Amendment's Due Process Clause means in different contexts. Adhering to **[—95—]** the Fifth Amendment's original meaning steers us clear of these problematic results.

V.

The Supreme Court has never interpreted the Fifth Amendment's Due Process Clause with respect to personal jurisdiction. The Court has expressly left the question open. It is our duty to offer an answer. But the majority opinion simply copies and pastes inapplicable modern Supreme Court case law expounding on the Fourteenth Amendment, as if the Fourteenth Amendment imbues the Fifth Amendment with new meaning. In my view, we should not put new wine in an old wineskin. There is no substitute for a diligent inquiry into the original public meaning of the Fifth Amendment's Due Process Clause. As originally understood and applied (or rather, *not* applied), the Fifth Amendment imposed no significant restriction on Congress's ability to authorize service of process abroad, and hence, to expand federal courts' personal jurisdiction. **{–282–}**

VI.

I would hold that the district court in this case had personal jurisdiction over NYK and remand for further proceedings. Therefore, I respectfully dissent.

(Reporter's Note: Dissenting opinion follows on p. 253).

[—96—] **{-282-}** **HIGGINSON,** Circuit Judge, dissenting:

I agree with the dissent's conclusion that the district court had adjudicative jurisdiction over NYK. I write separately to highlight that by importing Fourteenth Amendment constraints on personal jurisdiction, born out of federalism concerns, into process due to foreign corporations in global disputes, where those concerns don't exist, our court makes several mistakes.

First, the Supreme Court has been explicit it has not done this cross-incorporation. *See Bristol-Myers Squibb Co. v. Superior Ct. of Cal.*, 137 S. Ct. 1773, 1783-84 (2017) ("[S]ince our decision concerns the due process limits on the exercise of specific jurisdiction by a State, we leave open the question whether the Fifth Amendment imposes the same restrictions on the exercise of personal jurisdiction by a federal court."); *see also Omni Capital Int'l, Ltd. v. Rudolf Wolff & Co.*, 484 U.S. 97, 102 n.5 (1987); *J. McIntyre Mach., Ltd. v. Nicastro*, 564 U.S. 873, 885 (2011) (plurality opinion); *Asahi Metal Indus. Co. v. Superior Court*, 480 U.S. 102, 113 n.* (1987) (opinion of O'Connor, J.).

Second, as valiantly explicated in the principal dissent, discerning historical purpose to justify cross-incorporation of the 1868 meaning of "due process" in the Fourteenth Amendment, protecting all persons from state government depredation, back a century to 1791 and what the framers of the Fifth Amendment meant protecting "person[s]" from federal government overreach, all in effort to divine what process is constitutionally due foreign companies in 21st century global disputes, is an originalist mismatch that should call to mind Justice Jackson's reminder three-quarters of a century ago that "[j]ust what our forefathers did envision, or would have envisioned had they foreseen modern conditions, must be divined from materials almost as enigmatic as the dreams Joseph was called upon to interpret for Pharaoh." *Youngstown Sheet & Tube Co. v. Sawyer*, 343 U.S. 579, 634 (1952) (Jackson, J., concurring). Indeed, academics have regretted that "'existing records offer **[—97—]** no evidence of any debate on the due process clause in the Congress . . . or in the state legislatures that ratified' the Bill of Rights." Chimène I. Keitner, *Personal Jurisdiction and Fifth Amendment Due Process Revisited, in* THE RESTATEMENT AND BEYOND: THE PAST, PRESENT, AND FUTURE OF U.S. FOREIGN RELATIONS LAW 231, 236 n.20 (Paul B. Stephan & Sarah H. Cleveland eds., 2020) (alteration in original) (citing scholarship).[1]

Third, as the principal dissent and *amici* civil procedure scholars, not to mention practicing lawyers, observe, cross-incorporation has far-reaching, real-world implications.[2] Yet by importing the recently narrowed **{-283-}** "place of business" and "at home" Fourteenth Amendment requirement, which assigns cases to courts inside the United States, into a Fifth Amendment constitutional rule against access-to-justice in *any* United States court for ever-increasing transnational litigation, what we do is embroider five words written to *enhance* liberty in 1791 to send United States plaintiffs overseas in for hope of justice.[3] *See* Pamela K.

---

[1] My skepticism put to one side, I applaud the principal dissent for its consistency of constitutional effort.

[2] *See, e.g.*, Brief of *Amicus Curiae* for Civil Procedure Law Professors, at 3-4 ("If, as the district court held, the Due Process Clause applicable to state courts applies in equal measure to the federal courts, then Rule 4(k)(2) becomes useless. Indeed, because the negligence that plaintiffs allege in this case also seriously damages the Navy ship on which they were serving, that rationale would foreclose a damages suit by the United States Government from being heard in any federal court in the United States. Congress did not intend such an unjust result, and the Constitution does not require it.").

[3] It is unsurprising that corporations will calibrate knowledgeably around jurisdictional leaps like ours today. *See, e.g.*, Catherine A. Spicer et al., *Home Is Where You're Incorporated: The US Supreme Court Limits Forum Shopping*, ASSOCIATION OF CORPORATE COUNSEL DOCKET, (Dec. 18, 2020), https://docket.acc.com/home-where-youre-incorporated-us-supreme-court-limits-forum-shopping ("Some businesses considering this question may prefer to eliminate the possibility of being subject to general personal jurisdiction in the United States altogether. A multinational company that is incorporated under the laws of another

Bookman, *Toward the Fifth Restatement of* **[—98—]** *U.S. Foreign Relations Law: The Future of Adjudicative Jurisdiction under Public International Law*, *in* THE RESTATEMENT AND BEYOND, *supra*, at 335, 341 (describing "litigation isolationism" trend in doctrine—of course without anticipating our leap today cross-incorporating *Daimler*'s inapt federalism-based constriction to curtail application of federal law to multinational corporate defendants altogether); *see also* Pamela K. Bookman, *Litigation Isolationism*, 67 STAN. L. REV. 1081 (2015); Pamela K. Bookman, *Doubling Down on Litigation Isolationism*, 110 AJIL UNBOUND 57 (2016). When a defendant is a foreign corporation, even doing continuous and immense commerce in the United States, if it stays purposively not "at home" in any state, then its actions that infringe federal law across the globe yet without specific jurisdiction case-link, cannot be heard. *See also* Aaron D. Simowitz, *Legislating Transnational Jurisdiction*, 57 VA. J. INT'L L. 325, 327-28 (2018) (describing how the United States has become one of the most "jurisdictionally stingy" countries in the world—again, of course, without anticipating our further leap).

Fourth, cross-incorporation of bedrock fair notice due to "persons" in *interstate* cases, a federalism-centered and court-preserving inquiry, to fairness owed overseas corporations in *international* cases, I think overlooks the Supreme Court's distinct, foreign powers and sovereign state-centered comity approach confirmed in *Daimler AG v. Bauman* itself. 571 U.S. 117, 140-42 (2014). That inquiry, broadly described, resembles Fourteenth Amendment doctrinal constriction in outcome—redirecting litigation among courts—but, to my eye, is based neither on international law nor extrapolation from the Fifth Amendment. Instead, the Court assesses litigation in the international setting with use of the canon of statutory **[—99—]** interpretation known as the presumption against extraterritoriality, premised itself on the separation of powers truth that our political branches possess foreign relations powers hence courts should not apply United States statutes prescriptively when doing so might infringe the sovereignty of foreign nations unless Congress has made that intent clear. *See RJR Nabisco, Inc. v. European Cmty.*, 579 U.S. 325 (2016); **{-284-}** *Morrison v. Nat'l Austl. Bank Ltd.*, 561 U.S. 247 (2010); *EEOC v. Arabian Am. Oil Co.*, 499 U.S. 244 (1991).

Finally, the distinction that the Supreme Court has preserved, which we erase with cross-incorporation, is delineation that scholars, not only of constitutional law, *supra*, but also of foreign relations law, have discussed for years. *See, e.g.* THE RESTATEMENT AND BEYOND, *supra*. Much of this discussion is at the heart of The Restatement of the Foreign Relations Law of the United States, *see* FOURTH RESTATEMENT OF FOREIGN RELATIONS LAW §§ 401, 422, unacknowledged by us too, even as we redirect United States citizen-plaintiffs—asserting United States federal law claims and invoking United States federal law service of process—offshore, often to countries with far less developed legal systems than Japan.[4]

With the above in mind, I am confident that when the Supreme Court revisits the distinction it carefully has preserved, it will

nation and with its principal headquarters beyond **[—98—]** US borders will be "at home" nowhere in the United States. Claims against such a company could therefore be brought only pursuant to a court's specific jurisdiction.").

[4] At minimum, in this area of international comity and sensitivity, it would be important to know the views of the Solicitor General, or those of the Legal Advisor to the Department of State, as to what nexus is sufficient for federal courts to assert adjudicative jurisdiction without entangling our legal system with those of other nations. Though the Acting Solicitor General declined to file a brief in this case, in other cases, the United States has asked for special solicitude for its own sovereignty on the international stage. *See, e.g.*, Brief of the United States as *Amicus Curiae* at 32, *Ford Motor Co. v. Mont. Eighth Jud. Dist. Ct.*, 141 S. Ct. 1017 (2021) (Nos. 19-368, 19-369), 2020 WL 1478612, at *32 ("In addition, the United States' constitutional powers and special competence in matters of foreign affairs and international commerce, in contrast to the limited and geographically cabined sovereignty of each of the several States, would permit the exercise of federal judicial power in ways that have no analogue at the state level.").

take cognizance of all **[—100—]** pertinent scholarship, constitutional and foreign relations law. And I am confident it will consider the real world consequences the *amici* civil procedure professors highlight to urge, based both on Supreme Court precedent and also Congress's Rule 4(k)(2), that, in cases arising under federal law, the Fifth Amendment allows more flexibility than the Fourteenth Amendment, permitting "jurisdiction over a non-US defendant that does 'systematic and continuous' business in the United States." Here, that test is certainly met given NYK's extensive business and frequent litigation in the United States, hence I would find jurisdiction.

(Reporter's Note: Dissenting opinion follows on p. 256).

[—101—] {-284-} **OLDHAM,** Circuit Judge, dissenting:

This case should be resolved by two propositions. First, the Supreme Court has never answered—in fact, it has expressly left "open"—"the question whether the Fifth Amendment imposes the same restrictions [as the Fourteenth] on the exercise of personal jurisdiction by a federal court." *Bristol-Myers Squibb Co. v. Super. Ct. of Cal.*, 137 S. Ct. 1773, 1784 (2017); *see also J. McIntyre Mach., Ltd. v. Nicastro*, 564 U.S. 873, 885 (2011) (plurality op.); *Omni Cap. Int'l, Ltd. v. Rudolf Wolff & Co.*, 484 U.S. 97, 102 n.5 (1987). Second, as originally understood, the Fifth Amendment did not impose any limits on the personal jurisdiction of the federal courts. Instead, it was up to Congress to impose such limits by statute. *See, e.g.*, Stephen E. Sachs, *The Unlimited Jurisdiction of the Federal Courts*, 106 VA. L. REV. 1703, 1717–27 (2020); *Picquet v. Swan*, 19 F. Cas. 609, 615 (C.C.D. Mass. 1828) (No. 11,134) (Story, J.); *see also ante*, at 54–61 (Elrod, J., dissenting). That should've been the end of the case. {-285-}

With all respect for my esteemed colleagues, I do not understand how this case implicates (1) "linguistic drift." *See ante*, at 43–44, 63 (Elrod, J., dissenting). Nor do I see how the Supreme Court's (2) "longstanding incorporation jurisprudence" or (3) unenumerated-rights precedents prevent us from adopting the originalist answer here. *See ante*, at 31–32 (Ho, J., concurring).

1.

Start with linguistic drift. The theory appears to be that "due process of law" could've had one original public meaning when the People ratified the Fifth Amendment in 1791, and it could've "drifted" to some different original public meaning in 1868 when the People ratified the Fourteenth Amendment. *See ante*, at 43–44, 63 (Elrod, J., dissenting). Maybe it did. Maybe it didn't. All I know is that "linguistic drift" is irrelevant here. [—102—]

The Supreme Court has confessed that its Fourteenth Amendment personal jurisdiction precedents do not rest on original public meaning. *See Ford Motor Co. v. Mont. Eighth Jud. Dist. Ct.*, 141 S. Ct. 1017, 1036–39 (2021) (Gorsuch, J., concurring in the judgment); *id.* at 1032 (Alito, J., concurring in the judgment) (agreeing that "there are grounds for questioning the standard that the Court adopted in *International Shoe*" as an original matter); *id.* at 1025 n.2 (majority op.) (effectively conceding as much). With no originalist endpoint, there's nothing for the Fifth Amendment's original public meaning to "drift" to.

And it's particularly odd to inject into this case a theory of *reverse* drift. I do not understand how or why we'd take an *un*originalist interpretation of the Fourteenth Amendment, pull it back in time to 1791, and use it to blind ourselves to an *originalist* interpretation of the Fifth Amendment. *Ante*, at 32–33 (Ho, J., concurring). I am unaware of any case from any court that obligates us to do that—especially to answer a question that the Supreme Court has insisted is "open." *Bristol-Myers*, 137 S. Ct. at 1784.

2.

Next, incorporation. Here, the theory appears to be that incorporation doctrine obligates us to apply the same body of law to the federal and state governments. So, the theory goes, we must use the same non-originalist understanding of "due process of law" for both the Fifth and Fourteenth Amendments. *See ante*, at 34–35 (Ho, J., concurring).

I recognize that Judge Ho invokes incorporation as yet another reason for rejecting the principal dissent's theory of "linguistic drift."[1] It [—103—] nonetheless

[1] I also take it that Judge Ho invites other arguments for applying different bodies of personal-jurisdiction law to the federal and state governments. *See ante*, at 35 (Ho, J., concurring). One argument is that *none* of the personal-jurisdiction limits—for *any* government, state or federal—come from the Fifth or Fourteenth Amendments. *See* Sachs, [—103—] *supra*, at 1722–24. They instead come from the common law, which

bears emphasis, however, that incorporation does nothing to prevent us from adopting an originalist understanding of the Fifth Amendment's Due Process Clause—even in the face of the Court's non-originalist understanding of the Fourteenth Amendment.

Any suggestion to the contrary conflates procedural and "substantive" due process. Personal jurisdiction—which is all that matters here—is a question of "*procedural* due process." **{–286–}** *Phillips Petrol. Co. v. Shutts*, 472 U.S. 797, 812 (1985) (emphasis added). Incorporation, by contrast, is a question of "*substantive*" due process. *See Dobbs v. Jackson Women's Health Org.*, 142 S. Ct. 2228, 2246 (2022). That is, the Court's incorporation precedents take the substantive constitutional rights guaranteed by the first eight amendments and then use the Fourteenth Amendment's Due Process Clause to make those rights applicable against the States. It's of course true that the *substantive* rights are the same, regardless of whether the plaintiff sues a federal or state defendant. *McDonald v. City of Chicago*, 561 U.S. 742, 765 (2010); *N.Y. State Rifle & Pistol Ass'n v. Bruen*, 142 S. Ct. 2111, 2137 (2022). But that says nothing about whether the same *procedural* restrictions apply to the federal and state governments. That's presumably why, again, the Court has insisted the Fifth Amendment *procedural* due process question is "open," *Bristol-Myers*, 137 S. Ct. at 1784, notwithstanding the *substantive* rights guaranteed by incorporation doctrine.[2] **[—104—]**

obviously could place different limits on the reach of the federal and state sovereigns.

[2] It's no answer to say that the Supreme Court first left open the Fifth Amendment procedural due process question before it started incorporating the Bill of Rights against the States. *See ante*, at 29 (Ho, J., concurring) ("But *French* [*v. Barber Asphalt Paving Co.*, 181 U.S. 324 (1901),] was issued before the Court embraced the doctrine of incorporation."). *Bristol-Myers* (2017), *McIntyre* (2011), and *Omni* (1987) were all decided long after. The Court was surely aware of its incorporation doctrine in 2017, 2011, and 1987.

3.

Finally, a word about unenumerated rights. *Ante*, at 31 (Ho, J., concurring) (relying on *Gonzales v. Carhart*, 550 U.S. 124 (2007)). In *Carhart*, the Court upheld a federal-law abortion restriction without considering whether the Fifth and Fourteenth Amendments require different *substantive* frameworks for abortion. 550 U.S. at 132–68. From that, my esteemed colleague infers that both amendments must impose identical *procedural* frameworks for personal jurisdiction. *See ante*, at 31 (Ho, J., concurring).

That's a *non sequitur*. And it's easy to understand why no one swerved out of the way to address irrelevant procedural arguments while considering the invocation of an unenumerated "substantive" due process claim in 2007.

First, the Court did not purport to ground its preexisting abortion doctrine in originalism. *E.g.*, *Planned Parenthood of Southeastern Pennsylvania v. Casey*, 505 U.S. 833, 847–49 (1992) (plurality op.); *see also Dobbs*, 142 S. Ct. at 2317–50 (dissenting op.) (not defending *Roe* or *Casey* on originalist grounds). So it's unsurprising that the *Carhart* litigants said nothing about the original public meaning of any part of the Constitution.

Second, and in any event, long before *Gonzales*, the Supreme Court held that the same substantive framework applies to unenumerated rights under both the Fifth and Fourteenth Amendments' Due Process Clauses. *See, e.g.*, *Reno v. Flores*, 507 U.S. 292, 301–03 (1993); *United States v. Salerno*, 481 U.S. 739, 746 (1987). That obviously mattered in *Gonzales*. And it obviously doesn't matter where, as here, no one invokes "substantive" due process. In short, "[t]he non-discussion of an irrelevant question in an unrelated case does not prevent us from reaching the right answer to a constitutional **{–287–}** question that the Supreme Court has expressly left open." *Ante*, at 45 n.4 (Elrod, J., dissenting).

United States Court of Appeals
for the Fifth Circuit

No. 21-30573

LOGGERHEAD HOLDINGS, INC.
vs.
BP, P.L.C.

Appeal from the United States District Court for the Eastern District of Louisiana

Decided: September 2, 2022

Citation: 48 F.4th 378, 10 Adm. R. 258 (5th Cir. 2022).

Before **KING, ELROD,** and **SOUTHWICK,** Circuit Judges.

[—1—] {-380-} SOUTHWICK, Circuit Judge:

Loggerhead Holdings, Inc., a holding company that owned a scuba diving cruise business, was one of many plaintiffs who brought suit against an oil company because of the explosion of an offshore drilling rig and the **[—2—]** resulting discharge of a massive quantity of oil into the Gulf of Mexico. Loggerhead's claims were dismissed on summary judgment. We AFFIRM in part, REVERSE in part, and REMAND.

FACTUAL AND PROCEDURAL BACKGROUND

Loggerhead Holdings, Inc. began operating a scuba diving cruise business in 1986. The business relied on two special-purpose vessels named the *Nekton Pilot* and *Nekton Rorqual* that facilitated scuba expeditions. Beginning sometime after 2010, Loggerhead operated out of Fort Lauderdale on Florida's Atlantic shore and offered scuba-diving cruises for tourists in and around the Caribbean through its subsidiary, "Nekton Diving Cruises."

Loggerhead does not dispute that it suffered business setbacks in the late 2000s. Nekton's bookings declined significantly from 2008 to 2010. Loggerhead reported declining receipts and mounting net income losses from 2007 to 2009. Further, even though Loggerhead calculated positive earnings before interest, taxes, depreciation, and amortization ("EBITDA") throughout this period, it is apparent that its cruise business was encountering significant problems. In September 2009, Loggerhead put one of its vessels, the *Pilot*, into dry dock at Port St. Joe, Florida, for a refit of the vessel. Loggerhead's president, John Dixon, testified that the vessel was to be returned to service in June 2010. Despite that testimony, by April 2010, Loggerhead was not accepting bookings. Dixon testified that only $30,000 out of a projected $180,000 had been spent on parts for the *Pilot*.

About the same time, the *Rorqual* experienced problems of its own. Around April 10, 2010, the *Rorqual*'s starboard generator "had a casualty that was quickly fixed by installing a replacement generator." That same week, though, the replacement generator "had a low-oil pressure warning indication," and "Loggerhead limited its operation as a protective measure until the low-oil pressure condition could be diagnosed at Loggerhead's Port **[—3—]** St. Joe facility." Loggerhead thus planned to return the *Rorqual* to Port St. Joe at the completion of its final winter itinerary on April **{-381-}** 24, 2010. To facilitate the generator warranty check, Loggerhead canceled and allegedly rescheduled two weeks of summer cruises that were planned to depart on May 8 and May 15.

On April 20, 2010, *Deepwater Horizon*, a mobile offshore drilling unit hired by BP to drill the Macondo Well in the Gulf of Mexico, suffered a blowout, causing what would become an 87-day discharge of oil into the Gulf. Not long thereafter, the *Rorqual* went from the Turks and Caicos Islands to Port St. Joe on Florida's Gulf Coast. Dixon, in an affidavit, alleged that on the evening of May 2, 2010—one day before arriving at Port St. Joe—the *Rorqual* encountered oil from the Macondo Well. The oil damaged the vessel's main engines, generators, reverse osmosis water makers, HVAC, grey, sanitary, and ballast water systems. Dixon asserted he "personally observed Macondo oil on the vessel." He acknowledged, though, that he did not have the oil tested to determine if it could be matched to the oil from the Macondo Well. BP asserted in district court, and Loggerhead did not contest, that "it is possible to 'fingerprint' petroleum through the use of gas chromatography in order to determine the source of the crude oil." Dixon's response was that he was unaware of any other wells that were leaking, and thus his "deduction" was that the oil must have come from BP's well.

On May 17, 2010, Loggerhead announced on its website it was ceasing cruising operations, giving several reasons but making no reference to the *Deepwater Horizon* disaster. Loggerhead did not return the $417,000 in deposits paid by its customers, and its Nekton Diving Cruises subsidiary soon filed an assignment for the benefit of its creditors. Shortly after, other diving companies offered credit to Nekton's customers for diving trips with them. **[—4—]**

On August 10, 2010, the Judicial Panel on Multidistrict Litigation centralized all federal actions in the United States District Court for the Eastern District of Louisiana. *In re Oil Spill by Oil Rig "Deepwater Horizon,"* 910 F. Supp. 2d 891, 900 (E.D. La. 2012); *see* 28 U.S.C. § 1407. In 2012, BP entered two class settlements: one for medical claims and another for economic claims. *See In re Deepwater Horizon*, 723 F. App'x 247, 248 (5th Cir. 2018). Under the terms of the settlement for economic damages, class members released their claims in exchange for payment through a court supervised settlement program. *In re Oil Spill*, 910 F. Supp. 2d at 903. Loggerhead opted out of the settlement on September 19, 2012.

In 2013, Loggerhead sued a variety of BP entities in the United States District Court for the Southern District of Texas for claims arising from the *Deepwater Horizon* disaster. The suit was transferred to the Eastern District of Louisiana to join the others in that multidistrict litigation ("MDL"). Complying with a pretrial order, Loggerhead filed a new complaint in May 2016, asserting claims under the Oil Pollution Act ("OPA") for economic and physical damages. *See* 33 U.S.C. § 2702(b)(2)(B), (E). It also asserted a claim for compensatory and punitive damages under maritime law.

Following the close of the limited discovery allowed, BP moved for summary judgment. BP argued that Loggerhead failed to create a genuine factual issue that the *Deepwater Horizon* disaster caused it economic injury; thus, no reasonable jury could rule in Loggerhead's favor under the OPA or maritime law. BP also argued that Loggerhead's claim for damages due to physical injury failed because there was no evidence that the *Rorqual* had encountered oil discharged from the Macondo Well. Loggerhead's response included its **{–382–}** tax returns from 2007-2014, along with a new declaration from Dixon. Loggerhead argued its economic losses were caused by the oil from the *Deepwater Horizon* and it could prove its economic losses with reasonable certainty through its financial statements. Regarding the claim for damages **[—5—]** due to physical injury, Loggerhead responded that Dixon's deposition and affidavit established a genuine dispute of material fact as to whether oil from BP's well was what fouled the *Rorqual*'s engines and other systems.

The district court granted BP's motion for summary judgment on all claims. On the Section 2702(b)(2)(E) claim, the district court found that no jury could find Loggerhead's business failed because of the *Deepwater Horizon* disaster: "The evidence all points in one direction: that Loggerhead's business was going to fail in the Summer of 2010 regardless of whether the oil spill happened." The district court also held that no evidence supported Loggerhead suffered any loss in earnings resulting from "the injury, destruction, or loss of real property, personal property, or natural resources" as required by Section 2702(b)(2)(E). The court granted summary judgment on the claim. On the Section 2702(b)(2)(B) claim for "[d]amages for injury to, or economic losses resulting from destruction of, real or personal property," the district court assumed for summary judgment purposes that there may be a question of material fact regarding whether the *Rorqual* had been damaged from encountering BP's oil in the water. Still, the district court granted summary judgment on the claim because the only damages Loggerhead could recover under the statute would be "the cost of repairing the vessel's oil-damaged components, if any" and Loggerhead had not set out "such repair costs among its itemized list of damages."[1]

Loggerhead timely appealed. **[—6—]**

DISCUSSION

In reviewing an award of summary judgment *de novo*, we apply the same standard used by the district court. *Rogers v. Bromac Title Servs., L.L.C.*, 755 F.3d 347, 350 (5th Cir. 2014). With a motion for summary judgment, we ask whether, construing the facts in the light most favorable to the nonmoving party, the evidence is sufficient for a reasonable jury to find for the nonmovant. *Sierra Club, Inc. v. Sandy Creek Energy Assocs., L.P.*, 627 F.3d 134, 138 (5th Cir. 2010); *Cuadra v. Houston Indep. Sch. Dist.*, 626 F.3d 808, 812 (5th Cir. 2010). Summary judgment is appropriate "if the movant shows that there is no genuine dispute as to any material fact and the movant is entitled to judgment as a matter of law." FED. R. CIV. P. 56(a). "An issue is material if its resolution could affect the outcome of the action." *Sierra Club, Inc.*, 627 F.3d at 138 (quotation marks and citation omitted). Summary judgment should be granted "where critical evidence is so weak or tenuous on an essential fact that it could not support a judgment in favor of the nonmovant." *McCarty v. Hillstone Rest. Grp., Inc.*, 864 F.3d 354, 358 (5th Cir. 2017) (quotation marks and citations omitted).

A party can present critical evidence, though, in many forms, even self-serving affidavits: "'[S]elf-serving' affidavits and depositions may create fact issues even if not supported by the rest of the record." *Guzman v. Allstate Assurance Co.*, 18 F.4th 157, 160 (5th Cir. 2021). It is **{-383-}** unremarkable that evidence submitted by one side at the summary judgment stage will be "self-serving"; the question is whether that self-serving evidence is "conclusory, vague, or not based on personal knowledge." *Id.* at 161.

I. 33 U.S.C. § 2702(b)(2)(E) claim for economic damages

We first address the district court's grant of summary judgment on the Section 2702(b)(2)(E) claim. Loggerhead argues the district court erred by: (1) applying the incorrect causation standard to the claim; (2) not finding **[—7—]** that Dixon's declaration created a question of material fact regarding the cause of Loggerhead's economic damages; (3) making impermissible credibility determinations regarding Dixon's testimony; and (4) stepping outside the bounds of the Rule 56 inquiry by considering the meaning of Loggerhead's statements regarding EBITDA.

We consider Loggerhead's arguments together. Section 2702(b)(2)(E) allows for recovery of economic losses without requiring a plaintiff to show any physical damage to the plaintiff's property. 33 U.S.C. § 2702(b)(2)(E). "The only restriction on such recovery is that the loss must be *due to* the injury, destruction, or loss of real property, personal property, or natural resources." *In re Settoon Towing, L.L.C.*, 859 F.3d 340, 345, 5 Adm. R. 266, 268 (5th Cir. 2017) (quotation marks omitted) (emphasis added).

The parties dispute the precise causal standard applying to claims under Section 2702(b)(2)(E). A reasonable approach would be to apply the substantial-nexus test employed by the Supreme Court in *Pacific Operators Offshore, LLP v. Valladolid*, 565 U.S. 207 (2012). In that case, the Court addressed a federal statute providing remedies for injuries "occurring as the result of operations" on the Outer Continental Shelf, and it endorsed a "'substantial-nexus' test" requiring a "significant causal link" between the employee's injury and the employer's conduct. *Id.* at 221-222. Accordingly, under the substantial-nexus test, a plaintiff seeking to recover damages under Section 2702(b)(2)(E) must demonstrate a significant causal connection between operations on the Outer Continental Shelf and its alleged loss of profits or impairment of earning capacity.

[1] The district court also granted summary judgment for BP on Loggerhead's claims under general maritime law "for the same reasons" discussed in the remainder of the opinion. Loggerhead does not raise any issue here as to the dismissal.

In a previous opinion in this MDL, the district court applied the substantial-nexus test to determine causation. *In re Oil Spill by Oil Rig "Deepwater Horizon,"* 558 F. Supp. 3d 331, 339 (E.D. La. 2021). The district court utilized a sliding scale approach: **[—8—]**

> [T]he test [for causation] will vary with the circumstances — e.g., what qualifies as a "significant causal link" in a massive oil spill may not qualify in a much smaller oil spill. As applied here, if a fact-finder determined that the oil spill's injury to water and/or beaches caused fewer tourists to travel to Panama City Beach and further determined that Classy Cycles lost profits because of the decline in tourists, then this Court would hold that the "substantial-nexus" test is satisfied.

Id. We are not certain how this sliding scale concept works in different circumstances. Without endorsing that variant, we conclude a substantial-nexus test should be applied to the Section 2702(b)(2)(E) claims.

The district court considered the following undisputed facts in holding that no reasonable jury could find Loggerhead's cruise business would have survived even without the *Deepwater Horizon* disaster. Loggerhead's revenues, bookings, and reported **{-384-}** profits had been in decline for years, with Loggerhead reporting net losses on its tax returns for the years 2007–2009. In the years prior to 2010, the Loggerhead subsidiary operating the diving cruises had accrued millions of dollars of debt, against which it sometimes made timely payments but sometimes did not. By April 2010, when the oil rig exploded, the *Pilot* had been drydocked for months for an extended refit, only limited work had been done, and reservations were not yet being taken for summer cruises on the vessel. Instead, Loggerhead asserts it was depending on revenue from the *Rorqual* to pay for the repairs to the *Pilot*; indeed, it "needed the *Rorqual* to be in service" to finish the refit of the *Pilot*.

The *Rorqual* suffered two mechanical failures between April 10 and 24, 2010, causing Loggerhead to cancel two weeks of cruises from May 8 through May 22. Loggerhead had already planned off-charter weeks of April 24 through May 8. Then on April 24, four days after the *Deepwater* **[—9—]** *Horizon* blowout, the *Rorqual* completed its scheduled itinerary and traveled to Port St. Joe, Florida.

Some additional facts are said to be disputed. First, BP contends that Loggerhead canceled—rather than rescheduled—the May 8 and 15 cruises. Certainly, Dixon stated in his February 2021 deposition that the May 8 and 15 cruises were "cancel[ed]." Dixon's May 2021 declaration, though, asserts that the May 8 and 15 cruises were "reschedule[d]." Loggerhead argues that canceling and rescheduling are not mutually exclusive; it asserts that the cruise operations for the weeks of May 8 and 15 were canceled and that the passengers who booked for those two weeks were rescheduled to future cruise weeks. Loggerhead contends that by canceling and rescheduling the cruises to a later date, this suggests Loggerhead's business would have survived but for the *Deepwater Horizon* explosion. The district court determined the cruises were "*de facto* cancelled," relying on the fact Loggerhead "does not say what dates these cruises were rescheduled or provide any documentary proof that they were rescheduled." As previously stated, though, a party's affidavits and depositions may create fact issues even without corroborating evidence. *See Guzman,* 18 F.4th at 160. We conclude that cancelling and rescheduling may simply be different points in time for the same event. A genuine dispute of material fact exists here.

Second, relying on Dixon's declaration, Loggerhead asserts the *Rorqual* was still fully operational prior to the *Deepwater Horizon* explosion, although it was experiencing a starboard generator problem for which it traveled to Port St. Joe. We are not certain BP actually disputes this, but regardless, Dixon's declaration is sufficient factual support for his version of the story.

Third, Dixon stated that on May 2, 2010, on the way to Port St. Joe, the *Rorqual* traveled through waters containing oil from the *Deepwater Horizon* explosion. That oil damaged the vessel's main engines, generators, **[—10—]** reverse osmosis water makers, air-conditioning, grey, sanitary, and ballast water systems. Dixon described his assertion about the source of the oil as a "deduction," one based on being unaware of any other wells that were leaking oil. He also argues that on summary judgment that is enough; the oil that had coated some of the *Rorqual* had been preserved and could now be tested.

At least part of that argument is incorrect. Once it is time for a court to make a ruling on summary judgment, its grant or denial turns on whether there is a genuine dispute of material fact based on evidence before the court—not evidence that might be developed later. It is true **{-385-}** that the evidence offered for summary judgment purposes need not yet be in a form admissible at trial, but the party offering the evidence needs to be able to demonstrate that it can be put into an admissible form by the time of a trial. *See Lee v. Offshore Logistical & Transport, L.L.C.*, 859 F.3d 353, 355, 5 Adm. R. 264, 264–65 (5th Cir. 2017). The question of sufficiency of the evidence to create a fact issue as to the source of the oil is not that Dixon's assertions are in the wrong form, but that they are supported only by Dixon's "deduction."

What did BP offer? It presented contemporaneous estimates from that National Oceanic and Atmospheric Administration that on May 2 and May 3, the eastern advance of the oil slick was considerably west of where the *Rorqual* allegedly encountered oil in the water on those dates. Loggerhead does not direct us to any evidence it offered to the contrary, so we are left only with the deduction. We will say, that even though it was Loggerhead's burden to produce some competent evidence that the oil it encountered was from the Macondo Well, BP did not attempt to offer another source as a possibility. Instead, BP disputes that the *Rorqual* encountered any oil.

The district court did not decide whether there was any genuine dispute of fact, which certainly would be material, as to whether the *Rorqual* was damaged by oil from the Macondo Well. After identifying the dispute, the **[—11—]** court concluded that "no reasonable jury could conclude that the oil" from the *Deepwater Horizon* disaster "caused Loggerhead's business to fail. The evidence all points in one direction," that Loggerhead's business was collapsing at that time independently of anything for which BP was responsible.

Because we have the *discretion* to affirm on any basis supported by the record, *Rutila v. Dept. of Transp.*, 12 F.4th 509, 511 n.3 (5th Cir. 2021), we consider as an alternative ground that Loggerhead offered no competent summary judgment evidence identifying the source of any oil that the *Rorqual* encountered. Again, Loggerhead offered Dixon's *deduction* that it was the only possible source. Another way to put the argument is that based on the direct evidence that an oil slick for which BP was responsible was moving east in the Gulf, on the uncertainties that could be accepted as applying to governmental forecasts of how far this oil spread, and on the absence of evidence of any other well leaking oil that could explain the *Rorqual*'s encountering it, there was circumstantial evidence from which jurors could themselves deduce that the Macondo Well provided the oil that fouled the *Rorqual*. Jurors, of course, would first need to accept that the *Rorqual* encountered any oil.

BP is certainly correct that Loggerhead's evidence is exceedingly weak that any oil in the water that damaged the *Rorqual* came from the Macondo Well. Nonetheless, the district court, whose familiarity with the *Deepwater Horizon* disaster and any factual questions that exist about its effects has been hard earned, decided not to determine whether there was a genuine dispute of material fact about damage to the *Rorqual*. We thus decline to exercise our discretion to consider affirming on the basis that no genuine factual dispute exists about the cause of damage to the *Rorqual*.

Fourth, Dixon's declaration asserts that after the disaster, Loggerhead had trouble attracting and retaining future customers because of the ongoing Gulf of Mexico clean-up effort, water closures, and presence of **[—12—]** oil on the water which caused guests to cancel their reservations. BP insists these explanations are contrary to Loggerhead's announcement of cessation of operations on May 17, in which it did **{-386-}** not refer to the *Deepwater Horizon* disaster: "Due to the continually increasing cost of operations, decreased discretionary income of consumers, and overall economic difficulty, Nekton is unable to restart cruise operations at this time."

Certainly, it is undisputed that Loggerhead had millions of dollars in debt and limited assets at the time of the assignment for the benefit of creditors. Loggerhead asserts, though, that its demise was not a certainty prior to the *Deepwater Horizon* disaster. The firm had positive EBITDA for the years prior to 2010 and then diminished bookings after *Deepwater Horizon*. Of course, Nekton suffered serious business setbacks before the *Rorqual*'s mechanical problems, had canceled all its May itineraries after sending the vessel to be repaired, shut down operations, and then completed an assignment for the benefit of creditors. Dixon's declaration, though, states the *Rorqual* was "fully operational" and yielding revenue at the time of the *Deepwater Horizon* explosion.

As we stated earlier, summary judgment is appropriate "where critical evidence is so weak or tenuous on an essential fact that it could not support a judgment in favor of the nonmovant." *McCarty*, 864 F.3d at 358. The district court's placing this evidence in that category is understandable. The company was in significant financial distress, its survival subject to serious question even without the *Deepwater Horizon* disaster. Nonetheless, Loggerhead had been able to continue operations for several years despite its fraught financial condition, and indeed despite reporting net losses on its taxes for the three years preceding the disastrous events of April 2010 in the Gulf. Whether it could have continued to survive, if not thrive, had the April events not occurred presents a fact question. **[—13—]**

We conclude that a reasonable factfinder could find the requisite causal link between the *Deepwater Horizon* disaster and Loggerhead's demise. Summary judgment should not have been granted.

II. 33 U.S.C. § 2702(b)(2)(B) claim for physical damages

Loggerhead also appeals the district court's holding that BP was entitled to summary judgment regarding Loggerhead's OPA Section 2702(b)(2)(B) claim. Section 2702(b)(2)(B) permits recovery for "[d]amages for injury to, or economic losses resulting from destruction of, real or personal property." 33 U.S.C. § 2702(b)(2)(B). Subsection (B) requires physical injury to the plaintiff's property before a plaintiff can recover. *See In re: Oil Spill by Oil Rig "Deepwater Horizon,"* 902 F. Supp. 2d 808, 817 (E.D. La. 2012).

The district court determined "[t]here is perhaps a genuine dispute of material fact over whether the RORQUAL was oiled," yet still dismissed the claim. That is because the district court understood "Loggerhead's entire argument concerning the purported oiling of the RORQUAL" to be "designed to establish a lost profits/impaired earning capacity claim." The district court was correct that "[t]he most Loggerhead could hope to recover under § 2702(b)(2)(B) in this circumstance would be the cost of repairing the vessel's oil-damaged components, if any" and that the list of damages provided in Dixon's declaration and the economic expert's opinion did not include repair costs for oil-damaged components. Seeing a mismatch between the remedy sought and the one available under the statute, the district court dismissed the Section 2702(b)(2)(B) claim.

Loggerhead argues this was error because the district court failed to consider **{-387-}** Dixon's declaration along with a previously submitted "expert evaluation" for the "repairs required for *Nekton Rorqual* after the May 2, **[—14—]** 2010 oiling" which Loggerhead claims were just shy of $7 million. Loggerhead asserts that it offered "a detailed damage report" which listed "all the supporting documents" reviewed by the damage expert.

Together, Loggerhead contends the district court overlooked these documents which Loggerhead believes create a genuine issue of material fact regarding its claim for Section 2702(b)(2)(B) damages.

BP responds that Loggerhead has failed to provide competent evidence of physical damage. Although Dixon's declaration mentioned "restart cost," it did not identify a claim for costs to repair physical damage to the *Rorqual*. BP also argues that because Loggerhead only referred to the expert materials in its opposition to summary judgment regarding claims under Section 2702(b)(2)(E), reliance on those materials is forfeited. Finally, BP is correct that the only evidence for physical damages to the *Rorqual* in the report is a line item under "vessel repairs" titled "*Nekton Rorqual*" citing a sum of just over $6.8 million.

We agree with BP that this is not enough to create a genuine dispute of material fact. Although the expert report catalogues the sources allegedly supporting its findings, the supporting documents are not included in what was submitted to the district court on summary judgment, and they were not referred to in relation to either the Section 2702(b)(2)(E) or Section 2702(b)(2)(B) claims. Because Loggerhead was not able to offer more than Dixon's allegations and an unsupported estimate—evidence "so weak or tenuous on an essential fact that it could not support a judgment in favor of the nonmovant"—the district court properly granted BP's motion for summary judgment on the Section 2702(b)(2)(B) claim. *See McCarty*, 864 F.3d at 358.

The district court's judgment is AFFIRMED in part, REVERSED in part, and REMANDED.

United States Court of Appeals for the Fifth Circuit

No. 22-40158

BG GULF COAST LNG, L.L.C.
vs.
SABINE-NECHES NAVIGATION DIST. OF JEFFERSON COUNTY, TEX.

Appeal from the United States District Court for the Eastern District of Texas

Decided: September 14, 2022

Citation: 49 F.4th 420, 10 Adm. R. 265 (5th Cir. 2022).

Before **STEWART**, **ELROD**, and **GRAVES**, Circuit Judges.

[—1—] {–421–} **ELROD**, Circuit Judge: **{–422–}**

The Sabine–Neches Waterway is located in the southeastern-most parts of Texas and the southwestern-most parts of Louisiana, providing passage from the Gulf of Mexico to Port Arthur, Beaumont, and Orange, Texas, and beyond. It is vitally important to the local, state, and federal economies. Despite its importance, sixty years have gone by without much effort to maintain or otherwise improve it. The Sabine–Neches Navigation District set out to change that. The price tag on the proposed improvements totaled roughly $1.1 billion. After some bureaucratic wrangling, Congress **[—2—]** covered most of the cost with the District left to cover the rest. The District planned to cover its share through port fees. But the same federal law that led to congressional funding also sets limits on how costs can be passed onto consumers by local entities. Two energy companies sued the District, claiming that the port fees exceeded those limits. The district court concluded that they failed to state plausible claims and dismissed the case. We AFFIRM.

I.

As waterways here in America go, the Sabine–Neches Waterway is one of our nation's most critical. Not only does it rank near the top in business and busyness, it is home to the U.S. military's largest strategic commercial seaport. But as ships became larger, the Sabine–Neches Waterway largely stayed the same. Its lack of depth and width poses a problem for many modern vessels.

To make the necessary improvements to the Waterway, the District needed funds. Congress opened up the federal purse for such projects through the Water Resources Development Act of 1986, 33 U.S.C. § 2201, *et seq*. In the years before the Act's passage, trying to improve waterways was a bureaucratic nightmare. *See New Orleans S.S. Ass'n v. Plaquemines Port, Harbor & Terminal Dist.*, 874 F.2d 1018, 1024–25 (5th Cir. 1989) (digesting the backstory of the Harbor Development and Navigation Improvement Act, which was passed as part of the Water Resources Development Act). It could take up to twenty-six years from first study to project completion, with as many as nineteen independent reviews along the way. *Id.* When Congress passed and President Reagan signed the Act, Congress had not approved a project in nearly two decades. *Id.* Through the Act, Congress streamlined the process and came up with a new way to finance waterway-construction and -improvement projects. *Id.* at 1025. Rather than rely only on the federal **[—3—]** fisc, the federal government would shoulder some or most of the cost and would share the rest with state and local entities. *Id.* Plus, state and local entities had a greater practical interest in the waterway development, so they were more likely to get it done faster. *Id.*

The process begins with a feasibility study by the U.S. Army Corps of Engineers. Once that is done, it is published in the Federal Register and the Secretary of the Army gives it to Congress. Congress then reviews the study and the projected costs and puts it to a vote. If it prevails and the President signs it, Congress gives the local entities money to cover the first phase of the project (called "new start" funds). The local entities then enter into a cooperative agreement with the Army Corps of Engineers covering the project, which includes "provid[ing] to the Federal Government the non-Federal share of all other costs of construction of [the] project." 33 U.S.C. § 2211(e)(3). *See also Air Liquid Am.*

Corp. v. U.S. Corps of Engineers, 359 F.3d 358, 361 (5th Cir. 2004) (describing process). **{-423-}**

The District prepared for years, but did not formally begin the Sabine–Neches Waterway Channel Improvement Project until 2011. The District worked with the Army Corps of Engineers, and the Corps completed its study in March of that year. The Corps concluded that Congress should fund the Project: deeper waterways means bigger ships which fit more cargo, which means fewer ships, which means less congestion. The Secretary of the Army transferred the Project to Congress, Congress passed it, *see* Water Resources Reform and Development Act of 2014, Pub. L. No. 113–121, 128 Stat. 1193, 1364, § 7002 (2014) ("WRDA-14"),[1] and President Obama signed **[—4—]** it into law.[2] The Project's price tag was just over $1.1 billion, with the federal government covering around $748 million and the District just under $366 million. *Id.* Congress then appropriated "new start" funds for the Project to get the ball rolling in 2019. *See* Energy and Water, Legislative Branch, and Military Construction and Veterans Affairs Appropriations Act, 2019, Pub. L. No. 115–244, 132 Stat. 2897, 2898–99 (2019). Those new-start funds would ultimately be used to complete the first part of the Project: the deepening of Anchorage Basin No. 1 from twenty feet to forty feet.

The District and the Corps then entered into the statutorily required agreement. *See* 33 U.S.C. § 2211(e)(3). The Agreement listed the projected cost at over $1.2 billion (up a bit from WRDA-14), with a $732 million/$488 million federal–District split (roughly 60%–40%). That number, of course, was a projection, and its fluidity becomes relevant later. The Agreement otherwise detailed the specifics on the deepening and widening of the Waterway and outlined the environmental effects of the Project.[3] **[—5—]**

So the District needed $488 million. The first $20 million in "new start" funds went to deepening Anchorage Basin No. 1—before it was twenty-feet deep, now it is forty-feet deep. Once that was done, the District proposed the User Fee. The User Fee would apply only to ships with drafts greater than twenty feet—in other words, **{-424-}** ships that were too big to use the Basin before the deepening. The Fee could change based on certain (unrelated) conditions, but the basics are as follows:

	hydrocarbon cargo	**non-hydrocarbon cargo**
minimum	$0.00 per short ton	$0.00 per short ton
starting rate	$0.20 per short ton	$0.02 per short ton
maximum	$0.35 per short ton	$0.035 per short ton

[1] Because each new project that goes through this process requires an act of Congress (literally), the parties refer to each new act as "WRDA" followed by a two-digit year, *e.g.*, "WRDA-14." They also refer to the 1986 Act (detailed above) as "WRDA-86." **[—4—]** For ease of reference, we refer to the 1986 Act as "the Act" and otherwise refer to any other project-approval act as "WRDA-##."

[2] *See* David Hudson, *President Obama Signs the Water Resources Reform and Development Act, and Honors the "Borinqueneers,"* The White House (June 10, 2014), https://obamawhitehouse.archives.gov/blog/2014/06/10/president-obama-signs-water-resources-reform-and-development-act-and-honors-borinque.

[3] "[D]eepening the Sabine Neches Waterway (SNWW) from 40 to 48 feet and the offshore channel from 42 to 50 feet in depth from offshore to the Port of Beaumont Turning Basin; extending the 50-foot deep offshore channel by approximately 13.2 miles to deep water in the Gulf, increasing the total length of the channel from approximately 64 to 77 miles; tapering and marking the Sabine Bank Channel from 800 feet wide to 700 feet wide; deepening and widening the Taylor Bayou channels and turning basins; easing selected bends on the Sabine-Neches Canal and Neches River Channel; constructing new and enlarging/deepening existing turning and anchorage basins on the Neches River Channel; beneficial use of dredged material features consisting of the restoration of 2,853 acres of emergent marsh, improvement of 871 acres of shallow water habitat, and nourishment of 1,234 acres of existing marsh in Texas; mitigation measures consisting of the restoration of **[—5—]** 2,783 acres of emergent marsh, improvement of 957 acres of shallow water habitat, and stabilization and nourishment of 4,355 acres of existing marsh; and post-construction monitoring and adaptive management of the beneficial use features and mitigation areas[.]"

Every short ton loaded onto a ship or unloaded from a ship is charged.[4] Key for our purposes, the ordinance says that the District would collect the Fee until the first of either (a) all construction costs are repaid, or (b) January 1, 2049.

Per the Act, the District published the proposed ordinance in the Federal Register and received public comment. 86 Fed. Reg. 7369-05 (Jan. 28, 2021).[5] After a hearing, the Commissioners of the District passed the **[—6—]** Ordinance, and the District began levying the fee against the bigger ships on May 1, 2021.

BG Gulf Coast LNG and Phillips 66 Company are energy companies. BG Gulf Coast has already paid well into the six figures because of the Ordinance. As of the filing of the Complaint, Phillips 66 had not yet sent any of its cargo on bigger ships. But it planned to. They both sued, alleging that the Ordinance violated several provisions of the Act. The District moved to dismiss under Rule 12(b)(6). The district court granted the motion on each claim, concluding that the District satisfied all of the requirements of the Act, including the requirement that any fees must be imposed "on a fair and equitable basis."[6] The district court then dismissed the case with prejudice. The energy companies (hereinafter "BG Gulf Coast") appealed. We subsequently granted the District's motion to expedite the appeal.

II.

We review *de novo* the grant of a motion to dismiss under Rule 12(b)(6). *Residents of Gordon Plaza, Inc. v. Cantrell*, 25 F.4th 288, 295 (5th Cir. 2022). "To survive a motion to dismiss, a complaint must contain sufficient factual matter, accepted as true, to 'state a claim to relief that is plausible on its face.'" *Ashcroft v. Iqbal*, 556 U.S. 662, 678 (2009) (quoting **{-425-}** *Bell Atl. Corp. v. Twombly*, 550 U.S. 544, 570 (2007)). "A claim has facial plausibility when the plaintiff pleads factual content that allows the **[—7—]** court to draw the reasonable inference that the defendant is liable for the misconduct alleged." *Id.* We accept all well-pleaded facts as true and draw all reasonable inferences in favor of the plaintiff. *Id.* But we do not presume that a complaint's legal conclusions are true, no matter how well they are pleaded. *Id.*

A.

Section 2236 of the Act sets limits on (among other things) how and when a non-federal interest can pass costs onto consumers vis-à-vis "[p]ort or harbor dues." One such condition is in § 2236(a)(1): "Port or harbor dues may be levied only in conjunction with a harbor navigation project whose construction is complete (including a usable increment of the project)[.]"

To BG Gulf Coast, this means that the District can only impose a fee for either (a) its share of the entire $1.1 billion project once it is completed, or (b) its share of a "usable increment" of the Project, provided that the fee is imposed for use of that usable increment. Put another way, the District cannot impose the User Fee on vessels and cargo because of Anchorage Basin No. 1 to pay for any other part of the project, let alone (as

---

[4] A "ton" in America and Canada is 2,000 lbs., while a "ton" in the United Kingdom is 2,240 lbs. To avoid confusion, "short ton" is used for something that is 2,000 lbs. and "long ton" for 2,240 lbs.

[5] The District actually went through notice and comment twice. The first proposed ordinance set a flat $0.35/short ton for hydrocarbon cargo and no fee at all for the non-hydrocarbon cargo. 85 Fed. Reg. 37,634, 37,635 (June 23, 2020). After a hearing and talking with the Corps, the District revised the ordinance to what it is today. *Id.*

[6] Dictionaries at the time the Act was passed defined "fair" as "[h]aving the qualities of impartiality and honesty; free from prejudice, favoritism, and self-interest," *Fair*, Black's Law Dictionary 534 (5th ed. 1979), and "equitable" as "[j]ust; conformable to the principles of justice and right," *Equitable*, Black's Law Dictionary 482 (5th ed. 1979). *See also* Webster's Third New International Dictionary 815 (1971) ("equitable" means "characterized by equity"). The most recent edition of Black's Law Dictionary includes this example for the term "fair": "everyone thought Judge Reavley to be fair." *Fair*, Black's Law Dictionary 715 (11th ed. 2019).

the Ordinance says) the District's entire share of the project. According to BG Gulf Coast, this follows textually from the words "in conjunction with" in subsection (a)(1). As well as by contextual inference from other parts of § 2236 in which Congress only allows fees for incurred costs, not speculative future costs. BG Gulf Coast finds some further support in certain language from *Plaquemines*, language which, it says, makes this an open-and-shut issue. *See* 874 F.2d at 1025.

The District says that BG Gulf Coast's reading of the statute stops too soon; the full condition reads: "in conjunction with a harbor navigation project whose construction is complete (including a usable increment of the project) and for the following purposes and in amounts not to exceed those **[—8—]** necessary to carry out those purposes: (A)(i) to finance the non-Federal share of construction and operation and maintenance costs of a navigation project for a harbor under the requirements of [33 U.S.C. § 2211]." § 2236(a)(1). According to the District, this means that once a usable increment of the project is done, it may then "finance" its "share of construction and operation and maintenance costs of" the Project. In contrast to BG Gulf Coast's reading—which requires the non-federal interest to build first and pay later—this allows for the process under the Act to work like this: (1) Congress funds the first phase of the project; (2) the non-federal interest, after going through notice and comment, imposes a fee to build revenue to cover its share; (3) the fee raises funds to pay for the next increment of the project; and (4) so on until the project is complete.

The district court agreed with the District. It concluded that BG Gulf Coast's approach was atextual, as it required reading that parenthetical "(including a usable increment of the project)" out of the statute. BG Gulf Coast's way around the parenthetical was to say that "harbor navigation project" in (a)(1) must mean the same thing as "navigation project for a harbor" under (a)(1)(A)(i), and thus a fee for "a usable increment of the project" in (a)(1) meant that a fee could only finance the same "usable increment." The district court concluded that, no, "a usable increment of the project" defines what it means for a project to be "complete," not what it means to be a harbor navigation project. As for *Plaquemines*, the district court concluded **{-426-}** that it did not apply as it was purely about subsection (a)(2) and emergency-service fees.

We agree with the district court. BG Gulf Coast's interpretation of "in conjunction with" is far too cramped. To be sure, "conjunction" was defined at the time as a "simultaneous occurrence in space or time." *Conjunction*, American Heritage Dictionary 311 (2d College ed. 1982). BG Gulf Coast says that the User Fee is being levied "in conjunction with" the **[—9—]** District's "***plan*** to construct the Project's remaining increments at some future date." But that argument fails because subsection (a)(1) allows fees for projects "whose construction is complete (including a usable increment of the project)." It also says that other subsections, like (a)(3)(B), contemplate using fees for "project features *constructed* under this subchapter," which shows that fees are only for "incurred costs." But subsection (a)(1) refers to "usable increment[s]," not "project features," and it has no similar past-tense "constructed" language. *See Christiana Tr. v. Riddle*, 911 F.3d 799, 805 (5th Cir. 2018) ("When Congress includes particular language in one section of a statute but omits it in another, we presume[] that Congress intended a difference in meaning." (quotation omitted)). So if anything, that cuts against its argument because Congress presumptively treated "usable increments" of projects differently than "project features," and thus fees are allowed under different circumstances and require consideration of completely different factors.

BG Gulf Coast again tries to tie fees to the specific "usable increment of the project," so that fees may only be used after-the-fact to pay for that increment. But to do so, it has to argue that "(including a usable increment of the project)" modifies "a harbor navigation project," so that later when subsection (a)(1)(A)(i) says "a navigation project for a harbor," it means "a usable increment of the project." But it makes far more sense that this language means that once a usable increment of the project is complete, a fee may be levied, not that a fee may only be levied to finance a usable increment of the project. *Cf.* Antonin Scalia & Bryan A. Garner, Reading Law: The Interpretation of Legal Texts 152–53 (2012) (the Nearest-Reasonable-Referent canon: "When the syntax involves something other than a parallel series of nouns or verbs, a prepositive or postpositive modifier normally applies only to the nearest reasonable referent."). **[—10—]**

At first blush, some language in *Plaquemines* supports BG Gulf Coast, but that case concerned an entirely different provision of the Act. *Knight v. Kirby Offshore Marine Pac., L.L.C.*, 983 F.3d 172, 177, 8 Adm. R. 254, 255 (5th Cir. 2020) ("A statement is dictum if it could have been deleted without seriously impairing the analytical foundations of the holding and[,] being peripheral, may not have received the full and careful consideration of the court that uttered it." (quoting *United States v. Segura*, 747 F.3d 323, 328–29 (5th Cir. 2014))). *Plaquemines* described § 2236(a)(1) as "forbid[ing] fees to finance harbor improvements until after the project is complete," but that case was actually about subsection (a)(2), and how the Act does not otherwise constrain a port's ability to assess a fee until a port "has undertaken a harbor improvement project." 874 F.2d at 1026, 1024–25. So *Plaquemines* is only relevant to the extent it holds that the Act applies once a project *begins*, not when it *ends*, and the fact that subsection (a)(1) was in no way raised or relevant to the bottom-line conclusion is dispositive. *See Knight*, 983 F.3d at 178, 8 Adm. R. at 255 (dicta is "peripheral" and "may not have received [our] careful consideration").

BG Gulf Coast's theory of subsection (a)(1) fails at every turn. The statute, properly **{–427–}** construed, allows the District to finance its share of the project once a usable increment of the project is completed. Because Anchorage Basin No. 1 has been completed, subsection (a)(1) permitted the District to pass the Ordinance containing the User Fee.

B.

As discussed, upon completion of a usable increment of the project, § 2236(a)(1)(A)(i) allows a non-federal interest to levy a harbor fee "in amounts not to exceed those necessary to carry out" the following purpose: "to finance the non-Federal share of construction and operation and maintenance costs of a navigation project for a harbor under the requirements **[—11—]** of [33 U.S.C. § 2211]." Section 2211(a)(1)(B) says that the non-federal interest "shall pay, during the period of construction of the project," 25% "of the cost of construction of the portion of the project which has a depth in excess of 20 feet but not in excess of 50 feet[.]"

BG Gulf Coast reads these provisions together to argue that "amounts not to exceed those necessary" means that the District may only use the fee to finance 25% of the Project, as (according to BG Gulf Coast) the District "voluntarily agreed to pay more than 25% of the Project's total cost[.]" The District agreed to cover around 40% of the project, but if the Project comes in under budget, BG Gulf Coast alleges that the District still plans to pay the amount it agreed to—in other words, it may end up covering 60%–80% of the Project. Because it voluntarily agreed to pay that much, "the additional amount above 25% is not a 'requirement' of [33 U.S.C. § 2211]," so the District has to cover anything above 25% with funds that do not come from the User Fee. Summing that up, BG Gulf Coast argues that § 2211(a)(1)(B) places a 25% cap on financing a non-federal interest's share of an improvement project because anything not "require[d]" by § 2211(a)(1)(B) is not "necessary."

The District responds with a different provision of § 2211. Subsection (e) says that before any construction begins on harbors, the Secretary of the Army and the non-federal interests "shall enter into a cooperative agreement" and that the non-federal interests "shall agree to" "provide to the Federal Government the non-Federal share of all other costs of construction" of the project. 33 U.S.C. § 2211(e)(4). So when § 2236(a)(1) says "amounts not to exceed those necessary to carry out" the financing of the Project, the District says that the cooperative agreement was necessary to carry out the Project, and so the User Fee can be used to cover its contractual obligation. **[—12—]**

The district court did not squarely address that argument because it held that the 25% "requirement" is a floor, not a ceiling or a set amount. As everyone agrees, the District may voluntarily assume more than 25% of the cost of the project, which necessarily means that 25% is not both a floor and a ceiling. *Shall* does not mean *shall only*, and the statute contains no "up to" or "at least" language either. BG Gulf Coast then must turn to § 2236(a)(1) which limits fees to the "amount not to exceed those necessary" under § 2211. The district court said that it "cannot be that Section 2211 imposes a cap for the fee-based non-Federal share but not the alternatively funded non-federal share because that reading would require an express statutory provision. Section 2236(a)(1)'s language—'amount not to exceed those necessary'—is not enough."

The question is what § 2236(a)(1)(A)(i) means when it says that fees must be "in amounts not to exceed those necessary to carry out" the purpose of "financ[ing]" the **{-428-}** Project "under the requirements of" § 2211. BG Gulf Coast says that the "necessary" amount under § 2211 is the 25% requirement in subsection (a). The District says that the "necessary" amount under § 2211 is the amount that the District agreed to cover in the cooperative agreement with the federal government in subsection (e). Sadly, Congress did not say what subsection it was thinking of when it said "under the requirements of" § 2211, and the most natural reading is that it meant all of its requirements.

The word "necessary" has been hard to pin down since *McCulloch v. Maryland*, 17 U.S. (4 Wheat.) 316, 414 (1819). Black's Law Dictionary, before even getting to what the definition is, opens with this warning: "This word must be considered in the connection in which it is used, as it is a word susceptible of various meanings. It may import absolute physical necessity or inevitability, or it may import that which is only convenient, useful, appropriate, suitable, or conducive to the end sought." *Necessary*, Black's **[—13—]** Law Dictionary 928 (5th ed. 1979). And between the two, at least in the legal context, courts "rarely use 'necessary' in the latter sense." *Payne v. United States*, 289 F.3d 377, 389 (5th Cir. 2002) (Garza, J., dissenting in part). The term "necessary" here "does not exist in a vacuum," and its meaning "must be determined in the context in which [it] appear[s]." *Texas v. E.P.A.*, 983 F.3d 826, 837, 837 n.2 (5th Cir. 2020).

Section 2236(a)(1) is concerned with fees being levied "for the following purposes and in amounts not to exceed those necessary to carry out those purposes." The purpose relevant here is "to finance." And what can it finance? The District's share of the "construction and operation and maintenance costs" of the Project "under the requirements of" § 2211. Section 2211 has many requirements about costs under different specific circumstances, but if the purpose is "to finance" the District's share of the Project, the focus should be on what it had to do to secure financing. So it is true that paying 25% of the costs was necessary to secure financing vis-à-vis the fees, but the District *also* had to secure an agreement with the federal government under § 2211(e).

As BG Gulf Coast concedes, the Act gives the District discretion to go beyond that 25% amount for costs; it only sets a maximum on what percentage the federal government can spend. *See* 33 U.S.C. § 2280. With that discretion, because the amount of fees must be necessary to secure financing, and because the District had discretion to vary upward on the percentage of costs it covers, the term "necessary" more likely accords with the more permissive definition of the term. *Texas*, 983 F.3d at 837. What follows is that "necessary" means something more like "convenient, useful, appropriate, suitable, or *conducive to the end sought*." Black's, *supra* at 928 (emphasis added). *Cf.* 33 U.S.C. § 2236(a)(1) ("*necessary to carry out those purposes*" (emphasis added)). In this light, while it may not be strictly necessary to cover 40% of the costs under § 2236(a)(1) and § 2211(a), it was

[—14—] convenient and conducive to financing the Project. Thus, the District did not violate the Act by pledging to cover the costs above 25% with the proceeds of the User Fee.

BG Gulf Coast's argument hinges on a strict reading of "necessary." But context is needed to determine whether "necessary" means "absolute physical necessity" or merely "conducive to the end sought." Under these circumstances, it is the latter. Thus, the District can cover more than 25% of the cost with the User Fee proceeds. **{–429–}**

C.

BG Gulf Coast briefed several other arguments regarding the legality of the District's imposition of the User Fee. In its thorough and well-reasoned opinion, the district court explained why those claims must be dismissed. We agree with the conclusions reached by the district court and thus we do not disturb its holdings on appeal.

* * *

Because the district court properly dismissed each of BG Gulf Coast's claims, we AFFIRM.

United States Court of Appeals
for the Fifth Circuit

No. 21-30636

SEVILLE
vs.
MAERSK LINE, LTD.

Appeal from the United States District Court for the Eastern District of Louisiana

Decided: November 18, 2022

Citation: 53 F.4th 890, 10 Adm. R. 272 (5th Cir. 2022).

Before **JONES**, **SOUTHWICK**, and **OLDHAM**, Circuit Judges.

[—1—] {–893–} OLDHAM, Circuit Judge:

Plaintiff filed suit in a district court that concededly had no personal jurisdiction over the defendant and no colorable basis for venue. The district court dismissed the suit and refused to transfer venue. We affirm.

I.

Peter Wojcikowski was a seaman employed by defendant-appellee Maersk Line, Ltd. (MLL). On October 28, 2017, while working aboard an MLL vessel berthed in Bahrain, he was involved in an accident and suffered **[—2—]** a back injury. He returned to the United States for treatment and, a few weeks later, died from a self-inflicted gunshot wound.

On October 6, 2020, acting as Mr. Wojcikowski's personal representative, plaintiff-appellant Stacy Seville filed this Jones Act negligence claim in the Eastern District of Louisiana. She argued Mr. Wojcikowski's back injury was the proximate cause of his death.

MLL moved to dismiss for lack of personal jurisdiction, arguing venue was improper because MLL is not subject to personal jurisdiction in the Eastern District of Louisiana. Seville opposed the motion without contesting any of MLL's jurisdictional arguments. Instead she requested transfer to the Eastern District of Virginia under 28 U.S.C. § 1406(a). The district court granted MLL's Rule 12(b)(2) motion to dismiss for lack of personal jurisdiction, denied Seville's request to transfer under § 1406(a), and entered final judgment in favor of MLL. Seville timely appealed.

II.

Everyone here agrees the Eastern District of Louisiana was not a proper venue for this lawsuit. Appellant says the district court nonetheless abused its discretion by denying the motion to transfer venue and dismissing the case. We disagree.

We (A) explain the venue and venue-transfer rules. Then we (B) explain why Seville failed to carry her burden to show transfer was warranted. Finally, we (C) hold the district court did not abuse its discretion in declining to transfer this case.

A.

In suits brought under the Jones Act, venue is "proper in any district in which the defendant is subject to personal jurisdiction." 1 ADMIRALTY AND MARITIME LAW § 6:20 (6th ed., Dec. 2021 update) (citing 28 U.S.C. **[—3—]** § 1391(c)); *see also* 28 U.S.C. § 1391(b)(1) ("A civil action may be brought in . . . a judicial district in which any defendant resides[.]"); *id.* § 1391(c)(2) ("[A]n entity with the capacity to sue and be sued in its common name under applicable law, whether or not incorporated, shall be deemed to reside, if a defendant, in any judicial district in which such defendant is subject to the court's personal jurisdiction **{–894–}** with respect to the civil action in question[.]").

Where venue is improper, the district court should generally dismiss the case. But the court retains discretion to transfer it to a proper venue if such a transfer would serve "the interest of justice." 28 U.S.C. § 1406(a) ("The district court of a district in which is filed a case laying venue in the wrong division or district shall dismiss, *or if it be in the interest of justice, transfer* such case to any district or division in which it could have been brought." (emphasis added)). Among the relevant considerations for determining whether transfer is in the interest of justice, courts examine the plaintiff's reasons for filing suit in the improper district in the first place and ask whether the "plaintiff's belief that venue was proper was in good faith and reasonable." 14D CHARLES ALAN WRIGHT ET AL., FEDERAL PRACTICE AND PROCEDURE § 3827 (4th ed. 2021) [hereinafter WRIGHT & MILLER].[1] And where a "plaintiff's attorney reasonably could have foreseen that the forum in which the suit was filed was improper," courts **[—4—]** "often dismiss rather than transfer under Section 1406(a)" on the idea "that similar conduct should be discouraged." *Ibid.* That's because it is "obviously not 'in the interest of justice' to allow [§ 1406(a)] to be used to aid a non-diligent plaintiff who knowingly files a case in the wrong district." *Dubin v. United States*, 380 F.2d 813, 816 n.5 (5th Cir. 1967).

That's true even where a statute of limitations might bar re-filing. Our court has long recognized that a district court retains discretion in such cases to deny a non-diligent plaintiff's request for transfer. *See, e.g., ibid.* ("[The] statute of limitations" would be "frustrated by" § 1406 if that statute could be "used to aid a non-diligent plaintiff[.]"). Numerous other courts agree.[2] The rule is clear and well-established: **{-895-}** A district court may deny a request for transfer under § 1406 and dismiss the case where transfer would reward the **[—5—]** plaintiff's lack of diligence—even if the dismissal means the plaintiff will be time-barred from filing again in a proper venue.

B.

Appellant failed to carry her burden to show transfer was warranted here. That's because (1) MLL is not subject to personal jurisdiction in the Eastern District of Louisiana and (2) that fact was entirely foreseeable to any attorney exercising any amount of diligence.

1.

The Eastern District of Louisiana cannot assert general personal jurisdiction over MLL. Nor can it assert specific personal jurisdiction

---

[1] The full paragraph reads: "In most cases of improper venue, the courts conclude that it is in the interest of justice to transfer to a proper forum rather than to dismiss the litigation. The reasons for doing so are especially compelling if the statute of limitations has run since the commencement of the action, so that dismissal might prevent the institution of a new suit by the plaintiff and a resolution on the merits, or if the defendant has misled the plaintiff on the facts relevant to venue. District courts also are likely to order transfer rather than dismissal if it would be more efficient or economical to do so or if the plaintiff's belief that venue was proper was in good faith and reasonable. These are far from the only reasons for a court to prefer transfer to dismissal. Indeed, it is enough simply that the district judge, in the sound exercise of discretion, concludes that transfer is in the interest of justice, as many courts have concluded." 14D WRIGHT & MILLER § 3827.

[2] *See, e.g., Stanifer v. Brannan*, 564 F.3d 455, 460 (6th Cir. 2009) (explaining court's discretion to deny transfer where there was no "assertion of . . . personal jurisdiction that provided some arguable basis for thinking that the action was properly brought in the district in which it was originally filed," even if re-filing is time-barred); *Nichols v. G.D. Searle & Co.*, 991 F.2d 1195, 1202 (4th Cir. 1993) ("[A] district court does not abuse its discretion when it denies, as not in the interest of justice, a plaintiff's [transfer request under § 1406] because the plaintiff's attorney could reasonably have foreseen that the forum in which he/she filed was improper."); *Spar, Inc. v. Info. Res., Inc.*, 956 F.2d 392, 394 (2d Cir. 1992) (denying transfer where plaintiff sought "to avoid a statute of limitations defect through a transfer of venue" because it "would reward plaintiffs for their lack of diligence"); *Cirafici v. City of Ithaca*, 968 F.2d 1220 (unpublished table decision), 1992 WL 149862, at *2 (9th Cir. 1992) (holding transfer not in the interest of justice where plaintiff "was not diligent in prosecuting his action," even though plaintiff's "action may be time-barred"); *Deleski v. Raymark Indus., Inc.*, 819 F.2d 377, 381 (3d Cir. 1987) ("It is not in the 'interest of justice' to transfer this case . . . upon appellant's tardy discovery that her complaint is time-barred."); *Coté v. Wadel*, 796 F.2d 981, 985 (7th Cir. 1986) (denying transfer request where limitations period had run and "[e]lementary prudence would have indicated to [plaintiff's] lawyer that he must file a protective suit" in the forum "where the plaintiff can get personal jurisdiction over the defendant before, not after, the statute of limitations runs").

over MLL. So MLL is not subject to personal jurisdiction in the district where appellant filed suit.

First, general personal jurisdiction. A court may assert general personal jurisdiction over foreign corporations "when their affiliations with the State are so continuous and systematic as to render them essentially at home in the forum State." *BNSF Ry. Co. v. Tyrrell*, 137 S. Ct. 1549, 1558, 5 Adm. R. 2, 6 (2017) (quotation omitted). There are two "paradigm" forums in which a corporate defendant is "at home." *Ibid.*, 5 Adm. R. at 6 (quotation omitted). They are (1) the corporation's place of incorporation and (2) its principal place of business. *See ibid.*, 5 Adm. R. at 6. Beyond those two "paradigm" forums, there may also be "exceptional case[s]" where the exercise of general jurisdiction is appropriate because a corporate defendant's operations are "so substantial and of such a nature as to render the corporation at home" in the forum State. *Ibid.*, 5 Adm. R. at 6 (quotation omitted). But it is "incredibly difficult to establish general jurisdiction in a forum other than the place of incorporation or principal place of business." *Frank v. P N K (Lake Charles) LLC*, 947 F.3d 331, 337 (5th Cir. 2020) (quotation omitted). **[—6—]**

MLL is incorporated in Delaware. Its principal place of business is in Virginia. And appellant offers no reason whatsoever to think this might be "the exceptional case" where MLL's activities in Louisiana are so substantial as to render it at home there. So MLL is not subject to general personal jurisdiction in the Eastern District of Louisiana.

Second, specific personal jurisdiction. Specific jurisdiction "focuses on the relationship among the defendant, the forum, and the litigation." *Walden v. Fiore*, 571 U.S. 277, 284 (2014) (quotation omitted). It "arises when a defendant's minimum contacts with a forum state are related to the pending lawsuit." *E. Concrete Materials, Inc. v. ACE Am. Ins. Co.*, 948 F.3d 289, 296 (5th Cir. 2020). Our court applies a three-prong analysis: We consider "(1) whether the defendant has minimum contacts with the forum [S]tate, i.e., whether it purposely directed its activities toward the forum [S]tate or purposefully availed itself of the privileges of conducting activities there." *Monkton Ins. Servs., Ltd. v. Ritter*, 768 F.3d 429, 433 (5th Cir. 2014) (quoting *Seiferth v. Helicopteros Atuneros, Inc.*, 472 F.3d 266, 271 (5th Cir. 2006)). Then we analyze "(2) whether the plaintiff's cause of action arises out of or results from the defendant's forum-related contacts." *Ibid.* Finally, we ask "(3) whether the exercise of personal jurisdiction is fair and reasonable." *Ibid.* It's the plaintiff's burden to establish the first two prongs. **{-896-}** *See E. Concrete Materials*, 948 F.3d at 296.

Appellant can't meet that burden. Her complaint alleged that MLL does business in Louisiana and is amenable to process there. But there is simply no basis to conclude appellant's cause of action arises out of those forum-related contacts. All agree the cause of action arises out of events that took place far from Louisiana in the waters of Bahrain, and appellant has made no effort to connect the accident in Bahrain to MLL's business in Louisiana. Absent any attempt to explain the relationship between the **[—7—]** defendant, the forum, and this litigation, there is no way for appellant to establish specific jurisdiction.

2.

A district court might excuse this sort of mistake where plaintiff's attorney could not reasonably have anticipated the venue problem. That's especially true if it becomes clear the defendant is at fault—where, for example, "the defendant has misled the plaintiff on the facts relevant to venue." 14D WRIGHT & MILLER § 3827. But where "the plaintiff's attorney reasonably could have foreseen that the forum in which the suit was filed was improper," *ibid.*, transfer is normally unwarranted. And here, it was entirely foreseeable that the Eastern District of Louisiana lacked personal jurisdiction over MLL.

It is evident from the face of the complaint that MLL is not subject to general jurisdiction in the Eastern District of Louisiana. The complaint alleged that MLL is a Delaware corporation with its principal place of business in Virginia. And the complaint is devoid of any allegations that come close to suggesting MLL's activities in Louisiana are so substantial as to render it at home there. So "elementary prudence" should have revealed to Seville's attorney that the Eastern District of Louisiana lacked general personal jurisdiction over MLL. *Coté v. Wadel*, 796 F.2d 981, 985 (7th Cir. 1986).

So too with specific jurisdiction. As already explained, nothing in appellant's filings suggests a connection between defendant's forum-related contacts and this litigation. Moreover, appellant openly *admitted* there was no basis for thinking such a connection existed: When asked at oral argument to identify the connection between this lawsuit and the chosen forum, appellant's attorney told us "there isn't a connection, other than that we [appellant's attorneys] actually practice here [in the Eastern District of **[—8—]** Louisiana]." Oral Arg. at 9:20–9:35. It should go without saying that an attorney cannot choose a venue based on personal convenience.

Nor can an attorney file in the wrong venue and hope his opponent doesn't object. At oral argument, appellant's counsel purported to justify filing in the wrong venue on the ground that personal jurisdiction is waivable. *See* Oral Arg. at 11:40–12:30 (Q: "So it's okay for your law firm to file any suit at all in the district where you practice and place the burden on the defendant to transfer to the proper venue at any time, is that what you think § 1406 says?" A: ". . . I'm saying yes to your question because there's always a chance that they waive the jurisdiction themselves."). It's true that personal jurisdiction is waivable. It's also irrelevant. That's because the Federal Rules of Civil Procedure require a good-faith and colorable basis for *every* representation made to a federal court—no matter whether the other side objects. Specifically:

> REPRESENTATIONS TO THE COURT. By presenting to the court a pleading, written motion, or other paper—whether by signing, filing, submitting, or later advocating it—an attorney or unrepresented party certifies that to the best of the person's knowledge, information, and belief, **{-897-}** formed after an inquiry reasonable under the circumstances:
>
> . . .
>
> (2) the claims, defenses, and other legal contentions are warranted by existing law or by a nonfrivolous argument for extending, modifying, or reversing existing law or for establishing new law[.]

FED. R. CIV. P. 11(b)(2).

Appellant's attorney filed the complaint in the Eastern District of Louisiana and represented that "MLL is subject to and within the jurisdiction and venue of [that] Court." Yet at oral argument, counsel stated **[—9—]** that he (1) believed he needed no colorable basis for filing in that district, (2) in fact had no colorable basis for the representation he made as to jurisdiction and venue, (3) had known from the start that his only real chance of establishing personal jurisdiction and venue was if the defendant failed to object, and (4) figured he could always obtain a transfer under § 1406 if it turned out defendant objected. Those statements are equal parts disturbing and surprising. Today we hold that such admissions not only foreclose transfer under § 1406, on defendant's objection, but also give rise to Rule 11 violations.

C.

Section 1406 "confer[s] broad discretion in ruling on a motion to transfer." *Stanifer v. Brannan*, 564 F.3d 455, 456–57 (6th Cir. 2009). And a district court's decision to deny a motion to transfer venue "will not be reversed on appeal absent an abuse of discretion." *Peteet v. Dow Chem. Co.*, 868 F.2d 1428, 1436 (5th Cir. 1989).

It was clearly not an abuse of discretion for the district court to deny appellant's motion to transfer venue in this case. Appellant's attorney, by his own admission, knew there was no colorable basis for laying venue in the Eastern District of Louisiana. We have long made clear that it is "obviously not in the interest of justice to allow [§ 1406] to be used to aid a non-diligent plaintiff who knowingly files a case in the wrong district." *Dubin*, 380 F.2d at 816 n.5 (quotation omitted).

* * *

For these reasons, we AFFIRM the district court's order dismissing the case for lack of personal jurisdiction and denying appellant's request to transfer under 28 U.S.C. § 1406.

United States Court of Appeals for the Ninth Circuit

United States Court of Appeals
for the Ninth Circuit

No. 20-35818

ICTSI OREGON, INC.
vs.
INTERNATIONAL LONGSHORE & WAREHOUSE UNION

Appeal from the United States District Court for the District of Oregon

Decided: January 18, 2022

Citation: 22 F.4th 1125, 10 Adm. R. 278 (9th Cir. 2022).

Before **O'SCANNLAIN**, **CLIFTON**, and **NGUYEN**, Circuit Judges.

[—5—] **{-1127-}** **O'SCANNLAIN**, Circuit Judge: **{-1128-}**

This case arises out of the high-profile labor dispute that led to the closing of Terminal 6 of the Port of Portland to ocean-going cargo for more than a year.

I

A

On the west coast of the United States, the work of loading and unloading containers on and off international ocean-going vessels is typically performed by members of local unions affiliated with International Longshore and Warehouse Union ("ILWU National"). *Shipowners' Ass'n of the Pac. Coast*, 7 NLRB 1002, 1007–14 (1938). Some of the containers are refrigerated and are known as "reefers." While a reefer is off the vessel, it must be connected to a power source to maintain refrigeration. Handling reefers while they are off the vessels is known as "reefer work." Under the collective-bargaining agreement between ILWU National and Pacific Maritime Association ("PMA"), when a PMA member has the right to assign reefer work, it must assign it to a union affiliated with ILWU National. **[—6—]**

Before 2010, the Port of Portland ("the Port"), not a PMA member, had been assigning reefer work to members of International Brotherhood of Electrical Workers ("IBEW"), a different union. In 2010, marine terminal operator ICTSI Oregon, Inc. ("ICTSI"), a PMA member, leased Terminal 6 from the Port. However, under the lease, the Port retained control over the reefer work and continued assigning it to members of IBEW.

In 2012, upset by this arrangement, ILWU National and its affiliate, International Longshore and Warehouse Union Local 8 (collectively "ILWU") engaged in high-profile work stoppages, slowdowns, and other coercive activity at Terminal 6. *See, e.g.*, Richard Read, *Port of Portland's Troubled Terminal 6 Shuts for Second Day in a Row, Following Altercation*, The Oregonian (Mar. 5, 2014, 8:30 p.m.), https://www.oregonlive.com/business/2014/03/troubled_port_of_portland_cont.html. **{-1129-}** The ocean-going cargo traffic ceased for more than a year. By 2017, ILWU's actions forced ICTSI to buy back the remainder of its lease from the Port and to leave Terminal 6.

B

1

In response to these actions, ICTSI filed charges against ILWU with the National Labor Relations Board ("NLRB"). The Administrative Law Judge ("ALJ") found that ICTSI was a neutral, or secondary employer for purposes of the reefer dispute because the dispute was between the Port and ILWU. *ILWU*, 363 NLRB No. 47 (Nov. 30, 2015); *ILWU*, 363 NLRB No. 12 (Sept. 24, 2015). Based on this finding, the agency held that, between May 2012 and August 2013, ILWU violated 29 U.S.C. § 158(b)(4)(B), prohibiting unions from interfering with secondary employers (ICTSI) with the **[—7—]** purpose of coercing them into pressuring primary employers (the Port) to satisfy unions' (ILWU) demands (assignment of reefer work). *ILWU*, 363 NLRB No. 47; *ILWU*, 363 NLRB No. 12. The DC Circuit affirmed. *ILWU v. NLRB*, 705 F. App'x 3, 4 (D.C. Cir. 2017); *ILWU v. NLRB*, 705 F. App'x 1, 2–3 (D.C. Cir. 2017).

2

In this action, ICTSI seeks damages from ILWU for its violation of § 158(b)(4)(B). Before trial, interpreting this court's decision in *Mead v. Retail Clerks Int'l Ass'n, Loc. Union No. 839*, 523 F.2d 1371 (9th Cir. 1975), the district court assigned ICTSI the burden of proving three elements: (1) "[ILWU] engaged in . . . coercive job activity;" (2) "[o]btaining the reefer work was a substantial factor motivating that coercive activity, making it unlawful secondary activity;" and (3) "unlawful secondary activity was a substantial factor in causing ICTSI's damages." In turn, ILWU was allocated the burden of showing that ICTSI's damages were attributable to other factors, such as lawful labor activity or outside causes, like lower customer demand. Further, if ILWU prevailed in showing that other factors caused ICTSI's damages, it would have to show that the damages caused by its unlawful conduct and those other factors could be divided.

After a ten-day trial, the jury returned a verdict for more than $93.5 million for ICTSI. Among other findings, the jurors concluded that all of ILWU's actions were unlawful and that those actions were the sole cause of ICTSI's damages. Accordingly, they did not reach the issue of divisibility.

Later, ILWU moved for judgment as a matter of law ("JMOL") and new trial or remittitur. It argued that ICTSI **[—8—]** failed to carry its burden of proof as to liability and damages. The court denied outright the motion for new trial as to liability and also as to damages but conditioned its denial on ICTSI's acceptance of remittitur to $19 million. ICTSI rejected remittitur of damages. The court denied all other motions.

Then, ILWU filed a motion asking the district court to certify its post-trial order for interlocutory appeal under 28 U.S.C. § 1292(b). The district court granted such motion. It found that two questions satisfied the jurisdictional requirements of that section. The first question was whether the district court "correctly interpreted *Mead*" when it assigned ILWU the burdens of proving apportionment and divisibility of damages. The second was whether "ICTSI lost its status as a 'secondary employer'" by entangling itself in the dispute between ILWU and the Port.

3

In this Court, ILWU filed a petition for permission to appeal the certified order as **{-1130-}** required for interlocutory appeal jurisdiction under § 1292(b). ICTSI filed an answer opposing ILWU's petition and, in the alternative, asking us for permission to cross-appeal. A motions panel of this Court granted permission to ILWU to appeal and to ICTSI to cross-appeal.

On this interlocutory appeal, ILWU challenges the district court's denial of JMOL and the jury instructions. On cross-appeal, ICTSI challenges the district court's grant of new trial conditioned on remittitur. **[—9—]**

II

As a threshold matter, we must decide if we have jurisdiction to hear this case. ILWU argues that the two questions identified by the district court satisfy the requirements for interlocutory appeal under § 1292(b) and, thus, grant us jurisdiction.

A

We tackle the second issue first. ILWU argues that the question of whether "ICSTI [sic] entangled itself in the 'vortex' of ILWU's dispute with the Port . . . to such a degree that ICTSI lost its status as a 'secondary employer'" satisfies the hallmarks of § 1292(b). We must decide whether ILWU has stated a question of law.

1

Under 28 U.S.C. § 1292(b) parties may take an interlocutory appeal when "exceptional circumstances justify a departure from the basic policy of postponing appellate review until after the entry of a final judgment." *Coopers & Lybrand v. Livesay*, 437 U.S. 463, 475 (1978); *see also U.S. Rubber Co. v. Wright*, 359 F.2d 784, 785 (9th Cir. 1966) (per curiam).

Broadly, there are two requirements that must be met before we can assert jurisdiction over an interlocutory appeal.

a

The first jurisdictional requirement is that the district court must certify its order for appeal. To do so, it must determine that the order meets the three certification requirements outlined in § 1292(b): "(1) that there be a controlling question of law, (2) that there be substantial **[—10—]** grounds for difference of opinion [as to that question], and (3) that an immediate [resolution of that question] may materially advance the ultimate termination of the litigation." *In re Cement Antitrust Litig. (MDL No. 296)*, 673 F.2d 1020, 1026 (9th Cir. 1981).

A controlling question of law must be one of law—not fact—and its resolution must "materially affect the outcome of litigation in the district court." *Id.* at 1026; *see also Northwestern Ohio Adm'rs v. Walcher & Fox*, 270 F.3d 1018, 1023 (6th Cir. 2001) ("Because this is an interlocutory appeal, we have no authority to review the district court's findings of fact, but must confine our review to . . . questions of law."); *Clark-Dietz & Assocs.-Eng'rs v. Basic Const.*, 702 F.2d 67, 69 (5th Cir. 1983) ("[F]act-review questions [are] inappropriate for § 1292(b) review.").

The "substantial grounds" prong is satisfied when "novel legal issues are presented, on which fair-minded jurists might reach contradictory conclusions." *Reese v. BP Expl. (Alaska) Inc.*, 643 F.3d 681, 688 (9th Cir. 2011). For example, this prong is satisfied if "the circuits are in dispute on the question and the court of appeals of the circuit has not spoken on the point, if complicated questions arise under foreign law, or if novel and difficult questions of first impression are presented." *Couch v. Telescope Inc.*, 611 F.3d 629, 633 (9th Cir. 2010). However, the district court need not "await[] development of contradictory precedent" before concluding that the question presents a "substantial **{-1131-}** ground for difference of opinion." *Reese*, 643 F.3d at 688.

Finally, the "materially advance" prong is satisfied when the resolution of the question "may appreciably shorten the time, effort, or expense of conducting" the district court proceedings. *In re Cement*, 673 F.2d at 1027. As to the **[—11—]** timing of certification, the district court may certify the order for interlocutory appeal in the text of that order or in a separate order, known as the certification order. *In re Benny*, 812 F.2d 1133, 1136–37 (9th Cir. 1987).

b

The second jurisdictional requirement is that the party seeking appeal must make an "application . . . [to this court] within ten days after the entry of the [certification] order." 28 U.S.C. § 1292(b). The clock starts ticking from the moment the district court certifies the order, and not from the moment the order is issued. *In re Benny*, 812 F.2d at 1137. Typically, a motions panel of this court will then decide whether to grant or deny the application. *See, e.g., Reese*, 643 F.3d at 688; *Couch*, 611 F.3d at 632; *Kuehner v. Dickinson & Co.*, 84 F.3d 316, 318–19 (9th Cir. 1996). If the application is granted, the case will be assigned to a merits panel.

The merits panel then must agree that the requirements of § 1292(b) are met. "The opinion of the district judge that a controlling question is involved, while deserving of careful consideration, is not binding upon this court . . . ." *United States v. Woodbury*, 263 F.2d 784, 786 (9th Cir. 1959). Similarly, although we "[do] not lightly overturn a decision made by a motions panel during the course of the same appeal, we do not apply the law of the case doctrine . . . strictly in that instance." *United States v. Houser*, 804 F.2d 565, 568 (9th Cir. 1986), *abrogated on other grounds by Christianson v. Colt Indus. Operating Corp.*, 486 U.S. 800, 816–817 & n.5 (1988); *see also Kuehner*, 84 F.3d at 318–19. **[—12—]**

c

Even when this court has jurisdiction over an issue under § 1292(b), it enjoys broad discretion to refuse to accept it. "[T]he appellant . . . 'has the burden of persuading the court of appeals that exceptional circumstances justify a departure from the basic policy of postponing appellate review until after the entry of a final judgment.'" *Coopers*, 437 U.S. at 475. Although there is little guiding that discretion in the text of § 1292(b) or our caselaw, it has been compared to the discretion the Supreme Court enjoys when reviewing petitions for certiorari. *In re Convertible Rowing Exerciser Patent Litig.*, 903 F.2d 822, 822 (Fed. Cir. 1990). For example, this court may decline to exercise jurisdiction for reasons having little to do with the appeal itself, such as docket congestion. *Coopers*, 437 U.S. at 475. Indeed, it need not offer any reason at all. 16 Wright & Miller, *Federal Practice and Procedure* § 3929 (3d ed. 1998) ("[P]ermission might be denied without specifying reasons . . . ."). Similarly, nothing precludes this court from declining to assert jurisdiction after oral arguments. *Molybdenum Corp. of Am. v. Kasey*, 279 F.2d 216, 217 (9th Cir. 1960) (per curiam). Or from hearing some of the issues, but not others—including refusing to decide the question that provided the basis for certification. *Yamaha Motor Corp., U.S.A. v. Calhoun*, 516 U.S. 199, 203–04 (1996). Thus, even when this court has interlocutory jurisdiction, it is free to decline to hear some or all the issues the parties raise on appeal.

2

Taking the foregoing into consideration, we must conclude that the question **{-1132-}** that ILWU relies on is a question of fact, not "of law." *See* 28 U.S.C. § 1292(b). As is evident from the plain text of § 1292(b), for a question to confer **[—13—]** interlocutory jurisdiction on this court it must be a "question of law." *Id.*; *see also Walcher & Fox*, 270 F.3d at 1023; *Clark-Dietz*, 702 F.2d at 69; Wright & Miller § 3930. The dispute between the parties is not about whether primary—as opposed to secondary—employers can recover damages for violation of § 158(b)(4)(B) (a question of law); rather the dispute is about whether ICTSI became a primary employer under the circumstances of this case (a question of fact). Ruling on this issue, the district court primarily relied on facts from the record. So did ILWU's analysis in its opening and reply briefs and ICTSI's in its answer.

Indeed, such question does not present a substantial ground for disagreement as to the question of law. As we have explained, "[c]ourts traditionally will find that a substantial ground for difference of opinion exists where 'the circuits are in dispute on the question and the court of appeals of the circuit has not spoken on the point, if complicated questions arise under foreign law, or if novel and difficult questions of first impression are presented.'" *Couch*, 611 F.3d at 633. That is not the case here, and ILWU does not argue otherwise. Such question, therefore, does not satisfy the requirements of § 1292(b) and cannot be the basis for jurisdiction in this Court.

B

ILWU also contends that there is another basis for jurisdiction: the separate question of whether the district court "correctly interpreted *Mead*" when it assigned ILWU the burdens of proving apportionment and divisibility of damages.

The district court acknowledged and the parties do not dispute that the *Mead* question is not addressed in the four corners of the certified order. In that order, the district court **[—14—]** did not revisit its pre-trial rulings allocating the burdens of proof in view of *Mead*. As the court acknowledged, "[t]he two citations to *Mead* in the Post-Trial Opinion are not related to the Court's interpretation of *Mead* currently challenged by ILWU related to . . . divisibility and apportionment of damages." Nor did ILWU challenge those rulings in its post-trial motions.

ILWU, however, argues that we may reach the *Mead* issue under *In re Cinematronics*, 916 F.2d 1444 (9th Cir. 1990) and *Canela v. Costco Wholesale*, 971 F.3d 845 (9th Cir. 2020). The narrow issue before us is, then, whether a question not decided within the four corners of the certified order can confer jurisdiction on this court over such order.

1

When this court concludes that the question identified by the district court satisfies the requirements of § 1292(b), we have jurisdiction over *any* question within the four corners of the certified order—not just the identified controlling question. *Yamaha*, 516 U.S. at 205. Importantly, however, jurisdiction does not extend to other orders entered in the same case. *Id.* ("The court of appeals may not reach beyond the certified order to address other orders made in the case."); *Deutsche Bank v. FDIC*, 744 F.3d 1124, 1134–35 (9th Cir. 2014) ("In keeping with the letter and spirit of § 1292(b), our precedent, and Supreme Court guidance, we limit the scope of this appeal to the certified order and decline to reach any issues that are not encompassed within the certified order issued by the district court.").

We have recognized an exception to the statute's jurisdictional ambit: our interlocutory jurisdiction extends to a question outside the order when such **{-1133-}** question is "material" to the certified order. *Cinematronics*, 916 F.2d at 1449. **[—15—]** *Cinematronics* concerned a bankruptcy proceeding. *Id.* at 1446–47. In a first order, the bankruptcy court held that the claims before it were part of the "core bankruptcy proceedings" and, thus, it could issue "a final and binding judgment." *Id.* at 1447. It also found that the litigants had a right to jury trial on those claims. *Id.* However, it doubted that it had the authority to conduct a jury trial and asked the district court to do it instead. *Id.* In a second order, the district court found "that bankruptcy courts have authority to conduct jury trials in core proceedings." *Id.* at 1448. It did not, however, revisit the bankruptcy court's holding that the claims were part of core proceedings. *Id.* The district court then certified its order for interlocutory appeal to this court. *Id.*

We held that we had jurisdiction under § 1292(b) to review the bankruptcy court's conclusion that the claims were part of the core proceedings even though that holding was not part of the order certified by the district court. *Id.* at 1449. We observed that "the validity of the district court's decision . . . is inextricably tied to the bankruptcy judge's earlier ruling that . . . [the] claims constitute core bankruptcy proceedings." *Id.* The court summarized its reading of § 1292(b) by noting that in "a situation[] where reconsideration of a ruling material to an order provides grounds for reversal of the *entire* order," this court may address issues outside the four corners of the properly certified order. *Id.* (emphasis added).

Relying on *Cinematronics*, this court also reached outside the certified order in *Canela*. In that case, the district court decided, in a first order, that it had subject matter jurisdiction over the lawsuit. *Id.* at 848. In a second order, it denied Costco's motion for partial summary judgment on the issue of whether Canela had Article III standing to pursue **[—16—]** some of its claims. *Id.* The district court then certified the second order for interlocutory appeal after determining that the standing question passed the § 1292(b) test. *Canela v. Costco Wholesale Corp.*, No. 13-CV-03598-BLF, 2018 WL 3008532, at *1–3 (N.D. Cal. June 15, 2018). On appeal, this court concluded that it had jurisdiction to review the district court's jurisdictional ruling, made in the first order. *Canela*, 917 F.3d at 849. "Because the district court's subject matter jurisdiction is '*material*' to the summary judgment before us, we address it here," the court noted. *Id.* (quoting *Cinematronics*, 916 F.2d at 1449). This conclusion was consistent with *Cinematronics* because, just as in that case, reversing the district court's subject matter jurisdiction decision would have nullified the certified order. *Cinematronics*, 916 F.2d at 1449.

Thus, *Cinematronics* and *Canela* allow panels to assert interlocutory jurisdiction over issues not included in the four corners of the properly certified order when such issues are "material" to such order. *Id.*

2

However, the posture of this interlocutory appeal is unlike those of the appeals in *Cinematronics* and *Canela*. In those cases, as discussed above, the district court identified questions that properly satisfied the requirements of § 1292(b) within the four corners of the certified orders. For example, in *Cinematronics*, the district court certified the order based on the question of whether "bankruptcy courts have authority to conduct jury trials in core proceedings." *Cinematronics*, 916 F.2d at 1448. Similarly, in *Canela*, the controlling question in the order was whether Canela had Article III standing. *Canela*, 2018 WL 3008532, at *1–3. Once this court had jurisdiction to "permit an appeal to be taken from such order," **{-1134-}** 28 U.S.C. § 1292(b), based on those **[—17—]** questions, it was able to *extend* its interlocutory jurisdiction to the bankruptcy court's determination that the "claims constitute[d] core bankruptcy proceedings," *Cinematronics*, 916 F.2d at 1449, and to the district court's conclusion that it had subject matter jurisdiction, *Canela*, 971 F.3d at 849.

Here, by contrast, the only question in the four corners of the certified order that purportedly satisfies § 1292(b) is the "secondary employer" question. As discussed above, that question fails because it is not a question of law. Thus, unlike in *Cinematronics* and *Canela*, we cannot establish jurisdiction over the certified post-trial order. It follows that we cannot extend that jurisdiction to the *Mead* issue decided in the pre-trial ruling. The two precedents ILWU is relying on are, therefore, inapplicable here.

Accordingly, we lack jurisdiction under § 1292(b) to consider this question. In light of our disposition, the parties will have to continue their litigation in the district court, at least for now.

III

The appeals are **DISMISSED** for lack of jurisdiction.[1, 2]

---

[1] Even assuming we had jurisdiction, we would be inclined to exercise our discretion not to hear this case as the issues raised by the parties are factual, focusing on damages rather than liability. *Cf. Coopers*, 437 U.S. at 475.

[2] PMA's motion for leave to file an *amicus curiae* brief in support of ILWU is **GRANTED**.

United States Court of Appeals
for the Ninth Circuit

No. 18-15499

COUNTY OF SAN MATEO
vs.
CHEVRON CORP.

On Remand from the United States Supreme Court

Decided: April 19, 2022

Citation: 32 F.4th 733, 10 Adm. R. 284 (9th Cir. 2022).

Before **IKUTA, CHRISTEN,** and **LEE,** Circuit Judges.

[—17—] {-743-} IKUTA, Circuit Judge: **{-744-}**

This appeal requires us to determine whether a district court erred in remanding the plaintiffs' global-warming related complaints to state court after they were removed by the energy company defendants. On appeal, the defendants argue that the district court had removal jurisdiction over these complaints on multiple grounds, including federal question and federal enclave jurisdiction under 28 U.S.C. § 1331, federal officer removal jurisdiction under 28 U.S.C. § 1442(a)(1), bankruptcy jurisdiction under 28 U.S.C. § 1452(a) and 28 U.S.C. § 1334(b), and admiralty jurisdiction under 28 U.S.C. § 1333(1). Because the district court did not err in concluding that it lacked subject matter jurisdiction under any of these asserted grounds, we affirm.

I

The County of San Mateo, the County of Marin, and the City of Imperial Beach filed three materially similar complaints in California state court against more than 30 energy companies in July 2017.[1] The complaints allege that the Energy Companies' "extraction, refining, and/or formulation of fossil fuel products; their introduction of fossil fuel products into the stream of commerce; their wrongful promotion of their fossil fuel products and concealment of known hazards associated with use of those products; and their failure to pursue less hazardous alternatives available to them; is a substantial factor in causing the increase in global **[—18—]** mean temperature and consequent increase in global mean sea surface height." Further, according to the complaints, the Counties "have already incurred, and will foreseeably continue to incur, injuries and damages because of sea level rise caused by [the Energy Companies'] conduct." Such "sea level rise-related injuries and damages" include flooding that causes injury and damages to real property and its improvements, and prevents the "free passage on, use of, and normal enjoyment of that real property, or permanently [destroys] it." For instance, the Counties allege that Surfer's Beach near the city of Half Moon Bay "has lost 140 feet of accessible beach since 1964 due to erosion, which has been exacerbated and substantially contributed to by sea level rise and increased extreme weather." Other injuries caused by sea level rise, according to the Counties, include "infrastructural repair and reinforcement of roads and beach access." Based on these allegations, the complaints assert causes of action for public and private nuisance, strict liability for failure to warn, strict liability for design defect, negligence, negligent failure to warn, and trespass.

The Energy Companies removed the three complaints to federal court, asserting multiple bases for subject matter jurisdiction: (1) the Counties' claims raise disputed and substantial federal issues, *see Grable & Sons Metal Prods., Inc. v. Darue Eng'g & Mfg.*, 545 U.S. 308 (2005); (2) the Counties' claims are "completely preempted" by federal law; (3) the Counties' claims arose on "federal enclaves"; (4) the Counties' claims arise out of operations on the outer Continental Shelf, *see* 43 U.S.C. § 1349(b); (5) the Counties' claims arise from actions **{-745-}** that were taken by the Energy Companies pursuant to a federal officer's directions, *see* 28 U.S.C. § 1442(a); and (6) the Counties' claims are related to bankruptcy cases, *see* 28 U.S.C. §§ 1452(a), 1334(b). **[—19—]**

Shortly after the complaints were filed, the County of Santa Cruz, the City of Santa Cruz,

[1] We refer to the plaintiffs collectively as the "Counties" and to the defendants collectively as the "Energy Companies."

and the City of Richmond filed materially similar complaints in California state court. The Energy Companies removed these cases to federal court as well, asserting the same six bases for subject matter jurisdiction. Marathon Petroleum Corporation raised an additional ground for removal: the complaints raised issues concerning maritime activities, giving rise to admiralty jurisdiction. *See* 28 U.S.C. § 1333. These cases were assigned to the same district judge.

The Counties moved to remand each case to state court based on a lack of subject matter jurisdiction. In a reasoned opinion, the district court rejected all the grounds on which the Energy Companies relied for subject matter jurisdiction, but stayed its remand orders to give the Energy Companies an opportunity to appeal.

The Energy Companies appealed, and we affirmed the district court's determination that no subject matter jurisdiction existed under the federal-officer removal statute. *County of San Mateo v. Chevron Corp.*, 960 F.3d 586, 603 (9th Cir. 2020), *vacated*, 141 S. Ct. 2666 (2021) (mem.). We dismissed the rest of the appeal for lack of appellate jurisdiction. *Id.* Under 28 U.S.C. § 1447(d), "[1] [a]n order remanding a case to the State court from which it was removed is not reviewable on appeal or otherwise [(referred to as the "non-reviewability clause")], [2] except that an order remanding a case to the State court from which it was removed pursuant to section 1442 or 1443 of this title shall be reviewable by appeal or otherwise [(referred to as the **[—20—]** "exceptions clause")]."[2] We concluded that we lacked authority to review the remand order under the non- reviewability clause because the district court's order remanded the complaints on subject matter jurisdiction grounds, and the non-reviewability clause applies when a district court bases its remand order on subject matter jurisdiction or nonjurisdictional defects. *San Mateo*, 960 F.3d at 594–95 (citing *Atl. Nat'l Tr. LLC v. Mt. Hawley Ins. Co.*, 621 F.3d 931, 934 (9th Cir. 2010)). We also concluded that we lacked authority to review the remand order under the exceptions clause because we were bound by our precedent, *see Patel v. Del Taco, Inc.*, 446 F.3d 996, 998 (9th Cir. 2006), which indicated we had the authority to review only the portion of the district court's remand order that addressed 28 U.S.C. § 1442(a), federal officer removal, but lacked jurisdiction to review the appeal from the portions of the remand order that considered the other bases for subject matter jurisdiction, *San Mateo*, 960 F.3d at 595–96. Therefore, we rejected the Energy Companies' argument that 28 U.S.C. § 1447(d) gave us the authority to conduct plenary review of the district court's remand order and did not address the other bases for removal. *Id.* at 603.

The Energy Companies sought review by the Supreme Court. While the Energy Companies' petition for certiorari was pending, the Supreme Court decided *BP p.l.c. v. Mayor & City Council of Baltimore*, 141 S. Ct. 1532 (2021). *Baltimore* interpreted § 1447(d) as permitting appellate review of **{–746–}** all the defendants' grounds for removal under that section, and overruled the Fourth Circuit's interpretation of **[—21—]** § 1447(d) as limiting appellate review of a remand order to "the *part* of the district court's remand order" discussing § 1442 or 1443. *See Baltimore*, 141 S. Ct. at 1537. The Supreme Court then granted the petition for writ of certiorari in *San Mateo*, vacated judgment, and remanded for further consideration in light of *Baltimore*. *Chevron Corp. v. San Mateo County, California*, 141 S. Ct. 2666 (2021).

On remand, we conclude that *Baltimore* has effectively abrogated *Patel*'s reasoning and holding "in such a way that the cases are clearly irreconcilable." *Miller v. Gammie*, 335 F.3d 889, 900 (9th Cir. 2003) (en banc). Because *Baltimore* held that § 1447(d) gives us the authority to review the district court's entire remand order, 141 S. Ct. at 1538, we now consider all bases for removal raised by the defendants, rather than addressing only federal officer removal.

[2] 28 U.S.C. § 1442 relates to removal of an action against an agency or an officer of the United States, or "any person acting under that officer," and 28 U.S.C. § 1443 relates to civil rights cases.

We have jurisdiction under 28 U.S.C. § 1291. We review questions of statutory construction and subject matter jurisdiction de novo. *Ritchey v. Upjohn Drug Co.*, 139 F.3d 1313, 1315 (9th Cir. 1998). The defendant has the burden of proving by a preponderance of the evidence that the requirements for removal jurisdiction have been met. *Leite v. Crane Co.*, 749 F.3d 1117, 1122 (9th Cir. 2014).

II

A

We start with the Energy Companies' argument that the district court erred in rejecting its claims that it had federal-question jurisdiction under 28 U.S.C. § 1331, which provides that "district courts shall have original jurisdiction of all civil **[—22—]** actions arising under the Constitution, laws, or treaties of the United States." 28 U.S.C. §1331.

At the time of removal, the Counties' complaints asserted only state-law claims against the Energy Companies. Under the well-pleaded complaint rule, the plaintiff is "the 'master of the claim'" and can generally avoid federal jurisdiction if a federal question does not appear on the face of the complaint. *City of Oakland v. BP PLC*, 969 F.3d 895, 904 (9th Cir. 2020) (quoting *Caterpillar Inc. v. Williams*, 482 U.S. 386, 392 (1987)). The Energy Companies argue that the Counties' global-warming claims arise under federal common law and are removable under two exceptions to the well-pleaded complaint rule: (1) the exception articulated in *Grable*; and (2) the doctrine of complete preemption. We consider each in turn.

1

Grable affirmed a long line of Supreme Court cases that recognized an exception to the well-pleaded complaint rule when "federal law is a necessary element of the [plaintiff's] claim for relief." *Oakland*, 969 F.3d at 904 (cleaned up). "Only a few cases" have ever fallen into this narrow category. *Id.* Under this exception, "federal jurisdiction over a state law claim will lie if a federal issue is: (1) necessarily raised, (2) actually disputed, (3) substantial, and (4) capable of resolution in federal court without disrupting the federal-state balance approved by Congress." *Gunn v. Minton*, 568 U.S. 251, 258 (2013). If those requirements are met, federal jurisdiction exists "because there is a 'serious federal interest in claiming the advantages thought to be inherent in a federal forum,' which can be vindicated without disrupting Congress's **{-747-}** intended division of labor between state and **[—23—]** federal courts." *Id.* (quoting *Grable*, 545 U.S. at 313–14). The inquiry under *Grable* often focuses on the third requirement, which asks whether the case "turn[s] on substantial questions of federal law." *Oakland*, 969 F.3d at 905 (quoting *Grable*, 545 U.S. at 312).

In *Oakland*, we considered a similar issue. In that case, two cities sued various energy companies in state court, raising a state-law claim for public nuisance based on "production and promotion of massive quantities of fossil fuels" which "caused or contributed to 'global warming-induced sea level rise,'" and in turn led to injuries to the cities' wastewater treatment systems and stormwater infrastructure, as well as other injuries. *Id.* at 901–02. The energy companies argued that we had federal jurisdiction over the state complaint under the exception to the well-pleaded complaint rule for substantial federal questions. *Id.* at 902.

We rejected this argument, holding that even assuming that the complaint "could give rise to a cognizable claim for public nuisance under federal common law," the state law claim in that case did not raise a substantial federal question because "the claim neither requires an interpretation of a federal statute . . . nor challenges a federal statute's constitutionality," nor identifies "a legal issue necessarily raised by the claim that, if decided, will be controlling in numerous other cases." *Id.* at 906 (cleaned up). Further, as we explained:

> [I]t is not clear that the claim requires an interpretation or application of federal law at all, because the Supreme

> Court has not yet determined that there is a federal common law **[—24—]** of public nuisance relating to interstate pollution, and we have held that federal public-nuisance claims aimed at imposing liability on energy producers for acting in concert to create, contribute to, and maintain global warming and conspiring to mislead the public about the science of global warming, are displaced by the Clean Air Act.

Id. (cleaned up).

We also rejected the energy companies' argument that because the complaint "implicates a variety of 'federal interests,'" including energy policy, national security, and foreign policy, the complaint necessarily raised a substantial federal question. *Id.* at 906–07. Although we acknowledged that the "question whether the Energy Companies can be held liable for public nuisance based on production and promotion of the use of fossil fuels and be required to spend billions of dollars on abatement is no doubt an important policy question," we concluded it "does not raise a substantial question of federal law for the purpose of determining whether there is jurisdiction under § 1331." *Id.* at 907. Finally, we noted that a court's evaluation of the cities' public nuisance claim would require a fact-intensive and situation specific analysis, which "is not the type of claim for which federal-question jurisdiction lies" under *Grable*. *Id.* Therefore, we concluded that because the plaintiffs' claim did not raise a substantial federal issue, it did not fit within the exception to the well-pleaded complaint rule articulated in *Grable*. *Id.*

The same analysis applies here. Although in *Oakland* the plaintiffs raised a single public nuisance claim, while here the **[—25—]** Counties allege multiple state tort theories, including public nuisance, failure to warn, design defect, private nuisance, negligence, and trespass, the substance of their claims is the same as in *Oakland*: tortious conduct by the Energy Companies in the course of producing, selling, and promoting the use of fossil fuels contributed **{-748-}** to global warming and sea-level rise, which led to property damage and other injuries to the Counties. Therefore, even if we assume that the Counties' complaints "could give rise to a cognizable claim" under federal common law, *id.* at 906, the global-warming-related tort claims do not "require resolution of a substantial question of federal law" because they do not require any interpretation of a federal statutory or constitutional issue, and are "displaced by the Clean Air Act." *Id.* And as in *Oakland*, even if the complaints raise federal policy issues that are national and international in scope, implicate foreign affairs and negotiations with other nations, and require uniform standards, they do not "raise a substantial question of federal law for the purpose of determining whether there is jurisdiction under § 1331." *Id.* at 907. Finally, as in *Oakland*, the Counties' tort claims require a fact-intensive and situation-specific analysis, which "is not the type of claim for which federal-question jurisdiction lies." *Id.*

Therefore, the exception to the well-pleaded complaint rule for substantial federal questions under *Grable* does not apply to the Counties' claims.

2

Second, the Energy Companies argue that the Counties' state law claims fall under the "artful-pleading doctrine," another exception to the well-pleaded complaint rule. *Oakland*, 969 F.3d at 905. Under this doctrine, a federal **[—26—]** statute's preemptive force is "so 'extraordinary' that it 'converts an ordinary state common-law complaint into one stating a federal claim for purposes of the well-pleaded complaint rule.'" *Caterpillar*, 482 U.S. at 393 (quoting *Metro. Life Ins. Co. v. Taylor*, 481 U.S. 58, 65 (1987)). Once a federal statute completely preempts an area of state law, then "any claim purportedly based on that pre-empted state law is considered, from its inception, a federal claim, and therefore arises under federal law." *Id.* (citation omitted). We have held that complete preemption applies when Congress "(1) intended to displace a state-law cause of action, and (2) provided a substitute cause of action." *Oakland*, 969 F.3d at 906 (citations omitted). The Supreme Court has recognized only three statutes for which complete preemption applies: (1) § 301 of the Labor Management Relations Act, (2) § 502(a) of the Employee Retirement Income Security Act of 1974, and (3) §§ 85 and 86 of the National Bank Act. *See id.* at 905–906 (citations omitted).

The Energy Companies assert that the Counties' state-law claims are "completely preempted by the Clean Air Act and/or other federal statutes and the United States Constitution." We rejected this precise argument in *Oakland*, observing that "[t]he Clean Air Act is not one of the three statutes that the Supreme Court has determined has extraordinary preemptive force" and concluding that it does not "meet either of the two requirements for complete preemption." *Id.* at 907. The Energy Companies do not identify any other federal statute that completely preempts the state-law claims here. Therefore, the complete preemption exception to the well-pleaded complaint rule does not apply. **[—27—]**

3

We next turn to the Energy Companies' argument that the Counties' complaints arise under federal law for purposes of § 1331 because the tort claims at issue arose on a federal enclave.

The removal of a claim brought in state court under the federal enclave doctrine is premised on the following legal framework. First, a state law claim brought in **{-749-}** state court is removable under § 1331 when "federal law is a necessary element of the [plaintiff's] claim for relief." *Oakland*, 969 F.3d at 904 (cleaned up). The Constitution establishes the principle that federal law applies in federal enclaves:

> Congress shall have Power . . . [t]o exercise exclusive Legislation in all Cases whatsoever, over such District[s] . . . as may, by Cession of particular States, and the Acceptance of Congress, become the Seat of the Government of the United States, and to exercise like Authority over all Places purchased by the Consent of the Legislature of the State in which the Same shall be, for the Erection of Forts, Magazines, Arsenals, dock-Yards, and other needful Buildings.

U.S. Const. art. I, § 8, cl. 17.

As this clause has been interpreted, when the federal government purchases state land with the consent of the state legislature, "any law existing [on that land] must derive its authority and force from the United States and is for that reason federal law." *Mater v. Holley*, 200 F.2d 123, 124 (5th **[—28—]** Cir. 1952).[3] Accordingly, unless an exception applies, any conduct on a federal enclave is governed by federal law. *Id.*[4] Because federal law governs disputes arising from such conduct, federal courts have the "power to adjudicate controversies arising" on federal enclaves. *Id.* If federal law applies to a legal controversy arising on federal enclaves, then such a controversy necessarily "arises under the laws of the United States, within the meaning of 28 U.S.C. § 1331." *Id.* at 125. In sum, because conduct on a federal enclave is generally subject to federal law, a claim based on injuries stemming from such conduct arises under federal law, and a court has jurisdiction over such a claim under § 1331.[5]

We have referenced this framework for federal enclave jurisdiction in several cases. In *Willis v. Craig*, a civilian employee who was injured while working at a federal naval center brought a negligence action in federal

---

[3] We have said that *Mater* contains "[t]he best reasoning on [federal enclave jurisdiction]." *Willis v. Craig*, 555 F.2d 724, 726 n.4 (9th Cir. 1977) (per curiam).

[4] The state law that previously governed the territory "remain[s] operative as federal law" so long as it is consistent with federal law. *Mater*, 200 F.2d at 124. State law directly applies in federal enclaves only under one of three narrow exceptions, none of which is relevant here. *See Paul v. United States*, 371 U.S. 245, 268–69 (1963); *Goodyear Atomic Corp. v. Miller*, 486 U.S. 174, 180 (1988).

[5] Where such an action is transitory and a state court has personal jurisdiction over the defendant, the state court may also hear the action. *Mater*, 200 F.2d at 123 (citing *Ohio River Cont. Co. v. Gordon*, 244 U.S. 68 (1917)).

court. *See* 555 F.2d 724, 725 (9th Cir. 1977) (per curiam). We held that federal jurisdiction was proper if the employee's accident occurred on property that qualified as a federal enclave. *Id.* **[—29—]** at 726. In *Durham v. Lockheed Martin Corp.*, we noted in passing that federal courts would have federal question jurisdiction over an employee's claim arising from exposure to asbestos during his work on federal enclaves. 445 F.3d 1247, 1250 (9th Cir. 2006); *see also Alvares v. Erickson*, 514 F.2d 156, 160 (9th Cir. 1975) (noting in passing that in federal enclave cases, the jurisdiction of a federal court depends on "the locus in which the claim arose").

In this case, the Counties have not alleged that their claims are based on torts taking place on a federal enclave. Rather, their complaint raises state-law claims arising from injuries to real property and **{-750-}** infrastructure within their local jurisdictions. For instance, San Mateo's alleged injuries flow from its claim of trespass to land, i.e., that the Energy Companies' petroleum activities ultimately led to a sea-level rise that caused water to enter San Mateo property in violation of trespass law and caused various damages and nuisances there, including the destruction of real property and infrastructure within its borders.[6] **[—30—]**

Therefore, we turn to the question whether the Counties' tort claims arose from actions and injuries that occurred on federal enclaves and thus were governed by federal law. The Energy Companies argue that "pertinent" or "substantial" events giving rise to the complaints took place on federal enclaves. Specifically, they contend that Standard Oil Co. (Chevron's predecessor) operated Elk Hills Naval Petroleum Reserve, a federal enclave, for many decades, and CITGO distributed gasoline and diesel under its contracts with the government to multiple naval installations that are federal enclaves. Relying on several district court opinions, the Energy Companies contend that because federal law applied to these activities on federal enclaves, federal law applies to the Counties' claims, which are therefore removable under § 1331.

We disagree. Unlike in *Willis*, where the accident that resulted in the plaintiff's injury occurred on a federal enclave, or in *Durham*, where the exposure that resulted in the plaintiff's injury occurred on a federal enclave, the Energy Companies allege only that some of the defendants engaged **[—31—]** in some conduct on federal enclaves that may have contributed to global warming, which allegedly caused the rising sea levels that resulted in the injuries that are the basis for the Counties' claims. The Energy Companies do not allege how much of that conduct occurred on federal enclaves. The connection between conduct on federal enclaves and the Counties' alleged injuries is too attenuated and remote to establish that the Counties' cause of action is governed by the federal law

---

[6] The other claims raised by the Counties are analogous. For its trespass claim, San Mateo claims that the Energy Companies caused "ocean waters to enter" city property, without the city's consent, "permanently submerging real property owned by [San Mateo], causing flooding which have [sic] invaded and threatens to invade real property owned by [San Mateo] and rendered it unusable, and causing storm surges which have invaded and threatened to invade real Property owned by [San Mateo] and rendered it unusable." For its nuisance claims, San Mateo alleges that the condition of flooding and storms is "harmful and dangerous to human health," "indecent and offensive to the senses of the ordinary person," "obstruct[s] and threaten[s] to obstruct the free use of the People's property," and "obstruct[s] and threaten[s] to obstruct the . . . use of [various areas] within San Mateo County." San Mateo specifies that "the ultimate nature of the harm is the destruction of real and personal **[—30—]** property," and that "the interference borne is the loss of property and infrastructure within San Mateo County."

For its failure to warn claim, San Mateo alleges that the Energy Companies "failed to adequately warn customers, consumers, elected officials and regulators of known and foreseeable risk of climate change and the consequences that inevitably flow from the normal, intended use and foreseeable misuse of [their] fossil fuel products," which caused "damage to publicly owned infrastructure and real property, and the creation and maintenance of a nuisance that interferes with the rights of the County, its residents, and of the People." Finally, for its design defect claim, San Mateo alleges that the Energy Companies' "fossil fuel products are defective because the risks they pose to consumers and to the public, including and especially to [San Mateo] outweigh their benefits."

applicable to any federal enclave. As a result, the Energy Companies have failed to establish that a federal issue is "necessarily raised" by the complaints. **{-751-}** *Gunn*, 568 U.S. at 258.[7] We therefore reject this basis for removal jurisdiction.

B

The Energy Companies next argue that the Counties' claims were removable under the Outer Continental Shelf Lands Act (OCSLA). OCSLA gives federal courts jurisdiction over actions "arising out of, or in connection with (A) any operation conducted on the outer Continental Shelf which involves exploration, development, or production of the minerals, of the subsoil and seabed of the outer **[—32—]** Continental Shelf, or which involves rights to such minerals."[8]

According to the Energy Companies, the Counties' tort claims fall within this jurisdictional grant. The Energy Companies reason as follows: The Counties allege that their injuries were caused in part by the Energy Companies' cumulative fossil-fuel extraction; and a portion of this extraction took place on the outer Continental Shelf (OCS) because some of the Energy Companies have conducted (and continue to conduct) petroleum exploration, development, and production on the outer Continental Shelf.[9] Therefore, the Energy Companies argue, the Counties' claims "aris[e] **[—33—]** out of, or in connection with" the Energy Companies' operations on the outer Continental Shelf.

In evaluating the Energy Companies' argument, we begin with the text of the jurisdictional statute, 43 U.S.C. § 1349(b)(1). The terms "aris[e] out of, or in connection with" are not defined in the statute. Nor are the dictionary definitions helpful. According to the dictionary definitions around the time OCSLA was enacted, "arise" in this context means to "spring up; originate," and "connection" means "[r]elationship by causality, mutual dependence, logical sequence, or the like." Webster's New Int'l Dictionary of the English Language (2d ed. 1952). As these definitions indicate, both terms are broad and indeterminate, and do not incorporate any principle that would limit federal jurisdiction. When interpreting phrases such as these, which lack a definite or fixed ending point, we must identify "a limiting principle consistent with the structure of the statute and its other provisions." *Maracich v. Spears*, 570 U.S. 48, 60 (2013) (interpreting the phrase "in connection with"); *see also* **{-752-}** *Cal. Div. of Lab. Standards Enf't v. Dillingham Constr., N.A., Inc.*, 519 U.S. 316, 335 (1997) (Scalia, J., concurring) ("But applying the 'relate to' provision according to its terms was a project doomed to failure, since, as many a curbstone philosopher has observed, everything is related to everything else."). Thus, in interpreting terms such as "relates to," "in connection with," or "in reference to," a court

[7] We reject the Energy Companies' passing argument that federal enclave jurisdiction extends to complaints implicating "powerful federal interests." The constitutional basis for federal enclave jurisdiction is Congress's power to exercise exclusive legislation over federal enclaves, U.S. Const. art I, § 8, cl. 17, and we have no authority to extend federal enclave jurisdiction beyond such limitations.

[8] 43 U.S.C. § 1349(b)(1) provides in full:

> Except as provided in subsection (c) of this section [regarding the federal government's leasing program on the outer Continental Shelf], the district courts of the United States shall have jurisdiction of cases and controversies arising out of, or in connection with (A) any operation conducted on the outer Continental Shelf which involves exploration, development, or production of the minerals, of the subsoil and seabed of the outer Continental Shelf, or which involves rights to such minerals, or (B) the cancellation, suspension, or termination of a lease or permit under this subchapter. Proceedings with respect to any such case or controversy may be instituted in the judicial district in which any defendant resides or may be found, or in the judicial district of the State nearest the place the cause of action arose.

[9] The outer Continental Shelf is defined as "all submerged lands lying seaward and outside of the area of lands beneath navigable waters . . . and of which the subsoil and seabed appertain to the United States and are subject to its jurisdiction and control." 43 U.S.C. § 1331(a).

must "go beyond the unhelpful text and the frustrating difficulty of defining its key term, and look instead to the objectives" of the statute as a guide to its scope. *N.Y. State Conf. of Blue Cross & Blue Shield Plans v. Travelers Ins. Co.*, 514 U.S. 645, 656 (1995). The Supreme Court has approved this approach to interpreting OCSLA, acknowledging that terms which have "indeterminacy in isolation" should be **[—34—]** "interpreted in light of the entire statute." *Parker Drilling Mgmt. Servs., Ltd. v. Newton*, 139 S. Ct. 1881, 1888, 7 Adm. R. 36, 38 (2019).

Applying this interpretive approach, we turn to the structure and purpose of OCSLA as a whole. The Supreme Court has explained that "the purpose of OCSLA was 'to assert the exclusive jurisdiction and control of the Federal Government of the United States over the seabed and subsoil of the outer Continental Shelf, and to provide for the development of its vast mineral resources.'" *Gulf Offshore Co. v. Mobil Oil Corp.*, 453 U.S. 473, 479 n.7 (1981) (citation omitted). According to the Supreme Court's historical review of OCSLA, Congress was concerned about the extensive activity taking place on the outer Continental Shelf, and the need to identify with clarity the body of law that would govern such activities. *See Rodrigue v. Aetna Cas. & Sur. Co.*, 395 U.S. 352, 358 (1969). Congress recognized that "the full development of the estimated values in the shelf area [would] require the efforts and the physical presence of thousands of workers on fixed structures in the shelf area," and that "[i]ndustrial accidents, accidental death, peace, and order present problems requiring a body of law for their solution." *Id.* (cleaned up). After debating whether federal or state law should be applicable to the platforms and artificial islands created in the outer Continental Shelf (and to the workers present there), *see id.* at 363–64, Congress determined that federal law should "be applicable in the area, but that where there is a void, the State law may be applicable," *id.* at 358 (citation omitted).

To implement this determination, Congress expressly adopted "the federal enclave model" for OCSLA. *Parker Drilling*, 139 S. Ct. at 1890, 7 Adm. R. at 40. It did so by enacting 43 U.S.C. § 1333, which provides that "[t]he Constitution and laws and **[—35—]** civil and political jurisdiction of the United States are extended, *to the same extent as if the outer Continental Shelf were an area of exclusive Federal jurisdiction located within a State*" to all areas of the outer Continental Shelf where operations could occur, including the "subsoil and seabed" of the outer Continental Shelf, any artificial islands, installations attached to the seabed "erected thereon for the purpose of exploring for, developing, or producing resources," or any other installations or devices needed to transport the resources. 43 U.S.C. § 1333(a)(1)(A) (emphasis added). This language ensured that drilling rigs and equipment on the outer Continental Shelf were treated "as though they were federal enclaves in an upland State." *Rodrigue*, 395 U.S. at 355.

The "textual connection between the OCSLA and the federal enclave model" as set out in § 1333 "suggests that, **{-753-}** like the generally applicable enclave rule, the OCSLA sought to make all OCS law federal yet also 'provide a sufficiently detailed legal framework to govern life' on the OCS." *Parker Drilling*, 139 S. Ct. at 1890, 7 Adm. R. at 40 (citation omitted). Because § 1333 adopted the federal enclave model's legal framework for the outer Continental Shelf, we read § 1349(b) as according federal courts the same jurisdiction over actions and injuries on the outer Continental Shelf as they would have in other federal enclaves.[10] As explained above, *supra* at Section II(A)(3), federal courts have federal enclave jurisdiction over tort claims regarding actions and injuries **[—36—]** that occur on federal enclaves. Therefore, we read the phrase "aris[e] out of, or in connection with" in § 1349(b)(1) as granting federal courts jurisdiction over tort claims only when those claims arise from actions or injuries occurring on the outer Continental Shelf.

[10] We presume that Congress was familiar with the scope of federal jurisdiction over federal enclaves when enacting OCSLA. *See Goodyear Atomic Corp. v. Miller*, 486 U.S. 174, 184–85 (1988) ("We generally presume that Congress is knowledgeable about existing law pertinent to the legislation it enacts.").

Reading the phrase "aris[e] out of, or in connection with" in § 1349(b)(1) as consistent with federal enclave jurisdiction provides "a limiting principle consistent with the structure of the statute and its other provisions," *Maracich*, 570 U.S. at 60, including OCSLA's purpose of addressing "industrial accidents, accidental death, peace, and order," given "the physical presence of thousands of workers on fixed structures in the shelf area," *Rodrigue*, 395 U.S. at 358 (cleaned up). Our interpretation of § 1349(b)(1) is also consistent with the Supreme Court's references to the scope of federal court jurisdiction under OCSLA. As the Supreme Court has explained, "a personal injury action *involving events occurring on the Shelf* is governed by federal law, the content of which is borrowed from the law of the adjacent State, here Louisiana." *Gulf Offshore Co.*, 453 U.S. at 481 (emphasis added); *see also id.* (describing OCSLA's legal framework by analogizing to a statute providing federal enclave jurisdiction over "personal injury and wrongful-death actions *involving events occurring within a national park or other place subject to the exclusive jurisdiction of the United States*, within the exterior boundaries of any State" (emphasis added) (internal quotation marks omitted)).

Three of our sister circuits have "deem[ed] § 1349 to require only a 'but-for' connection" between operations on the outer Continental Shelf and a plaintiff's alleged injuries. *See In re Deepwater Horizon*, 745 F.3d 157, 163–64, 2 Adm. R. 171, 173 (5th Cir. 2014) (citation omitted) (collecting cases); *see also Bd. of* **[—37—]** *Cnty. Comm'rs of Boulder Cnty. v. Suncor Energy (U.S.A.) Inc.*, 25 F.4th 1238, 1273 (10th Cir. 2022) (adopting the Fifth Circuit's approach); *Mayor & City Council of Baltimore v. BP P.L.C.*, 2022 WL 1039685, at *21 (4th Cir. Apr. 7, 2022) (following the Fifth and Tenth Circuits in concluding that "invoking jurisdiction under § 1349(b)(1) requires a but-for connection between a claimant's cause of action and operations on the OCS"). The Energy Companies argue that this analysis is contrary to *Ford Motor Co. v. Montana Eighth Judicial District Court*, which held that the "requirement of a 'connection' between a plaintiff's suit and a defendant's activities" in order for a court to assert specific personal jurisdiction over a defendant is not synonymous with but-for causation. 141 S. Ct. 1017, 1019 (2021) (citation omitted). **{-754-}** While we are skeptical that *Ford Motor Co.*'s interpretation of judicial rules delineating the scope of a court's specific personal jurisdiction is pertinent in this different statutory context, we agree that the language of § 1349(b), "aris[e] out of, or in connection with," does not necessarily require but- for causation.[11] **[—38—]**

Despite our different approach to construing § 1349(b), our sister circuits' application of § 1349(b)(1) leads to a materially similar result, because "[t]he decisions finding jurisdiction under § 1349" feature "either claims with a direct physical connection to an OCS operation (collision, death, personal injury, loss of wildlife, toxic exposure) or a contract or property dispute directly related to an OCS operation." *Bd. of Cnty. Comm'rs of Boulder Cnty.*, 25 F.4th at 1273 (collecting cases). Therefore, "despite the seemingly broad 'but-for' test," adopted by our sister circuits, "courts have made it clear that a dispute must have a sufficient nexus to an operation on the OCS to fall within the jurisdictional reach of the OCSLA." *Id.* (cleaned up); *see also Mayor & City Council of*

---

[11] The Fifth Circuit's conclusion to the contrary is not based on its construction of the text of § 1349(b), but rather relies on cases construing 43 U.S.C. § 1333(b) (providing that a specified form of compensation was payable "[w]ith respect to disability or death of an employee resulting from any injury occurring as *the result of* operations conducted on the outer Continental Shelf" (emphasis added)). The Fifth Circuit "adopted a 'but for' test of causation in determining whether a particular injury was *the result of* operations on the shelf," *Herb's Welding v. Gray*, 766 F.2d 898, 900 (5th Cir. 1985) (emphasis added) (citation omitted), and then applied this "but for" test to § 1349(b)(1) without addressing the differences between the text of those provisions, *see Recar v. CNG Producing Co.*, 853 F.2d 367, 369 (5th Cir. 1988) (stating that "we have established a 'but for' test to resolve" the question whether a case "aris[es] out of or in connection with" operations on the OCS" for purposes of **[—38—]** § 1349(b), but citing only the line of cases construing § 1333(b) (cleaned up)).

Baltimore, 2022 WL 1039685 at *21 ("[A] 'mere connection' between a claimant's case and operations on the OCS is insufficient to show federal jurisdiction if the relationship is 'too remote.'").[12]

We now apply our rule to the Energy Companies' assertions here. The Energy Companies argue that because the Counties assert that their injuries were caused in part by the Energy Companies' cumulative fossil-fuel extraction, and because a portion of this extraction took place on the outer Continental Shelf, the Counties' claims "aris[e] out of, or in **[—39—]** connection with" the Energy Companies' operations on the outer Continental Shelf. We reject this argument, because the connection between such conduct and the injuries alleged by the plaintiffs here is too attenuated to give rise to jurisdiction. First, the Counties' complaints allege injuries occurring exclusively within their local jurisdictions, not on the outer Continental Shelf. Second, instead of alleging wrongful *actions* on the outer Continental Shelf, the Counties' claims focus on the defective nature of the Energy Companies' fossil fuel products, the Energy Companies' knowledge and awareness of the harmful effects of those products, and their "concerted campaign" to prevent the public from **{-755-}** recognizing those dangers. These allegations do not refer to actions taken on the outer Continental Shelf. For these reasons, the Energy Companies have failed to establish that the Counties' tort claims "aris[e] out of, or in connection with" the Energy Companies' operations on the outer Continental Shelf for purposes of jurisdiction under § 1349(b)(1).[13] **[—40—]**

C

We now turn to the Energy Companies' claim that the district court had subject matter jurisdiction under the federal-officer removal statute, 28 U.S.C. § 1442(a)(1).[14]

As currently drafted, § 1442(a)(1) provides for removal of:

> A civil action . . . that is against or directed to . . . [t]he United States or any agency thereof or any officer (or any person acting under that officer) of the United States or of any agency thereof, in an official or individual capacity, for or relating to any act under color of such office or on account of any right, title or authority claimed under any Act of Congress for the apprehension or punishment of criminals or the collection of the revenue.

28 U.S.C § 1442.

In order to invoke § 1442(a)(1), a private person must establish: "(a) it is a person within the meaning of the statute; (b) there is a causal nexus between its actions, taken pursuant to a federal officer's directions, and [the] plaintiff's claims; and (c) it can assert a colorable federal defense." *Riggs v. Airbus Helicopters, Inc.*, 939 F.3d 981, 986–87 (9th Cir. **[—41—]** 2019) (quoting *Fidelitad, Inc. v. Insitu, Inc.*, 904 F.3d 1095, 1099 (9th Cir. 2018)). To demonstrate a causal nexus, the private person must show: (1) that the person

[12] Indeed, in *Ford Motor Co.*, the Supreme Court acknowledged the need to impose limiting principles on indeterminate jurisdictional language, stating that "the phrase 'relate to'" in the judge-made rule requiring a lawsuit to "arise out of *or relate to* the defendant's contacts with the forum," before a court can assert specific personal jurisdiction "incorporates real limits, as it must to adequately protect defendants foreign to a forum." 141 S. Ct. at 1026 (citation omitted).

[13] Relatedly, we also reject the Energy Companies' claim that § 1349(b)(1) gives federal courts jurisdiction over any claim that threatens to impair the recovery of federally owned minerals from the outer Continental Shelf, or that otherwise might affect the oil industry. This interpretation would give federal courts jurisdiction over any claim that might affect the finances of an energy company that engaged in operations there, even if the claim had no direct connection to events on the outer Continental Shelf, and is contrary to the federal enclave model. *See Bd. of Cnty. Comm'rs of Boulder Cnty.*, 25 F.4th at 1275 (rejecting an identical argument).

[14] The Supreme Court vacated our prior opinion, *County of San Mateo v. Chevron Corp.*, 960 F.3d 586 (9th Cir. 2020), but did not address our reasoning regarding the federal officer removal statute. *See Baltimore*, 141 S. Ct. at 1543. Therefore, we largely reprise our reasoning in our prior opinion on this issue.

was "acting under" a federal officer in performing some "act under color of federal office," and (2) that such action is causally connected with the plaintiff's claims against it. *See Goncalves ex rel. Goncalves v. Rady Child.'s Hosp. San Diego*, 865 F.3d 1237, 1244–50 (9th Cir. 2017).

The parties focus on the first prong: whether the Energy Companies were "acting under" a federal officer's directions. We begin by providing some background. The federal officer removal statute has existed in some version since 1815. *Willingham v. Morgan*, 395 U.S. 402, 405 (1969). Although Congress has amended the statute on a number of occasions, *see Watson v. Philip Morris Cos.*, 551 U.S. 142, 147–49 (2007), most recently in 2011, *see* Removal Clarification Act of 2011 § 2, the purpose of the statute has remained essentially the same: its "basic purpose is to protect the Federal Government from the interference with its operations that would ensue were a State **{-756-}** able, for example, to arrest and bring to trial in a State court for an alleged offense against the law of the State, officers and agents of the Government acting . . . within the scope of their authority." *Watson*, 551 U.S. at 150 (cleaned up) (quoting *Willingham*, 395 U.S. at 406). Congress thought that allowing a federal officer to remove a state action was necessary because "[s]tate-court proceedings may reflect 'local prejudice' against unpopular federal laws or federal officials" and "deprive federal officials of a federal forum in which to assert federal immunity defenses." *Id.* (citation omitted). Moreover, state-court proceedings may have the effect of impeding or delaying the enforcement of federal law. *Id.* The federal officer removal statute should be "liberally construed" to fulfill its purpose of allowing federal **[—42—]** officials and agents who are being prosecuted in state court for acts taken in their federal authority to remove the case to federal court. *Id.* at 147 (citation omitted).

When Congress first enacted § 1442(a)(1), the phrase "officer of the United States" was generally understood as a term of art that referred to federal officers who "exercis[ed] significant authority." *Int'l Primate Prot. League v. Adm'rs of Tulane Educ. Fund*, 500 U.S. 72, 81 (1991) (quoting *Buckley v. Valeo*, 424 U.S. 1, 126 (1976)). In 1948, Congress amended the statute to include the language "person[s] acting under" any officer of the United States. Act of June 25, 1948, ch. 646, § 1442, 62 Stat. 869, 938 (codified at 28 U.S.C. § 1442). At the time, this change was understood as extending the section to apply to employees, as well as officers. *Int'l Primate Prot. League*, 500 U.S. at 84 (quoting H.R. Rep. No. 80-308, at A134 (1947)).

The Supreme Court subsequently interpreted the term "person acting under that officer" as extending to a "private person" who has certain types of close relationships with the federal government. *See Watson*, 551 U.S. at 152–53. The Supreme Court has identified a number of factors courts should consider in determining whether a private person is "acting under" a federal officer for purposes of § 1442(a)(1). Among other things, the Court considers whether the person is acting on behalf of the officer in a manner akin to an agency relationship. *See id.* at 151 (private person must be authorized to act "with or for [federal officers]" (alteration in original) (citation omitted)); *see also Goncalves*, 865 F.3d at 1246–47 (holding that a private person qualified as "acting under" a federal officer when it was "serving as the government's agent"); *Cabalce v. Thomas E. Blanchard & Assocs., Inc.*, 797 F.3d 720, 729 (9th Cir. 2015) (noting that **[—43—]** a company's independent-contractor status supported the conclusion that it was not acting under a federal officer). The Court also considers whether the person is subject to the officer's close direction, such as acting under the "subjection, guidance, or control" of the officer, or in a relationship which "is an unusually close one involving detailed regulation, monitoring, or supervision." *Watson*, 551 U.S. at 151, 153 (citation omitted); *see also Leite*, 749 F.3d at 1120, 1124 (holding that a defense contractor properly removed a case under § 1442(a)(1) based, in part, on "the Navy's detailed specifications regulating the warnings that equipment manufacturers were required to provide"). Third, the Court considers whether the private person is assisting the federal officer in fulfilling "basic governmental tasks" that "the Government itself would have had to perform" if it had not contracted with a private firm. **{-757-}** *Watson*, 551 U.S. at 153–54; *see also Goncalves*, 865 F.3d at 1246–47 (holding that private person fulfilled a basic governmental task by pursuing subrogation claims on behalf of a government agency). Finally, taking into account the purpose of §1442(a)(1), the Court has considered whether the private person's activity is so closely related to the government's implementation of its federal duties that the private person faces "a significant risk of state-court 'prejudice,'" just as a government employee would in similar circumstances, and may have difficulty in raising an immunity defense in state court. *Watson*, 551 U.S. at 152 (citation omitted).

As the Supreme Court has indicated, and circuit courts have held, a government contractor qualifies as a person "acting under" an officer under certain circumstances. *See id.* at 153–54. *Watson* cited with approval a Fifth Circuit case, *Winters v. Diamond Shamrock Chemical Co.*, which held that a government contractor could remove a state action under **[—44—]** § 1442(a) because the contractor was acting on behalf of the government to produce Agent Orange, a carcinogenic herbicide used as part of the war strategy in Vietnam, and was acting under the close direction of the federal government which had provided "detailed specifications concerning the make-up, packaging, and delivery of Agent Orange," as well as "on-going supervision . . . over the formulation, packaging, and delivery of Agent Orange." 149 F.3d 387, 399–400 (5th Cir. 1998), *overruled by Latiolais v. Huntington Ingalls, Inc.*, 951 F.3d 286, 8 Adm. R. 155 (5th Cir. 2020) (en banc). Further, the contractor provided a product that was "used to help conduct a war" and at least arguably "performed a job that, in the absence of a contract with a private firm, the Government itself would have had to perform." *Watson*, 551 U.S. at 154; *see also Goncalves*, 865 F.3d at 1246–47 (holding that a private contractor was "acting under" a federal officer when it was serving as an agent for the government and assisting the government in fulfilling basic duties).

By contrast, a person is not "acting under" a federal officer when the person enters into an arm's-length business arrangement with the federal government or supplies it with widely available commercial products or services. *See Cabalce*, 797 F.3d at 727–29; *cf. Goncalves*, 865 F.3d at 1244–47; *Winters*, 149 F.3d at 398–400. Nor does a person's "*compliance* with the law (or *acquiescence* to an order)" amount to "'acting under' a federal official who is giving an order or enforcing the law." *Watson*, 551 U.S. at 152. This is true "even if the regulation is highly detailed and even if the private firm's activities are highly supervised and monitored." *Id.* at 153. We may not interpret § 1442(a) so as to "expand the scope of the statute considerably, potentially bringing within its scope state-court actions filed against private firms in many highly regulated industries." *Id.* **[—45—]**

The Energy Companies argue that they meet the criteria under § 1442(a) to remove the Counties' complaints because they were "persons acting under" a federal officer based on three agreements with the government.[15] They also argue that there is a causal nexus between their actions under those agreements and the Counties' claims. We consider each of these agreements in turn.

We first consider CITGO's fuel supply agreements with the Navy Exchange Service Command (NEXCOM). **{-758-}** Under these contracts, CITGO agreed to supply gasoline and diesel fuel to NEXCOM for service stations on approximately forty U.S. Navy installations. The government resold the CITGO fuel at NEXCOM facilities to individual service members. The Energy Companies point to three sets of contractual requirements in the fuel supply agreements which they claim establish the "subjection, guidance or control" necessary to invoke federal jurisdiction, namely: (1) "fuel specifications" that required compliance with specified American Society for Testing and Material Standards and required that

[15] We have held that corporations are "person[s]" under § 1442(a)(1), *Goncalves*, 865 F.3d at 1244, so there is no dispute that the Energy Companies meet this requirement.

NEXCOM have a qualified independent source analyze the products for compliance with those specifications; (2) provisions that give the Navy the right to inspect delivery, site, and operations; and (3) branding and advertising requirements.[16] **[—46—]**

This argument fails. The contracts evince an arm's-length business relationship to supply NEXCOM with generally available commercial products. Supplying gasoline to the Navy for resale to its employees is not an activity so closely related to the government's implementation of federal law that the person faces "a significant risk of state-court 'prejudice.'" *Watson*, 551 U.S. at 152 (citation omitted). Accordingly, we hold that CITGO was not "acting under" a federal officer by supplying gasoline and diesel fuel to NEXCOM pursuant to fuel supply contracts.

Second, the Energy Companies point to the 1994 unit agreement[17] for the petroleum reserves at Elk Hills between Standard Oil Company of California (Chevron Corporation's **[—47—]** predecessor in interest) and the U.S. Navy. We have detailed the history of this unit agreement at length in our prior decisions. *See Standard Oil Co. of Cal.*, 545 F.2d at 626–28. In brief, Standard owned one-fifth and the Navy owned four-fifths of the approximately 46,000 acres comprising the Elk Hills reserves. As is common in the oil exploration and production industry, the two landowners entered into a unit agreement to coordinate operations in the oil field and production of the oil. Because the Navy sought to limit oil production in order to ensure the availability of oil reserves in the event of a **{-759-}** national emergency, the unit agreement required that both Standard and the Navy curtail their production and gave the Navy "exclusive control over the exploration, prospecting, development, and operation of the Reserve." To compensate Standard for reducing production, the unit agreement gave Standard the right to produce a specified amount of oil per day (an average of 15,000 barrels per day). Both parties could dispose of the oil they extracted as they saw fit, and neither had a "preferential right to purchase any portion of the other's share of [the] production."

Standard's activities under the unit agreement did not give rise to a relationship where Standard was "acting under" a federal officer for purposes of § 1442. Standard was not acting on behalf of the federal government in order to assist the government in performing a basic government function. Rather, Standard and the government reached an agreement that allowed them to coordinate their use of the oil reserve in a way that would benefit both parties: the government maintained oil reserves for emergencies, and Standard ensured its ability to produce oil for sale. When Standard extracted oil from the reserve, Standard was acting independently, *see Cabalce*, 797 F.3d at

[16] The Energy Companies cite the following sections in the fuel supply agreements. First, the fuel specification provisions require CITGO to "provide high quality gasoline product identical to or the same product as supplied [by] the contractor[']s commercially operated gasoline service stations [(e.g., regular leaded, regular unleaded, and premium unleaded)]." The "[m]otor fuel products supplied" by CITGO were required to comply **[—46—]** with the generic standards promulgated by the American Society for Testing and Materials, and the Navy agreed to "have a qualified independent source analyze the products provided [by CITGO]," including any product that was "suspected of being faulty/inferior." Second, the inspection provisions gave the Navy the right to "visually check truck compartment(s) before and after deliveries" of fuel, and to conduct "general operational reviews," which "might also include inspections of . . . vehicles." Third, the branding provisions require CITGO to "supply all necessary equipment, including signage, for each facility," to "incorporate the Government logo on at least three . . . provided signage fixtures," and to supply "[a] standard service station rotating-fixed neon or incandescent street corner station identification sign . . . for each Government fueling station." And CITGO could submit "proposals on [CITGO] branded product[s]," but the government was not obligated to market "said product under [CITGO's] brand or trade name."

[17] "A unit agreement was at that time and still is a common arrangement in the petroleum industry where two or more owners have interests in a common pool. Under such an arrangement, the pool is operated as a unit and the parties share production and costs in agreed-upon proportions." *United States v. Standard Oil Co. of Cal.*, 545 F.2d 624, 627 (9th Cir. 1976) (per curiam).

728–29, not as the Navy's "agent," *Goncalves*, 865 F.3d at 1246; *see also* H.R. **[—48—]** Rep. No. 112-17, pt. 1, at 3 (2011) ("Removal is allowed only when the acts of Federal defendants are essentially ordered or demanded by Federal authority . . ."). And Standard's arm's-length business arrangement with the Navy does not involve conduct so closely related to the government's implementation of federal law that the Energy Companies would face "a significant risk of state-court 'prejudice.'" *Watson*, 551 U.S. at 152 (citation omitted).[18]

Finally, we consider the Energy Companies' lease agreements, entitled "Oil and Gas Lease of Submerged Lands Under the Outer Continental Shelf Lands Act." Under these standard-form leases, the government grants the lessee the right to explore and produce oil and gas resources in the submerged lands of the outer Continental Shelf, and in exchange the lessee agrees to pay the government rents and royalties. The Energy Companies argue that the lessee Energy Companies were "acting under" a federal officer because the leases require that the lessees drill for oil and gas pursuant to government-approved exploration plans and that the lessees sell some of their production to certain buyers; specifically, lessees must offer twenty percent of their **[—49—]** production to "small or independent refiners," and must give the United States the right of first refusal in time of war or "when the President of the United States shall so prescribe."

This argument also fails. The leases do not require that lessees act on behalf of the federal government, under its close direction, or to fulfill basic governmental duties. Nor are lessees engaged in an activity so closely related to the government's **{–760–}** function that the lessee faces "a significant risk of state-court 'prejudice.'" *Watson*, 551 U.S. at 152 (citation omitted). In fact, the lease requirements largely track statutory requirements, for instance, that the lessee offer 20 percent of the "crude oil, condensate, and natural gas liquids produced on [the] lease . . . to small or independent refiners," 43 U.S.C. § 1337(b)(7), and that "[i]n time of war, or when the President shall so prescribe, the United States shall have the right of first refusal to purchase at the market price all or any portion of any mineral produced from the outer Continental Shelf," § 1341(b). Mere "compl[iance] with the law, even if the laws are 'highly detailed' and thus leave [an] entity 'highly regulated,'" does not show that the entity is "acting under" a federal officer. *Goncalves*, 865 F.3d at 1245 (quoting *Watson*, 551 U.S. at 151–53). We conclude that the federal government's willingness to lease federal property or minimal rights to a private entity for that entity's commercial purposes does not, without more, constitute the kind of assistance required to establish that the private entity is "acting under" a federal officer. Accordingly, the leases on which the defendants rely do not give rise to the "unusually close" relationship where the lessee was "acting under" a federal officer. *Watson*, 551 U.S. at 153. **[—50—]**

Because we conclude that the Energy Companies have not carried their burden of proving by a preponderance of the evidence that they were "acting under" a federal officer, we do not reach the question whether actions pursuant to the fuel supply agreement, unit agreement, or lease agreement had a causal nexus with the Counties' complaints, or whether the Energy Companies can assert a colorable federal defense. *See Fidelitad*, 904 F.3d at 1099.

---

[18] At oral argument, the Energy Companies argued for the first time that Standard was "acting under" a federal officer pursuant to the Naval Petroleum Reserves Production Act of 1976, Pub. L. 94-258, § 201, 90 Stat. 303 (1976), which directed the Secretary of the Navy to "produce such reserves [including the Elk Hill reserve] at the maximum efficient rate consistent with sound engineering practices for a period not to exceed six years" and to "sell or otherwise dispose of the United States share of such petroleum produced from such reserves." § 201, 90 Stat. at 308. Nothing in the record indicates that the Secretary of the Navy "ordered or demanded," H.R. Rep. No. 112-17, pt. 1, at 3 (2011), *reprinted in* 2011 U.S.C.C.A.N. 420, 422, that Standard produce oil on behalf of the Navy. Therefore, the Energy Companies' reliance on this Act is misplaced.

D

We turn next to the Energy Companies' argument that the district court had removal jurisdiction over the complaints under 28 U.S.C. § 1452(a) because they are related to bankruptcy cases involving Peabody Energy Corp., Arch Coal, and Texaco, Inc.

Under § 1452(a), "[a] party may remove any claim or cause of action in a civil action" (subject to certain exceptions) if the district court "has jurisdiction of such claim or cause of action under [28 U.S.C. § 1334]." Under § 1334(b), in turn, "the district courts shall have original but not exclusive jurisdiction of all civil proceedings arising under title 11, or arising in or related to cases under title 11," again with exceptions not applicable here.[19] In sum, a **[—51—]** defendant may remove a civil action if the district court has jurisdiction over the civil action because it is "related to cases under title 11." *Id.*

In defining the term "related to" in this context, we have differentiated between bankruptcy cases that are pending before a plan has been confirmed and bankruptcy cases where the plan has been confirmed and the debtor discharged from bankruptcy. *See In re Pegasus Gold Corp.*, 394 F.3d 1189, 1193–94 (9th Cir. 2005). While a bankruptcy case is pending, we **{–761–}** have defined "related to" broadly: A proceeding is "related to" a bankruptcy case when "*the outcome of the proceeding could conceivably have any effect on the estate being administered in bankruptcy.*" *In re Fietz*, 852 F.2d 455, 457 (9th Cir. 1988) (citation omitted). But the same term "related to" has a more limited meaning after a plan has been confirmed. *See Pegasus Gold*, 394 F.3d at 1194. A proceeding that arises after a plan has been confirmed is "related to" a bankruptcy case only if there is "a close nexus to the bankruptcy plan or proceeding." *Id.* at 1194 (quoting *In re Resorts Int'l, Inc.*, 372 F.3d 154, 167 (3d Cir. 2004)). In defining "close nexus," we have indicated that "matters affecting 'the interpretation, implementation, consummation, execution, or administration of the confirmed plan will typically have the requisite close nexus'" to a bankruptcy case. *Id.* at 1194 (quoting *Resorts Int'l*, 372 F.3d at 167).

We take a holistic approach to determining whether a proceeding that arises after a plan has been confirmed has a close nexus to that plan. We have explained that the close nexus test "requires particularized consideration of the facts **[—52—]** and posture of each case," and "can only be properly applied by looking at the whole picture." *In re Wilshire Courtyard*, 729 F.3d 1279, 1289 (9th Cir. 2013). At the same time, we recognize that it is necessary to avoid an interpretation of "related to" in the post-confirmation context that "could endlessly stretch a bankruptcy court's jurisdiction." *Pegasus Gold*, 394 F.3d at 1194 n.1; *see also Resorts Int'l*, 372 F.3d at 164 (holding that "bankruptcy court jurisdiction 'must be confined within appropriate limits and does not extend indefinitely, particularly after the confirmation of a plan and the closing of a case'" (citation omitted)). Thus, we have held that a "bankruptcy court did not retain 'related to' jurisdiction for [a] breach of contract action that could have existed entirely apart from the bankruptcy proceeding and did not necessarily depend upon resolution of a substantial question of bankruptcy law." *In re Ray*, 624 F.3d 1124, 1135 (9th Cir. 2010).

We now turn to the Energy Companies' claims that the Counties' complaints have a sufficiently close nexus to the Peabody Energy and Texaco, Inc. bankruptcy cases.[20] First, the Energy Companies claim that the Counties' complaints have a sufficiently close nexus to the Peabody Energy Corp.'s

[19] 28 U.S.C. § 1334(b) provides:

> Except as provided in subsection (e)(2) [(relating to claims arising from employment of professionals under 11 U.S.C. § 327)], and notwithstanding any Act of Congress that confers exclusive jurisdiction on a court or courts other than the district courts, the district courts shall have original but not exclusive jurisdiction of all **[—51—]** civil proceedings arising under title 11, or arising in or related to cases under title 11.

[20] The Energy Companies do not raise a distinct argument as to Arch Coal, so we do not address this issue.

bankruptcy case because the complaints require an interpretation of Peabody's bankruptcy plan. According to the Energy Companies, a bankruptcy court has already interpreted the plan in response to the Counties' complaints. Specifically, the Counties here filed their complaints a few months after Peabody's bankruptcy plan was confirmed and became effective in April 2017. *In re Peabody Energy Corp.*, No. 16-42529-399, 2017 WL 4843724 at *1 (Bankr. E.D. Mo. **[—53—]** Oct. 24, 2017). In July 2017, Peabody filed a motion to enjoin the Counties from prosecuting their complaint against Peabody and to dismiss those actions with prejudice on the ground that their claims had been discharged in bankruptcy. *Id.* The bankruptcy court granted the motion and directed the Counties to dismiss their causes of action against Peabody Energy with prejudice. *See id.*[21] The Energy Companies **{–762–}** allege that given the bankruptcy court's need to interpret Peabody Energy's confirmed plan, there is a close nexus between the plan and the Counties' complaints.

We disagree. As stated above, we take a holistic look at "the whole picture." *Wilshire Courtyard*, 729 F.3d at 1289. As a general rule, proceedings that merely require the court to read a confirmed plan to determine whether it bars certain claims that arose before the confirmation date are not proceedings "*affecting* the interpretation [or] implementation" of a plan. *Pegasus Gold*, 394 F.3d at 1194 (cleaned up) (emphasis added). Typically, where the district court's review of a plan involves merely the application of the plan's plain or undisputed language, and does not require any resolution of disputes over the meaning of the plan's terms, the review does not "depend upon resolution of a substantial question of bankruptcy law." *Ray*, 624 F.3d at 1135. **[—54—]** Therefore, in the usual case, such a review would lack the close nexus with the bankruptcy case necessary for "related to" jurisdiction.

Here, the Energy Companies have not argued that the district court would have to interpret disputed language in Peabody Energy's confirmed plan in order to determine whether the Counties' complaints were barred. Nor could they, because at the time of removal, Peabody Energy had already elected to seek an order enforcing the discharge and injunction provisions of the Chapter 11 plan in bankruptcy court. This means that at the time of removal, the district court was not presented with any matters requiring interpretation of the confirmed plan, which was taking place on a different jurisdictional pathway. And even if the district court had been required to review a plan, the Energy Companies have not argued that such a review would "depend upon resolution of a substantial question of bankruptcy law." *Id.* Accordingly, under the circumstances of this case, the complaints before the district court were not "related to" Peabody Energy's bankruptcy case for purposes of § 1334(b), and the district court did not have removal jurisdiction over the complaints under § 1452 on that basis.

We next turn to the Energy Companies' argument that the Counties' complaints have a sufficiently close nexus to Texaco, Inc.'s bankruptcy case. According to the Energy Companies, Texaco, Inc.'s plan (which was confirmed some time in the 1980s) bars various claims arising against Texaco prior to March 15, 1988, so the Counties' proceedings would involve interpretation of Texaco's plan. Again, we disagree. As with Peabody Energy, the Energy Companies have not argued that the district court would have to interpret disputed language in Texaco's confirmed plan in order to determine **[—55—]** whether the Counties' complaints were barred. Moreover, Texaco's relationship to the complaints is attenuated: the Counties have not named

---

[21] The Eighth Circuit affirmed this ruling on appeal. *See In re Peabody Energy Corp.*, 958 F.3d 717 (8th Cir. 2020). The Counties therefore dismissed Peabody Energy and Arch Coal from the complaint in June 2020. But at the time of the district court's remand order (on July 10, 2018), the Counties were still appealing the bankruptcy court's order directing the Counties to dismiss their complaint against Peabody. In determining whether the district court had removal jurisdiction, we must consider the events at the time of its ruling. *See Spencer v. U.S. Dist. Ct. for the N. Dist. of Cal.*, 393 F.3d 867, 871 (9th Cir. 2004); *County of San Mateo v. Chevron Corp.*, 294 F. Supp. 3d 934 (N.D. Cal. 2018).

Texaco in their complaints, and the Energy Companies claim Texaco is a defendant only because the complaints allege that Chevron's subsidiaries also engaged in culpable conduct. The district court would not have occasion to look at Texaco's plan unless it first determined that Texaco was a proper defendant who was liable for damages, and also determined **{-763-}** that the Counties' claims arose before 1988. Under our "particularized consideration of the facts and posture" of this case, *Wilshire Courtyard*, 729 F.3d at 1289, we conclude that the Counties' case does not have the close nexus to Texaco's confirmed plan necessary to give the district court jurisdiction under § 1334(b) or removal jurisdiction under § 1452. Therefore, we reject this basis of jurisdiction.[22]

E

Finally, we turn to the Energy Companies' argument that the district court had admiralty jurisdiction over this case. Only Marathon Petroleum Corporation preserved this argument by raising admiralty jurisdiction as a basis for **[—56—]** removal in its notice of removal.[23] According to Marathon, because the Counties' claims are based on fossil fuel extraction that occurs on vessels engaged in maritime activities, they fall within the Constitution's grant of original jurisdiction over "all Cases of admiralty and maritime Jurisdiction." U.S. Const. art. III, § 2, cl.1; *see also* 28 U.S.C. § 1333(1).[24]

We reject this argument because maritime claims brought in state court are not removable to federal court absent an independent jurisdictional basis. The relevant jurisdictional statute, 28 U.S.C. § 1333(1), gives a district court original jurisdiction of "[a]ny civil case of admiralty or maritime jurisdiction, saving to suitors in all cases all other remedies to which they are otherwise entitled." 28 U.S.C. § 1333(1). The "saving to suitors" clause of § 1333(1) "leave[s] state courts 'competent' to adjudicate maritime causes of action in proceedings 'in personam,' that is, where the defendant is a person, not a ship or some other instrument of navigation." **[—57—]** *Ghotra by Ghotra v. Bandila Shipping, Inc.*, 113 F.3d 1050, 1054 (9th Cir. 1997) (quoting *Madruga v. Superior Ct. of Cal.*, 346 U.S. 556, 560–61 (1954)). This means that when a plaintiff brings a maritime cause of action against a person in state court, a federal court lacks admiralty jurisdiction over that claim. *See id.* at 1055–56. In order to remove such a claim to federal court, the defendant must assert some other basis of jurisdiction, such as diversity jurisdiction. *See id.*; *see also Morris v. Princess Cruises, Inc.*, 236 F.3d 1061, 1069 (9th Cir. 2001).

Even assuming that the Counties' claims in this case qualify as maritime claims, the Counties chose to bring these claims in state court. Under the "saving to suitors" clause, these maritime claims are **{-764-}** not removable to federal court based on admiralty jurisdiction alone.[25]

---

[22] Because we decide on this ground, we need not reach the question whether removal of the claim under § 1334 is barred by § 1452(a), which prohibits the removal of a civil action by a governmental unit "to enforce such governmental unit's police or regulatory power." Nor do we need to address 28 U.S.C. § 1334(c)(2), which provides that "[u]pon timely motion of a party" the district court must abstain from hearing a proceeding based on a state law claim where the only source of jurisdiction is § 1334.

[23] The other Energy Companies failed to invoke admiralty jurisdiction and therefore forfeited this ground of removal. Contrary to the Energy Companies' argument, their reference to "federal common law" in their notice of removal is insufficient to invoke this basis of jurisdiction. *See O'Halloran v. Univ. of Wash.*, 856 F.2d 1375, 1381 (9th Cir. 1988); *see also* 28 U.S.C. § 1446(a) (requiring that a notice of removal contain "a short and plain statement of the grounds for removal").

[24] 28 U.S.C. § 1333(1) provides:

> The district courts shall have original jurisdiction, exclusive of the courts of the States, of:
>
> (1) Any civil case of admiralty or maritime jurisdiction, saving to suitors in all cases all other remedies to which they are otherwise entitled.

[25] The Energy Companies do not "specifically and distinctly," *United States v. Kama*, 394 F.3d 1236, 1238 (9th Cir. 2005), argue that the "saving to suitors" clause only preserved the right to pursue non-maritime remedies, or that the Federal Courts

III

We have long held that "removal statutes should be construed narrowly in favor of remand to protect the jurisdiction of state courts." *Harris v. Bankers Life and Cas. Co.*, 425 F.3d 689, 698 (9th Cir. 2005). This rule of construction is based on the long-standing principle that "[d]ue regard for the rightful independence of state governments, which should actuate federal courts, requires that they scrupulously confine their own jurisdiction to the **[—58—]** precise limits which the statute [authorizing removal jurisdiction] has defined." *Healy v. Ratta*, 292 U.S. 263, 270 (1934). In keeping with these principles, the Supreme Court has repeatedly affirmed its "deeply felt and traditional reluctance . . . to expand the jurisdiction of federal courts through a broad reading of jurisdictional statutes." *Merrill Lynch, Pierce, Fenner & Smith Inc. v. Manning*, 578 U.S. 374, 389–90 (2016) (citation omitted). Our adherence to this doctrine does not change merely because plaintiffs raise novel and sweeping causes of action. We therefore reject the broad interpretations of removal jurisdiction urged on us by the Energy Companies and affirm the district court's remand order.

AFFIRMED.

Jurisdiction and Venue Clarification Act of 2011 amended the removal statute, 28 U.S.C. § 1441, so as to allow removal based on admiralty jurisdiction alone. Therefore, those arguments are waived. *See id.*

United States Court of Appeals
for the Ninth Circuit

No. 20-17412

SAN FRANCISCO HERRING ASS'N
VS.
U.S. DEP'T OF THE INTERIOR

Appeal from the United States District Court for the Northern District of California

Decided: May 10, 2022

Citation: 33 F.4th 1146, 10 Adm. R. 302 (9th Cir. 2022).

Before **WALLACE** and **BRESS,** Circuit Judges, and **ENGLAND,*** District Judge.

* The Honorable Morrison C. England, Jr., United States District Judge for the Eastern District of California, sitting by designation.

[—4—] {-1147-} BRESS, Circuit Judge: **{-1148-}**

In 1972, Congress created the Golden Gate National Recreation Area (GGNRA), establishing a portion of San Francisco Bay as part of the National Park System. Congress included within the geographic boundaries of the GGNRA certain navigable waters that were already subject to the jurisdiction of the United States. The question in this case is whether the National Park Service may enforce in these offshore waters a prohibition on commercial fishing that applies generally in national parks. The answer to that question turns on whether Congress in the GGNRA's enabling act gave the Park Service statutory authority to administer the disputed waters of San Francisco Bay.

It quite clearly did. The text and structure of the GGNRA Act confirm that Congress has given the Park Service administrative jurisdiction over the waters in question. The contrary position of appellant San Francisco Herring Association, meanwhile, is untenable. The Association would have us hold that the Park Service could only administer the navigable waters of the GGNRA if the Service acquired a formal property interest in those waters from the State of California. But nothing in the GGNRA Act imposes such an unusual (and potentially unachievable) condition precedent upon the Park Service's usual authority over navigable waters within park boundaries. The language and context of the GGNRA Act instead reflect the commonsense conclusion that Congress did not include navigable waters within the boundaries of the GGNRA and direct their protection, only to severely hamstring the Park Service in accomplishing that objective. We therefore affirm the district court's summary judgment to the Park Service. **[—5—]**

I

A

In 1916, Congress enacted the National Park Service Organic Act (Organic Act), ordering the Secretary of the Interior, through the Director of the National Park Service, to administer the National Park System "to conserve the scenery, natural and historic objects, and wild life in the System units and to provide for the enjoyment of [the same] in such manner and by such means as will leave them unimpaired for the enjoyment of future generations." 54 U.S.C. § 100101. "The System shall include any area of land and water administered by the Secretary, acting through the Director, for park, monument, historic, parkway, recreational, or other purposes." *Id.* § 100501.

To achieve these preservation objectives, the Organic Act delegated to the Secretary the authority to "prescribe such regulations as the Secretary considers necessary or proper for the use and management of System units." *Id.* § 100751(a). Relevant here, Congress in 1976 amended the Organic Act to clarify the Secretary's authority to "prescribe regulations . . . concerning boating and other activities on or relating to water located within System units, including water subject to the jurisdiction of the United States." *Id.* § 100751(b); *see also* Pub. L. No. 94-458, sec. 1, 90 Stat. 1939 (1976).

The Park Service has adopted a host of regulations governing activities within national **{-1149-}** park units. These Park Service regulations apply, *inter alia*, within "[t]he boundaries of federally owned lands and waters administered by the National Park Service" and within "[w]aters subject to the jurisdiction of the United States **[—6—]** located within the boundaries of the National Park System, including navigable waters." 36 C.F.R. §§ 1.2(a)(1), (3).

Park Service regulations generally do not apply to "non-federally owned lands and waters . . . located within National Park System boundaries." *Id.* § 1.2(b). However, for waters subject to the jurisdiction of the United States located within park boundaries, including navigable waters, the regulations apply "except in Alaska, without regard to the ownership of submerged lands, tidelands, or lowlands."[1] *Id.* § 1.2(a)(3). Under the regulations, and as relevant here, "boundary" "means the limits of lands or waters administered by the National Park Service as specified by Congress." *Id.* § 1.4(a).

In 1972, Congress established the GGNRA as part of the National Park System. Pub. L. No. 92-589, 86 Stat. 1299 (1972) (codified at 16 U.S.C. § 460bb *et seq.*). Covering land and waters in San Francisco Bay that Congress deemed to "possess[] outstanding natural, historic, scenic, and recreational values," the GGNRA Act provides that "the Secretary shall preserve the recreation area, as far as possible, in its natural setting, and protect it from development and uses which would destroy the scenic beauty and natural character of the area." 16 U.S.C. § 460bb. In managing the GGNRA, the Secretary "shall utilize the resources in a manner which will provide for the recreation and educational opportunities consistent with sound principles of land use planning and management." *Id.* **[—7—]**

Because this case concerns the Park Service's authority under the GGNRA Act, it is necessary to explain the relevant provisions in some detail. Section § 460bb-1 defines the physical boundaries of the GGNRA. *Id.* § 460bb-1(a). The Recreation Area is comprised of "the lands, waters, and submerged lands" within its drawn boundaries, as specifically identified on certain property records and referenced maps. *Id.* Section 460bb-1(a)(1), entitled "Initial lands," largely identifies lands and waters that were part of the GGNRA at the time of the Act's passage in 1972. *Compare* Pub. L. No. 92-589, § 2, 86 Stat. 1299 (1972) *with* Pub. L. No. 109-131, sec. 202, § 2(a), 119 Stat. 2566 (2005). Section § 460bb-1(a)(2), entitled "Additional lands," lists various lands and waters that have been added to the GGNRA over time. *See* Pub. L. No. 93-544, § 2, 88 Stat. 1741 (1974); Pub. L. No. 95-625, sec. 317(a), § 2, 92 Stat. 3467 (1978); Pub. L. No. 96-199, sec. 103(a), § 2, 94 Stat. 67 (1980); Pub. L. No. 96-344, sec. 4(1), § 2, 94 Stat. 1133 (1980); Pub. L. No. 96-607, sec. 1001(1), § 2, 94 Stat. 3539 (1980); Pub. L. No. 102-299, sec. 2(b), § 2, 106 Stat. 236 (1992); Pub. L. No. 106-350, sec. 2, § 2, 114 Stat. 1361 (2000); Pub. L. No. 109-131, sec. 202, § 2, 119 Stat. 2566 (2005).

As relevant here, the boundaries of the GGNRA extend one-quarter mile offshore from Sausalito to Bolinas Bay in Marin County, around Alcatraz Island, and from Fort Mason to below Ocean Beach in San Francisco County. *See* 16 U.S.C. § 460bb-1(a)(1). This map in the record shows the relevant offshore boundaries: **[—8—] {-1150-}**

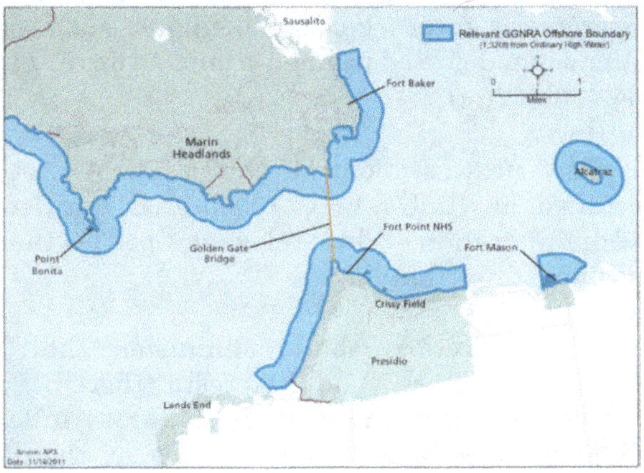

The majority of these quarter-mile offshore areas were part of the GGNRA upon its enactment in 1972. *See* H.R. Rep. No. 92-1391, at 53–55 (1972) (appended maps of GGNRA's original boundaries).

[1] The "Alaska exception" was added to the regulation after the Supreme Court's decision in *Sturgeon v. Frost*, 139 S. Ct. 1066, 7 Adm. R. 11 (2019), a case we discuss further below. *See* 5 Fed. Reg. 72956-01 (Nov. 16, 2020).

The next section of the Act, codified at 16 U.S.C. § 460bb-2, is entitled "Acquisition policy." This section provides details on which federal properties would be transferred to the GGNRA upon enactment and how the Secretary may acquire additional lands, including non-federal lands, that lie within the boundaries of the GGNRA. 16 U.S.C. § 460bb-2(a). Specifically, "[e]xcept as herein-after provided, Federal property within the boundaries of the recreation area is hereby transferred without consideration to the administrative jurisdiction of the Secretary for the purposes of this subchapter," subject to certain agreements between the Secretary and the agency formerly having jurisdiction over the property. *Id.* In considerable detail, § 460bb-2 then discusses the transfer of **[—9—]** various military properties, such as former forts and airfield space, into the GGNRA. *Id.* §§ 460bb-2(b)–(h).

With respect to future acquisitions, § 460bb-2 provides, in pertinent part, that "[w]ithin the boundaries of the recreation area, the Secretary may acquire lands, improvements, waters, or interests therein, by donation, purchase, exchange, or transfer." *Id.* § 460bb-2(a). However, "[a]ny lands, or interests therein, owned by the State of California or any political subdivision thereof, may be acquired only by donation." *Id.* The remainder of § 460bb-2 contains extensive provisions spelling out the mechanics of the Secretary's future land acquisitions, such as financing, deferred payments, and so forth. *Id.* §§ 460bb-2(m), (o).

The next section of the GGNRA Act, codified at 16 U.S.C. § 460bb-3, is entitled "Administration." In relevant part, this section states that:

> The Secretary shall administer the lands, waters, and interests therein acquired for the recreation area in accordance with the provisions of the [NPS Organic Act], as amended and supplemented, and the Secretary may utilize such statutory authority available to him for the conservation and management of wildlife and natural resources as he **{-1151-}** deems appropriate to carry out the purposes of this subchapter.

Id. § 460bb-3(a). As we will see, this provision is central to the Association's argument that the Park Service must acquire a formal property interest in navigable waters before it may administer them. **[—10—]**

B

The San Francisco Herring Association is a California-based non-profit group composed of small business owners who fish in the Bay Area. Suing on behalf of its members, the Association seeks to prevent the Department of Interior, the Park Service, and various agency officials (collectively, the Park Service) from enforcing in the GGNRA a commercial fishing prohibition that applies generally in national park units. The regulation at issue, which was promulgated in 1983, prohibits "[c]ommercial fishing, except where specifically authorized by Federal statutory law." 36 C.F.R. § 2.3(d)(4). Violations of this prohibition are punishable by fine and up to six months in prison. *See id.* § 1.3(a).

Each year from approximately November to March, herring enter San Francisco Bay to spawn, concentrating along the shores of Sausalito and Tiburon. Fishermen have caught herring from the Bay since at least the mid-nineteenth century, but more specialized fishing did not begin for herring roe, or eggs, until the 1960s. According to the Association, the waters at issue in this case are essential to the roe fishery because fishing is concentrated in discrete spawning areas near the shore.

The California Department of Fish and Wildlife (CDFW) has extensively regulated the herring roe fishery since 1973 to ensure that the fishery is safe and sustainable. Each year, prior to the beginning of the fishing season, CDFW issues an information packet to fishermen. Although the parties dispute when the Park Service began to assert administrative jurisdiction over the navigable waters in the GGNRA, by 2007 CDFW was including a formal notice in its information packet stating that the National Park Service

[—11—] had "exclusive jurisdiction" over the shoreline waters in question.

In 2013, the Association filed this lawsuit against the Park Service, alleging that the Service lacked the statutory authority to prohibit commercial herring fishing in the GGNRA. The district court disagreed and granted summary judgment for the government.

In two previous appeals, we held first that the district court lacked subject matter jurisdiction over the case because the Association had failed to identify any final agency action under the Administrative Procedure Act (APA), *see San Francisco Herring Ass'n v. U.S. Dep't of Interior (Herring I)*, 683 F. App'x 579, 580 (9th Cir. 2017), and then that the Association had later sufficiently alleged final agency action based on new allegations of specific enforcement efforts against individual fishermen. *See San Francisco Herring Ass'n v. U.S. Dep't of Interior (Herring II)*, 946 F.3d 564, 576–77 (9th Cir. 2019). On remand from *Herring II*, the district court then granted summary judgment to the Park Service, essentially reinstating its original decision that led to *Herring I*.

The Association has appealed for a third time. With the final agency action issue settled, we now confront the merits of the Association's statutory argument, reviewing the district court's grant of summary judgment de novo. *Ctr. for Biological Diversity v. Esper*, 958 F.3d 895, 903 (9th Cir. 2020).

II

Under the APA, a court may set aside final agency action if it determines {-1152-} that the action is "in excess of statutory jurisdiction, authority, or limitations, or short of statutory [—12—] right." 5 U.S.C. § 706(2)(C). In this case, the Association maintains that, under the GGNRA Act, the Park Service lacks the authority to enforce its commercial fishing prohibition on navigable waters within the GGNRA's boundaries. "When a party challenges agency action as inconsistent with the terms of a statute, courts apply the familiar analytical framework set forth in *Chevron, U.S.A., Inc. v. Natural Resources Defense Council, Inc.*, 467 U.S. 837 [] (1984)." *Corrigan v. Haaland*, 12 F.4th 901, 906–07 (9th Cir. 2021). Under *Chevron*, "[i]f the intent of Congress is clear, that is the end of the matter; for the court, as well as the agency must give effect to the unambiguously expressed intent of Congress." *Chevron*, 467 U.S. at 842–43.

In conducting this inquiry, we employ "traditional tools of statutory construction." *Id.* at 843 n.9. We construe a statute "in accordance with its ordinary and natural meaning," *N.L. v. Credit One Bank, N.A.*, 960 F.3d 1164, 1167 (9th Cir. 2020), recognizing that "[i]t is a fundamental canon of statutory construction that the words of a statute must be read in their context and with a view to their place in the overall statutory scheme," *Davis v. Mich. Dep't of Treasury*, 489 U.S. 803, 809 (1989). *See also Nken v. Holder*, 556 U.S. 418, 426 (2009) ("[S]tatutory interpretation turns on the language itself, the specific context in which that language is used, and the broader context of the statute as a whole." (quotations omitted)).

We hold that based on its language and structure, the GGNRA Act authorizes the Park Service to administer the navigable waters within the Recreation Area's boundaries one-quarter mile offshore. The Park Service may therefore enforce its generally applicable commercial fishing prohibition in the disputed waters of the GGNRA. [—13—]

A

Based on the statutory provisions as we set them out above, one might naturally assume that the Park Service of course has the statutory authority to administer navigable waters within the GGRNA's drawn geographic boundaries. But the Association argues otherwise, pointing specifically to § 460bb-3(a). That provision states in pertinent that "[t]he Secretary shall administer the lands, waters and interests *therein acquired* for the recreation area." 16 U.S.C. § 460bb-3(a) (emphasis added). The Association argues that for the Park Service to be able to "administer" the waters in question, it must first have "acquired" a formal property interest in them. Any such interest, the Association contends, is held by the State of California based on its alleged ownership of the submerged lands beneath the waters. Because the Park Service has not acquired from California any formal property interest in the disputed waters, the Association maintains that the Park Service lacks the power to administer these waters, with the result that it may not enforce its commercial fishing prohibition.

We do not think the Association's argument reflects the best reading of the statutory text. It is not disputed that the navigable waters at issue here are already within the jurisdiction of the United States, *i.e.*, subject to federal regulation. *See, e.g.*, *United States v. Rands*, 389 U.S. 121, 122–23 (1967) (discussing congressional power over navigable waters); *see also* **{-1153-}** *Utah Div. of State Lands v. United States*, 482 U.S. 193, 202 (1987) ("[E]ven if the land under navigable water passes to the State, the Federal Government may still control, develop, and use the waters for its own purposes."). And the Organic Act specifically gives the Secretary authority to "prescribe regulations . . . concerning boating and other activities on or relating to **[—14—]** water located within System units, *including water subject to the jurisdiction of the United States*." 54 U.S.C. § 100751(b) (emphasis added). As the Supreme Court has explained, the Organic Act's "statutory grants of power make no distinctions based on the ownership of either lands or waters (or lands beneath waters)" within park boundaries. *Sturgeon v. Frost*, 139 S. Ct. 1066, 1076, 7 Adm. R. 11, 14 (2019); *see also* 36 C.F.R. § 1.2(a)(3). The Park Service's general rules and regulations apply unless a park-specific law is "in conflict" with the Organic Act. 54 U.S.C. § 100755(a).

There is no such conflict here. Congress in the GGNRA Act squarely placed the navigable waters at issue here within the boundary lines of the Recreation Area. *See* 16 U.S.C. § 460bb-1(a) (referenced maps). Indeed, Congress intentionally incorporated maps that extended a defined quarter-mile-deep zone into the navigable waters of San Francisco Bay specifically to ensure that those waters would be regarded as part of the GGNRA. *Id.* Congress then expressly provided that in "carrying out the provisions of this subchapter, the Secretary shall preserve the recreation area, *as far as possible*, in its natural setting, and protect it from development and uses which would destroy the scenic beauty and natural character of the area." *Id.* § 460bb (emphasis added). Congress further directed the Secretary to "utilize such statutory authority available to him for the conservation and management of wildlife and natural resources as he deems appropriate to carry out the purposes of this subchapter." *Id.* § 460bb-3(a).

Read together, these provisions show that Congress granted the Secretary the authority to administer navigable waters within the Recreation Area's boundaries that were already subject to federal jurisdiction. To "acquire" means "[t]o gain possession or control of." *Acquire*, Black's Law **[—15—]** Dictionary (8th ed. 2004). It is well established that "running waters cannot be owned—whether by a government or by a private party." *Sturgeon*, 139 S. Ct. at 1078, 7 Adm. R. at 16 (citing *Fed. Power Comm'n v. Mohawk Power Corp.*, 347 U.S. 239, 247 n.10 (1954)). With that legal backdrop, of which Congress is presumed to be aware, *see, e.g.*, *Goodyear Atomic Corp. v. Miller*, 486 U.S. 174, 184–85 (1988), when Congress placed the disputed navigable waters within the boundaries of the GGNRA and directed their protection, the Park Service necessarily gained control over them, which is to say that it sufficiently "acquired" them for the purpose of administering them. 16 U.S.C. § 460bb-3(a). There was quite clearly a transfer of authority over these waters to the Park Service. *See id.* §§ 460bb, -2(a). Thus, there was no requirement for the Park Service to further "acquire" some formal property interest in navigable waters that are already subject to the jurisdiction of the United States; that are specifically delineated as part of the GGNRA; and that cannot even be "owned" in the traditional sense. *Sturgeon*, 139 S. Ct. at 1078, 7 Adm. R. at 16.

The GGNRA's differential treatment of land and navigable waters confirms our reading of the statute. In setting the boundaries of the GGNRA, Congress transferred existing federal lands into the GGNRA but also included within the boundaries of the Recreation Area nonfederal lands over which the Park Service **{-1154-}** otherwise lacked jurisdiction. *See* 16 U.S.C. §§ 460bb-1, -2. Congress then included extensive provisions for how the Secretary may acquire *land* but said nothing about how the Secretary might acquire *navigable waters*. For example, with respect to property held by California, § 460bb-2(a) provides that "[a]ny lands, or interests therein, owned by the State of California or any political subdivision thereof, may be acquired only by donation," without making any mention of **[—16—]** the Secretary acquiring interests in navigable waters from the State. *Id.* § 460bb-2(a).

Other provisions are to similar effect. Section 460bb-2(m), for example, provides detailed provisions for how the Secretary may finance land acquisitions but provides no guidance for acquiring rights in navigable waters. Similarly, § 460bb-2(o), entitled "Payment deferral; scheduling; interest rate," explains that *"[i]n acquiring those lands* authorized by the Ninety-fifth Congress for the purposes of this subchapter, the Secretary may, when agreed upon by *the landowner involved*, defer payment or schedule payments." *Id.* § 460bb-2(o) (emphasis added). Notably absent is any comparable provision addressing payment deferral and scheduling of acquisitions of navigable waters—for waters that Congress specifically included in the GGNRA, no less. Taken together, these provisions lend additional support to the Park Service's basic point that Congress did not envision the Secretary having to further acquire from California formal property rights in navigable waters that were already subject to federal jurisdiction and specifically included in park boundaries.

Finally, the Association's position is not only an inferior reading of the statutory text but could result in a significant implausibility. The GGNRA Act prevents the Secretary from acquiring property through eminent domain. *Id.* § 460bb-2(a). And within the GGNRA the Secretary may only acquire land interests from California by donation. *Id.* Under the California Constitution, however, the State may not alienate property rights held in the public trust for purposes of fishing and navigation. *See* Cal. Const. Art. I, § 25, Art. X, § 4. The Association's position thus leads to the apparent outcome that Congress included the waters at issue within the boundaries of the Recreation Area, directed **[—17—]** the Secretary to "preserve the recreation area, *as far as possible*," 16 U.S.C. § 460-bb (emphasis added), and then made it potentially impossible for the Secretary to do so. In its first amended complaint, the Association in fact affirmatively alleged that "the State of California could not have granted Defendants the right to prohibit fishing in the waters in question."

The Association now suggests in its briefing that there is "some conveyance" that would allow the Service to "administer the waters generally" "without offending public trust rights, and thus give the GGNRA Act meaning and effect." But the Association has not sufficiently demonstrated how such a transaction with the State would work or whether it could even be accomplished when the waters themselves cannot be owned. The principal case the Association cites concerned an action "by the state of California to quiet its title to certain *lands*." *People v. Cal. Fish Co.*, 138 P. 79, 81 (Cal. 1913) (emphasis added). And even if the Association's contemplated conveyance were possible, the lack of any provision in the GGNRA for such a novel "acquisition" convinces us that this is not what Congress had in mind when it included the disputed waters within park boundaries and ordered the Park Service to protect the area to the fullest extent possible.

B

In its reply brief, the Association for the first time argued that the Supreme Court's **{-1155-}** decision in *Sturgeon* supports its interpretation of the GGNRA. We disagree. *Sturgeon* is distinguishable. In fact, if anything, *Sturgeon* confirms that the Park Service's position here is the better one.

The dispute in *Sturgeon* arose from the Park Service's attempt to apply its regulation banning hovercrafts, **[—18—]** 36 C.F.R. § 2.17(e), to a portion of the Nation River in the Yukon-Charley Rivers National Preserve, a park system unit in Alaska. *Sturgeon*, 139 S. Ct. at 1072, 7 Adm. R. at 11. Sturgeon, a hovercraft-traveling moose hunter, argued that under the Alaska National Interest Lands Conversation Act (ANILCA), 16 U.S.C. § 3101 *et seq.*, the Park Service could not enforce its hovercraft ban in the disputed waters because in Alaska, "the Park Service has no power to regulate lands or waters that the Federal Government does not own." 139 S. Ct. at 1073, 7 Adm. R. at 11.

National Park system units in Alaska—comprising nearly 44 million acres—are drawn based on geographical boundaries that include land held by the State, Indian tribes, and private landowners. *Id.* at 1076–77, 7 Adm. R. at 14–15. In the usual course, "inholdings" such as these would typically be subject to Park Service regulations because under the Organic Act and implementing regulations, the Park Service is authorized to regulate within park boundaries without regard to ownership of the lands or waters. *Id.* at 1076, 7 Adm. R. at 14 (citing 54 U.S.C. §§ 100751(a), 100751(b); 36 C.F.R. §§ 1.2(a)(3), 6.2). But the Supreme Court held that the Park Service could not apply its hovercraft ban to the disputed waters within park boundaries in Alaska because of statutory language unique to ANILCA, which was itself borne out of Alaska's unique history and geography. *Id.* at 1073–77, 7 Adm. R. at 11–15.

The unique statutory language is found in Section 103(c) of ANILCA, which provides, in pertinent part, that "[o]nly those lands within the boundaries of any conservation system unit which are *public lands* (as such term is defined in this Act) shall be *deemed* to be included as a portion of such unit." 16 U.S.C. § 3103(c) (emphasis added). "[C]rucially," the Supreme Court explained in *Sturgeon*, 139 S. Ct. at 1076, 7 Adm. R. at 14–15, the term "land" in ANILCA is defined to **[—19—]** mean "lands, *waters*, and interests therein." 16 U.S.C. § 3102(1) (emphasis added). And "public lands" means "lands *the title* to which is in the United States." *Id.* § 3102(2) (emphasis added); *see also id.* § 3102(3).

Based on this language, *Sturgeon* held, "[a]s a matter of geography, both public and non-public lands fall inside those parks' boundaries," but "as a matter of law, only public lands would be viewed as doing so." *Sturgeon*, 139 S. Ct. at 1081, 7 Adm. R. at 18. *Sturgeon* thus held that the Park Service could not regulate the waters within the Yukon-Charley Rivers National Preserve. The United States did not own "title" to the Nation River because, as we have noted, "running waters cannot be owned—whether by a government or by a private party." *Id.* at 1078, 7 Adm. R. at 16. And Alaska owned title to the lands beneath the river. *Id.*, 7 Adm. R. at 16.[2] **{-1156-}**

The Association argues that § 460bb-3 in the GGNRA, which contains the alleged property interest acquisition requirement, is equivalent to Section 103(c) of ANILCA. But, in fact, § 460bb-3 differs meaningfully from Section 103(c). The latter is explicit that "[o]nly" the "public lands" within any system unit's boundaries would be "deemed" a part of that unit. 16 U.S.C. § 3103(c). And unlike the **[—20—]** GGNRA Act, ANILCA expressly defines "lands" to include water. *Id.* § 3102(1). ANILCA is also clear that determining whether lands (or waters) are "public lands" depends on whether the United States has "the title" to them. *Id.* § 3102(2).

---

[2] We need not resolve the complex dispute between the parties over who owns the submerged lands under the waters at issue here. Resolution of that disagreement would not answer the ultimate question of whether Congress specified that the Secretary had to further acquire a formal property interest in the navigable waters of San Francisco Bay before it could regulate them. And if, as we hold today, Congress did give the Secretary authority to administer the navigable waters without requiring the Park Service to acquire a formal property interest from California, under the Organic Act and Park Service regulations formal ownership of the land beneath the waters is irrelevant. *See Sturgeon*, 139 S. Ct. at 1076, 7 Adm. R. at 14; 36 C.F.R. § 1.2(a)(3).

The GGNRA Act does not use similar language, nor does it explicitly "deem" waters inside the Recreation Area's boundaries as outside the National Park System entirely. *See Sturgeon*, 139 S. Ct. at 1081, 7 Adm. R. at 18 ("The key word here is 'deemed.'"). Instead, the GGNRA reflects the opposite approach: the disputed navigable waters of San Francisco Bay are affirmatively part of the park, with no further requirement that anything more be done to make them so. That makes some sense considering that whereas ANILCA drew national park boundaries around *44 million acres* in Alaska—of which *18 million* were not owned by the federal government, *id.* at 1075, 7 Adm. R. at 13—we are considering here a drastically smaller quarter-mile offshore zone that was specifically included as part of the GGNRA's boundaries. Congress did not draw a massive circle around San Francisco Bay that happened to include these waters; it instead intentionally identified specific quarter-mile offshore areas for designated inclusion in the park.

Moreover, while the GGNRA Act reflects an analogous approach to ANILCA when it comes to non-federal *land*, the GGNRA Act differs from ANILCA when it comes to navigable waters: it does not equate "land" with "navigable waters" for legal purposes. *Cf. id.* at 1086, 7 Adm. R. at 22 ("ANILCA does not readily allow the decoupling of navigable waters from other non-federally owned areas in Alaskan national parks for regulatory . . . purposes."). Although "we must read ANILCA as treating identically solid ground and flowing water," *id.*, 7 Adm. R. at 23, the text of the GGNRA Act does not reflect that **[—21—]** same approach. That is because, as we explained above, the GGNRA Act makes extensive provision for the acquisition of non-federal lands and discusses at length particular properties for inclusion, but says nothing about acquiring property interests in navigable waters.

In short, *Sturgeon* shows that when Congress wants to disallow the Park Service from exercising its usual authority over navigable waters falling within the drawn boundaries of a national park system unit, Congress makes that intention clear. As the Supreme Court noted, "[i]f Sturgeon lived in any other State, his suit would not have a prayer of success." *Id.* at 1080, 7 Adm. R. at 18; *see also id.* at 1075, 7 Adm. R. at 13 (explaining that in ANILCA, "Congress set aside extensive land for national parks and preserves—but on terms different from those governing such areas in the rest of the country"); *id.* at 1087, 7 Adm. R. at 23 ("ANILCA recognized that when it came to navigable waters—just as to non-federal lands—in the new parks, Alaska should be the exception, not the rule." (quotations omitted)).

The Supreme Court in *Sturgeon* also made clear that its construction of ANILCA still "le[ft] the Park Service with multiple tools to 'protect' rivers in Alaskan national parks," including purchasing the submerged lands from Alaska. *Id.* at 1086–87, 7 Adm. R. at 23 (citing 16 U.S.C. § 3103(c)). But as discussed above, the GGRNA Act disallows such purchases from California, 16 U.S.C. § 460bb-2(a), and the Association maintains that California law would impose its own **{–1157–}** set of restrictions on the alienation of rights held in the public trust, Cal. Const. Art. I, § 25, Art. X, § 4. Unlike in *Sturgeon*, the Association's argument, if accepted, would make the Park Service's ability to protect the navigable waters in the GGNRA far more doubtful.

The substantial textual differences between ANILCA and the GGNRA Act thus confirm that *Sturgeon* does not **[—22—]** assist the Association, but instead supports the government. While Congress in ANILCA "created an Alaska-specific exception" to the Park Service's usual authority, *id.* at 1072, 7 Adm. R. at 11, we conclude it did not create such an exception for the disputed navigable waters in San Francisco Bay. We therefore hold that the Park Service may administer the navigable waters of San Francisco Bay within the GGNRA, with the consequence that it may enforce its commercial fishing rules in those waters.[3]

[3] Because we agree reviewing de novo that the Park Service prevails under the GGNRA Act, we do not address whether the Service's interpretation would be entitled to *Chevron* deference. And

AFFIRMED.

because we do not locate the Service's authority over the disputed waters in the National Park System Organic Act, we do not reach the Association's arguments regarding the canon against implied repeals.

United States Court of Appeals for the Ninth Circuit

No. 20-35985

MARTZ
vs.
HORAZDOVSKY

Appeal from the United States District Court for the District of Alaska

Decided: May 10, 2022

Citation: 33 F.4th 1157, 10 Adm. R. 311 (9th Cir. 2022).

Before **WARDLAW, MILLER,** and **BADE,** Circuit Judges.

[—5—] {-1160-} MILLER, Circuit Judge:

When a vessel is involved in an accident, the Shipowner's Limitation of Liability Act allows the owner to limit its liability to the value of the vessel and pending freight. 46 U.S.C. § 30505. To enjoy the benefit of that limit, the owner must bring a separate limitation-of-liability action **[—6—]** "within 6 months after a claimant gives the owner written notice of a claim." 46 U.S.C. § 30511(a).

In each of these two cases, which we have consolidated for decision, counsel for a victim of a maritime accident wrote to the vessel owners and suggested that the victim might be interested in pursuing litigation against the responsible parties. The owners then brought a limitation-of-liability action, but they did not do so until more than six months after receiving the letter. In each case, the district court determined that the letter constituted "written notice of a claim" and dismissed the action as untimely.

These cases present two issues of first impression in this circuit: first, whether the six-month statute of limitations in section 30511(a) is a jurisdictional rule, and **{-1161-}** second, what constitutes "written notice of a claim" sufficient to start the running of the limitations period. Reviewing the grant of summary judgment de novo, *Yu v. Albany Ins. Co.*, 281 F.3d 803, 806 (9th Cir. 2002), we hold that the statute of limitations is not jurisdictional and that a "written notice of a claim" has three elements: the notice must (1) be in writing, (2) clearly state that the victim intends to bring a claim or claims against the owner, and (3) include at least one claim that is reasonably likely to be covered by the Limitation Act. Because neither of the letters at issue informed the vessel owners of the claimant's intention to bring a covered claim against the owners, neither constituted "written notice of a claim" that started the running of the limitations period. It follows that both limitation-of-liability actions were timely. We therefore reverse in both cases and remand for further proceedings. **[—7—]**

I

A

On June 9, 2018, Reagan Martz was operating his parents' boat on Flat Lake, Alaska, when he collided with an inflatable raft being towed by another vessel. The collision killed Jennifer Horazdovsky, one of the occupants of the raft.

Over the next few weeks, two different lawyers representing Jennifer Horazdovsky's husband, Andrew Horazdovsky, wrote to the Martz family's lawyer asking for Reagan Martz's insurance information. Horazdovsky then retained a third lawyer, Robert Stone, and on December 4, 2018, Stone sent a three-page letter to the Martzes' lawyer with the subject line "Re: Horazdovsky v. Reagan Martz, William and Jane Martz." In the letter, Stone described the facts underlying the accident as he understood them. He wrote that "Reagan Martz, son of William and Jane Martz, was drinking heavily at a party sponsored by William and Jane Martz" and that "Reagan was a permissive user of a boat owned by his parents." To Stone, the facts "suggest[ed] that Reagan Martz was severely intoxicated, and that as a result of such intoxication, he collided with a raft occupied by Jennifer Horazdovsky"; he added that "Reagan Martz fled the scene, changed from the boat to a jet ski, and continued to flee the scene until he was ultimately apprehended." But Stone said that he was "not yet certain whether William Martz or Jane Martz bear any responsibility." Noting that he "would like to avoid unnecessarily naming parties to a lawsuit," he requested information about the ownership of the relevant property at Flat Lake and any insurance policies covering the Martzes. The Martzes' lawyer responded a few days later, stating that Reagan Martz had no relevant insurance coverage, that "[t]here is no basis for William and Jane Martz having any liability for this accident," and that **[—8—]** "we have not tendered this claim to any insurance companies."

On June 4, 2020, Andrew Horazdovsky, individually and as the personal representative of Jennifer Horazdovsky's estate, sued Reagan, William, and Jane Martz in Alaska state court, seeking damages under various tort theories. Two weeks later, William and Jane Martz brought an action in the District of Alaska for limitation of liability under section 30511(a). Horazdovsky moved for summary judgment on the ground that the action was untimely.

The district court granted the motion. It held that written notice of a claim "need not make an unequivocal demand to the vessel owner for compensation for a loss; it is enough if the notice presents a reasonable possibility of a claim subject to limitation." Applying that rule, the court noted that the correspondence to the Martzes **{–1162–}** came "by way of [Horazdovsky's] attorneys, immediately lending it some formality and import," and that Stone's letter was "captioned with reference to the adversarial posture of the parties." The court also observed that Stone's letter "outline[d] a theory of liability that implicates the vessel owners." Although acknowledging that Stone's letter was "tentative" in that it referred only to the possibility of legal action, the court reasoned that when read in its entirety, the letter constituted notice of a claim. Because the Martzes did not file their limitation action until more than a year after they received Stone's letter, the court concluded that the action was untimely.

B

On January 5, 2019, 13-year-old T.T. drowned during an open-ocean scuba-diving excursion near Honolulu. The excursion was conducted by Honu Watersports LLC, doing **[—9—]** business as Island Divers Hawaii, on a vessel owned by Fish N Dive LLC; both companies are controlled by an entity owned by Matthew Zimmerman.

Two days after the accident, Loretta Sheehan, an attorney representing T.T.'s family, wrote to Zimmerman to inform him that Sheehan had "been retained to investigate the death of [T.T.] on January 5, 2019, while he was participating in a drift dive with . . . Island Divers Hawaii," and to request that Zimmerman preserve "any and all evidence potentially related to this incident" including "photographs, videos, logs, [and] captain manifests." The letter warned that T.T.'s family would "consider it spoliation of evidence if Island Divers Hawaii alters, modifies, or destroys the evidence involved in this accident." Zimmerman's counsel acknowledged receipt of the letter and advised Sheehan to direct further communications to counsel and not to Zimmerman or any employees of Honu Watersports.

On September 19, 2019, T.T.'s estate and family sued Zimmerman, Honu Watersports, and Fish N Dive in Hawaii state court, seeking damages based on the accident. On November 5, 2019, Fish N Dive brought this action in the District of Hawaii for limitation of liability under section 30511(a).

We pause at this point to observe that the designation of the parties in actions of this kind can be confusing. Like the Martzes in the Alaska case, Fish N Dive is the defendant in the state-court tort action but the plaintiff in the federal limitation-of-liability proceeding. Courts often refer to such parties as the "limitation plaintiffs," but we think it is clearer to call them the "vessel owners" and to describe their adversaries as the "claimants." **[—10—]**

Arguing that the limitation-of-liability action was untimely under section 30511(a),

T.T.'s estate and family moved to dismiss for lack of subject-matter jurisdiction or, in the alternative, for summary judgment.

The district court denied the motion to dismiss. Noting that "[t]here is no clear jurisdictional language in the text of § 35011(a)," the court concluded that the limitations period in the statute "is a claims processing rule, not a jurisdictional requirement." It therefore held that the timeliness of the limitation action "will be determined under the summary judgment standard."

The district court granted the motion for summary judgment. The court held that to constitute "written notice of a claim," a communication must "inform[] the shipowner of an actual or potential claim." The court considered the reference to "spoilation of evidence" and the statement that the firm had been "retained to investigate **{–1163–}** the death of [T.T.]" sufficient to satisfy that requirement. And it concluded that the letter conveyed a claim reasonably subject to limitation because a wrongful death claim would necessarily have exceeded the value of the vessel, which was only $40,000. Because Fish N Dive had filed its limitation-of-liability action almost a year after it received the evidence-preservation letter, the court concluded that its claim was untimely.

II

Before we determine what events start the running of the limitations period in section 30511(a), we consider whether that provision limits the district court's jurisdiction or whether it is merely a claim-processing rule. If the statute is jurisdictional, then the untimeliness of a limitation-of-liability action would appropriately be asserted in a motion **[—11—]** to dismiss under Federal Rule of Civil Procedure 12(b)(1), like that brought by the claimants in the Hawaii case. *See Thornhill Publ'g Co. v. General Tel. & Elec. Corp.*, 594 F.2d 730, 733 (9th Cir. 1979). In addition, a district court would have a duty to consider the timeliness of such an action sua sponte. *See Pacific Choice Seafood Co. v. Ross*, 976 F.3d 932, 938, 8 Adm. R. 324, 327 (9th Cir. 2020).

Courts of appeals have disagreed about whether section 30511(a) is jurisdictional. *See Cincinnati Gas & Elec. Co. v. Abel*, 533 F.2d 1001, 1003 (6th Cir. 1976) (treating the time limit as jurisdictional); *Petition of Spearin, Preston & Burrows, Inc.*, 190 F.2d 684, 685–86 (2d Cir. 1951) (same); *In re Bonvillian Marine Serv., Inc.*, 19 F.4th 787, 793–94, 9 Adm. R. 273, 276–77 (5th Cir. 2021) (treating the time limit as not jurisdictional); *Orion Marine Constr., Inc. v. Carroll*, 918 F.3d 1323, 1328–29, 7 Adm. R. 463, 465–67 (11th Cir. 2019) (same). We agree with those courts that have held that section 30511(a) is an ordinary statute of limitations and is not jurisdictional.

The Supreme Court has held that only when Congress "clearly states that a threshold limitation on a statute's scope shall count as jurisdictional" should it be treated as jurisdictional. *Arbaugh v. Y & H Corp.*, 546 U.S. 500, 515–16 (2006); *see Al-Qarqani v. Chevron Corp.*, 8 F.4th 1018, 1024 (9th Cir. 2021). Statutory time limits, in particular, are jurisdictional "only if Congress has 'clearly state[d]' as much." *United States v. Wong*, 575 U.S. 402, 409 (2015) (alteration in original) (quoting *Sebelius v. Auburn Reg'l Med. Ctr.*, 568 U.S. 145, 153 (2013)). And "most time bars are nonjurisdictional" because they are merely "'claim-processing rules,' which 'seek to promote the orderly progress of litigation,' but do not deprive a court of authority to hear a case." *Id.* at 410 (quoting *Henderson v. Shinseki*, 562 U.S. 428, 435 (2011)). **[—12—]**

Section 30511(a) states that "[t]he action must be brought within 6 months after a claimant gives the owner written notice of a claim." It does not refer to the court's jurisdiction or otherwise suggest that it limits the court's adjudicatory power. Such "mundane statute-of-limitations language" does not create a jurisdictional limitation. *Wong*, 575 U.S. at 410; *see also Gonzalez v. Thaler*, 565 U.S. 134, 146 (2012). We therefore conclude that section 30511(a) is not jurisdictional. So, as both district courts below recognized, the untimeliness of a limitation-of-liability action is a merits issue appropriately raised in a motion for summary judgment. **{–1164–}**

III

Both of these appeals turn on what constitutes "written notice of a claim" under section 30511(a) and therefore starts the running of the statute of limitations. The district court in the Alaska case held that the key requirement is that the claimant communicate "the reasonable possibility of a claim." The district court in the Hawaii case took a similar view, concluding that the limitations period begins to run when the claimant "informs the shipowner of an actual or potential claim." In our view, both of those statements are overly expansive.

We begin our analysis with the statutory text. *See Van Buren v. United States*, 141 S. Ct. 1648, 1654 (2021); *Hall v. United States Dep't of Agric.*, 984 F.3d 825, 837 (9th Cir. 2020). Section 30511(a) contains two sentences. The first allows a vessel owner to bring a limitation-of-liability action: "The owner of a vessel may bring a civil action in a district court of the United States for limitation of liability under this chapter." And the second sets out the statute of limitations that governs such an action: "The action must be brought within 6 months after a claimant gives the owner **[—13—]** written notice of a claim." We hold that the phrase "written notice of a claim" imposes three requirements: the notice must (1) be in writing, (2) clearly state that the victim intends to bring a claim or claims against the owner, and (3) include at least one claim that is reasonably likely to be covered by the Limitation Act.

First, the statute requires "written notice." Because the notice must be written, it is the text of the writing—and not the extrinsic circumstances of its delivery—that determines whether a vessel owner has received notice of a claim. The claimants are therefore incorrect when they suggest that the "factual circumstances" of an accident can be sufficient to alert vessel owners of an impending claim. Modern American society is sufficiently litigious that anyone involved in an accident should be aware that claims for damages are a reasonable possibility. But the statute requires something more: "written notice." We therefore agree with the Eleventh Circuit that "[t]he Act's plain text . . . requires that the claimant provide written notice to the [vessel] owner." *Orion Marine Constr.*, 918 F.3d at 1333 n.4, 7 Adm. R. at 470 n.4 (emphasis omitted). Thus, "even actual knowledge of alleged damage is no substitute for the *written* notice required by the Act." *Id.*, 7 Adm. R. at 470 n.4.

To be sure, the notice need not be a formal complaint, and it need not employ any particular form of words. The statute does not require that the claimant "file" a notice of a claim—a verb that would suggest some level of formality—but only that it "give" notice. For that reason, courts have agreed "that letters sent by claimants to vessel owners may constitute notice of claim." *Doxsee Sea Clam Co. v. Brown*, 13 F.3d 550, 554 (2d Cir. 1994); *accord Orion Marine Constr.*, 918 F.3d at 1333 n.4, 7 Adm. R. at 470 n.4 (noting "that *informal* written notice, such as a letter sent by a claimant or his attorney, will **[—14—]** suffice under the Act in lieu of a formal complaint"). And by referring to "written notice," not "*a* written notice," the statute allows notice to be provided in multiple documents. *In re Complaint of RLB Contracting, Inc.*, 773 F.3d 596, 603–04, 2 Adm. R. 378, 382 (5th Cir. 2014), *overruled on other grounds by Bonvillian Marine Serv.*, 19 F.4th at 790, 9 Adm. R. at 274; *see Niz-Chavez v. Garland*, 141 S. Ct. 1474, 1480–81 (2021) (relying on the indefinite article "a" in the phrase "a notice to appear," 8 U.S.C. § 1229(a), to hold that the notice must be contained in a single document). **{-1165-}**

Second, the notice must be of a "claim." The word "claim" means "a demand of a right or supposed right" or "a demand for compensation, benefits, or payment"—a meaning that is essentially unchanged since 1936, when the statute of limitations was first enacted. *Webster's Third New International Dictionary* 414 (2002); *accord Black's Law Dictionary* 311 (11th ed. 2019) (an "assertion of an existing right"); *see* 46 U.S.C. § 185 (1940) ("The vessel owner, within six months after a claimant shall have given to or filed with such owner written notice of claim, may petition a district court of the United States of competent jurisdiction for limitation . . . .");

Webster's Second New International Dictionary 493 (1934). And in construing the word "claim" in other statutes, we have recognized that it "contemplates, in general usage, a demand for payment or relief, and, unless it is a claim *for* something, is no claim at all." *Avril v. United States*, 461 F.2d 1090, 1091 (9th Cir. 1972); *see also Avery v. United States*, 680 F.2d 608, 609–11 (9th Cir. 1982). Thus, for a writing to constitute "notice of a claim," it must be formulated to "actually inform a shipowner of the claimant's intentions to seek recovery from the owner." *In re Complaint of N.Y.T.R. Transp. Corp.*, 105 F.R.D. 144, 146 (E.D.N.Y. 1985); *accord In re Complaint of Okeanos Ocean Rsch. Found., Inc.*, 704 F. Supp. 412, 414 (S.D.N.Y. 1989) ("[T]he **[—15—]** notice must inform the owner of a claimant's intention to seek damages."). A vessel owner is not required to guess the claimant's intentions, and a tentative statement, or one that merely hints at the possibility of asserting a claim, is not enough.

Third, as we have previously held, the statute requires notice not just of any kind of claim, but of a claim for which the vessel owner could reasonably seek limitation of liability. *See Jung Hyun Sook v. Great Pac. Shipping Co.*, 632 F.2d 100, 102 (9th Cir. 1980); *see also In re Complaint of McCarthy Bros. Co./Clark Bridge*, 83 F.3d 821, 829 (7th Cir. 1996); *In re Complaint of Tom-Mac, Inc.*, 76 F.3d 678, 683 (5th Cir. 1996). If the value of the claim described in the notice is less than the value of the vessel and its pending freight, or if the claim is not subject to limitation under the Limitation Act, then the vessel owner has not received "written notice of a claim" that is relevant to section 30511(a).

The key difference between our interpretation of the statute and that of the district courts in these cases concerns the second part of the test, requiring that the writing inform the vessel owner that the claimant intends to seek a recovery from the owner. The district courts held that notice of "the reasonable possibility of a claim" or a "potential claim" was sufficient to start the running of the limitations period. But as we have explained, a "reasonable possibility" of a claim or a "potential claim" is not enough. Rather, the writing must convey to the vessel owner the claimant's actual intent to initiate a claim.

In reaching a contrary conclusion, the district courts applied language that has been used by other courts of appeals. Under the test used in the Second, Seventh, and Eleventh Circuits, for example, "a letter sent to a shipowner **[—16—]** by a claimant is sufficient to trigger the six-month period if (1) it informs the shipowner of an *actual or potential claim* (2) which may exceed the value of the vessel (3) and . . . reveal[s] a 'reasonable possibility' that the claim made is one subject to limitation." *McCarthy Bros.*, 83 F.3d at 829 (emphasis added) (quoting *Tom-Mac*, 76 F.3d at 683); *accord Doxsee Sea Clam Co.*, 13 F.3d at 554; *Orion Marine Const.*, 918 F.3d at 1331, 7 Adm. R. at 468. Similarly, the Fifth Circuit asks "(1) whether the writing communicates the *reasonable possibility* of a claim, and (2) **{–1166–}** whether it communicates the *reasonable possibility* of damages in excess of the vessel's value." *RLB Contracting*, 773 F.3d at 602, 2 Adm. R. at 381; *see also In re Eckstein Marine Serv. LLC*, 672 F.3d 310, 317 (5th Cir. 2012), *overruled on other grounds by Bonvillian Marine Serv.*, 19 F.4th at 790, 9 Adm. R. at 274.

Some of those cases, however, did not turn on the distinction between an actual claim and a "potential claim" or the "possibility of a claim." Instead, they involved communications that unambiguously asserted a claim, and the disputes focused on whether the claim was likely subject to limitation. *See, e.g., McCarthy Bros.*, 83 F.3d at 829; *Doxsee Sea Clam Co.*, 13 F.3d at 552, 554. Thus, it is possible that those courts of appeals, if confronted with the question, would agree with our conclusion that an actual claim is required. But to the extent our position differs from that of other circuits, we think it is compelled by the statutory text, which refers simply to a "claim," not a "possible" or "potential" claim.

The claimants resist this interpretation, urging that section 30511(a) should be "strictly construed." In support of that argument, they correctly observe that we have previously described the Limitation Act as "a relic of an earlier era." *Esta Later Charters, Inc. v. Ignacio*, 875 F.2d **[—17—]** 234, 239 (9th Cir. 1989). Indeed, more than 60 years ago, Judge Learned Hand suggested that "it is at least doubtful whether the motives that originally lay behind the limitation are not now obsolete." *In re United States Dredging Corp.*, 264 F.2d 339, 341 (2d Cir. 1959). And we have proposed that "Congress might be well advised to examine other approaches or to consider whether the rationale underlying the Liability Act continues to have vitality." *Esta Later Charters*, 875 F.2d at 239. But the critical word in that proposal is the first one: It is for Congress, not the courts, to repeal or amend statutes that have become obsolete. *Cf. Bostock v. Clayton Cnty.*, 140 S. Ct. 1731, 1738 (2020). And just as we may not repeal statutes that we consider outmoded, neither should we adopt special rules of strict construction to narrow their effect.

In any event, whatever might be said about the purposes of the Limitation Act as a whole, we do not believe that our interpretation disserves the purposes of its statute of limitations. Congress enacted the Limitation Act in 1851 in response to multiple incidents in which a vessel owner was "held liable for significant damage amounts under the common law rule of common carrier liability, which did not require proof that the owner was negligent or at fault." *Joyce v. Joyce*, 975 F.2d 379, 383 (7th Cir. 1992); *see Norwich & N.Y. Transp. Co. v. Wright*, 80 U.S. 104, 108–10 (1871). Its apparent goal was to protect investments in shipbuilding so that the American shipping industry could compete with that of Great Britain. *See Norwich*, 80 U.S. at 121–22; *Joyce*, 975 F.2d at 383–84.

In 1936, Congress added the six-month limitations period. Act of June 5, 1936, ch. 521, 49 Stat. 1480. Like all statutes of limitations—indeed, like all statutes generally—it reflects a balance between competing considerations. On **[—18—]** the one hand, a strict limitations period would prevent vessel owners from waiting until after a judgment has been issued against them to petition to limit liability, thereby unnecessarily wasting the time and resources of claimants. *See The Fred Smartley, Jr.*, 108 F.2d 603, 607 (4th Cir. 1940); *Complaint of N.Y.T.R. Transp. Corp.*, 105 F.R.D. at 145.

On the other hand, a more generous limitations period would reduce the burden on vessel owners. To bring a limitation-of-liability action, the vessel owner must either **{-1167-}** transfer "the owner's interest in the vessel and pending freight" to a trustee appointed by the court or deposit with the court an amount equal to that value. 46 U.S.C. § 30511(b). That is a costly step "to require . . . of [a vessel owner] upon penalty of losing his privilege when the claimant's position is equivocal." *In re Allen N. Spooner & Sons, Inc.*, 253 F.2d 584, 586 (2d Cir. 1958) (Hand, J., concurring). In addition, Congress could have been concerned that if a mere suggestion of a claim were enough to start the six-month clock, claimants would be encouraged to be ambiguous in their communications with vessel owners. *See McCarthy Bros.*, 83 F.3d at 829–30 ("The real danger in failing to hold claimants to a fairly high level of specificity in letters is that the claimant may nullify a shipowner's right to file a limitation action by sending a cryptic letter and then waiting more than six months to file a complaint.").

We conclude that "[a]s usual, there are (at least) two sides to the policy questions before us" and that "a rational Congress could reach the policy judgment the statutory text suggests it did." *Niz-Chavez*, 141 S. Ct. at 1486. Whether or not we would reach the same judgment ourselves, "no amount of policy-talk can overcome a plain statutory **[—19—]** command." *Id.* Policy arguments provide no reason to deviate from our interpretation of the statutory language.

IV

Applying our interpretation of section 30511(a), we conclude that neither claimant provided written notice of a claim to the vessel owner before filing suit in state court.

A

In the Alaska case, the claimant's attorneys sent three letters to the vessel owners, William and Jane Martz. But the first two letters discussed only Reagan Martz's potential liability for the accident, and Reagan Martz was not a vessel owner. Although the Martzes acknowledge that we must consider all three letters together, the first two add little to the third, which was Stone's letter of December 4, 2018. Like the district court, we therefore focus on that letter.

Stone's letter did not give notice of a claim against the vessel owners, William and Jane Martz. Specifically, it fell short because it did not state that Horazdovsky intended to seek a recovery from the Martzes. To be sure, the letter did outline a potential theory of liability whereby William and Jane Martz might be held liable for negligently entrusting the boat to Reagan. And its subject line—"Horazdovsky v. Reagan Martz, William and Jane Martz"—suggested the possibility of an adversarial proceeding. But the letter did not take a position on whether Horazdovsky intended to include William and Jane Martz in such a proceeding. To the contrary, it stated that Horazdovsky was "not yet certain whether William Martz or Jane Martz bear any responsibility" for the accident and wished to "avoid unnecessarily naming parties to a lawsuit." In other words, the letter equivocated on whether Horazdovsky intended to **[—20—]** assert a claim against William and Jane Martz. It did not demand anything from William and Jane Martz or assert an entitlement to any recovery from them. It therefore did not constitute "written notice of a claim" under section 30511(a).

Horazdovsky points out that when the Martzes' attorney responded to Stone's letter, he said that they had "not tendered this claim to any insurance companies." Based on that statement, Horazdovsky reasons that the Martzes "clearly understood" that Stone's letter "communicated written notice of a claim." But the statute **{–1168–}** creates an objective test, and what matters is what the written communication says, not how the recipient perceives it. Whatever the Martzes' attorney may have meant by the reference to a "claim," Stone's letter itself did not provide notice of a claim.

Because Stone's letter was not "written notice of a claim," Horazdovsky's state court complaint was the first written notice of a claim that the Martzes received. The Martzes filed their limitation-of-liability action two weeks after the state court action was filed, so the action was timely.

B

For similar reasons, we conclude that the evidence-preservation letter in the Hawaii case was also inadequate to start the running of the statute of limitations. That letter, too, did not state any intention to bring a claim against the vessel owners. It used legal terms such as "evidence," "spoliation," and "waiver," but it said only that an investigation was ongoing and that evidence related to T.T.'s death must be preserved. References to legal concepts without a definite statement of an intent to file suit—or to assert a legal right **[—21—]** in some other way—are insufficient to provide notice of a claim.

Although that determination is sufficient by itself to conclude that the letter did not start the running of the limitations period, there is also reason to doubt whether any claim in the letter would have been reasonably likely to be subject to limitation. While the district court was correct to note that any claim arising from T.T.'s death was likely to exceed the value of the vessel, our precedent requires that the claim be likely subject to limitation not only because of its value but also because it is covered by the Limitation Act. *See Jung Hyun Sook*, 632 F.2d at 102–04. The Limitation Act applies to claims arising out of a person's ownership of a vessel, including, in particular, claims for "loss, damage, or injury by collision," 46 U.S.C. § 30505(b); *see id.* § 30512, and it limits the owner's liability for the negligence of crew members and for the unseaworthiness of the vessel, *see In re Complaint of Messina*, 574 F.3d 119, 126–27 (2d Cir. 2009). It is not clear that it would extend to scuba diving accidents underwater that do not directly involve the vessel. *See* 46 U.S.C. § 30505(b); *cf. Delgado v. Reef Resort Ltd.*, 364 F.3d 642, 645–46 (5th Cir. 2004) (scuba diving is not a traditional maritime activity).

The letter described T.T.'s death as occurring "while he was participating in a drift dive with your company, Island Divers Hawaii." It did not mention the involvement of any vessel in T.T.'s death. Even assuming that the letter could be read to give notice of a claim against Honu Watersports and Matthew Zimmerman, it would be a claim against them for operating the scuba diving experience that resulted in T.T.'s death—not for their ownership of the vessel. As T.T.'s estate and family concede, such a claim would not be subject to **[—22—]** limitation under the Limitation Act. *See* 46 U.S.C. § 30505(b).

In sum, Fish N Dive did not receive written notice of a claim under section 30511(a) until the state court complaint was filed. Fish N Dive filed its limitation-of-liability action within six months of the state court action, so the limitation-of-liability action was timely.

REVERSED and REMANDED.

United States Court of Appeals
for the Ninth Circuit

No. 19-50268

UNITED STATES
vs.
DOMINGUEZ-CAICEDO

Appeal from the United States District Court for the Southern District of California

Decided: July 18, 2022

Citation: 40 F.4th 938, 10 Adm. R. 319 (9th Cir. 2022).

Before **SMITH** and **LEE**, Circuit Judges, and **ROBRENO**,* District Judge.

* The Honorable Eduardo C. Robreno, United States District Judge for the Eastern District of Pennsylvania, sitting by designation.

[—10—] **{–944–}** **SMITH**, Circuit Judge: **{–945–}**

The defendants in these three consolidated cases—Adrian Andres Cortez-Quinonez, Segundo Marcial Dominguez-Caicedo, and Victor Gaspar Chichande—were convicted of conspiring to distribute cocaine on board a vessel, possession of cocaine with intent to distribute on board a vessel, and aiding and abetting. In this appeal, they challenge the district court's denial of their pre-trial motions to dismiss the indictment. Defendants also argue that the prosecutor committed misconduct in his closing argument. Individually, Dominguez-Caicedo contends that the district court improperly excluded expert testimony that supported his duress defense. Cortez-Quinonez individually appeals the district court's decision not to suppress his post-arrest statements. He also argues that the prosecutor committed misconduct by arguing at his sentencing that Cortez-Quinonez was the ringleader, after arguing at trial that Dominguez-Caicedo was in charge. Finally, all three defendants argue that the district court erred by not granting them minor role reductions at sentencing. We have jurisdiction pursuant to 28 U.S.C. § 1291, and we affirm the defendants' convictions and Dominguez-Caicedo's and Cortez-Quinonez's sentences. We vacate Chichande's sentence and remand for resentencing.

FACTUAL AND PROCEDURAL BACKGROUND

On December 31, 2017, the Coast Guard cutter Stratton spotted a suspicious vessel—a 30- to 40-foot "panga" boat—carrying the three defendants near the Galapagos Islands. The Coast Guard observed the vessel and determined that it had no indicia of nationality. From a Coast Guard helicopter, Officer Charles Arena activated the helicopter's **[—11—]** blue law-enforcement lights and broadcast a message to the boat via maritime radio in English and Spanish, informing the vessel that the United States Coast Guard was ordering them to halt. When the panga did not stop, Arena ordered the "precision marksman" onboard the helicopter to fire warning shots into the water in front of the panga, some of which contained an orange tracer that makes the shots more visible. After discharging the warning shots, Arena observed "the occupants onboard start to throw items overboard," including "packages that were tied together." The Coast Guard later determined that the packages were attached to a "GPS buoy" that was also thrown overboard. When the panga still did not stop, the marksman fired two more warning shots into the water aft of the panga's engine, apparently to signal that those on board should move away from the engine, and then shot out the engine. Dominguez-Caicedo testified that by the time he saw the helicopter, it was shooting at the panga. He did not know that it was a U.S. Coast Guard helicopter. Cortez-Quinonez stated that he thought the shots from the helicopter were going to kill them.

Three officers from the Coast Guard then boarded the panga. Dominguez-Caicedo told the officers who boarded the panga **{–946–}** that they had been out fishing. Cortez-Quinonez identified himself as the "master" of the vessel through an interpreter, to one of the Coast Guard officers. Cortez-Quinonez gave the officers his Ecuadorian identification card. The other two defendants said that they did not have any identification with them. The Coast Guard then detained the three defendants and transferred them to the Stratton. Several days later, on January 2,

2018, they were transferred to the Northland, another Coast Guard vessel, where they were detained until January 3. **[—12—]**

On board the Stratton, according to Officer Welzant of the Coast Guard, the standard protocol dictates that each detainee is given an initial medical screening by the medical corpsman—essentially a nurse. They are not told where they are headed, they do not get an opportunity to contact their families, and they do not know how long they will be on board. Detainees are chained to a cable that runs the length of the deck inside the helicopter hangar (emptied of helicopters). Each detainee is chained to the cable using an eighteen-inch ankle shackle. The detainees remain chained at all times of the day and night, except for trips to the bathroom and approximately one hour per day of exercise time, during which the detainees are permitted to walk freely on the deck. Detainees can shower periodically. Cortez-Quinonez testified that he was forced to shower with the other two defendants while officers laughed at their "private parts and how [they] were naked," though it was not clear on which cutter this allegedly occurred. Welzant stated that there were no group showers on the Stratton. Welzant testified that detainees are escorted to use the restroom upon request, unless the crew is launching a helicopter or a small boat, which would take approximately ten minutes. However, the Stratton's detainee logbook showed that the three defendants were rarely taken to the restroom between 6:30 p.m. and 7:00 a.m. the next morning. When the three defendants in this case were detained, there were thirty-seven total detainees on board the Stratton.

Welzant testified that Defendants were provided with mats approximately half an inch thick on which to sleep. The Coast Guard confiscated the clothes that the defendants were wearing and gave them disposable Tyvek painters' coveralls to wear instead. These coveralls often ripped and exposed detainees. Each person also routinely receives a blanket. Detainees are fed three meals per day, primarily **[—13—]** consisting of rice and beans, supplemented with fruit approximately every other day. A jug of water is accessible to detainees at all times. Welzant stated that the detainees are also provided with dominoes, cards, and Spanish-language Bibles. Officer Jordan Groff testified to the conditions aboard the Northland, which were substantially similar to those on board the Stratton, except that the detainees ate eggs, potatoes, toast, enchiladas, spaghetti, and chicken, rather than rice and beans.

On January 3, 2018, the defendants were transferred to another Coast Guard cutter, the Mohawk. The defendants were transferred to the Mohawk—which was heading for Florida—because the Coast Guard suspected that the Department of Justice would prosecute the case in Florida. On the Mohawk, the detainees were kept on the top deck, exposed to the elements. According to Coast Guard officer Kristopher Meyer, the crew erects a tent on that deck while detainees are on-board to provide some shelter from the elements. The Mohawk crew does not provide any sleeping mats, though they do give each detainee a blanket and a towel.

While the defendants were on the Mohawk, there were numerous rain squalls, which caused the deck to become wet. When it rained during the night, the detainees **{–947–}** would either have to stand up or try to sleep while laying on the wet deck. On the Mohawk, detainees were served rice and beans for every meal. The defendants testified that the rice and beans were very undercooked, and that these meals resulted in them suffering gastrointestinal distress. The Mohawk's detainee log shows that Gaspar Chichande refused five meals in a row, and that Cortez-Quinonez and Dominguez-Caicedo refused three meals in a row. Cortez-Quinonez **[—14—]** testified that he was denied medical care on board the Mohawk, despite complaining of pain.

The defendants were aboard the Mohawk for five days. On January 8, 2018, they were transferred back to the Stratton—which was heading to California—because the Department of Justice had designated the Southern District of California as the prosecuting district. If the defendants had remained on the Mohawk, they would have arrived in Florida on January 17, 2018. However, the Coast Guard determined that there was no aircraft available to fly the defendants from Florida to California to prosecute them in the designated district.

On January 16, 2018, the defendants were transferred from the Stratton to their final cutter, the Active. The conditions of confinement on the Active were similar to those on the Stratton, except that the area where the defendants were shackled was protected from the elements only by a canvas tarp, and the sleeping mats provided were an inch-and-a-half thick. In addition, the temperature dropped as low as 50 degrees during the time the defendants were onboard the Active. Dominguez-Caicedo testified that he was extremely cold on the Active.

Dominguez-Caicedo and Cortez-Quinonez testified that the shackles and living conditions onboard the cutters caused them significant physical pain. A psychologist, Dr. Julia Kuck, testified as an expert witness at the defendants' motion to dismiss hearing. Dr. Kuck had interviewed Gaspar Chichande and diagnosed him with post-traumatic stress disorder (PTSD) with dissociative symptoms and panic attacks. This diagnosis was based on antecedent traumatic events such as childhood neglect, abandonment, and trauma. Dr. Kuck testified that the "primary triggering event" for Gaspar Chichande's PTSD was the Coast Guard **[—15—]** helicopter firing its gun at the panga. She also referred to the treatment aboard the Coast Guard cutters as psychological torture due to "unrelenting cold," "wet conditions on deck," "feral treatment of individuals," and "induced desperation."

The Coast Guard had intended to land the Active in San Diego, but due to bad weather, it was prevented from doing so. Instead, the Active landed in Long Beach on January 22, 2018, where DEA Agent Brandon Pullen met the ship and took custody of the defendants. Pullen testified that none of the three defendants appeared to be ill or under the influence of drugs or alcohol. Pullen had each defendant sign a Rule 5 waiver that allowed them to be transferred to San Diego instead of going before a magistrate judge in Long Beach. The waivers also advised Defendants that they were entitled to remain silent and to have an attorney appointed to represent them.

Pullen then advised each defendant of his *Miranda* rights in Spanish through another DEA agent, who served as an interpreter. Each defendant signed a *Miranda* waiver. After signing the waiver, Cortez-Quinonez made incriminating statements that suggested he knew that he was transporting drugs. At a pre-trial hearing, Cortez-Quinonez testified that at the time he signed the *Miranda* form, he did not understand that a lawyer could be appointed for him free of charge; the form does **{–948–}** not specify that the appointed attorney would be free of charge. The statements were nonetheless introduced at trial. The jury convicted the defendants on all charges.

STANDARDS OF REVIEW

We review de novo the district court's decision on the motion to dismiss for outrageous government conduct, and we review for abuse of discretion the district court's decision **[—16—]** not to use its supervisory powers to dismiss the indictment. *United States v. Restrepo*, 930 F.2d 705, 712 (9th Cir. 1991). We review "a district court's finding that a pre-arraignment delay was reasonable for clear error." *United States v. Liera*, 585 F.3d 1237, 1242 (9th Cir. 2009) (citation omitted).

In reviewing alleged prosecutorial misconduct to which a defendant objected at trial, we review under the harmless error standard. *United States v. Alcantara-Castillo*, 788 F.3d 1186, 1190 (9th Cir. 2015). Under the harmless error standard, we must view "the challenged conduct in the entire context of the trial, and reverse only if it appears more probable than not that prosecutorial misconduct materially affected the fairness of the trial." *Id.* (citation and internal quotation marks omitted). If the defendant does not contemporaneously object, we review the alleged misconduct for plain error. *Id.* Under plain error, "[w]e may reverse if (1) there was error; (2) it was plain; (3) it affected the defendant's substantial rights; and (4) viewed in the context of the entire trial, the impropriety seriously affected the fairness, integrity, or public reputation of judicial proceedings." *Id.* at 1190–91 (citation and internal quotation marks omitted). Furthermore, where a defendant alleges multiple instances of misconduct, we must consider the combined prejudicial effect of the misconduct. *Berger v. United States*, 295 U.S. 78, 89 (1935). In considering the cumulative effect of alleged misconduct, where the defendant objected to some—but not all—of the alleged misconduct, we review for plain error. *Alcantara-Castillo*, 788 F.3d at 1191. **[—17—]**

ANALYSIS

A

Prior to trial, the defendants moved to dismiss the indictment for outrageous government conduct based on their treatment aboard the Coast Guard cutters. They also sought to dismiss the indictment for violation of Federal Rule of Criminal Procedure 5, which requires that the Government bring defendants before a magistrate judge without unnecessary delay.

"The argument that an indictment must be dismissed because of outrageous government conduct is derived from a comment by the Supreme Court in *United States v. Russell*, 411 U.S. 423 (1973)," in which the Court distinguished a claim of outrageous government conduct from a claim of entrapment. *Restrepo*, 930 F.2d at 712. While entrapment depends on the defendant's criminal predisposition, "[a]n indictment may be set aside because of outrageous government conduct whether or not the defendant was predisposed to engage in criminal activity." *Id.* (citation omitted).

"In order to show outrageous government conduct, defendants must show conduct that violates due process in such a way that it is 'so grossly shocking and so outrageous as to violate the universal sense of justice.'" *United States v. Stinson*, 647 F.3d 1196, 1209 (9th Cir. 2011) (quoting *Restrepo*, 930 F.2d at 712). A claim of outrageous government conduct is "a claim that government conduct *in securing an indictment* was so shocking to due process values that the indictment **{-949-}** must be dismissed." *United States v. Nickerson*, 731 F.3d 1009, 1015 (9th Cir. 2013) (citation omitted). Therefore, in order to secure dismissal of an indictment due to outrageous government conduct, a **[—18—]** defendant must show a nexus between the conduct and either "securing the indictment or [] procuring the conviction." *Id.*

Defendants claim that the nexus between the Government's conduct and securing the indictment is satisfied because "if the Coast Guard had chosen to treat Appellants and other detainees humanely, they simply couldn't have conducted their Pacific operations." Specifically,

> [o]ne officer testified that feeding rice and beans [to the detainees] was the only affordable way for the Coast Guard to accomplish its mission. Another testified that the excessive restraint of defendants resulted from too few watchmen and too many detainees. Coast Guard testified that it couldn't get detainees to shore because its helicopters were old and didn't have long range. They claimed they couldn't wait for diplomatic clearance to get people off the cutters because it would upset the ability to patrol the ocean.

This is not the type of nexus that we generally consider sufficient to establish outrageous government conduct requiring dismissal of an indictment. For example, in *Nickerson*, the defendant argued that her indictment should have been dismissed based on "outrageous government conduct of videotaping her while she was using the toilet in a holding cell at the police station." 731 F.3d at 1014. The video camera that captured the defendant in *Nickerson* served a variety of purposes, including "medical and security concerns, such as if a detainee attempts suicide, if a physical altercation occurs between detainees, or if a detainee **[—19—]** becomes progressively more intoxicated or sick in the holding cell and needs medical attention." *Id.* at 1011.

Furthermore, the cameras "deter abusive police conduct[.]" *Id.* We held that "there was no nexus between that conduct and the criminal proceeding at issue." *Id.* at 1015. Accepting Dominguez-Caicedo's logic would have compelled the opposite conclusion. After all, if a medical or security concern resulted in the death of an arrested person, that would preclude the prosecutor from securing an indictment against that person. In other words, nearly all police actions are broadly connected to securing indictments. That cannot mean that all police actions have a nexus within the meaning of the outrageous government conduct doctrine.

We have dismissed an indictment due to outrageous government conduct in a published opinion only once, in *Greene v. United States*, 454 F.2d 783 (9th Cir. 1971). In *Greene*, "the government supplied the equipment and raw material for a bootlegging operation and was the defendant's sole customer." *United States v. Mayer*, 503 F.3d 740, 754 (9th Cir. 2007). We held that the government could not "involve itself so directly and continuously over such a long period of time in the creation and maintenance of criminal operations, and yet prosecute its collaborators." *Greene*, 454 F.2d at 787. The type of nexus in *Greene* between the allegedly outrageous conduct and securing an indictment or conviction is not present in this case.

Indeed, the development of the outrageous government conduct concept suggests that it does not even apply to conditions of pre-trial detention. For that reason, the Eleventh Circuit has rejected claims similar to those Defendants raise here. *See United States v. Jayyousi*, 657 F.3d 1085, 1112 (11th Cir. 2011) (holding that the outrageous government conduct doctrine "does not apply" to **[—20—]** alleged mistreatment between arrest and indictment). Unlike the Eleventh Circuit, our **{-950-}** circuit appears to have assumed without deciding that outrageous government conduct *could* apply to conditions of confinement, so long as there is a nexus between the conduct and securing the indictment or conviction. *E.g.*, *Nickerson*, 731 F.3d at 1015. Because there is no nexus here, it is unnecessary to revisit that conclusion.

Separate from the outrageous government conduct claim, federal courts also "have inherent supervisory powers to order dismissal of prosecutions" for three reasons: (1) to remedy "the violation of a recognized statutory or constitutional right"; (2) to ensure "that a conviction rests on appropriate considerations validly before a jury"; and (3) "to deter future illegal conduct." *United States v. Matta-Ballesteros*, 71 F.3d 754, 763 (9th Cir. 1995) (citation omitted). Defendants argue that even if outrageous government conduct does not require dismissal of the indictment, the district court should have used its supervisory powers to provide the same remedy. Their reasoning rests on the assertion that the "government should tread lightly in international waters, and the court should not condone mistreatment of foreigners with no connection to the United States." Pursuant to *Matta-Ballesteros*, that is not a sufficient reason to hold that the district court abused its discretion by not dismissing the indictment. Therefore, we affirm the district court's denial of Defendants' motions to dismiss for outrageous government conduct.

B

Defendants' joint Rule 5 claim requires us to determine (1) whether dismissal of an indictment is a remedy available for violation of Rule 5; and (2) if so, whether Defendants have shown that they are entitled to this remedy. We hold **[—21—]** that a court has the power to dismiss an indictment for egregious violations of Rule 5, but that the Government did not violate Rule 5 in this case.

1

"A person making an arrest outside the United States must take the defendant without unnecessary delay before a magistrate judge[.]" Fed. R. Crim. P. 5(a)(1)(B). This is termed the "'presentment' requirement," and it is meant "to prevent secret detention" and "inform a suspect of the charges against him[.]" *Corley v. United States*, 556 U.S. 303, 306 (2009). The predecessor to Rule 5(a) was *McNabb v. United States*, 318 U.S. 332 (1943), in which the Supreme Court held that "unwarranted detention" between arrest and presentment "led to tempting utilization of intensive interrogation." *Mallory v. United States*, 354 U.S. 449, 453 (1957). "[I]t was deemed necessary to render inadmissible incriminating statements elicited from defendants during a period of unlawful detention." *Id.* Thus, the normal remedy for violation of Rule 5 is suppression of statements made during the unnecessary delay. *Id.* When an individual does *not* make any incriminating statements during the delay in presentment, we have previously suggested that vacating the conviction and dismissing the indictment is a "drastic remedy" that the court can "invoke." *United States v. Jernigan*, 582 F.2d 1211, 1214 (9th Cir. 1978). However, we appear never to have granted that remedy in any prior case.

In *Bayless v. United States*, 381 F.2d 67, 70–71 (9th Cir. 1967), we affirmed the district court's denial of a motion to dismiss based on violation of Rule 5(a). We held that because the Government did not obtain any incriminating evidence between arrest and presentment, the defendant was not prejudiced by the Government's violation **{-951-}** of Rule 5(a). **[—22—]** *Id.* at 71. Consequently, the motion to dismiss the indictment "was correctly denied." *Id.*; *see United States v. Mejia*, 39 F. App'x 568, 569–70 (9th Cir. Apr. 29, 2002) (finding that a thirteen-day delay in presentment, while "reprehensible," did not warrant dismissal of the indictment). Conversely, in *United States v. Osunde*, 638 F. Supp. 171, 176 (N.D. Cal. 1986), the Northern District of California reasoned that a 106-day delay between arrest and presentment was a "flagrant" violation of Rule 5(a). And "[a]lthough the Court [could not] point to case law supporting dismissal, rather than suppression of evidence, for flagrant violations of Rule 5(a)," it held that Osunde's lengthy delay—with no incriminating evidence to suppress—made dismissal of the indictment appropriate. *Id.* at 176–77.

The Second and Eighth Circuits have outright rejected dismissal of the indictment as a remedy for violation of Rule 5, with holdings that appear to foreclose dismissal even in egregious circumstances. *United States v. Peeples*, 962 F.3d 677, 687–88 (2d Cir. 2020); *United States v. Cooke*, 853 F.3d 464, 471 (8th Cir. 2017) (holding that because the purpose of Rule 5 is to deter purposeful delay in presentment in order to extract a confession, "the appropriate remedy for a violation of Rule 5(a)(1)(A) is not dismissal of an indictment, but suppression of evidence illegally obtained as a result of the violation."). However, we are bound by *Bayless* and *Jernigan*, both of which determined that dismissal could be a remedy for particularly egregious violations of Rule 5 where no other relief is available. Thus, we examine whether the Government violated Rule 5. Because we conclude that it did not, we need not reach the question of whether the district court should have dismissed the indictment on that basis. **[—23—]**

2

Defendants argue that the Government violated Rule 5(a) by (1) having Defendants travel to California instead of Florida; and (2) having Defendants sign Rule 5 waivers that then allowed the Government to interrogate them before presentment, which took place the day after they arrived in the United States.

"Whether or not undue delay occurred . . . must be determined upon the individual facts of each case." *Gray v. United States*, 394 F.2d 96, 100 (9th Cir. 1967). The district court found that "the 23-day delay [between interdiction and arraignment] was reasonable" because "[o]n average, it takes 20 days to transport a detained individual from the Eastern Pacific to the U.S." Further, the district court stated, "the coast guard needed to determine which district in the United States would be responsible for the prosecution of the case and, therefore[,] where the defendants would be transported." According to the district court, the officer in charge of "figuring out how to transport the defendants to this district as quickly as possible" considered several options, including taking the defendants by ship to Florida, with a connecting flight to San Diego. However, because "[e]ach of these options had drawbacks," the officer "determined that transporting via coast guard cutter [to San Diego] was the most expeditious way of transporting [the defendants]." Finally, the district court stated that the timeline of transportation to San Diego and presentment the next morning constituted "bringing the defendants before a magistrate judge without unnecessary delay."

i

First, Defendants contend that the district court engaged in the wrong inquiry when examining their transportation **{–952–}** to **[—24—]** California. Instead of asking whether the Government transported Defendants *to the prosecuting district* without unnecessary delay, Defendants claim that the district court should have asked whether the Government transported Defendants *to a magistrate judge* without unnecessary delay.[1] It is undisputed that Defendants could have arrived in Florida five days earlier than they arrived in California. The issue is whether delay caused by the choice to transport Defendants directly to the prosecuting district (California, in this case) is an "unnecessary" delay for Rule 5 purposes. The district court implicitly held that it was not, and we agree.

Until now, we have not addressed whether a delay in arraignment caused by the Government's choice to send a defendant interdicted on the high seas directly to the prosecuting district (rather than the closest magistrate judge) is "unnecessary delay." In the Fourth Amendment unreasonable seizure context, the Supreme Court has stated that "[e]xamples of unreasonable delay [in presentment] are delays for the purpose of gathering additional evidence to justify the arrest, a delay motivated by ill will against the arrested individual, or delay for delay's sake." *Cnty. of Riverside v. McLaughlin*, 500 U.S. 44, 56 (1991). In *McLaughlin*, the Court specifically cited the "often unavoidable delays in transporting arrested persons from one facility to another" as a "practical realit[y]" that would not qualify as unreasonable. *Id.* at 57. **[—25—]**

Other courts that have addressed delays in presentment of defendants arrested on the high seas have uniformly held that such delays are reasonable. *See, e.g., United States v. Savchenko*, 201 F.R.D. 503, 506 (S.D. Cal. 2001) (holding that sixteen days to transport defendants apprehended 500 nautical miles from Mexico to the Southern District of California was reasonable); *United States v. Barahona-Estupinan*, 2004 WL 7333779, at *5 (S.D. Cal. Mar. 19. 2004) (six days to transport Defendants from near the Mexico-Guatemala border to San Diego was not unreasonable); *United States v. Torres-Iturre*, 2016 WL 2757283, at *3–4 (S.D. Cal. May 12, 2016) (twenty-one days to transport Defendants 2439 nautical miles to San Diego was reasonable); *United States v. Aragon*, 2017 WL 2889499, at *14 (S.D.N.Y. Jul. 5, 2017) (sixteen-day delay caused by transporting Defendants from the Pacific Ocean to New York for prosecution was not unreasonable).

Importantly, none of these cases compare the time it took the Government to bring the defendants to the prosecuting district to the time it *would* have taken to bring the defendants to the *closest* district. The Eleventh Circuit addressed this distinction, writing that "the MDLEA does not prohibit the government from taking offenders to Florida rather than California" because "[a] person violating the MDLEA may be tried in any district, if the offense was begun or committed upon the high seas." *United States v. Cabezas-Montano*, 949 F.3d 567, 591, 8 Adm. R. 364, 376 (11th Cir. 2020) (citation and internal quotation marks omitted). Therefore, the Eleventh Circuit said, "the issue here is not *where* the defendant was taken, but *why* it took the government 49 days to present the defendant arrested outside the United States before a magistrate judge in the United States for a probable cause hearing." *Id.*, 8 Adm. R. at 376. The court then applied the Eleventh **{–953–}** Circuit's test for determining whether a particular delay was

[1] Defendants' joint brief incorrectly states that Rule 5(a) requires transportation to "the nearest available magistrate." This was the language in an outdated version of Rule 5. The current language does not require that Defendants be transported to the nearest magistrate, only that they are transported to one without unnecessary delay.

[—26—] unnecessary. *Id.* at 591–92, 8 Adm. R. at 376–77. Like the Eleventh Circuit, we hold that the proper inquiry is whether transportation to the United States as a whole was unnecessarily delayed, rather than whether there was some other district in the United States in which the defendant could have been brought before a magistrate judge more quickly.

The district court did not clearly err in its determination that twenty-three days was not an unnecessary delay, given that the Coast Guard needed to transport Defendants from near the Galapagos Islands to San Diego. In fact, Defendants do not contend that twenty-three days was an unreasonable amount of time to reach California. We therefore conclude that the Coast Guard's decision to take Defendants to California, rather than Florida, did not violate Rule 5.

ii

There was a second period of delay between Defendants arriving in Long Beach and their presentment in San Diego. Defendants argue that this period of delay also violated Rule 5. Although they signed Rule 5 waivers in Long Beach, Defendants say that this was involuntary. Defendants also contend that the waiver only excused the Government from presenting them to a magistrate judge in Long Beach; it did not allow delay of presentment once Defendants arrived in San Diego.

Defendants arrived in Long Beach on January 22 at approximately 11:30 a.m., and cleared customs at 11:50 a.m. Agent Pullen took Defendants to the San Diego DEA office, arriving about 3:00 p.m. (with a stop for food at In-N-Out). That morning or the day before, Pullen had made an appointment for the 5:30 p.m. booking window for the defendants at the prison in San Diego. After *Miranda*izing Defendants, Pullen conducted brief interviews with each (ten [—27—] to twenty minutes), and then took them to the prison for booking. They went before a magistrate judge the next morning, January 23.

We have never addressed whether the standard procedures for booking arrestees in the Southern District of California violate Rule 5. However, numerous district courts have concluded that they do not. In *United States v. Lauina*, 2016 WL 1573195, at *1 (S.D. Cal. Apr. 18, 2016), the district court found "it necessary to revisit the current presentment procedures" because "certain detainees are still not presented on either the day of their arrest or the day following their arrest." The court explained, "In this district, rather than transporting detainees directly to a Magistrate Judge, arresting agents take detainees to the Metropolitan Correctional Center ("MCC") for initial processing." *Id.* This is because "the MCC provides the necessary function of organizing detainees prior to their initial appearance." *Id.* The court wrote that "bringing detainees directly to the Court would likely be disorganized, cause unsafe conditions, and be an inefficient use of the Court's time." *Id.* At the time of *Lauina*, "[t]he MCC maintain[ed] three booking windows each day at approximately 9:00 a.m., 12:30 p.m., and 5:00 p.m." *Id.* at *2.

Following *Lauina*, in *United States v. Portocarrero-Angulo*, 2017 WL 3283856, at *8 (S.D. Cal. Aug. 1, 2017), the district court rejected an international-waters defendant's argument that a Friday-to-Monday delay between arrival in San Diego and presentment was unnecessary. The court wrote, "General Order No. 605 of this Court requires the Department of Justice, through the Bureau of Prisons and the U.S. Marshal Service, to ensure that every detainee being brought before the Court has been screened for and determined not to have transmittable tuberculosis {-954-}." *Id.* The [—28—] court went on to state that "[t]he need to complete this screening makes the delay between Defendant's arrival in San Diego on Friday afternoon and his presentment the next Monday reasonable." *Id.*

Defendants arrived in Long Beach around 11:50 a.m., so the 5:30 p.m. booking window was the earliest available. Although Cortez-Quinonez states that the Magistrate Judge was arraigning defendants until "at least 5 p.m.," that does not support the contention that Defendants could have been arraigned after their tuberculosis screening at 5:30 p.m.

Furthermore, there is no evidence that Pullen purposely delayed the booking and presentment to interrogate the defendants. Under these circumstances, the district court's finding that the delays in presentment were reasonable was not clearly erroneous. Because we hold that the Government did not violate Rule 5, we need not examine whether Defendants voluntarily signed their Rule 5 waivers, or whether the facts of this case present a Rule 5 violation that warrants dismissal of the indictment.

C

Cortez-Quinonez also argues that in the event we find that there was no Rule 5 violation, his statement still should have been suppressed because it was involuntary.

Upon arrival at the DEA office in San Diego, Cortez-Quinonez and the Spanish-language interpreter had the following exchange in Spanish, which has been translated into English. Per the court translator, "Non-standard spelling, word choice and grammar in English reflect the manner of the Spanish spoken, and have been underlined. Ambiguous utterances have been rendered with different **[—29—]** possibilities (or inferred meaning) in brackets."[2] Additionally, words the agent spoke in English are italicized.

> Agent: *Okay*. Before doing it any questions, you have to understand your rights. You have... right to... remeintz silent. Anything that you say can be useds against you. Before of a kert. Before doing it any questions, you have the right to consult an attorney. You have the right to have an attorney present during the ... inter-egation. In the event of not being able to pay for the services of a attorney, and if you so wish, an [would/were to] be... appointed... before doing it any questions. Have you understood [his/her/its/your] rights?
>
> Cortez-Quinonez: Yes.
>
> Agent: *Okay*. Are you availab-, wel-, willing to answer somes questions, or do you want an attorney?
>
> Cortez-Quinonez: Yes, I am willing to... to the questions, because... now, being here—you do understand me?—one, one's family members—you understand me?—things, how they are in [one's] country... when one suffers from hardship... **[—30—]**
>
> Agent: Yes, but, are you sure, or, or... do you want an attorney?
>
> Cortez-Quinonez: [Okay.../What?] There, there isn't, there isn't any money to pay an...
>
> Agent: That's fine. The, uh, here, in this country, they give you an... attorney. You don't have to pay.
>
> [pause]
>
> Agent: *So,* so, do you want to talk, or [does he/does she/do you] want to wait? Until speaking with your attorney.
>
> Cortez-Quinonez: But, the attorney, [until when/for how long]? This morning? **{-955-}**
>
> Agent: Yes, but... [that's that/nothing can be done]. You can't... leave. You do understand me?
>
> [pause]
>
> Agent: *So*, do you want to wai' for, for... an attorney?
>
> Cortez-Quinonez: No, well, my buddy doesn't have [enough] for... an attorney neither, just the... the **questions**—you do understand me?
>
> Agent: *Okay, so,* you want to talk? **[—31—]**
>
> [pause]

[2] We have reproduced the translation of the transcript exactly as it appears in the record. The translation appears to be a literal word-for-word substitution of English for Spanish.

> Agent: *Okay.* so put yours... initials here, at each point. And then, "have you... uh, understood [his/her/its/their/your] rights?" put "yes." And then "are you are willid to asnwer somes questions", "yes." *Okay? So,* initials, at each point...
>
> Cortez-Quinonez: [UI] the, of my first name, or—
>
> Agent: —Mm-hmm—
>
> Cortez-Quinonez: —of my last name?
>
> Agent: Yes. Your, uh, first name.
>
> Cortez-Quinonez: My first name. Like that, like it is here, written down?
>
> Agent: Yes. Mm-hmm.
>
> . . . .
>
> Agent: And then, here, uh... that "yes," you have understood.
>
> [pause]
>
> Agent: And then, here, that "yes," you want to talk.
>
> [pause] **[—32—]**
>
> Agent: Initials, at each point.
>
> Cortez-Quinonez: Just of my name?—
>
> Agent: —Yes.
>
> [pause]
>
> Agent: Okay, and the [Ø] goes; put your signature, here.
>
> [pause]
>
> Agent: Thank you.

Cortez-Quinonez then gave an incriminating statement that was used against him at trial.

Pursuant to the Due Process Clause, a statement is voluntary only if it is "the product of a rational intellect and a free will." *Blackburn v. Alabama*, 361 U.S. 199, 208 (1960). "[T]he characteristics of the accused and the details of the interrogation" are relevant considerations. *United States v. Kelley*, 953 F.2d 562, 564–65 (9th Cir. 1992). However, introduction of a statement at trial that was given without "coercive government misconduct" does not violate the Due Process Clause. *Colorado v. Connelly*, 479 U.S. 157, 163 (1986). It appears that the only coercive government misconduct Cortez-Quinonez has alleged is his treatment on board the Coast Guard cutter. However, at the time Cortez-Quinonez gave his statement, he was no longer experiencing this treatment. Cortez-Quinonez was advised of his rights, indicated he understood them, asked a clarifying question about his right to counsel, and then gave an inculpatory statement. The district court did not err by **[—33—]** finding that the statement was voluntary under the Due Process Clause.

D

1

We turn next to Defendants' prosecutorial misconduct claims. In closing argument, the prosecutor stated, "when the coast guard showed up, [Defendants] had to pull from the drug trafficker's playbook. Play number one. You saw it on the video. Don't move. They might not spot you." After defense counsel objected, and the court overruled the objection, the prosecutor clarified, "I'm not talking about a playbook somewhere. I'm talking about what they did and what the facts in evidence show. Okay? Just so we're clear." The prosecutor went on to discuss "Plan B. Act normal. Nothing to see here," "Plan C, speed away," and "Plan D," which "was **{-956-}** throw the drugs overboard." After Plan D, "there's more in the playbook," because "Plan E" is to "deceive." Finally, "Plan F" was "[t]hings that they have said" at trial—namely, that they were forced to transport the narcotics. The prosecutor returned to the playbook analogy several times.

Defense counsel objected to the prosecutor's use of the playbook analogy, so we review under the harmless error standard. First, we must determine whether the reference to a playbook was error. *Alcantara-Castillo*, 788 F.3d at 1190. Defendants characterize the prosecutor's alleged misconduct as stating facts that were not in evidence—namely, that there was a drug trafficker's playbook that Defendants were following.

The prosecutor's reference to the playbook analogy is distinct from statements of facts not in evidence that this **[—34—]** court has held to be misconduct requiring reversal. *See, e.g., United States v. Toomey*, 764 F.2d 678, 681 (9th Cir. 1985) (holding that a prosecutor's statement that "[w]e know that the delivery of heroin base . . . occurred on April 28" when there was no evidence that the package contained heroin base was harmless); *United States v. Wilkes*, 662 F.3d 524, 540 (9th Cir. 2011) (holding that a prosecutor's statement that a defense witness lied because he "has an ax to grind" was not improper reference to facts not in evidence).

In this case, the prosecutor's references to a "playbook" clearly were not meant to imply that there was an actual playbook in evidence that listed Plans A–F.[3] Instead, the prosecutor was using the playbook analogy to provide a framework to consider Defendants' different actions during the Coast Guard's interdiction.

Defendants also argue that the prosecutor's use of the playbook analogy constituted improper vouching and implied extra-record knowledge not available to the jury. The transcript of the prosecutor's closing argument simply does not bear this out. As stated above, the playbook analogy was used to explain why the defendants did what they did, creating an overarching narrative for the video showing the interdiction. The prosecutor's argument was based on the facts in evidence. We hold that this argument did not constitute prosecutorial misconduct, and so we do not address whether the referenced misconduct was harmless error. **[—35—]**

2

Defendants also contend that the prosecutor committed misconduct by arguing in closing that Dominguez-Caicedo was in charge but arguing at sentencing that Cortez-Quinonez was the leader.

In closing, the prosecutor said:

> Here is [Gaspar Chichande's] testimony from this trial. "In fact, you indicated Mr. Cortez was the captain, he was in charge, didn't you?" And he said, "Well, because he had a device with him, and that's why I said he was the captain." "But he had a device, and he would tell you to drive such and such route?" "Yes, sir." "And in fact, you specifically called him the captain?" "Yes, sir." "Because he was in charge?" And he says, "I think so." Right? He thinks he's in charge because he's manning the engines, but you know from watching the video that Mr. Dominguez is the one calling the shots. You see it. He's this one that turns around and gives the order. **{–957–}**

The prosecutor also stated "Mr. Dominguez [is] the man giving the order for the boat to take off[.]" In other words, Gaspar Chichande testified that he believed Cortez-Quinonez was the captain of the boat, but the video of the interdiction showed that Dominguez-Caicedo gave the order for the boat to take off.

At Cortez-Quinonez's sentencing, the district court began by giving counsel his tentative on the sentence—240 months. Cortez-Quinonez's attorney "strongly urge[d]" **[—36—]** the court to "come off [its] tentative" based on the argument that Cortez-Quinonez was more similar to Gaspar Chichande (who got 180 months) in terms of relative culpability than he was to Dominguez-Caicedo (who got 216 months). The court stated, "I

[3] This contrasts with the case Defendants cite, *United States v. McGill*, 815 F.3d 846 (D.C. Cir. 2016), in which the court held that a prosecutor committed misconduct by arguing that the defendant's letters from jail constituted a "playbook" that the defense attorney and witnesses all consulted in order to put on a false defense.

haven't disregarded your arguments yet, but so far, it kind of has struck me that it's Mr. Cortez that really was the one that was most culpable and most in charge." The prosecutor then argued:

> In terms of the suggestion that [Cortez-Quinonez] wasn't in charge, our trial strategy is not what is necessarily 100 percent what actually is—who's in charge, right?
>
> The fact that we may highlight a particular person in closing argument is a trial strategy in light of how the trial played out and the evidence, but what we do know—so I wouldn't take too much from that.
>
> But what we do know is that Mr. Gaspar Chichande testified, and he said that it was Mr. Cortez who had the GPS communication device. . . . Mr. Cortez says in his post-arrest statement that, in fact, [the bosses] were telling him—giving instructions, that sort of stuff [through the device].
>
> He's also the one who instructs Mr. Gaspar Chichande to activate the GPS device. That's testimony that's uncontroverted in the trial. . . . When the coast guard comes onboard, who is it that says he's the captain? It's Mr. Cortez. **[—37—]**

In context, it is clear that the prosecutor did not argue facts in closing that he knew were untrue. The trial evidence showed both that Dominguez-Caicedo gave the order for the boat to take off, attempting to outrun the Coast Guard, *and* that Cortez-Quinonez was driving the boat, communicating with the bosses back in South America, and gave the order for Gaspar Chichande to activate the GPS buoy before throwing the narcotics overboard. It was not inconsistent for the prosecutor to point out all of these facts, both in closing argument and at sentencing. We hold that this alleged misconduct also does not constitute error.

3

Cortez-Quinonez argues that the prosecutor's alleged misconduct resulted in depriving him of a minor role reduction, violating his right to due process. However, for the same reasons that the prosecutorial misconduct claim fails, Cortez-Quinonez's due process claim also fails—the prosecutor highlighted different facts that were not inconsistent with each other at different stages of the proceeding.

4

In closing argument, the prosecutor said, "Ladies and gentlemen, throwing cocaine overboard on a vessel is knowing possession of cocaine. All right? Just watch this [video] clip. That's the element in a heartbeat." Defense counsel objected, and the district court overruled the objection. The prosecutor then immediately clarified:

> The evidence shows that what they're doing is knowing possession of the cocaine. They know that it's there, they have control of it, and they're throwing it overboard, and you **[—38—]** infer from their **{-958-}** actions that they know it's cocaine or some other drug . . . and clearly when the coast guard comes, they don't throw the fuel barrels and all that overboard. They're throwing the cocaine overboard.

Defendants argue that although "the prosecutor softened the categorical nature of this incorrect statement of the law," "that softening came too late," resulting in the jury being "most likely left with the incorrect view of the law that simply possessing something that turned out to be cocaine is sufficient to prove knowing possession under the law."

The jury was instructed that "an act is done knowingly if the defendant is aware of the act and does not act through ignorance, mistake, or accident. . . . You may consider evidence of the defendant's words, acts, or omissions along with all the other evidence in deciding whether the defendant acted knowingly." Although it is true that throwing wrapped bales overboard without knowing that there is cocaine inside is not in itself enough to establish knowing possession, the prosecutor immediately clarified that he meant the jury could infer knowledge of the contents of the packages based on their throwing them overboard. This error was harmless in the context of the entire trial.

E

Dominguez-Caicedo attempted to call an expert witness, Diego Alexander Marinez, an attorney in Colombia. Mr. Marinez grew up approximately 40 miles from the area where Dominguez-Caicedo lived (Barbacoas). He travels to Barbacoas at least once per month for work. According to the offer of proof submitted to the district court, Mr. Marinez was prepared to testify that he is familiar with armed criminal paramilitary groups in that area. He also would **[—39—]** have testified that he "is aware" that these groups kidnap, intimidate, and use violence to further their criminal enterprises, including drug trafficking. Mr. Marinez also stated that he "is aware" that these groups dress in military garb and carry assault rifles in broad daylight in the area.

Mr. Marinez's testimony would have been offered to corroborate Dominguez-Caicedo's duress defense. At trial, Dominguez-Caicedo testified that five paramilitary members carrying machine guns kidnapped him and forced him to transport narcotics. However, the district court excluded Mr. Marinez's expert testimony on the grounds that it was not "based on sufficient facts or data which is the product of reliable principles and methods" and that the witness had not "applied the principles and methods reliably to the facts in the case." The district court continued:

> I can't find what principles and methods the supposed expert would use. I don't even know what he's an expert in. There's no indicia that any other experts would accept the principles or the opinions or conclusions that this so-called expert would proffer. I don't know what his educational background is on the subject. I don't know of any publications or other certifications or professional memberships that he belongs to that would allow him to express an opinion on any of the things that he has proffered. I don't know what materials he may have received or reviewed. I don't know his prior experience as an expert in the area. I don't know what records he may have reviewed, what procedures, and what methodology did he use once in arriving at this so-called **[—40—]** opinion, what examinations, what research, what testing, what surveys, or what verifications were used. I don't know what, if anything, he did to, for example, try to disprove any hypothetical or ultimate conclusion that he has reached. I don't know, in fact, looking at this, any of this, whether he really has any knowledge **{-959-}** whatsoever of any of the things that [he] has testified or proposes to testify to.

In all, the district court found "absolutely no indicia whatsoever of reliability," and that the testimony would not be helpful.

Dominguez-Caicedo contends that the district court's focus on the *Daubert* factors of reliable principles and methods was misplaced. Instead, Dominguez-Caicedo argues that the district court's focus should have been on the "knowledge and experience" of the expert, since the subject of the expert's testimony was to be his knowledge and experience, rather than his scientific analyses.

In *Daubert v. Merrell Dow Pharmaceuticals, Inc.*, 509 U.S. 579 (1993), the Supreme Court listed several relevant factors for assessing the reliability of scientific expert testimony under Federal Rule of Evidence 702. Among these were whether the expert's theory or technique has been tested; whether it "has been subjected to peer review and publication"; the "error rate" of "a particular scientific technique"; and the general acceptance of a theory or technique within the scientific community. 509 U.S. at 593–94. Then, in *Kumho Tire*, the Supreme Court discussed how to apply *Daubert* to expert testimony that was not scientific in nature: **[—41—]**

> We conclude that *Daubert*'s general holding—setting forth the trial judge's general "gatekeeping" obligation—applies not only to testimony based on "scientific" knowledge, but also to testimony based on "technical" and "other specialized" knowledge. We also conclude that a trial court *may* consider one or more of the more specific factors that *Daubert* mentioned when doing so will help determine that testimony's reliability. But, as the Court stated in *Daubert*, the test of reliability is "flexible," and *Daubert*'s list of specific factors neither necessarily nor exclusively applies to all experts or in every case. Rather, the law grants a district court the same broad latitude when it decides *how* to determine reliability as it enjoys in respect to its ultimate reliability determination.

Kumho Tire Co. v. Carmichael, 526 U.S. 137, 141–42 (1999) (internal citations omitted).

Although some of the factors the district court listed are not obviously relevant to Mr. Marinez, some are. For example, Mr. Marinez's offer of proof omits *how* Mr. Marinez "is aware" of the activities of FARC. As the district court stated, then, there is no indicia that other experts on FARC would agree with Mr. Marinez's opinion that FARC uses "intimidation and violence in the town of Barabaoas [sic] and its surrounding area to further their criminal enterprises" and that "these armed groups do little to hide their existence in the town of Barbacoas." It was also unclear "what, if anything," Mr. Marinez did to try to disprove his opinion that these individuals are part of FARC. **[—42—]** In short, the offer of proof fell short of showing the basis for Mr. Marinez's expert opinion that Dominguez-Caicedo's testimony about FARC kidnapping him was plausible.

Dominguez-Caicedo is correct in that the factors the district court listed apply more directly to testimony of a scientific nature, which Mr. Marinez's was not. However, given the extremely broad latitude the Supreme Court has said district courts have in conducting this inquiry, we hold the district court did not abuse its discretion by looking at these particular factors and finding Mr. Marinez's testimony wanting. *See Kumho Tire*, 526 U.S. at 142.

F

All three defendants challenge the district court's denial of their requests for minor role reductions at sentencing. When **{-960-}** reviewing sentencing decisions, we review the district court's identification of the relevant legal standard de novo, its factual findings for clear error, and its application of the legal standard to the facts for abuse of discretion. *United States v. Gasca-Ruiz*, 852 F.3d 1167, 1170 (9th Cir. 2017) (en banc). We begin by clarifying how district courts should conduct the minor role analysis before turning to each defendant's specific arguments.

1

A defendant who is "plainly among the least culpable of those involved in the conduct of a group" may receive a "minimal" role adjustment, which comes with a Sentencing Guidelines reduction of at least four levels.[4] U.S.S.G. **[—43—]** § 3B1.2(a), cmt. 4. A defendant "who is less culpable than most other participants in the criminal activity, but whose role could not be described as minimal" may receive a "minor" role adjustment, which provides a reduction of at least two levels. *Id.* at cmt. 5. To be eligible for either adjustment, the defendant must also be "substantially less culpable than the average participant in the criminal activity." *Id.* at cmt. 3(A).

The relevant comparison is to the other participants in the defendant's crime, not to typical defendants who commit similar crimes.[5] *See United States v. Diaz*, 884 F.3d

[4] We say "at least" because a mitigating role adjustment can interact with other provisions of the Sentencing Guidelines to trigger additional adjustments. *See, e.g.*, U.S.S.G. § 2D1.1(a)(5).

[5] In the past we have referred to these typical defendants as "hypothetical average participants," but we use the term "typical defendant" here

911, 916 (9th Cir. 2018). Thus, in this case, the district court was required to compare the defendants to the other participants in their crimes, not to typical defendants occupying their roles, such as typical drug transporters. Further, when the mitigating role commentary instructs courts to compare the defendant's culpability to that of "the average participant in the criminal activity," it is not referring to the actual level of culpability of any single participant. It is instead referring to the mathematical average, *i.e.,* a "single value that represents the midpoint of a broad sample of subjects." *Average*, *Black's Law Dictionary* (11th ed. 2019). Thus, "*all* likely participants in the criminal scheme" must be included in calculating the average. *Diaz*, 884 F.3d at 916–17 (emphasis added); *United States v. Rojas-Millan*, 234 F.3d 464, 472 (9th Cir. 2000).

To determine whether a defendant is substantially less culpable than the average participant in the offense, a district **[—44—]** court must proceed in three steps. First, the court must identify all of the individuals for whom there is "sufficient evidence of their existence and participation in the overall scheme." *Rojas-Millan*, 234 F.3d at 474. Second, the court must calculate a rough average level of culpability for these individuals, taking into consideration the five factors in comment 3(C) to the Mitigating Role Guideline. *See Diaz*, 884 F.3d at 916. Third, the court must compare the defendant's culpability to that average. If the defendant is substantially less culpable than that average and meets the other criteria, he should be granted a mitigating role adjustment. If the defendant is not substantially less culpable than that average, he is not eligible for the adjustment.

The Government and some district courts appear to have interpreted *United States v. Hurtado*, 760 F.3d 1065, 1069 (9th Cir. 2014), *overruled on other grounds by Gasca-Ruiz*, 852 F.3d at 1174, to suggest **{–961–}** that a court must first identify all participants in the crime and then disregard participants of above-average culpability (and, presumably, those of below-average culpability) and compare the defendant's culpability only to the remaining individuals whom the district court deems to be of average culpability. A court following this approach compares the defendant's culpability to only the *median* participants' actual level of culpability instead of comparing the defendant's culpability to the average level of culpability of all the participants in the offense.

This understanding of *Hurtado* is incorrect. At the outset, we note that much of *Hurtado* has been overruled or **[—45—]** abrogated.[6] But to the extent anything remains of *Hurtado*, it simply stands for the proposition that comparing a defendant to only the most culpable subset of the participants in the offense does not demonstrate that the defendant is entitled to a minor role reduction. Instead, the district court must compare the defendant's culpability with the average level of culpability of *all* of the participants in the crime. *Hurtado* did not set forth an entirely different method of performing the minor role analysis.

because it is more precise, and it avoids confusion with our discussion of the "average participant" referred to in comment 3(A).

[6] For instance, *Hurtado* states that the district court "did not clearly err when it found that Hurtado was a typical commercial drug smuggler—no better, no worse,—and not entitled to a minor role reduction" and that "[t]he district court was not clearly erroneous in finding that although Hurtado may have been a cog in some larger wheel, he was an *essential* cog who . . . knowingly smuggled a large quantity of narcotics into the United States . . . ." 760 F.3d at 1067. But the 2015 amendments to the mitigating role commentary made clear that the relevant comparison is to other participants in the defendant's crime, not to "typical" defendants committing similar crimes, and that "[t]he fact that a defendant performs an essential or indispensable role in the criminal activity is not determinative." U.S.S.G § 3B1.2 cmt. n.3(C). Similarly, *Hurtado* suggested that various factors "alone" could "justify denial of minor role" but we have since held that "the assessment of a defendant's eligibility for a minor-role adjustment must include consideration of the factors identified by the Amendment, not merely the benchmarks established by our caselaw that pre-dates Amendment 794's effective date." *Diaz*, 884 F.3d at 916. We have also since held that *Hurtado* applied the wrong standard of review. *See Gasca-Ruiz*, 852 F.3d at 1174.

Nor could it have. Fourteen years earlier, we held that courts should compare a defendant's culpability to "all participants in the criminal scheme for which he was charged" even if those co-participants are not charged. *Rojas-Millan*, 234 F.3d at 472. There, the Nevada Highway Patrol stopped Rojas-Millan as he was couriering drugs east from Los Angeles to Nevada. *Id.* at 467–68. In the car with **[—46—]** him was Jorge Adame-Farias. *Id.* After being convicted of various drug crimes, Rojas-Millan sought a minor role reduction, which the district court denied. *Id.* at 472. The district court concluded that Rojas-Millan was not substantially less culpable than Adame-Farias, who was charged alongside Rojas-Millan, and that it could not compare Rojas-Millan's conduct against the drug supplier in Los Angeles and the recipient in Nevada because they were not charged. *Id.*

We vacated the sentence and remanded, holding that "the district court should have evaluated [Rojas-Millan's] role relative to all participants in the criminal scheme for which he was charged." *Id.* We explained that "ignoring the actions of other participants . . . subjects less culpable defendants to longer sentences simply because their more involved co-conspirators managed to escape arrest or were tried separately. We see no reason why the Guidelines would sanction such a regime, and we find confirmation in the language of § 3B1.2 that the intent was not to do so." **{-962-}** *Id.* at 473. We thus vacated Rojas-Millan's sentence and remanded for the district court to compare Rojas-Millan's culpability "relative to the involvement of other likely actors, such as the alleged Los Angeles supplier and the Reno distributor . . . if the district court found sufficient evidence of their existence and participation." *Id.* at 473–74. The only limit on the comparison group we recognized in *Rojas-Millan* was that the district court was required to find "sufficient evidence of [the comparators'] existence and participation" in the crime. *Id.* at 474. If the district court found on remand that the Los Angeles supplier and Reno distributor participated, it was required to compare Rojas-Millan's culpability to theirs. *Id.* at 473–74. We did not hold that the district court could decline to consider the Los Angeles and Reno participants' culpability if it determined **[—47—]** that they were leaders or organizers or were otherwise of "above-average" culpability. Indeed, to do so would be inconsistent with our observation that "ignoring the actions of other participants" undermines the purpose of the minor role reduction because doing so "subjects less culpable defendants to longer sentences simply because their more involved co-conspirators managed to escape arrest or were tried separately." *Id.* at 473.

Since we already held in *Rojas-Millan* that "all participants in the criminal scheme" must be included in the comparison, we could not have departed from that rule in *Hurtado* to require district courts to exclude the most highly culpable participants. *See Miller v. Gammie*, 335 F.3d 889, 900 (9th Cir. 2003) (en banc). Further, while the "median" approach does not turn on who is charged, it is even less consistent with the purposes of the minor role reduction than the approach we disapproved of in *Rojas-Millan* because it would exclude the most culpable participants *in every case*, even if they were charged, simply because they are highly culpable. This approach grossly distorts the court's assessment of the defendant's relative role. Finally, in the eight years since it was decided, we have never cited *Hurtado* in a published opinion for the proposition that district courts may exclude highly culpable participants from the comparison.

In sum, *Hurtado* did not change our longstanding approach to the mitigating role analysis, which requires district courts to include "all participants in the criminal scheme" in the comparison. *Rojas-Millan*, 234 F.3d at 472; *see also Diaz*, 884 F.3d at 916–17. With these clarifications in mind, we turn to each defendant's arguments. **[—48—]**

2

Chichande argues that the district court erred by excluding his recruiter from the comparison. We agree. The district court concluded that Chichande's recruiter existed and participated, yet it excluded him from the comparison group. The court stated at sentencing:

> So the defendant has to show me well, who's the average participant so that I can then make a determination as to whether or not the defendant is, in fact, substantially less culpable than the average participant . . . . So what do we know? Well, we know this gentleman was recruited by someone who, in my opinion, if that individual were before me, would receive an aggravated role for being a leader/organizer. We have the people with the guns . . . . So taking a look at the people that are involved, there are three people on the boat. I believe, frankly, that probably one of them is somewhat more culpable than the other two. And I do believe that this defendant, given the fact that he was more candid and forthright, probably deserves a break in that regard. It doesn't really affect my assessment of **{-963-}** minor role . . . . So what do I know? I know that there were men with guns. I know that there was a recruiter or someone that got this fellow into this venture. But I don't know who the average participant would be. And I don't know that this defendant would be substantially less culpable than whoever that average participant is. **[—49—]**

This discussion shows that the district court attempted to identify a single "average participant" with whom to compare Chichande. When the district court could not identify such an individual, it denied the minor role adjustment, apparently without comparing Chichande's culpability with anyone's. At a minimum, the court excluded the recruiter. This analysis was erroneous. As we have explained, the proper comparison is to the average of *all* of the individuals who participated in Chichande's offense, including those that the district court believed were leaders or organizers or who were otherwise highly culpable. Because the district court misunderstood the appropriate legal standard, we vacate Chichande's sentence and remand for the district court to conduct the minor role analysis applying the correct legal standard.

The Government argues that any error in the district court's minor role analysis was harmless because the district court made an alternative Guidelines calculation assuming it granted Chichande a minor role reduction and stated that it would impose the same "sentence regardless of whether [it] gave him minor role." We disagree.

"A mistake in calculating the recommended Guidelines sentencing range is a significant procedural error that requires us to remand for resentencing." *United States v. Munoz-Camarena*, 631 F.3d 1028, 1030 (9th Cir. 2011). "When a defendant is sentenced under an incorrect Guidelines range—whether or not the defendant's ultimate sentence falls within the correct range—the error itself can, and most often will, be sufficient to show a reasonable probability of a different outcome absent the error." *Molina-Martinez v. United States*, 136 S. Ct. 1338, 1345 (2016). Accordingly, we have vacated sentences and remanded for resentencing when district courts have misunderstood the **[—50—]** law governing the minor role reduction. *See, e.g., Diaz*, 884 F.3d at 918; *Rojas-Millan*, 234 F.3d at 475. At the same time, a sentencing error can be harmless. *See Munoz-Camarena*, 631 F.3d at 1030 n.5. To establish harmlessness, the Government must show that "it is more probable than not" that the error did not affect the sentence. *United States v. Morales*, 108 F.3d 1031, 1040 (9th Cir. 1997) (en banc); *see also United States v. Olano*, 507 U.S. 725, 734 (1993).

A "district court's mere statement that it would impose the same . . . sentence no matter what the correct calculation cannot, without more, insulate the sentence from remand." *Munoz-Camarena*, 631 F.3d at 1031; *see also United States v. Williams*, 5 F.4th 973, 978 (9th Cir. 2021). This is because a district court's analysis must "flow from an initial determination of the correct Guidelines range," *id.* at 1031, and the district court must keep that range "in mind throughout the process," *id.* at 1030 (quoting *United States v. Carty*, 520 F.3d 984, 991 (9th Cir. 2008)). At the same time, a sentencing error may be harmless if the district court "acknowledges that the correct Guidelines range is in dispute and performs [its] sentencing analysis twice, beginning with both the correct and incorrect range." *Id.* at 1030 n.5.

The Government argues that that is what the district court did here. We disagree. When it came time to impose the **{-964-}** sentence, the district court started by determining that Chichande's criminal history category was I, his base offense level was 38, and a two-level upward adjustment was warranted because he co-piloted the boat, for a total offense level of 40. This yielded a Guidelines range of 292 to 365 months. *See* U.S.S.G. Manual Ch. 5 Pt. A (U.S. Sent'g Comm'n 2018). The district court then concluded that a 292-month sentence "would be excessive" because Chichande was a first-time offender, discussed the 18 U.S.C. **[—51—]** § 3553(a) factors, and ultimately imposed a sentence of 180 months. After imposing the sentence, the district court provided Chichande with a copy of the supervised release conditions and informed him that he could appeal. Immediately afterward the following exchange occurred:

> **Counsel for Chichande:** Yes, I've told him that I will file that Notice of Appeal this morning.
>
> **The Court:** All right. Is there anything else I need to address? Is there anything – well, I guess for purposes of making sure we all understand – by the way, I did do a guideline calculation assuming that I gave him minor role. I think that would have resulted in, if I'm not mistaken, a range of 121 to 151 months. I think I did a calculation giving him acceptance. That would result in 97 to 121 months.
>
> But as I said, my sentence was based on [the] 3553(a) factors. Given the seriousness of the offense and the nature of the offense, the circumstances of the offense, the amount of the drugs, the fact that a shooting was required, I think 180 months is a reasonable sentence, and I would impose that sentence regardless of whether I gave him minor role. In that case, I would be varying up. In this case, I'm varying down. Anything else I've missed?

The district court's discussion of the alternative ranges at the very end of the sentencing hearing does not **[—52—]** demonstrate that the district court conducted the sentencing a second time starting with the correct range and keeping it in mind throughout the process. The conclusory nature of this discussion, and the fact that it occurred *after* the district court had already imposed Chichande's sentence and only in response to Chichande's declaration that he would appeal suggest that the district court did not meaningfully consider this range in arriving at its sentence. Since the Government has not met its burden of establishing that any error was harmless, we vacate Chichande's sentence and remand for resentencing so that the district court may apply the correct legal standard.

3

Cortez-Quinonez argues that the district court erred because it "expressly acknowledged the existence of a Pablo-Escobar-type drug lord" and "a giant, complex drug-trafficking organization" but nevertheless refused to include members of that organization in the comparison. In the district court, Cortez-Quinonez cited a report that the Sentencing Commission sent to Congress listing roles of individuals often involved in drug trafficking organizations in order of their typical culpability and argued that the court was required to compare his conduct to individuals occupying those roles who "likely" were involved in his crime.

The fact that illicit drugs are often traceable to larger drug trafficking organizations does not mean that district courts must compare the conduct of each defendant convicted of a drug crime to that of every hypothetical member of a typical drug trafficking organization. *See* **{-965-}** *United States v. Rosas*, 615 F.3d 1058, 1068 (9th Cir. 2010) ("Every drug trafficking defendant could point to an unknown network preceding them in the drug trade. Such an **[—53—]** argument will normally be ineffective when considering whether the defendant is entitled to a mitigating role reduction."). We have repeatedly held that the relevant comparators are the *actual* participants in the defendant's crime. *See, e.g., Diaz*, 884 F.3d at 916–18; *United States v. Benitez*, 34 F.3d 1489, 1498 (9th Cir. 1994); *United States v. Petti*, 973 F.2d 1441, 1447 (9th Cir. 1992). The 2015 Amendments to the mitigating role commentary confirmed that interpretation. *See United States v. Quintero-Leyva*, 823 F.3d 519, 522–23 (9th Cir. 2016). By "actual participants," we mean only participants for whom there is "sufficient evidence of their existence and participation." *Rojas-Millan*, 234 F.3d at 474. Even if one can *assume* based on how drug trafficking organizations typically operate that it is likely that another unidentified person participated in the crime, the district court is not required to compare the defendant's culpability with that of the unidentified person. Indeed, without evidence of the proposed comparator's existence or participation the district court has nothing against which to compare the defendant's conduct. In this case, for example, Cortez-Quinonez invited the district court to speculate about what roles hypothetical participants in drug trafficking organizations typically occupy and to compare those hypothetical participants' imagined conduct to his own. We have repeatedly rejected these kinds of comparisons in the past, and we do so again today. *See Diaz*, 884 F.3d at 913–18 (holding that district court properly limited the comparison group to Diaz's recruiter and co-participant and properly declined to compare Diaz's culpability to that of "'unknown' individuals who 'have to exist in order for a drug trafficking organization to function'"); *Rosas*, 615 F.3d at 1068 (holding that district court properly limited the comparison group to Rosas' two co-participants and properly declined to compare him to "unknown participants in the drug chain, **[—54—]** including 'the source of the marijuana, distributors, packagers, sellers, etc.'").

In arguing to the contrary, Cortez-Quinonez relies heavily on our statements in *Diaz* and *Rojas-Millan* instructing district courts to consider "likely" participants. But Cortez-Quinonez takes the word "likely" out of context. We have referred to likely participants to make clear that the defendant does not necessarily need to know the participant's name or see the participant for there to be sufficient evidence of that person's participation in the offense. *See Diaz*, 884 F.3d at 917; *Rojas-Millan*, 234 F.3d at 473–74. But we have never required a comparison to unknown persons one might *assume* participated but about whom there is no evidence of their *actual* participation. Therefore, the district court did not err by declining to compare Cortez-Quinonez's culpability to the unknown "Pablo-Escobar-type drug lord" and unknown members of "a giant, complex drug-trafficking organization" that may have been involved in the manufacture and distribution of the drugs Cortez-Quinonez was transporting.

Cortez-Quinonez next argues that the district court erred by "ignor[ing] [his] lack of ownership in the drugs and his relatively low compensation." But the district court heard argument regarding this factor, stated that it considered all "five nonexhaustive factors," and ultimately adopted the Government's analysis of them. And even if the district court erroneously weighed that factor against Cortez-Quinonez, that one of the five factors in comment 3(C) weighed in favor of Cortez-Quinonez does not mean that the district court abused its discretion in denying the **{–966–}** minor role adjustment. *See Quintero-Leyva*, 823 F.3d at 523. **[—55—]**

4

Dominguez-Caicedo's arguments are similar. He claims that the district court identified "the man who commandeered Mr. Dominguez into participating in this offense" and "the 'guys with the guns' who approached Dominguez" as "potential likely participants" but nevertheless improperly refused to compare his culpability to theirs. He also argues that the district court improperly "overlooked" "all the persons" the Government identified in its pre-trial expert disclosure, "those who actually own the cocaine at the heart of this case," and "those who recruited and tricked Mr. Dominguez's co-defendants." Once again, we disagree.

With respect to the "guys with guns" and "man who commandeered Mr. Dominguez into participating in this offense" Dominguez-Caicedo's characterization is not consistent with the record. Dominguez-Caicedo testified at trial that while he was harvesting bananas in rural Colombia, he was kidnapped by five armed men wearing hoodies and masks who told him they needed him for a mission. He testified that these men eventually placed him on the boat carrying the drugs at issue here. At sentencing, the district court made clear that it did not believe Dominguez-Caicedo's account and did not find these individuals to be likely participants in the offense. The court explained: "I mean, Mr. Dominguez-Caicedo was hoping that by telling his story, he was going to [be] able to convince the jury that he was acting under duress. The jury didn't believe it. It's a self-serving statement that I frankly – I don't buy, either. I don't accept it." Therefore, contrary to Dominguez-Caicedo's argument, the district court did not determine that the "guys with guns" and the "man who commandeered **[—56—]** Mr. Dominguez" were "likely participants," and therefore did not err by excluding them from the comparison.

Next, the district court was not required to address the people the Government identified in its pre-trial expert disclosure, the people who allegedly owned the cocaine, and the people who allegedly recruited Dominguez-Caicedo's co-defendants because Dominguez-Caicedo failed to object to the Presentence Report's (PSR) conclusion that he did not provide evidence of their existence and participation in the offense.

The PSR concludes that "the defendant has presented no information supporting the fact that he was substantially less culpable than the other identified participants in this offense as he appears to have held the same role as CORTEZ and GASPAR." It also says that "Defense counsel . . . believes a minor role adjustment is appropriate, but did not provide any basis for it." Federal Rule of Criminal Procedure 32(f)(1) requires parties to "state in writing any objections, including objections to material information . . . contained in or omitted from the [PSR]." If a party objects to a material factual assertion in or omission from the PSR, the district court must rule on the objection. Fed. R. Crim. P. 32(i)(3)(B); *see also United States v. Petri*, 731 F.3d 833, 837–39 (9th Cir. 2013). But if a party does not object, the district court is not required to address factual assertions raised for the first time in a sentencing memorandum or at the sentencing hearing. *Petri,* 731 F.3d at 841.

Petri is illustrative. There, Petri objected to the PSR's recommendation that the district court deny Petri's request for a minor role reduction because, among other things, he alleged that he was "used by the more sophisticated individuals in the scheme, including a man named 'Sorin,' whom Petri identified as the ringleader." **{-967-}** *Id.* at 836. But **[—57—]** while Petri cited Sorin's alleged involvement in support of his objection to the PSR's recommendation to deny him a minor role reduction, he did not specifically object to the omission of factual information about Sorin in the PSR. *Id.* at 836, 841. In other words, Petri objected to the probation officer's ultimate recommendation that the court deny the minor role reduction but did not specifically object to the probation officer's decision not to include "any factual assertion regarding whether 'Sorin' manipulated or coerced Petri into complicity." *Id.* at 841. In his sentencing memorandum and during the sentencing hearing, Petri's attorney attempted to supplement the record with details about Sorin's alleged coercion and argued that recently discovered documents showed Sorin was involved. *Id.* at 836–37. The district court ultimately denied the minor role reduction without addressing whether Sorin coerced Petri. *Id.* at 837. On appeal, we held that the district court "had no responsibility to rule on . . . if 'Sorin' coerced" Petri because Petri's objection to the PSR was not specifically directed at the alleged factual omissions in the PSR. *Id.* at 841.

Dominguez-Caicedo did not properly object to his presentence report at all.[7] Therefore,

[7] Dominguez-Caicedo included a footnote in his sentencing memorandum citing to Cortez-Quinonez's objections to *his* PSR and stated that

the district court was **[—58—]** not required to address his argument raised for the first time in his sentencing memorandum—and never mentioned during the sentencing hearing—that there was sufficient evidence that the individuals he identified were involved in the crime.

CONCLUSION

We affirm all three defendants' convictions, and Dominguez-Caicedo's and Cortez-Quinonez's sentences. We vacate Chichande's sentence and remand for resentencing consistent with this opinion.

AFFIRMED in part, and VACATED and REMANDED in part.

"Mr. Dominguez joins in his co-defendant's analysis regarding the applicability of a mitigating role adjustment in this case." Dominguez-Caicedo's footnote is not a proper objection to the PSR. First, it does not dispute any of the factual assertions or alleged omissions in his own PSR. Second, we held in *Petri* that an argument in a sentencing memorandum does not constitute an objection to a PSR. Third, Dominguez-Caicedo filed his sentencing memorandum after the deadline for objecting to the PSR. The deadline for objecting to the PSR is "14 days after receiving" it, Fed. R. Crim. P. 32(f)(1), and Dominguez- **[—58—]** Caicedo filed his sentencing memorandum 28 days after the PSR was filed. For each of these reasons, Dominguez-Caicedo's footnote was not a proper objection to the PSR, and it did not require the district court to address whether these individuals participated in the crime.

This page intentionally left blank

United States Court of Appeals for the Eleventh Circuit

United States Court of Appeals
for the Eleventh Circuit

No. 20-11789

C&W FACILITY SERVS., INC.
VS.
SECRETARY OF LABOR

Petition for Review of a Decision of the Occupational Safety and Health Review Commission

Decided: January 13, 2022

Citation: 22 F.4th 1284, 10 Adm. R. 342 (11th Cir. 2022).

Before **PRYOR,** Chief Judge, **GRANT,** and **HULL,** Circuit Judges.

[—2—] {–1285–} PRYOR, Chief Judge:

This petition for review requires us to decide whether the Occupational Safety and Health Review Commission erred when it decided that C&W Facility Services, Inc., violated a regulatory requirement, 29 C.F.R. § 1910.132(a), by failing "to provide and require the use of personal protective equipment . . . in the form of [personal flotation devices] to an employee pressure washing a boat dock." Our precedents required the Secretary to prove either that the provision and use of personal protective equipment is industry custom or that "the employer ha[d] actual knowledge that a hazard requires the use of . . . [the] personal protective equipment." *Fla. Mach. & Foundry, Inc. v. Occupational Safety & Health Rev. Comm'n*, 693 F.2d 119, 120 (11th Cir. 1982). But the Secretary presented no evidence of an industry custom requiring the use of personal flotation devices and no substantial evidence that C&W had actual knowledge that pressure washing its boat dock required the use of those devices. The Commission decided that the Secretary satisfied his burden by proving only that C&W was aware of the conditions that made the boat dock hazardous. Because the Commission failed to apply the correct standard and the record lacks substantial evidence of actual knowledge under that standard, we grant the petition for review, set aside the order of the Commission, and vacate the citation. **[—3—]**

I. BACKGROUND

Johnnie Norton operated a pressure washer with a rotary scrubber on a dock at the Tampa Convention Center as part of his normal job duties. The concrete dock **{–1286–}** was approximately 289 feet and 7 inches long by 10 feet and 2 inches wide. The dock had no guardrails or barricades and was surrounded on three sides by water. At the edge of the dock where Norton was pressure washing, the bay was approximately 19 feet deep. Norton fell into the bay while performing his work and drowned. Norton was wearing rubber boots and was not wearing a personal flotation device. Norton had been working at the Tampa Convention Center for about a year.

Upon receiving reports of Norton's death, the Occupational Safety and Health Administration sent Compliance Officer Marrero to investigate. Officer Marrero examined the scene of the accident and conducted a series of interviews with other employees. During his investigation, Officer Marrero did not identify any incidents of employees falling off the dock and into the water before Norton's fatal accident, but he did identify two employees who pressure washed the same dock as Norton in the years leading up to his death who voluntarily wore personal flotation devices. Several witnesses told Officer Marrero that one employee would always wear a personal flotation device while working close to the water because he had a fear of water. The other employee, who once pressure washed the dock when Norton was out sick, told Officer Marrero that although no supervisor instructed him to do so **[—4—]** and he was able to swim, he went to the warehouse and acquired a life jacket to wear while he washed the dock. Mike Sheehan, an operations manager at the Convention Center, asked Norton if he could swim before Norton took over the task of pressure washing the docks from the employee who always wore a personal flotation device. Norton told Sheehan that he could do so.

As a result of Officer Marrero's inspection, the Administration issued a citation to C&W for its failure to provide and require the use of a personal flotation device to an employee who was pressure washing the dock in violation of federal health and safety regulations. The Administration classified the citation as "serious" because it involved a fatality, and proposed a $12,675 penalty.

C&W contested the citation, but an administrative law judge affirmed the citation after a three-day hearing. The administrative law judge concluded that Norton was C&W's "employee" within the meaning of the Occupational Safety and Health Act, 29 U.S.C. § 652. The administrative law judge concluded, in the alternative, that C&W was properly cited as the "controlling employer" under the Administration's Multi-Employer Citation Policy. See OCCUPATIONAL SAFETY & HEALTH ADMIN., DIRECTIVE CPL 2-0.124 (1999). And the administrative law judge found that the Secretary had satisfied his burden of proving a violation of section 1910.132(a), including that C&W had the requisite knowledge to be held liable.

The administrative law judge acknowledged that our precedents required the Secretary to prove either that the use of personal **[—5—]** flotation devices was an industry custom or that C&W had "clear actual knowledge that personal protective equipment was necessary under the circumstances." *S&H Riggers & Erectors, Inc. v. Occupational Safety & Health Rev. Comm'n*, 659 F.2d 1273, 1285 (5th Cir. Unit B Oct. 1981). Because the Secretary did not present any evidence of industry custom at the hearing, the administrative law judge considered only whether C&W had actual knowledge. The administrative law judge relied on a decision from the Tenth Circuit, *Jake's Fireworks Inc. v. Acosta*, 893 F.3d 1248, 1260 (10th Cir. 2018), to assert that "[t]he Secretary need not show that an employer understood or acknowledged **{-1287-}** that the physical conditions were actually hazardous" but "only that the employer was aware of the physical conditions that constitute a violation."

The administrative law judge found that C&W had "clear actual knowledge that [personal protective equipment] was necessary under the circumstances" because "[t]he circumstances (that the dock was unguarded and surrounded on three sides by the Tampa Bay, and that there were no ladders extending off the dock) are facts that existed before Mr. Norton drowned" and because the fact that Sheehan asked Norton if he could swim proved that C&W was "aware of these 'circumstances.'" The administrative law judge also found that "[C&W] had specific confirmed knowledge that [personal flotation devices] were warranted because C&W Supervisor Sheehan specifically asked Mr. Norton if he could swim." He reasoned that "Sheehan's query . . . is evidence of actual knowledge that pressure washing the boat dock at the [Tampa **[—6—]** Convention Center] without a [personal flotation device] being issued and worn presented a drowning hazard." The administrative law judge gave heavy weight to the evidence that two other employees who pressure washed the dock voluntarily wore life jackets while doing so. And he described "[o]perating a pressure washer and rotary scrubber on an unguarded dock close to water" as "an open and obvious hazard," citing deposition testimony asserting that "anyone tasked with using a pressure washer to clean the dock would have to get the entire dock, including the very edge of the dock that abuts the water."

C&W appealed the decision of the administrative law judge to the Commission, which declined to review the decision. So, the decision of the administrative law judge became a final order of the Commission. *See* 29 U.S.C. § 661(j).

II. STANDARDS OF REVIEW

We will set aside an order of the Commission only if it is arbitrary and capricious, an abuse of discretion, or otherwise not in accordance with the law. 5 U.S.C. § 706(2)(A); *Fluor Daniel v. Occupational Safety & Health Rev. Comm'n*, 295 F.3d 1232, 1236 (11th Cir. 2002). Factual findings of the Commission are conclusive so long as they are supported by "substantial evidence" in the record. 29 U.S.C. § 660(a); *Fluor Daniel*, 295 F.3d at 1236. "Substantial evidence is more than a scintilla and is such relevant evidence as a reasonable person would accept as adequate to support a conclusion." *J.A.M. Builders, Inc. v. Herman*, 233 F.3d 1350, 1352 (11th Cir. 2000) (internal quotation marks omitted). **[—7—]**

III. DISCUSSION

The Administration cited C&W for violating section 1910.132(a), which provides that protective equipment must be provided by employers and used by employees "wherever it is necessary by reason of hazards." *See* 29 C.F.R. § 1910.132(a). Section 1910.132(a) is a "performance standard," which means that it identifies its objective but does not prescribe the means for or the specific obligations of the employer to comply with the objective. Because "[d]ue process mandates that an employer receive notice of the requirements of any [Administration] regulation before he is cited for an alleged violation," performance standards can create problems of fair notice. *S&H Riggers*, 659 F.2d at 1279; accord *Owens-Corning Fiberglass Corp. v. Donovan*, 659 F.2d 1285, 1288 (5th Cir. Unit B Oct. 1981) ("Due process requires that employers be given reasonably clear advance notice of what is required of them by [Administration] regulations.").

In the context of performance standards like section 1910.132(a), settled precedent resolves the problem of fair notice **{-1288-}** with a heightened knowledge requirement. That is, to hold an employer liable under a performance standard, the Secretary must prove either that the protective measure is industry custom or that the employer had "actual knowledge that a hazard requires the use of some other or additional personal protective equipment." *Fla. Mach. & Foundry*, 693 F.2d at 120. The Secretary concedes that "no evidence demonstrating an industry custom of requiring [personal flotation devices] for workers doing pressure washing on docks was **[—8—]** introduced before the [administrative law judge]," so the only dispute is whether C&W had "actual knowledge."

We divide our discussion in two parts. First, we explain that the Commission misapplied the standard for actual knowledge. Second, we explain that there is no substantial evidence to support a finding that C&W had actual knowledge of the requirement to provide and require the use of personal flotation devices for employees when they are pressure washing the dock.

A. The Commission Misapplied the Standard for "Actual Knowledge."

Our precedent is clear: to hold an employer liable under section 1910.132(a) in the absence of an industry custom, the Secretary must prove that the employer had "actual knowledge that personal protective equipment is necessary to protect its employees from a particular hazard." *S&H Riggers*, 659 F.2d at 1278. Actual knowledge cannot be "implied from voluntary safety efforts standing alone," but "an employer's safety program may be considered in support of a finding of knowledge along with other factors indicating to the employer the need for particular safety equipment." *Owens-Corning*, 659 F.2d at 1288. Instead, our precedent demands "evidence in the record of a specific, confirmed knowledge on [the employer's] part regarding a hazard warranting a [personal protective equipment] requirement." *Cotter & Co. v. Occupational Safety & Health Rev. Comm'n*, 598 F.2d 911, 915 (5th Cir. 1979). In determining whether there is substantial evidence of actual knowledge, we have paid close attention to previous workplace **[—9—]** accidents, *see id.* at 914, the extent to which employees demand protective equipment, *see Owens-Corning*, 659 F.2d at 1289, and the obviousness of the hazard, *see S&H Riggers*, 659 F.2d at 1282–83.

Our requirements for "actual knowledge" are illustrated in three decisions of our predecessor circuit. In *Cotter & Co. v. Occupational Safety & Health Review Commission*, our predecessor circuit reversed an order of the Commission holding an employer liable under section 1910.132(a) for failing to require employees to wear steel-toed shoes on a shipping and receiving dock. 598 F.2d at 912. There, the employer had a program through which employees could voluntarily buy steel-toed shoes, but the shoes were not required in the workplace. *Id.* In the two years preceding the Administration's inspection, "[o]nly one injury . . . would have been prevented or mitigated by steel-toed shoes." *Id.* at 914. The court determined that the company did not have actual knowledge because it found "no evidence in the record of a specific, confirmed knowledge on the employer's part regarding a hazard warranting a steel-toed shoe requirement." *Id.* at 915. The court also warned against "the folly of discouraging an employer, by expanding the scope of his liability beyond what it would otherwise be, from exhorting employees to take every possible safety precaution in the development of a superior industrial safety program." *Id.*

In *Owens-Corning Fiberglass Corp. v. Donovan*, our predecessor circuit affirmed an order of the Commission holding an **{-1289-}** employer liable for failing to require employees to wear gloves when **[—10—]** handling fiberglass insulation. 659 F.2d at 1286. The court concluded that there was substantial evidence to support the administrative law judge's determination that the employer had actual knowledge that gloves were "necessary to protect its employees from fiberglass itch" because the employer had been aware "for at least [the previous] thirty years that many, if not most, employees exposed to fiberglass develop fiberglass itch . . . and that wearing gloves [was] the only way to prevent fiberglass itch." *Id.* at 1288–89. The court clarified that although "[k]nowledge that personal protective equipment is required may not be implied from voluntary safety efforts standing alone[,] . . . an employer's safety program may be considered in support a finding of knowledge along with other factors indicating to the employer the need for particular safety equipment." *Id.* at 1288. The Court assessed the proportion of employees that took advantage of the voluntary program and considered it important that, unlike in *Cotter*, where the voluntary steel-toed shoes program served only to accommodate the preferences of individual employees, it was "apparent from the record . . . that [the employer's] glove program resulted from its employees' demands, through their union, that [the employer] provide gloves to all who desired them." *Id.* at 1289.

In *S&H Riggers & Erectors, Inc. v. Occupational Safety & Health Review Commission*, our predecessor circuit reversed an order of the Commission holding an employer liable for failing to require employees to use safety belts on the roof of a multi-story building. 659 F.2d at 1275–76. The court held that there was not **[—11—]** substantial evidence that the employer had actual knowledge of the requirement, even though the company "did not contest a previous citation for . . . failure to require safety belts." *Id.* at 1284. And the Court rejected the Secretary's "faulty premise that the presence of an 'obvious' hazard by itself gives notice of the need to provide safety belts or other protective equipment." *Id.* at 1282. In fact, "the very 'obviousness' of a hazard" such as an unguarded, open roof might "lead a reasonable employer to conclude that no further safety precautions are necessary" because the workers would have a "constant awareness of the danger of falling." *Id.* at 1283. Although *S&H Riggers* involved an alleged violation of section 1926.28(a), not section 1910.132(a), the actual-knowledge requirements for the two regulations are the same. *Id.* at 1275 n.2, 1278.

The administrative law judge misapplied this standard. Although the administrative law judge cited the correct standard from *S&H Riggers*, he also incorrectly asserted that "[t]he Secretary need not show that an employer understood or acknowledged that the physical conditions were actually hazardous" but "must show only that the employer was aware of the physical conditions that constitute a violation." These statements directly conflict with our precedents, which require both actual knowledge of the hazard and actual knowledge that the hazard requires the provision and use of personal protective equipment. *See Cotter*, 598 F.2d at 915; *Owens-Corning*, 659 F.2d at 1290; *S&H Riggers*, 659 F.2d at 1278, 1285. This heightened knowledge requirement is a requirement of due process, and the administrative law judge's failure to apply it means **[—12—]** that the decision was "not in accordance with law." *See* 5 U.S.C. § 706(2)(A).

B. The Record Lacks Substantial Evidence of Actual Knowledge.

The record also lacks substantial evidence to support a finding that C&W had actual knowledge. Under our precedents, **{-1290-}** the evidence relied on by the administrative law judge—the condition of the dock, Sheehan's query whether Norton could swim, the two instances of voluntary personal-flotation-device use, and the "open and obvious" nature of the hazard—cannot sustain a finding of actual knowledge of the requirement to provide and require the use of personal flotation devices. Because there is not more than a "scintilla" of evidence to support a finding of actual knowledge, *see J.A.M. Builders*, 233 F.3d at 1352, we set aside the order of the Commission.

C&W's awareness of the circumstances of Norton's work on the dock is insufficient to support a finding of actual knowledge. In both *Cotter* and *S&H Riggers*, the employers were aware of the conditions under which their employees worked. But this awareness did not constitute "specific, confirmed knowledge . . . regarding a hazard warranting a [personal protective equipment] requirement." *Cotter*, 598 F.2d at 915; *accord S&H Riggers*, 659 F.2d at 1285.

Likewise, Sheehan's question to Norton about his ability to swim does not support a finding of actual knowledge that personal flotation devices were required. At most, this evidence supports a **[—13—]** finding that C&W was aware of a possible hazard for employees who could not swim. It also evidences that C&W may have concluded that an employee's ability to swim negated the possible hazard. As the Court explained in *Owens-Corning*, "[a]n employer may be aware of a possible hazard, yet still lack notice that mandatory personal protective equipment is necessary, if the hazard has never given rise to an injury." 659 F.2d at 1290. In the absence of evidence of prior incidents of employees falling off the dock, C&W's awareness of a possible hazard for employees unable to swim does not support a finding of "actual knowledge that [the] hazard require[d] the use of [personal flotation devices]." *See Fla. Mach. & Foundry, Inc.*, 693 F.2d at 120; *see also Owens-Corning*, 659 F.2d at 1290 ("[A] very low injury rate has a definite bearing on the question whether an employer has notice that personal protective equipment is necessary under a general regulation such as [section] 1910.132(a).").

The voluntary use of personal flotation devices by two other employees also does not support a finding of actual knowledge that personal flotation devices were *required* to abate the hazard. Like the voluntary steel-toed shoes program in *Cotter*, the voluntary safety precautions of two employees are evidence only that the preferences of these employees were accommodated, "rather than . . . reflect[ing] the knowledge of the employer that the [personal flotation devices] were necessary precautions." *See* 598 F.2d at 914–15. The administrative law judge's attempt to distinguish *Cotter* on the ground that the employer there encouraged employees "to **[—14—]** take every possible safety precaution" is unavailing. *See id.* at 915. C&W's failure to encourage its employees to "take every possible safety precaution" cannot be evidence that C&W knew that personal flotation devices were necessary. If anything, it suggests a lack of that knowledge.

Finally, the "obviousness" of a hazard is not evidence of actual knowledge and does not absolve the Secretary of his burden, especially when the obviousness of the hazard would put employees on notice of the potential risk. *See S&H Riggers*, 659 F.2d at 1282–83. "In the absence of an industry custom or standard requiring the use of [personal flotation devices], or a history of fall accidents, [C&W] . . . could [have] reasonably conclude[d] that employees' constant awareness of the danger of falling provides adequate protection against falls from flat, open surfaces." *See id.* at 1283. Like C&W's failure to encourage **{-1291-}** its employees to "take every possible safety precaution," the "open and obvious" nature of the hazard on the dock might cut against a finding of actual knowledge that personal flotation devices were necessary.

Because substantial evidence does not support a finding that C&W had actual knowledge of the requirement to provide and require the use of personal flotation devices for employees pressure washing the dock, we grant the petition for review, "set[] aside . . . the order of the Commission," and vacate the citation. *See* 29 U.S.C. § 660(a). "If the evidence would support but not compel a finding of actual knowledge, a remand would be required in order to permit the Commission to complete the factfinding process" **[—15—]** under the correct standard. *S&H Riggers*, 659 F.2d at 1284. But "[b]ecause we hold that a finding of actual knowledge would not be supported by substantial evidence in the record" even if the administrative law judge applied the correct standard, "a remand would be inappropriate." *Id.* And because we have vacated the citation, we need not discuss whether Norton was an "employee" of C&W within the meaning of the Occupational Safety and Health Act or whether C&W was the "controlling employer" within the meaning of the Administration's Multi-Employer Citation Policy.

IV. CONCLUSION

The petition for review is **GRANTED**, the order of the Commission is **SET ASIDE**, and the citation is **VACATED**.

United States Court of Appeals
for the Eleventh Circuit

No. 21-10745

SAVAGE SERVS. CORP.
vs.
UNITED STATES

Appeal from the United States District Court for the Southern District of Alabama

Decided: February 8, 2022

Citation: 25 F.4th 925, 10 Adm. R. 348 (11th Cir. 2022).

Before **ROSENBAUM** and **PRYOR**, Circuit Judges, and **ALTMAN**,* District Judge.

* The Honorable Roy K. Altman, United States District Judge for the Southern District of Florida, sitting by designation.

[—2—] {-927-} ALTMAN, District Judge:

In the wake of the Exxon Valdez oil spill, which saw millions of gallons of oil pour into the waters off Alaska's coast, Congress passed the Oil Pollution Act of 1990 (the "OPA"). The OPA creates a comprehensive remedial scheme that governs—and apportions liability for—oil-removal costs. The statute holds oil spillers strictly liable *upfront* for oil-removal expenses and then carefully incentivizes their good behavior by allowing them, if they meet certain requirements, (1) to avail themselves of one of three liability defenses and (2) to seek contribution on the *back end* from other culpable parties.

In our case, the M/V SAVAGE VOYAGER was transporting oil through a Mississippi waterway when an accident at a boat lift—operated by the U.S. Army Corps of Engineers—caused a rupture in the SAVAGE VOYAGER's hull, through which thousands of gallons of oil poured into the river. Blaming the Government, the owners of the vessel sued the United States. Critically, though, they sued, not under the OPA, but under the common-law admiralty regime that has persisted for centuries. And, hoping to pierce the **[—3—]** Government's sovereign immunity, they relied on the Suits in Admiralty Act (the "SAA"), a 1920 law by which Congress generally waived sovereign immunity for most admiralty claims.

This case—hinging on the interplay between the OPA and the SAA—presents an issue of first impression in the federal courts. The district court dismissed the vessel owner's claims for *removal* costs in two steps. *First*, the court held that the **{-928-}** OPA authorizes no claim against the Government for oil-removal damages. *Second*, it concluded that the OPA's comprehensive remedial scheme displaced the SAA's more general sovereign-immunity waiver. We agree and now affirm. **[—4—]**

BACKGROUND

I. The Spill

We start at the beginning—with an oil spill in the Tennessee-Tombigbee Waterway, a manmade system of canals, locks, and dams linking the Tennessee River in Mississippi with the Tombigbee River in Alabama. Here's a map of the Waterway:

On September 8, 2019, the M/V SAVAGE VOYAGER was pushing two tank barges along the Tennessee-Tombigbee Waterway.[1] Our Plaintiffs—Savage Services Corp. and Savage Inland **[—5—]** Marine LLC—owned the vessel.[2] Along its journey, the vessel approached the Jamie Whitten Lock, a boat lift operated by the U.S. Army Corps of Engineers (the "Army Corps").

Things quickly devolved from there. On Savage's account, when the barge entered the lock, the lock master "began de-watering the lock chamber without notice or warning to the crew" and without "confirm[ing] the tug and tow were within the miter walls." At that point, the vessel's crew noticed that the "rake end" of one of the barges was caught on the north miter wall. The crew immediately relayed this information to the lock master. But, by then, it was too late. The lock chamber descended nearly sixty feet—and, as the water in the chamber fell, the barge rose **{–929–}** out of the water until the angle became so steep that the barge fell off the miter wall. The weight of the barge caused the rake end of the barge to bend upward. According to Savage, the distorted rake "punctured a cargo tank . . ., resulting in a release of crude oil into the lock chamber." In the end, the barge looked like this: **[—6—]**

Savage alleges that the Army Corps was "solely responsible" for the accident and that "[t]here was nothing the SAVAGE VOYAGER could have done to avoid the accident." Savage also says that, as a result of the Army Corps's sole negligence, Savage suffered $4 million in damages—mostly due to the time-consuming process of removing oil from the Waterway. Hoping to recover these costs, Savage sued the United States in admiralty, relying in large measure on the Suits in Admiralty Act of 1920. In the SAA, the United States waived its sovereign immunity for most admiralty claims. *See* 46 U.S.C. § 30903(a) ("In a case in which, . . . if a private person or property were involved, a civil action in admiralty could be maintained, a civil action in admiralty *in personam* may be brought against the United States or a federally-owned corporation."). **[—7—]**

II. The Federal Water Pollution Control Act

Before the Oil Pollution Act of 1990—the law that *now* governs oil-removal liability—there was the Clean Water Act, more formally known as the Federal Water Pollution Control Act Amendments of 1972 (the "FWPCA"). The FWPCA was the cornerstone of a fractured liability scheme. *See* J.B. Ruhl & Michael J. Jewell, *Oil Pollution Act of 1990: Opening a New Era in Federal and Texas Regulation of Oil Spill Prevention, Containment and Cleanup, and Liability*, 32 S. TEX. L. REV. 475, 481 (1991) ("The cornerstone of pre-OPA federal oil spill liability law was found in the Federal Water Pollution Control Act[.] Supplementing that central provision in specified, limited contexts were the Trans-Alaska Pipeline Authorization Act, the Deepwater Port Act of 1974, and the Outer Continental Shelf Lands Act[.]"). **{–930–}**

The default under the FWPCA was for the federal government to take the lead on oil-spill removal. In the event of an oil spill, the law authorized the President of the United States "to act to remove or arrange for the removal of such oil or substance at any time, unless he determines such removal will be done properly by the owner or operator of the vessel . . . from which the discharge occurs." 33 U.S.C. § 1321(c)(1) (1988).

As to liability, the FWPCA provided that the "owner or operator of any vessel from

[1] Tank barges are non-self-propelled vessels that carry liquids—including oil.

[2] For simplicity's sake, we'll refer to Savage Services Corp. and Savage Inland Marine LLC (collectively) as "Savage."

which oil . . . is discharged . . . shall . . . be liable to the United States Government for the actual costs . . . for the removal of such oil or substance by the United States **[—8—]** Government." *Id.* § 1321(f)(1). The vessel owner was strictly liable for those costs, subject to certain complete defenses. Those defenses allowed the owner to avoid liability by "prov[ing] that a discharge was caused solely by (A) an act of God, (B) an act of war, (C) *negligence on the part of the United States Government*, or (D) an act or omission of a third party without regard to whether any such act or omission was or was not negligent, or any combination of the foregoing clauses." *Id.* (emphasis added). Remember the emphasized portion of this last sentence because it will become very important to our overall story. The United States could seek the "full amount" of its oil-removal costs if it could "show that such discharge was the result of willful negligence or willful misconduct within the privity and knowledge of the owner." *Id.* Otherwise, the owner's liability was capped by the vessel's typology and its size. *Id.*

On top of allowing *complete* defenses, the FWPCA left the door open for responsible parties to bring contribution claims against third parties: "The liabilities established by this section shall in no way affect any rights which . . . the owner or operator of a vessel . . . may have against any third party whose acts may in any way have caused or contributed to such discharge." *Id.* § 1321(h). The FWPCA also created a "revolving fund" to finance government-cleanup efforts: "[t]here is hereby authorized to be appropriated to a revolving fund to be established in the Treasury such sums as may be necessary to maintain such fund at a level of $35,000,000." *Id.* § 1321(k). **[—9—]**

III. The Oil Pollution Act of 1990

Congress passed the Oil Pollution Act of 1990 in the aftermath of the Exxon Valdez oil spill, which had resulted in more than 11 million gallons of crude oil spilling into Alaska's waters. S. REP. NO. 101-99, at 1 (1989). After Exxon Valdez, Congress concluded that "the costs of spilling [oil] and paying for its clean-up and damage is not high enough to encourage greater industry efforts to prevent spills and develop effective techniques to contain them." S. REP. NO. 101-94, at 3 (1989). Congress also found fault in the "fragmented collection of Federal and State laws providing inadequate cleanup and damage remedies"—along with the "taxpayer subsidies to cover cleanup costs." *Id.* at 1. The FWPCA, Congress felt, "set[] inappropriately low limits of liability." *Id.* And its revolving fund was entirely inadequate: "Between 1971 and 1982 the United States Government obligated $124 million from the ... revolving fund, but recovered only $49 million from spillers, for a total expenditure of $75 million in national funds. . . . [S]ince the fund is appropriated from the Treasury, it undercuts budget reduction goals and runs counter to cost internalization policies." *Id.* at 3. The "purpose" of the OPA was "to establish a comprehensive system of liability and compensation for damages caused by oil pollution," H.R. REP. NO. 101-242, pt. 2, at 31 (1989), and to "internalize those costs [associated with oil-spill cleanup] **{-931-}** within the oil industry and its transportation sector," S. REP. NO. 101-94, at 2. **[—10—]**

To effectuate those ends, the OPA—which amends the FWPCA[3]—sets out a comprehensive scheme that apportions liability for oil-cleanup costs and damages. For starters, the OPA defines the "responsible party" in any oil spill as the "person owning, operating, or demise chartering the vessel." 33 U.S.C. § 2701(32)(A). In the event of an oil spill, the OPA requires the executive branch to identify the responsible party. *Id.* § 2714(a) ("When the President receives information of an incident, the President shall, where possible and appropriate, designate the source or sources of the discharge or threat."). The responsible party is then strictly liable—at

[3] *See United States v. Am. Com. Lines, L.L.C.*, 759 F.3d 420, 422, 2 Adm. R. 283, 283 (5th Cir. 2014) (noting that the "Clean Water Act ('CWA'), also known as the Federal Water Pollution Control Act ('FWPCA'), 33 U.S.C. [§] 1321, [was] amended by OPA"); *Water Quality Ins. Syndicate v. United States*, 522 F. Supp. 2d 220, 231 (D.D.C. 2007) (explaining that the "predecessor statute to the OPA [was] the Federal Water Pollution Control Act").

least in the first instance—for any oil-removal costs or damages: "Notwithstanding any other provision or rule of law, . . . each responsible party for a vessel . . . from which oil is discharged . . . is liable for the removal costs and damages . . . that result from such incident." *Id.* § 2702(a).

In exchange for this *initial* liability, the OPA offers vessel owners significant financial incentives to encourage them to fully perform their obligations. *First,* the OPA provides a *complete* defense to liability "if the responsible party establishes, by a preponderance of the evidence, that the discharge . . . of oil and the **[—11—]** resulting damages or removal costs were caused solely by . . . (1) an act of God; (2) an act of war; (3) an act or omission of a third party . . . ; or (4) any combination of paragraphs (1), (2), and (3)." *Id.* § 2703(a). Note the conspicuous absence of the third clause we highlighted earlier—which allowed for a complete defense under the FWPCA in cases where the *federal government* was negligent. *Second,* the OPA establishes limitations on the responsible party's liability. The liability of the owner of a double-hull tank vessel weighing less than 3,000 gross tons, for example, would be limited to the greater of $1,900 per gross ton or $4 million. *Id.* § 2704(a). But these benefits (the complete defenses and the liability limits) are available to responsible vessel owners *only if* they "report the incident as required" and "provide all reasonable cooperation and assistance . . . in connection with removal activities." *Id.* §§ 2703(c), 2704(c)(2). The liability limits are unavailable if the responsible party's "gross negligence or willful misconduct" caused the spill. *Id.* § 2704(c)(1).

In addition to supplying complete defenses to liability, the OPA also allows—in a carefully worded provision—responsible vessel owners to seek contribution from *other* culpable parties: a "person may bring a civil action," the law says, "for contribution against any other person who is liable or potentially liable under this Act or another law." *Id.* § 2709. The statute defines the term "person" to mean "an individual, corporation, partnership, association, State, municipality, commission, or political subdivision of a **[—12—]** State, or any interstate body." *Id.* at § 2701(27). This definition (notably) *does not* include the United States Government. *Id.*

Through the OPA, Congress created the Oil Spill Liability Trust Fund. The Fund's resources come from (among other things) (1) environmental taxes on crude oil and certain petroleum products and (2) government collections from specified environmental **{-932-}** fines and penalties. 26 U.S.C. § 9509. The Fund works like an insurance pool: When a responsible party is entitled to a complete "defense to liability" or a "limitation of liability," the Fund will *both* reimburse the responsible party for payments made *and* cover any additional removal costs and damages. 33 U.S.C. § 2708(a). Similarly, if a responsible party fails to timely pay a claim for removal costs or damages, the entity that *does* pay those costs may present its claim for reimbursement to the Fund. *Id.* § 2713(a), (c) (noting that a claimant who first presents its claim to the responsible party may then "present the claim to the Fund" if the responsible party "denies all liability" or does not "settle[]" the claim "within 90 days").[4] **[—13—]**

IV. The District Court's Order

In response to Savage's amended complaint, the Government filed a partial motion to dismiss, contending that the United States has not waived its sovereign immunity for Savage's "spill removal cost claim." The Government didn't move to dismiss Savage's claims for *other* damages—*e.g.*, its claims for barge-repair, loss-of-use, and lost-cargo costs.[5]

---

[4] *See generally* Cynthia M. Wilkinson *et al.*, *Slick Work: An Analysis of the Oil Pollution Act of 1990*, 12 J. ENERGY NAT. RES. & ENV'T L. 181, 207 (1992) ("The Federal Oil Spill Liability Trust Fund (Federal Fund), is available to pay for oil-spill related costs when the spiller cannot be identified, when the spiller can successfully defend against a charge of liability, when the spiller can invoke liability limits and claims exceed those limits, when the spiller is not subject to United States jurisdiction (a foreign spiller), or when a spiller is insolvent or otherwise cannot make good on its obligations under the OPA.").

[5] The United States also filed a counterclaim for about $150,000 in "monitoring costs." The

Savage, in turn, moved for partial summary judgment, seeking an affirmative ruling that the United States has waived its sovereign immunity as to those same oil-removal claims.

The district court granted the Government's motion to dismiss and denied Savage's motion for summary judgment. As the court put it: "Congress has enacted a specific, detailed statute assigning responsibility for oil-spill cleanup costs (at the initial payee level, and beyond) that lacks any waiver of sovereign immunity applicable to the events pleaded in the Amended Complaint." "In so doing," the district court held, "Congress has expressed its intent to effect an implied repeal of the general sovereign immunity provision in the [SAA] as it pertains to oil-spill cleanup damages." Savage timely appealed. **[—14—]**

STANDARD OF REVIEW

We review the district court's order granting the motion to dismiss and denying the motion for summary judgment *de novo*. *See Sun Life Assurance Co. of Can. v. Imperial Premium Fin., LLC*, 904 F.3d 1197, 1207 (11th Cir. 2018).

DISCUSSION

This case is hard in part because (at least at first glance) it seems to fall squarely at the intersection between two well-established canons. On the one hand, we are "heirs to a system in which the sovereign, the king, was not amenable to suit." ANTONIN SCALIA & BRYAN A. GARNER, READING LAW: THE INTERPRETATION OF LEGAL TEXTS 281 (2012) [hereinafter READING LAW]. Tracking that tradition, "[a]bsent a **{-933-}** waiver, sovereign immunity shields the Federal Government and its agencies from suit." *F.D.I.C. v. Meyer*, 510 U.S. 471, 475 (1994); *see also United States v. Mitchell*, 463 U.S. 206, 212 (1983) ("It is axiomatic that the United States may not be sued without its consent and that the existence of consent is a prerequisite for jurisdiction."). "Waivers of the Government's sovereign immunity, to be effective, must be unequivocally expressed." *United States v. Nordic Vill. Inc.*, 503 U.S. 30, 33 (1992) (internal quotation marks omitted). Indeed, "[a]ny ambiguities in the statutory language are to be construed in favor of immunity[.]" *F.A.A. v. Cooper*, 566 U.S. 284, 290 (2012).

On the other hand, "[c]ourts generally adhere to the principle that statutes relating to the same subject matter should be **[—15—]** construed harmoniously if possible, and if not, that more recent or specific statutes should prevail over older or more general ones." *Tug Allie-B, Inc. v. United States*, 273 F.3d 936, 941 (11th Cir. 2001) (quoting *S. Nat. Gas Co. v. Land, Cullman Cnty.*, 197 F.3d 1368, 1373 (11th Cir. 1999)). In other words, while recognizing that what's new and specific trumps what's old and more general, we've also warned that "[t]he conclusion that two statutes conflict . . . is one that courts must not reach lightly." *Miccosukee Tribe of Indians of Fla. v. U.S. Army Corps of Eng'rs*, 619 F.3d 1289, 1299 (11th Cir. 2010). "Courts must first 'assiduously attempt' to try to construe two statutes in harmony before concluding that one impliedly repeals the other." *Id.* (quoting *Tug Allie-B*, 273 F.3d at 952 (Black, J., concurring)). While this "canon is hardly absolute," a "doctrine of readily implied repealer would repeatedly place earlier enactments in doubt." READING LAW at 327–28.

The problem, as the parties present it, is that these presumptions pull (or *seem* to pull) in opposite directions in our case. The Government, guided by the presumption against waivers of sovereign immunity, says that the OPA sets out a comprehensive remedial scheme that *doesn't* allow responsible parties to sue the United States. Savage, by contrast, contends that the OPA, especially when read together with the SAA, *does* create a cause of action against the United States—or (alternatively) that it authorizes responsible parties to bring common-law

Government alleges that it incurred these costs "[i]n responding to this incident"—specifically, when "the U.S. Coast Guard closed the Tennessee-Tombigbee Waterway between mile markers 410 and 414 and established a Unified Command to direct cleanup efforts."

admiralty claims against the federal government. **[—16—]**

"In ascertaining the plain meaning of the statute, the court must look to the particular statutory language at issue, as well as the language and design of the statute as a whole." *K Mart Corp. v. Cartier, Inc.*, 486 U.S. 281, 291 (1988). In our view, the OPA's text and structure squarely foreclose the kind of oil-removal claim Savage has advanced here.

I. The OPA Does Not Create a Cause of Action Against the United States

We begin with the easier call: the OPA doesn't create a cause of action for oil spillers to seek contribution from the United States. The OPA, recall, provides that "[a] person may bring a civil action for contribution against any other person who is liable or potentially liable under this Act or another law." 33 U.S.C. § 2709. The OPA defines "person" to include an "individual, corporation, partnership, association, State, municipality, commission, or political subdivision of a State, or any interstate body." *Id.* § 2701(27). As we've said, the United States is conspicuously absent from this list. Because the United States is not a "person" under the plain **{–934–}** language of the statute—and since the contribution provision allows for contribution claims only against "any other *person*"—the OPA doesn't authorize Savage to seek contribution from the Government. And this plain-text reading of the statute is further strengthened by "our longstanding interpretive presumption that 'person' does not include the sovereign," *Vt. Agency of Nat. Res. v. U.S. ex rel. Stevens*, 529 U.S. 765, 780 (2000), a presumption that's at its acme in cases like ours "where the statute imposes a burden or **[—17—]** limitation, as distinguished from conferring a benefit or advantage," on the sovereign, *Wilson v. Omaha Indian Tribe*, 442 U.S. 653, 667 (1979).

Pushing back, Savage argues that we should interpret the word "State" to include the United States because those terms are defined coextensively in the OPA.[6] Savage is right that the OPA provides one definition for both terms. It says:

> "United States" and "State" mean the several States of the United States, the District of Columbia, the Commonwealth of Puerto Rico, Guam, American Samoa, the United States Virgin Islands, the Commonwealth of the Northern Marianas, and any other territory or possession of the United States[.]

33 U.S.C. § 2701(36). But this definition doesn't give us the answer Savage is hoping for. Instead, it does little more than explain that the "United States" and "States" are meant to include all U.S. *properties*—both those that are technically states and those that are just territories or protectorates. So, for example, when the OPA defines "onshore facility" to mean a facility on "any land within the United **[—18—]** States," that includes facilities in Puerto Rico. *Id.* § 2701(24). And, when the OPA discusses "removal costs incurred by . . . a state," that includes losses incurred by Guam. *Id.* § 2702(b)(1). For several reasons, though, it would strain language and logic to conclude that, when Congress included "States" (but not "United States") within its definition of "person," it actually meant both individual states *and* the United States.

First, when Congress intended for a provision to apply to both the states and the United States, it referred to each separately—often pointing expressly to the "United States Government." *See, e.g., id.* § 2706(a) ("In the case of natural resource damages . . . , liability shall be-- (1) to the United States Government for natural

[6] Savage also points us to the fact that the OPA allows responsible parties to pursue contribution actions against a "person" under "another law" and contends that "[c]learly 'another law' includes the SAA." Fair enough. But that doesn't answer the threshold question of whether the United States is a "person" that *can* be sued under "another law." It also fails to account for the OPA's "[n]otwithstanding" clause, 33 U.S.C. § 2702(a). *See infra* at Section III.B.

resources belonging to, managed by, controlled by, or appertaining to the United States [or] (2) to any State for natural resources belonging to, managed by, controlled by, or appertaining to such State[.]"); *id.* § 2712(f) ("Payment of any claim or obligation by the Fund under this Act shall be subject to the United States Government acquiring by subrogation all rights of the claimant or State to recover from the responsible party.").[7] Why would **[—19—]** **{-935-}** Congress have used the terms "United States" and "States" separately if they meant the same thing? It wouldn't have. Savage's interpretation collides head-on, then, with the surplusage canon, which cautions courts to "avoid a reading that renders some words altogether redundant." READING LAW at 176; *see also In Re Shek*, 947 F.3d 770, 777 (11th Cir. 2020) ("This surplusage canon obliges us, whenever possible, to disfavor an interpretation when that interpretation would render a clause, sentence, or word superfluous, void, or insignificant." (cleaned up)).

Second, when Congress waived sovereign immunity in the contribution provisions of other statutes, it did so much more explicitly. Take, for instance, the Comprehensive Environmental Response, Compensation and Liability Act of 1980 ("CERCLA")—a strikingly similar statute with a modified strict-liability scheme for (non-oil-related) hazardous spills. CERCLA, like the OPA, defines "United States" and "State" together. *See* 42 U.S.C. § 9601(27) ("The terms 'United States' and 'State' include the several States of the United States, the District of Columbia, the Commonwealth of Puerto Rico, Guam, American Samoa, the United States Virgin Islands, the Commonwealth of the Northern Marianas, and any other territory or possession over which the United States has **[—20—]** jurisdiction."). And, like the OPA, CERCLA provides that "[a]ny person may seek contribution from *any other person* who is liable or potentially liable." *Id.* § 9613(f)(1) (emphasis added). But, unlike the OPA, CERCLA plainly opens the United States up to liability in contribution by defining a "person" as including *both* the United States *and* the individual states. *Id.* § 9601(21) ("The term 'person' means an individual, firm, corporation, association, partnership, consortium, joint venture, commercial entity, *United States Government*, State, municipality, commission, political subdivision of a State, or any interstate body." (emphasis added)). Given how similar these two statutes (CERCLA and OPA) are, we think it extremely telling that, in the latter, Congress decided to *delete* the United States from the OPA's definition of "person[s]" who could be sued.

And CERCLA's not alone on this front. In crafting one provision of the Clean Water Act—housed in the same title of the Code as the OPA—Congress provided that "any citizen may commence a civil action on his own behalf . . . against any person . . . including . . . the United States"—again, unambiguously waiving its immunity with respect to civil actions. 33 U.S.C. § 1365(a). And the Resource Conservation and Recovery Act ("RCRA") says that "any person may commence a civil action on his own behalf . . . against any person, including the United States and any other governmental instrumentality or agency." 42 U.S.C. § 6972(a)(1)(B). Congress, in short, knows how to waive sovereign immunity when it wants to. And, unfortunately for Savage, it chose *not* to include **[—21—]** these well-hashed sovereign-immunity waivers in the OPA. *See generally Pinares v. United Techs. Corp.*, 973 F.3d 1254, 1262 (11th Cir. 2020) ("Where Congress knows how to say

[7] *See also, e.g.*, 33 U.S.C. § 2701(29) ("'public vessel' means a vessel owned or bareboat chartered and operated by the United States, or by a State or political subdivision thereof, or by a foreign nation, except when the vessel is engaged in commerce"); *id.* § 2702(b)(1)(A) ("removal costs" include "all removal costs incurred by the United States, a State, or an Indian tribe"); *id.* § 2702(b)(2)(A) ("damages" include damages to natural resources, "which shall be recoverable by a United States trustee, a State trustee, an Indian tribe trustee, or a foreign **[—19—]** trustee"); *id.* § 2702(b)(2)(D) ("damages" include lost tax revenues, "which shall be recoverable by the Government of the United States, a State, or a political subdivision thereof"); *id.* § 2704(c)(3) (the owner or operator of an Outer Continental Shelf facility or vessel shall be liable for "all removal costs incurred by the United States Government or any State or local official or agency").

something but chooses not to, its silence is controlling." (quoting *Animal Legal Def. Fund v. U.S. Dep't of Agric.*, 789 F.3d 1206, 1217 (11th Cir. 2015))). **{–936–}**

Third, courts are "especially reluctant to read 'person' to mean the sovereign where, as here, such a reading is 'decidedly awkward.'" *Int'l Primate Prot. League v. Adm'rs of Tulane Educ. Fund*, 500 U.S. 72, 83 (1991) (quoting *Will v. Mich. Dep't of State Police*, 491 U.S. 58, 64 (1989)). And there's no two ways about it: Savage's proposal to treat the United States as a "person" would lead to implausible results. For example, the OPA makes "[a]ny person" who fails to comply with certain "financial responsibility" requirements "liable to the United States for a civil penalty, not to exceed $25,000 per day of violation." 33 U.S.C. § 2617a(a). Savage's reading would thus make the United States liable *to itself* for civil sanctions. Imagine for a moment what that would look like: with the Environmental Torts Section of the Department of Justice working both sides of the same case at the same time—both prosecuting the United States for, and defending the United States against, those civil penalties. Given everything we've said thus far, there's no reason to believe that Congress intended for such an awkward result.

Fourth, in defining "person" under the OPA, Congress set out a careful list of governmental entities: States, municipalities, **[—22—]** political subdivisions of a State. 33 U.S.C. § 2701(27). But it didn't include the United States Government. The Supreme Court—invoking (though not by name) the canon of *expressio unius est exclusio alterius*—held (in a similar context) that, "[w]hile both [statutes at issue] define 'person' to cover States, subdivisions of States, municipalities, and interstate bodies . . . , neither statute defines 'person' to include the United States. Its omission has to be seen as a pointed one when so many other governmental entities are specified[.]" *U.S. Dep't of Energy v. Ohio*, 503 U.S. 607, 617–18 (1992); *see also* NORMAN SINGER & SHAMBIE SINGER, 2A SUTHERLAND STATUTORY CONSTRUCTION § 47:23 (7th ed. updated Nov. 2021) [hereinafter SUTHERLAND STATUTORY CONSTRUCTION] ("*Expressio unius* instructs that, where a statute designates a form of conduct, the manner of its performance and operation, and the persons and things to which it refers, courts should infer that all omissions were intentional exclusions.").

The OPA, in short, doesn't create a cause of action by which oil spillers can seek contribution from the United States for oil-removal costs.

II. The OPA Does Not Provide a Complete Defense to Liability for Governmental Negligence

Nor does the OPA allow a responsible party to escape *all* liability by pointing to the federal government's negligence. As we've noted, "courts have held that the enumerated defenses of other strict liability schemes are exclusive and should be narrowly **[—23—]** construed." *Tug Allie-B*, 273 F.3d at 943 n.7 (collecting cases). The OPA, recall, provides a complete defense to liability "if the responsible party establishes, by a preponderance of the evidence, that the discharge . . . of oil and the resulting damages or removal costs were caused solely by (1) an act of God; (2) an act of war; (3) an act or omission of a third party ...; or (4) any combination of paragraphs (1), (2), and (3)." 33 U.S.C. § 2703(a).

As this list makes pellucid, there's no *explicit* defense for negligence on the part of the federal government. And, while the OPA does reference "an act or omission of a third party," we simply cannot construe this exception to strict liability as including the United States. Why? Because a third party is a "party or person besides the two **{–937–}** primarily concerned, as in a law case or the like." *Third Party*, OXFORD ENGLISH DICTIONARY,https://www.oed.com/view/Entry/200849?redirectedFrom=third+party#eid (last visited Feb. 7, 2022); *see also Third Party*, BLACK'S LAW DICTIONARY (11th ed. 2019) (defining "third party" as "someone other than the principal parties"). Looking at the OPA's design, it'd be hard to conclude that the first and second parties are anyone other than the responsible party (on the one hand) and the United States (on the other). The OPA, after all, divvies up—amongst those two "principal" parties—the liability for an oil spill, the responsibility for remedying an oil spill, and the authority for directing oil-spill cleanups.

And we're not alone in saying so. In *In re Glacier Bay*, 71 F.3d 1447 (9th Cir. 1995), the Ninth Circuit tackled a massive oil-spill action that had been brought under the FWPCA, the OPA's **[—24—]** predecessor. That statute, in detailing a spiller's rights against those "who caused or contributed to [the] discharge," provided that "[t]he liabilities established by this section shall in no way affect any rights which . . . the owner or operator of a vessel . . . may have against any *third party* whose acts may in any way have caused or contributed to such discharge." 33 U.S.C. § 1321(h) (emphasis added). And, like Savage, the owner of the oil tanker there contended "that the term 'third party' . . . may include the United States government." *Glacier Bay*, 71 F.3d at 1455. The Ninth Circuit made quick work of this argument:

> We cannot reconcile [the spiller's] reading with the structure of the statute. Read as a whole, [the FWPCA] sets out the rights and responsibilities of discharging vessel owners and the United States government vis-a-vis each other. These are the parties of the first and second parts. The term "third party" is used to refer [to] parties *other than* these two[.]

Id. We reach the same conclusion here.

The OPA's amendments to the FWPCA only further support our view that Congress removed governmental negligence as a complete defense to liability. As we've said, the FWPCA expressly allowed vessel owners to recover reasonable oil-removal costs from the United States if the "discharge was caused solely by (A) an act of God, (B) an act of war, (C) *negligence on the part of the United States Government*, or (D) an act or omission of a third party without regard to whether such act or omission was or was **[—25—]** not negligent, or of any combination of the foregoing causes." 33 U.S.C. § 1321(i) (emphasis added). The OPA—as the Government points out—reduced these complete defenses from four to three, eliminating the defense for "negligence on the part of the United States Government." *Id.* § 2703(a). The ineluctable inference we draw from this deletion is that Congress *intentionally* eliminated the erstwhile defense for governmental negligence.

Nonplussed, Savage argues that, even as Congress was removing the governmental-negligence defense, it tacitly (and simultaneously) restored that defense by transforming the United States into a "third party" under the third-party-defense clause. But there are several problems with this theory. For one thing, it violates the surplusage canon by needlessly forcing us to suppose that the FWPCA's governmental-negligence defense is (and long has been) redundant given the availability of the third-party defense. *Cf. Nat'l Ass'n of Home Builders v. Defs. of Wildlife*, 551 U.S. 644, 669 (2007) ("[W]e have cautioned against reading a text in a way that makes part of it redundant."). For another, when "Congress acts to amend a statute, we **{-938-}** presume it intends its amendment to have real and substantial effect." *Husky Int'l Elecs., Inc. v. Ritz*, 578 U.S. 356, 359–60 (2016) (quoting *United States v. Quality Stores, Inc.*, 572 U.S. 141, 148 (2014)); *see also* READING LAW at 256 ("If the legislature amends or reenacts a provision . . . , a significant change in language is presumed to entail a change in meaning."). Savage, though, would have us conclude that, when Congress eliminated "negligence on the part of the United States Government" as a **[—26—]** defense, it never (actually) eliminated the governmental-negligence defense. In fact, Savage would have us believe that Congress's amendment did nothing at all. That can't be right. A third problem with Savage's construction is that it flouts the dispositive English-usage problems the Ninth Circuit identified almost thirty years ago. *See In re Glacier*, 71 F.3d at 1455 (observing that "discharging vessel owners and the United States government . . . are the parties of the first and second parts" and that, as a result, "third party" could *not* refer to the United States).

For all these reasons, we conclude that the OPA includes no complete defense for governmental negligence.

III. The OPA is Exclusive

So where does that leave us? The SAA "broadly waives the Government's sovereign immunity" for admiralty claims. *Henderson v. United States*, 517 U.S. 654, 656 (1996); *see also Kasprik v. United States*, 87 F.3d 462, 465 (11th Cir. 1996) ("The SAA does not provide a cause of action against the United States but rather constitutes the United States' limited waiver of sovereign immunity with respect to admiralty suits."). And the OPA, as we've now learned, is a specific statute that governs liability for oil-spill **[—27—]** removals and which does *not* create a right of action for suits against the United States.[8] But that's really only half the problem.

The heart of the parties' disagreement lies here—on this question: is the OPA *exclusive*? Savage maintains that, even if the OPA may not *itself* contain a waiver of sovereign immunity, vessel owners may still go after the United States for removal costs and damages by bringing common-law admiralty claims against the Government pursuant to the SAA's sovereign-immunity waiver. The Government, for its part, contends that the OPA provides a comprehensive—and exclusive—remedy for oil-spill-removal claims, displacing any cause of action Savage could've brought under the common law (or the SAA). We think the Government has the better side of this argument.

A. A Detailed Statute Preempts General Remedies

As an initial matter, our analysis is governed by "the well-established principle that, in most contexts, 'a precisely drawn, detailed statute pre-empts more general remedies.'" *Hinck v. United States*, 550 U.S. 501, 506 (2007) (quoting **{-939-}** *EC Term of Years Tr. v.* **[—28—]** *United States*, 550 U.S. 429, 433 (2007)). The Supreme Court has held, for instance, that "whe[re] Congress enacts a specific remedy . . . when previous remedies were 'problematic,' the remedy provided is generally regarded as exclusive." *Id.* (quoting *Block v. N.D. ex rel. Bd. of Univ. & Sch. Lands*, 461 U.S. 273, 285 (1983)). And that makes sense: when the legislature has attacked a specific problem—and crafted a detailed and precise remedy to address that problem—we should generally assume that the law represents Congress's considered and exclusive judgment on that issue.

Imagine a local municipality that promulgates two ordinances. The first provides a cause of action for trespass against any *person* who encroaches on private land. The second provides a cause of action for trespass against any *police officer* and outlines a limited set of circumstances in which the cause of action may be asserted—*e.g.*, only when the officer was operating outside of his jurisdiction, was off duty, or was acting in violation of constitutional constraints. We think it beyond peradventure to say that a plaintiff in our city looking to sue a *police officer* for trespass could assert a claim only under the latter (more specific) ordinance—and not under the general trespass law. Otherwise, what purpose would the second ordinance serve?

And that's pretty much what happened here. In 1990, Congress enacted a detailed—and precisely drawn—statute that governed almost every aspect of an oil-spill cleanup. As we've explained, the OPA assigns initial liability to the vessel owner, 33 U.S.C. § 2702; places caps on—and offers complete defenses to— **[—29—]** that liability for parties who act responsibly, *id.* §§ 2703, 2704; outlines the contours of available contribution claims, *id.*

[8] We'd note, by the way, that the only courts to have considered *this* question—whether the Government waived its sovereign immunity under the OPA—have agreed that the OPA contains no such waiver. *See Rick Franklin Corp. v. U.S. Dep't of Homeland Sec.*, 2008 WL 337978, at *3 (D. Or. Feb. 4, 2008) ("The OPA does not contain a waiver of the government's sovereign immunity from suit."); *Int'l Marine Carriers v. Oil Spill Liab. Tr. Fund*, 903 F. Supp. 1097, 1102 (S.D. Tex. 1994) ("Nothing in OPA section[s] 2712, 2713, or 2715 can be construed as a waiver of sovereign immunity.").

§ 2709; creates an industry-financed Fund to limit the burden on taxpayers, *id.* § 2712; and assigns jurisdiction, venue, and time limitations for claims arising under the statute, *id.* § 2717. Congress didn't draw up this carefully balanced design—a veritable super-structure of oil-cleanup rights, duties, and obligations—for no reason. It did it to strike the right incentives within the oil industry itself—incentives the previous regime had, in Congress's estimation, failed to drive home. This detailed scheme thus preempts the general oil-removal remedies that might've been available under either the common law or the SAA.

In similar circumstances, courts have routinely reached this same conclusion. Take *United States v. Bormes*, 568 U.S. 6 (2012), for instance. There, the plaintiff sued the government under the Fair Credit Reporting Act. In doing so, the plaintiff attempted to invoke a waiver of sovereign immunity from a different statute, the Little Tucker Act. The Little Tucker Act, like the SAA, doesn't create a cause of action against the federal government—but only waives sovereign immunity for certain "claim[s] against the United States, not exceeding $10,000." 28 U.S.C. § 1346(a)(2). Given the comprehensiveness of the FCRA's remedial scheme, the Supreme Court refused to allow the plaintiff to sue the United States. In this way, it recognized—as we do—that "a precisely drawn, detailed statute pre-empts more general remedies." *Bormes*, 568 U.S. at 12–13. It then found that the FCRA created just such a "detailed **[—30—]** remedial scheme" because its provisions "set out a carefully circumscribed, time-limited, plaintiff-specific cause of action," "precisely define the appropriate forum," prescribe "a specified limitations period," and vest "jurisdiction" in certain courts. *Id.* at 15 (cleaned up). It concluded:

> [O]ur precedents collectively stand for a more basic proposition: Where a specific statutory scheme provides the accoutrements **{-940-}** of a judicial action, the metes and bounds of the liability Congress intended to create can only be divined from the text of the statute itself.... Since FCRA is a detailed remedial scheme, only *its own* text can determine whether the damages liability Congress crafted extends to the Federal Government. To hold otherwise—to permit plaintiffs to remedy the absence of a waiver of sovereign immunity in specific, detailed statutes by pleading general Tucker Act jurisdiction—would transform the sovereign-immunity landscape.

Id. at 14–15.

Our case is just the same. The OPA is a "detailed remedial scheme" that "provides the accoutrements of a judicial action." It carefully balances (and neatly circumscribes) liability for oil-removal claims. *See generally* 33 U.S.C. §§ 2702, 2703, 2704, 2709. It mandates time limits for bringing covered claims under the statute. *Id.* § 2717(f) (prescribing a three-year statute of limitations for "an action for damages under this Act," "[a]n action for recovery of **[—31—]** removal costs," an "action for contribution for any removal costs or damages," and an "action based on rights subrogated pursuant to this Act"). It precisely defines the forum in which any such action must be brought, noting that "[v]enue shall lie in any district in which the discharge or injury or damages occurred, or in which the defendant resides, may be found, has its principal office, or has appointed an agent for service of process." *Id.* § 2717(b). And it lists the courts that may lawfully exercise subject-matter jurisdiction over its claims, providing (for instance) that "the United States district courts shall have exclusive original jurisdiction over all controversies arising under this Act, without regard to the citizenship of the parties or the amount in controversy." *Id.* Like the statute at issue in *Bormes*, then, the OPA is a "detailed remedial scheme" that constitutes the exclusive source of liability for oil-removal claims. Whether oil-spill liability extends to the federal government, in other words, must be determined by the OPA's *own text*.[9] **[—32—]**

---

9 There is, it's true, one difference between our case and *Bormes*—one neither party seems to notice. In *Bormes*, the plaintiff brought his case under the FCRA and attempted to "mix and match"

Or take the Supreme Court's decision in *Brown v. General Services Administration*, 425 U.S. 820 (1976). That case required the Court to decide whether Title VII of the Civil Rights Act of 1964 "provides the exclusive judicial remedy for claims of discrimination in federal employment." *Id.* at 821. After a deep-dive into the law and its history, the Court determined that the "structure of the [statute] fully confirms the conclusion that Congress intended it to be exclusive and pre-emptive." *Id.* at 829. In reaching this result, the Court pointed to the "balance, completeness, and structural integrity" of the statutory scheme and noted that the law "proscribes federal employment **{–941–}** discrimination and establishes an administrative and judicial enforcement system," which includes—for instance—"certain preconditions" (like EEOC exhaustion). *Id.* at 832.

The OPA does all of those things. As we've said, it prescribes *where* to sue and *when*. 33 U.S.C. § 2717. But it does much more than that: It sets out a detailed "[c]laims procedure" that governs actions against responsible parties, requiring that (other than in limited circumstances) "all claims for removal costs or damages shall be presented first to the responsible party" before the claimant can present its claim in court or to the Fund in a manner approved by the President. *Id.* § 2713(a), (e); *see generally* 33 C.F.R. § 136.105 (setting out the "[g]eneral requirements for a claim" under the **[—33—]** OPA). On Savage's view, however, a claimant can avoid all of these steps by simply asserting its claims under general admiralty law in federal court. To quote the Supreme Court: "[i]t would require the suspension of disbelief to ascribe to Congress the design to allow its careful and thorough remedial scheme to be circumvented by artful pleading." *Brown*, 425 U.S. at 833.

B. The "Notwithstanding" Clause

The OPA's text—always a good place to start and end—like- wise suggests that the law's remedial scheme is exclusive. *Cf.* READING LAW at 56 ("The words of a governing text are of paramount concern, and what they convey, in their context, is what the text means."). In assigning liability, the very first (substantive) provision of the OPA says:

> *Notwithstanding any other provision or rule of law*, and subject to the provisions of this Act, each responsible party for a vessel or a facility from which oil is discharged, or which poses the substantial threat of a discharge of oil, into or upon the navigable waters or adjoining shorelines or the exclusive economic zone is liable for the removal costs and damages specified in subsection (b) that result from such incident.

33 U.S.C. § 2702(a). We've previously held that a "notwithstanding" clause is "Congress's indication that the statute containing that language is intended to take precedence over any preexisting or subsequently-enacted legislation on the same subject." **[—34—]** *Miccosukee*, 619 F.3d at 1298 (cleaned up) (quoting *Castro v. Sec'y of Homeland Sec.*, 472 F.3d 1334, 1337 (11th Cir. 2006)).[10] Of course, such a clause "must be read in the context of the entire statute." *Id.* at 1300. But, for all the

---

its FCRA cause of action with the Little Tucker Act's sovereign-immunity waiver. Our Plaintiff, by contrast, doesn't assert any claim under the OPA. Instead, it advances a claim under federal maritime law and relies on the SAA for its waiver of sovereign immunity—something it unquestionably *can* do as a general matter. This, though, is a difference without much significance—at least for our purposes. That's because *Bormes* turned on the longstanding (and broader) rule that a precisely drawn and detailed statutory scheme preempts an older, more-general set of remedies. And that's exactly what happened in our case: once the precisely **[—32—]** drawn—and detailed—OPA came into being, plaintiffs like Savage could no longer invoke general maritime law (in conjunction with the SAA) to create a cause of action for oil-removal costs against the federal government.

[10] It's worth focusing on that language for a moment. The OPA says that a responsible party "is liable for the removal costs and damages" provided for under the Act, "[n]otwithstanding any other provision or rule of law, and subject to the provisions of this Act[.]" 33 U.S.C. § 2702(a). If Savage could escape liability under *another* "provision or rule of law," *see supra* at note 6, this language would be reduced to meaning nothing at all. We don't read statutes that way.

reasons we've outlined, we think *that* context—from the detailed remedial scheme, to the specific attention to oil removal, to the problems Congress intended to fix—supports our reading of the OPA's exclusivity.

Savage disagrees. In its view, the OPA's "savings" clause leaves available to responsible parties certain alternative causes of action, not found in the OPA—like, for instance, the common-law maritime claims Savage has advanced here. The OPA's savings clause is fairly straightforward. It reads: "Except as otherwise provided in this Act, this Act does not affect . . . admiralty and maritime law." 33 U.S.C. § 2751(e). Relying on *dicta* from a district-court decision in Louisiana, Savage contends **{-942-}** that, through the OPA's savings clause, Congress intended to "preserve[] existing maritime law except where OPA contains a specific provision *to the contrary*." *In re Oil Spill by Oil Rig "Deepwater Horizon" in Gulf of Mex., on Apr. 20, 2010*, 496 F. Supp. 3d 989, 1001 (E.D. La. 2020). The *Deepwater Horizon* Court reached this conclusion (which it notably **[—35—]** described as "dicta" and characterized as "not part of the Court's holding") by relying on a congressional Conference Report, in which the Conference Committee had described the savings clause to mean that "there is no change in current law unless there is a *specific* provision to the contrary." *Id.* at 1000 (emphasis added) (quoting H.R. REP. NO. 101-653 (1990) (Conf. Rep.)).

There are a few things to say about this. *First*, "legislative history is not the law," and "even those of us who believe that clear legislative history can illuminate ambiguous text won't allow ambiguous legislative history to muddy clear statutory language." *Azar v. Allina Health Servs.*, 139 S. Ct. 1804, 1814 (2019) (cleaned up); *see also Ratzlaf v. United States*, 510 U.S. 135, 147–48 (1994) ("There are, we recognize, contrary indications in the statute's legislative history. But we do not resort to legislative history to cloud a statutory text that is clear."); *Harris v. Garner*, 216 F.3d 970, 976 (11th Cir. 2000) (en banc) ("When the import of the words Congress has used is clear, as it is here, we need not resort to legislative history, and we certainly should not do so to undermine the plain meaning of the statutory language."); Alexander Hamilton, Final Version of an Opinion on the Constitutionality of an Act to Establish a Bank, *in* 8 THE PAPERS OF ALEXANDER HAMILTON 97, 111 (Harold C. Syrett ed., 1965) (Feb. 23, 1791) ("[W]hatever may have been the intention of the framers of a constitution, or of a law, that intention is to be sought for in the instrument itself[.]").

Second, the text of the OPA *is* unambiguous. After all, "except as otherwise provided" *does not* mean, as the *Deepwater* **[—36—]** *Horizon* Court supposed, "except as *specifically* provided otherwise" (whatever that might mean). And the fact is that the OPA *has* "provided otherwise." The OPA is a detailed and comprehensive framework for apportioning oil-spill liability. Through its many parts, Congress chose *not* to afford vessel owners any cause of action against the United States. Quite the contrary: It eliminated, as we've said, a provision—present in the OPA's predecessor statute—that would've allowed vessel owners to skirt liability in the case of governmental negligence. And it strayed from similar statutory schemes (like CERCLA and RCRA) that expressly allow for contribution claims against the federal government. The plain import of these unambiguous decisions, then, is that Congress *has* provided otherwise—by making clear that the Government is *not* liable for oil-removal costs. And at least one of our sister circuits has adopted this commonsense interpretation of the law—*viz.*, that the OPA's savings clause "shows that the admiralty claims that are preserved are those that are not addressed in the OPA." *In re Settoon Towing, L.L.C.*, 859 F.3d 340, 351, 5 Adm. R. 266, 274 (5th Cir. 2017).

An everyday example might help us clarify this point. Your friend, who's organizing a picnic, sends a group of people some rules, including this one: "Except as otherwise provided in this text message string, you can bring a sandwich to the picnic." Just before the picnic, your friend texts the group a second rule: "You can bring a turkey bacon sandwich if it has lettuce, tomatoes, and onions." If you arrive at the picnic with a turkey bacon **{-943-}** sandwich that has *nothing* on it—*i.e.*, *no* lettuce, tomatoes, and onions—have you **[—37—]** violated your friend's rules? Under the tenets of ordinary English usage, it would sure seem so. And the same common English usage dictates the result here. Our statute says (in effect): "You can assert a contribution claim if you bring it against a 'person.'" If you bring a contribution claim against *not* a person—against the United States, for example—you've violated the obvious import of the statute. *Cf.* READING LAW at 107 ("When a car dealer promises a low financing rate to 'purchasers with good credit,' it is entirely clear that the rate is not available to purchasers with spotty credit.").

C. Other Circuits

While the interplay between the OPA and the SAA presents an issue of first impression across the federal courts, we're not painting on a blank canvas. That's because our sister circuits have universally concluded that the OPA embodies the exclusive remedy for oil-removal claims that fall within the statute's ambit. In *United States v. American Commercial Lines, L.L.C.*, 759 F.3d 420, 2 Adm. R. 283 (5th Cir. 2014), for example, the Fifth Circuit held that the OPA's "balanced and comprehensive remedial scheme provides the exclusive remedy for a claimant to recover statutory removal costs from a responsible party." *Id.* at 425, 2 Adm. R. at 286. Why? Because, "when Congress enacts a carefully calibrated liability scheme with respect to specific remedies, 'the structure of the remedies suggests that Congress intended for the statutory remedies to be exclusive.'" *Id.* at 424, 2 Adm. R. at 285 (quoting *United States v. M/V BIG SAM*, 681 F.2d 432, 441 (5th Cir. 1982)). The OPA meets each of those criteria. **[—38—]**

Nor is the Fifth Circuit alone in saying so. *See S. Port Marine, LLC v. Gulf Oil Ltd. P'ship*, 234 F.3d 58 (1st Cir. 2000). In *South Port Marine*, the First Circuit embarked on "a straightforward inquiry into whether Congress intended the enactment of the OPA to supplant the existing general admiralty and maritime law, which allowed punitive damages under certain circumstances in the area of oil pollution" and "conclude[d] that Congress did so intend." *Id.* at 65; *see also id.* ("Congress intended the OPA to be the exclusive federal law governing oil spills[.]" (cleaned up)). Starting with "the text of the statute itself," the court found that the "scheme is comprehensive." *Id.* "We think," it said, "that the OPA embodies Congress's attempt to balance the various concerns at issue, and trust that the resolution of these difficult policy questions is better suited to the political mechanisms of the legislature than to our deliberative process." *Id.* at 66. We agree and thus reject Savage's attempt to have us disturb the comprehensive scheme Congress created—and to tip the careful balance Congress designed. *See also Ironshore Specialty Ins. Co. v. United States*, 871 F.3d 131, 139, 5 Adm. R. 49, 54 (1st Cir. 2017) ("[W]e acknowledged in *South Port Marine* that the OPA supplants general admiralty and maritime law when the OPA is triggered[.]").

And those decisions are just the tip of the iceberg. Long before the OPA was on anyone's radar, courts—including the Supreme Court—had held that the FWPCA (the OPA's predecessor) constituted the exclusive remedy for removal costs and damages. In the Supreme Court's words: **[—39—]**

> Congress' intent in enacting the [FWPCA] was clearly to establish an all-encompassing program of water pollution regulation. *Every* point source discharge is prohibited unless covered by a permit, which directly subjects the discharger to the administrative apparatus established by Congress to achieve its goals. The "major purpose" of the [FWPCA] was "to establish a *comprehensive* **{-944-}** long-range policy for the elimination of water pollution." S. REP. NO. 92-414, at 95. No Congressman's remarks on the legislation were complete without reference to the "comprehensive" nature of the [FWPCA].

City of Milwaukee v. Illinois & Michigan, 451 U.S. 304, 318 (1981) (holding that the FWPCA displaced a common-law nuisance claim);[11] *see also, e.g., United States v. Dixie Carriers, Inc.*, 627 F.2d **[—40—]** 736, 737 (5th Cir. 1980) ("[W]e conclude that Congress intended for the Federal Water Pollution Control Act (FWPCA) to provide the exclusive legal remedy for the government to recover its oil spill cleanup costs[.]"); *Steuart Transp. Co. v. Allied Towing Corp.*, 596 F.2d 609, 618 (4th Cir. 1979) ("We therefore conclude that [the FWPCA] was designed to replace, rather than to supplement, the judicial remedies developed in the absence of a comprehensive statute. Since the judicial remedies are inconsistent with the statute, the statute provides the sole means for the federal government to recover oil removal costs.").[12] **[—41—] {-945-}**

And, as the Supreme Court has explained, "Congress is presumed to be aware of an administrative or judicial interpretation of a statute and to adopt that interpretation when it re-enacts a statute without change." *Lorillard v. Pons*, 434 U.S. 575, 580 (1978); *see also Keene Corp. v. United States*, 508 U.S. 200, 212 (1993) ("[W]e apply the presumption that Congress was aware of these earlier judicial interpretations and, in effect, adopted them."). We can assume, in other words, that, when it enacted the OPA in 1990, Congress knew that courts—including the U.S. Supreme Court—had routinely interpreted the FWPCA as providing the exclusive **[—42—]** remedy for removal costs. If Congress thought these interpretations were wrong, it could've easily corrected the error by making clear that the OPA was *not* to be similarly construed. But it didn't—precisely because

---

[11] To the extent it matters, that same legislative history—emphasizing the comprehensiveness of the legislation—dominates the OPA. *See, e.g.*, S. REP. NO. 101-94 (stating that the OPA "builds upon section 311 of the Clean Water Act to create *a single Federal law* providing cleanup authority, penalties, and liability for oil pollution" (emphasis added)); H.R. REP. NO. 101-242, pt. 2, at 31 ("The purpose of this legislation is to establish a comprehensive system of liability and compensation for damages caused by oil pollution[.]"); 135 CONG. REC. S9690 (daily ed. Aug. 3, 1989) (statement of Sen. Baucus) (referring to "[t]his comprehensive bill"); 135 CONG. REC. H7894 (daily ed. Nov. 1, 1989) (statement of Rep. Quillen) (calling the OPA a "much needed comprehensive oilspill bill"); 136 CONG. REC. S11536 (daily ed. Aug. 2, 1990) (statement of Sen. Mitchell) ("As the author of the Senate bill, I am pleased we are finally enacting **[—40—]** a tough, comprehensive bill."); *cf.* Patrick Nash, *The Adequacy of the Oil Pollution Act's Compensation Scheme in the Case of a Catastrophic Oil Spill*, 7 J. MIN. L. & POL'Y 105, 108 (1991) ("As was the case with the floor debate for FWPCA, the floor debate regarding OPA was replete with redundant exclamations of 'comprehensive[ness].'").

[12] Savage insists that the Supreme Court's decision in *Exxon Shipping Co. v. Baker*, 554 U.S. 471 (2008), suggests otherwise. There, the Court held that the "[FWPCA]'s penalties for water pollution . . . [do not] preempt the common law punitive-damages remedies at issue here." *Id.* at 488. For three reasons, *Baker* is inapposite.

First, the FWPCA addressed the "actual costs incurred . . . for the removal of such oil or substance by the United States Government." 33 U.S.C. § 1321(f) (1998). But it didn't address the punitive-damages remedies the Court refused to strike down in *Baker*. The OPA, by contrast, governs the very sort of costs Savage incurred in this case—including, for instance, "all removal costs," "[d]amages for injury to . . . natural resources," "[d]amages for injury to . . . real or personal property," and "[d]amages for loss of subsistence use of **[—41—]** natural resources." 33 U.S.C. § 2702(b). As to the kinds of damages it actually covers, in other words, the OPA *is exclusive*.

Second, *Baker* noted that the FWPCA has a "saving clause reserving 'obligations . . . under any provision of law for damages to any publicly owned or privately owned property resulting from a discharge of any oil.'" *Baker*, 554 U.S. at 488 (quoting 33 U.S.C. § 1321(o)). But our savings clause is materially different because it *doesn't* broadly reserve pre-existing property claims. Instead, it prefaces any "savings" with the crucial phrase: "[e]xcept as otherwise provided in this Act," 33 U.S.C. § 2751(e)—a phrase that didn't appear in the FWPCA. And, as we've said, Congress *has* provided otherwise in the OPA by foreclosing any oil-removal claims against the Government.

Third, as *Baker* rightly observed, it's "hard to conclude that a statute expressly geared to protecting 'water,' 'shorelines,' and 'natural resources' was intended to eliminate *sub silentio* oil companies' common law duties to refrain from injuring the bodies and livelihoods of private individuals." *Baker*, 554 U.S. at 488–89. Here, the equities are just the reverse: it'd be hard to conclude that a statute geared to shifting oil-pollution costs from the taxpayer to the oil industry would allow the oil industry to turn around and recover those same costs from the taxpayer. *Baker*, in short, is neither here nor there.

Congress agreed, as we do, that the OPA (like the FWPCA before it) provides the *exclusive* remedy for oil-removal costs.

D. Policy

Still resisting, Savage says that it would be unfair "to protect the Government from the consequences of its decisions when acting . . . as a tortfeasor that causes millions of dollars of property damage and environmental cleanup costs." Two thoughts on this. *First*, it simply isn't our place to second-guess the legislature's fairness determinations or to supplant its considered judgment with our own. *See Mamani v. Berzain*, 825 F.3d 1304, 1310 (11th Cir. 2016) ("[U]nless and until the first and third branches of government swap duties and responsibilities, we cannot rewrite statutes."). *Second*, there's plenty of reason to believe that the first branch *did* hope to narrowly tailor the taxpayer's burden in the event of an oil spill. The OPA, after all, puts the vessel owner first in line to pay any removal costs. 33 U.S.C. § 2702. It also employs a Fund—financed largely by taxes and penalties on the oil industry—to cover, among other things, excess costs and damages. *Id.* § 2712. And it raised the limits on oil-spill liability. *Id.* § 2704. To the extent we can divine some congressional purpose from these decisions, it would appear that one (primary) purpose was to force the oil industry to internalize the negative externalities of its business— **[—43—]** *i.e.*, to incentivize the oil industry to avoid financially and environmentally costly oil spills in the first instance.

Relying on legislative history, Savage maintains that the OPA was not meant to permanently shift liability from the Government to a vessel owner—but simply (in Savage's words) to "close[] a loophole in the patchwork of predecessor statutes whereby the owner of a vessel leaking oil could deny liability long enough to force the Government to coordinate and fund the emergency response to a fast-expanding environmental disaster[.]" As we've said, however, we needn't wade into the murky waters of the statute's legislative history because "a law is the best expositor of itself." *Pennington v. Coxe*, 6 U.S. 33, 52 (1804) (Marshall, C.J.).[13] And, through the OPA, Congress exposited itself rather clearly. **[—44—] {-946-}**

IV. Implied Repeal

Which takes us back to where we started. Savage sees this case through the lens of the repeal-by-implication doctrine, which instructs that "[c]ourts must first 'assiduously attempt' to try to construe two statutes in harmony before concluding that one impliedly repeals the other." *Miccosukee*, 619 F.3d at 1299 (quoting *Tug Allie-B*, 273 F.3d at 952 (Black, J., concurring)).

We very much doubt that this implied-repeal lens is the right way to view our case. The Supreme Court has recognized that "the expectation that there would be some

---

[13] Even if we were to accept Savage's invitation, we think *that* history may well tell a different story. Congress enacted the OPA in the wake of "[t]he 11-million gallon spill from the Exxon Valdez in Prince William Sound, Alaska, and the three spills within a 24-hour period just months later in the coastal waters of Rhode Island, the Delaware River and the Houston Ship Channel." S. Rep. No. 101-94, at 2. Congress concluded that those "four major oil spills within a three-month period suggest that spills are still too much of an accepted cost of doing business for the oil shipping industry" and that "the costs of spilling and paying for its clean-up and damage is not high enough to encourage greater industry efforts to prevent spills and develop effective techniques to contain them." *Id.* at 3. "Sound public policy," Congress made clear, "requires reversal of these relative costs." *Id.*

And the then-extant federal laws weren't doing the trick. The Senate Report noted that, "[b]etween 1971 and 1982 the United States Government [—44—] obligated $124 million from the Clean Water Act's section 311(k) revolving fund, but recovered only $49 million from spillers, for a total expenditure of $75 million in national funds." *Id.* The Report also signaled Congress's intent to move away from "taxpayer subsidies to cover cleanup costs" and towards "internaliz[ing] those costs within the oil industry and its transportation sector." *Id.* at 2. By shifting the burden of cleanup costs onto the oil industry—and by precluding the oil industry from seeking contribution payments from the Government (read: taxpayers)—the OPA seems to further, rather than to frustrate, each of these objectives.

expression of an intent to 'repeal' is particularly strong in a case . . . in which the 'repeal' would extend to virtually every case to which the statute had application." *United States v. United Cont'l Tuna Corp.*, 425 U.S. 164, 169 (1976). But the converse is also true: when a highly specific statute narrowly displaces a general one, it's not at all clear that the presumption against implied repeal applies. *See Harris v. Owens*, **[—45—]** 264 F.3d 1282, 1296 (10th Cir. 2001) ("The later statute simply addresses one particular application and carves out an exception. We see no repeal-by-implication problem."); *see also* 1A SUTHERLAND STATUTORY CONSTRUCTION § 23:16 ("Where a later special or local statute is not irreconcilable with a general statute to the degree that both statutes cannot have a coincident operation, the general statute is not repealed, and the special or local statute exists as an exception to its terms."); READING LAW at 183 (explaining that, under the general/specific canon, "the specific provision is treated as an exception to the general rule"). The reasoning behind this interpretive canon is sound: When Congress undermines an *entire* statute, we tend to view that statute as *repealed*, and we generally expect Congress to *say* that it intended so drastic a result. But when the legislature merely carves out a narrow exception to an old provision by addressing a discrete sub-issue in the original statute—think: a law specifically targeting the Carolina northern flying squirrel against the backdrop of the Endangered Species Act—it's not at all clear that the legislature is *repealing* anything. And, in this circumstance at least, we wouldn't necessarily expect Congress to *say* that it was.[14] **[—46—]** **{-947-}**

The OPA is a lot like the Carolina-northern-flying-squirrel statute we just invented—and the SAA serves as a useful substitute for the Endangered Species Act. For starters, the SAA broadly applies to admiralty claims against the Government. It governs, for instance, when a passenger on a "boat [is] swept over a dam" and injured due to the "failure of the Corps of Engineers to post properly located signs warning water craft of the dam." *Beeler v. United States*, 338 F.2d 687, 688 (3d Cir. 1964). Or when a "longshoreman" falls through the "pad-eye" of a public vessel. *Grillea v. United States*, 232 F.2d 919, 922 (2d Cir. 1956) (Hand, J.). Or when someone "tubing on the Missouri River . . . alide[s] with a submerged buoy placed in the river by the United States Coast Guard." *Harrell v. United States*, 443 F.3d 1231, 1234 (10th Cir. 2006) (cleaned up). Or when a "seaman" for the Coast Guard returns to a drydock late at night and—"in the condition for which seamen are famed"—turns some valves and sinks the drydock. *Ira S. Bushey & Sons, Inc. v. United States*, 398 F.2d 167, 169 (2d Cir. 1968) (Friendly, J.). Or any of the other countless claims that might arise on the sea.[15] The OPA, covering a mere subset of admiralty **[—47—]** claims—*viz.*, those involving oil-spill liability—addresses only a *small* piece of that much larger maritime mosaic. Far from repealing the SAA, then, the OPA simply carves out a narrow exception that governs only one of the SAA's many applications. We thus wouldn't really expect Congress to say that the OPA "repealed" anything at all.[16] **[—48—]** **{-948-}**

---

[14] Here's a hypothetical to bring this point home. Imagine a scenario in which Congress repealed the OPA tomorrow—thus ridding the U.S. Code of the OPA's detailed (and exclusive) framework for oil-removal claims. Wouldn't vessel owners (like Savage) then be able to bring common-law oil-removal claims against the United States under the SAA's general provisions? We don't see why not. And, if that's right, then it seems clear that Congress didn't *repeal* **[—46—]** any part of the SAA when it promulgated the OPA—because, if it had, there'd be no SAA to revert to once the OPA was erased. *Cf.* READING LAW at 334 ("When a statute is repealed, it falls irretrievably into oblivion. It is not half-buried in expectation of resurrection. Hence a repeal of a repealer does not revivify the statutory corpse.").

[15] Including, by the way, cases just like ours. The Government doesn't disagree, remember, that Savage *can* pursue its common-law claim against the **[—47—]** United States for costs that fall beyond the OPA's grasp—things like damage to the barge, loss of use, and lost cargo.

[16] Even if Savage were right that the Government's position amounts to a contention that the OPA impliedly repealed the SAA (to some limited extent), that implied repeal wouldn't save Savage here. Courts have long held that "Congress's intent to effect an implied repeal can be inferred when a later statute conflicts with or is repugnant to an earlier statute; or when a newer

Other courts have tackled the repeal-by-implication doctrine in precisely this way. Take the Fourth Circuit's ruling in *Strawser v. Atkins*, 290 F.3d 720 (4th Cir. 2002). That case

statute covers the whole subject of the earlier one, and clearly is intended as a substitute." *Miccosukee*, 619 F.3d at 1299; *see also King v. Cornell*, 106 U.S. 395, 396 (1882) ("While repeals by implication are not favored, it is well settled that where two acts are not in all respects repugnant, if the later act covers the whole subject of the earlier, and embraces new provisions which plainly show that the last was intended as a substitute for the first, it will operate as a repeal.").

Our decision in *Tug Allie-B* is on point. In that case, a commercial tugboat "ran aground and collided with coral reefs in the vicinity of Ledbury Reef in Biscayne National Park." *Tug Allie-B*, 273 F.3d at 936. The vessel owner filed a claim under the Limitation of Liability Act, which "limits a vessel owner's liability for any damages arising from a maritime accident to the post-accident value of the vessel and its pending freight." *Id.* at 939. The United States filed a counterclaim under the Park System Resources Protection Act (the "PSRPA"), "claiming that, pursuant to the PSRPA, it was entitled to all damages due to injuries to resources in the National Park as a result of the grounding." *Id.* Looking to the language of the statutes, this Court found that, **[—48—]** "in the absence of any explicit statutory language limiting damages under the PSRPA, . . . Congress contemplated that the Government could seek full recovery under the statute for accidents causing injury to park lands." *Id.* at 942. On the other hand, the Limitation of Liability Act "provides for a limitation on the total of all recoverable damages in a marine accident." *Id.* In light of this "conflict," we applied the PSRPA—which had no cap on damages—concluding that the "most recent" and "more specific" statute "controls." *Id.* at 949.

Our case, of course, is all-the-more compelling. While the SAA generally waives sovereign immunity for admiralty claims, the OPA doesn't. In enacting a *comprehensive* framework for oil-spill-cleanup liability, the OPA not only has no explicit waiver of sovereign immunity. It also eliminated a complete defense to liability premised on governmental negligence, and it defined "person"—in stark contrast to similar statutes like CERCLA—as including just about every governmental entity one could think of *other than* the federal government. In this way, our position is even stronger than it was in *Tug- Allie-B*, where we were left only with "silence" on the part of Congress. As in that case, then, the OPA—the statute that's both more specific and more recent—controls.

arose out of litigation between several U.S. states and most of the major tobacco companies. After the states and the tobacco companies settled, a class of Medicaid recipients who had received medical assistance for tobacco-related complications sued the states, contending that the "usual provisions for distribution of Medicaid recoveries [under 42 U.S.C. § 1396k(b)] apply to the funds the states receive from the [settlement agreement], so that . . . they have a federal right to a share of those funds." *Id.* at 728. On appeal, the Fourth Circuit **[—49—]** found that this more-general rule was preempted by a 1999 Medicaid amendment, which "expressly provide[d] that 'a State may use amounts recovered or paid to the State' under the [settlement agreement] 'for any expenditures determined appropriate by the State.'" *Id.* at 730 (quoting 42 U.S.C. § 1396b(d)(3)(B)(ii)).

In doing so, the Fourth Circuit concluded that the repeal-by-implication doctrine was inapposite. It distinguished run-of-the-mill implied-repeal decisions by observing that those "cases in- volve[d] repeals of *entire* statutes or rules." *Id.* at 733 (emphasis added). "By contrast, the effect of the 1999 amendment is highly specific. The amendment does not repeal the general operation of § 1396k(b)." *Id.* In fact, "[e]very Medicaid recipient—except those seeking tobacco money from the states—has the same rights under § 1396k(b) after the 1999 amendment as he or she had before it." *Id.* "Rather than repeal by implication a general statute (§ 1396k(b)), the 1999 amendment simply created a specific, discrete exception to that statute." *Id.* Our case is on all fours. The OPA is "highly specific." And every maritime plaintiff—except for an oil spiller—"has the same rights" after the OPA as it did before. Rather than repeal by implication the (general) SAA, the (specific) OPA simply created a discrete exception to it. As in *Strawser*, then, the repeal-by-implication doctrine is sort of beside the point.

***

Through the OPA, Congress struck a balance between the obligations of oil-vessel owners and the rights those owners might have to seek reimbursement for their oil-removal costs. Whether **[—50—]** that balance was the right one, it isn't for us to say. After careful review, we **AFFIRM**.

United States Court of Appeals
for the Eleventh Circuit

No. 21-10955

NEWBAUER
vs.
CARNIVAL CORP.

Appeal from the United States District Court for the Southern District of Florida

Decided: February 28, 2022

Citation: 26 F.4th 931, 10 Adm. R. 367 (11th Cir. 2022).

Before **WILSON, LUCK,** and **LAGOA,** Circuit Judges.

[—2—] {-932-} **LAGOA,** Circuit Judge:

Michelle Newbauer appeals from the district court's dismissal of her complaint against Carnival Corporation for failure to state a claim. Newbauer contends that the district court erred in its dismissal because she pleaded sufficient facts to support the constructive notice element of her negligence claims. Alternatively, Newbauer argues that the district court erred in dismissing her complaint without first giving her an opportunity to amend. After careful review, and with the benefit of oral argument, we affirm the district court's dismissal. **{-933-}**

I. FACTUAL AND PROCEDURAL BACKGROUND[1]

Carnival, a Panamanian corporation with its principal place of business in Miami, Florida, operates a number of cruise ships, including the *Magic*. Newbauer, a passenger onboard the *Magic*, "was walking on the Lido Deck of the vessel, near the Red Frog Bar, when she slipped on a liquid or wet, slippery transitory substance near the bar and fell." As a result of this fall, she sustained **[—3—]** "serious injuries including a patellar subluxation and a lateral meniscus tear of the right knee, which was surgically repaired."

Newbauer filed a complaint against Carnival in the Southern District of Florida, asserting claims for negligent failure to maintain and negligent failure to warn. She alleged that "the liquid or wet, slippery transitory substance" she slipped on "was located in an area of the ship that was a high traffic dining area" such that Carnival "knew or should have known of the presence of the . . . substance." Newbauer further alleged that the substance "had existed for a sufficient period of time before [her] fall" such that Carnival had actual or constructive knowledge of its presence and the opportunity to correct or warn about the hazard. In the alternative, Newbauer alleged that Carnival had actual or constructive knowledge of the substance because of "the regularly and frequently recurring nature of the hazard in that area."

Carnival filed a motion to dismiss pursuant to Rule 12(b)(6), arguing that Newbauer failed to properly plead a negligence claim. Carnival contended that Newbauer's allegations were "insufficient, without more, to put Carnival on notice of the specific alleged dangerous condition" and did "not put forward any allegations as to the open and obvious nature of the hazard pled." Instead, Carnival argued that Newbauer's allegations were "nothing more than a boilerplate recitation of the elements [of a negligence claim] followed by mere conclusory statements," which were "wholly insufficient." Newbauer opposed Carnival's motion. **[—4—]**

The district court granted Carnival's motion to dismiss. The district court found that Newbauer "failed to allege that Carnival was on either actual or constructive notice of the hazard in question" and thus failed to satisfy the pleading standards set forth in *Bell Atlantic Corp. v. Twombly*, 550 U.S. 544 (2007), and *Ashcroft v. Iqbal*, 556 U.S. 662 (2009). The district court noted that Newbauer had not alleged any facts in support of her claim that there were prior slip and fall incidents where she fell. As to her allegation about the highly trafficked dining area, the

[1] Because the procedural posture of this case involves a Federal Rule of Civil Procedure 12(b)(6) motion, we must accept the allegations of plaintiff's complaint as true. *See Chaparro v. Carnival Corp.*, 693 F.3d 1333, 1335 (11th Cir. 2012). The facts set forth in this section of the opinion therefore are taken from the complaint and construed in the light most favorable to the plaintiff.

district court found that Newbauer mistakenly conflated foreseeability with actual or constructive notice and that she had not sufficiently pled that the high trafficked area gave Carnival actual or constructive notice of the wet substance at issue. And, as to her allegation about the length of time the hazard had been present, the district court determined that it was impossible to tell, based on Newbauer's sole conclusory statement, if the condition was present for seconds, minutes, or hours. Thus, the district court explained that while Newbauer's complaint made clear that it was "*possible*" Carnival **{–934–}** was on notice, the complaint did not allege sufficient facts to state a claim that were "*plausible* on [their] face sufficient to survive a motion to dismiss." This appeal ensued.

II. STANDARD OF REVIEW

"We review *de novo* the district court's grant of a Rule 12(b)(6) motion to dismiss for failure to state a claim, accepting the complaint's allegations as true and construing them in the light most favorable to the plaintiff." *Chaparro v. Carnival Corp.*, 693 **[—5—]** F.3d 1333, 1335 (11th Cir. 2012) (quoting *Cinotto v. Delta Air Lines Inc.*, 674 F.3d 1285, 1291 (11th Cir. 2012)).

III. ANALYSIS

On appeal, Newbauer contends that the district court erred in dismissing her complaint for failure to state a claim. Newbauer asserts that she pleaded sufficient facts under Rule 8(a)(2) to support the constructive notice element of her negligence claims. She also asserts that the district court applied a heightened pleading standard in contravention of Rule 8(a)(2).

Federal Rule of Civil Procedure 8(a)(2) requires a complaint to provide "a short and plain statement of the claim showing that the pleader is entitled to relief." The pleading standard in Rule 8 "does not require 'detailed factual allegations,' but it demands more than an unadorned, the-defendant-unlawfully-harmed-me accusation." *Chaparro*, 693 F.3d at 1337 (quoting *Iqbal*, 556 U.S. at 678). Thus, "[a] complaint that provides 'labels and conclusions' or 'a formulaic recitation of the elements of a cause of action' is not adequate to survive a Rule 12(b)(6) motion to dismiss." *Id.* (quoting *Twombly*, 550 U.S. at 555). Instead, the complaint "must contain sufficient factual matter, accepted as true, to 'state a claim to relief that is plausible on its face.'" *Id.* (quoting *Iqbal*, 556 U.S. at 678). To do so, "[a] facially plausible claim must allege facts that are more than merely *possible*," and a plaintiff's factual allegations that are "'merely consistent with' a defendant's liability" will not be considered facially plausible. *Id.* (emphasis added) (quoting *Iqbal*, 556 U.S. at 678). Indeed, "[a] claim has facial plausibility when **[—6—]** the plaintiff pleads factual content that allows the court to draw the reasonable inference that the defendant is liable for the misconduct alleged." *Iqbal*, 556 U.S. at 678. And "if allegations are indeed more conclusory than factual, then the court does not have to assume their truth." *Chaparro*, 693 F.3d at 1337.

While "[t]he plausibility standard is not akin to a 'probability requirement,' . . . it asks for more than a sheer possibility that a defendant has acted unlawfully." *Iqbal*, 556 U.S. at 678 (quoting *Twombly*, 550 U.S. at 556). This analysis is not formulaic; instead, "[d]etermining whether a complaint states a plausible claim for relief [is] . . . a context-specific task that requires the reviewing court to draw on its judicial experience and common sense" in reviewing the plaintiff's allegations. *Id.* at 679. Additionally, "[t]hreadbare recitals of the elements of a cause of action" and "conclusory statements" are insufficient. *Id.* at 678 (citing *Twombly*, 550 U.S. at 555). When evaluating a motion to dismiss, the first step is to "eliminate any allegations in the complaint that are merely legal conclusions." *Am. Dental Ass'n v. Cigna Corp.*, 605 F.3d 1283, 1290 (11th Cir. 2010). The second step is to assume the veracity of well-pleaded factual allegations and "then **{–935–}** determine whether they plausibly give rise to an entitlement to relief." *Id.*

"Maritime law governs actions arising from alleged torts committed aboard a ship sailing in navigable waters," and we "'rely on general principles of negligence law'" in analyzing those actions. *Guevara v. NCL (Bahamas) Ltd.*, 920 F.3d 710, 720, 7 Adm. R. 476, 481 (11th Cir. 2019) (quoting *Chaparro*, 693 F.3d at 1336). The elements of a negligence **[—7—]** claim are well settled: "a plaintiff must allege that (1) the defendant had a duty to protect the plaintiff from a particular injury; (2) the defendant breached that duty; (3) the breach actually and proximately caused the plaintiff's injury; and (4) the plaintiff suffered actual harm." *Franza v. Royal Caribbean Cruises, Ltd.*, 772 F.3d 1225, 1253, 2 Adm. R. 582, 603 (11th Cir. 2014) (quoting *Chaparro*, 693 F.3d at 1336). "With respect to the duty element in a maritime context, 'a shipowner owes the duty of exercising reasonable care towards those lawfully aboard the vessel who are not members of the crew.'" *Guevara*, 920 F.3d at 720, 7 Adm. R. at 481 (quoting *Kermarec v. Compagnie Generale Transatlantique*, 358 U.S. 625, 630 (1959)). "This standard 'requires, as a prerequisite to imposing liability, that the carrier have had actual or constructive notice of [a] risk-creating condition, at least where, as here, the menace is one commonly encountered on land and not clearly linked to nautical adventure.'" *Id.*, 7 Adm. R. at 481 (alteration in original) (quoting *Keefe v. Bahama Cruise Line, Inc.*, 867 F.2d 1318, 1322 (11th Cir. 1989)); *see also Kornberg v. Carnival Cruise Lines, Inc.*, 741 F.2d 1332, 1334 (11th Cir. 1984) (explaining that a shipowner "is not liable to passengers as an insurer, but only for its negligence"). In order to survive Carnival's motion to dismiss, Newbauer therefore had to plead sufficient facts to support each element of her claim, including that Carnival had actual or constructive notice about the dangerous condition. *Amy v. Carnival Corp.*, 961 F.3d 1303, 1308, 8 Adm. R. 424, 426–27 (11th Cir. 2020).

Actual notice exists when the defendant knows about the dangerous condition, and constructive notice exists where "the **[—8—]** shipowner ought to have known of the peril to its passengers." *Keefe*, 867 F.2d at 1322. A plaintiff "can establish constructive notice with evidence that the 'defective condition exist[ed] for a sufficient period of time to invite corrective measures.'" *Guevara*, 920 F.3d at 720, 7 Adm. R. at 481 (alteration in original) (quoting *Monteleone v. Bahama Cruise Line, Inc.*, 838 F.2d 63, 65 (2d Cir. 1988)). "Alternatively, a plaintiff can establish constructive notice with evidence of substantially similar incidents in which 'conditions substantially similar to the occurrence in question must have caused the prior accident.'" *Id.* (quoting *Jones v. Otis Elevator Co.*, 861 F.2d 655, 661–62 (11th Cir. 1988)).

This appeal requires us to determine whether Newbauer alleged a facially plausible claim that Carnival knew or "ought to have known of" the hazardous wet surface that caused her to slip. *Keefe*, 867 F.2d at 1322. Reviewing Newbauer's complaint and accepting her allegations as true, we conclude that Newbauer failed to include any factual allegations that were sufficient to satisfy the pleading standard set forth in *Iqbal* and *Twombly* such that it is facially plausible that Carnival had actual or constructive notice of the dangerous condition. Rather, her complaint contains only conclusory allegations as to actual or constructive notice. For example, Newbauer alleged in her complaint that Carnival had constructive notice of the wet substance on the deck because it was in a "high traffic dining area," but she failed to provide any factual allegations supporting the notion that high traffic in the area gave Carnival notice of the condition. Similarly, **{-936-}** while Newbauer alleged in **[—9—]** her complaint that the substance "had existed for a sufficient period of time before [her] fall" such that Carnival had constructive notice of its presence, she failed to allege any facts in support of this conclusory allegation. Likewise, Newbauer failed to allege a sufficient factual basis to support her conclusory allegation that Carnival had actual or constructive knowledge of the hazard based on the "regularly and frequently recurring nature of the hazard in that area." And "[w]hile legal conclusions can provide the framework of a complaint, they must be supported by factual allegations," which are noticeably absent from Newbauer's complaint. *Iqbal*, 556 U.S. at 679.

Newbauer argues, however, that her allegation that the wet substance was in a high traffic area supports the following series of inferences: (1) because the area was highly trafficked, crewmembers working in the nearby bars and restaurants would be present there; (2) before and at the time of her fall, crewmembers were staffing the surrounding bar and dining areas; and (3) those crewmembers had a clear, unobstructed view of the area in which she fell. Based on these inferences, Newbauer contends that Carnival had constructive notice of the wet substance on the deck.

Newbauer's argument is unpersuasive because she failed to allege any facts suggesting the amount of time the hazard existed on the deck before she fell or that there were crewmembers monitoring the area. Indeed, Newbauer's complaint did not allege any facts supporting the conclusions that the substance had been on the floor for a sufficient period of time to create constructive notice, **[—10—]** that this was a recurring issue, or that there may have been employees in the area who observed the hazard and failed to take corrective action.

Additionally, we conclude that Newbauer's reliance on this Court's decision in *Yusko v. NCL (Bahamas), Ltd.*, 4 F.4th 1164, 9 Adm. R. 403 (11th Cir. 2021), is misplaced. *Yusko* reaffirmed that where, as here, a plaintiff is proceeding on a theory of direct liability against the shipowner for the negligent maintenance of the premises, the plaintiff must establish notice as part of her negligence claim. *Id.* at 1167–69, 9 Adm. R. at 404–06. Here, Newbauer sued Carnival directly for negligent maintenance and failure to warn and has not raised any negligence claims under the theory of vicarious liability.

Finally, Newbauer asserts that the district court erred by not granting her leave to amend *sua sponte* before dismissing the complaint. But our precedent is clear that "[a] district court is not required to grant a plaintiff leave to amend [her] complaint sua sponte when the plaintiff, who is represented by counsel, never filed a motion to amend nor requested leave to amend before the district court." *Wagner v. Daewoo Heavy Indus. Am. Corp.*, 314 F.3d 541, 542 (11th Cir. 2002) (en banc). Because Newbauer never sought leave to amend the complaint, we conclude that there was no error.

IV. CONCLUSION

Accordingly, for the reasons stated, we conclude that the district court did not err in dismissing Newbauer's complaint, and we **[—11—]** affirm the district court's dismissal of Newbauer's complaint for failure to state a claim.

AFFIRMED.

United States Court of Appeals
for the Eleventh Circuit

No. 20-14639

FUENTES
VS.
CLASSICA CRUISE OPERATOR LTD

Appeal from the United States District Court for the Southern District of Florida

Decided: May 3, 2022

Citation: 32 F.4th 1311, 10 Adm. R. 371 (11th Cir. 2022).

Before **JORDAN**, **PRYOR**, and **MARCUS**, Circuit Judges.

[—2—] {-1315-} JORDAN, Circuit Judge:

Under maritime law, a ship owner in "navigable waters owes to all who are on board for purposes not inimical to [its] legitimate interests the duty of exercising reasonable care under the circumstances of each case." *Kermarec v. Compagnie Generale de Transatlantique*, 358 U.S. 625, 632 (1959). In this case, which arises in a summary judgment posture, a cruise ship passenger and one of his friends assaulted another passenger, Reinier Fuentes, during disembarkation. Our main task, applying *Kermarec* and its progeny, is to determine what duty the cruise line, Classica Cruise Operator Ltd., owed to Mr. Fuentes under maritime law. *See The Admiral Peoples*, 295 U.S. 649, 654 (1935) (injury suffered by a passenger when falling from the gangplank during disembarkation "presented a case within the jurisdiction of admiralty"); *Minott v. M/Y BRUNELLO*, 891 F.3d 1277, 1283, 6 Adm. R. 450, 453 (11th Cir. 2018) ("An injury caused by a vessel in navigable waters is a maritime tort.").[1]

I

As this appeal arises from the district court's grant of summary judgment in favor of Classica, our review is de novo, and **[—3—]** we view the facts and inferences in Mr. Fuentes' favor. *See Taylor v. Rojas*, 141 S. Ct. 52, 53 n.1 (2020); *Tolan v. Cotton*, 572 U.S. 650, 657 (2014); *Jenkins v. Nell*, 26 F.4th 1243, 1249 (11th Cir. 2022). Viewed in that light, here is what the record shows.

Mr. Fuentes and his wife were passengers on a two-night cruise aboard the *Grand Classica*, a ship operated by Classica. On the evening of May 12, 2018, they were playing foosball on the ship when they were interrupted by Clynt Hadley, another passenger. According to Mr. Fuentes, Mr. Hadley intentionally bumped into the foosball table and made a comment directed at his wife. Mr. Fuentes did not respond to Mr. Hadley's comment and did not report the encounter to any of Classica's employees.

The next morning, after the *Grand Classica* docked, Customs and Border Protection **{-1316-}** stopped the disembarkation process, causing the lobby on Deck 5 to become crowded. At the time, Mr. Fuentes estimates there were approximately 20 passengers— including himself and his wife—cueing up in the immigration line waiting to disembark.

Mr. Fuentes noticed Mr. Hadley attempting to cut in front of them. He told Mr. Hadley that he should go to the back of the line and not attempt to "skip" in front of the other passengers. A verbal altercation between Mr. Fuentes and Mr. Hadley then ensued.

Sayyed Azzad Alam, a *Grand Classica* security officer, was standing nearby when the verbal exchange began and radioed the **[—4—]** chief of security for help. Mr. Azzad Alam then approached Mr. Fuentes and Mr. Hadley—who were about four to five feet apart—stepped between them and asked that they "calm down." D.E. 48-1 at 112, 116. After Mr. Azzad Alam spoke to Mr. Hadley, he then turned to speak to Mr. Fuentes. At that point,

[1] We also address a second issue—whether the district court erred by denying Mr. Fuentes' motion for sanctions based on Classica's alleged failure to prepare its designee for his Rule 30(b)(6) deposition.

Mr. Hadley "blindsided" Mr. Fuentes by punching him in the face and charging at him. *Id.* at 117; *see id.* at 110, 113. Mr. Fuentes tried to grab Mr. Hadley in a headlock, but Mr. Hadley and one of his friends knocked Mr. Fuentes to the ground, injuring his right elbow in the process. *See id.* at 114, 117-18, 121. The takedown, according to Mr. Fuentes, was a "spur of the moment type of thing." *Id.* at 121.

Customs personnel responded to the scene, and then two of the ship's security officers, including the chief of security, arrived. *See id.* at 126-28. Police were called, and Mr. Fuentes received first aid. He later underwent surgery and was hospitalized for several days.

In his complaint, Mr. Fuentes alleged that Classica was negligent, and responsible for his injuries, because it failed to (a) reasonably and properly train security personnel; (b) have adequate security measures, including adequate security presence and surveillance cameras; (c) warn him of the danger of being physically assaulted while onboard the vessel; (d) promulgate and enforce policies and procedures designed to prevent passengers from physically assaulting other passengers; and (e) exercise reasonable care under the circumstances. The district court granted sum- **[—5—]** mary judgment in favor of Classica, ruling that there was no evidence suggesting that Classica had actual or constructive notice of the risk of harm to someone like Mr. Fuentes.

II

As noted, federal maritime law governs this action because Mr. Fuentes was injured while waiting to disembark the *Grand Classica*. *See The Admiral Peoples*, 295 U.S. at 654; *Minott*, 891 F.3d at 1283, 6 Adm. R. at 453. We therefore dismiss Mr. Fuentes' contention, *see* Appellant's Br. at 25 n.8, that we are required to apply state law given the diversity of the parties. *See Pope & Talbot v. Hawn*, 346 U.S. 406, 410–11 (1953) (rejecting the contention that a maritime tort is controlled by state law when the parties are diverse).

When "analyzing a maritime tort case, we rely on general principles of negligence law." *Chaparro v. Carnival Corp.*, 693 F.3d 1333, 1336 (11th Cir. 2012) (internal quotation marks omitted). To prevail on his negligence claims, Mr. Fuentes had to establish that (1) Classica had a duty to protect him from a particular injury; (2) Classica breached that duty; (3) the breach actually and proximately caused his injury; and (4) he suffered actual harm. *See Carroll v. Carnival Corp.*, 955 F.3d 1260, 1264, 8 Adm. R. 412, 413 (11th Cir. 2020). This appeal concerns the duty element, which presents a question of **{–1317–}** law. *See Coumou v. United States*, 107 F.3d 290, 295 (5th Cir. 1997), *opinion withdrawn and superseded in part on reh'g*, 114 F.3d 64 (5th Cir. 1997); *Sutton v. Earles*, 26 F.3d 903, 912 n.8 (9th Cir. 1994); *Matter of Flowers*, 526 F.2d 242, 244 (8th Cir. 1975). **[—6—]**

A

A cruise line like Classica owes its passengers "a 'duty of reasonable care' under the circumstances." *Sorrels v. NCL (Bahamas) Ltd.*, 796 F.3d 1275, 1279, 3 Adm. R. 659, 659 (11th Cir. 2015). Generally speaking, a duty of care exists under maritime law "when injury is foreseeable or when contractual or other relations of the parties impose it. In determining the existence of [a] duty a court must examine and weigh the probability of an accident, the potential extent of the injury, and the cost of adequate precautions." 1 Thomas Schoenbaum, Admiralty and Maritime Law § 5:4 (6th ed. & 2021 update) (footnotes omitted).

Our cases reflect the same understanding. For example, we have held that "[l]iability [under maritime law] for a failure to warn . . . arises from foreseeability, or the knowledge that particular conduct will create danger." *Daigle v. Point Landing, Inc.*, 616 F.2d 825, 827 (5th Cir. 1980). *See also* 1 Robert Force & Martin J. Norris, The Law of Maritime Personal Injuries § 8:8 (5th ed. & Dec. 2021 update) ("The duty of care includes the duty to anticipate danger that is reasonably foreseeable."); Restatement (Third) of Torts: Liab. for Physical & Emotional Harm § 7(a) (Am. L. Inst. 2010) ("An actor ordinarily has a duty to exercise reasonable care when the actor's conduct creates a risk of physical harm.").

"In this circuit, the maritime standard of reasonable care usually requires that the cruise [line] have actual or constructive knowledge of the risk-creating condition." *Sorrels*, 796 F.3d at 1286, 3 Adm. R. at 665. Classica's duty and potential liability therefore "'hinge[ ] on **[—7—]** whether it knew or should have known' of the dangerous condition." *Carroll*, 955 F.3d at 1264, 8 Adm. R. at 413 (quoting *Keefe v. Bahama Cruise Line, Inc.*, 867 F.2d 1318, 1322 (11th Cir. 1989). Mr. Fuentes recognizes this, as he acknowledges that "this is a case about notice." Appellant's Br. at 2.[2]

This case involves an attack on one passenger by other passengers. In the context of passenger-on-passenger violence, a cruise line has a duty to warn and/or protect when it or its employees reasonably apprehend the danger such that the attack was foreseeable. *See, e.g., Colavito v. Gonzales*, 1981 WL 164457, at *4 (S.D. Tex. Feb. 25, 1981) (cited with approval in 1 Schoenbaum, Admiralty and Maritime Law, at § 5:11); *Doe v. NCL (Bahamas) Ltd.*, 2012 WL 5512314, at *4 (S.D. Fla. Nov. 14, 2012); 1 Force & Norris, The Law of Maritime Personal Injuries, at § 9:16 (citing cases). *See also H.S. ex rel. R.S. v. Carnival Corp.*, 727 F. App'x 1003, 1006 (11th Cir. 2018) (unpublished) ("Because the proximate cause of H.S.'s injury was an intervening criminal act **[—8—]** by 'a fellow passenger,' Carnival could not be liable in negligence unless the 'injury by its nature could have been reasonably anticipated **{–1318–}** or naturally expected to occur or reasonably foreseen in time [for it] to have prevented the injury."); Restatement (Third) of Torts: Physical and Emotional Harm, at § 19 ("The conduct of a defendant can lack reasonable care insofar as it foreseeably combines with or permits the improper conduct of the plaintiff or a third party.").

Before reviewing the evidence as to notice, we address Mr. Fuentes' framing of the foreseeability inquiry. Mr. Fuentes argues that the district court erred in viewing "the alleged harm" as physical altercations during the disembarkation of cruise ships. *See* Appellant's Br. at 9. As he sees things, Classica had a duty to warn about or prevent Mr. Hadley's "foreseeable attack" because it knows that verbal disputes between passengers—no matter the circumstances in which they occur—can lead to physical altercations. *See id.* at 9, 11, 18, 22.

Assuming that Mr. Fuentes is correct that, as a behavioral and social matter, verbal disagreements can turn into physical confrontations, the foreseeability analysis that he advocates is described at too high a level of generality and ignores too many variables. Cruise ships carry hundreds (and sometimes thousands) of passengers on each voyage, and those persons physically congregate and interact with each other in countless numbers of ways during the trip (at dinner, at poolside, at shows, at the bar, at the casino, at the shops, at excursions, at the nightclub, etc.). Because **[—9—]** a cruise line is not "an insurer" of its passengers' safety, *see Keefe*, 867 at 1322, the foreseeability determination must have some connection to the events that gave rise to the negligence claim. After all, a cruise line's duty is to protect its passengers "from a *particular* injury." *Chaparro*, 693 F.3d at 1336 (emphasis added). As one district court has put it, a plaintiff in a maritime tort case "cannot avoid summary judgment on some generalized theory of foreseeability that is divorced from the particular events in question." *Weiner v. Carnival Cruise Lines*, 2012 WL 5199604, at *4 (S.D. Fla. Oct. 22, 2012). *See also* Restatement (Third) of Torts: Physical and Emotional Harm, at § 7(a),

[2] Based on the Supreme Court's decision in *New Jersey Steam-Boat Co. v. Brockett*, 121 U.S. 637, 645–46 (1887), we have held that where a crewmember assaults a passenger, the *Kermarec* "reasonable care" standard does not apply, and the owner of the ship is strictly and vicariously liable. *See Doe v. Celebrity Cruises, Inc.*, 394 F.3d 891, 908–09, 913 (11th Cir. 2004). *Accord* 1 Schoenbaum, Admiralty and Maritime Law, at § 5:11 (a vessel owner "is liable without negligence if the injury to a passenger is caused by the intentional misconduct of the crew"). Because Mr. Fuentes was assaulted by fellow passengers, *Doe* is not applicable and we apply the "reasonable care" standard.

comment j ("The extent of foreseeable risk depends on the specific facts of the case and cannot be usefully assessed for a category of cases.").

Take *K.T. v. Royal Caribbean Cruises, Ltd.*, 931 F.3d 1041, 1043, 7 Adm. R. 507, 507 (11th Cir. 2019), which involved a maritime negligence claim against a cruise line by a minor who was sexually assaulted by other passengers. In addressing the issue of notice at the motion to dismiss stage, we focused on incidents involving the same type of harm suffered by the plaintiff and held that the allegations in the complaint were "enough to establish that the danger of sexual assault in general and of sexual assault on minors in particular was foreseeable, and indeed was known" to the cruise line. *See id.* at 1044, 7 Adm. R. at 508.

A similar case is *Chaparro*, 693 F.3d at 1335-37, where the claim was that a cruise line failed to warn passengers of dangers at Coki Beach in St. Thomas, one of the ship's ports of call. Shots **[—10—]** were fired during a gang member's funeral, and a passenger who was on the way back to the ship after visiting Coki Beach was killed by gunfire. *See id.* at 1335. After holding that a cruise line has a duty to warn passengers of known dangers at ports of call, we explained that the complaint was sufficient to state a plausible claim for negligent failure to warn because it alleged that the cruise line generally knew of gang violence and public shootings in St. Thomas; knew of Coki Beach's reputation for drug sales, theft, and gang violence; knew or should have known about the gang member's funeral **{-1319-}** taking place near Coki Beach; encouraged passengers to visit Coki Beach; and failed to warn passengers of the dangers there. *See id.* at 1337.

B

"Actual notice exists when the defendant knows about the dangerous condition[.]" *Newbauer v. Carnival Corp.*, 26 F.4th 931, 935, 10 Adm. R. 367, 369 (11th Cir. 2022). Mr. Fuentes argues that Classica had actual notice that Mr. Hadley was going to attack him because it "had multiple security officers present during the several-minutes long verbal dispute . . . but failed to timely intervene" and because it hired a security company, G4S, to help with crowd control. *See* Appellant's Br. at 9, 13. These assertions fail for a few reasons.

First, although the presence of a security officer (or an outside security company) during disembarkation connotes some awareness of the need to maintain order, a verbal dispute does not provide actual notice that a physical assault is to follow. *See, e.g., Amy v. Carnival Corp.*, 961 F.3d 1303, 8 Adm. R. 424 (11th Cir. 2020) (decid- **[—11—]** ing whether the record contained evidence from which a reasonable jury could conclude that Carnival knew or should have known that children could climb or pass through the Deck 14 guard rail). Verbal disputes occur every day in various walks of life, but thankfully they do not always lead to violent altercations. *See* Restatement (Third) of Torts: Physical and Emotional Harm, at § 19, comment f ("In many situations, the possibility of criminal misconduct is so slight that an actor is not negligent for failing to take the possibility into account.").

Second, contrary to Mr. Fuentes' claim, the security officer who was at Deck 5 intervened before the assault. He separated Mr. Fuentes and Mr. Hadley, told the men to calm down, and called for additional help. As Mr. Fuentes himself acknowledged, he was "blind-sided" by Mr. Hadley's punch, and the attack was a "spur of the moment type of thing." D.E. 48-1 at 116–121. Under the circumstances, Classica could not have foreseen the assault on Mr. Fuentes. *See Colavito*, 1981 WL 164457, at *2–*3.

Third, there is no evidence suggesting that Classica had reason to believe that Mr. Hadley posed a specific danger to Mr. Fuentes or any other passenger. Neither Mr. Fuentes nor Mr. Hadley reported their encounter at the foosball table the previous night to Classica.

In sum, Mr. Fuentes has not presented sufficient evidence to create an issue of fact as to whether Classica had actual notice that Mr.

Hadley or other passengers would attack him during disembarkation. **[—12—]**

C

Mr. Fuentes also contends that Classica had constructive notice of a dangerous or risk-creating condition. Constructive notice may be established through evidence of previous similar incidents or the cruise line's prior warnings regarding the specific danger. *See, e.g., Sorrels*, 796 F.3d at 1288–1289, 3 Adm. R. at 666–67 (holding that testimony the ship's employees would post a warning sign on the pool deck after it rained was enough to create an issue of material fact as to whether there was notice that the deck was slippery when wet).

The most important aspect of the summary judgment record, in our view, is that there is not a single documented violent altercation between passengers during disembarkation aboard the *Grand Classica* or any of Classica's other cruise ships. Indeed, the only incident in the record of passenger-on-passenger violence aboard any ship in the Classica fleet (under any circumstances) involved a domestic dispute between a husband and wife inside of a **{–1320–}** private stateroom cabin. This single incident, which is different in kind from the assault on Mr. Fuentes, did not constitute constructive notice to Classica about the likelihood of physical altercations during disembarkation.

Based on the deposition testimony of Classica's chief of security, it is reasonable to infer that some disputes had occurred on prior voyages during disembarkation. Mr. Fuentes argues that it is also reasonable to infer that these disputes were physical alter- **[—13—]** cations, but the excerpt he relies on does not support that contention. Here is the excerpt:

> Q: Is there anything that you yourself or your staff that you wish were done differently to prevent the physical assault of Mr. Fuentes?
>
> [. . .]
>
> THE WITNESS: It was a daily routine. And as I said, it is cruse ship, people are disembarking on the line. And when there was a small argument, the security staff went and did what they are to do. They separated and removed the – they deescalated the matter.

D.E. 48-3 at 116. Mr. Fuentes says that the phrase "when there was" indicates that physical altercations between passengers were a regular occurrence. *See* Appellant's Br. at 16. We disagree, for the question posed to the chief security officer was about the attack on Mr. Fuentes, and not about attacks against other passengers on different occasions. And insofar as the chief security officer explained that "things happen" during disembarkation, *see* D.E. 48-3 at 116, there is no indication that "things" referred to physical violence between passengers. And no fair inference to that effect can be drawn from that single ambiguous statement.

Mr. Fuentes also points to prior incidents involving aggressive, intoxicated male passengers on another Classica ship. *See* Appellant's Br. at 9. Those incidents, however, did not escalate **[—14—]** into physical violence, and therefore did not provide constructive notice.

Mr. Fuentes cites to *Carideo v. Whet Travel, Inc.*, 2018 WL 1461678 (S.D. Fla. March 23, 2018), which also involved an assault by some passengers against another. In that case, the district court ruled that the plaintiff "barely" survived a motion for summary judgment with respect to notice on his claim that the cruise line was negligent due to a lack of preparation for, and deterrence of, attacks in general. *See id.* at *8, *12. The salient facts in *Carideo* were, however, very different: the voyage was a three-day groove/electronic music cruise catering to 2,200 young adults; the cruise line advertised and served large amounts of alcohol (it had bar stations all over the ship, sold buckets of beer, and promoted discounts on multiple-beer purchases); there was evidence of five prior passenger-on-passenger assaults on the cruise line's ships in the previous three years; and the cruise line's director of security testified in another case about repeated demands for more security officers aboard ships. *See id.* at *3, *7. Without passing on the correctness of *Carideo,* we believe it is factually distinguishable.

D

Mr. Fuentes contends that the district court improperly disregarded certain opinions of his expert, Kim Peterson. *See* Appellant's Br. at 14. As relevant here, Mr. Peterson stated in his report that Classica "failed to follow the ship's usual and customary protocol for passenger debarkation, i.e., passengers queue-up to ap- **[—15—]** proach the gangway guard station via two stateroom passageways directly outside the debarkation gangway guard station," which "clearly was intended to avoid the potential **{-1321-}** for a chaotic and threatening environment." D.E. 48-9 at 8.[3]

Whatever its merit, this opinion by Mr. Petersen did not address the issue of notice, which as Mr. Fuentes acknowledges is the critical question on appeal. It went, instead, to whether Classica was actively negligent—and created a dangerous condition— by failing to follow its own disembarkation procedures (a theory Mr. Fuentes has not pursued on appeal). To the extent that the district court may have erred by dismissing or ignoring Mr. Petersen's opinion, any such error was harmless. *Cf. Colan v. Mesa Petroleum Co.,* 951 F.2d 1512, 1518 (9th Cir. 1991) ("Because our review is independent, any error committed by the district court in weighing the evidence, discerning inferences from disputed facts, and in determining credibility was harmless.").

III

Mr. Fuentes asserts that Grant Plummer, Classica's corporate representative, was not adequately prepared for his Rule 30(b)(6) deposition on two topics—prior incidents of "aggressive behavior" on ships in Classica's fleet over the past three years, and how many security officers were present on Deck 5 when the as- **[—16—]** sault occurred. He argues that the magistrate judge and the district court erred in denying his motion for sanctions, which requested attorney's fees and sought to bind Classica to the answers given by Mr. Plummer during his deposition. He adds that, to make matters worse, after the Rule 30(b)(6) deposition Classica provided a security log indicating that multiple security officers were present, and Mr. Plummer submitted a declaration addressing whether there had been any incidents of passenger-on-passenger violence on Classica's ships. The district court, he says, considered these submissions in its summary judgment order. *See* Appellant's Br. at 19-26.

A

We review a district court's order denying a motion for sanctions for abuse of discretion. *See Beck v. Prupis,* 162 F.3d 1090, 1100 (11th Cir. 1998). This standard gives the district court a "range of choice . . . so long as that choice does not constitute a clear error of judgment." *United States v. Frazier,* 387 F.3d 1244, 1259 (11th Cir. 2004) (en banc) (internal quotation marks and citation omitted). In other words, a district court has "broad, yet not unbridled, discretion" in deciding whether to impose evidentiary sanctions. *Citronelle-Mobile Gathering, Inc. v. Watkins,* 943 F.2d 1297, 1305 (11th Cir. 1991) (internal quotation Marks omitted).

Rule 30(b)(6) allows a party to depose a corporation. The rule requires that party, "[i]n its notice or subpoena[,]" to "describe with reasonable particularity the matters for examination." Fed. R. Civ. P. 30(b)(6). Once properly noticed, the corporation **[—17—]** must designate a person (or persons) "who consent to testify on its behalf" and "may set out the matters on which each person will testify." *Id.* During the deposition, the designee is required to "testify about information known or reasonably available to the [corporation]." *Id.*

[3] Mr. Peterson's opinion does not appear to take into account that Customs and Border Protection stopped the disembarkation process on the morning of the incident, causing Deck 5 to become crowded. *See* D.E. 48-3 at 81.

The corporation's duty to prepare a Rule 30(b)(6) witness extends, "beyond matters personally known to [the] designee," to all information reasonably available to the corporation, "whether from **{–1322–}** documents, past employees, or other sources." *Brazos River Auth. v. GE Ionics, Inc.*, 469 F.3d 416, 433 (5th Cir. 2006); *Kartagener v. Carnival Corp.*, 380 F. Supp. 3d 1290, 1294 (S.D. Fla. 2019). If the designee is not able to answer questions regarding the subject matter he was designated to testify about, the corporation has failed to satisfy its obligation to prepare the designee and may be subject to sanctions. *See Black Horse Lane Ass'n, L.P. v. Dow Chem. Corp.*, 228 F.3d 275, 304 (3d Cir. 2000).

But a Rule 30(b)(6) deposition is not a memory test, and "[a]bsolute perfection is not required of a . . . witness." *QBE Ins. Corp. v. Jorda Enters., Inc.*, 277 F.R.D. 676, 691 (S.D. Fla. 2012). Accordingly, the "fact that a designee could not answer every question on a certain topic does not necessarily mean that the corporation failed to comply with its obligation[s]." *Id. See also Dapron v. Spire, Inc.*, 329 F.R.D. 223, 227 (E.D. Mo. 2019) (explaining that a "deposing party may not demand that a corporate designee be prepared to speak with encyclopedic authority"). **[—18—]**

B

We start with Mr. Plummer's testimony about how many security officers were at Deck 5 when Mr. Fuentes was assaulted. The district court, by affirming the magistrate judge's order denying sanctions, essentially concluded that Mr. Plummer's testimony, though imprecise, was not so inconsistent with the incident log discovered and produced after his deposition that it rose to the level of sanctionable failure to prepare under Rule 30(b)(6). *See* D.E. 74 at 11; D.E. 88 at 2.

Mr. Fuentes argues that Mr. Plummer was not adequately prepared because he answered that Classica was "unaware" whether any of its security officers were present when the heated verbal exchange with Mr. Hadley began. *See* Appellant's Br. at 22. But the deposition transcript tells a different story:

Q: So[,] the incident report indicates that there was no employee present in the area attempting to defuse the situation.

A: What I remember is that security got involved.

Q: Okay.

A: Security was there[,] and they tried to get involved, and then they had to contact the – the police, shoreside authorities to come on.

[. . .] **[—19—]**

Q: -- do you even know in this lobby where people congregate whether or not there was [*sic*] even employees in the area?

A: As I've already stated, there were multiple employees in the area.

Q: How do you know that?

A: How I know that [*sic*], because we have a whole process that we follow.

Q: How do you know the process was being followed?

A: We have reports of the crew members that it was being followed.

D.E. 48-5 at 40–42.

Mr. Plummer's statements do not differ substantively from the account that appears in the incident report produced by Classica after the Rule 30(b)(6) deposition. In that report, Mr. Azzad Alam—the security officer who initially intervened in the scuffle—wrote that Mr. Fuentes and Mr. Hadley "were using abusive language, [and] before the matter get heat up [*sic*] [he] intervene[d] and tr[ied] to separate [them.]" D.E. 43-1. Mr. Azzad Alam also wrote that he called for the chief of security to assist him and that "he arrived [on] the scene immediately and tr[ied] to pacify **{-1323-}** the guest, but . . . Mr. Hadley . . . gave a punch [*sic*] to guest . . . Mr. Fuentes[.]" *Id.* Mr. Plummer's statements on Clas- **[—20—]** sica's behalf, however sparse, do not contradict this telling. At the very least, there was no abuse of discretion in ruling that Mr. Plummer's testimony on this point was not sanctionable failure under Rule 30(b)(6).

C

That leaves Mr. Plummer's testimony about eight prior incidents of "aggressive behavior" on Classica's ships. Mr. Plummer said that he had no knowledge as to seven of those incidents involving passengers on other Classica ships, and Mr. Fuentes focuses on his lack of information about an incident on May 11, 2018. This incident, according to Mr. Plummer's subsequent declaration, involved the domestic dispute between a husband and wife in their stateroom that turned into a physical altercation. *See* D.E. 36-2 at 2.

The district court, again affirming the magistrate judge's order, concluded that Mr. Plummer's testimony, when viewed in the context of the extensive deposition as a whole, was a lapse of preparation that did not rise to the level of sanctionable conduct. *See* D.E. 74 at 10; D.E. 88 at 2. Again, we perceive no abuse of discretion.

As the magistrate judge explained, Mr. Plummer's inability to answer questions regarding an exhibit listing prior incidents of "aggressive behavior" on Classica ships was not sanctionable because Mr. Fuentes only listed "prior physical assaults" as an area of inquiry on the notice of deposition. *See King v. Pratt & Whit-* **[—21—]** *ney*, 161 F.R.D. 475, 476 (S.D. Fla. 1995) (holding that a corporate designee is not obligated to answer questions outside of the scope of noticed areas of examination), *aff'd sub nom., King v. Pratt & Whitney*, 213 F.3d 646 (11th Cir. 2000). The incidents listed on the exhibit, except the one discussed below, involved conflicts that did not rise to the level of physical assaults.

With respect to the sole incident listed in the exhibit that involved a "physical assault"—the domestic dispute between a husband and wife in their stateroom—Mr. Plummer did not know the details during his deposition and only provided specifics in his subsequent declaration. The magistrate judge and the district court could have sanctioned Classica for that failure, but under the abuse of discretion standard, their refusal to do so does not constitute reversible error. *Cf. Lebron v. Royal Caribbean Cruises, Ltd.*, 2018 WL 4258269, at *9 (S.D. Fla. Sept. 6, 2018) ("[T]he occasional 'I don't know' in the context of [a] massively broad deposition does not itself reveal a Rule 30(b)(6) violation, if the witness otherwise took reasonable steps to prepare.").

As one leading treatise has put it, disputes about compliance with Rule 30(b)(6) are seldom clear cut: "More often, there is considerable room for disagreement about whether [Rule 30(b)(6)'s] requirements have been satisfied, and what remedy should be employed if they have not been satisfied." 8A Charles Alan Wright, Arthur R. Miller & Richard Marcus, Federal Practice and Procedure § 2103 (3d ed. & April 2021 update). That is the case here. The range of choice afforded by the abuse of discretion **[—22—]** standard calls for affirmance of the denial of Mr. Fuentes' motion for sanctions.[4] **{-1324-}**

[4] As noted, Mr. Fuentes takes issue with the fact that Classica filed a post-deposition declaration by Mr. Plummer in support of its motion for summary judgment. In that declaration, as set out in the text, Mr. Plummer provided details concerning the physical altercation that he could not recall during the deposition (the one between the husband and wife). The magistrate judge correctly observed, however, that nothing in the record suggests that Mr. Plummer's declaration regarding the details of that incident is inaccurate. If Mr. Fuentes doubted the veracity of Mr. Plummer's declaration, or felt prejudiced by it, he was not without recourse. He could have sought permission to redepose Mr. Plummer or another Classica designee as to that incident under Rule 30(b)(6), maybe even at Classica's expense, and that remedy would have been appropriate under

V

We affirm the grant of summary judgment in favor of Classica and the denial of Mr. Fuentes' motion for sanctions.

AFFIRMED.

the circumstances. He also could have moved to strike the declaration as improper. But he did not seek either option, and as a result, it was permissible for the district court to rely on the declaration in its order granting summary judgment.

United States Court of Appeals
for the Eleventh Circuit

No. 21-10772

BRADY
vs.
CARNIVAL CORP.

Appeal from the United States District Court for the Southern District of Florida

Decided: May 5, 2022

Citation: 33 F.4th 1278, 10 Adm. R. 380 (11th Cir. 2022).

Before **NEWSOM** and **MARCUS**, Circuit Judges, and **LAWSON**,* District Judge.

* The Honorable Hugh Lawson, United States District Judge for the Middle District of Georgia, sitting by designation.

[—2—] {-1280-} **NEWSOM**, Circuit Judge:

This is a slip-and-fall case arising under admiralty law. In a nutshell, Mary Brady slipped on a puddle of water and broke her hip shortly after boarding a Carnival cruise ship. She then sued the cruise line for negligence. The district court granted summary judgment for Carnival, holding that it lacked a duty to protect Brady because its crewmembers had neither actual nor constructive notice of the particular puddle that caused her fall. For the following reasons, we reverse and remand for further proceedings consistent with this opinion.

I

The facts, taken in the light most favorable to Brady, as the summary-judgment loser, are as follows: On the afternoon of August 18, 2018, the weather was hot and dry in Cape Canaveral, Florida. Brady boarded the Carnival "Sunshine" for a cruise vacation with her family and friends. She immediately proceeded to the ship's Lido Deck to meet other members of her party and grab some lunch. The scene was what one would expect at the beginning of a cruise: The sun was shining, music was playing, and it **[—3—]** was "really crowded" on the deck because the passengers weren't yet allowed in their cabins.

After a few minutes, Brady found the group she was searching for and began walking toward them. Brady was looking straight ahead at her friend, Jessica Chasen, and didn't see a patch of colorless liquid on the deck. Brady stepped in the puddle and her foot came out from under her. She "went flying up in the air" and landed "really hard on [her] back," with her "feet [coming] down afterwards." The impact fractured Brady's hip, and the injury would require Brady to leave the ship and undergo hip-replacement surgery.

Although Carnival claimed—in both an interrogatory answer and a casualty report submitted to the Bahamas Maritime Authority—that there was a caution sign in place, Brady said there weren't any warning signs in the immediate vicinity of her fall. There appears to be some truth to both positions, as a photo that Carnival took of the scene depicts a caution sign on the Lido Deck some 20 feet away from the puddle on which Brady slipped.

Brady sued Carnival in admiralty for negligence. Following discovery, the district **{-1281-}** court granted Carnival's motion for summary judgment on the basis that Brady failed to show that Carnival had knowledge of the particular puddle that caused Brady's fall. After the court denied Brady's Rule 59 motion for reconsideration, she timely appealed. **[—4—]**

II

"We review a district court's grant of summary judgment *de novo*, considering the facts and drawing all reasonable inferences in the light most favorable to the non-moving party." *Melton v. Abston*, 841 F.3d 1207, 1219 (11th Cir. 2016) (per curiam). Summary judgment is proper if the movant shows that "there is no genuine dispute as to any material fact and the movant is entitled to judgment as a matter of law." Fed. R. Civ. P. 56(a). "[T]he substantive law will identify which facts are material." *Anderson v. Liberty Lobby, Inc.*, 477 U.S. 242, 248 (1986). And a "genuine" dispute exists if "a jury applying [the applicable] evidentiary standard could reasonably find for either the plaintiff or the defendant" as to the material fact. *Id.* at 255.

III.

Maritime law governs the liability of a cruise ship for a passenger's slip and fall. *Everett v. Carnival Cruise Lines*, 912 F.2d 1355, 1358 (11th Cir. 1990). That cousin of the common law, however, draws heavily "on general principles of negligence law." *Carroll v. Carnival Corp.*, 955 F.3d 1260, 1264, 8 Adm. R. 412, 413 (11th Cir. 2020) (quotation omitted). Consistent with those principles, Brady must make four showings in order to prevail: "(1) Carnival had a duty to protect her from a particular injury; (2) Carnival breached that duty; (3) the breach actually and proximately caused her injury; and (4) she suffered actual harm." *Id.*, 8 Adm. R. at 413. **[—5—]**

This appeal implicates only the first element. As to that one, Carnival owed Brady "a duty of 'ordinary reasonable care under the circumstances, a standard which requires, as a prerequisite to imposing liability, that the carrier have had actual or constructive notice of the risk-creating condition.'" *K.T. v. Royal Caribbean Cruises, Ltd.*, 931 F.3d 1041, 1044, 7 Adm. R. 507, 508 (11th Cir. 2019) (quoting *Keefe v. Bahama Cruise Line, Inc.*, 867 F.2d 1318, 1322 (11th Cir. 1989) (per curiam)).

A

At the outset, we clarify what, under our precedent, the relevant "risk-creating condition" was here. It was not, as the district court suggested, the presence of the particular "puddle on which [Brady] slipped." Order at 3. Rather, the salient issue is whether Carnival knew, more generally, that the area of the deck where Brady fell had a reasonable tendency to become slippery—and thus dangerous to passengers—due to wetness from the pool.

This much is dictated by our decision in *Carroll*. There, the plaintiff was crossing Deck 11 of another Carnival cruise ship. *See* 955 F.3d at 1262–63, 8 Adm. R. at 412. "While Mrs. Carroll was walking behind her husband, her right foot clipped the leg of one of the lounge chairs" on the deck, "causing her to fall and suffer injuries." *Id.* at 1263, 8 Adm. R. at 412. There was no evidence—at least none cited by the court or the parties—that Carnival was aware that the *specific* chair that caused Carroll's fall was protruding into the walkway. Yet in reversing on the issue of notice, this Court relied on more general "evidence reflecting that Carnival took corrective measures to prevent people **[—6—]** from tripping over *the lounge chairs in the walkway on Deck 11*." *Id.* at 1265, 8 Adm. R. at 415 (emphasis added). For instance, "one of Carnival's **{-1282-}** pool deck supervisors . . . testified that the lounge chairs on Deck 11 were supposed to be arranged in the upright position, and he was instructed (and trained other employees that he supervised) to make sure that the chairs were not protruding into or blocking the walkway." *Id.* at 1266, 8 Adm. R. at 415. Another employee "testified that part of her duties included patrolling Deck 11 and moving any lounge chairs that were blocking the walkway." *Id.*, 8 Adm. R. at 415. And a third "testified that because passengers sometimes pull out chairs and do not put them back in place, they can create an 'unsafe condition,' so it is part of the staff's duties to take corrective action and remove that hazard." *Id.*, 8 Adm. R. at 415. Because this testimony showed that Carnival had "taken corrective measures"—repositioning the lounge chairs on Deck 11 to maintain a clear walkway—we held that the protruding chair that injured Carroll was a "known danger." *Id.*, 8 Adm. R. at 415. This was "enough to withstand summary judgment on the issue of Carnival's notice," despite a lack of evidence that Carnival knew that the specific injury-causing chair was jutting out into the walkway. *Id.*, 8 Adm. R. at 415.

Carroll is a published decision, and "we are bound by the prior-precedent rule to follow" it. *Arias v. Cameron*, 776 F.3d 1262, 1275 (11th Cir. 2015). That is, "even if we disagree[] with [*Carroll*]," we are "required to be faithful to it." *Id.* **[—7—]**

Here, the district court failed to faithfully follow *Carroll.*[1] The court ruled for Carnival because "[t]here is no evidence in the record that any Carnival crewmember was notified or was otherwise aware of the existence of *the puddle on which [Brady] slipped*." Order at 3 (emphasis added); *see also id.* at 5 ("There is no evidence Carnival knew of the existence of this puddle of water."); *id.* at 6 (focusing on "whether Carnival had constructive notice of the puddle on the deck"). While that may be true, it misses the relevant question. Under *Carroll,* the issue of notice turns more broadly on (1) whether Carnival had notice that the area where Brady fell had a reasonable tendency to become wet, *see Carroll,* 955 F.3d at 1266, 8 Adm. R. at 415, and (2) whether it "had actual or constructive knowledge that the pool deck where [Brady] fell could be slippery (and therefore dangerous) when wet," *Sorrels v. NCL (Bahamas) Ltd.,* 796 F.3d 1275, 1288, 3 Adm. R. 659, 667 (11th Cir. 2015).

B

Taking all reasonable inferences and construing the evidence in Brady's favor, we hold that a rational jury could find for her on both questions. **[—8—]**

Start with whether Carnival knew that the deck area was reasonably likely to become wet. Carnival's representative, Maurice Vega, admitted in an interrogatory that "the mid ship open Lido Deck area"—*i.e.*, where Brady fell—"is reasonably expected to become wet due to . . . passengers' use of the swimming pool." The interrogatory continued on to note that, nevertheless, "yellow caution cones were in place." Such a warning sign is visible in the background of one of the photos, about 20 feet from the location of Brady's fall. And Chasen overheard a crewmember provide a statement that there were "safety cones on the deck" in the vicinity "where [Brady] fell." The cruise line's casualty report similarly claims that a "caution sign was in place." A rational factfinder could conclude from this **{–1283–}** evidence that a warning sign was indeed in place on the pool deck—or was meant to be—near the location of the incident. So too, a rational factfinder could draw the inference from Carnival's admissions and its placement of a warning sign near its pool that it knew that the area would frequently become wet from its passengers' normal use of the pool. *See Carroll,* 955 F.3d at 1266, 8 Adm. R. at 415.

In response, Carnival insists that Vega "clarified" at his deposition that the warning signs weren't related to wetness on the deck, but rather, were "placed as a general reminder to passengers to be careful." Br. of Appellee at 29. That is one view of the evidence. "At the summary judgment stage, however, we must view all evidence and factual inferences in favor of [Brady]." *Guevara v. NCL (Bahamas) Ltd.,* 920 F.3d 710, 722, 7 Adm. R. 476, 482 (11th Cir. 2019). When **[—9—]** read in the light most favorable to her, both Carnival's interrogatory response and its casualty report link the placement of the caution sign to the expectation of wet conditions on the pool deck. To elevate Vega's deposition testimony over these documentary sources would be to invade the jury's province as the finder of fact. *See Anderson,* 477 U.S. at 255 ("Credibility determinations, the weighing of the evidence, and the drawing of legitimate inferences from the facts are jury functions, not those of a judge[.]"). Particularly when Carnival's admissions are viewed alongside the sign's proximity to the pool, a reasonable jury could find a "connection between the warning and the danger." *Guevara,* 920 F.3d at 721, 7 Adm. R. at 482; *see Amy v. Carnival Corp.,* 961 F.3d 1303, 1309, 8 Adm. R. 424, 427 (11th Cir. 2020).

That leaves the question whether Carnival "had actual or constructive knowledge that the pool deck where [Brady] fell could be *slippery* (and therefore dangerous) when wet." *Sorrels,* 796 F.3d at 1288, 3 Adm. R. at 667 (emphasis added). As we've explained before, "[e]vidence that a ship owner has taken corrective action can establish notice of a

---

[1] In fairness to the district court, neither side cited *Carroll* in their summary judgment briefs. But the fact that the parties have failed to identify a binding decision doesn't make it any less binding. Between the closing of briefing and oral argument in this Court, we sought and received supplemental briefing on *Carroll*'s application.

dangerous or defective condition." *Carroll*, 955 F.3d at 1265, 8 Adm. R. at 414. And that's just what we have here. The fact that warning signs were "posted on the pool deck" in the general area of Brady's fall, when "viewed in the light most favorable to [Brady], is enough to withstand summary judgment as to notice." *Sorrels*, 796 F.3d at 1289, 3 Adm. R. at 667. That's because a reasonable inference from the placement of the caution sign is that Carnival knew that the Lido Deck would become slippery when wet. *See id.* at 1288, 3 Adm. R. at 667 (permitting this inference where a crewmember "would sometimes post warning signs **[—10—]** on the pool deck after it had rained" and "had been told to post warning signs in the restaurant whenever there was water or some other liquid on the floor . . . because it was known to her supervisors that the teak floor could be slippery when wet"); *Mabrey v. Carnival Cruise Lines, Inc.*, 438 So. 2d 937, 938 (Fla. Dist. Ct. App. 1983) (holding that evidence of a "Slippery When Wet" sign at the entrance to a deck of the cruise ship precluded a directed verdict). In other words, a jury could reasonably find that placing a warning sign on the deck served as Carnival's acknowledgment of the danger. Even the district court seems to have accepted this inference. It just erred (for reasons already explained) in its framing of the relevant hazard.

At the same time, it doesn't matter that the caution sign wasn't placed exactly where Brady fell. The deck in both locations—which are fairly close to one another—is made of the same material. So, if a jury believes that the sign indicates that Carnival had notice that the deck would become slippery when wet, then it could reasonably infer that Carnival knew that the area where Brady slipped would pose that same hazard. **{-1284-}**

"To be clear, a reasonable jury also could see other evidence to indicate that Carnival lacked notice." *Amy*, 961 F.3d at 1310, 8 Adm. R. at 428. For example, one interrogatory response from Carnival claims that the "deck material" is "appropriate for the mid ship open Lido Deck area." But weighing this conflicting evidence is a "task . . . for the jury." *Id.*, 8 Adm. R. at 428. Based on Carnival's repeated admissions that warning signs were present in the area, we hold that there is a genuine issue **[—11—]** of material fact as to Carnival's notice. *See id.* at 1309, 8 Adm. at 428; *Carroll*, 955 F.3d at 1266, 8 Adm. R. at 415; *Sorrels*, 796 F.3d at 1289, 3 Adm. R. at 667; *Mabrey*, 438 So. 2d at 938. Accordingly, the district court's grant of summary judgment on the basis that Carnival lacked notice was improper.[2]

* * *

We **REVERSE** and **REMAND** for the district court to address, in the first instance, Carnival's alternative argument with respect to the alleged open-and-obvious nature of the hazard.

---

[2] In so holding, we don't foreclose the possibility of Carnival "showing that it did not *breach* its duty to warn because" the alleged "sign provided passengers with a sufficient warning about the dangerous condition in the area." *Guevara*, 920 F.3d at 722, 7 Adm. R. at 483 (emphasis added). The issue of breach, however, isn't before us.

United States Court of Appeals
for the Eleventh Circuit

No. 20-14728

GLOBAL MARINE EXPLORATION, INC.
VS.
REPUBLIC OF FRANCE

Appeal from the United States District Court for the Northern District of Florida

Decided: May 12, 2022

Citation: 33 F.4th 1312, 10 Adm. R. 384 (11th Cir. 2022).

Before **LAGOA, BRASHER,** and **TJOFLAT,** Circuit Judges.

[—2—] {-1314-} LAGOA, Circuit Judge:

This case arises out of the discovery of several shipwrecks found off the coast of Cape Canaveral, Florida, including *La Trinité*, the flagship of the 1565 fleet of the Royal Navy of France, which was captained by Jean Ribault. In 1565, Ribault was dispatched by the French Admiral Gaspard II de Coligny to reinforce the French Huguenot settlement of Fort Caroline located on the St. Johns River near what is now Jacksonville, Florida. The Spanish, however, also laid claim to what they called La Florida, and Pedro Menéndez de Avilés had founded the Spanish settlement of St. Augustine near the French Fort Caroline. King Phillip II of Spain ordered Menéndez de Avilés to destroy the French settlement. Following a skirmish at the mouth of the St. Johns River with Spanish ships, Ribault left in pursuit of the Spanish flagship, the *San Pelayo*. Ribault encountered a hurricane which destroyed his fleet and drove Ribault and his surviving crew members ashore. That same hurricane allowed Menéndez de Avilés to succeed in capturing Fort Caroline after an overland expedition from St. Augustine. After Fort Caroline was destroyed, no further French settlements were established in Florida.

Global Marine Exploration, Inc. ("GME"), conducts marine salvage activities and discovers historic shipwreck sites in Florida's coastal waters. GME entered into authorization agreements with the Florida Department of State, Division of Historical Resources ("FDOS"), to conduct salvage activities in Florida coastal waters off **[—3—]** Cape Canaveral. Following a 2015 agreement between GME and FDOS, GME discovered several shipwreck sites and informed FDOS of its discovery. Soon after, however, GME learned that FDOS was in contact with the Republic of France to recover the shipwreck sites, assuming that one of the sites was *La Trinité*. GME subsequently filed an *in rem* admiralty action against the "Unidentified, Wrecked and (for Finders-Right Purposes) Abandoned Sailing Vessel" in federal court. FDOS and France became parties to that action, and the Middle District of Florida concluded that the identity of the *res* was *La Trinité* and that *La Trinité* is France's sovereign property. GME did not appeal the *in rem* action. *See Glob. Marine Expl., Inc. v. Unidentified, Wrecked & (for Finders-Right Purposes) Abandoned Sailing Vessel* ("*GME I*"), 348 F. Supp. 3d 1221 (M.D. Fla. 2018).

Following *GME I*, GME sued France, alleging claims for an *in personam* lien **{-1315-}** award, unjust enrichment, misappropriation of trade secret information, and interference with its rights and relations. France moved to dismiss GME's amended complaint under Federal Rule of Civil Procedure 12(b)(1), arguing that the district court lacked subject matter jurisdiction under the Foreign Sovereign Immunities Act ("FSIA"), 28 U.S.C. §§ 1602–11, and that the commercial activity exception to the FSIA, 28 U.S.C. § 1605(a)(2), was inapplicable. The district court agreed with France, finding that the FSIA's commercial activity exception did not apply, and dismissed GME's claims. GME now appeals the district court's **[—4—]** dismissal, contending that France engaged in commercial activity such that the FSIA's commercial activity exception applies.

For the reasons discussed below, and with the benefit of oral argument, we conclude that the FSIA's commercial activity exception applies. Accordingly, we reverse the district court's Rule 12(b)(1) dismissal and remand for further proceedings.

I. FACTUAL AND PROCEDURAL BACKGROUND

GME is a Florida corporation that conducts marine salvage activities and discovers historic shipwreck sites in Florida's coastal waters. GME conducts its salvage activities under authorization agreements with FDOS. In these agreements, Florida granted GME a fixed-term "cultural resource recovery easement for salvage exploration and operational purposes" on Florida-owned submerged lands, as well as permits for GME to use those submerged lands and navigable waters for construction work. GME then "undertook prolonged and expensive research, survey, reporting, and identification of shipwrecked sites," including artifacts, "with reasonable investment-backed expectation[s] and program assurances that its salvage activity" would be fully compensated in line with the value of the discovered sites. In doing so, "GME expended millions of dollars and enormous time and effort."

In 2014, FDOS and GME entered into six agreements governing salvage activity for six different, three-square mile areas off the coast of Cape Canaveral. On August 14, 2015, FDOS and GME entered into a seventh agreement—designated as Permit No. 2015- **[—5—]** 03—authorizing GME to survey another designated three-square mile area off Cape Canaveral and to locate and report any shipwreck sites discovered. GME discovered five separate shipwrecks and six historic shipwreck sites in this designated area, and GME's mapped conclusions of the area were provided as part of its report and request to FDOS for approval to proceed with recovery. GME also excavated small artifact items (and took photos and videos as identification of other monuments) from one of the shipwreck sites. GME provided FDOS with the photos and videos. And FDOS directed GME to submit the location coordinate information incident to the agency's oversight and inventory of historical resources division. According to GME, the coordinate information would remain confidential and would be commercially used only by GME.

At some point, GME learned that FDOS was "collaborating and negotiating" with France to recover the shipwreck sites discovered by GME without its involvement, as FDOS and France believed that the shipwreck was France's *La Trinité*—the flagship of the 1565 fleet of the Royal Navy of France that sank during a hurricane off the coast of Florida. Concerned by this development, GME filed the *in rem* admiralty action—*GME I*—in September 2016, and FDOS and France became parties to that action. *See* 348 F. Supp. 3d at 1224. In connection with filing that *in rem* action, GME deposited with the district **{-1316-}** court several small artifacts (e.g., ballast stones) from the site. **[—6—]**

The next month, FDOS demanded GME turn over those same artifacts to it, suspended GME's salvage activity permit, and prohibited GME from proceeding with full recovery of the discovered shipwreck sites. The *GME I* district court later conferred temporary *in rem* custody to FDOS and precluded any shipwreck recovery pending its decision. Ultimately, the *GME I* district court granted France's motion to dismiss the action for lack of subject matter jurisdiction because it concluded that the *res* at issue was *La Trinité*, which was France's sovereign property. *See id.* at 1242. GME did not appeal that order.

Following *GME I*, France and FDOS entered into a "Declaration of Intention Between the State of Florida and the Republic of France On the shipwrecks of Jean Ribault's fleet" (the "Declaration of Intent"). The Declaration of Intent stated that, as a result of the district court's decision in *GME I*, France was authorized "to begin recovery operations" of *La Trinité* and that the signatories would cooperate "concerning research on, and protection and preservation of" *La Trinité*. FDOS and France further agreed to: (1) protect the shipwreck sites "to prevent any form of plundering"; (2) recover the shipwreck sites and present those discoveries to the public in Florida, e.g., through exhibitions or publications; (3) promote the common history of the United States and France in Florida; and (4) identify, evaluate, mobilize, and oversee resources and organizations to fulfill the Declaration of Intent's objectives. The

Declaration of Intent also established a steering committee to implement the agreement. **[—7—]**

In April 2020, GME sued France, alleging that "France is sending missions to Florida to oversee the project and provide scientific expertise" under the Declaration of Intent and that "work is on-going." GME also asserted that France was performing commercial activity in Florida through France's agreement with FDOS and others, "and by activities undertaken or to be undertaken, in relation to GME's discovered shipwreck sites for which GME claims rights and interest."

GME asserted four claims against France: (1) an *in personam* salvage lien; (2) "quasi contract/unjust enrichment"; (3) misappropriation of GME's trade secret information; and (4) interference with GME's rights and relations. As to its lien claim, GME alleged that it was entitled to compensation because without GME's services the shipwreck sites would not have been discovered and therefore GME's services significantly benefit any "full recovery of the historic shipwreck sites." In its count for unjust enrichment, GME asserted that it had conferred a substantial benefit to France based on its services related to the shipwreck sites. As to its misappropriation of trade secret claim, GME alleged that "[t]he precise locations of GME's discovered shipwreck sites and the methods used to identify those locations were proprietary and confidential information owned by GME" and that France's use of that information was unauthorized and without GME's consent. And, as to its interference claim, GME alleged that France knew of GME's contractual rights and advantageous business and contractual relations with FDOS but intentionally acted to influence, induce, and **[—8—]** collaborate with FDOS for the latter to abrogate its obligations to, and relations with, GME.

France moved to dismiss GME's amended complaint under Rule 12(b)(1), arguing that the district court lacked subject matter jurisdiction under the FSIA and that GME failed to show that the commercial activity exception to the FSIA applied. In particular, France contended that the core **{-1317-}** conduct at issue was its "intergovernmental cooperation for the historic preservation of [its] military vessel," which was manifestly a governmental function. France submitted a declaration from Florence Hermite, a "Magistrat de Liaison – Legal Attaché," who attested that France entered into the Declaration of Intent under the Heritage Code of France Section L522-1, which provides, as translated into English, that France "prescribes measures aimed at the detection, conservation of safeguarding by scientific study of the heritage archaeological, designates the scientific manager of any preventative archeology operation and carries out control and evaluation missions for these operations."

The district court granted France's motion to dismiss. The district court explained that the commercial activity exception had three components: whether "(1) the action is based upon (2) a commercial activity (3) carried on in the United States by a foreign state." The district court concluded that the action at issue was "France's intergovernmental declaration with Florida—and its overall relationship with Florida regarding the shipwreck sites," which "lack[ed] . . . a commercial nature" because France was not **[—9—]** involved in "the type of actions by which a private party engages in trade and traffic or commerce." While noting that private actors sometimes engage in marine exploration and shipwreck recovery and preservation efforts, the district court reasoned "that alone did not make France's activities commercial." The district court explained that "the nature of France's activity is the recovery and disposition of its own sovereign military property" and that its choice to recover or preserve the property was not like "entering a market and behaving as a private person would." The district court noted that the Declaration of Intent, signed by government actors, showed that France and FDOS were working together to protect and preserve *La Trinité* and that, as such, France had not entered the market or engaged in trade or commerce.

The district court also concluded that, even if France's activities were commercial in nature, GME's claims against France were not "based upon" those activities. The district court determined that "the foundation" for GME's alleged injuries was not France's intergovernmental declaration with Florida or activities related to that declaration, i.e., GME was not injured by the fact that France sought to preserve its culture or recover its shipwreck's artifacts. Rather, the district court reasoned GME's injuries were based upon the fact that France took ownership of *La Trinité*, which occurred in *GME I*, and that GME could not claim ownership of the *res*. The district court therefore concluded it lacked subject matter jurisdiction under the FSIA.

This timely appeal ensued. **[—10—]**

II. STANDARD OF REVIEW

"When evaluating a district court's conclusions on a Rule 12(b)(1) motion, '[w]e review the district court's legal conclusions *de novo* and its factual findings for clear error.'" *Odyssey Marine Expl., Inc. v. Unidentified Shipwrecked Vessel*, 657 F.3d 1159, 1169 (11th Cir. 2011) (alteration in original) (quoting *Carmichael v. Kellogg, Brown & Root Servs., Inc.*, 572 F.3d 1271, 1279 (11th Cir. 2009)). And we review *de novo* a district court's determination of whether it had jurisdiction under the FSIA. *Devengoechea v. Bolivarian Republic of Venezuela*, 889 F.3d 1213, 1220 (11th Cir. 2018).

III. ANALYSIS

On appeal, GME argues that the district court erred in dismissing its amended complaint for two reasons. First, GME asserts **{-1318-}** that the district court erroneously determined that the FSIA's commercial activity exception to foreign sovereign immunity did not apply to France's activities in the case. Second, GME contends that its action against France was "based upon" France's commercial activities such that subject matter jurisdiction existed under the FSIA. We address these arguments in turn.

A. Whether France's activities are "commercial activities" under the FSIA

The FSIA "supplies the ground rules for 'obtaining jurisdiction over a foreign state in the courts of this country.'" *Federal Republic of Germany v. Philipp*, 141 S. Ct. 703, 709 (2021) (quoting *Argentine Republic v. Amerada Hess Shipping Corp.*, 488 U.S. 428, **[—11—]** 443 (1989)). The FSIA "creates a baseline of immunity from suit," *id.*; *accord* 28 U.S.C. § 1604, and "unless a specified exception applies, a federal court lacks subject-matter jurisdiction over a claim against a foreign state," *Saudi Arabia v. Nelson*, 507 U.S. 349, 355 (1993).

One such exception is the "commercial activity" exception contained in the first clause of 28 U.S.C. § 1605(a)(2). The exception provides that "[a] foreign state shall not be immune from the jurisdiction of courts of the United States or of the States in any case . . . in which the action is based upon a commercial activity carried on in the United States by the foreign state." § 1605(a)(2). Title 28 U.S.C. § 1603(d) defines "commercial activity" as "either a regular course of commercial conduct or a particular commercial transaction or act," and states that "[t]he commercial character of an activity shall be determined by reference to the nature of the course of conduct or particular transaction or act, rather than by reference to its purpose."

While the definition in § 1603(d) "leaves the critical term 'commercial' largely undefined," the Supreme Court has explained that "when a foreign government acts, not as regulator of a market, but in the manner of a private player within it, the foreign sovereign's actions are 'commercial' within the meaning of the FSIA." *Republic of Argentina v. Weltover, Inc.*, 504 U.S. 607, 612, 614 (1992). Additionally, because the FSIA "provides that the commercial character of an act is to be determined by reference to its 'nature' rather than its 'purpose,' the question is not whether the **[—12—]** foreign government is acting with a profit motive or instead with the aim of fulfilling uniquely sovereign objectives." *Id.* at 614 (quoting § 1603(d)).

Instead, we must determine "whether the particular actions that the foreign state performs (whatever the motive behind them) are the *type* of actions by which a private party engages in 'trade and traffic or commerce.'" *Id.* (quoting Black's Law Dictionary 270 (6th ed. 1990)). Thus, whether a foreign state is acting in the manner of a private party "is a question of behavior, not motivation." *Nelson*, 507 U.S. at 360. For example, a foreign state's "issuance of regulations limiting foreign currency exchange is a sovereign activity, because such authoritative control of commerce cannot be exercised by a private party" while "a contract to buy army boots or even bullets is a 'commercial' activity, because private companies can similarly use sales contracts to acquire goods." *Weltover*, 504 U.S. at 614–15.

In *Weltover*, the Supreme Court concluded that Argentina's issuance of bonds as part of a plan to stabilize its currency **{-1319-}** was a commercial activity within the meaning of the FSIA. *Id.* at 620. The Court explained that the "commercial character" of the bonds was demonstrated by the fact that they were "in almost all respects garden-variety debt instruments," e.g., "[t]hey [could] be held by private parties, they [were] negotiable and [could] be traded on the international market[,] . . . and they promise[d] a future stream of cash income." *Id.* at 615. And the Court rejected Argentina's argument that "the line between 'nature' and 'purpose' rests upon a 'formalistic distinction [that] simply is neither useful nor **[—13—]** warranted'" because that argument was "squarely foreclosed by the language of the FSIA." *Id.* at 617. It was thus "irrelevant *why* Argentina participated in the bond market in the manner of a private actor; it matter[ed] only that it did so." *Id.*

Subsequently, in *Nelson*, the Supreme Court found that, unlike Argentina's activities in *Weltover*, the intentional conduct alleged by the plaintiffs—"wrongful arrest, imprisonment, and torture" by the Saudi Government—did not qualify as commercial activity because the conduct at issue "boil[ed] down to abuse of the power of its police by the Saudi Government" and "a foreign state's exercise of the power of its police has long been understood for purposes of the restrictive theory as peculiarly sovereign in nature." 507 U.S. at 361. The Court explained that "[s]uch acts as legislation, or the expulsion of an alien, or a denial of justice, cannot be performed by an individual acting in his own name," and "can be performed only by the state acting as such." *Id.* at 362 (quoting Hersch Lauterpacht, *The Problem of Jurisdictional Immunities of Foreign States*, 28 Brit. Y.B. Int'l L. 220, 225 (1952)). Thus, the Court concluded that the "[e]xercise of the powers of police and penal officers is not the sort of action by which private parties can engage in commerce." *Id.* And regardless of the Saudi Government's motivation for its allegedly abusive treatment of the plaintiff, e.g., to resolve commercial disputes, the Court explained that argument went to the activity's purpose, which was "irrelevant to the question of an activity's commercial character" under the FSIA. *Id.* at 362–63; *accord Honduras Aircraft Registry, Ltd. v.* **[—14—]** *Government of Honduras*, 129 F.3d 543, 548 (11th Cir. 1997) ("[I]n ascertaining whether the FSIA commercial exception applies, it is irrelevant that Honduras may have had a possible profit motive or that Honduras may have intended only to fulfill its unique sovereign objectives.").

We have since applied the principles of *Weltover* and *Nelson* several times in analyzing whether a foreign state's activities are commercial activities under the FSIA. For example, in *Honduras Aircraft*, Honduras had decided to "upgrade and modernize" its "civil aeronautics program to comply with international aviation laws." 129 F.3d at 545. In so doing, Honduras contracted with the plaintiffs to provide goods and services to help Honduras achieve this goal, including setting up a data base for Honduras's aircraft registry, writing regulations, training government personnel, and providing "the other things needed to register, inspect and certify aircraft." *Id.* at 547. Ultimately, Honduras breached the contract, and plaintiffs sued. Honduras moved to dismiss for lack of subject matter jurisdiction, arguing that the FSIA's commercial activity exception did not apply because "the inspection and registration of aircraft are powers peculiar to sovereigns, as private persons cannot grant airworthiness certificates and register aircraft." *Id.* We disagreed, explaining that while "registering aircraft under the Honduras flag is an act peculiar to its **{-1320-}** sovereignty," plaintiffs were not contending that the contract at issue "gave them the right to register aircraft." *Id.* at 548. Rather, the plaintiffs sought to enforce their contract with Honduras, in which "they contracted to provide **[—15—]** goods and services to Honduras in connection with its expanded civil air program by inspecting and certifying aircraft airworthiness so that Honduras would be able to appropriately register the aircraft under its flag." *Id.* Indeed, the contract provided "only that plaintiffs would provide the means and do the technical work," and we reasoned that "[a]ny party, sovereign or not, could contract for those goods and services." *Id.* Thus, we explained that Honduras commercially entered the market as a private player to secure technical assistance and upgrades for its civil air program. *Id.* at 548–49.

Similarly, in *Guevara v. Republic of Peru*, 468 F.3d 1289 (11th Cir. 2006), we addressed "whether a foreign state's offer of a reward in return for information enabling it to locate and capture a fugitive" fell within FSIA's commercial activity exception and we concluded that it did so. *Id.* at 1292. We noted that "[t]he location and capture of a fugitive by law enforcement officials of a country may be a sovereign act." *Id.* at 1298. But we explained that the reward offer at issue "did not promise that in return for the information it was seeking Peru would locate and capture" the fugitive, and the plaintiff was not seeking to compel the fugitive's capture. *Id.* at 1298–99. Instead, the plaintiff sought the monetary reward that Peru offered in exchange to anyone who furnished information "that enabled Peru to capture" the fugitive. *Id.* at 1299. We found the facts in *Guevara* similar enough to those in *Honduras Aircraft* to compel the same result—instead of using its sovereign powers to search for the fugitive, Peru ventured into the **[—16—]** marketplace to buy the information needed to locate the fugitive. *Id.* The plaintiff provided that information for a price—Peru's monetary reward offer. *Id.* Thus, we concluded that "[t]he underlying activity at issue—the exchange of money for information—[was] 'commercial in nature and of the type negotiable among private parties.'" *Id.* (quoting *Honduras Aircraft*, 129 F.3d at 547); *see also Devengoechea*, 889 F.3d at 1221, 1224 (explaining that the plaintiff's claims based on Venezuela's failure to pay the plaintiff for artifacts was commercial activity because, similar to a private purchaser, Venezuela met with the seller, examined the artifacts, and negotiated to examine them further and to possibly purchase them). We also rejected Peru's argument that "commercial activity" only included activities "done for a profit motive," as "a 'motive' test tread[ed] too closely to an examination of 'purpose.'" *Guevara,* 468 F.3d at 1302.

By contrast, in *Beg v. Islamic Republic of Pakistan*, 353 F.3d 1323, 1326 (11th Cir. 2003), we concluded that the Pakistani government's alleged actions of expropriating Plaintiff's land involved the power of eminent domain—a sovereign power—and were therefore not commercial. We explained that "[c]onfiscation of real property is a public act because private actors are not allowed to engage in 'takings' in the manner that governments are" and that "[d]etermining whether or how to compensate property owners for takings is also a sovereign function, not a market transaction." *Id.* at 1326–27. Thus, even though the Pakistani government allegedly failed to provide the plaintiff with alternative property, **[—17—]** "the *nature* of the foreign government's act is public and not commercial." *Id.* at 1327.

And, in *Odyssey*, a shipwreck recovery business, Odyssey, discovered the remains of a Spanish vessel in international waters and filed an *in rem* admiralty action **{-1321-}** against the vessel and its cargo. 657 F.3d at 1166. *Odyssey* did not concern the FSIA's commercial activity exception in § 1605(a) but rather 28 U.S.C. § 1609, the section of the FSIA that provides that a foreign state's property in the United States "shall be immune from attachment[,] arrest[,] and execution except as provided in [28 U.S.C. §§]

1610 and 1611." *See Odyssey*, 657 F.3d at 1175–76. Odyssey, however, did not invoke the exceptions provided in §§ 1610 or 1611; instead, it argued for "a commercial activity exception to § 1609's immunity to arrest." *Id.* at 1176. This Court rejected Odyssey's argument, as the international treaty that Odyssey asserted was incorporated into § 1609 did not "appear to create a commercial activity exception to § 1609's immunity to arrest." *Id.* We also noted that, even if such an exception existed, the Spanish vessel at issue was not engaged in commercial activity, as defined by § 1603(d), because it was not acting like an ordinary private person in the marketplace. *See id.* at 1176–77. We explained that at the time it sank the ship "was 'act[ing] . . . like a sovereign' by transporting [Spanish coins and cargo] during a time of threatened war" as part of the Spanish Navy. *See id.* at 1177 (some alterations in original) (quoting *Guevara*, 468 F.3d at 1298). **[—18—]**

With these precedents in mind, we turn to the case before us. In its dismissal order, the district court determined that France's activities in the case consisted of "France's intergovernmental declaration with Florida—and its overall relationship with Florida regarding the shipwreck sites"—and that these activities were not commercial in nature. While recognizing that private actors engage in marine exploration activities and shipwreck recovery efforts, the district court reasoned that those activities alone did not make the nature of France's activities commercial, comparing the case to mail service, which can take both governmental and commercial forms. The district court construed "the nature of France's activity [as] the recovery and disposition of its own sovereign military property" and explained that, regardless of whether France chose to recover its property or work with Florida to preserve it, France was "not entering a market and behaving as a private person would." The district court also reasoned that it mattered "to some extent" that France's agreement was with Florida, not a private actor.

GME contends that the district court erred in finding that France's activities—a "marine archeological recovery project for recovery of six historical shipwreck sites in Florida"—did not constitute "commercial activity" under the FSIA. GME argues that the "what" of France's activity—effecting archaeological salvage recovery of historic shipwreck sites—and the "means" employed for the activity—e.g., negotiating agreements with Florida and others; directing, coordinating, and participating in recovery efforts; **[—19—]** securing private and grant source fundings; and conserving and arranging for the exhibition of artifacts—are commercial in nature. GME notes that similar types of activity are performed in commerce by private entities, including GME itself, "with which [FDOS] proposed to 'partner' for the same project." And GME asserts that the district court improperly looked to the "governmental direction or purpose" of France's activities, which is irrelevant to the question of an activity's commercial nature.

We agree with GME and conclude that the nature of France's activities here are commercial under the FSIA. As set forth by the Declaration of Intent, France, in cooperation with FDOS, planned to engage **{-1322-}** in a marine archaeological recovery project of the shipwreck sites off the coast of Cape Canaveral. And the Declaration of Intent provides that, to conduct this project, France will identify, evaluate, mobilize, and oversee "public and/or private resources and organizations." In other words, France, along with FDOS, planned to acquire funding and to hire organizations or businesses to conduct its shipwreck recovery efforts. And, according to GME's amended complaint, France has performed actions and entered into agreements with FDOS and others in connection with the shipwreck recovery project. These actions—fundraising, contracting with organizations and businesses to carry out excavations of shipwreck sites (i.e., asset recovery), and overseeing the logistics of the project—are "commercial in nature and of the type negotiable among private parties." *Guevara*, 468 F.3d at 1299 (quoting *Honduras Aircraft*, 129 F.3d at 547). **[—20—]**

The district court focused on the fact that France had entered into the Declaration of Intent with another sovereign power (Florida) in order to recover and preserve the shipwreck sites, including *La Trinité*, and to promote the shared history of the United States and France in Florida. But the district court's analysis of France's activities was too narrow and "purpose" oriented. "[T]he question is not whether the foreign government is acting with a profit motive or . . . with the aim of fulfilling uniquely sovereign objectives." *Guevara*, 468 F.3d at 1298 (quoting *Weltover*, 504 U.S. at 614). "Rather the issue is whether the particular actions that the foreign state performs . . . are the *type* of actions by which a private party engages in 'trade and traffic or commerce.'" *Id.* (quoting *Weltover*, 504 U.S. at 614). Therefore, although the purpose of France's shipwreck recovery efforts may be to protect, recover, and preserve the shipwreck sites, and to promote its common history with the United States in Florida, "it is irrelevant *why* [France engaged in this shipwreck recovery project] in the manner of a private actor; it matters only that it did so." *Weltover*, 504 U.S. at 617.

France, however, argues that its activities are not commercial in nature because they are "required by the patrimony laws of France," as explained by the Hermite declaration it submitted in support of its motion to dismiss. In support of its position, France relies on the Second Circuit's decision in *Barnet v. Ministry of Culture & Sports of the Hellenic Republic*, 961 F.3d 193 (2d Cir. 2020), which the district court also relied on in dismissing GME's amended complaint. In *Barnet*, the Second Circuit faced the **[—21—]** question of whether Greece's assertion of ownership over an ancient Greek artifact constituted commercial activity under the FSIA. *Id.* at 195. An auction house announced it planned to auction the Greek artifact on behalf of a trust. When Greek officials learned of the auction, they emailed the auction house a demand letter, stating that the artifact belonged to Greece under its "patrimony laws" that declared Greek artifacts to be Greece's property. *Id.* The auction house withdrew the artifact from the auction, and both the trust and auction house filed suit against Greece, seeking declaratory relief on the disputed issue of ownership and asserting that the commercial activity exception—specifically, the third clause of § 1605(a)(2)—to the FSIA applied. *Id.*; *see* § 1605(a)(2) ("A foreign state shall not be immune from the jurisdiction of courts of the United States . . . in which the action is based ... upon an act outside of the United States in connection with a commercial activity of the foreign state elsewhere and that act causes a direct effect in the United States."). **{-1323-}**

On appeal, the Second Circuit explained that Greece's predicate act—sending its demand letter to the auction house—was not taken "in connection with a commercial activity" by Greece outside of the United States. *Barnet*, 961 F.3d at 200 (quoting § 1605(a)(2)). The Second Circuit explained that "Greece undertook the act of sending the letter in connection with its claim of ownership over the figurine pursuant to its patrimony laws" and found that this act was sovereign in nature—Greece claimed ownership of the artifact "by adopting legislation that nationalizes **[—22—]** historical artifacts and by enforcing those patrimony laws." *Id.* at 200–01. The Second Circuit reasoned that "[n]ationalizing property is a distinctly sovereign act" and that Greece was "acting in a sovereign capacity by enforcing laws that regulate ownership and export of nationalized artifacts." *Id.* at 201. And the Second Circuit found that Greece's "insistence on recognition of and obedience to its patrimony laws [were] not 'the *type* of actions by which a private party engages in trade and traffic or commerce,'" nor "analogous to a private commercial transaction." *Id.* (quoting *Weltover*, 504 U.S. at 614, 616). Thus, the Second Circuit concluded that the adoption and pursuit of compliance with patrimony laws established that the nature of Greece's "activity was sovereign rather than commercial." *Id.* at 201–02.

But France's activities here are not like Greece's activity in *Barnet*. Therefore, we do not find *Barnet* persuasive here. To begin with, the activity at issue in *Barnet*—the sending of a letter claiming ownership of an artifact—is both narrower in scope and different in type than France's activities here, i.e., planning and executing a shipwreck recovery project with FDOS. More critically, we find that focusing on the foreign state's "patrimony laws" in this case would be akin to the "motive" test we warned of in *Guevara* that "treads too closely to an examination of 'purpose.'" 468 F.3d at 1302. While France's motive in pursuing the shipwreck recovery project may be to comply with its patrimony laws, "the Supreme Court has instructed us that the FSIA 'unmistakably commands' that we consider the nature, rather than the purpose of a **[—23—]** transaction." *Id.* at 1302. We must therefore look to the nature of underlying activity and determine whether it is commercial in nature, e.g., the type of activity that is "negotiable among private parties." *Id.* at 1299 (quoting *Honduras Aircraft*, 129 F.3d at 547); *see Devengoechea*, 889 F.3d at 1221 ("[W]hether a foreign government acts out of a profit motive or out of a desire to fulfill 'uniquely sovereign objectives' is entirely irrelevant to the analysis of whether an activity qualifies as 'commercial.'" (quoting *Weltover*, 504 U.S. at 614)). And as we have already discussed, fundraising, entering into contracts with third parties to engage in marine excavation and asset recovery, and overseeing the logistics of that project are commercial in nature, as they are the type of activities that private parties (including GME) engage in.

France further relies on *Odyssey*, but that case is also distinguishable from the case before us. As explained above, in *Odyssey*, we faced an *in rem* action to determine ownership of a shipwreck and the application of § 1609, not § 1605, of the FSIA. Odyssey asked us to create a commercial activities exception to § 1609's immunity to arrest, arguing that the Spanish ship was engaged in commercial activity when it sank. In rejecting this argument, we concluded that there was not "a commercial activity exception to § 1609's immunity to arrest." *Odyssey*, 657 F.3d at 1176. We also noted that, even if such an exception existed, Spain's activities in operating the ship, during the late 18th and early 19th centuries, were sovereign in **{-1324-}** nature. *Id.* at 1176–77. Unlike *Odyssey*, GME's claims concern France's current-day activities in pursuing recovery **[—24—]** efforts with FDOS of the shipwreck sites—the same activities GME was pursuing with FDOS—not the military activities that France was pursuing when *La Trinité* and other ships of the Royal Navy of France sank in 1565. Thus, while *Odyssey* may have some relevance to *GME I*—the earlier *in rem* proceeding—it does not apply to this case where GME seeks damages based on the nature of France's present-day activities.

We therefore conclude that France's activities here are commercial activities under the FSIA.

B. Whether GME's action is "based upon" France's commercial activities

Although we conclude that France's activities are commercial under the FSIA, our inquiry under § 1605's commercial activity exception does not end there. Under § 1605(a)(2), we must also determine whether GME's action is "based upon" France's commercial activities. *See Nelson*, 507 U.S. at 356. To do so, "we must identify the conduct upon which the suit is based" by looking at "the 'particular conduct' that constitutes the 'gravamen' of the suit," i.e., "the 'core' of the suit." *Devengoechea*, 889 F.3d at 1222 (quoting *OBB Personenverkehr AG v. Sachs*, 577 U.S. 27, 35 (2015)); *see also Nelson*, 507 U.S. at 358 (explaining that the only reasonable reading of the term "based upon" is that it "calls for something more than a mere connection with, or relation to, commercial activity."). But we do not undertake an "exhaustive claim-by-claim, element-by-element analysis" of the plaintiff's cause of action. *Sachs*, 577 U.S. at 34. **[—25—]**

For example, in *Devengoechea*, the plaintiff filed suit against Venezuela for failing to pay for or return to him artifacts belonging to Simón Bolívar. 889 F.3d at 1217. In determining whether the plaintiff's action was "based upon" Venezuela's commercial activity, we explained that the conduct that injured the plaintiff—and made up the gravamen of his suit—was Venezuela's failure to pay for or return the artifacts. *Id.* at 1223.

Here, the district court assumed, for the sake of this part of its analysis, that France's activities were commercial in nature and found that GME's injury was not "based on" the Declaration of Intent and that France's activities were not related to the Declaration, i.e., the shipwreck recovery project. Rather, the district court found that GME's action was "based upon the fact that France took ownership of the ship," which "occurred the moment the [*GME I* district court] concluded that the *res* was *La Trinité* and belonged to France." GME contends that this characterization of its suit against France was in error. Rather, GME argues, the gravamen of its suit is France's activities related to the shipwreck recovery project and France's failure to compensate GME for a substantial benefit it conferred to France—the value of its services that led to the discovery of the shipwreck sites including *La Trinité*. And GME argues that, without its services, France could not have undertaken the shipwreck recovery project.

While we pass no judgment on the merits of GME's claims, we find that the "gravamen" of GME's suit is France's activities in executing the shipwreck recovery project and its failure to **[—26—]** compensate GME for the value of the services. Indeed, the core of GME's claims against France—claims for an *in personam* salvage lien award, unjust enrichment, misappropriation of **{–1325–}** trade secret information, and interference with its rights and relations—is France's failure to compensate GME for the value of GME's salvaging services. *See Devengoechea*, 889 F.3d at 1223 ("The conduct that actually injured Devengoechea—and therefore that makes up the gravamen of Devengoechea's lawsuit—is Venezuela's failure to return the Bolívar Collection to Devengoechea or to pay him for it."). GME's salvage services led to the discovery of *La Trinité* and the other shipwreck sites, which, in turn, led to France's joint shipwreck recovery project with FDOS, as set forth by the Declaration of Intent. And, as explained above, France's activities in planning and executing the shipwreck recovery project qualify as "commercial activity."

We therefore hold that the FSIA's commercial activity exception to foreign sovereign immunity applies because GME's action is "based upon" France's commercial activity in the United States. Accordingly, the district court had subject matter jurisdiction over GME's suit against France.

IV. CONCLUSION

For these reasons, we reverse the district court's order dismissing GME's amended complaint for lack of subject matter jurisdiction and remand for further proceedings.

REVERSED and REMANDED.

United States Court of Appeals
for the Eleventh Circuit

No. 20-14517

GREAT LAKES INS. SE
vs.
WAVE CRUISER LLC

Appeal from the United States District Court for the Southern District of Florida

Decided: June 15, 2022

Citation: 36 F.4th 1346, 10 Adm. R. 394 (11th Cir. 2022).

Before JORDAN, PRYOR, and MARCUS, Circuit Judges.

[—2—] **{–1349–}** PRYOR, Circuit Judge:

This case arises out of an insurance dispute between Great Lakes Insurance SE ("Great Lakes") and Wave Cruiser LLC ("Wave Cruiser"). Wave Cruiser purchased an "all risks" insurance policy from Great Lakes covering a vessel that Wave Cruiser had recently acquired. The policy did not cover engine damage unless an accidental external event caused the damage. After Wave Cruiser purchased the policy, the vessel suffered catastrophic engine failure. Wave Cruiser submitted a claim on its policy. Great Lakes denied the claim, explaining that Wave Cruiser had not shown that an external event caused the engine damage.

Great Lakes filed suit for a declaratory judgment that Wave Cruiser's policy did not afford coverage for the loss. Wave Cruiser filed counterclaims for breach of contract and breach of the duty of good faith and fair dealing. The district court granted summary judgment to Great Lakes. The district court concluded that Wave Cruiser failed to come forward with evidence that an external event caused the engine damage.

On appeal, Wave Cruiser argues that the district court incorrectly placed the burden on it to prove at trial that an external event caused the engine damage. Wave Cruiser also argues that the district court abused its discretion by considering expert testimony from a lay witness. After careful consideration, and with the benefit **[—3—]** of oral argument, we affirm. We agree with the district court that Wave Cruiser had the burden to come forward with evidence that an external event caused the engine failure. We also conclude that although the district court incorrectly considered **{–1350–}** expert opinion from a lay witness, summary judgment was appropriate because Wave Cruiser failed to create a genuine dispute of material fact as to whether an external event caused the engine failure.

I. BACKGROUND

We begin by describing the insurance policy that Wave Cruiser purchased from Great Lakes. We then turn to the incident that caused Wave Cruiser to make a claim on that policy and the litigation that followed.

A. The Insurance Policy

Great Lakes issued policy No. CSRYP/175137 (the "Policy") to Wave Cruiser. The Policy provided $310,000 in coverage for Wave Cruiser's 2003 45' Viking (the "vessel") and ran from April 25, 2019 to April 25, 2020. The Policy was "an 'all risks' form of marine insurance policy" that covered "any loss and or damage" to the vessel that was "accidental, fortuitous in nature and . . . incidental" to the vessel's use. Doc. 25-1 at 22.[1] But the Policy did not provide coverage for all types of damage and contained several exclusion provisions identifying types of damage the Policy did not cover. Under Exclusion r, the Policy provided no coverage for **[—4—]** "[d]amage to the Scheduled Vessel's engines . . . unless caused by an accidental external event such as collision, impact with a fixed or floating object, grounding, stranding, ingestion of foreign object, lightning strike or fire." *Id.* at 6.

The Policy also included a choice of law provision. This provision provided that "entrenched principles and precedents of substantive United States Federal Admiralty law" would govern disputes under the Policy.

[1] "Doc." numbers refer to district court docket entries.

Doc. 25-1 at 16. If no entrenched federal admiralty principles or precedents existed, then the Policy called for the application of New York substantive law.

B. The Vessel's Engine Failure

Before Wave Cruiser purchased the vessel, a surveyor completed a prepurchase report on it. The surveyor concluded that the vessel and its machinery were "primarily sound." Doc. 22-3 at 13. He also recommended that the engines be inspected to make sure they worked properly. At some point a marine diesel technician performed a 2500-hour service inspection on the vessel's engines and reported that they were in "great shape." Doc. 25-5 at 3. A few months later, however, the vessel's port engine suffered catastrophic engine failure.[2] The vessel's engines had operated for 17 **[—5—]** hours between the surveyor's prepurchase inspection and the port engine failure. The captain of the vessel did not report rough weather or anything else unusual and described the engine failure "as sudden and unexpected." Doc. 25-5 at 2.

Wave Cruiser's agent reported the engine failure to Great Lakes. Great Lakes' **{-1351-}** underwriter assigned Arnold & Arnold Inc. to investigate the claim. An Arnold & Arnold surveyor named Captain Ian Allen inspected the vessel. Allen had been a surveyor for Arnold & Arnold since 2012, but he had no "training or certification on the type of" engine that failed in the vessel. Doc. 49-1 at 8. He also did not consider himself an expert on internal combustion engines or, more specifically, diesel engines.

After his inspection, Allen issued his "First Report." Doc. 22-5 at 1. In the report, Allen determined that the cause of the engine failure could only be determined by removing and dissembling the engine. He found no evidence of an external cause but did posit some "possible causes" and noted that the "most likely" cause of the damage was "fatigue failure of one or more parts." Doc. 25-5 at 4. After completing his inspection, Allen sent Wave Cruiser a letter **[—6—]** explaining that Great Lakes reserved its right to deny coverage for the claim under the policy's Exclusion r.

Wave Cruiser notified Allen that it had removed the damaged port engine from the vessel and invited him to examine it again. Allen submitted another report after inspecting the engine. *See* Doc. 25-7. In this report, he observed that the gaskets for the engine's cylinder heads and oil pan were old. He noted there were clamshells on the intake side of the engine's water pump, but he could not explain how the clamshells entered the water pump because the intake strainer was intact. He noted that although clams could restrict intake flow, "there was no evidence of the engine overheating." Doc. 25-7 at 2. Allen next examined engine cylinder parts that had come off the engine when it failed. He observed "elongation of a connecting rod top" on one of the engine's cylinders and reported that "[e]llongation is generally a type of damage that would occur over a period of time, rather than in a sudden failure." Doc. 25-7 at 2. Allen ended his report by stating that he could not determine with certainty which engine part failed first. But he concluded that "we can say with certainty that there was excess friction at the cylinder one and six connecting rod journal, and an internal engine failure did occur in this area." *Id.* at 3. During his deposition, Allen testified that he "could not find evidence of an external event that would have precipitated the" engine failure. Doc. 49-1 at 6.

---

[2] In its brief, Wave Cruiser states that "[t]he engine's failure occurred well before the end of the engine's projected lifespan" but does not cite anything in the record to support this statement. Appellant Br. at 11. Wave Cruiser submitted a "Statement of Material Facts" to the district court alongside its motion for summary judgment which also stated that the engine failed before the **[—5—]** end of its lifespan. Doc. 22 at 2. This document does not provide a record cite to support this statement. A review of the record also provides no support for this statement. Under Southern District of Florida Local Rules, a fact in a statement of material facts can only be admitted if it is supported by properly cited record evidence. S.D. Fla. L.R. 56.1(c). Because the statement concerning the engine's lifespan was not supported by record evidence, we will not consider it.

Allen recommended that Great Lakes continue to reserve its right to deny coverage under the Policy. A short time later, Allen **[—7—]** sent Wave Cruiser a letter denying its claim. The letter stated that there was no evidence of an external cause for the engine failure. Citing Exclusion r, the letter explained that the Policy did not cover engine damage unless caused by an accidental external event.[3]

C. Procedural History

Great Lakes brought this action seeking a declaratory judgment that the Policy did not cover the vessel's damaged engine. Wave Cruiser filed a counterclaim alleging that Great Lakes breached the terms of the Policy by failing to investigate the claim fully and cover the loss. The counterclaim also alleged that Great Lakes breached its duty of good faith and fair dealing. **{-1352-}**

Wave Cruiser filed a motion for summary judgment on its breach-of-contract counterclaim. Great Lakes filed a motion for summary judgment on its declaratory-judgment claim. In its motion, Great Lakes argued that it "remains Capt. Allen's expert opinion that there was no evidence that an external event caused the failure of the port engine." Doc. 24 at 2. Wave Cruiser then filed a motion to strike Allen as an expert witness because Great Lakes failed to disclose that he was an expert in accordance with Federal Rule of Civil Procedure 26(a)(2)(B). The district court denied the **[—8—]** motion but ordered that Wave Cruiser depose Allen. During his deposition, Allen testified that he did not have expert knowledge about engines and did not consider himself an expert witness. After the deposition, Great Lakes filed a notice withdrawing Allen as an expert. Great Lakes argued that "[i]nstead, the evidence offered by Capt. Allen should be considered merely as the evidence of a lay witness." Doc. 48 at 1.

The district court issued an order granting Great Lakes' motion for summary judgment and denying Wave Cruiser's motion for summary judgment. The district court applied a three-part burden shifting framework to determine whether the Policy covered Wave Cruiser's claim. Under this framework, Wave Cruiser had the initial burden to present evidence that it suffered a fortuitous loss within the Policy period. Once Wave Cruiser did this, the burden would shift to Great Lakes to establish that a policy exclusion applied. If Great Lakes established an applicable exclusion, the burden would return to Wave Cruiser to produce evidence that an exception to the policy exclusion applied.

The district court determined that Wave Cruiser met its initial burden by presenting evidence that the vessel was well maintained and recently serviced and that the engine failed suddenly and unexpectedly. The district court then considered whether Great Lakes could show that an exclusion to the Policy applied. Great Lakes argued that Exclusion r applied because it excluded engine damage unless caused by an external event, and the district court agreed. The district court rejected Wave Cruiser's argument that **[—9—]** Great Lakes—and not Wave Cruiser—had to prove the cause of the engine damage. Instead, the district court shifted the burden back to Wave Cruiser to present evidence that the exception to Exclusion r—engine damage caused by an external event—applied. The district court concluded that Wave Cruiser failed to carry its burden of proof, stating that the "total absence of evidence showing an external event necessarily means that there is no evidence triggering the exception to Exclusion r[.]" Doc. 56 at 23. Thus, the district court concluded, Great Lakes was entitled to summary judgment.[4]

[3] The letter also cited Exclusion b which denies coverage for losses "due to wear and tear, gradual deterioration, . . . [and] weathering[.]" Although Wave Cruiser argued that there was no evidence that the engine failure was caused by the losses included in Exclusion b, *see* Appellant Br. at 14, it does not cite to any evidence for that proposition nor does it discuss it further in its briefing.

[4] After determining that the Policy did not cover Wave Cruiser's claim, the district court dismissed Wave Cruiser's counterclaim for breach of covenant of good faith and fair dealing.

The district court entered final judgment in favor of Great Lakes. Wave Cruiser timely appealed to this Court.

II. STANDARD OF REVIEW

We review the district court's grant of summary judgment *de novo*, applying the same legal standards as the district court. *Hurlbert v. St. Mary's Health Care Sys., Inc.*, 439 F.3d 1286, 1293 (11th Cir. 2006). Summary judgment is appropriate only "if the movant shows that there is no genuine dispute as to any material fact and the movant is entitled to judgment as a matter of law." Fed. R. Civ. P. 56(a). The court must draw all reasonable inferences in favor of the non-moving **{-1353-}** party. *Welch v. Celotex Corp.*, 951 F.2d 1235, 1237 (11th Cir. 1992). **[—10—]**

We review a district court's evidentiary rulings for abuse of discretion. *Cook ex rel. Est. of Tessier v. Sheriff of Monroe Cnty.*, 402 F.3d 1092, 1103 (11th Cir. 2005). "However, even a clearly erroneous evidentiary ruling will be affirmed if harmless." *Furcron v. Mail Ctrs. Plus, LLC*, 843 F.3d 1295, 1304 (11th Cir. 2016).

III. DISCUSSION

Wave Cruiser contends that the district court erred in granting summary judgment to Great Lakes because it incorrectly placed the burden on Wave Cruiser to prove that an external event caused the engine failure. In addition, it argues that the district court abused its discretion by considering expert opinion evidence from Allen, who conceded that he was not an expert.

After careful review, we conclude that the district court properly granted summary judgment to Great Lakes. Wave Cruiser bore the burden to prove at trial that an external event caused the engine failure, and it failed to come forward at summary judgment with evidence to meet this burden. And although the district court erred by considering Allen's opinion testimony, we nonetheless hold that the error was harmless.

A. The District Court Correctly Granted Summary Judgment Because Wave Cruiser Failed to Come Forward with Evidence to Meet Its Burden to Prove that an External Event Caused the Engine Failure.

Wave Cruiser contends it did not have to prove that an external event caused the vessel's engine failure. Instead, it argues, to establish that Exclusion r applied, Great Lakes bore the burden of **[—11—]** proving that an internal event caused the engine failure. Before we can resolve which party had the burden to prove what caused the vessel's engine to fail, we must determine what law applies.

1. Applying the Parties' Choice of Law, Wave Cruiser Had the Burden to Prove that an External Event Caused the Engine Failure.

Because the Policy provides for marine insurance, it "give[s] rise to admiralty jurisdiction." *St. Paul Fire & Marine Ins. Co. v. Lago Canyon, Inc.*, 561 F.3d 1181, 1184 (11th Cir. 2009). "When admiralty jurisdiction is invoked, a uniform body of federal maritime law applies." *Aqua Log, Inc. v. Lost & Abandoned Pre-Cut Logs & Rafts of Logs*, 709 F.3d 1055, 1061, 1 Adm. R. 448, 452 (11th Cir. 2013). The Policy's choice-of-law provision states that disputes should be "adjudicated according to well established, entrenched principles and precedents of substantive United States Federal Admiralty law and practice but where no such well established, entrenched precedent exists, this insuring agreement is subject to the substantive laws of" New York. Doc. 22-1 at 16. Our Circuit has never examined whether a choice-of-law provision is enforceable under federal maritime law, making this a question of first impression. Other circuits have enforced choice-of-law agreements in maritime contracts, however.[5] *See e.g.*, **{-1354-}** *Chan v.*

[5] Although we have never decided whether a choice-of-law clause is enforceable under federal maritime choice-of-law rules, we have suggested in dicta that they are. In *GEICO Marine Insurance Company v. Shackleford*, 945 F.3d 1135, **[—12—]** 1137, 7 Adm. R. 528, 528 (11th Cir. 2019), we

Soc'y Expeditions, Inc., 123 F.3d **[—12—]** 1287, 1296–97 (9th Cir. 1997) ("[W]here the parties specify in their contractual agreement which law will apply, admiralty courts will generally give effect to that choice."). Indeed, the Fifth and Third Circuits have enforced choice-of-law provisions with the exact same language as the provision at issue here. *See Great Lakes Reinsurance (UK) PLC v. Durham Auctions, Inc.*, 585 F.3d 236, 245 (5th Cir. 2009) ("[E]ither the general maritime law . . . or New York law, . . . governs the parties' rights under the instant marine insurance policy."); *AGF Marine Aviation & Transp. v. Cassin*, 544 F.3d 255, 261 (3rd Cir. 2008) ("[T]he Policy, and its choice of law provision, was in effect at the time the Yacht sank, and governs this dispute."). We see no reason to depart from our sister circuits by declining to enforce the parties' choice-of-law agreement in this case. We note that the Fifth Circuit applied the choice-of-law provision in *Durham Auctions* because no party showed that its application "would be unreasonable or unjust." 585 F.3d at 244. We have no occasion today to decide whether we would refuse to enforce a choice-of-law clause in a maritime contract if its enforcement would be unreasonable or unjust because neither party argues that here.

The Policy's choice-of-law provision first directs us to determine whether there are any entrenched principles or precedents of **[—13—]** admiralty law that would govern this dispute. Wave Cruiser points to two published maritime-law decisions, arguing they establish that for Exclusion r to apply and bar coverage of Wave Cruiser's claim, Great Lakes had to prove the cause of the vessel's engine failure. Upon review, we do not believe they answer the question before us.

Wave Cruiser's argument relies primarily on *Morrison Grain Co., Inc. v. Utica Mutual Insurance Co.*, 632 F.2d 424 (5th Cir. 1980).[6] That case arose out of an insurer's refusal to pay its insured's claim for damage to a ship's cargo. *Id.* at 426–27. The policy at issue insured "against all risks of physical loss or damage to property from any external cause." *Id.* at 427 (internal quotation marks omitted). The insured sued; the district court concluded that the insurer had to pay the insured's claim for the damaged cargo. *Id.* at 428. On appeal, the Fifth Circuit had to determine the "respective burdens of proof" under the policy of the insurer and the insured. *Id.* at 427.

The insurer argued that for coverage to apply, the insured had the burden to prove that something external damaged the cargo. *Id.* at 429. The Fifth Circuit disagreed, reasoning that "[i]t would seem to be inconsistent with the broad protective purposes of 'all risk' insurance to impose on the insured . . . the burden of **[—14—]** proving the precise cause of the loss or damage." *Id.* at 430. The court held that an insured under an all-risk policy had the "not . . . particularly onerous" burden to show a fortuitous loss. *Id.* The insured could meet this burden by showing that the cargo was in good condition when the insurance company issued the policy and was found to be damaged when it was unloaded from the vessel. *Id.* at 431. Once the insured made this showing, then the burden shifted to the insurer to establish the applicability of any exclusions to coverage. *Id.*

Wave Cruiser also points to **{-1355-}** *Banco Nacional De Nicaragua v. Argonaut Insurance Co.*, 681 F.2d 1337 (11th Cir. 1982), decided a few years later. That case likewise involved an insurance policy that covered "all risks of physical harm to [certain cargo] caused by any external force, subject to certain exceptions." *Id.* at 1339. The insurer denied coverage for the loss and the insured filed suit. *Id.* On appeal, we reiterated the burden-shifting framework from *Morrison Grain*. *Id.* The insured had the initial burden to show that a fortuitous loss occurred within the policy period. *Id.* at 1340. The burden then shifted to the insurer to show that an exclusion to coverage applied. *Id.*

---

examined whether a marine insurance policy covered damage to a yacht. We applied federal maritime law, noting that "[t]he parties could have included a choice-of-law provision selecting state law over federal law[.]" *Id.* at 1143, 7 Adm. R. at 533.

[6] In *Bonner v. City of Prichard*, 661 F.2d 1206, 1209 (11th Cir.1981) (en banc), we adopted as binding precedent all decisions of the former Fifth Circuit handed down prior to October 1, 1981.

According to Wave Cruiser, these two cases establish that it did not have the burden to prove that an external event caused the vessel's engine failure. The problem for Wave Cruiser is that *Morrison Grain* and *Banco Nacional De Nicaragua* do not answer the ultimate question in this case. Both cases addressed the parties' respective burdens under an "all risk" policy, holding that insured **[—15—]** parties do not have to show the cause of damage to meet their initial fortuitous-loss burden under such policies. Neither case examined a policy with an exclusion that was subject to an exception. In contrast, here, Exclusion r states that the Policy does not cover engine damage "unless caused by an accidental external event[.]" Doc. 25-1 at 6. Our review of federal admiralty law has uncovered no authority or principle to guide us on who bears the burden to prove the cause of the loss under an exclusion like this one.

Because federal admiralty precedent sheds no light on how Exclusion r allocates the burden of proof, the Policy's choice-of-law provision points us to New York law. The Court of Appeals of New York has examined policy exclusion provisions that include exceptions. *See Northville Indus. Corp. v. Nat'l Union Fire Ins. Co. of Pittsburgh*, 679 N.E.2d 1044 (N.Y. 1997). We find its analysis instructive.

Northville Industries concerned general liability insurance purchased by a gasoline-storage business. *Id.* at 1046. The policy contained an exclusion provision barring coverage for damages "arising out of the discharge, dispersal, release or escape of toxic chemicals, liquids or other pollutants into or upon land but this exclusion does not apply if such discharge, dispersal, release or escape is *sudden and accidental*." *Id.* (alterations adopted) (emphasis in original). Two of the insured's facilities released gasoline into the groundwater. *Id.* Neighboring properties sued. *Id.* When the insured sought coverage under the policy, the insurer refused, citing the exclusion. *Id.* The insured brought a declaratory judgment **[—16—]** action to establish that its insurer had an obligation to defend and indemnify it. *Id.* On appeal, the Court of Appeals of New York had to determine whether the exclusion foreclosed coverage. *Id.* at 1047–49. The court held that once the insurer showed the exclusion precluded coverage, "the burden shift[ed] to the insured to demonstrate" that an exception to the exclusion applied. *Id.* at 1048; *see also Ment Bros. Iron Works Co., v. Interstate Fire & Cas. Co.*, 702 F.3d 118, 121 (2d Cir. 2012) ("Once the insurer establishes that an exclusion applies, however, New York law has evolved to place the burden of proof on the insured to establish the applicability of an *exception to the exclusion*." (emphasis in original)).

The court's analysis in *Northville Industries* is easily applied to Exclusion r. Great Lakes had the burden to establish that Exclusion r precluded the claim because the claim was for engine damage. Then the burden shifted back to Wave **{–1356–}** Cruiser to prove that the exception to Exclusion r applied because an accidental external event caused the loss.

To sum up, the Policy's choice-of-law provision first points us to federal admiralty law, which provides that under an all-risk maritime insurance policy an insured has the initial burden to provide evidence that a fortuitous loss occurred within the policy period. *Morrison Grain Co., Inc.*, 632 F.2d at 430–31; *Banco Nacional De Nicaragua*, 681 F.2d at 1339–40. The burden then shifts to the insurer to demonstrate that an exclusion provision forecloses coverage. *Morrison Grain Co., Inc.*, 632 F.2d at 431. Federal admiralty law is silent, however, when it comes to which party has the **[—17—]** burden to prove that an exception to the exclusion applies. In the absence of governing federal admiralty law, the Policy's choice-of-law provision directs us to apply New York law, which places this burden on the insured. *Northville Indus. Corp.*, 679 N.E.2d at 1048. We conclude that the district court did not err in placing the burden on Wave Cruiser to prove that an external event caused the engine failure, and therefore the damage fell within the exclusion's exception.

2. Summary Judgment was Appropriate Because Wave Cruiser Failed to Come Forward with Evidence that an External Event Caused the Engine Failure.

Applying the burden shifting framework established by New York law, we conclude that Wave Cruiser offered sufficient evidence to meet its initial burden. Great Lakes then met its burden under the framework to demonstrate that Exclusion r applied. But Wave Cruiser failed to come forward with evidence to create a genuine issue of material fact on the ultimate issue—on which it bore the burden of proof at trial—of whether an external event caused the engine failure.

As an initial matter, Wave Cruiser had to demonstrate that the vessel's engine failure was a fortuitous loss under the Policy. The evidence shows that a marine diesel technician performed a 2500-hour inspection on the engines and found them to be in great shape. The vessel's port "engine was operated seventeen hours between the time of survey and the time of engine failure." Doc. 25-5 at 2. The failure was "sudden and unexpected." *Id.* In *Morrison* **[—18—]** *Grain*, we held that the insured demonstrated a fortuitous loss by presenting evidence that the cargo was in good condition when the ship departed and in a damaged condition when the ship arrived. *Morrison Grain*, 632 F.2d at 431–33. Likewise, here, Wave Cruiser presented evidence that the engine was in good condition at the time the Policy attached and then stopped working unexpectedly. This is enough at the summary judgment stage for Wave Cruiser to meet its "not . . . particularly onerous" burden to provide evidence of a fortuitous loss. *Id.* at 430.

The burden then shifted to Great Lakes to establish that Exclusion r applied. Because Exclusion r unambiguously precluded coverage for damage to the vessel's engine "unless caused by an accidental external event," Great Lakes met this burden by showing that Wave Cruiser's claimed loss was engine damage. Doc. 25-1 at 6.

Wave Cruiser then bore the burden to prove that the exception to the exclusion applied. "To survive summary judgment, the nonmoving party bearing the ultimate burden of proof at trial must come forward with evidence sufficient to withstand a directed verdict motion." *Hickson Corp. v. N. Crossarm Co., Inc.*, 357 F.3d 1256, 1260 (11th Cir. 2004). Wave **{-1357-}** Cruiser did not present any evidence identifying what caused the engine failure. Instead, Wave Cruiser argues that the same evidence that satisfied its fortuitous-loss burden also created a genuine dispute of material fact concerning whether an external event caused the engine failure. We disagree. To survive summary judgment on its fortuitous-loss burden, **[—19—]** Wave Cruiser did not have to create a genuine dispute of material fact concerning the "cause of the loss." *Morrison Grain*, 632 F.2d at 430. But that is precisely what it had to do once the burden shifted back to Wave Cruiser to prove that the exception to Exclusion r applied. The evidence that the vessel received a 2500-hour inspection and was found to be in great shape says nothing about what caused the engine failure; thus, it did not create a genuine dispute of fact on this issue. To hold otherwise would collapse Wave Cruiser's two separate burdens into one, with the effect that Exclusion r would, essentially, be read out of the Policy.

Neither party in this case has submitted evidence of what caused the engine failure. But Wave Cruiser had the burden at trial to prove that an external event caused the port engine to fail. "Where, as here, the non-moving party bears the burden of proof on an issue at trial, the moving party" may prevail on summary judgment by "show[ing] that the non-moving party has no evidence to support its case[.]" *Hammer v. Slater*, 20 F.3d 1137, 1141 (11th Cir. 1994). Great Lakes has shown that Wave Cruiser has no evidence that an external event caused the engine failure, so the district court properly granted summary judgment to Great Lakes.[7] **[—20—]**

---

[7] Wave Cruiser argues that Allen testified that the engine failure had an external cause, and that Great Lakes improperly changed this testimony with an errata sheet. Great Lakes' errata sheet sought to make four changes that substituted the word "external" for the word "internal" or made similar alterations. Great Lakes maintains that the

B. The Court Abused Its Discretion by Considering Expert Opinion Evidence from Allen, But this Error was Harmless.

Wave Cruiser also argues that the district court abused its discretion by considering expert opinion evidence from Allen's survey reports and his deposition. Great Lakes withdrew Allen as an expert witness, but the district court considered his testimony and survey reports as lay opinion evidence under Federal Rule of Evidence 701. We conclude that the district court abused its discretion by considering Allen's opinions, but this error was harmless.

Under Federal Rule of Evidence 701, "a lay witness may offer opinions that are: '(a) rationally based on the perception of the witness, (b) helpful to a clear understanding of the witness' testimony or the determination of a fact in issue, and (c) not based on scientific, technical, or other specialized knowledge within the scope of Rule 702.'" *United States v. Hill*, 643 F.3d 807, 840–41 (11th Cir. 2011) (quoting Fed. R. Evid. 701). "This rule of evidence is designed to prevent parties from proffering an expert in lay witness clothing by ensuring that testimony that is actually expert passes the strictures **{-1358-}** of Rule 702." *Lebron v. Sec'y of Fla. Dep't of Child. & Fams.*, 772 F.3d 1352, 1372 (11th Cir. 2014) (internal quotation **[—21—]** marks omitted). Lay opinion testimony cannot "provide specialized explanations or interpretations that an untrained layman could not make if perceiving the same acts or events." *United States v. Peoples*, 250 F.3d 630, 641 (8th Cir. 2001).

In this case, the district court noted Allen's observation regarding the clamshells found on the intake side of the pump and his speculation that although "such marine organisms would restrict intake flow," these clams likely did not since "there was no evidence of the engine overheating." Doc. 56 at 5. It also considered Allen's opinion that the elongation of one of the engine's connecting rods was the kind of damage that occurred over a period of time. In addition, the district court took into account Allen's opinion that "there was excess friction at the cylinder one and six connecting rod journal and an internal engine failure did occur in this area." Doc. 56 at 6. The district court correctly considered Allen's testimony about the presence of clams and that the connecting rod was elongated because this testimony was "based on [his] firsthand knowledge" and observations. *United States v. Rivera*, 780 F.3d 1084, 1094 (11th Cir. 2015) (internal quotation marks omitted). Likewise, it was within the district court's discretion to consider Allen's statement that there was excess friction on cylinders one and six because it, too, was based on his observations of the engine parts. But the inferences Allen drew, that the clams did not cause the engine to overheat and fail, that the elongation took place over a period of time, and that the excess friction at cylinders one and six was connected to the engine failure, "blurs into supposition and **[—22—]** extrapolation [which] crosses the line into expertise." *Lebron*, 772 F.3d at 1372. To be admissible, these opinions would have to be based on "specialized knowledge." Fed. R. Evid. 701. By his own admission, Allen does not have specialized knowledge about the engine in this case or internal combustion engines in general. The district court therefore abused its discretion by considering Allen's opinions about the cause of the engine failure.

Although the district court abused its discretion, we conclude that this error was harmless. The district court's grant of summary judgment to Great Lakes was appropriate because Wave Cruiser failed to produce evidence to create a genuine dispute of material fact concerning whether an external event caused the vessel's port engine

---

changes corrected transcription errors. **[—20—]** "[A] change of substance which actually contradicts the transcript is impermissible unless it can plausibly be represented as the correction of an error in transcription, such as dropping a 'not.'" *Thorn v. Sundstrand Aerospace Corp.*, 207 F.3d 383, 389 (7th Cir. 2000). We need not decide which party is correct about the errata, however, because, as we explain below, Wave Cruiser is correct that Allen's opinions on the cause of the engine failure are inadmissible.

failure. The inadmissibility of Allen's opinions does not change this.

IV. CONCLUSION

We conclude that (1) the district court did not err by placing the burden on Wave Cruiser to provide evidence that an external event caused the vessel's port engine to fail, and (2) the district court committed harmless error by considering inadmissible expert opinion testimony. Accordingly, we affirm the judgment of the district court.

AFFIRMED.

United States Court of Appeals
for the Eleventh Circuit

No. 21-10298

HOLLAND
vs.
CARNIVAL CORP.

Appeal from the United States District Court for the Southern District of Florida

Decided: October 4, 2022

Citation: 50 F.4th 1088, 10 Adm. R. 403 (11th Cir. 2022).

Before **WILSON**, **LUCK**, and **LAGOA**, Circuit Judges.

[—2—] {–1091–} LAGOA, Circuit Judge:

Donnie Holland appeals the district court's dismissal of his amended complaint against Carnival Corporation for failure to state a claim under Federal Rule of Civil Procedure 12(b)(6). Holland contends that the district court erred in finding that his amended complaint failed to allege sufficient facts in support of his negligence claims to show that Carnival was on notice of the alleged hazard. After careful review and with the benefit of oral argument, we conclude that the district court's dismissal was proper and affirm.

I. FACTUAL AND PROCEDURAL BACKGROUND[1]

Carnival, a Panamanian corporation with its principal place of business in Miami, Florida, operates a number of cruise ships, including the *Horizon*. Holland, a passenger onboard the *Horizon*, "was descending the glass stairs from Deck 5 to Deck 4[,] when he slipped on a wet or slippery transient foreign substance." As a result, Holland "sustained serious injuries, including a complete **[—3—]** rupture of the right knee patella tendon and an avulsion fracture of the tibial tubercle necessitating open surgical repair and extensive physical therapy."

Holland filed an action against Carnival in the Southern District of Florida. In his amended complaint, Holland alleged that Carnival "had actual and/or constructive notice of the dangerous condition" he slipped on, i.e., the "wet or slippery transient foreign substance" on the glass staircase. He alleged that the glass staircase was "one of the most highly trafficked areas of the ship," as it was "flanked by shops on either side staffed by dozens of crewmembers" and opened up to a casino and approximately six different bars and dining areas. Holland also alleged that "[s]everal hundred passengers and crew-members traverse[d]" the glass stairway "every day, many of whom [were] carrying drinks," that the "[c]rewmembers in the surrounding shops have a clear unobstructed view of the staircase," and that there were "frequently spills on the staircase," **{–1092–}** which Carnival was "aware of due to the frequent nature of prior slip and fall incidents on this staircase." And Holland alleged that, at the time of his fall, "the surrounding shops were staffed with crewmembers who had been present in their shops for approximately four hours or more," meaning that Carnival "knew or should have known that the particular wet, foreign or transitory substance upon which [he] fell was present prior to [him] falling." Holland also claimed that various safety agencies had "developed safety standards applicable to [the] staircase [at **[—4—]** issue]," which "in and of themselves constitute[d] constructive notice that conditions in violation of th[ose] standards are hazardous."

Holland's amended complaint asserted two negligence claims against Carnival: (1) vicarious liability for negligent maintenance; and (2) vicarious liability for negligent failure to warn of a hazard. As to the negligent maintenance claim, Holland alleged that Carnival had actual or constructive knowledge of the hazardous condition and that its crewmembers failed to "conduct sufficient routine inspections of the area," to "maintain

[1] Because the procedural posture of this case involves a Federal Rule of Civil Procedure 12(b)(6) motion, we must accept the allegations of plaintiff's complaint as true and construe them in the light most favorable to the plaintiff. *See Chaparro v. Carnival Corp.*, 693 F.3d 1333, 1335 (11th Cir. 2012). The facts set forth in this section of the opinion therefore are taken from the complaint and construed in the light most favorable to the plaintiff.

the glass stairs in a reasonably safe condition," and to "properly clean and dry the glass stairs." As to the negligent failure to warn claim, Holland asserted that Carnival had actual or constructive knowledge of the dangerous condition and that its crewmembers failed to adequately warn Holland of the condition before he fell "by appropriate signs, markings, written or oral warnings, or otherwise."

Carnival filed a motion to dismiss pursuant to Rule 12(b)(6), arguing that Holland failed to raise a plausible negligence claim because he "fail[ed] to allege adequate evidence that Carnival had actual or constructive notice of a risk creating condition." Carnival further argued that Holland's mere conclusory allegations as to whether Carnival was or should have been aware of the specific, alleged hazard were insufficient to impute notice to it. Holland opposed Carnival's motion.

The district court granted Carnival's motion to dismiss. The district court found that Holland "failed to allege that Carnival was on either actual or constructive notice of the hazard in question" **[—5—]** and thus failed to satisfy the pleading standards set forth in *Bell Atlantic Corp. v. Twombly*, 550 U.S. 544 (2007), and *Ashcroft v. Iqbal*, 556 U.S. 662 (2009). The district court found that Holland failed to provide any facts in support of his bare allegation that there were frequent, prior slip and fall incidents on the specific glass staircase, such that this allegation failed to establish constructive notice. The district court also found that Holland's allegation that the glass staircase was highly trafficked failed because that allegation did not support a conclusion that Carnival should have known of the alleged condition at the time of Holland's injury. The district court explained that the totality of Holland's allegations was that certain Carnival employees "may have been in a position to see that there was a liquid on the stairs in question," which were in a high traffic area of the ship, but that "it [was] impossible . . . to tell if the hazardous condition . . . complain[ed] of was present for five second[s], five minutes, or five hours." Therefore, while the amended complaint made clear it was "*possible* that Carnival was on notice," it did "not state a claim that [was] *plausible* on its face sufficient to survive a motion to dismiss." And the district court rejected Holland's argument that certain safety regulations ipso facto established constructive notice. Accordingly, because Holland failed to allege that Carnival was on actual or constructive notice of the "wet or slippery transient foreign substance," **{-1093-}** the district court dismissed Holland's amended complaint. This appeal ensued. **[—6—]**

II. STANDARD OF REVIEW

"We review *de novo* the district court's grant of a Rule 12(b)(6) motion to dismiss for failure to state a claim, accepting the complaint's allegations as true and construing them in the light most favorable to the plaintiff." *Chaparro v. Carnival Corp.*, 693 F.3d 1333, 1335 (11th Cir. 2012) (quoting *Cinotto v. Delta Air Lines Inc.*, 674 F.3d 1285, 1291 (11th Cir. 2012)). However, "the tenet that a court must accept as true all of the allegations contained in a complaint is inapplicable to legal conclusions." *Iqbal*, 556 U.S. at 678.

III. ANALYSIS

On appeal, Holland argues that the district court erred in dismissing his negligence claims against Carnival for failure to state a plausible claim—specifically, that Holland failed to plausibly allege that Carnival had actual or constructive notice of the alleged hazardous condition. We disagree.

Federal Rule of Civil Procedure 8(a)(2) requires a plaintiff's complaint to provide "a short and plain statement of the claim showing that the pleader is entitled to relief." This pleading standard requires that a plaintiff allege "enough facts to state a claim to relief that is plausible on its face," i.e., facts that will "nudge[] [a plaintiff's] claims across the line from conceivable to plausible." *Twombly*, 550 U.S. at 570. "A claim has facial plausibility when the plaintiff pleads factual content that allows the court to draw the **[—7—]** reasonable inference that the defendant is liable for the misconduct alleged." *Iqbal*, 556 U.S. at 678.

While "[t]he plausibility standard is not akin to a 'probability requirement,' . . . it asks for more than a sheer possibility that a defendant has acted unlawfully." *Id.* (quoting *Twombly*, 550 U.S. at 556). This analysis is not formulaic; instead, "[d]etermining whether a complaint states a plausible claim for relief [is] . . . a context-specific task that requires the reviewing court to draw on its judicial experience and common sense" in reviewing the plaintiff's allegations. *Id.* at 679. Additionally, "[t]hreadbare recitals of the elements of a cause of action" and "conclusory statements" are insufficient. *Id.* at 678 (citing *Twombly*, 550 U.S. at 555). To that end, we have counseled that the first step in evaluating a motion to dismiss is to "eliminate any allegations in the complaint that are merely legal conclusions." *Am. Dental Ass'n v. Cigna Corp.*, 605 F.3d 1283, 1290 (11th Cir. 2010); *accord Iqbal*, 556 U.S. at 678 ("Where a complaint pleads facts that are 'merely consistent with' a defendant's liability, it 'stops short of the line between possibility and plausibility of "entitlement to relief."'" (quoting *Twombly*, 550 U.S. at 557)).

"Maritime law governs actions arising from alleged torts committed aboard a ship sailing in navigable waters," and we "rely on general principles of negligence law" in analyzing those actions. *Guevara v. NCL (Bahamas) Ltd.*, 920 F.3d 710, 720, 7 Adm. R. 476, 481 (11th Cir. 2019) (quoting *Chaparro*, 693 F.3d at 1336). General principles of negligence law, as applied in the maritime context, recognize a claim **[—8—]** based on a shipowner's direct liability for its own negligence or a claim based on a shipowner's vicarious liability for another's negligence. Direct liability and vicarious liability are very different concepts, and as discussed below, Holland has improperly tried to **{–1094–}** blend them into a single theory of liability against Carnival.

The elements of a negligence claim based on a shipowner's direct liability for its own negligence are well settled: "a plaintiff must allege that (1) the defendant had a duty to protect the plaintiff from a particular injury; (2) the defendant breached that duty; (3) the breach actually and proximately caused the plaintiff's injury; and (4) the plaintiff suffered actual harm." *Franza v. Royal Caribbean Cruises, Ltd.*, 772 F.3d 1225, 1253, 2 Adm. R. 582, 603 (11th Cir. 2014) (quoting *Chaparro*, 693 F.3d at 1336). "With respect to the duty element in a maritime context, 'a shipowner owes the duty of exercising reasonable care towards those lawfully aboard the vessel who are not members of the crew.'" *Guevara*, 920 F.3d at 720, 7 Adm. R. at 481 (quoting *Kermarec v. Compagnie Generale Transatlantique*, 358 U.S. 625, 630 (1959)). "This standard 'requires, as a prerequisite to imposing liability, that the carrier have had actual or constructive notice of [a] risk-creating condition, at least where, as here, the menace is one commonly encountered on land and not clearly linked to nautical adventure.'" *Id.*, 7 Adm. R. at 481 (alteration in original) (quoting *Keefe v. Bahama Cruise Line, Inc.*, 867 F.2d 1318, 1322 (11th Cir. 1989)); *see also Kornberg v. Carnival Cruise Lines, Inc.*, 741 F.2d 1332, 1334 (11th Cir. 1984) (explaining that a shipowner "is not liable to passengers as an insurer, but only for its negligence"). Thus, a shipowner's **[—9—]** actual or constructive knowledge of the hazardous condition arises as part of the duty element in a claim seeking to hold the shipowner directly liable for its own negligence.

In contrast, a shipowner's duty to a plaintiff is not relevant to a claim based on vicarious liability. When the tortfeasor is an employee, the principle of vicarious liability allows "an otherwise non-faulty employer" to be held liable "for the negligent acts of [that] employee acting within the scope of employment." *Langfitt v. Fed. Marine Terminals, Inc.*, 647 F.3d 1116, 1121 (11th Cir. 2011) (citation omitted). In other words, liability for the agent's negligence is legally imputed to the non-negligent principal. *See Meyer v. Holley*, 537 U.S. 280, 285–86 (2003) ("The principal is liable for the acts and negligence of the agent in the course of his employment, although he did not authorize or did not know of the acts complained of." (quoting parenthetically *New Orleans, M. & C.R. Co. v. Hanning*, 82 U.S. 649, 657 (1872))).

In his amended complaint, Holland denominated each count as a claim for vicarious liability and alleged in each count that Carnival "was vicariously liable for any negligence or failure to exercise reasonable care by its crewmembers" to maintain a hazard-free stairway or to warn of any hazardous condition on the stairway. But other than the claims' titles and the conclusory allegation asserting that Carnival was vicariously liable, there is nothing in Holland's complaint that would lead one to understand his claims as seeking to impose liability on an otherwise nonfaulty Carnival for an employee's negligence. First, Holland did not identify any **[—10—]** specific crewmember whose negligence caused Holland's injury, much less a specific crewmember whose negligence occurred while acting within the scope of his employment—essential parts of any claim seeking to impose vicarious liability on an employer for an employee's negligence. *See Langfitt*, 647 F.3d at 1121. Second, in each count, Holland alleged that Carnival owed him, "as a fare paying passenger lawfully on board its vessel, a duty of reasonable care for his safety," and that Carnival "had actual and/or constructive notice of the **{-1095-}** dangerous condition" on the glass staircase. Neither of those allegations is relevant to a claim based on vicarious liability, but both are relevant to a claim based on Carnival's direct liability for its own negligence. Finally, both before the district court and on appeal before this Court, Holland focused his argument on the sufficiency of his allegations regarding Carnival's actual or constructive notice of the allegedly dangerous condition on the staircase—allegations only relevant to the duty element of a claim seeking to hold Carnival directly liable for its own negligence.

It is thus apparent that, despite what he has called his claims, Holland seeks to hold Carnival directly liable for its own negligence and not vicariously liable for a specific employee's negligence. Under a theory of direct liability, in order to survive Carnival's motion to dismiss, Holland had to plead sufficient facts to support each element of his claim, including that Carnival had actual or constructive notice about the dangerous condition. **[—11—]**

Actual notice exists when the defendant knows about the dangerous condition. *See Keefe*, 867 F.2d at 1322; *Guevara*, 920 F.3d at 720, 7 Adm. R. at 481. Constructive notice exists where "the shipowner ought to have known of the peril to its passengers, the hazard having been present for a period of time so lengthy as to invite corrective measures." *Keefe*, 867 F.2d at 1322. A plaintiff can establish constructive notice by alleging "that the 'defective condition exist[ed] for a sufficient period of time to invite corrective measures.'" *Guevara*, 920 F.3d at 720, 7 Adm. R. at 481 (alteration in original) (quoting *Monteleone v. Bahama Cruise Line, Inc.*, 838 F.2d 63, 65 (2d Cir. 1988)). A plaintiff can also establish constructive notice by alleging "substantially similar incidents in which 'conditions substantially similar to the occurrence in question must have caused the prior accident.'" *Id.*, 7 Adm. R. at 481 (quoting *Jones v. Otis Elevator Co.*, 861 F.2d 655, 661–62 (11th Cir. 1988)). On appeal, Holland relies only on constructive notice and has abandoned any argument as to actual notice. We therefore will focus our analysis on whether Holland alleged a facially plausible claim that Carnival "ought to have known of" the hazardous wet or slippery surface that caused him to slip. *See Keefe*, 867 F.2d at 1322.

Turning to Holland's amended complaint, and accepting his allegations as true, we conclude that Holland failed to include factual allegations that plausibly suggest Carnival had constructive notice of the dangerous condition. Therefore, Holland has failed to satisfy the pleading standard set forth in *Iqbal* and *Twombly*. Rather, Holland's amended complaint contains only conclusory **[—12—]** allegations as to constructive notice. For example, Holland only set forth the following factual allegations as to notice. The glass staircase, on which Holland slipped and fell due to a hazardous sub-stance, was in a highly trafficked area of the *Horizon*. Several hundred passengers and crewmembers traversed the staircase every day, many of whom carried drinks. Crewmembers working in shops surrounding the staircase had "a clear unobstructed view of the staircase," and there were "frequently spills on the staircase," which Holland contended Carnival was "aware of due to the frequent nature of prior slip and fall incidents on this staircase." Thus, those crewmembers "can see spills as they happen and can see foreign substances left on the staircase by spills," and at the time of Holland's fall, "the surrounding shops were staffed with crewmembers who had been present in their shops for approximately four hours or more." Finally, Holland alleged that safety agencies had "developed safety standards applicable to this staircase." In sum, Holland alleged that the hazard occurred on a **{–1096–}** highly trafficked staircase that was potentially visible to many crewmembers and was subject to the regulation of safety agencies.

But while Holland alleges facts that establish the *possibility* that Carnival had constructive notice of the hazardous substance on the staircase as to invite corrective measures, a claim only has facial *plausibility* when the plaintiff's allegations allow "the court to draw the reasonable inference that the defendant is liable for the misconduct alleged." *See Iqbal*, 556 U.S. at 678. As to constructive notice, Holland was required to plausibly allege that either (1) the **[—13—]** hazardous substance existed on the staircase for a sufficient length of time, *see Keefe*, 867 F.2d at 1322, or (2) substantially similar incidents occurred in which "conditions substantially similar to the occurrence in question must have caused the prior accident," *Guevara*, 920 F.3d at 720, 7 Adm. R. at 481 (quoting *Jones*, 861 F.2d at 661–62).

As to whether there were substantially similar incidents, Holland's conclusory allegations that "[t]here are frequently spills on the staircase" and "prior slip and fall incidents on this staircase" are insufficient. *See Iqbal*, 556 U.S. at 678 ("[C]onclusory statements[] do not suffice."); *see also Am. Dental Ass'n*, 605 F.3d at 1293–94. And Holland has not alleged any facts concerning a substantially similar incident to the one at issue. Therefore, Holland has not plausibly alleged that Carnival had constructive knowledge based on a substantially similar incident.

As to the length of time the alleged hazardous substance was on the staircase, we conclude that the inferential leap from Holland's premise—that the staircase is highly visible and well-trodden—to his conclusion—that the hazard existed for a sufficient length of time—is too great. Indeed, Holland's amended complaint lacks any allegation as to how long the "wet or slippery transient foreign substance" existed on the glass staircase. Nor does the amended complaint allege any factual allegations describing that substance in a way that would suggest it existed on the staircase for a sufficient period of time such that Carnival should have been aware of it or that would tend to show that the liquid was on the staircase for an amount of time sufficient to impute constructive **[—14—]** notice to Carnival. And the amount of time that the hazard existed is a key factor for a plaintiff, such as Holland, to establish that a defendant such as Carnival had constructive notice of the hazard.

Furthermore, while Holland alleges that there were crewmembers in the surrounding shops, he does not allege that there were any crewmembers in the immediate area of the glass staircase that could have observed or warned him of the hazard. Simply put, Holland's allegations do not cross the line from possibility to plausibility of entitlement to relief. *See Iqbal*, 556 U.S. at 678.

Finally, we conclude that Holland's reliance on this Court's decision in *Yusko v. NCL (Bahamas), Ltd.*, 4 F.4th 1164, 9 Adm. R. at 403 (11th Cir. 2021) is misplaced. In *Yusko*, the cruise ship's employee—a professional dancer—was partnered with the plaintiff in a dance competition during a cruise. *Id.* at 1166, 9 Adm. R. at 403. During their performance, the cruise ship's employee released the plaintiff's hands as she leaned away during a dance move, causing her to fall and hit her head on the deck. *Id.*, 9 Adm. R. at 403. In analyzing the plaintiff's negligence claim, which was brought under a theory of vicarious liability, we held that "a passenger need not establish that a shipowner had actual or constructive notice of a risk-creating condition to hold a shipowner liable for the negligent acts of its employees." *Id.* at 1170, 9 Adm. R. at 407. But *Yusko* also reaffirmed that **{-1097-}** where, as here, a plaintiff is relying on a theory of direct liability "to hold a shipowner liable for maintaining dangerous premises" or "for failing to warn of dangerous conditions," the plaintiff must establish notice to the shipowner as a part of those claims. *See id.*, 9 Adm. R. at 407. Indeed, we cited with approval both *Keefe* **[—15—]** and our decision in *Everett v. Carnival Cruise Lines*, 912 F.2d 1355 (11th Cir. 1990), in which we held that "for the passenger's negligence claim to succeed, the shipowner must 'have had actual or constructive notice of the risk-creating condition.'" *Yusko*, 4 F.4th at 1168, 9 Adm. R. at 405 (quoting *Everett*, 912 F.2d at 1358).

And although we stated in *Yusko* that a plaintiff "may choose to proceed under a theory of direct liability, vicarious liability, or both," we noted that "common sense suggests that there will be just as many occasions where passengers are limited to a theory of direct liability" and that "[s]ometimes, as in *Keefe*, a passenger will not be able to identify any specific employee whose negligence caused her injury." *Id.* at 1170, 9 Adm. R. at 407. This case is exactly the type of case described in *Yusko* where a passenger is limited to a theory of direct liability. Unlike the plaintiff in *Yusko*, Holland has not identified any specific Carnival employee's negligent action that caused his fall. And nothing in *Yusko* suggests that Holland can avoid pleading the elements necessary to allege Carnival's direct liability for negligent maintenance and failure to warn by titling his claims as claims for vicarious liability and asserting in a conclusory allegation that Carnival was vicariously liable for any negligent action by any of its crewmembers. We thus conclude that this case is like our decisions in *Keefe* and *Everett*, and we decline to apply and extend *Yusko* here. We therefore hold that Holland has failed to state plausible claims of negligence against Carnival.

IV. CONCLUSION [—16—]

For the reasons stated, we affirm the district court's dismissal of Holland's amended complaint for failure to state a claim.

AFFIRMED.

United States Court of Appeals
for the Eleventh Circuit

No. 21-12729

NORWEGIAN CRUISE LINE HOLDINGS LTD
vs.
STATE SURGEON GEN.

Appeal from the United States District Court for the Southern District of Florida

Decided: October 6, 2022

Citation: 50 F.4th 1126, 10 Adm. R. 409 (11th Cir. 2022).

Before **PRYOR,** Chief Judge, **ROSENBAUM,** and **BRASHER,** Circuit Judges.

[—2—] {-1129-} **PRYOR,** Chief Judge: **{-1130-}**

This appeal concerns whether a Florida statute that prohibits all businesses operating in the state from requiring customers to provide documentary proof that they are vaccinated against COVID-19 violates the Free Speech and Commerce Clauses of the Constitution. Norwegian Cruise Line Holdings Ltd., a corporation headquartered in Florida, operates cruise ships that travel around the world. Norwegian requires everyone on board its ships to be vaccinated against COVID-19. To enforce that policy, Norwegian requires its customers to provide proof of vaccination. Florida sought to protect its residents from that kind of discrimination by enacting a statute that prohibits businesses from "requir[ing] patrons or customers to provide any documentation certifying COVID-19 vaccination or post-infection recovery to gain access to, entry upon, or service from the business operations in [Florida]." **[—3—]** FLA. STAT. ANN. § 381.00316(1). Norwegian sued Florida's Surgeon General and moved for a preliminary injunction. The district court entered a preliminary injunction on the grounds that the statute likely violates Norwegian's right to speak freely, *see* U.S. CONST. amends. I, XIV, and likely unduly burdens interstate commerce, *see* U.S. CONST. art. I, § 8, cl. 3.

We vacate the preliminary injunction. Florida's statute is a regulation of economic conduct that only incidentally burdens speech, which does not implicate the First Amendment. And its burdens on interstate commerce do not exceed the benefits of furthering Florida's substantial interests in protecting its residents from discrimination and invasions of privacy.

I. BACKGROUND

After March 2020, the COVID-19 pandemic took a substantial toll on the cruise industry. Although some cruise lines voluntarily suspended operations, not all did. *See* 85 FED. REG. 16628, 16631 (Mar. 24, 2020). As a result, the federal government published a No Sail Order and generally prohibited cruise-ship operations. *Id.* For more than a year, Norwegian's "entire 28-vessel fleet was docked and inactive" because of the pandemic. And the halt of operations in that time allegedly cost Norwegian more than $6 billion.

Later that year, the Centers for Disease Control and Prevention published another order that "establishe[d] a framework for a phased approach to resuming cruise ship passenger operations in **[—4—]** U.S. waters." 85 FED. REG. 70153, 70153 (Nov. 4, 2020). The conditional sailing order included the "[e]stablishment of laboratory testing of crew onboard cruise ships in U.S. waters"; "simulated voyages designed to test a cruise ship operators' ability to mitigate COVID-19 onboard cruise ships"; "a certification process"; and "a return to passenger voyages in a manner that mitigates the risk of COVID-19 introduction, transmission, or spread among passengers and crew onboard ships and ashore to communities." *Id.* And the order "contain[ed] requirements for . . . [s]horeside COVID-19 laboratory screening testing of all crew"; "onboard diagnostic testing capabilities for symptomatic travelers"; "shoreside COVID-19 laboratory screening testing of all newly embarking crew"; and "continued compliance with complete, accurate, and acknowledged, No Sail Order Response Plans." *Id.*

In April 2021, the Centers sent a letter to "Cruise Industry Colleagues." The letter included updates for fully vaccinated passengers and crew. "In lieu of conducting a simulated voyage" as announced in the phased approach, cruise ship operators could "submit to [the Centers] a clear and **{-1131-}** specific vaccination plan and timeline to limit cruise ship sailings to 95 percent of passengers who have been verified by the cruise ship operator as fully vaccinated prior to sailing."

The State of Florida sued the Centers and moved for a preliminary injunction on the ground that the conditional sailing order and the later instructions were unlawful. *See Florida v. Becerra*, 544 F. Supp. 3d 1241, 1246–47 (M.D. Fla. 2021). The district court **[—5—]** preliminarily enjoined the Centers "from enforcing against a cruise ship arriving in, within, or departing from a port in Florida the conditional sailing order and the later measures." *Id.* at 1305. The Centers appealed to this Court and requested a stay of the injunction. After we first granted that request, we *sua sponte* vacated our initial order and denied the Centers' request for a stay. *See Florida v. Sec'y, Dep't of Health & Hum. Servs.*, No. 21-12243 (11th Cir. July 23, 2021). This year, the Centers moved to voluntarily dismiss the appeal and we granted that motion. So, the conditional sailing order and later instructions are now non-binding guidelines, but all cruise lines operating in Florida have voluntarily complied.

Norwegian planned to resume sailing from Florida for the first time "aboard the *Norwegian Gem*." On July 9, 2021, the Centers approved Norwegian's application for a conditional sailing certificate. Norwegian "attested to [the Centers] . . . that at least 95% of passengers and 95% of its crew on its upcoming cruise will be confirmed as fully vaccinated prior to sailing." (Internal quotation marks omitted.) When Norwegian submitted its attestation, it "planned—and continues to plan—to 'confirm[]' passengers' and the crews' COVID-19 vaccination status through documentation, which [it] understand[s] to be the only reliable way of confirming vaccination status in this context."

Florida acted to discourage and prohibit businesses from requiring vaccination documents as a condition of service. Governor Ron DeSantis issued an executive order declaring that "[b]usinesses in Florida are prohibited from requiring patrons or customers to **[—6—]** provide any documentation certifying COVID-19 vaccination or post-transmission recovery to gain access to, entry upon, or service from the business." Fla. Exec. Order No. 21-81 § 2 (Apr. 2, 2021). The order required that businesses comply "to be eligible for grants or contracts funded through state revenue." *Id.* § 4. The Governor explained that "many Floridians have not yet had the opportunity to obtain a COVID-19 vaccination, some have infection-acquired immunity, and others may be unable to obtain a COVID-19 vaccination due to health, religious, or other reasons." *Id.* at 1. The order also stated that "individual COVID-19 vaccination records are private health information which should not be shared by mandate" and that "COVID-19 vaccine passports reduce individual freedom and will harm patient privacy." *Id.*

The next month, the Florida Legislature enacted a statute that is substantively identical to section 2 of the executive order. The statute prohibits vaccine-documentation requirements as follows:

> [A]ny business operating in this state . . . may not require patrons or customers to provide any documentation certifying COVID-19 vaccination or postinfection recovery to gain access to, entry upon, or service from the business operations in this state. This subsection does not otherwise restrict businesses from instituting screening protocols consistent with authoritative or controlling government-issued guidance to protect public health. **[—7—]** **{-1132-}**

FLA. STAT. ANN. § 381.00316(1). The statute further declares that the State "may impose a fine not to exceed $5,000 per violation." *Id.* § 381.00316(4). The statute became effective on July 1, 2021.

The proponents of the legislation based their support on reasons like those of the Governor. In the House, Representative Tom Leek—the sponsor of the bill and the chairman of the Pandemics Committee—reasoned that the statute would protect a substantial minority population from discrimination:

> We must recognize that vaccine hesitancy is real and understandable. Don't get me wrong: . . . get vaccinated. Please! Get vaccinated; let's return to normal. But recognize that it is fair for certain segments of our community to be hesitant about getting the vaccine, and that it is absolutely true that the largest segment of our community that is vaccination-hesitant is our minority population. It was not anti-freedom nor wrong when the State stepped in and said that employers could not discriminate on the basis of race. It was not anti-freedom nor wrong when the State told landlords that they could not discriminate against people with disabilities. And it is right today for the State to tell businesses that they may not—may not—enact policies that unfairly and disparately discriminate against our minority populations.

House Session, FLA. HOUSE OF REPRESENTATIVES, at 2:28:28–2:29:37 (Apr. 28, 2021), https://www.flsenate.gov/media/Video-Player?EventID=1_2usodgs8-202104281030&Redirect=true. Representative Leek also explained that the "bill protects the rights of **[—8—]** a material portion of our minority population who remains vaccine hesitant." *Id.* at 2:30:45–2:30:56. Representative Mike Beltran explained that news reports confirmed the existence of discrimination against people based on vaccination status and concluded that "we have people discriminating against you if you're not vaccinated. Why are we doing this?" *Id.* at 2:24:25–2:24:59.

In the Senate, Senator Danny Burgess reasoned along similar lines. He explained that the Legislature was "making sure there's not a chilling effect for those who . . . have religious reasons for not getting [the vaccine] or health reasons for not wanting to get it." Senate Session, FLA. SENATE, at 6:24:00–6:24:10, (Apr. 29, 2021), https://www.flsenate.gov/media/VideoPlayer?Even-tID=1_3wpkrnbb-202104291000&Redirect=true. He added that the "vaccine is not mandated and we have exemptions already when it comes to religious beliefs, so I think that we're just in line with . . . those policies." *Id.* at 6:24:08–6:24:19. And when asked "about . . . cruise ship[s]" specifically, Senator Burgess explained that "we're making a public policy call here in Florida that . . . if you operate a business here in Florida you cannot require one to have a vaccine . . . to gain entry." *Id.* at 6:30:36–6:30:57.

The cruise industry did not uniformly adopt a vaccination requirement for all passengers. Carnival Cruise Line, Royal Caribbean International, Celebrity Cruises, and MSC Cruises each "allowed at least some unvaccinated passengers to sail, although the policy regarding the number of unvaccinated passengers permitted to sail on each ship varie[d] by company." Some of these cruise **[—9—]** lines "required vessels to sail with at least 95 percent of their passengers fully vaccinated" and required "[v]accinated passengers" to provide proof of their vaccination status at the terminal. "Other companies, such as MSC, have not required ships to sail with a set percentage of vaccinated guests." Norwegian took a more restrictive approach that would exclude all unvaccinated persons from their **{–1133–}** cruises. Indeed, Norwegian "promised its passengers 100% vaccinated cruises *before* [the statute] was enacted on May 3, 2021, and before it took effect on July 1, 2021." (Emphasis added.)

Norwegian and several of its wholly owned subsidiaries sued the Surgeon General of Florida in his official capacity and moved for "[p]reliminary and permanent injunctive relief preventing [the Surgeon General] from enforcing Florida Statute § 381.00316 against [Norwegian], including any subsidiaries, operators or agents" and a "declaration that [the statute] is unlawful as applied to" Norwegian. Norwegian complained that "[w]hile [it] [intended to] require documentation confirming that its passengers have been vaccinated," the State "enacted a law . . . that expressly *prohibits* [Norwegian] from requiring such documentation." Norwegian asserted that the statute "blocks communications between a business and its customers . . . in violation of the First Amendment" and "profoundly disrupts the proper flow of interstate and international commerce without advancing any substantial state interest . . . in violation of the Dormant Commerce Clause."

To support its claims, Norwegian alleged that its ships "sail to interstate and foreign ports" and that "[m]any such ports require **[—10—]** proof of vaccination to enter, proof of vaccination to enter without a mandatory quarantine, or proof of vaccination to enter without testing." Norwegian "scheduled several upcoming voyages to foreign ports that require proof of vaccination to enter *without testing*, including Belize, Bahamas, British Virgin Islands, and Honduras." (Emphasis added.) "As such, [Norwegian] . . . planned cruises requiring proof that 100% of passengers and crew have been vaccinated against COVID-19." Norwegian alleged that it "cannot verify its passengers' COVID-19 vaccination status unless it can require passengers to show documentation certifying that they are fully vaccinated" because "[t]here is no adequate substitute for documentary proof when it comes to confirming vaccination status." Because "the only way for [Norwegian] to require vaccine documentation . . . would be by eschewing operations in Florida," Norwegian alleged that its "operations will be impaired and it will lose substantial revenue." It alleged that "Florida's [statute] threatens to disrupt and even shut down the interstate and foreign cruise operations of [Norwegian]." And the statute allegedly burdens Norwegian's speech because it "restricts the transmission of information based on its content, as it expressly prohibits transmission only of documentation 'certifying COVID-19 vaccination or postinfection recovery.'" (Quoting FLA. STAT. ANN. § 381.00316(1).)

In an affidavit Norwegian filed in the district court, Dr. Stephen Ostroff explained that "[r]equiring that all passengers and crew be fully vaccinated is the single best way to guard against COVID-19 transmission on cruise ships." He added that "cruise **[—11—]** lines [cannot] effectively implement passenger and crew vaccination requirements" without "an adequate way to verify vaccination status" because "it is not uncommon for individuals to attempt to evade public health screening protocols."

Norwegian's Chief Executive Officer, Frank J. Del Rio, explained in an affidavit that "80% of cruise passengers would prefer fully vaccinated voyages" and that "[t]he maintenance of consumer confidence and goodwill is essential for sustainable business success in the cruise industry." He also explained that "requiring full vaccination for 100% of passengers and crew is consistent with the vaccination protocols required by many foreign ports where [Norwegian] ships are scheduled to visit." **{-1134-}** He reported that "[n]o other jurisdiction that [Norwegian] operates in around the world prohibits documenting passengers' vaccination status as Florida now does." And he attested that "[t]he loss of revenue caused by the [statute] in calendar year 2021 could exceed $100 million and could also result in a loss or diminishment of employment for [Norwegian] employees in South Florida."

Norwegian moved for a preliminary injunction, which the district court granted. The district court enjoined the Surgeon General "from enforcing [s]ection 381.00316 against [Norwegian] pending resolution of the merits of this case." It "f[ound] that [Norwegian] [was] entitled to a preliminary injunction because [it] ha[d] shown: (1) a substantial likelihood of success on the merits of [its] First Amendment and [D]ormant Commerce Clause claims; (2) that [it] would suffer irreparable injury absent an injunction; and **[—12—]** (3) that the equities and public interest weigh in favor of an injunction." On the First Amendment claim, the district court ruled that section 381.00316 is a content-based restriction; it rejected the argument that section 381.00316 is an economic regulation of conduct that only incidentally burdens speech; and it held that the statute fails to survive heightened scrutiny. On the

Dormant Commerce Clause claim, it ruled that section 381.00316 "does not directly regulate, or affirmatively discriminate against, interstate commerce" and that the "[s]tatute is applicable to both out-of-state and in-state business entities that operate in the State of Florida." The district court concluded—and the parties agreed—that the statute "does not implicate concerns about local economic protectionism raised by courts that" enjoin statutes that do. It applied the balancing test of *Pike v. Bruce Church, Inc.*, 397 U.S. 137 (1970). It ruled that the Surgeon General "failed to articulate how the goals of medical privacy and antidiscrimination are fulfilled by the express terms of the [s]tatute." And it ruled that the burdens on interstate commerce are likely to be clearly excessive in relation to the putative local benefits of the statute.

After the Surgeon General filed this appeal, Norwegian identified two destinations that had since required all passengers aged 12 and older to be fully vaccinated for ships to enter port—the Bahamas and the United States Virgin Islands. But before oral argument, the Surgeon General notified this Court that the governments of those destinations now allow unvaccinated persons to enter with negative COVID-19 tests. *See* Emergency Powers (Covid- **[—13—]** 19 Pandemic) (Management and Recovery) (No.2) (Amendment) (No. 8) Order, 2021, at 2–3, PRIME MINISTER OF THE BAHAMAS (Aug. 19, 2021) (specifying that the order is "[e]ffective the 3rd day of September, 2021 until the 1st day of November, 2021"); *Travel Protocols*, THE BAHAMAS (Apr. 2, 2022), https://travel.gov.bs/file/travelProtocols; Thirty-Fifth Supplemental Executive Order and Proclamation by the Governor of the United States Virgin Islands § 4, at 7–8, OFFICE OF THE GOVERNOR (Feb. 28, 2022).

II. STANDARD OF REVIEW

"We review a district court's grant of a preliminary injunction for abuse of discretion." *Fed. Trade Comm'n v. On Point Cap. Partners LLC*, 17 F.4th 1066, 1077 (11th Cir. 2021). "We review the preliminary injunction's underlying legal conclusions *de novo* and its findings of fact for clear error." *Id.* at 1078.

III. DISCUSSION

"A preliminary injunction is an extraordinary remedy never awarded as of **{-1135-}** right," *id.* at 1077 (internal quotation marks omitted), and the party seeking that remedy must satisfy a four-part test, *Otto v. City of Boca Raton*, 981 F.3d 854, 860 (11th Cir. 2020). First, it must prove that "it has a substantial likelihood of success on the merits." *Id.* (internal quotation marks omitted). Second, it must prove that it will suffer irreparable injury unless the injunction issues. *Id.* Third, it must prove that the injury that threatens it "outweighs whatever damage the proposed injunction may cause the opposing party." *Id.* (internal quotation marks omitted). Finally, it **[—14—]** must prove that "the injunction would not be adverse to the public interest" if issued. *Id.* (internal quotation marks omitted).

We divide our discussion in two parts. First, we explain that Norwegian is unlikely to succeed on the merits of its First Amendment claim. Second, we explain that Norwegian is unlikely to succeed on the merits of its Dormant Commerce Clause claim.

A. Norwegian Is Unlikely to Succeed on the Merits of Its First Amendment Claim.

"The First Amendment, applicable to the States through the Fourteenth Amendment," *Reed v. Town of Gilbert*, 576 U.S. 155, 163 (2015), provides that governments "shall make no law . . . abridging the freedom of speech," U.S. CONST. amend. I. That command generally removes from governments the "power to restrict expression because of its message, its ideas, its subject matter, or its content." *Reed*, 576 U.S. at 163 (internal quotation marks omitted). Statutes "that target speech based on its communicative content" are "presumptively unconstitutional and may be justified only if the government proves that they are narrowly tailored to serve compelling state interests." *Id.* And "regulation[s] of speech [are] content based if

[they] appl[y] to particular speech because of the topic discussed or the idea or message expressed." *Id.*

The parties disagree about whether section 381.00316(1) is a content-based restriction of speech subject to heightened scrutiny. The Surgeon General argues that the statute is not subject to the First Amendment because it is a regulation of economic *conduct* **[—15—]** that only incidentally burdens speech. Norwegian argues that the statute is a content-based restriction of *speech* that cannot survive strict or intermediate scrutiny.

We agree with the Surgeon General. "In cases at the margin, it may sometimes be difficult to figure out what constitutes speech protected by the First Amendment. But this is not a hard case in that respect." *See Wollschlaeger v. Governor*, Fla., 848 F.3d 1293, 1307 (11th Cir. 2017) (en banc).

Statutes that regulate non-expressive conduct do "not implicate the First Amendment at all" even if they incidentally burden speech. *See Otto*, 981 F.3d at 861, 865. "[R]estrictions on protected expression are distinct from restrictions on economic activity or, more generally, on nonexpressive conduct." *Sorrell v. IMS Health Inc.*, 564 U.S. 552, 567 (2011). "[T]he First Amendment does not prevent restrictions directed at commerce or conduct from imposing incidental burdens on speech." *Id.* The Supreme Court has long acknowledged that making "a course of conduct illegal" is not "an abridgment of freedom of speech . . . merely because the conduct was in part initiated, evidenced, or carried out by means of language, either spoken, written, or printed." *Ohralik v. Ohio State Bar Ass'n*, 436 U.S. 447, 456 (1978) (quoting **{-1136-}** *Giboney v. Empire Storage & Ice Co.*, 336 U.S. 490, 502 (1949)). It has affirmed that "the State does not lose its power to regulate commercial activity deemed harmful to the public whenever speech is a component of the activity." *Id.* And it has rejected the contention "that the constitutional freedom for speech . . . extends its immunity to speech **[—16—]** or writing used as an integral part of conduct in violation of a valid criminal statute." *Giboney*, 336 U.S. at 498. That "expansive interpretation" of the First Amendment "would make it practically impossible ever to enforce laws against agreements in restraint of trade as well as many other agreements and conspiracies deemed injurious to society." *Id.* at 502. So, if section 381.00316 regulates non-expressive economic conduct that only incidentally burdens speech, then it does "not implicate the First Amendment at all." *See Otto*, 981 F.3d at 861, 865.

Anti-discrimination statutes ordinarily regulate non-expressive conduct. The "focal point" for their prohibitions is "on the *act* of discriminating against individuals in the provision of publicly available goods, privileges, and services on the proscribed grounds." *Hurley v. Irish-Am. Gay, Lesbian & Bisexual Grp. of Bos., Inc.*, 515 U.S. 557, 572 (1995) (emphasis added). Enacting anti-discrimination statutes is "well within the State's usual power . . . when a legislature has reason to believe that a given group is the target of discrimination, and . . . do[es] not, as a general matter, violate the First or Fourteenth Amendments." *Id.* For that reason, "philosophical objections" do not generally "allow business owners and other actors in the economy and in society to deny protected persons equal access to goods and services under a neutral and generally applicable public accommodations law." *Masterpiece Cakeshop, Ltd. v. Colo. C.R. Comm'n*, 138 S. Ct. 1719, 1727 (2018). "Where the government does not target conduct on the basis of its expressive content, acts are not shielded from regulation merely **[—17—]** because they express a discriminatory idea or philosophy." *R.A.V. v. City of St. Paul*, 505 U.S. 377, 390 (1992). And the Supreme Court has repeatedly applied these principles in rejecting First Amendment challenges to anti-discrimination statutes. *See, e.g., Wisconsin v. Mitchell*, 508 U.S. 476, 487 (1993); *Hishon v. King & Spalding*, 467 U.S. 69, 78 (1984) (rejecting the argument "that application of Title VII . . . would infringe constitutional rights of expression" because "invidious private discrimination . . . has never been accorded affirmative constitutional protections" (alteration adopted) (internal quotation marks omitted)); *Runyon v. McCrary*, 427 U.S. 160,

176 (1976) (explaining that although "parents have a First Amendment right to send their children to educational institutions that promote the belief that racial segregation is desirable, . . . it does not follow that the *practice* of excluding racial minorities from such institutions is also protected").

Section 381.00316 is an anti-discrimination statute that regulates non-expressive economic conduct. The statute prohibits "any business operating in" Florida from "requir[ing] patrons or customers to provide any documentation certifying COVID-19 vaccination or postinfection recovery to gain access to, entry upon, or service from the business operations in [Florida]." FLA. STAT. ANN. § 381.00316(1). A "requirement" is "[t]he *act* of establishing something as a need or necessity." *See Requirement*, BLACK'S LAW DICTIONARY **{-1137-}** (11th ed. 2019) (emphasis added). The plain meaning of the statute prohibits the same action as any run-of-the-mill anti-discrimination statute: closing the business's doors to a class of **[—18—]** persons based "on . . . proscribed grounds." *See Hurley*, 515 U.S. at 572. A business violates section 381.00316 when it commits the "act," *see id.*, of "deny[ing]" patrons or customers "access to goods and services," *Masterpiece*, 138 S. Ct. at 1727, based on their failure to prove that they are not members of the protected class. *See* FLA. STAT. ANN. § 381.00316(1). It prohibits businesses from discriminating by "treat[ing] differently" vaccinated and unvaccinated persons based on a condition that members of only one class can satisfy. *See Wollschlaeger*, 848 F.3d at 1317. And it protects conduct for those who either cannot or desire not to comply with the proscribed condition. *See* FLA. STAT. ANN. § 381.00316(1). So, section 381.00316(1) targets "the *practice* of excluding [persons] from" businesses and prohibits their exclusion. *See Runyon*, 427 U.S. at 176.

Section 381.00316(1) does "not implicate the First Amendment at all." *See Otto*, 981 F.3d at 861. Section 381.00316(1) "appl[ies] to non-expressive conduct such as failing to," *see Wollschlaeger*, 848 F.3d at 1317, grant persons who are unwilling or unable to verify their vaccination status "access to, entry upon, or service from the business operations," FLA. STAT. ANN. § 381.00316(1). And when the statute regulates non-expressive conduct in that way, "there is no First Amendment problem." *Wollschlaeger*, 848 F.3d at 1317.

Norwegian argues that the statute regulates communications between businesses and customers. It argues that "Florida's [b]an restricts the free flow of vital, potentially life-saving **[—19—]** information by targeting only one type of *written* information exchange." It adopts the view of the district court that section 381.00316 "regulates speech because it restricts the free flow of information by rendering the *exchange* permissible in some circumstances but impermissible in others." And it maintains that "[t]he [b]an is triggered by a specific mode (documentary) of conveying specific information (vaccination against COVID-19) between a specific speaker and audience (customer to business)" because "[o]nly if a business first engages in this communicative exchange can its ensuing conduct (restricting access) violate the [b]an." We disagree.

Section 381.00316(1) limits no communications between customers and businesses. Norwegian concedes that the statute does not prohibit businesses from *asking* customers about their vaccination status. *See Greater Phila. Chamber of Com. v. City of Phila.*, 949 F.3d 116, 135–36 (3d Cir. 2020) (holding that a provision "clearly regulate[d] speech because it prevent[ed] employers from asking potential applicants specific questions" about wage history but holding that a provision that prohibits "the act of *relying* on wage history to set a salary" regulated conduct). And the statute does not prohibit customers from *responding*—orally or in writing—with that information and proof. *Cf. Wollschlaeger*, 848 F.3d at 1307 (holding that provisions "trigger[ed] First Amendment scrutiny" because they "expressly limit[ed] the ability of certain speakers—doctors and medical professionals—to write and speak about **[—20—]** a certain topic—the ownership of firearms—and thereby restrict[ed] their ability to communicate and/or convey a message").

What businesses may *not* do is close their doors to customers who decline to present private medical documentation. *See* FLA. STAT. ANN. 381.00316(1). The act of closing the doors to those persons is prohibited, not any communicative exchange **{-1138-}** between them and the businesses that would like to discriminate against them "on the proscribed grounds." *See Hurley*, 515 U.S. at 572. Section 381.00316(1) is distinguishable from "speaker-focused and content-based restrictions on speech" that "limit a category of people—[such as businesses]—from communicating a particular message." *Cf. Otto*, 981 F.3d at 863 (internal quotation marks omitted) (holding that regulations of therapists were speaker-focused and content-based restrictions because they expressly restricted therapists "from communicating a particular message").

To be sure, Norwegian correctly asserts that the statute does not prohibit requiring oral verification of vaccination status, *see* FLA. STAT. ANN. § 381.00316(1), but that fact means only that the statute does not prohibit all conceivable discriminatory conduct against unvaccinated and privacy-concerned persons. Likewise, a statute that prohibits "any business" from "requir[ing] patrons or customers to provide any documentation certifying" that they are American born "to gain access to, entry upon, or service from the business," *see id.*, would not prohibit all discriminatory conduct against foreigners, but it would proscribe a subset of that kind of non-expressive conduct. *Cf., e.g.*, 42 U.S.C. § 2000e-2(a), (a)(1) ("It **[—21—]** shall be an unlawful employment practice for an employer . . . to fail or refuse to hire or to discharge any individual . . . because of such individual's . . . national origin."); 42 U.S.C. § 2000d ("No person in the United States shall, on the ground of . . . national origin, be excluded from participation in, be denied the benefits of, or be subjected to discrimination under any program or activity receiving Federal financial assistance."). Different statutes can target different instances of the same kind of evil. And governments need not eliminate all discrimination whenever they wish to eliminate any. *See Katzenbach v. Morgan*, 384 U.S. 641, 657 (1966) ("[I]n deciding the constitutional propriety of the limitations in . . . a[n anti-discrimination] measure we are guided by the familiar principles that a statute is not invalid under the Constitution because it might have gone farther than it did, that a legislature need not strike at all evils at the same time, and that reform may take one step at a time, addressing itself to the phase of the problem which seems most acute to the legislative mind." (citations and internal quotation marks omitted)).

The only speech that section 381.00316(1) burdens is incidental to its direct prohibition of the discriminatory conduct of excluding persons the statute protects. "We recognize . . . the long-standing principle that valid regulations of conduct might sweep up some speech at their margins." *Otto*, 981 F.3d at 865. Although businesses may request documentary proof of vaccination status, they cannot use words to exclude people who decline that request—"in that case, sir, you may not enter." But burdens to that **[—22—]** kind of speech are precisely those that do not implicate the First Amendment when the statute is "directed at commerce or conduct." *Sorrell*, 564 U.S. at 567. "That is why a ban on race-based hiring may require employers to remove 'White Applicants Only' signs." *Id.* (internal quotation marks omitted). Norwegian likewise cannot put up a sign that says, "No Vaccine Passport, No Entry." That sign—analogous in this context to "a supervisor's statement 'sleep with me or you're fired'[—]may be proscribed not on the ground of any expressive idea that the statement communicates, but rather because it facilitates the threat of discriminatory conduct." *See Saxe v. State Coll. Area Sch. Dist.*, 240 F.3d 200, 208 (3d Cir. 2001) (Alito, J.). "Despite the purely verbal [or **{-1139-}** written] quality of such a threat, it surely is no more 'speech' for First Amendment purposes than the robber's demand 'your money or your life.'" *See id.*

To be sure, anti-discrimination statutes can sometimes offend the First Amendment. *See Wollschlaeger*, 848 F.3d at 1317. Anti-discrimination statutes offend the First Amendment when they "declar[e] [another's] speech . . . to be the public accommodation" to which protected persons must be given access for their own expression. *Hurley*, 515 U.S. at 573 (holding that "state courts' application of [an anti-discrimination] statute had the effect of declaring" a parade that had an "expressive character . . . to be [a] public accommodation"). And they can also give offense if the regulated conduct is, as Norwegian argues here, expressive. **[—23—]**

Section 381.00316(1) does not burden speech or expressive conduct in those forbidden ways. The statute does not "requir[e] [Norwegian] to alter the expressive content of" its speech in the way that adding an unwanted message to a parade would do. *See id.* at 572–73. And the Supreme Court has "extended First Amendment protection only to conduct that is *inherently* expressive." *Rumsfeld v. F. for Acad. & Institutional Rts., Inc. (FAIR)*, 547 U.S. 47, 66 (2006) (emphasis added). "An observer who sees" a patron board cruise A instead of B "has no way of knowing whether" B "is expressing its disapproval of the" unvaccinated passengers, "all [B's] rooms are full, or the [patron] decided for reasons of their own that they would rather" go on A. *See id.* "The expressive component" of Norwegian's "actions is not created by the conduct itself but by the speech that accompanies it," and "[t]he fact that such explanatory speech is necessary is strong evidence that the conduct at issue here"—denying service to people—"is not so inherently expressive that it warrants protection." *See id.*; *see also id.* ("If combining speech and conduct were enough to create expressive conduct, a regulated party could always transform conduct into 'speech' simply by talking about it."). The "objections" Norwegian has and can publicly announce consistent with section 381.00316(1) "do not allow [it] . . . to deny protected persons equal access to goods and services." *Masterpiece*, 138 S. Ct. at 1727. And its cruise-line "services lack the expressive quality of a parade, a newsletter, or the editorial page of a newspaper," *see FAIR*, 547 U.S. at 64, even if Norwegian "intends" by those services "to express an idea," *see United States v. O'Brien*, 391 U.S. 367, 376 (1968). **[—24—]**

Supreme Court precedent confirms our conclusion that section 381.00316(1) regulates economic conduct. In *Rumsfeld v. Forum for Academic and Institutional Rights, Inc.*, the Supreme Court considered a statute that "prevents an institution from receiving certain federal funding if it prohibits military recruiters from gaining access to campuses, or access to students on campuses, for purposes of military recruiting in a manner that is at least equal in quality and scope" to other employers. 547 U.S. at 54 (alteration adopted) (internal quotation marks omitted). Law schools that sought to exclude for political reasons military recruiters from their campuses argued that the statute violates the First Amendment. *Id.* at 52–53. The Supreme Court rejected that contention. Like section 381.00316(1) in relation to businesses, the Supreme Court explained that the statute in *FAIR* "neither limits what law schools may say nor requires them to say anything." *See id.* at 60. The Court held that the statute in *FAIR* "regulates conduct, not speech" because "[i]t **{-1140-}** affects what law schools must *do*—afford equal access to military recruiters—not what they may or may not *say*." *Id.* And it likened the statute to permissible anti-discrimination statutes that regulate conduct. *Id.* at 62. The same reasoning establishes that section 381.00316(1) does not implicate the First Amendment: it affects what Norwegian "must *do*—afford equal access to" those who cannot or do not disclose their own private medical documentation—"not what [Norwegian] may or may not *say*." *See id.* at 60. **[—25—]**

Our en banc decision in *Wollschlaeger v. Governor* also establishes that section 381.00316(1) regulates non-expressive conduct. In that decision, we considered a Florida statute that "prohibits discrimination 'against a patient based solely' on his or her ownership and possession of a firearm." 848 F.3d at 1317 (quoting FLA. STAT. ANN. § 790.338(5)). We upheld the statute because it "appl[ies] to non-expressive conduct such as failing to return messages, charging more for the same services, declining reasonable appointment times, not providing test results on a timely basis, or delaying treatment because a patient (or a parent of a patient) owns firearms." *Id.* And we can similarly uphold section 381.00316(1) because it regulates non-expressive conduct such as "failing to" admit someone who lacks vaccination documentation on board a cruise ship. *See id.*

Norwegian's reliance on *Sorrell v. IMS Health Inc.*, 564 U.S. 552, and *Expressions Hair Design v. Schneiderman*, 137 S. Ct. 1144 (2017), is unavailing. Both decisions involved statutes that prohibited speakers from conveying information in particular ways. And neither is on point because section 381.00316(1) includes no similar prohibition.

In *Sorrell*, the Supreme Court invalidated a state statute that prohibited "pharmacies, health insurers, and similar entities from selling prescriber-identifying information . . . to pharmaceutical marketers"; that prohibited those businesses "from disclosing" the information "for marketing"; and that "bar[red] pharmaceutical manufacturers and detailers from using the information for **[—26—]** marketing." 564 U.S. at 563. The Court reasoned that the statute "prohibits pharmaceutical manufacturers from using the information for . . . marketing, that is, speech with a particular content." *Id.* at 564. It explained that the statute prohibits the sale of that information to recipients who will use it for marketing, but not to "those who wish to engage in certain educational communications." *Id.* (internal quotation marks omitted). And the Supreme Court confronted "a case in which the government [had] prohibit[ed] a speaker from conveying information that the speaker *already possesse[d]*," a prohibition that "implicated" "[a]n individual's right to speak." *Id.* at 568 (emphasis added) (internal quotation marks omitted).

Section 381.00316(1), by contrast, does not prohibit the conveyance of any information in either direction, and it in no way subjects to any restraints the communication of any information already in Norwegian's or its customers' possession. *Sorrell* is inapposite.

Norwegian's reliance on *Expressions Hair Design* is similarly unavailing. In that decision, the Supreme Court held that a statute that prohibited merchants from imposing a surcharge on credit card users but did not prohibit them from offering discounts for the use of cash regulated speech, not merely conduct. *See* 137 S. Ct. at 1146–47. The Court explained that "typical price regulation[s]" regulate the "seller's conduct" and only "indirectly dictate **{-1141-}** the content of [his] speech." *Id.* at 1150–51. If, for example, the price regulation declares that a sandwich shop must charge $10 for **[—27—]** sandwiches, the regulation would regulate "the amount that a store could collect," and would incidentally involve communicating to customers that the price for a sandwich is $10. *Id.* But the ban on surcharges told "merchants nothing about the amount they [were] allowed to collect from a cash or credit card payer." *Id.* at 1151. Instead, the ban "regulate[d] . . . how sellers [could] communicate their prices." *Id.* A seller could communicate that the price is $10.30, with a $0.30 cash discount, but could not communicate that the price is $10.00, plus $0.30 for credit card users. *Id.* "In regulating the communication of prices rather than prices themselves, [the statute] regulate[d] speech." *Id.* Section 381.00316(1), by contrast, does not tell businesses how they may describe permissible conduct to customers. *Cf. Dana's R.R. Supply v. Att'y Gen.*, 807 F.3d 1235, 1245 (11th Cir. 2015) ("Calling [a Florida statute] a 'no-surcharge law,' then, is something of a misnomer. The statute targets expression alone. More accurately, it should be a 'surcharges-are-fine-just-don't-call-them-that law.'").

We conclude that section 381.00316(1) does "not implicate the First Amendment at all," *see Otto*, 981 F.3d at 861, because it regulates non-expressive economic conduct. And "run-of-the-mill economic regulations [are] assessed under rational-basis review." *Dana's R.R. Supply*, 807 F.3d at 1251. "It is enough that there is an evil at hand for correction, and that it might be thought that the particular legislative measure was a rational way to correct it." *Williamson v. Lee Optical of Okla., Inc.*, 348 U.S. 483, 488 (1955). Section 381.00316(1) bears a rational relationship to the State's **[—28—]** substantial interests in protecting its residents from discrimination and burdens to privacy because it prohibits businesses from excluding people who cannot or wish not to produce private medical documentation.

B. Norwegian Is Unlikely to Succeed on the Merits of Its Dormant Commerce Clause Claim.

The Commerce Clause provides that "Congress shall have Power . . . [t]o regulate Commerce with foreign Nations, and among the several States." U.S. CONST. art. I, § 8, cl. 3. Although this clause expressly concerns Congress's power, the Supreme Court has discerned a dormant or negative aspect that limits the power of the "several States," *id.*, to burden foreign or interstate commerce. "The Dormant Commerce Clause prohibits regulatory measures designed to benefit in-state economic interests by burdening out-of-state competitors." *Island Silver & Spice, Inc. v. Islamorada*, 542 F.3d 844, 846 (11th Cir. 2008) (internal quotation marks omitted). And there are only two ways a statute can violate the Dormant Commerce Clause: "by discriminating against interstate commerce or . . . by unduly burdening interstate commerce." *Fla. Transp. Servs., Inc. v. Miami-Dade Cnty.*, 703 F.3d 1230, 1244 (11th Cir. 2012).

A regulation violates the Dormant Commerce Clause only if it fails either one of two tests. *See Islamorada*, 542 F.3d at 846. First, protectionist regulations that directly discriminate against interstate commerce, or that have "the effect of favoring in-state economic interests," are invalid unless they "advance a legitimate local **[—29—]** purpose that cannot be adequately served by reasonable nondiscriminatory alternatives." *Id.* (alteration adopted) (internal quotation marks omitted). These regulations are unconstitutional if the State cannot satisfy that narrow exception. **{–1142–}** *Fla. Transp. Servs., Inc.*, 703 F.3d at 1244. Second, "if the law or regulation advances a legitimate local interest and has only indirect effects on interstate commerce, we apply the balancing test from *Pike*." *Id.* at 1244 (internal quotation marks omitted).

The district court correctly ruled that section 381.00316(1) neither directly nor indirectly discriminates against interstate commerce. *Accord* Dissenting Op. at 13 n.20. Indeed, the statute expressly regulates all and only "business[es] operating in [Florida]"—both local and out-of-state—for their "business operations in [Florida]." *See* FLA. STAT. ANN. § 381.00316(1). And the parties agree that the statute survives this test.

The sole question then is whether section 381.00316(1) satisfies *Pike*'s balancing test: "Where the statute regulates even-handedly to effectuate a legitimate local public interest, and its effects on interstate commerce are only incidental, it will be upheld unless the burden imposed on such commerce is clearly excessive in relation to the putative local benefits." *Pike*, 397 U.S. at 142. Under this test, we must first determine whether "a legitimate local purpose" for section 381.00316 exists. *See id.* If the State has a legitimate local purpose in enacting section 381.00316(1), we weigh the local benefits of enforcing the statute against the burdens imposed on interstate commerce. *Id.* Only if the burdens on interstate commerce **[—30—]** clearly exceed the local benefits of section 381.00316 will we invalidate that statute. *See Fla. Transp. Servs.*, 703 F.3d at 1244. "And the extent of the burden that will be tolerated will of course depend on the nature of the local interest involved, and on whether it could be promoted *as well* with a lesser impact on interstate activities." *Pike*, 397 U.S. at 142 (emphasis added).

The Surgeon General asserts two state interests. First, the Surgeon General asserts that Florida has an interest in ensuring that businesses operating within the state do not discriminate against its citizens for failure to provide documentation of vaccination status. Second, the Surgeon General asserts that Florida has an interest in protecting the medical privacy of its residents.

Protecting residents from economic discrimination is a substantial interest. That interest derives from the State's traditional "police powers to protect" the well-being of its residents. *See Medtronic, Inc. v. Lohr*, 518 U.S. 470, 475 (1996). "The States traditionally have had great latitude under their police powers to legislate as to the protection of the lives, limbs, health, comfort, and quiet of all persons"—latitude that includes regulating economic relationships. *See Metro. Life Ins. Co. v. Massachusetts*, 471 U.S. 724, 756 (1985) (internal quotation marks omitted); *see also id.* (explaining that "States possess broad authority under their police powers to regulate the employment relationship" (internal quotation marks omitted)). "[T]he regulation of health and safety matters is primarily, and historically, a matter of local concern." *Hillsborough Cnty. v. Automated Med. Lab'ys, Inc.*, 471 U.S. 707, 719 (1985). The **[—31—]** Supreme Court has "long recognized that a State's interests in the health and well-being of its residents extend beyond mere physical interests to economic and commercial interests." *See Alfred L. Snapp & Son, Inc. v. Puerto Rico ex rel. Barez*, 458 U.S. 592, 609 (1982); *see also id.* at 608 (acknowledging "the State's interest in the removal of barriers to the participation by its residents in the free flow of interstate **{–1143–}** commerce"). And the Supreme Court has also "recognize[d] a similar state interest in securing residents from the harmful effects of discrimination," "a substantial interest" that consists in "assuring its residents that it will act to protect them from" that discrimination. *See id.* at 609; *Wollschlaeger*, 848 F.3d at 1314 (explaining that the State "has a substantial interest in making sure that its residents are able to obtain health care without discrimination"). So protecting residents from being excluded from access to goods and services by businesses that operate within the State is a substantial interest weightier than a "legitimate local" one. *See Pike*, 397 U.S. at 142.

It is true, as the dissent states, that deference is not warranted whenever a state asserts that it is promoting its economy or protecting a domestic industry. Dissenting Op. at 24. But this statute directly protects a class of individuals from being ostracized. Like any antidiscrimination statute, it protects these individuals by preventing businesses from excluding them from the market. *See Alfred L. Snapp & Son, Inc.*, 458 U.S. at 609; *Wollschlaeger*, 848 F.3d at 1314. The statute prevents real harm, not some abstract economic impact. Without this statute, unvaccinated Floridians **[—32—]** risk being turned away from the businesses that make their lives possible—grocery stores, restaurants, fitness gyms, clothing stores, barber shops and hair salons, and even pharmacies. After all, the statute covers "any business operating in [Florida]," not just luxury ocean liners. FLA. STAT. ANN. § 381.00316(1). The dissent's attempt to artificially limit the State's interest to the protection of cruise ship passengers is, therefore, not persuasive. Dissenting Op. at 1 n.1. Florida's interest in protecting the unvaccinated from discrimination—not generally promoting its economy—is legitimate.

In similar fashion, the dissent relies on a footnote in the Supreme Court's decision in *Head v. New Mexico Board of Examiners in Optometry*, 374 U.S. 424, 428 n.4 (1963), to argue that the State's interest is insubstantial because economic well-being has an attenuated connection to public health. Dissenting Op. at 25. But *Head* supports our position. For one, *Head* upheld the statute at issue: a New Mexico law that prevented the publication of price advertising of eyeglasses by a local newspaper and radio station. 374 U.S. at 429. For another, in doing so, *Head* recognized the "legitimacy of state legislation" to protect public health. *Id.* at 428. In reaching this conclusion, *Head* acknowledged that "[t]he case is not one . . . in which the State seeks to justify a statute as a health measure on the attenuated theory that the economic well-being of a profession or industry will assure better performance in the public interest." *Id.* at 428 n.4. So too here. The Florida statute was not designed to protect a discrete profession or industry. Instead, the statute serves the State's legitimate interest in prohibiting businesses **[—33—]** from excluding its citizens from the interstate market. The Supreme Court has already recognized this interest is a substantial one, *Barez*, 458 U.S. at 609, and *Head* says nothing to the contrary.

The state interest in protecting the privacy of residents is also substantial. "We recognize that protection of individual privacy is a substantial government interest." *Wollschlaeger*, 848 F.3d at 1314. Supreme Court "precedents leave no room for doubt that 'the protection of potential clients' privacy is a substantial [and traditional] state interest.'" *See* **{-1144-}** *Florida Bar v. Went For It, Inc.*, 515 U.S. 618, 625 (1995) (quoting *Edenfield v. Fane*, 507 U.S. 761, 769 (1993)); *cf. also Cal. Democratic Party v. Jones*, 530 U.S. 567, 585 (2000) (explaining that "the State's interest in assuring the privacy of" party affiliation is not "a 'compelling' one" because that "specific privacy interest is not [like] the confidentiality of medical records or personal finances").

Taken together, the two state interests are plainly weighty. That is, Florida has a substantial interest in protecting its residents from economic ostracism based on their hesitancy to divulge to businesses private medical information. And that weighty state interest is dispositive here.

Because Florida's substantial interests are in matters traditionally of state concern, the burdens section 381.00316(1) imposes on interstate commerce do not clearly exceed its putative local benefits. The Supreme Court has explained "that a State's power to regulate commerce is never greater than in matters traditionally of local concern." *Kassel v. Consol. Freightways Corp.*, 450 U.S. 662, **[—34—]** 670 (1981) (plurality opinion). One "example" is "regulations that touch upon safety," regulations that "the Court has been most reluctant to invalidate." *Id.* (internal quotation marks omitted). And "if safety justifications are not illusory, the Court will not second-guess legislative judgment about their importance in comparison with related burdens on interstate commerce." *Id.* (internal quotation marks omitted). The rationale for that strong deference to legislative judgments applies to other "example[s]" of "a State's power to regulate commerce . . . in matters traditionally of local concern," *id.*, such as regulations that touch upon the health and economic well-being of residents, *Barez*, 458 U.S. at 609; *Hillsborough*, 471 U.S. at 719. To be sure, "the incantation of a purpose to promote the public health or safety does not insulate a state law from Commerce Clause attack[s]" if "[r]egulations designed for that salutary purpose nevertheless . . . further the purpose . . . marginally," while "interfer[ing] with commerce . . . substantially." *Kassel*, 450 U.S. at 670. But if "[w]e cannot say that the Florida legislature's [traditional] justification[s] w[ere] merely illusory" in that way, we also cannot "second guess the legislature's judgment as to the relative importance of [those] justifications versus any burdens imposed on interstate commerce." *Locke v. Shore*, 634 F.3d 1185, 1194–95 (11th Cir. 2011).

The dissent attempts to evade the fact that section 381.00316(1) is a traditional well-being regulation by implicitly relying on the false premise that such a regulation would have to promote residents' physical health and safety. The dissent asserts that **[—35—]** the statute "cannot seriously be described as a" safety regulation, Dissenting Op. at 33, but the Supreme Court has made clear that the traditional police power of the state includes promoting residents' *economic* health and safety, *Barez*, 458 U.S. at 609. Florida is entitled to promote that interest over possible benefits to residents' *physical* health and safety. And the dissent ignores the secondary health effects of economic harm of which the Legislature can take account. *Cf.* FLA. STAT. § 252.311(4) (explaining that it is "the intent of the Legislature to minimize the negative effects of an extended emergency" such as "the COVID-19 pandemic").

The decision of the Supreme Court in *Minnesota v. Clover Leaf Creamery Co.*, 449 U.S. 456 (1981), illustrates the substantial deference **{-1145-}** owed to state legislative judgments. In that case, "the Minnesota Legislature enacted a statute banning the retail sale of milk in plastic nonreturnable, nonrefillable containers, but permitting such sale in other nonreturnable, nonrefillable containers, such as paperboard milk cartons." *Id.* at 458. "Proponents of the legislation argued that it would promote resource conservation, ease solid waste disposal problems, and conserve energy." *Id.* at 459. After a dairy sued seeking an injunction for violating the Equal Protection, Due Process, and Dormant Commerce Clauses, the trial court invalidated the Act on all three theories because it found as a fact that "the Act w[ould] not succeed in effecting the Legislature's published policy goals." *Id.* at 460. The Supreme Court of Minnesota affirmed "on the federal equal protection and due process grounds" based on that finding. *Id.* at 460–61 (internal **[—36—]** quotation marks omitted). And the Supreme Court reversed. *Id.* at 461. It held that any burden to interstate commerce was "not clearly excessive in light of the substantial state interest in promoting conservation of energy and other natural resources and easing solid waste disposal problems, which [it] ha[d] already reviewed in the context of [its] equal protection analysis." *Id.* at 473 (citing *id.* at 465–70) (internal quotation marks omitted); *see also id.* at 470–71 n.14; *contra* Dissenting Op. at 19 (faulting this opinion for citing the equal-protection analysis that the Supreme Court itself cited in its Commerce Clause analysis).

The Supreme Court made clear the great deference owed to legislatures when their asserted interests are substantial. "Whether *in fact* the Act will promote more environmentally desirable milk packaging is not the question"; the question is whether the "Legislature *could rationally have decided* that its ban on plastic nonreturnable milk jugs might foster greater use of environmentally desirable alternatives." *Id.* at 466. The Court explained that the state courts' finding "that the Act is not a sensible means of conserving energy" was of no moment because "it is up to legislatures, not courts, to decide on the wisdom and utility of legislation," and because "the question clearly is at least debatable, the Minnesota Supreme Court erred in substituting its judgment for that of the legislature." *Id.* at 469 (citation omitted) (internal quotation marks omitted). And importantly, "it is not the function of the courts to substitute their evaluation of legislative facts for that of the legislature." *Id.* at 470. **[—37—]**

Both *Kassel v. Consolidated Freightways Corp.* and *Clover Leaf Creamery* make clear that we owe strong deference to the Florida Legislature when it exercises its traditional police powers to promote traditional local interests based on justifications that are not illusory. And the State's justifications are not illusory if applying section 381.00316(1) "as written" would "rationally contribute to [the State's] purported local benefits." *See Fla. Transp. Servs.*, 703 F.3d at 1260. Section 381.00316(1) clears that low bar.

Our dissenting colleague argues that *Clover Leaf* does not govern because there "the Court didn't need to engage in further analysis of the local-benefits side of *Pike*'s balance" because further analysis would not have made a difference to the balancing outcome since the law there imposed only a "minor" burden on commerce. Dissenting Op. at 57. But the problem with our dissenting colleague's argument is that the Court *did* engage in that analysis. *Clover Leaf Creamery Co.*, 449 U.S. at 470. In doing so, the Court offered **{-1146-}** a deferential approach toward state legislation that cannot be reconciled with the dissent's analysis. The Court's reasoning was echoed in *Kassel*, which the dissent does not suggest involved a "minor" burden on commerce. Indeed, *Kassel* addressed regulations that "impair[ed] significantly the federal interest." 450 U.S. at 671. And this Court has already read *Kassel* to command substantial deference to states without any caveat for a "minor" burden on commerce. *Locke*, 634 F.3d at 1194–95 (citing *Kassel*, 450 U.S. at 670)). **[—38—]**

Applying section 381.00316(1) as written would rationally contribute to the State's purported local benefits. Those benefits include protecting its unvaccinated and privacy-minded residents from discrimination and required disclosures of private medical information—benefits that implicate traditional and substantial state interests. The statute rationally contributes to those interests by outlawing conduct by businesses that would directly discriminate against the unvaccinated, indirectly discriminate against minority communities that are disproportionately vaccine-hesitant, and require all residents—vaccinated or not—to disclose to businesses their private medical records.

These "point[s] w[ere] stressed by [section 381.00316(1)'s] proponents in the legislature," evidencing that they were among "the legislature's major concerns." *Clover Leaf Creamery Co.*, 449 U.S. at 468–69. "As

Representative [Leek], chief sponsor of the bill in the House of Representatives, explained," *see id.* at 467, "the largest segment of our community that is vaccination-hesitant is our minority population," which is why "the State [should] tell businesses that they may not . . . enact policies that unfairly and disparately discriminate against our minority populations." *House Session, supra,* at 2:28:00–2:31:11. "Representative [Beltran] asked rhetorically, 'Why [are we doing this]?'," *see Clover Leaf Creamery Co.,* 449 U.S. at 469–70, after he reported that "we have people discriminating against you if you're not vaccinated." *House Session, supra,* at 2:24:20–2:25:00. And the Legislature passed the bill over **[—39—]** objections about the cruise industry. *See Senate Session, supra,* at 6:30:30–6:31:03.

The dissent dismisses this evidence of the Legislature's concerns, but its reasoning is unavailing. We, of course, share the dissent's concerns about the difficulties of discerning collective legislative intent—at least when trying to interpret a statute. Dissenting Op. at 39–40. But as the dissent concedes, we must look to legislative history because the Supreme Court has done so in this context. *Id.* at 39. Here, we are not using legislative history to determine what the statute means but to ensure that it serves a constitutional purpose. Legislative history is often used this way, *see, e.g., Church of the Lukumi Babalu Aye, Inc. v. City of Hialeah,* 508 U.S. 520, 534 (1993); *Wallace v. Jaffree,* 472 U.S. 38, 58 (1985); *Village of Arlington Heights v. Metropolitan Housing Development Corp.,* 429 U.S. 252, 266 (1977), and its limited application in this context avoids the pitfalls that Justice Scalia identified. The decision cited by the dissent, *New England Power Co. v. New Hampshire,* 455 U.S. 331 (1982), illustrates this exact distinction. In *New England Power,* the Court did not rely upon legislative history because it had to discern the meaning of a law passed by Congress to decide whether *Congress* had altered the limits of state power. *Id.* at 341. *New England Power* did not involve the deferential task of assessing **{-1147-}** whether a *state* law served a constitutional purpose. *Id.* So it is inapposite.

The dissent complains that we rely "exclusively" on Representative Leek's concern about Florida's vaccine-hesitant minority **[—40—]** populations, Dissenting Op. at 38, while ignoring the fact that he was the "chief sponsor of the bill in the House of Representatives," *see Clover Leaf Creamery Co.,* 449 U.S. at 467, and the Chairman of the Pandemics Committee. Instead of crediting his statements, the dissent uncharitably contorts another of Representative Leek's statements to imagine contradiction where none exists. When asked if any other state statute "created a new protected class that has not been addressed through constitutional law," Representative Leek responded that state law has indeed created protected classes but that "[t]hat is not addressed in this bill." Dissenting Op. at 37. That statement—that the creation of a new protected class is not addressed in the bill—does not mean, as the dissent asserts, that the bill has nothing whatever to do with protecting minority populations. *Id.* at 38. We decline the dissent's invitation to assume legislative mendacity with no evidence of it.

The dissent also latches on to our conclusion that the State's justifications were "rational" and erroneously argues that we have applied rational basis review to the State's arguments. *Id.* at 58. Both *Kassel* and *Clover Leaf Creamery* make clear that we must assess whether the State's justifications are illusory. *See Locke,* 634 F.3d at 1194–95. Only after determining whether deference is owed do we defer to the State's rational view. *Id.* Under rational basis review, by contrast, we do not assess whether the State's justifications are illusory. Instead, we defer to any "reasonably conceivable" facts or purposes that could support a classification, even if they are not the actual rationales behind the legislation. *F.C.C. v.* **[—41—]** *Beach Comm., Inc.,* 508 U.S. 307, 313 (1993). These are two different standards, and we have correctly applied the former by determining that the State's justifications are not illusory.

The district court also second-guessed Florida's legitimate justifications. Like the trial court in *Clover Leaf Creamery Co.,* 449 U.S. at 460, the district court found that "the record" establishes that section 381.00316(1) "is materially [in]effective at" advancing the State's interests. It reasoned that "nothing in the statute appears to prohibit businesses from imposing a vaccination requirement" in another form, such as by demanding *oral* verification. *See also* Dissenting Op. at 47 (explaining that the statute does not prohibit requiring oral verification of vaccination status). It also reasoned that "Florida's failure to regulate employers, COVID-19 test results, and other medical documentation—including documentary proof-of-vaccination requirements for schoolchildren—conflicts with its purported desire to protect medical privacy." And it concluded that "[t]he statute also does not actually protect against" discrimination against unvaccinated persons because businesses may still differentiate between the vaccinated and unvaccinated in implementing other practices.

The district court erred for two reasons. First, the Supreme Court "has made clear that a legislature need not strike at all evils at the same time or in the same way." *Cloverleaf Creamery Co.*, 449 U.S. at 466 (internal quotation marks omitted). Indeed, "a legislature may implement its program step by step, adopting regulations that only partially ameliorate a perceived evil and deferring **[—42—]** complete elimination of the evil to future regulations." **{-1148-}** *Id.* (alterations adopted) (internal quotation marks omitted). The district court erred by subjecting the statute to a kind of means-end scrutiny that would require that it eliminate all conceivable discrimination and burdens of medical privacy if it wishes to eliminate any.

Second, the district court failed to give the Legislature the deference it was due. It is "at least debatable," *id.* at 469 (internal quotation marks omitted), whether the *direct* regulation of one kind of discrimination would *indirectly* discourage the other kinds that the district court identified. For example, Norwegian itself concedes that "[t]here is no adequate substitute for documentary proof when it comes to confirming vaccination status" and that businesses like Norwegian "cannot verify [their] [customers'] COVID-19 vaccination status unless [they] can require passengers to show documentation certifying that they are fully vaccinated." If so, it is rational to suppose that section 381.00316(1) would discourage businesses from engaging in what Norwegian concedes are exercises in futility. The Legislature *"could rationally have decided," id.* at 466, to prohibit what in its view is the worst species of the kinds of evils it targeted *and* that its prohibition would discourage or eliminate other species in addition. And as for the conduct the statute directly prohibits, it is incontrovertible that it will succeed at reducing or eliminating that conduct. Without section 381.00316(1), some businesses would indeed discriminate as Norwegian itself did. **[—43—]**

Florida is on firmer ground than Minnesota was in *Clover Leaf Creamery Co.* Although Minnesota's putative benefits depended on the truth of empirical claims, such as whether a particular ban would conserve energy, *id.* at 459–60, Norwegian concedes that section 381.00316(1) would stop businesses like Norwegian from requiring vaccine documentation as a condition of service. And no amount of empirical evidence is needed to understand that preventing compelled disclosures of medical documentation held by only one class of persons prevents instances of both discrimination and required disclosures of private medical documentation that would otherwise occur. *Contra* Dissenting Op. at 17 (relying on a decision in which the State's asserted physical-safety interests were subject to empirical disconfirmation).

The dissent insinuates that section 381.00316(1) is not a true antidiscrimination statute because discrimination based on vaccination status "contrasts sharply" with the "'invidious discrimination' that 'frequently occurs along ethnic lines.'" *Id.* at 48; *see also id.* at 33 (quoting *Barez*, 458 U.S. at 609). The dissent contests that comparison because it concludes that Norwegian does not "seek to invidiously discriminate against unvaccinated people; it seeks to distinguish between vaccinated and unvaccinated people to ensure the health and safety of its passengers." *Id.* at 45.

We disagree. Florida clearly sought to prevent discrimination *against* unvaccinated people by prohibiting businesses from distinguishing *between* vaccinated and unvaccinated people. The dissent resists this conclusion by arguing that "[i]n practice, the **[—44—]** statute protects only unvaccinated people against discrimination." *Id.* at 40. But the State need not protect vaccinated and unvaccinated people from discrimination equally. After all, Section 381.00316(1) does not involve a constitutionally protected class or anything like selective protection of one such class over others. *Cf. City of New Orleans v. Dukes*, 427 U.S. 297, 303 (1976) ("[T]he judiciary may not sit as a superlegislature to judge the wisdom or desirability **{–1149–}** of legislative policy determinations made in areas that neither affect fundamental rights nor proceed along suspect lines."). More analogous examples abound. Consider a statute that prohibits employers from relying on the wage history of prospective employees to set wages. *See Greater Phila. Chamber of Com.*, 949 F.3d at 134–36. Or consider another statute that prohibits employers from requiring prospective employees to provide wage-related information. Those statutes target wage discrimination even if they leave untouched other forms of discrimination against the poor. And they are anti-discrimination statutes even if they "protect[] only [poor] people against discrimination" who have suffered from wage discrimination. *See* Dissenting Op. at 47.

The Supreme Court has rejected the dissent's view that statutes must strike at all forms of discrimination if they strike at any to count as anti-discrimination statutes. *See Katzenbach*, 384 U.S. at 656–57 (rejecting an argument that a statute "itself works an invidious discrimination . . . by prohibiting the enforcement of [an] English literacy requirement only for those educated in American-flag schools . . . in which the language of instruction was other than **[—45—]** English" because anti-discrimination statutes "need not strike at all evils at the same time" and "reform may take one step at a time" (internal quotation marks omitted)). A legislature can conclude that one kind of discrimination involving a non-suspect class is more pressing than discrimination against another non-suspect class. And the Florida Legislature could have sensibly supposed that discrimination against the unvaccinated was a serious problem requiring legislative interposition but that discrimination against the vaccinated was not. *Cf. id.* at 657 (explaining that anti-discrimination "reform may take one step at a time, addressing itself to the phase of the problem which seems most acute to the legislative mind" (internal quotation marks omitted)). Indeed, the evidence the dissent marshals suggests that the Legislature was unmoved by arguments that discrimination against vaccinated people was a problem that needed the same remedy. Dissenting Op. at 47–48 (discussing floor statements citing an apparent example of discrimination against vaccinated people). So Florida has the discretion to determine that the differences between vaccinated and unvaccinated people do not reasonably justify the economic ostracism to which the Legislature found the latter would otherwise be subjected.

The dissent's distinction between invidious and non-invidious discrimination is also mistaken. *Id.* at 42–43. For one, the dissent assumes that the statute has nothing to do with protecting minority populations, but the statute, as Representative Leek stated, indirectly protects minority communities who are vaccine hesitant. **[—46—]** *Supra* at 7. In any event, the dissent fails to acknowledge that the State may recognize new protected classes beyond federal law. As the "double security" of a "compound republic," states can do more than federal law to ensure "security for civil rights." The Federalist No. 51 at 320 (James Madison) (Clinton Rossiter ed., 1961). For example, states may protect the indigent, the disabled, and the elderly from discrimination even though these classes are not constitutionally protected. The dissent ignores this basic point. Instead, it substitutes its own intuitions to conclude that Florida's interests are illusory because the statute only protects against (what it labels) "non-pejorative" or "neutral" discrimination (whatever those labels mean). Dissenting Op. at 34, 45–46.

The dissent has it backwards. The State—not an Article III court—has the **{-1150-}** constitutional authority to determine what is and is not a "reasonable distinction" between its citizens and what qualifies as discrimination worth remedying. *Id.* at 42. In doing so, the State may find, as a matter of fact, that it needs to protect the unvaccinated from being excluded from the market. The dissent's approach would flip the script and allow Article III judges to decide which of Florida's citizens deserve protection. And that approach would threaten the State's authority to protect its citizens from various forms of discrimination. We decline the dissent's invitation to put these policy decisions in the hands of unelected federal judges. The states are in a better position to make "reasonable distinctions" between their citizens and to secure their civil rights. For that **[—47—]** reason, the Constitution affords state legislatures great deference in this area. *Clover Leaf Creamery Co.*, 449 U.S. at 466.

The dissent's dismissal of Florida's substantial interest in protecting privacy is similarly unpersuasive. The dissent concludes that section 381.00316(1) "does not meaningfully promote privacy." *Id.* at 53. The dissent reasons that "the state itself requires Floridians to present proof of vaccination against diseases other than COVID-19 to attend schools at the very same time that Section 381.00316(1) prohibits cruise lines from requiring documentation of COVID-19 vaccination." *Id.* at 56. But the dissent's argument again rests on an unstated and false premise that legislatures must treat all diseases as though they are equal. The Legislature could have sensibly determined that the effects of polio on children justify burdening privacy but that the effects of COVID-19 on children do not. The Legislature expressly considered that *other* diseases warrant vaccination requirements in schools despite burdens to privacy. That kind of line-drawing is quintessentially one for legislatures, not this Court. And that a legislature might weigh health benefits against privacy interests differently for different diseases does not mean that it advances privacy interests "trivially" when it prohibits compelled disclosures whenever it decides that the privacy side of the scale is weightier.

We conclude that applying section 381.00316(1) "as written" would "rationally contribute to [the State's] purported local benefits." *See Fla. Transp. Servs.*, 703 F.3d at 1260. And because "[w]e cannot say that the Florida legislature's [traditional] justification[s] **[—48—]** w[ere] merely illusory," we also cannot "second guess the legislature's judgment as to the relative importance of [those] justifications versus any burdens imposed on interstate commerce." *Locke*, 634 F.3d at 1194–95. So, at the very least, Norwegian "must overcome a strong presumption of validity" that favors section 381.00316(1). *See Kassel*, 450 U.S. at 670 (internal quotation marks omitted).

Despite the evidence that it will suffer economically if it complies with section 381.00316(1), Norwegian cannot overcome that strong presumption of validity. Norwegian can travel with unvaccinated passengers to ports. Although the Bahamas and the United States Virgin Islands once required all passengers aged 12 and older to be vaccinated, the governments of those destinations have since revised their protocols to allow unvaccinated persons to enter with negative COVID-19 tests. Norwegian concedes that other foreign ports similarly allow unvaccinated passengers to enter with negative testing. And Norwegian's Chief Executive Officer testified that Norwegian "plann[ed] to require that passengers . . . test negative for COVID-19 before boarding [its] cruises" in any event. Even so, Norwegian relies on evidence that compliance with **{-1151-}** section 381.00316(1) would burden its operations. The district court concluded that "documentary proof of vaccination w[ould] expedite passengers' entry into virtually every single country and port where [Norwegian] intend[s] to sail." And it concluded that without such proof, other protocols would be "impractical" and "financially, legally, and logistically onerous" for Norwegian. But **[—49—]** these burdens to Norwegian are not "clearly excessive in relation to" the benefits of furthering the

State's substantial anti-discrimination and privacy interests. *See Pike*, 397 U.S. at 142.

The Commerce Clause does not necessarily protect Norwegian against prohibitive burdens imposed by local law. "[T]he Commerce Clause protects the interstate market, not particular interstate firms, from prohibitive or burdensome regulations." *Clover Leaf Creamery Co.*, 449 U.S. at 474 (internal quotation marks omitted). So, "nondiscriminatory regulation[s] serving substantial state purposes [are] not invalid simply because [they] cause[] some business to shift from a predominantly out-of-state industry to a predominantly in-state industry." *Id.* The effect of prohibitive or burdensome regulations on individual firms ordinarily "relates to the wisdom of the statute, not to its burden on commerce." *Exxon Corp. v. Governor of Maryland*, 437 U.S. 117, 128 (1978). To be sure, burdens to individual firms can sometimes be unduly burdensome if, against the facts here, the putative local benefits are illusory or insubstantial. In *Pike*, for example, "the State's tenuous interest in having the company's [products] identified as originating in [the State] c[ould not] constitutionally justify the requirement that the company build and operate an unneeded $200,000 . . . plant in the State." 397 U.S. at 145. But the *Pike* Court did not "deal[] . . . with state legislation in [a] field where the propriety of local regulation has long been recognized," *id.* at 143 (internal quotation marks omitted), and it instead dealt with a regulation "requiring business operations to be performed in the home State **[—50—]** that could more efficiently be performed elsewhere," a kind of "burden on commerce [that] has been declared to be virtually *per se* illegal," *id.* at 145. Because the State's interests here are substantial and long recognized, the statute can subject some businesses to prohibitive or burdensome regulations.

Section 381.00316(1) also does not unduly burden out-of-state firms any more than domestic ones. The statute does not prohibit foreign cruise lines from imposing their preferred vaccination requirements when conducting business elsewhere, and those cruise lines that do impose their preferences abroad "may continue to move freely across the [Florida] border" on other trips. *Clover Leaf Creamery Co.*, 449 U.S. at 472. Compliance with the statute may very well impose additional costs on certain cruise lines, "but there is no reason to suspect that the gainers will be [Florida] firms, or the losers out-of-state firms." *See id.* at 472–73; *see also id.* at 473 n.17 ("The existence of major in-state interests adversely affected by [a statute] is a powerful safeguard against legislative abuse."). Indeed, Norwegian is headquartered in Florida. And the strong deference ordinarily due to the Legislature remains if the statute is burdensome to domestic and foreign businesses alike. *Cf. Kassel*, 450 U.S. at 675–76 ("Less deference to the legislative judgment is due . . . where the local regulation bears disproportionately on out-of-state residents and businesses."). "[B]ecause this burden is one shared by Florida and out-of-state firms alike, the burden is not clearly excessive **{–1152–}** in relation to the requirement's local benefit." *Locke*, 634 F.3d at 1195. **[—51—]**

Norwegian also may choose to "eschew[] operations in Florida" if it is forced to comply with section 381.00316(1), but that choice would not establish a burden that is clearly excessive in relation to the State's substantial interests. Although "[s]ome [businesses] may choose to withdraw entirely from the [Florida] market, . . . interstate commerce is not subjected to an impermissible burden simply because an otherwise valid regulation causes some business to shift from one interstate [business] to another." *Exxon*, 437 U.S. at 127. The district court acknowledged that some cruise lines do not impose the kind of requirement that Norwegian would like to impose. And those other cruise lines that maintain operations in Florida may, consistent with section 381.00316(1), continue to require compliance with other restrictions for the unvaccinated, such as COVID-19 testing.

Finally, neither the district court nor Norwegian has identified a less burdensome regulation that would "promote[] as well" the State's substantial interests. *See Pike*, 397

U.S. at 142. Norwegian argues that "Florida could have adopted a narrow carveout that specifically exempts cruise line operators or interstate activities and services, such as international cruises." (Internal quotation marks omitted.) The district court used the same examples and reasoned that the State's "failure to adopt a less restrictive alternative . . . undermine[s] the survival of [s]ection 381.00316 when applying the *Pike* balancing test." But there is no reason to believe that any less burdensome alternatives would have promoted the State's interest "as well" as section 381.00316(1). *Id.* For example, an **[—52—]** exemption for specific industries would allow businesses within them to discriminate against and require disclosures of private medical documentation from customers and patrons. It is hard to see how that state of affairs promotes anti-discrimination and privacy interests as well as an outright ban. Indeed, the district court faulted the State for not enacting a statute that more effectively promotes those interests by extending the ban to employer-employee relationships.

Norwegian and the district court "have suggested several alternative statutory schemes, but these alternatives are either more burdensome on commerce than [section 381.00316(1)] (as, for example, banning all [vaccination requirements]) or less likely to be effective (as, for example, providing" exemptions). *See Clover Leaf Creamery Co.*, 449 U.S. at 473–74. That reasoning would turn the *Pike* test on its head. Instead of a test designed to be deferential to nondiscriminatory state laws, the test would require invalidating all such laws. Every statute that incidentally burdens interstate commerce can have gerrymandered exemptions to prevent burdensome effects in particular industries or to particular firms, but *Pike* tells us that those effects are ordinarily permissible.

One final argument merits attention. "Because foreign commerce is at stake," Norwegian argues that "weightier justification is required from the State." "In the unique context of foreign commerce, a State's power is further constrained because of the special need for federal uniformity." *Barclays Bank PLC v. Franchise Tax Bd.*, 512 U.S. 298, 311 (1994) (internal quotation marks omitted). **[—53—]** This consideration is typically implicated in the context of "state tax[es] on the instrumentalities of foreign commerce," *see Japan Line, Ltd. v. Cnty. of Los Angeles*, 441 U.S. 434, 448 (1979); *see also* **{-1153-}** *Wardair Can. Inc. v. Fla. Dep't of Rev.*, 477 U.S. 1, 8 (1986), but it is also implicated in the context of foreign trade and discriminatory "export restrictions," *S.-Cent. Timber Dev., Inc. v. Wunnicke*, 467 U.S. 82, 99–101 (1984) (invalidating a "protectionist" and "naked restraint on export of unprocessed [timber]" to a foreign country in part because "foreign commerce [was] burdened by the restriction"). Those contexts concern "international relations" and "foreign intercourse and trade," contexts in which "the people of the United States act through a single government with unified and adequate national power." *Japan Line, Ltd.*, 441 U.S. at 448 (internal quotation marks omitted).

By contrast, any burdens imposed by section 381.00316(1) result incidentally from matters traditionally of local concern. As we have explained, section 381.00316(1) is a "regulation of health and safety," "matters [that are] primarily, and historically, ... matter[s] of local concern," *Hillsborough*, 471 U.S. at 719, not a tax or restraint on imports and exports. And it is not the case that Congress has given "substantial attention" to the kind of regulation at issue, which does not "regulat[e] commercial relations with foreign governments." *See Wunnicke*, 467 U.S. at 99–100 (internal quotation marks omitted). So the incidental burdens imposed on foreign commerce are not "clearly excessive in relation to the putative local benefits," *Pike*, 397 U.S. at 142, that result from Florida's **[—54—]** traditional power to pass local well-being regulations to further substantial local interests. *Cf. S. Pac. Co. v. Ariz. ex rel. Sullivan*, 325 U.S. 761, 783 (1945) (explaining that "[r]egulations affecting the safety of the[] use [of highways] . . . affect[s] alike shippers in interstate and intrastate commerce" and are "akin to quarantine measures, game laws, and like local regulations of rivers, harbors, piers, and docks, with respect to which the state has exceptional scope for the exercise of its regulatory power, and which, Congress not acting, have been sustained even though they materially interfere with interstate commerce").

We conclude that Norwegian is unlikely to succeed on the merits of its Commerce Clause claim. Florida has a substantial interest in protecting its "residents from the harmful effects of discrimination," *see Barez*, 458 U.S. at 609, and in protecting the medical privacy of its residents, *Wollschlaeger*, 848 F.3d at 1314. And Florida has sought to further those interests by enacting a statute that proscribes businesses from subjecting an entire class of residents—including a substantial minority population—to economic ostracism by requiring that they produce medical documentation they either do not have or would like not to convey. *Cf. Barez*, 458 U.S. at 609. Because these justifications are not illusory, this Court cannot "second guess the legislature's judgment as to the relative importance of [those] justifications versus any burdens imposed on interstate commerce." *Locke*, 634 F.3d at 1195. It follows that "the burden on interstate commerce" does not "clearly outweigh[] the State's legitimate purposes," *Clover Leaf Creamery Co.*, 449 U.S. **[—55—]** at 474, especially where, as here, "the interests on both sides are incomemensurate"; "more like judging whether a particular line is longer than a particular rock is heavy," *Bendix Autolite Corp. v. Midwesco Enters., Inc.*, 486 U.S. 888, 897 (1988) (Scalia, J., concurring in the judgment). Florida may, consistent with the Commerce Clause, "remov[e] ... barriers to the participation by its residents in the free flow of interstate **{–1154–}** commerce." *Barez*, 458 U.S. at 608.

IV. CONCLUSION

We **VACATE** the preliminary injunction against the Surgeon General.

(Reporter's Note: Dissenting opinion follows on p. 430).

[—1—] {-1154-} **ROSENBAUM,** Circuit Judge, dissenting:

Today the Majority Opinion validates an unconstitutional Florida law—Florida Statutes Section 381.00316(1), which prohibits businesses from requiring patrons to show proof of vaccination to receive services—as that law applies to the cruise industry.[1] It does so by effectively applying only half of the dormant Commerce Clause analysis that Supreme Court precedent requires—and not even applying that half correctly. For dormant Commerce Clause challenges to state laws, Supreme Court precedent requires us to balance the local benefits a state's law brings against the burdens that law imposes on interstate and foreign commerce. When the burdens clearly exceed the benefits, the law violates the dormant Commerce Clause. Four major mistakes plague the Majority Opinion's application of the dormant Commerce Clause test.

First, the Majority Opinion shortcuts the balancing process by mislabeling Section 381.00316(1) a health and safety regulation. **[—2—]** It does so because state laws that meaningfully promote public health and safety receive "strong deference" from federal courts balancing a law's local benefits against the burdens that law imposes on interstate and foreign commerce. But a regulation qualifies for that kind of deference under dormant Commerce Clause analysis only if it actually "touch[es] upon safety," Maj. Op. at 34 (quoting *Kassel v. Consol. Freightways Corp.*, 450 U.S. 662, 670 (1981) (plurality opinion)), and meaningfully advances the state's interest in promoting health and safety. Here, though, the only way Section 381.00316(1) "touch[es] upon safety" is to wallop it.

Indeed, Florida's law is the exact opposite of a law that meaningfully promotes health and safety: it will facilitate the spread of COVID-19 onboard cruise ships by depriving cruise lines of the ability to verify passengers' vaccination statuses, a resource Norwegian's[2] Chief Executive Officer has described as the company's most valuable tool for preventing the spread of COVID-19 onboard. The Majority Opinion doesn't let that pesky little fact stop it from treating Florida's law like it promotes health and safety, though, so the law can benefit from (undeserved) "strong deference." **[—3—]**

Second, contrary to Supreme Court precedent, the Majority Opinion does not assess whether (and, if so, to what extent) applying Section 381.00316(1) to the cruise industry *actually* furthers Florida's **{-1155-}** claimed interests. As the Supreme Court has explained, a state's interest is "illusory" when the law "further[s]" the state's claimed interest only "marginally," *Kassel*, 450 U.S. at 670 (plurality opinion); *see also id.* at 691 (Rehnquist, J., dissenting). But the Majority Opinion never determines whether applying Section 381.00316(1) to the cruise industry actually furthers Florida's claimed interests. Instead, the Majority Opinion just evaluates Florida's claimed interests in the abstract. And that allows it to improperly equate Florida's interest in preventing cruise lines from distinguishing between vaccinated and unvaccinated customers for health reasons with a state's interest in remedying invidious discrimination along racial, ethnic, religious, or gender lines. By engaging in this false equivalency, the Majority Opinion artificially inflates the nature of Florida's actual interest (which is relatively weak, particularly in the

---

[1] Plaintiffs-Appellants Norwegian Entities "br[ought] this [case as an] as-applied constitutional challenge," and the district court enjoined Florida "from enforcing Section 381.00316 against Plaintiffs [Norwegian entities]" only. *Norwegian Cruise Line Holdings, Ltd. v. Rivkees*, 553 F. Supp. 3d 1143, 1148, 1180 (S.D. Fla. 2021). Yet the Majority Opinion refuses to recognize that this appeal raises only an as-applied challenge. *See* Maj. Op. at 31–32 (insisting on analyzing the statute facially and discussing its application to "grocery stores, restaurants, fitness gyms, clothing stores, barber shops and hair salons, and even pharmacies"). Perhaps that's because it recognizes the weakness of its arguments as they relate to this appeal as it was in fact brought. More on this later. *See infra* at 49–50.

[2] I use "Norwegian" to refer collectively to the plaintiffs-appellants: Norwegian Cruise Line Holdings Ltd.; NCL (Bahamas) Ltd., d/b/a Norwegian Cruise Line; Seven Seas Cruises S. De R.L., d/b/a Regent Seven Seas Cruises; and Oceania Cruises S. De R.L., d/b/a Oceania Cruises.

context of the cruise industry) to be as robust as a state's truly strong interest in preventing invidious discrimination.

Third, the Majority Opinion affords strong weight to Florida's goal of protecting the privacy of those who wish not to disclose their COVID-19 vaccination status, even though Florida itself requires proof of vaccination against many other infectious and potentially deadly and debilitating diseases to attend school and partake in other public services. In so doing, the Majority Opinion **[—4—]** ignores that such a "distinction is at variance with [Florida's] asserted legislative purpose, and tends to undermine [Florida's] justification for the burden the statute imposes on interstate commerce." *Edgar v. MITE Corp.*, 457 U.S. 624, 644 (1982).

Each of these three errors piles false weight upon false weight upon false weight on the local-benefits side of the balance so that validation of Florida's law under the Commerce Clause is a foregone (but false) conclusion. And then, for good measure, the Majority Opinion makes its fourth major error, all but ignoring the substantial burdens Section 381.00316(1) imposes on interstate and foreign commerce by facilitating the spread of COVID-19 aboard cruise ships and worldwide—burdens that damage the supply chain and significantly affect commerce otherwise.

The Majority Opinion's insistence on effectively ending its analysis with its (incorrect) assessment of the local benefits and then declaring the law valid under the Commerce Clause—rather than weighing the actual (minimal) benefits the law bestows against the true and heavy burden the law imposes on commerce—leaves the analysis half-done (and wrongly so on the done half). And it's a lot like leaving the house wearing a misbuttoned tuxedo shirt and tails, while barefoot and pantless, and declaring yourself to be formally attired. For everyone's sake, neither should occur.

Instead of the Majority's half-dressed analysis, we must correctly evaluate the local benefits—that is, we must discern the precise interests that Section 381.00316(1) furthers when applied to the cruise industry. And then, as the term "balancing test" conveys, **[—5—]** we must balance those local benefits against the burdens the law inflicts on both interstate and foreign commerce. When we do that, it's clear that the heavy burdens the law imposes on commerce far outweigh any minimal benefits in the context of the cruise industry. So Section 381.00316(1) violates the Commerce Clause as applied to Plaintiff-Appellant Norwegian. And the district court did not abuse its discretion in preliminarily enjoining the law.

I begin my analysis in Section I where the Majority Opinion left off: by noting **{–1156–}** the heavy burdens Section 381.00316(1) imposes on interstate and foreign commerce because of its significant role in the particular context of the cruise industry in facilitating and spreading COVID-19 around the globe. With that in mind, I then examine the governing standards for reviewing a preliminary injunction and for reviewing a challenge under the dormant Commerce Clause in Sections II and III, respectively. In Section IV, I explain why Florida's statute imparts few local benefits. Section V weighs any local benefits of the law against the substantial burden it inflicts on interstate and foreign commerce and shows that Norwegian is likely to succeed on the merits.[3] And Section VI shows why Norwegian meets the remaining requirements for a preliminary injunction. **[—6—]**

I. COVID-19 has exacted and continues to exact a heavy toll on commerce, which Section 381.00316(1) significantly exacerbates by facilitating the spread of COVID-19 on cruise ships and around the world.

The damage COVID-19 has wrought did not end with the tragic deaths of more than 6-and-a-half million people worldwide, including

[3] Because Section 381.00316(1) is unconstitutional under the dormant Commerce Clause, I do not consider whether it is also unconstitutional under the First Amendment.

those of the million-plus in the United States.[4] Among other legacies of COVID-19 the world lives with, we must now deal with "long COVID," a grave and widespread condition. More than one-fifth of the roughly 609 million people who survived COVID-19—about 121 million globally and almost 19 million in the United States alone—suffer from some form of long COVID.[5] According to the CDC, long COVID can cause "brain fog," debilitating fatigue, heart palpitations, shortness of breath, sleep problems, diarrhea, depression, chest pain, and joint and muscle pain.[6] **[—7—]** Worse still, these symptoms result from biological and chemical changes in the body.[7]

Take "brain fog," for instance. Stanford researchers studying mouse brains found that, after a COVID-19 infection, an abnormal increase in activity of certain brain cells had contributed to higher inflammation in the brain.[8] In fact, "[t]he genes expressed . . . after COVID-19 overlapped closely with those expressed . . . in neurological conditions such as Alzheimer's disease."[9]

That's right—Alzheimer's. And with long COVID, it's not just mouse brains that show signs of Alzheimer's; it's human **{-1157-}** brains, too.[10] Not only that, but "the acquired dementia that these patients get tends to be lasting and very problematic."[11] And kids who've suffered COVID-19 have been found twice as likely to **[—8—]** experience seizures and three times as likely to have psychotic disorders as kids who haven't had COVID-19.[12]

Nor do long COVID's profound effects stop there. Some long-haulers have problems with multiple organ systems or even experience autoimmune conditions that increase their risks of developing diabetes, heart conditions, or neurological conditions.[13]

But vaccines can prevent many of these problems. First off, vaccinated people are "markedly" less likely to contract COVID-19 than unvaccinated people.[14] And among those who get COVID- 19, vaccinated people are *twelve times less likely* to endure severe disease and require hospitalization than those who are unvaccinated.[15] Vaccinated people are also only *half as likely* to develop long COVID if they do fall ill.[16] **[—9—]**

Plus, vaccines protect more than just those who receive them. Studies show that

---

[4] World Health Organization, *WHO Coronavirus (COVID-19) Dashboard*, https://covid19.who.int/ (last visited Oct. 5, 2022).

[5] *See* Lara Bull-Otterson et al., *Post–COVID Conditions Among Adult COVID-19 Survivors Aged 18–64 and ≥65 Years — United States, March 2020–November 2021*, Centers for Disease Control and Prevention — Morbidity and Mortality Weekly Report (May 27, 2022), https://www.cdc.gov/mmwr/volumes/71/wr/mm7121e1.htm; *see also* World Health Organization, *WHO Coronavirus (COVID-19) Dashboard, supra.*

[6] *See Long COVID or Post-COVID Conditions*, Centers for Disease Control and Prevention, https://www.cdc.gov/coronavirus/2019-ncov/long-term- effects/index.html (last visited Oct. 5, 2022).

[7] *See id.*

[8] *See* Erin Digitale, *Brain Fog After COVID-19 has Similarities to 'Chemo Brain,' Stanford-Led Study Finds*, Stanford Medicine — News Center (June 13, 2022), https://med.stanford.edu/news/all-news/2022/06/brain-fog-covid- chemo-brain.html.

[9] *Id.*

[10] *Id.*

[11] Elizabeth Cooney, *Risk of 'brain fog' and other conditions persists up to two years after Covid infection*, Stat https://www.statnews.com/2022/08/17/risk-of-brain-fog-and-other-conditions-persists-up-to- two-years-after-covid-infection/ (quoting Dr. Wes Ely) (last visited Oct. 5, 2022).

[12] *Id.*

[13] *See supra*, note 5.

[14] *See* David N. Fisman et al., *Impact of Population Mixing Between Vaccinated and Unvaccinated Subpopulations on Infectious Disease Dynamics: Implications for SARS-CoV-2 Transmission*, Canadian Medical Association Journal (Apr. 25, 2022), https://www.cmaj.ca/content/194/16/E573.

[15] *See COVID-19 Vaccines Continue to Protect Against Hospitalization and Death Among Adults*, Centers for Disease Control and Prevention (Mar. 18, 2022), https://www.cdc.gov/media/releases/2022/s0318-COVID-19- vaccines-protect.html.

[16] *See UKHSA Review Shows Vaccinated Less Likely to Have Long COVID than Unvaccinated*, GOV.UK (Feb. 15, 2022), https://www.gov.uk/government/news/ukhsa-review-shows-vaccinated-less-likely-to-have-long-covid-than-unvaccinated.

unvaccinated people contribute disproportionately to the spread of COVID-19 to others—including to vaccinated individuals.[17] In fact, the district court here found that vaccines "reduce the risk of transmission from a fully vaccinated person by 80 to 90 percent." *Norwegian Cruise Line Holdings, Ltd.*, 553 F. Supp. 3d at 1150. So a vaccinated person is both less likely to develop COVID-19 herself and also less likely to spread COVID-19 to others than is an unvaccinated person.

This disparity is especially significant in the context of cruises, where hundreds—if not thousands—of people congregate in close quarters for several days or weeks at a time. As the CDC has recognized, "COVID-19 spreads easily between people in close quarters on board ships."[18] And when passengers disembark from the cruise, they enter other countries and eventually return home to different states and countries around the world, carrying with them and further spreading any infections they contracted on the ship.

Vaccines have been an important development in combatting our ongoing COVID-19 problem. Still, some may have valid **[—10—] {-1158-}** reasons for not getting vaccinated, and judging those reasons is not what this case is about.

Instead, this case is about the destruction that COVID-19 has exacted and continues to exact on national and foreign commerce: the obvious and hefty costs to economic output. Just consider the harm the pandemic has caused to the supply chain.[19] When we view COVID-19 through this lens, it is undeniable that more cases of COVID-19 mean even more damage to commerce.

Yet Section 381.00316(1) prohibits almost all businesses, including cruise lines like Norwegian, from, before serving patrons, requiring them to show proof that they are vaccinated. In this way, the statute compounds the burdens COVID-19 inflicts on interstate and foreign commerce because unvaccinated people are significantly more likely to develop (and therefore transmit) COVID-19 than vaccinated people, especially in a cruise setting. The district court found that obtaining proof of vaccination from passengers is the most important safeguard to prevent the spread of COVID-19 through cruises.

But because of Section 381.00316(1), cruise lines can't do that. So they have no way to mitigate the spread of COVID-19 on **[—11—]** that important basis. And because the extended time in close quarters on cruises fuels the transmission of COVID-19 by unvaccinated people, more passengers will develop COVID-19. That increased transmission creates problems not only for Norwegian's onboard medical services—which can become overrun with COVID-19 patients, obstructing medical care for other illnesses and conditions—but also for the passengers onboard, the inhabitants of the cities and ports the ships visit, and those people whom passengers encounter on their journeys home and in their communities, all of whom are now more likely to contract COVID-19 and possibly develop long COVID. In turn, that imposes far-reaching costs on interstate and foreign commerce for Norwegian, which suffers injuries to its goodwill and its business. And it inflicts even greater burdens on interstate and foreign commerce generally by removing workers from the workforce, which decreases consumers' spending power and causes interstate and foreign commerce to contract.

II. Standard of Review

With those burdens in mind, I turn to the standards that govern our review of the district court's decision to impose a preliminary injunction. We review a district court's

---

17 *See* Fisman, *supra*.

18 *See Cruise Ship Travel During COVID-19*, Centers for Disease Control and Prevention (last updated July 18, 2022), https://www.cdc.gov/coronavirus/2019-ncov/travelers/cruise-travel-during-covid19.html.

19 *See, e.g.*, Sean Harapko, *How COVID-19 Impacted Supply Chains and What Comes Next*, EY (Feb. 18, 2021), https://www.ey.com/en_us/supply-chain/how-covid-19-impacted-supply-chains-and-what-comes-next ("The COVID-19 pandemic has posed significant challenges for supply chains globally.").

order on a motion for preliminary injunction for abuse of discretion. *Alabama v. U.S. Army Corps of Eng'rs*, 424 F.3d 1117, 1129 (11th Cir. 2005). When conducting our evaluation, we review a district court's conclusions of law de novo and "findings of fact underlying the grant of an **[—12—]** injunction for clear error," *Am.'s Health Ins. Plans v. Hudgens*, 742 F.3d 1319, 1329 (11th Cir. 2014).

And when, as here, constitutional rights are at stake, our deference to the district court is great: even if "the underlying constitutional question is close," "we should uphold the injunction and remand for trial on the merits." *Ashcroft v. ACLU*, 542 U.S. 656, 664–65 (2004). So "if the district court's analysis of the preliminary injunction factors reflects a reasonable conclusion about a close question of constitutional law," "novel **{-1159-}** and difficult constitutional questions [should be] settled at a later stage, with the benefit of further factual and legal development" *Gordon v. Holder*, 721 F.3d 638, 644–45 (D.C. Cir. 2013), *overruled on other grounds by South Dakota v. Wayfair, Inc.*, 138 S. Ct. 2080, 2099 (2018); *see also Valle Del Sol Inc. v. Whiting*, 709 F.3d 808, 817 (9th Cir. 2013).

We consider four factors when determining the propriety of preliminary injunction relief: (1) whether the party seeking the injunction has shown a substantial likelihood of success on the merits, (2) whether the party seeking the injunction will suffer irreparable harm without the injunction, (3) whether the balance of the equities favors an injunction, and (4) whether an injunction serves the public interest. *Gonzalez v. Governor of Ga.*, 978 F.3d 1266, 1270–71 (11th Cir. 2020). "The third and fourth factors 'merge' when, as here, the government is the opposing party." *Id.* at 1271 (11th Cir. 2020) (cleaned up). Likelihood of success on the merits "is 'generally the most important' of the four factors." *Id.* at 1271 **[—13—]** n.12 (quoting *Schiavo ex rel. Schindler v. Schiavo*, 403 F.3d 1223, 1232 (11th Cir. 2005)).

III. The Dormant Commerce Clause

This deferential standard of review governs our consideration of the district court's conclusion that Section 381.00316(1), as applied to the cruise industry, violates the Commerce Clause. The Commerce Clause empowers Congress "to regulate commerce with foreign nations, and among the several states, and with the Indian tribes." U.S. Const. art. I, § 8, cl. 3.

Besides conferring that power on Congress, the Clause also invalidates state laws that "impos[e] substantial burdens" on interstate and foreign commerce. *Dennis v. Higgins*, 498 U.S. 439, 448 (1991) (citation and quotation marks omitted).[20] We sometimes refer to this "implicit restraint" of the Commerce Clause as the "dormant" Commerce Clause. *United Haulers Ass'n, Inc. v. Oneida-Herkimer Solid Waste Mgmt. Auth.*, 550 U.S. 330, 338, 343 **[—14—]** (2007). The so-called dormant Commerce Clause invalidates state legislation that "unduly burdens" interstate and foreign commerce. *Fla Transp. Servs., Inc.*, 703 F.3d at 1245.

Whether a law unduly burdens commerce turns on the balancing test that *Pike v. Bruce Church, Inc.*, 397 U.S. 137 (1970), sets forth. Under that test, a state law violates the dormant Commerce Clause when "the burden imposed on" foreign and interstate "commerce is clearly excessive in relation to the putative local benefits." *Id.* at 142.

To state the obvious, the *Pike* balancing test is a balancing test. So it's worth emphasizing that, in evaluating whether Section 381.00316(1) survives that test, we must *balance* the burden that the law imposes

[20] This "dormant" aspect of the Commerce Clause also prohibits state action that discriminates against interstate commerce. *See, e.g., Fla. Transp. Servs., Inc. v. Miami-Dade Cnty.*, 703 F.3d 1230, 1243 (11th Cir. 2012). So we generally use a "two-tiered analysis" to evaluate state action challenged under the dormant Commerce Clause. *Id.* Here, though, I agree with the Majority that Section 381.00316(1) survives scrutiny under the first tier of that analysis—the statute does not discriminate against out-of-state commerce. *See* Maj. Op. at 29. For that reason, I limit my discussion to the second tier, which focuses on whether Section 381.00316(1) unduly burdens interstate commerce. *See Fla. Transp. Servs.*, 703 F.3d at 1244.

on interstate and foreign commerce against the local benefits the law yields to further the State's asserted interests. **{–1160–}** Even if the state had a rational basis for believing its legislation would accomplish a stated purpose, that is not enough, contrary to the Majority Opinion's suggestion, *see* Maj. Op. at 36, to uphold the law under the Commerce Clause.[21] Rather, even if the state had a rational basis, we still must weigh the law's local benefits against the burden it imposes on commerce. Again, *Pike* imposes a *balancing* test. **[—15—]**

I begin with what we must balance on the state-interest side (local benefits) of the scale. On this side of the balance, *Pike* and its progeny require two inquiries. First, we must identify the true legislative purpose of the law, and second, we must determine whether and how much the law actually furthers the true purpose.

Starting with the first inquiry, we can often just accept a state's asserted purpose at face value. But we can't do that when the legislative scheme and history show that the state's asserted purpose "could not have been a goal of the legislation." *Clover Leaf Creamery Co.*, 449 U.S. 456, 463 n.7 (1981) (quoting *Weinberger v. Wiesenfeld*, 420 U.S. 636, 648, n.16 (1975)); *see also Locke v. Shore*, 634 F.3d 1185, 1194 (11th Cir. 2011) (accepting a state's asserted safety interest when "the legislative history confirm[ed] that the legislature highlighted safety concerns").

Pike shows how this inquiry works. There, Arizona enforced one of its laws in a way that prohibited a farming company from transporting uncrated cantaloupes from its Arizona ranch to its packing and processing facility in California. *Pike*, 397 U.S. at 138. That law's "core" provision required that fruits shipped from Arizona "be packed" so that the visible fruits did "not 'materially misrepresent' the quality of the lot as a whole." *Id.* at 142–43. The "impetus" for that requirement was Arizona's "fear that some growers were shipping inferior or deceptively packaged produce," which caused "the reputation of Arizona growers" to suffer. *Id.* at 143. Arizona "stipulated that [the law's] primary purpose [was] to promote and preserve the reputation of Arizona growers"—which, **[—16—]** in the abstract, the Supreme Court observed, were "surely legitimate state interest[s]." *Id.*

But as instructive here, the Court did not just accept Arizona's *asserted* interest and balance it against the burdens the law imposed on commerce. Rather, the Court observed that "application of the Act" to the farming-company plaintiff had "a far different impact, and quite a different purpose." *Id.* at 144. That farming company grew cantaloupes "of exceptionally high quality." *Id.* So applying the law to this company—and thus preventing the company from packing its fruit outside Arizona—did not serve "the purpose of keeping the reputation of [Arizona] growers unsullied," *id.* Instead, this application "served to enhance" the "reputation" of Arizona growers by informing consumers that the company's "high quality" cantaloupes were "grown in Arizona." *Id.* And the Court held that, though the law's claimed purpose encompassed "legitimate state interests[,]" *id.* at 143, "the State's interest [as applied in that particular case was] minimal at best," *id.* at 145–46. In fact, that "tenuous interest" failed to justify even the "incidental consequence" the law imposed on the farming-company plaintiff. *Id.* **{–1161–}**

Among other things, *Pike* teaches us we don't just blindly accept the state's asserted interest. Rather, we must discern the state's interest by actually looking at the law as applied to the litigant challenging the state's law. Only then can we see what interests the state's law serves in the particular context where it is being challenged. **[—17—]**

Once we discern the state's interest as applied to the litigant challenging the state's law, we move to the second step of the "local benefits" analysis. At this point, "the question becomes one of degree." *Id.* at 142. So we focus on how well the state's law furthers its purpose. In many cases, state laws "designed for" a "salutary purpose" still fail under the

[21] As I explain later, *see infra* at 53–58, the Majority Opinion's suggestion that the second tier of the *Pike* test requires only rational-basis review on the local-benefits side of the test is incorrect. *See* Maj. Op. at 37–38 (suggesting as much).

Pike test because those laws "further the purpose so marginally." *Kassel*, 450 U.S. at 670 (plurality opinion); *see also id.* at 691 (Rehnquist, J., dissenting) (explaining that a State's "asserted safety justification, although rational," will often fail under *Pike* when the law yields "safety benefits" that "are demonstrably trivial").

And the Supreme Court has repeatedly invalidated state laws under the dormant Commerce Clause when those laws further their purpose only marginally. In *Raymond Motor Transportation, Inc. v. Rice*, 434 U.S. 429 (1978), for example, the Court invalidated a Minnesota highway safety law because the challengers "produced a massive array of evidence to disprove the state's assertion that the regulations ma[de] some contribution to highway safety." *Id.* at 445.

The Court again invalidated a law that furthered its purpose only marginally in *Bibb v. Navajo Freight Lines, Inc.*, 359 U.S. 520 (1959). There, the Court invalidated an Illinois highway safety law because the plaintiffs "conclusively show[ed]" that the law had no safety "advantages," and "testimony" revealed that the measure "create[d] hazards previously unknown to those using the highways." *Id.* at 525. *See also S. Pac. Co. v. Ariz. ex rel. Sullivan*, 325 **[—18—]** U.S. 761, 779 (1945) (invalidating Arizona safety measure that increased hazards and afforded "at most slight and dubious" safety benefits); *Fla. Transp. Servs., Inc.*, 703 F.3d at 1261 (invalidating County permitting practices that "did not further, but if anything disserved, the County's purported purposes and benefits"). As these cases illustrate, a state's interest is "illusory"—and accorded only slight weight—when the record shows that the law furthers its purpose only marginally. *See Kassel*, 450 U.S. at 671 (plurality opinion); *id.* at 692 (Rehnquist, J., dissenting).

In sum, the state-interest side of the scale demands two inquiries. First, we discern the state's true interest or purpose as the law is applied. And second, we analyze how well the law furthers those interests. We describe the product of these inquiries, taken together, as the "local benefits" that flow from the state's law.

Next, we balance those local benefits against the burdens the law imposes on interstate and foreign commerce. In so doing, we must remember that "the critical consideration is the overall effect of the statute on both local and interstate activity." *Brown-Forman Distillers Corp. v. N.Y. State Liquor Auth.*, 476 U.S. 573, 579 (1986). In this sense, striking a balance under *Pike* requires "a sensitive, case-by-case analysis of purposes and effects," *South Dakota v. Wayfair, Inc.*, 139 S. Ct. 2080, 2094 (2018) (quoting **{–1162–}** *W. Lynn Creamery, Inc. v. Healy*, 512 U.S. 186, 201 (1994)).

Take *Clover Leaf Creamery*, for example—the case on which the Majority Opinion effectively rests its analysis. In that case, the Court reviewed a Minnesota law, which prohibited **[—19—]** retailers from selling milk bottled in single-use plastic bottles, under both the Equal Protection and Commerce Clauses. 449 U.S. at 458. The parties agreed that the State's asserted interests of conserving resources and waste-disposal problems "[we]re legitimate state purposes." *Id.* at 462. In its equal-protection analysis, the Court applied rational-basis review and sustained the law because the State's ban on single-use plastic milk containers bore "a rational relation to the State's objectives." *Id.* at 470.

Then the Court turned to the dormant Commerce Clause analysis. That analysis, unlike the Equal Protection Clause analysis, required a balancing of the local benefits against the burdens the law imposed on interstate commerce. The Court determined that the "burden imposed on interstate commerce by the statute [was] relatively minor." *Id.* at 472. Emphasizing just how minimal that burden was, the Court noted that the law required only that milk producers package their products in something other than single-use plastics—say, cardboard, or glass, or recyclables. And "most dairies package[d] their products in more than one type of container," anyway. *Id.* So that burden, the Court explained, was "not 'clearly excessive' in light of the substantial state interest in promoting conservation of energy and other natural resources and easing solid waste disposal problems." *Id.* at 473.

Under those circumstances, it made no difference that the law bore only a rational relation to the state's legitimate interest. And that, of course, makes sense: when a law imposes only a minor burden on commerce, that law "cannot" inflict "a burden on **[—20—]** interstate commerce that is 'clearly excessive in relation to the putative local benefits' under *Pike*." *Nat'l Ass'n of Optometrists & Opticians v. Harris*, 682 F.3d 1144, 1155 (9th Cir. 2012). And "we need not examine the actual putative benefits of the challenged statute[]." *Id.* By logical extension, then, a law that imposes only a minor burden on commerce will necessarily survive review under the Commerce Clause if it also survives rational-basis review under the Equal Protection Clause (as was the case in *Clover Leaf Creamery*).

But that calculus changes when the law inflicts real burdens on commerce. *See Pike*, 397 U.S. at 140 (invalidating Arizona's law because it imposed an excessive burden on interstate commerce by requiring a farmer to "build packing facilities" at a "cost" of "approximately $200,000"). In that case, we must carefully consider the local benefits that the state law returns and weigh them against its burdens. *See Town of Southold v. Town of E. Hampton*, 477 F.3d 38, 52 (2d Cir. 2007) (explaining the need to "remand[] for further discovery or trial where a party has offered a credible expert affidavit alleging a burden on interstate commerce and challenging the proposed benefits of the law."). Greater burdens on commerce require greater local benefits. *Pike*, 397 U.S. at 142.

And when the state's law also burdens foreign commerce, even a relatively minor burden can invalidate the law. Under those circumstances, we must apply the "well-accepted rule that state restrictions burdening foreign commerce are subjected to a more rigorous and searching scrutiny." **{-1163-}** *S.-Cent. Timber Dev., Inc. v.* **[—21—]** *Wunnicke*, 467 U.S. 82, 101 (1984). Here, as I've explained, *see supra* Section I, there's no question that Section 381.00316(1) burdens foreign commerce and relations.

Even the Majority Opinion concedes that this rule of scrutiny applies to "restraint[s] on imports and exports." Maj. Op. at 53. And of course, the cruise industry exports tourism when it annually takes millions of passengers from the United States to ports and cities around the world.[22] Section 381.00316(1) restrains that export by requiring cruise ships to carry unvaccinated passengers. As I've mentioned, that restraint is incredibly burdensome: cruises must, for example, allocate additional resources to their onboard medical facilities because those facilities are more likely to become inundated with COVID-19 outbreaks.

Plus, local populations in foreign countries—many of whom "lack access to healthcare and other resources" needed to combat COVID-19, Del Rio Aff. ¶ 19—must endure heightened COVID-19 transmission rates because cruise ship from Florida must carry **[—22—]** unvaccinated passengers to those locations. Then, after their cruises, when passengers from around the world return home, those who've contracted COVID-19 spread it to others on their journeys home and in their communities. And as I've explained, COVID-19 and long COVID inflict a huge toll not just on the cruise lines in these ways but also on commerce around the world—by removing workers from the supply chain and consumers from the market. For these reasons, we must subject Florida's law

[22] *See* Statista, *Cruise industry in the United States—statistics & facts* (July 18, 2022), https://www.statista.com/statistics/1251080/number-of-cruise-passengers-from-north-america/ (noting that more than 15 million cruise passengers left from ports in North America in 2019). Indeed, PortMiami is the Cruise Capital of the world. *See PortMiami*, Florida Ports Council, https://flaports.org/ports/portmiami/. "Port Canaveral is perhaps best known as the second busiest cruise port in the world," *see Port Canaveral*, Florida Ports Council, https://flaports.org/ports/port-canaveral/. And Port Everglades is the third busiest cruise port in the world. *Port Everglades*, Florida Ports Council, https://flaports.org/ports/port-everglades/.

"to a more rigorous and searching scrutiny." *Wunnicke*, 467 U.S. at 101.

When we do that, as I explain in Sections IV and V, we must conclude that Section 381.00316(1) cannot survive dormant Commerce Clause scrutiny under the *Pike* balancing test.

IV. The local benefits Section 381.00316(1) delivers are minimal at best in the context of the cruise industry.

In defense of its law, Florida asserts as the law's purposes (1) "preventing discrimination" against and (2) "promoting privacy" for those who wish not to disclose their COVID-19 vaccine documents. Fla.'s Initial Br. at 29. On that basis, both Florida and the Majority Opinion describe Section 381.00316(1) as a regulation of "health and safety." Fla.'s Initial Br. at 40; Maj. Op. at 53. From there, the Majority Opinion concludes that we owe "strong deference to the Florida Legislature" because Florida *"could rationally have decided"* that its law yields the putative benefits that the state proffers. *See* Maj. Op. at 36 (quoting *Clover Leaf Creamery*, 449 U.S. at 461–70); *see also id.* at 42. **[—23—]**

That approach is backwards. As I explain in Subsection A, we grant state laws "strong deference" only when they actually promote health and safety. Section 381.00316(1) does no such thing. So the "strong deference" we reserve for health-and-safety regulations does not attach to Section 381.03316(1). And while Florida's **{-1164-}** asserted interests in preventing discrimination and protecting privacy are legitimate state interests in theory, they are both illusory on this record as applied to the cruise industry, which I explain in Subsections B and C, respectively.

A. *Although Florida describes Section 381.00316(1) as an exercise of police power to safeguard the public health and safety, it is not a law that furthers genuine health and safety interests, as the law yields no safety benefits, but meaningfully increases hazards as it applies to the cruise industry.*

The Majority Opinion first goes awry by extolling Florida's law as a regulation of health and safety, a status it then uses to cloak the law with the "strong deference" that we ordinarily reserve for laws that actually promote public health and safety. Yet even the Majority Opinion knows it can't reasonably characterize Section 381.00316(1)—which facilitates the spread of COVID-19—as a regulation that furthers health and safety. *See* Maj. Op. at 34–35 (implicitly conceding that Section 381.00316(1) does not further "physical health and safety"). So after granting Section 381.00316(1) "strong deference" as if that law furthers a genuine interest in promoting health and safety, the Majority Opinion then promptly disowns any safety-and-health purpose attributable to Florida's law. **[—24—]** Instead, it explains, Florida's law need not actually "promote residents' physical health and safety" to be an exercise of the police power to safeguard public health and safety. *Id.* at 34. The illogic of this "logic" speaks for itself.

Apparently sensing this, the Majority Opinion makes another move: it argues that Florida's law promotes "residents' *economic* health and safety," so it is entitled to the "strong deference" generally reserved for regulations that genuinely protect health and safety. *Id.* at 35. But that's just wrong. And it enables the Majority Opinion to impermissibly hide the ball.

Florida certainly has a legitimate interest in promoting its residents' economic well-being. But that interest, by itself, does not necessarily warrant "strong deference" for the purpose of the dormant Commerce Clause analysis like a state's interest in promoting its residents' health and safety does. Rather, the Majority Opinion's sleight-of-hand improperly cloaks Florida's interest in furthering Floridians' economic well-being with the deference meant for a state's interest in promoting its residents' physical health and safety. And that illegitimate move proves outcome-determinative for the Majority Opinion's analysis.

To be sure, the Majority Opinion later acknowledges "the evidence" that Norwegian "will suffer economically if it complies with section 381.00316(1)." Maj. Op. at 48. But it upholds Florida's law by relying on the "strong presumption of validity" that the dormant Commerce Clause reserves for laws that actually promote public health and safety. *Id.* Yet that "strong presumption of **[—25—]** validity" disappears once we establish that Florida's law does not further health and safety.

i. Although regulations that meaningfully further health and safety warrant strong deference for the purpose of the dormant Commerce Clause analysis, economic-well-being regulations do not necessarily justify that same strong deference.

A law that promotes Floridians' economic well-being does not necessarily warrant the same deference that a law that meaningfully promotes Floridians' health and safety does. As the Supreme Court has explained, a statute "directly addressed to **{-1165-}** the protection of public health," which "falls within the most traditional concept" of a state's police power, differs from a statute that a state labels "a health measure on the attenuated theory that" it promotes the "economic well-being" of its residents. *Head v. New Mexico Bd. of Exam'rs in Optometry*, 374 U.S. 424, 428 & n.4 (1963); *see also Raymond Motor Transp.*, 434 U.S. at 448–449 (Blackman, J., concurring) (explaining that a state's economic interests receive less deference than a state's safety interest under *Pike*).[23]

In fact, this basic distinction explains the outcome in *Pike*—the fruit-shipping case. Arizona's asserted interest in *Pike* did "not" implicate "state legislation in the field of safety where the propriety of local regulation has long been recognized." 397 U.S. at 143. **[—26—]** Rather, Arizona asserted an economic well-being justification to "preserve the reputation of Arizona growers by prohibiting deceptive packaging" because some growers were hiding rotten fruit in packaging where it was not visible. *Id.* at 142–43. But the farming-company plaintiff packed high-quality produce. *Id.* So applying the law's requirement that the fruit be packaged in Arizona to that company enhanced (rather than preserved) Arizona's reputation for produce. And the Court held that this particular "interest [was] minimal at best—certainly less substantial than a State's interest in securing employment for its people." *Id.* at 146.

To summarize, then, the *Pike* Court distinguished not only between laws promoting safety and those promoting economic well-being, but also between different laws promoting economic well-being and even between the different economic well-being interests that a single law protected. In this respect, the *Pike* Court found some economic interests are more important—and therefore more worthy of deference—than others. The upshot of this is that, contrary to the Majority Opinion's suggestion, no one-size-fits-all approach exists for affording weight to a state's economic-well-being justifications.

Nor can the Majority Opinion's misleading citation clauses alter this principle. The Majority Opinion Frankensteins citations together to justify its conclusion that "strong deference" applies with equal force to laws that meaningfully further health and safety and those that further economic well-being—meaningfully or not. *See* Maj. Op. at 34. In so doing, the Majority Opinion creates its **[—27—]** own monster of a rule that robotically accords "strong deference" to any state interest that is conceivably related to the state's residents' well-being in any way. But that bloated view of a state's police powers is wrong.

[23] Chief Justice Burger and Justices Brennan and Rehnquist joined Justice Blackman's concurrence. Justice Stevens did not participate in the case.

We agree, the Majority and I, that a state has a quasi-sovereign interest—rather than a proprietary or sovereign interest—in the "well-being" of its citizens. *Id.* at 31 (citing *Alfred L. Snapp & Son, Inc. v. Puerto Rico ex rel. Barez,* 458 U.S. 592, 609 (1982)). And a state's "quasi-sovereign" interest encompasses its citizens' economic and physical well-being. *Barez,* 458 U.S. at 609. But a state's "quasi-sovereign" interest merely invests it with "standing under the *parens patriae* doctrine." *Id.* That fact is totally separate from and unrelated to the deference we afford to different interests in a dormant Commerce Clause analysis.

In the dormant Commerce Clause context, the Supreme Court has told us to **{-1166-}** give greater deference to regulations that meaningfully further health and safety than to economic-well-being regulations—to treat, in other words, these two interests differently. As the Court has noted, there is "no field" where "deference to state regulation has been greater than that of highway safety regulation." *Raymond Motor Transp.,* 434 U.S. at 443. And in *Pike,* as I just discussed, the Court distinguished "state legislation in the field of safety" from state legislation designed to enhance the economic well-being of its residents. 397 U.S. at 143. It further distinguished among the strengths of different economic-well-being interests. **[—28—]**

In sum, *Pike* requires "a sensitive, case-by-case analysis of purposes and effects," *Wayfair,* 139 S. Ct. at 2094 (quoting *Healy,* 512 U.S. at 201). And the Majority Opinion's one-size-fits-all approach, which accords strong deference upon a state's "incantation of a purpose to promote" its residents' well-being in any conceivable way, *Kassel,* 450 U.S. at 670, contradicts the Supreme Court's distinction between a state's interests in meaningfully promoting health and safety and in promoting different types of economic well-being. So even assuming that Section 381.00316(1) furthers Floridians' economic well-being, it does not follow that "strong deference" attaches to that law unless it meaningfully advances health and safety.

And regardless of whether we view the distinction between meaningful health-and-safety regulations, on the one hand, and economic regulations, on the other, as a feature or flaw, it is an essential element of our constitutional system. Of course, "[e]conomic welfare is always related to health, for there can be no health if men are starving." *Baldwin v. G.A.F. Seelig, Inc.,* 294 U.S. 511, 523 (1935) (Cardozo, J.). But even so, the "chief occasion" for the Commerce Clause was to invest the *federal* government—not the several states—with power to regulate the national economy. *Id.* at 522. "This principle that our economic unit is the Nation, which alone has the gamut of powers necessary to control the economy," has a corollary: "the states are not separable economic units." *H.P Hood & Sons, Inc. v. Du Mond,* 336 U.S. 525, 537–38 (1949) (Jackson, J.). And if we recede from that principle and necessarily accord **[—29—]** "strong deference" to states' economic-welfare justifications, *see* Maj. Op. at 34, we will "invite a speedy end of our national solidarity." *Baldwin,* 294 U.S. at 523.

To preserve that national solidarity, we must distinguish between regulations that meaningfully further health and safety, which warrant "strong deference," and economic well-being regulations, which are more likely to unduly burden interstate and foreign commerce. Florida's law is not one that meaningfully furthers health and safety (just the opposite). So it does not necessarily demand the "strong deference" that the Majority Opinion surrenders to the state.

ii. Florida's law does not warrant strong deference because it does not meaningfully advance health or safety and in fact harms them.

That said, both Florida and the Majority Opinion describe Section 381.00316(1) as an exercise of the state's "traditional police power" to safeguard both the "public health and safety *and* the economic well-being of its citizens," meaning that we must analyze both interests under *Pike.* Fla.'s Initial Br. at 1, 40; *see also* Maj. Op. at 35. They make this move, it seems, because the Supreme Court "has been **{-1167-}** most reluctant to invalidate" "regulations that touch upon safety," *id.* at 34 (quoting *Kassel*, 450 U.S. at 670); *see also* Fla.'s Initial Br. at 40. But Section 381.00316(1) is no safety regulation.

As I've noted, *Pike* requires that we scrutinize the legislature's actual interest—not simply accept its stated interest at face **[—30—]** value. *Clover Leaf Creamery Co.*, 449 U.S. at 463 n.7. And no one can seriously contend that Section 381.00316(1) furthers the public's health or safety. On the contrary, the law, which makes it impossible for cruise lines to ensure their passengers are vaccinated, endangers the health and safety of Norwegian's passengers and the community at large. After all, the district court found that vaccines "reduce the risk of transmission from a fully vaccinated person by 80 to 90 percent." *Norwegian*, 553 F. Supp. 3d at 1150. As Del Rio tells it, vaccination is the "most effective way to protect passengers, crews, and locals from the spread of COVID-19." Del Rio Aff. ¶ 27. So, he said, "verifying the vaccination status of cruise passengers" is the best safeguard against COVID-19 transmission aboard the company's cruises.[24] Del Rio Aff. ¶ 26. By removing this tool from the cruise industry, Section 381.00316(1) ensures more transmission of COVID-19 and decreases public safety.

We, of course, owe deference to the district court's factual findings. But it's not just the district court and Del Rio who think vaccination plays a critical role in stemming COVID-19 transmission. Scientific evidence verifies the important role that vaccination plays in stemming the transmission of COVID-19—especially in close quarters like cruise ships. *See supra* at pp. 8–9. **[—31—]**

Plus, here, the legislative history confirms that Florida neither consulted with medical experts nor reviewed scientific evidence when it enacted Section 381.00316(1). For example, during floor debates, Florida Senator Danny Burgess, who introduced the amendment that ultimately became Section 381.00316(1), *see* S.B. 2006, Amendment 330036, 2021 Leg. Sess. (Fla. 2021), resisted reference to any health- or safety-related evidence, reminding his colleagues at least twice that he had "no medical background." *See, e.g., Senate Session*, FLA. SENATE, at 6:20:51–6:20:56 (Apr. 29, 2021), https://www.flsenate.gov/media/VideoPlayer?EventID=1_q42x9ekw-202104291000&Redirect=true. When Senator Doug Broxson asked,

> "I think most of us feel fairly confident that the vaccine is working, so technically ... if you go on a cruise ship and 95% of the people have taken the vaccine, the 5% that did not would be exposing the other 5%. Is that a fair analogy, that what we're doing is letting people that choose not to have a vaccine to be exposed by the other people who are choosing not to have a vaccine?"

Id. at 6:34:30–6:35:03. Senator Burgess responded, "Again, not having a medical background but **understanding kind of the ... maybe unscientific approach**, I would agree. I think that's fair." *Id.* at 6:35:09–6:35:19 (emphasis added).

But unfortunately, Senator Broxson got the science wrong: unvaccinated people transmit COVID-19 to both unvaccinated *and* **[—32—]** *vaccinated* people. *See* Fisman, *supra*. And unvaccinated people infect more **{-1168-}** people, on a *pro rata* basis, than vaccinated people. *See id.* So Senator Broxson was mistaken: the bill doesn't just facilitate transmission of COVID-19 from unvaccinated people to other unvaccinated people—it also facilitates transmission of COVID-19 from unvaccinated people to vaccinated people.

In this respect, this case is just like *Raymond Motor Transportation*, where the Court invalidated Wisconsin's so-called highway-safety regulation because "a massive array of evidence" disproved "the State's assertion that the regulations ma[d]e some contribution to highway safety." 434 U.S. at

[24] To be sure, the district court found that "testing is an important adjunct measure." *Norwegian*, 553 F. Supp. 3d at 1174. But it concluded that testing "cannot serve as a substitute for vaccination because tests are susceptible to false positive and false negative results, even when repeated testing is done." *Id.*

444. In an even more extreme way, the evidence here shows that Section 381.00316(1) does not safeguard the public health and safety but rather jeopardizes it.

But Section 381.00316(1)'s violation of the dormant Commerce Clause is even more obvious than that of the law at issue in *Raymond Motor Transportation*. There, Wisconsin's asserted interest was "promot[ing] highway safety." *Id.* at 442. And as the Supreme Court explained, there is "no field" where "deference to state regulation has been greater than that of highway safety regulation." *Id.* at 443. Section 381.00316(1), though, is not a health-and-safety regulation—let alone a highway-safety regulation. So it is entitled to less deference than the "safety regulation" in *Raymond Motor Transportation*.

Even if we assumed that same deference attached to Section 381.00316(1), though, a "massive array of evidence" still **[—33—]** "disprove[s] the State's assertion that the regulations make some contribution" to health and safety. Instead, Section 381.00316(1) undermines public health and safety. *Id.* at 444. So Section 381.00316(1) cannot seriously be described as a "bona fide safety regulation[.]" *Kassel*, 450 U.S. at 670 (plurality opinion). And Florida's asserted interest in "safeguarding public health and safety," Fla.'s Initial Br. at 1, is therefore "illusory," *Kassel*, 450 U.S. at 671 (plurality opinion); *see also id.* at 691 (Rehnquist, J., dissenting).

B. Section 381.00316(1) does not prevent discrimination.

I next turn to Florida's first of two asserted interests in promoting the economic well-being of its citizens. Florida first asserts an interest in "preventing discrimination for failure to provide documentation evidencing COVID-19 vaccination." Fla.'s Initial Br. at 2–3. But as I've noted, the first task in evaluating a state's interest under *Pike* is to discern the state's true interest. That is key here because "discrimination" can connote several meanings. *See, e.g., Discrimination, Black's Law Dictionary* (11th ed. 2019); Bryan A. Garner, *Garner's Modern English Usage* 287–88 (4th ed. 2016). And identifying the accurate use of the term here transforms the rest of the analysis.

Skipping that step, the Majority Opinion equates discrimination based on vaccination status with "invidious discrimination" that "frequently occurs along ethnic lines." *See* Maj. Op. at 30–31 (quoting *Barez*, 458 U.S. at 609); *Barez*, 458 U.S. at 609. From there, the Majority Opinion assumes parity between Florida's interest in remedying noninvidious discrimination based on vaccination **[—34—]** status and a state's interest in remedying invidious discrimination based on ethnicity. No matter the evil, the Majority announces, a state's interest in remedying "discrimination" is always "substantial" and always "weightier" than a mere "legitimate" interest. Maj. Op. at 31.

But the problem for the Majority Opinion is that, as *Black's Law Dictionary* **{-1169-}** unambiguously explains, invidious discrimination and noninvidious discrimination are two entirely different things. *See Discrimination, Black's Law Dictionary, supra*; Garner, *supra*, at 287–88. And the weight of a state's interest in remedying discrimination varies "depend[ing] on the nature" of the discrimination in need of remedying. *Pike*, 397 U.S. at 142. After all, the "question" of how much weight to accord a state's legitimate interest is necessarily "one of degree." *Id.* That makes it crucial to discern the type of discrimination that Florida's law tries to remedy before assigning weight to Florida's interest in remedying discrimination.

I start by defining "discrimination." In the dictionary sense, discrimination connotes the "intellectual faculty of noting differences and similarities." *Discrimination, Black's Law Dictionary, supra* (definition 1). That use of "'discrimination' is neutral" and not in any way considered pejorative. *Id.* But "the current political use of the term is frequently non-neutral, pejorative." *Id.*

On that score, *Black's Law Dictionary* defines "discrimination" in the pejorative sense in two ways: (1) "The effect of a law or established practice that confers privileges on a certain class or **[—35—]** that denies privileges to a certain class because of race, age, sex, nationality, religion, or disability"; and (2) "Differential treatment; esp., a failure to treat all persons equally when no reasonable distinction can be found between those favored and those not favored." *Id.* (definitions 2 and 3).

i. Florida's law does not remedy discrimination based on race, age, sex, nationality, religion, or disability.

At times, both Florida and the Majority Opinion seemingly invoke the first of those pejorative uses of the term, suggesting that Florida's interest lies in remedying discrimination against its "minority populations" because those communities are more likely to face vaccine hesitancy. *See* Maj. Op. at 38; *see also id.* at 7, 45; Fla.'s Initial Br. at 29, 45 ("Through the statute, Florida is protecting its vulnerable minority populations . . . ."). But even though some "minority populations" have faced discrimination from certain parts of the medical community for decades, thus understandably prompting vaccine hesitancy of some in those populations, it's hard to take this description of *Florida's interest* at face value given the evidence (or more accurately, lack of it) supporting that assertion.

That evidence, on which Florida and the Majority Opinion rely exclusively, is a single comment Representative Tom Leek made on the legislature's floor on April 28, 2021. Aside from that remark, the legislative history lacks any evidence that the state intended Section 381.00316(1) as antidiscrimination legislation to protect Florida's "minority populations." No other representative or senator made comments to that effect. Nor do any one of the **[—36—]** six analyses of SB 2006 (the bill that became Section 381.00316) from the Florida Senate's Committees on Rules, Appropriations, and Military and Veterans Affairs, Space, and Domestic Security say the first thing about protecting Florida's "minority populations," even though many of those analyses discuss the bill's purported intent.

And Representative Leek disavowed any such legislative intent the day before he made the statement on which Florida and the Majority Opinion rely as proof that Florida enacted Section 381.00316(1) to protect its minority populations. During the House session on April 27, 2021, the following exchange occurred when Representative Michael Grieco asked Representative Leek about the provision that eventually became Section 381.00316(1): **{-1170-}**

Grieco: Chair Leek, are you familiar with what is a protected class for purposes of private businesses being unable to discriminate against them?

Leek: . . . ***That's outside the scope of this bill***, but the answer is yes, I'm familiar.

Grieco: With that familiarity, specifically as it applies to people that can't be discriminated [against] based on age, disability, gender, race, religion, are you familiar with anywhere else in state statute where we have created a new protected class that has not been addressed through constitutional law? **[—37—]**

Leek: ***We're pretty far afield from what's in this bill***. But there are protected classes created by federal law, state law, etc. So I hope that addresses your question. Just understand: ***that is not addressed in this bill***.

House Session, FLA. HOUSE OF REPRESENTATIVES, at 3:00:16–3:01:17 (Apr. 27, 2021) (emphasis added), https://www.flsenate.gov/media/VideoPlayer?EventID=1_ggkot7ka-202104271030&Redirect=true. In other words, Representative Leek appeared to deny that the bill's purpose is to protect Florida's "minority populations" from discrimination. In fact, Representative Leek said, "That's outside the scope of this bill," "We're pretty far afield from what's in this bill," and "That is not addressed in this bill." Three times Representative Leek declined to link what became Section 381.00316(1) with protecting "minority populations." *But see* Maj. Op. at 39–40 (selectively quoting Representative Leek to avoid grappling with this fact).[25] **[—38—]**

To reiterate, then, the contention that Florida enacted Section 381.00316(1) as civil-rights legislation to protect "minority populations" relies exclusively on Representative Leek's statement, which he made the day after disavowing any link between Florida's law and discrimination based on age, disability, gender, race, or religion. To be sure, I do not attribute "legislative mendacity" to Representative Leek for his contradictory statement the next day. Maj. Op. at 40. On the contrary, I assume that Representative Leek reflected on Representative Grieco's question the prior day and then concluded and asserted in good faith the next day that the bill protects "minority populations." There's certainly nothing wrong with that.

But Representative Leek's individual revelation doesn't make protecting "minority populations" the intent of the Florida legislature in enacting Section 381.00316(1). Nothing else from the legislative record—neither from the multiple floor debates, Committee reports, nor any **{-1171-}** other part of the legislative history—echoes Representative Leek's statement on April 28 that the intent of the statute was to protect "minority populations." And "[w]hat **[—39—]** motivates one legislator to make a speech about a statute is not necessarily what motivates scores of others to enact it." *Dobbs v. Jackson Women's Health Org.*, 142 S. Ct. 2228, 2255 (2022) (citation and quotation marks omitted). After all, one legislator's reconsidered view alone is not the *legislature's* view.

Rather than engage with this truth, the Majority Opinion faults me for "ignoring the fact that [Representative Leek] was the 'chief sponsor of the bill in the House of Representatives," Maj. Op. at 40 (quoting *Clover Leaf Creamery*, 449 U.S. at 467). Yet even the case on which the Majority Opinion relies for that claim shows that a single legislator—even a bill's chief sponsor—does not speak for the legislature. *See Clover Leaf Creamery*, 449 U.S. at 467 (citing statements from three senators on top of a statement from the bill's chief sponsor in the House to divine legislative purpose). Indeed, as the Supreme Court has explained, relying "on a single statement made on the floor of the House of Representatives" to "divine" legislative purpose, even in the Commerce Clause context, "is an exercise fraught with hazards," *New England Power Co. v. New Hampshire*, 455 U.S. 331, 341–42 (1982). And that is especially so when, as here, the bill's sponsor so clearly comes to his revelation about the bill's purpose for the first time after the bill has left the committee.

So while a dormant Commerce Clause analysis necessarily relies in part on legislative history, this particular use of legislative history is the very evil that Justice Scalia warned against when he explained that "Judge Harold Leventhal used to describe the use of **[—40—]** legislative history as the equivalent of entering a crowded cocktail

[25] No one disputes that Florida "may recognize new protected classes beyond federal law." Maj. Op. at 46. But Representative Leek, whom the Majority Opinion relies on exclusively to discern Florida's legislative intent, explicitly denied doing so. On the contrary, he explained that recognizing a new protected class beyond federal law was "not addressed in this bill," and the Majority Opinion twice concedes as much. *Id.* at 40 ("[T]he creation of a new protected class is not addressed in the bill[.]"); *id.* at 44 ("Section 381.00316(1) does not involve a constitutionally protected class[.]"). By ignoring what Representative Leek actually said and attributing that purpose to Florida's law, anyway, the Majority Opinion "substitutes its own intuitions" for those of the Florida legislature. *Id.* at 46. Even so, even assuming (contrary to **[—38—]** Representative Leek's repeated denials) that Florida had recognized a new protected class beyond those recognized by federal law, the law creating that class would still have to comply with the Constitution and federal law. *See, e.g.*, U.S. Const. art. VI. So even if Florida passed a law recognizing a new protected class for unvaccinated persons, that law would be unconstitutional if it imposed burdens on commerce that clearly exceeded its benefits. *Pike*, 397 U.S. at 142. The Majority Opinion "ignores" these "basic point[s]." Maj. Op. at 46.

party and looking over the heads of the guests for one's friends," *Conroy v. Aniskoff*, 507 U.S. 511, 519 (1993) (Scalia, J., concurring)—or more accurately in this case, for "one's [sole and fair-weather] friend[]." Justice Scalia would be disappointed.

The Majority Opinion responds to that criticism with a *non sequitur*: It's permissible, we are told, to rely on a *single legislator's* statement—which contradicted that legislator's statement from the day before—as evidence of the *legislature's* purpose (even though the legislature is composed of 160 legislators) because the Majority Opinion uses that evidence not "to determine what the statute means but to ensure that it serves a constitutional purpose." Maj. Op. at 39. That makes no sense.[26] The whole point here is to identify the intent of the *legislature*—no matter how the Majority Opinion describes our exercise.[27] And Justice Scalia's concern **{-1172-}** was **[—41—]** that a single legislator's statement (even when he doesn't say the opposite the preceding day) does not reveal the entire legislature's intent. And it's hard to imagine a more graphic illustration of the problem Justice Scalia pointed out than the Majority Opinion's efforts to identify the Florida legislature's intent based solely on one of two contradictory statements a single representative made on the floor.

At bottom, there is no evidence that the *legislature*'s intent in enacting Section 381.00316(1) was to prevent discrimination against Florida's minority populations.

ii. <u>Nor does Florida's law remedy any other type of invidious discrimination.</u>

Nor does the second pejorative use of the term "discrimination" capture the interest that Florida asserts. To reiterate, that definition describes the "failure to treat all persons equally ***when no reasonable distinction can be found between those favored and those not favored***." *Discrimination, Black's Law Dictionary, supra* (definition 3) (emphasis added); *see also CSX Transp., Inc. v.* **[—42—]** *Alabama Dep't of Revenue*, 562 U.S. 277, 287 (2011) (describing this definition as the "ordinary meaning" of discrimination). Applying this definition of "discrimination," the Supreme Court hypothesized that taxing "one group of taxpayers a 2% rate and another group a 4% rate, ***if the groups are the same in all respects***, is to discriminate against the latter." *Id.* (emphasis added). And of course, remedying this type of *invidious* discrimination is a substantial state interest.

But that's not a problem here. In fact, the record lacks any evidence of businesses' use of vaccination status as a proxy for a person's disability, religion, or race. Rather, the evidence established that Norwegian sought proof of passengers' vaccination statuses only because that is the "most effective way to protect passengers, crews, and locals from the spread of COVID-19." Del Rio Aff. ¶ 27. Put

---

[26] It's also misleadingly imprecise. To be sure, in performing the *Pike* dormant Commerce Clause balancing test, we look to see whether the law has a constitutional purpose in that if the law passes the balancing test, it comports with constitutional requirements under the dormant Commerce Clause. But our inquiry under the local-benefits side of the *Pike* balancing test is not whether the state's purpose was constitutional in a generic sense. Even assuming it was, the state's purpose can still fail the *Pike* balancing test. That is so because, as I've explained, once we identify the state's actual interest as applied to the complaining plaintiff, we must weigh the benefits that flow from the nature of that interest against the burdens the law imposes on commerce.

[27] The Majority Opinion insists that *New England Power* proves that there's something meaningfully different about relying on a single legislator's remarks to ascertain the legislative purpose when evaluating the local benefits **[—41—]** to the state under the *Pike* balancing test versus when determining what a statute means. *See* Maj. Op. at 39. It misses the point. Of course, we often do not rely at all on legislative history in ascertaining statutory intent, while the *Pike* balancing test requires us to consider legislative history in identifying the local benefits to the state. But that difference does not change the fact that—no matter the context in which it is wielded—a single legislator's uncorroborated (and self-contradictory) statement simply cannot speak for the intent of the legislature as a whole. Not surprisingly, the Majority Opinion cites absolutely nothing for its novel premise to the contrary.

simply, differential treatment because of vaccination status rests on a "reasonable distinction" between vaccinated and unvaccinated people. *Discrimination*, *Black's Law Dictionary*, *supra* (definition 3). The distinction is reasonable because unvaccinated people are substantially more likely to transmit COVID-19 than vaccinated people, especially in the context of a cruise ship. *See Norwegian*, 553 F. Supp. 3d at 1150.

Ignoring the reason behind Norwegian's distinction between vaccinated and unvaccinated passengers, the Majority Opinion appears to incorrectly suggest that Florida enacted Section 381.00316(1) to protect against invidious discrimination against unvaccinated people. Maj. Op. at 46; *see also id.* at 31. But this **[—43—]** betrays a misunderstanding of invidious discrimination—that is, discrimination when no reasonable distinction can be found between those favored and those not favored. *See Loving v. Virginia*, 388 U.S. 1, 10 (1967) (equating "invidious discrimination" with "arbitrary **{-1173-}** . . . discrimination"). Nor does the Majority Opinion marshal any evidence in the record to prove otherwise. The record is bereft, for example, of any evidence that Norwegian desires to act with "class-based, invidiously discriminatory animus" towards unvaccinated passengers. *Bray v. Alexandria Women's Health Clinic*, 506 U.S. 263, 272–73 (1993) (citation omitted). That's so because Norwegian's distinction between vaccinated and unvaccinated passengers is "reasonable rather than arbitrary and invidious." *McLaughlin v. Florida*, 379 U.S. 184, 191 (1964). Norwegian's distinction rests on the science of infectious-disease transmission.

Consider again why Norwegian would draw such a distinction: when hundreds of passengers, including unvaccinated passengers, congregate onboard a cruise to eat, socialize, and vacation in close quarters for several days, that translates to more COVID-19 cases than would be the case without vaccinated passengers. *See Norwegian*, 553 F. Supp. 3d at 1150–51, 1179. And that, in turn, means cruise operators must spend more to treat those who develop COVID-19 onboard. They also must cope with COVID-19 outbreaks that inundate their limited health services onboard, leaving little bandwidth to deal with other health emergencies. More cases of COVID-19 also mean that fewer passengers can enjoy their vacations, making them less likely to be return customers. And **[—44—]** some passengers who become ill may die or develop long COVID after disembarking, causing them to suffer from debilitating, long-term effects for years to come. Not only that, but cruise passengers who spread COVID-19 in foreign ports create additional problems for cruise lines (not to mention for those who frequent those foreign ports).

The Majority Opinion responds that I "ha[ve] it backwards" and that "[t]he State—not an Article III court—has the constitutional authority to determine what is and is not a 'reasonable distinction' between its citizens and what qualifies as discrimination worth remedying." Maj. Op. at 46. It continues, "declin[ing] [my alleged] invitation to put . . . policy decisions in the hands of unelected federal judges." *Id.* That sure sounds like a good invitation to decline. But it's not one I make. Once again, the Majority Opinion contorts my analysis, fails to apply the proper test under the dormant Commerce Clause, and then faults me for applying that test, which Supreme Court jurisprudence requires.

Of course, the state can determine "what qualifies as discrimination worth remedying." *Id.* But as *Pike* and its progeny show, that doesn't absolve us of evaluating the nature of that interest. So for example, in *Pike*, the Court disregarded Arizona's asserted interest because "application of the act" to the farming-company plaintiff there had "a far different impact, and quite a different purpose." 397 U.S. at 144. *See also Clover Leaf Creamery*, 449 U.S. at 463 n.7 (explaining the need to disregard a state's asserted interest when it "could not have been a goal of the legislation." (quoting **[—45—]** *Weinberger*, 420 U.S. at 648 n.16)). Indeed, as I've explained, the *Pike* Court's evaluation of the nature of the state's interest revealed that the state's *asserted* interest—"protect[ing] and enhanc[ing] the reputation of growers within the

State" by preventing fruit packers from packaging fruit in a way that misrepresented the fruit's quality—was significantly more substantial than the nature of the state's *actual* interest in applying its law to the farming-company plaintiff. *See* 397 U.S. at 143–46. And perhaps unlike its asserted interest, its actual **{–1174–}** interest was not enough to justify the burdens on commerce. *Id.* at 146.

As *Pike* itself shows, evaluating the nature of the state's actual interest is critical to proper application of the *Pike* balancing test because it allows us to ensure proper weight on the local-benefits side of the balance. And it's simply reality that Norwegian's use of vaccination status to make scientifically supported, health-based decisions is just not the same thing at all as invidious ethnic or racial discrimination. So the use of Section 381.00316(1) to prevent Norwegian from requiring proof of vaccination to board a multi-day cruise to foreign ports is not entitled to the same weight on the local-benefits side of the analysis as a state law that prohibits invidious discrimination.

The bottom line is that Norwegian does not seek to invidiously discriminate against unvaccinated people; it seeks to distinguish between vaccinated and unvaccinated people to ensure the health and safety of its passengers. And that non-pejorative "discrimination" is noninvidious. It is therefore a far cry from the **[—46—]** discrimination that occurs when a doctor refuses or delays "treatment [merely] because a patient (or a parent of a patient) owns firearms." *Wollschlaeger v. Florida*, 848 F.3d 1293, 1314, 1317 (11th Cir. 2017) (en banc)—a false equivalence the Majority Opinion suggests. *See* Maj. Op. at 31–32. Nor does distinguishing between vaccinated and unvaccinated people for health and safety purposes even vaguely resemble the "evils" of the "invidious discrimination" that "frequently occurs along ethnic lines." *Barez*, 458 U.S. at 609. And we must reject the Majority Opinion's unfortunate efforts to equate them. *See* Maj. Op. at 32 (treating a state's interest in remedying both these forms of discrimination as equal); *id.* at 43 (defending this false equivalence).

iii. Even assuming that Florida's law remedies non-pejorative discrimination, that interest is trivial at best.

That brings us back to the first, non-pejorative definition of discrimination: at best, Section 381.00316(1) remedies the "intellectual faculty of noting differences and similarities," *Discrimination*, Black's Law Dictionary, *supra* (definition 1), by preventing businesses from denying services to unvaccinated people, *see* Maj. Op. at 38 (reciting Representative Mike Beltran's statement that "we have people discriminating against you if you're not vaccinated," (quoting *House Session*, FLA. HOUSE OF REPRESENTATIVES, at 2:24:20–2:25:00 (Apr. 28, 2021), https://www.flsenate.gov/media/VideoPlayer?EventID=1_rch640e3-202104281030&Redirect=true). **[—47—]**

And because we must evaluate the nature of the interest the state claims, it's important to identify that interest precisely. *See Pike*, 397 U.S. at 145–146 (evaluating the state's interest as the law applied to the company that sued in that case). Although Section 381.00316(1) seems on its face like it protects *both* vaccinated and unvaccinated people from discrimination for failure to produce documentation of vaccination, that's not so. In practice, the statute protects only unvaccinated people against discrimination. Only unvaccinated people cannot produce documentation that they are vaccinated. And in any case, the statute punishes businesses only for requiring customers to provide "documentation certifying COVID-19 vaccination or postinfection recovery"—not for requiring proof that customers are unvaccinated. Fla. Stat. § 381.00316(1).

In fact, the Florida Legislature even voted against an amendment that would **{–1175–}** have protected vaccinated people from discrimination. During the debate on the bill that became Section 381.00316(1), Senator Jason Pizzo voiced concerns about this kind of discrimination. He pointed to a Miami school, for example, that warned students and teachers not to get vaccinated because "they could be contracting something … called shedding, which is disrupting and interrupting women's menstrual cycles, their reproductive systems." *Senate Session*, FLA. SENATE, at 6:04:22–6:06:30 (Apr. 29, 2021). "That's a teacher telling a student to stay away from their parents if they've been vaccinated[,]" he said. *Id.* "Did you honestly think that there was gonna be a—I didn't—a business **[—48—]** that would say, 'You cannot work here anymore, Teachers'; telling your teachers that if you choose to get vaccinated, you are not allowed to work here anymore?" *Id.*

Nor was Senator Pizzo alone in voicing these concerns. Representative Grieco also remarked that the same Miami school, which received public funds, had adopted a policy preventing its teachers from being vaccinated and prohibiting vaccinated people from interacting with students. *House Session*, FLA. HOUSE OF REPRESENTATIVES, at 3:02:50–3:03:19 (Apr. 27, 2021). Yet the state chose not to realize an interest in preventing this type of discrimination. And when Senator Pizzo proposed an amendment to address this issue,[28] the Senate voted it down.

In any case, I assume that Florida's interest in protecting only unvaccinated people from "the intellectual faculty of noting differences and similarities" is a legitimate state interest. *Discrimination*, *Black's Law Dictionary*, *supra* (definition 1). But of course, the nature of that evil contrasts sharply with the "evils" of the "invidious discrimination" that "frequently occurs along ethnic lines." *Barez*, 458 U.S. at 609. Yet the Majority Opinion treats a state's interest in remedying both evils as one and the same. *See* Maj. Op. at 30–31. That's obviously a false equivalence. And discarding it **[—49—]** reveals that Florida's interest is not "a substantial interest [that is] weightier than a 'legitimate local' one." *Id.* at 31.

That's especially so when we consider that Norwegian challenges Section 381.00316(1) only as it applies to cruise ships. Apparently aware of this problem for its analysis, the Majority Opinion relies on "grocery stores, restaurants, fitness gyms, clothing stores, barber shops and hair salons, and even pharmacies," Maj. Op. at 32, to argue Florida's interest here is substantial. But those establishments are irrelevant to this case because Norwegian challenges the law only as applied to cruise ships. Unlike cruise ships, those businesses do not transit international waters with their patrons in close quarters for days or weeks at a time. And they do not drop off their patrons in foreign countries or regularly have their patrons leave for other states or countries upon completing their business.

In short, they do not present the same infectious-disease-transmission problems that cruises do. Yet even Florida has recognized that infectious-disease-transmission issues as they relate to COVID-19 are not the same in all business contexts. *See* Section 381.00316(5) (excepting "health care provider[s]" from complying with Section 381.00316(1)). For the reasons the district court found and I've explained, the cruise context is one industry where infectious-disease-transmission **{–1176–}** problems are especially significant and different than the infectious-disease-transmission problems in contexts like the Majority Opinion relies on. **[—50—]**

The Majority Opinion's refusal to address the challenge that is actually before the Court betrays its lack of confidence that Section 381.00316(1) survives dormant Commerce Clause analysis as applied to the cruise industry.

iv. Because Florida's law furthers its interest in preventing discrimination only marginally, that interest is illusory.

As I have mentioned, the extent to which an interest can justify burdening interstate and foreign commerce "will of course depend on the nature of the local interest involved," *Pike*, 397 U.S. at 142. And in considering the nature of that interest, we must also

[28] The proposed amendment provided, "A business, a governmental entity, or an educational institution may not reject, restrict, obstruct, interfere, prevent, or deny a person access to, entry upon, or services from a business, a governmental entity, or an educational institution because the person is vaccinated against COVID-19."

remember that this is an as-applied challenge that seeks to enjoin Section 381.00316(1) only as it applies to the cruise industry.

To that end, there's no question that Florida's law furthers its interest in preventing discrimination (if at all) only marginally. And that's the death knell for Florida's law, for a state's interest is "illusory" when the law, though "designed for" a "salutary purpose," "further[s] that purpose" only "marginally," *Kassel*, 450 U.S. at 671 (1981) (plurality opinion); *see also id.* at 691 (Rehnquist, J., dissenting). That's the case here for two interrelated reasons.

To begin with, this law applies to millions of cruise passengers, and only a small subset of those passengers are Floridians. While the cruise industry serves some Floridians, it also attracts many passengers from the other forty-nine states and around the world. As I've noted, Florida boasts the three biggest cruise ports in the world, and PortMiami is among "the cruise industry's largest **[—51—]** and most essential international ports."[29] Cruise passengers travel to Florida from across the globe. Many of those passengers remain in Florida for only the time necessary to get to and board the cruise ship, before leaving Florida, often sailing to international destinations, and then, right after their cruises, returning to their homes outside the state. So any local benefits from Section 381.00316(1)'s application to the cruise-ship industry are minimal and short-lived.

Second, those benefits, minimal as they are to begin with, vanish soon after the cruise leaves port. Suppose a cruise ship departing from Florida does not require proof of vaccination to board the cruise. Instead, after leaving port, the cruise ship requires proof of vaccination to enter and use the common facilities. And those who refuse to present vaccine documents must use separately designated and inferior facilities. *See Norwegian*, 553 F. Supp. 3d at 1155 (explaining that some cruise lines have already implemented similar practices).[30] **[—52—] {-1177-}**

Even the Majority Opinion concedes that Florida's laws could do nothing about this. *See* Maj. Op. at 50 (accepting that cruise lines that "impose their [vaccine requirement] preferences abroad 'may continue to move freely across the Florida border'"). And the Majority Opinion is right to make that concession because a state's law is "invalid" under the Commerce Clause when "the practical effect of the regulation is to control conduct beyond the boundaries of the State." *Healy v. Beer Inst., Inc.*, 491 U.S. 324, 336 (1989).

As applied to the cruise industry, then, Section 381.00316(1) protects unvaccinated Floridians from the "intellectual faculty of noting differences and similarities" only at the time of boarding and disembarking. *Discrimination, Black's Law Dictionary, supra* (definition 1). After that, cruise lines are free to differentiate between vaccinated and unvaccinated persons at their leisure. So the conclusion that Florida's law furthers its purpose only "marginally" is inescapable. *Kassel*, 450 U.S. at 670–71 (plurality opinion); *see also id.* at 691 (Rehnquist, J., dissenting). And Florida's interest in preventing discrimination is thus "illusory," *id.* at 671 (plurality opinion). **[—53—]**

---

[29] *See supra* at note 22.

[30] Even if a cruise line took this approach, it could not avoid close contact between vaccinated and unvaccinated people at the beginning and end of the cruise—while the cruise line was subject to Florida's law. And the crew, who would have to serve both unvaccinated and vaccinated people onboard the same ship, would also be exposed to both unvaccinated and vaccinated people. That problem only compounds after crew members interact with unvaccinated passengers because "the crew typically live and eat in small congregate places." *Norwegian*, 553 F. Supp. 3d at 1151. So such an approach would not protect against transmission of COVID-19 from unvaccinated people to vaccinated people in the same way that verifying vaccination status would. For the same reasons, it would not protect people in foreign cities from COVID- **[—52—]** 19 transmitted by those who leave cruise ships to visit those cities. And of course, it would not prevent COVID-19 cases from overrunning the medical services onboard and obstructing medical care for other illnesses and conditions. So such a practice would not avoid the great burdens on interstate and foreign commerce that Section 381.00316(1) imposes.

To all that, the Majority Opinion's only retort is to accuse me of "artificially limit[ing] the State's interest" by focusing only on Section 381.00316(1)'s application to "luxury ocean liners." Maj. Op. at 32. But focusing on Section 381.00316(1)'s application to "luxury ocean liners" is precisely what *Pike* requires. *See Pike*, 397 U.S. at 144 (disregarding Arizona's asserted interest because "application of the act" to the farming-company plaintiff had "a far different impact, and quite a different purpose."); *see also Norwegian*, 553 F. Supp. 3d at 1180 (enjoining Florida "from enforcing Section 381.00316 against [Norwegian]" only). And adhering to *Pike* reveals that Florida's interest in preventing discrimination is, to quote the Majority, "artificial[]" because it is illusory. Maj. Op. at 32.

C. Section 381.00316(1) does not meaningfully promote privacy.

Florida's final asserted justification for the statute is one in "promoting privacy" for those who wish not to disclose their COVID-19 vaccine documents. There is no doubt that protecting privacy is a legitimate state interest.

But Florida has indicated that that privacy interest is significantly less substantial in the context of requiring proof of vaccination against deadly diseases. As Senator Tina Polsky pointed out during the bill's floor debates, Section 381.00316 prohibits businesses and schools from requiring proof of vaccination for COVID-19—even though businesses and schools can require, for instance, proof of vaccination for measles, mumps, and rubella. *See Senate* **[—54—]** *Session*, FLA. SENATE., at 6:18:00–6:18:18; 6:19:53–6:20:19; 6:20:43–6:20:49 (Apr. 29, 2021).[31] **{-1178-}**

Time and again the Supreme Court has made clear that, when a state contradicts its asserted interest in other contexts, that fact "tends to undermine" the state's "justification for the burdens" its law "imposes on interstate commerce." *MITE Corp.*, 457 U.S. at 644. In *Raymond Motor Transportation*, for example, the Court invalidated a Wisconsin statute that generally prohibited trucks exceeding fifty-five feet in length from operating on the state's highways. 434 U.S. at 432. In so doing, the Court concluded that Wisconsin's "assertion that the challenged regulations contribute to highway safety" was "undercut by the maze of exemptions from the general truck-length limit that the State itself allow[ed]." *Id.* at 443, 445.

The same issue arose in *Edgar v. MITE Corp.* There, Illinois enacted a law requiring that certain tender offers be registered with **[—55—]** the Secretary of State. 457 U.S. at 626–27. Illinois's asserted purpose for this law was to provide greater protections for resident security holders than federal securities laws afforded. *Id.* at 644. But the law also "completely exempt[ed] from coverage a corporation's acquisition of its own shares." *Id.* As a result, a company could make a tender offer for its own stock without complying with the law, leaving that company's shareholders to depend on only federal securities laws. *Id.* Yet Illinois clearly viewed those provisions as inadequate to protect investors in other contexts. *Id.* "This distinction [wa]s at variance with Illinois' asserted legislative purpose," the Court said, "and it tend[ed] to undermine [the State's] justification for the burdens the statute impose[d] on interstate commerce." *Id.*

This case is no different. In all three circumstances, the state contradicted its

[31] As with those vaccinations, COVID-19 vaccines have obtained full authorization from the FDA. *See* U.S. Food and Drug Administration, *FDA Approves First COVID-19 Vaccine* (Aug. 23, 2021), https://www.fda.gov/news-events/press-announcements/fda-approves-first-covid-19-vaccine (announc- ing FDA full approval for Pfizer-BioNTech COVID-19 vaccine for those 16 and older); U.S. Food and Drug Administration, *Coronavirus (COVID-19) Update: FDA Takes Key Action by Approving Second COVID-19 Vaccine* (Jan. 31, 2022), https://www.fda.gov/news-events/press-announcements/corona-virus-covid-19-update-fda-takes-key-action-approving-second-covid-19-vac- cine (announcing FDA full approval for Moderna COVID-19 vaccine for those 18 and older). So vaccines for COVID-19 stand on the same footing as FDA-approved vaccines for other diseases.

asserted interest in other contexts, thus undermining the weight of the state's interest. And that makes sense: when the legislature treats the same alleged problem differently—here, Florida's inconsistent treatment of the alleged lack of privacy that attends a requirement to show documentation of vaccination for an infectious, highly contagious, potentially deadly and debilitating disease at business and public institutions where people must interact and share contact with one another—it suggests that the state's claimed interest in remedying that problem is not as important as if the state addressed that interest uniformly.

So here, as in *MITE Corp.* and *Raymond Motor Transportation*, Florida has undermined its asserted interest in protecting **[—56—]** Floridians' privacy by contradicting that interest. Florida contradicted its privacy interest because the state itself requires Floridians to present proof of vaccination against diseases other than COVID-19 to attend schools at the very same time that Section 381.00316(1) prohibits cruise lines from requiring documentation of COVID-19 vaccination. "This distinction is at variance with [Florida's] asserted legislative purpose, and tends to undermine [Florida's] justification for the burdens the statute imposes on interstate [and foreign] commerce." *MITE Corp.*, 457 U.S. at 644.

The Majority Opinion simply ignores *MITE Corp.* and **{-1179-}** *Raymond Motor Transportation*. It doesn't even mention them at all. Instead, the Majority Opinion says it is irrelevant that Florida requires disclosure of vaccination documentation for other infectious, potentially deadly, or debilitating diseases to attend school and other venues, while it espouses an interest in protecting the privacy of COVID-19 vaccination documentation. *See* Maj. Op. at 47. Yet while that distinction might be irrelevant when we subject state laws to rational-basis review (under equal-protection or due-process analysis, for example), that distinction is very relevant when we review state laws challenged under the dormant Commerce Clause.

To support its contrary claim, the Majority Opinion relies exclusively on the *Clover Leaf Creamery* Court's *equal-protection* analysis. *See* Maj. Op. at 41 (asserting "that a legislature need not strike at all evils at the same time or in the same way" (quoting *Clover Leaf Creamery*, 449 U.S. at 466)). The Majority Opinion **[—57—]** justifies this move, it seems, because the *Clover Leaf Creamery* Court relied on its analysis of Minnesota's asserted interests, which it had "already reviewed" during its equal-protection analysis, for the purpose of its dormant Commerce Clause analysis. 449 U.S. at 473.

But the Majority Opinion's reliance on *Clover Leaf Creamery*'s equal-protection analysis is wrong for three reasons. *First*, because the Minnesota law in *Clover Leaf Creamery* imposed only a "minor" burden on commerce, *id.* at 472, the Court didn't need to engage in further analysis of the local-benefits side of *Pike*'s balance. Indeed, when a law imposes only a minor burden on commerce, "it follows that there cannot be a burden on interstate commerce that is 'clearly excessive in relation to the putative local benefits' under *Pike*." *Nat'l Ass'n of Optometrists & Opticians*, 682 F.3d at 1155. But when a law imposes more than a minor burden on commerce—and especially when a law imposes a burden on foreign commerce, *see Wunnicke*, 467 U.S. at 101—we must carefully consider the local benefits that the state law produces, before weighing those benefits against the law's burdens. *See Town of Southold*, 477 F.3d at 52 (explaining the need to "remand[] for further discovery or trial where a party has offered a credible expert affidavit alleging a burden on interstate commerce and challenging the proposed benefits of the law.").

Second, as far as I can tell, there's not a single other Supreme Court or Eleventh Circuit case that both applies *Pike* and employs **[—58—]** rational-basis scrutiny on the local-benefits side of the equation.[32]

[32] When we analyze laws the United States Congress has enacted, we ask whether Congress could have had a rational basis for concluding that a regulated activity sufficiently affected interstate commerce to assess the constitutionality of the statute under the Commerce Clause. *United States*

Perhaps that explains the Majority Opinion's choice to retcon dormant Commerce Clause cases to support its mistaken application of rational-basis review when analyzing Section 381.00316(1)'s local benefits. But as I am about to explain, the Majority Opinion fails to cite a single case that actually supports its incorrect contention that courts engage in rational-basis review when analyzing the local-benefits side of the scale under *Pike*. **{-1180-}**

The Majority Opinion first revises *Florida Transportation Services* to support the proposition that Florida's "justifications are not illusory if applying section 381.00316(1) 'as written' would 'rationally contribute to [Florida's] purported local benefits.'" Maj. Op. at 37 (quoting *Fla. Transp. Servs.*, 703 F.3d at 1260); *see also id.* at 47. In essence, the Majority Opinion says that a state's justifications are not illusory if the state had a rational basis for believing that its law would "contribute to the State's purported local benefits." *Id.* at 38 (alterations adopted). But *Florida Transportation* **[—59—]** *Services* never said that a state's asserted justifications are not illusory if the state had a rational basis for believing that its law would contribute to the state's purported benefits.

In fact, we never mentioned the term "rational basis" in that entire opinion. Nor did we cite *Clover Leaf Creamery*. Instead, we cited *Raymond Motor Transportation*, among other cases. And we explained that Miami-Dade's "permitting practices did not further, but if anything rather disserved, the County's purported purposes and benefits." *Fla. Transp. Servs.*, 703 F.3d at 1261. So, we reasoned, "while the local benefits identified by the County [we]re legitimate, the Port Director's permitting practices d[id] not rationally contribute to these purported local benefits." *Id.* at 1260. In other words, we used "rationally" in the sense that the state's challenged practices did not *actually* further its justifications for those practices—not as code that we were engaging in rational-basis review.

In the same way, the Majority Opinion distorts *Kassel v. Consolidated Freightways* to justify applying rational-basis review to the local-benefits side of the *Pike* scale. Maj. Op. at 37 (quoting *Kassel*, 450 U.S. at 671). But *Kassel* did not, as the Majority Opinion claims, "echo[]" *Clover Leaf Creamery. Id.* On the contrary, *Kassel* dealt with an Iowa highway-safety law that "tend[ed] to *increase* the number of accidents," prompting the Court to find that Iowa's asserted "safety interest" was "illusory," 450 U.S. at 671, 675 (plurality opinion). That fact, coupled with Iowa's "statutory exemptions," suggested that "the deference traditionally accorded a **[—60—]** State's safety judgment [was] not warranted." *Id.* at 678 (citing *Raymond Motor Transp.*, 434 U.S. at 444 & n.18, 446–47). And because Iowa's law also imposed a substantial burden on interstate commerce, the Court held that it "violate[d] the Commerce Clause." *Id.* at 678–79. In short, *Kassel* dealt with a law that imposed substantial burdens on commerce. For that reason, the Court had no choice but to determine whether Iowa's law produced any benefits. And because the law did not produce any benefits, the Court held that Iowa's asserted safety justification was illusory.

Nor have we ever read, as the Majority Opinion suggests, "*Kassel* to command substantial deference" when a state's safety benefits were illusory. Maj. Op. at 37. On the contrary, *Florida Transportation Services* applied *Kassel* to hold that Miami-Dade's permitting practices failed the dormant Commerce Clause because they were, in effect, illusory, as they "did not further, but if anything rather disserved, the County's purported purposes and benefits." *Fla. Transp. Servs.*, 703 F.3d at 1261 (citing *Kassel*, 460 U.S. at 670).

And *third*, *Raymond Motor Transportation* preceded, and *MITE* followed, *Clover Leaf Creamery*. And they both teach that a state

v. Lopez, 514 U.S. 549, 556–57 (1995). And when the Supreme Court used to evaluate state taxes that discriminated against those out of state (the first tier of the *Pike* analysis), it used to consider whether the state's justification had a rational basis. *Fulton Corp. v. Faulkner*, 516 U.S. 325, 345–46 (1996). But it no longer does that. *Id.* Of course, this case involves neither of these situations, in any case.

undercuts the weight of its asserted interest by contradicting that interest in other contexts. Plus, as I've mentioned, as far as I can tell, in the forty-one years **{–1181–}** since the Supreme Court issued *Clover Leaf Creamery*, no Supreme Court case has employed rational-basis review to analyze a law's local benefits under *Pike*. Nor does **[—61—]** any Supreme Court case abrogate or limit *Raymond Motor Transportation*'s and *MITE*'s analyses in this respect.

The clear import of these facts is that *Clover Leaf Creamery* relied on its equal-protection analysis of the state's interests for the purpose of its dormant Commerce Clause analysis of those interests because the law imposed only a "minor" burden on commerce. 449 U.S. at 473. So the Court did not need to further explore the local-benefits side of the analysis because it could make no difference to the outcome. After all, the minor burden couldn't outweigh the local benefits, in any case.

Put simply, *Clover Leaf Creamery* did not somehow silently add or substitute rational-basis review for the *Pike* balancing test or for any part of that test under dormant Commerce Clause jurisprudence. And the Majority Opinion's efforts to rewrite the *Pike* balancing test to the contrary are inconsistent with dormant Commerce Clause jurisprudence.

Because this case demands application of the *Pike* balancing test rather than rational-basis review, the question is whether Florida's law imposes a burden on commerce that clearly exceeds its local benefits. And both *MITE Corp.* and *Raymond Motor Transportation* demand the conclusion that, by requiring Floridians to present proof of vaccination against other infectious, potentially deadly or debilitating diseases to attend school, Florida has undermined any substantiality its asserted interest in protecting Floridians' privacy in this context may have otherwise had. For that **[—62—]** reason, Florida's asserted privacy interest warrants less weight on the local-benefits side of the *Pike* balancing scale.

V. The substantial burden Section 381.00316(1) imposes on domestic and foreign commerce clearly exceeds any local benefits the law bestows.

As Section IV of this dissent shows, Florida's justifications for Section 381.00316(1) are illusory. But even if we assume Section 381.00316(1) could "rationally" further the interests Florida claims, again, a "determination that a state law is a rational safety measure does not end the Commerce Clause inquiry." *Kassell*, 450 U.S. at 691 (Rehnquist, J., dissenting); *see also id.* at 670 (plurality opinion); *Raymond Motor Transp.*, 434 U.S. at 443. Rather, even a safety measure may be "rational" and still fail under *Pike* if it yields demonstrably trivial safety benefits while imposing a meaningful burden on commerce. And Section 381.00316(1) goes a step beyond that—it imposes substantial burdens on commerce.

As is clear by now, the law makes the spread of COVID-19 significantly more likely—especially in the cruise setting, where, as the district court found, "a large volume of individuals in close quarters" spend an extended period together, presenting "many opportunities for person-to-person contact in crowded or indoor settings, such as group and buffet dining, entertainment events, and excursions." *Norwegian*, 553 F. Supp. 3d at 1151. Del Rio also explained that infected passengers (whose infection may not show up on a COVID-19 test) can expose the local populations to **[—63—]** COVID-19 when other countries allow cruise passengers to disembark. Del Rio Aff. ¶ 19. "[M]any of these populations lack the access to healthcare and other resources," so they "may be badly damaged and they may understandably blame [Norwegian] for it." *Id.* **{–1182–}**

But Section 381.00316(1) doesn't just increase COVID-19 cases onboard and in foreign ports. It also increases COVID-19 cases around the United States and the world. "[O]nce a cruise concludes, passengers may engage in air transportation or other types of common transports to return home." *Norwegian*, 553 F. Supp. 3d at 1151. As a result, infected passengers can cause "widespread transmission and possibly 'super spreader' events" after they disembark from the cruise and reach their homes. *Id.* So Florida's law doesn't impact *just* Floridians—it has a nationwide and even worldwide impact.

And the more people who are infected with COVID-19, the greater the burden on commerce. That's because people who are confined to beds and hospitals or who are otherwise unable to work because of the lingering effects of COVID-19 and long COVID—not to mention those who die from the virus—cannot participate in commerce as they would if they were not infected. They cannot go to their jobs and schools, consume goods and services, or participate in many other commercial activities. And at the risk of stating the obvious, dead people can't participate in commerce at all. Nor can people who are on ventilators or in the intensive care unit. Plus, when there are COVID-19 surges **[—64—]** (especially because of ever-more-transmissible and dangerous variants), even healthy people are more reluctant to go to work, to school, or on vacation.

We need only look to the well-known effects of COVID-19 on the supply chain to understand the size of the impact large numbers of COVID-19 cases have on both interstate and foreign commerce. *See, e.g.*, Sean Harapko, *How COVID-19 Impacted Supply Chains and What Comes Next*, EY (Feb. 18, 2021), https://www.ey.com/en_us/supply-chain/how-covid-19-impacted-supply-chains-and-what-comes-next ("The COVID-19 pandemic has posed significant challenges for supply chains globally."). COVID-19, in short, dramatically impacted interstate commerce by killing and temporarily (and permanently, in many cases) disabling millions of people, keeping them out of work, school, and leisure activity and gravely affecting the economy.

By exacerbating the COVID-19 problem, Section 381.00316(1) appreciably increases these harms nationwide (and worldwide) while bestowing negligible (if any) local benefits. So the provision doesn't survive review under the dormant Commerce Clause when we balance the law's trifling benefits against the enormous costs it inflicts on interstate and foreign commerce. "[W]here, as here, the State's safety interest has been found to be illusory, and its regulations impair significantly the federal interest in efficient and safe interstate [and foreign] transportation, the state law cannot be harmonized with the Commerce Clause." *Kassel*, **[—65—]** 450 U.S. at 671 (plurality opinion); *see also id.*. at 691 (Rehnquist, J., dissenting).

For these reasons, the district court did not abuse its discretion in finding that Norwegian established a substantial likelihood of success on its dormant Commerce Clause claim.

VI. The remaining preliminary injunction factors also favor the district court's entry of its preliminary injunction.

Finally, I consider the remaining preliminary-injunction factors. As with the first and most important criterion, the district court did not abuse its discretion in concluding that Norwegian established that irreparable harm and the equities and public interest favored injunction.

First, without a preliminary injunction, Norwegian will endure irreparable harm, "the sine qua non of injunctive relief." **{-1183-}** *Siegel v. LePore*, 234 F.3d 1163, 1176 (11th Cir. 2000) (quoting *Ne. Fla. Chapter of the Ass'n of Gen. Contractors v. City of Jacksonville*, 896 F.2d 1283, 1285 (11th Cir. 1990)). As the district court noted, the undisputed record shows that, without being able to credibly verify vaccination status, Norwegian will suffer injury to its "reputation, trust, and goodwill." *Norwegian*, 553 F. Supp. 3d at 1178. Florida has presented no evidence to refute Norwegian's assertions in these regards.

On appeal, Florida suggests that Norwegian chose to stake its reputation on requiring vaccine documentation. But that suggestion conflicts with the uncontradicted proof that Norwegian's **[—66—]** vaccination protocols are integral to its longstanding brand, reputation, and customer base. As Norwegian explained, it and its passengers prize safety, hygiene, and comfort. That's why passengers choose to cruise with Norwegian. And less than 100% vaccination virtually ensures more COVID-19 cases and all the ill effects on safety, hygiene, and comfort that come with that. Florida also disregards that Norwegian sold at least some of its tickets for 100%-vaccinated cruises before the legislature enacted Section 381.00316(1).

Beyond these harms, Norwegian would suffer monetary losses that it couldn't recover from the state because of its sovereign immunity, thus rendering the harm suffered irreparable. *See Odebrecht Constr., Inc. v. Sec'y, Fla. Dep't of Transp.*, 715 F.3d 1268, 1289 (11th Cir. 2013) ("[A]bsent waiver by the State or valid congressional override, the Eleventh Amendment bars a damages action against a State in federal court." (quoting *Kentucky v. Graham*, 473 U.S. 159, 169 (1985))). Florida has not rebutted Norwegian's assertion that, without an injunction, it is likely to suffer significant financial losses.

Finally, putting the general public—including Norwegian's passengers and employees, the populations who greet them, and those around them when they travel home—at risk of exposure to COVID-19 poses the worst form of irreparable harm. Florida denies neither that vaccines best protect against COVID-19, nor that vaccine documentation best confirms vaccination status. Nor can Florida seriously deny that COVID-19 and long COVID can be **[—67—]** serious—and even fatal. *See Ala. Ass'n of Realtors v. Dep't of Health & Hum. Servs.*, 141 S. Ct. 2485, 2490 (2021) ("[T]he public has a strong interest in combating the spread of the COVID-19 Delta variant."). In sum, there is no shortage of irreparable injury here.

The equities and public interest favor an injunction, too. Because Norwegian has established likely success on its constitutional challenge under the dormant Commerce Clause, the balance of harm and the public interest weigh in its favor because "[t]he public has no interest in the enforcement of what is very likely an unconstitutional statute." *Odebrecht*, 715 F.3d at 1290; *see also KH Outdoor, LLC v. City of Trussville*, 458 F.3d 1261, 1272 (11th Cir. 2006). Plus, the more people incapacitated with COVID-19 and long COVID, the worse the effect on interstate and foreign commerce. And that is certainly not in the public interest.

As to the equities, as I have mentioned, Norwegian has shown that it is likely to suffer significant financial and reputational harms without an injunction, and it has also shown that public health will be jeopardized.

By contrast, Florida has identified no public benefit from the continued enforcement of the statute against Norwegian, other than those that I've previously explained are not sufficient even to get the **{–1184–}** statute past dormant Commerce Clause review. To be sure, Florida asserts that it suffers an "ongoing irreparable injury" whenever it is "'enjoined by a court from effectuating [a] statute[] enacted by representatives of its people,'" invoking its "sovereign **[—68—]** capacity" and "traditional police powers." Fla.'s Initial Br. at 44–45 (first quoting *Maryland v. King*, 567 U.S. 1301, 1303 (2012) (Roberts, C.J., in chambers); then citing *Hand v. Scott*, 888 F.3d 1206, 1214 (11th Cir. 2018)). But those interests can be used to defend virtually any state statute, no matter how patently unconstitutional or noxious. And Florida does not deny that "the public interest is served when constitutional rights are protected." *Democratic Exec. Comm. of Fla. v. Lee*, 915 F.3d 1312, 1327 (11th Cir. 2019).

In sum, the district court did not abuse its discretion in preliminarily enjoining the operation of Section 381.00316(1) as applied to Norwegian.

VII. Conclusion

For all these reasons, I would affirm the district court's order granting a preliminary injunction of Section 381.00316(1) as applied to Norwegian. Because, in my view, the Majority Opinion incorrectly reaches the opposite conclusion, I respectfully dissent.

United States Court of Appeals
for the Eleventh Circuit

No. 20-14047

UNITED STATES
VS.
F.E.B. CORP.

Appeal from the United States District Court for the Southern District of Florida

Decided: November 1, 2022

Citation: 52 F.4th 916, 10 Adm. R. 456 (11th Cir. 2022).

Before **WILSON** and **ROSENBAUM**, Circuit Judges, and **CONWAY**,* District Judge.

* The Honorable Anne C. Conway, United States District Judge for the Middle District of Florida, sitting by designation.

[—2—] {-919-} ROSENBAUM, Circuit Judge:

A small island lies just off Key West, Florida. It was not born in the usual way. No volcanic lava plumes rose from the sea and created it. Rather, about a hundred years ago, the United States labored to dredge oceanic soil from Key West Harbor, which it piled up on the ocean floor. Later, during World War II, the United States conducted further dredging operations in the area and again dumped the soil it collected in the same area in Key West Harbor. At some point during these operations, Wisteria Island was born.

After Wisteria Island's birth, Congress ceded title to all lands within three miles of the United States's coast to the states, except for lands that were (1) "built up," "filled in," "or otherwise reclaimed" (2) by the United States (3) for the United States's use. We must determine whether Wisteria Island satisfies this exception. Only the third requirement is at issue in this appeal: whether the United States created Wisteria Island for its "use."

Plaintiff-Counterdefendant-Appellee United States says that it created Wisteria Island to store dredged soil. Defendant-Counter-claimant-Appellant **{-920-}** F.E.B., which claims to own the island, **[—3—]** rejects the United States's assertion that it built Wisteria Island for its "use." According to F.E.B., the island arose simply as a result of the United States's discarding of the soil it dredged from the channel. After all, F.E.B. says, merely dumping soil in a pile isn't *using* it.

We agree with the United States that, if it created Wisteria Island as a place to store dredged soil, then the United States built up or filled in Wisteria Island for the United States's use. But on this record, we find a genuine issue of material fact exists as to why the United States created the island. So after a thorough review of the record and with the benefit of oral argument, we affirm in part and vacate in part the district court's grant of summary judgment to the United States and denial of summary judgment to F.E.B., and we remand this case for a factual determination of why the United States created Wisteria Island.

I. FACTUAL BACKGROUND

A. The Creation of Wisteria Island

The United States received the land that became Florida—then known as "La Florida"—from Spain in the 1818 Adams-Onis Treaty. *See* Treaty of Amity, Settlement, and Limits, Between the United States of America and His Catholic Majesty, Spain-U.S., Feb. 22, 1819, 8 Stat. 252.

Just over twenty-five years later, in 1845, Florida officially became a state. *An Act for the Admission of the States of Iowa and Florida into the Union*, Pub. L. 28-48, 5 Stat. 742 (Mar. 3, 1845). **[—4—]** The Florida Keys, a chain of islands south of mainland Florida, is a part of the state of Florida. Key West lies at the southwest end of the Keys. The same year that Florida became a state, President Polk reserved the "shoals" of Key West for "military purposes."

Eventually, in the early 1920s, the United States "dredged"—or removed soil from the ocean floor—in Key West Harbor, piling the dredged oceanic soil (also called "spoils" or "spoilage") up until it became an island.[1] Just before that, during a hurricane in 1919, a 150-foot ship called the *Wisteria* sank near the shallow ocean floor upon which Wisteria Island was later built. In recognition of that event, the island that the United States created in that area was called Wisteria Island.

After the dredging was complete, two men applied to buy the island for $500. The Florida Trustees of Internal Improvement Fund published a notice that it intended to sell the island. But the Navy Department objected that the island belonged to the United States and therefore was not Florida's to sell. The Trustees withdrew the notice and rejected the application. In the meantime, the Navy Department asked the Secretary of the Interior for an executive order reserving the island for military use because the island was "directly under the guns of Fort Taylor" and, if privately developed, might "become a constant source of expense on account of claims by private parties for damages incidental to gun fire." In **[—5—]** addition, it said, "[i]f in the future Key West defenses are to be modernized, these areas would be of great value in connection with outer defense works . . . . In view of their strategic location for naval purposes . . . it is desired to have them formally reserved for naval purposes." Just a month later, President Coolidge issued an executive order reserving, **{-921-}** for naval purposes, this area near Key West, including Wisteria Island.

This is a map depicting Wisteria Island in relation to Key West. A red arrow points to Wisteria Island.

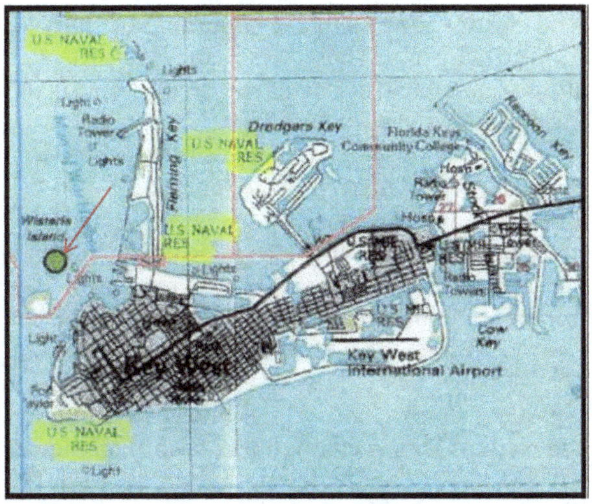

[—6—]

The record is silent about what happened to Wisteria Island between the 1920s and 1940s. But after World War II broke out, the United States began a "huge dredging contract" to "provide adequate seaplane landing and take-off areas," moving some 5.4 million cubic yards of spoils over two years. The project also deepened the "submarine basin" to twenty-two feet and "the main ship channel" to thirty feet. During that period, the United States again dumped the dredge spoils where it had in the 1920s. As a result, Wisteria Island expanded to its current size,[2] about twenty-one acres above water and eighteen below, for a total of thirty-nine acres.

The United States intended the maximum fill height—meaning how tall the island would be—to be five feet over the mean high-water line. But if the available material on the island were leveled, Wisteria Island's flattened elevation would be only three feet over the mean high-water line.

One of F.E.B.'s expert witnesses, geotechnical engineer Mr. Roberto Balbis, submitted a report stating that "[i]t appears that the discharge area was not walled off to help contain the discharge and maximize the amount of fill retained" and that the filling of

[1] The parties dispute whether the spoils location was above or below the water line, but that distinction is irrelevant for purposes of this appeal.

[2] It's possible that the island was originally larger and shrank because of erosion over time. And while that fact may be relevant at trial, the precise details aren't relevant to this appeal.

Wisteria Island was "haphazard." In his view, "the haphazard **{-922-}** manner of **[—7—]** filling suggests that Wisteria [Island] was simply a place to discard excess spoil not needed for any purpose."

B. Legal Developments

Shortly after Wisteria Island reached its current size, oil was discovered in the undersea floor just off the West Coast of the United States. *United States v. California*, 332 U.S. 19, 23 (1947) ("*California I*"). Unsurprisingly, both the United States and the coastal states claimed ownership of the oil. *Id.* In 1947, the Supreme Court settled the dispute by holding that the near-offshore undersea floor belonged to the United States. *Id.* at 40. In response, Congress considered ceding some of the near-offshore undersea floor to the coastal states—the question was how much. *See F.E.B. Corp. v. United States*, 818 F.3d 681, 687 (11th Cir. 2016) ("*F.E.B. I*").

During the legislative process, Secretary of the Navy Robert Anderson testified before Congress that petroleum was crucial to the military and also that the military had bases and other improvements on near-offshore islands. *Submerged Lands: Hearings on S.J. Res. 13, S. 294, S. 107, S. 107 Amendment, and S.J. Res. 18 Before the S. Comm. on Interior & Insular Affs.*, 83rd Cong. 545 (1953) (statement of Robert B. Anderson, Secretary of the Navy). He expressed concern that "in some of the proposed bills[,] title of the United States would be relinquished to all lands beneath navigable waters within State boundaries[,] which is defined to include filled in, made or reclaimed lands." *Id.* at 546. The problem, Secretary Anderson said, was that a "substantial number of military **[—8—]** and naval installations are located on filled in lands and have been improved by the erection of permanent buildings and other structures at a cost to the Government of many millions of dollars." *Id.* So, he concluded, it was "essential that any legislation that would affect lands or installations of the nature described herein should contain appropriate provisions confirming title to and reserving title in the United States to such lands and improvements. In Secretary Anderson's view, then, "[t]hese lands with their structures are truly property which has been developed by the Federal Government and bear no immediate relation to the matter you now have under consideration." *Id.*

One Senator asked Secretary Anderson whether he had a list of the places that should be excluded because they had such improvements. *Id.* at 547. Secretary Anderson responded that he would prefer that "the title to military shore installations could be protected by a general provision." *Id.* But, he said, "[i]f . . . Congress found that it could not properly be so protected, we would be glad to submit such descriptions as you would think appropriate." *Id.* Rear Admiral Ira Nunn, the Judge Advocate General of the Navy, submitted a partial list of such places. *Id.* at 550; *see Bills to Promote the Exploration, Development, and Conservation of Certain Resources in the Submerged Lands and to Provide for the Use, Control, and Disposition of the Lands and Resources of the Lands Beneath Inland Waters and In the Continental Shelf: Hearings on H.R. 2948 and Similar Bills Before the Subcomm. No. 1 of the H. Comm. on the Judiciary*, 83rd Cong. 201 (1953)) (Statement **[—9—]** of Ira Nunn, Judge Advocate General of the Navy). Among those listed was Naval Base Key West.

Attorney General Herbert Brownell, Jr., also testified. *Submerged Lands: Hearings on S.J. Res. 13, S. 294, S. 107, S. 107 Amendment, and S.J. Res. 18 Before the S. Comm. on Interior & Insular Affs.*, 83rd Cong. 925 (1953) (Statement of Herbert Brownell, Attorney General). In his opening **{-923-}** statement, he emphasized that the Department of Justice hoped the eventual law would "make certain that all installations on submerged, reclaimed, or filled or other lands" by "the Federal Government" "belong[ed] to [the Federal Government]." *Id.* at 926.

In 1953, Congress passed the Submerged Lands Act (the "Act"), 43 U.S.C. §§ 1301–15, *et seq.*, which transferred to states the title and ownership of "lands beneath navigable waters" within the boundaries of states and all lands beneath navigable waters within three geographical miles of the state's coast.

Id. §§ 1301(a)(1)–(2), 1311. But Congress expressly excepted from this grant "all lands filled in, built up, or otherwise reclaimed by the United States for its own use." *Id.* § 1313(a).

C. Selling Wisteria Island

Meanwhile, two years earlier, in 1951, Florida again noticed its intent to sell Wisteria Island—this time via a quitclaim deed (one with no warranties of title) to a private buyer. *F.E.B. I.*, 818 F.3d at 684. The United States objected to the sale, claiming that the federal government, not the state of Florida, owned Wisteria Island. *Id.* The sale went through, anyway. *Id.* **[—10—]**

In 1954, the Navy asked the Bureau of Land Management about its claim to Wisteria Island, explaining that Wisteria Island and the area around Frankfort Bank were of "great strategic importance." The Navy asserted that Wisteria Island was close to "highly classified Naval activities," and it would be a "security risk to allow the island to fall into the hands of private individuals."

Nonetheless, in 1967, F.E.B. acquired the title to Wisteria Island. *Id.* Wisteria Island experienced (legally speaking) a still breeze until 2011. And then the legal clouds began to gather.

II. PROCEDURAL HISTORY

A. F.E.B. I

In 2011, the United States asserted ownership over Wisteria Island. *Id.* In response, F.E.B. sued under the Quiet Title Act, 28 U.S.C. § 2409a, arguing that it owned the island. *Id.* at 684–85. The district court held that F.E.B.'s action was time-barred and dismissed the case for lack of subject-matter jurisdiction. *Id.* at 685.

On appeal, we affirmed. Under the Quiet Title Act, a cause of action accrues when "the plaintiff or his predecessor in interest knew or should have known of the claim of the United States" to the real property. *Id.* (citing 28 U.S.C. § 2409a(g)). Florida—F.E.B.'s predecessor in interest—knew of the United States's claim in 1951 because the United States had objected to the sale and claimed ownership at that time. *Id.* So, we said, the twelve-year statute of limitations began in 1951 and ran in 1963, nearly fifty years before F.E.B.'s 2011 lawsuit. *Id.* **[—11—]**

We rejected F.E.B.'s argument that the United States had acquiesced in F.E.B.'s ownership or, through the 1953 passage of the Act, abandoned the 1951 claim of ownership so as to reset the statute of limitations. *Id.* at 687. We reasoned that the United States couldn't abandon property without an affirmative congressional act, which needed to be "clear and unequivocal," and the Act did not rise to that level. *Id.* at 688. This was so, we said, because the Act released only *some* submerged lands and excepted those that were filled in, built up, or otherwise reclaimed by the United States for its own use. *Id.* As we explained, the Act wasn't a clear and unequivocal retraction of the United States's claim to Wisteria Island because it wasn't apparent whether Wisteria Island satisfied the filled-in land exception. *Id.* **{-924-}**

We abstained from resolving the merits question: whether Wisteria Island *was* "filled in, built up, or otherwise reclaimed by the United States for its own use." *Id.* at 693. Rather, we said "only that, given the undisputed and well-known facts of Wisteria Island's creation, the plain language of the [Act's] exception for lands 'built up by the United States for its own use,' gave rise to an open and obvious question as to whether the [Act] applied in this case." *Id.* (citation omitted). "The title dispute," we concluded, "remains unresolved." *Id.* at 694 (citations omitted).

B. The Proceedings in District Court in this Case

Following F.E.B.'s lawsuit, in 2018, the United States sued F.E.B., seeking a declaratory judgment that the United States, not F.E.B., held title to the thirty-nine acres—twenty acres above sea **[—12—]** level and nineteen below—that made up Wisteria Island. In its answer, F.E.B. disputed that the property at issue was thirty-nine acres, arguing that a little over seventeen acres were not subject to the Act's exception.

The parties filed cross motions for summary judgment. For its part, the United States—seeking summary judgment as to all thirty-nine acres—submitted evidence that the United States had used Wisteria Island "[a]t various times before 1953 . . . as a protective barrier for naval operations . . . ; as a spoil area; and for operational purposes." It argued that there was no factual dispute that the island was created by dredging and used as a spoils location. Wisteria Island, the United States said, was built up by the United States for the United States's use. The United States also said that *F.E.B. I*'s holding—that the United States hadn't clearly and unequivocally conveyed title to Wisteria Island to Florida—required the court to find for the government. Finally, the United States pointed out that the Navy had explicitly referenced Key West Naval Base as a location it wanted protected in a report to Congress while Congress was writing the Act.

F.E.B. responded that Wisteria Island didn't fit in the Act's exception for lands "filled in, built up, or otherwise reclaimed by the United States for its own use" because the Navy had simply discarded the dredged soil there and hadn't done anything on Wisteria Island—flattened the top, built anything on it, or even protected it from erosion. F.E.B. pointed to a 1956 report from the Commander of the Key West Naval Base explaining that "the **[—13—]** deposit of spoil that created Wisteria was 'incidental to the deepening of the ship channel' and that 'there [was] nothing on record locally as to the intention of the Navy to use the Island after it was created." It also relied on testimony from Secretary Anderson, Rear Admiral Nunn, and Attorney General Brownell, Jr., to support its claim that Congress never intended to reserve its claim to Wisteria Island because the executive officers were concerned with retaining lands that the United States had improved, and the United States didn't improve Wisteria Island.

Second, F.E.B. said our decision in *F.E.B. I* didn't control the outcome because we had explicitly left open whether Wisteria Island fit within the Act's exception. F.E.B. also attached numerous expert reports, including an expert report from grammarian Mr. Bryan Garner, linguist Dr. Barry Schein, and surveyor Mr. Michael Finkbeiner. Mr. Garner's and Dr. Schein's reports—as well as parts of Mr. Finkbeiner's report—concluded that the phrase "for its own use" in the Act must have independent meaning from "built up or filled in" because the language would otherwise be surplusage. F.E.B. didn't argue that summary judgment was improper **{-925-}** for all thirty-nine acres because part of Wisteria Island wasn't subject to the Act's exception, as it wasn't made of dredge spoils.

The United States moved to exclude the expert reports as improper expert opinions because they purported to analyze and interpret statutes. Thus, the United States argued, the reports invaded the province of the judge. For its part, F.E.B. asserted that the expert-witness testimony wasn't excludable because it was **[—14—]** helpful in analyzing the grammatical structure of the statute, even if it went to the ultimate issue.

The district court entered summary judgment for the United States. It began by defining the question at summary judgment: whether the "incidental but deliberate creation" of Wisteria Island was "for [the United States's] own use." Next, the district court concluded that *F.E.B. I* was persuasive, but not binding, authority that Wisteria Island was created for a distinct purpose. That Wisteria Island had no future use, the district court reasoned, wasn't relevant because the word "future" was not in the statute. The district court declined to rely on the grammarian expert reports because, it said, statutory interpretation is the exclusive province of the court and, if there were any ambiguity, the district court was required here to construe the statute in favor of the United States.

After the district court granted the United States's summary-judgment motion, the United States submitted a proposed judgment decreeing that the United States owned all thirty-nine acres of Wisteria Island. F.E.B. objected. In its view, only the twenty acres above sea level could be characterized as "filled in" under the Act's exception. The district court entered judgment against F.E.B., awarding all thirty-nine acres of Wisteria Island to the United States.

F.E.B. reiterated its argument that some of the land wasn't "filled in" in Rule 59(e), Fed. R. Civ. P., and Rule 60, Fed. R. Civ. P., motions. The district court ordered the parties to address **[—15—]** whether F.E.B. abandoned or waived the argument in its Rule 59(e) and Rule 60 motions when it failed to make it in response to the United States's motion for summary judgment.

In response, the United States said that F.E.B. had waived the argument because it had agreed that the "Subject Property" was thirty-nine acres and that the relevant question was whether the Act applied to those thirty-nine acres. F.E.B. took the opposite position. It reasoned that it had preserved its argument through its expert reports showing that not all of the thirty-nine acres were made of dredged soil. The district court denied F.E.B.'s Rule 59(e) and Rule 60 motions for three reasons. It concluded that F.E.B. hadn't preserved the argument through references in some expert reports, that F.E.B. had invited the error in framing its summary-judgment briefing, and, that, on the merits, the Act applied to land in question.

F.E.B. now appeals both the entry of summary judgment and the denial of its post-judgment motions.

III. STANDARD OF REVIEW

We review the grant or denial of summary judgment de novo. *B&G Enters., Ltd. v. United States*, 220 F.3d 1318, 1322 (11th Cir. 2000).

As for the district court's decisions about "the admissibility of expert testimony and the reliability of an expert opinion," we review them for abuse of discretion. *United States v. Frazier*, 387 F.3d 1244, 1258 (11th Cir. 2004) (en banc). Under this standard, **[—16—]** "we must affirm unless we find that the district court has made a **{-926-}** clear error of judgment, or has applied the wrong legal standard." *Id.* at 1259.

We likewise review for abuse of discretion the district court's denial of a Rule 60(b) motion for relief from a judgment or order. *Arthur v. Thomas*, 739 F.3d 611, 628 (11th Cir. 2014). The same is true of our review of the district court's denial of a Rule 59(e) motion to alter or amend a judgment. *Stone v. Wall*, 135 F.3d 1438, 1442 (11th Cir. 1998).

IV. DISCUSSION

F.E.B. makes three arguments on appeal. First, F.E.B. asserts that the district court erred in entering summary judgment for the United States because Wisteria Island wasn't created for the United States's "own use." Second, F.E.B. claims that the district court erred in disregarding F.E.B.'s expert witnesses' reports on the statutory interpretation of the Act. And third, F.E.B. contends that the district court erred in denying its post-judgment motions to amend or otherwise relieve F.E.B. of the district court's judgment here.

A. Submerged Lands Act

We first must decide whether the Submerged Land Act's exception for land "created for [the United States's] own use" applies to Wisteria Island.

Because this is a case about the meaning of a statute, we begin "with the statutory text, and end[] there as well if the text is **[—17—]** unambiguous." *BedRoc Ltd., LLC v. United States*, 541 U.S. 176, 183 (2004). The Supreme Court has instructed that we should generally construe words "as taking their ordinary meaning at the time Congress enacted the statute." *New Prime Inc. v. Oliveira*, 139 S. Ct. 532, 539 (2019) (alterations adopted and internal citations omitted). Here, Congress passed the Act in 1953, so we consult contemporaneous dictionaries. *Id.*

We begin with the word "for." "For" in this context requires intent. The fourth edition of *Black's Law Dictionary*—published in 1951—defined "for" at least in part as "[t]he cause, motive or occasion of an act, state[,] or condition." *For, Black's Law Dictionary* (4th ed. 1951). And the *New International Dictionary* of the same era described it similarly. *For, New International Dictionary* (1952) ("having as goal or object; in order to be, become, or act as"). *Cf. Textron Lycoming Reciprocating Engine Div., Avco Corp. v. United Auto. Aerospace & Agric. Implement Workers Loc. 787*, 523 U.S. 653, 656 (1998) ("It is true enough … that one of the numerous definitions of the word 'for' is . . . '[w]ith the purpose or object of.'") (citation omitted). The contemporaneous dictionaries then, establish that land is filled in "for" the United States's use when the land is filled in "with the purpose or object" that the United States will use it—in other words, not accidentally.

The other key word is "use." "Use," in the 1950s, had a broad definition. The fourth edition of *Black's Law Dictionary* defined "use" as "to make use of, to convert to one's service, to avail one's self of, to employ" and as the "act of employing everything, **[—18—]** or state of being employed, application; employment, as the use of a pen, or his machines are in use. Also the fact of being used or employed habitually[.]" *Use, Black's Law Dictionary* (4th ed. 1951). The 1952 *New International Dictionary* defined "use" as "to convert to one's service, to avail oneself of"; to "engage in, carry one, indulge in" and "function." *Use, New International Dictionary* (1952). "Use" then, can really mean any utility, **{-927-}** any way in which the filled in land is "convert[ed]" to the United States's "service."

Applying those definitions here, we derive three principles. First, because of the presence of the word "for," the filling in or building up must have some intentionality to it—it cannot be accidental. *Id.* The United States does not "build up" an island *for* its own use accidentally. Second, "use" is a broad term—converting to service or employing (again, *for* a purpose). And third, we note that the Act does not require *actual* use. That is, the text does not demand that the use be employed. As long as the land was created to be used, it doesn't matter whether the United States actually used the land.

The question, then, is whether the United States had an intended use for Wisteria Island when the United States created it. "As a general rule, a party's state of mind (such as knowledge or intent) is a question of fact for the factfinder, to be determined after trial." *Chanel, Inc. v. Italian Activewear of Fla., Inc.*, 931 F.2d 1472, 1476 (11th Cir. 1991). Both parties have submitted evidence supporting their positions. On this record, we cannot say that **[—19—]** evidence necessarily resolves the question in one party's favor. So we hold that a factfinder must determine the United States's intent in creating Wisteria Island.

The United States argues that Wisteria Island was created for the "use" of storing dredged soil. As the United States explains the island's history, the United States completed a dredging project in the 1920s, dumping spoils in the area that became known as Wisteria Island. But that wasn't the only time the United States deposited spoils there. Twenty years later, the United States carried out another dredging project and again dumped the spoils in the same area—this time on top of the older spoils. The United States suggests that, when Wisteria Island was created, it served as a designated storage site for dredging spoils extracted from the Key West area.

We agree that, if true, this purpose could fit within the Act's "for its own use" exception. "Storage" is a use. So if that was the United States's intent in creating Wisteria Island—to establish a storage location for spoils from the Key West area at the time of the original buildup in the 1920s and also beyond—the United States "convert[ed] [the soil] to [its] service." *Use, New International Dictionary* (1952).

But uncritically accepting the premise that the concept of "storage" fits within "use" would eviscerate the meaning of the latter term. That is, the United States could argue that anytime it put dredge spoils (or even trash) in a spot, and those deposits created land, it was "storing" the spoils or trash there. Under that theory, **[—20—]** *all* filled-in or built-up lands would be created for the "use" of storing dredged spoils. The phrase "for its own use" would be surplusage—a result we strive to avoid. *See* A. Scalia & B. Garner, *Reading Law: The Interpretation of Legal Texts* 174 (2012) ("[No words] should needlessly be given an interpretation that causes it to duplicate another provision or to have no consequence.").

So how do we draw the line between storage that is "use" and simple dumping? Speaking in normal parlance, when we put soil (or anything else) in a particular place, sometimes we are storing it and other times we are disposing of it. The difference between storage and discarding is, in our view, an intent of future use.[3] For instance, **{-928-}** when we put unwanted trash in the trashcan, we are disposing of it because we don't want it anymore and don't intend to use it; we aren't "storing" it there. On the other hand, when we leave the car in the garage, we are storing it (not disposing of it) because we are going to use it in the future.

Applying that logic here, we consider the United States's intentions when it built up what became known as Wisteria Island. If, at that time, the United States intended to use it not just then but also in the future as a designated place to put dredge spoils from the Key West area, then it created Wisteria Island for its own use—namely as a location to store dredging spoils. But if the United States just dumped the spoils in the area with no intention of ever **[—21—]** depositing further dredge spoils (or otherwise using Wisteria Island), then the United States did not create Wisteria Island "for its own use." Rather, it just discarded the spoils in a pile that became known as Wisteria Island. And that does not qualify as "for its own use."

The Supreme Court's decision interpreting the Act, *California ex rel. State Lands Commission v. United States*, 457 U.S. 273 (1982) ("*California II*"), reinforces this analysis. In *California II*, the United States had built protective barriers at the entrance of Humboldt Bay. Over time, as the bay's tides moved sand, that water movement caused sand to build up around the barriers, creating dry land. *Id.* at 275. The United States and California debated who owned land that had accreted around the jetties.[4] *Id.* at 276. The Supreme Court resolved the case on choice-of-law and riparian-law grounds. It concluded that, under applicable federal law, accreted lands belonged to the upland owner, the United States. *Id.* at 285–86.

But California also made a second, independent argument. It contended that, even if the accreted land belonged to the United **[—22—]** States, the Act constituted an express surrender of the title. *Id.* at 286. The Supreme Court rejected this argument because the Act didn't apply to accreted land. *Id.* at 287 ("We do not read this provision of the Act as applying to the gradual process by which sand accumulated along the shore, although caused by a jetty affecting the action of the sea."). And even if the Act had applied, the Supreme Court said, the accretions fit the exception for "all lands filled in, built up, or otherwise reclaimed by the United States for its own use." *Id.* at 287.

While this final statement is dicta,[5] it is Supreme Court dicta. So we apply it as

---

[3] Still, as we have noted, there is no requirement that the United States *actually* use the land in the future.

[4] "Accretion" occurs when water "gradual[ly] and imperceptibl[y]" deposits silt, sand, soil, or sediment on an existing structure "so as to create new dry land in an area that was previously covered by water." *Proof of Accretion or Avulsion in Title and Boundary Disputes Over Additions to Riparian Land*, 73 *Am. Jur. Proof of Facts* 3d 167 (Sept. 2022 Update), I.B., § 6.

A jetty is a barrier projecting into the sea or other body of water to protect a harbor. *Webster's Universal College Dictionary* (1st ed. 1997).

[5] That statement is dicta for two reasons. First, we so characterized it in our prior appellate decision interpreting this statute. *See F.E.B. I*, 818 F.3d at 689 ("*In California II*, the Supreme Court stated in dicta that the SLA exception for land built up by the United States 'for its own use' would apply to coastline that had slowly accreted after the United States constructed jetties nearby[.]"). We are bound by that determination here. *Smith v.*

{–929–} much as the text of the statute allows. *See Schwab v. Crosby*, 451 F.3d 1308, 1325 (11th Cir. 2006) ("[T]here is dicta and then there is dicta, and then there is Supreme Court dicta."). Applying those facts here, if the unintentional accretion of **[—23—]** land around a jetty that the government built for its own use could qualify for the Act's "use" exception, then if the United States intended what eventually became Wisteria Island to serve as a location for dredging-spoil deposits, that land purposefully piled into a particular place would also qualify.[6] **[—24—]**

F.E.B. rejects this conclusion, relying on an expert witness (Mr. Balbis) who said that "[i]t appears that the discharge area was not walled off to help contain the discharge and maximize the amount of fill retained" and that the filling of Wisteria Island was "haphazard." Mr. Balbis continued that "the haphazard manner of filling suggests that Wisteria [Island] was simply a place to discard excess spoil not needed for any purpose." Maybe so. But even if it was, that does not necessarily mean that the United States did not create Wisteria Island "for its own use." As we've explained, if the United States created the land with the intent of designating a dredge-spoils dumping ground (or a place to "store" the dredge spoils, as the United States describes it)—not just for the original dredging project in the 1920s but for other dredging projects in Key West Harbor in the future—then it created the island "for its own use."

On this record, we can't tell. To be sure, the United States argues that it built Wisteria Island for the purpose of storing dredge spoils. And the United States did, in fact, later use Wisteria Island for the dumping of additional dredge spoils. But as we've noted, F.E.B. has also presented evidence from its experts that a factfinder could find supports the notion that the United States had no plan for future use of Wisteria Island when it created the land. So on this record, it's not clear to us what **{–930–}** the United States's intent was at the time it built up what became known as Wisteria Island. For that reason, a factfinder must determine what the United States's intent was. *Williams v. Obstfeld*, 314 F.3d 1270, 1277 (11th Cir. **[—25—]** 2002) ("[T]he existence of knowledge or intent is a question of fact for the factfinder, to be determined after trial.").[7]

GTE Corp., 236 F.3d 1292, 1304 (11th Cir. 2001) (explaining that the prior panel precedent rule applies to the earlier case's "reasoning and result"). Second, because the Supreme Court held that the Act didn't apply, its statement that an exception to the Act would apply wasn't necessary to decide the case. *Jordan v. Hamlett*, 312 F.2d 121, 124 (5th Cir. 1963) ("In any event, what was said there in this regard was not necessary to the holding[] and was dictum."). The Supreme Court's decision would be unchanged if the sentence about the Act's exception were eliminated because the Supreme Court held that the Act didn't apply at all.

[6] Some might suggest that *California II* could be read as creating a rule that the Act does not require an intended use for the land at all. After all, the land accreted around the jetties in *California II* inadvertently—the United States did not fill it in for its own use (though, of course, the United States did build for its own use the jetties around which the land accreted). But we don't read *California II* this way because it would cause the language in the Act—"filled in *for* the [United States's] *use*"—to be surplusage. That is so because, if inadvertently created land were land created "for the United States's use," then *all* land would qualify under the exception, and the "for its own use" phrase would be meaningless.

The Supreme Court in *California II* had no occasion to consider whether the Act included a use requirement because it held the Act didn't apply at all to the land in question and devoted only a paragraph to the topic. *See Schwab*, 451 F.3d at 1325 (following dicta because "[t]his is not subordinate clause, negative pregnant, devoid-of-analysis, throw-away kind of dicta. It is well thought out, thoroughly reasoned, and carefully articulated analysis by the Supreme Court describing the scope of one of its own decisions").

We are duty-bound to follow the Supreme Court's decisions but we don't unnecessarily follow dicta to the point at which the result would conflict with the express text of a statute. *See, e.g., Oklahoma v. Castro-Huerta*, 142 S. Ct. 2486, 2498 (2022) ("Dicta that does not analyze the relevant statutory provision cannot be said to have resolved the statute's meaning. . . . [T]he Court's dicta, even if repeated, does not constitute precedent and does not alter the plain text of the General Crimes Act[.]").

[7] The trial will be a bench trial because neither side demanded a jury trial. *See* Fed. R. Civ. P. 38 (d) ("A party waives a jury trial unless its demand is properly served and filed."); *cf. United States v. Florida*, 482 F.2d 205, 207 (5th Cir. 1973) (holding

The parties argue instead that each is entitled to full summary judgment. We are not persuaded.

First, we reject the United States's argument that we are bound by *F.E.B. I* 's statement that "Wisteria Island's origin is undisputed: It was built up by Navy contractors, who used the land for the government's purpose and benefit of storing fill accumulated from nearby dredging operations." *F.E.B. I,* 818 F.3d at 688. To the contrary, *F.E.B. I* explicitly declined to decide whether the Act's exception applied to Wisteria Island. *Id.* at 693 (holding that the facts of Wisteria Island's creation "gave rise to an open and obvious question as to whether the [Act] applied" leaving "further explication of these issues to future cases").

Second, we find unpersuasive the United States's appeal to the presumption that "grants of federal property are construed strictly in favor of the United States." *F.E.B. I,* 818 F.3d at 689. The presumption is that "nothing passes except what is conveyed in **[—26—]** clear language." *United States v. Union Pac. R.R. Co.,* 353 U.S. 112, 116 (1957). But here, the Act is an explicit textual grant of federal property. The only question is whether Wisteria Island fits within an exception to that clear grant. That answer turns not on the clarity of the textual grant but on the facts about the purpose (or lack thereof) underlying Wisteria Island's creation.

And *third,* the United States points out that, when asked for a list of "filled in" lands, Rear Admiral Nunn submitted a list to Congress that included the naval station at Key West. That fact might well be evidence that the factfinder could consider. But Rear Admiral Nunn's submission—as a member of the executive branch—is evidence of executive intent, not legislative intent. The United States hasn't directed us to—nor have we found—a congressional report or committee report that Congress specifically intended to retain title to Wisteria Island—only that the executive branch wanted Congress to do so. *See Demby v. Schweiker,* 671 F.2d 507, 511 (D.C. Cir. 1981) (rejecting "the contention that the views of an officer of the Executive Branch . . . constitute evidence probative of congressional intent under the circumstances here").

In short, the United States has submitted only enough evidence that it created Wisteria Island for its own use to get to a trial—not for judgment as a matter of law.

F.E.B.'s arguments fare no better. *First,* F.E.B. contends that "dredging is not a use." This is so, F.E.B. says, because all dredged lands are filled-in lands. So F.E.B. posits that if dredged lands were "lands filled in, built up, or otherwise reclaimed by the United **[—27—]** States *for its own use,*"43 U.S.C. § 1313(a) (emphasis added), **{-931-}** merely because the United States had dredged them, then "for its own use" would be redundant of "lands filled in, built up, or otherwise reclaimed by the United States." Put simply, F.E.B. reasons, the phrase would lack meaning.

We agree that, if the United States's discarding of spoils—never intended for any future purpose—constituted use, then the word "use" would be surplusage. But as we've explained, if the United States intended to use what became Wisteria Island as a designated dumping location for future dredge spoils, that's a "use" in the same way that a garbage dump is a "use" of the land on which it is located.

Second, F.E.B. emphasizes that the United States never used Wisteria Island in a more traditional sense. That is, the military never built a structure on it and the United States never otherwise improved it in any way. But because our focus must center on why the land was built, post-creation use (or lack thereof) isn't dispositive. What matters is why (at the time of filing in or building up) the land was reclaimed. Was it accidental or was it for a reason? To be sure, that the United States never built an installation on the island may

non-jury trial where United States filed a declaratory judgment action to quiet title). In addition, F.E.B. was not entitled to a jury trial because it counterclaimed against the United States. *See* 28 U.S.C. § 2409a ("A civil action against the United States under this section shall be tried by the court without a jury.").

be probative of the fact that the United States didn't "fill in" Wisteria Island for use as a military base. But it isn't probative of whether the United States built Wisteria Island *at the time* for a purpose. Besides, the record shows that the United States did deposit additional dredge spoils about twenty years after it originally filled in the area. So again, if the United States created the island as **[—28—]** place for contemporaneous and future dredge-spoil deposits, that still would be "for its own use."

Third, F.E.B. relies on legislative history to show that Congress never intended for the Act to cover Wisteria Island. It cites the testimony of Secretary of the Navy Robert Anderson, Rear Admiral Ira Nunn, and Attorney General Herbert Brownell, Jr. But none of the three were members of the legislative branch, so their views can tell us little about what *Congress* intended. *See Demby*, 671 F.2d at 511.

As the District of Columbia Circuit has put it, "[executive officials'] views are binding neither upon Congress nor the courts in determining the meaning of this congressional enactment. They are, in essence, no more than free advice on the subject of how Congress might, if it chose, achieve a particular end." *Id.* Rather, "Congress' acceptance or rejection of such counsel suggests little about its true legislative intent. The only value of such comment is as an interpretation by an administrative official." *Id.* We agree.

On this record, there is a genuine dispute of fact about whether the United States created Wisteria Island for its own use or whether Wisteria Island's creation was an accident. Given that a genuine dispute of material fact exists, we must vacate the district court's entry of summary judgment and remand for trial.

B. Expert Witnesses

F.E.B. also raises some arguments about its experts. First, it asserts that the district court abused its discretion in excluding **[—29—]** F.E.B.'s expert witnesses' testimony on the meaning of "for its own use." And second, F.E.B. contends that the district court abused its discretion when it excluded the report of Mr. Finkbeiner, its expert surveyor, because, in F.E.B.'s view, the report would have been helpful. We disagree.

Under Federal Rule of Evidence 702, a witness with particular "knowledge, skill, experience, training, or education" may offer opinion testimony if that witness's knowledge "will help *the trier of fact* to **{-932-}** understand the evidence or to determine a fact in issue[.]" Fed. R. Evid. 702 (emphasis added).

The district court did not abuse its discretion in excluding F.E.B.'s experts because statutory interpretation is a legal question for a judge, not a factual question for the trier of fact. *Commodores Ent. Corp. v. McClary*, 879 F.3d 1114, 1129 (11th Cir. 2018). And at summary judgment, there is no trier of fact. Rather, the district court answers legal questions and determines whether enough evidence allows for a rational trier of fact to find for the non-moving party. *See* Fed. R. Civ. P. 56; *Fernandez v. Bankers Nat'l Life Ins. Co.*, 906 F.2d 559, 569 (11th Cir. 1990) ("[T]he district court inappropriately acted as the trier of fact and erred in granting summary judgment to Bankers."). While expert witnesses may offer opinions on an "ultimate issue" in a case, they may not offer "legal conclusions." *Commodores*, 879 F.3d at 1128–29. In *Commodores Entertainment Corporation*, for instance, the excluded expert report opined that the "original members 'owned the underlying **[—30—]** marks jointly as tenants in common.'" *Id.* at 1129. We said this legal conclusion was "properly struck." *Id.*

Assuming without deciding that legal-conclusion expert reports may be admissible in limited circumstances,[8] the district court didn't abuse its discretion in excluding the reports here.

[8] We can imagine circumstances in which such testimony—say, about foreign law or about the historical underpinnings of a term or phrase—might be helpful. *See, e.g.*, *District of Columbia v. Heller*, 554 U.S. 570, 605 (2008) (analyzing the original public meaning of the Second Amendment).

Mr. Garner's expert report was explicitly a legal opinion. He acknowledged that, "[a]s a textualist, [he] abstain[ed] from using legislative history." Then he told the district court that he "believe[d]" his opinions "accord[ed] with sound principles of textual interpretation, and in [his] opinion the provision in question is unambiguous." Given that which interpretive sources to use and the ambiguity of a statutory provision are unquestionably matters of statutory interpretation, the district court did not abuse its discretion in excluding the report.

Dr. Schein's report is perhaps a slightly closer call (but not much). Dr. Schein offered background principles of English grammar, explaining how causative verbs function. But Dr. Schein also characterized his retention as an expert as being "to interpret sections of the Submerged Lands Act." As we have discussed, though, statutory interpretation is a matter for a judge. So we cannot say **[—31—]** that the district court exceeded the bounds of its discretion in excluding Dr. Schein's report.

Finally, F.E.B. asserts that the district court abused its discretion when it struck parts of the report of F.E.B.'s expert surveyor, Michael Finkbeiner.[9] We disagree.

The district court did not err in striking the parts of the report that it excluded because Finkbeiner (1) defined legal terms; (2) opined on whether the United States in fact "filled in" the subject property **{-933-}** or (3) explained the legal history of Wisteria Island. The district court did not need any assistance in finding or applying legal definitions. *See Commodores*, 879 F.3d at 1128–29. It therefore did not abuse its discretion in excluding parts of the surveyor's report.

[9] We aren't sure whether the district court actually excluded the report. The district court did not reference Finkbeiner's report. Nor did it describe the surveyor Finkbeiner in the excluding language of its order—referring to only "[l]inguists, legal lexicographers, and grammarians." But it granted the United States's motion—which sought to exclude parts of Finkbeiner's report—in full. So we proceed as if the district court excluded the requested portions of Finkbeiner's report.

C. Reconsideration

Finally, F.E.B. argues that the district court erred in awarding all thirty-nine acres of Wisteria Island to the United States because the land below the water line is not "filled in" land. It says that the only competent evidence—a surveyor's report—described the submerged land as "non-filled seabed." F.E.B. also claims that **[—32—]** it preserved the argument when, in its answer to the United States's complaint, it denied that all thirty-nine acres were subject to the Act. Because submerged land cannot be considered "filled in," F.E.B. reasons, the district court clearly erred in awarding the United States title to those parts of Wisteria Island. We are not persuaded.

The district court did not abuse its discretion in denying F.E.B.'s motions because F.E.B. failed to preserve the issue. Litigants cannot use a Rule 59(e) motion to "raise argument or present evidence that could have been raised prior to the entry of judgment." *Michael Linet, Inc. v. Vill. of Wellington*, 408 F.3d 757, 763 (11th Cir. 2005). The same goes for Rule 60(b). *Arthur*, 739 F.3d at 628.

Here, the United States sued for a declaration that it owned *all* thirty-nine acres of Wisteria Island. It also moved for summary judgment as to *all* thirty-nine acres of Wisteria Island. F.E.B. did not respond by arguing that summary judgment as to all thirty-nine acres would be improper; it argued only that Wisteria Island wasn't "filled in or built up" for the United States's own use within the meaning of the statute. F.E.B. never asserted that below-sea-level spoils weren't "built up." Because F.E.B. didn't develop this argument before the district court granted summary judgment, the district court didn't abuse its discretion in denying the motions.

To be sure, F.E.B. mentioned this distinction in three places: (1) in one paragraph of its Answer; (2) in one sentence of its own motion for summary judgment; (3) in one sentence of one expert **[—33—]** report. But those three snippets cannot preserve the issue. District courts resolving summary-judgment motions are not on buried-treasure hunts. And "[a] passing reference to an issue in a brief is not enough[.]" *Hamilton v. Southland Christian Sch., Inc.*, 680 F.3d 1316, 1319 (11th Cir. 2012). When the United States moved for summary judgment as to all thirty-nine acres, F.E.B. had to "plainly and prominently" clarify that it (thought that it) had title to the underwater acres regardless of the status of the above-sea-level land. *United States v. Willis*, 649 F.3d 1248, 1254 (11th Cir. 2011). It did not do so. For that reason, the district court did not abuse its discretion in refusing to consider F.E.B.'s fallback position.

V. CONCLUSION

If Wisteria Island was "filled in" or "built up" *for* the United States's "use," then it belongs to the United States. But on this record, we are unsure of the United States's intent in creating Wisteria Island. The reason the United States created Wisteria Island remains the subject of a genuine question of fact that must be answered by a trier of fact. So we affirm in part and vacate in part, remanding for further proceedings consistent with this opinion.

AFFIRMED IN PART and VACATED AND REMANDED IN PART.

United States Court of Appeals
for the Eleventh Circuit

No. 21-12729

NORWEGIAN CRUISE LINE HOLDINGS LTD
vs.
STATE SURGEON GEN.

Appeal from the United States District Court for the Southern District of Florida

Decided: December 22, 2022

Citation: 55 F.4th 1312, 10 Adm. R. 469 (11th Cir. 2022).

Before **PRYOR,** Chief Judge, **ROSENBAUM,** and **BRASHER,** Circuit Judges.

[—2—] {–1313–} PRYOR, Chief Judge: **{–1314–}**

We must consider whether this appeal of a preliminary injunction is moot. Norwegian Cruise Lines Ltd. obtained the injunction barring the Florida Surgeon General from enforcing a prohibition against businesses requiring proof of vaccination as a condition of service. But Norwegian recently filed a suggestion of mootness stating that it no longer requires proof of vaccinations on its cruises. Yet, Norwegian's filings make clear that it has not suspended its vaccination requirements permanently or categorically. It also continues to defend its entitlement to equitable relief by asking us to leave the preliminary injunction intact. Based on these filings, Norwegian has not met its heavy burden of establishing that this appeal is moot.

I. BACKGROUND

In July 2021, Norwegian challenged the enforcement of a Florida law prohibiting any business operating in the state from "requir[ing] patrons or customers to provide any documentation **[—3—]** certifying COVID-19 vaccination." FLA. STAT. § 381.00316(1). *See generally Norwegian Cruise Line Holdings Ltd. v. State Surgeon Gen.*, 50 F.4th 1126, 10 Adm. R. 409 (11th Cir. 2022). Norwegian argued that the state statute violated the First Amendment and Dormant Commerce Clause. And it moved to enjoin the Surgeon General from enforcing the statute against Norwegian and to obtain a "declaration that [the statute] is unlawful as applied to" Norwegian.

The district court preliminarily enjoined the Surgeon General "from enforcing [the statute] against [Norwegian] pending resolution of the merits of this case." Florida appealed, and Norwegian defended the preliminary injunction. We heard oral argument in May 2022.

On October 4, Norwegian filed a "suggestion of mootness," which we construed as a motion to dismiss the appeal as moot. Norwegian simultaneously filed a motion for an indicative ruling in the district court to lift the preliminary injunction. Norwegian maintained that it had "remov[ed] all COVID-19 testing, masking and vaccination requirements for its cruises." (Citation and internal quotation marks omitted). As a result, Norwegian argued that the appeal was "likely moot." Florida responded and opposed Norwegian's suggestion of mootness. On October 6, we issued a published opinion vacating the preliminary injunction on the merits. *See Norwegian*, 50 F.4th at 1130, 10 Adm. R. at 409. We withheld the mandate and requested supplemental briefing on whether the appeal was moot.

Norwegian continued to argue that the appeal is moot. It stated that the "dissipation of the COVID-19 pandemic" had **[—4—]** allowed it to "relax[] . . . [its] institutional protocols" and remove its vaccination requirements. It argued that these "changed circumstances" ended a "live controversy" between the parties. Norwegian acknowledged that its revised policy "does not supersede country specific requirements," meaning that should a country reimpose a vaccine mandate, Norwegian would too. But it maintained that "no country-specific **{–1315–}** requirements have implicated any cruises departing from Florida."

In its supplemental briefing, Norwegian abandoned its suggestion that the preliminary injunction should be lifted. Norwegian instead argued that the preliminary injunction should remain in place. Norwegian stated that "[t]his appeal should be dismissed *without* vacating the district court's order." (Emphasis added.) It doubled down on that position in its reply brief by maintaining that we should leave the preliminary injunction "undisturbed." And Norwegian has never moved to dismiss the underlying case. Although Norwegian has argued that this *appeal* is moot and should be dismissed, Norwegian has not moved to dismiss the *action*.

The Surgeon General responded that the appeal is not moot. He argued that "Norwegian has not entirely rescinded its vaccination documentation policy" because Norwegian "g[ave] no assurances that [it] will not reimplement the policy with full force" and its removal of the vaccination requirements was "not categorical." The Surgeon General pointed out that Norwegian still maintained the authority to "den[y] boarding if all country specific requirements are not met." He also argued that Norwegian, "[a]s the **[—5—]** prevailing party in the district court, [could not] voluntarily rescind its offending policy to moot [the] appeal" and preserve the judgment in its favor below.

II. DISCUSSION

This dispute concerns the "constitutional command that the federal judiciary hear only 'Cases' and 'Controversies.'" *Vital Pharms., Inc. v. Alfieri*, 23 F.4th 1282, 1288 (11th Cir. 2022) (quoting U.S. CONST. art. III, § 2). "[B]ecause a case or controversy must exist throughout all stages of litigation, we must ensure—up until the moment our mandate issues—that intervening events have not mooted the appeal ...." *Id.* (internal quotation marks and citations omitted). "A case becomes moot—and therefore no longer a 'Case' or 'Controversy' for purposes of Article III—'when the issues presented are no longer live or the parties lack a legally cognizable interest in the outcome.'" *Already, LLC v. Nike, Inc.*, 568 U.S. 85, 91 (2013) (quoting *Murphy v. Hunt*, 455 U.S. 478, 481 (1982)). The "party seeking dismissal," *World Wide Supply OU v. Quail Cruises Ship Mgmt.*, 802 F.3d 1255, 1259, 3 Adm. R. 668, 670 (11th Cir. 2015) (internal quotation marks omitted), bears the "heavy" "burden" of establishing mootness, *Cnty. of Los Angeles v. Davis*, 440 U.S. 625, 631 (1979). For the following reasons, Norwegian has not met that heavy burden.

We agree with the Surgeon General that a "live dispute" exists because Norwegian has not established that it has relaxed its vaccination requirements permanently or categorically. "The possibility that [a party] may change its mind in the future is sufficient **[—6—]** to preclude a finding of mootness." *United States v. Generix Drug Corp.*, 460 U.S. 453, 456 n.6 (1983). Norwegian has offered no evidence of its vaccine policies or its intentions for the future beyond the boilerplate statement that it is not requiring COVID-19 vaccination "for now and for the foreseeable future." Indeed, Norwegian appears to concede that it "has not 'abolished its policy forevermore.'" We see no reason to believe that Norwegian will not seek to reinstate its policy given its continued insistence that the Florida law is unconstitutional. *See Jager v. Douglas Cnty. Sch. Dist.*, 862 F.2d 824, 833–34 (11th Cir. 1989) (finding no mootness when defendants "never promised not to resume the prior practice" and "continue[d] to press on appeal that the voluntarily ceased **{–1316–}** conduct should be declared constitutional"). For all we know, with COVID-19 cases currently rising, Norwegian may do so.

Norwegian's removal of its vaccination requirements is also not categorical, which reduces the likelihood that its protocols have been permanently changed. As the Surgeon General argues, and Norwegian concedes, the revised policy "does not supersede country specific requirements." Norwegian will defer to other countries as to whether proof certifying COVID-19 vaccination is required on its cruises—a decision outside its control.

We have held that an appeal is not moot where the defendant might exercise its "discretion to change its policy" back while continuing to press the old policy's validity. *ACLU v. Fla. Bar*, 999 F.2d 1486, 1494–95 (11th Cir. 1993). So it is here. Given that Norwegian has acknowledged that it must change its vaccine protocols **[—7—]** to accommodate "country specific requirements," it has necessarily asserted discretion to reimpose its vaccination requirements. Only one country that Norwegian visits needs to require vaccines for it to do so. Given the rapidly shifting nature of the pandemic, Norwegian has not persuaded us that it is an "exceedingly remote" possibility that some countries—and, thus, Norwegian—will reimpose vaccine requirements.

Norwegian's filings establish that the appeal is not moot. Norwegian has never argued that the *case* itself is moot. That is, Norwegian has not expressed any intent to dismiss the action were we to remand. Norwegian has had multiple opportunities to clarify its position. After Norwegian stated in its "suggestion of mootness" that it would move to lift the stay, we asked the parties for supplemental briefing. Norwegian told us in both of its supplemental briefs that the preliminary injunction should not be vacated. Norwegian stated that the injunction should be left "undisturbed." *Cf. Frank v. Minn. Newspaper Ass'n, Inc.*, 490 U.S. 225, 227 (1989) (finding an appeal moot when "appellee, the original plaintiff in the case, state[d] its willingness to forego any further claim to the declaratory and equitable relief sought in its complaint"). We take Norwegian at its word.

How can it be that a case Norwegian does not want dismissed involving a preliminary injunction that Norwegian does not want vacated is moot? Norwegian has offered no explanation for this position. The most plausible one is that Norwegian believes **[—8—]** there is a reasonable chance it will reinstate its vaccination policy and benefit from the preliminary injunction.

Our dissenting colleague maintains that the appeal is moot because Norwegian told the district court "that the preliminary injunction should now be lifted." Dissenting Op. at 12; *see also* Dissenting Op. at 6–7. But the district court denied Norwegian's motion in the light of our decision on the merits. After all, this matter was on appeal and there had been no docket activity in the district court since October 2021. When the district court denied Norwegian's motion for an indicative ruling, Norwegian could have asked us to vacate the preliminary injunction. It did the opposite. It suggested we should leave the preliminary injunction "undisturbed."

For similar reasons, even if Norwegian's conduct otherwise met the criteria for mootness, the voluntary cessation exception to mootness applies. A case is moot when "there is no reasonable expectation that the wrong will be repeated." *City of Erie v. Pap's A.M.*, 529 U.S. 277, 287 (2000) (citation omitted). So, the "[m]ere voluntary cessation of allegedly illegal conduct does not moot a case." **{–1317–}** *Troiano v. Supervisor of Elections*, 382 F.3d 1276, 1282 (11th Cir. 2004) (citation omitted). If it did, parties could evade our jurisdiction and remain "free to return to [their] old ways." *Id.* at 1282–83 (citation omitted). To moot an appeal, the party that voluntarily ceased the challenged conduct must make it "absolutely clear that the . . . behavior could not reasonably be expected to recur." *United States v. Concentrated Phosphate Exp. Ass'n, Inc.*, 393 U.S. **[—9—]** 199, 203 (1968); *see also City of Erie*, 529 U.S. at 288. Otherwise, the appeal is not moot.

Norwegian has not established that it is "absolutely clear" that it will not reimpose the vaccine protocols on its cruises. *Concentrated Phosphate Export Ass'n*, 393 U.S. at 203. Norwegian has not permanently abolished the challenged policy and maintains the discretion to reinstate it at the whims of various destination countries. Norwegian continues to insist that its vaccination requirements were valid. *Jager*, 862 F.2d at 833–34. And it adopts the highly unusual position that the preliminary injunction should continue to bind the Surgeon General, while never suggesting that the action should be dismissed. These filings do not make it "absolutely clear" that Norwegian will not reimpose a vaccine requirement on its cruises. If anything, they suggest the opposite inference.

Norwegian and the dissent resist this conclusion by suggesting that the voluntary cessation exception does not apply to plaintiffs in these circumstances. Dissenting Op. at 9. Not so. In *City of Erie v. Pap's A.M.*, the Supreme Court held that a case was not moot based on the plaintiff's cessation of its challenged conduct. 529 U.S. at 288. There, a business challenged the constitutionality of a municipal ordinance banning public nudity and obtained an injunction against its enforcement. *Id.* at 283–86. But after the Supreme Court granted certiorari, the business moved to dismiss the case as moot and submitted an affidavit that it was no longer operating as a nude dancing club. *Id.* at 287. The Supreme Court denied the motion. *Id.* **[—10—]**

The Supreme Court acknowledged that "this [was] not a run of the mill voluntary cessation case," because it was the "plaintiff who, having prevailed below, now seeks to have the case declared moot." *Id.* at 288. But the Supreme Court concluded that the appeal was not moot under the voluntary cessation exception. It held that—although the business no longer existed, its building had been sold to a real estate developer, and the 72-year-old owner swore that he had no interest in reopening the business—the business had not established that it was "absolutely clear" that it would not "resum[e] operations." *Id.*; *see also id.* at 302–03 (Scalia, J., concurring in the judgment). The Supreme Court concluded that the business maintained "a concrete stake in the outcome of this case because, to the extent [the business] ha[d] an interest in resuming operations, it ha[d] an interest in preserving the judgment of the [court below]." *Id.* at 288. The Supreme Court also held that "[t]he city ha[d] an ongoing injury because it [wa]s barred from enforcing" its ordinance due to the injunction. *Id.*

At least one of our sister circuits has applied the *City of Erie* framework and found an appeal not moot, even when the plaintiff voluntarily ceased the challenged conduct. In *Borden v. School District of the Township of East Brunswick*, a high school football coach sued the local school district and sought a declaration that the district's policy prohibiting faculty participation in student-initiated prayer was unconstitutional. 523 F.3d 153, 158–59 (3d Cir. 2008). The district court sided with the coach and entered judgment in his favor. **{-1318-}** *Id.* at 164. On appeal, the coach argued that the **[—11—]** case became moot because he "only sought relief for the 2006 season" and "his coaching contract [wa]s subject to annual renewal." *Id.* at 164 n.6. The Third Circuit disagreed.

Citing *City of Erie*, the Third Circuit concluded that the appeal "contains the factors necessary to warrant a finding that it is not moot." *Id.* First, because the coach was a tenured teacher who had been rehired for the previous twenty-five years, the Third Circuit concluded that he had not made it absolutely clear that he would cease the challenged conduct. *Id.* The coach "continue[d] to have an interest in the ... case." *Id.* Second, the school district had an "ongoing injury" because the district court had issued a declaratory judgment invalidating the school district's policy. *Id.* The Third Circuit concluded the case was not moot. *Id.*

This case also contains both elements necessary to find that it is not moot. Because Norwegian has not established that it is "absolutely clear" that it will not reimpose the vaccine protocols on its cruises, Norwegian has "a concrete stake in the outcome of this case." *City of Erie*, 529 U.S. at 288. In the event Norwegian requires passengers on its cruises to present documentation of their vaccination status, it "has an interest in preserving the judgment of the" district court. *Id.* Reflecting this "interest," Norwegian continues to defend its entitlement to equitable relief. The Surgeon General also has an ongoing injury. Because Norwegian has not "forgo[ne] . . . [its] claim to the declaratory and equitable relief," *Frank*, 490 U.S. at 227, the Surgeon General cannot enforce the state statute against Norwegian and is "under the weight of an adverse judgment," *City* **[—12—]** *News & Novelty, Inc. v. City of Waukesha*, 531 U.S. 278, 284 (2001). Both sides have the requisite interest to bar a finding of mootness.

The voluntary cessation doctrine is designed to "prevent[] litigants from attempting to manipulate the Court's jurisdiction to insulate a favorable decision from review." *City of Erie*, 529 U.S. at 288. Ordinarily, defendants have this incentive. If not for the voluntary cessation doctrine, defendants could promise to stop the challenged practice, moot the case, and then "return to [their] old ways." *Friends of the Earth, Inc. v. Laidlaw Env't Servs. (TOC), Inc.*, 528 U.S. 167, 189 (2000) (citation omitted). But, as *City of Erie* illustrates, in cases in which the plaintiff obtains an injunction against a defendant, the roles reverse on appeal. With an injunction in place, the plaintiff has the incentive to temporarily cease its practice to moot the appeal and leave the injunction intact, before returning to its "old ways." *Id.*

This appeal presents a textbook application of that strategy. With the case on the eve of decision, Norwegian told us it will stop requiring passengers to present proof of their vaccination status and filed a suggestion of mootness. But it continues to defend the preliminary injunction on the merits and asks us to leave it intact. All the while, it maintains the discretion to reimpose vaccine requirements. Norwegian, in short, has done little—certainly far less than the business in *City of Erie*—to convince us that it is absolutely clear that it will not reimpose its vaccine requirements. As a result, we conclude that the appeal is not moot. **[—13—]**

III. CONCLUSION

We **DENY** the motion to dismiss the appeal as moot.

(Reporter's Note: Dissenting opinion follows on p. 474).

[—1—] {-1318-} ROSENBAUM, Circuit Judge, dissenting: {-1319-}

An appeal is moot when an appellate court cannot award the prevailing party any meaningful relief. This is an appeal from an order preliminarily enjoining Florida from enforcing Florida Statute § 381.00316(1), which prohibits businesses from requiring their customers to present proof of vaccination, against Norwegian.[1] But two days before we issued our opinion in this appeal, Norwegian asked the district court to lift the preliminary injunction. As a result, we could no longer award either party meaningful relief, and this appeal was moot before our opinion issued.

The Majority Opinion's contrary conclusion depends entirely on smoke and mirrors. Although the Majority Opinion insists that Norwegian wishes for the preliminary injunction to "remain in place," Maj. Op. at 4, Norwegian told the district court "that the preliminary injunction should now be lifted." ECF No. 53 ¶ 5. And while the Majority Opinion now characterizes Norwegian's vaccine policy as "the challenged policy," Maj. Op. at 9, Norwegian was the plaintiff here, and it's difficult to imagine how it could make a constitutional challenge to its own policy. Indeed, the Majority Opinion addressing the merits in this appeal previously conceded that Florida's statute (not Norwegian's vaccine [—2—] policy) is the challenged practice in this case. *See Norwegian Cruise Line Holdings Ltd. v. State Surgeon Gen.*, 50 F.4th 1126, 1130, 10 Adm. R. 409, 409 (11th Cir. 2022) (Pryor, C.J.) ("This appeal concerns whether a Florida statute . . . violates the Free Speech and Commerce Clauses of the Constitution.").

When we dispense with the Majority Opinion's counterfactual, the mootness analysis in this case is simple: Once Norwegian asked the district court to lift the preliminary injunction, our Court could no longer award Florida any relief. Indeed, the only relief we ever could have awarded Florida in this appeal was an order vacating the district court's preliminary injunction. And if we did that and Norwegian later reimposed its vaccine policy, the company would face fines under Florida Statute § 381.00316(4)—just like it would if it reinstituted its vaccine policy after the district court lifted the preliminary injunction in accordance with Norwegian's request. So any decision on the merits of this appeal cannot affect the litigants' rights. "That kind of advisory opinion is beyond the power of federal courts." *Jacobson v. Fla. Sec'y of State*, 974 F.3d 1236, 1269 (11th Cir. 2020) (Pryor, C.J.).

Insisting that this appeal is not moot, the Majority Opinion asserts that Norwegian "has not suspended its vaccination requirements permanently or categorically." Maj. Op. at 2; *see also id.* at 5. But that assertion is a red herring. In this case, where all that is at issue is the constitutionality of Florida's statute, we cannot grant Florida relief by requiring Norwegian to suspend its vaccination requirements permanently or categorically. So whether Norwegian [—3—] might later reimpose its vaccine policy is therefore irrelevant to the mootness analysis.

It is equally irrelevant to the question of whether this appeal is moot that Norwegian urged us to address the second-order question—whether, if this appeal is moot, we should vacate the district court's preliminary-injunction order—by declining to vacate the district court's order. The question of whether an appeal is moot is separate and distinct from the question of {-1320-} whether, when an appeal is moot, the district court's order should be vacated.

When interlocutory appeals (like this one) become moot before we can rule on them, our "usual practice is just to dismiss the appeal as moot and not vacate the order appealed from." *Democratic Exec. Comm. of Fla. v. Nat'l Republican Senatorial Comm.*, 950 F.3d 790, 795 (11th Cir. 2020) (quoting *Brooks v. Ga. State Bd. of Elections*, 59 F.3d 1114, 1122 (11th Cir. 1995)). So it's no surprise that Norwegian has asked us to follow that course

[1] I use "Norwegian" to refer collectively to the plaintiff-appellants: Norwegian Cruise Line Holdings Ltd.; NCL (Bahamas) Ltd., d/b/a Norwegian Cruise Line; Seven Seas Cruises S. De. R.L., d/b/a Regent Seven Seas Cruises; and Oceana Cruises S. De R.L., d/b/a Oceana Cruises.

here. And as in other appeals from interlocutory orders that have become moot before we can rule on them, Norwegian's argument about vacatur doesn't mean, contrary to the Majority Opinion's suggestion, that Norwegian wants the *preliminary injunction* to remain in place. Rather, Norwegian is simply asking us not to vacate the order that previously imposed the preliminary injunction, which Norwegian has since asked the district court to lift.

That said, vacatur is an equitable remedy, meaning the decision whether to vacate turns on the circumstances in each case. Because Norwegian mooted this appeal unilaterally—*i.e.*, by **[—4—]** asking the district court to lift the preliminary injunction—after prevailing in the district court, Supreme Court precedent requires us to vacate the district court's opinion. Therefore, I would both find that this appeal is moot and vacate the district court's opinion.

Because the Majority Opinion's conclusion to the contrary eviscerates this Court's Article III jurisprudence, I respectfully urge the Court to rehear this matter en banc.

I.

This lawsuit arose when Norwegian sued Florida, seeking a declaration that Florida Statute § 381.00316 is unlawful and an injunction preventing Florida from enforcing that law against Norwegian. The district court granted Norwegian's motion for a preliminary injunction, enjoining Florida from "enforcing Section 381.00316 against [Norwegian] pending the resolution of the merits of this case." *Norwegian Cruise Line Holdings, Ltd. v. Rivkees*, 553 F. Supp. 3d 1143, 1180 (S.D. Fla. 2021). Florida then appealed.

On October 3, 2022, NCL "remov[ed] all COVID-19 testing, masking and vaccination requirements effective Oct. 4, 2022."[2] The next day, Norwegian filed a motion for an indicative ruling in **[—5—]** the district court,[3] asking the district court to lift its preliminary injunction. ECF No. 53. In that motion, Norwegian explained that the district court "preliminarily enjoined a statute that prohibits a business practice that NCL[] is no longer engaging in, for now and the foreseeable future." *Id.* ¶ 5. On the same day, Norwegian filed a "suggestion of mootness" in this Court, which we construed **{–1321–}** as a motion to dismiss the appeal as moot.

But two days after NCL filed its motion asking the district court to lift the preliminary injunction, we issued a published opinion vacating the preliminary injunction on the merits. *See Norwegian Cruise Line Holdings Ltd.*, 50 F.4th at 1126, 10 Adm. R. at 409. We then withheld the mandate and asked the parties to submit briefs addressing whether this appeal was moot when our opinion issued.

II. [—6—]

The Constitution limits the power of federal courts to deciding only "[c]ases" and "[c]ontroversies." U.S. Const. art. III, § 2. That limit on our power "goes to the heart of our constitutional doctrine of the separation of powers and the proper role of the judiciary." *Djadju v. Vega*, 32 F.4th 1102, 1108 (11th Cir. 2022) (quoting *Troiano v. Supervisor of Elections*, 382 F.3d 1276, 1282 (11th Cir. 2004)). Among the rules that enforce that

[2] Press Release, Norwegian Cruise Line, Norwegian Cruise Line to Eliminate COVID-19 Testing, Masking and Vaccination Requirements Beginning Oct. 4, 2022 (Oct. 3, 2022), https://www.ncl.com/newsroom/norwegian-cruise-line-to-eliminate-covid-19-testing-masking-and-vaccination-requirements-beginning-oct-4-2022.

[3] When a litigant moves in the district court while "an appeal" is "docketed and is pending," Federal Rule of Civil Procedure 62.1(a)(3) authorizes a district court to issue an indicative ruling, stating "that it would grant the motion if the court of appeals remands for that purpose . . . ." When a district court "states that it would grant" such a motion, the Federal Rules of Appellate Procedure permit a court of appeals "to remand for further proceedings" while retaining jurisdiction over the appeal. FED. R. APP. P. 12.1(b); *see also Carver Middle Sch. Gay-Straight All. v. Sch. Bd. of Lake Cnty.*, 842 F.3d 1324, 1331 (11th Cir. 2016) (W. Pryor, J.) ("When an appeal presents a contested issue of mootness, we have allowed the district court the opportunity to address that issue first.").

limit on our power is the doctrine of mootness. *Id.*

The doctrine of "mootness concerns the availability of relief," *Wood v. Raffensperger*, 981 F.3d 1307, 1317 (11th Cir. 2020) (Pryor, C.J.) (citation omitted), meaning that an issue becomes moot when "it no longer presents a live controversy with respect to which the court can give meaningful relief." *Id.* at 1316 (quoting *Christian Coal. of Fla., Inc. v. United States*, 662 F.3d 1182, 1189 (11th Cir. 2011)); *see also, e.g., Chafin v. Chafin*, 568 U.S. 165, 172 (2013) (explaining that a case becomes moot "when it is impossible for a court to grant any effectual relief whatever to the prevailing party" (quoting *Knox v. Serv. Emps.*, 567 U.S. 298, 307 (2012))); *Djadju*, 32 F.4th at 1108 (explaining that an appeal becomes moot when the court cannot grant an "appellant meaningful relief" (quoting *Troiano*, 382 F.3d at 1282)).

This appeal is moot because we are unable to grant either party any relief. After the district court preliminarily enjoined Florida from enforcing Section 381.00316 against Norwegian, Florida appealed, seeking relief in the form of an order from this Court vacating the district court's order and permitting Florida to enforce **[—7—]** its law against Norwegian. But Norwegian asked the district court to lift the preliminary injunction while Florida's appeal was pending before us. ECF No. 53. And from that point forward, assuming the district court would have granted Norwegian's request and lifted the preliminary injunction,[4] Florida could have enforced its law against Norwegian. So once Norwegian asked the district court to lift the preliminary injunction, this appeal stopped presenting a "live controversy with respect to which" this Court could have "give[n] meaningful relief." *Wood*, 981 F.3d at 1316.

Even granting the Majority Opinion's speculation that Norwegian "has not suspended its vaccination requirements permanently or categorically," Maj. Op. at 2; *see also id.* at 5, that fact says nothing about whether this appeal is moot. We can award no relief in this appeal that will prevent Florida from "permanently or categorically" suspending its vaccine requirements. This appeal only ever presented us with a binary choice for relief: Either affirm the district court's preliminary injunction, thus enjoining Florida from enforcing **{–1322–}** its law against Norwegian, or vacate the district court's preliminary injunction, thus allowing Florida to enforce its law **[—8—]** against Norwegian. Neither choice would require Norwegian to "permanently or categorically" suspend its vaccine requirements.

To be sure, Norwegian would face fines under Section 381.00316(4) if we reversed the district court's preliminary injunction and Norwegian later reimposed its vaccine policy. But as I've noted, the result would be the same once the district court granted Norwegian's request to lift the preliminary injunction. ECF No. 53. And even if we affirmed the district court's preliminary injunction, the result would still be the same because, again, Norwegian has asked the district court to lift the preliminary injunction. In short, "a decision by this court affirming or vacating the defunct injunction cannot affect the rights of the litigants." *Vital Pharms., Inc. v. Alfieri*, 23 F.4th 1282, 1289 (11th Cir. 2022) (Pryor, C.J.) (quoting *United States v. Sec'y, Fla. Dep't of Corr.*, 778 F.3d 1223, 1229 (11th Cir. 2015)). So a decision either way would be purely advisory.

It's no response at all to say, as the Majority Opinion does, that "the district court denied Norwegian's request to lift the preliminary injunction in light of our decision on the merits." Maj. Op. at 8. For starters, the district court denied the motion for indicative ruling *solely because* we issued our opinion.[5] *See* ECF No. 55. Not only that but

[4] To the extent that this assumption is contestable, the appropriate step is to "remand to the district court" and permit it to rule on Norwegian's request to lift the preliminary injunction. *Carver Middle Sch. Gay-Straight All.*, 842 F.3d at 1331 (W. Pryor, J.) ("When an appeal presents a contested issue of mootness, we have allowed the district court the opportunity to address that issue first."); *see also infra* n.3.

[5] So to state the obvious, the district court's order leaves no basis for concluding that the district court would have denied Norwegian's motion for indicative ruling on the merits.

the Majority Opinion's response merely begs **[—9—]** the question because it assumes we can resurrect an appeal that is otherwise moot by issuing an opinion addressing the appeal's merits. Worse still, that response concedes that this appeal was moot when our opinion issued. And it posits that the appeal suddenly awoke from the dead like some type of zombie eight days later, when the district court denied Norwegian's request to lift the preliminary injunction as moot because our merits decision rendered the motion moot. This type of circular reasoning cannot provide jurisdiction where none exists.

Nor does the voluntary-cessation exception to the mootness doctrine apply. Maj. Op. at 8–12. The voluntary-cessation doctrine holds "that 'a *defendant's* voluntary cessation of a *challenged practice* does not deprive a federal court of its power to determine the legality of the practice.'" *Friends of the Earth, Inc. v. Laidlaw Env't Servs. (TOC), Inc.*, 528 U.S. 167, 189 (2000) (emphasis added) (quoting *City of Mesquite v. Aladdin's Castle, Inc.*, 455 U.S. 283, 289 (1982)). But Norwegian is not a defendant, and its vaccine policy is not the challenged practice in this case, regardless of what the Majority Opinion says now. *See* Maj. Op. at 9 (characterizing Norwegian's vaccine policy as "the challenged policy"). Indeed, the Majority Opinion addressing the merits in this appeal conceded as much: "This appeal concerns whether a Florida statute that prohibits all businesses operating in the state from requiring customers to provide documentary proof that they are vaccinated against COVID-19 *violates the Free Speech and Commerce Clauses of the Constitution.*" *Norwegian Cruise Lines Holdings Ltd.*, 50 F.4th at **[—10—]** 1130, 10 Adm. R. at 409 (emphasis added). Rather than asking us "to determine the legality" of Norwegian's vaccine policy, this appeal required us "to determine the legality" of Section 381.00316(1).

Resisting this conclusion, the Majority Opinion claims that the voluntary-cessation doctrine can apply to a plaintiff under these circumstances. Maj. Op. at 9–11. **{-1323-}** To support that claim, the Majority Opinion cites the Supreme Court's decision in *City of Erie v. Pap's A.M.*, 529 U.S. 277 (2000). There, a municipality in Pennsylvania enacted an ordinance banning public nudity. *Id.* at 283. The plaintiff, a nude-dancing establishment located in the municipality, challenged the ordinance in state court, arguing that it violated the First Amendment. The Pennsylvania Supreme Court agreed and invalidated parts of the ordinance. *Id.* at 286. After the Supreme Court granted the petition to review the state-court judgment, the appellee-plaintiff submitted an affidavit asserting that it had ceased operating a nude dancing establishment in the municipality and, on that basis, asserted that the case was moot. *Id.* at 287. But the Supreme Court disagreed, explaining that the municipality had an "ongoing injury" because the state-court judgment "barred" the city "from enforcing the public nudity provisions of its ordinance." *Id.* at 288. "If the challenged ordinance is found constitutional," the Court explained, then the appellant-municipality could "enforce it, and the availability of such relief is sufficient to prevent the case from becoming moot." *Id.*

But this appeal differs materially from *City of Erie* because we cannot grant any relief that will prevent this appeal from **[—11—]** becoming moot. The district court's preliminary injunction here prohibits Florida from enforcing Section 381.00316(1) against only Norwegian and its subsidiaries. *See Rivkees*, 553 F. Supp. 3d at 1180. But Norwegian has asked the district court to lift the preliminary injunction, so Florida would no longer be enjoined from enforcing its law against even Norwegian and its subsidiaries.

In contrast, the state-court judgment in *City of Erie* invalidated the municipality's nudity provisions altogether, meaning that the municipality could not enforce its ordinance against anyone—the appellee-plaintiff there or anyone else. *See City News & Novelty, Inc. v. City of Waukesha*, 531 U.S. 278, 284 (2001) ("[H]ad we declared *Erie* moot, the defendant municipality would have been saddled with an 'ongoing injury,' *i.e.*, the judgment striking its law." (citing *City of Erie*, 529 U.S. at 288)).

Given that Norwegian has asked the district court to lift the preliminary injunction, Florida (unlike the municipality in *City of Erie*) has no ongoing injury at all. In *City of Erie*, the Supreme Court emphasized that a favorable decision would once again enable the defendant-municipality to enforce its law, "and the availability of such relief [was] sufficient to prevent the case from becoming moot." 529 U.S. at 288. But here, dismissing Florida's appeal as moot would not leave the state burdened with the district court's preliminary injunction because, as I've noted, Norwegian asked the district court to lift that preliminary injunction. *See City News & Novelty*, 531 U.S. at 283 (distinguishing *City of Erie* since **[—12—]** "dismissal" for mootness would "not keep" the municipal defendant "under the weight of an adverse judgment").

In sum, this appeal from the district court's order granting Norwegian a preliminary injunction became moot when Norwegian told the district court "that the preliminary injunction should now be lifted." ECF No. 53 ¶ 5.

III.

Concluding that this appeal is moot does not end the matter; the Supreme Court's decision in *United States v. Munsingwear, Inc.*, 340 U.S. 36 (1950), "always requires appellate courts to consider whether vacatur is appropriate when the requirements of Article III are **{-1324-}** no longer met because one party is no longer able to obtain relief on the merits." *Democratic Exec. Comm. of Fla.*, 950 F.3d at 794.

As for this issue, Florida and Norwegian both agree on two general propositions. First, when an appeal becomes moot before we can rule on it, we generally dismiss the appeal and vacate the underlying judgment. *See* Fla.'s Suppl. Letter Resp. at 9 (citing *Sec'y, Fla. Dep't of Corr.*, 778 F.3d at 1229–30); Norwegian's Suppl. Letter Reply at 9–10. Second, in cases involving appeals from preliminary injunctions, this court's "usual practice" is to dismiss the appeal without vacating the underlying district court order. Fla.'s Suppl. Letter Resp. at 9 (citing *Brooks*, 59 F.3d at 1122); Norwegian's Suppl. Letter Br. at 9–10 (quoting *Brooks*, 59 F.3d at 1122). As far as vacatur goes, the parties disagree about only which of **[—13—]** these two general propositions applies if we find that this appeal is moot.

The Majority Opinion, on the other hand, muddies the waters, insisting that Norwegian's vacatur-related arguments prove that the company wishes for the preliminary injunction to "remain in place." Maj. Op. at 4. In so doing, the Majority Opinion conflates the question of mootness with the second-order question—whether, when an appeal is moot, to vacate the underlying district court judgment. But make no mistake: As far as the question of mootness is concerned, Norwegian told the district court "that the preliminary injunction should now be lifted." ECF No. 53 ¶ 5. From that point forward, we could not issue any decision affecting the litigants' rights. The only question that remains is whether to vacate the district court's judgment.

And that question is an easy one in this case because Supreme Court precedent ties our hands. True, in appeals from interlocutory orders, our "usual practice is just to dismiss the appeal as moot and not vacate the order appealed from." *Democratic Exec. Comm. of Fla.*, 950 F.3d at 794 (quoting *Brooks*, 59 F.3d at 1122). But vacatur "is rooted in equity," meaning that "the decision whether to vacate turns on 'the conditions and circumstances of the particular case.'" *Azar v. Garza*, 138 S. Ct. 1790, 1792 (2018) (per curiam) (quoting *United States v. Hamburg-Amerikanische Packetfahrt-Actien Gesellschaft*, 239 U.S. 466, 478 (1916)). "One clear example where 'vacatur'" is necessary arises when the appeal becomes moot from "the 'unilateral action of the party who **[—14—]** prevailed in the lower court.'" *Id.* (alteration adopted) (quoting *Arizonans for Off. English v. Arizona*, 520 U.S. 43, 71–72 (1997)).

Vacatur is clearly necessary here because Norwegian, after successfully procuring a preliminary injunction in the district court, unilaterally mooted this appeal by asking the district court to lift the preliminary injunction. For this reason, in addition to vacating our October 6, 2022, opinion as moot, I would vacate the district court's order enjoining Florida from enforcing Section 381.00316 against Norwegian until what turned out to be October 4, 2022.

IV.

"For a court to pronounce upon the constitutionality of a state or federal law when it has no jurisdiction to do so is, by very definition, for a court to act ultra vires." *Jacobson*, 974 F.3d at 1245 (Pryor, C.J.) (alteration adopted) (quoting *Steel Co. v. Citizens for a Better Env't*, 523 U.S. 83, 101–102 (1998)). But the Majority Opinion does just that in this appeal by deciding on the constitutionality of Section 381.00316, even **{–1325–}** though that decision cannot afford either party any meaningful relief.

In so doing, the Majority Opinion exercises power that Article III of the Constitution does not authorize. Because this ultra vires power grab tramples Article III's case-or-controversy limitation on our jurisdiction, I respectfully dissent. And because today's opinion hopelessly confuses our mootness precedent and violates the separation of powers, I respectfully urge the Court to revisit this matter en banc.

This page intentionally left blank

United States Court of Appeals for the District of Columbia Circuit

United States Court of Appeals
for the District of Columbia Circuit

No. 21-5120

OCEANA, INC.
vs.
RAIMONDO

Appeal from the United States District Court for the District of Columbia

Decided: June 7, 2022

Citation: 35 F.4th 904, 10 Adm. R. 482 (D.C. Cir. 2022).

Before **ROGERS** and **RAO,** Circuit Judges and **RANDOLPH,** Senior Circuit Judge.

[—2—] {-905-} RANDOLPH, Senior Circuit Judge:

This appeal from the judgment of the district court (Cooper, J.) presents issues regarding a federal agency's amendments to its fisheries management plan for tuna, swordfish and sharks that migrate along the Atlantic coast.

I.

Oceana, Inc., an organization dedicated to protecting oceans of the world, brought this action claiming that the agency's rulemaking failed to provide sufficient protection for the dusky shark (*Carcharhinus obscurus*). Oceana's standing is unchallenged and rests on affidavits from its members. **{-906-}**

The federal agency is the National Marine Fisheries Service, an agency in the Department of Commerce. The Fisheries Service is responsible for administering the Fishery Conservation and Management Act of 1976, Pub. L. No. 94-265, 90 Stat. 331, commonly known as the Magnuson-Stevens Act. The Act is intended to "promote domestic commercial and recreational fishing under sound conservation and management principles," 16 U.S.C § 1801(b)(3), in the "exclusive economic zone" of the United States, *id.* § 1801(b)(1), an area extending 200 nautical miles seaward from each State's coastline, *see* Proclamation No. 5030, 48 Fed. Reg. 10,605 (Mar. 10, 1983). Within each coastal State's territorial sea, which generally extends three geographic miles from its coastline, the State has jurisdiction to regulate fishing. *See United States v. Maine*, 469 U.S. 504, 513 (1985).

There are eight regional Fishery Management Councils for the coastal fisheries in the Atlantic and Pacific. *See Anglers Conservation Network v. Pritzker*, 809 F.3d 664, 667 (D.C. Cir. **[—3—]** 2016). With respect to "highly migratory species"[1] that travel across the Councils' regional boundaries in the Atlantic,[2] the Fisheries Service directly undertakes management of the fishery. 16 U.S.C. § 1852(a)(3).

The dusky shark is such a "highly migratory species." This shark inhabits temperate and tropical coastal seas throughout the world. Distinct dusky shark populations in the western Atlantic Ocean travel north in the spring as far as the coast of Massachusetts and then, in the fall, southward as far as the Gulf of Mexico and the Caribbean. Along the coast, these sharks are found in the surf and seaward as far as the Continental Shelf.

Dusky sharks may grow as large as twelve feet in length and weigh as much as 400 pounds. The "biology of this species . . . is characterized by very late age at first reproduction (~ 20 years), high longevity (> 40 years), and very limited reproductive potential, which result in low population growth rates and long generation times (30 years)." E. CORTÉS ET AL., STOCK ASSESSMENT OF DUSKY SHARK IN THE U.S. ATLANTIC AND GULF OF MEXICO 49 (2006). The shark bears small litters after a long gestation period, estimated to "be as long as 22–24 months."[3] **[—4—]**

---

[1] The Act defines "highly migratory species" as "tuna species, marlin (Tetrapturus spp. and Makaira spp.), oceanic sharks, sailfishes (Istiophorus spp.), and swordfish (Xiphias gladius)." 16 U.S.C. § 1802(21).

[2] The boundaries, that is, of the following: the New England Council, Mid-Atlantic Council, South Atlantic Council, Gulf Council, and Caribbean Council. 16 U.S.C. § 1852(a)(3).

[3] Merry Camhi et al., *Dusky Shark, in* SHARKS, RAYS AND CHIMAERAS: THE STATUS OF THE

To know this is to understand why commercial fishermen landing unlimited numbers of dusky sharks in the coastal Atlantic Ocean pose a threat to the species in that region. One might wonder why commercial fishermen would, as they had for decades, even bother to target dusky sharks. By all accounts shark meat is barely palatable. Fishermen nevertheless sought out this species to satisfy the demand for shark-fin soup. This is a Chinese dish, for centuries considered a delicacy,[4] **{–907–}** selling at one time in fancy restaurants in California and elsewhere for as much as $100 a bowl, most of which consisted of chicken stock. It apparently did not matter that shark fins, like those of the dusky shark, have no taste and no nutritional benefit.

Overfishing of the dusky sharks in the Atlantic regions threatened the species. *See* Endangered and Threatened Wildlife and Plants; Notice of 12-Month Finding on Petitions to List the Northwest Atlantic Population of the Dusky Shark as Threatened or Endangered Under the Endangered Species Act (ESA), 79 Fed. Reg. 74,684, 74,688 (Dec. 16, 2014). Congress and the Fisheries Service, over the years, have taken actions that have protected the Atlantic dusky shark population. In 1993, the Fisheries Service banned "shark finning" in the Atlantic fishery. *See* Atlantic Highly Migratory Species (HMS) Fisheries; Fishery Management Plan (FMP), Plan Amendment, and Consolidation of Regulations, 64 Fed. Reg. 29,090, 29,108 (May 28, 1999); *see also* 50 C.F.R. § 678.21(a) (1993). Seven years later, Congress passed the Shark Finning Prohibition Act, Pub. L. No. 106-557, 114 Stat. 2772 (2000), which amended the Magnuson-Stevens Act to prohibit the removal of "any of the fins of a shark **[—5—]** (including the tail) at sea." 16 U.S.C. § 1857(1)(P)(i); *see also Chinatown Neighborhood Ass'n v. Harris*, 794 F.3d 1136, 1140, 3 Adm. R. 582, 583 (9th Cir. 2015).[5]

In 1999, the Fisheries Service amended the Atlantic Fisheries Management Plan for highly migratory species to prohibit vessel operators from retaining dusky sharks. *See* 50 C.F.R. § 635.22(c) (2000); 50 C.F.R. pt. 635, app. A (2000); Amendments to the Fishery Management Plan for Atlantic Tunas, Swordfish, and Sharks and the Fishery Management Plan for Atlantic Billfish, 71 Fed. Reg. 58,058, 58,142 (Oct. 2, 2006); 64 Fed. Reg. at 29,108–09, 29,160. In other words, the annual catch limit for dusky sharks became zero. *See Oceana, Inc. v. Raimondo (Oceana II)*, 530 F. Supp. 3d 16, 19, 21 (D.D.C. 2021). The prohibition on vessel operators retaining, possessing, landing, selling, or purchasing dusky sharks remains in effect. 50 C.F.R. § 635.24(a)(5); 50 C.F.R. pt. 635, app. A (2016). In 2006, the Service took the added step of prohibiting fishing for and possessing sandbar sharks, "a doppelganger of the dusky whose targeting had resulted in sizable dusky shark bycatch." *Oceana II*, 530 F. Supp. 3d at 19. The Service adopted this measure because most dusky-shark bycatch was occurring in longline fishing, especially for sandbar sharks and **[—6—]** other large coastal sharks.[6]

CHONDRICHTHYAN FISHES 298 (Fowler et al. eds., 2005) (citation omitted).

[4] "The rapid expansion of the commercial shark fishery in the US in the late 1980s was fuelled in large part by the demand for shark fins in the markets of Asia. Duskies have one of the most sought after fins for shark fin soup because of their large size and high fin needle content (ceratotrichia) . . .." *Id.* at 299 (citations omitted).

[5] No fewer than sixteen states and three territories impose some prohibition on shark finning or possession of shark fins. *See* AM. SAMOA CODE ANN. § 24.0961; CAL. FISH & GAME CODE §§ 2021, 2021.5, 7704(c); DEL. CODE ANN. tit. 7, § 928A; FLA. STAT. ANN. § 379.2426; 5 GUAM CODE ANN. § 63114.1; HAW. REV. STAT. § 188-40.7; 515 ILL. COMP. STAT. § 5/5-30; LA. STAT. ANN § 56:326(E); MD. CODE ANN. NAT. RES. § 4-747; MASS. GEN. LAWS ANN. ch. 130, § 106; NEV. REV. STAT. ANN. § 597.905(1); N.M. STAT. ANN. §§ 17-10-2(A), 17-10-3(A); N.J. STAT. ANN. § 23:2B-23; N.Y. ENV'T. CONSERV. LAW § 13-0338; 2 N. MAR. I. CODE § 5651; OR. REV. STAT. ANN. § 509.160; 20 R.I. GEN. LAWS ANN. § 20-1-29; TEX. PARKS & WILD. CODE ANN. § 66.2161; WASH. REV. CODE ANN. § 77.15.770.

[6] The Act defines "bycatch" as "fish which are harvested in a fishery, but which are not sold or kept for personal use, and includes economic discards and regulatory discards. Such term does not include fish released alive under a recreational catch and release fishery management program." 16 U.S.C. § 1802(2).

Also, in 2003, the Fisheries Service closed a large area in the mid-Atlantic off the coast of North Carolina to bottom longline fishing from January 1st through **{-908-}** July 31st of each year "in part, because of high bycatch and mortality rates of dusky sharks on bottom longline gear in that area." Appellee Br. 9 (citing Atlantic Highly Migratory Species; Atlantic Shark Management Measures, 68 Fed. Reg. 74,746, 74,760–63 (Dec. 24, 2003)).

Even so, pelagic (open ocean) longline fishing[7] and bottom longline fishing[8] continued to pose a threat to the dusky shark. This type of fishing in the Atlantic and adjacent regions concentrates on tuna and swordfish. Fishermen determine where to fish by locating temperature fronts between cooler and warmer water masses. Vessels deploy lines five to forty miles long across these fronts. The mainline is rigged with gangions—leaders attached to the main line—containing baited hooks. If the intended catch is swordfish, the line will usually **[—7—]** be put out at dusk and retrieved at dawn;[9] if the target is tuna, the line will be put out at dawn and picked up at dusk.[10] *See Oceana, Inc. v. Gutierrez (Oceana I)*, 488 F.3d 1020, 1021 (D.C. Cir. 2007).

Although dusky sharks can no longer be the target of longline fishermen, they remain a "bycatch." Based on a 2016 updated stock assessment, the Fisheries Service found that dusky shark bycatch mortality had to be reduced by thirty-five percent of 2015 levels for the population to recover by 2107. *See* Atlantic Highly Migratory Species; Atlantic Shark Management Measures; Final Amendment 5b, 82 Fed. Reg. 16,478, 16,479 (Apr. 4, 2017). The 2016 study showed significant progress in reducing overfishing of dusky sharks. Nonetheless, the study determined that a further twelve percent-median reduction in mortality from 2015 levels was needed to end overfishing.

In response, the Service amended its 2006 Fisheries Management Plan for Atlantic highly migratory species. The amendments, collectively called Amendment 5b, reconfirmed the closure of the dusky-shark fishery and the annual catch limit of zero. *Id.* at 16,484. In addition, Amendment 5b added greater training and certification requirements for fishermen to **[—8—]** identify dusky sharks,[11] new protocols for releasing hooked sharks; a requirement to use circle hooks for bottom-longline fisheries; and communication protocols for fishermen to alert others to avoid areas where dusky sharks are encountered.[12] *Id.* at 16,479. **{-909-}**

On circle hooks, "the point is turned perpendicularly back to the shank to form a generally circular, or oval, shape." 50 C.F.R. § 635.2. They are so designed to catch the lip of the fish and, unlike traditional J-hooks, circle hooks rarely result in gut-hooking. Circle hooks will therefore decrease post-release mortality as compared to J-hooks. *See* 82 Fed. Reg. at 16,479–80; *see also* J.A. 687.

Circle hooks had already been mandated for pelagic longline fishing in the Atlantic in order to protect leatherback sea turtles and

7 "Pelagic longline means a longline that is suspended by floats in the water column and that is not fixed to or in contact with the ocean bottom." 50 C.F.R. § 635.2.

8 "Bottom longline means a longline that is deployed with enough weights and/or anchors to maintain contact with the ocean bottom." *Id.*

9 Swordfish feed at night. *See* Peter Ward et al., *A Fish Lost at Sea: The Effect of Soak Time on Pelagic Longline Catches*, 102 FISHERY BULL. 179, 179, 182 (2005). Studies in the coastal Pacific Ocean found that a "soak time of 5 hours and 3500 hooks (if that were possible) would result in a total catch of about two swordfish." *Id.* at 187.

10 *Id.* at 182.

11 *See* 82 Fed. Reg. at 16,479, 16,488; *see also* J.A. 580, 594. Receiving the certification needed to retain non-prohibited sharks from recreational, vessel-based fishing will include taking a training course focused on "shark identification and regulation." 82 Fed. Reg. at 16,488; *see also* J.A. 580, 694.

12 Under the regulations, vessels must relocate "at least one nautical mile away from the location" where a dusky shark is encountered. *Oceana II*, 530 F. Supp. 3d at 51; *see* 50 C.F.R. § 635.21(c)(6)(ii), (d)(2)(iii). This is typical for regulations regarding protected species. For instance, the Service requires vessels to move at least one nautical mile away from a location where sea turtles or smalltooth sawfish are caught. *See* 50 C.F.R. § 635.21(b)(3).

facilitate their release when they became entangled in the lines and foul-hooked. *See Oceana I*, 488 F.3d at 1022–23. As a bycatch mitigation measure, Amendment 5b applied the same requirement to bottom longline fishing for tuna and swordfish. **[—9—]**

The hooks for pelagic and bottom landline fishing must be non-stainless steel and thus corrodible. This too is an important bycatch-mortality mitigation measure. Pursuant to Amendment 5b, each vessel must have on board dehooker devices so that dusky sharks (and other species) may be released while they are still in the water. If the devices fail, the crew member must free the shark by cutting the gangion—the leader attached to the main line—"so that less than three feet (91.4 cm) of line remains attached to the hook." 50 C.F.R. § 635.21(c)(6)(i). The shark will then swim away with a hook attached to its jaws and a short run of line. The hook will then corrode quickly in saltwater, thus "minimizing injuries to released sharks." J.A. 602.[13]

This brings us to the procedural setting of the case. District Judge Cooper issued two comprehensive opinions. In the first, "the Court questioned [the Fisheries Service's] exclusion of logbook data from its assessment of the magnitude of the dusky shark bycatch problem and found that these issues warranted remand." *Oceana II*, 530 F. Supp. 3d at 23.[14] On remand the Service explained why there was "no scientifically valid basis to extrapolate dusky shark bycatch data from logbooks and other sources to estimate the total amount of dusky shark bycatch." *Id.* at 24. **[—10—]**

Oceana then renewed its challenge to Amendment 5b. The court found the Service's treatment of the data unproblematic. Judge Cooper also concluded that the Service did not violate the Magnuson-Stevens Act by failing to enact stricter regulations. *Id.* at 30–54.

II.

Oceana describes its appeal as raising two issues.

A.

Oceana's first issue is whether the Fisheries Service violated the Magnuson-Stevens Act "by failing to actually limit bycatch of the overfished dusky shark or hold fisheries accountable to any level of dusky shark bycatch, despite the fact that bycatch is the cause of dusky shark overfishing and the sole impediment to rebuilding the population?" **{-910-}**

Oceana's arguments on this issue are muddled. For more than two decades, the "annual catch limit" for dusky sharks has been zero. In its opening brief, Oceana complained that the Fisheries Service violated section 1853(a)(15)[15] because it failed to include bycatch within the annual zero catch limit. In response, the Fisheries Service's brief pointed out that it did indeed include bycatch: "the annual catch limit of zero applies not just to landing, retention, possession, and sale of dusky sharks, but also to bycatch of dusky sharks resulting in **[—11—]** mortality."[16] Appellee Br. 30; *see* 50 C.F.R. § 600.310(f)(1)(i).

In its reply brief, Oceana tried to recover from its error. Oceana's argument became that although the Service included bycatch mortality in the annual catch limit, this did

[13] Our discussion centers on the regulations applied to longline commercial fishermen. The Service also regulates gill-netting (50 C.F.R. § 635.21(g)) and recreational fishing. Rod-and-reel fishing for non-prohibited sharks, for example, may be done only with "non-offset, corrodible circle hooks," 50 C.F.R. § 635.22(c)(1), "except when fishing with flies or artificial lures." *Id.* § 635.21(f)(2). The same requirements apply to handline fishing. *Id.* § 635.21(k); *see also id.* § 635.22(c)(1).

[14] We have sustained the Service's reliance on logbooks in assessing bycatch. *See Oceana I*, 488 F.3d at 1024–25.

[15] Each fisheries management plan must "establish a mechanism for specifying annual catch limits in the plan (including a multiyear plan), implementing regulations, or annual specifications, at a level such that overfishing does not occur in the fishery, including measures to ensure accountability." 16 U.S.C. § 1853(a)(15).

[16] *See* 50 C.F.R. § 600.310(f)(1)(i) ("Catch includes fish that are retained for any purpose, as well as mortality of fish that are discarded.").

not count. Why? Because "[i]f bycatch mortality is always above zero, then the catch limit of zero does not act as a numerical limit on bycatch mortality." In other words, if the speed limit is set at 60 m.p.h. and drivers exceed it, there really is no speed limit.

We sought clarification at oral argument. Oceana's counsel conceded that under the Act "catch" includes bycatch mortality, but not other bycatch (*e.g.*, live dusky sharks that are released by dehooking or cutting the leader). *See* Oral Argument Recording, *Oceana, Inc. v. Raimondo*, No. 21-5120, at 1:50–2:22 (Mar. 18, 2022).

So we move on to the remainder of Oceana's first issue—namely, whether the Fisheries Service has implemented any accountability measures to enforce the zero catch limit for dusky sharks.

Oceana views the new protocols in Amendment 5b—such as the training and circle-hook requirements—not as "accountability" measures, but as "conservation and management"[17] measures under 16 U.S.C. § 1851(a). It suggests those measures cannot qualify as "accountability" measures because they may not succeed in holding fisherman to the zero **[—12—]** catch limit. That is, the measures do not hold fisherman "accountable" to the limit. This argument makes the same error as Oceana's "limit" argument. Ticketing speeders is an accountability measure even though drivers sometimes speed. So too with the measures in Amendment 5b, including closure of the dusky-shark fishery—if fisherman are not permitted to fish for dusky sharks this will implement the zero catch limit. That at least is how the Fisheries Service views its actions. *See* 82 Fed. Reg. at 16,484. Further, Amendment 5b provides additional measures to "reduce dusky shark mortality" through "bycatch reduction." J.A. 701. These measures supplement the Fisheries Service's preexisting measures to curb the overfishing of dusky sharks by reducing bycatch. *See, e.g.*, J.A. 345.

It is important to keep in mind that the rules of the Fisheries Service under this Act are directed not at lawyers and bureaucrats, but at captains of fishing ships and their crews. Those subject to the rules would find it difficult to see a material difference in the ends sought by accountability **{-911-}** measures and those sought by conservation-and-management measures. The Act's overall aim is to prevent overfishing. *See, e.g.*, 16 U.S.C. § 1801(a); 50 C.F.R. § 600.310(b)(2)(ii)–(iii). Sections 1851(a) and 1853(a)(15), for instance, each call for measures to help prevent overfishing. *Compare* 16 U.S.C. § 1851(a)(1), *with id.* § 1853(a)(15). Given this common goal, one would expect accountability measures and conservation-and-management measures to overlap. The training requirements, for example, could be both a management measure—seeking to limit bycatch—and an accountability measure—removing an excuse for thinking that a dusky shark is another species. In terms of preserving and enhancing the dusky shark population in the western Atlantic, nothing much—including the legality of Amendment 5b—turns on how one protective measure or another is pigeon-holed. **[—13—]**

B.

Oceana's second issue is whether the Fisheries Service violated the Magnuson-Stevens Act "when it failed to establish a reasonable likelihood that training measures, communication protocols, and minor gear changes would reduce dusky shark bycatch by 35 percent, the minimum reduction needed to meet the statutory requirement to rebuild the population?"

Relying on *Natural Resources Defense Council, Inc. v. Daley*, 209 F.3d 747, 753–56 (D.C. Cir. 2000), Oceana argues that the Service had to show that Amendment 5b would result in at least a fifty percent chance that the Atlantic dusky shark population would rebound. In *Daley*, the Service set a harvest quota for summer flounder that appeared too high to prevent overfishing. *Id.*

Daley does not control here. The Service is not attempting to balance a catch quota with

[17] Oceana also cites 16 U.S.C. § 1853(a)(1), which calls for conservation-and-management measures.

preventing overfishing. *See id.* at 754. Rather, the Service has closed the dusky-shark fishery and set the lowest possible number of allowable catches: zero. 82 Fed. Reg. at 16,484. In short, unlike in *Daley*, the Service here is not promoting an overly optimistic sustainability projection to justify a more liberal fishing quota.

Oceana also criticizes the studies and evaluations the Service relied upon in adopting its Amendment 5b protocols. In what is an all-too-familiar mode of appellate brief writing, Oceana wastes space plucking quotations from our court's opinions and stringing them together without analysis. Thus, Oceana reminds us, as if we needed reminding, that our court does not "rubber-stamp" agency action, that we do not "accept bare conclusory allegations as fact," and that we do not defer to "unsupported suppositions." Appellant Br. 49–50 (internal quotation marks omitted). **[—14—]**

Oceana should be reassured, although assurances are not needed, that we have never used or even owned a rubber stamp, that we have never, ever considered an allegation alone to be a fact, and that we have never credited a "supposition" that was lacking in support. *See Oceana, Inc. v. Ross*, 920 F.3d 855, 863 (D.C. Cir. 2019).

As to the regulations regarding hooks, the Service relied on evidence supporting its conclusion that circle-hook usage will decrease dusky-shark mortality. The Service found that twenty-five percent of bottom longline vessels did not use circle hooks. Oceana cites a study finding no significant difference in mortality rates between the use of circle hooks and J-hooks to argue that the requirement will have no appreciable impact. *See* J.A. 464. But the Service cited multiple studies finding reduced at-vessel shark mortality when circle hooks were used instead of J-hooks. *See* 82 Fed. Reg. at 16,491; *see also* J.A. 376–77, 687. The Service's reliance on the **{-912-}** cited studies, J.A. 599, its acknowledgment of contrary evidence, J.A. 687, and its stated reasons for reaching its conclusions, J.A. 599, 687, amount to decisionmaking based on reasoning having reliable evidentiary support. *See Shafer & Freeman Lakes Env't Conservation Corp. v. FERC*, 992 F.3d 1071, 1093 (D.C. Cir. 2021). No more is required.

Oceana also blames the Service for failing to show that Amendment 5b's new training requirements will be efficacious. The Service explained that the requirements should help recreational fishermen identify and properly handle caught dusky sharks. 82 Fed. Reg. at 16,488; J.A. 595. The Service recognized that it could not "quantify the total mortality reduction" that this particular measure would bring. J.A. 682. But the Service cited two studies in concluding that "education to fishermen can significantly improve compliance rates, reduce mistaken/illegal landings, [and] reduce post-release mortality **[—15—]** rates . . .." *Id.* The Service therefore had solid grounds on which to conclude that the training-and-certification requirements would reduce dusky-shark mortality. *See Oceana I*, 488 F.3d at 1025.

The judgment of the district court is affirmed.

United States Court of Appeals
for the District of Columbia Circuit

No. 21-5166

LOPER BRIGHT ENTERS., INC.
VS.
RAIMONDO

Appeal from the United States District Court for the District of Columbia

Decided: August 12, 2022

Citation: 45 F.4th 359, 10 Adm. R. 488 (D.C. Cir. 2022).

Before **SRINIVASAN***, Chief Judge, **ROGERS** and **WALKER**, Circuit Judges.

* Chief Judge Srinivasan was drawn to replace Judge Jackson, now Justice Jackson, who heard argument and did not participate in this opinion.

[—2—] {-363-} ROGERS, Circuit Judge:

In implementing an Omnibus Amendment that establishes industry-funded monitoring programs in New England fishery management plans, the National Marine Fisheries Service promulgated a rule that required industry to fund at-sea monitoring programs. A group of commercial herring fishing companies contend that the statute does not specify that industry may be required to bear such costs and that the process by which the Service approved the Omnibus Amendment and promulgated the Final Rule was improper. We affirm the district court's grant of summary judgment to the Service based on its reasonable interpretation of its authority and its adoption of the Amendment and the Rule through a process that afforded the requisite notice and opportunity to comment.

I.

The Magnuson-Stevens Fishery Conservation and Management Act of 1976 (the "Act"), 16 U.S.C. §§ 1801–1884, in furtherance of its goal "to conserve and manage the fishery resources . . . of the United States," 16 U.S.C. § 1801(b)(1), authorizes the Secretary of Commerce, and the National Marine Fisheries Service ("the Service") as the Secretary's delegee, to implement a comprehensive fishery management program, *id.* § 1801(a)(6); *see id.* §§ 1854, **[—3—]** 1855(d). Key to the statutory scheme is the promulgation and enforcement of "fishery management plans." Plans and periodic amendments are developed by regional fishery management councils, *id.* § 1852(h)(1), and include measures "necessary and appropriate for the conservation and management of the fishery," *id.* § 1853(a)(1)(A). The proposing council may include specific conservation **{-364-}** and management measures enumerated in 16 U.S.C. § 1853(b), as well as any other measures "determined to be necessary and appropriate," *id.* § 1853(b)(14). In addition, the council may propose implementing regulations. *Id.* § 1853(c).

Nine fisheries, including the Atlantic herring fishery, are managed by the New England Fishery Management Council (the "Council"). *Id.* § 1852(a)(1)(A), (h)(1). The Council submitted the Omnibus Amendment to the Service, which published a notice of availability and subsequently opened a comment period. Notice of Availability, 83 Fed. Reg. 47,326 (Sept. 19, 2018); Notice of Proposed Rulemaking ("NPRM"), 83 Fed. Reg. 55,665 (Nov. 7, 2018). The Service approved the Omnibus Amendment on December 18, 2018, and published the Final Rule on February 7, 2020.[1] The Amendment and the Rule set out a standardized process to implement and revise industry-funded monitoring programs in the New England fisheries. Omnibus Amendment at v; Final Rule, 85 Fed. Reg. at 7,414–17. Plan coverage requirements may be waived if monitoring is unavailable or certain exemptions based on use of monitoring equipment or catch size apply. *See* Final Rule, 85 Fed. Reg. at 7,417, 7,419–20. **[—4—]**

[1] *Industry-Funded Monitoring: An Omnibus Amendment to the Fishery Management Plans of the New England Fishery Management Council* (2018) ("Omnibus Amendment"); Magnuson-Stevens Fishery Conservation and Management Act Provisions; Fisheries of the Northeastern United States; Industry-Funded Monitoring Final Rule, 85 Fed. Reg. 7,414 (Feb. 7, 2020) ("Final Rule").

The monitoring program for the Atlantic herring fishery covers 50 percent of herring trips. The 50-percent coverage target is met through a combination of limited Service-funded monitoring pursuant to the fishery management plan, *see* 16 U.S.C. § 1853(a)(11), and, for the difference between the target and Service-funded monitoring, industry-funded monitoring, with owners of vessels selected by the Service to carry an industry-funded monitor and pay the associated costs (other than administrative costs). Final Rule, 85 Fed. Reg. at 7,417. The Service estimated industry costs to the herring fishery "at $710 per day," which in the aggregate could reduce annual returns by "approximately 20 percent." *Id.* at 7,418.

Appellants are commercial fishermen who regularly participate in the Atlantic herring fishery. They filed a lawsuit alleging, as relevant, that the Act did not authorize the Service to create industry-funded monitoring requirements and that the rulemaking process was procedurally irregular. The district court ruled on the parties' cross-motions for summary judgment in the government's favor. *Loper Bright Enters., Inc. v. Raimondo*, 544 F. Supp. 3d 82, 127 (D.D.C. 2021).

II.

On appeal, appellants' challenge to the Final Rule presents the question how clearly Congress must state an agency's authority to adopt a course of action. This court is aware of the Supreme Court precedent that Congress must clearly indicate its intention to delegate authority to take action that will have major and far-reaching economic consequences. *Util. Air Regul. Grp. v. EPA*, 573 U.S. 302, 323–24 (2014). But that "major questions doctrine" applies only in those "'extraordinary cases' in which the 'history and breadth of the authority that [the agency] has asserted,' and the 'economic and political significance' of that assertion, provide a 'reason to hesitate **[—5—]** before concluding that Congress' meant to **{–365–}** confer such authority." *West Virginia v. EPA*, 142 S. Ct. 2587, 2595 (2022) (alteration in original) (quoting *FDA v. Brown & Williamson Tobacco Corp.*, 529 U.S. 120, 159–60 (2000)). Here, the Service's challenged actions are distinct. Congress has delegated broad authority to an agency with expertise and experience within a specific industry, and the agency action is so confined, claiming no broader power to regulate the national economy. The court's review thus is limited to the familiar questions of whether Congress has spoken clearly, and if not, whether the implementing agency's interpretation is reasonable. *See Chevron U.S.A., Inc. v. Nat. Res. Def. Council*, 467 U.S. 837, 842–43 (1984). Although the Act may not unambiguously resolve whether the Service can require industry-funded monitoring, the Service's interpretation of the Act as allowing it to do so is reasonable.

A.

Appellants contend the Act permits the Service to require at-sea monitors but prohibits any industry-funded monitoring programs beyond three circumstances. The Service responds that the Act unambiguously authorizes it to implement industry-funded monitoring requirements. The court applies the familiar two-step *Chevron* framework. *See, e.g., Cigar Ass'n of Am. v. FDA*, 5 F.4th 68, 77 (D.C. Cir. 2021) (citing *Chevron*, 467 U.S. at 842–43). At *Chevron* Step One, the court, "employing traditional tools of statutory interpretation," evaluates "whether Congress has directly spoken to the precise question at issue." *Chevron*, 467 U.S. at 842–43 & n.9. "If the intent of Congress is clear, that is the end of the matter; for the court, as well as the agency, must give effect to the unambiguously expressed intent of Congress." *Id.* at 842–43. If the statute considered as a whole is ambiguous, then at *Chevron* Step Two the court defers to any "permissible **[—6—]** construction of the statute" adopted by the agency. *Cigar Ass'n of Am.*, 5 F.4th at 77 (quoting *Chevron*, 467 U.S. at 843).

At *Chevron* Step One, the court "begin[s] with the language employed by Congress and the assumption that the ordinary meaning of that language accurately expresses the legislative purpose." *Engine Mfrs. Ass'n v. S. Coast Air Quality Mgmt. Dist.*, 541 U.S. 246, 252 (2004) (internal quotation marks omitted). Section 1853(b)(8) provides fishery management plans may "require that one or more observers be carried on board a vessel . . . for the purpose of collecting data necessary for the conservation and management of the fishery." That text makes clear the Service may direct vessels to carry at-sea monitors but leaves unanswered whether the Service must pay for those monitors or may require industry to bear the costs of at-sea monitoring mandated by a fishery management plan. When Congress has not "directly spoken to the precise question at issue," the agency may fill this gap with a reasonable interpretation of the statutory text. *Chevron*, 467 U.S. at 842.

The Service maintains that two additional features of the Act, when paired with Section 1853(b)(8), unambiguously establish authority to require industry-funded monitoring. First, Section 1853 contains two "necessary and appropriate" clauses that permit plans approved by the Service to "prescribe such other measures, requirements, or conditions and restrictions as are determined to be necessary and appropriate for the conservation and management of the fishery." *Id.* § 1853(b)(14); **{-366-}** *see also id.* § 1853(a)(1)(A) (mandating "measures . . . necessary and appropriate for the conservation and management of the fishery"). Second, the penalty provisions allow the Service to impose permit sanctions for failure to make "any payment required for observer services provided to or contracted by an owner or operator," *id.* § 1858(g)(1)(D), and make unlawful various acts committed against "any data collector employed **[—7—]** by the [Service] or under contract to any person to carry out responsibilities under [the Act]," *id.* § 1857(1)(L).

Taken together, these provisions of the Act signal the Service may approve fishery management plans that mandate at-sea monitoring for a statutory purpose. Section 1853(b)(8) grants authority to require that vessels carry at-sea monitors. Sections 1853(a)(1)(A) and (b)(14) grant authority to implement measures "necessary and appropriate"—a "capacious[]" grant of power that "leaves agencies with flexibility," *Michigan v. EPA*, 135 S. Ct. 2699, 2707 (2015)—to achieve the Act's conservation and management goals. The penalties in Sections 1857 and 1858 further indicate that Congress anticipated industry's use of private contractors. Still unresolved, however, is the question of whether the Service may require industry to bear the costs of at-sea monitoring mandated by a fishery management plan.

When an agency establishes regulatory requirements, regulated parties generally bear the costs of complying with them. In *Michigan v. EPA*, 135 S. Ct. 2699, 2711 (2015), the Supreme Court held that an agency implementing a policy under wide-ranging "necessary and appropriate" authority must consider the costs of compliance. That principle presupposes that a "necessary and appropriate" clause vests an agency with some authority to impose compliance costs. Here, the Act's national standards for fishery management plans direct the Service to "minimize costs" of conservation and management measures, 16 U.S.C. § 1851(a)(7), and to "minimize adverse economic impacts" of such measures "on [fishing] communities," *id.* § 1851(a)(8). Those statutory admonitions to reduce costs seem to presume that the Service may impose some costs, as "minimize" does not mean eliminate entirely. In addition, neither Section 1853(b)(8) nor any other provision of the Act imposes a funding-related **[—8—]** restriction on the Service's authority to require monitoring in a plan. That also suggests the Act permits the Service to require industry-funded monitoring.

The inference that the Service may require fishing vessels to incur costs associated with meeting the 50-percent monitoring coverage target is not, however, wholly unambiguous. Nothing in the record definitively establishes whether at-sea monitors are the type of regulatory compliance cost that might fall on fishing vessels by default or whether Congress would have legislated with that assumption. Absent such an indication, the court cannot presume that Section 1853(b)(8), even paired with the Act's "necessary and appropriate" and penalty provisions, unambiguously affords the Service power to mandate that vessels pay for monitors. *See N.Y. Stock Exch. LLC v. SEC*, 962 F.3d 541, 554 (D.C. Cir. 2020).

Appellants maintain that Sections 1821, 1853a(e), and 1862, which create monitoring programs with some similarities to the Omnibus Amendment's monitoring program, give rise by negative implication to the inference that the Act unambiguously deprives the Service of authority to create additional industry-funded monitoring requirements. This *expressio unius* reasoning, "when countervailed by a broad grant of authority contained within the same statutory scheme, **{-367-}** . . . is a poor indicator of Congress' intent." *Adirondack Med. Ctr. v. Sebelius*, 740 F.3d 692, 697 (D.C. Cir. 2014). Examination of each of the three monitoring programs further illustrates why appellants' view is unfounded.

First, the limited access privilege program created in Section 1853a(e) authorizes a council to establish "a program of fees . . . that will cover the costs of management, data collection and analysis, and enforcement activities." It does not list monitoring as a covered activity. *See id.* Although **[—9—]** monitoring might qualify as "data collection and analysis," this provision does not speak directly to this point, nor does it say anything about who may fund observers. The canon that "the specific governs the general," *RadLAX Gateway Hotel, LLC v. Amalg. Bank*, 566 U.S. 639, 645 (2012); *see Genus Med. Techs. LLC v. FDA*, 994 F.3d 631, 638 (D.C. Cir. 2021), is unhelpful to appellants in this context because there is no relevant "conflict" between statutory terms that do not address the same subject, *Genus Med. Techs.*, 994 F.3d at 638–39. Section 1853a(e) therefore does not suggest any limitation on the Service's discretion to impose monitoring costs on industry under Section 1853(b)(8).

Second, the North Pacific Council monitoring program created by Section 1862, which "requires that observers be stationed on fishing vessels" and "establishes a system . . . of fees . . . to pay for the cost of implementing the plan," 16 U.S.C. § 1862(a)(1)–(2), is similarly distinguishable. These fees are to be "collected" by the Service, *id.* § 1862(b)(2), and deposited into a North Pacific Fishery Observer Fund established by the Act and "in the Treasury," *id.* § 1862(d), for disbursement to cover the costs of the monitoring program, *see id.* § 1862(a), (e). This special fee program also does not suggest that the Service lacks authority to require industry-funded observers in all other fisheries. The fee program in Section 1862 institutes a different funding mechanism from that of the Omnibus Amendment and Final Rule: under Section 1862, money collected from regulated parties passes through government coffers, while under the Omnibus Amendment and Final Rule, regulated vessel owners pay third-party monitors directly to supply services required for regulatory compliance. Congress's specific authorization of a single fishery program funded by fees paid to the government does not unambiguously demonstrate that the Act prohibits the Service from implementing **[—10—]** a separate program in which industry pays the costs of compliance to service providers without any government pass-through.

Section 1821 creates a foreign fishing vessel monitoring program, which authorizes the Secretary to impose a "surcharge" to "cover all the costs of providing a United States observer" aboard foreign vessels. *Id.* § 1821(h)(4). Generally, observers on foreign vessels are funded through "surcharges [to owners] collected by the Secretary" and deposited in an earmarked U.S. government fund, *id.*, a fee program roughly analogous to the North Pacific Council monitoring program. In the event of insufficient appropriations, however, Section 1821 establishes a "supplementary observer program" by which "certified observers or their agents" are "paid by the owners and operators of foreign fishing vessels for observer services." *Id.* § 1821(h)(6). This provision for industry-funded observers in the foreign-fishing section of the Act, does not show that Congress implicitly intended to preclude the Service from requiring any other industry-funded monitoring. *See Util. Air Regul. Grp.*, 573 U.S. at 323–24. Its contingency plan for monitoring in the foreign-fishing context has no unambiguous **{-368-}** consequences for the Service's authority to implement industry-funded monitoring in other contexts. By providing for industry-funded observers as part of a contingency in the foreign-fishing provisions of the Act, it appears doubtful that Congress intended implicitly to preclude the Service from requiring industry-funded monitoring in all other circumstances. Further, the Act's penalty provisions offset negative inferences that might be drawn from Section 1821. *See* 16 U.S.C. §§ 1857(1)(L), 1858(g)(1)(D). Rather, these broad provisions indicate that Congress anticipated the use of privately retained contractors to comply with the Act's requirements. And the penalties in a broadly applicable section of the Act appear to recognize the possibility of industry-contracted and funded observers beyond the foreign-vessel **[—11—]** context. If Congress had intended for penalties associated with industry-funded monitoring to apply only in the foreign fishing context, the court would expect that Congress in the penalty provisions would have specifically referenced foreign vessels or included a cross-reference to the foreign fishing provision.

Finally, appellants claim that, given the substantial costs of industry-funded monitoring to herring fishing companies, "Congress would not have delegated 'a decision of such economic and political significance to an agency in so cryptic a fashion'" as reliance on "necessary and appropriate" authority. Appellants' Br. 41 (quoting *Brown & Williamson Tobacco Corp.*, 529 U.S. at 160). Indeed, an agency may not rely on a "necessary and appropriate" clause to claim implicitly delegated authority beyond its regulatory lane or inconsistent with statutory limitations or directives. *See, e.g., Ala. Ass'n of Realtors v. HHS*, 141 S. Ct. 2485, 2487–88 (2021); *Michigan*, 135 S. Ct. at 2707–08; *N.Y. Stock Exch.*, 962 F.3d at 554–55. The Service does not do so here because its interpretation falls within the boundaries set by the Act. Section 1853(b)(8) expressly envisions that monitoring programs will be created and, through its silence, leaves room for agency discretion as to the design of such programs. In addition, at-sea monitoring relates to the Service's interest in fishery management and the Act contains no bar on industry-funded monitoring programs, instead permitting plans to "prescribe such other measures, requirements, or conditions and restrictions" as are "necessary and appropriate for the conservation and management of the fishery," *id.* § 1853(b)(14); *see id.* § 1853(a)(1)(A). The Service's understanding of Section 1853(b)(8) and the "necessary and appropriate" clauses as encompassing industry-funded monitoring thus does not exceed statutory limits.

Nonetheless, the text does not compel the Service's interpretation of the Act as granting authority by omission to **[—12—]** require industry-funded monitoring. Courts "construe [a statute's] silence as exactly that: silence." *EEOC v. Abercrombie & Fitch Stores, Inc.*, 135 S. Ct. 2028, 2033 (2015). Neither Section 1853(b)(8) nor any other provision of the Act explicitly allows the Service to pass on to industry the costs of monitoring requirements included in fishery management plans. Nor do the traditional tools of statutory interpretation provide another basis on which to conclude that the Act unambiguously supports the Service's interpretation. Congress has thus provided no wholly unambiguous answer at *Chevron* Step One as to whether the Service may require industry-funded monitoring in the Omnibus Amendment and Final Rule. Although an agency's interpretation need not be compelled by the text for it to **{–369–}** prevail at Step One, here, where there may be some question as to Congress's intent, particularly in view of appellants' cost objection, it behooves the court to proceed to Step Two of the *Chevron* analysis.

Pursuant to Step Two, an agency's interpretation can prevail if it is a "reasonable resolution of an ambiguity in a statute that the agency administers," *Michigan*, 135 S. Ct. at 2707, and "the agency has offered a reasoned explanation for why it chose that interpretation," *Cigar Ass'n of Am.*, 5 F.4th at 77 (internal quotation marks omitted). Under this deferential standard, the Service's interpretation of the Act as authorizing additional industry-funded monitoring programs is reasonable. Section 1853(b)(8), paired with the Act's "necessary and appropriate" clauses, demonstrates that the Act considers monitoring "necessary and appropriate" to further the Act's conservation and management goals. That conclusion provides a reasonable basis for the Service to infer that the practical steps to implement a monitoring program, including the choice of funding mechanism and cost-shifting determinations, are likewise "necessary and appropriate" to implementation of the Act. *See* Final Rule, 85 Fed. Reg. at 7,422–23. **[—13—]**

In addition, the Final Rule provides a reasoned explanation for the Service's interpretation. The Rule noted that Section 1853(b)(8) authorizes the Service to require at-sea monitors "for the purpose of collecting data necessary for the conservation and management of the fishery. *Id.* at 7,422 (quoting 16 U.S.C. § 1853(b)(8)). It further explained that industry-funded monitoring to reach the new 50-percent coverage target would best serve the Act's conservation and management goals. In particular, increased monitoring would permit the Service "to assess the amount and type of catch, to more accurately monitor annual catch limits, and/or provide other information for management." *Id.* at 7,423. The Rule also stated that industry-funded monitoring was consistent with other provisions of the Act that impose compliance costs on industry. *Id.* at 7,422. This explanation reasonably tied the industry-funded monitoring requirement to the Act's purposes. The Service's interpretation of the Act is therefore owed deference at *Chevron* Step Two.

Our dissenting colleague agrees that the *Chevron* framework governs this case but disagrees about how it applies, asserting that the court should reach *Chevron* Step Two only if "the statute is ambiguous" *and* "Congress either explicitly or implicitly delegated authority to cure that ambiguity." Dis. Op. at 5 (internal quotation marks omitted); *see id.* at 5 n.16. The dissent suggests that "Congress's silence on a given issue . . . [generally] indicates a lack of authority," *id.* at 6, but *Chevron* instructs that judicial deference is appropriate "if the statute is silent *or* ambiguous with respect to the specific issue," 467 U.S. at 843 (emphasis added). The Supreme Court has affirmed its *Chevron* analysis, *see, e.g., City of Arlington v. FCC*, 569 U.S. 290, 296 (2013), and this court has reacknowledged its binding force, *see, e.g., Sierra Club v. EPA*, 21 F.4th 815, 818–19 (D.C. Cir. 2021). The dissent's reference to recent cases in which the Supreme Court has not applied the **[—14—]** framework, *see* Dis. Op. at 5 & n.6, does not affect the obligation of this court to "leav[e] to [the Supreme] Court the prerogative of overruling its own decisions," *Agri Processor Co. v. NLRB*, 514 F.3d 1, 8 (D.C. Cir. 2008) (second alteration in original) (quoting *Rodriguez de Quijas v. Shearson/Am. Express, Inc.*, 490 U.S. 477, 484 (1989)). **{-370-}**

Not every statutory silence functions as an implicit delegation. *See U.S. Telecom Ass'n v. FCC*, 359 F.3d 554, 566 (D.C. Cir. 2004). But Section 1853(b)(8)'s silence on the issue of cost of at-sea monitoring provides no basis for applying different standards of review here. Dis. Op. at 8–9. Under *Chevron*, such silence in the context of a comprehensive statutory fishery management program for the Service to implement, 16 U.S.C. §§ 1801(a)(6), 1854, 1855(d), is a lawful delegation, *Chevron,* 467 U.S. at 842–44. Furthermore, the Supreme Court has instructed that a broad "necessary and appropriate" provision, as appears in the Act, "leaves agencies with flexibility" to act in furtherance of statutory goals, *Michigan*, 135 S. Ct. at 2707, and here the Service pointed to the Act's conservation and management goals. Speculation that the Service's interpretation of its authority may lead to exorbitant regulatory costs to industry, *see* Dis. Op. at 11, overlooks *Chevron* Step Two's reasonableness limitation. Nor, in these circumstances, is Congress's provision for industry-funded monitoring in three unique situations properly understood to eliminate the Service's authority to create industry-funded monitoring programs in any other situation, *see id.* at 12–14. Under the well-established *Chevron* Step Two framework, the Service's interpretation of the Act to allow industry-funded monitoring was reasonable. **[—15—]**

B.

Appellants' alternative challenge emphasizes that this court reviews the grant of summary judgment *de novo* and the Omnibus Amendment and Final Rule were enacted and adopted pursuant to the Administrative Procedure Act ("APA"). Under the APA's deferential standard, the court upholds agency action unless it is "arbitrary, capricious, an abuse of discretion, or otherwise not in accordance with law." 5 U.S.C. § 706(2)(A); *see Cigar Ass'n of Am*, 5 F.4th at 74. "An agency is owed no deference," however, "if it has no delegated authority from Congress to act." *N.Y. Stock Exch.*, 962 F.3d at 553. The court "determines whether the resulting regulation exceeds the agency's statutory authority" before it determines whether the regulation "is arbitrary or capricious," *id.* at 546 (citing *Sullivan v. Zebley*, 493 U.S. 521, 528 (1990)), as is addressed in subsection A.

Appellants urge that the Omnibus Amendment and Final Rule are arbitrary and capricious, even if statutorily authorized, "because they do not adequately account for the economic cost" of industry-funded monitoring for participants in the Atlantic herring fishery. Appellants' Br. 55. To survive arbitrary and capricious review, an agency "may not 'entirely fai[l] to consider an important aspect of the problem' when deciding whether regulation is appropriate." *Michigan*, 135 S. Ct. at 2707 (alteration in original) (quoting *Motor Vehicle Mfrs. Ass'n of U.S., Inc. v. State Farm Mut. Auto. Ins. Co.*, 463 U.S. 29, 43 (1983)). Cost is such a factor in view of the Act's directive that fishery management plans minimize adverse effects and costs to the fishing community wherever possible. *See* 16 U.S.C. § 1851(a)(7), (8).

The record shows the Service took note of evidence that the Atlantic herring industry-funded monitoring program costs **[—16—]** impacted vessels $710 per day and could reduce annual returns by approximately 20 percent. Final Rule, 85 Fed. Reg. at 7,418. It evaluated the economic impacts of the program in detail, *see id.* at 7,417–22, 7,428–29, responded to comments raising cost-related concerns, *see id.* at 7,424–26, **{-371-}** and described its efforts to minimize economic impacts on herring fishery participants, *see id.* at 7,429–30. For example, vessel owners may request waivers of industry-funded monitoring coverage on trips intending to land less than 50 metric tons of herring, and midwater trawl vessels may comply with the requirement through electronic monitoring instead of retaining a private monitor. *Id.* at 7,430. Further, in the Rule, the Service explained its choice of a 50-percent coverage target as "balanc[ing] the benefit of additional monitoring with the costs associated with additional monitoring," *id.* at 7,425, and adopted exemptions designed to address adverse effects on smaller vessels, *see id.* at 7,419–20, 7,425, 7,430. So, the Service's decision to proceed with an industry-funded monitoring requirement after extensive deliberations on the question of cost was not arbitrary or capricious.

C.

Finally, appellants contend that promulgation of the Omnibus Amendment and the Final Rule was procedurally improper. Specifically, appellants challenge the Service's failure to comply with the Act's timeline for review of the Amendment, *see* 16 U.S.C. §§ 1853, 1854, and its use of overlapping comment periods for the Amendment and the Rule. Neither contention is persuasive.

That the Service did not follow the Act's timeline provides no basis for relief here. The Service published the notice of availability for the Omnibus Amendment three days after the statutory deadline, *see* 16 U.S.C. § 1854(a)(1)(A)–(B), (5), and **[—17—]** adopted the Final Rule more than a year after its comment period ended, *see* Final Rule, 85 Fed. Reg. at 7,414, contrary to the requirement that implementing regulations be promulgated within thirty days of the close of their comment period, *see* 16 U.S.C. § 1854(b)(3). Procedural errors that are "technical" in nature and "therefore harmless" are "not grounds for vacating or remanding." *Int'l Bhd. of Teamsters v. U.S. Dep't of Transp.*, 724 F.3d 206, 217 (D.C. Cir. 2013); *see Nevada v. Dep't of Energy*, 457 F.3d 78, 90 (D.C. Cir. 2006). Appellants do not identify any harm or prejudice resulting from the alleged delay. In addition, "if a statute does not specify a consequence for noncompliance with statutory timing provisions, the federal courts will not in the ordinary course impose their own coercive sanction." *Barnhart v. Peabody Coal Co.*, 537 U.S. 149, 159 (2003) (internal quotation marks omitted); *see Transp. Div. of Int'l Ass'n of Sheet Metal, Air, Rail & Transp. Workers v. Fed. R.R. Admin.*, 10 F.4th 869, 873–74 (D.C. Cir. 2021). The Act does not penalize missed deadlines, and appellants do not point to any basis for this court *sua sponte* to vacate the Final Rule.

Appellants' suggestion that the Service "prejudged the legality" of the Omnibus Amendment through its use of overlapping comment periods with the Final Rule fares no better. The Act requires that notice and comment on a plan amendment and its accompanying regulations occur in tandem. *See* 16 U.S.C. §§ 1853(c)(1), 1854(a)(1), (5), 1854(b)(1)(A). Even if the statutory text did not control, the Service may initiate implementing regulations of its own accord, subject to APA notice-and-comment requirements that it "publish [a] notice of proposed rulemaking in the Federal Register and . . . accept and consider public comments on its proposal." *Mendoza v. Perez*, 754 F.3d 1002, 1020 (D.C. Cir. 2014) (citing 5 U.S.C. § 553). Here, the Service set comment periods of sixty and forty-five days, respectively, for the Omnibus Amendment and the Final Rule and **{-372-}** stated that it would **[—18—]** consider comments received on either document in its decision to approve the Amendment. NPRM, 83 Fed. Reg. at 55,667. The Act does not require publication of approval of plan amendments. *See* 16 U.S.C. § 1854(a)(3). So, the Service could address public comments on the Omnibus Amendment upon promulgation of the Final Rule, *see* 85 Fed. Reg. at 7,422–27. In view of Congress's expectation that the Service would consider comments on plan amendments and implementing regulations at the same time, *see* 16 U.S.C. §§ 1853(c)(1), 1854(a)(1), (5), 1854(b)(1)(A), appellants fail to show a lack of fair notice and a meaningful opportunity to comment as the APA requires. *See, e.g., Conn. Light & Power Co. v. Nuclear Regul. Comm'n*, 673 F.2d 525, 528 (D.C. Cir. 1982).

Accordingly, the court affirms the district court's grant of summary judgment to the Service and denial of summary judgment to appellants.

(Reporter's Note: Dissenting opinion follows on *p. 496).*

[—1—] {-372-} **WALKER,** Circuit Judge, dissenting:

Did Congress authorize the National Marine Fisheries Service to make herring fishermen in the Atlantic pay the wages of federal monitors who inspect them at sea?

Congress unambiguously did not.

I

A fishery is both a group of fish and the fishing for that group.[1] The Magnuson-Stevens Act governs all fisheries in federal waters.[2] Its goal is to keep the fisheries healthy so that Americans can enjoy the economic, recreational, and nutritional benefits of a marine ecosystem.[3]

In pursuit of that goal, the Act allows the National Marine Fisheries Service to approve fishery management plans, which set rules for the fisheries they govern.[4] Those plans are developed by regional councils and include provisions specifying things like the number of fish that will be harvested in the fishery, the type of fishing gear to be used, and the reporting methods required.[5] When a plan needs updating, the [—2—] relevant council submits a proposed amendment to the Fisheries Service for review.[6] The council may also propose corresponding implementing regulations.[7] Then the Fisheries Service must publish those proposals, take comments, and approve or disapprove of the proposals.[8] If it approves, it will promulgate them as final regulations.[9]

That's what happened here. The New England Council amended the Atlantic herring fishery management plan to require that fishermen allow at-sea monitors on many of their fishing trips, and the Fisheries Service approved its amendment. {-373-} [10] The at-sea monitors are third-party inspectors who go aboard fishing vessels to keep an eye on operations. They track things like how many of which fish are being caught with what gear. No one disputes that the Magnuson-Stevens Act allows the Fisheries Service to impose this monitoring requirement.

But providing a monitor for a days-long fishing voyage can get expensive, and the Fisheries Service has had trouble affording its preferred monitoring programs with just its congressionally appropriated funds.[11] Add to that a further [—3—] problem for the Fisheries Service: Congress generally prohibits an agency from collecting fees and keeping the money from those fees for the agency's own purposes.[12] Instead, absent

---

[1] 16 U.S.C. § 1802(13).

[2] *Id.* § 1801 *et seq.*

[3] *Id.* § 1801(b).

[4] *Id.* §§ 1853, 1854(a). The Fisheries Service's authority is delegated from the Secretary of Commerce. Although the Appellees also include the Secretary of Commerce, the Department of Commerce, and officials in the National Oceanic and Atmospheric Administration, I refer to the appellees as the "Fisheries Service" because they are the most direct regulators in this matter.

[5] *Id.* § 1853(a)(4)-(5), (a)(11), (b)(4). The regional councils were established by the Magnuson-Stevens Act and are made up of representatives from various interested sectors (commercial, recreational, governmental, and academic). *Id.* § 1852.

[6] *Id.* § 1852(h)(1).

[7] *Id.* § 1853(c).

[8] *Id.* § 1854(a).

[9] *Id.* § 1854(b)(3).

[10] Magnuson-Stevens Fishery Conservation and Management Act Provisions; Fisheries of the Northeastern United States; Industry Funded Monitoring, 85 Fed. Reg. 7417 (Feb. 7, 2020).

[11] Fisheries of the Northeastern United States; Atlantic Herring Fishery; Amendment 5, 79 Fed. Reg. 8,786, 8,792-93 (Feb. 13, 2014) (The Fisheries Service has been working since at least 2013 to find a legal way to use industry funding to increase observer coverage as [—3—] "[b]udget uncertainties prevent [the Fisheries Service] from being able to commit to paying for increased observer coverage in the herring fishery."); *see also* Fisheries of the Northeastern United States; Atlantic Mackerel, Squid, and Butterfish Fisheries; Amendment 14, 79 Fed. Reg. 10,029, 10,038 (Feb. 24, 2014) (Without industry funding, "increased observer coverage levels would amount to an unfunded mandate, meaning regulations would obligate [the Fisheries Service] to implement something it cannot pay for.").

[12] 31 U.S.C. § 3302(b) (With one unrelated exception, "an official or agent of the Government receiving money for the Government from any source shall deposit the money in the Treasury as

express statutory authority to keep and spend that money, agencies can only spend as much money as Congress appropriates.[13]

Here, the Fisheries Service attempted a workaround. It decided to make fishing companies, like Loper Bright Enterprises, hire and pay for their own at-sea monitors. The Fisheries Service estimates that for the Atlantic Herring fishery, those monitors will cost more than $700 per day and could reduce financial returns to the fishermen by twenty percent.

The fishermen challenged the amendment and the implementing regulations in district court and now appeal the **[—4—]** court's decision granting summary judgment for the Fisheries Service.[14]

I would reverse the judgment of the district court because the Magnuson-Stevens Act unambiguously does not authorize the Fisheries Service to force the fishermen to pay the wages of federally mandated monitors.

II

Agencies are creatures of Congress, so they have no authority apart from what Congress bestows.[15] **{-374-}**

The Fisheries Service points to the Magnuson-Stevens Act as its source of authority for requiring fishermen to pay for at-sea monitors. We review the Fisheries Service's interpretation **[—5—]** of that statute under the two-step *Chevron* framework.[16] First, we ask "whether Congress has directly spoken to the precise question at issue" or "left a gap for the agency to fill."[17] At that stage, in searching for direction from Congress, we empty our interpretive toolkit.[18] And if it's clear that the text does not authorize the agency's action, the analysis ends, and the agency loses.[19] Only if the statute is ambiguous, and only if "Congress either explicitly or implicitly delegated authority to cure that ambiguity," do we proceed to *Chevron*'s second step and defer to the agency's reasonable interpretation of the ambiguity.[20] **[—6—]**

---

soon as practicable without deduction for any charge or claim.").

[13] *Id.* § 1341(a)(1) ("An officer or employee of the United States Government or of the District of Columbia government may not—(A) make or authorize an expenditure or obligation exceeding an amount available in an appropriation or fund for the expenditure or obligation").

[14] *Loper Bright Enterprises, LLC v. Raimondo*, 544 F. Supp. 3d 82, 127 (D.D.C. 2021).

[15] *Louisiana Public Service Commission v. FCC,* 476 U.S. 355, 374 (1986) ("an agency literally has no power to act . . . unless and until Congress confers power upon it"); *Motion Picture Association of America, Inc. v. FCC*, 309 F.3d 796, 801 (D.C. Cir. 2002) ("An agency may not promulgate even reasonable regulations that claim a force of law without delegated authority from Congress."); *Railway Labor Executives' Association v. National Mediation Board*, 29 F.3d 655, 670 (D.C. Cir.), *amended*, 38 F.3d 1224 (D.C. Cir. 1994) ("Agencies owe their capacity to act to the delegation of authority, either express or implied, from the legislature."); *Bowen v. Georgetown University Hospital,* 488 U.S. 204, 208 (1988) ("It is axiomatic that an administrative agency's power to promulgate legislative regulations is limited to the authority delegated by Congress.").

[16] *Chevron U.S.A., Inc. v. NRDC, Inc.*, 467 U.S. 837, 842-44 (1984). *But see Becerra v. Empire Health Foundation*, 142 S. Ct. 2354 (2022) (not mentioning *Chevron*); *National Federation of Independent Business v. OSHA*, 142 S. Ct. 661 (2022) (same); *BNSF Railway Co. v. Loos*, 139 S. Ct. 893 (2019) (same); *Pereira v. Sessions*, 138 S. Ct. 2105, 2121 (2018) (Kennedy, J., concurring) ("Given the concerns raised by some Members of this Court, it seems necessary and appropriate to reconsider, in an appropriate case, the premises that underlie *Chevron* and how courts have implemented that decision." (citations omitted)).

[17] *Chevron*, 467 U.S. at 842-43.

[18] *Arizona Public Service Co. v. EPA*, 211 F.3d 1280, 1287 (D.C. Cir. 2000).

[19] *Chevron*, 467 U.S. at 842-43; *see also Virginia Uranium, Inc. v. Warren*, 139 S. Ct. 1894, 1900 (2019) (plurality opinion) ("in any field of statutory interpretation, it is our duty to respect not only what Congress wrote but, as importantly, what it didn't write").

[20] *Hearth, Patio & Barbecue Association v. United States Department of Energy*, 706 F.3d 499, 504 (D.C. Cir. 2013) ("The ambiguity must be such as to make it appear that Congress either explicitly or implicitly delegated authority to cure that ambiguity. Mere ambiguity in a statute is not evidence of congressional delegation of authority." (quoting *American Bar Association v. Federal Trade Commission*, 430 F.3d 457, 469 (D.C. Cir. 2005))).

Congress's silence on a given issue does not automatically create such ambiguity or give an agency carte blanche to speak in Congress's place.[21] In fact, all else equal, silence indicates a lack of authority.[22]

That means that when agency action is challenged, it is not the challenger's job to show that Congress has specifically prohibited the challenged action.[23] Holding **{-375-}** challengers to that burden would be "entirely untenable."[24] Instead, an agency must positively demonstrate where Congress explicitly or implicitly empowered it to act. **[—7—]**

III

Both sides agree that nowhere in the Magnuson-Stevens Act does Congress explicitly empower the Fisheries Service to require the Atlantic herring fishermen to fund an at-sea monitoring program. So to prevail, the Fisheries Service must point to some implicit delegation of that authority.

It has failed to do so. The Act unambiguously does not authorize the Fisheries Service to require these fishermen to pay the wages of at-sea monitors.[25]

A

The Fisheries Service first relies on 16 U.S.C. § 1853(b)(8), which provides that fishery management plans may:

> **require that one or more observers be carried on board a vessel** of the United States engaged in fishing for species that are subject to the plan, for the purpose **[—8—]** of collecting data necessary for the conservation and management of the fishery.[26]

That provision allows the agency to require that fishermen give at-sea monitors a place on their vessels—the fishermen must let the monitor "be carried."

The Fisheries Service argues that such authority implicitly includes the authority to make the fishermen pay the monitors' wages because the wages are simply an incidental cost of complying with the duty to allow monitors onboard. In the agency's eyes, it's no different than, say, the cost of buying statutorily-required fishing gear.

---

21 *United States Telecom Association v. FCC*, 359 F.3d 554, 566 (D.C. Cir. 2004) ("the failure of Congress to use 'Thou Shalt Not' language doesn't create a statutory ambiguity of the sort that triggers *Chevron* deference"); *American Petroleum Institute v. EPA*, 52 F.3d 1113, 1120 (D.C. Cir. 1995) ("we will not presume a delegation of power based solely on the fact that there is not an express withholding of such power").

22 *United States Telecom Association*, 359 F.3d at 566 ("The statutory 'silence' simply leaves that lack of authority untouched.").

23 *Bais Yaakov of Spring Valley v. FCC*, 852 F.3d 1078, 1082 (D.C. Cir. 2017) ("The [agency] and the dissent seem to suggest that the agency may take an action . . . so long as Congress has not *prohibited* the agency action in question. That theory has it backwards as a matter of basic separation of powers and administrative law. The [agency] may only take action that Congress has *authorized*."); *Railway Labor Executives' Association*, 29 F.3d at 671 ("Were courts to *presume* a delegation of power absent an express *withholding* of such power, agencies would enjoy virtually limitless hegemony, a result plainly out of keeping with *Chevron* and quite likely with the Constitution as well.").

24 *Motion Picture Association*, 309 F.3d at 805-06; *see also Gulf Fishermens Association v. National Marine Fisheries Service*, 968 F.3d 454, 456 (5th Cir. 2020), *as revised* (Aug. 4, 2020) ("Congress does not delegate authority merely by not withholding it").

25 *But see Relentless Inc. v. United States Department of Commerce*, 561 F. Supp. 3d 226, 238 (D.R.I. 2021) (Another group of herring fishermen challenged the same industry-funding provision, and citing our district court, the District of Rhode Island found that the Fisheries Service "reasonably interpreted" the Magnuson-Stevens Act "to authorize" industry-funded monitors in the Atlantic herring fishery.); *Goethel v. Pritzker*, No. 15-CV-497-JL, 2016 WL 4076831, at *6 (D.N.H. July 29, 2016), *aff'd sub nom. Goethel v. United States Department of Commerce.*, 854 F.3d 106, 108, 5 Adm. R. 21, 21 (1st Cir. 2017) (The district court found that the Magnuson-Stevens Act authorized a similar industry-funding scheme in a different fishery, but the First Circuit affirmed on timeliness grounds, expressly declining to decide whether industry funding violated the Act.).

26 16 U.S.C. § 1853(b)(8) (emphasis added).

But that analogy doesn't hold up.

First, the Act's language meaningfully differs in its treatment of gear and observers. Section 1853(b)(4) allows plans to "require the use" of certain fishing gear. If the Act similarly allowed plans to *require the use* of an at-sea monitor, perhaps the Fisheries Service could argue that the cost of procuring the monitor was incidental to that command. But § 1853(b)(8) doesn't allow plans to require that fishermen use observers. It only allows them to require that fishermen let observers "be carried on board." **{-376-}**

A cost incidental to *carrying* an observer might include the additional fuel costs of a marginally heavier boat or the opportunity cost of giving to the monitor a bunk that would otherwise be occupied by a working fisherman. Those are costs that necessarily follow when a fisherman lets a monitor on his boat. By contrast, there is no inherent, or even intuitive, **[—9—]** connection between paying a monitor's wage and providing him passage.

Second, inspection requirements and gear requirements are different classes of impositions on regulated parties, and they carry different expectations.[27] Regulatory mandates, such as gear requirements, often carry compliance costs. But the Fisheries Service has identified no other context in which an agency, without express direction from Congress, requires an industry to fund its inspection regime.

Even if the Fisheries Service had found a few outliers, it is not usual to require a regulated party to pay the wages of its monitor when the statute is silent. Nor is it expected. In short, it is not the type of thing that goes without saying. And here, Congress didn't say it.[28]

[27] Those expectations, of course, inform our interpretation of how "ordinary people understand the rules that govern them." *Niz-Chavez v. Garland*, 141 S. Ct. 1474, 1485 (2021).

[28] *See Mozilla Corp. v. FCC*, 940 F.3d 1, 83 (D.C. Cir. 2019) ("No matter how desirous of protecting their policy judgments, agency officials cannot invest themselves with power that Congress has not conferred." (citations omitted)).

B

The Fisheries Service next asks us to find its authority in § 1853's "necessary and appropriate" clauses.[29] The first such clause, § 1853(a)(1)(A), says that fishery management plans:

> **shall contain the conservation and management measures**, applicable to foreign fishing and fishing by vessels of the United States, **which are necessary [—10—] and appropriate** for the conservation and management of the fishery, to prevent overfishing and rebuild overfished stocks, and to protect, restore, and promote the long-term health and stability of the fishery.[30]

And the second such clause, § 1853(b)(14), similarly says that fishery management plans:

> **may prescribe such other measures**, requirements, or conditions and restrictions **as are determined to be necessary and appropriate** for the conservation and management of the fishery.[31]

The Fisheries Service argues that because the monitors' data collection is important and because the Fisheries Service can't afford it, it is necessary and appropriate to make the fishermen fund it.

For three reasons, I disagree.

First, context tells us that the Fisheries Service's capacious reading is wrong. Section 1853(a) says that fishery management plans must, for example, describe the fishery, specify a reporting methodology, and identify essential fish habitats.[32] And § 1853(b) says that fishery management plans may, for example, designate protected coral zones, limit the type and amount of fish to be caught, and assess the effect of plan measures on certain fish stocks.[33] **{-377-}** Those and the

[29] 16 U.S.C. § 1853(a)(1)(A), (b)(14).

[30] *Id.* § 1853(a)(1)(A) (emphases added).

[31] *Id.* § 1853(b)(14) (emphases added).

[32] *Id.* § 1853(a)(2), (a)(11), (a)(7).

[33] *Id.* § 1853(b)(2)(B), (b)(3)(A), (b)(9).

other measures surrounding the "necessary and appropriate" **[—11—]** provisions "inform[] the grant of authority by illustrating the kinds of measures that could be necessary" or appropriate.[34] And none of the measures in those sections look anything like the funding scheme that the Fisheries Service contemplates here.

Second, the logic of the Fisheries Service's argument could lead to strange results.[35] Could the agency require the fishermen to drive regulators to their government offices if gas gets too expensive? Having the agency officials at work may be "appropriate" for "management of the fishery." Yet I doubt that Congress meant to allow for free fisherman chauffeurs.

Or what if Congress were to entirely defund the compliance components of the Fisheries Service—could the agency continue to operate by requiring the industry to fund a legion of independent contractors to replace the federal employees? That generous interpretation of "necessary and **[—12—]** appropriate" could undermine Congress's power of the purse.[36] So although the words "necessary and appropriate" may be broad, they cannot be as limitless as the Fisheries Service suggests.[37]

Third, if Congress had wanted to allow industry funding of at-sea monitors in the Atlantic herring fishery, it could have said so. But it instead chose to expressly provide for it in only certain *other* contexts.[38] The existence of specific provisions **[—13—]** **{-378-}** for industry funding elsewhere — for only certain North Pacific fisheries, foreign fishing, and limited access privilege programs — suggests that the Fisheries Service can't turn to a catchall "necessary and appropriate" prerogative to implicitly authorize industry funding in the Atlantic herring fishery.[39]

---

[34] *Alabama Association of Realtors v. Department of Health & Human Services*, 141 S. Ct. 2485, 2488 (2021); *see also Washington State Department of Social & Health Services v. Guardianship Estate of Keffeler*, 537 U.S. 371, 384 (2003) ("under the established interpretative canons of *noscitur a sociis* and *ejusdem generis*, where general words follow specific words in a statutory enumeration, the general words are construed to embrace only objects similar in nature to those objects enumerated by the preceding specific words" (cleaned up)); *see also NASDAQ Stock Market, LLC v. SEC*, 961 F.3d 421, 428 (D.C. Cir. 2020) (applying the canon to reject an agency interpretation within the *Chevron* framework).

[35] *Merck & Co., Inc., v. United States Department of Health & Human Services*, 962 F.3d 531, 541 (D.C. Cir. 2020) ("the breadth of the Secretary's asserted authority is measured not only by the specific application at issue, but also by the implications of the authority claimed").

[36] *See, e.g.*, John Holland & Laura Allen, *An Analysis of Factors Responsible for the Decline of the U.S. Horse Industry: Why Horse Slaughter Is Not the Solution*, 5 Kentucky Journal of Equine, Agriculture, and Natural Resources Law 225, 225-27 (2013) (Congress used its funding power in its effort to end commercial horse slaughter by defunding the requisite ante-mortem inspections.).

[37] *See Alabama Association of Realtors*, 141 S. Ct. at 2489 ("It is hard to see what measures this interpretation would place outside the CDC's reach, and the Government has identified no limit . . . beyond the requirement that the CDC deem a measure necessary." (cleaned up)); *Mozilla Corp.*, 940 F.3d at 75 ("even the allowance of wide latitude in the exercise of delegated powers is not the equivalent of untrammeled freedom to regulate activities over which the statute fails to confer, or explicitly denies, Commission authority" (cleaned up)).

[38] 16 U.S.C. § 1862(a) (North Pacific fishery), § 1821(h)(4) (foreign fishing), § 1853a(e)(2) (limited access privilege programs). A limited access privilege program is one in which an entity is permitted to catch a specified portion of the total allowable catch for all the fishermen per fishing season. Although the fee provision for limited access privilege programs does not itself mention observers, it nevertheless covers them. Section 1853a(c)(1)(H) instructs that a limited access privilege program shall "include an effective system for enforcement, monitoring, and management of the program, including the use of observers," and subsection (e) instructs that **[—13—]** "fees paid by limited access privilege holders . . . will cover the costs of management, data collection and analysis, and enforcement activities."

[39] *Sebelius v. Cloer*, 569 U.S. 369, 378 (2013) ("We have long held that where Congress includes particular language in one section of a statute but omits it in another section of the same Act, it is generally presumed that Congress acts intentionally and purposely in the disparate inclusion or exclusion." (cleaned up)).

Take for example the provision governing the North Pacific fisheries. The statute says that the relevant council may, in certain North Pacific fisheries, "require[] that observers be stationed on fishing vessels" and "establish[] a system . . . of fees . . . to pay for the cost of implementing the plan."[40]

That provision and the "necessary and appropriate" provisions were enacted at the same time.[41] It is hard to believe that, when Congress decided to *explicitly* allow industry-funding for observers in one way (fees) in one place (the North Pacific), it also decided to *silently* allow all fisheries to fund observers in any other way they choose.[42] The plainer reading **[—14—]** of the text is that Congress's authorization for industry funding was limited to what it expressly authorized.[43]

In its briefing, the Fisheries Service tried to explain away the existence of this specific industry-funding provision by arguing that Congress merely wanted to "mandate" a certain solution in the North Pacific.[44] But that's not what Congress did. The language of the fee provision in the North Pacific is discretionary, not mandatory.[45]

The Fisheries Service also tries to draw a distinction between (1) making fishermen pay for monitors through a "fee" program like the program used in the North Pacific — where the money goes to the government, and the government then uses that money to pay the monitors' wages—and (2) making the fishermen pay the monitors directly, as here, without the government as a middleman.[46] **[—15—]** But if the Fisheries **{-379-}** Service is correct that the two schemes *aren't* analogous, that shows the novelty of the Fisheries Service's scheme for the Atlantic herring fishery — a novelty that cuts even more against the Fisheries Service's reliance on an authority either implied or provided by the catch-all "necessary and appropriate" clauses. And on the other hand, if the two schemes *are* analogous, that suggests that Congress made a deliberate choice when it expressly approved fishermen-funded monitoring only for the North Pacific, foreign fishing, and limited access privilege programs—and not here.[47] **[—16—]**

---

40 16 U.S.C. § 1862(a).

41 Fishery Conservation Amendments of 1990, Pub. L. No. 101-627, § 109(b)(2), 104 Stat. 4436, 4448 (codified at 16 U.S.C. § 1853(b)(8)); *id.* § 118(a), 104 Stat. 4457 (codified at 16 U.S.C. § 1862).

42 *Gross v. FBL Financial Services, Inc*, 557 U.S. 167, 175 (2009) ("negative implications raised by disparate provisions are strongest where the provisions were considered simultaneously" (cleaned up)).

43 *See NASDAQ Stock Market LLC v. SEC*, No. 21-1167, 2022 WL 2431638, at *6 (D.C. Cir July 5, 2022) (Although our Circuit has, at times, been skeptical of the *expressio unius* canon, when "a grant of authority . . . reasonably impl[ies] the preclusion of alternatives, the canon is a useful aide." (cleaned up)).

44 Government Brief 44 ("In this situation, 'the contrast between Congress's mandate in one context with its silence in another suggests not a prohibition but simply a decision *not to mandate* any solution in the second context, i.e., to leave the question to agency discretion.'" (quoting *Cheney Railroad Co. v Interstate Commerce Commission*, 902 F.2d 66, 69 (D.C. Cir. 1990))).

45 16 U.S.C. § 1862(a)(2) ("The North Pacific council *may* . . . require[] that observers be stationed on fishing vessels" and "establish[] a system . . . of fees . . . to pay for the cost of implementing the plan." (emphasis added)).

46 The Fisheries Service is not eager to highlight that the North Pacific and limited-access schemes are not at all analogous to the **[—15—]** scheme at issue here in at least one respect: their cost. In the North Pacific, if fees are set as a fixed percentage, they may not exceed two percent of the value of what the ship brings in on a trip. 16 U.S.C. § 1862(b)(2)(E). And in the context of limited access privilege programs, the cap is three percent. *Id.* § 1854(d)(2)(B). But here, the required payments to at-sea monitors could reduce the fishermen's financial returns by twenty percent.

47 To the extent there is a meaningful difference between paying fees to the government and paying observers directly, the Magnuson-Stevens Act already, explicitly, contemplates both. The Act creates more traditional fee programs in the North Pacific, limited access privilege programs, and foreign fishing generally. But when the Fisheries Service has "insufficient appropriations" to provide full observer coverage for foreign fishing, the Act calls for the implementation of a supplementary observer

* * *

Fishing is a hard way to earn a living.[48] And Congress can make profitable fishing even harder by forcing fishermen to spend a fifth of their revenue on the wages of federal monitors embedded by regulation onto their ships.

But until Congress does that, the Fisheries Service cannot.

I respectfully dissent.

---

program under which "certified observers" are "paid by the owners and operators of foreign fishing vessels for observer services." 16 U.S.C. § 1821(h)(6)(C). So we know that Congress is (1) aware of the possibility that appropriations are sometimes insufficient to cover observer programs and (2) capable of creating industry-funding schemes to resolve that dilemma. And the Fisheries Service itself acknowledges both of those points in a document currently posted on its website regarding limited access privilege programs. United States Department of Commerce, National Oceanic and Atmospheric **[—16—]** Administration & National Marine Fisheries Service, The Design and Use of Limited Access Privilege Programs 3 (Lee G. Anderson & Mark C. Holliday eds., 2007), https://www.fisheries.noaa.gov/resource/document/design-and-use-limited-access-privilege-programs (last updated June 13, 2019) ("In times of constant or shrinking federal budgets, obtaining the funds to pay for new management plans is a real concern. Congress implicitly took this into consideration by mandating a cost recovery program for LAP programs. **Funds to cover the additional costs of the LAP program will have to come from the current appropriations.** This means that there will have to be cuts elsewhere. The [councils'] decisions should ensure that the costs of implementation and operation do not exceed the appropriated and cost-recovered funds available. Regardless of whether it is a LAP program, the alternative is the potential disapproval of a [fishery management plan] (or part of it) where funds are insufficient to carry out a management choice." (emphasis added)).

[48] *Cf.* Ernest Hemingway, The Old Man and the Sea (1952); Herman Melville, Moby Dick (1851); The Perfect Storm (Warner Bros. Pictures 2000); Billy Joel, The Downeaster "Alexa" (1990); *The Deadliest Catch* (Discovery Channel 2005-present); Letter from Vincent Van Gogh to Theo Van Gogh (on or about May 16, 1882), https://vangoghletters.org/vg/letters/let228/letter.html ("The fishermen know that the sea is dangerous and the storm fearsome, but could never see that the dangers were a reason to continue strolling on the beach." (emphasis omitted)).

United States Court of Appeals
for the District of Columbia Circuit

No. 21-7036

ESTATE OF LEVIN
vs.
WELLS FARGO BANK, N.A.

Appeal from the United States District Court for the District of Columbia

Decided: August 16, 2022

Citation: 45 F.4th 416, 10 Adm. R. 503 (D.C. Cir. 2022).

Before **PILLARD** and **WALKER,** Circuit Judges and **RANDOLPH,** Senior Circuit Judge.

[—2—] {-417-} RANDOLPH, Senior Circuit Judge:

These consolidated cases, on appeal from a judgment of the district court, present competing claims to a blocked electronic funds transfer. The parties are, on one side, the United States, which blocked the transaction because terrorists initiated it. On the other side are victims of Iran-sponsored terrorism who have obtained multi-million dollar judgments against the Iranian government.

Taif Mining Services, LLC, an Omani company, initiated the electronic transfer to consummate its purchase of the *Nautic*, an oil tanker registered in Liberia. Crystal Holdings Limited, a Liberian subsidiary of a Greek company, was the seller. A law firm, Holman Fenwick Willan LLP, based in London, facilitated **[—3—]** the sale.

The U.S. Treasury Department's Office of Foreign Assets Control ("OFAC") maintains a list of "Specially Designated Nationals and Blocked Persons." *See* Exec. Order No. 13,224 (2001), *as amended by* Exec. Order No. 13,886 (2019); 31 C.F.R. § 594.201. OFAC listed the Islamic Revolutionary Guard Corps. Two members of the Iranian Revolutionary Guard formed Taif Mining in an apparent attempt to hide its affiliation with the Islamic Republic of Iran. Taif Mining itself is now on OFAC's list. **{-418-}**

Taif Mining initiated its electronic funds transfers to Crystal Holdings pursuant to a sales agreement for the *Nautic*. The Holman Fenwick law firm served as the parties' escrow agent. Taif's downpayment of $2.34 million moved through the international financial system in September 2019 and reached Crystal Holdings' Swiss bank account without interruption.

In October 2019, Taif Mining wired Holman Fenwick $9.98 million, the balance of the *Nautic*'s purchase price. Holman Fenwick deposited the funds in its escrow account at Lloyds Bank PLC, in London. Taif directed the law firm to send, "[f]or and on behalf of Taif," the $9.98 million to the Credit Suisse account of Crystal Holdings in Switzerland. Taif also instructed Holman Fenwick to use Bank of New York Mellon as the "intermediary bank" for the transfer. Whether Holman Fenwick relayed this instruction to Lloyds Bank is not clear.

We have described before how funds are transferred electronically through intermediary banks when the parties to the financial transaction have accounts at different banks. *See Heiser v. Islamic Republic of Iran*, 735 F.3d 934, 936 (D.C. Cir. **[—4—]** 2013).[1] Here, the bridge between the Lloyds Bank of London and the Credit Suisse Bank in

[1] *Heiser* described the role of intermediary banks with this example:

> Suppose O wants to transfer $100 to B. If O and B have an account at Bank X, then the transaction is simple. O can instruct Bank X, which will debit O's account and credit B's account with $100. But suppose O has an account at Bank X, and B has an account at Bank Y. Unless Banks X and Y are members of the same lending consortium, they must involve a third "intermediary" bank with which Banks X and Y both have accounts. The transaction would proceed as follows: (1) O instructs Bank X to pay B; (2) Bank X debits O's account and forwards instructions to the intermediary bank; (3) the intermediary bank debits Bank X's account, credits Bank Y's account, and forwards instructions to Bank Y; and (4) Bank Y credits B's account.

735 F.3d at 936.

Switzerland was the Wells Fargo bank in New York.

The $9.98 million electronic funds transfer was blocked in the instant after Wells Fargo debited its Lloyds account but before it credited its Credit Suisse account. The blocking was done pursuant to 50 U.S.C. § 1702, and Executive Order No. 13,224 (2001), *as amended by* Executive Order No. 13,886 (2019).[2] How federal authorities were able to anticipate the transfer and act before its completion is not disclosed. After blocking the transfer, Wells Fargo placed the funds in an account in South Dakota, as the bank apparently does with all **[—5—]** blocked assets.

Months later, in May 2020, the United States filed a forfeiture action for the blocked funds. *United States v. $2,340,000.00 Associated with Petroleum Tanker Nautic*, No. 20-cv-1139 (D.D.C. filed May 1, 2020); *see* 18 U.S.C. § 981(a)(1)(A), (C), (G)(i).[3] The Wall Street Journal reported the government's forfeiture action and its indictment of the two Iranians who were behind Taif. Mengqi Sun & Dylan Tokar, *U.S. Charges Two Iranians over Oil Tanker Purchase, Seeking $12 Million Forfeiture*, WALL ST. J. (May 2, 2020), https://perma.cc/B75B-KMVT. The article stated that the funds were being held at Wells Fargo. *Id.*

After learning of the government's forfeiture action, attorneys for two groups of **{-419-}** victims of Iranian terrorism and their relatives, holding judgments against Iran, filed separate writs of attachment in the United States District Court for the District of Columbia. The *Owens* plaintiffs are victims of al-Qaeda's 1998 bombings of the U.S. embassies in Kenya and Tanzania. They have nearly $1 billion in judgments against Iran. *See* Order, *Owens v. Republic of Sudan*, No. 01-cv-2244 (D.D.C. Mar. 28, 2014), R. Doc. 301; Order, *Mwila v. Islamic Republic of Iran*, No. 08-cv-1377 (D.D.C. Mar. 28, 2014), R. Doc. 88; Order, *Khaliq v. Republic of Sudan*, No. 10-cv-356 (D.D.C. Mar. 28, 2014), R. Doc. 40. The *Levin* plaintiffs obtained nearly $30 million in judgments against Iran for the 1984 kidnapping and torture of Jeremy Levin by Iran-backed Hezbollah. *Levin v. Islamic Republic of Iran*, No. 05-cv-2494, 2008 WL 11493474 **[—6—]** (D.D.C. Jan. 14, 2008).[4]

Plaintiffs sought to attach the funds at Wells Fargo pursuant to two federal statutes. The first, 28 U.S.C. § 1610(g) of the Foreign Sovereign Immunities Act ("FSIA"), "subject[s] to attachment" "the property of a foreign state . . . and the property of an agency or instrumentality of such a state" against which a plaintiff holds a judgment under 28 U.S.C. § 1605A. The second, § 201(a) of the Terrorism Risk Insurance Act of 2002 ("TRIA"), Pub. L. No. 107–297, 116 Stat. 2322, 2337 (codified at 28 U.S.C. § 1610 Note "Satisfaction of Judgments from Blocked Assets of Terrorists, Terrorist Organizations, and State Sponsors of Terrorism"), "subject[s] to execution or attachment" "the blocked assets of [a] terrorist party (including the blocked assets of any agency or instrumentality of that terrorist party)" against which a plaintiff holds a judgment under 28 U.S.C. §§ 1605(a)(7) or 1605A. Section 201(a) specifies that such assets can be attached "[n]otwithstanding any other provision of law."

The United States intervened in both cases and moved to quash plaintiffs' writs of attachment. The government also asserted that plaintiffs were attempting to circumvent the "orderly administration" of the United States Victims of State Sponsored Terrorism Fund. *See* 34 U.S.C. § 20144.[5]

---

[2] The Treasury Secretary's authority to block terrorist transactions has been delegated to the Director of OFAC. 31 C.F.R. § 594.802.

[3] As is evident from the case title, the United States also sought forfeiture of Taif's downpayment, which is now in Crystal's possession.

[4] The *Levin* plaintiffs also filed writs of attachment in South Dakota and in the Southern District of New York. Those proceedings have been stayed pending the outcome of this case.

[5] The Fund provides a means for victims of state-sponsored terrorism to collect on their unpaid judgments through money the federal government obtains from terrorist states and actors, including through forfeiture proceedings. 34 U.S.C. § 20144.

After consolidating the cases, the district court ruled that **[—7—]** Iran lacked any property interest in the blocked funds held by Wells Fargo. The court therefore quashed plaintiffs' writs of attachment. *See Levin v. Islamic Republic of Iran*, 523 F. Supp. 3d 14 (D.D.C. 2021). The court based its ruling on the Uniform Commercial Code Article 4A, and our opinion in *Heiser*, of which more in a moment.

The district court treated each transaction in this electronic funds transfer as "a stand-alone agreement between sender and recipient." *Id.* at 21. By this the court meant that when an electronic funds transfer is unsuccessful and an intermediary bank is involved, the intermediary bank "is obligated to refund payment only to the immediately prior sender." *Id.* at 22. Thus, the intermediary bank "has no obligation to" the entity that initiated the transfer (the "originator"). *Id.* The originator must recover from its own bank, that is, the bank that sent payment to the intermediary bank. *Id.* **{–420–}**

But for the blocking, the electronic funds transfer would have moved this way:[6]

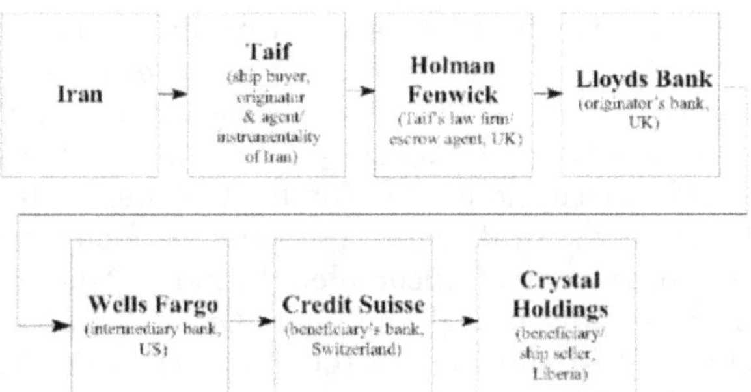

[—8—] Relying on Uniform Commercial Code Article 4A, and especially § 4A-402, the district court "assume[d]" that Taif, rather than the Holman Fenwick law firm, was the "originator" of the funds transfer. *Levin*, 523 F. Supp. 3d at 21. The court concluded that Iran (via Taif) had no claim to the funds at Wells Fargo, and therefore had "no property interest" in them. *Id.* at 21–22. This was because Taif was not "the entity immediately preceding the bank 'holding' the EFT in the transaction chain." *Id.* at 21 (quoting *Calderon-Cardona v. Bank of N.Y. Mellon*, 770 F.3d 993, 1002 (2d Cir. 2014)). That entity was Lloyds Bank. *Id.* And so the district court held that in the absence of any Iranian property interest (through Taif Mining) in the funds, plaintiffs could not attach them under § 201 or § 1610(g) to collect their judgments against Iran. *Id.* at 20.

Both sides in this appeal, relying on *Heiser*, have set forth opposing views on whether, in light of U.C.C. Article 4A, Iran has a "sufficient property interest" in the blocked funds.[7] A "sufficient property interest," that is, to warrant plaintiffs' attachments under § 201 and § 1610(g).

The focus on *Heiser* is understandable. That case is similar to this one. In both, OFAC blocked an electronic funds transfer **[—9—]** when it reached an intermediary U.S. bank. And in *Heiser*, as here, the plaintiffs relied on § 201 and § 1610(g) to collect their judgments. But there the material similarities end.

Unlike this case, the plaintiffs in *Heiser* were seeking to attach funds at intermediary banks under § 201 and § 1610(g) because the beneficiary's bank was Iranian. OFAC's blocking had prevented the funds from reaching the Iranian bank. This is why we described the Iranian banks as having only "a contingent future possessory interest in the funds." *Heiser*, 735 F.3d at 937.[8] **{–421–}**

---

[6] This graphic is drawn from page 7 of the Commercial Law Professors' *Amicus* Brief.

[7] The *Owens* plaintiffs argue in the alternative that the U.C.C. does not apply:

> The U.C.C. was not designed to address terrorist behavior, and Article 4A was specifically drafted to prevent the interruption of funds transfers. But halting transfers is the entire point of sanctions blocking, and that is precisely what OFAC did in this case. As a result, Article 4A is ill-equipped to address the issues of ownership here.

Owens Appellants' Br. 20.

[8] The intermediary banks in *Heiser* never contested that funds blocked at an intermediary bank, where the originator or the originator's bank was or may have been an agency or instrumentality of Iran, could be attached using § 201 and

Pursuant to the U.C.C. Article 4A, the Iranian bank in *Heiser* "was not the beneficiary or originator" and under "the principles of Article 4A," the blocking foreclosed any claim that legal title had passed to the Iranian bank. *Id.* at 941. For this reason and in view of settled common law principles,[9] we ruled **[—10—]** against the plaintiffs. In our view Congress, in § 201 of TRIA and § 1610(g) of FSIA, could not possibly have "intended judgment creditors of foreign states to be able to attach property those states do not own." *Id.* at 938.

These differences between *Heiser* and this case are significant. As Professor Paul Mishkin, a "thoughtful legal scholar[],"[10] put it, when federal courts incorporate state law as federal common law, such incorporation must be done "as to a single issue at a time" and the court must consider whether the "issue's outcome" is consistent with the "federal program." Paul J. Mishkin, *The Variousness of "Federal Law": Competence and Discretion in the Choice of National and State Rules for Decision,* 105 U. PA. L. REV. 797, 804–06 (1957); *see* Caleb Nelson, *The Persistence of General Law*, 106 COLUM. L. REV. 503, 510–11 & n.33 (2006). It follows that we may use Article 4A if and only if, on the issue presented, doing so would be consistent with TRIA § 201 and FSIA § 1610(g). *Boyle v. United Techs. Corp.*, 487 U.S. 500, 507–13 (1988); *Burks v. Lasker,* 441 U.S. 471, 479–80 (1979). As we held in *Heiser*, "Article 4A does not apply of its own force. . . . Federal law, specifically § 201 and § 1610(g), is controlling." 735 F.3d at 940. **[—11—]**

To sum up thus far, *Heiser* did not settle whether U.C.C. Article 4A, or any provisions of it, would apply in a case such as this as matter of "federal common law."[11] Henry J. Friendly, *In Praise of* Erie*—and of the New Federal Common Law*, 39 N.Y.U. L. REV. 383, 410 (1964)); *see Clearfield Tr. Co. v. United States*, 318 U.S. 363, 366–68 (1943); Caleb Nelson, *The Legitimacy of (Some) Federal Common Law*, 101 VA. L. REV. 1, 35–36, 63 & n.220 (2015).

Most of what is set forth in the lengthy U.C.C. Article 4A and its Commentaries, **{-422-}** entitled "Funds Transfers," deals with technical banking subjects, of no concern here. The parties in this case naturally focus on § 4A-402, the section dealing with electronic funds transfers that have miscarried. This section, like other Article 4A sections, seeks to avoid disruptions to funds transfers. Its function is to allocate risks and to facilitate the unwinding of uncompleted funds transfers in a fair and orderly manner. *Grain Traders, Inc. v. Citibank, N.A.*, 160 F.3d 97, 101 (2d Cir. 1998).[12]

---

§ 1610(g). *Heiser*, 735 F.3d at 936 n.3. In fact, there were many "*uncontested* accounts" with those characteristics that the banks requested the district court turn over to terrorist victim plaintiffs. *Id.*; *see* Joint Appendix at 160–61, 257, 277–78, *Heiser v. Islamic Republic of Iran*, 735 F.3d 934 (D.C. Cir. 2013) (No. 12-7101); Third Party Petition Alleging Claims in the Nature of Interpleader at 3–4, *Heiser v. Islamic Republic of Iran*, 00-cv-2329 (D.D.C. Aug. 31, 2012), R. Doc. 235.

[9] We described the common law thus:

> If a debtor merely holds property as an intermediary for a third party, but does not own the property, then a creditor cannot attach it. *See Carpenter v. Nat'l City Bank of Chi.*, 48 App. D.C. 133, 134–35, 136 [—10—] (D.C. Cir. 1918). These principles carry significant weight because "statutes should be interpreted consistently with the common law." *Manoharan v. Rajapaksa*, 711 F.3d 178, 179 (D.C. Cir. 2013) (per curiam) (quoting *Samantar v. Yousuf*, 560 U.S. 305, 320 (2010)).

Heiser, 735 F.3d at 938.

[10] *Danforth v. Minnesota*, 552 U.S. 264, 275 n.12 (2008); *id.* at 294–95 (Roberts, C.J., dissenting).

[11] We acknowledge that the Second Circuit appears to have adopted U.C.C. Article 4A, or at least New York's version of it, as federal common law for all electronic funds transfers in cases such as this one within its non-diversity jurisdiction. *See, e.g., Doe v. JPMorgan Chase Bank, N.A.*, 899 F.3d 152, 156–57 (2d Cir. 2018). We also acknowledge that our opinion aligns with the dissenting opinion in that case. *Id.* at 158–62 (Chin, J., dissenting).

[12] *Grain Traders* is not a federal common law case; it is a diversity case that applies New York law, specifically New York's version of Article 4A. 160 F.3d at 98.

As applied in this case, the objectives of U.C.C. § 4A-402 and OFAC's blocking are incompatible. While § 4A-402 seeks to minimize disruptions in electronic funds transfers, OFAC's blocking does the opposite – its purpose is to disrupt terrorist **[—12—]** electronic fund transactions. While § 4A-402 is designed to govern the unraveling of uncompleted electronic transfers,[13] when OFAC blocks electronic funds transfers there will be no unraveling.[14] That is the point of blocking. Thus, the Permanent Editorial Board for the Uniform Commercial Code,[15] in its Commentary No. 16, concluded that Article 4A should not be "honored" when "a regulation of the Treasury Department's Office of Foreign Assets Control ('OFAC')" disrupts an **[—13—]** electronic transfer.[16] That of course describes this case.

[13] A funds transfer may not be completed because the intermediary bank becomes insolvent after the originator's bank credits the intermediary's account, there is a mistake in the payment order, or a bank accidentally sends a duplicate payment order. 3 JAMES J. WHITE ET AL., UNIFORM COMMERCIAL CODE § 23:15, 21 (6th ed. 2014).

[14] At least not in the United States. We have no information on potential causes of action in foreign jurisdictions.

[15] The Permanent Editorial Board

> is a joint committee of the American Law Institute and the Uniform Law Commission (also known as the National Conference of Commissioners on Uniform State Laws) that assists in attaining and maintaining uniformity in state statutes governing commercial transactions by discouraging non-uniform amendments to the Uniform Commercial Code by the states, and by approving and promulgating amendments to the UCC when necessary.

Export–Import Bank of the U.S. v. Asia Pulp & Paper Co., 609 F.3d 111, 119 n.8 (2d Cir. 2010) (internal quotation marks omitted).

[16] The district court relied on Commentary No. 16 in concluding that Iran (through Taif) had no property interest in the $9.98 million held at Wells Fargo. *Levin*, 523 F. Supp. 3d at 21. The court may not have been aware of the Permanent Editorial Board's caveat regarding OFAC, quoted in the text above.

When one steps back from § 4A-402's elaborate – but inapplicable – methods for unwinding misfired electronic transfers, the path to our judgment seems clear. OFAC's blocking is aimed at terrorists and their financial transactions. The TRIA "subject[s] to execution or attachment" "the blocked assets of [a] terrorist party," such as a State Sponsor of Terrorism like Iran, "including the blocked assets of any agency or instrumentality of that terrorist party" against which plaintiffs hold a judgment under 28 U.S.C. §§ 1605(a)(7) or 1605A. § 201(a), 116 Stat. 2337. Again, section 201(a) specifies that such assets can be attached "[n]otwithstanding any other provision of law."

Wells Fargo Bank is merely a stakeholder. It risks no financial loss. Lloyds Bank is not on the hook – it received $9.98 million from the Holman law firm and it transmitted $9.98 million to Wells Fargo. The Holman law firm held the $9.98 million as an escrow agent; it never owned the **{-423-}** money.[17] The only entity that is out of pocket as a result of OFAC's blocking is the Iranian front Taif,[18] and that is because it is subject to U.S. sanctions. In terms of the TRIA, just quoted, the $9.98 million **[—14—]** therefore represents "blocked assets of [a] terrorist party."[19]

The opposition of the United States rests on U.C.C. Article 4A, which we find inapplicable. The government agrees with the district court's decision to apply Article 4A and the conclusion reached. There is another problem with the position of the United States. The government's argument here and the district court's holding[20] that Iran (Taif) has no property interest in the blocked funds "is inherently at odds with OFAC regulations that require the 'property and interests in property' of [Specially Designated Global

[17] Since these are for the most part instant transactions we disregard the effect of interest on the funds.

[18] At least according to U.S. law, which to our analysis is all that matters.

[19] Because the funds can be attached using the TRIA, we need not decide whether attachment is permissible under § 1610(g) of the FSIA.

[20] *Levin*, 523 F. Supp. 3d at 21.

Terrorists] to be blocked in the first place. *See* 31 C.F.R. § 594.201(a). If [a terrorist's] interest in funds is, in effect, entirely extinguished while temporarily midstream, there would be no authorization to block those midstream funds as 'property [or] interests in property' of a designated terrorist party because that property would belong *solely* to the intermediary bank, not a designated terrorist party." *Doe*, 899 F.3d at 161 (Chin, J., dissenting) (third and fourth alterations in original).

Since U.C.C. Article 4A does not apply, the next question is what does. Our answer is that under § 201, which deals only with assets that have already been blocked by the United States, terrorist victims may attach OFAC blocked electronic funds transfers if those funds can be traced to a terrorist owner.

Tracing is used throughout federal law to attach consequences to those having or having had interests in property. The Supreme Court has commented: "Courts use tracing rules in cases involving fraud, pension rights, bankruptcy, trusts, etc." **[—15—]** *Luis v. United States*, 578 U.S. 5, 22 (2016) (plurality opinion) (per curiam). The federal forfeiture statutes expressly incorporate tracing. *See, e.g.*, 18 U.S.C. §§ 981, 982; 21 U.S.C. § 881(a)(6); *United States v. Daccarett*, 6 F.3d 37, 55 (2d Cir. 1993).[21] Consistent with other situations when tracing is used, innocent third parties must be protected. Therefore, blocked funds can be attached only if no intermediary or upstream bank asserts an interest as an innocent third party. *See Heiser*, 735 F.3d at 938–39; *Doe*, 899 F.3d at 160–61 (Chin, J., dissenting).

Tracing resolves this case in plaintiffs' favor. The government admits that the $9.98 million blocked funds at Wells Fargo "are traceable to Taif" and thus to Iran. United States Br. 47. The premise of the government's forfeiture action is that the funds are traceable to Iran. *See* J.A. 51 ¶¶ 1–2; *id.* at 58–60 ¶¶ 47–59. Neither Wells Fargo nor Lloyds has asserted a claim to the blocked funds. The district **{-424-}** court therefore erred in concluding that the plaintiffs had failed to show that the blocked funds were, under § 201(a) of the TRIA, "the blocked assets of [a] terrorist party (including the blocked assets of any agency or instrumentality of that terrorist party)." 116 Stat. 2337. The district court's judgment rested entirely on this holding and its decision is all that we have addressed.

Reversed and remanded. **[—16—]**

EPILOGUE

In January 2020 the United Arab Emirates seized the *Nautic* pursuant to a civil court order. Crystal initiated an arbitration against Taif Mining to collect the $9.98 million balance. While the arbitration was pending, and while the *Nautic* was moored off the UAE coast, Iranians hijacked the ship.

(Reporter's Note: Concurring opinion follows on p. 509).

[21] The U.C.C.'s Permanent Editorial Board, in its Commentary No. 16, indicated that Article 4A does not apply in drug forfeiture cases, and that with respect to blocked electronic funds, the "*Daccarett* court, as appropriate in a forfeiture case, identified the amount of the funds as 'traceable' to an illicit activity and therefore subject to attachment under 21 U.S.C. § 881(a)."

[—1—] {-424-} PILLARD, Circuit Judge, concurring:

I agree with the majority that the Uniform Commercial Code's Article 4A is an inappropriate rule of decision for determining whether funds owned by a terrorist party that initiates an EFT, during which the government blocks the funds based on 31 C.F.R. § 594.201, are property "of" a terrorist party for purposes of TRIA § 201. But in the place of Article 4A, I would make explicit that common-law ownership and agency principles apply instead of or in addition to tracing. Because the majority's rule apparently produces the same result in this case, I concur.

No party proposed we adopt tracing alone as our rule of decision in this context, and for good reason. That approach does not fulfill a key requirement of TRIA that we highlighted in *Heiser v. Islamic Republic of Iran*: that the terrorist party be shown to have "an ownership interest" in the funds sought. 735 F.3d 934, 941 (D.C. Cir. 2013); *see id.* at 938-40. Tracing typically involves a sort of forensic accounting—a process of identifying how an asset has been transformed, transferred, or substituted such that a claim against the asset can instead be made against the new one. "With the help of [tracing] rules, the victim of a robbery, for example, will likely obtain the car that the robber used stolen money to buy." *Luis v. United States*, 578 U.S. 5, 22 (2016). But tracing presupposes ownership; it does not identify any legal rule for establishing ownership, or even require that ownership be shown. The majority's holding that the relevant funds may be attached so long as they are "traceable to Taif," *supra* at 15, stops short of specifying any rule of decision to substitute for U.C.C. Article 4A in providing the statutorily required showing of ownership under *Heiser*.

Specifying only the tracing approach creates needless uncertainty. As we observed in *Heiser*, "[t]he blocking regulations cast a wide net," and are "not based on legal ownership." 735 F.3d at 936. The fact that the government has blocked funds is not itself assurance that the funds are or were **[—2—]** owned by terrorists. Victims of terrorism seeking to attach OFAC blocked electronic funds must also show the funds can be traced to a terrorist *owner*, *id.* at 941, a showing the government itself need not make prior to the blocking.

The court's opinion helpfully limits its tracing-based TRIA rule to circumstances in which "no intermediary or upstream bank asserts an interest as an innocent third party," *supra* at 15. But it does not explain the legal basis of that limitation. And it leaves unclear, for example, whether a bank could make such an assertion after the TRIA plaintiffs had recovered against the property. We must avoid a rule that "risks punishing innocent third parties"—the result *Heiser* read TRIA to **{-425-}** prevent. 735 F.3d at 939 (citing cases establishing that we strictly construe attachment statutes to protect innocent parties).

In a case in which the tracing rule alone does not eliminate such risk, an apt federal rule of decision was presented to us: the application of common-law ownership and agency principles in lieu of the U.C.C. Article 4A-based rule applied in *Heiser*. *See Owens* Appellants' Br. 36-40. The relevant TRIA provision seeks to hold terrorist parties accountable by subjecting their assets to attachment. Treating banks effectuating EFTs as agents rather than owners in this context would ensure that even in financial transactions like EFTs that are designed to be quick and difficult to interrupt, that design does not defeat the ability of TRIA claimants to reach funds during terrorist-initiated EFTs that the blocking regime succeeds in interrupting. This rule would allow the law to keep its eye on the ball as Congress plainly intended: The banks are just the tools for carrying out the transaction. Whether it is transferred by EFT or some more traditional means like a check, property in a transaction that a terrorist party funds, **[—3—]** initiates, and primarily benefits from is appropriately subject to claims under TRIA.

The logic of this approach echoes the common law's treatment of certain banking relationships in the decades before the U.C.C. added specialized treatment of electronic fund transfers. In *Commercial National Bank v. Armstrong*, for example, the Supreme Court recognized that "the relation created between the banks as to [a check to be cashed] was that of principal and agent," which created a "trust obligation" over the funds to be transferred and permitted those funds to be "specifically trac[ed]" back to the principal's rightful ownership. 148 U.S. 50, 56 (1893). Because of that agency relationship,

> [w]hether it be said that such funds are specifically traceable in the possession of the subagent, or that the agent has never reduced those funds to possession, or put itself in a position where it could rightfully claim that it has changed the relation of agent to that of debtor, the result [was] the same.

Id. at 57. The result was that traceable funds intended as cash payment on that check belonged to the principal, rather than the agent bank, even if those funds were stopped mid-transfer. *Id.* at 57-58; *see also, e.g.*, *City of Miami v. First Nat. Bank*, 58 F.2d 561 (5th Cir. 1932).

Under that approach, for purposes of TRIA § 201, plaintiffs must establish not only that funds have been blocked based on "any interest" that a terrorist party may have in them, 50 U.S.C. § 1702(a)(1)(B), but also that the funds are owned by the terrorist—not by an innocent EFT initiator, *see Heiser*, 735 F.3d at 936, or other innocent party. Any bank **[—4—]** downstream from a terrorist party originator of an EFT, for example, is not treated as owner of the funds, as it would be under U.C.C. Article 4A. Rather, under general common law rules applicable to non-EFT money transfers, it would be treated as an agent or subagent of the originator-owner. Here, Taif was the owner of the funds it asked Holman Fenwick to electronically transfer, and for current purposes it thus retained ownership of the contested funds, even as the funds passed through the hands of its agents and subagents until they were frozen in Wells Fargo's possession. Thus, applying common law ownership and agency principles would treat Taif—and only Taif—as holding an ownership interest in the blocked funds. **{-426-}**

I therefore concur in reversing the district court's determination that the blocked funds were not "of" a terrorist party. *Supra* at 15. I write separately to emphasize that, in my view, tracing alone is a conceptually incomplete rule of decision. But I do not take the court's tracing approach to be inconsistent with additional reliance on a federal rule based on common-law ownership and agency principles—to the extent it might be needed in future litigation—to harmonize today's decision with *Heiser* and reduce legal uncertainty for innocent owners and third parties like Wells Fargo.

United States Court of Appeals
for the District of Columbia Circuit

No. 20-1411

EVERPORT TERMINAL SERVS., INC.
VS.
NATIONAL LABOR RELATIONS BD.

On Petitions for Review and Cross Application for Enforcement of an Order of the National Labor Relations Board

Decided: August 26, 2022

Citation: 47 F.4th 782, 10 Adm. R. 511 (D.C. Cir. 2022).

Before **SRINIVASAN,** Chief Judge, **RAO,** Circuit Judge, and **EDWARDS,** Senior Circuit Judge.

[—2—] {-784-} RAO, Circuit Judge:

This case arises from a dispute over which union—the International Association of Machinists ("IAM") or the International Longshore and Warehouse Union ("ILWU")—is entitled to represent the mechanic workforce at the Ben Nutter Terminal in Oakland, California. For many years, the Terminal's mechanics **{-785-}** were represented by the IAM. In 2015, Everport Terminal Services, Inc., took over the Terminal's operation and decided to hire a new workforce. As a member of the multi-employer Pacific Maritime Association ("PMA"), Everport was party to a collective bargaining agreement negotiated between the PMA and the ILWU. As Everport read that agreement, it required Everport to prioritize ILWU applicants in hiring its new mechanics and to recognize the ILWU as their representative. Everport therefore gave qualified ILWU applicants first choice of the available mechanic positions, filling the remaining vacancies with **[—3—]** applicants from the Terminal's existing, IAM-represented workforce.

After the IAM cried foul, the National Labor Relations Board ("Board") found that Everport had unlawfully discriminated against the Terminal's incumbent mechanics on the basis of their IAM affiliation; that it had violated its statutory obligation to recognize and bargain with the incumbent mechanics' chosen union, the IAM; and that it had prematurely recognized the ILWU as the representative of the Terminal's mechanics. The Board also found the ILWU had unlawfully demanded and accepted recognition from Everport. In its order, the Board did not dispute—or even engage with—Everport's reading of the PMA-ILWU agreement, instead dismissing it as a "red herring." Because that was arbitrary, we grant the petitions for review and vacate the Board's order.

I.

A.

Workers at West Coast ports have historically bargained with their employers on a coastwide basis. In 1938, the Board certified the ILWU as the bargaining representative for "all the workers employed at longshore labor in the Pacific Coast ports of the United States." *Shipowners' Ass'n of the Pac. Coast*, 7 NLRB 1002, 1022 (1938). Coastwide representation was necessary, the Board found, because employers were coordinating workers' terms of employment on a coastwide basis. *See id.* at 1023–24; *see also Cal. Cartage Co. v. NLRB*, 822 F.2d 1203, 1206 (D.C. Cir. 1987) (explaining the Board's decision in *Shipowners*). Since 1949, West Coast port operators have bargained with the ILWU through the Pacific Maritime Association, a "multi-employer bargaining representative ... with the primary purpose of negotiating, executing, and administering collective bargaining agreements." *PMA v.* **[—4—]** *NLRB*, 967 F.3d 878, 881, 8 Adm. R. 549, 549 (D.C. Cir. 2020). ILWU members will work only for port operators that are in the PMA, and because of the Board's decision to certify a coastwide bargaining unit, the ILWU represents virtually all skilled longshoremen on the West Coast.

All PMA employers are bound by the terms of a collective bargaining agreement negotiated between the PMA and the ILWU, the Pacific Coast Longshore Contract Document ("Longshore Contract"). The Longshore Contract specifies the longshore jobs PMA employers must give to ILWU members. It also sets the terms of employment for those workers—the wages and benefits they receive, the process through which they are hired, and the reasons for which they may be fired.

The Longshore Contract's scope is broad, reaching "[v]irtually all longshore work at West Coast ports," *ILWU v. NLRB* (*"Kinder Morgan"*), 978 F.3d 625, 630, 8 Adm. R. 334, 335 (9th Cir. 2020), and the Board has upheld many of its jurisdiction setting provisions as consistent with the National Labor Relations Act, *see PMA*, 256 NLRB 769, 770 (1981); *cf. IAM, Loc. Lodge No. 1484 v. ILWU, Loc. 13*, 781 F.2d 685, 688 n.2 (9th Cir. 1986). In its earliest iterations, it covered stevedore work—i.e., loading and unloading ships. Later, the PMA **{-786-}** and the ILWU expanded the Longshore Contract to cover mechanics—the workers who maintain and repair the equipment used to load and unload ships—but agreed that PMA members who had employed non-ILWU mechanics before 1978 could continue doing so. *PMA*, 256 NLRB at 769–70. The parties again modified the Longshore Contract in 2008, making clear that mechanic work at "all new marine terminal facilities that commence operations after July 1, 2008, shall be assigned to the ILWU." As before, however, they made an exception for terminals where non-ILWU mechanics were employed before 2008—sites the parties designated as "red-circled." Thus, if **[—5—]** non-ILWU mechanics had been employed at a terminal since before 1978, the Longshore Contract's amendments permit PMA members to continue employing them.

For all work that falls within its scope, the Longshore Contract sets out a hiring process that PMA members must follow. At each port on the West Coast, the ILWU maintains dispatch halls where ILWU jobseekers may submit applications. PMA members may hire only from these dispatch halls and must allocate work based on applicants' qualifications, skills, and seniority. The PMA and the ILWU, however, have historically made a limited exception for mechanics. If there are too few ILWU members seeking mechanic work at the relevant dispatch hall, then after offering jobs to all of the hall's qualified mechanics, a PMA member may fill any remaining vacancies "off the street." These non-ILWU hires are onboarded through the so-called "Herman-Flynn process." Off-the-street hires are subjected to a ninety-day probationary period, after which they become "registered" employees that are entitled to the same benefits as ILWU members and are required to pay ILWU dues.

B.

This case centers on twenty-seven mechanic positions at the Ben Nutter Terminal. The Terminal was "red-circled" in 2008 because non-ILWU mechanics had been working there since before 1978.

For many decades, the Terminal was operated by two PMA members—Marine Terminals Corporation ("Marine") and its subsidiary, Miles Motor Transport System ("Miles")—whose stevedores were represented by the ILWU and whose **[—6—]** mechanics were represented by the IAM.[1] In 2002, Evergreen Marine Corporation acquired the right to operate the Terminal and then subcontracted the Terminal's operation to Marine and Miles. In 2012, Evergreen entrusted the Terminal's operation to its subsidiary, Everport, which again rehired Marine and Miles to run the Terminal. The same workforce remained at the Terminal—Marine and Miles continued using ILWU-represented stevedores and IAM-represented mechanics—and Everport had no direct relationship with these workers.

In 2015, dissatisfied with the state of the Terminal's operations, Everport resolved to operate the Terminal itself and informed Marine and Miles that their contract would end on December 4, 2015. Everport needed to hire stevedores from the ILWU to run the Terminal, so it joined the PMA in June 2015. Everport explored subcontracting the Terminal's mechanic work, but ultimately

[1] The mechanics employed by Marine and Miles were divided into two separate IAM-affiliated bargaining units, but for the purposes of this opinion we refer to them as a single bargaining "unit."

decided to employ the Terminal's mechanics directly.

The ILWU informed Everport that if it chose to employ its own mechanics, it would need to hire them from the local **{–787–}** dispatch hall. "[T]he 'red-circle' waiver at the [Terminal] is fully based on the direct bargaining relationship between [Marine and Miles] and IAM," the ILWU explained. "Upon termination of the subcontracting relationship with [Marine and Miles], the 'red circle' waiver no longer applies." After Marine and Miles ceased operations, the Terminal would become a "new marine terminal"—which the Longshore Contract defined to include "vacated facilities." As such, its red-circle status would lapse and the Terminal's mechanic jobs would come within the ILWU's jurisdiction. Therefore, **[—7—]** according to the ILWU, Everport was obligated to hire its mechanics from the ILWU dispatch hall and, if necessary, through the Herman-Flynn process. The ILWU was clear that "failure to comply with the full terms of the [Longshore Contract] will result in the Union pursuing all available remedies."

Unsure of its obligations, Everport consulted the PMA, which corroborated the ILWU's reading of the Longshore Contract. According to the PMA, after Marine and Miles ceased operations at the Terminal, it would "no longer [be] a red-circle facility because Everport had no prior agreement with any union at the Terminal and the Terminal was [being] vacated." Based on the PMA and the ILWU's mutual understanding of their contract, Everport told the ILWU that "qualified [ILWU] workers will receive first consideration for steady mechanic jobs." Everport indicated that if vacancies remained after exhausting the pool of qualified ILWU applicants, it would try to rehire the mechanics currently working for Marine and Miles.

After learning of Everport's job postings at the ILWU dispatch hall, the IAM demanded that Everport recognize it as the rightful bargaining representative of the Terminal's mechanics. In response, Everport explained its interpretation of the Longshore Contract and why it had to prioritize ILWU applicants for the Terminal's mechanic positions after the Terminal's red-circle designation lapsed.

Everport began hiring mechanics in late November. It first interviewed candidates who had submitted applications through the ILWU hiring hall; afterwards, it considered Marine and Miles' employees, treating them as off-the-street, potential Herman-Flynn hires. Everport's interviewers kept notes about which applicants were ILWU-represented and which were not. **[—8—]** Everport ultimately hired fifteen ILWU applicants and twelve applicants from Marine and Miles' mechanic workforce.

The Terminal reopened under Everport's operation in December 2015. Pursuant to the Herman-Flynn process, Everport treated Marine and Miles' former mechanics as new hires, which meant they lost the seniority-based benefits they had formerly received from Marine and Miles as IAM members. With minor exceptions, Everport's mechanics did the same work, in the same conditions, as their predecessors.

C.

Soon after Everport reopened the Terminal, the IAM filed charges, arguing that Everport and the ILWU had colluded to discriminate against Marine and Miles' mechanics—depriving some of them of their jobs, unilaterally changing their terms and conditions of employment, and violating their right to be represented by the union of their choice. After investigating, the Board's General Counsel filed a complaint against Everport and the ILWU.

The administrative law judge ("ALJ") sided with the IAM. *See Everport Terminal Servs., Inc.*, 370 NLRB No. 28, slip op. at 45–46 (Sept. 30, 2020). Specifically, she found that Everport had unlawfully **{–788–}** discriminated against IAM-represented mechanics on the basis of their union affiliation, *see* 29 U.S.C. § 158(a)(1), (3), and had prematurely recognized and bargained with the ILWU before it was clear that Everport's mechanics would choose to be ILWU-represented, *see id.*

§ 158(a)(1)–(2). The ALJ also found that Everport was a "successor employer" of Marine and Miles under *NLRB v. Burns International Security Services*, 406 U.S. 272 (1972). Everport therefore had a duty to bargain with the incumbent mechanics' chosen union, a duty it breached by refusing to recognize the IAM. *See* 29 U.S.C. § 158(a)(1), (5). Further, the ALJ found that because **[—9—]** Everport's hiring process was infused by a general "animus" towards the IAM, it was also a "perfectly clear" successor under *Burns*, and therefore lost the right to set its mechanics' terms and conditions of employment. *Everport*, slip op. at 33; *see also Karl Kallmann ("Love's Barbeque")*, 245 NLRB 78, 82 (1979), *enf'd in relevant part*, 640 F.2d 1094 (9th Cir. 1981). Everport's unilateral imposition of the Longshore Contract's terms onto the Terminal's existing workforce was therefore unlawful. *See* 29 U.S.C. § 158(a)(1), (5). Finally, the ALJ found that the ILWU had demanded recognition "before Everport began operations and when it did not represent an uncoerced majority of the [Terminal's mechanics]," and had unlawfully induced Everport to discriminate against the incumbent mechanics based on their IAM affiliation. *Everport*, slip op. at 46 (finding violations of 29 U.S.C. § 158(b)(1)(A), (b)(2)).

After Everport and the ILWU appealed, a three-member panel of the Board adopted the ALJ's findings and conclusions. *See id.* at 1–2. With respect to the conclusion that Everport had unlawfully imposed the Longshore Contract on the Terminal's mechanics, the panel split as to the ALJ's reasoning. Two of the Board members agreed with the ALJ that because Everport had "used a general discriminatory hiring plan applicable to *all* applicants from the predecessor workforce," it was not only a *Burns* successor, but had also forfeited the right to set its mechanics' initial terms and conditions of employment.[2] *Id.* at 1 n.4. In the alternative, however, all three Board members agreed that even if Everport had retained the right to set its mechanics' initial terms of employment, its recognition of the **[—10—]** ILWU as its mechanics' representative was still premature, and so its imposition of the Longshore Contract onto those mechanics was unlawful.

The Board ordered Everport to revoke its recognition of the ILWU, cease applying the Longshore Contract to its mechanics, recognize and bargain with the IAM, and offer to rehire any IAM mechanics who had lost their jobs. It also ordered Everport and the ILWU to make whole any workers who were financially harmed by the unfair labor practices.

Everport and the ILWU each timely petitioned for review, challenging the Board's conclusions as arbitrary and capricious in violation of the Administrative Procedure Act. 5 U.S.C. § 706(2)(A). The Board filed a cross application, asking this court to enforce its order, and the IAM intervened on the Board's behalf. We have jurisdiction under 29 U.S.C. § 160(e), (f). **{-789-}**

II.

We begin with the Board's finding that Everport was a successor employer to Marine and Miles' mechanics and that it unlawfully refused to recognize their chosen union, the IAM.

It is an "unfair labor practice for an employer ... to refuse to bargain collectively with the representatives of his employees." *Id.* § 158(a)(5). When a business with unionized employees changes hands, the new owner ordinarily has no duty to recognize the union that represented the predecessors' employees: unless rehired, they are not "*his* employees." *Id.* (emphasis added); *see Burns*, 406 U.S. at 280 n.5; *cf. Howard Johnson Co. v. Detroit Loc. Joint Exec. Bd.*, 417 U.S. 249, 261 (1974) ("[N]othing in the federal labor laws requires that an employer who purchases the assets of a business ... hire all of the employees of the predecessor.") (cleaned up). But "[i]f the **[—11—]** new employer makes a conscious decision to maintain generally the same business and to hire a majority of its

[2] Member Emanuel would have found that Everport retained the right to set its mechanics' terms of employment. In his view, it was not clear that but for Everport's discrimination, all or substantially all of the Terminal's incumbent mechanics would have retained their jobs.

employees from the predecessor," the employer also inherits his predecessor's duty to bargain with the incumbent union. *Fall River Dyeing & Finishing Corp. v. NLRB*, 482 U.S. 27, 41 (1987).

A new business owner inherits its predecessor's duty to bargain, in other words, if (1) its employees continue to perform substantially the same work after the handover; (2) the existing bargaining unit remains appropriate; and (3) "the majority of its employees were employed by its predecessor." *Id.*; *see also Trident Seafoods, Inc. v. NLRB*, 101 F.3d 111, 114 (D.C. Cir. 1996). The third requirement can also be satisfied even where the predecessor's employees do not constitute a majority of the successor's employees. If the Board finds that antiunion animus distorted its hiring process, "the Board presumes that but for such discrimination, the successor would have hired a majority of incumbent employees." *NLRB v. CNN Am., Inc.*, 865 F.3d 740, 752 (D.C. Cir. 2017) (cleaned up). By contrast, if the employer relies on "valid business reason[s]" in hiring its new workforce, it does not inherit any bargaining obligation. *Love's Barbeque*, 245 NLRB at 81.

Here, the Board found that (1) the Terminal's mechanics continued to do substantially the same work after Everport began directing the Terminal's operations; (2) a mechanic-specific bargaining unit remained appropriate; and (3) Everport's hiring process was marred by animus towards the IAM. Everport therefore had a duty to bargain with the incumbent union, and its refusal to do so was unlawful. Everport and the ILWU do not contest the Board's first finding, but argue that the second and third were arbitrary and capricious. We agree. **[—12—]**

A.

In holding that a mechanic-specific bargaining unit remained appropriate after Everport took over the Terminal's operation, the Board arbitrarily ignored its precedents and the language of the Longshore Contract.

Before any unionization vote can take place, the Board must determine "the unit appropriate for the purposes of collective bargaining." 29 U.S.C. § 159(b). Unit-appropriateness determinations are fact specific, so we generally defer to the "broad discretion" of the Board. *United Food & Com. Workers v. NLRB*, 519 F.3d 490, 494 (D.C. Cir. 2008). But a "bargaining unit determination will not stand if arbitrary." *Cleveland Constr., Inc. v. NLRB*, 44 F.3d 1010, 1014 (D.C. Cir. 1995). **{–790–}**

In successorship cases, the Board presumes that a "change in ownership should not uproot bargaining units that have enjoyed a history of collective bargaining unless the units no longer conform reasonably well to other standards of appropriateness." *Cadillac Asphalt Paving Co.*, 349 NLRB 6, 9 (2007) (cleaned up). To rebut that presumption, the new owner must identify "compelling circumstances sufficient to overcome the significance of bargaining history," *Cmty. Hosps. of Cent. Cal. v. NLRB*, 335 F.3d 1079, 1085 (D.C. Cir. 2003) (cleaned up)—for instance, that the existing unit has become "repugnant to Board policy," *Trident Seafoods*, 101 F.3d at 118 (cleaned up).

In this case, Everport told the Board that, as a PMA member, it was bound by the Longshore Contract's terms, and that because the Terminal's red-circle status had lapsed, it was obligated to recognize the ILWU as the bargaining representative of all its employees at the Terminal, mechanics included. Under Everport's reading of the Longshore Contract, **[—13—]** in other words, a mechanic-specific bargaining unit was "inappropriate as a matter of law."

If Everport's interpretation of the Longshore Contract were correct, the only unit appropriate for the Terminal's mechanic workforce was the coastwide one created in *Shipowners* and reinforced in subsequent Board decisions. In *Shipowners*, the Board determined that a coastwide unit was appropriate for all longshoremen on the West Coast. *See* 7 NLRB at 1022–25. As a result of that decision, all PMA members' employees who come within the Longshore Contract's scope can be represented only by the ILWU. Furthermore, in *PMA*, the Board found that, subject to narrow exceptions, the Longshore Contract's "clear" terms assign all mechanic work at PMA-operated terminals to the ILWU. 256 NLRB at 770; *cf. Kinder Morgan*, 978 F.3d at 642, 8 Adm. R. at 346 (concluding that "the plain language of the [Longshore Contract] unambiguously assigns to the [ILWU] all [mechanic] work, on all present and future stevedore cargo handling equipment ... for all PMA members, at all West Coast ports," subject to the exceptions inserted in 1978 and 2008). On Everport's understanding that the Terminal's red-circle status had lapsed, if Everport had recognized a mechanic-specific unit and continued to bargain with the IAM, it would have violated its duty under the Longshore Contract to bargain only with the ILWU's coastwide unit.

Nevertheless, the Board found that a mechanic-specific bargaining unit remained appropriate after Everport took over Terminal operations. To explain this decision, it was necessary for the Board to answer the objections of Everport and the ILWU on the merits, particularly as the Board gives "controlling weight" to the parties' interpretation of their collective bargaining agreement. *Mining Specialists, Inc.*, 314 NLRB 268, 268 (1994). The Board, however, refused to **[—14—]** engage Everport's reading of the Longshore Contract, dismissing the question of whether the Terminal remained red-circled as a "red herring." *Everport*, slip op. at 43. Before this court, the Board again represented that Everport's obligations as a PMA member were "irrelevant" to the successorship question. The Board gave two reasons for this position, but neither is persuasive.

First, the Board argued that Everport's PMA membership was irrelevant because the IAM was "not a party to the PMA-ILWU Agreement, so it did not agree to [the red-circle] provisions." *Id.* But while the Board ordinarily seeks to keep intact long-established bargaining units, its precedents require it to ensure that any established unit "remains appropriate *for the* **{-791-}** *successor employer*." *Walden Sec., Inc.*, 366 NLRB No. 44, slip op. at 11 (Mar. 23, 2018) (emphasis added). To determine whether a mechanic-specific unit was appropriate for Everport, the Board had to analyze whether bargaining with such a unit would have been consistent with Everport's obligations under the Longshore Contract. The Board cannot simply label a substantial contractual argument a "red herring" in order to avoid addressing it. *Everport*, slip op. at 43.

Second, the Board intimated in its order that the Longshore Contract actually permitted Everport to bargain with a mechanic-specific unit, irrespective of whether the Terminal remained red-circled. For instance, it claimed that "[t]he red-circle language ... recognizes that a number of [mechanic] units were not historically represented by ILWU." *Id.* at 41. But the fact that a number of units were not historically represented by the ILWU does not support the conclusion that Everport could bargain with a mechanic-specific unit even if the Terminal's red-circle status lapsed. The Longshore Contract clearly covers mechanics unless a relevant exception applies. Therefore, only if the Terminal remained red-circled could **[—15—]** Everport bargain with a mechanic-specific unit, but that was the question the Board refused to answer.

The Board also sought to rely on the fact that Everport considered hiring a subcontractor that could retain Marine and Miles' mechanics, claiming that such actions were "contradictory to Everport's position that the red circle language no longer applied" after it joined the PMA. *Id.* at 39. Everport's behavior, however, was entirely consistent with its reading of the Longshore Contract. If Everport had found a subcontractor to oversee mechanic work at the Terminal, and if that subcontractor was not a PMA member, then the subcontractor could potentially have rehired Marine and Miles' workers and recognized the IAM as their representative. Here again, the Board's reason for ignoring Everport's contractual obligations was unfounded.

Finally, although *PMA* held the Longshore Contract clearly assigns all mechanic work at

PMA-operated terminals to the ILWU, so long as no exception applies, the Board argued that *PMA* was not controlling because that case "had no successorship issues." *Everport*, slip op. at 41. The Board cannot evade its precedents so easily. That the Longshore Contract's "clear" terms require PMA members to hire their mechanics from the ILWU, absent an applicable exception, was central to the Board's conclusion in *PMA*. 256 NLRB at 770. The Board also deflected by arguing that the version of the Longshore Contract at issue in *PMA* was "superseded in 2008 with [the] red circle language." *Everport*, slip op. at 41. That is true, but it does not excuse the Board's failure to assess whether the Terminal in fact remained red-circled. If the red-circle status had lapsed before Everport began operations, Everport would have had a "clear" duty to bargain with the coastwide ILWU unit. *PMA*, 256 NLRB at 770. In other words, without showing why Everport's reading of the Longshore **[—16—]** Contract was in error, the Board could not square its unit-appropriateness finding with *PMA*.

In "certify[ing] appropriate bargaining units ... the Board cannot ignore its own relevant precedent but must explain why it is not controlling." *LeMoyne-Owen Coll. v. NLRB*, 357 F.3d 55, 60 (D.C. Cir. 2004) (cleaned up). Here, both *Shipowners* and *PMA* required Everport to recognize the ILWU as the sole representative of all employees that came within the Longshore Contract's scope. The Board could not find that a mechanic-specific unit was appropriate, therefore, without determining whether the Terminal's mechanics were covered **{-792-}** by the Longshore Contract. Because the Board "entirely failed to consider [that] important aspect of the problem," its selection of a mechanic-specific bargaining unit was unreasonable. *Motor Vehicle Mfrs. Ass'n of U.S., Inc. v. State Farm Mut. Auto. Ins. Co.*, 463 U.S. 29, 43 (1983).

B.

The Board also concluded that Everport's hiring process was distorted by animus towards the IAM. That too was arbitrary.

As explained above, the third prong of the *Burns* successorship test is satisfied if the Board finds that a new employer's hiring decisions were motivated by antiunion animus. *Love's Barbeque*, 245 NLRB at 82; *Cap. Cleaning Contractors, Inc. v. NLRB*, 147 F.3d 999, 1005 (D.C. Cir. 1998). In other words, a new business owner cannot evade the duty to bargain by refusing to hire its predecessors' employees because of their union affiliation. To establish whether a new employer's refusal to hire its predecessor's employees was driven by antiunion animus, the Board relies on the test set out in *Wright Line*, 251 NLRB 1083 (1980). Under *Wright Line*, "the General Counsel must [first] make a prima facie showing **[—17—]** sufficient to support the inference that protected [union] conduct was a motivating factor behind the [employer's action]." *Wendt Corp. v. NLRB*, 26 F.4th 1002, 1010 (D.C. Cir. 2022) (cleaned up). "Once a prima facie case has been established, the burden shifts to the company to show that it would have taken the same action in the absence of the unlawful motive." *Ozburn-Hessey Logistics, LLC v. NLRB*, 833 F.3d 210, 218 (D.C. Cir. 2016) (cleaned up). If the employer's reasons are pretextual, they do not rebut the prima facie showing of animus. *See id.* at 219–20.

As prima facie evidence of animus against the IAM, the Board pointed to two sets of facts. First, it found Everport had intentionally prioritized job applicants from the ILWU over those from the IAM in various ways—telling the ILWU about its vacant mechanic positions before the IAM; interviewing the ILWU's candidates before the IAM's; hiring less experienced ILWU applicants instead of better qualified IAM ones; and, on at least one occasion, telling an IAM applicant he could not be hired because of his union affiliation. Second, the Board found that Everport had used a secret hiring quota. Based on the testimony of three IAM-represented applicants, the Board determined Everport had resolved to give fifty-one percent of the available mechanic positions to ILWU-represented applicants and forty-nine percent to Marine and Miles' employees, so that a majority of its mechanics would be ILWU-represented. Everport and the ILWU do not contest these findings.

In response, Everport argued its hiring process was not discriminatory when properly viewed in light of the Longshore Contract. In staffing the Terminal, Everport's "only duty" was to hire its employees on "a basis other than hostility to a union," *Sierra Realty Corp. v. NLRB*, 82 F.3d 494, 496 (D.C. Cir. 1996), and it must be the case that the requirements of a Board- **[—18—]** sanctioned collective bargaining agreement can furnish a non-discriminatory rationale for a company's hiring decisions. The Board did not find, and does not argue, that Everport's initial decision to join the PMA was motivated by animus against the IAM. And as a general matter, the Board conceded that Everport's hiring process was "consistent" with the one required by the Longshore Contract. *Everport*, slip op. at 18. Therefore, if Everport's interpretation of the Longshore Contract were correct—if the Terminal's red-circle status had lapsed, requiring Everport to prioritize mechanic applicants from the ILWU and **{-793-}** fill remaining vacancies through the Herman-Flynn process—it had a valid business reason for preferring ILWU applicants over IAM-represented ones.

Nevertheless, the Board explicitly declined to engage with Everport's reading of the Longshore Contract. The Board claimed Everport's invocation of its contract obligations was "pretextual," since it "did not remain neutral" and its "actions were pro-ILWU." *Id.* at 36–37. As evidence of Everport's bias, however, the Board pointed to the fact that it followed the hiring process required by the Longshore Contract. The Board's circular conclusion, in other words, was that Everport's asserted reason for prioritizing ILWU-represented job applicants could not be credited because Everport had prioritized ILWU-represented job applicants. That is not reasoned decisionmaking.

That leaves the Board's finding that Everport secretly employed a hiring quota. Since the Longshore Contract does not require quota-based hiring, Everport could not justify its decision to use one by pointing to its PMA membership.[3] The **[—19—]** Board, however, failed to explain why a finding of animus towards the IAM necessarily followed from its finding that Everport used a quota. When viewed in context, it is possible that Everport adopted the quota in order to discriminate against the IAM's applicants. But the opposite conclusion is plausible too.

The record indicates that Everport more than once declined to hire qualified ILWU applicants, instead hiring better-qualified IAM ones.[4] The record also shows that "Everport's internal documentation [indicated] a preference for keeping the mechanic units as they existed" before the handover. *Id.* at 37. In light of these facts, it is at least possible that Everport used the hiring quota to hire *more* of the Terminal's incumbent mechanics than the Longshore Contract's terms allowed, but not so many as to trigger a clash for recognition between the ILWU and the IAM. If that were so, then Everport adopted the quota not from animus towards the IAM, but to favor IAM applicants in the hiring process.

The Board was required to set out "a rational connection between the facts found and the choice made." *State Farm,* 463 U.S. at 43 (cleaned up). Here, it failed to reasonably explain why Everport's quota, viewed in light of the Longshore Contract, supported an inference of animus against the IAM. Instead, without explanation, it chose to ignore the substantial evidence that undercut its conclusion. *Cf. Lakeland Bus Lines, Inc. v. NLRB*, 347 F.3d 955, 963 (D.C. Cir. 2003) (holding that **[—20—]** the Board's "clipped view of the record" did not support its finding that the employer had committed unfair labor practices). We therefore conclude that "the process by which the agency reached its judgment was neither logical nor rational."

[3] The Longshore Contract does not require quotas for hiring mechanics. Rather, as explained above, it simply obligates PMA **[—19—]** members to exhaust all qualified ILWU applicants before offering vacancies to any non-ILWU applicant.

[4] Although the issue is not before us, we note the ILWU could have raised a claim that Everport violated the Longshore Contract by rejecting qualified ILWU applicants in order to hire Marine and Miles' former mechanics.

Fox v. Clinton, 684 F.3d 67, 80 (D.C. Cir. 2012) (cleaned up); *see also Allentown Mack Sales & Serv., Inc. v. NLRB*, 522 U.S. 359, 374 (1998) ("Not only must an agency's decreed result be within the scope of its lawful authority, but the process by which it reaches that result must be logical and rational.").[5] **{-794-}**

* * *

The Board did not reasonably explain its conclusion that Everport was a *Burns* successor with a duty to bargain with the IAM. Therefore, its finding that Everport unlawfully refused to bargain with the IAM was arbitrary and must be vacated.

III.

We next address the Board's finding that Everport prematurely recognized the ILWU as its mechanics' representative and that the ILWU unlawfully accepted its recognition.

In most cases, an employer who recognizes a union before it employs a "substantial and representative complement of its projected work force" and is "engaged in normal business operations" commits an unfair labor practice. *Elmhurst Care Ctr.*, 345 NLRB 1176, 1177 (2005); *see generally Int'l Ladies Garment Workers' Union v. NLRB*, 366 U.S. 731, 737–40 (1961). Here, the Board found that Everport recognized the **[—21—]** ILWU repeatedly throughout the summer and fall of 2015, before it "employ[ed] any mechanics at the Terminal" or was "engaged in normal business operations." *Everport*, slip op. at 39. Therefore, the Board found that Everport's recognition of the ILWU as its mechanics' representative was premature.

Given the unique bargaining landscape in which Everport was operating, however, the Board needed to explain its decision to apply a rigid version of the premature recognition test to Everport and the ILWU. The Board has long permitted groups of employers to negotiate with their employees collectively through multiemployer bargaining units. *See Arbor Constr. Pers., Inc.*, 343 NLRB 257, 257–58 (2004); *cf. Brown v. Pro Football, Inc.*, 518 U.S. 231, 240 (1996) ("Multiemployer bargaining ... is a well-established, important, pervasive method of collective bargaining."). The Board has recognized the PMA as the "multiemployer bargaining association" responsible for negotiating with the ILWU. *ILWU Loc. 19*, 266 NLRB 193, 194 (1983). It is undisputed that because of the Board's decision in *Shipowners*, it is not feasible to operate a West Coast port without joining the PMA. Finally, all PMA members are required to recognize the ILWU as their employees' bargaining representative. *See PMA*, 256 NLRB at 770 ("[E]mployers who join the PMA after the execution of the bargaining agreement are subject to its terms.").

If the Board's rigid view of the premature recognition test applied in this context, then *every* employer who joins the PMA—thereby committing to hire its longshoremen from the ILWU and to recognize the ILWU as their representative—commits an unfair labor practice the moment it joins. But that would make the system of collective bargaining the Board sanctioned in *Shipowners* nonsensical and unworkable: a port operator could not lawfully join the PMA before hiring its **[—22—]** workforce and it could not hire a workforce before joining the PMA. The Board neither acknowledged nor explained this apparent Catch-22, which is a telltale sign of arbitrary and capricious agency action. *See Advanced Life Sys. Inc. v. NLRB*, 898 F.3d 38, 49 (D.C. Cir. 2018) (vacating a Board order that left the employer "in a Catch-22").

IV.

Finally, the Board found that Everport committed an unfair labor practice when it imposed the Longshore Contract's terms on the Terminal's mechanics. For the reasons given above, neither of the Board's justifications for this conclusion was reasonable. First, the Board claimed that Everport lost the right to set its mechanics' initial terms and conditions of employment because it "used a general discriminatory **{-795-}** hiring plan,

[5] For the reasons given in this subsection, the Board's conclusions that Everport discriminated against the IAM, and that the ILWU encouraged it to do so, must also be set aside.

applicable to *all* applicants from the predecessor workforce," which made it a "perfectly clear" *Burns* successor. *Everport*, slip op. 1 n.4. The Board's successorship finding was not reasonably supported, *see supra* Part II, so its ancillary finding that Everport was a perfectly clear successor was arbitrary *a fortiori*. Alternatively, the Board claimed that the terms and conditions imposed on the Terminal's mechanics were unlawful because they stemmed from Everport's premature recognition of the ILWU. Because the Board's purported application of the premature recognition test was unfounded and left Everport in an untenable Catch-22, the Board's alternative basis for its decision does not pass muster. *See FCC v. Fox Television Stations, Inc.*, 556 U.S. 502, 515 (2009) (holding that agencies may not change their policies "*sub silentio*"). **[—23—]**

* * *

For the foregoing reasons we grant the petitions for review, deny the Board's cross application for enforcement, and vacate the Board's order.

So ordered.

Tables of Authority

This page intentionally left blank

Table of Cases

This page intentionally left blank

TABLE OF CASES[1]

PAGE

A

[1] Cases named solely after ships, *see, e.g.*, *The Pennsylvania*, 86 U.S. (19 Wall.) 125 (1873), are alphabetized under the letter "T." Cases where the United States is the plaintiff are alphabetized by defendant under the letter "U."

C

D

E

F

G

H

I

J

K

L

M

N

O

P

Q

R

S

T

U

V

W

X

Y

Z

This page intentionally left blank

Table of Statutes and Rules

This page intentionally left blank

TABLE OF STATUTES AND RULES[1]

PAGE

TREATIES/INTERNATIONAL

FEDERAL

CONSTITUTION

MISCELLANEOUS

[1] As cited in the opinions reported.

STATUTES

Rules

REGULATIONS

STATE AND U.S. TERRITORIES

This page intentionally left blank

Index

This page intentionally left blank

INDEX

PAGE

A

B

C

D

E

F

G

I

J

L

M

N

O

P

R

S

T

V

W

Y

Z

This page intentionally left blank

www.ingramcontent.com/pod-product-compliance
Lightning Source LLC
LaVergne TN
LVHW060013210926
848481LV00013B/3698
9781733779081